Marketing Research

Marketing Research

Eric Shiu, Joseph Hair, Robert Bush and David Ortinau

McGraw-Hill
Higher Education

London Boston Burr Ridge, IL Dubuque, IA Madison, WI New York San Francisco
St. Louis Bangkok Bogotá Caracas Kuala Lumpur Lisbon Madrid Mexico City Milan
Montreal New Delhi Santiago Seoul Singapore Sydney Taipei Toronto

Marketing Research
Shiu, Hair, Bush and Ortinau
ISBN-13 978-0-07-711706-1
ISBN-10 0-07-711706-9

McGraw-Hill
Higher Education

Published by McGraw-Hill Education
Shoppenhangers Road
Maidenhead
Berkshire
SL6 2QL
Telephone: 44 (0) 1628 502 500
Fax: 44 (0) 1628 770 224
Website: www.mcgraw-hill.co.uk

British Library Cataloguing in Publication Data
A catalogue record for this book is available from the British Library

Library of Congress Cataloguing in Publication Data
The Library of Congress data for this book has been applied for from the Library of Congress

Acquisitions Editor: Rachel Gear
Development Editor: Jennifer Rotherham
Marketing Manager: Alice Duijser
Senior Production Editor: James Bishop

Cover design by Adam Renvoize
Printed and bound in Italy by Rotolito Lombarda

ISBN-13 978-0-07-711706-1
ISBN-10 0-07-711706-9

Dedicated to my parents, Wanfei and Kwaiying, and my wife Peihsiuan.
Their love and support make what I am today and make
my involvement in this text possible.

Brief Table of Contents

Detailed Table of Contents

Preface

I feel honoured to have been given the chance to adapt *Marketing Research* by Professor Joseph Hair, Robert Bush and David Ortinau for the European market.

This new text differs from similar texts on the high street in many ways. Research is all about choice. That is, marketing researchers always need to analyse the unique circumstance they face at different stages of the marketing research process, and strive to make the most appropriate choices at each stage. In order to help readers, many of whom are would-be marketing practitioners needing to be involved in marketing research from time to time, to be analytical enough to make choices as best as they can, this text has been written with an analytical perspective in order to nurture the reader's analytical mindset.

Since the 1980s, technological advances have exerted a big impact on marketing research practices. However, there is no one text that elaborates the relationship between marketing research and technology in sufficient detail. In this text we place a strong emphasis on illustrating how technology has helped the industry practice and how it will continue to shape marketing research in future. We include the discussion of technology-enabled market intelligence, geographic information systems, social network websites such as Facebook and Second Life and a new electronic form of consumer data called consumer-generated media (CGM), to name just a few. You will find a separate chapter dedicated to discussing the deployment of technology in marketing research.

This text is European in context. Cases or examples from different European countries have been used to illustrate different marketing research concepts and practices. These countries span the continent from the UK in the west to Turkey in the east, as well as from Norway in the north to Spain in the south.

We have also used numerous European companies and real life events throughout the book in order to bring concepts to life and stimulate the reader's interest in what is traditionally regarded as a relatively difficult and boring subject. This will enable the reader to gain a more effective understanding of marketing research. The companies and real-life events featured in this text include Guinness, Nokia, IKEA, Red Bull and the FIFA World Cup in Germany, to name a few.

As SPSS is arguably the most popular statistical software in Europe, in both the school and office context, we incorporate its use in Chapter 1 to introduce the software. It is then used in all six chapters in Part 4 so that readers can if they wish access the SPSS environment, follow the explanations in the text and readily apply the concepts of the different analytical techniques that they learn to practise.

In addition to the numerous one-off cases provided throughout the book, we have introduced a continuing case in the first chapter, and it reappears at various points throughout the book to help readers understand important marketing research concepts and learn how to use SPSS appropriately in different analysis situations. We feel this continuing case study, based on a real-life European company (albeit with a fictitious dataset for obvious business confidentiality reasons), will give readers a real sense of the relationship between what they are learning and what is actually happening in business life. The familiarity and continuity provided by the continuing case will help readers to integrate their understanding of different concepts and tools across chapters, so that they can subsequently broaden and deepen their understanding of the subject.

We stress the equal importance of qualitative and quantitative research methods. Whether we should use one or the other, or both, should be dependent on the objectives of the research project concerned. Therefore we aim at achieving a fine balance between qualitative and quantitative research methods in this text. Aside from secondary research, which we regard as one of the research methods, we have two 'qualitative' and two 'quantitative' chapters. A chapter specifically on observation techniques, which can be qualitative or quantitative, is also included.

For some marketing practitioners, data analysis is probably one of the most complicated parts of the research process. In the four data analysis chapters (Chapters 16–19), we introduce at least one example for each major analytical technique that we have covered. Many of the examples given are derived from either the authors' own research projects or other researchers' work published in quality journals. By learning different analytical techniques through these examples, readers should find it easier to absorb the knowledge and be more able to apply the knowledge to practice.

Content and Organization

We have divided the text into four Parts. Part 1 (Chapters 1–3) introduces the reader to the world of marketing research by illustrating the value of marketing research, describing the marketing research industry and its players, systematically explaining the marketing research process in its totality, and elaborating how technology is and will be deployed in marketing research. The last topic on technology deployment in Part 1 of the book may be particularly illuminating because it gives readers possible new dimensions for approaching their research in future.

Part 2 (Chapters 4–9) explains the different major research methods that marketing researchers can adopt for their research project. We categorize secondary research as one of the research methods. This may sound different from the organization of other marketing research texts on the high street, but we believe that secondary research itself can generate information useful for meeting part of or even all the objectives of a research project. Indeed different researchers have different levels of capability in the use of the secondary research method. In this Part, we include all the major research methods that researchers can consider for their work. We keep a balance in introducing different qualitative and quantitative research methods, and try not to overemphasize one over the other. With this in mind, there are two chapters covering qualitative methods and two covering quantitative ones. From our teaching experience, some students experience difficulty in identifying whether observation techniques are qualitative or quantitative, and a review of current marketing research texts shows that opinions are divided on how best to place the discussion of observation techniques in the text. We believe that observation techniques, as opposed to all other major research methods, can be either qualitative or quantitative. Accordingly, a separate chapter has been specifically assigned for the discussion of observation. For Part 2, please see the following diagram which outlines the qualitative and quantitative research methods covered in this text.

Qualitative and Quantitative Research Methods Covered in this Text

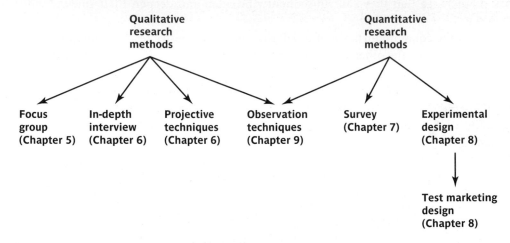

Part 3 (Chapters 10–14) is all about what marketing researchers can do in order to increase the accuracy of the data they are going to collect. In this part, we explain how to design a good questionnaire. We also elaborate how to develop an abstract construct and different types of scale measurement. Considering that attitudinal data is one of the most sought-after types of data in marketing research, we assign a separate chapter discussing all the major issues surrounding the design of attitude scales. Sampling is one of the most influential factors of accuracy in a marketing research project, and we therefore devote two chapters to illustrating sampling-related concepts and techniques, from sampling theory to the determination of sample size.

Part 4 (Chapters 15–20), the last part, is concerned with the preparation and analysis of the data we've collected at earlier stages of the marketing research process. After disseminating the knowledge regarding how to prepare the collected data prior to immediate analysis, chapters 16 to 19 introduce and explain all the major and popular data analysis techniques in marketing research. These include elementary analysis, hypothesis testing, bivariate correlation, and regression analysis, as well as different multivariate techniques including structural equation modelling. To give readers the opportunity to practise while working through these data analysis chapters, we use the continuing Jimmy Spice's case study to demonstrate how to use the different data analysis techniques that we cover through SPSS. The last chapter is devoted to the preparation and presentation of marketing research reports. Graphic and presentation aids will highlight the discussion in this chapter.

Many chapters concludes with an illustrative example entitled 'Marketing Research in Action' which counts to facilitate the reader's understanding of chapter topics and to provide the reader with a 'how-to' approach for conducting marketing research in real life.

Dr Eric Shiu
The University of Birmingham
UK

Guided Tour

This book offers a wealth of pedagogical features to help bring marketing research to life and make the subject more accessible to students. Key features of this text include:

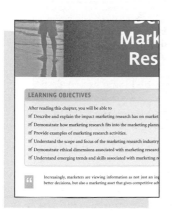

Learning Objectives:

Each chapter begins with clear learning objectives that students can use to gauge their expectations for the chapter discussion in view of the nature and importance of the chapter's material.

Real-World Chapter Openers:

Each chapter opens with an interesting and relevant example of a real world business situation that illustrates the focus and significance of the chapter's material. Examples include Adidas, Nokia and Rexona.

Key Terms and Concepts:

These are bold faced in the text and defined in the glossary. They are also listed at the end of the chapters along with page numbers to make reviewing easier and included in the Glossary at the end of the book.

A Closer Look at Research:

These illustrative boxes are found frequently throughout the chapters and come in three categories: Technology, Small Business and In the Field. Each example exposes the student to real-world marketing research issues.

though, lies in the restrictions on the types of data that can be collected example, it is difficult to use multiple levels of agreement/disagreement, like all but impossible to accurately ask a brand image question that would ent to answer using a semantic differential scale (see Chapter 13).

ETHICS
Conducting Marketing Research for Non-Research Purpose
When a marketing research project is carried out, the tacit agreement betwe the respondents/interviewees is that the project should be for research purp to Marketing Research Society, UK, a 'research purpose' is where informatio to enhance understanding in a way that provides robust information on th study. It does not include data collection intended directly to create sales or s ions of the respondents/interviewees. Nor does it include data collection as tion gathering for use on future sales or direct marketing activities, such as sales leads, contact details, or related details a particular respondent's/inte consumption patterns. Direct action should not be taken in relation to name viewees as a result of the marketing research project.

On some occasions, market research companies may carry out a resea research purpose, which is when data is collected for reasons other than for defined above. For example, an office equipment supplier approaches a rese of business contacts which the office equipment supplier can target for its p of this project is to build a marketing list for direct marketing purpose. The devise a questionnaire together with a prize draw that can be administered s

In the above case, proper procedures should be undertaken by the resear form to the marketing research ethical standard. The Marketing Research Soc conducting projects for non-research purpose, an ethical and responsible ensure that:

• the questions are fit for purpose and clients have been advised accordi

Ethics:

These boxes make students aware of the ethical issues that face market researchers.

Global Insights:

These boxes encourage the student to see the international implications of, and opportunities for, marketing research.

the last chapter – the nature of the measurement scales will d nique is appropriate to analyse data.

Selection of a proper technique requires consideration of t dependent and independent sets of variables. When the dep metrically, a suitable technique could be discriminant analysi measured metrically, eligible techniques include multiple re Multiple regression and discriminant analysis typically require use non-metric dummy variables. ANOVA and MANOVA are a pendent variables. For the interdependence techniques of fact default, researchers should use metrically measured variables, b acceptable.

Multivariate statistical techniques help marketers make bet univariate or bivariate statistics. But regardless of which type come of the analysis is the key point. Review the Global Insig change across markets.

Global Insights
Analysis from Global Research May Yield Interesti
Just Kids Inc., a marketing research firm specializing in the 2- some interesting findings among youngsters in Great Britain. shed their childhood much earlier than their peers elsewhere. sally loved, but the same advertising that attracts a 9-year-old 9-year-old British counterpart. Asked to identify their favo

2 Given the general questions that the owner has cited above, are there questions that you would suggest to the owner when designing for activities?

Summary of Learning Objectives

■ **Describe and explain the impact marketing research has on mark** Marketing research is the set of activities central to all marketing less of the complexity or focus of the decision. Marketing research ing managers with accurate, relevant, and timely information marketing decisions with a high degree of confidence. Within the ning, marketing research is responsible for the tasks, methods, an use to implement and direct its strategic plan.

■ **Demonstrate how marketing research fits into the marketing plan** Marketing research is the backbone of any relationship marketi marketing research facilitates the implementation of the process th customer/market knowledge, data integration, information techno customer profiles. The key to successful marketing planning is Information related to product performance, distribution efficien promotional efforts is crucial for developing the strategic plan. T of any marketing research endeavour is to design a project that information possible in aiding the development of a marketing pla

■ **Provide examples of marketing research activities.** The scope of marketing research activities extends far beyond es characteristics. The major categories of marketing research activi limited to, (1) situation research efforts (which include opportuni studies, benefit and lifestyle studies, and importance-performance design-driven research efforts (which include target market analy

Chapter Summaries:

The detailed chapter summaries provide links to the learning objectives to help students remember key facts, concepts and issues. They also serve as an excellent study and revision guide.

Questions for Review and Discussion:

The Review Questions and Discussion Questions are carefully designed to enhance the learning process and to encourage the application of concepts learned in the chapter to real business situations.

Review Questions
1 Provide three examples of how marketing research helps marketing personne make sound managerial decisions.
2 What improvements in market planning can be attributed to the results obtaine from customer satisfaction studies?
3 List the three basic approaches used in the collection of marketing researc information. Briefly describe each method and comment on its application.
4 Discuss the importance of target market analysis. How does it affect the deve opment of market planning for a particular company?
5 What are the advantages and disadvantages for companies maintaining an inter nal marketing research department? What advantages and disadvantages can b attributed to the hiring of an external marketing research supplier?
6 As the marketing research industry expands in the new century, what skills wi future executives need to possess? How do these skills differ from those cur rently needed to function successfully in the marketing research field?
7 Identify and explain four potential unethical practices within the marketin research process and their contribution to 'deceptive research results.'

Discussion Questions
1 **Experience the Internet.** Go online to one of your favourite search engine ('Yahoo!, Google, etc.) and enter the following search term: marketing research From the results, access a directory of marketing research firms. Select a particula firm and comment on the types of marketing research studies it performs.
2 **Experience the Internet.** Using the Yahoo! search engine, specifically the Ge Local section, select the closest major city in your area and search for the num ber of marketing research firms there. Select a company, email that compan and ask to have any job descriptions for positions in that company emailed bac to you. Once you obtain the descriptions, discuss the particular qualities neede to perform each job.
3 You have been hired by McDonald's to lead a mystery shopper team. The goal o your research is to improve the service quality at the McDonald's restaurant i your area. What attributes of service quality will you attempt to measure? Wha customer or employee behaviours will you closely monitor?
4 Contact a local business and interview the owner/manager about the types o marketing research performed for that business. Determine whether the busi ness has its own marketing research department, or if it hires an outside agenc Also, determine whether the company takes a one-shot approach to particula problems or a systematic over a long period of time.
5 **Experience the Internet.** As the Internet continues to grow as a medium fo

Marketing Research in Action:

The cases found at the end of the chapters provide students with additional insights into how key concepts in each chapter can be applied to real world situations. These cases can serve as class discussion tools or applied case exercises.

Jimmy Spice's restaurant continuing case study is a specially designed scenario embedded throughout the book for the purpose of questioning and illustrations about specific chapter topics. It provides students with an ongoing example for applying marketing research concepts and recognizing the challenges associated with them as they appear in the text. A data set accompanies this useful learning example.

Case 1: Red Bull
Dietrich Mateschitz founded the company, Red Bull, in Austria, his native country. As the son of humble primary school teachers, Mateschitz got his trade degree from the University of Vienna and worked at Unilever, Germany's Jacobs Coffee and Blendax for some time. His performance was noticeable such that within some years of service, he became the director of the International Marketing function at Blendax, which was later acquired by Procter & Gamble. His responsibility at Blendax took him to the far-off countries, including Thailand, where he discovered a Japanese syrup tonic drink that sold in pharmacies as a stimulating agent. After trying the tonic drink him self, he found a way to fight his jetlag. This is when Mateschitz decided to study the tonic market. 'I realized that these little syrups developed in Japan did extremely well all over Asia', he recalls. Mateschitz smelled the potential of the business in the unspoiled Western markets.

It took him three years to finalise the tonic drink formula. The top brand of tonic drink in the Thai market was called Krating Daeng, meaning 'Red Water Buffalo' in Thai. Mateschitz bor rowed this brand idea and decided to use the name 'Red Bull', which he believed was more prom ising for the Western markets. The drink was carbonated for Western palates and was packaged in a slim blue-silver can instead of a bottle. The three key ingredients of the Thai drink – an amino acid called taurine, caffeine, and glucuronolactone, a carbohydrate – were retained.

Before launching, marketing research with consumers was conducted. Results were less than promising. Red Bull was neither very appealing nor did it have a good taste. Some consumers commented that the berry-flavoured beverage tasted medicinal. Further, an 8.3-ounce can of Red Bull comes at a price that is double the price of a 12-ounce can of Coke.

However, Mateschitz decided to ignore the marketing research results and set up offices in Fuschl, a town just outside Salzburg, Austria. Since there was no existing market for Red Bull, but Red Bull will recalls, 'When we first started, we said there is no existing market for Red Bull, but Red Bull will

Technology to enhance learning and teaching

Online Learning Centre (OLC)

After completing each chapter, log on to the supporting Online Learning Centre website. Take advantage of the study tools offered to reinforce the material you have read in the text, and to develop your knowledge of marketing research.

CONTENT TBC

Resources for students include:

- Glossary
- Weblinks
- Cases

Also available for lecturers:

- Instructor's Manual
- PowerPoint presentations
- Additional care studies
- Solutions to questions in the book
- Additional exam questions
- SPSS Data sets

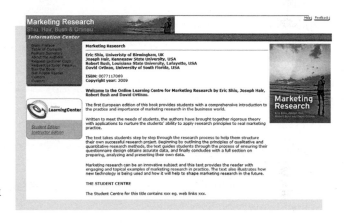

Custom Publishing Solutions: Let us help make our content your solution

At McGraw-Hill Education our aim is to help lecturers to find the most suitable content for their needs delivered to their students in the most appropriate way. Our **custom publishing solutions** offer the ideal combination of content delivered in the way which best suits lecturer and students.

Our custom publishing programme offers lecturers the opportunity select just the chapters or sections of material they wish to deliver to their students from a database called Primis at **www.primisonline.com**

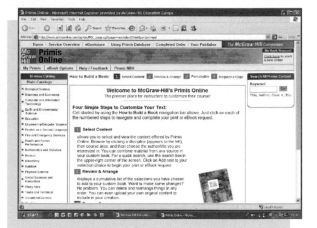

Primis contains over two million pages of content from:

- textbooks
- professional books
- case books – Harvard Articles, Insead, Ivey, Darden, Thunderbird and BusinessWeek
- Taking Sides – debate materials

Across the following imprints:

- McGraw-Hill Education
- Open University Press
- Harvard Business School Press
- US and European material

There is also the option to include additional material authored by lecturers in the custom product – this does not necessarily have to be in English.

We will take care of everything from start to finish in the process of developing and delivering a custom product to ensure that lecturers and students receive exactly the material needed in the most suitable way.

With a Custom Publishing Solution, students enjoy the best selection of material deemed to be the most suitable for learning everything they need for their courses – something of real value to support their learning. Teachers are able to use exactly the material they want, in the way they want, to support their teaching on the course.

Please contact your local **McGraw-Hill representative** with any questions or alternatively contact Warren Eels **e: warren_eels@mcgraw-hill.com**.

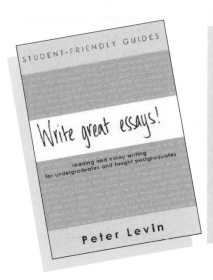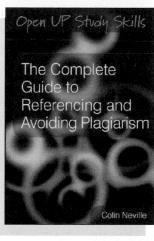

Acknowledgements

Our thanks go to the following reviewers for their comments at various stages in the text's development:

Theuns Kotze, University of Pretoria
Ralf van der Lans, Erasmus University
Erjen Van Nierop, University of Groningen
Nick Lee, Aston University
Niclas Ohman, Stockholm School of Economics
Yvonne Moogan, Liverpool John Moores
Martin Wetzels, Maastricht University
Donal Rogan, Institute of Technology, Tallaght, Dublin
Sonja Gensler, Vrije University

We would also like to extend our thanks to Rose Leahy and Nollaig O'Sullivan for kindly supplying the Guinness case in chapter one.

Author's Acknowledgements

In radically adapting and rewriting this text, I have been given a helping hand from many academic colleagues both inside and outside the University of Birmingham. My colleagues at McGraw-Hill, in particular Jennifer Rotherham, Melanie Havelock and Rachel Gear, have also been very helpful throughout the whole process. I'm much indebted to them all.

Every effort has been made to trace and acknowledge ownership of copyright and to clear permission for materials adopted or reproduced in this book. The publishers will be pleased to make suitable arrangements to clear permission with any copyright holders whom it has not been possible to contact.

Dr Eric Shiu lectures at the University of Birmingham, UK. He achieved an MA degree with distinction at Lancaster University. Afterwards, he underwent a doctoral research training programme through which he was awarded a MSc by Research degree, and then completed a doctorate at the University of Edinburgh. Prior to joining the University of Birmingham, Eric taught at the University of Edinburgh. He has received a Certificate of Award after successfully completing the International Teachers Programme organized by the International Schools of Business Management, and more recently has been awarded Postgraduate Certificate in Learning and Teaching in Higher Education by the University of Birmingham. Eric has accumulated more than ten years of research experience across academic, governmental and industry domains, which earned him a number of research awards. Additionally, a paper adapted from his PhD research has assisted him in receiving the first prize research award from the UK Online User Group. He has obtained a number of research-related grants, with the most recent one being from European Science Foundation. He currently teaches marketing research as well as product and innovation management at master degree levels, and has successfully nurtured a number of PhD graduates. Eric has published widely in quality journals, such as *International Journal of Market Research, The Service Industries Journal, Technovation,* and *Journal of Marketing Management.*

Joseph F. Hair, Jr., earned his Ph.D. in Marketing from the University of Florida, Gainesville. He currently holds the Alvin C. Copeland Endowed Chair of Franchising and is the Director, Entrepreneurship Institute, Ourso College of Business Administration, Louisiana State University. He has published over 25 books, including *Marketing,* 7th edition (SouthWestern, 2004); *Multivariate Data Analysis,* 6th edition (Prentice Hall, 2006); and *Essentials of Business Research Methods* (Wiley, 2003). He has also published numerous articles in academic journals, such as the *Journal of Marketing Research, Journal of Academy of Marketing Science, Journal of Business/ Chicago, Journal of Advertising Research, Journal of Business Research,* and others. He has consulted with many companies, provided expert testimony in litigation matters, and developed numerous executive education programs. In May 2004, he was given the Academy of Marketing Science Outstanding Marketing Teaching Excellence Award. Under his leadership in 2003 the LSU Entrepreneurship Institute was recognized by *Entrepreneurship Magazine* as one of the top 12 programs nationally. Joseph F. Hair, Jr., is often invited to give lectures on research techniques to graduate programs at universities in Europe and in other countries abroad.

Robert P. Bush earned a B.A. in Psychology and Economic History from St. Mary's University and an M.A. and Ph.D. in Marketing at Louisiana State University. He began his teaching career at the University of South Florida before moving on to the University of Mississippi, the University of Memphis, and then the University of Louisiana, Lafayette. He was chairman of the committee on Grants and Research for the Fogelman College of Business from 1991 to 1997 and Director of the Ph.D. program at Memphis from 1995 to 1997. He has been a consultant for a wide range of corporations and institutes, as well as for the U.S. Department of Defense. Robert P. Bush is the coauthor of *Retailing for the 21st Century* (Houghton Mifflin, 1993) and a coeditor of *Advances in*

Marketing (LSU Press, 1994). He is a regular contributor to such academic publications as *Journal of Advertising, Journal of Consumer Marketing, Journal of Marketing Education, Journal of Direct Marketing, Journal of Health Care Marketing, and Marketing Education Review.*

David J. Ortinau earned a B.S. in Management from Southern Illinois University, Carbondale, an M.A. in Business Administration, with a specialty in marketing research, from Illinois State University, and a Ph.D. in Marketing from Louisiana State University. He began his teaching career at Illinois State University and after completing his Ph.D. degree he moved to the University of South Florida, Tampa, where he continues to win awards for both outstanding research and for excellence in teaching. He has a wide range of research interests from research methodologies and scale measurement of attitude formation and perceptual differences in retailing and services marketing to interactive electronic marketing technologies and their impact on information research problems. He consults for a variety of corporations and small businesses, with specialties in customer satisfaction, customer service quality, customer service value, retail loyalty, and imagery. David J. Ortinau continues to serve as a member of the editorial review board for the *Journal of the Academy of Marketing Science (JAMS)* and the *Journal of Business Research (JBR)*. He was co-editor of *Marketing: Moving Toward the 21st Century* (SMA Press, 1996). He remains an active leader in the Marketing discipline. He has held many leadership positions in the Society for Marketing Advances (a.k.a. Southern Marketing Association), served as co-chair of the 1998 Southern Marketing Association's Doctoral Consortium in New Orleans and the 1999 Society for Marketing Advances' Doctoral Consortium in Atlanta. He is a past President of SMA and was recognized as the 2001 SMA Fellow. He is currently serving as the (2004–2006) President of the SMA Foundation and recently served as the 2004 Academy of Marketing Science Conference Program co-chair. He has presented numerous papers at academic meetings and has been a regular contributor to and referee for such prestigious publications as the *Journal of the Academy of Marketing (JAMS), Journal of Retailing (JR), Journal of Business Research (JBR), Journal of Marketing Education (JME), Journal of Health Care Marketing (JHCM), Journal of Services Marketing,* and others.

PART 1

Introduction to Marketing Research

Part contents

Chapter 1

Defining Marketing Research

LEARNING OBJECTIVES

After reading this chapter, you will be able to

☑ Describe and explain the impact marketing research has on marketing decision making.

☑ Demonstrate how marketing research fits into the marketing planning process.

☑ Provide examples of marketing research activities.

☑ Understand the scope and focus of the marketing research industry.

☑ Demonstrate ethical dimensions associated with marketing research.

☑ Understand emerging trends and skills associated with marketing research.

> " Increasingly, marketers are viewing information as not just an input for making better decisions, but also a marketing asset that gives competitive advantage. "
> –*Philip Kotler*

Using Marketing Research for Effectively Reaching and Managing Customers – Adidas's FIFA World Cup Marketing Research Project in France

As a major sponsor of the 2006 FIFA World Cup, Adidas was embarking on an aggressive market- ing research project a year before the kick off. The objective of this project was to measure the effectiveness of an integrated marketing campaign for Adidas in the French market. Through a better understanding of the contributions of different elements of the campaign, a better customer relationship management strategy could be devised. The integrated marketing campaign was aimed at matching the events around the French football team.

The project was a complicated one as it needed to measure twenty different channels of media contact. In order to incorporate all these different media channels in one questionnaire, the number of measurement metrics had to be small and manageable.

To measure the effectiveness of each media channel, the following simple set of metrics was used:

- Prompted brand recall in the past seven days;
- Promoted recall of the different points of media contact on which consumers were exposed to the brand in the past seven days;
- Appreciation of the campaign using a 6-point hedonic scale.

On the other hand, to measure the impact of the different media channels on the brand, the following metrics were used:

- Top of mind and spontaneous awareness of the brand;
- Preferred brand in football;
- Key image items;
- Claimed purchase of different types of Adidas products;
- Intention to recommend the brand;
- Intention to purchase products of the brand.

Respondents to the questionnaire were identified as young males aged 15 to 25 years. Completed questionnaires were collected from 120 to 150 targeted respondents every week within the 11-month period of the project. To communicate the ongoing results within Adidas's management and to help the company to be even more customer-centric than before, a management dashboard was created (see the Figure 1.1).

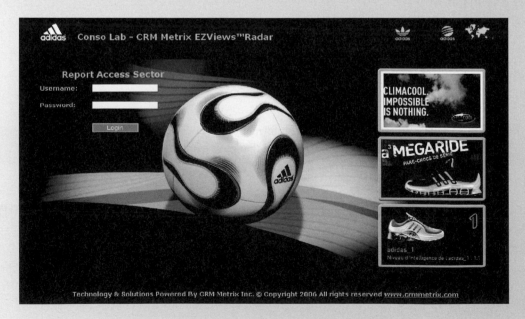

Figure 1.1 Adidas sponsoring FIFA World Cup and other football activities.

A number of insightful findings came with the final stage analysis of the questionnaire data. These findings demonstrate some innovative ideas for developing and implementing a more effective integrated marketing communication campaign, which in turn inform the desirable directions of the management of customer relationship in the future. For example, three major findings that can help managers for marketing communication and customer relationship management purposes are:

- Do your best to better know the best customers in your market. The best customers are those with the highest value and/or the most influential. You should know how they get information about their favourite brands, the types of media channels they use, and how they want to be connected with the brand.

- Create an integrated marketing campaign through which these target customers will have a maximum of opportunities to connect with the brand, preferably whenever and wherever they want.

- In light of the above two findings, increase the number of different media channel contacts to create a global brand experience. This can help to maximize the opportunity to consumers to be able to connect with the brand whenever and wherever they want.

Adapted from a business case written for ESOMAR by Laurent Flores (CEO and Founder of crmmetrix, France), Guillaume Weill (Managing Director of crmmetrix, France), Oliver Heck (Consumer Insight Manager of Adidas, France).

Definition and Usefulness of Marketing Research

The chapter opening example above illustrates how marketing research can operate to help businesses in various sectors. The example highlights the desirable linkage between marketing research and marketing. A sound marketing research project should be customer-centric throughout the whole research process, and should feed the results it generates from the process to the marketing programme, in order to increase customer satisfaction, customer trust and customer loyalty, which are important factors in the customer decision on which company and brand to choose.

The European Society for Opinion and Marketing Research (ESOMAR) formally defines **marketing research** as follows:

> Marketing research is a key element within the total field of marketing information. It links the consumer, customer and public to the marketer through information which is used to identify and define marketing opportunities and problems; generate, refine and evaluate marketing actions; improve understanding of marketing as a process and of the ways in which specific marketing activities can be made more effective. Marketing research specifies the information required to address these issues; designs the method for collecting information; manages and implements the data collection process; analyses the results; and communicates the findings and their implications.

Marketing research The function that links the consumer, customer and public to the marketer through information for marketing purposes.

Applying this definition to the chapter opening example, we can see that Adidas collected and used marketing research information in order to identify areas for improvement of customer relationship, as well as for development of an effective marketing campaign for their current and potential customers.

Marketing research is a systematic process. The tasks in this process include designing methods for collecting information, managing the information collection process, analysing and interpreting results and communicating findings to decision makers. This chapter provides an overview of marketing research as well as a fundamental understanding of its relationship to marketing practices. We first explain why firms use marketing research and give some examples of how marketing research can help companies make sound marketing decisions. Next we discuss who should use marketing research and when.

The chapter also provides a general description of the activities companies use to collect marketing research information. We present an overview of the marketing research industry in order to clarify the relationship between the providers and the users of marketing information. The chapter closes with a description of the role of ethics and good conduct in marketing research. It also includes an appendix on careers in marketing research (Appendix 1, page 691) as well as one on how to use the statistical analysis software package SPSS (Appendix 2, page 693).

Marketing Research and Marketing

As can be implied from the definition in the previous section, marketing research is concerned with research from the perspective of marketing. Then what is marketing exactly? **Marketing** is about the planning and execution of the pricing, promotion, and distribution of products and services in order to create exchanges that satisfy both the firm and its customers. The process of creating this exchange is the responsibility of the firm's marketing manager. Marketing managers attempt to facilitate the marketing process by following various decision criteria. More specifically, they focus on (1) getting the right goods and services (2) to the right people, (3) at the right place and time, (4) with the right price, and (5) through the use of the right blend of promotional techniques. Adhering to these criteria ultimately leads to the success of the marketing effort. However, the common denominator associated with each criterion is uncertainty. Uncertainty mainly lies in the fact that consumer behaviour is unpredictable. In order to reduce this uncertainty, marketing managers must have accurate, relevant, and timely information. Marketing research is the mechanism for generating that information.

> **Marketing** The process of planning and executing the pricing, promotion, and distribution of products and services in order to create exchanges that satisfy both the firm and its customers.

Marketing can be espoused from either a short-term or a long-term perspective. Companies adopting a short-term perspective of marketing focus on maximizing their short-term benefits, usually in the form of sales, market share and/or profit, through a series of marketing activities. However, companies taking a long-term perspective to market their products or services will usually be more successful and sustainable. They often follow a business strategy known as **relationship marketing**, which aims at building long-term relationships with customers by

> **Relationship marketing** The name of a strategy that entails forging long-term relationships with customers.

offering value and providing customer satisfaction. In return, these companies are rewarded with repeat sales, as well as continual increases in sales, market share and/or profits. Dell Computers, which serves the global computer market, focuses highly on relationship marketing. Dell sees its customers as individuals with unique desires. Its marketing research programme is directed towards measuring these aspects of the customer, then developing its entire marketing programme around such measures to build long-term relationships with customers.

The success of any relationship marketing programme depends on knowledge of the market, effective training programmes, and employee empowerment and teamwork:

- **Knowledge of the market.** For an organization focusing on building relationships with customers, it must know all relevant information pertaining to those customers. This implies that the company must have an obsession with understanding customer needs and behaviour and using that information to deliver satisfaction to the customer. Nowhere is this more important than in the marketing research responsibilities of the company.

- **Effective training programmes.** Building excellence in relationships begins with the employee. In the eyes of many consumers, the employee is the company. Therefore, it is critical, not only in a marketing research capacity, but throughout the entire company, that the actions and behaviours of employees be market-oriented. Many organizations such as McDonald's and Toyota have corporate universities designed to train employees in customer relations. Furthermore, many of these universities train employees in the proper techniques of gathering data from customers. Emphasizing informal customer comments, discussing issues on competing products and encouraging customers to use comment cards are some ways in which employees can be trained for enriching their data-gathering practices.

- **Employee empowerment and teamwork.** Many successful companies encourage their employees to be more proactive in solving customer problems. On-the-spot problem solving is known as empowerment. Additionally, organizations are now developing cross-functional teams dedicated to developing and delivering customer solutions. For example, in the Jeep Division of Daimler-Chrysler, employees within the marketing research and the engineering functions work together to better understand the requirements of their customers.

Empowerment and teamwork facilitate relationship building with customers. These two dimensions, along with training and knowledge of the market, form the catalyst for implementing a successful relationship-marketing strategy.

Companies espousing the spirit of relationship marketing should gather market-driven data to learn more about customers' needs and behaviours for the purpose of delivering added value and satisfaction to the customer. The data, in conjunction with information technology, is then used to develop stronger relationships with customers. Fundamentally, relationship marketing is based on a number of concepts focusing on the marketplace and the consumer. Specifically, these concepts address:

- **Customer/market knowledge:** This is the starting point of any relationship marketing strategy. Marketing researchers gather information from multiple sources as it pertains to the customer. Key data to be captured include demographics, psychographics, buying and service history, preferences, complaints and all other communications the customer has with the company. Data can be internal, through customers' interaction with the company, or external, through surveys or other data collection methods.

- **Data integration:** This process develops a data warehouse to integrate information from multiple sources into a single shared data source depository. The data, which are used to understand and predict customer behaviours, are then made available to all functional areas of the company so that anyone who interacts with the customer will have a complete history of the customer.

- **Information technology:** The process of data integration can be facilitated by the use of marketing research techniques that are driven by information technology. These techniques perform functions such as basic reporting on customers, data mining, statistical analysis procedures, and data visualization.

- **Creating customer profiles:** Collected and integrated data are used to develop customer profiles. These profiles are then made available to all functional areas of the company utilizing the appropriate information technology.

These concepts are embodied in a variety of outcomes based on the planning and decision making objectives of the company (e.g. introducing new products, developing new market segments, evaluating advertising campaigns). The overriding goal is to provide the necessary data and technology to monitor customer changes while building and maintaining long-term customer relationships.

Framework of Marketing Planning and Research Activities

To succeed in its relationship marketing strategy, a company must set up a sound framework for its marketing planning activities and make many appropriate decisions within the framework. Each marketing planning activity within the framework must be supported by corresponding marketing research activities. Execution of these marketing planning and research activities can then guarantee the generation of information and decisions as essential inputs for the implementation of the relationship marketing strategy.

Exhibit 1.1 lists the major marketing planning activities and their corresponding marketing research activities. One can see that some of these marketing planning activities are strategic in nature, while others are more tactical. The two can vary significantly in complexity and focus. As a rule of thumb, the more strategic the activities are, the more complex they become; the tactical activities, on the other hand, are more focused. Examples of the strategic marketing planning activities are to decide which new markets to penetrate, which products to introduce, and which new business opportunities to pursue. Such broad strategic decisions usually require decision makers to consider a variety of alternative approaches. Conversely, tactical decisions regarding advertising effectiveness, product positioning, and sales tracking, while still complex, are somewhat narrower in focus. Such decisions usually concentrate on a specific advertising campaign, a particular brand or a specific market segment. Such decisions often centre on monitoring performance or anticipating and initiating changes in a company's marketing practices.

Regardless of the complexity or focus of the marketing planning activities, managers must have accurate information to make the right decisions for the activities concerned. The entire marketing planning process is a series of decisions that must be made with high levels of confidence about the outcome. It is therefore not surprising to realize that a sound marketing research process is the nucleus for confident decisions made on marketing planning activities.

Although the list of activities listed in Exhibit 1.1 is by no means exhaustive, it does provide a general illustration of the relationship between marketing planning and marketing research. The following sections describe this relationship in more detail.

EXHIBIT 1.1 Marketing Planning and Corresponding Marketing Research Activities

Marketing Planning Activities	Marketing Research Activities
Situation Analysis	
Market analysis	Opportunity assessment
Market segmentation	Descriptive studies
	Benefit and lifestyle studies
Competition analysis	Importance-performance analysis
Programme Design	
Target marketing	Target market analysis
Positioning	Positioning
New product planning	Concept and product testing
	Test marketing
Programme Development	
Product portfolio decisions	Customer satisfaction studies
	Service quality studies
Distribution decisions	Cycle time research
	Retailing research
	Logistic assessment
Pricing decisions	Demand analysis
	Sales forecasting
Integrated marketing communication decisions	Advertising effectiveness studies
	Attitudinal research
	Sales tracking
Programme Tracking	
Programme control	Product analysis
	Environmental forecasting
Critical information analysis	Marketing decision support systems

Situation Analysis

The purpose of **situation analysis** is to monitor the appropriateness of a firm's marketing strategy and to determine whether changes to the strategy are necessary. A situation analysis includes three decision areas: market analysis, market segmentation and competition analysis. Within the context of the analysis, the purposes of marketing research are to

1 Locate and identify new market opportunities for a company (opportunity assessment).
2 Identify groups of customers in a product or service market who possess similar needs, characteristics and preferences (benefit and lifestyle studies, descriptive studies).
3 Identify existing and potential competitors' strengths and weaknesses (importance-performance analysis).

> **Situation analysis** To monitor the appropriateness of a firm's marketing strategy and to determine whether changes to the strategy are necessary.

A Closer Look at Research *(In the field)*

Situation Analysis Will Help Guinness Maintain Their Position at the Top of the World

Arthur Guinness began brewing at the famous St James' Gate in Dublin in 1759, signing a lease for 9000 years at €45 per annum. Initially he brewed ale, but in 1799 the decision was made to focus solely on brewing stout porter. During the nineteenth century St James' Gate Brewery became the largest brewery in Ireland and the Guinness trademark was introduced. By 1886 Guinness had become the largest brewery in the world, with an annual production of 1.2 million barrels. It appointed international quality controllers in the 1890s to ensure the Guinness sold outside Ireland was the same high quality as that found at home. Now owned by Diageo, Guinness continues to be the best selling stout in the world.

Ideally a pint of Guinness should be served in a slightly tulip shaped pint glass as opposed to the taller European tulip glass or 'Nonic' glass which contains a ridge approximately three quarters of the way up the glass. On the way to the tap, the beer is passed through a chiller and is forced through a five-hole disc restrictor plate in the end of the tap, which increases the fluid pressure and friction, forcing the creation of small bubbles which form a creamy head. Due to the forming action of the nitrogen, a 'double pour' is required, where the pint is three-quarters filled, allowed to settle and then topped up to the full pint. According to the company this 'double pour' should take 119.5 seconds. Guinness has promoted this wait with advertising campaigns such as 'good things come to those who wait'.

In Ireland, this 'double pour' of 'the perfect pint' is the norm, where all customers are familiar with the action and are prepared and even expect to wait the extra time while their pint of Guinness 'settles'. Outside of Ireland however, this 'double pour' action is often not the norm and instead the pint glass is quickly filled to the top and immediately given to the customer; essentially a 'fast-poured' Guinness. This is an issue of concern to Diageo who believe that 'the perfect pint' is a slow poured one.

Anecdotal evidence suggests that a lot of customers just want a fast beer and so bartenders in many situations will not do a 'double pour'. Other factors can also be seen to be at play here:

- Customers outside of Ireland may be unaware that a pint of Guinness should be poured in a 'double pour' action
- Contrary to the anecdotal evidence, customers outside of Ireland may be prepared to wait for a slow poured pint if they knew that it was considered 'the perfect pint'.
- Bartenders may be uneducated about the 'double pour' and/or may be unwilling to pull a slow pint of Guinness.

In examining this issue, Diageo believe that European-wide research among customers and bartenders is essential to inform their marketing strategy for Europe. While currently the best selling stout in the world, Diageo are conscious of changing trends in alcohol consumption and the growing popularity of lagers and wines across Europe which threatens sales of stout. To maintain Guinness at the top, Diageo believe that researching bartenders and customers thoughts on the 'double pour' in Europe is essential.

Written and kindly supplied by Rose Leahy and Nollaig O'Sullivan, Cork Institute of Technology, Ireland.
Sources: www.guinness.com and Irish Independent (2007).

Market Analysis

The research task related to market analysis is **opportunity assessment**. It involves collecting information on product or service markets for the purpose of forecasting how they would change. Companies gather information relevant to macroenvironmental trends (political and regulatory, economic and social, and cultural and technological) and assess how those trends would affect the product or service market.

> **Opportunity assessment** Involves collecting information on product or service markets for the purpose of forecasting how they would change.

The role of marketing research is to gather and categorize information relating to macroenvironmental variables, and then interpret the information in the context of strategic consequences to the firm. Marketing researchers use three common approaches in the collection of macroenvironmental information:

1 Content analysis, in which researchers analyse various information sources such as trade publications, newspaper articles, computer databases and academic literature for information on trends in a given industry.

2 In-depth interviews, in which researchers conduct formal and systematic in-depth interviews with experts in a given field.

3 Questionnaires, in which researchers use structured questionnaires to gather information on environmental occurrences.

These procedures will be discussed further in Chapters 11, 12, and 13.

 ## A Closer Look at Research *(In the field)*

Nokia Embraces a New Approach to Conduct Opportunity Assessment

Nokia, arguably the most notable Finnish company, is the world's largest mobile phone maker. It has a database containing information about its one billion customers – one-sixth of humanity.

One key strength of Nokia is its pursuit of new product opportunity that could continue to keep the company in the driving seat in the industry. Opportunity assessment becomes a crucial marketing research activity of the Finnish giant. This opportunity-chasing behaviour could be partly explained by Nokia's genes. Founded in 1865 as a timber company, its brand – now ranked fifth globally – was stamped on paper goods, wellington boots and television sets before the company focused on the mobile market 16 years ago.

In recent years, they have developed a new approach to collect valuable data for helping them in assessing new product opportunities. They have decided to make more intensive use of their vast customer database, by inviting their customers to consult on what works, what wows, and what doesn't.

'We realized in early 2005 that if we only focused on innovation from within, we were limiting our scope for real breakthroughs', Nokia's Chief Technology Officer Bob Iannucci said. 'We want more wild ideas.'

With this new concept in mind, Nokia has also invited bloggers and tech-savvy media specialists to brainstorm on future mobile products, some of which could be great product opportunities for the company. 'The ability to include larger numbers of users into the development cycle means you can have a much more collaborative approach to development and you can try ideas out, refine them and move forward – or fail fast and get out', said Bob Iannucci.

Source: European CEO, May/June 2008.

Market Segmentation

The research tasks useful for market segmentation are descriptive studies as well as benefit and lifestyle studies. The former involves collecting descriptive information about consumers, such as product purchase, gender, age, education, occupation, income and family size. The latter focuses on consumer lifestyle and the benefits consumers expect to attain from the product they purchase. Marketing researchers use the data collected from both types of study in order to identify segments within the market for the product or service in question.

> **Descriptive studies** and **Benefit and lifestyle studies** Collection of data of product purchase, consumer demographics, consumer lifestyle and expected product benefits.

Determining the significant consumer characteristics that can differentiate between heavy and light purchasers serves as the critical interaction between marketing research and marketing programme development. Chapter 9 will focus on this issue and examine, in detail, customer-driven marketing research approaches.

Competitive Analysis

A research task used in competitive analysis is **importance-performance analysis**, which is an approach for evaluating competitors' strategies, strengths and limitations. Importance-performance analysis asks consumers to identify key attributes that drive their purchase behaviour within a given industry. These attributes might include price, product performance, product quality, accuracy of shipping and delivery, and convenience of store location. Consumers are then asked to rank the importance of the attributes. They are also requested to score the performance of each of the key attributes for each competing firm, and these scores are then adjusted by considering the relative importance of each of the key attributes concerned.

> **Importance-performance analysis** A research approach for evaluating competitors' strategies, strengths, and limitations.

Following this data collection and adjustment process, researchers can objectively evaluate the competitors. Highly rated attributes are viewed as strengths, and lower ranked attributes are viewed as weaknesses. When the competing firms are analysed in aggregate, a company can see where its competitors are concentrating their marketing efforts and where they are falling below customer expectations.

Programme Design

Information collected during a marketing situation analysis is subsequently used to design a marketing strategy. At this stage of the planning and decision-making process, companies identify target markets, develop positioning strategies for products and brands, test new products and assess market potential.

Target Marketing

Target market analysis provides useful information for identifying those people (or companies) that an organization wishes to serve. In addition, it helps management determine the most efficient way of serving the targeted group. Target market analysis attempts to provide information on the following issues:

- Demographic and psychographic characteristics
- Cognition and affection
- Purchase decision process
- Product usage pattern

> **Target market analysis** Information for identifying those people (or companies) that an organization wishes to serve.

In order to provide such information, the marketing researcher must measure certain key variables as outlined in Exhibit 1.2.

Positioning

Positioning is a process in which a company seeks to establish a meaning or definition of its product offering that is consistent with customers' needs and preferences. Companies accomplish this task by combining elements of the marketing mix in a manner that meets or exceeds the expectations of targeted customers.

> **Positioning** A process in which a company seeks to establish a meaning or definition of its product offering that is consistent with customers' needs and preferences.

The task of the marketing researcher is to provide an overview of the comparison between competitive product offerings based on judgments of a sample of respondents who are familiar with the product category being investigated. Consumers are asked to indicate how they view the similarities and dissimilarities among relevant product attributes for a set of competing brands. For example, positioning among beers may indicate that customers decide between 'popular versus premium' and 'regional versus national' brands.

This information is then used to construct perceptual maps, which transform the positioning data into 'perceptual space'. Perceptual mapping reflects the dimensions on which brands are evaluated, typically representing product features, functions or benefits judged as important in the consumer selection process.

EXHIBIT 1.2 Target Market Characteristics and Associated Variables Measured in Target Market Analysis

Target Market Characteristics	Key Variables to Measure
Demographics	Gender, age, race, religion, income, occupation, family size and geographic location
Psychographics	Consumer activities, interests and opinions
Cognition and affection	Product/brand awareness, salient product attributes and level of brand loyalty
Purchase decision process	Product involvement, perceived risk of purchase, propensity to purchase, size and frequency of purchase
Product usage pattern	Occasion (e.g. special use, gift); situation (e.g. climate, time of day, place); and usage context (heavy, medium, or light)

New Product Planning

The research tasks related to new product planning are **concept and product testing** and **test marketing**, which give management the necessary information for decisions on product improvements and new product introductions. Concept and product testing attempts to answer two fundamental questions: 'How does a concept or product perform for the prospective customer?' and 'How can a concept or product be improved to meet or even exceed customer expectations?' Specifically, concept and product tests

1 Determine whether the prospective new product should replace the current product.

2 Identify new product concepts that are most preferred or actively sought.

3 Assess the appeal of the new concept or product for different target segments.

4 Provide necessary information for designing and redesigning new products.

> **Concept and product testing** and **Test marketing** Information for decisions on product improvements and new product introductions.

Test marketing, on the other hand, is concerned with testing of a finished new product on an actual market. It differs from concept and product testing in three aspects. First, in concept and product testing, the object under scrutiny is either just a new product concept or an unfinished product. Second, in test marketing, the people being tested are real consumers on the market spot, whilst in concept and product testing, they are only respondents recruited by the company. Third, the number of people being tested is much higher in test marketing than in concept and product testing.

Programme Development

The information requirements for programme development concentrate on all the components of the marketing mix: product, price, promotion, and distribution. Managers combine these components to form the total marketing effort for each market targeted. While at first sight this may appear to be an easy task, decision makers must remember that the success of the total marketing effort relies heavily on synergy. It is critical that the marketing mix not only contains the right elements but does so in the right amounts, at the right time, and in the proper sequence. Ensuring that this synergy occurs is the responsibility of market researchers.

Product Portfolio Analysis

Within product portfolio analysis, the total product line typically is the focal point of investigation. Market researchers design studies that help product managers make decisions about reducing costs, altering marketing mixes, and changing or deleting product lines. Two types of study are customer satisfaction studies and service quality studies.

Customer satisfaction studies assess the strengths and weaknesses customers perceive in a firm's marketing mix. While these studies are usually designed to analyse the marketing mix collectively, many firms elect to focus on customer responses to one element at a time (e.g. degree of satisfaction to the price). Regardless of their scope, customer satisfaction studies concentrate on measuring customer attitudes. Research indicates that customer attitudes are linked to perception of company image, purchase intentions, brand switching and brand loyalty. Attitude information allows management to make intelligent decisions regarding product or brand repositioning, new product introduction, pruning of ineffective products and new market segments. Chapters 11 and 12 discuss the design and development of attitudinal research studies.

> **Customer satisfaction studies** These studies assess the strengths and weaknesses that customers perceive in a firm's marketing mix.

Service quality studies are designed to measure the degree to which an organization conforms to the quality level customers expect. Service quality studies concentrate on physical facilities and equipment, appearance and behaviour of company personnel, and dependability of the company and its products. For example, employees will usually be rated on their general willingness to help customers and provide them with prompt and friendly treatment.

> **Service quality studies** Are designed to measure the degree to which an organization conforms to the quality level customers expect.

A popular service quality study is the mystery shopper study, in which trained professional shoppers visit, for example, retail stores and/or financial institutions, and 'shop' for various goods and services. Atmosphere, friendliness and customer appreciation are just a few of the dimensions evaluated by mystery shoppers. Some firms also patronize their competitors to see how their own performance compares. Data from service quality studies have been invaluable for decision making related to products or services. For example, firms can anticipate problems in product or service offerings before they get out of hand. Also, the data enable firms to assess themselves relative to competitors on key strengths and weaknesses.

Distribution Decisions

Distribution decisions take into account the distributors and retailers that link producers with end users. The distribution channel used by a producer can strongly influence a buyer's perception of the brand. For example, Rolex watches are distributed through a limited number of retailers that project a prestigious image consistent with the Rolex brand name. Three common types of distribution-related research methods are *cycle time research, retailing research*, and *logistic assessment*.

With many businesses moving to control inventory costs, automatic replenishment systems and electronic data interchange are becoming widely used. Closely associated with such inventory systems is **cycle time research**, which centres on reducing the time between the initial contact with a customer and the final delivery (or installation) of the product. This research is most often conducted for large distribution networks that consist of manufacturers, wholesalers, and retailers. Cycle time research does not ignore shorter channels of distribution (direct to retailer or end user), for in many cases, such as direct marketing, it becomes critical in exploring ways to increase customer satisfaction and fulfilment. Here marketing research makes contributions by collecting information that will help reduce costs in the total cycle time, as well as exploring alternative methods of distribution to reduce the time frame in the delivery and installation of goods.

> **Cycle time research** A research method that focuses on reducing the time between the initial contact and final delivery (or installation) of the product.

Two common research practices in this area are delivery expense studies and alternative delivery systems studies. The former seeks to obtain expense information for each delivery system being currently used, while the latter attempts to explore the viability of alternative delivery systems (e.g. post office, DHL). Both aim at providing a high degree of customer satisfaction in a cost-effective manner. Such studies rely heavily on internal company records or databases. Usually referred to as secondary research, these studies are becoming more common. Chapter 3 is devoted to information-gathering procedures at a secondary level.

Retailing research includes studies on a variety of topics. Because retailers are viewed as independent businesses, many of the studies we have discussed are applicable to the retail environment. Yet, at the same time, the information needs of retailers are unique. Market research studies peculiar to retailers include trade area analysis, store image/perception studies, in-store traffic pattern studies, and location analysis.

> **Retailing research** Studies on topics such as trade area analysis, store image/perception, in-store traffic patterns, and location analysis.

Because retailing is a high-customer-contact activity, much retailing research focuses on database development through optical scanning procedures. As illustrated in Exhibit 1.3, every time a salesperson records a transaction using an optical scanner, the scanner notes the type of product, its manufacturer and vendor and its size and price. Marketing research then

EXHIBIT 1.3 Information Collection Process through Retail Optical Scanning

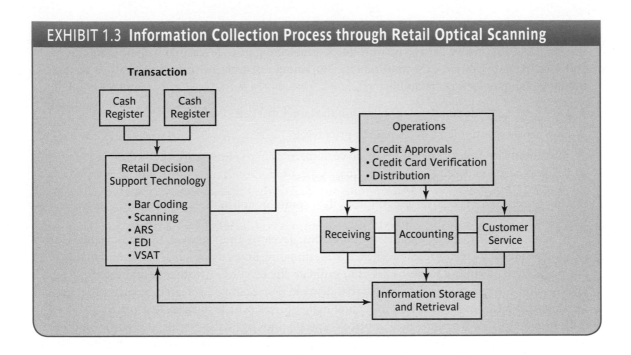

categorizes the data and combines it with other relevant information to form a database. As a result, retailers can find out what television programmes their customers watch, the kinds of neighbourhoods they live in, and the types of stores they prefer to patronize. Such information helps retailers determine what kind of merchandise to stock and what factors may influence purchase decisions.

Marketing research related to **logistic assessment** is an often overlooked area in distribution decisions. One reason for this is that it traditionally has been driven by secondary data, that is, information not gathered for the study at hand but for some other purpose. This type of information in logistics enables market researchers to conduct total cost analysis and service sensitivity analysis.

> **Logistic assessment** Information in logistics allows market researchers to conduct total cost analysis and service sensitivity analysis.

Total cost analysis explores the alternative logistic system designs a firm can use to achieve its performance objective at the lowest total cost. The role of marketing research is to develop an activity-based cost information system by identifying key factors that affect transportation, inventory, and warehousing costs.

Service sensitivity analysis helps organizations design basic customer service programmes by evaluating cost-to-service trade-offs. In conducting this type of analysis, market researchers look for ways to increase various basic services by making adjustments in transportation activities, inventory levels, or location planning. Each adjustment is analysed relative to its impact on corresponding total costs.

Pricing Decisions

Pricing decisions involve pricing new products, establishing price levels in test-market situations, and modifying prices for existing products. Marketing research must provide answers to such fundamental questions as the following:

1 How large is the demand potential within the target market?
2 How sensitive is demand to changes in price levels?
3 What nonprice factors are important to customers?
4 What are the sales forecasts at various price levels?

Pricing research can take a variety of forms. Two common approaches are *demand analysis* and *sales forecasting.*

When a company evaluates a new product idea, develops a test market, or plans changes for existing products, a critical research challenge is estimating how customers will respond to different price levels. **Demand analysis** seeks to estimate the level of customer demand for a given product and the underlying reasons for that demand. For example, research indicates that customers often buy more of certain products at higher prices, which suggests that price may be an indication of quality. The influence of price on perceptions of quality seems to occur most often when customers are unable to evaluate the product themselves. The chemical firm DuPont, using demand analysis, also obtains measures of nonprice factors for its products. Among those factors are delivery, service, innovation, brand name and quality.

> **Demand analysis** A research method that seeks to estimate the level of customer demand for a given product and the underlying reasons for that demand.

Demand analysis often incorporates a test marketing procedure. This involves the actual marketing of a product in one of several cities with the intent of measuring customer sensitivity to changes in a firm's marketing mix. Test marketing is discussed in detail in Chapter 8. Demand analysis can also incorporate end-user research studies and analysis of historical price and quality data for specific products.

Closely associated with demand analysis is **sales forecasting**. After demand analysis identifies the variables that affect customer demand, sales forecasting uses those variables to provide estimates of financial outcomes for different price strategies.

> **Sales forecasting** Uses variables that affect customer demand to provide estimates of financial outcomes for different price strategies.

Although a variety of sales forecasting techniques exist, most can be placed in one of two categories: qualitative or quantitative. Qualitative techniques include user expectation studies, sales-force composites, juries of executive opinion and Delphi techniques. Quantitative forecasting techniques include market testing, time series analysis, and statistical demand analysis.

Integrated Marketing Communication Decisions

Promotional decisions, many times viewed as integrated marketing communications, are important influences on any company's sales. Companies spend billions of dollars yearly on various promotional activities. Given the heavy level of expenditures devoted to promotional activities, it is essential that companies design studies that will generate optimum returns from the promotional investment.

Marketing research methods used to acquire information about the performance of a promotional programme must consider the entire programme. Employing the appropriate methodology, estimating adequate sample sizes, and developing the proper scaling techniques are just three key areas of promotional research. Each of these areas is used when considering the three most common research tasks of integrated marketing communications: advertising effectiveness studies, attitudinal research and sales tracking.

Because advertising serves so many purposes and covers so many objectives, advertising effectiveness studies often vary across situations. **Advertising effectiveness studies** may be qualitative, quantitative, or both. They may take place in laboratory-type settings or in real-life settings. Measures of the effectiveness of an advertisement may be taken before or at various times after media placement. Regardless, the key elements of advertising effectiveness studies are what is being measured, when the measurement is made, and which medium is being used.

> **Advertising effectiveness studies** Focus on what is being measured, when the measurement is made and which medium is being used.

Most advertising effectiveness studies focus on measuring a particular advertisement's ability to generate awareness, communicate product benefits, or create a favourable predisposition about a product. In attempting to accomplish such measurement objectives, market researchers usually include attitudinal research within the advertising effectiveness study.

Attitudinal research can be categorized into three types. First is the *cognitive approach*, which attempts to measure consumers' knowledge and opinions about a given product or brand. Second, *affect approaches* measure consumers' overall impressions of a product or brand. These impressions are usually associated with dimensions like good/bad, pleasant/unpleasant, or positive/negative. Third, *behavioural approaches* seek to measure consumers' specific behaviours (brand loyalty, brand switching, etc.) with regard to a given product or brand. Because many promotional strategies are designed to affect consumers' attitudes, the results of attitudinal research play an important role in the design and implementation of promotional programmes.

> **Attitudinal research** Can take a cognitive approach, affect approach or behavioural approach to measure consumer attitudes.

Personal selling also plays a major role in a firm's promotional mix. The objectives assigned to salespeople frequently involve expected sales results such as sales quotas. Nonsales objectives are also important and may include increasing new accounts, evaluating middlemen, or achieving set levels of customer service. Both forms of objectives are commonly tied to the evaluation of a salesperson's overall performance. Several variables must be considered in this evaluation process, which uses a technique commonly called **sales tracking**. From the standpoint of marketing research, key information must be gathered on salespeople and placed into the proper units of analysis in order to provide adjustments for factors beyond the control of individual salespeople. Sales-tracking procedures allow for this adjustment by assessing a combination of objective and subjective performance dimensions.

> **Sales tracking** Gather information on salespeople in order to provide adjustments for factors beyond the control of individual salespeople.

A sales-tracking form can be devised in order to capture the key information provided by salespeople. Typically the form includes standard industrial classification (SIC) codes, annual sales, and number of employees. The form also illustrates the effectiveness of the selling function by documenting who sold the product, the number of sales calls required to close the sale, and the profit generated. A well-designed sales tracking system such as this helps managers diagnose performance-related problems and determine corrective actions that may be necessary.

Programme Tracking

After the programme has been implemented, it needs systematic tracking in order to monitor the performance of the programme continuously, and if necessary, take appropriate action to adjust the contents of the programme for improving its performance. The role of marketing research here is to conduct a series of analyses of the performance of the programme concerned.

Programme Control

Two key areas of focus are product analysis and environmental forecasting. **Product analysis** attempts to identify the relative importance of product selection criteria to buyers and rate brands against these criteria. Such analysis is conducted throughout the life cycle of the product or brand. It is particularly useful when developing the strengths-and-weaknesses section of a marketing plan. Many of the standardized information services provided by marketing research firms, such as Information Resources and AC Nielsen, monitor the performance of competing brands across a wide variety of products.

> **Product analysis** Identifies the relative importance of product selection criteria to buyers and rates brands against these criteria.

Environmental forecasting is used to predict external occurrences that can affect the long-term strategy of a firm. This technique usually involves a three-phase process that begins with a survey of customers and industry experts. This is followed by a market test to measure customer response to a particular marketing programme and, finally, an analysis of internal company records to determine past buying behaviours. The net result is an accumulation of data

> **Environmental forecasting** A research method used to predict external occurrences that can affect the long-term strategy of a firm.

pertaining to industry trends, customer profiles, and environmental changes that allows a company to adapt its strategy to anticipated future events.

Critical Information Analysis

Critical information is concerned with the type of information that has the potential to help companies to develop a competitive advantage. For many companies, the task of critical information analysis is achieved through the development of a sophisticated **marketing decision support system (MDSS)**, a company-developed database used to analyse company performance and control marketing activities.

> **Marketing decision support system (MDSS)** A company-developed database used to analyse company performance and control marketing activities.

The MDSS includes standardized marketing research reports, sales and cost data, product-line sales, advertising data, and price information. This information is organized to correspond to specific units of analysis (market segments, geographic locations, particular vendors), and is used for various decisions from reordering inventory to launching new products. The value of the MDSS becomes most apparent when the system focuses on decision making at the strategic level.

One industry in which the MDSS has been popularly used is the airline industry. The MDSS adopted in this industry can usually provide the facility for the determination of mileage awards for frequent flyers and a reservation support database which is organized according to different market segments. Through the effective use of the system, airline companies would be able to locate the most important market segments so that they can put more emphasis on the needs of these segments. For example, an airline company may discover that the top 5 per cent of the customers account for almost 50 per cent of its sales. These key customers are highlighted on all service screens and reports. Ticket agents are alerted when one of these customers phones in or arrives, so they can offer a variety of special services, such as first-class upgrades.

New technologies for collecting, processing, and analysing market research data are rapidly changing organizations in a variety of ways. Many experts predict that technologies associated with the MDSS will reduce the need for primary data-collection methods in the future. The impact of the MDSS on marketing research will be discussed in Chapter 3.

The Marketing Research Industry

The marketing research industry has experienced healthy growth in recent years. According to ESOMAR, the industry's worldwide turnover in 2007 was €20.61 billion, which represented 3.8% inflation-adjusted growth over the previous year. Europe occupied the largest share (45%)

EXHIBIT 1.4 Top 20 Countries with Highest Market Research Spend per Capita in 2007

Country	Spend per Capita (€)
Sweden	33.87591
UK	33.24088
France	31.29197
Norway	24.63504
Germany	23.61314
Australia	21.67153
USA	21.09489
Finland	21
Denmark	20.9562
Switzerland	19.76642
Netherlands	17.67153
Ireland	17.57664
Canada	17.0146
New Zealand	16.73723
Belgium	13.32847
Austria	13.29927
Spain	11.86861
Italy	10.67153
Luxembourg	10.62774
Hong Kong	9.664234

Converted from US$ to € based on the exchange rate provided by IMF.

of the market, followed by North America (34%), Asia Pacific (14%), Central and Latin America (5%), and the Middle East and S Africa (2%).

The fact that Europe occupied nearly half of the global market research turnover is no surprise, as the fierce competition in various sectors and the cultural diversity among European countries force companies interested in the European market to conduct market research in order to have an accurate and comprehensive understanding of the competition they face and the consumers they target. Exhibit 1.4 shows that among the top 20 countries with highest market research spend per capita, 15 are European countries.

As shown in Exhibit 1.4, Sweden has the highest market research spend per capita, while the UK is the second highest. In comparison to all its neighbouring European countries, the UK generates the largest market research turnover. As of 2005, the top 20 marketing research companies in the UK are, in descending order, TNS, Ipsos MORI, Gfk (including NOP), Information Resources, Luminas, ORC International, Flamingo International, Lorien Research, Marketing Sciences, Quaestor, ESA Market Research, Nunwood, BDRC Group, RONIN Corporation, Conquest Research, RDSi (including Field Initiatives), mruk, Accent, Maven Management and Perspective.

According to Boddy's (2001) study, perceived reasons for the success of the UK market research industry are specialization and niche positioning, commercial orientation, well-organized selling, marketing orientation, corporate credibility, increasing need for market intelligence, international research coordination, branded market research products, individual researcher credibility and adherence to objective quality control measures.

In the long term, the global marketing research industry is expected to continue to grow steadily in mature markets such as the old EU countries and the US, and more rapidly in developing countries. The more rapid economic growth of an increasing number of developing countries, such as China and India, necessitates greater understanding of these previously less known markets and therefore presents numerous business opportunities to the marketing research industry.

In order to compete more successfully in the increasingly lucrative yet competitive market, marketing research companies have been engaged in mergers and acquisitions among themselves in recent years. As of 2007, the top 25 global marketing research companies are all from the US, the UK, Germany, France, Japan and Brazil, and the top 1000 clients now account for approximately 80 per cent of the global marketing research expenditure.

EXHIBIT 1.5 Top 25 Global Marketing Research Companies

Rank	Company	Headquarters	Parent Country
1	The Nielsen Company	Haarlem, New York, NY	USA
2	IMS Health Inc.	Norwalk, CT	USA
3	Taylor Nelson Sofres Plc.	London	UK
4	GfK AG	Nuremberg	Germany
5	The Kantar Group	Fairfield, CT, London	UK
6	Ipsos Group S.A.	Paris	France
7	Synovate	Chicago	USA
8	Information Resources Inc.	London	UK
9	Westat Inc.	Rockville, MD	USA
10	Arbitron Inc.	New York, NY	USA
11	INTAGE Inc.	Tokyo	Japan
12	J.D. Power and Associates	Fenton, NJ, Westlake Village, CA	USA
13	Harris Interactive Inc.	Westlake Village, CA, Rochester, NY	USA
14	Maritz Research	Rochester, NY, Fenton, NJ	USA
15	The NPD Group Inc.	Omaha, Nebraska, Port Washington, NY	USA
16	Opinion Research/Guideline Corp.	Tokyo, Princeton, NJ	USA
17	Video Research Ltd.	Tokyo, Port Washington, NY	Japan
18	IBOPE Group	São Paulo	Brazil
19	Lieberman Research Worldwide	Los Angeles, CA	USA
20	comScore Inc.	Reston, VA	USA
21	Cello Research & Consulting	London	UK
22	Market Strategies International	Los Angeles, CA	USA
23	BVA Group.	Paris	France
24	OTX	Los Angeles, CA	USA
25	Dentsu Research Inc.	Tokyo	Japan

Types of Marketing Research Firms

Marketing research providers can be classified as either internal or external, or custom or standardized. Internal research providers are normally organizational units that reside within a company. There are a number of benefits to keeping the marketing research function internal; these benefits include research method consistency, shared information across the company, minimized spending on research, and ability to produce actionable research results.

Other firms choose to use external sources for marketing research. External sources, usually referred to as marketing research suppliers, perform all aspects of the research, including study design, questionnaire production, interviewing, data analysis and report preparation. These firms operate on a fee basis and commonly submit a research proposal to be used by a client for evaluation and decision purposes. An actual example of a proposal is provided in the Marketing Research in Action at the end of Chapter 2.

Many companies use external research suppliers because, first, the suppliers can be more objective and less subject to company politics and regulations than internal suppliers. Second, many external suppliers provide specialized talents that, for the same cost, internal suppliers could not provide. And finally, companies can choose external suppliers on a study-by-study basis and thus gain greater flexibility in scheduling studies as well as matching specific project requirements to the talents of specific research firms.

Marketing research firms also can be considered customized or standardized. Customized research firms provide specialized, highly tailored services to the client. Many firms in this line of business concentrate their research activities in one specific area such as brand name testing, test marketing, or new product development. For example, Namestormers assists companies in brand name selection and recognition, Survey Sampling International concentrates on sampling development for client companies, and Uniscore conducts studies designed around retail scanning data. In contrast, standardized research firms provide more general services. These firms also follow a more common approach in research design so that the results of a study conducted for one client can be compared to norms established by studies done for other clients. Examples of these firms are Burke Market Research, which conducts day-after advertising recall; AC Nielsen (separate from Nielsen Media Research), which conducts store audits for a variety of retail firms; and Arbitron Ratings, which provides primary data collection regarding commercial television.

Many standardized research firms also provide syndicated business services, which include audits, purchase diary panels, and advertising recall data made or developed from a common data pool or database. A prime example of a syndicated business service is a database established through the retail optical scanner method. One such database, available from AC Nielsen and operated through the Scantrack system, tracks the retail sales of thousands of grocery brand-name products. This data can be customized for a variety of industries (confectionery, beverage, etc.) to indicate volume sales by channel, region or period of time in a given industry. The Closer Look at Research box illustrates further the Scantrack system and an example of results that it produces.

 ## A Closer Look at Research *(In the field)*
Scantrack: Scanning and Tracking UK Grocery Brands

Scantrack uses the retail optical scanner method to monitor weekly sales from a nationwide network of EPoS checkout scanners. Coverage includes grocery multiples, co-ops, multiple off-licences, independents, symbol groups and multiple forecourts, who will be sent back the Scantrack data for their category planning and marketing strategy purposes. Scantrack accounts for more than 80% of every £1 spent in UK grocery with full scanning inputs. Therefore, the information of the top 100 UK grocery brands (the following lists the top 30) compiled from the store audit data by Scantrack can be regarded as highly reliable.

Top 30 Grocery Brands in the UK

Brand	2006 Sales (£'000)	Year on Year Change
1. Coca Cola	942,391	5.0
2. Warburtons	514,341	17.7
3. Walkers	424,002	4.0
4. Hovis	403,126	16.1
5. Cadbury Dairy Milk	361,503	−2.5
6. Nescafe	331,265	−0.8
7. Andrex	326,646	5.2
8. Lucozade	296,216	16.5
9. Kingsmill	282,318	−4.9
10. Robinsons	277,285	4.6
11. Tropicana	222,471	27.4
12. Persil Laundry	217,010	−0.4
13. Pepsi	216,343	−4.8
14. Whiskas	216,126	9.8
15. Pedigree	191,990	2.5
16. Flora Spreads	185,237	3.4
17. Müller Corner	183,161	3.0
18. McCann Frozen Chips	182,249	7.3
19. Lurpak Spreads	175,838	6.8
20. Heinz Baked Beans	175,222	3.3
21. Ariel	174,211	−5.9
22. Bernard Matthews Cooked Meat	173,598	−6.5
23. Wrigley's Extra	169,397	2.0
24. Bold	166,915	10.2
25. Felix	161,476	−5.3
26. Galaxy	159,157	11.7
27. Birds Eye Frozen Fish	158,755	14.1
28. Heinz Soups	156,535	−2.4
29. Ribena	153,046	0.3
30. Volvic	148,214	13.1

Source: Adapted with permission from Nielsen, which owns Scantrack.

In addition, some firms act as either brokers or facilitators to provide marketing research services for their clients. **Brokers** provide the ancillary tasks that complement many marketing

Brokers Businesses that provide ancillary tasks to complement a specific marketing research study.

research studies. For example, marketing research suppliers and clients who do not have the resources for data entry, tabulation, or analysis will typically use a broker service to facilitate the data management process. Brokers usually offer specialized programming, canned statistical packages, and other data management tools at low cost.

Facilitators are businesses that perform marketing research functions as a supplement to a broader marketing research project. Advertising agencies, field service providers and independent consultants are usually classified as facilitators because they help companies complete broader marketing projects.

> **Facilitators** Businesses that perform marketing research functions as a supplement to a broader marketing research project.

Advertising agencies are in the business of designing, implementing, and evaluating advertising campaigns for individual clients. Many agencies use their own research services to guide the development of the campaign and test for effectiveness. In this instance, the advertising agency provides marketing research to facilitate the advertising campaign process.

> **Advertising agencies** Businesses that design, implement and evaluate advertising campaigns for individual clients; many of them use their own marketing research services to accomplish the advertising tasks assigned by clients.

The primary responsibilities of **field service providers** are to schedule, supervise, and complete a field work study by executing chosen methods such as focus groups, depth interviews and questionnaire survey. In essence, they perform primary data collection services required for a specific marketing research project.

> **Field service providers** Businesses that schedule, supervise and complete field work studies assigned by individual clients.

Independent consultants, the third kind of facilitators, are usually hired ad hoc by client companies to complement strategic planning activities for clients. Many consultants, offering unique and specialized research skills, are assigned the tasks to facilitate a total quality management programme, develop a marketing information system, or train employees in the procedures of marketing research.

> **Independent consultants** Businesses that are usually hired ad hoc by client companies to complement strategy planning activities for their clients.

As this discussion shows, marketing research is a diverse industry. Diversity, coupled with increased revenue growth in the industry, has created job opportunities for people with a variety of skills. Furthermore, as more and more marketing research projects take on an international flavour, these opportunities will continue to expand. The following section addresses what skills will be needed in the industry.

Changing Skills for a Changing Industry

Marketing research employees represent a vast diversity of cultures, technology and personalities. As marketing research companies, notably from Europe and USA, expand their geographic scope overseas, the requirements for successfully executing marketing research projects will change dramatically. Many fundamental skill requirements will remain in place, but new and innovative practices will require a totally unique skill base that is more comprehensive than ever before.

In a survey of 100 marketing research companies, basic fundamental business skills were rated high for potential employees. Communication skills (verbal and written), interpersonal skills (ability to work with others), and statistical skills were the leading attributes in basic job aptitude. More specifically, the top five skills these marketing research companies hope to find in candidates for marketing research positions are (1) the ability to understand and interpret secondary data, (2) presentation skills, (3) foreign language competency, (4) negotiation skills, and (5) computer proficiency. Results of this survey indicate there has been a shift from analytical to execution skill requirements in the marketing research industry. In the future, analysing existing databases, multicultural interaction, and negotiation are likely to be important characteristics of marketing researchers. Marketing research jobs are discussed further in Appendix 1 at page 691.

Ethics in Marketing Research Practices

There arc many opportunities for both ethical and unethical behaviours to occur in the research process. The major sources of ethical dilemmas in marketing research are the interactions among the three key groups: (1) the research provider (e.g. researcher, research organization, or its representatives); (2) the research user (e.g. client company, decision maker); and (3) the respondents (e.g. subjects under investigation).

 ## A Closer Look at Research *(In the field)*

Hotels in Britain and Ireland May Have Breached Ethics in Marketing Research Practices

Hotels could be breaking data protection laws by storing personal information about guests on computer files – ranging from details about home life to whether they misbehaved during their stay.

'This is potentially problematic', a spokeswoman for the Information Commissioner's office said.

Information stored includes marital status, number of children, age, nationality, home town, pastimes and occupation. Some hotels store names of guests' overnight companions and dining companions, whether they are heavy drinkers, have been rude or polite, whether they have paid for 'adult films', and whether they have used drugs or taken part in 'immoral activities' such as using prostitutes.

Less sensitive records are kept of interests such as favourite sports, films, plays, books, and newspapers. Hotels use Internet searches and information gleaned by staff to form files that are distributed to doormen, receptionists, waiters and chambermaids – usually with downloaded pictures.

Employees at Jumeirah Hotels are shown guest dossiers that are pinned to noticeboards in staff areas. 'We believe in a systematic approach to customer service', said David Picot, Jumeirah Hotels' regional general manager for Europe. 'Doormen don't just know guests' names, they have their resumes. We Google it. We build a profile for all guests: their job, family, how many days they usually stay.' He said that 'if a customer has misbehaved or done something that's immoral or illegal, like drugs, we'd store that.' Other hotel chains including Fairmount, Four Seasons, Inter-Continental, the Eton Collection, and Starwood keep guest histories.

A spokesman for the Dylan Hotel in Dublin said: 'a profile is kept on every guest', including who corporate clients have stayed overnight with and 'certain drinks they like'. The Inter-Continental Carlton Cannes has a database including details of favourite television channels. The Lace Market Hotel in Nottingham says that it uses Google to find images of guests.

Source: The Times, 2008.

Unethical Activities by the Research User

Decisions and practices of the research users present opportunities for unethical behaviour. One such behaviour is when they request a detailed research proposal from several competing research providers with no intention of selecting a firm to conduct the research. In this situation, they solicit the proposals for the purpose of learning how to conduct the necessary marketing research themselves. Research users can obtain first drafts of questionnaires, sampling frames and sampling procedures, and knowledge on data collection procedures. Then, unethically, they can use the information either to perform the research project themselves or bargain for a better price among interested research companies.

Unfortunately, another common behaviour of unethical clients or decision makers is promising a prospective research provider a long-term relationship or additional projects in order to obtain a very low price on the initial research project. Then, after the researcher completes the initial project, the research user forgets about the long-term promises.

Unethical Activities by the Research Provider

While there might be numerous opportunities for the researcher provider (the researcher, the research organization, or its representatives) to act unethically in the process of conducting a study, there are five major sources of unethical activities that can originate within the research organization. First, a policy of unethical pricing practices is a common source of conflict. For example, after quoting a set overall price for a proposed research project, the researcher may tell the decision maker that variable cost items such as travel expenses, monetary response incentives, or fees charged for computer time are extra, over and above the quoted price. Such 'soft' costs can be easily used to manipulate the total project cost.

Second, all too often research firms just simply do not provide the promised incentive (e.g. contest awards, gifts, even money) to respondents for completing the interviews or questionnaires. Also, many firms will delay indefinitely the fees owed to field workers (e.g. interviewers, data tabulators, data entry personnel). Usually, these parties are paid at the project's completion and thus lose any leverage they have with the research provider to collect on services rendered.

Third, it is not uncommon for the researcher or the organization to create respondent abuse. Research organizations have a tendency to state that interviews are very short when in reality they may last up to one hour. Other situations of known respondent abuse include selling the respondents' names and demographic data to other companies without their approval, using infrared dye on questionnaires to trace selective respondents for the purpose of making a sales call, or using hidden tape recorders in a personal interviewing situation without the respondent's permission.

Fourth, an unethical practice found all too often in marketing research is the selling of unnecessary or unwarranted research services. While it is perfectly acceptable to sell follow-up research that can aid the client's or decision maker's company, selling bogus services is completely unethical.

Lastly, there are several researcher-related unethical practices within the execution of the research design such as (1) falsifying data, (2) duplicating actual response data, and (3) consciously manipulating the data structures inappropriately.

A practice of data falsification known to many researchers and field interviewers is called curbstoning (or rocking-chair) interviewing. This occurs when the researcher's trained interviewers or observers, rather than conducting interviews or observing respondents' actions as directed in the study, will complete the interviews themselves or make up 'observed' respondents' behaviours. Other falsification practices include having friends and relatives fill out surveys, not using the designated sample of sample respondents but rather anyone who is conveniently available to complete the survey, or not following up on the established callback procedures indicated in the research procedure.

Another variation of data falsification is duplication of responses or the creation of 'phantom' respondents. This is a process whereby a researcher or field personnel (e.g. interviewer, field observer, or data entry personnel) will take an actual respondent's data and duplicate it to represent a second set of responses. This practice artificially creates data responses from people who were scheduled to be in the study but who for some reason were not actually interviewed. To minimize the likelihood of data falsification, research organizations typically randomly verify 10 to 15 per cent of the interviews. Finally, researchers act unethically when they consciously manipulate data structures from data analysis procedures for the purpose of reporting a biased picture to the decision maker, or do not report selected findings at all.

Unethical Activities by the Respondent

The primary unethical practice of respondents or subjects in any research endeavour is that of providing dishonest answers or of faking behaviour. The general expectation is that when a subject has freely consented to participate, they will provide truthful responses, but truthfulness might be more difficult to achieve than one thinks. Some procedures are available to researchers to help evaluate the honesty of respondents' answers or actions. For example, bipolar questioning is used as a consistency check in surveys. Here the first question is framed in a positive way and the second question is framed in a negative way. The respondent's answers, if consistent, would be inversely related.

Other areas of possible ethical dilemmas within a researcher–respondent relationship are (1) the respondent's right to privacy; (2) the need to disguise the true purpose of the research; and (3) the respondent's right to be informed about certain aspects of the research process, including the sponsorship of the research.

Marketing Research Codes of Ethics

Of increasing importance to today's ethical business decision-making processes is the establishment of company ethics programmes. These programmes offer perhaps a decent chance of minimizing unethical behaviour within the company concerned. Many marketing research companies have established internal company codes of ethics derived from the ethical codes formulated by larger institutions (ESOMAR as a main example) that govern today's marketing research industry. Exhibit 1.6 displays the rules of the International Code of Marketing and Social Research Practice developed by ICC (International Chamber of Commerce) and ESOMAR. This Code and its accompanying rules provide a framework for identifying ethical issues and arriving at ethical decisions in situations researchers sometimes face.

EXHIBIT 1.6 Rules of ICC/ESOMAR International Code of Marketing and Social Research Practice

A. General

1 Marketing research must be carried out objectively and in accordance with established scientific principles.

2 Marketing research must always conform to the national and international legislation which applies in those countries involved in a given research project.

B. The rights of respondents

3 Respondents' cooperation in a marketing research project is entirely voluntary at all stages. They must not be misled when being asked for their cooperation.

4 Respondents' anonymity must be strictly preserved. If the respondent on request from the researcher has given permission for data to be passed on in a form which allows that respondent to be personally identified:

(a) the respondent must first have been told to whom the information would be supplied and the purposes for which it will be used, and also

(b) the researcher must ensure that the information will not be used for any non-research purpose and that the recipient of the information has agreed to conform to the requirements of this Code.

5 The researcher must take all reasonable precautions to ensure that respondents are in no way directly harmed or adversely affected as a result of their participation in a marketing research project.

6 The researcher must take special care when interviewing children and young people. The informed consent of the parent or responsible adult must first be obtained for interviews with children.

7 Respondents must be told (normally at the beginning of the interview) if observation techniques or recording equipment are being used, except where these are used in a public place. If a respondent so wishes, the record or relevant section of it must be destroyed or deleted. Respondents' anonymity must not be infringed by the use of such methods.

8 Respondents must be enabled to check without difficulty the identity and bona fides of the researcher.

C. The professional responsibilities of researchers

9   Researchers must not, whether knowingly or negligently, act in any way which could bring discredit on the marketing research profession or lead to a loss of public confidence in it.

10   Researchers must not make false claims about their skills and experience or about those of their organization.

11   Researchers must not unjustifiably criticize or disparage other researchers.

12   Researchers must always strive to design research which is cost efficient and of adequate quality, and then to carry this out to the specifications agreed with the client.

13   Researchers must ensure the security of all research records in their possession.

14   Researchers must not knowingly allow the dissemination of conclusions from a marketing research project which are not adequately supported by the data. They must always be prepared to make available the technical information necessary to assess the validity of any published findings.

15   When acting in their capacity as researchers the latter must not undertake any non-research activities, for example database marketing involving data about individuals which will be used for direct marketing and promotional activities. Any such non-research activities must always, in the way they are organized and carried out, be clearly differentiated from marketing research activities.

D. The mutual rights and responsibilities of researchers and clients

16   These rights and responsibilities will normally be governed by a written contract between the researcher and the client. The parties may amend the provisions of Rules 19 – 23 below if they have agreed to this in writing beforehand, but the other requirements of his Code may not be altered in this way. Marketing research must also always be conducted according to the principles of fair competition, as generally understood and accepted.

17   The researcher must inform the client if the work to be carried out for that client is to be combined or syndicated in the same project with work for other clients but must not disclose the identity of such clients.

18   The researcher must inform the client as soon as possible in advance when any part of the work for that client is to be subcontracted outside the researcher's own organization (including the use of any outside consultants). On request the client must be told the identity of any such sub-contractor.

19   The client does not have the right, without prior agreement between parties involved, to exclusive use of the researcher's services or those of his organization, whether in whole or in part. In carrying out work for different clients, however, the researcher must endeavour to avoid possible clashes of interest between the services provided to those clients.

20   The following records remain the property of the client and must not be disclosed by the researcher to any third party without the client's permission:

   (a) marketing research briefs, specifications and other information provided by the client

   (b) the research data and findings from a marketing research project (except in the case of syndicated or multi-client projects or services where the same data are available to more than one client).

The client has however no right to know the names and addresses of respondents unless the latter's explicit permission for this has first been obtained by the researcher (this particular requirement cannot be altered under Rule 16).

▶ 21 Unless it is specifically agreed to the contrary, the following records remain the property of the researcher:

(a) marketing research proposals and cost quotations (unless these have been paid for by the client). They must not be disclosed by the client to any third party, other than to a consultant working for the client on that project (with the exception of any consultant working also for a competitor of the researcher). In particular, they must not be used by the client to influence research proposals or cost quotations from other researchers.

(b) the contents of a report in the case of syndicated and/or multi-client projects or services where the same data are available to more than one client and where it is clearly understood that the resulting reports are available for general purchase or subscription. The client may not disclose the findings of such research to any third party (other than to his own consultants and advisors for use in connection with his business) without the permission of the researcher.

(c) all other research records prepared by the researcher (with the exception in the case of non-syndicated projects of the report to the client, and also the research design and questionnaire where the costs of developing these are covered by the charges paid by the client).

22 The researcher must conform to currently agreed professional practice relating to the keeping of such records for an appropriate period of time after the end of the project. On request the researcher must supply the client with duplicate copies of such records provided that such duplicates do not breach anonymity and confidentiality requirements (Rule 4); that the request is made within the agreed time limit for keeping the records; and that the client pays the reasonable costs of providing the duplicates.

23 The researcher must not disclose the identity of the client (provided there is no legal obligation to do so), or any confidential information about the latter's business, to any third party without the client's permission.

24 The researcher must on request allow the client to arrange for checks on the quality of fieldwork and data preparation provided that the client pays any additional costs involved in this. Any such checks must conform to the requirements of Rule 4.

25 The researcher must provide the client with all appropriate technical details of any research project carried out for that client.

26 When reporting on the results of a marketing research project the researcher must make a clear distinction between the findings as such, the researcher's interpretation of these and any recommendations based on them.

27 Where any of the findings of a research project are published by the client the latter has a responsibility to ensure that these are not misleading. The researcher must be consulted and agree in advance the form and content of publication, and must take action to correct any misleading statements about the research and its findings.

28 Researchers must not allow their names to be used in connection with any research project as an assurance that the latter has been carried out in conformity with this Code unless they are confident that the project has in all respects met the Code's requirements.

29 Researchers must ensure that clients are aware of the existence of this Code and of the need to comply with its requirements.

Besides ESOMAR, the Market Research Society (MRS), which is based in London and has the largest number of members worldwide, has established its Code of Conduct. This will not be fully listed in the book because the Code is essentially based upon and fully compatible with the Code of ESOMAR. Instead the fundamental principles that govern the design of the MRS Code of Conduct are listed in Exhibit 1.7.

EXHIBIT 1.7 Fundamental Principles Governing the Marketing Research Society Code of Conduct

Research is founded upon the willing cooperation of the public and business organizations. It depends upon their confidence that it is conducted honestly, objectively, with unwelcome intrusion, and without harm to respondents. Its purpose is to collect and analyse information, and not directly to create sales, nor to influence the opinions of anyone participating in it. It is in this spirit that the Code of Conduct has been devised.

The general public and other interested parties shall be entitled to complete assurance that every research project is carried out strictly in accordance with this Code, and that their rights of privacy are respected.

In particular, they must be assured that no information that could be used to identify them will be made available without their agreement to anyone outside the agency responsible for conducting the research. They must also be assured that the information they supply will not be used for any purposes other than research and that they will not be adversely affected or embarrassed as a direct result of their participation in a research project.

Wherever possible, respondents must be informed as to the purpose of the research and the likely length of time necessary for the collection of the information. Finally, the research findings themselves must always be reported accurately and never used to mislead anyone, in any way.

Both ESOMAR and MRS believe that adherence to their Codes implies that research is conducted in accordance with the principles of data protection legislations, which are available in all those countries where protection of personal data is viewed as important and should be legally enforced. The first European country to have a law of data protection is Sweden, which was passed in 1973. It predated by one year the passage of similar legislation in the US – the Privacy Act of 1974. The Swedish law had, and continues to have, Far-reaching effects on record keeping and records management in Europe. Since then, many European countries, including Austria, Denmark, Germany, Norway, Belgium, Luxembourg, the Netherlands and the UK, have also passed their data protection laws. France has a very stringent data protection law. In Spain and Portugal, data protections are incorporated into their constitutions. Most of these laws reflect, to varying extents, the provisions of the Council of Europe's Data Protection Convection of 1981.

The data protection legislations in different European countries share largely the same spirit and have similar contents. The corresponding legislation in the UK is the Data Protection Act 1998. According to Data Protection Act 1998, personal data is referred to as data which relates to a living individual who can be identified from the data, or from the data and other information in the possession of, or likely to come into the possession of, the data controller. There are eight Principles in the Act which are described in Exhibit 1.8.

Research ethics is increasingly becoming an essential issue and all decent marketing researchers are expected to adhere to the relevant code and conduct when conducting their marketing research projects. Although the codes of ethics or conduct advocated by marketing research associations cannot guarantee continuous ethical behaviour in marketing research, they represent a big step forward by giving proactive guidance and the appearance of integrity to the marketing research industry.

Emerging Trends

Parallel with the recent and expected growth of the industry, a number of evolving trends have emerged, which present new opportunities and challenges to the professionals in the industry.

EXHIBIT 1.8 The Eight Principles of the UK Data Protection Act 1998

The First Principle

Personal data shall be processed fairly and lawfully.

The Second Principle

Personal data shall be obtained only for one or more specified and lawful purposes, and shall not be further processed in any manner incompatible with that purpose or those purposes.

Exemption: where personal data are not processed to support decisions affecting particular individuals, or in such a way as likely to cause substantial damage or distress to any data subject, such processing will not breach the Second Principle.

The Third Principle

Personal data shall be adequate, relevant and not excessive in relation to the purpose or purposes for which they are processed.

The Fourth Principle

Personal data shall be accurate and, where necessary, kept up to date.

The Fifth Principle

Personal data processed for any purpose or purposes shall not be kept longer than is necessary for that purpose or those purposes.

Exemption: under the circumstances described in Exemption of The Second Principle above, the data may be retained indefinitely despite the Fifth Principle.

The Sixth Principle

Personal data shall be processed in accordance with the rights of data subjects under this Act.

The Seventh Principle

Appropriate technical and organizational measures shall be taken against unauthorized or unlawful processing of personal data and against accidental loss or destruction of, or damage to, personal data.

The Eighth Principle

Personal data shall not be transferred to a country or territory outside the European Economic Area, unless that country or territory ensures an adequate level of protection for the rights and freedoms of data subjects in relation to the processing of personal data.

First, with the ever increasing volume of available secondary data – notably over the Internet – and the escalating cost of marketing research projects charged by reputable marketing research companies, there has been an increased emphasis on secondary data collection methods. Second, the continuous development of new technologies has given marketing researchers new tools to enable them to work more effectively and efficiently, and as a result, there has been a movement towards the adoption of technology-related data management, such as optical scanning data and database technology. Third, the continual development of new technologies also provides an opportunity for marketing research to make increased use of digital technology for information acquisition and retrieval. Fourth, the rapid economic growth of an increasing number of developing countries and the resulting need for marketing research information means that marketing research companies would be more likely than ever to have a broader international client base. Fifth, there has been an increasing emphasis on the provision of business intelligence and insight necessitated by integrated management and use of business information instead of pure data collection and analysis.

Case 1: Red Bull

Dietrich Mateschitz founded the company, Red Bull, in Austria, his native country. As the son of humble primary school teachers, Mateschitz got his trade degree from the University of Vienna and worked at Unilever, Germany's Jacobs Coffee and Blendax for some time. His performance was noticeable such that within seven years of service, he became the director of the International Marketing function at Blendax, which was later acquired by Procter & Gamble. His responsibility at Blendax took him to far-off countries, including Thailand, where he discovered a Japanese syrup tonic drink that sold in pharmacies as a revitalizing agent. After trying the tonic drink himself, he found a way to fight his jetlag. This is when Mateschitz decided to study the tonic market. 'I realized that these little syrups developed in Japan did extremely well all over Asia', he recalls. Mateschitz smelled the potential of the business in the unspoiled Western markets.

It took him three years to finalize the tonic drink formula. The top brand of tonic drink in the Thai market was called Krating Daeng, meaning 'Red Water Buffalo' in Thai. Mateschitz borrowed this brand idea and decided to use the name 'Red Bull', which he believed was more promising for the Western markets. The drink was carbonated for Western palates and was packaged in a slim blue-silver can instead of a bottle. The three key ingredients of the Thai drink – an amino acid called taurine, caffeine, and glucuronolactone, a carbohydrate – were retained.

Before launching, marketing research with consumers was conducted. Results were less than promising. Red Bull was neither very appealing nor did it have a good taste. Some consumers commented that the berry-flavoured beverage tasted medicinal. Further, an 8.3-ounce can of Red Bull comes at a price that is double the price of a 12-ounce can of Coke.

However, Mateschitz decided to ignore the marketing research results and set up offices in Fuschl, a town just outside Salzburg, Austria. Since then sales have been spectacular. Mateschitz recalls, 'When we first started, we said there is no existing market for Red Bull, but Red Bull will

Photography by David Price, Alamy

create it. And this is what finally became true'. He also commented 'There are times to listen to focus groups and times not to. There's a time to 'hear' and there's a time to go for it'. In retrospect, Mateschitz may be correct but taking such an emotional decision is a hard one to legitimize.

Questions

1 Mateschitz ignored the negative research results and went ahead with the launch of Red Bull, which subsequently became a big success in the highly competitive beverage market. Does it imply that marketing research is useless? Justify your answer.

2 In view of the increasingly fierce competition in the energy drink market, Red Bull is contemplating recruiting a marketing research talent who will take full charge of the company's marketing research activities. What necessary and desirable characteristics do you expect that an ideal candidate for the post should possess?

Case 2 (Continuing Case Study): Jimmy Spice's Restaurant

Jimmy Spice's restaurant was first established in Birmingham, UK in 2004. The restaurant serves foods of different ethnic origins, in particular Indian, Thai, Chinese and Italian foods. It is well located on Broad Street, the most popular street for dining, drinking and entertainment. Customer traffic is high, but competition is intense.

The restaurant concept is based on the provision of a wide array of popular ethnic foods, and customers can eat as much as they like at a fixed price. The owner emphasizes the food's exotic appeal by displaying maps, pictures and ingredients from the countries of origin throughout the setting. The restaurant also aims at instilling a fun, festive atmosphere, which is brightly lit and bustling with activity. Fast and friendly service is also part of the restaurant's appear. The target customers are mainly young professionals, university students and families who are looking for an enjoyable meal at an affordable price.

As the competition for dining customers in the city is increasingly intense, the owner of Jimmy Spice's restaurant needs to continuously improve restaurant operations. He needs information in order to better understand what aspects of the restaurant drive customer satisfaction and where it can improve. He has raised a few questions to be researched. Are the customers satisfied and if not, why not? Are there problems with the food, the atmosphere, or some other aspect of restaurant operations (e.g. employees or service)? Is the target market correctly defined or does it need to focus on a different niche? What are the common characteristics of satisfied customers? Answering these and other similar questions will help the owner focus the restaurant's marketing efforts, improve operations, and be in a clearer position to consider expanding the restaurant concept from the UK to other cities in Europe.

Accordingly, Jimmy Spice's restaurant has recruited a local marketing research company to organize for the implementation of a questionnaire survey on 400 customers, and the data

EXHIBIT 1.9 The Use of Jimmy Spice's Restaurant Case study in This Text

Chapter	Conceptual Understanding	SPSS Applications
1	Marketing research activities	Start-up procedures and click-through sequences for selected data analysis techniques
2	Problem definition; Research design	–
3	Database modelling; Technology-enabled market intelligence; Data warehouse; MDSS; GIS	–
4	Secondary research	–
5	–	–
6	In-depth interview	–
7	Survey	–
8	Experimental design	–
9	–	–
10	Questionnaire development via flowerpot approach	
11	Scale measurements	–
12	Attitude scale design	–
13	Sampling approach; Sampling techniques	–
14	Sampling design	–
15	–	Recording of responses to open-ended questions; Data coding; Error detection; Missing data; One-way tabulation; Cross-tabulation
16	–	Bar chart; Area Chart; Pie or round chart; Measures of central tendency; Measures of dispersion; Univariate tests of significance; Independent samples t-test; Paired samples t-test
17	–	Pearson correlation analysis; Spearman correlation analysis; coefficient of determination; bivariate regression analysis
18	–	Multiple regression analysis; Dummy variable; Multicollinearity; ANOVA; Discriminant analysis
19	–	Factor analysis; Cluster analysis
20	–	Illustration of data output; Writing up of conclusions

collected have been put into an SPSS enabled database. For the sake of business confidentiality, the data given here are fictitious. However, the database will serve our learning and teaching purposes, and will be referred to throughout the book.

Exhibit 1.9 shows how Jimmy Spice's restaurant case will be used in different chapters to help readers build up their understanding of marketing research concepts as well as SPSS applications.

Questions

1 Based on your understanding of Chapter 1, and specifically using Exhibit 1.1, what type(s) of marketing research activities should the owner of Jimmy Spice's restaurant consider?

2 Given the general questions that the owner has cited above, are there additional information/ questions that you would suggest to the owner when designing for their marketing research activities?

Summary of Learning Objectives

■ **Describe and explain the impact marketing research has on marketing decision making.**
Marketing research is the set of activities central to all marketing-related decisions regardless of the complexity or focus of the decision. Marketing research is responsible for providing managers with accurate, relevant, and timely information so that they can make marketing decisions with a high degree of confidence. Within the context of strategic planning, marketing research is responsible for the tasks, methods, and procedures a firm will use to implement and direct its strategic plan.

■ **Demonstrate how marketing research fits into the marketing planning process.**
Marketing research is the backbone of any relationship marketing strategy. Specifically, marketing research facilitates the implementation of the process through the generation of customer/market knowledge, data integration, information technology, and the creation of customer profiles. The key to successful marketing planning is accurate information. Information related to product performance, distribution efficiency, pricing policies, and promotional efforts is crucial for developing the strategic plan. The primary responsibility of any marketing research endeavour is to design a project that yields the most accurate information possible in aiding the development of a marketing plan.

■ **Provide examples of marketing research activities.**
The scope of marketing research activities extends far beyond examination of customer characteristics. The major categories of marketing research activities include, but are not limited to, (1) situation research efforts (which include opportunity assessment, descriptive studies, benefit and lifestyle studies, and importance-performance analysis); (2) programme design-driven research efforts (which include target market analysis, positioning, concept and product testing, and test marketing); (3) programme development research (which includes customer satisfaction studies, service quality studies, cycle time research, retailing research, logistic assessment, demand analysis, sales forecasting, advertising effectiveness studies, attitudinal research, and sales tracking); and (4) performance tracking analysis (which includes product analysis, environmental forecasting, and marketing decision support systems).

■ **Understand the scope and focus of the marketing research industry.**
Generally, marketing research projects can be conducted either internally by an in-house marketing research staff or externally by independent or facilitating marketing research firms. External research suppliers are normally classified as custom or standardized, or as brokers or facilitators.

■ **Demonstrate ethical dimensions associated with marketing research.**
Ethical decision making affects all industries, including marketing research. Ethical dilemmas in marketing research are likely to occur among the research provider, the research user, and the respondents. Specific unethical practices of research providers include unethical pricing practices, failure to meet obligations to respondents, respondent abuse, selling unnecessary services. Unethical behaviour by research users includes requesting research proposals with no intent to follow through and unethical practices to secure low-cost research services. The falsification of data and duplication of actual responses are unethical practices associated with the respondents.

■ **Understand emerging trends and skills associated with marketing research.**
Just as the dynamic business environment causes firms to modify and change practices, so does this environment dictate change to the marketing research industry. Specifically, technological changes have already shaped how marketing research is conducted, and will continue to affect marketing research practices in future. Necessary skills required to adapt to these changes include (1) the ability to understand and interpret secondary data, (2) presentation skills, (3) foreign-language competency, (4) negotiation skills, and (5) computer proficiency.

Key Terms and Concepts

Advertising agencies   26
Advertising effectiveness studies   19
Attitudinal research   19
Benefit and lifestyle studies   12
Brokers   25
Concept and product testing
   and test marketing   14
Customer satisfaction studies   15
Cycle time research   16
Demand analysis   18
Descriptive studies   12
Environmental forecasting   21
Field service providers   26
Facilitators   26
Importance-performance
   analysis   12

Independent consultants   26
Logistic assessment   17
Marketing   6
Marketing decision support
   system (MDSS)   21
Marketing research   5
Opportunity assessment   11
Positioning   13
Product analysis   20
Relationship marketing   6
Retailing research   16
Sales forecasting   18
Sales tracking   19
Service quality studies   15
Situation analysis   9
Target market analysis   13

Review Questions

1   Provide three examples of how marketing research helps marketing personnel make sound managerial decisions.

2   What improvements in market planning can be attributed to the results obtained from customer satisfaction studies?

3   List the three basic approaches used in the collection of marketing research information. Briefly describe each method and comment on its application.

4   Discuss the importance of target market analysis. How does it affect the development of market planning for a particular company?

5   What are the advantages and disadvantages for companies maintaining an internal marketing research department? What advantages and disadvantages can be attributed to the hiring of an external marketing research supplier?

6   As the marketing research industry expands in the new century, what skills will future executives need to possess? How do these skills differ from those currently needed to function successfully in the marketing research field?

7   Identify and explain four potential unethical practices within the marketing research process and their contribution to 'deceptive research results.'

Discussion Questions

1   **Experience the Internet.** Go online to one of your favourite search engines (Yahoo!, Google, etc.) and enter the following search term: marketing research. From the results, access a directory of marketing research firms. Select a particular firm and comment on the types of marketing research studies it performs.

2   **Experience the Internet.** Using the Yahoo! search engine, specifically the Get Local section, select the closest major city in your area and search for the number of marketing research firms there. Select a company, email that company, and ask to have any job descriptions for positions in that company emailed back to you. Once you obtain the descriptions, discuss the particular qualities needed to perform each job.

3   You have been hired by McDonald's to lead a mystery shopper team. The goal of your research is to improve the service quality at the McDonald's restaurant in your area. What attributes of service quality will you attempt to measure? What customer or employee behaviours will you closely monitor?

4   Contact a local business and interview the owner/manager about the types of marketing research performed for that business. Determine whether the business has its own marketing research department, or if it hires an outside agency. Also, determine whether the company takes a one-shot approach to particular problems or is systematic over a long period of time.

5   **Experience the Internet.** As the Internet continues to grow as a medium for conducting various types of marketing research studies, there is growing concern about ethical issues. Identify and discuss three ethical issues pertinent to research conducted using the Internet.

6   Identify and describe at least two situations in which marketing research should not be undertaken.

7   How is the Internet changing the field of marketing research?

8   Discuss how recent ethical developments are impacting the marketing research industry.

2

The Marketing Research Process

LEARNING OBJECTIVES

After reading this chapter, you will be able to

☑ Describe the major environmental factors influencing marketing research and explain their impacts on the research process.

☑ Discuss the phases and steps of the research process and explain some of the key activities within each step.

☑ Explain the differences between raw data, data structures and information, and describe the process by which raw data are transformed into information that managers can use.

☑ Illustrate and explain the critical elements of problem definition in marketing research.

☑ Distinguish between exploratory, descriptive and causal research designs.

☑ Identify and explain the major components of a research proposal.

 Information is of the prime importance in impacting on an organization's profit performance.
    –*McKinsey Global Survey on 3470 business professionals worldwide in March 2006*

Using the Research Process to Address Marketing Problems – Re-Launching the Rexona Brand in the French Deodorant Market

In the year prior to implementing a vigorous marketing research process, Rexona, a deodorant brand owned by Unilever, had lost market share points to a local L'Oréal brand, Narta, in France.

Rexona somehow seemed to have lost touch with consumers. What's more, its marketing teams were no longer talking a common language. They couldn't agree what was the underlying factor causing the problem, for example, whether functional credentials were not being communicated strongly enough or whether cultural factors were having a stronger influence. The challenging task for the research was to diagnose the levels at which the problem was occurring, i.e. functional, emotional, social and/or cultural, and to find a new way ahead in the market for Rexona.

An early stage of the marketing research process is to develop the research approach for the project concerned. Unilever adopted the RESC model (RESC stands for Rational, Emotional, Social and Cultural) as the theoretical framework upon which they carried out the research design for the project. Very briefly, the model involves examining consumer needs holistically by going beyond rational (R) and emotional (E) motivations, to look also at motivations at the social (S) and cultural (C) levels.

One major aspect of the research design was to determine the methods for data collection. In the first stage of data collection a fusion of qualitative methods were used, including stakeholder interviews, semiotic analysis, photo diaries and extended creativity groups. Together, these methods generated the main verbal and visual associations, social influences and cultural factors to be quantified.

In the second and final stage, 1000 online interviews were conducted in both France and the UK, the UK being included to provide a comparative context for the study. These online interviews used a variety of creative questions to measure emotional, social and cultural factors. These included projective storytelling to describe the modern woman; visual associations to quantify semiotic discourses; and the examination of cultural icons including local female personalities.

Results show that at a rational/functional level Rexona scored well, but there was little difference compared to Narta. Although Rexona was regarded as one of the ultimate efficacy brands, there was still room for improvement as consumers do not believe that any brand offers the ideal protection. In addition, Rexona was perceived as having a harsh fragrance. This opened up an avenue for Rexona to aim towards a less harsh positioning. Also the research indicated that the reassurance of efficacy needs to be based on more than just sportiness, particularly at the other RESC levels.

At the emotional level, Narta tended to be perceived as more celebratory, happy and cheerful. Rexona, on the other hand, tended to be more masculine and a bit more loud and brash. As the benchmark for comparison, an ideal deodorant brand was cited by respondents as being feminine, modern and young. At the social level, Narta was sociable, fun-loving and optimistic, while Rexona was more about meeting everyday challenge and survival.

However, it was at the cultural level that Unilever really saw the stark contrast between Rexona and Narta, with the latter far closer to the positioning of the ideal brand in this marketplace. While Narta was young, independent, ambitious, empowered, modern and fun-loving, Rexona was seen as tomboyish, competitive, sporty, stressed and playing men at their own game. These associations were strongly influenced by the brand's past advertising.

Thus a clear signal for Unilever was that the cultural content of the brand's past advertising had made Rexona more resonant with the 'Empowered Woman' reminiscent of the culture of the 1980s and 1990s than the woman at the new millennium. In response to the results of the research, Unilever decided to re-launch Rexona with a new concept, new pack design and graphics, new formulations and a new communication. The re-launch aimed to create a step change in women's perception of Rexona as a brand that is different, works better and unequivocally 'for me'.

Unilever also addressed the issue that Rexona was perceived as having a harsh fragrance by employing the technology of 'micro-capsules' and significantly improving the formulation. Consequently, Unilever was able to deliver the message that 'body responsive Rexona offers intelligent protection that works in sync with your body'.

In addition, Unilever made Rexona's packaging more appealing to women through the use of elegant curves, helping the brand to move closer to the attributes associated with the ideal brand of deodorant: feminine, modern and young.

The development of new communication was probably the most demanding part of the re-launch. Unilever realized that Rexona, as a cornerstone brand in the deodorant market, had to retain its associations with 'strength' and 'strong women'. However, being a 'strong woman' at the time of 'post-modern femininity' prevalent in the new millennium has little to do with physical strength and everything to do with emotional strength. The new strong woman is one who possesses passion, resourcefulness and intuition. Figure 2.1 describing the journey from traditional to post-modern woman was a great inspiration for Unilever. The company could visualize the new Rexona woman as the post-modern woman who wants to succeed in life but at the same time goes back to the past to tap into the more traditional expressions of femininity and uses that femininity in a strategic way.

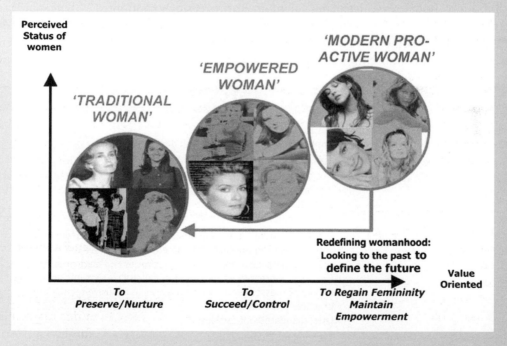

Figure 2.1 The journey from traditional to post-modern woman.

Portraying the new Rexona woman led to the development of the insight for the new communication campaign, 'I enjoy living life with intensity', and the discriminator 'Living with intensity doesn't have to make you sweat'. The brand mission has thus become 'to equip and empower women to live their lives to the fullest'.

Source: Adapted from a show case written for ESOMAR by Jaroslav Cir (Head of CMI (Deodorants Europe), Unilever Personal Care), John Pawle (Managing Director, QiQ International Ltd) and Simon Patterson (Managing Director, CRAM International Ltd)

Value of the Marketing Research Process

As the 'real world chapter opener' example illustrates, owners and managers frequently have marketing problems they need help to resolve. In such situations, additional information often is needed to make a decision or solve a problem. One solution is a marketing research project conducted following a standardized research process. This chapter uses an information perspective to explain the marketing research process. It begins with a discussion of the critical environmental factors that directly influence the scope of the research process. Much of the chapter provides an overview of the four basic phases that make up the research process and the specific steps involved in each phase, as well as activities and questions a researcher must address within each step. The final section of the chapter explains how to develop a marketing research proposal.

This chapter serves as a preview of some of the central topics in the text. Much of the discussion is descriptive in nature. Overall, this chapter provides the general blueprint for understanding the marketing research process. The topics introduced are discussed in much more detail in subsequent chapters.

Changing View of the Marketing Research Process

Organizations, both for-profit and not-for-profit, are increasingly confronted with new and more complex challenges and opportunities that are the result of changing legal, political, cultural, technological, and competitive issues. Exhibit 2.1 summarizes several key environmental factors that are significantly impacting business decision making and the marketing research process.

EXHIBIT 2.1 Environmental Factors That Affect Marketing Research Practices

Environmental Factors	Impact on Marketing Research and Examples
Internet and e-commerce	Revolutionizing the methods of collecting data and information. *Examples:* increased emphasis on secondary data structures; increases in the need for and integration of technology-driven online and offline databases; shorter acquisition and retrieval time requirements; greater proficiency in interactive multimedia systems.
Gatekeeper technologies and data privacy legislation	Raising concerns about consumers' right to privacy, to what extent consumer information can be shared, and increased difficulties of reaching people for their input on attitudes and behaviours. *Examples:* increased employment of caller ID, electronic answering, and voice messenger devices; increases in intrusive telemarketing practices and scam artists; stronger, more restrictive data privacy laws; mandated opt-out options.
Global market expansion	Creating multicultural interaction problems, opportunities, and questions for marketing decision makers as well as new language and measurement challenges for researchers. *Examples:* different cultural-based market needs and wants; different global data requirements for segmentation; use of different, yet compatible measurement schemes for market performance, attitude, and behaviour data.
Marketing research as a strategy	Leading businesses to reposition marketing research activities with more emphasis on strategic implications. *Examples:* use of marketing research for developing CRM and customer and competitor intelligence strategies; marketing researchers' deeper involvement in developing online/offline databases.

Perhaps the most influential factor is the **Internet**. It may be logical to think that the time before the Internet exists belongs to the previous generation, as the Web has very rapidly become an integral part of our everyday lives for many years. However, it is important to remember that in many ways this is still a new and comparatively young technology. For example, the ongoing rapid technological advances and growing use of the Internet by people worldwide are making it a driving force in many current and future developments in marketing research. Traditional research philosophies are being challenged as never before. For example, there is a growing emphasis on secondary data collection, analysis, and interpretation as a basis of making business decisions. **Secondary data** is information previously collected for some other problem or issue. In contrast, **primary data** is information collected for a current research problem or opportunity.

> **Internet** A network of computers and technology linking computers into an information superhighway.
>
> **Secondary data** Historical data structures of variables previously collected and assembled for some research problem or opportunity situation other than the current situation.
>
> **Primary data** Firsthand raw data and structures which have yet to receive any type of meaningful interpretation.

A by-product of the Internet is the ongoing collection of data that are placed in a data warehouse and are available as secondary data to help understand business problems and to make better decisions. Many of today's larger businesses (e.g. Tesco, Boots the Chemist, Wal-Mart) are using interlinkages between online scanning of customers' real-time purchase behaviour with offline customer profiles in the data warehouse to enhance their ability to understand shopping behaviour and better meet customer needs. But even medium- and small-sized companies are building databases of customer information to serve current customers more effectively and to attract new customers.

Second is **gatekeeper technologies** (e.g. caller ID and automated screening and answering devices) as a means of protecting one's privacy. These technologies are getting popular as more and more people are increasingly fed up by the escalating amount of commercial cold calls and unsolicited emails. Marketing researchers' ability to collect consumer data has then been limited by these gatekeeper devices. As a result, marketing researchers need to contact more people to complete a single interview. Similarly, online marketers and researchers must provide opt-in/opt-out options when soliciting business or collecting information. Advances in gatekeeper technologies will continue to challenge marketers to be more creative in developing new ways to reach respondents.

> **Gatekeeper technology** Advanced telecommunication technologies that allow a person to screen incoming contact messages from other people or organizations.

A third challenge facing marketing decision makers is the widespread expansion into global markets. Global expansion introduces marketing decision makers to new sets of cultural issues that force researchers to focus not only on data collection tasks, but also on data interpretation and information management activities. For example, one of the largest full-service global marketing information firms, NFO (National Family Opinion) Worldwide, Inc., with subsidiaries in Europe, North America, Australia, Asia and the Middle East, has adapted many of its measurement and brand tracking services to accommodate specific cultural and language differences encountered in global markets.

Fourth, marketing research is being repositioned in businesses to play a more important role in strategy development. Marketing research increasingly is being used to identify new business opportunities and to develop new product, service and delivery ideas. It also is being viewed not only as a mechanism to more efficiently execute CRM (customer relationship management) strategies, but also as a critical component in developing competitive intelligence. For example, Sony uses its Playstation website (www.playstation.com) to collect information on PlayStation gaming users and to build closer relationships. The PlayStation website is designed to create a community of users who can join PlayStation Underground where they will 'feel like they belong to a subculture of intense gamers'. To achieve this objective the website offers online shopping, opportunities to try new games, customer support, and information on news, events and promotions. Interactive features include online gaming and message boards, as well as other relationship-building aspects. Marketing researchers at Sony and other companies are becoming more like cross-functional information experts, assisting in collecting not only marketing information, but information on all types of business functions.

While many other factors are influencing the marketing research process, these are the key ones now forcing managers and researchers to view marketing research as an information management function. Indeed, the **marketing research process** is a systematic approach to collecting, analysing, interpreting, and transforming raw data into decision-making information. Understanding the process of transforming raw data into usable information from a broader information-processing framework expands the applicability of the research process in solving organizational problems and creating opportunities.

> **Marketing research process** The systematic task steps in the gathering, analysing, interpreting, and transforming of data structures and results into decision-making information.

Determining the Need for Marketing Research

Before we introduce and discuss the phases and specific steps of the marketing research process, it is important that you understand when the research process is needed and when it is not. Moreover, increasingly researchers must interact closely with managers in recognizing business problems, questions and opportunities.

While many marketing research texts suggest the first step in the marketing research process is for the researcher to establish the need for marketing research, this places a lot of responsibility and control in the hands of a person who might not be trained in understanding the management decision-making process. Decision makers and researchers frequently are trained differently in their approach to identifying and solving business problems, questions and opportunities, as illustrated in the 'A Closer Look at Research' box. Until decision makers and marketing researchers become closer in their thinking, the initial recognition of the existence of a problem or opportunity should be the primary responsibility of the decision maker, not the researcher.

To help prevent the differences between decision makers and researchers from complicating the initial business problem definition process, the decision makers should be given the responsibility of initiating the activities in recognizing and defining the problem or opportunity situation. For now, a good rule of thumb is to ask, 'Can the stated decision-making problem (or question) be resolved by using subjective information (e.g. past experience, gut feelings)?' If 'No' is the logical response, the marketing research process needs to be considered and perhaps implemented.

In most cases when some type of additional information is needed to address a problem, decision makers will need assistance in determining the problem, collecting and analysing the data, and interpreting that information. The need to activate the research process basically comes from decision makers' ability to recognize problem and opportunity situations as well as monitor market performance conditions.

A key to understanding when the marketing research process should be undertaken is the notion that marketing research no longer focuses on just the activities of collecting, analysing, and interpreting primary data for solving management's problems. Increasingly, secondary research and data warehouse information are being used to address decision-making situations. Technological advances in the Internet, high-speed communication systems, and faster secondary and primary data acquisition and retrieval systems are dramatically changing marketing research practices. As a result, the constraints used in determining whether to conduct research are less restrictive than in the past.

 ## A Closer Look at Research *(In the field)*
Management Decision Makers and Marketing Researchers

Management Decision Makers   Tend to be decision-oriented, intuitive thinkers who want information to confirm their decisions. They want additional information now or 'yesterday', as well as results about future market component behaviour ('What will sales be next year?'), while maintaining a frugal stance with regard to the cost of additional information. Decision makers tend to be results oriented, do not like surprises, and tend to reject the information when they are surprised. Their dominant concern is market performance ('Aren't we number one yet?'); they want information that allows certainty ('Is it or isn't it?'); and they advocate being proactive but often allow problems to force them into reactive decision-making modes.

Marketing Researchers   Tend to be scientific, technical, analytical thinkers who love to explore new phenomena; accept prolonged investigations to ensure completeness; focus on information about past behaviours ('Our trend has been …'); and are not cost conscious about additional information ('You get what you pay for'). Researchers are results oriented but love surprises; they tend to enjoy abstractions ('Our exponential gain …') and the probability of occurrences ('May be', 'Tends to suggest that …'); and they advocate the proactive need for continuous inquiries of market component changes, but feel most of the time that they are restricted to doing reactive ('quick and dirty') investigations due to management's lack of vision and planning.

There are four situations in which the decision to commission a marketing research project may be ill advised. These are listed and discussed in Exhibit 2.2. One of the shortcomings of this approach to deciding when to conduct research is that in each situation the decision maker is assumed to have prior knowledge about the 'true' availability of existing information, the necessary time and staff, adequate resources or clear insight into the expected value of the resulting information. As technology advances, these assumptions become more suspect.

EXHIBIT 2.2 Situations When Marketing Research Might Not Be Needed

When information already available When the decision maker has substantial knowledge about markets, products and services, and the competition, enough information may exist to make an informed decision without doing marketing research. Some experts believe advancements in computer and information processing technology increase the chance that the right information gets to the right decision makers in a timely fashion.

When insufficient time frames When the discovery of a problem situation leaves inadequate time to execute the necessary research activities, decision makers may have to use informed judgment. Competitive actions/reactions sometimes emerge so fast that formalized marketing research studies are not a feasible option.

When inadequate resources When there are significant limitations in money, manpower, and/or facilities, then marketing research typically is not feasible.

When costs outweigh the value When the benefits to be gained by conducting the research are not significantly greater than the costs, then marketing research is not feasible.

The main responsibility of today's decision makers is to initially determine if the research process should be used to collect the needed information. The initial question the decision maker must ask is: *Can the problem and/or opportunity be resolved using only subjective information?* Here the focus is on deciding what type of information (subjective, secondary, or primary) is required to answer the research question(s). In most cases, decision makers should undertake the marketing research process any time they have a question or problem or believe there is an opportunity, but either do not have the right subjective information or are unwilling to rely on subjective information to resolve the problem. In reality, conducting secondary and primary research studies costs time, effort, and money. Exhibit 2.3 displays a framework that illustrates the factors and examples of the questions that must be asked and answered to determine whether the research process is necessary.

After deciding that subjective information alone will not resolve the identified problem, the next question to be answered by the decision makers focuses on the nature of the decision: *Does the problem/opportunity situation have strategic or tactical importance?* Strategic decisions tend to have broader time horizons but are much more complex than tactical decisions. Most strategic decisions are critical to the company's operations and bottom-line profitability objectives. In turn, on the basis of the investment associated with a tactical decision, undertaking the research process might be the appropriate alternative for collecting data and information. For example, La Tasca, a popular Spanish tapas bar and restaurant chain in Europe, may decide to make a tactical decision to update its menu. Researching the opinions of known customers can prove helpful in determining new food items to be included and those items that should not be on the menu. Our suggestion is that if the problem situation has strategic or significant tactical importance, then a formal marketing research project should be carried out.

Another key managerial question deals with the availability of existing information. With the assistance of the research expert, decision makers face the next question: *Does adequate information for addressing the defined problem already exist within the company's internal record systems?*

In the past, if the necessary marketing information was not available in the firm's internal record system, then a customized marketing research project would be undertaken to produce and report the information. Today, advances in computer technology and changing management

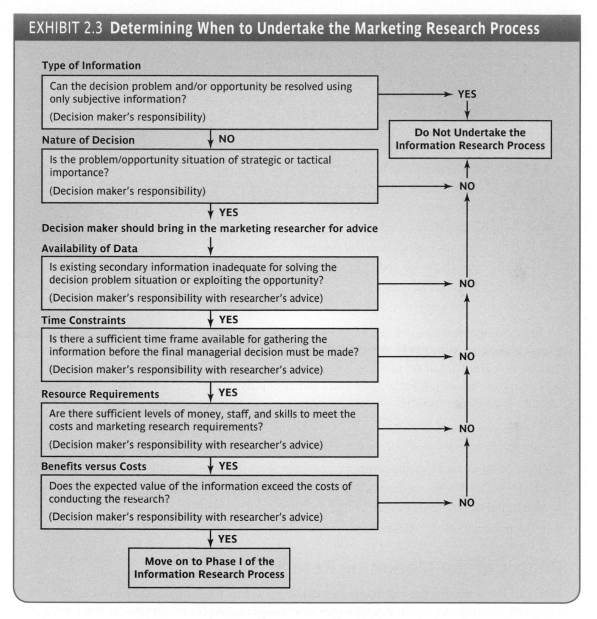

EXHIBIT 2.3 Determining When to Undertake the Marketing Research Process

philosophy towards the cross-functional sharing of information enable management to record, store, and retrieve huge amounts of operating data (e.g. sales, costs, and profitability by products, brands, sales region, customer groups) with greater ease and speed.

With input from the research expert, decision makers must assess the 'time constraints' associated with the problem/opportunity: *Is there enough time to conduct the necessary research before the final managerial decision must be made?* Today's decision makers often need information in real time. But in many cases, systematic research that delivers high-quality information may take several months. If the decision maker needs the information immediately, then there is insufficient time to complete the research process. Another fundamental question focuses on the availability of marketing resources (e.g. money, staff, skills, facilities): *Is money budgeted for doing formalized research?* For example, many small businesses simply lack the necessary funds to consider doing any type of formal research.

Some type of cost–benefit assessment should be made regarding the overall value of the research compared to the cost: *Do the benefits of having the additional information outweigh the costs of gathering the information?* This type of question remains a challenge for today's decision makers. While the cost of doing marketing research varies from project to project, generally it can be estimated accurately. Yet, predetermining the true value of the expected information remains somewhat subjective. In addition to the foregoing considerations that help to determine whether to use the research process, decision makers should give thought to the following set of evaluative questions:

- What is the perceived importance and complexity of the problem?
- Is the problem realistically researchable? Can the critical variables in the proposed research be adequately designed and measured?
- Will conducting the needed research give valuable information to the firm's competitors?
- Will the research findings be implemented?
- Will the research design and data represent reality?
- Will the research results and findings be used as legal evidence?
- Is the proposed research politically motivated?

In deciding whether to employ the research process, another useful approach involves an always elusive question: *Why should the decision maker conduct marketing research?* Although there is no agreed-upon set of rules for determining when to conduct research other than the general notion initially described, there are some conditional reasons to consider when deciding whether to conduct research:

1 If the information will clarify the problem or identify marketplace changes that directly influence the company's product/service responsibilities.

2 If the information helps the company to acquire meaningful competitive advantages within its market environment.

3 If the information leads to marketing actions that will achieve marketing objectives.

4 If the information provides proactive understanding of future market conditions.

Phases of the Marketing Research Process

The marketing research process is typically described as a set of standardized phases. In this text, we define it as consisting of four distinct yet interrelated phases: (1) determine the research problem, (2) select the appropriate research design, (3) execute the research design, and (4) communicate the research results (see Exhibit 2.4). Researchers must ensure that all phases of the process are completed properly if the best possible information is to be available for organizational decision makers. Each phase, however, should be viewed as a separate process that consists of a combination of integrated research steps.

The four phases are guided by the principles of the **scientific method**, which involves formalized research procedures that can be characterized as logical, objective, systematic, reliable, valid,

Scientific method Formalized research procedures that can be characterized as logical, objective, systematic, reliable, valid, impersonal and ongoing.

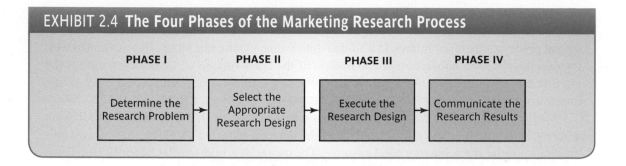

EXHIBIT 2.4 **The Four Phases of the Marketing Research Process**

PHASE I	PHASE II	PHASE III	PHASE IV
Determine the Research Problem	Select the Appropriate Research Design	Execute the Research Design	Communicate the Research Results

impersonal and ongoing. Traditional marketing research emphasizes the collection and analysis of primary data. But the marketing research process places equal emphasis on the use of secondary data.

Transforming Raw Data into Information

The primary goal of the marketing research process is to provide organizational decision makers with secondary or primary information that will enable them to resolve a problem, answer an existing question, or pursue an opportunity. Information is created only after the data have been collected, analysed, interpreted, and transformed into narrative expressions decision makers can understand and use. To understand this process, one must know the difference between raw data, data structures, and information.

First, **raw data** represent the actual firsthand responses that are obtained about an object or subject of investigation by asking questions or observing actions. These initial responses have not been analysed or given an interpretive meaning. Some examples of raw data are (1) the actual individual responses on a questionnaire; (2) the words recorded during a focus group interview; (3) the tally of vehicles that pass through a specified intersection; (4) the list of purchases, by product type, recorded by an electronic cash register at a local supermarket.

> **Raw data** Firsthand responses obtained about the subject of investigation.

All secondary and primary marketing information is derived from the following process: *gather raw responses; apply some form of data analysis to create usable data structures; and then have someone (a researcher or decision maker) interpret those data structures.*

Gather raw data → Create data structures → Provide interpretation

Data structures are the result of combining individual raw responses into groups of data using some type of quantitative or qualitative analysis procedure (e.g. content analysis, calculation of sample statistics). The results can reveal data patterns or trends, which in turn can be

> **Data structures** Results of combining raw data into groups using some type of quantitative or qualitative analysis.

simple or complex. Some examples are (1) the average number of times 500 moviegoers patronize their favourite cinemas; (2) the frequency distribution of 1,000 university students eating at several predetermined restaurants in a 30-day time frame; (3) the sampling error associated with the overall expressed satisfaction of 250 owners of the latest version of Toyota cars; and (4) the z-test results of comparing hotel selection criteria means for first-time and repeat patrons of a mid-market hotel.

Information is derived from data only when someone – either the researcher or the decision maker – takes the time and effort to interpret the data and attach a meaning. To illustrate this process, consider the following hotel example. The owner of a mid-market hotel, JP Hotel, was assessing ways to improve the firm's bottom-line profit figures. Specifically, they were seeking ways to cut operating costs. The finance manager of the hotel suggested cutting back on the 'quality of the bedding and towels' in the rooms. Before making a final decision, the hotel owner asked the marketing manager to organize a series of interviews with the hotel's business customers using a scientifically sound research process.

> **Information** The set of facts derived from data structures when someone – either the researcher or decision maker – interprets and attaches narrative meaning to the data structures.

Exhibit 2.5 summarizes the study's key results. In the study, 880 people were asked to indicate the degree of importance they placed on seven criteria when selecting a hotel. Respondents used a six-point importance scale ranging from (6) 'Extremely important' to (1) 'Not at all important'. The individual responses represent the raw data. The researcher used the raw data to calculate the overall average importance for each of the criteria using a simple 'mean analysis' procedure,

EXHIBIT 2.5 Summary of Overall Importance Differences of Selected Hotel Selection Criteria Used by First-Time and Repeat Business Patrons

Hotel Selection Criteria	Total (n = 880) Mean[a] Value	First-Time Patrons (n = 440) Mean Value	Repeat Patrons (n = 400) Mean Value	z Test
Cleanliness of the room	5.65	5.75	5.50	*
Good-quality bedding and towels	5.60	5.55	5.62	
Preferred guest card options	5.57	5.42	5.71	*
Friendly/courteous staff and employees	5.10	4.85	5.45	*
Free VIP services	5.06	4.35	5.38	*
Conveniently located for business	5.04	5.25	4.92	*
In-room movie entertainment	3.63	3.30	4.56	*

[a] Importance scale: a six-point scale ranging from 6 (extremely important) to 1 (not at all important).
* Mean importance difference between the two patron groups is significant at $p < .05$.

where the resulting means represent the data structures associated with each selection criterion across all respondents and for both first-time and repeat patrons. In fact, all the numbers are data structures. However, these results, by themselves, do not provide the management team with any meaningful information to assist in determining whether or not 'quality bedding and towels' should be cut back to reduce operating costs.

When the owner was shown the results, he asked this question: 'I see a lot of seemingly impressive numbers, but what are they really telling me?' The marketing manager quickly responded by explaining what the numbers concerning the 'quality bedding and towels' criterion were suggesting: 'Among our first-time and repeat business customers, they consider the quality of the hotel's bedding and towels one of the three most important selection criteria that impact their choice of a hotel to stay at when an overnight stay is required for business. In addition, business travellers feel the cleanliness of the room and offering preferred guest card options are equally important to the quality of bedding and towels criterion, yet first-time business patrons place significantly stronger importance on cleanliness of the room ($x = 5.75$) than do our repeat business patrons ($x = 5.50$). In turn, repeat business customers place significantly more importance on the availability of our preferred guest card options ($x = 5.71$) in their hotel selection process than do first-time business patrons ($x = 5.42$).' Upon understanding the information being provided by the data, the hotel owner decided it would not be wise to cut back on the quality of bedding or towels as a way to reduce operating expenses and improve profitability.

Interrelatedness of the Steps and the Research Process

As soon as decision makers recognize they need assistance, they should meet with the marketing researcher and begin executing a formalized, scientific research process. Exhibit 2.6 shows the interrelated steps included in the four phases of the research process. All these phases and steps are covered in this text. Although the chapters are not arranged in the same sequence as the steps shown here because the best sequence for learning is not the same as that for actually doing the research, the four Parts cover more or less the same material as the phases outlined here, with the first two phases covered in Parts 1 and 2 and the last two phases dealt with in Parts 3 and 4.

Although in most instances researchers would follow the four phases in order, the individual steps may be shifted or omitted. Often the complexity of the problem, the urgency for solving the problem, the cost of alternative approaches, and the clarification of information needs will directly impact how many of the steps are taken and in what order. For example, secondary data or 'off-the-shelf' research studies may be found that could eliminate the need to collect primary data, thus eliminating the need for a sampling plan. Similarly, pretesting the questionnaire (step 7) might reveal weaknesses in some of the scales being considered (step 6), resulting in further refinement of the scales or even selection of a new research design (back to step 4).

What might happen if the research process is not appropriately followed? Substantial time, energy and money can be spent with the result being incomplete, biased or wrong information for proper decision making. For example, a golf and country club wanted to determine its members' overall satisfaction with the 'beverage cart' services being provided on the golf course and gain insight to how to improve those services. Not knowing the research process, the committee instinctively designed a simple rating card asking members to rate the beverage cart service using a six-point scale ranging from (6) 'Outstanding' to (1) 'Terrible' and supplying a space for written comments. After reviewing only 50 cards returned, the committee found that members' comments suggested that there were several activities associated with the beverage cart operations

---

EXHIBIT 2.6 Phases and Steps in the Marketing Research Process

Phase	**I:**	**Determine the Research Problem**
Step	1:	Identify and clarify management's information needs
Step	2:	Specify the research questions and define the research problem
Step	3:	Confirm research objectives and assess the value of the information
Phase	**II:**	**Select the Appropriate Research Design**
Step	4:	Determine the research design and data sources
Step	5:	Develop the sampling design and sample size
Step	6:	Assess measurement issues and scales
Step	7:	Pretest the questionnaire
Phase	**III:**	**Execute the Research Design**
Step	8:	Collect and prepare data
Step	9:	Analyse data
Step	10:	Transform data structures into information
Phase	**IV:**	**Communicate the Research Results**
Step	11:	Prepare and present final report to management

---

that were associated with overall satisfaction. But the rating scheme was measuring overall performance rather than satisfaction. The committee did receive data and information about the beverage cart service, but it was not what they were looking for. Although the committee had blindly incorporated some of the key activities found within the marketing research process, the data did not help them address their initial problem.

Phase I: Determine the Research Problem

The process of determining the research problem involves three interrelated activities: (1) identify and clarify information needs; (2) specify the research questions and define the research problem; and (3) confirm research objectives and assess the value of the information. These activities bring researchers and decision makers together under the notion that management has recognized the need for some type of information to deal with an issue concerning firm performance.

Step 1: Identify and Clarify Management's Information Needs

Usually, before the researcher becomes involved, decision makers have prepared a formal statement of what they believe is the problem. At this point, researchers then assist decision makers in making sure the problem or opportunity has been correctly defined and that the decision maker is aware of the information requirements. Remember that a **decision problem** exists when management has established a specific objective that may be achieved through any of several courses of action. The question becomes: Which is the best option?

> **Decision problem** A situation in which a manager is not certain which course of action will help him or her accomplish a specific objective.

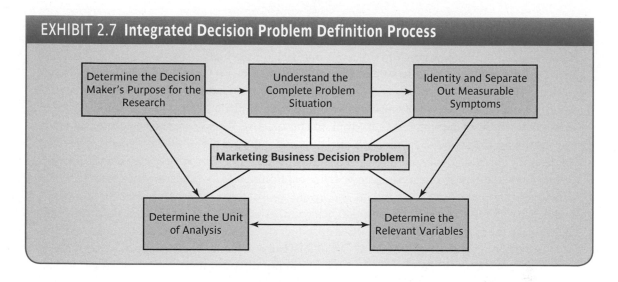

EXHIBIT 2.7 Integrated Decision Problem Definition Process

For researchers to gain a clear understanding of the decision problem, they must use an integrated problem definition process, as shown in Exhibit 2.7. There is no one best process. But any process undertaken should include the following activities: (1) determine the decision maker's purpose for the research; (2) understand the complete problem situation; (3) identify and separate out measurable symptoms; (4) determine the appropriate unit of analysis; and (5) determine the relevant variables. Being able to correctly define and understand the actual decision problem is an important first step in determining if it is really necessary to conduct research. A poorly defined decision problem can easily produce research results that are unlikely to have any value, as in the CocaCola versus Pepsi-Cola example, illustrated in the Closer Look at Research box.

A Closer Look at Research *(In the field)*
Global Taste Battle between Coca-Cola and Pepsi-Cola

In an effort to gain market share, the Pepsi-Cola Company conducted a series of blind taste tests and determined that soft-drink consumers preferred the sweetness of Pepsi to the crisper taste of Coke. On the basis of what was called the Pepsi Challenge, Pepsi developed a marketing programme concentrating on younger soft-drink customers and labelling them the Pepsi Generation.

The Coca-Cola company's initial response was to increase its advertising budget and develop a claim of product superiority. Nonetheless, Coke's own taste tests validated Pepsi's claims that customers preferred a sweeter product. Using information obtained in the development of Diet Coke, Coca-Cola created a new, sweeter Coke product and embarked on one of the most extensive marketing research programmes in the history of the soft-drink industry.

Coke's market research lasted three years and asked over 200,000 customers to participate in blind taste tests. The information research question that guided Coca-Cola's research programme was: 'What will be the ultimate consumer reactions to the taste of the new Coke product?' Results of the marketing research indicated that when asked to compare unmarked beverages, consumers favoured the new Coke formula over the original Coke product by a margin of 55 per cent to 45 per cent. When both soft drinks were identified, 53 per cent of those taking the test still preferred the new Coke formula over the original Coke.

Based on these research results, Coca-Cola decided to introduce a new sweeter-formula Coke. The product was introduced with the name New Coke and the original Coke was discontinued. Within three months, however, old Coke was put back on the market. By the end of the year, the new Coke formula, the one marketing research showed to be preferred by drinkers, was discontinued. What happened? Where did Coca-Cola go wrong? What should have been measured? What if Coca-Cola had put the new product under the old label? These remain good topics of discussion within marketing research. From one perspective, Coca-Cola can be accused of being too narrow in the scope of its research question and defining the problem so that researchers investigated and tested only one aspect – consumers' preferences of taste associated with cola soft drinks. In this situation, researchers can be criticized for not also investigating the extent to which consumers have emotional attachment and loyalty to existing brand names and the impact of such loyalty on purchase and consumption behaviour. Among other things, Coca-Cola's research failed to ask the respondents if the new Coke product should replace the original Coca-Cola. It is worth mentioning that a new product of Coca-Cola, Coke Zero, was launched in 2006. As opposed to the previous occasion, this time the company did not discontinue Coke or Diet Coke, and no disastrous outcome occurred. Coca-Cola might have learned from the previous mistake, and avoided making the same one this time.

Purpose of the Research Request

Determining the research purpose is the beginning of any good problem definition process. The decision maker has the initial responsibility of deciding there might be a need for the services of a researcher in addressing a recognized decision problem or opportunity. Once brought into the situation, the researcher begins the problem definition process by asking the decision maker to express their reasons for thinking there is a need to undertake research. Using this type of initial questioning procedure, researchers begin to develop insights as to what the decision maker believes to be the problem. Having some basic idea of why research is needed focuses attention on the circumstances surrounding the problem. The researcher then asks questions that distinguish between the symptoms and actual causal factors. One method that might be employed here is for researchers to familiarize the decision maker with the iceberg principle, displayed in Exhibit 2.8.

Understand the Complete Problem Situation

Both the decision maker and the researcher must understand the complete problem. This is easy to state but quite often difficult to execute. To gain such understanding, researchers and decision makers should perform a situation analysis of the circumstances surrounding the problem area. A **situation analysis** is a popular tool that focuses on the gathering of background information to familiarize the researcher with the overall complexity of the decision area. A situation analysis attempts to identify the events and factors that have led to the current decision problem situation, as well as any expected future consequences. Complete awareness of the problem situation provides better perspectives on (1) the decision maker's needs; (2) the complexity of the problem situation; and (3) the types of factors involved.

> **Situation analysis** A tool that focuses on the informal gathering of background information to familiarize the researcher with the overall complexity of the decision area.

EXHIBIT 2.8 The Iceberg Principle

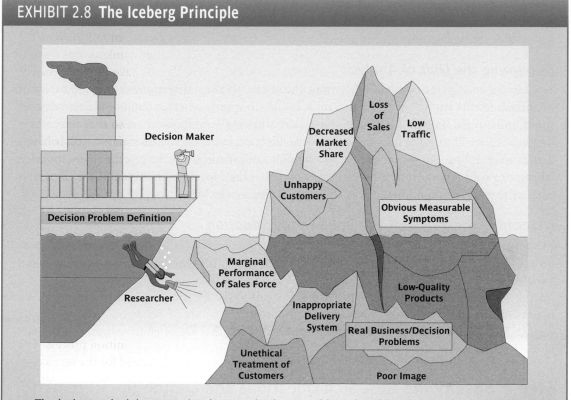

The iceberg principle states that in many business problem situations the decision maker is aware of only 10 per cent of the true problem. Often what is thought to be the problem is nothing more than an observable outcome or symptom (i.e. some type of measurable market performance factor), while 90 per cent of the problem is neither visible to nor clearly understood by decision makers. For example, the problem may be defined as 'loss of market share' when in fact the problem is ineffective advertising or a poorly trained sales force. The real problems are submerged below the waterline of observation. If the submerged portions of the problem are omitted from the problem definition and later from the research design, then decisions based on the research may be less than optimal.

Conducting a situation analysis can enhance communication between the researcher and the decision maker. The researcher must develop complete knowledge of the client's overall business. To objectively understand the client's situation (i.e. industry, competition, product lines, markets, and in some cases, production facilities), the researcher cannot rely solely on information provided by the client because many decision makers do not know or will not disclose all needed information. Only when the researcher sees the client's business practices objectively can the true problem be clarified. In short, researchers must develop expertise in the client's business.

Identify and Separate Out Measurable Symptoms

Once the researcher understands the overall problem situation, he or she must work with the decision maker to separate the root problems from the observable and measurable symptoms that may have been initially perceived as being the decision problem. For example, many times managers view declining sales or loss of market share as problems. After examining these issues, the researcher may see that they are the result of more concise issues such as poor advertising execution, lack of sales force motivation, or inadequate distribution. The challenge facing the researcher is one of clarifying the real decision problem by separating out possible causes from symptoms. Is a decline in sales truly the problem or merely a symptom of lack of planning, poor location, or ineffective sales management?

Determine the Unit of Analysis

As a fundamental part of problem definition, the researcher must determine the appropriate unit of analysis for the study. The researcher must be able to specify whether data should be collected about individuals, households, organizations, departments, geographical areas, or some combination of these. The unit of analysis will provide direction in later activities such as scale development and sampling. For example, in an automobile satisfaction study the researcher must decide whether to collect data from the purchaser (i.e. individual) of a specific vehicle or from a husband-wife dyad representing the household in which the vehicle is driven.

Determine the Relevant Variables to the Situation

The researcher and decision maker jointly determine the specific variables for the research questions that need to be answered. The primary focus is on identifying independent and dependent variables. Determination must be made as to the types of information (i.e. facts, predictions, relationships) and specific constructs that are relevant to the decision problem. A construct is a hypothetical variable consisting of several component responses or behaviours thought to be related. Exhibit 2.9 provides several examples of constructs that are often investigated with marketing research.

Step 2: Specify the Research Questions and Define the Research Problem

Next, the researcher must reformulate the problem in scientific terms. That is, the researcher must redefine the problem as a research question. This is necessary because scientific approaches are superior in executing a systematic approach to problem solving. This is the responsibility of the researcher. In fact, from here on the researcher assumes most of the responsibility for the satisfactory outcome of the research process.

EXHIBIT 2.9 Examples of Constructs Investigated in Marketing

Constructs	Operational Description
Brand awareness	The degree of awareness of a designated brand; awareness could be either unaided or aided
Attitudes towards a brand	The degree of intensity of consumers feeling positive or negative towards a specific brand
Purchase intentions	The likelihood of consumers planning to buy the specified object (e.g. product or service) within a designated time period
Importance of factors	The extent to which specific factors are influencing a consumer's purchase decision
Psychographics	The attitudes, interests, opinions, and lifestyle characteristics of consumers providing the information
Satisfaction	The evaluation of post-purchase consumption experience with a particular product, service, or company

Redefining the problem into a research question is the most critical step in the marketing research process, because how the research problem is defined greatly influences all of the remaining research steps. The researcher's task is to restate the initial variables associated with the problem in the form of one or more key question formats (how, what, where, when, or why). For example, the boss of a home improvement store chain was concerned about the corporate image of the company. The initial research question was, 'Do our marketing strategies need to be modified to increase satisfaction among our current and future customers?' For this purpose, a qualified marketing researcher was recruited to clarify the company's information needs. Having conducted some preliminary research, the researcher successfully translated the initial research question into a series of specific questions displayed in Exhibit 2.10. With assistance of the client company, the researcher then identified the attributes in each research question. For example, specific 'store/operation aspects' included convenient operating hours, friendly/courteous staff, and a wide assortment of products and services.

When research questions are written, two approaches can be taken to determine the level of detail to use. One approach is to phrase the question using a general focus that includes only the category of possible factors to develop the data requirements without specifying the actual individual factors. For example, with the demographic question in the home improvement store chain example, the phrasing is somewhat ambiguous because it expresses only the need for a 'demographic/psychographic profile' of customers without specifying which particular demographic characteristics (e.g. age, income, education level, marital status) or psychographic factors (e.g. price conscious, do-it-yourself, brand loyalist, information seeker) should be investigated. The other approach is to be much more specific in phrasing the research questions. For example, if the home improvement store chain is interested in determining the price range for a particular Black & Decker power drill, the research questions would be phrased as follows: (1) 'What are the price ranges customers expect to pay for the Black & Decker RX power drill?' and (2) 'What are the price ranges customers are willing to pay for the Black & Decker RX power drill?' Here each research question focuses on a specific data requirement – expected price ranges and then actual price ranges.

After redefining the problem into research questions and identifying the information requirements, the researcher must make initial assessments about the types of data (c.g. secondary or primary) that will best answer each research problem. Although final decisions on types of data are part of Step 4 (Determine the Research Design and Data Sources), the researcher begins the

---

EXHIBIT 2.10 Initial and Redefined Research Questions for the Home Improvement Store Chain

Initial research question:
Do our marketing strategies need to be modified to increase satisfaction among our current and future customer segments?

Redefined research questions:
What store/operation aspects do people believe are important in selecting a home improvement store?

How do customers evaluate the operation of our stores?

What are the perceived strengths and weaknesses of our store operations?

How do customers and non-customers compare our stores to other competitors' stores?

What is the demographic/psychographic profile of the people who patronize our stores?

process in Step 2. The researcher asks the question, 'Can the specific research question be addressed with data that already exist or does the question require new data?' To answer this fundamental question, researchers ask a series of additional questions concerning data availability, data quality, costs and time constraints.

Finally, Step 2 enables the researcher to determine whether the information being requested by management is necessary. This step must be completed before going on to Step 3.

Step 3: Confirm Research Objectives and Assess the Value of Information

The research objectives should be confirmed based on the definition of the research problem in Step 2. Formally stated research objectives provide guidelines for determining which other steps must be undertaken. The assumption is that if the objectives are achieved, the decision maker will have the information needed to solve the problem.

In some ways, research objectives serve as the justification for management and researchers to undertake a marketing research project. Consider the amphitheatre example in the Closer Look at Research box. Notice that the three research objectives listed at the end are different from the amphitheatre's statement of the research problem and the researcher's information problem. Before researchers move beyond Phase I of the research process, they must make sure a complete definition is given to each factor in the study. There also must be clear justification for the relevancy of each factor. For example, what does the amphitheatre design team really mean by 'protection'? Protection from what – rain or cold or snow, or perhaps something else?

A Closer Look at Research *(Small Business Implications)*
Design Features of a New Amphitheatre

A new amphitheatre, which would house a wide variety of performing arts events, is to be built in southern Europe. The amphitheatre design team is now facing some difficult decisions. They are not sure which design features should be included in the structure to handle different types of events (theatrical productions, music concerts, dance productions, etc.). Further, they can't decide if the structure should accommodate indoor events, outdoor events, or a combination. They question the seating capacity and are worried about ticket prices, parking requirements, availability of refreshments and types of events most desired by local residents and visitors. They subsequently hire a marketing research consultant to assist in gathering both primary and secondary data needed to address the team's questions and concerns. After several meetings with the design team, the researcher presents his research proposal, which states that the 'primary research objective focused on the collection of attitudinal and behavioural information to be used in addressing several questions posed by the amphitheatre design team. The questions focus on performing arts events and possible design features for the proposed amphitheatre structure.' Three of the key research questions are:

1 What type of performing arts programmes would residents and guests most prefer to see offered?

2 What prices should be charged for the various types of events?

3 What type of summer evening performing arts programmes would people prefer attending at an indoor versus outdoor facility? If outdoors, what type of protection should be provided to the audience and the performers?

Small Business Implications

These questions are then transformed into the following research objectives:

1 To determine how often people attended performing arts events in the past 12 months and which three types of events (dance productions, theatrical productions, music concerts, etc.) they would be most interested in attending.

2 To determine, by event type, the average price range a person would expect and be willing to pay for an adult-reserved-seat ticket to the events presented.

3 To determine the extent to which people would prefer to attend a specific type of event at an indoor or outdoor facility and the specific type of protection that should be offered the audience if the event was held at an outdoor facility.

Before moving to Phase II of the marketing research process, the decision maker and the researcher must evaluate the expected value of the information. This is not an easy task because a number of factors come into play. 'Best guess' answers have to be made to the following types of questions: (1) 'Can the information be collected at all?' (2) 'Can the information tell the decision maker something not already known?' (3) 'Will the information provide significant insights?' (4) 'What benefits will be delivered by this information?' In most cases, marketing research should be conducted only when the expected value of the information to be obtained exceeds the cost of doing the research.

Phase II: Select the Appropriate Research Design

The main focus of Phase II is to select the most appropriate research design for a given set of research objectives. The steps in this phase are briefly outlined below.

Step 4: Determine the Research Design and Data Sources

The research design serves as a master plan of the methods used to collect and analyse the data. Determining the most appropriate research design is a function of the marketing research objectives and the specific information requirements. In this plan, the researcher must consider the type of data, the data collection approach (survey, observation, etc.), the sampling method, the schedule and the budget. Although every research problem is unique, most research objectives can be met by using one of three types of research designs: exploratory, descriptive and causal.

Exploratory Research Designs

Exploratory research focuses on collecting either secondary or primary data and using an unstructured format to interpret them. Of the three types of research designs, exploratory research includes the fewest characteristics of the scientific method. It often is used simply to classify the problems or opportunities and is not intended to provide conclusive information to determine a course of action. Some examples of exploratory research techniques are focus-group

> **Exploratory research** Research that focuses on collecting either secondary or primary data and using an unstructured format or informal procedures to interpret them.

interviews, in-depth interviews and pilot studies. Exploratory research also may use some forms of secondary data (e.g. online databases). Exploratory research can be somewhat intuitive and is used by many decision makers who monitor market performance measures for their company or industry. Exploratory designs will be treated in more detail in Chapter 6.

Descriptive Research Designs

Descriptive research uses a set of scientific methods and procedures to collect raw data and create data structures that describe the existing characteristics (e.g. attitudes, intentions, preferences, purchase behaviours, evaluations of current marketing mix strategies) of a defined target group. Descriptive research designs are appropriate when the research objectives include determining the degree to which marketing variables are related to actual market phenomena. Here, the researcher looks for answers to the who, what, when, where and how questions.

> **Descriptive research** Research that uses a set of scientific methods and procedures to collect raw data and create data structures that describe the existing characteristics of a defined target population or market structure.

Descriptive studies provide information about customers, competitors, target markets, environmental factors, or other phenomena of concern. For example, there is a growing trend among chain restaurants to conduct annual studies that describe customers' attitudes, feelings and patronage behaviour towards their restaurants as well as towards the main competitors. These studies, referred to as either image assessment surveys or customer satisfaction surveys, describe how customers rate different restaurants' customer service, convenience of location, food quality, overall quality and so on. Information generated from descriptive designs provides decision makers with information to select a course of action. Descriptive designs will be discussed further in Chapter 7.

Causal Research Designs

Causal research is designed to collect raw data and create data structures that will enable the decision maker to determine cause-and-effect relationships between two or more decision variables. Causal research is most appropriate when the research objectives include the need to understand which decision variables (e.g. advertising) are the cause of the dependent phenomenon (e.g. sales) defined in the research problem.

> **Causal research** Research designed to collect raw data and create data structures and information that will allow the researcher to model cause-and-effect relationships between two or more market (or decision) variables.

Causal research can be used to understand the relationships between the causal factors and the outcome predicted. This type of research design enables decision makers to gain the highest level of understanding in the research process. In addition, understanding the cause–effect relationships among market performance factors enables the decision maker to make 'If–then' statements about the variables. For example, after the completion of a causal research study, the owner of a men's casual clothing store in Milan might be able to say, 'If I expand the assortment of brand-name shirts, increase my advertising budget by 15 per cent, have an introductory 30 per cent-off sale on the new shirts, and keep the rest of my marketing mix strategies unchanged, then overall sales volume can be predicted to increase by 40 per cent.'

While causal research designs provide an opportunity to assess and explain causality among critical market factors, they tend to be complex, expensive and time-consuming. Experimental designs have the greatest potential for establishing cause–effect relationships because they enable researchers to examine changes in one variable while manipulating one or more other variables under controlled conditions. Causal research designs are treated in more depth in Chapter 8.

Secondary and Primary Data Sources

The sources of data structures and information needed to solve marketing research problems can be classified as either secondary or primary, determination of which is based on three fundamental dimensions: (1) whether the data already exist in some type of recognizable format, (2) the degree to which the data have been interpreted by someone, and (3) the extent to which the researcher or decision maker understands the reason(s) why the data were collected and assembled. Sources of secondary data include inside a company, at public libraries and universities, on Internet websites, purchased from firms specializing in providing secondary information and so on. Chapters 3 through 5 cover secondary data and sources.

Primary data represent 'firsthand' raw data and data structures that have not had any type of meaningful interpretation. Primary data are the result of conducting some type of exploratory, descriptive, or causal research project that employs mainly surveys, focus groups, depth interviews or observation to collect the data. Primary data are collected and assembled specifically for a current marketing research problem. The nature and collection of primary data are covered in Chapters 6 to 13.

Step 5: Determine the Sampling Plan and Sample Size

If the decision is made to conduct some type of secondary research, then Step 5 (sampling) is not directly undertaken by the researcher. The researcher must still determine what population is being represented by the secondary data and decide if that population is relevant to the current research problem. Relevancy of secondary data is covered in Chapter 3. When conducting primary research, consideration must be given to sampling issues.

If predictions are to be made about market phenomena, the sample and its representativeness must be clearly understood. Typically, marketing decision makers are most interested in identifying and resolving problems associated with their target markets. Therefore, researchers need to identify the relevant **target population**. In collecting data, researchers can choose between two basic approaches. The first is referred to as a census of the target population. This may be the preferred approach for a small population. In a **census**, the researcher attempts to question or observe all the members of a defined target population.

Target population A specified group of people or objects for which questions can be asked or observations made to develop required data structures and information.

Census A procedure in which the researcher attempts to question or observe all the members of a defined target population.

EXHIBIT 2.11 Critical Questions and Issues in the Development of a Sampling Plan

- Given the problem, research objectives, and information requirements, who would be the best person (or object) to question or observe?
- What demographic (e.g. gender, occupation, age, marital status, income levels, education) and/or behavioural traits (e.g. regular/occasional/nonshopper; heavy user/light user/nonuser; customer/non-customer) should be used to identify population membership?
- How many population elements must be in the sample to ensure it is representative of the population?
- How reliable does the information have to be for the decision maker?
- What are the data quality factors and acceptable levels of sampling error?
- What technique should be used in the actual selection of sampling units?
- What are the time and cost constraints associated with executing the appropriate sampling plan?

The second approach, used when the defined target population is large, involves the selection of a **sample** from the overall membership pool of a defined target population. Researchers must use a representative sample of the population so the resulting information is generalizable. To achieve this objective, researchers develop a sampling plan as part of the overall research design. A sampling plan serves as the blueprint for defining the appropriate target population, identifying the possible respondents, establishing the procedures for selecting the sample, and determining the appropriate size of the sample. Exhibit 2.11 lists the critical questions and issues researchers typically faced when developing a sampling plan.

> **Sample** A randomly selected subgroup of people or objects from the overall membership pool of a defined target population.

Sampling plans can be classified into two general types: probability and nonprobability. In probability sampling, each member of the defined target population has a known chance of being selected. Also, probability sampling gives the researcher the opportunity to assess the sampling error. In contrast, nonprobability sampling plans cannot measure sampling error and limit the generalizability of any information to the population.

Sample size affects data quality and generalizability. Researchers must therefore determine how many people to include or how many objects to investigate. Chapters 9 and 10 discuss sampling in more detail.

Step 6: Assess Measurement Issues and Scales

Step 6 is the second most important step in the research process. This step focuses on identifying the dimensions to investigate and measuring the variables that underlie the problem. The measurement process determines how much raw data can be collected and also the amount of information that can be inferred from the data.

Given the importance of measurement to the process of creating information, researchers must be able to answer questions such as: (1) What level of information is needed from a variable? (2) How reliable does the information need to be? (3) How valid does the information need to be? (4) How does one ensure that the scale measurements are reliable and valid? (5) What dimensions underlie the critical factors being investigated? and (6) Should single measures or multi-item measures be used to collect the data? For example, researchers must know what scaling assumptions or properties must be built into a scale design to ensure management's information needs are met. Chapters 11 and 12 discuss measurement and scale design procedures as well as other important measurement issues.

Although most of the specific activities involved in Step 6 are related to primary research, understanding these activities is important in secondary research studies as well. For example, in executing data mining with database variables, researchers must consider the basic measurement issues involved with the database. They must have an understanding of the measurement principles that were used in creating the database as well as the potential biases associated with the data. Lack of understanding can easily lead to misinterpretation of the secondary data and reporting of inappropriate or inaccurate information.

Step 7: Pretest the Questionnaire

Researchers must always pretest the questionnaire. Pretesting is done with individuals representative of those who will be asked to actually complete the survey. In a pretest respondents are asked to complete the questionnaire and comment on issues like clarity of instructions and questions, sequence of the topics and questions, and anything that is potentially difficult or confusing.

Phase III: Execute the Research Design

The execution phase is the heart of the research process. The main objectives of this phase are to finalize all necessary data collection forms, gather and prepare the data, analyse the data and create appropriate data structures, and interpret those structures to understand the initial problem. To achieve this overall objective, researchers must execute the next three interactive steps of the research process: (8) data collection and preparation, (9) data analysis, and (10) transforming data structures into information. As in the first two phases, researchers here must be cautious to ensure potential biases or errors are either eliminated or at least minimized.

Step 8: Collect and Prepare Data
Data Collection Methods

There are two fundamental approaches to gathering raw data. One is to have interviewers and/or devices ask questions about variables and market phenomena or to use self-completion questionnaires. The other is to observe individuals or market phenomena. Some of the major tools available in these two fundamental approaches are listed in Exhibit 2.12.

A major advantage of questioning approaches over observation is they enable the researcher to collect a wider array of data. Survey data can pertain not only to current behaviour but also to state of mind or intentions. In short, it can be used to answer why people are behaving as they are, not just how.

EXHIBIT 2.12 Data Collection Tools Used in Marketing Research

Questioning Tool	Description
Trained interviewers	Highly trained people who ask respondents specific questions and accurately record their responses. *Examples:* face-to-face interviewers, telephone interviewers, focus group moderators who pose questions to the participants.
Interviewers with electronic devices	Highly skilled people who use high-technology devices during encounters with respondents. *Examples:* interviewers handling computer-assisted personal interviews and computer-assisted telephone interviews.
Fully automatic devices	High-technology devices that interact with respondents without the presence of a trained interviewer. *Examples:* on-site fully automatic interviews, fully automatic telephone interviews, computer-disk mail surveys, electronic-mail surveys, computer-generated fax surveys, Internet surveys.
Observation Tool	
Trained observers	Highly skilled people who use their senses (sight, hearing, smell, touch, taste) to observe and record physical phenomena. *Examples:* mystery shoppers, traffic counters, focus-group moderators who observe non-verbal communication clues of the participants.
Mechanical/ electronic devices	High-technology instruments that can artificially observe and record physical phenomena. *Examples:* security cameras, videotaping equipment, scanning devices, Internet technology, tape recorders, air-hose traffic counters.

Observation methods can be characterized as natural or contrived; disguised or undisguised; structured or unstructured; direct or indirect; and human, electronic, or mechanical. For example, researchers might use trained human observers or a variety of mechanical devices such as a video camera, tape recorder, audiometer, eye camera, or pupilometer to record behaviour or events.

As technology advances continue, researchers are moving towards integrating the benefits of technology with existing questioning tools that enable faster data acquisition. Online primary data studies (e.g. email surveys, online focus-group interviews, Internet surveys) are increasing as well as secondary database research studies. Data collection instruments and methods are covered in Chapters 6, 7, 8, 12, and 13.

Preparation of Data

Once the primary data are collected, the researcher must perform several activities before doing data analysis. A coding scheme is needed so the raw data can be entered into computer files. Typically, researchers assign a logical numerical descriptor (code value) to all response categories. After the responses are entered, the researcher inspects the computer files to verify they are accurate. The researcher then must clean the data for coding or data-entry errors. As part of the data-cleaning process, each variable's data structure is tabulated. Chapter 14 discusses data preparation.

Data preparation in secondary research studies is somewhat different from that used with primary research. Researchers focus on evaluating the use of a single or multiple databases to obtain the needed information. When the data exist in multiple databases, different databases must be merged into one comprehensive database, or accessible via Internet connections. At times, overlaying one database on another can be very challenging and may require restructuring of one or more databases to achieve compatibility. Another activity is determining which data should be included in the analysis. Chapter 5 covers secondary data preparation and other key issues.

Step 9: Analyse Data

In Step 9, the researcher begins the process of turning raw data into data structures that can be used to generate useful information for the decision maker. The researcher analyses the data and creates data structures that combine two or more variables into indexes, ratios, constructs and so on. Analysis procedures vary widely in sophistication and complexity, from simple frequency distributions (percentages) to sample statistics (e.g. mean, median, mode) and perhaps even multivariate data analysis for data mining. Different procedures enable the researcher to (1) statistically test hypotheses for significant differences or correlations among several variables, (2) evaluate data quality, and (3) test models of cause–effect relationships. Chapters 15 to 17 provide an overview of data analysis techniques.

Step 10: Transform Data Structures into Information

Information is created for decision makers in Step 10. Researchers, or in some cases, the decision maker interpret the results of the statistical analysis. This does not mean a simple narrative description of the results. Interpretation means integrating several aspects of the findings into statements that can be used to answer the initial question. The data are similar to colours that can be used to paint a comprehensive picture.

Phase IV: Communicate the Research Results

The last phase of the marketing research process focuses on reporting the research findings and newly created information to management. The overall objective is to develop a report that is useful to a non-research-oriented person.

Step 11: Prepare and Present the Final Report to Management

Step 11 is preparing and presenting the final research report to management. The importance of this step cannot be overstated. There are some sections that should be included in any research report (e.g. executive summary, introduction, problem definition and objectives, methodology, results and findings and limitations of study). The researcher asks the decision maker whether specific sections need to be included or expanded, such as recommendations for future actions or further information needs. In some cases, the researcher not only submits a written report but also makes an oral presentation of the major findings. Chapter 18 describes how to write and present research reports.

Develop a Marketing Research Proposal

By understanding the four phases of the research process, a researcher can develop a research proposal that communicates the research framework to the decision maker. A **research proposal**

Research proposal A specific document that serves as a written contract between the decision maker and the researcher.

is a specific document that serves as a written contract between the decision maker and the researcher. It lists the activities that will be undertaken to develop the needed information, the research deliverables, how long it will take and what it will cost.

The research proposal is not the same as a final research report. But some of the sections appear similar. There is no best way to write a research proposal. Exhibit 2.13 shows the sections that should be included in most research proposals. The exhibit presents only a general outline, but an actual proposal can be found in the Marketing Research in Action at the end of this chapter. Additional examples of research proposals are available at www.mhhe.com/shiu09.

EXHIBIT 2.13 General Outline of a Research Proposal

TITLE OF THE RESEARCH PROPOSAL

I. Purpose of the Proposed Research Project
Includes a description of the decision problem and specific research objectives.

II. Type of Study
Includes discussions of the type of research design (i.e. exploratory, descriptive, causal), and secondary versus primary data requirements, with some justification of choice.

III. Definition of the Target Population and Sample Size
Describes the overall target population to be studied and determination of the appropriate sample size, including a justification of the size.

IV. Sampling Design, Technique and Data Collection Method
Includes a substantial discussion regarding the sampling technique used, the actual method for collecting the data (e.g. observation or survey), incentive plans, and justifications.

V. Specific Research Instruments
Discusses the method used to collect the needed data, including the various types of scales.

VI. Potential Managerial Benefits of the Proposed Study
Discusses the expected values of the information to management and how the initial problem might be resolved, including the study's limitations.

VII. Proposed Cost for the Whole Project
Itemizes the expected costs associated with conducting the research project, including a total cost figure and anticipated completion time frames.

VIII. Profile of the Research Company Capabilities
Briefly describes the main researchers and their qualifications as well as a general overview of the company.

IX. Optional Dummy Tables of the Projected Results
Offers examples of how the data might be presented in the final report.

The JP Hotel Preferred Guest Card Marketing Research Proposal

Purpose of the Proposed Research Project

The purpose of this proposed research project is to collect attitudinal, behavioural, motivational and general demographic information to address several key questions concerning the JP Hotel Preferred Guest Card, a recently implemented marketing strategy. The key questions are as follows:

1 Is the Preferred Guest Card being used by cardholders?

2 How do cardholders evaluate the privileges associated with the card?

3 What are the perceived benefits and weaknesses of the card, and why?

4 To what extent does the Preferred Guest Card serve as an important factor in selecting a hotel?

5 How often do the cardholders use their Preferred Guest Card?

6 When do the cardholders use the card?

7 Of those who have used the card, what privileges have been used and how often?

8 What general or specific improvements should be made regarding the card or the extended privileges?

9 How did the cardholders obtain the card?

10 Should the Preferred Guest Card membership be complimentary or should cardholders pay an annual fee?

11 If there should be an annual fee, how much should it be? What would a cardholder be willing to pay?

12 What is the demographic profile of the people who have the JP Hotel Preferred Guest Card?

Type of Project

To collect the data needed to address the above-mentioned managerial questions, the research should be of a structured, nondisguised design characterized as exploratory and descriptive. The project will be descriptive to the extent that most of the questions focus on identifying the perceived awareness, attitudes, and usage patterns of the JP Hotel Preferred Guest Card as well as the demographic profiles of the current cardholders. It will be exploratory with regard to the investigation of possible improvements to the card and its privileges, the pricing structure and the perceived benefits and weaknesses of the current card's features.

Definition of the Target Population and Sample Size

The target population to be studied consists of 20,000 or so individuals who are current holders of the JP Hotel Preferred Guest Card. Statistically, a conservative sample size would be 384. But realistically, a sample of approximately 1,500 should be used to enable examination of sample subgroups. The bases for this approximation are (1) the likely response rate based on the sampling method and questionnaire design; (2) a predetermined level of precision of ±5 per cent sampling error and a desired confidence level of 95 per cent; (3) general administrative costs and trade-offs; and (4) the desirability of having a prespecified minimum number of randomly selected cardholders for the data analyses.

Sampling Design, Technique and Data Collection Method

A probabilistic random sampling technique will be used to draw the needed sample for the project. Using a mail survey, cardholders randomly selected as prospective respondents will be mailed a personalized self-administered questionnaire. Attached to the questionnaire will be a carefully designed cover letter that explains the generalities of the study as well as inducements for respondent participation. Given the nature of the study, the perceived type of cardholder, the general trade-offs regarding costs and time considerations, and the utilization of updated incentives to induce respondent participation, a mail survey would be more appropriate than other methods.

The Questionnaire

The questionnaire will be self-administered. That is, respondents will fill out the survey in the privacy of their home and without the presence of an interviewer. All the questions in the survey will be pretested by a convenience sample to assess clarity of instructions, questions, and administrative time dimensions. Response scales used in the actual questions will conform to standard questionnaire design guidelines and industry wisdom.

Potential Managerial Benefits of the Proposed Study

Given the scope and nature of this proposed research project, the study's findings will enable JP Hotel's management to answer questions regarding the Preferred Guest Card as well as other marketing strategy issues. Specifically, the proposed study will help JP management to

- Better understand the types of people that hold and use the Preferred Guest Card and the extent of that usage.
- Identify specific feature problems that could serve as indicators for evaluating (and possibly modifying) current marketing strategies or tactics as they relate to the card and its privileges.
- Develop specific insights concerning the promotion and distribution of the card to additional segments.

Additionally, the proposed research project will initiate a customer-oriented database and collection system to assist JP Hotel in better understanding its customers' service needs and wants in the future. Customer-oriented databases will be useful in developing promotional strategies as well as pricing and service approaches.

Proposed Project Costs

Questionnaire/cover letter design and reproduction costs	€1,400
Development	
Typing	
Pretest	
Reproduction (1,500)	
Envelopes (3,000)	
Sample design and plan costs	€ 810
Administration/data collection costs	€1,920
Questionnaire packet assembly	
Postage and PO box	
Address labels	

Coding and predata analysis costs	€ 2,000
Coding and setting of final codes	
Data entry	
Tab development	
Computer programming requirements	
Computer time	
Data analysis and interpretation costs	€ 3,250
Written report and presentation costs	€ 1,425
Total maximum proposed project cost*	€10,805

* Costing policy: Some costs may be less than what is stated on the proposal. Cost reductions, if any, will be passed on to the client. Additionally, there is a ± 10 per cent cost margin associated with the pre- and actual data analysis activities depending on client changes of the original tab and analyses requirements.

Principal Researcher's Profile

The research for this proposed project will be conducted by MRG, a research firm that specializes in a wide array of research approaches. MRG has conducted numerous marketing research studies for many Fortune 1000 companies. The principal researcher and project coordinator will be Dr Alex Smith, Senior Project Director at MRG. Dr Smith holds a PhD in Marketing and also an MBA. With 25 years of marketing research experience, he has conducted numerous projects within the consumer packaged-goods products, hotel/resort, retail banking, automobile and insurance industries, to name a few. He specializes in projects that focus on customer satisfaction, service/product quality, market segmentation, and general consumer attitudes and behaviour patterns as well as interactive electronic marketing technologies. In addition, he has published numerous articles on theoretical and pragmatic researching topics.

A Dummy Table Example of Findings

In an effort to illustrate the potential types of findings that can be expected from the proposed research, a dummy data table, which has been shown in Exhibit 2.5 above (see p. 52) is provided in this proposal. The dummy data table is used to illustrate the type of data table that would be useful in addressing the research question: 'To what extent does the Preferred Guest Card serve as an important factor in selecting a hotel?'

Questions

1 If this research proposal is implemented, will it achieve the purposes of the management of JP Hotel?

2 Is the target population being interviewed the appropriate one? Why or why not?

3 Are there any other questions you believe should be included in the project?

Summary of Learning Objectives

■ **Describe the major environmental factors influencing marketing research and explain their impacts on the research process.**
Several key environmental factors have significant impacts on the tasks, responsibilities and efforts associated with marketing research practices. The Internet and e-commerce, gatekeeper

technologies and data privacy legislation, new global market expansion, and repositioning marketing research as a strategy are forcing researchers to balance their use of secondary and primary data to assist decision makers in solving decision problems and taking advantage of opportunities. Researchers are required to continuously improve their ability to use technology-driven tools and databases. There are also greater needs for faster acquisition, retrieval, analysis and interpretation of cross-functional data and information among decision-making teams within global market environments.

- **Discuss the phases and steps of the research process and explain some of the key activities within each step.**
  The marketing research process was discussed in terms of four major phases, identified as (1) determination of the research problem; (2) development of the appropriate research design; (3) execution of the research design; and (4) communication of the results. To achieve the overall objectives of each phase, researchers must be able to successfully execute 10 interrelated task steps: (1) determine and clarify management's information needs; (2) redefine the decision problem as a research problem; (3) establish research objectives and determine the value of the information; (4) determine and evaluate the research design and data sources; (5) determine the sampling plan and sample size; (6) determine the measurement issues and scales; (7) collect and process data; (8) analyse data; (9) transform data structures into information; and (10) prepare and present the final report to management. The overview of the steps highlights the importance of each step and showed how it is related to the other steps in the research process.

- **Explain the differences between raw data, data structures and information and describe the process by which raw data are transformed into information that managers can use.**
  Researchers and decision makers must understand that raw data, data structures and information are different constructs. Raw data consist of the responses obtained by either questioning or observing people or physical phenomena. Data structures are created by submitting the raw data to some type of analysis procedure. In turn, information is created only when either the researcher or decision maker interprets the data structures.

- **Illustrate and explain the critical elements of problem definition in marketing research.**
  Phase I of the research process consists of three important task steps: (1) determine and clarify management's information needs; (2) redefine the decision problem as a research problem; and (3) establish research objectives and evaluate the value of information. The most critical step for the success of any research endeavour is the second one. Before redefining the initial decision problem as a research problem, the decision maker needs to work with the researcher to determine and clarify the true information needs of the situation. Defining the decision problem correctly requires the use of a five-step model that includes uncovering the decision maker's purpose, understanding the complete problem situation, separating out the measurable symptoms, determining the appropriate unit of analysis, and determining the most relevant factors of the situation. Defining decision problems as research problems allows the researcher to focus on the how, what, which, who, when, where and why questions needed to guide the formulation of the research objectives and clarify the pertinent information requirements. All the effort, time and money spent to execute marketing research will be wasted if the true marketing research problems are misunderstood.

- **Distinguish between exploratory, descriptive and causal research designs.**
  The main objective of exploratory research designs is to create information that the researcher or decision maker can use to (1) gain a clearer understanding of the decision

problem; (2) define or redefine the initial problem, separating the symptom variables from the independent and dependent factors; (3) crystallize the problem and the objective; or (4) identify the specific information requirements (e.g. facts, estimates, predictions, variable relationships). Exploratory research designs are not intended to provide conclusive information.

Descriptive research designs focus on using a set of quantitative methods to collect raw data and create data structures that are used to describe the existing characteristics (e.g. attitudes, intentions, preferences, purchase behaviours, evaluations of current marketing mix strategies) of a defined target population. The researcher looks for answers to how, who, what, when and where questions. Information from this type of research design allows decision makers to draw inferences about their customers, competitors, target markets or other phenomena of concern.

Finally, causal research designs are useful when the research objectives include the need to understand why particular market phenomena happen. The focus of this type of research design is to collect raw data and generate data structures and information that will allow the decision maker or researcher to model cause-and-effect relationships between two or more variables.

■ **Identify and explain the major components of a research proposal.**
Once the researcher understands the different phases and task steps of the marketing research process, they can develop a research proposal. The proposal serves as a contract between the researcher and the decision maker. There are nine sections suggested for inclusion: (1) purpose of the proposed research project; (2) type of study; (3) definition of the target population and sample size; (4) sampling design, technique and data collection method; (5) specific research instruments; (6) potential managerial benefits of the proposed study; (7) proposed cost for the whole project; (8) profile of the researcher and company; and (9) optional dummy tables of the projected results.

Key Terms and Concepts

Causal research 62	Internet 45
Census 63	Primary data 45
Data structures 51	Raw data 51
Decision problem 54	Research proposal 67
Descriptive research 62	Sample 64
Exploratory research 61	Scientific method 50
Gatekeeper technologies 45	Secondary data 45
Information 52	Situation analysis 56
Marketing research process 46	Target population 63

Review Questions

1 Identify the significant changes taking place in today's business environment that are forcing management decision makers to rethink their views of marketing research. Also discuss the potential impact that these changes might have on marketing research activities.

2 In the business world of the twenty-first century, will it be possible to make critical marketing decisions without marketing research? Why or why not?

3 How are management decision makers and marketing researchers alike? How are they different? How might the differences between these two types of professionals be reduced?

4 Explain the specific differences that exist between raw data, data structures and information. Discuss how marketing research practices are used to transform raw data into meaningful bits of information.

5 Comment on the following statements:

a The primary responsibility for determining whether marketing research activities are necessary is that of the marketing research specialist.

b The marketing research process serves as a blueprint for reducing risks in making marketing decisions.

c Selecting the most appropriate research design is the most critical task in the research process.

6 How can you determine when marketing research might be needed to solve a problem or pursue an opportunity?

7 Why is determining the decision problem as a research problem the most critical step in any research endeavour?

8 Discuss the activities involved in the problem definition process. What should be the researcher's responsibilities in that process?

9 How can the iceberg principle be used to help decision makers gain a clearer understanding of their decision problem? What are the major differences between problem symptoms and decision problems?

10 Explain the value of preparing a research proposal.

Discussion Questions

1 For each of the four phases of the marketing research process, identify the corresponding steps and develop a set of questions that a researcher should attempt to answer.

2 What are the differences in the main research objectives of exploratory, descriptive, and causal research designs? Which design type would be most appropriate to address the following question: 'How satisfied or dissatisfied are customers with the automobile repair service offerings of the dealership from which they purchased the latest version of Toyota cars?'

3 When should a researcher use a probability sampling method rather than a non-probability method?

4 **Experience the Internet**. Using your Internet browser and a search engine, go to the Gallup Poll Organization's page at **http://poll.gallup.com/**. Select the 'International Polls' option. Click on 'The Gallup Poll of Iraq' and then click on 'how the Gallup Poll of Iraq was conducted'. Read and comment on the research process used.

5 Using McDonald's as a case company, discuss how doing a situation analysis can help the researcher in determining a marketing research problem.

6 The programme manager at the BBC (British Broadcasting Corporation) would like to know how many viewers are likely to tune in to a new series of 'The Apprentice' TV programme. Identify three situations in which doing a marketing research study to address the programme manager's question might prove to be inappropriate, and explain why.

7 What kind of research design would be best for a Jimmy Spice's restaurant project whose purpose is to learn more about what current customers like or dislike about the restaurant?

8 How would you define the problem facing the owners of Jimmy Spice's restaurant?

Chapter 3

Marketing Research and Technology

> You know more about my customers after three months than I know after thirty years.
>
> *—Lord Maclaurin, Former Tesco chairman referring to the decision support system supported by Tesco Clubcard data*

Technology-Enabled Market Intelligence Allows AirMiles to Compete Better in the Air

AirMiles is equipped with a 13-strong customer insight team, which was set up in 2005, to enhance the company's relationship with its customers.

The company has about 8.5 million customers, of which 2.5 million are active. Although it has access to an enormous amount of behavioural data arising from its loyalty programme, AirMiles is concerned that this alone is not always enough to get to grips with its customers.

AirMiles recently conducted a large online market research project by emailing a questionnaire to 520,000 customers, both active and inactive. Seventy-one thousand of them responded. They replied with information about their likelihood to switch behaviour, which was married with their current behaviour, such as shopping at Tesco and holding a Clubcard, but not converting Clubcard points to AirMiles.

The data obtained from the project were analysed through the use of a statistical software package, in order to establish propensity models across AirMiles' active customer base. These models were used for the purposes of acquisition and cross-selling of collection partners. Communication with respondents was then tailed to show the Company had listened to them, understood their viewpoints and increased the degree of content relevancy for them.

The insights derived from the survey data were also passed electronically to the Company's communication channels, such as AirMiles' call centre and direct mail campaigns, in order to increase their effectiveness in optimizing the Company's marketing strategy.

Courtesy of Martin Evans of Cardiff Business School notifying the authors of this case study. Adapted from Marketing Direct Magazine, 2007.

Introduction

The real-world chapter opener illustrates how technology can be effectively deployed to collect data via the loyalty card programme and the Internet, to establish propensity models, and to share market intelligence information between different departments of the company. The importance of technologies in marketing research will become clear as you read this book. In the chapter on survey method, for example, online survey has been made possible through the advent of Internet technology. Also in many chapters, SPSS, a product of statistical software package technology advancement, has been used to facilitate the analysis of collected data.

This chapter does not intend to repeat the discussion of the technologies that are introduced in other chapters. Instead the chapter will focus first on the technologies that can be deployed for more strategic marketing research purposes. These include, among others, the use of technology for building up a market intelligence enterprise, a marketing research database, and a marketing decision support system. The chapter will then finish with the introduction of emerging technologies that could become highly influential in the marketing research industry in the near

EXHIBIT 3.1 **Some Crucial Topics Covered in this Chapter**

Telephone-enabled market intelligence
Telephone-enabled business intelligence
Data management process, including:
    Data warehousing
    Marketing research database
    Data mining
    Database modelling
Marketing decision support system, including
    Geographic information system
Other emerging technological trends
    Web 2.0
    Second Life

future. Exhibit 3.1 lists some of the crucial topics covered in this chapter, all of which are either facilitated (such as market intelligence and business intelligence) or driven (such as MDSS and geographic information system) by today's technologies.

Technology-Enabled Market Intelligence

A primary function of marketing research is to collect, store and analyse customer interaction information (customer knowledge). To do so, the practice of marketing research has to be transformed into one of **technology-enabled market intelligence**, which goes beyond the traditional market research practice of data gathering to one where data acquisition is strategic and transactional in focus. In short, technology-enabled market intelligence is based on real-time customer information that can be made possible only by the deployment of appropriate technology.

> **Technology-enabled market intelligence** The use of real-time customer information (customer knowledge) to achieve a competitive advantage, which can be made possible only by the deployment of appropriate technology.

Technology-enabled market intelligence begins with the notion of customer knowledge. An enterprise cannot meet its customers' needs and wants, and thereby offer value, unless it understands clearly the evolution and change of the customer. A major use of customer knowledge is to assess profitability and provide increased value to targeted customer segments.

Therefore, for effective use of the concept of technology-enabled market intelligence, the major questions to answer are:

1 What kind of relationship will add value to the enterprise's customers (loyalty programmes, preferred customer status, etc.)?

2 What is the value perception of the customer segment, and how can the value be enhanced (direct communication to customers, new services, etc.)?

3 What products and services, and what mode of delivery, have value to the customer segment (e.g. stock market alerts via Web-enabled cell phones)?

4 What are customers' responses to marketing and sales campaigns?

To answer these questions, marketing researchers capture and integrate information about consumers from multiple sources. This includes demographic and psychographic data, behavioural and preference data, complaint behaviour, and all other direct and indirect communications with the enterprise. Data of this nature are used for two purposes: to create customer profiles that can be used to tailor interactions with customers; and to segment customers in order to develop appropriate product and service offerings, marketing campaigns and growth and retention programmes.

Collecting and capturing the information involves the development of a technology-enabled market intelligence culture. This culture ensures that collected data are integrated into all facets of the enterprise. Most customer data in an enterprise exist in **silos**. That is, data that are exclusive to one functional area of the enterprise are not shared with other areas of the enterprise. For example, late payment notices from accounting are often not shared with customer service departments attempting to introduce customers to a new product or programme. Data such as these should be shared with all departments of the business so that an informed understanding of the customer is gained by all who interact with them. This level of knowledge and integration comes about only through technology-enabled market intelligence.

> **Silo** Data in one functional area of a business not shared with other areas exist in silos.

Transforming Marketing Research into Technology-Enabled Market Intelligence

A well-known premise in business is that approximately 20 per cent of a company's customer base provides a significantly high percentage of revenues and profit. For example, Coca-Cola found that one-third of its Diet Coke drinkers consumed 84 per cent of total Diet Coke sales. On the basis of this type of data, companies are fighting to increase profits from high-consumption customers. Like Coca-Cola, many companies are following an enterprise-wide focus, examining all organizational departments for the purpose of sharing and leveraging information. The goal of this process is to transform the company from a marketing research, information-acquisition company, to a technology-enabled market intelligence enterprise that shares information for the purpose of being connected, responsive and proactive to customers.

The technology-enabled market intelligence enterprise follows a different business model from traditional companies. The model provides a competitive advantage by using customer information at the **granular data** level. That is, data are detailed, highly personalized and specifically

> **Granular data** Highly detailed, highly personalized data specifically structured around an individual customer.

structured around the individual customer. The enterprise embraces the vision that targeting customers is not sufficient – capturing and retaining customers is the overall goal. On the basis of granular customer information, technology-enabled market intelligence enterprises anticipate the desires of the customer and refine their offerings according to this anticipation. This is commonly referred to as a customer-centric approach. A **customer-centric approach** facilitates convenience and efficiency for customers in their interactions with the enterprise. Interactions are used to obtain information from the customer in order to build and solidify a relationship. The Closer Look at Research box illustrates how the process works in the financial services industry.

> **Customer-centric approach** Use of granular data to anticipate and fulfil customers' desires.

The technology-enabled market intelligence enterprise has four unique characteristics that shape and define its character. These characteristics are (1) the strategic use of customer information; (2) information largely based on a transactional focus; (3) enterprisewide approach to the use of information; and crucially (4) the deployment of appropriate technology.

A Closer Look at Research *(In the field)*

Collecting Technology-Enabled Market Intelligence Data in the Financial Services Industry

Egg, an online bank based in the UK, embarked on a proactive technology-enabled market intelligence data collection programme in April 2005. It surveyed customers at risk of losing control of their debts. The objective of the survey was not to exert pressure on the debt-burdened customers to pay up, but to find out more about them and strengthen their ties to the bank.

The data gathered from the customers was transmitted to the Borrowing Management team of the bank. For any customer who had expressed dissatisfaction in the survey, an alert would automatically be generated in the call centre, which would make a follow-up call to the dissatisfied customer in order to try to resolve any problem issue. Egg would then close the loop by resurveying the customer as necessary, in order to ensure that the programme has effectively worked in the case.

Results of the proactive programme have been very encouraging. Follow-up survey data indicated that customers 'feel more in control of their finances since Egg began the programme' and are happier with the bank. Response rate to the survey of the programme increases to 10 per cent, which is much higher than the norm, and nearly 1,000 customers per month participate in the survey.

Source: Adapted from Admap, 2006.

Strategic Use of Customer Information

Two key questions driving technology-enabled market intelligence data collection programmes are 'What does my customer value?' and 'What is the value of my customer?' An enterprise driven by technology-enabled market intelligence addresses these questions through its unending effort to strategically use customer information to sort customers into profitable and unprofitable segments. Information from various sources both within and outside the enterprise must be organized and categorized into the firm's data warehouse. The primary information collected includes, among others, customer information from transactions (e.g. purchase frequency, purchase amount), salespeople (e.g. competitive information), call centres (e.g. customer feedback), sales promotion (e.g. tools used, results), survey data (e.g. customer satisfaction), in-store interactions, the Internet and database marketing companies. The enterprise then performs statistical analysis of a customer's value, likes and dislikes, lifetime value and profitability. Using this information, the enterprise refines its product and service offering to meet the needs of the most profitable customer segments, build loyalty among these customers, and manage positive relationships with them.

In the consumer electronics industry, for example, young single adults purchase DVD players for their homes and automobiles; new parents often want camcorders; and established families look for multiple televisions. Retired adults buy leisure products; divorced couples spend to set up new households. This is the type of information that can be profitable to a technology-enabled market intelligence enterprise.

Information Based on a Transactional Focus

In every contact with customers an opportunity exists to capture customer information, invest in the customer relationship and build loyalty. Real-time communication between the buyer and the enterprise enables the firm to enhance its positive interaction with the customer. During real-time communication, the enterprise has the opportunity to capture information beyond the transaction, for example, not just what the customer purchases when a desired item is not available (e.g. having to buy a Pepsi when a Coke is not available), but what each customer actually desires and why. The enterprise then shares that information throughout product planning and production to respond to the reason for needing the product or service.

Beyond the transaction, enterprises can collect information relating to the context of the interaction. Through contextual marketing, a bank, for example, might learn that a particular customer generally phones the bank's call centre on Sunday evenings. When the bank wants to communicate with that customer, that would be a good time and the telephone would be an excellent way of conducting the interaction.

Enterprise-wide Approach to the Use of Information

The process of gathering information during each transaction or at each contact with the customer and using that information is critical to the success of a technology-enabled market intelligence data collection programme. It is also critical that the information does not remain in the hands of marketing or advertising but is disseminated throughout the enterprise. Successful enterprises use information across all business units to manage the supply chain, create customized products and pricing structures, acquire new customers and improve service and quality. This is referred to as 'information at every **touchpoint**'. That is, all individuals in the enterprise having direct or indirect contact with the customer must be exposed to the identical level of information

Touchpoint　Specific customer information gathered and shared by all individuals in an enterprise.

pertaining to that customer. All business units – accounting, engineering, production, marketing, distribution, and so on – not only share information about customers, but share the same information about customers. This level of shared information must even extend beyond the firm to include all facets of the enterprise – suppliers, independent contractors, facilitating agencies and retailers.

Deployment of Appropriate Technology

Technology support makes it possible to develop a strategic, information-rich market intelligence programme. Technology provides the platform for turning customer data into customer knowledge. In short, information technology enables companies to maximize profitability through precise targeting of market segments. We are in a new era of marketing research that leverages relationships through the use of technology. For example, an enterprise collects customer data relating to demographics, billings, transactions, satisfaction levels and service quality. These data, with additional primary and secondary data, are integrated and stored in a centralized database called a data warehouse. The data are then analysed through such techniques as data mining. With powerful new technological approaches, companies are now leveraging technology so that information itself becomes a primary product. For example, Wal-Mart, the largest retailer in the world, requires all suppliers not only to access and use information in their data warehouse, but to cooperate in capturing information by using RFID (Radio Frequency Identification tags) tracking technology to manage the supply chain.

Data Collection in a Technology-Enabled Market Intelligence Environment

Growth in the electronic marketplace and the resultant increase in the availability of customer data have been major drivers of the accelerated pace at which enterprises are adopting technology-based solutions for developing their market intelligence environment. Technology is the driving force behind not only the integration and sharing of data, but also the collection of the data. In most technology-enabled market intelligence programmes, data are tracked at the point of customer interaction. This may occur at point-of-sale terminals or on the Web. Regardless of the source, the goal is to collect all relevant customer interaction data, store the data in the data warehouse, and subsequently analyse the data to develop profitable customer profiles.

Technology-Enabled Business Intelligence

Companies aiming at seeing a bigger picture may like to convert their enterprise from one of technology-enabled market intelligence to one of technology-enabled business intelligence. If so, they need to deploy the appropriate mix of technologies in order to develop and run a business intelligence programme (BIP). A BIP is a formal, continuously evolving process by which a business assesses the evolution of its industry, the trend in the market, as well as the capabilities of current and potential competitors to nurture a competitive advantage. It is not infeasible to develop and run a BIP without using advanced technology. However, technological advances, such as in computing speed, storage space, integration of different technological domains and virtualization, have made the nourishment and implementation of a BIP much more efficient, the data (both input and output) more accurate, and the result potentially more insightful.

Based on its BIP needs, a company gathers BIP data from its sales force and marketing research staff, customers, industry periodicals, competitors' promotional material, analysis of competitors' products and annual reports, trade shows, and distributors.

Approaches for Gathering BIP Data

Although a variety of approaches can be used to gather BIP data, the most appropriate one depends on the objective of the business intelligence programme. The following eight approaches are used for gathering BIP data:

1 **Governmental agencies.** Government sources can yield valuable data for the BIP, but their use may be limited by the excessive lead time involved.

2 **Online databases.** With increasing sophistication and affordability of information technology, this approach will proliferate as a data gathering method.

3 **Company and investment community resources.** Some types of data that are not widely available from databases can be obtained by contacting a particular corporation or investment community sources.

4 **Surveys and interviews.** Surveys can yield data about competitors and products, while interviews can provide more in-depth perspectives from a limited sample.

5 **Drive-by and on-site observations.** Observing competitors' parking spaces, new construction in progress, customer service at retail stores, volume and patterns of trucking activities, and so on, can provide useful BIP data about the state of a competitor's business.

6 **Benchmarking.** A leading competitor is identified and its operations are analysed and compared with the business's own operations.

7 **Defensive competitive intelligence.** A company monitors and analyses its own business activities as competitors and outsiders see them.

8 **Reverse engineering.** Unravelling of competitors' products and services may provide important information about their quality and costs.

Technology-Enabled Data Management Process

As illustrated in the chapter opening example, the foundation of any good technology-enabled market intelligence programme is its ability to provide shared information across the organization in order to serve their individual customers in the best possible manner. For this to occur the organization should make the fullest exploitation of appropriate technologies for developing and maintaining a vigorous customer data management process. This process includes collecting and storing customer data in a data warehouse, partitioning and categorizing the data in a marketing research database and utilizing data analysis techniques including data mining, to profile individual customers and react to their desires. In today's marketing research world an increasing amount of customer data can be retrieved through surfing the Internet, so we will begin this section by introducing the different types of Internet-generated customer data.

Internet-Generated Customer Data

Many customers surf the Internet under the illusion that their activities are private and anonymous. Signing onto the Internet, visiting virtual storefronts, sending and receiving email or chatting in newsgroups – all these activities are increasingly being tracked by various businesses. Many businesses search for valuable data about current or prospective customers through the Internet. These data can be classified as passive, active, or directed.

Passive Data

Passive data, frequently referred to as automatic data, are automatically given to a business once a consumer visits a particular website. The data obtained by the business is the Internet address, and it can appear in two forms. The Internet protocol (IP) address is the numeric location of a computer physically attached to the Internet. Each computer has its own unique and individualized IP address. The domain name (DN) is the second form of data obtained over the Internet. This type of data combines geographical and specific user information. For example, look at Dirk@uva.nl. Dirk is the user name, uva (Universiteit van Amsterdam) is the server name, and nl (the Netherlands) is the location.

> **Passive data** Data supplied to a business when a consumer visits the company's website.

Passively gathered data can be used by businesses for segmentation purpose. The information a surfer leaves by just visiting a site can easily be used to categorize individuals into segments. The business can narrow its customer demographic base by determining if there are any commonalities in the domain location of the customers and can target advertising or promotional material to this common domain.

Active Data

Active data are acquired by a business when customers interact with the business's website. Through the use of 'cookies' or online application forms filled out by the customer, a tremendous amount of information about the customer can be obtained. A cookie is a small piece of information a Web server can store with a Web browser and later read back from that browser. The user cookie is a unique identifier, assigned by the Web server and saved on a customer's computer that is provided back to the Web server upon request. Using this technology, a business can track a customer's progress through a website page by page. Once a customer visits a website, the customer will have the business added to his or her cookie file, indicating that this was a visited site.

Consequently, every time the customer accesses the business's website, the business will have the customer's information and will then be able to track the number of times that customer searched that website.

> **Active data** Data acquired by a business when customers interact with the business's website.

Added to passive data, active data increase the level of customer knowledge for the enterprise. Email addresses, other volunteered information and surfing patterns tracked through cookies can be used to enhance knowledge of the customer. The information can also be used to predict the tastes, desires, preferences, and buying patterns of the customer. For example, a customer can visit IKEA's website, the popular Swedish furniture seller, and select items such as desk lamps, light bulbs, book shelves, cupboards, or kitchen appliances. As the customer adds these items to the shopping cart on the website, the list of these items is kept in the customer's browser's cookie file so that all the items can be paid for at once at the end of the shopping experience. Of course, if the customer makes a purchase, email addresses, credit card information and geographic location of the customer are also retained in the file. On the basis of a simple shopping trip, IKEA now knows who the customer is, where the customer lives, various forms of financial information, what was bought and in what quantity and how to contact this customer for future communications. The interactive nature of this data collection method enables companies to use the information obtained to target market efforts so narrowly that marketing efforts can be personalized for each individual customer.

Directed Data

Directed data are comprehensive data available on customers through the use of computers. Directed data are not necessarily new information on customers but can be considered newly accessed information on customers. For example, businesses can use the online services provided by Experian, one of the leading credit information providers in the world, to find the customer's full name, full address, postcode and credit purchase history.

> **Directed data** Comprehensive data about customers collected through the use of computers.

This type of data can yield rich information about a customer. As another example, directed data can be used to track a person's visits on the Web and buying habits, and even generate a complete profile of the individual. In fact, technologies have been developed to log and analyse a person's browser patterns. Businesses buying into these technologies can collect valuable data about their customers and potential customers.

We now move on to discuss the four pillars of technology-enabled data management process. These are data warehousing, marketing research database, data mining, and database modelling.

Data Warehousing

A **data warehouse** is a central repository for the information an organization collects. Data from various functions of the organization are stored in a central computer so that the information can be shared across all functional departments of the business. The major significance of a data warehouse is its purposes. From the standpoint of data collection, a data warehouse serves two purposes. First, the data warehouse collects and stores data for the daily operation of the business. This type of data is called **operational data** and the system used to collect operational data is online transaction processing, known as OLTP. Operational data represent not only information collected from customers, but also data collected from suppliers and vendors.

> **Data warehouse** Central repository for all significant parts of information that an organization collects.
>
> **Operational data** Data for the daily operation of the business.

The second purpose of the data warehouse is to collect, organize and make data available for analysis. This enables the business to use the data warehouse as a decision-making tool for marketing programmes. This type of data is commonly referred to as **informational data** and the system used to collect and organize informational data is online analytical processing, known as OLAP. This process involves the development of customer categories based on relationships among the data. For example, purchase history, patronage frequency, store choice, and brand preference may all share a common relationship among a group of customers and are therefore grouped and categorized to form a profile of a particular customer group, similar to that of a market segment profile. The data warehouse provides the company with a system that is driven toward shared information; that is, information that can be used by any and all functional departments of the business.

> **Informational data** Data available for analysis purposes.

A data warehouse is comparable to a campus library, both as a resource for and as a service to the entire university. The value of your campus library resource is determined by the variety and assortment of books, periodicals and professional information it contains. The value of your campus library service is based on how quickly and easily the staff can assist you in finding and using what you need.

In a data warehouse, the value of the resource is determined by the amount and variety of data collected and stored in the warehouse. The value of the service is determined by the ease of use and the extent to which the information can be shared throughout the entire business.

Types of Customer Data in Data Warehouse

The type of data collected and stored is a key determinant of the success of any data warehouse. Data collected for a warehouse is highly specific to the business, yet the common feature of all data, regardless of the business, is that it is centred on the customer. Hospitals collect data on patient procedures, financial institutions collect data on financial services used, and insurance companies collect data on types of policies and risk associated with types of events that might occur. Although all three differ in their product/service offerings, they are similar in collecting data related to the customer. Aside from secondary and primary data stored in the warehouse, two unique types of customer data most commonly collected for a data warehouse are (1) real-time transactional data and (2) customer-volunteered data.

Real-time transactional data are collected at the point of sale. This type of data is usually collected through a customer loyalty programme. Customer loyalty cards identify who the customer is, what the customer is buying and in what quantity and frequency, and at what type of retail outlet. The key dimension is that data are collected at the time of purchase, so manufacturers can identify how customers respond to a specific marketing programme being used at that point in time. For example, sales of Stella Artois beer may be tracked via point-of-sale data where price may vary over certain days along with point-of-sale promotional activities. In this case, the retailer can identify the impact of price and promotional variations on the sale of Stella Artois beer.

> **Real-time transactional data** Data that are collected at the point of sale.

Customer-volunteered information is provided by the customer without any solicitation. This type of data can be offline or online. Examples are customer comment cards or complaints, customer communications via online chat rooms and data obtained through customer groups.

> **Customer-volunteered information** Data that are provided by the customer without any solicitation.

In the US, Wal-Mart has both real-time transactional data and customer-volunteer information in its data warehouse. Its data warehouse, second in size only to the Pentagon, contains over 200 terabytes (trillions of characters) of transactional data. Among other things, Wal-Mart uses its warehouse database to help stores select and adapt merchandising mixes to match local neighbourhood preferences. In the UK, through its Clubcard loyalty programme, Tesco also has huge amount of customer data that can track the shopping habits of up to 13 million British families for more than a decade.

Marketing Research Database

A marketing research database is a central repository of all relevant information concerning a company's customers. Specifically, a **marketing research database** is a collection of information indicating what customers are purchasing, how often they purchase and the amount they purchase. A well-designed marketing research database incorporates information from a multitude of diverse sources, including actual transactions, history of promotional effectiveness, consumer surveys, secondary data and other past marketing research project data. Unlike operational databases that reflect accounting and financial data, a marketing research database enables users to analyse purchase behaviour over some predetermined time frame, event, or business situation.

> **Marketing research database** Collection of information indicating what customers are purchasing, how often they purchase, and the amount they purchase.

A typical marketing research database is structured around transactional information that is chronologically arranged to reflect each purchase occasion. Additional information (demographics, lifestyles, media habits) is entered into the transactional data so a company can develop a complete picture of its customers. The outcome is a complete customer profile based on actual purchase frequency and amount at any given point in time. When categorized effectively, the information provides a company with a total customer portfolio to be used in making product or brand decisions, resource allocations and decisions on communication tools and distribution channels.

The information in a marketing research database is generated by the customer via sales invoices, warranty cards, telephone calls, market research projects and so forth. The information is then logically arranged to allow for instant access whenever the customer contacts a company or vice versa.

Such databases typically are linked to an interactive computer system that can automatically display a customer profile on demand. This enables the user of the database to recognize customers by name, purchase history, general interests and product uses, as well as future product needs. In addition, many marketing research databases are complemented with information pertaining to a company's total product mix. This tells the database user exactly what a company makes or sells, which items are the most popular, and which are most suitable for certain customers.

At the core of the database is a network that provides specific information on each and every product or service provided by the company. With such information companies can tell customers which replacement parts to order for their dishwasher, how to change a filter on their air conditioner, what games are available for their Nintendo system and what each would cost. Even technical questions, such as those regarding installation of a home television satellite system, can be routed to a company expert.

Airlines and travel agencies provide excellent examples of marketing research database development and usage. These service providers take the concept of the marketing research database further by being able to book customers on complicated tours around the world; have hotel rooms and rental cars waiting at each destination; and deliver tickets, boarding passes and itineraries overnight. This happens because of a networked database that links airlines, hotels, car rental services and express delivery systems. With database information, the service provider knows a particular customer prefers a window seat, usually travels with Lufthansa, always flies first class and uses Hertz Number One Gold Club Auto Rentals. The service provider knows the address to which the tickets are to be delivered, the spouse's name and the home and office phone numbers. All of the customer's information is stored in the database and can be accessed instantly anytime the service provider needs it.

 ## A Closer Look at Research (*In the field*)

Relying on External Database Expert Companies – the UK Business Universe™

Because of expertise, time, financial or other constraints, some companies may decide not to develop the marketing research database themselves, and instead rely on external database expert companies. One such company is Blue Sheep, an important business-to-business marketing services provider, based in Cheltenham, UK, which has launched the UK Business Universe. It is an aggregated database of various different data sources about the UK workplace market, which can be very useful for business-to-business marketing purpose. Information from over 8 million workplace locations is brought together in a single file leading to a consolidated database of nearly 5 million workplace records suitable for analysis purpose and over 4 million workplace records that can be used straight for direct marketing campaigns.

The file is updated monthly. Each data supplier provides Blue Sheep with a fresh copy of their database. The company then conducts over 1.8 billion matches to make sure the file is as up to date as possible. With over 450,000 amendments made by the data suppliers to their databases, the need to reflect these continual amendments in the company's consolidated database is crucial.

The Venn diagram below shows the overlap of records from five of the company's data suppliers after matching. In this sample, only 32,000 out of the 4.3 million records are present in all the five databases. Such a lack of overlap highlights the significant benefit derived from the consolidation of diverse customer data sources.

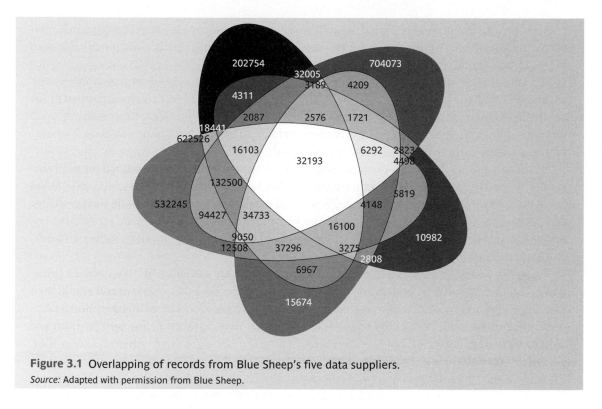

Figure 3.1 Overlapping of records from Blue Sheep's five data suppliers.
Source: Adapted with permission from Blue Sheep.

Purposes of a Marketing Research Database

In the broadest sense, the purpose of any marketing research database is to help a firm develop meaningful, personal communication with its customers. This level of communication deals with the proper products or brands, the various prices of the product offering and the level of customer service to be built into the total offering. In short, a marketing research database allows a company to communicate at the right place, at the right time, with the right product, to the right customer. Lands' End, Dell, Nike, Coca-Cola, Procter and Gamble, BMW, Cath Kidston and many other consumer goods companies have extensive databases to better serve their customers.

More specific purposes of the marketing research database are (1) to improve the efficiency of market segmentation; (2) to increase the probability of repeat purchase behaviour; and (3) to enhance sales and media effectiveness. To fulfil these purposes, the successful marketing research database must enable users to measure, track, and analyse customer buying behaviours. The role of marketing research, then, becomes one of generating, developing and sustaining the database.

Marketing research databases are constructed to achieve or enhance customer relationships. The databases bring back the level of individual service lost due to mass merchandising. In the past, local retailers knew each customer and their family members. They established a bond with customers that included two-way communication, instilled customer loyalty, increased customer satisfaction and fostered the growth of the business. Mass merchandising and modern retailing ended this relationship. Price, not loyalty, began to drive customers' purchase decisions. While quality of merchandise went up, personal service went down. Today the situation is reversing itself. By giving a firm access to information on each customer's family demographics, leisure activities, purchase history, media interests and personal socioeconomic factors, the modern database can help that firm recreate personal service.

Four fundamental areas in which the database benefits the firm are (1) exchanging information with customers, (2) determining heavy users, (3) determining lifetime customer value, and (4) building segment profiles.

One of the most valuable benefits of a database involves the exchange of information between a firm and its customers. Information on product availability, special features, competitive product comparisons, repairs and warranties is critical for customer service. Most businesses, through internal secondary data, have this information available. The task becomes providing it to customers to allow them better decision-making capabilities.

At the same time, customers possess a wealth of information absolutely essential for any business. Why do customers buy a certain product? What features and benefits do they seek? What other products are they likely to purchase? Successful databases constantly provide such exchange of information. Every contact with a customer becomes an occasion to provide more information to a database. Also, as a business learns more about its customers, it understands what information customers want from it.

Information exchange tells a business that all customers are not alike. With a database, businesses can distinguish heavy, medium and light users of their product or service and adjust their strategy accordingly. The database's ranking system for all customers can help the business tailor products, benefits and services to each class to keep heavy users loyal and stimulate medium and light users to buy more.

Within each user class, the business can also determine the expected lifetime value per customer. When a customer is acquired, the database enables the business to determine what it can expect from that customer. Calculating contribution to profit and overhead for a customer's lifetime with the company is a major task. Using this lifetime value, the company can determine how much to spend on marketing activities to keep the customer satisfied and loyal.

Finally, a marketing research database enables the business to answer the crucial question: 'Why do some consumers buy our products or services regularly, while others do not?' The simple premise behind a database is that consumers themselves can provide the information necessary to answer this question. Other questions that can be answered using the database include:

- How do our products compare with the competition?
- What is the relationship between perceived value and price of the product?
- How satisfied are customers with the service level and support for the product?
- What are the comparisons among demographics, lifestyles, attitudes, and media habits between different buyers and users of the product?

Through various modelling techniques, individuals can be profiled on the basis of selected characteristics that will likely distinguish buyers from non-buyers, as well as heavier from lighter users.

Data Enhancement

The primary role of a database is to serve as an information and intelligence resource for a company. Central to this objective is the process of **data enhancement**, which is defined as the overlay

> **Data enhancement** The overlay or partitioning of information about new or existing customers for the purpose of better determining their responsiveness to marketing programmes.

(adding) of information about customers to better determine their responsiveness to marketing programmes. Data enhancement gives organizations three distinct advantages:

1 **More knowledge of customers.** Knowing exactly who buys products or services is extremely valuable in adjusting a company's marketing plan. Most databases are built with this purpose and concentrate on internal company data for current users of a product or service. Data enhancement enables external primary data to be woven into current internal data to gain a more accurate categorization of customers based on their true value to the company. The external data normally contain, but are not limited to, demographic, psychographic, behavioural and motivational data about various consumers.

2 **Increased effectiveness of marketing programmes.** Through data enhancement, the marketing function of an organization can gain greater insights into communications, distribution and new product development. When internal data about customers are enhanced with external data, usage profiles by consumer can be tailored to reflect the unique desires of various customer groups.

3 **Better prediction of response to new marketing programmes.** Having concise information on various customer groups allows for increased targeting efficiency. Efficiency is increased when current customer profiles are used to predict the probability of targeting new yet similar customers with a new marketing plan. In short, the probability of success regarding new programmes and procedures can be calculated according to the enhanced data.

Effective Development of Enhanced Databases

A typical database contains three critical data units that can be interactively categorized for unique customer profile reports: geodemographic, attribute and target market dimensions. Exhibit 3.2 shows the interactive properties of these data units.

Two levels of geodemographic factors are generally used: geographic market and residential area. At the residential level, information requirements centre on the individual, the household and the postcode where current customers reside. The geographic market level requires data at a more aggregate level representing metropolitan or regional market areas.

Typically, attitudinal data reflect an individual's preferences, views and feelings toward a particular product or service offering. Attitudinal data reflect a person's overall attitude towards the product, specific brands and product features and are an important component of database

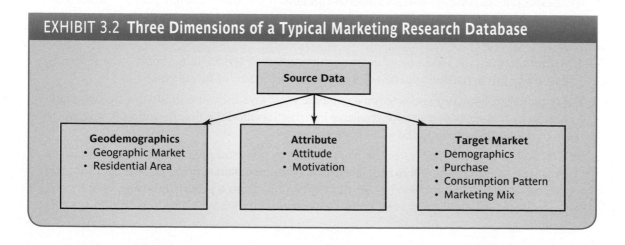

EXHIBIT 3.2 Three Dimensions of a Typical Marketing Research Database

development because they are related to purchase behaviour. When individuals have a positive attitude towards a product or brand, they are more inclined to buy it than when they have neutral or negative attitude.

Motivational data refer to the drive, desire, or impulse that channels an individual's behaviour towards a goal. Motivational data typically involve those factors behind why people behave as they do. Seeking particular product benefits, shopping at stores that are convenient and comfortable, or simply enjoying the interaction with certain salespeople may all constitute motivational characteristics that drive a purchase decision. In short, motivational data reflect the activities behind the purchase. Whether the issue is store loyalty, brand loyalty, or media influence, motivational data describe those circumstances that direct a customer's behaviour towards a goal.

Target market characteristics describe heavy product users versus light users on such dimensions as demographics, purchase volume and purchase frequency. Other data reveal household consumption patterns, shopping patterns, advertising effectiveness and price sensitivity information.

The key to database enhancement, of course, is the availability of data to increase the interactive efficiency of the data units. In most database development, the geodemographic unit is called the driver dimension because it determines (or drives) the type and amount of additional data that can be generated for cross-reference purposes. For example, a company may have a limited database of its current customers. But it wants to use a promotional campaign to increase awareness of its product offering among potential new users. Analysis of its database based on geodemographic factors reveals useful information on where current customers reside. However, it provides little value regarding the targeting of new customers except for similar residential locations. Therefore, the data requirement shifts to obtaining external data on attributes and target market characteristics of current users in order to enhance the transferability of current customer profiles to potential new customers.

In this simple example, geodemographic data served as the driver for determining additional data requirements. Depending on the level and amount of information available on a geodemographic level, additional data requirements are then determined.

The Dynamics of Database Development

A database is 'a comprehensive collection of interrelated data'. The data comes from many sources both internal and external to the company. Regardless of where the information comes from, a database is only as good as the information it contains. If the information required to make marketing decisions is not in the database, the database is useless. From a marketing perspective, information generated for a database must possess the following:

1 **Affinity.** Data must reflect prior usage of the product or service in question. Data reflecting past usage by current customers is one of the best predictors of future purchases.

2 **Frequency.** Information reflected in a database must give users the ability to categorize customers by frequency of purchase. Available information should reflect the amount of business each individual has conducted with the company.

3 **Recency.** Length of time between purchases is a very powerful predictor of future purchases. Because of this, recency of purchase is a critical factor in database dynamics. Recency assumes that a customer who purchased a non-durable product from a particular business last month has a greater probability of repurchase than a customer whose last purchase occurred six months ago.

Using recency, customers are profiled on the basis of their most recent purchase, the most recent having the highest probability and the least recent having the lowest probability of repurchase. Each customer is assigned a recency code (1=most recent, 5=least recent, for example) and sorted into groups based on the assigned codes.

Once these profiles are established, decision makers view these customers in a totally different light. Certain customer groups can receive new product promotions, while others may be targeted with specially designed marketing efforts to increase repeat purchases. Recency allows the business to build better relationships with different customer classes. It enables the researcher to determine which ones are most important and which groups need additional cultivation.

4 **Amount.** How much a customer purchases from any one company is a good predictor of future usage status. Therefore, the data must facilitate categorization of customers into specific usage groups (light, medium, heavy users).

Many companies go beyond the above guidelines and consider profitability as well. Customers may purchase frequently and in large amounts, but if they purchase only items that are on sale or deeply discounted they are less profitable to the firm. In the banking sector, some company divides its customers into 10 segments based on profitability. Customers in the more profitable segments are called by relationship managers to make them aware of new products and services. Less profitable customers are encouraged to use less costly approaches like the Internet.

While it is important to realize that the information for a database must contain certain characteristics, researchers must never lose sight of the fact that database development is unique to each company. The amount and type of information relevant to one business may not be relevant to another. Database development is highly specific, yet within this specificity lies the art of maximizing the relevancy of the information.

Rules of Thumb in Database Development

Given the value a well-developed database can add to a company, management should view the total process of database development as a commitment to a long-term data acquisition plan. Thus, the development of a database should be budgeted as a multiyear process. Researchers should begin with collecting the data that will have the greatest amount of predictive power.

Second, management should view the data acquisition process in terms of the width and depth of the database. **Depth** refers to the overall number of key data fields or variables that make up the data record (all data pertaining to the individual or company). **Width**, in contrast, refers to the total number of records contained in the database (total number of individuals or companies in the database).

Depth The overall number of key data fields or key variables that will make up the data record.

Width The total number of records contained in the database (also referred to as sample size).

Finally, companies should avoid jumping onto the database bandwagon (i.e. developing a database just because everyone else is) and then failing to commit the necessary resources. A marketing research database is a constant and ongoing process. A database will not succeed unless the company makes a commitment to long-term data acquisition and enhancement.

Database Technology

Many companies have data on almost every aspect of their operations. They even have data on how much data they have. What are data? Data are verbal or numerical facts that can be used for reasoning or calculating. In database terminology, a **data field** is a basic characteristic about a customer or client (e.g. gender, age, name, address).

> **Data field** A basic characteristic about a customer.

Data fields have little value when treated individually. But when they are combined in a manner that makes them useful for making decisions, they acquire value and can be regarded as information. **Database technology** refers to the tools used to transform data into information. Database technology processes data and stores it in a single databank. It consists of two unique features: a database management system and a data dictionary. A database management system is a computer programme that creates, modifies and controls access to the data in the database. Users of these programmes follow basic instructions to combine data and produce a desired output. The output of a typical database management system is shown in Exhibit 3.3. A data dictionary provides descriptions of the data in the database. It formats the data and assigns meaning to the data fields or variables. Together, the database management system and data dictionary constitute what is called the database processing system.

> **Database technology** The tools that are used to transform data into information.

Two types of database processing systems exist: sequential and relational. A **sequential database system** organizes data in a very simple pattern; that is, a simple path, linkage, or network. In a sequential database only two single data fields can be paired. Once paired, they can be linked to a third data field. Once this group is connected, it can be linked to a fourth, and then to a fifth, and so on, as illustrated in Exhibit 3.4.

> **Sequential database system** Data in a very simple pattern; that is, a simple path, linkage, or network.

Many companies choose to develop sequential databases because they allow users to easily access detailed data linked to a specific data field or variable (e.g. region shipped). Also, database systems are commonly used by companies that require reports based on consistent data in a given format, which can be easily prepared by a sequential database system.

EXHIBIT 3.3 Typical Output of a Database Management System

PRIMARY BUSINESS	CONTACT PERSON	ADDRESS	PHONE	FAX	EMAIL	CUSTOMER NO.
Banking	Douglas Jones					521170
Banking	Ernest Stevens					299568
Food	Denny Taveres					572117
Computer	Richard Trotter					342422
Food	John Richards					595710
Food	Clare Thomson					127397
Computer	Dale Cowart					376271
Computer	Daniel Grant					222620
Cosmetics	George Michie					542005
Cosmetics	Lucy Chen					109800
Cosmetics	Frank Terry					961758
Cosmetics	Benson Shiu					485416
Cosmetics	Jenny Sepulveda					485414
Cosmetics	Jerry Wooster					600671
Computer	Millos Cikasa					535822
Computer	Olivier Dulaun					407602
Computer	Patricia Sugar					780000
Computer	Louise Allen					740005
Computer	Michael Jones					145560
Computer	Mark Mika					397700
Banking	Bill Tomlinson					194076
Banking	Carol Collins					488978
Cosmetics	Gordon Canning					431884
Cosmetics	Paul Morgan					420092
Cosmetics	Allen Ransom					312743
Food	Marilyn White					375954
Food	Gemma Nicholson					383478
Food	Philip Crouch					360140
Food	Elizabeth McClaren					403937
Food	Royce Shafer					957600
Cosmetics	Malcolm Green					383478
Cosmetics	Leslie Wong					429606
Food	Candy Lee					375954
Food	Bruce Fisher					997554
Food	Dan Premus					596553
Food	Bruce Fisher					325766
Food	Edward Cassateri					189319
Banking	David Whelan					550691
Banking	Nancy Holland					568613
Banking	Sarah Lampard					222430
Cosmetics	Roland Gage					787745
Food	Wayne West					984813
Food	Christine Allen					494287

For privacy reason, contact details including addresses, phone numbers, fax numbers and email addresses are not shown.

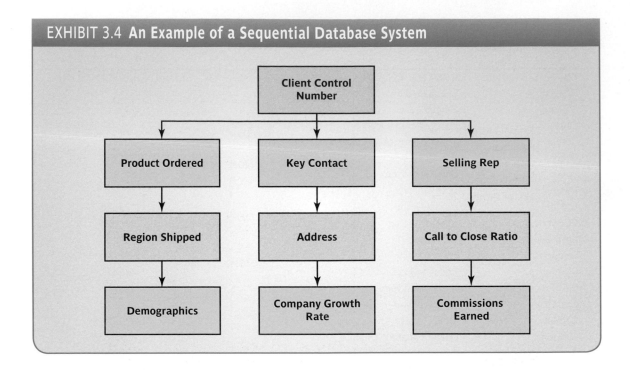

EXHIBIT 3.4 An Example of a Sequential Database System

A **relational database system** operates somewhat differently from a sequential database system. The major difference is that relational databases require no direct relationship between data fields or variables. Data are structured in tables with rows and columns, with the tables (not the data fields) being linked together depending on the output desired. With a relational database system, the table becomes an individual file, rows correspond to records (width), and columns represent data fields or variables (depth) within each record.

> **Relational database system** A system that structures a database in tables with rows and columns, with the tables (not data fields) being linked together depending on the output desired.

In Exhibit 3.5, for example, each row represents the number of customers for that particular field. The 'primary market served' attribute, for example, is divided into regional, national and international fields. Each column contains the breakdown of each customer by primary business (bakery, snack food, medicine, etc.). The rows and columns together constitute the table, which profiles customers by industry segment.

Relational databases offer greater flexibility than sequential databases in examining complex data relationships. In addition, relational databases enable the analyst to look at all data fields or variables simultaneously rather than one variable at a time. Overall, relational databases are best for dynamic situations in which the database must expand over time and in which multiple variable applications are needed.

EXHIBIT 3.5 A Relational Database Showing a Customer Profile by Industry Segment

	Bakery (15)	Snack food (42)	Medicine (35)	Chemical (7)	Other (11)
Primary Market Served					
Regional	1(6.7)	3(7.1)		1(14.3)	1(9.1)
National		37(88.1)	7(20.0)	2(28.6)	3(27.3)
International	3(20.0)		8(22.9)	2(28.6)	5(45.5)
No. of Product Lines					
One	1(6.7)		1(2.9)	1(14.3)	3(27.3)
Two	6(40.0)	2(4.8)	2(5.7)		2(18.2)
Three		1(2.4)	5(14.3)	1(14.3)	1(9.1)
Four	1(6.7)	4(9.5)	4(11.4)	3(42.9)	
Five				1(2.9)	
Six	1(6.7)				1(9.1)
Seven					
Region					
North East	5(33.3)	9(21.4)	13(37.1)		2(18.2)
South East	1(1.7)	1(2.4)	4(11.4)	6(85.7)	5(45.5)
North West	4(26.7)	23(54.8)	3(8.6)	1(14.3)	2(18.2)
South West	5(33.3)	2(4.8)	1(2.9)		2(18.2)
Central		7(16.7)	13(37.1)		

Data Mining

Many businesses have implemented systematic processes for collecting data from a variety of sources. Justification for these efforts focuses on specific marketing questions facing the business. Data warehouses are designed to answer marketing questions. Many businesses are drowning in data while starving for useful information about customers. This data overload has led to widespread interest in data mining.

Data mining is the process of finding hidden relationships among variables contained in data stored in the data warehouse. Data mining is an analysis procedure known primarily for the recognition of significant patterns of data for particular customers or customer groups. Marketing researchers have used data mining for many years, but the procedures usually were performed on small data sets containing 1,000 or fewer respondent records. Today, with the development of sophisticated data warehouses, the size of data sets being analysed has increased to thousands, even millions of respondent records. For example, Tesco's Clubcard database has up to 13 million, while AirMiles database has approximately 8.5 million. Special data mining tools have been developed for the specific purpose of analysing customer patterns found in very large databases.

Data mining Process of finding hidden patterns and relationships among variables/characteristics contained in data stored in the data warehouse.

Data mining finds not easily identifiable relationships among several customer dimensions within large data warehouses. The procedure is conducted when the market researcher has limited knowledge of a particular subject. For example, management in a casino business may ask the question, 'What are the characteristics of the gaming customers who spent the most in our casino last year?' Data mining techniques are used to search the data warehouse, capture the relevant data, categorize the significant characteristics and develop a profile of the high-budget gambler.

The Data Mining Process

Exhibit 3.6 illustrates a framework of what is involved in the data mining process. This framework focuses on four elements: the marketing research question, data mining approaches, data mining implementation and visual data mining.

Marketing Research Question

This is the starting point in any data mining analysis. For example, management may want answers to questions such as 'Which customers are most likely to visit our casino in the month of July?' To provide an answer, data mining tools analyse two key requirements: description and prediction.

Description is the process of discovering patterns and relationships among key customer characteristics such as demographic variables, gambling expenditures, frequency of casino visits,

> **Description** The process of discovering patterns and relationships among key customer characteristics.

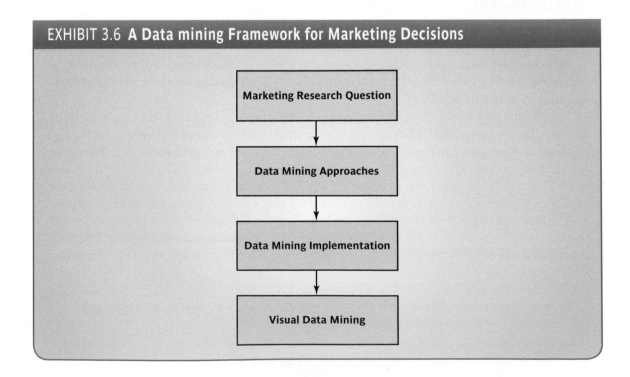

EXHIBIT 3.6 A Data mining Framework for Marketing Decisions

Marketing Research Question

↓

Data Mining Approaches

↓

Data Mining Implementation

↓

Visual Data Mining

amount of money won/lost, month, day of week, time of day, number of hours engaged in gambling. **Prediction** uses these patterns and relationships to predict future trends and behaviours, such as which customers will visit during a given month and how much they are likely to gamble during the month.

> **Prediction** Uses patterns and relationships to predict future trends and behaviours.

Data Mining Approaches

Data mining uses several approaches for description and prediction. One or more of these approaches can be used, for example, to profile groups based on gender, age, income, race and lifestyle using consistent or sequential behaviour patterns, or to predict customer satisfaction levels based on friendliness of employees, cleanliness of surroundings, quality of services and reputation of the business. The choice of approach depends on the research question, as well as on how the data contained in the warehouse are stored and categorized.

Exhibit 3.7 lists the most commonly used data mining approaches and two business applications, one in retailing and another one in direct mailing. These approaches can also be applied to non-business applications, such as in medical, as illustrated in the same Exhibit.

EXHIBIT 3.7 Most Commonly Used Approaches in Data Mining

Decision Trees

This is a set of rules that uses a tree-like structure to classify customers into segments or other relevant groups. Examples of this approach include:

Retailing: What are the differences between frequent and infrequent shoppers at Carrefour?

Medical: Which factors affect kidney transplant survival rates?

Direct mailing: Which prospects are good risks and therefore an attempt should be made to sell them a mortgage?

Rule Induction

This process develops 'If ... then ...' rules to classify individuals in a database. While decision trees use a set of rules, rule induction methods generate a set of independent rules that are unlikely to form a tree and may form better classification patterns. Examples include:

Retailing: Will the likelihood of purchase of a one-year extended warranty on a new digital camera be greater than, equal to, or less than 10 per cent?

Medical: What are the 'good risk' criteria that must be met before trying a particular treatment on a cancer patient?

Direct mailing: Will the response to a mail campaign for Wagamama be greater than 5 per cent?

Neural Networking

This is a nonlinear predictive model that learns how to detect patterns that match a particular profile. The name comes from the fact that the process resembles that of the human brain. The results typically are based on clustering or sequencing of patterns. Examples include:

Retailing: Which brand of DVD player is a prospect most likely to purchase?

▶

Medical: What disease is a person likely to contract?

Direct Mailing: Who will respond to a particular mailing?

Fuzzy Logic

This approach handles imprecise concepts like 'large, small, old, young, high, and low' and is more flexible. It examines fuzzy types of data classifications rather than those with more precise boundaries.

Retailing: Who is a likely customer for our new line of HDTV products?

Medical: Which smokers are likely to develop lung cancer?

Direct Mailing: Who might be a likely person to respond to our new promotional campaign?

Genetic Algorithms

These are not used to find patterns, but rather to guide the learning process of neural networking. The approach loosely follows the pattern of biological evolution in which members of one generation compete to pass on their characteristics to the next generation until the best model is found. Examples include:

Retailing: What is the optimal store layout for a particular location?

Medical: What is the optimal treatment for a particular disease?

Direct Mailing: What is the optimal demographic profile of an individual who is likely to invest €10,000 or more in a mutual fund this year?

Data Mining Implementation

During this process, with the help of powerful data mining software, the research carries out the data mining process. The process is most likely to be a trial and error one, and the expected outcome is to derive the most sensible model or results.

Visual Data Mining

No matter which data mining approach is used, deciding how the results will be presented is a critical part of any data mining activity. A data mining approach may be very good at discovering patterns, but if those patterns are not effectively visualized, the power to make strategic decisions using the information is lost. Thus, the success of any data mining procedure relies heavily on the ability of the researcher to comprehend and present the results of the analysis relative to the marketing question being answered.

Database Modelling

The usual ultimate purpose of marketing research database and data mining is to try to build up a reliable model that the organization can utilize for their decision-making process. Before conducting any modelling, the researcher needs to review, refine and format the raw data so it can be easily processed using statistical packages. This data interface process is necessary for successful query and modelling activities.

A Closer Look at Research *(In the field)*

Experian Introduces The National Canvasse, an Extended Version of the Electoral Register

The National Canvasse is Experian's consumer database, providing a more up-to-date dataset than the Electoral Register alone.

It brings together numerous data sources to fill the gap left out by those who opt out of the Electoral Register. Currently about 30 per cent of the electorate opt out and the rate may continue to increase annually. This means the database derived from the Electoral Register misses out on data of about 30 per cent of the population, and is in this sense significantly incomplete.

The National Canvasse fills this gap by sourcing additional data besides the Electoral Register. These additional data include Experian's Canvasse Lifestyle data, Directors data, Shareholder data and Contributor data sources. The contributors are referred to companies with large commercial databases built from customer transactions. These databases provide data for individuals who have not opted out of third party marketing activity. Through this gap filling work, the National Canvasse can provide over 90 per cent coverage of the Electoral Register opt-outs equating to a massive 11.6 million records.

The National Canvasse is claimed to be the most widely covered consumer database, and is a useful source for database modelling purposes. A simple use of the National Canvasse is the QuickAddress Locator, which enables organizations to generate postcode and address details quickly and accurately from a grid reference. The Locator will either return the single address or postcode, or all of the postcodes within the area that the organization selects. If a grid reference does not coincide with a postcode area, the Locator will find the nearest postcode to the grid reference and reports the distance from the reference. When used in conjunction with a front-end GIS mapping package, a complete and verified address can be returned by simply clicking on a map.

Source: www.qas.co.uk

Database modelling is designed to summarize what companies already know about their customers and use this knowledge to predict their future behaviour. When a database model fails to predict a customer's future behaviour, the database analyst needs to ask whether the company truly knows enough about its customers.

The Closer Look at Research box highlights a widely covered consumer database that can be very useful for direct marketing or other marketing purposes. Many companies find themselves data rich and information poor. The process of customer modelling often points to a company's information shortages and triggers new ideas for future marketing research endeavours. An effective approach to handling database modelling is to start where the process will end and then work backwards. The question then becomes: 'How will the information be used?' or 'What will the information enable us to do?' With this approach the researcher knows how the modelling output will be usable for the decision maker, and can then work backwards to collect the required input data. Among the many modelling procedures that exist in database analysis, two of the more traditional are scoring models and lifetime value models.

Scoring Models

Scoring models are used to predict consumption behaviour. Each individual in the database is assigned a score based on his or her propensity to respond to a marketing variable or make an

EXHIBIT 3.8 An Example of a Gains Table

Group Number	Number of Customers	Percentage of Customers	Cumulative Number of Customers	Cumulative Percentage of Customers	Average profit per Customer	Predicted Profit	Cumulative Average Profit per Customer	Cumulative Predicted Profit
1	100,000	20%	100,000	20%	€20	€2,000,000	€20.00	€2,000,000
2	100,000	20	200,000	40	15	1,500,000	17.50	3,500,000
3	100,000	20	300,000	60	10	1,000,000	3.50	4,500,000
4	100,000	20	400,000	80	5	500,000	1.25	5,000,000
5	100,000	20	500,000	100	1	100,000	.20	5,100,000

actual purchase. High scores are indications of very desirable customers; low scores represent less desirable segments. The initial objective is to rank customer segments based on their potential profitability to the company. The primary feature of scoring models is called the gains table. An example of a gains table is presented in Exhibit 3.8.

> **Scoring models** Database models used to predict consumption behaviour; each individual in the database is assigned a score based on their propensity to respond to a marketing variable or make an actual purchase.

Using a gains table, a database analyst can project and manage the profitability of various customer segments. For example, according to the data in Exhibit 3.8, the customer base is composed of 500,000 persons divided into five equal segments of 100,000, or five segments of 20 per cent of the market. The gains table ranks each of these segments based on its profit potential. Group 1 customers have the highest profit potential, and group 5 the lowest. Group 1 is estimated to draw approximately €2 million in future profit, or an estimated €20 per customer, and so on. Combined, groups 1, 2, and 3 are expected to generate €4.5 million in total future profits, or an estimated €20, €17.50, and €3.50, respectively, per customer. As you move through the gains table, the percentage of profitability per segment begins to decrease. This approach reinforces the basic marketing principle that customers are not homogeneous and, more specifically, the conventional wisdom that, generally speaking, 20 per cent of customers can represent 80 per cent of a company's profit. In the case of Exhibit 3.8, 40 per cent of customers generate approximately 70 per cent of total profit.

Key Variables in Scoring Models

Key variables in the scoring model enable researchers to determine which factors can be used to separate customers into purchase groups. Scoring models use weights to multiply assigned values in each customer's record. For example, suppose five factors are useful in separating heavy users from light users of hair spray – age, income, occupation, number of children under 18 and home value. On the basis of customer characteristics in the database, the scoring model determines that for heavy users of hair spray, the variables are arranged in the following order and assigned a corresponding weight: home value, .130; age, .050; occupation, .042; number of children under 18, .022; and income, .012. Obviously, the real weights produced by the model would be quite different, since they are to be multiplied by numbers (e.g. age in years, occupation in assigned coded value, income in thousands). For our discussion, however, let's assume these are real values.

In this example, home value is an important factor, with income being a less important factor for classifying customers into a heavy user group. The model permits a researcher to run a programme that takes each of the relevant factors in the customer record and multiplies it by the appropriate weight. The multiplied values are then added together to get an overall score. The score represents the likelihood of a customer being a heavy user (or a medium user, etc.) of the product.

Variables used to generate scoring model gains tables should be from actual purchase behaviour data. Key variables include mainly demographics, psychographics, lifestyle data and purchase habits including frequency, volume and amount spent at a given time. Categories of these variables are then assigned weights depending on their ability to predict purchase behaviour. For example, men may purchase more power tools than women. Therefore, on the basis of the single demographic variable of gender, men can be assigned a 10, women a 4. The weight structure for two customer groups based on gender might look like the following:

Table 3.1 Scoring model – weight structure for two gender-based customer groups

Customer Group A		Customer Group B	
Gender: Female	4 pts	Gender: Male	10 pts
Frequency: 2 months	4 pts	Frequency: 1 month	8 pts
Amount: €100	5 pts	Amount: €50	10 pts
Age group: 50 plus	2 pts	Age group: 30–50	10 pts
Total:	15 pts	Total:	38 pts

As can be seen, Group B (with 38 points) has better matching variables than Group A (with only 15 points). The total scores for each group are then converted to the currency. So 38 points would become €38 and 15 points would become €15. This conversion becomes the foundation for predicting future profitability in gains table analysis.

Scoring models have a limited period of effectiveness. The life of the model is directly related to changes in customer demand. Therefore, scoring models need to be revised as the market changes.

Lifetime Value Models

The fundamental premise behind **lifetime value models** is that customers, just like physical and tangible machinery, represent company assets. Moreover, customers represent a continuous stream of cash flow based on transactions they conduct with the business. All too often, the outcome of many marketing research projects is to obtain information that can be used to generate new customers only. Lifetime value models demonstrate that it is more valuable for businesses to concentrate on qualified customers first, then focus on growing them rather than constantly seeking new customers. Database information in most lifetime value models includes the following:

1 **Price variables:** The initial product or service cost and any price changes that occur.

2 **Sales promotional variables:** Type used, cost of the incentive.

3 **Advertising variables:** Type used, cost of the incentive.

4 **Product costs:** Direct costs, plus quality of goods/services.

5 **Relationship-building efforts:** Type and cost of relationship-building devices, expected value of building long-term relationships.

> **Lifetime value models** Database models developed on historical data, using actual purchase behaviour, not probability estimates, to predict future actions.

Database information is used to identify the most profitable customers. Exhibit 3.9 represents the output from a hypothetical lifetime value model for a fast food restaurant. In this example 10,000 new customers are targeted for the marketing effort. The average amount spent by customers is about €4.30, and a free sandwich (with a cost of 90 pence) is the incentive to attract the customers. Therefore, the estimated real revenue is €34,000. Expenses amount to 60 per cent of the revenue. Total expenses are thus €20,400.

The business averages a 35 per cent return rate of its customers. Therefore, mailing out 10,000 free sandwich coupons should yield 3,500 responses at a cost of €3,800. Total expenses for this planned effort are estimated at €24,200. With an initial investment of €3,800, the total contribution should result in a €9,800 return to the business. This, in turn, equates to a total lifetime

EXHIBIT 3.9 A Hypothetical Lifetime Value Model for a Fast Food Restaurant

PERIOD	1	2	3	4
CUSTOMERS	10,000			
REPEAT		3,500	1,225	428
REPEAT %		35%	35%	35%
REVENUE				
AVERAGE AMOUNT	€4.30	€4.50	€4.75	€4.75
COST OF INCENTIVE	0.90			
TOTAL	34,000	15,750	5,818	2,033
EXPENSES				
DIRECT COST	60%	60%	60%	60%
TOTAL	20,400	9,450	3,491	1,219
REPEAT EFFORT				
TARGET	10,000	3,500	1,225	428
REPEAT %	35%	35%	35%	35%
RATE	3,500	1,225	428	150
TOTAL MAIL	10,000	3,500	1,225	428
COST	€3,800	€1,330	€465	€162
TOTAL EXPENSES	€24,200	€10,780	€3,956	€1,381
CONTRIBUTION	9,800	4,970	1,862	652
INVESTMENT	3,800	1,330	465	162
TOTAL LIFETIME VALUE	€6,000	€9,460	€11,037	€11,527
CUSTOMER VALUE	€0.60	€0.96	€1.10	€1.15

customer value of €6,000, or 60 pence per customer during the first period of the promotion. Given expected rates of return for customers over the next three promotional periods, total contribution would fall to €652, with investment costs down to €162. Total lifetime value over four periods would increase to €11,527. The four-period lifetime value for an individual customer is €1.15.

To summarize, as a database tool lifetime value models examine the asset value of customers. In contrast to purchase intention data, lifetime value models are based on actual purchase data, which is often a better predictor of customer behaviour.

The Marketing Decision Support System

More and more businesses – including the small to medium-sized enterprises in the UK and the multinational retailers in Europe overall, as introduced in the two 'A Closer Look at Research' boxes below – are using technology to better align their operations, resources and strategies to maximize the value customers derive from their products and services. Applications have focused on automating customer operational procedures for the purpose of interaction and data collection. However, 'customer-centric' businesses are increasingly embracing a view that goes beyond the functionality of such applications to include a full range of support system components. These approaches foster the creation of a closed-loop decision support system.

A Closer Look at Research (Using Technology)
Reaping the Benefits of Systematization of Business and Customer Data in UK SMEs

Many UK small to medium-sized enterprises (SMEs) are failing to maximize their marketing opportunities, largely because they have neither the time nor ability to systematize and fully utilize relevant business and customer data for informing their marketing decisions. However, there are an increasing number of UK SMEs which have successfully established some form of marketing decision support systems that have greatly benefited their growth.

Bentley Designs, a UK furniture manufacturer, importer and distributor based in Middlesex, has solicited the assistance of IRIS, a specialist software business based in Datchet, Berkshire, and accordingly installed a small-scale marketing decision support system to target profitable customers, ensure timely internal control and streamline day to day operations.

With better knowledge of their customers, Bentley Designs is consciously reducing its customer base while selectively growing business based on higher margin products with targeted customers. Understanding where the higher margin products and the target customers are, the company can then confidently aim at moving its target market from the low to middle tier of retailers to the middle to top end. This aim is being met by improving the company's product design and quality.

By using the system to flag up sales orders and invoices for margin, Bentley Designs has regained a significant amount of revenue that would previously have been lost.

With the product stock information in the system, the company is automatically supplied with reports on stock levels of product lines due to be discontinued. The system also allows Bentley Designs to replace hand-crafted reports and spreadsheets created over time with a single, integrated and accurate source of business information. Therefore, previous manual processes – from multiple entries of the same information to repeated attempts at making diverse information sources agree – can be discarded.

Caroline Donovan, General Manager of Bentley Designs, said, 'In what is rapidly becoming a challenging retail environment, detailed business insight and early warning of changes in financial or stock status is vital'.

Listed below are a number of simple steps that can be taken to move towards the maximization of marketing opportunities. Note that all these steps can be easily integrated into a marketing decision support system.

- Enable real-time access to relevant business and customer data
- Utilize exception reporting and alerts for real-time management
- Automate reporting processes to reduce time spent on report generation
- Empower responsible staff with real-time access to business and customer data
- Reduce paper and streamline processes to reduce costs.

A Closer Look at Research *(Using Technology)*
Consolidating Data for Real-Time Decisions in European Multinational Retailers

With the continuing growth of the customer base and the product portfolios offered, more and more European multinational retailers were and still are facing the issue of consolidating their customer data. Before installing a decision support system, a retailer often didn't know which of its customers were the same people. Under the same retailer's umbrella, customers could get a credit card, then use it to buy clothes from a catalogue. They could have their hair dyed red, then have their picture taken. Each purchase record appeared in a different database, and therefore eight separate transactions would appear to be from eight different people. The retailer needed to tie together the records that made up individual customer profiles, but first it had to figure out which records belonged to the same person.

To complicate the problem further, system consistency had to be superimposed because the data sources had different underlying structures: the hair salon indexed records by home phone number; the credit card database identified customers by name. The retailer had to standardize and make sense of all the data. The decision support system known as 'unified data view' seemed to be the answer. The system allowed the retailer to build a single picture of each customer, creating a powerful decision tool to improve service and increase customer retention.

Customer retention is a goal for both retailers and manufacturers. The advent of more powerful support tools, advanced analytical processes such as data mining and rich customer data sources is powering this business trend. The benefit of these technologies is realized when data associated with the customer is merged with data generated by ongoing business operations. This infrastructure is known as a decision support system, and it is increasingly being used by successful companies in Europe and beyond.

A **marketing decision support system (MDSS)** is a computer-based system used by marketing personnel at any functional level (e.g. sales, product or brand management, advertising). The output is special reports, mathematical simulations, or tracking devices.

Marketing decision support system (MDSS)   A computer-based system intended for use by particular marketing personnel at any functional level for the purpose of solving semistructured problems.

The MDSS and the marketing information system (MIS) have been viewed as almost identical. With the emergence of new technology, however, the two systems have evolved into unique research tools. The MDSS, in contrast to the MIS, possesses several unique characteristics:

1 It focuses on specific research problems to support individual marketing personnel.

2 It provides information to facilitate a specific decision (new product planning, advertising effectiveness, distribution alternatives).

3 Its primary purpose is to evaluate alternative solutions to marketing-related problems and to identify the best course of action.

4 It solves more limited problems such as facilitating the design of sales territories, evaluating outcomes of new product or brand launches, or even profiling specific target markets for marketing actions.

5 Its emphasis is twofold: information storage and categorization and resultant solutions.

RMS, a UK company designing and implementing planning and scheduling solutions since 1993, has a wide customer base across Europe and the US. In 1995, it formed a highly successful association with Preactor International and became a Preactor solutions provider. Preactor is an advanced planning scheduling software product for manufacturing companies and is an example of MDSS solution. Another MDSS solution is Factivity from MDSS in the US. It is designed specifically to integrate with Preactor, and can be used to control shop floor labour and work-in-process production as well as provide real-time data collection for a MDSS database that can be used to manage supply chain issues. In 2007, RMS and MDSS entered into partnership to broaden the support capability of these two MDSS solutions providers.

Marketing Decision Support Systems, Inc. is another major international supplier of MDSS solutions. Examples of how it has helped clients solve MDSS problems include: developing a marketing database for a consumer electronics company to track sales patterns and sales force productivity; setting up a system for a durable goods manufacturer that uses monthly industry forecasts to decide on factory production schedules; and helping a household goods manufacturer analyse data from its numerous product registration forms so it could distribute marketing information to the dealers that sell its products.

A Marketing Decision Support System Diagram

Exhibit 3.10 illustrates how a MDSS supports marketing personnel in various capacities. The MDSS stores and categorizes three groups of marketing information: environmental, transactional and business intelligence. This information is contained within an information processing system consisting of a computer, a marketing research database and specialized software. This information processing system enables the user to examine information and obtain output in the form of specialized reports, responses to database queries and model simulations. Reports and database queries are used most often to identify market-related problems. Simulations are helpful in planning alternative solutions to problems.

The purpose of this section is to acquaint the reader with how a MDSS is used. With the discussion of information technology and database development in this chapter, and secondary data in the following chapter, these different domains of knowledge together form the foundation for understanding the MDSS.

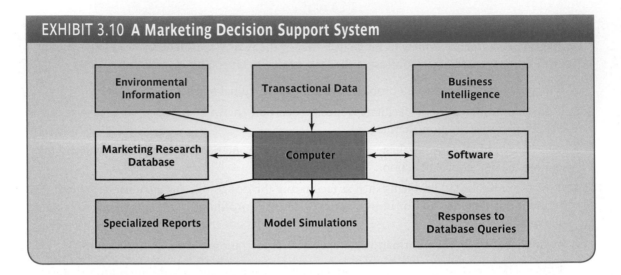

EXHIBIT 3.10 **A Marketing Decision Support System**

Information Requirements

Much of the information in the MDSS is secondary. The MDSS is designed to provide solutions to current problems in the marketplace. It contains actual market data, not intentions or attitudes. Information used in the MDSS provides marketing personnel with a picture of what happened in the past, so the present and the future can be put in perspective. Market activities are reported quickly, as they actually happen, so marketing personnel can act accordingly. For example, when Miller Brewing Company introduced its Miller Red Beer, managers needed to know how the beer was selling at different stores, at different price points, under different promotional campaigns. Corrective actions to change or enhance the marketing effort had to take place immediately. Here the very valuable data were the direct, point-of-sale, transactional data linked into the MDSS from various store locations. Transactional data revealed that sales were less than estimated at convenience stores in some particular region. It happened that Budweiser was doing a massive point-of-sale campaign for its Michelob brand, undermining all marketing efforts by Miller. Within 24 hours, Miller distributors were instructed to contact convenience store managers in the region and offer them financial incentive if they would remove all Michelob promotions and exclusively promote Miller.

On the basis of a simulation of transactional data, Miller estimated the sales increase would more than offset the lost revenue resulting from the cost of financial incentive provided to convenience stores which cooperated. Armed with this data, distributors were able to persuade convenience store managers to change their emphasis to Miller. This rapid reaction would not have been possible without point-of-sale data and MDSS simulations. The key to the success of this decision was showing managers at Miller what happened in the past, what was happening today, and what would happen tomorrow.

Environmental Information

Within the context of the MDSS, **environmental information** is that pertaining to suppliers and distributors. Information on suppliers is particularly important, because cooperation and

Environmental information Information pertaining to suppliers and distributors.

coordination of activities with these firms ensure that a company has the necessary raw materials and services to react to changes in the market. Specifically, companies must have reliable information on supply considerations such as cost, quality and product reliability.

In an MDSS, suppliers are often ranked by the monetary amount of business they do with a company. A series of other related criteria can be established and stored within the information processing unit of the MDSS. Examples of the criteria that can be used with supplier processing software to evaluate all suppliers are as follows:

1 Monetary amount of business by season and year.
2 Growth or shrinkage of annual monetary amount of business.
3 Accuracy of shipping and billing.
4 Timeliness of deliveries.
5 Price terms and allowance.
6 Returns and procedures.

A sample output of supplier processing software is shown in Exhibit 3.11. Perhaps the greatest advantage of such a system is that a supplier can be selected or replaced immediately so that the company can avoid shortages or excessive inventory and, ultimately, customer dissatisfaction.

Distribution Partners

Distributors are typically referred to as service wholesalers. They are businesses that secure products from the manufacturer and sell them to retailers. Service wholesalers are widely used

---

EXHIBIT 3.11 Example of Output from Supplier Processing Software

Supplier

Activity (Manufacturer, Jobber, Importer, etc.)

Merchandise   Top Grade _____ Medium _____ Low-End _____

Sales Office Address   Telephone _____

Factory or Warehouse Address

Company Officers and Titles

Buyer Contacts – State peculiarities or special handling required by
   a. Sales Office   b. Factory or Warehouse

Rating – Dun & Bradstreet

Ethics of Firm

Ranking in Industry

Vendor Importance to Store

Store Importance to Vendor

Record of All Arrangements (Terms, Trade Discounts, Cash Discounts, Cooperative Advertising, etc.)

Remarks (State clearly any additional information not covered above that will guide any member of our organization who may have to deal with this vendor.)

Date   By Whom

because they offer many advantages over selling direct to retail. For example, they offer packaging and shipping services, reduce inventory carrying needs, reduce credit risks and simplify bookkeeping. Many businesses, such as grocery stores and convenience stores, have no choice but to use wholesalers due to the wide merchandise variety they must maintain. Thus, the profitability of the use of service wholesalers is continually evaluated. Hard data related to wholesalers should include:

1 Levels of inventory carried by various wholesalers.

2 On-time delivery performance.

3 Minimum ordering requirements.

4 Transportation costs.

5 Repairs, allowances, and adjustments.

6 Level of service (e.g. automatic merchandise replacement, inventory management).

Exhibit 3.12 shows a document from a wholesaler evaluation system, included in many marketing decision support systems. As you can see, the system allows for efficient comparative evaluation among wholesalers. Here again, the accuracy and timeliness of data are necessary in order for the system to be effective in the decision making process.

EXHIBIT 3.12 Example of Wholesaler Evaluation System

```
WHOLESALER INQUIRY                              PROGRAMME-NAME: 201U5031
                                                PFKEY  1 - RESTART
   DEPARTMENT    20    LADIES SPORTSWEAR         PFKEY  16 - EXIT
   WHOLESALER  437801  LONGROAD INDUSTRIES,LTD.
        DATE  01/07/07


   RECEIPTS:                   MARKDOWNS:
      UNITS     420               UNITS     56    ADVERTISE CONTRIBUTION  .00
      @ RETAIL  6715.80           @ RETAIL  280.23
      @ COST    3156.45                            # ORDERS PLACED: 6


                              PURCHASES:

   SALES:                                          # SHIPMENTS:      5
                                 @ RETAIL  7438.20
      UNITS     324              @ COST    4462.92   OVER SHIPMENTS: 0
      @ RETAIL  5389.77
      @ COST    3108.45       INVOICED AMOUNT:       UNDER SHIPMENTS: 1


   RETURNS:                      INVOICE   3782.40
                                 DISCOUNT   231.18
      UNITS      23              FREIGHT     45.20
      @ RETAIL  367.77          RETAIL    6715.80

                                           Press "ENTER" to continue *
```

Business Intelligence

An additional informational requirement of a marketing decision support system is **business intelligence**, which often comes from a business intelligence programme introduced earlier in this chapter. Business intelligence activities lack the structure and rigour of more formal information gathering practices associated with suppliers and distributors, but they represent an important informational input to the MDSS.

> **Business intelligence** Information about the industry evolution, market trend and competition often collected through a business intelligence programme.

Transactional Data

Transactional data is information resulting from a transaction usually between a customer and a retailer. New methods of collecting transactional data are emerging and will significantly change the practice of marketing research. Today, five technologies interact to help researchers collect and maintain transactional data: *bar coding, optical scanning, automatic replenishment, electronic data interchange* and *reader sorters*.

> **Transactional data** Information resulting from a transaction usually between a customer and a retailer.

Bar coding is a pattern of varied-width bars and spaces that represents a code of numbers and letters. When decoded through an optical scanning device, the code points to important product information. Brand name, style, size, colour and price are some of the data represented by bar codes. Bar codes also provide data on inventory levels, percentage of markup on the item, stock turnover rate and quantity levels necessary for reordering.

> **Bar coding** A pattern of varied-width bars and spaces that represents a code of numbers and letters.

Bar coding operates in conjunction with optical scanners. An **optical scanner** is a light-sensitive device that 'reads' bar codes; that is, it captures and translates unique bar code numbers into product information and thus facilitates data entry into the MDSS. Two scanning techniques are commonly employed. First, the universal product code (UPC) is a generally accepted bar code for the retail industry. A UPC is a 12-digit number used for merchandise identification. Second is the shipper container marking (SCM). An SCM is a bar code that facilitates the identification and shipping of containers between manufacturers, distributors, and retailers. UPCs and SCMs can

> **Optical scanner** A light-sensitive device that 'reads' bar codes; that is, captures unique bar code numbers and translates them into product information.

be read by a variety of optical scanners. Stores like Carrefour and Wal-Mart use handheld scanners for speed and convenience. Optical scanning wands are used predominantly by department stores because of loosely attached price tags. Flatbed scanners or in-line conveyers are used mainly by supermarkets due to the volume of items and coupons that need scanning.

Every time an optical scanner reads a bar code, it electronically records what was bought, the manufacturer and supplier, the size and price. This information is then archived in a database and enhanced with market intelligence and other research-related information. The resulting database has the potential to reveal what consumers watch on television, what type of neighbourhood they live in and what kinds of stores they shop at.

Exhibit 3.13 illustrates an example of how scanner data can be cross-referenced as well as the value it holds for marketing researchers. Information in the exhibit is based on AC Nielsen Homescan, a consumer packaged goods purchase information service with key consumer insights in 18 countries, based on consumer purchase information from over 126,000 households globally.

An **automatic replenishment system (ARS)** is a continuous, automated system designed to analyse inventory levels, merchandise order lead times and forecasted sales. It also generates purchase orders for merchandise that needs quick replenishment. Automatic replenishment systems

> **Automatic replenishment system (ARS)** A continuous automated system designed to analyse inventory levels, merchandise order lead times, and forecasted sales.

EXHIBIT 3.13 Homescan: Scanner Data for Decision Making

Homescan allows marketing and sales teams to compare and contrast basic shopping measures across channel shoppers and category buyers within key retail channels and accounts.

Retailers can no longer think that their competition is limited to their specific channel. Manufacturers need to partner with retailers in developing a category strategy to establish the most effective merchandising, promotional and pricing levels to drive increased category and brand volume.

For example, although more category buyers shop in Retailer A (17.091 million), only 11% buy Category Z there. Retailer A should have the potential to convert at least as many category buyers as Retailer B (29%).

Buyer Conversion	Category Z		
	Retailer A	Retailer B	Retailer C
Retailer Shoppers (000)	70,300	62,300	37,900
Category Buyers Who Shop in Account (000)	17,091	15,537	8,771
Category Buyers Who Buy Category in Account (000)	1,873	4,429	495
Buyer Conversion (per cent Ctgy Buyers Who Shop in Acct AND Buy Ctgy in Acct.)	11%	29%	6%
Category Dollars/Category Buyer	€8.60	€22.60	€4.81

Converting 29 per cent of Retailer A shoppers to purchase Category Z represents a €26.47 million opportunity for Retailer A (29% – 11% = 18% incremental conversion * 17.1 million households * €8.60/ per household = €26.47 million opportunity). There is additional opportunity through improved category buying rate (€8.60 – €22.60).

Spending Power	Total Account Dollars		
	Retailer A	Retailer B	Retailer C
Shopping Dollars/ Account Shoppers	€224.62	€575.13	€251.95
Shopping Dollars Among Category Z Buyers Who Shop in Account	€258.91	€690.49	€265.19
Spending Power Index	115	120	105

Category Z buyers display strong spending power relative to the average account shopper, especially in Retailer B.

help firms carry the lowest possible levels of inventory while still maintaining a sufficient quantity to avoid stock-outs. Inventory levels are optimized because order quantities are smaller and ordering is more frequent. In addition, inventory movement is improved because reordering is automatic, stock turnover rates are higher, and the cost of spoilage and shrinkage is decreased dramatically.

Electronic data interchange (EDI) is a computerized system that speeds the flow of information and products from producer to distributor to retailer, contributing to increased sales, reduced markdowns and lowered inventory carrying costs. EDI differs from an ARS in that additional benefits are derived from reductions in costs of clerical and administrative activities associated with merchandise ordering. Electronic data interchange centres mainly on electronic exchange of information such as purchase orders, invoices, advanced shipping notices, and product return notices. In essence, EDI is the information arm of an automatic replenishment system.

Electronic data interchange (EDI) A computerized system designed to speed the flow of information and products from producer to distributor to retailer.

EDI is available in two formats: direct data interchange among producers, distributors and retailers and third-party networks, which operate as clearing houses or electronic mailboxes for retailers. While slight differences exist between these two formats, their benefits are much the same. Electronic data interchange reduces the costs of clerical work and data entry, postage, handling and form printing. The speed of communication reduces inventory carrying costs, improving the efficiency of relevant parties in the supply chain.

Automatic replenishment systems and electronic data interchange are keys to the MDSS. Toys 'R' Us, for example, is a multi-billion euro business with approximately 1,500 stores worldwide that is networked to over 500 suppliers. Being a highly seasonal company with much of the sales occurring around the Christmas period, Toys 'R' Us relies heavily on inventory control for its survival. It attributes its growth and profitability to the inventory and information components of the MDSS. Transmitted data include orders and shipment confirmations. Sales and inventory records are also transmitted, providing information on which toys are sold at which stores worldwide and when the items need to be replenished. More specifically, through EDI Toys 'R' Us can monitor sales trends and communicate with vendors automatically.

The final element used in generating transactional data is the **reader-sorter**. The reader-sorter is a computerized device located at the point of sale that resembles a miniature automated teller machine (ATM). It enables customers to pay for transactions with credit or debit cards. The magnetic strip on the back of each card contains a wealth of customer data. On this tiny strip an individual's personal, historical data are stored, along with other relevant data such as at which store the card was used, what was actually purchased and when, along with significant demographic and lifestyle data.

> **Reader-sorter** A computerized device located at the point of sale that resembles a miniature automated teller machine (ATM); it enables customers to pay for transactions with credit or debit cards.

At the point of sale, when a consumer uses the reader-sorter as a payment method, data from both the magnetic strip and the current purchase are automatically collected. The optical scanner (via a bar code) is collecting and recording product purchases while the reader-sorter (via the credit or debit card) is collecting and recording information on who is making the purchase. Both groups of information are then stored in the central database of the MDSS. When compiled with other customer purchases, a specific product-related profile can be generated based on store activities over a period of time.

Exhibit 3.14 contains a sample MDSS report on individuals who purchased Pepsi products at a particular supermarket. On the basis of the database information, we learn these individuals

EXHIBIT 3.14 **Sample MDSS Report on Pepsi Buyers**

	TARGET LIFESTYLES FOR HEAVY PEPSI USERS						
	Penetration				**Penetration**		
Lifestyles	**Total**	**Target**	**Index**	**Lifestyles**	**Total**	**Target**	**Index**
Bought Heavy Rock Music	7.76	13.11	109	Joggers/Runners	9.16	12.61	138
Bought Rock Music	15.90	24.85	156	Drink Vodka	18.74	22.24	115
Attended Pop/Rock Concerts	8.91	13.53	152	Go Bicycling	16.77	19.63	117
Ride Motorcycles	3.71	5.46	147	Bought Music CDs	23.44	27.26	116
Bought Soul/R&B/Black Music	8.13	11.65	143	Bought Film DVDs	48.06	35.70	115
Downhill Skiers	3.98	5.65	143	Bought Traditional/ Cntmpry jazz	5.97	6.81	114
Bought Pop Music	17.10	24.18	141	Bought New Foreign Cars	12.28	13.85	113
Do Weight Training	9.84	13.87	141	Smoke Menthol Cigarettes	9.15	10.26	112

also listen to rock music, bought film DVDs, do weight training, go skiing and drink vodka. Our knowledge of the lifestyles of heavy Pepsi users is therefore significantly increased.

With this information Pepsi can anticipate daily sales, plan in-store promotional activities, anticipate reactions to price and packaging changes, and maintain an accurate description of its target market. Since the data were generated on actual product purchases, not propensity to purchase Pepsi, the information has high predictive accuracy. Thus, the benefits of a MDSS are not only its ability to collect and categorize relevant customer information, but also to predict based on the information-processing element of the MDSS. Many large consumer packaged good companies use this kind of information in their MDSS systems.

Information Processing and the MDSS

The three key elements of the information processing component of the MDSS are the database, the computer facilities and the software system. We have already discussed database development, so our focus here is on the computer and the software system.

The computer and the software system serve one primary function in the MDSS: to produce reports valuable to the decision maker. The computer and software system of the MDSS should:

- Reflect the needs for the user, not the analyst.
- Provide reports for the user within minutes.
- Sort and print highly specific report data.
- Be easy to read, use and manipulate.
- Be custom-made versus prewritten. While prewritten systems are less expensive, if the system does not meet the user's needs, it is useless.

Two general types of software systems exist for MDSS: statistical software systems and managerial function software systems.

Statistical Software Systems

Statistical software systems analyse large volumes of data and compute basic statistics such as means and standard deviations. They also compare sets of numbers and use such tests as t-tests and chi-square tests to determine how similar or different the numbers are. More sophisticated routines are also available.

> **Statistical software systems** MDSS systems that analyse large volumes of data and compute basic and more sophisticated statistics.

While a variety of statistical software systems exist, SAS (www.sas.com) and SPSS (www.spss.com) are the most robust packages for the MDSS, and are usually the favourite choice of the research analyst. Statistical knowledge is needed to understand the statistical rationales behind the use of these packages.

Managerial Function Software Systems

In the MDSS environment, three **managerial function software systems** are commonly employed: forecasting systems, product/brand management systems and promotional budget systems.

> **Managerial function software systems** MDSS systems used by managers; these include forecasting systems, product/brand management systems and promotional budget systems.

Many forecasting systems enable sales or marketing managers to project future occurrences. They all use the types of data described earlier as a basis for predicting sales. For example, if transactional data indicate that purchases increase with increased presence of the product at retail, the relationship could be stated in mathematical (i.e. modelled) terms. Forecasting systems usually produce sales or profitability projections in a report form such as the one in Exhibit 3.15.

Product/brand management software systems enable managers to plan for new product introduction. One such package, called brand planning, is based on a critical path analysis and displays the output in the form of a Gantt chart. The brand planning package plans the sequencing of activities (production, packaging, sales, etc.) that must be performed in order to have a successful product launch.

Promotional budget systems enable managers to predict and control promotional expenditures. Limits are set for each element of the promotional budget. Reports are issued on a monthly basis indicating how actual expenses relate to budget projections. An example of a promotional budget system is the ADBUG. This model evaluates sales response to advertising. Conceptually, the system is quite simple in that it examines what is happening to an entire industry, product class, or even brand within the class. The system uses what-if assumptions and performs a series of sensitivity analyses to measure sales response based on the effects of advertising expenses, product seasonality, general trends, competition and price.

In order to develop the sales response function, the ADBUG user makes a number of assumptions. These include:

1 A certain level of advertising expenditures will maintain brand share at some given level.

2 A floor exists where brand share will fall by a fixed amount with zero advertising.

3 A ceiling exists where brand share will increase given large advertising expenditures.

The ADBUG system has two main objectives: (1) to determine the optimum level of advertising expenditures for achieving a desired level of sales at a point of time and (2) to determine how to change advertising expenditures over time to maximize profits.

Regardless of which MDSS software system is used, the goal is to produce information from data in order to facilitate decisions. The common denominator of all MDSS software systems is that modelling capabilities are used to provide direct support to the manager for solving problems. Therefore, before we cover MDSS output we provide a brief discussion of models.

MDSS Models and Output

When the information contained in the MDSS is classified by the software system, the result is some form of output for the decision maker. When the output provides a solution to the problem, it is most likely generated by a modelling technique. A model is an abstraction that explains some phenomenon or activity. For example, a model is a way to explain how a company's sales fluctuate in response to advertising expenditures. Modelling capabilities enable the MDSS to produce output. The most common types of MDSS outputs are reports, simulations and queries.

EXHIBIT 3.15 Illustration of Output from Sales Forecasting System

PROJECTS QUOTED RECAP: September
RECAP BY INDUSTRY:

		Total w/Revisions by Industry and Type	Total w/Revisions by Industry	Total Complete by Industry and Type	Total Complete by Industry	No. of Quotes
BAKING	Systems (S)	€550,004.00		€2,398,425.00		3
	Screeners (CS)	€38,761.91		€38,761.91		1
	Rotary Valves (CV)	€0.00		€0.00		0
	Miscellaneous (M)	€0.00	€588,765.91	€0.00	€2,437,186.91	0
PLASTIC	Systems (S)	€0.00		€0.00		0
	Screeners (CS)	€0.00		€0.00		0
	Rotary Valves (CV)	€0.00		€0.00		0
	Miscellaneous (M)	€0.00	€0.00	€0.00	€0.00	0
CHEMICAL	Systems (S)	€314,980.00		€559,519.00		4
	Screeners (CS)	€19,140.00		€19,140.00		3
	Rotary Valves (CV)	€10,860.00		€10,860.00		2
	Miscellaneous (M)	€0.00	€344,980.00	€0.00	€589,519.00	0
PHARMACEUTICAL	Systems (S)	€69,918.00		€129,918.00		4
	Screeners (CS)	€0.00		€0.00		0
	Rotary Valves (CV)	€0.00		€0.00		0
	Miscellaneous (M)	€200,000.00	€269,918.00	€252,000.00	€381,918.00	2
FOOD	Systems (S)	€13,670,547.00		€22,409,527.00		12
	Screeners (CS)	€155,667.00		€155,667.00		6
	Rotary Valves (CV)	€28,120.00		€28,120.00		3
	Miscellaneous (M)	(€67,100.00)	€13,787,234.00	€317,200.00	€22,910,514.00	1
DAIRY	Systems (S)	€0.00		€0.00		0
	Screeners (CS)	€13,374.00		€13,374.00		1
	Rotary Valves (CV)	€0.00		€0.00		0
	Miscellaneous (M)	€0.00	€13,374.00	€0.00	€13,374.00	0
PARTS	General (Parts)	€0.00	€0.00	€0.00	€0.00	0
Powder Paint	Systems (S)	€0.00		€0.00		0
	Screeners (CS)	€46,065.00		€97,584.00		3
	Rotary Valves (CV)	€0.00		€0.00		0
	Miscellaneous (M)	€0.00	€46,065.00	€0.00	€97,584.00	0
		€15,050,336.91	€15,050,336.91	€26,430,095.91	€26,430,095.91	45

Total w/ Revisions by Industry	Total Complete by Industry	No. of Quotes
€311,987.91	€363,506.91	19
€0.00	€0.00	0
€138,918.00	€138,918.00	3
€13,485,890.00	€21,758,234.00	7
€655,000.00	€655,000.00	2
€458,541.00	€3,514,437.00	14
€0.00	€0.00	0
€0.00	€0.00	0
€0.00	€0.00	0
€15,050,336.91	€26,430,095.91	45

A MDSS Sales Analysis Output Example

An example of MDSS output is a series of sales analysis reports produced from accounting and sales transaction data. The data used in preparing the records are sorted into various sequences to provide a sales manager with information describing the firm's sales by customer, region and salesperson. A sales-by-customer report is shown in Exhibit 3.16. Customers are listed in descending order based on year-to-date sales and percentage contribution to total sales. This enables the sales manager to analyse customers on a percentage-of-sales basis. The same technique is used in the sales-by-region report in Exhibit 3.17. The sales manager can then analyse sales made by salespeople within their region.

Geographic Information Systems

Most MDSS models have simulation capability. A commonly used MDSS simulation is a geographic information system (GIS). A geographic information systems uses spatial modelling in conjunction with data drawn from the MDSS. It enables users to display spatial data organized as map layers. With the technological advance in satellite imagery, the use of GIS for all sorts of purposes including marketing research purposes has been increasing. Availability of satellite images as a data source will lead to more sophisticated use of global positioning systems (GPS) to find the best locations.

Geographic information system market areas are analysed to learn where defined demographic characteristics overlap. In fact, neighbourhoods can be clustered into categories and defined by both demographic and lifestyle data. The data is then linked to household information to produce neighbourhood profiles that are useful for sales planning. An example of GIS is described as a European case study at the end of this chapter.

EXHIBIT 3.16 Output of Sales-by-Customer Report for System Products

Customer	Region	Sales €	Per cent of Sales	Per cent of System Sales
Allied Materials	NE	€3,272,48	21.6%	31.2%
Thomson Building Materials	NE	1,067,051	7.0%	10.2%
Global Drug	SE	1,038,019	6.8%	9.9%
Continental Biscuits	SW	776,218	5.1%	7.4%
Golden Electronics	SE	632,505	4.2%	6.0%
Floor to Go	NW	590,717	3.9%	5.6%
Warner Dairy Products	C	330,270	2.2%	3.1%
Look International	C	300,830	2.0%	2.9%
Contemporary Design	NW	252,122	1.7%	2.4%
Sky Pictures	SW	233,028	1.5%	2.2%
Pink Pizza	C	178,000	1.2%	1.7%
Uniform Sports	SW	172,725	1.1%	1.6%
BHI International	NE	147,868	1.0%	1.4%
Classical Publishing	SE	145,560	1.0%	1.4%
Emerald Furniture	NE	125,688	0.8%	1.2%
Sharp Liquour	NW	117,644	0.8%	1.1%
Parallel Measuring Equipment	C	106,678	0.7%	1.0%

EXHIBIT 3.17 Output of Sales-by-Region Report for Northeast Region

Customer	Product	Sales €	Per cent of Sales	Per cent of System Sales
Snyders of Harwich	sys	€632,505	4.2%	26.6%
Scholes Foods	sys	252,122	1.7%	10.6%
Stirling Drug	sys	233,028	1.5%	9.8%
Silver Flake	sys	178,000	1.2%	7.5%
M&M Mars	sys	172,725	1.1%	7.3%
Glaxo	sys	147,868	1.0%	6.2%
Reading Chemical	sys	117,644	0.8%	4.9%
Guildford Software	sys	98,806	0.7%	4.2%
Configuration Corporation	engr	74,000	0.5%	3.1%
Hershey Chocolate	sys	66,939	0.4%	2.8%
MFI Furniture	sys	63,801	0.4%	2.7%
Weight Watchers	inst	60,850	0.4%	2.6%
Bryan Meyers	sys	59,667	0.4%	2.5%
Keyman Process	sys	31,050	0.2%	1.3%
Unique Carbide	vlv	30,050	0.2%	1.3%
Wascagen Foods	vlv	18,982	0.1%	0.8%
Giant Air Technology	vlv	18,523	0.1%	0.8%
A & E Machine	scr	15,073	0.1%	0.6%
Snicker Chocolate	vlv	15,062	0.1%	0.6%
EDF Energy	vlv	15,025	0.1%	0.6%

Using GIS, geographic parameters are examined to identify regions or locations based on spatial coincidence of relevant factors. For example, GIS can be used to examine environmental, economic and political factors for identifying potential store location sites as well as the environmental impact of a proposed site development. The main advantage of GIS is its ability to pose what-if scenarios. Actually GIS has become one of the most important tools for applications of 'niche' marketing strategies and it has applications in a wide variety of industries. In fact, GIS can facilitate problem solving and decision making in many areas of marketing, resource management, planning and environmental monitoring. A geographic information system combines layers of information about a place to give you a better understanding of that place. The layers of information you combine depend on your purpose – finding the best location for a new store, analysing environmental impact, viewing similar social activities in a city to detect a pattern, and so on.

Like most tools, however, GIS is only as good as the person using it. Using word-processing software, for example, does not make one an accomplished writer. Effective use of GIS requires an understanding of the fundamental concepts of geographic data and systems, map coordinate systems, data integrity and accuracy, overlay analysis and database manipulation. Geographic information system technology integrates spatial modelling, database management and computer graphics in a system for managing and manipulating geographic data. Exhibit 3.18 shows the four major components of a GIS: data input, data analysis, data management system and data output.

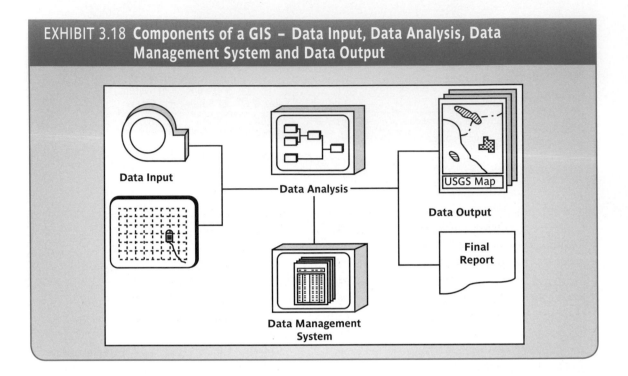

EXHIBIT 3.18 Components of a GIS – Data Input, Data Analysis, Data Management System and Data Output

The key to proper application of GIS technology is the database. Attribute GIS application typically uses a relational database management system to manipulate attribute information.

The GIS database contains map layers representing geographic themes organized in a digital format. The map layers, which are geocoded to a standard coordinate system, can be conceptualized as a stack of floating maps tied to a common map base, as shown in Exhibit 3.18. Each map layer can be independently accessed. When combined, information and related attributes from individual layers (such as Land use and Hydrography in Exhibit 3.19) can be referenced to one

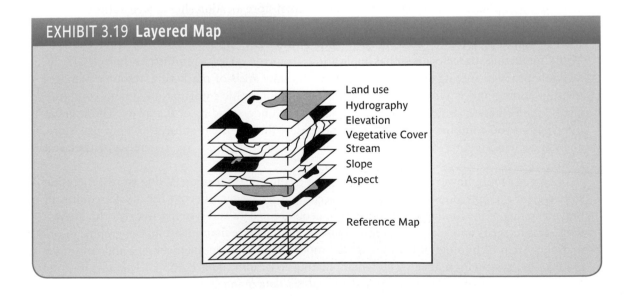

EXHIBIT 3.19 Layered Map

another from a spatial standpoint. In this sense, a GIS database can be conceptualized as a stack of floating map layers registered to a common map base.

In addition to the map layers, a GIS database also includes a data file containing attribute information about features indicated on each map layer. For example, the data for a map layer of the road network of Majorca, Spain, may include information such as road name, road type, physical distance and address range. Geographic system information spatial analysis involves manipulation of map layers, individually or in combination, to derive solutions to spatial problems that assist the user in decision making.

Applications

A geographic information system enables marketers to 'layer' information within a neighbourhood or larger geographic areas. Market areas can be examined to learn where defined demographic characteristics – gender, age, income and race, for example – overlap. Neighbourhoods are then 'clustered' into categories and defined by demographic data and lifestyle information. Moreover, geodemographic information is linked with other types of household information to produce sophisticated profiles of neighbourhoods that are a valuable tool for all types of target marketing. Some marketing research firms offer databases that allow businesses to look at their market area in levels as fine as several blocks of residence.

If applied effectively, GIS can be a very useful planning tool for marketers, resource scientists and land use planners. The availability and expanded use of satellite imagery for GIS applications will have a marked effect on GIS technology. Further integration of GIS applications with remote sensing technology is foreseen. There will also be expanded and more sophisticated use of the Global Positioning System (GPS) in data location and registration.

MDSS and Queries as an Output Resource

A **query** is another component of the MDSS that facilitates data retrieval. It enables the user to retrieve information from the system without having to use special software. The response, either on screen or in hard-copy form, has the same general appearance as a regular MDSS report.

> **Query** A segment of the MDSS that enables the user to retrieve information from the system without having to use special software.

The unique feature of MDSS queries is they arise after data are provided to the analyst, that is, the need to use query operations arises after the analyst reviews the results of an earlier report. For example, a loan manager interested in cross-selling bank services can request a display of customer use of banking products (e.g. loans, credit cards, savings accounts), which would then be used to formulate detailed queries about the customer's financial information. This would enable the manager to view various services the customer may not be using, hence providing a cross-selling opportunity for the bank. A query enables the analyst to combine input and output forms, so that inputs (new bank services to cross-sell) are always given in the context of the previous MDSS output (current product use). Additionally, the analyst can fill in or select inputs that can modify the current output or result in different output altogether, such as selection/evaluation criteria for new product offerings.

Other Emerging Technological Trends

There have been numerous established technological trends occurring since the 1980s, such as the continuing advancement of computer technology, the increasing capabilities of statistical software packages, the advent of the Internet and the launch of the loyalty card system, which have changed marketing research practice.

This section does not intend to cover all those technological trends that have already been established by the marketing research industry. Instead we will cover some of those that are still emergent, which have not yet been well utilized or defined in the marketing research industry, but are potentially revolutionary. We will discuss Facebook and Second Life, two trends which are hugely popular in society across the globe and are made possible by the continuing advancement of technology, and their relevance to marketing research. Both Facebook and Second Life are made possible by the concept of Web 2.0, which is introduced below.

Web 2.0

Web 2.0 is a concept describing the trend in the use of Web technology and Web design that strives to enhance information sharing and collaboration among users. The complex and continually evolving technology infrastructure of Web 2.0 comprises server-software, content-syndication, messaging-protocols, standards-oriented browsers with plug-ins and extensions, as well as different kinds of client-applications. Integrating all these elements enables the provision of Web 2.0 sites with information creation, storage and dissemination challenges and capabilities that go beyond what the so-called Web 1.0 can provide.

For users, Web 2.0 allows them to do more than just retrieve information from the computer screen. They can build on the interactive facilities of Web 1.0 to provide network-as-platform computing. Users can own data on a Web 2.0 site and exercise control over that data, such as in Facebook and Second Life. This is in sharp contrast to Web 1.0 sites where users are much more restricted in what they can view. They are also not allowed to modify the site content.

As the technology infrastructure enabling the Web 2.0 concept has become available, it has been rapidly embraced by society. As a result, information such as media information is increasingly being pulled by consumers, rather than being pushed at them. Consumers are becoming in total control of what and how much information they wish to see, whom they like to share their information with, as well as whom they are willing to collaborate with in creating and modifying information. This is an open, democratic and liberal use of information which we have never seen before. Exploitation of the Web 2.0 concept makes possible the emergence of Facebook and Second Life, both of which provide marketing researchers with new thinking on how to do marketing research.

Facebook

Facebook is a social networking website which was launched on 4 February 2004. On the website, users can join networks through which to connect and interact with other people. They can add friends and send them messages. They can update their personal profiles whenever they want and notify their network members about themselves. Facebook is so popular that in the month of April 2008 alone more than 70 million people had been to the website.

The popularity of Facebook has prompted marketing researchers to ponder its potential in their professional work. Historically marketing researchers have to follow the standard procedures of discussing the marketing research brief and marketing research proposal with the clients, identifying an appropriate sample, collecting data from the sample, analysing the findings, and disseminating the results. Technological advances, such as the advent of the Internet, have allowed for the possibility of conducting questionnaire surveys online, and have made the marketing research process more efficient, but the process hasn't changed significantly in essence.

One thing that Facebook can offer marketing researchers is its Facebook Polling facility. Through Facebook Polling, marketing researchers can get responses very quickly. They can set up the questions they wish to address, identify the sample size they need, pay about €25 for every 100 completed responses, and can wait for the results to be in their Facebook account within a few hours. These Facebook Polling results cannot replace the results that we get from a proper research design and a more representative sample. However, with a moderate expense of say €100 to €200, marketing researchers can obtain quick primary data which they can use to potentially redefine their marketing research problem and fine tune the scope of their marketing research project.

Therefore, the conventional marketing research process is problem definition followed by secondary research, which is followed by primary research. Facebook Polling facilitates an early-stage primary research even before the marketing research problem has been vigorously defined. It allows for more iteration between the steps of the marketing research process, served by, in principle, as many Facebook Pollings as the marketing researcher wishes.

Second Life

Second Life is the Internet-based virtual three-dimensional world where millions of people around the globe are leading an alternative existence. Since its launch in 2003, Second Life has been hugely popular and inhabited by millions of people, called residents, from all corners of the globe. These residents, once entering the Second Life world, will find a large digital continent, other fellow residents, and their creations.

With the vast resident base in Second Life, some companies have been considering it for marketing research purposes. One company that has put ideas into practice is British Telecom (BT). The company has entered the Second Life world by owning an island there called Area 21. It has been using Second Life to conduct a market potential test of its new communication technology, called AvaTalk, which uses the company's global IP platform, Web21C, to carry calls and transmit SMS messages to mobile networks around the world. With this technology, users of virtual worlds can call or SMS their colleagues and friends in the real world.

In a one-month long market potential test starting on 26 March 2008, BT offered its Avatalk phone and text services for free to all Second Life residents, who are then able to make 10 free calls of up to one hour each and send 10 SMS messages from inside Second Life to almost anywhere in the world. These calls can be made from red BT phone boxes, which are put in six locations in the Second Life world. They are Idearium, Italy Island Resort, Nuova Sicilia, Style Magazine, Torino Vera, and Venice Italy.

At the phone box all the resident users need to do is click either the Call symbol or SMS symbol. They will be asked to make their Avatar say 'Yes' to confirm that they have read and agreed to the trial terms and conditions. They will then be asked to enter the phone number that they wish to use from BT AvaTalk. In case any resident user wants to use BT AvaTalk wherever their avatar goes, they can use a BT AvaTalk Head up Display. This can be worn by their avatar so that it appears in the peripheral vision of the avatar.

With BT offering the virtual-to-real communication service free to all Second Life residents for a whole month, it allows a large number of resident users enough time to try out the new communication technology. This will provide BT with a first-hand understanding of the demand for virtual-to-real world communications and other valuable insights into the expected market potential of the technology.

Other Marketing Research Uses

Web 2.0-enabled online social networks, including Facebook, Second Life, MySpace, etc., are also potentially a medium through which marketing researchers can solve their sampling problems. By accessing these networks, researchers could reach hard-to-secure demographic groups and discover hard-to-discover insights arising from traces of information left on the networks.

Online social networking has attracted particularly young and active online users. For years the marketing research industry has struggled to recruit panels of this type of consumer. The rise of online social networks has dramatically made this panel recruitment task much easier. Indeed a number of marketing researcher companies have managed with success to recruit thousands of young and active online users in just a few months.

For instance, Face Group has launched a project called Headbox, which uses online social networks to investigate the opinions of 16–25-year-old youngsters. This demographic group has shown that they are happy to communicate with their friends, social groups and even strangers via the online social networks. With a target of a final sample size of 30,000 youngsters in mind, Headbox conducted focus groups over online social networks to find out what the youngsters think about certain topics that Face Group aims to investigate.

Job Muscroft, the managing director at Face Group, contends that this new data collection method, i.e. focus groups over online social networks, is much better for them than the traditional face-to-face focus group method. 'We can host groups from people anywhere in the UK, create an ongoing dialogue. With traditional groups, it's almost impossible to get the guys back in the room again when you have finished the first session. We've interested in involving them in the whole creative process, not just in researching one thing. So we can come back to them and say, "What do you think of this?"' (*Source:* Research Magazine, www.research-live.com).

Case 1: Marketing Research Databases in the European Banking Industry

Leading with Data

The continual widening of the Eastern European markets and the integration through the European Union movement have enlarged the European banking market. Concurrently, mergers and acquisitions are not uncommon, and competition for the enlarged banking market is increasingly fierce. There is also increasing concern about the risk of bank failure among European policymakers. Effective management and utilization of customer data is a good way for European banks to compete successfully and minimize the risk of failure.

Therefore, European bankers have increasing appetites for customer data and are using it to drive their businesses. The importance of the knowledge about customers is further fuelled by the e-transition of the banking industry. New electronic delivery channels are changing traditional banker–client relationships, replacing them with a fluid market system in which consumers can shop for products and services on price. Loyalty is difficult to come by, as products become increasingly commoditized, and channels of delivery more abundant. In this environment, banks are grooming a new breed of data-savvy executives who can lead by following the data trail.

Courting Profitable Customers

Different bankers are at different levels in their mastery of the data basics of segmentation and data enhancement. But competition is forcing quick transformations of those who are not on board. The collection, integration, enhancement, and analysis of customer data have become must-do disciplines for improving marketing efficiency.

Many banks are concerned with the warehousing of multiple streams of customer and prospect data and with providing analytical tools to their executives to support customer acquisition and retention efforts. Some of this work is being outsourced to service bureaus and consultants to help bring projects to rapid completion. And new data service providers are cropping up in unexpected places. MasterCard International, for example, has thousands of member banks that access consumer transaction data by account number.

While data is driving more acquisition and retention programmes, only a minority of banks use data for the more sophisticated profitability analysis at the account or household level. Profitability analysis involves obtaining operating costs, by product, identifying profit components from each transaction file, creating a formula for each product, and validating the accuracy of the calculated data. It can be used to measure a customer's return.

Take an hypothetical example. A bank's initial profitability analysis showed that 20 per cent of customers were very profitable, 20 per cent were very unprofitable, and 60 per cent were marginal. Going further, the bank analysed two of its branches. Branch 'A' is in an affluent neighbourhood and very profitable, while Branch 'B' is in a blue-collar area and losing money. To the bank's surprise, the two branches were comparable in loan ratios and all other areas except one: no-fee checking. That product alone pushed Branch 'B' into the red. This knowledge allowed the bank manager to change the minimum balance, raise fees, and use other alternatives to improve the profitability of both the accounts and the branch. Conventional wisdom holds that blue-collar customers are a bank's bread and butter because affluent customers often establish more than one banking relationship, but analysis showed that wasn't true in this case. Because the affluent customers' balances were so much higher – double that of other households, even without the total banking relationship – they produced a much better return.

marketing research in action

Mastering the Basics

Banks are recommended the following 'rules' when working with their customer databases:

- **RFM segmentation.** Segmenting customers by the three key variables of behaviour: recency, frequency, and monetary value (RFM). Transaction data remains the most powerful predictor of future behaviour and can help banks identify the best prospects and possible defectors.

- **Data enhancement.** Appending demographic and geographic data to customer records permits various modelling and mining efforts to be undertaken, including:

  1 **Profiling.** Create a profile of individual customers and households in each of your key segments, comparing the incidence of a particular type of buyer in your customer universe to the larger marketplace.

  2 **Cross-selling the existing customer base.** Identify the best customers and target those who are prime candidates for additional products and services. Analytical models pinpoint variables that will lift response – which means you can mail to fewer people and get a greater response.

  3 **Upselling or reactivating customers.** Low-balance customers can be upgraded to more profitable status with appropriate product targeting. Inactive customers may likewise be viable prospects for other offerings.

  4 **Retention.** Reduce churn in your customer base by identifying factors predictive of defection and taking remedial actions to turn likely defectors into your loyal customers.

  5 **Acquisition.** Data can be used in various ways to improve acquisition. Your profile of your best customers points the way to the prospect most likely to respond and be profitable over time. This data can drive your offer, your creativity, and your media selection.

The Loyalty Connection

Developing deeper customer loyalty is an ongoing challenge for every financial institution. It is compounded by the industry's increasing reliance on technology, both for developing products and executing transactions. As reliance on brick-and-mortar branch infrastructures and personal relationships lessens, low-cost, high-tech options such as automated teller machines (ATMs) and online banking are increasingly homogenizing product offerings, and banks may lose the opportunity to cross-sell and up-sell to their own customers because newcomers, not tied to banking's traditional branch infrastructure, can deliver services more cheaply. While it may be hard to think of bank products and services as commodities that we can shop around for like bread or milk, that mindset is changing.

Newcomers to banking such as Egg Banking plc and Intelligent Finance in the UK are making some inroads with Internet-happy customers. But there is an upside for established players who are expanding their own online offerings. Electronic transactions generate transactional data that, when handled proactively, can help banks stand out from the crowd.

Designing Win-Win Situations

Leading with data in financial services is not without its challenges. One of the key problems is that a model profitable customer – one who runs high balances on credit cards or other loan programmes – is also a model candidate for bankruptcy. That problem has been worsened by industry practices in issuing preapproved credit cards, which has contributed to rising bad debts.

The delinquency crunch has attracted some nonbank innovators to the marketplace. For example, Merchandise cataloger Fingerhut in the US decided to pursue high-risk customers as a lucrative credit card market. Using the company's catalog database containing 500 pieces of information on the cataloger's 50-million-name file, Fingerhut opened 670,000 credit card accounts with about £250 million in receivables in less than a year, making it one of the largest card issuers in the US. Factoring in the inherent risk of extending credit to low- to middle-income families, Fingerhut allowed a 6 per cent write-off for bad debt and a competitive interest rate on its co-branded Visa and MasterCards. Fingerhut attributed the company's success to data – 'It all goes back to the database,' said their chief executive officer.

Data can also help bankers to think about customers in fresh ways. Data helps banks to develop traditional or emerging channels and to glean all the information they possibly can. For example, banks can add a relational database field to track which customers opened savings accounts for their children, and market to them at an appropriate time in future.

Conclusions

Banks are entering a new era of relationship-building strategies. Intensely transaction-driven, they have realized that product-oriented strategies will give way to more targeted and focused marketing efforts. What follows are the main benefits banks derive as they adopt relationship-building strategies that lead with data:

- They can more easily and effectively carry out segmentation and cross-selling strategies.
- They can more efficiently sell the maximum amount of the banking products targeted to the right segments of their databases.
- They can build multiple product relationships with targeted customer segments, as sophisticated modelling techniques and profitability analysis allow customized value offerings and pricing.

Questions

1 Using the knowledge you acquired in this chapter, suggest ways banks and other companies can use databases to better serve their customers.

2 What are the limitations of the use of these databases in the banking industry?

Case 2: Baltic Sea Region Geographic Information System

The Baltic Drainage Basin Project has established a GIS database, which mainly focuses upon land cover, land use and population. The Project was a multi-disciplinary research project under the EU Environmental Research Programme. The resulting GIS database was developed as a joint effort between the Beijer Institute, Stockholm; the Department of Systems Ecology, Stockholm University; and UNEP/GRID-Arendal. At first sight, this GIS database seems to be less relevant to businesses. In reality, some information such as population density, arable lands, pasture lands and land cover, are useful for a deeper understanding of the region or a specified part of the region. This information would be particularly useful for the agribusiness sector. In its full use,

GIS can operate to provide businesses with crucial location information and, hence, actual location decisions. Exhibit 3.20 shows the output of population distribution from the Baltic Sea Region GIS.

EXHIBIT 3.20 **The Baltic Sea Region GIS Showing the Population Distribution within the Baltic Sea Drainage Basin**

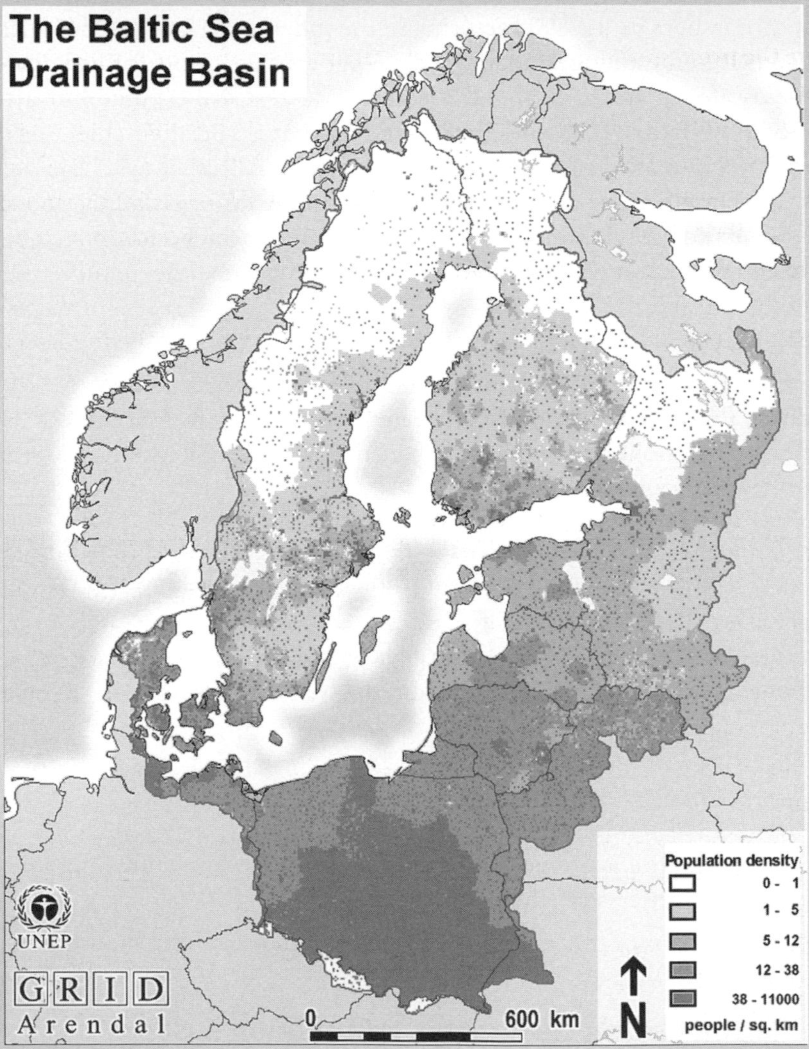

Questions

1 Illustrate the use of the Baltic Sea Region for marketing research purposes?
2 How could GIS be used to identify a location for a new Carrefour hypermarket?
3 Could GIS be used by a sales manager to design sales territories for sales people? How?
4 What are some other examples of how GIS could be used in marketing research?

Summary of Learning Objectives

- **Understand the meaning of technology-enabled market intelligence.**

  The technology-enabled market intelligence enterprise follows a business model different from that of the more traditional companies. This model promotes a competitive advantage by using customer information at the 'granular' level; that is, data that are highly detailed, highly personalized and specifically structured around the individual customer. This enterprise embraces the vision that targeting customers is not sufficient; capturing customers is the goal.

- **Illustrate the process of data collection for a technology-enabled market intelligence programme.**

  In these programmes data are tracked at the point of customer interaction. This may occur at point-of-sale terminals or on the Web. Regardless of the source, the goal is to collect all relevant customer interaction data, store the data in the data warehouse, and subsequently analyse the data to render profitable customer profiles.

- **Illustrate and define a marketing research database.**

  A marketing research database is a central repository of customer information such as on what customers are purchasing, how often, and in what amount. The fundamental purpose of any customer database is to help a firm develop meaningful, personal communication with its customers. Other more specific purposes of this database are to improve efficiency of market segment construction, increase the probability of repeat purchase behaviour, and enhance sales and media effectiveness.

- **Illustrate the development and purposes of a data warehouse.**

  A data warehouse is a central repository for all significant parts of information that an organization collects. Data from various major functions of the organization are inventoried on a central mainframe computer so that information can be shared across all functional departments of the business. There are two major purposes of a data warehouse. First is to collect and store data for the daily operation of the business, and second is to collect, organize and make data available for analysis purpose.

- **Explain the process of data mining as it relates to the data warehouse.**

  Data mining is the process of finding hidden relationships among variables contained in data stored in the data warehouse. Data mining is a data analysis procedure known primarily for the recognition of significant patterns of data as they pertain to particular customers or customer groups.

- **Understand the role of modelling in database analysis.**

  The purpose of database modelling is twofold: (1) to summarize what companies already know about their customers, and (2) to show companies what they need to learn about their customers. Two common modelling techniques exist in database analysis. Scoring models, using a gains table, are designed to predict consumption behaviour. Lifetime value models measure the value a customer represents to the firm. Both models rely on actual purchase behaviour, not probability estimates based on purchase intentions.

- **Understand the purpose of a marketing decision support system (MDSS).**

  A MDSS is designed to help marketing personnel with decision making activities. These activities are highly focused on a specific problem and information required to solve that problem. With proper information, a MDSS allows the manager to identify the best course of action in solving market related problems. Therefore, the primary purpose of a MDSS is to manipulate information so as to provide problem solutions.

■ **Describe the various information requirements used to design a MDSS.**

The bulk of the information contained in a MDSS comes from secondary data. The common forms of information used in a MDSS are environmental information, transactional data and business intelligence.

■ **Understand the role of transactional data in a MDSS.**

Considered the most important information requirement, transactional data provide information resulting from point-of-sale transactions. This information allows managers to track and react to daily sales fluctuations, evaluate the effectiveness of marketing activities, and develop predictive models based on actual product sales data.

■ **Explain the relationship between information processing and MDSS.**

The key elements of the information processing components of a MDSS are the database, the computer facilities, and the software system. Collectively these elements can provide the manager or user with the capability to produce timely and accurate reports. The driving force behind report generation is the specific software system employed by the MDSS. The two most common forms of software systems are statistical software systems and managerial function software systems.

■ **Provide examples of output from a MDSS.**

The most common forms of MDSS output are reports, simulations, and queries. Normally the reports are generated for determining profitability or performance measures on the marketing mix. Simulations are used to produce what-if scenarios. A valuable simulation for many MDSS users is the geographic information system (GIS). Finally, queries enable users to retrieve information from the system without having to use a unique software programme.

■ **Discuss the relationship that exists between marketing decision support system and business intelligence.**

Information from business intelligence programmes is a key input to marketing decision support systems. The groundwork for a business intelligence programme is accomplished through a business intelligence audit, which is primarily a review of operations of a business and its competitors.

■ **Illustrate and define a geographic information system.**

'Geographic information system' (GIS) is a commonly used MDSS simulation. GIS uses spatial modelling in conjunction with data drawn from the MDSS, enabling uses to display spatial data organized as map layers. It contains four major components: data input, data analysis, data management system, and data output.

■ **Appreciate the potential role of emerging technologies in marketing research process**

Technological advances have already brought significant impacts on the marketing research industry over the past decades, but the advances are unstoppable and emerging technologies will continue to play a potentially revolutionary impact on the marketing research process. One type of emerging technologies that has been earmarked to possess such revolutionary potential is Web 2.0. Facebook and Second Life, two of the popular applications of Web 2.0, have already begun to mark their influence in the marketing research industry.

Key Terms and Concepts

Active data   84

Automatic replenishment
system (ARS)   112

Bar coding   111

Business intelligence   111

Customer-centric approach   80

Customer-volunteered
information   87

Database technology   94

Data enhancement   90

Data field   94

Data mining   97

Data warehouse   85

Depth   93

Description   98

Directed data   85

Electronic data interchange
(EDI)   113

Environmental information   108

Granular data   79

Informational data   86

Lifetime value models   104

Managerial function software
systems   116

Marketing decision support system
(MDSS)   106

Marketing research database   87

Operational data   85

Optical scanner   111

Query   121

Passive data   84

Prediction   99

Reader-sorter   114

Real-time transactional data   86

Relational database system   96

Scoring models   102

Sequential database system   94

Silo   79

Statistical software systems   115

Technology-enabled market
intelligence   78

Touchpoint   81

Transactional data   111

Width   93

Review Questions

1 Briefly describe the basic essentials of a technology-enabled market intelligence programme.

2 Briefly explain the following concepts as they apply to a technology-enabled market intelligence environment: the strategic use of customer information, information based on a transactional focus, enterprise-wide approach to the use of information, and deployment of appropriate technology.

3 What role does technology play in a market intelligence programme?

4 Describe the significant implications that exist when companies collect the following data: active data, passive data, and directed data.

5 List the three advantages that data enhancement provides and explain how Adidas could use each one.

6 Explain the differences between a sequential database and a relational database. What advantages are associated with each?

7 Describe how data mining works and how it is helping companies to improve their decision making.

8 What is the value of database modelling in understanding customer behaviour?

9 What advantages of a marketing decision support system are not present in a management information system?

10 Why is it important to use secondary marketing information in a marketing decision support system?

11 List the five methods of collecting and maintaining transactional data, and provide an explanation of how each method can affect a company's marketing strategy.

12 What ethical implications are associated with the use of electronic scanning devices and electronic information storage procedures?

13 What are the three key elements that make up the information-processing component of the MDSS?

14 What is the purpose of a business intelligence programme?

15 What is the value of a business intelligence audit?

Discussion Questions

1 Describe the technology-enabled market intelligence programme and discuss the potential contributions this kind of programme has for a business enterprise.

2 **Experience the Internet.** Conduct an Internet search on firms that are involved in the data mining business. Select one of these firms and provide a brief write-up on what that firm provides regarding data mining.

3 Why are transactional data collection techniques important to Holsten-Brauerei AG, the long-standing beer brewery in Hamburg's Altona district?

4 Briefly describe the differences between scoring models and lifetime value models. In what situations would each modelling procedure be most appropriate?

5 Could Jimmy Spice's restaurant benefit from using database modelling in its operations? If so, how?

6 Would the application of the technology-enabled market intelligence concept improve Jimmy Spice's restaurant operations? If so, how?

7 What are the major types of information Jimmy Spice's Restaurant should include in building a data warehouse?

8 **Experience the Internet.** Go to www.yahoo.com and search for companies that use and develop MDSSs. Provide a brief report on the number of companies that develop the systems and the applications for which they are used. Now try www.google.com and see if your results differ.

9 **Experience the Internet.** Go to www.gis.com. What is the purpose of this Web site? How would it help someone interested in GIS?

10 Discuss the differences associated with statistical software systems and managerial function software systems. Why are managerial function software systems used more frequently in actual business situations?

11 What is the most important advantage of a geographic information system (GIS)? What information would a GIS provide for an agribusiness seeking to a location? Explain.

12 Could Jimmy Spice's restaurant benefit from using a MDSS in its operations? If so, how?

13 Would the application of geographic information system (GIS) principles improve Jimmy Spice's restaurant operations? If so, how?

14 What are the major types of business intelligence Jimmy Spice's restaurant should be collecting for its MDSS?

PART 2

Research Methods

Part contents

Secondary Research

LEARNING OBJECTIVES

After reading this chapter, you will be able to

☑ Illustrate and define consumer-generated media.

☑ Understand how secondary data fit into the marketing research process.

☑ Demonstrate how secondary data can be used in problem solving.

☑ List sources of traditional internal secondary data.

☑ Know how to use and extract external secondary data.

☑ Identify sources of external secondary data.

☑ Understand the availability and use of syndicated sources of secondary data.

☑ Understand the impacts of computerization of secondary data.

> " In today's competitive environment, the key word is fast. Faster in obtaining results, faster in disseminating results. Therefore, we now conduct marketing research with priority given to secondary data.
>
> Why? It's faster. "
>
> *–Robert Bengen*
> *Director of Marketing and Research, Samsonite Corporation*

Know Your Customer: Making the Most of an Information-Rich Environment

Canon, a Japanese electronics giant, has created a blogging platform for their Canon Creativity Centre. Similar initiatives have also been taken by Xerox, Nintendo Wii and Sony Ericsson. The blog messages left by customers and the public can then be monitored by respective companies for tracking the market trends and understanding who's saying what about the company's brands and products. This is called buzz monitoring. The company can then evaluate the sentiment of its brand and the level of influence the blog messages have. If the sentiment is encouraging, the company can continuously monitor it and could do something in order to benefit from it. If the sentiment is negative, then the company may need to take proactive and corrective action before it spreads further.

Consumer-Generated Media – an Emerging Form of Secondary Data

The examples of Canon and the other companies in the opening example may not at first appear to fully illustrate the traditional notion of using secondary data. Yet they illustrate the use of an emerging form of secondary data, referred to as **consumer-generated media (CGM)**. It has recorded the fastest growth among the whole range of media. In the blogpulse portal alone, there are more than 43 million English language blogs at the time of publishing, with up to a million new posts observed each day. More amazing still, these figures represent only one CGM platform in one language! Given the new information technology available, many companies are now using a variety of techniques to collect, store and categorize customer data for future marketing decisions. Information gathered from blogs, podcasts, Internet forums, online communities and online social networks (Exhibit 4.1) is increasingly used to exploit a data-rich environment based on customer interaction. As more and more such data become available, many companies are realizing they can be used to make sound marketing decisions. Data of this nature are unique in that they are unprompted and extremely raw. They are more readily available, often more valid, and usually less expensive to secure than company-gathered primary data.

> **Consumer-generated media (CGM)** A collective name applied to different forms of digital communications whereby consumers openly share their opinions and experiences, often about their reactions to products and services.

This chapter focuses on the types of secondary data available, how they can be used, the benefits they offer, and the impact of the Internet on the use of secondary data.

EXHIBIT 4.1 Some Major Forms of Consumer-Generated Media

Form	Meaning
Blog	A user-generated website where entries, which contain commentary or news on a particular subject, are made in journal style and displayed in a reverse chronological order
Podcast	An audio (or occasionally video) recording available on an Internet source (website, blog, etc.) for real-time listening or downloading
Internet forum	A web application for holding discussions and posting user-generated content

Online community	A group of people that primarily interact via a computer network
Online social network	A collection of various web-based ways for users to interact, such as chat, messaging, email, video, voice chat, file sharing, blogging and discussion groups

A Closer Look at Research *(Using Technology)*

Assessing the Marketing Impacts of Direct versus Indirect Exposures to Consumer-Generated Media among the Belgian Online Population

An important outcome trend of the different forms of consumer-generated media is what today's marketers call 'word of mouse' (WoNo). Verhaeghe et al. (2007) defined it as 'the act of a consumer receiving, creating and/or distributing marketing-relevant content through online channels (both textual and audio-visual)'.

Until recently, word of mouse was measured only from the perspective of direct exposure, by registering the click through or forward rates. Although these secondary data are useful, they are mechanical and ignore the underlying behavioural and attitudinal processes undertaken by the consumers. These processes, whereby a consumer converses and interacts with others regarding the contents to which he/she was directly exposed on the Internet, imply these other consumers are indirectly exposed to the same online contents. The potential impact of this kind of indirect exposure was largely ignored until recently.

Dove, a global brand of cleansing and personal care products owned by Unilever, was concerned that the portrayal of female beauty in popular culture has been helping to perpetuate an idea of beauty that is neither authentic nor attainable in real life. This distorted perception could impact on women's well-being, happiness and self-esteem.

In order to help rectify this, Dove commissioned a 75-second viral film called 'Evolution'. In this film, Dove captivatingly shows how distorted our perceptions of beauty are. The film was posted in various forms on the Internet, including on YouTube and an email with a link to the film and sent to a large number of people.

Data on the effects of the direct and indirect exposures of the film were then collected via the Belgian Internet access panel of XL Online Panels. In total 1,503 panel members participated in the respective survey. Collected data were weighted to the Belgian online population so as they could be representative in terms of language spoken, gender, age, education and professional status, as well as Internet usage intensity.

Results show that 42 per cent of respondents who were directly exposed to the film had more sympathy for the Dove brand, while 32 per cent of respondents being indirectly exposed had the same attitude. Even more interesting, 32 per cent of indirectly exposed respondents, compared to 15 per cent of directly exposed respondents, would talk to others about Dove in a more positive way. The indirectly exposed people were also more likely than their directly exposed counterparts to have taken a closer look at Dove products (15 per cent versus 11 per cent), and to be going to watch more closely for other marketing communications by Dove (24 per cent versus 14 per cent).

These results suggest that indirect exposure could pose more significant marketing impacts than direct exposure. Information about direct exposure can be obtained in the form of secondary data (click through or forward rates), but the 'indirectly exposed' kind of data can only be accessed through primary research such as in a survey. More often than not, a marketing research project necessitates the use of both secondary and primary data.

Source: Adapted from a business case by de Ruyck, Schillewaert, van Belleghem and Distave, 2007.

The Nature and Scope of Secondary Data

One of the basic tasks of marketing research is to obtain information that helps a company's management make the best possible decisions. Focusing on the particular marketing problem to be analysed, the researcher needs to determine whether useful information already exists, how relevant the information is, and how it should be obtained. Existing sources of information are more widespread than one might expect, as illustrated in the chapter opening example, and should always be considered first in any data collection procedure.

The term **secondary data** refers to data not gathered for the immediate study at hand but for some other purpose. There are two types of secondary data – internal and external. **Internal secondary data** are data collected by a company for accounting purposes, marketing activity reports and customer knowledge. **Customer knowledge information** is provided by customers for purposes that may be outside the marketing function of an organization. For example, information may be provided to engineers, logistical support personnel, or information technology departments for issues relating to product improvement, packaging, or Web registration. Nonetheless, data of this type, if properly warehoused and categorized, can be an invaluable form of secondary data for marketing decisions as they relate to customer relationship management (CRM). Customer relationship management focuses on customer involvement and interactions throughout many of the processes of an organization.

> **Secondary data** Data not gathered for the immediate study at hand but for some other purpose.
>
> **Internal secondary data** Data collected by the individual company for accounting purposes, marketing activity reports and customer knowledge.
>
> **Customer knowledge information** Information provided by customers that is unsolicited and can be used for marketing planning purposes.

External secondary data consist of data supplied by outside entities mainly including the national government, foreign governments, non-governmental organizations (NGOs), academic institutions, research institutions, industry associations, commercial organizations and private individuals. External secondary data may be in the form of standardized marketing research services such as store audits and consumer purchase panels provided by NPD Group, and European Grocery Retailing report published by the Institute of Grocery Distribution. Increasingly external

> **External secondary data** Data supplied by outside entities.

secondary data can be obtained from computerized data sources. These may include computerized data sets, websites managed by public organizations and private business organizations and customer volunteered information.

The Role of Secondary Data in Marketing Research

The role of secondary data in the marketing research process has changed in recent years. Traditionally, research based on secondary data was viewed as nonoriginal. It often was outsourced to a corporate librarian, syndicated data collection firm, or junior research analyst. The main functions of secondary data research were to provide historical background for a current primary research endeavour and to allow longitudinal trend analysis within an industry. In other words, secondary data research was viewed as the filler, attachment, or appendix to the formal primary research report. With the increased emphasis on business and competitive intelligence and the ever-increasing availability of information from proprietary online databases, secondary data research is gaining importance in the marketing research process.

The secondary research method is increasingly applied to specific marketing problems due to the relative speed and cost-effectiveness of gathering secondary data. Many large corporations are redefining the role of the secondary research analyst to that of a business unit information professional or specialist linked to the information technology area. This individual creates contact and sales databases, prepares competitive trend reports, develops customer retention strategies, and so forth.

Secondary Data and Customer-Centric Organizations

More and more forward looking organizations are adopting a customer-centric, data-driven initiative to manage their business. They place their current and potential customers at the centre of whatever nature or level of business decision they make, in order to get customers, retain customers and expand customers for the benefit of their business. To achieve this, they have to learn about customers' needs and behaviours as accurately and in as much detail as possible. For this relevant data is needed, much of which is secondary data.

In order to exploit effectively their available secondary data, the organization should use a combination of technology and human resources to collect, organize, analyse and present the data, so as to gain insights into the behaviours of customers and the value those customers hold for the organization. For any customer-centric, data-driven initiative to be effective, an organization must first decide what kind of customer data it is looking for and what it intends to do with those data. For example, financial institutions can keep track of customer life cycle stages in order to determine the right time to market appropriate banking products like retirement planning products.

The organization must then examine all the different ways customer data comes into the business, where and how the data are stored, and how data are currently being used. For example, one company may interact with customers in a variety of ways including mail campaigns, websites, brick and mortar stores, call centres, salespersons and advertising efforts. It should use appropriate technology and human resources to link these sources of secondary data. The data then flow between operational systems (e.g. sales and inventory systems) and analytical systems that help sort through them for customer patterns. The organization then combs through the data to obtain an overall view of each customer and pinpoint areas where service enhancements are needed.

Secondary Data Research Tasks and the Marketing Research Process

In many areas of marketing research, secondary research plays a subordinate role to primary research. In concept testing, product testing and measurement of customer satisfaction, only primary research is needed to provide answers to marketing problems. Yet when the data are appropriately selected for specific situations, secondary data research can not only save time and money, but also provide the researcher with a broad avenue of answers. In many instances, secondary data can be used to directly assess the research problem at hand. Indeed secondary data collection can be the starting point in defining the actual research that needs to be conducted. If the problem can be solved based on available secondary data alone, then the company can save time, money and effort. If the level of secondary data is not sufficient to solve the specific research problems, then primary data collection needs to be considered.

Exhibit 4.2 illustrates the functional roles of secondary data research. These roles typically are viewed in terms of their focus and value. If the focus of the research project is on external market dynamics, it will likely be a secondary research responsibility. One task of secondary research is trend analysis, which uses past market data to project future changes in a dynamic marketplace. Additionally, secondary data collection is a vital support task in providing business and competitive intelligence. Both tasks involve the acquisition of secondary data and information about all aspects of a competitor's marketing and business activities. In short, external market dynamics is an area that requires proactive secondary research.

If the research focus is on the external customer, secondary research adds value to the research process. Researchers may, for example, use internal company documents to profile the current customer base. This existing customer base can then be projected to identify significant characteristics of potential new customers. Finally, needs analysis, which identifies critical problems or requirements of specific customer groups, is an additional secondary research task. Customer volunteered information shared on the Web could be a very good source of secondary data for needs analysis.

The third type of secondary research involves providing internal support data for the company. Here the focus switches to providing support for primary research activities, sales presentations and decision-making functions. For example, internal and external secondary data on the change in the market and the possible factors of the market change can be collected and analysed

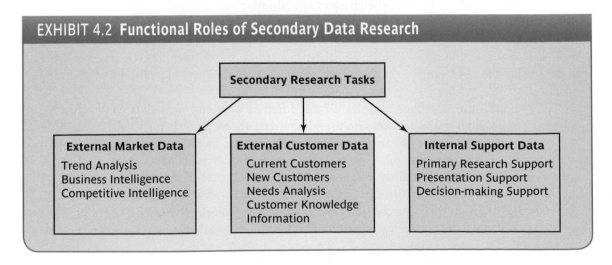

EXHIBIT 4.2 Functional Roles of Secondary Data Research

Secondary Research Tasks		
External Market Data	**External Customer Data**	**Internal Support Data**
Trend Analysis	Current Customers	Primary Research Support
Business Intelligence	New Customers	Presentation Support
Competitive Intelligence	Needs Analysis	Decision-making Support
	Customer Knowledge	
	Information	

for the problem definition process of a marketing research project or for deciding on the marketing strategy to be adopted.

Use and Evaluation of Secondary Data Sources

The primary reason for using secondary data is to save the researcher time and money. Secondary data collection involves locating the appropriate source or sources, extracting the necessary data, and recording the data for the research purpose in question. This usually takes only several days and in some cases only a few hours. Primary data, in contrast, can take months to accurately collect. When you consider the process of designing and testing questionnaires, developing a sampling plan, actually collecting the data and then analysing and tabulating them, you can see that primary data collection can be a time consuming procedure.

In addition to taking a long time, primary data collection can be costly. Fees for services rendered by market research firms usually start at thousands of Euros. Clearly, the scope and magnitude of the research project play a significant role in the fee charged for a particular project. Generally speaking, for any primary data collection project it is difficult to avoid wages, expenses, transportation costs, field work costs and clerical charges. In contrast, with many secondary data sources such costs are nonexistent or minimal.

Because of time and cost savings, the first general rule of thumb associated with any research endeavour is to exhaust all potential sources of secondary data. In today's environment of information abundance, many firms, both consumer and industrial, are finding secondary data sources adequate for solving many of their marketing research problems. Indeed, by 2010 almost half of all marketing research objectives are expected to be accomplished using secondary data.

As information becomes more abundant, and technology allows for greater refinement and categorization of the information, the emphasis on secondary data is likely to increase. In addition, secondary data are likely to become more accurate. Bar coding, optical scanning and database point-of-purchase data often provide companies with all the information they need for much of their marketing research.

With the increasing emphasis on secondary data, researchers will develop better procedures to evaluate the quality of information obtained via secondary data sources. The new procedures should be based on six fundamental principles:

1   **Purpose.** Since most secondary data are collected for purposes other than the one at hand, the data must be carefully evaluated on how they relate to the current research objective. Many times the original collection of the data is not consistent with a particular market research study. For example, in the UK National Food Survey, food expenditure and consumption data are collected and provided at household level. If a researcher is interested in correlating these data to demographic data at an individual level, they need to look for other sources of secondary data, or have to make either of the following two assumptions: that food expenditure and consumption do not differ significantly among members of the same household, or that the difference of food expenditure and consumption between the head of household and the rest of the household is generally the same across all the households in the survey. This researcher can then go on to correlate the demographic data of the head of household to the food expenditure and consumption per capita of the household.

2   **Accuracy.** When assessing secondary data, researchers need to keep in mind whether the study that generated the secondary data was designed properly. For example, was the most appropriate research methodology adopted? Was the data collection method the most appropriate for

the purpose of the study? If a questionnaire was used, was the questionnaire properly designed? Were the measures for the questions used developed properly, such as whether the dichotomous forced choice question, instead of the interval scale question, was used to measure consumer attitude towards foreign automobile imports? Was the proper sampling method, which influences the generalizability of the data, used? Who are the respondents? Are they from certain groups or randomly from the population? All these questions shed light on whether the study was properly designed, which in turn affects the accuracy of the data.

In addition, the researcher should pay attention to the time when the secondary data being considered were collected. Data that are a few years old are more likely to be inaccurate because of the potential problem of obsoleteness than those that were collected more recently.

3 **Consistency.** When evaluating any source of secondary data, a good strategy is to seek out multiple sources of the same data to assure consistency. For example, when evaluating the economic characteristics of a foreign market, a researcher may try to gather the same information from government sources, private business publications *(Fortune, BusinessWeek)* and speciality import/export trade publications.

4 **Credibility.** Researchers should always question the credibility of the secondary data source. Technical competence, service quality, reputation and training and expertise of personnel representing the organization are some of the measures of credibility.

5 **Methodology.** The quality of secondary data is only as good as the methodology employed to gather it. Flaws in methodological procedures can produce results that are invalid, unreliable, or not generalizable beyond the study itself. Therefore, the researcher must evaluate the size and description of the sample, the response rate, the questionnaire and the method for collecting the data (telephone, Internet, or personal interview).

6 **Bias.** Researchers must try to determine the underlying motivation or hidden agenda, if any, behind secondary data. It is not uncommon to find secondary data sources published to advance the interests of commercial, political, or other special interest groups. Sometimes secondary data are published to incite controversy or refute other data sources. Researchers must try to determine if the organization reporting the data is motivated by a certain purpose.

Traditional Internal Sources of Secondary Data

The logical starting point in searching for secondary data is the company's own internal information. Many organizations fail to realize the wealth of information their own records contain. Additionally, internal data are the most readily available and can be accessed at little or no cost at all. Yet, while this appears to be an overwhelming rationale for using traditional internal data, researchers must realize that the majority of this comes from past business activities. This is not to say that internal data are not usable for future business decisions. As will be evident in the following discussion, internal data sources can be highly effective in helping decision makers plan new product introductions or new distribution outlets.

Types of Internal Secondary Data

Generally, internal data will consist of sales or cost information. Data of this type are commonly found in internal accounting or financial records. The two most useful sources of information are sales invoices and accounts receivable reports. But quarterly sales reports and sales activity reports are also useful. Exhibit 4.3 lists key variables found in each of these internal sources of secondary data.

> ## EXHIBIT 4.3 Common Sources of Internal Secondary Data and Their Respective Key Variables
>
> 1. **Sales invoices**
>   a. Customer name
>   b. Address
>   c. Product/service sold
>   d. Price by unit
>   e. Salesperson
>   f. Terms of sales
>   g. Shipment point
>
> 2. **Accounts receivable reports**
>   a. Customer name
>   b. Products/services purchased
>   c. Total units and amount of sales
>   d. Customer as percentage of total sales
>   e. Customer as percentage of regional sales
>   f. Profit margin
>   g. Credit rating
>   h. Items returned
>   i. Reasons for return
>
> 3. **Quarterly sales reports**
>   a. Total units and amount of sale by:
>   Customer   Geographic segment
>   Customer segment   Sales territory
>   Product   Salesperson
>   b. Total sales against planned objective
>   c. Total sales against budget
>   d. Total sales against prior periods
>   e. Actual sales percentage increase/decrease
>   f. Contribution trends
>
> 4. **Sales activity reports**
>   a. Classification of customer account:
>   Mega
>   Large
>   Medium
>   Small
>   b. Available sales potential
>   c. Current sales penetration
>   d. Existing bids/contracts by:
>   Customer
>   Product

Sales Invoices

Sales invoices contain a wealth of data pertaining to both current and past customers. As a secondary data research tool, such invoices can provide customer profiles, sales trends, unit sales history and other key items of information.

Accounts Receivable Reports

Accounts receivable reports contain information relative to both past and current customers. They also provide information on relative profit margins; reasons behind customer returns; and revenues by industry, segment, or geographic location. With such information, accounts receivable reports can provide partial measures of customer satisfaction/dissatisfaction, price tactics and sales history.

Quarterly Sales Reports

Quarterly sales reports normally illustrate planned sales activities relative to actual sales results. These reports are invaluable sources of information on sales territories, effective sales techniques and competitive intelligence. The information is often useful in sales training and presentation planning.

Sales Activity Reports

Sales activity reports typically are prepared each month by individual sales representatives and usually contain data on sales, competition, territory activities and changes in the marketplace.

EXHIBIT 4.4 Additional Sources of Secondary Data

Source	Information
Customer letters	General satisfaction/dissatisfaction data
Customer comment cards	Overall performance data
Mail-order forms	Customer names, addresses, items purchased, cycle time of order
Credit applications	Detailed biography (demographic, socioeconomic, credit usage, credit ratings) of customers
Cash register receipts	Sales amount, merchandise type, salesperson, vendor, manufacturer
Salesperson expense reports	Sales activities, competitor activities in market
Employee exit interviews	General internal satisfaction/dissatisfaction data, internal company performance data
Warranty cards	Names, addresses, postcodes, items purchased, sales amount, reasons for product return
Past marketing research studies	A variety of data pertaining to the situation in which marketing research was conducted
Internet-provided information	Customer registration information, tracking, Web site visits, email correspondence

In general, most selling organizations require their sales personnel to include competitive activities on these reports, making them an excellent source of data for competitive intelligence.

Other Types

Other types of internal data that exist among company records can be used to complement the information thus far discussed. Exhibit 4.4 outlines other potential sources of internal secondary data.

A lot of internal company data is available for marketing research activities. If maintained and categorized properly, these data can be used for analysing product performance, customer satisfaction and target market strategies. They are also useful for planning new product introductions, product deletions, promotional strategies and customer service tactics.

Using and Extracting External Sources of Secondary Data

After searching for internal secondary data, the next logical step for the researcher to focus on is external secondary data. This section will first focus on the more conventional types of external secondary data such as government documents, business information and syndicated sources. We then discuss the Internet as an increasingly popular source of secondary data.

Planning for the External Secondary Data Search

The major challenge associated with external secondary data is finding and securing the appropriate sources from which to extract the data. During this process, the problem may not be about finding out whether information exists, but about finding out where the information resides.

When seeking secondary data sources, it is best to follow some sort of plan. A simple procedure when searching for secondary data is the 'GO-CART approach' (for goals, objectives, characteristics, activities, reliability and tabulation).

1 **Goals.** Focus your information search on topics and concepts relevant to the specific research question at hand. If the research question is how to develop market or target market profiles, seek out information relevant to this topic (demographics, socioeconomic data, etc.). If the research question is how to understand customer satisfaction as it relates to product usage, seek out information on the product, for example, how it is manufactured, distributed and transported. Let this information point to potential reasons for satisfaction or dissatisfaction.

2 **Objectives.** Seek out as much information as you can on the topic. Then check all references and citations that may enable you to address more specific topics. Backtracking through references and citations will allow you to narrow down the information.

3 **Characteristics.** Always define the specific characteristics of information you are seeking. For example, if you are seeking psychographic data, identify the specific characteristics of the data you wish to uncover. Are you looking for activities, interests, opinions (i.e. lifestyles)? If so, relative to what topics? Television viewing patterns, product usage, political affiliations, and so on? Focus your data search on a list of characteristics you're seeking as an aid in answering the research question.

4 **Activities.** Outline the places, people, events and tasks that will be part of your secondary data search. You will probably need to visit libraries and speak with reference librarians. You may need to go to local government offices, trade associations, newspaper file rooms, or even seminars. Document what needs to be done, where you need to do it and who can help you along the way.

5 **Reliability.** Try to find several data sources on the same topic. This will enable you to assess consistency and be confident of the reliability of the data.

6 **Tabulation.** Document all sources of your data search. If possible, cross-reference the various sources. Finally, verify that what you have collected is indeed what needs to be collected to answer the research question at hand. If not, an additional data search may be necessary.

The GO-CART approach for planning a secondary data search is by no means the only way to collect secondary data. It does, however, provide an agenda to follow in order to prioritize elements of the search process. Because the search for secondary data can range from very simple to highly complicated, a specific plan for a data search is necessary for each situation the researcher faces. Without any type of plan, the time and cost benefits typically associated with secondary data may not be realized.

Key Sources of External Secondary Data

The amount of secondary information is indeed vast. But the information needs of many researchers are often connected by some common themes. Data most often sought by researchers include demographics, employment characteristics, economic data, competitive and supply characteristics, regulations, and international market characteristics. Exhibit 4.5 provides examples of some key variables within these categories.

EXHIBIT 4.5 Some Key Variables Sought in Secondary Data Search

Demographics
Population growth: actual and projected
Population density
In-migration and out-migration patterns
Population trends by age and race

Employment Characteristics
Labour force growth
Unemployment levels
Employment by industry
Employment by occupation category

Economic Data
Income levels
Industry output
Retail sales

Competitive Characteristics
Number of competitors
Advertising levels

Supply Characteristics
Provision of distribution facilities
Provision of air, rail, road and water transportation
Expenditure on new infrastructure projects

Regulations
Taxes
Wages
Licensing

International Market Characteristics
Culture patterns
Social customs
Religious and moral backgrounds
Business philosophies
Political climates
Legal systems
Trade barriers
Export and transportation requirements

Several key sources of secondary data enable the researcher to create a hierarchy of information sources to guide secondary data search. Developing a hierarchy of secondary data sources is consistent with the second task of the GO-CART approach – initially look for as much information as can be obtained easily and quickly. Then work to tailor your data search to specific needs. Several broad to narrow data sources are described below to help guide the researcher through the jungle of secondary information.

International Standard Industrial Classification of All Economic Activities (ISIC)

A proper step when conducting secondary research at an industry level across countries is to refer to the numeric listings of the **International Standard Industrial Classification of All Economic Activities (ISIC) codes.** Every industry has been assigned an ISIC code. Businesses within each industry report all activities (production, sales, etc.) according to their code. Currently, there are 21 one-digit industry section and 88 two-digit industry division codes representing everything from crop production and animal hunting to activities of extraterritorial organizations and bodies. Each two-digit industry division code is divided into a number of three-digit industry

---

International Standard Industrial Classification of All Economic Activities (ISIC) codes
Numerical industrial listings designed to promote uniformity in data reporting procedures by governments and businesses in different countries.

group codes, which add up to 238 and are further categorized into four-digit industry class codes. It is at this four-digit level, which includes altogether 420 industry classes, that researchers usually focus because they provide the most detailed and often the most useful industry data.

These ISIC codes were designed to promote uniformity in industry data reporting by governments and businesses in different countries. They have been developed and occasionally revised by the United Nations Statistics Division. Wide use of them has been made by researchers, officials and business practitioners, both nationally and internationally. Exhibit 4.6 presents the latest version of the ISIC codes.

EXHIBIT 4.6 International Standard Industrial Classification of All Economic Activities (ISIC) Draft Revision 4 at One- and Two- Digit Levels

A	**Agriculture, forestry and fishing**	
01	Crop and animal production, hunting and related service activities	
02	Forestry and logging	
03	Fishing and aquaculture	
B	**Mining and quarrying**	
05	Mining of coal and lignite	
06	Extraction of crude petroleum and natural gas	
07	Mining of metal ores	
08	Other mining and quarrying	
09	Mining support service activities	
C	**Manufacturing**	
10	Manufacture of food products	
11	Manufacture of beverages	
12	Manufacture of tobacco products	
13	Manufacture of textiles	
14	Manufacture of wearing apparel	
15	Manufacture of leather and related products	
16	Manufacture of wood and of products of wood and cork, except furniture; manufacture of articles of straw and plaiting materials	
17	Manufacture of paper and paper products	
18	Printing and reproduction of recorded media	
19	Manufacture of coke and refined petroleum products	
20	Manufacture of chemicals and chemical products	
21	Manufacture of basic pharmaceutical products and pharmaceutical preparations	
22	Manufacture of rubber and plastics products	
23	Manufacture of other non-metallic mineral products	
24	Manufacture of basic metals	
25	Manufacture of fabricated metal products, except machinery and equipment	
26	Manufacture of computer, electronic and optical products	
27	Manufacture of electric equipment	
28	Manufacture of machinery and equipment n.e.c.	
29	Manufacture of motor vehicles, trailers and semi-trailers	

30	Manufacture of other transport equipment
31	Manufacture of furniture
32	Other manufacturing
33	Repair and installation of machinery and equipment
D	**Electricity, gas, steam and air conditioning supply**
35	Electricity, gas, steam and air conditioning supply
E	**Water supply sewerage, waste management and remediation activities**
36	Water collection, treatment and supply
37	Sewerage
38	Waste collection, treatment and disposal activities; materials recovery
39	Remediation activities and other waste management services
F	**Construction**
41	Construction of buildings
42	Civil engineering
43	Specialized construction activities
G	**Wholesale and retail trade; repair of motor vehicles and motorcycles**
45	Wholesale and retail trade and repair of motor vehicles and motorcycles
46	Wholesale trade, except of motor vehicles and motorcycles
47	Retail trade, except of motor vehicles and motorcycles
H	**Transportation and storage**
49	Land transport and transport via pipelines
50	Water transport
51	Air transport
52	Warehousing and support activities for transportation
53	Postal and courier activities
I	**Accommodation and food service activities**
55	Accommodation
56	Food and beverage service activities
J	**Information and communication**
58	Publishing activities
59	Motion picture, video and television programme production, sound recording and music publishing activities
60	Programming and broadcasting activities
61	Telecommunications
62	Computer programming, consultancy and related activities
63	Information service activities
K	**Financial and insurance activities**
64	Financial service activities, except insurance and pension funding
65	Insurance, reinsurance and pension funding, except compulsory social security
66	Activities auxiliary to financial service and insurance activities
L	**Real estate activities**
68	Real estate activities
M	**Professional, scientific and technical activities**
69	Legal and accounting activities
70	Activities of head offices; management consultancy activities

71	Architectural and engineering activities; technical testing and analysis
72	Scientific research and development
73	Advertising and market research
74	Other professional, scientific and technical activities
75	Veterinary activities
N	**Administrative and support service activities**
77	Rental and leasing activities
78	Employment activities
79	Travel agency, tour operator, reservation service and related activities
80	Security and investigation activities
81	Services to buildings and landscape activities
82	Office administrative, office support and other business support activities
O	**Public administration and defence; compulsory social security**
84	Public administration and defence; compulsory social security
P	**Education**
85	Education
Q	**Human health and social work activities**
86	Human health activities
87	Residential care activities
88	Social work activities without accommodation
R	**Arts, entertainment and recreation**
90	Creative, arts and entertainment activities
91	Libraries, archives, museums and other cultural activities
92	Gambling and betting activities
93	Sports activities and amusement and recreation activities
S	**Other service activities**
94	Activities of membership organizations
95	Repair of computers and personal and household goods
96	Other personal service activities
T	**Activities of households as employers; undifferentiated goods- and services-producing activities of households for own use**
97	Activities of households as employers of domestic personnel
98	Undifferentiated goods- and services-producing activities of private households for own use
U	**Activities of extraterritorial organizations and bodies**
99	Activities of extraterritorial organizations and bodies

Source: United Nations Statistics Division, 2007.

Government Documents

Detail, completeness and consistency are major reasons for using government documents. The best of these is the census derived from a nationwide survey. It is the only survey which provides a detailed and complete picture of the entire population, and it is unique because it attempts to include everyone at the same time and asks the same core questions everywhere. In the UK, it has been conducted every ten years since 1801.

There are two notes of caution about census data. First, they are collected only every 10 years with slight periodic updates, so researchers always need to be aware of the timeliness issue of census data. Second, they can be misleading. Not every person or household is reflected in census data. Those who have recently changed residences or were simply not available for contact at census time are not included in census data.

In between the two censuses, there are also many updated documents provided by the government. The prominent repository of these government documents in the UK is the Office for National Statistics, whose publications are the foundation for most of the information available on the country's population, economic, social and other major activities. Exhibit 4.7 lists some of the common sources of secondary data available from the Office.

For government documents in Europe, Eurostat, the Statistical Office of the European Community based in Luxemburg, is an ideal target. It provides statistical information on a wide range of topics, covering the entire European Union, the euro-zone, candidate countries and

EXHIBIT 4.7 Selected Government Documents Published for the UK

Themes	Publications
Agriculture, fishing and forestry	Agricultural census summary sheets by geographic area
	Weekly market report on prices of agricultural outputs
	Family food: annual report on food expenditure, consumption and nutrient intakes
Commerce, energy and industry	Product sales and trade manufacture
	E-commerce survey of business
	Annual business inquiry
Economy	UK economic and financial data
	National statistics annual report
	United Kingdom economic accounts
	Retail prices index: annual index numbers of retail prices
	Profitability of UK companies
	Regional competitiveness and state of the regions
	Overseas trade statistics
	Relative regional consumer price levels
Education and training	Region in figures
	Public resources for teaching and student numbers in HEFCE-funded institutions
Labour market	Public sector employment
	Average weekly earnings
	Annual local area Labour Force Survey
	Labour market statistics
	Trade union membership
Population and migration	Population trends
	Population estimates for UK, England and Wales, Scotland and Northern Ireland
Social and welfare	Social trends
	Focus on ethnicity and identity
	Focus on religion

EXHIBIT 4.8 The Nine Broad Themes and Some of Their Key Publications Provided by Eurostat

Theme	Publication
General statistics	Eurostat yearbook
	Regions: statistical yearbook
Economy and finance	European Union foreign direct investment yearbook
	Economic portrait of the European Union
Population and social conditions	The life of women and men in Europe – a statistical portrait
	European social statistics
Industry, trade and services	European business – facts and figures
	Business in candidate countries – facts and figures
Agriculture and fisheries	Fisheries yearbook
	Agricultural statistics data
External trade	External and intra-European Union trade – statistical yearbook
Transport	Panorama of transport – statistical overview of transport in the European Union
	Aviation and maritime statistics in the candidate countries
Environment and energy	Gas and electricity market statistics
	Environmental pressure indicators for the European Union
Science and technology	Statistics on science and technology in Europe
	Research and development – annual statistics

selected countries outside the European Union. This statistical information can be categorized into nine broad themes. Exhibit 4.8 lists some key publications under each of these themes.

Secondary Sources of Business Data

The amount of secondary data available from businesses is virtually unlimited. Researchers can use directories to conduct secondary business data research in a more convenient and systematic way. They can also consult professional associations, leading newspapers and prominent commercial periodicals as part of their research. The following are some commonly used sources of business information mainly for the UK, European and international markets:

Marketing Handbook

Marketing and Creative Handbook

Outdoor Advertising Association

Institute of Practitioners in Advertising

Direct Marketing Association

Institute of Sales Promotion

Chartered Institute of Public Relations

Datamonitor

Euromonitor

Mintel

The Financial Times

The Economist

DM Weekly

Marketing Week

Marketing

Marketing Direct

Precision marketing

New Media Age

Campaign

Revolution

Another good source of business information is the ABI/INFORM Complete™, which is one of the most comprehensive business databases on the market today. The database covers business and economic conditions, corporate strategies and management techniques, as well as competitive and product information. Its international coverage can help researchers to grasp a basic and broad picture of companies and business trends in many parts of the world.

For budget conscious marketing researchers, the marketing pocket book series published by WARC can be an inexpensive source of secondary data. These are concisely loaded with lots of general marketing information in specified regions. For example, *The European Marketing Pocket Book*, in addition to having a pan-European section, provides economic, demographic, marketing, media and advertising data on each of the 33 European countries, which include all the member states of the European Union. *The UK Marketing Pocket Book*, on the other hand, contains over 60,000 facts and figures related to marketing in the UK. The WARC marketing pocket book series extends beyond Europe and UK, and covers Americas and Asia Pacific. *The Americas Marketing Pocket Book* is a recent addition to the series, which provides marketing and media data in each of the 19 countries on North and South America. *The Asia Pacific Marketing Pocket Book* covers as many as 36 countries in Asia Pacific, Africa and the Middle East.

 A Closer Look at Research *(In the field)*

Utilizing Secondary Data to Place a Value on Each Customer

Organizations are now treating secondary data as a valuable balance sheet asset. They try to utilize the data in order to place a clear value on each of their customers. This can help them to size and prioritize their investment in customer-centric activities.

In directing their customer-centric investment, Lands' End, an international catalogue retailer, uses vast amounts of secondary data to calculate the lifetime value of customers. Knowing, for example, that a specific type of customer is likely to spend €1,000 on merchandise over ten transactions allows these companies to place a clear value on the relationship with this customer type, and then appropriately budget for customer-centric activities that can retain or enhance this customer relationship value. Analytical applications that improve data quality, such as data warehousing and data mining, are of course critical components of the process.

Statistical Sources of Secondary Data

Some popular statistical sources of secondary data have been introduced in the previous section. These statistical data can be presented in processed format on a table or report, or in raw format on a spreadsheet. The former form is ready made and easier to be read by researchers. The latter, on the other hand, is more complicated as it can contain raw data from each of the thousands of respondents. However, if the researcher is equipped with sufficient data analysis skill and has the time required for the analysis, the data in raw form can provide a much better prospect for the researcher to meet their research objective, enrich their findings and sometimes discover something out of serendipity.

The UK Data Archive is the curator of the largest collection of research-led secondary datasets in raw format in social sciences and humanities in the UK. Many of the datasets could be requested by researchers at commercial organizations. Some of the major datasets held are as follows:

Expenditure and Food Survey

Family Resources Survey

General Household Survey

British Household Panel Survey

Newspapers and Commercial Periodicals

Some of the established newspapers and commercial periodicals, such as the *Financial Times* and the *Economist*, have been introduced earlier in this chapter. As these kinds of publications are circulated regularly and frequently – usually on a daily, weekly or monthly basis – the information provided is very recent. However, the information they contain is usually of a large volume, and researchers need time to search for articles that are suitable for their research projects.

Nowadays, more and more of these newspapers and commercial periodicals have been archived in some manner, allowing the researcher access to historical information. For example, if the researcher is interested in understanding the new product launch trend in the UK food market, they can subscribe to the Grocer Archive. At less than €20 a month, he can conduct search on all national launches of new food products over the past year from the archive.

Syndicated Sources of Secondary Data

An important trend in marketing research is towards a greater dependency on syndicated secondary data sources. There are two main reasons for this. First, companies can obtain substantial information from a variety of industries at a relatively low cost. Second, because most of the data contained in these sources was collected at the point of purchase, the information represents actual purchase behaviour, which is more accurate than the data on purchase intentions usually pursued in a questionnaire survey. The following will first define syndicated data and then discuss the methods usually used by marketing research companies for collecting these data.

Characteristics of Syndicated Data Sources

Syndicated data normally consist of data that have been collected and compiled according to some standardized procedure. In many cases these data are collected for particular companies, with a specific purpose motivating the data collection procedure. This information is then sold to different client companies in the form of tabulated results, or reports prepared specifically for a client's research needs. In the latter case, the reports are personalized and tailored to the client by reporting units. For example, reports can be organized by geographic region, sales territory, market segment, product class, or brand. In order for these data sources to be effective, suppliers of syndicated data must have in-depth knowledge of the industry and generate timely data. Suppliers have traditionally employed one of two methods of data collection: consumer panels and store audits. A third method that is gaining ground – optical scanner technology – will be discussed in a later chapter.

> **Syndicated data** Data that have been collected and compiled according to some standardized procedure; provides customized data for companies, such as sales trend, market share and advertising effectiveness.

Consumer Panels

Consumer panels consist of large samples of households that have agreed to provide specific, detailed data for an extended period of time. Data provided by these panels usually consist of product purchase information or media habits. Information typically is reported on a particular consumer package goods industry.

> **Consumer panels** Large samples of households that provide specific, detailed data for an extended period of time.

Panels typically are designed and developed by marketing research firms. A rigorous data collection approach is adopted. Panel participants are required to record detailed behaviours at the time of occurrence on a highly structured questionnaire. The questionnaire contains a large number of questions related directly to actual product purchase and/or media exposure. This is usually an ongoing procedure whereby respondents report data back to the company on a weekly or monthly basis.

Panel data are then sold to a variety of clients after being personalized and tailored to the client's research needs. A variety of benefits are associated with panel data. These include (1) lower cost than primary data collection methods; (2) rapid availability and timeliness; (3) accurate reporting of socially sensitive expenditures (i.e. products may include beer, liquor and cigarettes); and (4) high level of specificity (i.e. data pertain to actual products purchased or media used, not merely intentions to purchase or use). However they are not without problems. When selecting a consumer panel data source, researchers should consider the following three possible primary weaknesses:

1 **Sampling error.** Most consumer panels underrepresent minorities. In fact, many panels report a sampling distribution that is highly skewed to white, middle-class respondents.

2 **Turnover.** No one panel member is obligated to stay on the panel for the entire duration. Members can decide to quit the panel, have other family members perform the response activities, or simply don't respond at all. This feature seriously jeopardizes the representativeness and internal validity of the data.

3 **Response bias.** Many panel respondents have a tendency to answer questions in a socially desirable manner, knowing their purchases are being scrutinized. They may also be unable to answer ambiguous questions and forget brand names or product characteristics. As a result, they may leave certain questions blank and record wrong answers, leading to high levels of response bias among the panel data.

There are two types of panel-based data sources: those reflecting actual purchases of products and services and those reflecting media habits. The discussion below provides some examples of both types.

Examples of Consumer Panel Data Sources

A variety of companies offer panel-based purchasing data. One such company is National Family Opinion (NFO), which has set up consumer panels across different countries, including the UK, Germany, Portugal, the US, Canada, Australia, and so on. It is also equipped with a number of specialist consumer panels, including the kids and teenagers panel, the IT and technology panel and the entertainment panel. The company maintains these consumer panels to conduct a variety of studies, such as product tests, concept tests, awareness tests, attitude studies and brand-usage studies. In connection with these panels, NFO offers a proprietary software programme called Smart-System. This system enables clients to access and analyse complex information quickly, with easy cross-referencing on major data variables.

Another major company is AC Nielsen, which recruits over 260,000 households as members of its consumer panels in 27 different countries. Data obtained from these panels can offer key consumer insights in the respective countries.

AC Nielsen has recently set up an innovative consumer panel, called MyScan, in the UK market. It aims to tap information from the increasingly important convenience sector. Following a successful pilot panel of 500 individuals in 2004, sponsored by major clients including Unilever Bestfoods, Britvic, Nestlé Rowntree and Kraft Food, the company has subsequently developed a 4,500 strong panel of consumers, aged between 11 and 64 who continuously record their out of home consumption.

The main characteristic of MyScan is the use of miniature portable key fob scanners. They are used to record individuals' purchases for out of home consumption captured at the point of sale, thereby eliminating the need for diaries or recall. MyScan can understand which products were purchased by which consumers through which channels, at what date and time. It can even capture where each product was stocked, where it was consumed and who consumed it.

Examples of Media Panel Data Sources

Media panels and consumer panels are similar in procedure, panel composition and design. They differ only in that media panels primarily measure media consumption habits as opposed to product or brand consumption. As with consumer panels, a multitude of media panels exist. This section provides examples of the more commonly used syndicated media panel data sources.

Arbitron Inc. is primarily an international media research firm that conducts ongoing data collection for a wide variety of clients including mainly radio broadcasters, radio networks, cable companies, advertisers, advertising agencies, out of home advertising companies and the online radio industries. The company's media data collection has been made much more accurate and efficient with the development of the Portable People Meter (PPM) system, which it started to develop as the new multimedia measurement system in 1992. The PPM is a unique, versatile audience measurement system that can track consumer exposure to any broadcast signal. It can determine what consumers listen on the radio, what they watch on broadcast, cable and satellite television, what media they stream on the Internet, as well as what they hear in stores and entertainment venues.

In June 2007, the PPM technology successfully acquired an additional major client – the radio industry in Denmark. The industry has signed a contract to adopt Arbitron PPM system as their electronic audience measurement system. As a result, a national panel of 750 Danish consumers will be equipped with the Arbitron PPM to collect overnight radio listening data. Danish broadcasters will analyse the ratings at one-minute increments and use the data for commercial sales and programme planning. The PPM system will be able to provide the Danish radio industry with more specific information on the types and numbers of people who are listening to the various programmes.

Nielsen Media Research is another company involved in the provision of media panel data. It is mainly based in the US, and its flagship service of Nielsen is the National Television Index (NIT). Based on a 5,000-household sample, the NIT provides an estimation of national television audiences measuring 'ratings' and 'share'. Ratings refer to the percentage of households that have at least one television set tuned to a programme for at least 6 of every 15 minutes a programme is aired. Share constitutes the percentage of households that have a television tuned to one specific programme at one specific time. Data are collected on television, cable and home video viewing habits through an electronic device, called a people meter, connected to a television set. The people meter continuously monitors and records when a television set is turned on, what channels are being viewed, how much time is spent on each channel and who is watching. The data are communicated back to the central computer by telephone.

The primary purpose of the NIT data is to assist media planners in determining audience volume, demographics and viewing habits. This information is then used to calculate media efficiency measured as cost per thousand (CPM); that is, how much it costs to reach 1,000 viewers. CPM measures a programme's ability to deliver the largest target audience at the lowest cost.

While most data are collected by the people meter, Nielsen still maintains diary panels in 211 local markets measuring the same media habits.

Store Audits

Store audits consist of formal examination and verification of how much of a particular product or brand has been sold at the retail level. Based on a collection of participating retailers, audits are performed on product and brand movements in return for detailed activity reports and cash compensation to the retailer. The audits then operate as a secondary data source. Clients can

> **Store audits** Formal examination and verification of how much of a particular product or brand has been sold at the retail level.

acquire the data relative to industry, competition, product, or specific brand. Store audits provide two unique benefits: precision and timeliness. Many of the biases of consumer panels are not found in store audits. By design, store audits measure product and brand movements directly at the point of sale (usually at the retail level). Also, sales and competitive activities are reported when the audit is completed, making the data timely and readily available to potential users.

An inherent problem of the traditional store audit, which uses humans to record the audit information in store, is representativeness. Rarely can this traditional type of audit be performed at all stores in any given area. Therefore, what is reported can be somewhat misleading. Areas in which product sales are extremely high or low may be ignored for the audit process. While this may not affect inferences regarding national sales averages, it can distort sales figures at the regional or local level.

Data Gathering in the Store Audit

Key variables being measured in the store audit typically include beginning and ending inventory levels, sales receipts, price levels, local advertising and point-of-purchase (POP) displays. Collectively, these data allow users of store audit services to generate information on the following factors:

1 Product/brand sales in relation to competition.
2 Inventory levels at retail.
3 Effectiveness of shelf space, shelf location and POP displays.
4 Sales at various price levels.
5 Effectiveness of coupons and in-store promotions.
6 Competitive marketing practices.
7 Sales by store type, location, territory and region.

With the continual development of retail technology and the cooperation of more and more retailers, today's store audit can provide much more accurate and representative information than the traditional store audit. One such major provider of this modern store audit is Nielsen's Scantrack Service, which has been introduced in Chapter 1.

The Internet as a Growing Source of Secondary Data

The Internet has dramatically accelerated the speed at which anyone can obtain useful secondary information. Websites describe products and services and provide information that can be used to evaluate corporate structures and strategies. Finding a company's webpage can be fairly easy when companies use their name as the URL.

In addition to factual information, more subjective information such as consumer opinions about specific companies, products or issues can also be found on the Internet.

One of the popular sources of marketing-related secondary data on the Internet is Marketing UK (Exhibit 4.9). It continuously provides updated news on business and finance, marketing, advertising and the economy. Users can also find the popular Internet links to directories and associations, major market research companies, newspapers, commercial periodicals and CRM-related information.

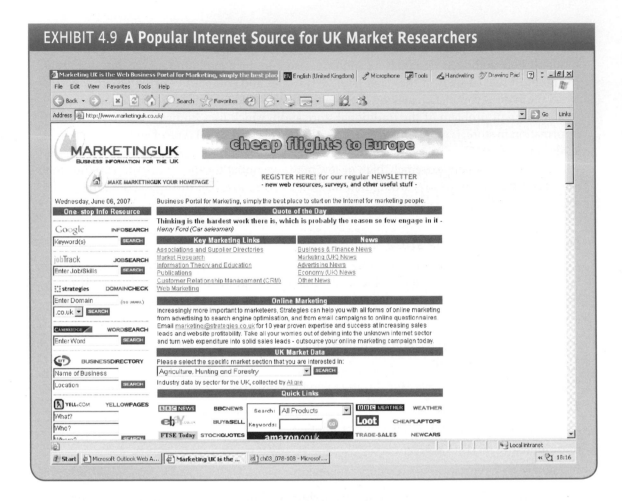

EXHIBIT 4.9 A Popular Internet Source for UK Market Researchers

Another very good website is www.corporateinformation.com (Exhibit 4.10). This provides global corporate information on the leading companies in over 60 countries. Over 32,000 companies are included in its database.

A Closer Look at Research *(In the field)*

Computer Technology and Real-Time Data

As computer technology continues to advance and more people become versed in search strategies for Internet information, the role of secondary research will continue to change. Secondary data researchers will become more involved with a company's internal data technology-related department as they begin to tap into real-time inventory and client or production systems to add more customization of information to the secondary data that they find online. Try it for yourself. Go to www.freeedgar.com. You can find hundreds of documents on companies (mainly US, but including other countries such as UK and Japan) that are not only continuously updated but also highly customized from a secondary data perspective.

Perhaps one of the greatest assets of the Internet is the various search engines. Sites such as AltaVista, Excite, Google and Yahoo! are very popular with researchers looking for secondary data on the Internet. These organizations offer search engines that scan the Internet looking for

EXHIBIT 4.10 A Global Corporation Information Website

information on a designated topic. Each search engine uses its own indexing system to locate relevant information. However, remember that the Internet has no restrictions on what is published there. Search engines yield files with a wide range of quality from a variety of searches. Try multiple sites when researching a particular topic.

There is no question the Internet has become a significant tool and is likely to be the overwhelming source needed to supply information for a business intelligence programme (BIP). Exhibit 4.11 provides additional sources of BIP information on the Internet.

The Future of Secondary Data Sources

As the technology of information and database management is continuously developed and becomes more accessible, more and more secondary data will be available at the push of a computer key. This is already happening, and is more fully described in Chapter 5. Furthermore, as communication technology begins to merge with computer technology (e.g. interactive television and shopping, two-way satellite communication, at-home on-demand shopping), the amount of secondary data is expected to mushroom. Although this increase may not be the main purpose of the technology, it will be the result of the interaction process. More actual purchase information than ever before will become available in a timely and cost-efficient manner.

As more and more organizations begin to realize the full value of information and database management, they will be more able to customize secondary data sources.

EXHIBIT 4.11 Selected Internet Information Sources for Marketing Research

Source	Description of Data	Web Address
European Research Gateway Online	Stores 60,000 records of R&D projects currently in operation in Europe	www.cordis.lu/ergo/home
International Business Resource	Provides human intelligence-based and expert-based categorization of international business resources	www.globaledge.msu.edu
B2B Marketing Online	Supplies information for the business-to-business marketing community worldwide	www.b2bm.biz
Internet Intelligence Index	Over 600 intelligence-related Internet sites from macro economic data to individual patent and stock quote information	www.fuld.com
PR Web Press Release Newswire	Online news and press release distribution to 90,000 customers worldwide	www.prweb.com
Global Market Information Database	Web-based access to Euromonitor's entire reference and source data covering different countries and markets	www.gmid.euromonitor.com
Key Note Market Information Centre	Publishes market research report across 29 market sectors	www.keynote.co.uk
Mad.co.uk	Delivers business insight to professionals in marketing, media, new media, advertising and design	www.mad.co.uk
Altema	Is a very useful resource for anyone researching French markets	www.altema.com/altema/
Communications Market Reports	Cover developments in the electronic communications sector in the UK and beyond	http://www.ofcom.org.uk/research/cm/
Economist Intelligence Unit	Inject a constant flow of analysis and forecasts on more than 200 countries and eight key industries	http://www.eiu.com
Ipsos	Publish market reports and surveys in France	http://www.ipsos.fr/
Grocery Manufacturers/Food Products Association	Supply industry data from the world's preeminent association of the food, beverage, and consumer packaged goods industry	http://www.gmabrands.com/

Case 1: Secondary Research for Spain's Supermarket Chain Sector – the Role of Geodemographic Segmentation in Retail Location Strategy

Geodemographic segmentation refers to the classification of consumers by the type of residential area in which they live. It is therefore based on the differentiation of residential areas according to the demographic, socio-economic or even psychographic characteristics of their residents. The first underlying principle is that similar residential areas have similar shopping needs and habits and, consequently, similar response patterns to marketing stimuli. The second underlying idea is that individuals with similar characteristics tend to reside in the same areas and share the same environments – that is to say, residential areas tend to be internally homogeneous so that their residents do not differ significantly from a mean profile.

The potential utility of geodemographic segmentation has led to the commercialization of several standard geodemographic classifications that embrace almost the entire urban geography of developed countries, which are available for sale as an important source of secondary data for marketing research purposes. Widely known examples are ACORN from CACI and MOSAIC from CCN Systems. In Spain, MOSAIC Iberia S.A. launched the first geodemographic typology of the Spanish urban geography. The last version of this taxonomy is now offered for public sale by EXPERIAN.

One popular application of these geodemographic data is in helping retailers select retail site locations that are the most suitable for them. The utility of geodemographic segmentation as an analytic tool in retail site selection is based on its capacity to differentiate geographic markets in terms of the quality of the consumers. The idea is to select possible locations not only in terms of the quantity of consumers but also the fit between these consumers and the retailer in question. The market area should include those consumers whose shopping needs and habits match the assortment and services provided by the retailer. This European case, which is based on the work published by Gonzalez-Benito and Gonzalez-Benito (2005) is about a study looking into the use of the readily available secondary data to perform geodemographic segmentation analysis for cross-checking with the retail location strategy of the top ten supermarket chains in Spain (see Exhibit 4.12). Specifically, the relationship between supermarket chains and the geodemographic profile of their market areas is analysed. Confirmation of this probable relationship would imply the effectiveness of the use of readily available secondary geodemographic data in helping Spanish supermarket chains to identify their respective spatial markets.

To conduct this study, data about each supermarket chain, which are available from the Censo de Supermercados (Supermarket Census) of Publicaciones Alimarket in November 2001, were required. The data include chain, group, address, size of sales area and retail format. Besides, the geodemographic classification MOSAIC was used to characterize each of the supermarket chains being studied. MOSAIC divides the Spanish urban geography into 506,329 areas classified into 14 groups and 48 typologies. Technical data analysis details behind these MOSAIC classifications will be illustrated in Chapter 19.

Chi-square test results indicate the presence of a significant relationship between the top ten supermarket chains and MOSAIC geodemographic groups. This means their retail location strategies reflect the selection of spatial markets with specific geodemographic profiles. Further chi-square test results prove that, in most of the cases, these chains differ from each other in terms of the type of spatial markets selected to locate their store networks. The following summarizes the typical and atypical geodemographic groups for each chain.

EXHIBIT 4.12 The Top Ten Supermarket Chains in Spain

Supermarket Chain	Number of Stores	Mean Size	Standard Deviation Size
Caprabo	350	889.29	776.55
Champion	153	1696.60	714.36
Charter	171	286.15	137.36
Consum	715	715.50	342.39
Dia	2316	258.29	169.88
El Arbol	618	531.73	257.40
Lidl	323	784.37	129.99
Mercadona	558	1058.58	380.56
Plus Superdescuento	172	720.03	80.01
Supersol	467	740.00	499.98
Total	5843	577.03	478.24

Caprabo. Typical groups: elite, urban well-off, qualified professionals and tourist. Atypical groups: mid-level professionals, non-qualified, diversified rural and agricultural.

Champion. Typical groups: elite and tourist. Atypical groups: consolidated and agricultural.

Charter. Typical groups: qualified professionals, mid-level professionals, industrial and sectorial mix. Atypical groups: provincial well-off, consolidated, non-qualified, security and defence, non-residential areas.

Consum. Typical groups: provincial well-off and tourist.

Dia. Typical groups: passive areas. Atypical groups: tourist.

El Arbol. Typical groups: provincial well-off, sectorial mix, agricultural. Atypical groups: tourist, industrial.

Lidl. Typical groups: non-residential areas. Atypical groups: qualified professionals.

Mercadona. Typical groups: qualified professionals.

Plus superdescuento. Typical groups: diversified rural and non-residential areas. Atypical groups: urban well-off, sectorial mix.

Supersol. Typical groups: consolidated, non-qualified, security and defence. Atypical groups: industrial.

Source: Based on an adaptation of a study by Oscar Gonzalez-Benito and Javier Gonzalez-Benito (2005).

Questions

1 The above European case shows how a marketing research study can be conducted by relying solely on the use of secondary data. What are the conditions under which purely secondary data research can be used for a marketing research project?

2 What are the drawbacks of the approach used to conduct this European case study illustrated above?

Case 2: Jimmy Spice's Restaurant Anticipating Expansion

As you recall from Chapter 1, Jimmy Spice's restaurant has been operating in Birmingham, UK since 2004. The owners of the restaurant, when developing their five-year plan, anticipated the opening of two additional locations in the country after five years of successful operation at the Birmingham location. The owners were planning to expand to Manchester and Edinburgh.

After revisiting the five-year plan, the owners have realized they lack data and information relevant to these two cities. In fact, the only information they have are the population size and growth of these two cities. Realizing this, they have decided to develop an area profile of Manchester and Edinburgh relative to the restaurant market.

Key secondary data must be collected. Population characteristics, economic conditions, competitive trends in the restaurant industry and market factors appear to be the starting point of the secondary data search. The owners, realizing these factors may be too broad for facilitating an expansion decision, have requested the help of a local university marketing research class to conduct a secondary data search for specific information on Manchester and Edinburgh. At this point, the owners need your help in the secondary data search – designing the approach, deciding on the types of data needed, collecting the data and presenting conclusive evidence.

Questions

1 Develop a list of the specific variables that need to be examined regarding demographic characteristics, economic characteristics, competitive dimensions of the restaurant market and other relevant customer data pertaining to Manchester and Edinburgh.

2 Based on the information and what you've learned in the chapter, perform a secondary data search on all key variables you identified in your answer to question 1.

3 Develop a comparative profile of the two cities (Manchester, Edinburgh) based on your secondary data and provide the owners with a report showing evidence that one, both, or neither of the cities would be desirable for possible restaurant expansion.

Summary of Learning Objectives

■ **Illustrate and define consumer-generated media.**
Given new information technology available, many companies are now using a variety of techniques to collect, store and categorize customer data for future marketing decisions. Information gathered from blogs, podcasts, Internet forums, online communities and online social networks – collectively called consumer-generated media – is increasingly used to exploit a data-rich environment based on customer interaction. Data of this nature are unique in that they are unprompted and extremely raw.

■ **Understand how secondary data fit into the marketing research process.**
The task of a marketing researcher is to solve the problem in the shortest time, at the least cost, with the highest level of accuracy. Therefore, before any marketing research project is conducted, the researcher must seek out existing information that may facilitate a decision or outcome for a company. Existing data are commonly called secondary data.

■ **Demonstrate how secondary data can be used in problem solving.**
If secondary data are to be used to assist the decision-making process or problem-solving ability of the manager, they need to be evaluated on six fundamental principles: (1) purpose (how relevant are the data to achieving the specific research objectives at hand?); (2) accuracy (are the data collected, measured, and reported in a manner consistent with quality research practices?); (3) consistency (do multiple sources of the data exist?); (4) credibility (how were the data obtained? what is the source of the data?); (5) methodology (will the methods used to collect the data produce high-quality data?); and (6) bias (was the data-reporting procedure tainted by some hidden agenda or underlying motivation to advance some public or private concern?).

■ **List sources of traditional internal secondary data.**
Internal secondary data are usually sorted into four major categories, including sales invoices, accounts receivable reports, quarterly sales reports and sales activity reports. Other forms of internal data include customer letters, customer comment cards, mail-order forms, etc.

■ **Know how to use and extract external secondary data.**
Because of the volume of external data available, researchers need to ensure that the right data are located and extracted. A simple guideline to follow is called the GO-CART approach: define *goals* the secondary data need to achieve; specify *objectives* behind the secondary research process; define specific *characteristics* of data that are to be extracted; document all *activities* necessary to find, locate and extract the data sources; focus on *reliable* sources of data; and *tabulate* all the data extracted.

■ **Identify sources of external secondary data.**
External secondary data can be obtained from a wide variety of sources. The most common forms of external data are International Standard Industrial Classification of All Economic Activities (ISIC) codes, government documents (which include census reports), business directories, professional associations, business databases, statistical sources, newspapers, commercial periodicals and other commercial publications.

■ **Understand the availability and use of syndicated sources of secondary data.**
Syndicated (or commercial) data sources consist of data that have been systematically collected and compiled according to some standardized procedure. Suppliers of syndicated data have traditionally used one of two approaches in collecting data: consumer panels and store audits. There is indeed a third approach, which relies on the use of optical-scanner technology, and which has been discussed in the preceding chapter. With most syndicated data sources, the objective is quite clear: to measure point-of-sale purchase behaviours or to measure media habits.

■ **Understand the impacts of computerization of secondary data.**
The computerization of secondary data is revolutionizing the marketing research industry. Online services are making more data available that are more applicable to business needs than ever before. In addition, databases and information systems are bringing the use of secondary data to monumental proportions. Technology will make secondary data more customized and applicable for many businesses.

Key Terms and Concepts

Consumer-generated media
  (CGM)   138
Consumer panels   156
Customer knowledge information   140
External secondary data   140
Internal secondary data   140

International Standard Industrial
Classification of All Economic
  Activities (ISIC) codes   148
Secondary data   148
Store audits   158
Syndicated (or commercial) data   156

Review Questions

1 What characteristic separates secondary data from primary data? What are three sources of secondary data?
2 Explain why a company should use all potential sources of secondary data before initiating primary data collection procedures.
3 List the six fundamental principles used to assess the validity of secondary data.
4 List the three methods of data collection typically used by the suppliers of commercial data sources, and discuss the advantages and disadvantages associated with each.
5 How can information from a sales activity report be used to improve a company's marketing research efforts?
6 Briefly discuss the GO-CART approach of secondary data search management.
7 How is the Internet changing the nature and use of secondary data?

Discussion Questions

1 **Experience the Internet.** Go online to your favourite browser and find the County or City Council home page for your particular region of residence. For example, www.sheffield.gov.uk would get you to the home page for Sheffield City Council. Once there, seek out the demographic and socioeconomic data available that can be useful for marketing research purpose. Provide a demographic profile of the residents in your region of residence.
2 **Experience the Internet.** Go to the home page of the UK census, www.statistics. gov.uk/census2001. Select the category Economy and browse the data provided. How useful these data are in helping you to understand the general economic environment?
3 Aldi, a discount supermarket chain based in Germany, is planning to explore the Asian market where it has not yet established any store. What specific country information are needed to assist the management team of Aldi in deciding on which Asian country should be selected for its international expansion?
4 You are planning to open a coffee shop in one of two areas in your local community. Conduct a secondary data search on key variables that would allow you to make a logical decision on which area is best suited for your proposed coffee shop.
5 Using the data you collected in the MRIA exercise in this chapter, should Jimmy Spice's open restaurants in other markets?
6 What is the value of panel data in making marketing research decisions?

Chapter 5

Qualitative Research Methods: An Overview and Focus Group

LEARNING OBJECTIVES

After reading this chapter, you will be able to

- ☑ Identify the fundamental differences between qualitative and quantitative research methods and explain their appropriateness in collecting useful data.

- ☑ Explain the advantages and disadvantages of qualitative research methods for data collection purposes.

- ☑ Describe and explain the focus group method used in gathering primary data.

- ☑ Explain the phases that should be followed in order to conduct a focus group properly.

- ☑ Understand online focus groups and how they compare to traditional offline focus groups.

> " We couldn't afford to sit back and rely on gut instinct. In an ever-changing media environment, it is important for us as a company to know our customers and what value they are to us and our advertisers.
>
> —*Scott Longstaff*
> *Head of Sales at Future Publishing, Bath, England*

Using Focus Groups and In-Depth Interviews to Understand Computer Gamers

Future Publishing, one of the UK's leading computer games magazine publishers, wanted to identify the role that specialist games magazines play within the gaming community. It was particularly interested in the extent to which games magazines can influence the decision-making process for games purchases, as well as how influential are these magazines in generate positive word-of-mouth recommendations.

The intuitive feeling was that specialist games magazines could be very influential. However, the dynamics of the gaming community and the way in which information is shared and exchanged among the community participants were not fully understood. By exploring this area further, Future Publishing hoped to be able to advise advertisers on how to use their media-spend for exerting the greatest impact on the gaming community at large. Should the advertisers target specific groups directly, or should they focus on other gamers by leveraging on the word-of-mouth power?

Future Publishing commissioned Continental Research, based in London, to conduct this research. Qualitative research, including both focus groups and triad in-depth interviews, was conducted with active gamers. Continental conducted triads among teenagers because they are typically less comfortable and forthcoming in a large group. Using the triads approach was deemed appropriate in trying to understand the dynamics and lines of communication among a close-knit group of friends.

Gamers had no trouble in warming to the topic of conversation. However, it quickly became clear that gaming is a very competitive activity for some, which can be examined further through focus groups and triad in-depth interviews.

For example, there was talk of dusk-till-dawn gaming sessions; of the 'friend' who could complete four games within one day; and of the teenager whose mum had to write him a sick note because his thumbs ached and his vision went blurry after a heavy gaming session! Such stories gave an indication of the obsession with gaming, particularly among teenagers.

It was also interesting to realize that, despite some posturing, all gamers admitted to knowing somebody who was a games guru while none admitted to being at that level themselves.

The key role of this qualitative research was to identify different gaming typologies in terms of not only their gaming activity, but also – more importantly – their communication role in the gaming world. Once different typologies had been identified, Continental was able to hypothesize about the likelihood of communication between different types of gamers, which would be tested through the next phase of quantitative research.

Source: Research Magazine, News Archive, www.research-live.com

The Value of Qualitative Research

The computer gamers opening example illustrates several important issues business decision makers must be aware of to resolve marketing problems and questions. First, management quite often is faced with problem situations where important questions cannot be adequately addressed or resolved merely with secondary information. Meaningful insights can be gained only through the collection of primary data. Recall that primary data typically are collected using a set of formal procedures in which researchers question or observe individuals and record their findings. Second, quite often collecting only qualitative data does not ensure management will fully understand the problem. Collecting quantitative data might be necessary as well.

As we continue our examination of the research process, attention turns away from research activities that emphasize secondary data. This chapter begins a series of three that discuss the three basic types of research design (exploratory, descriptive and causal) used to collect primary data. As discussed in earlier chapters, the research objectives and information requirements are the keys to determining the type of research design that is most appropriate in collecting data. For example, exploratory research is used when the research objectives focus on clarifying the research problems, creating hypotheses and establishing research priorities. Descriptive designs are used when the research objectives emphasize describing and measuring marketing issues at a particular point in time. Data from a descriptive design provide answers to research questions framed in who, what, where, when, how many, how much and how often formats as they relate to management's initial decision problem situation. But descriptive designs often are not as useful in collecting primary data to explain why the marketing phenomena are happening. As discussed in Chapter 2, information for addressing many 'why' questions is obtained with causal research designs. Causal research designs are used to determine causality in relationships between marketing factors and research problems as well as testing 'if-then' statements about the various issues being investigated.

At this stage, recall two important points. First, although exploratory, descriptive and causal research designs might appear to be mutually exclusive, in many cases it is the complete set of research questions that will determine whether one particular research design or a combination of designs will be used to collect the appropriate data. A second point to remember is that although the research process may implicitly suggest that exploratory research should always be undertaken before descriptive or causal research, there are cases in which exploratory research is used after some other design. For example, Shiu (2003) found that, from questionnaire survey data, in terms of proportion of population segment, traditional markets in Britain were visited most often by older males aged 60 or above. This is an unexpected finding. Explorative research using focus groups and in-depth interviews would be an appropriate follow-up procedure to identify what motivates this particular group to patronise traditional markets more often than others.

At the heart of any research design are the methods actually used to collect the required data. Methods for collecting data have typically been classified into two very broad categories: qualitative and quantitative. This chapter and Chapter 6 will introduce several qualitative research methods used to collect qualitative, or 'soft', data structures. In contrast, Chapters 7 and 8 will focus on the different quantitative methods (e.g. surveys) used by researchers in collecting data which are mostly about figures. Finally, in Chapter 9, we will specifically illustrate the observation method, which cannot be categorized into qualitative or quantitative because it can be either depending on the objectives of the research project being undertaken. However, readers should keep in mind that in order to achieve the totality of objectives set up by a particular research project, it is never unusual for the researcher to use a multiple-methods approach, where data are collected using both qualitative and quantitative research methods.

An Overview of Qualitative and Quantitative Research Methods

Prior to discussing the qualitative techniques normally used in exploratory research designs, we will identify some of the fundamental differences between qualitative and quantitative research

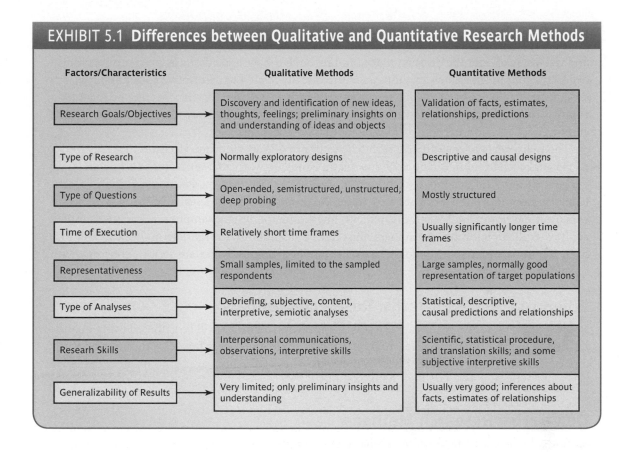

EXHIBIT 5.1 **Differences between Qualitative and Quantitative Research Methods**

Factors/Characteristics	Qualitative Methods	Quantitative Methods
Research Goals/Objectives	Discovery and identification of new ideas, thoughts, feelings; preliminary insights on and understanding of ideas and objects	Validation of facts, estimates, relationships, predictions
Type of Research	Normally exploratory designs	Descriptive and causal designs
Type of Questions	Open-ended, semistructured, unstructured, deep probing	Mostly structured
Time of Execution	Relatively short time frames	Usually significantly longer time frames
Representativeness	Small samples, limited to the sampled respondents	Large samples, normally good representation of target populations
Type of Analyses	Debriefing, subjective, content, interpretive, semiotic analyses	Statistical, descriptive, causal predictions and relationships
Research Skills	Interpersonal communications, observations, interpretive skills	Scientific, statistical procedure, and translation skills; and some subjective interpretive skills
Generalizability of Results	Very limited; only preliminary insights and understanding	Usually very good; inferences about facts, estimates of relationships

methods. Although there are vast differences between the two approaches, there is no single agreed-on set of factors that distinguishes them as being mutually exclusive. The factors listed in Exhibit 5.1 offer some insights on the general differences.

Quantitative Research Methods

Quantitative research is commonly associated with surveys or experiments and is considered the mainstay of the research industry for collecting marketing data. **Quantitative research** places heavy emphasis on using formalized questions and predetermined response options in questionnaires administered to large numbers of respondents. For example, when you consider quantitative research, think of Renault conducting a nationwide mail survey in France on customer satisfaction among new car purchasers or Trailfinders Express doing a nationwide survey on travel behaviours with telephone interviews. In certain situations, however, observation

> **Quantitative research** Research that places heavy emphasis on using formalized standard questions and predetermined response options in questionnaires or surveys administered to large numbers of respondents.

techniques are also used to collect nonverbal and/or behavioural data from respondents during the questioning process. With quantitative research, the research problems typically are specific and well defined, and the decision maker and researcher have agreed on the precise information needs. Quantitative research methods are more directly related to descriptive and causal research designs but can be associated with exploratory designs as well. Success in collecting primary data is more a function of correctly designing and administering the survey instrument than of the communication and interpretive skills of an interviewer or observer.

The main goals of quantitative research are to provide specific facts decision makers can use to (1) make accurate predictions about relationships between market factors and behaviours, (2) gain meaningful insights into those relationships, (3) validate the existing relationships and (4) test various types of hypotheses. In quantitative research practices, researchers are well trained in construct development, scale measurement, questionnaire design, sampling and statistical data analysis skills. In addition, researchers must have a solid ability to translate numerical data into meaningful narrative information. Data reliability and validity issues are serious concerns with quantitative research.

When to Use Quantitative Research Methods

In most descriptive and many causal research endeavours, the data will be gathered using quantitative data collection approaches. Exhibit 5.2 lists some guidelines for determining when it is appropriate to use quantitative research methods. These guidelines are by no means exhaustive and will be discussed in detail in Chapters 7 and 8.

Qualitative Research Methods

As noted before, **qualitative research** has come to refer to selected research methods normally used in exploratory research designs. One of the main objectives of qualitative research is to gain *preliminary insights* into research problems. On the surface, qualitative research methods incorporate some scientific elements but normally lack the critical elements of true reliability.

EXHIBIT 5.2 **Guidelines for Using Quantitative Research Methods**

Quantitative research methods are appropriate when decision makers or researchers are:

- Validating or answering a business problem or opportunity situation or information requirements.
- Obtaining detailed descriptions or conclusive insights into the personality, attitudinal, emotional and motivational factors that influence marketplace behaviours.
- Testing theories and models to explain marketplace behaviours or relationships between two or more marketing constructs.
- Testing and assessing the reliability and validity of scale measurements for investigating specific market factors, consumer qualities (e.g. perceptions, attitudes, emotional feelings, preferences, beliefs) and behavioural outcomes.
- Assessing the effectiveness of their marketing strategies on actual marketplace behaviours.
- Gaining conclusive insights into new product or service development.
- Determine repositioning strategies of current products or service images.
- Segmenting the market.

Qualitative research tends to focus on the collection of detailed amounts of primary data from relatively small samples of subjects by asking questions or observing behaviour. Researchers well trained in interpersonal communication and interpretive skills use either open-ended questions that allow for in-depth probing of the subjects' initial responses or specific observational techniques that allow for analysis of behaviours. In some cases, qualitative data can be collected within relatively short periods of time, but it is difficult to summarize the data into meaningful findings quickly. Qualitative data analysis may involve subjective content, interpretation or semiotic analysis procedures that the researcher should be alert to.

> **Qualitative research** Research used in exploratory designs to gain preliminary insights into decision problems and opportunities.

The nonstructured format of the questions and the small sample size tend to limit the researcher's ability to generalize (or infer) qualitative data to the population. Nevertheless, qualitative data have important uses in understanding and resolving business problems, especially in the areas of initial discovery and preliminary explanation of marketplace or customer behaviour and decision processes. For example, qualitative data can be invaluable in providing researchers with initial ideas about specific problems or opportunities; theories, models, or constructs; or the designing of new, specific scale measurements. Yet qualitative data generally is not solely relied on in recommending a final course of action.

When to Use Qualitative Research Methods

In most exploratory research projects, the raw data is gathered through qualitative data collection practices. Exhibit 5.3 lists some guidelines for determining when it is appropriate to use qualitative research methods for collecting information with exploratory designs.

EXHIBIT 5.3 Guidelines for Using Qualitative Research Methods

Qualitative research methods are appropriate when decision makers or researchers are:

- Identifying a business problem, opportunity situation, or establishing information requirements.
- Obtaining preliminary insights into the personality, attitudinal, emotional and motivational factors that influence marketplace behaviours.
- Building theories and models to explain marketplace behaviours or relationships between two or more marketing constructs.
- Developing reliable and valid scale measurements for investigating specific market factors, consumer qualities (e.g. perceptions, attitudes, emotional feelings, preferences, beliefs) and behavioural outcomes.
- Trying to determine the preliminary effectiveness of their marketing strategies on actual marketplace behaviours.
- Gaining preliminary or conclusive insights into new product or service development.
- Developing a preliminary idea for the repositioning strategies of current products or service images.

EXHIBIT 5.4 **Advantages and Disadvantages of Using Qualitative Research Methods**

Advantages of Qualitative Methods	Disadvantages of Qualitative Methods
Economical and timely data collection	Lack of generalizability
Richness of the data	Inability to distinguish small differences
Accuracy of recording marketplace behaviours	Difficulty in establishing reliability and validity
Preliminary insights into building models and scale measurements	Difficulty in finding well-trained interviewers and observers

Advantages and Disadvantages of Qualitative Research Methods

Like other primary data collection techniques, qualitative research methods offer several advantages to today's researchers. Exhibit 5.4 summarizes the main advantages and disadvantages.

Major Advantages

One general advantage of qualitative research methods is that they are both *economical and timely* compared to most quantitative methods. Due in part to the use of small samples, researchers can complete their investigations quicker and at a significantly lower cost. Another advantage is the *richness of the data.* The unstructured nature of qualitative techniques enables the researcher to collect in-depth data about the subjects' perceptions, attitudes, emotions and beliefs, all of which may strongly influence their observable market behaviours. Such in-depth data can be invaluable in gaining a preliminary understanding of those behaviours. Some qualitative techniques allow decision makers to gain first hand *experiences* with customers and can provide very revealing information about their thinking patterns. The richness of the qualitative data can often supplement the facts gathered through other primary data collection techniques. Some qualitative methods enable the investigator to accurately record *actual behaviours,* not just reported behaviours.

Some qualitative research methods provide researchers with excellent preliminary insights into building marketing models and scale measurements. In addition, qualitative data play a critical role in *identifying marketing problems.* The in-depth information enhances the researcher's ability to predict consumer behaviour in the marketplace, as well as to develop better marketing constructs and more reliable and valid scale measurements of those constructs.

Major Disadvantages

Although qualitative research produces useful information, it has a number of disadvantages. First, qualitative data normally *lack generalizability* (or representativeness). That is to say, due to the use of small, nonrandom samples, the information generated by qualitative research techniques cannot be generalized to larger groups of individuals. This *lack of representativeness* of the defined target population severely limits the use of qualitative information in helping decision makers select and implement final action strategies. For example, the attitudes and behaviours of a group of 8 to 12 university students specializing in the study of marketing are unlikely to be representative of all university students in the UK, of students at a particular university, of students pursuing a business degree or business discipline (including marketing) at that university, or even of their classmates (i.e. students also specializing in the study of marketing). Small sample sizes make it virtually impossible for researchers to extend findings beyond the group used to collect the data.

Another disadvantage is the raw data generated through qualitative methods are limited by their *inability to distinguish small differences.* Many times marketing successes and failures are based on small differences in marketing mix strategies. Using small samples of subjects to provide critical information does not allow researchers to evaluate the impact of small differences. Moreover, researchers are often forced to analyse qualitative data at aggregate, not disaggregate, levels. Aggregation of the findings eliminates the opportunity to study individual differences. In most cases, the reliability of data collected using qualitative research methods cannot be assessed. Decision makers often are reluctant to use information that cannot be assessed for reliability.

Compared to studies that use quantitative research, there is much more *difficulty in establishing reliability and validity* in qualitative research. There is a set of well-developed procedures that researchers can choose from for examining the reliability and validity of the quantitative studies they are conducting. It is not entirely impossible to determine the reliability and validity in qualitative research. Indeed these issues have been increasingly dealt with in recent years and a number of concepts have been developed, but it is still fair to say that qualitative researchers always face an uphill task to prove the reliability and validity of their studies.

Finally, the *difficulty in finding well-trained interviewers and observers* to conduct qualitative research can be a potential disadvantage. With the informal, unstructured nature of obtaining qualitative data, few researchers have the extensive formal training needed to be an expert in the qualitative field. Moreover, it is difficult for the unsuspecting practitioner to discern the researcher's qualifications or the quality of the research.

Focus Group Method

Nature of Focus Group Method

As the most popular qualitative research method, the focus group method will be covered in this chapter. Other popular qualitative research methods will be dealt with in Chapter 6.

Focus group research involves bringing a small group of people together for an interactive and spontaneous discussion of a particular topic or concept. Focus groups normally consist of 8 to 12 participants who are guided by a professional moderator through a detailed discussion that typically lasts about one and a half hours. By getting the group members to talk in detail about a topic, the moderator draws out as many ideas, attitudes and experiences as possible about the specified issue.

> **Focus group research** A formalized process of bringing a small group of people together for an interactive, spontaneous discussion on one particular topic or concept.

The overall goal of focus group research is to give researchers, and ultimately decision makers, as much information as possible about how people regard the topic of interest. That topic is typically a product, service, concept, or organization. Unlike many other types of questioning techniques, focus group research is not restricted to just asking and answering questions posed by an interviewer. Its success relies heavily on the group dynamics, the willingness of members to engage in an interactive dialogue, and the professional moderator's ability to keep the discussion on track. The fundamental idea behind the focus group approach is that one person's response will spark comments from other members, thus generating a spontaneous interplay among all of the participants.

EXHIBIT 5.5 Some Pertinent Uses of Focus Group Research

1 To provide data for defining and redefining marketing problems.

2 To identify specific hidden information requirements.

3 To provide data for better understanding results from other quantitative studies.

4 To reveal consumers' perceptions, attitudes, feelings, motives, hidden needs and behaviours regarding products, services, or practices.

5 To generate new ideas about products, services, or practices such as delivery methods.

6 To discover new constructs and measurement methods.

7 To help explain changing consumer preferences.

8 To generate or assess new product or service ideas.

Uses of Focus Group Research

There are many reasons focus group research is the most popular qualitative research method. As noted earlier, data collected in focus groups can offer preliminary insights into hidden marketing phenomena. Exhibit 5.5 lists some other pertinent uses of focus group research. Each of these is described in more detail below.

To Provide Data for Defining and Redefining Marketing Problems

In those situations where managers or researchers experience difficulties in identifying and understanding a specific marketing problem, focus groups can help distinguish the differences between symptoms and problems. For example, the chairperson of a business management faculty at a major English university was not sure why undergraduate enrolment levels were continually declining. The chairperson called for a faculty meeting using a focus group format. The discussion revealed several unexpected factors that provided preliminary insights into why enrolment levels were declining. One of these had to do with whether the current curriculum was offering students the kinds of skills currently demanded by businesses. The faculty investigated this issue and found significant gaps between the faculty's perspective and the business world's as to which skills the students needed. The faculty began a reassessment of its curriculum in an attempt to realign the skills being taught to those being mandated by the business world.

To Identify Specific Hidden Information Requirements

In some situations decision makers and researchers are not totally sure what specific types of data should be investigated. In these situations, focus groups can reveal unexpected aspects of the problem and thus can directly help researchers determine what specific data should be collected. For example, Leicester's New Performing Arts Centre might be faced with the difficulty of deciding what design features should be included in the construction of the new centre. Their research team could conduct several focus groups consisting of local residents and seasonal visitors. From the groups' spontaneous, unstructured discussions, specific features and concerns such as different types of indoor and outdoor events, parking requirements, availability of refreshments, seating design and capacity, pricing of tickets and protection from bad weather might be revealed as being important factors that need further understanding.

To Provide Data for Better Understanding Results from Other Quantitative Studies

There are situations where quantitative research investigations leave the decision maker or researcher asking why the results came out the way they did. Focus groups can be conducted to help explain the findings of other surveys. For example, corporate management of JP Hotels, Inc. conducted a survey among business guests at its hotels concerning free in-room entertainment services. The results indicated that 85 per cent of the business guests were aware of the availability of the entertainment services but only 15 per cent actually used them. Not understanding what caused this gap between awareness and actual use, JP Hotels conducted several focus groups among its business guests regarding these services. The focus group discussions revealed that business travellers were either too busy or too exhausted to watch any type of TV at night. They preferred to read or listen to music as a means of relaxing after a long workday.

To Reveal Consumers' Perceptions, Attitudes, Feelings, Motives, Hidden Needs and Behaviours Regarding Products, Services or Practices

Focus groups provide researchers with excellent opportunities to gain preliminary insights into what consumers think or feel about a wide array of products, services or practices. For example, a manufacturer like Procter & Gamble uses focus groups to obtain data that reveal consumers' attitudes for and against using Crest toothpaste. These data help the company understand how consumer brand loyalty is developed and what marketing factors are necessary to reinforce it.

A Closer Look at Research *(In the field)*
Using Focus Groups to Identify Potential Critical Success Factors of Re-innovation

Re-innovation, as opposed to radical innovation and incremental innovation, has received scant attention in the academic world. Studies on its definition, construct measurement, antecedents and critical success factors are far few and between. Yet re-innovation is an important phenomenon in the business world. Examples include the launch of Apple iPod and Honda CRV.

To redress this imbalance in innovation research, Dr Colin Cheng and Dr Eric Shiu at the University of Birmingham in England used the focus group method to attempt to identify potential critical success factors of re-innovation.

Four high-tech industries – namely software, information technology, telecommunications and consumer electronics – were selected from which potential focus group participants were recruited. These industries were chosen because evidence shows that they launch new products more often than many other industries.

Possible participants were first contacted by phone in order to gauge their willingness to participate as well as to ascertain whether they were suitable participants. The three criteria for assessing their suitability were (1) they must have been involved in new product development in any of the four industries for at least five years; (2) they must now be in a management position responsible for new product development; and (3) they must have the experience in developing and launching re-innovative products during the past five years. Subsequently, 71 people who had met all these three criteria were recruited.

The 71 participants were assigned into eight different focus groups whose sizes ranged from eight to ten. In order to reduce dominance by a few participants in focus group discussions, participants from the same company were allocated to different groups.

Prior to the convening of the focus groups, an interview guide was developed by the researchers. Detailed instructions about the topic to be discussed and the planned procedures during focus group sessions were sent to the participants. All focus group discussions were carried out during weekends because participants said that this was the most convenient timing for them. Each focus group session was held in a dedicated conference room with a one-way mirror. All participants were informed that the one-way mirror would be used for observation and the observation was for this research only. Nametags were provided, and drinks and light snacks were served in order to make participants feel comfortable.

On average, each focus group lasted 92 minutes, with a minimum of 81 minutes and a maximum of 104 minutes. After finishing all the focus group sessions, a number of follow-up telephone interviews were held in order to clarify some issues or explore them in greater detail. The focus group transcripts were vigorously checked to ensure their validity and reliability. They were then ready to be analysed.

Results have led to the development of a conceptual framework of critical success factors of re-innovation. The framework comprises five sets of main factors: (1) development process, (2) manufacturing process, (3) product features, (4) organizational integration and (5) launch timing, which is moderated by the moderating factor of competitive response. Some of these factors consist of multiple items. For example, 'customization', 'relative advantage', and 'added value' are classed under the factor of 'product features'. With this conceptual framework, a series of propositions were established, which were later tested by using a large-scale questionnaire survey.

To Generate New Ideas about Products or Services

This particular objective of focus groups has long been a mainstay among decision makers and researchers. Here, focus groups generate interactive discussions about new or existing products and services. Data collected through these discussions provides valuable preliminary insights into ideas for radically innovated or really new products, new usages of existing products and services, possible changes for improving products or services, or identifying better delivery systems. A classic example is how Arm & Hammer, a US-based multinational enterprise, discovered new in-home uses for baking soda. Periodically, the company conducts focus groups among known users of Arm & Hammer baking soda. Data generated from these discussions has revealed that baking soda is used for such things as cleaning kitchens and bathrooms, cleaning around babies, deodorizing everything from carpets to cat litter boxes, freshening laundry, soothing and conditioning skin and cleaning teeth. Today, Arm & Hammer baking soda is marketed as a natural product with 'a houseful of uses'.

To Discover New Constructs and Measurement Methods

For academicians and practitioners alike, focus groups play a critical role in the process of developing new marketing constructs and creating reliable and valid construct measurement scales. In the exploratory stage of construct development, researchers may conduct focus groups concerning a particular marketing idea to reveal additional insights into the underlying dimensions that may make up the construct. These insights can help researchers develop scales that can be tested and refined through larger survey research designs. Take the important construct of service quality, for example. Researchers have been trying to refine the measurement of this construct since the mid-1980s. They continue to ask such questions as 'What does service quality mean to consumers, practitioners, and academicians?' 'What is the underlying dimensionality of the construct – is it unidimensional or multidimensional?' and 'What is the most appropriate way of measuring service quality?'

To Help Explain Changing Consumer Preferences

This objective refers to the use of focus groups to collect data that can be useful in understanding how customers describe their experiences with different products and services. This type of qualitative data can be valuable in improving marketing communications as well as in creating more effective marketing segmentation strategies. For example, a manufacturer of a brand-name line of lawn care products may be interested in such questions as 'What do consumers like about lawn care and gardening?' 'What words or terms do they use in describing lawn care/gardening products and their use?' 'Why do they do their own lawn work?' and 'How do they take care of their lawns and gardens?'

Conducting Focus Groups

While there is no one particular way of conducting focus groups that is acceptable to all researchers, focus groups can be viewed as a process divided into three logical phases: planning the study, conducting the focus group discussion, and analysing and reporting the results (see Exhibit 5.6).

Phase 1: Planning the Focus Group Study

As with most other types of marketing research, the planning phase is most critical for successful focus groups. In this phase, researchers and decision makers must have a clear understanding of the purpose of the study, a precise definition of the problem and specific data requirements. There must be agreement to such questions as: 'Why should such a study be conducted?' 'What

---

EXHIBIT 5.6 The Three-Phase Process for Conducting a Focus Group

Phase 1: Planning the Focus Group Study
- This is the most critical phase.
- Researchers must have an understanding of the purpose of the study, a precise definition of the problem and specific data requirements.
- Key decisions focus on who the appropriate participants would be; how to recruit and select participants; what size the focus group should be; and where to have the session.

Phase 2: Conducting the Focus Group Discussion
- One of the key players in this phase is the focus group moderator.
- To ensure a successful interactive session, the moderator's role and pertinent characteristics must be clearly understood by everyone involved.
- A necessary activity in this phase is the development of a moderator's guide that outlines the topics, questions and sub-questions that will be used in the session.
- The actual focus group session should be structured with beginning, main and closing sections.

Phase 3: Analysing and Reporting the Results
- After the actual session is completed, the researcher should conduct a debriefing analysis with all the key players involved to compare notes.
- The researcher should conduct a content analysis on the raw data obtained from the participants during the session and write a formal report that communicates the findings.
- Key to the researcher here is to remember who will be the reading audience, the purpose of the report and an appropriate report style format.

kinds of information will be produced?' 'What types of information are of particular importance?' 'How will the information be used?' and 'Who wants the information?' Answers to these types of questions can help eliminate the obstacles (organizational politics, incomplete disclosure and hidden personal agendas) that can delay agreement and create problems between decision makers and researchers. Other important decisions in the planning phase relate to who the participants should be, how to select and recruit respondents, size of the group and where to have the focus group sessions.

Focus Group Participants

In deciding who should be included as participants in a focus group, researchers must give strong consideration to the purpose of the study and think about who can best provide the necessary information. While there is no one set of human characteristics that can guarantee the right group dynamics, the focus group must be as homogeneous as possible but with enough variation to allow for contrasting opinions. Key factors in the selection process are the potential group dynamics and the willingness of members to engage in dialogue. Desirable commonalities among participants may include gender, age, educational level, occupation, family structure, as well as past use of a product, service, or programme. The underlying concern is the degree to which these factors influence members' willingness to share ideas within group discussions. Having a homogeneous focus group in which participants recognize their common factors and feel comfortable with one another is likely to create a more natural and relaxed group environment than having a heterogeneous group. Furthermore, participants in homogeneous focus groups are less likely to be eager to present contrived or socially acceptable responses just to impress other group members or the moderator. Researchers need to remember that in most cases, focus group participants are neither friends nor even acquaintances but typically strangers. Many people can feel intimidated or hesitant to voice their opinions, feelings, or suggestions to strangers.

A factor often overlooked in the selection of focus group participants is that of individuals' existing knowledge level of the topic. Researchers must determine whether prospective participants have some prior knowledge about the topics to be discussed in the focus group. Lack of knowledge on the part of participants severely limits the opportunities for creating spontaneous, interactive discussions that will provide detailed data about a specific topic. For example, bringing together a group of people who sell women's shoes for a discussion about the operation of a nuclear power plant is likely to produce few meaningful insights pertinent to that topic.

Recruitment and Selection of Participants

Recruiting and selecting appropriate participants is essential for the success of any focus group. We have already noted the necessity for homogeneous groups. Now it becomes critical to understand the general makeup of the target audience that needs to be represented by the focus group. Exhibit 5.7 lists some general rules for the selection process.

Screening for Eligible Participants. To select participants for a focus group, the researcher must first develop a screening form that specifies the characteristics respondents must have to qualify for group membership. Researchers also must choose a method for contacting prospective participants. They can use lists of potential participants supplied by either the company sponsoring the research project, a screening company that specializes in focus groups, or a direct mail list company. Other methods are piggyback focus groups, on-location interviews, snowball sampling, random telephone screening and placing advertisements in newspapers and on bulletin boards. Regardless of the method used to obtain the names of prospective participants, the key to

EXHIBIT 5.7 General Rules for the Selection of Focus Group Participants

General Rule Factors	Description of Rule Guidelines
Specify exact selection criteria	Interacting with the decision maker, the researcher needs to identify, as precisely as possible, all the desired characteristics of the group members.
Maintain control of the selection process	The researcher must maintain control of the selection process. A screening mechanism that contains the key demographic and/or socioeconomic characteristics must be developed and used to ensure consistency in the selection process. In those situations where the researcher allows someone else to do the selection, precise instructions and training must be given to that individual.
Beware of potential selection bias	Selection bias tends to be overlooked by researchers and decision makers alike. Biases can develop in subtle ways and seriously erode the quality of the data collected. Beware of participants picked from memory, or because they expressed an interest or concerns about the topic, or because they are clones of the person doing the selection.
Incorporate randomization	Whenever possible, randomize the process. It will help attain a nonbiased sample of prospective participants. This will work only if the pool of respondents meets the established selection criteria.
Check respondents' knowledge	For any given topic, prospective participants may differ in knowledge and experience. Lack of experience and knowledge may directly affect respondents' abilities to engage in spontaneous topical discussions.
Keep in mind that no process is perfect	Researchers have to make the best choices they can with the knowledge they have at the time of selection. The process may overlook certain aspects of the problem and inadvertently neglect individuals with unique points of view.

qualifying a person is the screening form. A sample telephone screening form is shown in Exhibit 5.8. This form illustrates the format, key questions and screening instructions.

Issue of Sampling in Focus Groups. The issue of sampling requires some special thought when planning focus groups. Traditionally, researchers try to randomize the process of identifying prospective subjects. While randomization is critical in quantitative surveys, it is not as necessary in qualitative studies. Focus groups tend to require a more flexible research design. While a degree of randomization is desirable, it is not the primary factor in selection. Participant credibility during the focus group discussions is one of the key factors researchers want to achieve. Randomization can help reduce the selection bias inherent in some forms of personal recruitment, but there is never total assurance.

Recruitment of Participants. Once a prospective participant is identified, contacted and qualified for group membership, the task becomes one of obtaining that person's willingness to actually join

EXHIBIT 5.8 Telephone Screening Questionnaire to Recruit Focus Group Participants: Leicester's New Performing Arts Centre

Respondent's Name: _____   Date: _____

Mailing Address: _____   Phone #: _____

_____   Fax #: _____

(City)   (County)   (Postcode)

Hello, my name is _____, and I'm calling for Leicester's New Performing Arts Centre. We are conducting a short interesting survey and would like to include your opinions. The questions will take less than two minutes. Let me begin by asking …

1   Do you or any member of your immediate household work for a research firm, advertising agency, or a firm that produces or markets performing arts programmes or events?

  (__) Yes **[THANK THE PERSON AND TERMINATE AND TALLY]**

  (__) No **[CONTINUE]**

2   Have you attended a performing arts event in the past month?

  (__) Yes **[CONTINUE]**

  (__) No **[THANK THE PERSON AND TERMINATE AND TALLY]**

3   Are you a resident of _____ county?

  (__) Yes **[CONTINUE]**

  (__) No **[THANK THE PERSON AND TERMINATE AND TALLY]**

4   Are you currently employed full-time or part-time outside the home?

  (__) Full-time **[CONTINUE]**

  (__) Part-time **[THANK THE PERSON AND TERMINATE AND TALLY]**

  (__) Not currently employed **[THANK THE PERSON AND TERMINATE AND TALLY]**

5   Please stop me when I come to the age category to which you belong.

  (__) Under 20 **[THANK THE PERSON AND TERMINATE AND TALLY]**

  (__) 21 to 35 **[RECRUIT AT LEAST 12]**

  (__) 36 to 50 **[RECRUIT AT LEAST 12]**

  (__) 51 to 65 **[RECRUIT AT LEAST 12]**

  (__) Over 65 **[THANK THE PERSON AND TERMINATE AND TALLY]**

[PARTICIPANT RECRUITMENT PART – READ BY INTERVIEWER]

(Mr, Mrs, Ms) **(Person's Last Name Here)**, the **Leicester's New Performing Arts Centre** is sponsoring a meeting with people, like yourself, to discuss performing arts programmes and events. We understand that **many people are busy yet enjoy attending performing arts events and have opinions about different topics concerning the performing arts**. We would like you to join a group of people, like yourself, to **discuss** and **get your opinions** about some performing arts topics. This **a** a sales meeting, **but strictly a research project**. The group will meet on **Wednesday evening, 15 August, at the Royal Academy of Arts in London**. We would like you to be our guest. The **session will start promptly at 7:00 pm**, there will be refreshments **and the session will be over by 9:30 pm**. Those people **who participate will receive €75** as our token of appreciation for participating in this important discussion session. Will you be able to attend?

(__) Yes **[CONFIRM NAME, ADDRESS, PHONE, AND FAX NUMBERS]**

(__) No **[THANK THE PERSON AND TERMINATE AND TALLY]**

[If YES], I will be sending you a **letter and information packet in a few days confirming the meeting and your participation**.

If you have **any questions or need to cancel**, please telephone our office at **[GIVE OFFICE PHONE NUMBER]**. On behalf of Leicester's New Performing Arts Centre, **thank you and have a pleasant (day or evening)**.

Note: The items that absolutely must be included in a screening form are in bold type.

the group. Securing the respondent's willingness to participate is not an easy process. The researcher must invite the respondent to participate in the discussion of an interesting and important topic. There is no one best method of achieving this task, but there are some key factors that must be incorporated in the process. The researcher should use only professionally trained people as recruiters. They must have good interpersonal communication skills, as well as such characteristics as a positive, pleasant voice, a professional appearance, polite and friendly manners and a 'people-to-people' personality. The recruiter must establish a comfort zone with the respondent as quickly as possible.

To bring legitimacy to the research project, the recruiter must be able to clearly articulate the general interest and importance of the topic. It must be made clear to the respondent that because of the small group size, their opinions and feelings on the topic are very important to the success of the project. The recruiter must make it clear that the group meeting is not a sales meeting, but strictly a research project. Other information that must be included are the date, starting/ending times, location of the focus group, the incentives for participating and a method of contacting the recruiter if the prospective participant has any questions or problems concerning the meeting.

After the respondent commits to participating in the focus group, the researcher must send out a formal confirmation/invitation letter that includes all the critical information about the focus group meeting. The main purpose of this type of letter is to reinforce the person's commitment to participate in the focus group. Exhibit 5.9 displays a hypothetical confirmation letter. The last activity in the recruiting process is that of calling the respondent the day before (or the morning of) the actual focus group session to further reinforce their commitment to participate in the session.

Size of the Focus Group

Most experts agree that the optimal number of participants in any type of focus group is from eight to twelve. Any size smaller than eight participants is not likely to generate the right type of group dynamics or energy necessary for a beneficial group session. Also there is the increased probability of the moderator having to become too active and talkative to keep the discussions flowing. In contrast, having too many participants can easily limit each person's opportunity to contribute insights and observations.

One of the reasons for the wide range of members (eight to twelve) directly relates to the fact that it is difficult to predict just how many respondents will actually show up at the focus group session. It is not uncommon for twelve people to agree to participate but for only eight to show up. Some researchers may try to hedge on actual response rates by inviting more people than necessary, in the hope that only the right number will show up. In cases where too many respondents show up, the researcher is forced to decide whether or not to send some home. The greatest fear of a focus group researcher is that no one will show up for the session, despite promises to the contrary.

Focus Group Incentives. While using screening forms, professionally trained recruiters, personalized invitations and follow-up phone calls can help secure a person's willingness to participate, incentives are also needed because participation requires both time and effort. Participants usually must reserve time out of a busy schedule and are likely to incur expenses such as for child care, travel and meals. Finally, participants will typically spend time (often between 90 minutes and two hours) in the actual session. In some cases the total time is three hours – two hours for the session and an additional hour for pre- and post-interviewing activities. Consequently, group members need to be remunerated for their willingness to participate.

The incentive can be treated as a stimulus to get prospective participants to attend the scheduled session on time. Focus group incentives can remind people that their commitment to participate is worth the effort, incline them to keep the promised time slot from being preempted

EXHIBIT 5.9 Sample of Confirmation/Invitation Letter to Focus Group Members

[ORGANIZATION OFFICIAL LETTERHEAD]

[Date]
[Name of the Participant]
[Mailing Address]
[City, County, Postcode]

Dear **[First Name of Participant]:**

Thank you for accepting our invitation to attend the discussion on Performing Arts Programme and Events at the Royal Academy of Arts in London, on Wednesday evening, 15 August. The Royal Academy of Arts is **located** at Burlington House, Piccadilly W1J 0BD. For your convenience, **please find the enclosed map and specific directions to the Academy,** if needed. We would like **you to be at** the Academy **between 6:45 pm and 7:00 pm;** the discussion session **will begin at 7:00 pm.** There will be refreshments and the **session will end by 9:30 pm.**

Since we are talking to a limited number of people, t**he success and quality** of the discussion **will be based on the cooperation and participation of the people who attend.** Your opinions and feelings are **very important, and attendance** at the session will help **make the research project a success.**

As mentioned during our earlier telephone conversation, the discussion will focus on several critical issues and topics concerning Performing Arts Programmes and Events, and **we would like to get your opinions and feelings on these topics.** Your **candid thoughts on the topics** will be **very important to the success of the study.** Remember, this session is **strictly a research project,** and **no sales or solicitations** will be made. At the **conclusion** of the discussion session, we will be **giving you €75** to cover your expenses in attending. If necessary, child care will be provided. If **by chance you find you are not able** to attend the session or **have any questions,** please call us to let us know **as soon as possible** at our office. That **phone number is (020)7300-8000.**

Again, on behalf of Leicester's New Performing Arts Centre I thank you for your willingness to participate in the study. I am looking forward to meeting you on 15 August and sharing your important thoughts and feelings on the performing arts topics.

Sincerely,

Thomas G. Smith
Moderator

Note: All parts that are in bold type show information that must be included in the letter.

by other factors, and help to communicate to the participants that the discussion session is important. While different types of incentives have different effects on participation, money is by far the best incentive choice. The advantages of using money as an incentive are that (1) it is immediately recognized and understood by the participants, (2) it is portable and fits into small spaces, (3) most people like to receive immediate cash, and (4) it has a proven track record of working. The money amount per participant will vary from project to project, with many ranging between €50 and €100.

Number of Focus Group Sessions. Depending on the complexity of the issues to be discussed, one or more focus group sessions must be held. 'Just how many sessions should be conducted?' is an elusive question. There is no set standard. The rule of thumb is there should be a minimum of two sessions but that sessions should continue until no more new ideas, thoughts, or feelings are offered by different groups of respondents.

Focus Group Locations

The last element in the planning phase is where to hold the focus group sessions. This component is important partly because of the length of the discussions. Since a focus group session can last between 90 minutes and two hours, it is necessary to ensure that the setting is comfortable, uncrowded and conducive to spontaneous, unrestricted dialogue among all group members – such as a large room that allows for a roundtable format and is quiet enough so that at least audiotaping can take place with minimum disturbances. Depending on the researcher's budget constraints, focus groups can be held in such locations as the client's conference room, the moderator's home, a meeting room at a church or civic organization and an office or hotel meeting room, to name a few.

While all of the sites listed above are adequate, in most instances the best location is a professional focus group facility. Such facilities offer a set of specially designed rooms for conducting focus group interviews. Normally, each room has a large table and comfortable chairs for up to 13 people (12 participants and a moderator), a relaxing atmosphere, built-in recording equipment, and usually a one-way mirror so that researchers or decision makers can view and hear the discussions without being seen. Also available is videotaping equipment used to capture the participants' nonverbal communication behaviours. Using a professional focus group facility usually adds to the overall data collection costs.

Phase 2: Conducting the Focus Group Discussions

The success of the actual focus group session depends heavily on the moderator and their communication, interpersonal, probing, observation, and interpretive skills. The moderator must be able not only to ask the right questions but also to stimulate and control the direction of the participants' discussions over a variety of predetermined topics.

The Focus Group Moderator

The **focus group moderator** is well trained in interpersonal communication skills and professional manners. Moderators draw from the participants the best and most innovative ideas about the assigned topic or question. The moderator's objectives are to seek the best ideas from each group member and to stimulate spontaneous interactive and detailed discussions. The moderator is responsible for creating positive group dynamics and a comfort zone between himself or herself and each group member as well as among the members themselves. Although there is no one set of traits or characteristics that describe the type of person who would make the best focus group moderator, Exhibit 5.10 lists some of the traits researchers have used in selecting focus group moderators.

> **Focus group moderator** A special person who is well trained in interpersonal communication skills and professional manners.

EXHIBIT 5.10 Important Traits of a Focus Group Moderator

The following descriptions represent some of the important traits that a researcher must consider in the selection of an excellent moderator for the focus group session:

1   The person must be well trained in interpersonal communications and have excellent listening, observation and interpretive skills.

2   The moderator must display professional mannerisms, have a good memory for names, create positive group dynamics and a comfort zone for spontaneous and interactive dialogue.

3   The moderator must be comfortable and familiar with group dynamics and processes, and must be able to exercise mild, unobtrusive control over participants.

4   The moderator must have good understanding and background knowledge of the specified topics and questions.

5   The person must be well trained in asking follow-up probing questions, and must demonstrate respect and sensitivity for the participants and their expressed opinions and feelings.

6   The moderator must be able to communicate clearly and precisely both verbally and in writing, and must be objective, self-disciplined and focused.

7   The person should exhibit a friendly, courteous, enthusiastic, and adaptive personality, along with a sense of humour.

8   The person should be experienced in focus group research.

9   The moderator must have a quick mind capable of noting new ideas that come from the group.

10   The moderator must know how and when to bring closure to one topic and move the discussion to the next.

Moderator's Characteristics and Role.   Moderators must be comfortable and familiar with group dynamics and processes. The moderator must manage the participants and be able to guide them from one topic to the next while maintaining group enthusiasm and interest for the topic. Successful moderating requires knowing when to bring closure to one topic and move on to the next. The moderator should not only have a good understanding of the specified topics and questions but also demonstrate a curiosity toward each topic and each participant's response. This curiosity may result in follow-up probing questions that uncover ideas, avenues, or connections that shed new light on the topic. Another important trait is that of demonstrating respect and sensitivity for participants and their expressed opinions and feelings on the topic. Showing respect for the group members can directly affect the value and quality of the data collected.

The moderator must have sufficient background knowledge of the topic to place all comments in perspective and follow up with appropriate questions. Moreover, the moderator must be able to communicate clearly and precisely both verbally and in writing. Moderating the session requires objectivity, self-discipline, concentration and careful listening on the part of the moderator. He or she must guard against interjecting personal opinions about the topic or a participant's response, and must instead focus on eliciting the perceptions of the group members. In addition, the moderator must be mentally prepared and completely familiar with the questioning route, yet flexible enough to allow follow-up probing questions.

A Closer Look at Research
Moderator's Guide for Leicester's New Performing Arts Centre Focus Group Sessions

I. **INTRODUCTION**

   a. Welcome the participants.

   b. Briefly highlight the focus group format … get consent forms signed and turned in (if necessary).

   c. Explain ground rules for session:

> No correct answers – only your opinions and feelings … you are speaking for other people like yourself … want to hear from everyone.
>
> Briefly explain the audiotaping of the session and why … so I don't have to take many notes. If necessary, mention the one-way mirror and that some of my colleagues are observing the session … because they are extremely interested in your opinions.
>
> Only one speaks at a time … please no side discussions … I do not want to miss anyone's comments.
>
> Do not worry if you do not know much about a particular topic we talk about … it is OK and important for me to know … if your views are different from someone else's that's all right … it is important for me to know that too … please do not be afraid of having different opinions, just express them … remember there is no one right answer.
>
> This is an informal discussion … a research project, not a sales meeting … I will not be contacting you later on to try to sell you anything … I want you to be comfortable and relax … just express your opinions and feelings.

   d. Any questions? [Answer all questions of participants.] Let's begin.

II. **WARMUP** [Use opening question format.]

Tell us your name and one or two things about yourself. [Ask this of each participant.] (Build group dynamics and comfort zone among group members.)

III. **INTRODUCE FIRST TOPIC**

[Use an introductory question format.]

'FROM YOUR VIEWPOINT, TO WHAT EXTENT DO YOU ENJOY ATTENDING PERFORMING ARTS PROGRAMMES AND/OR ENTERTAINMENT EVENTS?'
Probe for:

   a. Types of programmes and events that have been attended in the past and would attend in the future.

   b. Types of programmes and events most preferred to see offered in Leicester's New Performing Arts Centre. [Use transition question format to move to next topic.]

IV. **SECOND MAJOR TOPIC**

[Use a critical question format.]
Now I want you to think about how people make their decisions to attend performing arts programmes and events.

'WHAT PERFORMING ARTS/ENTERTAINMENT FEATURES DO PEOPLE DEEM IMPORTANT IN DECIDING TO ATTEND A PARTICULAR PROGRAMME OR EVENT?'
Probe for:

a. Detail and clarification of features.

b. Understanding of importance of identified features. [Use transition question format to move to the next topic.]

V. SPECIFIC DESIGN FEATURES

[Use a critical question format.]
Now think about the facilities used to present performing arts programmes and events.
'WHAT FACTORS SHOULD BE INCLUDED IN FACILITY STRUCTURE DESIGN?'
Probe for:

a. Specific design features and why.

b. Thoughts and feelings about indoor versus outdoor programme/event capabilities.

c. Types of protection features for outdoor events for the audience and the performers. [Use transition question format to move to closure of session.]

VI. CLOSE SESSION WITH SUGGESTIONS AND FINAL THOUGHTS

[Use ending question format.]
'TAKING INTO CONSIDERATION OUR DISCUSSIONS, WHAT SPECIFIC ACTIONS WOULD YOU SUGGEST OR RECOMMEND TO THE RESEARCH TEAM TO HELP MAKE LEICESTER'S NEW PERFORMING ARTS CENTRE FACILITY THE BEST POSSIBLE?'
Probe for clarity of specific ideas and details as to why.

Features: ___ structure designs

        ___ seating requirements

        ___ theatre style vs. auditorium style

        ___ quality of sound system/acoustics

        ___ outdoor event protection features

'ANY LAST THOUGHTS, FEELINGS, OR COMMENTS?'
[Ask and probe for each participant.]

VII. END THE SESSION

a. Thank the participants for their cooperation and input.

b. Give each participant his or her gift of appreciation.

c. Extend a warm wish of a safe journey home to them all.

Preparing a Moderator's Guide. To ensure that the actual focus group session is productive, it is necessary to prepare a detailed moderator's guide. A **moderator's guide** represents a detailed outline of the topics and questions that will serve as the basis for generating the spontaneous interactive dialogue among the group participants. The nearby Closer Look at Research box shows a moderator's guide that was incorporated in the Leicester's New Performing Arts Centre example mentioned earlier. Using a structured outline format, a sequence is established for asking a series of opening, introductory, transition and ending questions. Opening questions are asked at the beginning of the focus group and can be answered quickly to identify characteristics participants have in common. These questions are normally factual and are important in establishing the group's comfort zone and internal dynamics. Introductory questions are also used to introduce the general topic of discussion as well as provide group members with the opportunity to reflect on past experiences and their connection with the overall topic. Typically, these questions are not critical to the final analysis but are important in creating spontaneous, interactive discussions. The objective of transition questions is to direct the conversation toward the main topics of interest. Transition questions help group members view the topic in a broader scope and let the participants know how others feel about the topic. In general, these questions serve as the logical link between introductory and substantive questions. From a content perspective, substantive questions drive the overall study. The moderator uses these questions to get to the heart of discussing the critical issues underlying the topics of interest. Finally, ending questions are asked to bring closure to the discussion. They allow participants to reflect on previous comments and feelings, and they encourage members to summarize any final thoughts.

> **Moderator's guide**   A detailed outline of the topics, questions, and subquestions used by the moderator to lead the focus group session.

The Actual Focus Group Session

Beginning the Session. As the participants arrive for the session, they should be warmly greeted by the moderator and made to feel comfortable. If name cards have not been prepared in advance, participants should be instructed to write their first names, in large letters, on the cards. Before the participants sit down, there should be an opportunity (about 10 minutes) for sociable small talk, coupled with refreshments. The purpose of these pre-session activities is to create a friendly, warm, comfortable environment in which participants feel at ease. During the socializing period, the moderator should use their observation skills to notice how well group members interact and talk with one another. If the moderator can identify dominant talkers and shy listeners, this can be used to place members strategically around the table.

If consent forms are required, participants should sign them and give them to the moderator before the session begins. The moderator should briefly discuss the ground rules for the session: only one person should speak at a time, everyone should understand the purpose of the session and act accordingly, and so on. In some cases, a brief mention of the sponsoring client is in order (e.g. the sponsoring client looks forward to the group's discussion on the topic as a way to decide on an important issue). In most cases, the sponsoring client is not identified to avoid introducing bias into the discussion. If the situation requires the use of a one-way mirror or audio/video equipment for taping purposes, the moderator should tell participants and briefly explain their logical use in the session. Sometimes group members are asked to introduce themselves with a few short remarks. This approach breaks the ice, gets each participant to talk, and continues the process of building positive group dynamics and comfort zones. After completing the ground rules and introductions, the moderator asks the first question using an opening question format. This question is designed to engage all participants in the discussion.

Main Session. Using the moderator's guide, the first topic area is introduced to the participants. As the discussion unfolds, the moderator must be able to use probing techniques to gain as many details as possible. If there is a good rapport between group members and the moderator, it should not be necessary for the moderator to spend a lot of time merely asking selected questions and receiving answers. Because there are no hard-and-fast rules on how long the discussion should last on any one particular topic, the moderator must use their judgment in deciding when to bring closure to one topic and move on to the next. In general, the session should move toward the study's critical questions at a pace that ensures enough time for depth probing of as many ideas and opinions as possible.

Closing the Session. After all of the prespecified topics have been covered, participants should be asked an ending question that encourages them to express final ideas or opinions. The moderator can briefly summarize the group's main points and ask if these are accurate. During the summary activities, the moderator should observe the body language of the participants for signs of agreement, disagreement, hesitation, or confusion. For example, it would be appropriate for the moderator to present a final overview of the discussion and then ask the participants, 'Have we missed anything?' or 'Do you think we've missed anything in the discussion?' Responses to these types of closing questions may reveal some thoughts that were not anticipated. Upon final closure, participants should be given a short debriefing of the session, thanked for participating, given the promised incentive gift or cash, and wished a safe journey home.

Phase 3: Analysing and Reporting the Results
Analysis Techniques

Debriefing Analysis.   If the researcher or the sponsoring client's representatives are present, they and the moderator should conduct a **debriefing analysis** and wrap-up activities immediately after the focus group members leave the session. These activities give the researcher, moderator, and client a chance to compare notes. The key players who have heard the discussion need to know how their impressions compare to each other. Insights and perceptions can be expressed concerning the major ideas, thoughts, feelings and suggestions from the session.

> **Debriefing analysis** An interactive procedure in which the researcher, moderator and client discuss the subjects' responses to the topics of the focus group session.

Ideas for improving the session can be uncovered and applied to further focus group sessions. For example, strong points can be identified and emphasized and errors noted, while they are still fresh in everyone's mind. Some researchers like to use debriefing analysis because it (1) provides an opportunity to include the opinions of the moderator with those of practicing experts in the business area concerned; (2) allows the researcher or sponsoring client's representatives to learn, understand and react to the moderator's top-of-mind perceptions about what was said in the group discussion; and (3) can offer opportunities for brainstorming new ideas and implications of the main points expressed in the discussion. In contrast, potential shortcomings of debriefing include (1) a clear possibility of creating interpretive bias; (2) faulty recall on the part of the moderator due to recency or limited memory capabilities; and (3) misconceptions due to lack of time for reflecting on what was actually said by the participants.

Content Analysis.   Although **content analysis** is an appropriate analysis tool to use in any type of qualitative research, it is probably the most widely used formalized procedure by qualitative researchers in their efforts to create meaningful findings from focus group discussions.

This procedure requires the researcher to implement a systematic procedure of taking individual responses and categorizing them into larger theme categories or patterns.

> **Content analysis** The systematic procedure of taking individual responses and grouping them into larger theme categories or patterns.

Depending on how the group discussion was recorded and translated (e.g. transcript, audio-tape, videotape, session notes), the researcher reviews the participants' raw comments and creates a report according to common themes or patterns. This process requires the researcher to consider several analysis and interpretive factors (see Exhibit 5.11).

EXHIBIT 5.11 Important Analysis and Interpretive Factors When Analysing Focus Group Data

Analysis/Interpretive Factors	Description and Comments
Consider the words	Thought must be given to both the words used by the participants and the meanings of those words. Because there will be a variety of words and phrases used by the group members, the researcher will have to determine the degree of similarity and classify them accordingly. It should be remembered that editing messy quotations is a difficult but necessary task.
Consider the context	The researcher will have to gain an understanding of the context in which participants expressed key words and phrases. The context includes the actual words as well as their tone and intensity (voice inflection). It must be remembered that nonverbal communication (body language) can also provide meaningful bits of data worth analysing.
Consider the extensiveness and frequency of participants' comments	In most situations, some of the topics presented in the session will be discussed by more participants (extensiveness) and some comments made more often (frequency) than others. The researcher should not assume that extensiveness and frequency of comments are directly related to their importance.
Consider the intensity of comments	Sometimes group members will talk about specific aspects of a topic with passion or deep feelings. While left undetected in transcripts alone, the intensity factor can be uncovered in audio- or videotapes by changes in voice tone, talking speed and emphasis placed on certain words or phrases.
Consider the specificity of responses	Those responses that are associated with some emotional first hand experience probably are more valuable than responses that are more vague and impersonal. For example, 'I feel that the new Aldi's cheese scone is a ripoff because I ate one and it tasted just terrible, especially at the price they are charging' should be given more weight than 'The new Aldi's cheese scone does not taste very good, considering what it costs.'
Consider the big picture	Because data from focus groups come in many different forms (words, body language, intensity, etc.), the researcher needs to construct an aggregate theme or message of what is being portrayed. Painting a bigger picture of what group members are actually saying can provide preliminary insights into how consumers view the specified product, service, or programme. Caution should be used when trying to quantify the data. Use of numbers can inappropriately convey the impression that the results can be projected to a target population, which is not within the capabilities of qualitative data.

Reporting Focus Group Results

To properly report the findings, the researcher must understand the audience, the purpose of the report, and the expected format. The researcher must have a strong understanding of the people who will be using the results – their preferences in receiving information and their demographic profile, including age, educational level and occupation, to name only a few factors. Overall, the report should stress clarity and understanding and should support the findings. In many cases, the writing style can be informal and the vocabulary familiar. The researcher should use active rather than passive voice and incorporate quotations, illustrations and examples where appropriate.

In writing the report, the researcher must be aware of its basic purpose. First, the report should communicate useful insights and information to the audience. It should be a clear and precise presentation tailored to the individual information needs of the specific users. It must offer a logical sequence of findings, insights and recommendations. The researcher should also keep in mind the report will serve as a historical record that will likely be reviewed at some point in the future.

Format of the Report

Traditionally, focus group reports have been presented in a narrative style that uses complete sentences supported by direct quotes from the group discussion. An alternative is to use an outline format supported with bulleted statements that use key words or phrases to highlight the critical points from the group discussion. Regardless of the style, the report must be written in a clear, logical fashion and must look professional. Although there is no one best format, Exhibit 5.12 describes the essential components of a typical report.

EXHIBIT 5.12 Components of a Written Focus Group Research Report

Components of the Report	Description
Cover page	The front cover should include the title, the names of people receiving or commissioning the report, the names of the researchers and the date the report is submitted.
Executive summary	A brief, well-written executive summary should describe why the focus group session was conducted and list the major insights and recommendations. It should be limited to two pages and be able to stand alone.
Table of contents	This section provides the reader with information on how the report is organized and where various parts can be located. (It is optional for short reports.)
Statement of purpose and procedural design	This section describes the purpose of the study and includes a brief description of the focus groups held, critical questions, the number of focus group sessions, the methods of selecting participants and the number of people included in each session.
Results and findings	The results derived from the findings are most often organized by critical questions or overall ideas. The results can be presented in a number of ways using narrative formats or bulleted lists, listing raw data, summarizing the discussion, or using an interpretative approach.
Summary of themes	Statements in this section are not limited to specific questions but rather connect several questions into a larger picture.

Limitations and alternative explanations	This section can be placed within the results section, if it is brief. Limitations reflect those aspects of the study that reduce the application of the findings or affect different interpretations of the findings.
Recommendations	This optional section is not automatically included in all focus group reports. The recommendations suggest what can be done with the results.
Appendix	The appendix should include any additional materials that might be helpful to the reader. A copy of the moderator's guide, screening form, or other relevant material would go into the appendix.

Advantages of Focus Groups

With an understanding of the process and activities of conducting focus groups, we can see the advantages and disadvantages associated with this popular qualitative research method. There are basically five major advantages to using the focus group method: they stimulate new ideas, thoughts, and feelings about a topic; foster understanding of why people hold belief or behave in certain market situations; allow client participation; elicit wide-ranging participant responses; and can bring together hard-to-reach subject groups.

New Ideas, Thoughts and Feelings

The spontaneous, unrestricted interaction among focus group participants during discussions can stimulate new ideas, thoughts and feelings that may not be raised in one-on-one interviews. There is a high likelihood that respondents will offer creative opinions about a subject topic. With an effective moderator, participants are more at ease in expressing their candid opinions than in a one-on-one situation with an interviewer. In a spontaneous, interactive environment, participants are encouraged to freely engage in group creativity that induces a 'snowballing' process where additional responses are triggered by someone else's comments.

Underlying Reasons for Behaviour

Focus groups allow researchers to collect detailed data about the underlying reasons people think or act as they do in different market situations. A trained moderator can help in directing the focus group discussion so that participants feel comfortable in expressing why they hold certain beliefs or feel the way they do about particular discussion topics such as the product's attributes, service components, brand images, or particular marketing practices, to name a few.

Client Participation

Focus groups offer another advantage by allowing the decision makers the opportunity to be involved in the overall process from start to finish. Clients can have an interactive role in creating the research objectives and setting the focus groups' overall agenda and initial research questions. The energetic atmosphere during the actual sessions enables the client's representatives and researchers to observe first hand (from behind a one-way mirror) the group dynamics and how participants respond to information on the topics and questions of interest. This participation can lead to impressions and results that suggest specific actions. In some cases, clients formulate and begin action plans based on their observations even before the data are analysed and submitted as a final report.

Breadth of Topics Covered

Focus groups can range over an unlimited number of topics and management issues as well as very diverse groups of subjects like children, teenagers, senior citizens, and so on. Sessions can incorporate prototypes of new products to be demonstrated or advertising copy being evaluated. In addition, other types of projective data collection methods could be included (e.g. balloon tests, role-playing activities, word association tests, picture tests) to stimulate spontaneous discussion of a topic. Recent technology has added new flexibility to the process by allowing clients located in different geographic regions to participate in and observe the live sessions without having to be at the specific facility location.

Special Market Segments

Another advantage is the technique's unique ability to bring together groups of individuals, such as doctors, lawyers, and engineers, to name a few, who might not otherwise be willing to participate in a study. The focus group format allows these hard-to-interview individuals an opportunity to interact with their peers and compare thoughts and feelings on common topics and issues of interest.

Disadvantages of Focus Groups

As with any exploratory research design, focus groups are not a perfect research method. The major weaknesses of focus groups are inherently similar to all qualitative methods: the findings lack generalizability to the target population, the reliability of the data is questionable, the interpretation is subjective and the cost per participant is high.

Low Generalizability of Results

As with any qualitative method, the findings developed from focus groups tend to lack representativeness with regard to the target population. This makes it very difficult, if not impossible, for the researcher to generalize the results to larger market segments. For example, Procter & Gamble's brand manager of Crest toothpaste as well as the researcher might run substantial risks in believing that the attitudes and feelings toward a new formula change in the product obtained from 12 Crest users in a focus group are truly representative of the typical attitudes and feelings of the millions of Crest users in the market.

Questions of Data Reliability

Given the type of data collected in focus groups, data reliability is a potentially big issue of concern. In addition to having to deal with very small sample sizes, the unstructured nature of the data (nominal nature of the verbalized comments and nonverbal body language) precludes analyzing the results in standard statistical formats (e.g. percentage and mean values). Adding to this weakness is the possibility that some degree of the known 'Hawthorne effect' has impacted the data collected from the participants: the focus group process can easily create an environment that makes some of the participants think they are 'special' and act accordingly when offering their comments.

Another potential problem relates to effects of moderator interaction bias. Because of the social interaction in focus groups, the moderator must guard against behaving in ways that might prejudice participants' responses. For example, a moderator who is aggressive or confronting in nature could systematically lead participants to say whatever they think the moderator wants to hear. In contrast, a moderator's attempts to play dumb or too supportive of participants' comments may create a sense of phoniness on the moderator's part, thus causing some respondents to stop making comments. While difficult to measure, these conditions may reduce the reliability of the data.

Subjectivity of Interpretations

Given the nature of the data collected, selective use of the data by either the researcher or the client's representatives can create problems. For example, if the client enters the focus group process with preconceived ideas of what will emerge from a focus group, that client often can find something in the data (e.g. participants' comments) that can be subjectively interpreted as being supportive of these views while ignoring any opposing data. In addition, there is always the possibility of moderator interpretation bias, which can quickly reduce the trustworthiness of the information being provided to marketing decision makers.

High Cost Per Participant

The costs of identifying, recruiting and compensating focus group participants along with the costs of the moderator(s) and facilities are overall quite high, resulting in a high-cost-per-participant average. Sometimes the average cost per participant even exceeds the cost of having a one-on-one in-depth interview.

Despite all the above disadvantages, focus groups are often regarded as a very good method for many research topics and are popular not only in Europe, but globally. The European and Asian Insights box describes a pan-European study relying on the focus group method and the difference between the West and the East when conducting focus groups.

European Insights

Focus Groups with European Citizens in Sixteen Countries

EuroPHEN (European Public Health Ethics Network), which was funded by European Commission Fifth Framework Programme, employed a market research company, TRBI, to conduct focus groups in each of the sixteen European countries. The research purpose was to examine how citizens in different countries and cultures weigh competing claims of private and public interest. Six focus groups were conducted in each country with an equal spread of participants who were male or female, in the age range of 20–35 or 45–60, married or single, with children or childless, with or without further education, and smokers or non-smokers. In addition, the focus groups were split between two sites in each country, e.g. London and Glasgow in the UK, Amsterdam and Eindhoven in the Netherlands. The intention was to establish the views of a greater diversity of people. Each focus group contained six to ten participants, and lasted one and a half to two hours.

Each focus group session was audio- and video-recorded. All these records were sent to the research team in Sheffield. The Sheffield team located transcribers who spoke each of the relevant European languages and the audio records were transcribed into their native language. These transcriptions were then transcribed into English. Translations were checked against the videos as a form of quality control.

The researchers in the Sheffield team then established the coding and carried out full in-depth analysis of the translations of the focus groups.

Asian Insights
Conducting Focus Groups in Oriental Countries

The culture of the respondents in relation to openness, honesty and disclosure warrants consideration. In many cultures, particularly in the West, people have less difficulty in sharing their view with others and engaging in debates where their views may differ from others within the group. The culture of free speech makes the focus group discussion come naturally. However, this cannot be assumed for all cultures.

In many oriental countries, to appear openly critical of products, services and suppliers cannot be assumed to be so easy. Oriental people are less open and have been conditioned to keep their opinions to themselves in order that they don't unintentionally insult others or cause others to 'lose face'. When an oriental person causes others to 'lose face', he exposes himself to a similar loss. Consequently the focus group moderator in Asia has to be very skilled, perhaps even more so than in the Western context, at encouraging participation, making participants feel comfortable and drawing out the quieter ones. The warm-up period is often longer in Asia. As many Asian countries such as Singapore, Indonesia and Malaysia speak different languages, having a multi-language skill is a definite plus.

The more casual way of life in countries such as Thailand, Malaysia and Indonesia means that keeping a commitment to turn up for a focus group is less likely than in the West. At the very mundane level, traffic jams in many Asian big cities are the norm. Getting six to ten people in one place at one time is always a challenge. A good strategy is to invite two to three more people than you need to the focus group.

Always allow more time for recruitment, transcription and analysis than you would in Western countries. The multitude of different accents and the use of varied local slang often make transcription a very time-consuming job.

Try to break up your focus groups according to age, social class and gender. It is usually considered rude in Asia for a younger person to even suggest they have a different opinion from either an older person or one who is more 'senior' or 'important'. The same problem can also occur with females in a group of males. Always keep your genders segregated, especially in places like Thailand and India.

In spite of the above potential problems, focus groups can be a particularly useful method of data collection in Asia due to Asian people's strong oral tradition. For most of them, talking and discussing comes naturally whether it is in the restaurant or on the mobile phone. Many Asians are naturally social. The exchange of information by word of mouth is central to not only their cultures, but also the way business is done there.

Furthermore, many Asian countries such as mainland China, India and Taiwan speak different dialects, and people in these countries can talk and converse in more than one dialect. However, reading and writing in those dialects is far more difficult. Therefore, translating questionnaires often results in changes to the 'meaning' of questions, resulting in misunderstanding and invalid results. The focus group setting can reduce a lot of these difficulties.

Source: Adapted with permission of Orient Pacific Century, which specializes in Asian business strategy, market research, branding strategy and business development, and is located in Kuala Lumpur, Malaysia.

Online Focus Groups

Few would argue that the future of the focus group method continues to be bright. Improved sophistication in the Internet, telecommunications and computer technology is leading the way toward new trends in conducting focus groups that will keep this qualitative data collection method popular well into the 2010s.

A high-tech version of focus groups, commonly termed **online focus groups**, is becoming more widely used. With this approach, a special group of service application providers (SAPs), not marketing researchers, have successfully integrated many of the benefits of the high-speed computer and telecommunication technologies into focus group research. For example, interactive marketing technologies (IMTs) facilitate conducting telephone, video and Internet focus groups through such formats as teleconference networks. TeleSessions, FocusVision Networks and itracks Internet software use videoconferencing and online Internet systems to complete focus groups. In addition, FocusVision Worldwide, Inc., Interactive Tracking Systems, Inc., and others offer interactive focus group research systems that allow customization of any business's needs, whether they involve testing new TV advertisements, product or advertising concepts, or observing consumers' reactions to words, phrases, or visuals.

> **Online focus group** Subjects are gathered and the session is carried in real time across the Internet to clients and researchers.

The rapid introduction and continuous improvements of Internet technologies are driving how, what, when, where and how fast qualitative data are collected, analysed and disseminated to researchers and decision makers. High-speed Internet-assisted approaches are making it easier to reach today's hard-to-reach subjects and are shortening the time cycle in completing focus group research projects, while allowing decision makers to interact with the process in real time.

Online Versus Offline Focus Group Research

Opinions differ on whether the future of focus group research will be online methods or offline practices, based on acknowledged new speed and flexibility requirements. For now, it is important to understand the driving forces behind online practices. The push is coming not from marketing researchers, but rather from the new breed of specialized focus group data collection facilities. Once limited to providing researchers with a 'professional' taping facility for conducting the actual focus group sessions, with the integration of high technology these service providers shorten the data acquisition, analysis, and reporting activities of focus groups. Decision makers are attracted by the real-time dimension and flexibility these service providers offer.

Overall, the processes, guidelines and decisions that are required in the 'planning' and 'execution' stages of an online focus group session are, for the most part, the same for conducting a traditional offline focus group session. For example, both methods require that the decision maker and researcher fully understand the nature of the focus group method and together develop the focus group objectives. Similar activities for identifying the appropriate type of people for inclusion in the focus group, the sampling, recruitment and selection of the prospective participants, as well as decisions concerning size and number of focus groups, incentives and location must be jointly undertaken by the researcher and decision maker regardless of the approach.

There are subtle differences between online and offline focus group research. For example, the technology driving the data-capturing activities during the focus group session is much more sophisticated for online than for offline methods, requiring online moderators to have a greater technological aptitude and understanding of the devices used to gather the data in real time. Online focus groups provide significantly greater flexibility to client participation before, during and after the session. Offline methods require that the client's representatives be at the focus group, located behind a one-way mirror, and communication capabilities with the moderator are limited and antiquated (e.g. handwritten notes, or specified breaks in the session). In contrast, online methods use advanced communication technologies that enable clients to directly participate from anywhere in the world – all they need is a computer and Internet access.

Offline focus groups have the advantage of gaining additional information from each of the participants through the moderators' and clients' ability to directly observe the participants' non-verbal communication habits and body language during the actual session. In certain forms of online group interviews (e.g. chat room discussions, bulletin boards, newsgroups, discussion lists, etc.) the lack of face-to-face interaction makes obtaining this type of additional information impossible. In turn, the lack of face-to-face exposure might well make online participants feel more comfortable in giving more candid responses than those in an offline group interview. In any of the online methods (excluding those that use some form of face-to-face interactions), incentives needed to recruit participants are normally less extensive than the incentives needed to secure participants in offline group interviews.

The greatest differences between the two methods are in the last phase of the process (analyzing and reporting of the results). Online focus groups allow for data manipulation, retrieval, and reporting of the qualitative data results in real time, whereas the offline version typically takes researchers days, if not weeks, to get and present the findings to decision makers. For more insights into online focus group research practices, visit the book's website at www.mhhe.com/shiu09.

Using Focus Group and In-Depth Interview Methods for *Kids' Market Research* in Ukraine

Marketing research in Ukraine was a developing industry in the decade after the country's independence from the former Union of Soviet Socialist Republics (USSR). Fast moving consumer goods (FMCG), pharmaceutical products, alcohol and tobacco were the most popular research areas.

Since the mid-1990s competition in the Ukrainian marketing research industry has become increasingly intense. A number of factors have contributed to this change in the competitive landscape. Traditionally, advertising agencies contracted marketing research work to a separate firm, but they had begun conducting their own marketing research in response to their customers' demands. There was less and less differentiation between advertising, branding and marketing research agencies, as they each worked to satisfy all of their clients' needs.

Other competition in the marketing research industry exists besides the large firms competing for contracts, such as independent consultants soliciting marketing research work. In between election periods, companies that conducted research for political blocs would conduct marketing research as well.

The major marketing research companies operating in Ukraine include Gfk-USM, *ACNielsen* Ukraine LLC, IPSOS S.A., Consumer Insights Ukraine (CIU) and Comcon Ukraine. While there are many niche players, none of the firms operating in Ukraine has been solely dedicated to marketing research focusing on children until the Natalia Berezovskaya founded *Kids Market Consulting* (KMC).

Berezovskaya started KMC in Kyiv, Ukraine in September 2002. Her studies in mass media and communications at Dnipropetrovsky State University sparked her interest in the marketing research industry. With more than 10 years' experience as a radio anchor for youth programmes, Berezovskaya was able to identify kids, tweens and teens as unserved segments in the Ukrainian marketplace.

Prior to starting at KMC, Berezovskaya made contact with marketing research firms serving the kids, tweens and teens segments in other countries, such as Yeladim, Teenage Research Unlimited and Doyle Research. Along with this research, Berezovskaya monitored media sources, such as magazines, the Internet and business publications, to determine the feasibility of setting up a similar niche marketing research firm in Ukraine. The presence of Western children's brands, the appearance of perceived low-quality national Ukrainian brands, as well as the general lack of information regarding the consumer psychology of children were encouraging indications of the success of such a niche business.

Challenges arose for KMC in the beginning, due to its first-mover position in the kids, tweens and teens niche. There was initially a low level of acknowledgement from potential clients, due to the lack of information surrounding this specific segment in Ukraine. In order to promote the business, KMC worked to increase prospects' knowledge about the advantages of marketing to children. KMC organized seminars and presentations and introduced child-target marketing at workshops. The company promoted consolidated research, whereby it offered one package of marketing research to several buyers. Traditional marketing research services are offered, with the focus of each service on kids, tweens and teens. Services include:

- Surveys and questionnaires for quantitative studies
- 'Delicate Age' study, a regular investigation of lifestyles and consumer preferences of children and teenagers

marketing research in action

- Focus group discussions
- One-on-one, in-depth interviews with children to better understand their feelings towards brands
- Child-and-parent pair interviews to understand the psychology of child-parent interaction in purchasing
- Creative groups (brainstorming groups with children to develop ideas about names, heroes, slogans, etc.)
- Observation and immersion experiences
- Desktop studies (analysis of secondary information and its assessment by different experts)
- Hall-test and home-test (assessment of the target group's reaction to the product at its point of sale, or practical use of the study subject in the target group's routine life)

Difficulties involved in working in this niche included collecting information from children, who were often unable to articulate their thoughts clearly. With the use of child psychologists specially trained by KMC in concepts of marketing research, KMC has been able to study the market awareness of kids, tweens and teens in Ukraine.

Seeing the potential of marketing research on kids, tweens and teens, non-specialized marketing research firms in Ukraine began competing for KMC's niche business.

Questions

1 *Kids Market Consulting* uses both qualitative and quantitative approaches to conduct research on the kids' market. Which approach would be more appropriate? Why?

2 Focus groups and in-depth interviews are two major research methods used by *Kids Market Consulting*. Which method would be better for this niche market? Why?

Summary of Learning Objectives

- **Identify the fundamental differences between qualitative and quantitative research methods and explain their appropriateness in collecting useful data.**

  In business situations where secondary information alone cannot answer management's questions, primary data must be collected and transformed into usable information. Researchers can choose between two types of research methods for data collection purposes: qualitative or quantitative. There are many differences between these two approaches with respect to their research objectives, type of research design, type of questions, time of execution, generalizability to target populations, type of analysis and researcher skill requirements.

  Qualitative research methods focus on generating exploratory, preliminary insights into decision problems. They focus on collecting detailed amounts of data from relatively small samples by questioning or observing what people do and say. These methods require the use of researchers well trained in interpersonal communication, observation, and interpretation. Data are normally collected using open-ended or non-structured questioning formats that allow for probing of hidden attitudes or behaviour patterns, or human/mechanical/electronic observation techniques for current behaviours or events.

In contrast, quantitative research methods place heavy emphasis on using formalized, structured questioning practices where the response options have been predetermined by the researcher. These questions tend to be administered to large numbers of respondents. Quantitative methods are directly related to descriptive and causal types of research projects where the objectives are either to validate the existence of relationships among defined variables or to make more accurate predictions of the impacts of market factors on specified behaviours. Quantitative researchers are well trained in construct development, scale measurements, questionnaire design, sampling and statistical data analysis.

- **Explain the advantages and disadvantages of qualitative research methods for data collection purposes.**
The general advantages of qualitative research methods include the economy and timeliness of data collection; richness of the data; accuracy of recording marketplace behaviours; and preliminary insights into building models and scale measurements. The potential disadvantages include the lack of generalizability of the data to larger target groups; inability of the data to distinguish small differences; lack of data reliability; and difficulty in finding well-trained investigators, moderators, interviewers, and observers.

- **Describe and explain the focus group method used in gathering primary data.**
While there are a number of qualitative research methods available for collecting primary data, this chapter focuses on focus groups. Focus groups involve bringing a small group of people together for an interactive and spontaneous discussion of a particular topic or concept. The success in focus groups relies on the group dynamics of the members, the willingness of members to engage in an interactive dialogue and the moderator's ability to keep the discussion on track.

Some pertinent uses of focus group research are: (1) to provide data for defining or redefining marketing problems; (2) to identify specific hidden information requirements; (3) to provide data for better understanding results from other qualitative studies; (4) to reveal consumers' perceptions, attitudes, feelings, motives, hidden needs, and behaviours regarding products, services, or practices; (5) to generate new ideas about products, services or practices; (6) to discover new constructs and measurement methods; (7) to help explain changing consumer preferences, and (8) to generate or assess new product or service ideas.

- **Explain the phases that should be followed in order to conduct a focus group properly.**
The three phases of a focus group study are planning the study, conducting the actual focus group discussion and analysing and reporting the results. In the planning of a focus group, decisions have to be made regarding who should participate; how to recruit and select the appropriate participants; what size the group should be; what incentives to offer to encourage and reinforce participants' willingness and commitment to participate; and where the group session should be held. In conducting the focus group discussion, the moderator's role is paramount. A moderator's guide should be in place, which serves as the basis for generating the spontaneous interactive dialogue among the group participants. Debriefing analysis and content analysis are common techniques used for analysing focus group results. To properly report the results, the researcher must understand the audience, the purpose of the report and the expected format of the report.

■ **Understand online focus groups and how they are compared to traditional offline focus groups.**

Online focus groups are a high-tech version of focus groups. In online focus groups, subjects are gathered and the session is carried in real time across the Internet to clients and researchers. Overall, the processes, guidelines and decisions that are required in the 'planning' and 'execution' stages of an online focus group session are, for the most part, the same for conducting a traditional offline focus group session. The greatest differences are in the last phase of the process (analysing and reporting the results). Online focus groups allow for data manipulation, retrieval and reporting of the results in real time, whereas the offline version typically takes researchers days, if not weeks, to get and present the findings to decision makers.

Key Terms and Concepts

Content analysis 191	Moderator's guide 189
Debriefing analysis 190	Online focus group 197
Focus group moderator 185	Qualitative research 173
Focus group research 175	Quantitative research 171

Review Questions

1 What are the major differences between quantitative and qualitative research methods? What skills must a researcher have to effectively use each of these two types of methods?

2 Explain the pros and cons of using qualitative research methods as the means of developing raw data structures for each of the following situations:

   a Adding carbonation to Innocent Smoothies and selling it as a true soft drink.

   b Finding new consumption usages for Arm & Hammer baking soda.

   c Inducing customers who have stopped shopping at Somerfield to return to Somerfield.

   d Advising a travel agency that wants to enter the cruise ship vacation market.

3 What are the characteristics of a good focus group moderator? What is the purpose of a moderator's guide?

4 Why is it important to have eight to twelve participants in a focus group? What difficulties might exist in meeting that objective?

5 Why are the screening activities so important in the selection of focus group participants?

6 Develop a screening form that would allow you to select participants for a focus group on the benefits and costs of leasing new automobiles.

7 What are the advantages and disadvantages of online focus groups compared to the offline version?

8 How are focus group participants recruited, and what are the common difficulties associated with the recruitment of these people?

Discussion Questions

1 Develop a moderator's guide that could be used in a focus group to investigate the following question: Why do 30 per cent of Sky subscribers discontinue their subscription after the initial three-month special package offer?

2 Thinking about how most participants are recruited for focus groups, identify and discuss three ethical issues that the researcher must consider when using the focus group method to collect primary data and information.

3 **Experience the Internet.** Go to the websites of different major market research companies. What are the different methods of focus groups these companies offer? If you are the developer of computer video games and want to use focus groups to develop greater understanding of the game customers/players, which focus group method would you prefer to use for the purpose, and why?

4 Conduct a focus group and write a brief summary report on the following decision question: 'What are the considerations mobile phone owners have when deciding whether to upgrade their phones or not?'

6

Qualitative Research Methods: In-Depth Interviews and Projective Techniques

LEARNING OBJECTIVES

After reading this chapter, you will be able to

☑ Understand the purposes behind the use of the in-depth interview method and the projective techniques.

☑ Illustrate the advantages and disadvantages of the in-depth interview method.

☑ Identify the steps required to conduct an in-depth interview.

☑ Describe the different special types of the in-depth interview method as well as the different types of projective techniques.

Large amounts of qualitative work have usually been prerequisite to fruitful quantification in the physical sciences.

−Thomas Kuhn

Making Full Use of In-Depth Interviews

A specialist marketing research company, Shopping Behaviour Xplained, has recently formed a new company, Xtraviews. This new company aims at making full use of the results gathered from in-depth interviews by not only analysing the contents of the interview, but also studying systematically and in as much detail as possible the psychological and physiological clues left by the respondent during the interview. The Xtraviews approach involves filming face-to-face interviews with respondents and analysing their body language, voice tone, as well as two other parameters which the company is keeping as business secrets.

Xtraviews said: 'If you want better answers to your research questions, then why not start by simply analysing more of the information interviewees provide by way of the responses they happily give you.'

Clients that have used the approach since it was introduced include Imperial Tobacco and B&Q.

Source: Research Magazine, News Archive, www.research-live.com

In-Depth Interviews

Thomas Kuhn, a worldwide prominent scholar in the philosophy of science stressed the importance of qualitative research in the physical sciences. Indeed qualitative research is equally important in the study of social sciences, including marketing research. If you come across research work in the field of marketing in the library or via the Internet, you will notice that qualitative work was often done before quantitative research was conducted for a research project.

On the other hand, the real-world chapter opener introduces the increasing popularity of a new approach that aims to broaden and deepen the capture of results obtained from in-depth interviews. It also demonstrates that, in spite of the dominance of the use of questionnaire survey in marketing research, qualitative research methods such as the in-depth interview are still espoused by many leading businesses. This chapter continues our qualitative research journey by focusing on the other two major methods – in-depth interview and projective techniques.

An **in-depth interview**, also referred to as a 'depth' or 'one-on-one' interview, represents a formal process in which a trained interviewer asks a subject a set of predetermined and probing questions usually in a face-to-face setting. Depending on the research objectives, the typical setting for this type of interview would be either the subject's home or office, or some type of centralized interviewing centre that is convenient for the subject. In special situations, in-depth interviews can be conducted by telephone or through a high-tech telecommunication system that allows face-to-face interchanges through a television or computer. Exhibit 6.1 lists some major uses of the in-depth interviewing method.

> **In-depth interview** A formalized process in which a well-trained interviewer asks a subject a set of predetermined and probing questions usually in a face-to-face setting.

EXHIBIT 6.1 Major Uses of In-Depth Interviewing

To gain preliminary insights into **what** the subject thinks or believes about the topic of concern or **why** the subject exhibits certain behaviours.

To obtain unrestricted and detailed comments revealing feelings, opinions or beliefs that can help the interviewer better understand the different elements of the subject's thoughts and the reasons they exist.

To have the respondent communicate as much detail as possible about his or her knowledge and behaviour towards a given topic or object.

In-depth interviewing allows the researcher to collect both attitudinal and behavioural data from the subject that spans all time frames (past, present and future). Let's say, for example, that corporate management of Thistle Hotels wants to understand how to deliver better on-site services to business customers. Thistle's researchers can conduct on-site, in-depth interviews with selected business travellers that include the following predetermined questions:

1 What were the specific factors you used in selecting Thistle for overnight accommodations during your business trip to London? (Motives)

2 What hotel services did you use during your stay? (Behaviour)

3 How satisfied or dissatisfied are you with those services? (Current feelings)

4 How likely are you to stay at a Thistle Hotel next time you are in London for business, and why? (Future intended behaviour)

A unique characteristic of this data collection method is that the interviewer uses *probing questions* as the mechanism to get more data on the topic from the subject. By taking the subject's initial response and turning it into a question, the interviewer encourages the subject to further explain the first response and creates natural opportunities for a more detailed discussion of the topic. The general rule of thumb is that the more a subject talks about a topic, the more likely he or she is to reveal underlying attitudes, emotions, motives and behaviours. To illustrate the technique of using probing questions, let's use the second question from the above Thistle example. The dialogue might go as follows:

Interviewer: What hotel services did you use during your stay?
Subject: I used the front desk quite often.
Interviewer: With regard to the front desk, what were some of the actual services you requested?
Subject: Well, besides checking in, I inquired about the availability of a fitness room and car rental.
Interviewer: Why were you interested in information about the hotel's fitness centre and car rental service?
Subject: When I am away on business, I enjoy a good workout to help relieve stress buildup and I find my energy level improves.
Interviewer: While at the hotel, how did renting a car fit into your plans?
Subject: I had a business meeting the next day at 9:30 am across town; afterward I planned to play a round of golf.
Interviewer: Which rental car company do you usually prefer to use?
Subject: Hertz – they are the best! I have Gold VIP status with them and I receive frequent flier miles.

Interviewer: Besides using the fitness centre and renting a car, what other hotel services might you request during your stay?

Subject: I might rent a movie at night.

Interviewer: Rent a movie? What kinds of movies do you prefer?

Subject: When away from home, I enjoy watching action-oriented movies as a means to relax after a long day on the road. I do not get much of a chance when I am at home with my wife and the kids.

Interviewer: Are there any other services you would consider using?

Subject: No. (With this response, the interviewer would move on to the next topic.)

By interpreting this dialogue and those involving other participants, the researcher can create theme categories that reveal not only what hotel services the guests used, but why those particular services were used during their stay at the Thistle. Here, management learns the property's fitness centre, on property car rental service and availability of in-room movie entertainment are some of the hotel features that must be in place to attract business travellers to the hotel. In addition, the fitness centre and movie entertainment features could be promoted with a theme towards 'stress reduction' activities during the customer's stay at the hotel.

A word of caution about probing questions: it is critically important that the interviewer avoid framing questions that allow the subject to reply with a simple but logical 'no'. Unless the interviewer intends to bring closure to the discussion, probing questions should not be framed in formats like 'Can you tell me more about that point?' 'Could you elaborate on that?' 'Do you have some specific reasons?' or 'Is there anything else?' All these formats allow the subject to logically say no. Once a no response is given, it becomes very difficult to continue probing the topic for more detailed data.

 ## A Closer Look at Research *(In the field)*

IKEA Gained Customer Insights through In-Depth Interviews

Since opening its first store in Almhult, Sweden in 1958, IKEA has emerged as a global furniture retailing giant. The company is shrewd in detecting the current and future consumption trends. In order to gain customer insights and correctly detect the trend of the time, the company relies on marketing research from time to time.

Recently the Swedish giant conducted in-depth interviews in England for the purpose of understanding how the English use their homes and what products they want in them. One of the interviewees, Boyd Chung, expressed his attitudes towards IKEA. 'It is easy to navigate', he said. The IKEA pathway, the line of bossy blue arrows that forces customers through the whole store, is much vilified. This giving of direction is precisely what many customers want. 'My friends and I go there once or twice a month, for recreation, window-shopping, inspiration and to see solutions to our problems,' says Chung. Interviewees in general have implicitly shown their desire to be told by IKEA what they can do with their homes.

Skills Required for Conducting an In-Depth Interview

For in-depth interviewing to be an effective data collection tool, interviewers must have excellent interpersonal communication and listening skills. **Interpersonal communication skills** relate to the interviewer's ability to ask questions in a desired manner so that the subject understands what she or he is expected to respond. **Listening skills** include the ability to accurately hear, record and interpret the subject's responses. Depending on the complexity of the topic and the desired data requirements, most interviewers ask permission from the subject to record the interview using either a tape recorder or possibly a video recorder rather than relying solely on handwritten notes.

Interpersonal communication skills The interviewer's ability to articulate questions in a desired manner.

Listening skills The interviewer's ability to accurately hear, record and interpret the subject's responses.

As mentioned above, without excellent probing skills, the interviewer may inadvertently allow the discussion of a specific topic to end before all the potential data are revealed. **Probing questions** need to be precise and include the subject's previous reply. Interpretive skills relate to the interviewer's ability to accurately understand and record the subject's responses. These skills play a critical role in the process of transforming the actual raw data into usable information. An interviewer's weak interpretive skills will have a negative impact on the quality of the data collected. For example, if the interviewer does not understand the subject's response, he or she is not likely to follow up with a probing question that will move the dialogue where it is intended to move. The resulting data may not be very meaningful to the initial area of inquiry. Finally, the personality of the interviewer plays a significant role in establishing a 'comfort zone' for the subject during the question/answer process. Interviewers should be easygoing, flexible, trustworthy and professional. Respondents who feel at ease with a person are more likely to reveal their hidden attitudes, feelings, motivations and behaviours.

Probing questions Questions that result when an interviewer takes the subject's initial response to a question and uses that response as the framework for the next question (the probing question) in order to gain more detailed responses.

Advantages of In-Depth Interviews

As a qualitative research method, in-depth interviewing offers researchers several benefits. First is flexibility. One-on-one personal interviews enable the researcher to ask questions on a wide variety of topics. The question-and-answer process gives the researcher the flexibility to collect data not only on the subject's activities and behaviour patterns, but also on the attitudes, opinions and motivations that underlie those reported behaviours. Probing questions allow researchers to collect highly detailed data from the subject regarding the topic at hand. Once a certain comfort zone is reached in the interviewer – subject relationship, subjects willingly reveal their inner thinking.

Disadvantages of In-Depth Interviews

Data collected by in-depth interviews is subject to the same general limitations as all qualitative research methods. Although in-depth interviews can generate a lot of detailed data, the findings lack generalizability, reliability, and the ability to distinguish small differences. Inaccurate findings may be caused by the introduction of interviewer – interviewee artifacts (e.g. interviewer illustrates empathy towards the respondent's answers); interviewee errors (e.g. faulty recall, concern with social acceptability, fatigue); or interviewer errors (e.g. inadequate listening, faulty recording procedures, fatigue).

Steps in Conducting an In-Depth Interview

In planning and conducting an in-depth interview, there are a number of logical and formalized steps. Exhibit 6.2 highlights those necessary steps.

EXHIBIT 6.2 Key Steps in Conducting an In-Depth Interview

Steps	Description and Comments
Step 1	**Understand Management's Initial Decision Problems/Questions**
	• Researcher must gain a complete understanding of management's critical initial problem situation and decision questions.
	• Researcher must engage in dialogue with the decision maker that focuses on bringing clarity and understanding of the current problem situation (factors, thoughts, concerns) that have led the decision maker to state their questions.
Step 2	**Create a Set of Appropriate Research Questions**
	• A set of appropriate research questions must be developed that will serve as the 'backbone' of the in-depth interview.
	• Using new-found understanding of the problem situation, the 'how, what, when, where, who, etc.' framing technique, the research questions should directly focus on the major elements of the initial decision problems or questions.
	• The research questions should be arranged using a logical flow from 'general' to 'specific'.
Step 3	**Decide on the Best Environment for Conducting the Interview**
	• Researcher must decide on the best location for the interview, understand the characteristics of the prospective subject and use a relaxed, comfortable interviewing setting.
	• The setting should allow for a private conversation without outside distractions.
Step 4	**Select, Screen and Secure the Prospective Subjects**
	• There is no one 'best' method for selecting potential subjects, but each must be screened to assure they meet some set of specified criteria for being the 'right person' to interview.
	• Decision maker and researcher make a joint decision on the critical qualifying criteria.
	• Sometimes particular demographic and/or behavioural factors are used.
Step 5	**Contact Prospective Subjects, Provide Guidelines and Create Comfort Zone**
	• Researcher (interviewer) meets the subject and provides the appropriate introductory guidelines for the interviewing process.
	• Obtains permission to tape-record the interview.
	• Spends the first few minutes prior to the start of the questioning process creating a 'comfort zone' for the subject, using warm-up questions.
Step 6	**Conduct the In-Depth Interview**
	• Begins the interview by asking the first listed research questions.
	• Using the subject's response to the initial research questions, researcher uses 'probing' questions to obtain as many details from the subject as possible on the topic before moving to the next question.
	• For each listed question, the researcher repeats the probing questioning technique, until the last question is discussed.
	• On completing the interview, thank the subject for participating and provide the predetermined incentives, if any.
Step 7	**Analyse the Subject's Narrative Responses**
	• Researcher begins interpreting the responses of each subject interviewed by either using predetermined classification systems or by using the raw responses to first create a classification system and then go back and code the raw responses.
	• This analysis is very similar to that of a focus group. For more guidelines, go to Exhibit 6.13.
Step 8	**Write a Summary Report of the Results**
	• Whether one or several interviews are conducted, writing up a summary report is very similar to writing a report for a 'focus group.' Refer to Exhibit 6.14 for the guidelines.

Special Types of In-Depth Interview Method

Executive Interview

An **executive interview** is a personal exchange with a business executive that usually takes place in the executive's office. In general, executive interviews focus on collecting primary data concerning the company, its products, and the industry in which it is doing business. Few executives are willing to share business hours to discuss non-business issues or personal preferences with the interviewer.

> **Executive interview** A personal exchange with a business executive usually conducted in his or her office.

Securing an appointment with a business executive can be a time-consuming process, and even then his or her commitment to disclose detailed information can be questionable. This type of interview requires the use of well-trained and experienced interviewers because the topics are often sensitive and highly technical. However, if conducted successfully, executive interviews can provide great insights about the company, its products and the industry.

Experience Interview

An **experience interview** gathers opinions and insights informally from people considered to be knowledgeable on the issues associated with the research problem. For example, if the research problem involves difficulties in purchasing do-it-yourself products online from B&Q, then interviews among dissatisfied online B&Q purchasers can be conducted. If a company like IKEA has a research problem that deals with estimating future demands for its newly created website, the company could begin by contacting several website 'experts' and asking their opinions on the issues concerned.

> **Experience interview** Informal gathering of information from individuals thought to be knowledgeable on the issues relevant to the research problem.

For the most part, experience interviews differ from other types of interviewing approaches in that there is no attempt to ensure that the findings are representative of any overall defined group of subjects. To illustrate this point, let's take a tutor at your university who is asked to teach a marketing research module for the first time. The fundamental research problem here simply deals with which topics should be covered in what detail within a specified time frame. The tutor could contact several other people inside and outside the university who have experience in teaching a marketing research module and ask their opinions about topics and depth of coverage. Although these 'experts' may provide useful information, there is a good chance their opinions and suggestions would differ from the collective thoughts of all people who have experience in teaching marketing research.

Protocol Interview

A **protocol interview** places a person in a specified decision-making situation and asks the person to verbally express the process and activities that are undertaken in making a decision. This technique is useful when the research problem focuses on selected aspects (e.g. motivational or procedural) of making a purchase decision. For example, Dell Computer Company wants to understand the difficulties associated with the various decision criteria customers use when making online purchases of Dell computers. By asking several Dell computer purchasers to verbalize the steps and activities they went through, the researcher is able to work backward and identify the different processes used in making online purchase decisions. This can provide the researcher with insights of those motivational and/or procedural activities that may be potential obstacles keeping other potential customers from making an online purchase from Dell.

> **Protocol interview** The subject is placed in a specified decision-making situation and asked to verbally express the process and activities that he or she would undertake to make a decision.

Articulative Interview

An **articulative interview** focuses on listening for and identifying of key conflicts in a person's orientation values towards products, services or concepts. This interview type gets subjects to articulate their orienting values as well as their inherent conflicts with those values that otherwise might seem inexpressible. An articulative interview is structured to elicit narratives as opposed to gaining factual truths. The interview focuses on uncovering what subjects find worthy and unworthy in their lives; how they live in particular roles and in certain domains of activity. The line of questioning used by an articulative interviewer requires the subjects to express a narrative that incorporates a past-present-future structure of the topic of concern. During the story-telling process, the interviewer raises questions about the parts of the story that were left out that tend to bring out expressions of conflict. By questioning the narrative context, the interviewer encourages subjects to describe how the roles they hold are in conflict resulting in seemingly insoluble dilemmas.

> **Articulative interview** A qualitative-oriented interviewing technique that focuses on the listening for and identifying of key conflicts in a person's orientation values towards products, services or concepts.

In conducting articulative interviews, the researcher must be able to achieve two goals: identify the subjects' orienting values towards the product, service, or concept being investigated and clarify existing value conflicts. To identify subjects' orienting values, the researcher must be able to (1) question the obvious and listen for differences; (2) study the present; (3) know the past; and (4) learn the descriptive vocabulary used by the subjects. For example, researchers studying parents from different cultures and economic classes about their values taught to their children initially found that most parents universally expressed: 'I want what is best for my children. And that is that they 'do well' in life'. By questioning the obvious, it was learned that among parents in middle-class Mexican culture, 'doing well' means visibly achieving the next economic class status, but in low-income Mexican culture, 'doing well' means the children will have their own home without regard to whether it came by good fortune or hard work.

As a result of articulative interviewing, the researcher is able to identify significantly different shadings of 'doing well'. In order to expose a participant's value conflicts, the researcher must be able to (1) listen for confusion, awkwardness, resignations and contradictions among the subjects;

(2) listen for invidious distinctions and self-righteous expressions; (3) identify the roles the subject plays in relation to the product or service category; and (4) elicit defining narratives of life changes.

To illustrate how to elicit defining narratives of life changes, take an example that the researcher was studying female university graduates regarding their orienting value of 'being taken seriously'. When asked to reflect back as university students, many of the subjects thought their future careers would mean everything to them. Being taken seriously meant doing anything to get ahead in a career. But after entering the workforce, a new value arose – being able to live a balanced, quality life. For many, this meant attaining a successful career, having a happy family, engaging in healthy physical activities, and taking vacations. To better understand the changing meaning of 'being taken seriously' and the conflicts of living a quality life, the researcher used follow-up questions such as 'Where do you see your professional lives moving in the future?' 'What do you wish you could keep from the old way of being serious?' 'How does having a family fit in?' and/or 'How do you view yourself in comparison to your mother?'

Projective Techniques

Projective techniques constitute a 'family' of qualitative data collection techniques where participants are asked to project themselves into specified buying situations, and are then asked to elaborate their responses about the situations. The underlying objective is to learn more about the participants in situations where they may not be able or willing to reveal their true thoughts under a direct questioning process. These techniques were initially developed in the motivational area of social and clinical psychology and include word association tests, sentence completion tests, picture tests, thematic apperception tests (TAT), cartoon or balloon tests, and role-playing activities.

> **Projective techniques** An indirect method of questioning that enables a subject to project beliefs and feelings onto a third party, into a task situation, or onto an inanimate object.

 ## A Closer Look at Research *(In the field)*

Using Projective Techniques to Portray the Perceived Image of a Modern Proactive French Woman

To identify cultural factors that might have impacted on the declining market share of Rexona, a major deodorant brand in France, researchers used the projective technique to ask female respondents what they thought of as the attributes possessed by a typical modern French woman. One respondent said:

'*There was a French woman: refined with her clothes, with her perfume, letting her hair float in the wind at the weekend and with a more strict hairdo at work. A dynamic person in regular contact with men who she doesn't have any problem to manage and respect her as an accomplished person. Married and a late mother because finding her place in the work life wasn't easy but once she managed that, her professional and personal relationship were in symbiosis. Sustained by an ever thoughtful husband/partner, her standing increased by him, confident now in that she is 30–35 years. This for me is the life of the ideal typical modern French woman! I think we all try to reach this life … with more or less success.*'

After analysing the quotes from all the respondents projecting their beliefs and feelings onto an ideal typical modern French woman, researchers could conclude that French women see themselves as discreet (natural and simple appearance), holistic about health and well-being, and dynamic (having energy and elegant).

The results helped the researchers conceptualize what a modern proactive French woman is like, and to re-launch the Rexona brand portraying the message that the new Rexona woman is the modern proactive woman.

Source: Printed with permission of Jaroslay Cir (Head of CMI Deodorants Europe, Unilever Personal Care), John Pawle (Managing Director, QiQ International Ltd) and Simon Patterson (Managing Director, CRAM International Ltd).

Word Association Test

In interviews using the **word association test**, a participant is read a word, or a pre-selected set of words or short phrases one at a time, and asked to respond with the first thing that comes to his or her mind regarding that word. For example, what comes to your mind when you hear the word 'red'? Some people may respond with hot; others might say danger, apple, stop, fire engine, or Santa Claus. After completing the list of words, researchers then look for hidden meanings and associations between the responses and the words being tested on the original list. Advertising researchers employ word association tests in efforts to develop a meaningful advertising copy a target market can quickly identify. HSBC, for example, launched an TV advertisement in which people from different parts of the world are being presented with the word 'tree' and then asked a word that first come across their mind. Through playing with this word association technique, a variety of tree-associated words are generated, including paper, nature, oxygen, and home. The purpose of this advertisement is to promote HSBC's image as a corporation determined to go green.

> **Word association test** A projective technique in which the subject is presented with a word, or a list of words or short phrases one at a time, and asked to respond with the first thing that comes to mind.

Sentence Completion Test

In a **sentence completion test**, respondents are given incomplete sentences and asked to complete them in their own words in hopes that the respondents will reveal some hidden aspects about their thoughts and feelings towards the investigated object. From the data collected, researchers interpret the completed sentences to identify meaningful themes or concepts. For example, let's say the local Balti restaurant in your area wants to find out what modifications to its current image are needed to attract a larger portion of the university student market segment. Researchers could interview university students in the area and ask them to complete the following sentences:

People who eat at Balti restaurants are _____.

Balti restaurants remind me of _____.

Balti restaurants are the place to be when _____.

University students go to Balti restaurants to _____.

My friends think Balti restaurants are _____.

> **Sentence completion test** A projective technique where subjects are given a set of incomplete sentences and asked to complete them in their own words.

While the researcher could (and should) separately identify different themes from the data provided from each question, integrating the data could reveal overall themes that might prove more useful in creating a dining experience likely to attract significantly more university students. For example, an interpretation of the data from the first sentence might reveal the theme of 'older, more mature restaurant patrons', suggesting that serious changes would be needed to attract those university students not interested in spending their dining experience in a restaurant setting where mature people eat. The theme for the second sentence might be 'family-oriented', suggesting that Balti restaurants are perceived as an eating establishment that may not appeal to many university students. The next sentence might support a theme of 'great place to take a date', indicating university students think of Balti restaurants as a place to eat dinner when out on a date. Data from the next sentence might suggest the theme of 'a place to hang out with friends'. Here it would be important for the restaurant to make sure its advertisements convey this theme to university students. The final sentence might generate data that supports the theme 'fun atmosphere', indicating that students like going to Balti restaurants when they want to have fun. Now combining the information, Balti restaurants' management will know the university market perceives the restaurant as being an enjoyable place to meet friends or have dinner with a date, but a place that is too family oriented and caters more to non-university patrons.

Picture Test

In a **picture test**, respondents are given a picture and instructed to describe their reactions by writing a short narrative story about the picture. Researchers then interpret the content of the written stories to identify the respondent's positive, neutral, or negative feelings or concerns generated by the picture. Traditionally, this method has proven very useful to advertising agencies testing the impact of pictures for use on product packaging, print advertisements and brochures. For example, a test print advertisement for a Virgin Mobile phone designed to possibly attract more university student consumers depicted a fogged-up back window of a car with the advertisement headline written on the window that said 'Hello lovers: get a hot Virgin Mobile phone for just €29'. A picture test may divulge some aspects about the advertisement that are not as intended by Virgin Mobile's advertising agency. Perhaps some university students might not make the connection because they do not have a significant other or they just went through a tough relationship breakup. Also, the €29 rate may not be seen as a bargain. Regardless of the stories communicated by the respondents, the picture test would be a useful method to assist management at Virgin Mobile in determining the audience's reactions to the advertisement.

> **Picture test** A qualitative interviewing method where subjects are given a picture and asked to describe their reactions by writing a short narrative story about the picture.

Thematic Apperception Test (TAT)

Similar to yet different from the picture test is the **thematic apperception test (TAT).** Instead of asking the participant to write a short story about what a single picture is communicating, the TAT presents participants with a series of pictures where the consumer and/or products/services are the main focus in each picture. Typically there is some level of continuity among the pictures. Participants are asked to provide their descriptive interpretation of what is happening in the pictures or a story about the pictures and what the people may do next. The researcher then conducts a content analysis of the descriptions and stories. The goal is to create interpretable themes based on the descriptions or stories attached to the pictures.

> **Thematic apperception test (TAT)** A specific projective technique that presents the subjects with a series of pictures and asks them to provide a description of or a story about the pictures.

One of the key success factors in using TAT is that pictures or cartoon stimuli must be sufficiently interesting to the participants to induce discussions, yet ambiguous enough not to give away the nature of the research project. It is important that hints not be given to the picture characters' positive or negative predispositions. For example, a designer clothing manufacturer wanting to test the potential of a new pair of jeans having a positive appeal to female university students may use TAT by showing selected females a set of pictures with the first one portraying three university age females at the local department store discussing the jeans. The second picture may show one of the females getting dressed in the jeans and the final picture might have a female dancing in the jeans at a party. After viewing the pictures, participants are asked to provide their interpretation of what is going on in each picture. The researcher then does a content analysis of the descriptions or stories to uncover latent themes that might represent either positive or negative elements of the jeans. While TATs are fun to do, the complexity factor of the picture or stimuli used can cause difficulties in analysis. Insights gained from TAT research can prove useful in better understanding the use of elements in product design, packaging, print advertisements and brochures.

Cartoon or Balloon Test

A **Cartoon (balloon) test** involves the use of cartoons for eliciting respondents' hidden thoughts. Typically, one or two characters are arranged in a setting, sometimes pre-described and at other times ambiguous. Normally the characters themselves are presented in a vague manner, without expression, to ensure the respondent is not given any clues regarding a suggested type of response. The researcher places an empty balloon above one or both of the characters and instructs respondents to write in the balloon(s) what they believe the character(s) are saying. The researcher then interprets these written thoughts to identify the respondent's latent feelings about the situation being portrayed in the cartoon. For example, when shown a cartoon situation of a male and female character in a pet store in which the female is making the statement, 'Here is a multilevel cat condominium on sale for €99', the respondent is asked how the male character in the drawing would respond and asked to write it in the balloon above the male character. After the response is provided, the researcher then uses their interpretive skills to evaluate the respondent's reactions.

> **Cartoon (balloon) test** A qualitative data collection method in which the subject is given a cartoon drawing and suggests the dialogue in which the character(s) might engage.

Role-Playing Activities

In **role-playing activities**, participants are asked to take on the identity of a third person, such as a neighbour or friend, placed in a specific, predetermined situation and then asked to verbalize how they would act in the situation. This participants-as-third-party approach would make the participants less defensive and more likely to expose their true conscious or hidden thoughts.

> **Role-playing activities** Subject is asked to act out someone else's behaviour in a specified setting.

marketing research in action

Using Projective Techniques for E-business Research in Ireland and New Zealand

Worldwide governments are generally in agreement that small and medium-sized enterprises (SMEs) must become involved in e-business for their survival. For example, the European Commission's Go-Digital Initiative (2002) is noted for its 'vision to create highly entrepreneurial and dynamic world class SMEs able to compete effectively in the globalised digital economy'.

However, despite Internet technologies, which enable e-business development, widely renowned as a facilitator for improved business practice, SMEs are not capitalizing on this new mode of conducting business. One main element needed to break down barriers to SMEs' uptake of e-business is support and leadership from government and educators to promote the value of e-business transformation. Realizing the importance of e-business development among SMEs and the role of the government in this development, Ramsey, Ibbotson and McCole (2006) undertook a study to investigate small and medium business owner-managers' perceptions of government support for e-business development in Ireland and New Zealand. These two countries were chosen because they possess similar characteristics in terms of culture, peripheral location and high dependence on small organizations. Also in both countries, despite their respective governments' e-business support initiatives, there is a significant technological lag in the 'level' of e-business activities among SMEs.

The research comprises two stages. Stage one involved an interview with each owner-manager in the sample to understand their current practice with regard to e-business development and solicitation of government support for the development. Altogether 46 owner-managers participated in the interview, with 12 of them from Northern Ireland, 14 from Republic of Ireland and the remaining 20 from New Zealand. Results show that the majority of the sample recognized the importance of employing Internet-based technologies to develop an e-business strategy for enhancing the way they operate. However, few were prepared to seek government support to develop e-business. Indeed, only 5 (2 in Northern Ireland, 2 in Republic of Ireland and 1 in New Zealand) of the sample of 46 had sought support from government sources.

In stage two of the research, projective techniques were used to uncover the owner-managers' perceptions of various issues affecting their decision on e-business development. While one-on-one interviews and focus groups are the usual settings in which projective techniques are applied, this research decided to administer the projective technique via post. This is because the owner-manager participants are generally time-poor and less able to go through a projective session in person. By contrast, the postal mode would be less intrusive and therefore provide participants with the alternative to complete the tests at a time convenient to them. Perhaps the best evidence for the use of the postal mode is the subsequent satisfactory response rate of 65 per cent, with 7 from Northern Ireland, 9 from Republic of Ireland and 14 from New Zealand.

Intent on building rigour into the analysis and interpretation of the data collated from the projective tests, both content analysis and the modified matrix technique were used to map and analyse the responses. Mapping the responses involved three steps. First is concept identification, with content analysis being utilized as a surfacing technique to search the responses for frequency of word usage. Step two is link description where concepts that are related are linked. The last

EXHIBIT 6.3 Descriptors of Repertory Cause-and-Effect Grid Variables

Grid Variable	Description
Innovation	Level of innovation propensity
Commitment	Owner-managers' commitment to Internet-based technologies
Resources	Financial ability to adopt and maintain Internet-based technologies
Government	Propensity to seek government support such as in finances and training initiatives
Technical	Level of technical competence
Product	New product development opportunities
Competition	Attitudes towards the threat of competition in the e-business environment
Uncertainty	Perception of risk in the business/e-business environment

step is property clarification – that is, the researcher looks at each concept and relationships that are linked to it and then explains the meaning of the concepts.

Next the modified matrix technique was used to uncover cause and effect beliefs that may influence perceptions and behaviour associated with the research problem. The half-grid approach was deemed more advantageous than a 2 x 2 approach as it reduces the number of times a relationship needs to be considered. A causal grid was created in which variables were listed in rows and columns. A '0' (zero) was entered if there was no relationship between the row variables and the column variables; an 'A' if the row variable caused a change in the column variable or a 'B' if the column variable caused a change in the row variable. Direction of the causal relationship would also be indicated with a '+' for a positive causal relationship and a '–' if it was a negative causal relationship. The variables listed in the grid below were drawn from the projective tests.

Maps for individual respondents were combined to depict an overall picture representing the sample. The main focus of the analysis is the calculation of an outdegree and an indegree score for each variable in the grid. The outdegree score is calculated to ascertain the number of paths leading from each variable in the grid. The higher the outdegree score the more a variable is seen to cause changes in the other variables. The indegree score measures how much a variable is influenced by other variables and is relative to the number of paths leading to a particular variable from other variables. A higher indegree score indicates that a variable is seen predominantly as an outcome or effect of changes in the other variables. The indegree and outdegree scores were then obtained by totalling the values in columns and rows, respectively, and their ranks were assigned.

The aggregated responses gleaned from the projective techniques, as shown in Exhibit 6.4, confirm that the variable government support has the lowest-ranking outdegree score of 2.57, from which it is inferred that government support is least likely to cause change in the e-business decisions of owner-managers. It is also inferred that, while technical skills ability is perceived by a majority of participants as being caused by the propensity to seek government support (0.70), the uncertainty (perception of risk) associated with e-business causes an increase in the propensity to seek government support (0.73), and appropriate resources (financial) fundamentally cause technical skills ability to increase (0.83), these factors have not, in practice, caused the

EXHIBIT 6.4 **Causal Relationships as Perceived by the Sample and Indegree and Outdegree Scores**

	Innovation	Commitment	Resources	Government	Technical	Product	Competition	Uncertainty	Outdegree Score	Rank
Innovation	0.00	0.75	0.35	0.60	0.30	0.73	0.58	−0.40	2.91	7
Commitment	0.80	0.00	−0.45	0.35	0.16	0.73	0.28	0.80	3.25	4
Resources	0.30	0.63	0.00	0.44	0.83	0.46	0.70	0.50	3.86	2
Government	0.40	0.12	−0.40	0.00	0.70	0.60	0.52	0.63	2.57	8
Technical	0.20	0.64	0.50	0.45	0.00	0.36	0.58	0.63	3.08	6
Product	0.50	0.33	0.85	0.60	0.45	0.00	−0.20	0.70	3.23	5
Competition	0.54	0.50	0.74	0.20	0.60	0.90	0.00	0.25	3.73	3
Uncertainty	0.93	0.72	0.60	0.73	0.60	0.13	0.30	0.00	4.41	1
Indegree Score	3.67	3.69	2.19	3.27	3.64	3.91	3.16	2.83		
Rank	3	2	8	5	4	1	6	7		

Numbers in cells indicate proportion that agreed; '−' indicates a negative relationship.

majority of these SMEs to seek government support. In fact, a negative relationship has been found between government support and resources (−0.40) and implies that funding for e-business from government sources does not cause SMEs to seek it.

The reasons for the aggregated scores discussed here are closely related to owner-managers' perceptions of the type of support that can be provided. This information on perceptions was captured through the word association test, which asked them to consider their respective governments' current supporting roles in providing them with information and practical help about how to develop an e-business. The word association tests included both positive and negative associations relative to perceptions of current e-business support, and consisted of words such as generalized, irrelevant, useful, complicated, patronizing and brilliant, with the option given to participants to add more appropriate words. The word association test resulted in 82 per cent of participants associating negative words with the level of help and support provided by governments. The most used associations were 'generalized', 'simplistic' and 'patronizing'.

Additionally the completion test was utilized to establish how the owner-managers perceive government bodies could be of better support to them in their existing and future e-business developments. The speech bubble of the government representative was completed and the following scenario accompanied the completion test.

SMEs may need support from public institutions to accelerate their uptake of Internet-based technologies.

Participants were then asked to consider the illustrations below and fill in the bubbles to depict what they thought the person was saying and thinking in response to the government representative.

Figure 6a: Government support completion test (present)

Figure 6b: Government support completion test (future)

The responses from the completion tests led to several issues being highlighted. These include SME e-business policy formation and information dissemination, e-business funding applications, a lack of trust in the judgement of government bodies and entrepreneurial bravado. Detailed analysis of these issues can be found in the article written by Ramsey et al. (2006) in Issue 5 of the *International Journal of Market Research*. For now you should be able to see that by combining the outcomes of the modified matrix with the qualitative responses achieved from the word association and completion tests, the various issues of concern were further reinforced and clarified.

Questions

1 Based on what you understand from this case study, to what extent did the choice of the research approach contribute to the success of this e-business research project?

2 What would be the other research approach that could also be appropriate for this research project? Compare and contrast the approach that you suggest and the approach that Ramsey, Ibbotson and McCole adopted?

Summary of Learning Objectives

■ **Understand the purposes behind the use of the in-depth interview method and the projective techniques.**
In-depth interviewing is a formal process in which a trained interviewer asks a subject a set of predetermined and probing questions usually in a face-to-face setting. This method can be used for a number of purposes, such as (1) to gain preliminary insights into what the subject thinks or believes about the topic of concern or why the subject exhibits certain behaviours; (2) to obtain unrestricted and detailed comments revealing feelings, opinions or beliefs that can help the interviewer better understand the different elements of the subject's thoughts and the reasons they exist; and (3) to have the respondent communicate as much detail as possible about their knowledge and behaviour towards a given topic or object. Successful implementation of this method depends heavily on the interviewer's interpersonal communication skills and listening skills.

In projective techniques, participants are asked to project themselves into specified situations, and are then asked to elaborate their responses about the situations. The underlying purpose is to learn more about the participants in situations where they may not be able or willing to reveal their true thoughts under a direct questioning process.

■ **Illustrate the advantages and disadvantages of the in-depth interview method.**
In-depth interviewing is renowned for its flexibility, capability to collect highly detailed data and potential to probe into the inner thinking of the interviewees. However, the method suffers from a lack of generalizability and reliability. It is also regarded as being less able to distinguish small differences. Sometimes the findings may even be inaccurate because of interviewer- or interviewee-induced errors.

■ **Identify the steps required to conduct an in-depth interview.**
There are eight typical steps involved in conducting an in-depth interview. They are (1) understanding management's initial decision problems/questions; (2) creating a set of appropriate research questions; (3) deciding on the best environment for conducting the interview; (4) selecting, screening and securing the prospective subjects; (5) contacting

prospective subjects, providing guidelines and creating a comfort zone; (6) conducting the in-depth interview; (7) analysing the subject's narrative responses; and (8) writing a summary report of the results.

- **Describe the different special types of the in-depth interview method as well as the different types of projective techniques.**

Four special types of in-depth interviewing were introduced in this chapter. In an executive interview, there is a personal exchange with a business executive usually conducted in their office. In an experience interview, the interviewer informally gathers information from individuals thought to be knowledgeable on the issues relevant to the research problem. To conduct a protocol interview, the subject is placed in a specified decision-making situation and asked to verbally express the process and activities that they would undertake to make a decision. An articulative interview focuses on the listening for and identifying of key conflicts in a person's orientation values towards products, services or concepts.

There are six types of projective techniques. In a word association test, the subject is presented with a word, or a list of words or short phrases one at a time and asked to respond with the first thing that comes to mind. In a sentence completion test, subjects are given a set of incomplete sentences and asked to complete them in their own words. In a picture test, a picture is given to the subject, who is asked to describe their reactions by writing a short narrative story about the picture. In a thematic apperception test, subjects are presented with a series of pictures and are then asked to provide a description of or a story about the pictures. In a cartoon (balloon) test, the subject is given a cartoon drawing and suggests the dialogue in which the character(s) might engage. In role playing activities, the subject is asked to act out someone else's behaviour in a specified setting.

Key Terms and Concepts

Articulative interview 211	Probing questions 208
Cartoon (balloon) test 215	Projective techniques 212
Executive interview 210	Protocol interview 211
Experience interview 210	Role-playing activities 215
In-depth interview 205	Sentence completion test 213
Interpersonal communication skills 208	Thematic apperception test (TAT) 214
Listening skills 208	Word association test 213
Picture test 214	

Review Questions

1. Compare and contrast the unique characteristics, main research objectives and advantages/disadvantages of the focus group and in-depth interviewing techniques.

2. What are the main differences between articulative interviews and in-depth interviews?

3. Develop a word association test that will provide some insight into the following research question: 'What are the students' perceptions of their university's student union?'

1   What type of exploratory research design (focus group, in-depth interview, observation, projective interview) would you suggest for each of the following situations and why?

   a   The research and development director at Calvin Klein suggests a new type of cologne for men that could be promoted by a sports celebrity like Michael Jordan.

   b   The manager of university accommodation services at your university proposes some significant changes to the physical configuration of the current rooms for students.

   c   The management of B&Q must decide on the best location for a new store in your home town.

   d   The senior design engineer for Fiat wishes to identify the most appropriate design changes to be integrated into the next generation of their automotives.

   e   The general manager at Nando Chickenland wishes to offer customers two 'new and exciting' menu items that would be a blend of chicken, spicy herbs and lemon.

   f   A retail supermarket manager would like to know the popularity of a new brand of cereal produced by Kellogg's.

2   Beefeater restaurant is concerned about the shifting attitudes and feelings of the public towards the consumption of red meat. Its owner thinks that the 'red meat' issues are not that important because his restaurant also serves fish and chicken meals. Select any two 'projective interviewing' techniques that you feel would be appropriate in collecting data for the above situation. First, defend your choice of each of your selected projective interviewing techniques. Second, describe in detail how each of your two chosen techniques would be applied to Beefeater's research problem at hand.

3   Refer to Jimmy Spice's restaurant case first presented at the end of Chapter 1. In their quest for better understanding consumers' attitudes and feelings towards casual dining-out experiences, the owner of Jimmy Spice's restaurant asked two important questions: (1) Do specific restaurant features differ in importance to consumers when deciding where to go for their casual dining? (2) Do consumers in general prefer dining out in a festive atmosphere or a quiet, romantic restaurant one? Using your understanding of the in-depth interviewing method, develop and execute a 45-minute in-depth interview that will allow you to capture the necessary information for answering the owner's two questions. After completing the interview, analyse your data and write a one- or two-page summary report that answers the owner's two questions.

Chapter 7

Quantitative Research Methods: Survey

LEARNING OBJECTIVES

After reading this chapter, you will be able to

☑ Explain the advantages and disadvantages of the survey method to collect primary data.

☑ Discuss the many types of survey method available to researchers. Identify and discuss the factors that drive the choice of different types of survey method.

☑ Explain how the electronic revolution is affecting the administration of survey research.

☑ Identify and describe the strengths and weaknesses of each type of survey method.

☑ Identify and explain the types of errors that can occur in survey research.

"
Consumer Market Tracker survey has proven to be a very efficient and complete tool to evaluate our performance in different parts of the world. It is helping us to have a global view of our business and, at the same time, to look at the local specific issues.
–Riccardo Brenna
Head of Research and Intelligence, Sony Ericsson
"

The Sony Ericsson Mobile Phone Market Study

Sony Ericsson, the joint venture of two high tech giants, necessitates continuous research to track the development of the Sony Ericsson brand, alongside the marketing investment made (e.g. advertising expenditure), in a very competitive and fast-evolving industry.

Additionally, since the 2000s, the mobile phone industry has been changing its focus: instead of selling handsets to first-time buyers, the majority of sales are now repeat buyers with more demanding requirements and higher expectations. In fact, the mobile phone replacement market now accounts for more than 50 per cent of purchases globally (around 250 million phones). Sony Ericsson needs market insight on how the renewal rate was evolving so that market forecast could be as accurate as possible.

Furthermore, with technology advancing alongside user sophistication, Sony Ericsson needs to monitor customer perceptions of mobile phone technological development, such as image, gaming, connectivity and convergence. To be successful, the brand needs to differentiate itself from other competitors and own its profitable territory. Sony Ericsson's international reach also means that it requires consistent, credible, meaningful and timely indexes on a global, regional and local level.

Against this backdrop of information requirement, Sony Ericsson cooperates with TNS to conduct continuous, large-scale and multi-country survey.

The overall objectives of the study are to:

- Generate company-wide performance indicators for brand health and identify the strengths and weaknesses of the Sony Ericsson brand in comparison to its competitors at global, regional and local market levels;
- Provide full visibility on market development and buying/renewal trends to facilitate market forecasting; and
- Monitor and review advertising effectiveness and changes in brand share over time to inform sales forecasting.

To achieve the above objectives, TNS conducts a questionnaire survey on more than 3,500 consumers across fourteen countries. These a multi-country samples can be used to represent their corresponding individual countries, and collectively can be largely representative of the global mobile phone population.

Telephoning is the most commonly used approach in most of the countries involved in this study. However, in countries where telephone penetration is low, the face-to-face approach is used. Random-route-sampling specific to each country is used to obtain a representative sample of the total population.

To maintain accuracy but minimize the time involved in data checking, a bespoke online editing tool, Webeditor, has been developed. Using this, local agencies are able to submit data to a centrally maintained checking programme. Only once the data has successfully passed this check is it forwarded to the central team for processing.

To further reduce the lead time from surveying to reporting, TNS uses its analysis and reporting platform, WEbMiriad, which enables the development of template research reports that are tailed to local and regional markets. When new monthly data is input all reports are automatically updated with the most recent results. This system means that local and regional reports can be accessed within one week following the completion of the fieldwork. With the inclusion of re-formatted back data from the Ericsson brand tracing study, trends for both the company and its competitors can be viewed back to the beginning of 1999.

Results of this study have been encouraging. They have been well communicated and are used throughout the company. Examples of use include the following:

- The results are used for annual target setting within the company;
- The results are used in customer presentations, boards meetings and employee meetings to show the development of the brand;

- The results of advertising campaigns around the world are measured through the study;
- The continuous research findings play an important role in forecasting;
- Correspondence analysis and key driver analysis have been used to understand more about the brand image and reasons for purchase of the main brands in the market.

Source: Research Magazine, News Archive, www.research-live.com

Value of Survey Method

The real-world chapter opener shows that sometimes the research problem requires primary data that can only be gathered by questioning a large number of respondents who are representative of the defined target population. Survey research can play an important role in providing the necessary information to guide a firm's development of new marketing strategies.

We begin this chapter by discussing the interrelatedness of the descriptive research design and the survey method. Then we provide an overview of the method and its main objectives. The next section examines the various types of survey method in more detail. This is followed by a discussion of factors in selecting among different types of survey method. The remainder of the chapter deals with types of errors common in survey research.

Interrelatedness of Descriptive Research Design and Survey Method

Before we discuss the methods employed in conducting descriptive research, it is necessary to understand the interrelationships among descriptive research design, quantitative research methods and survey method as well as how researchers interchange these concepts in their efforts to collect primary data. First, determination of whether the research design should be descriptive is based on three factors: (1) the nature of the initial decision problem/opportunity; (2) the set of research questions; and (3) the research objectives. When the nature of the initial research problem/ opportunity is either to describe specific characteristics of existing market situations or to evaluate current marketing mix strategies, then descriptive research design is an appropriate choice. Second, if the management's research questions focus on issues such as the who, what, where, when, and how elements of target populations or market structures, then a descriptive research design may be appropriate. Finally, if the task is to identify meaningful relationships, determine whether true differences exist, or verify the validity of relationships between the marketing phenomena, then descriptive research designs should be considered. Keep in mind that these factors do not by themselves automatically determine the need to use descriptive research designs.

Researchers must also give consideration to the quantitative aspects associated with descriptive research designs. Quantitative research practices are driven by the need to collect information from enough members of the target population so that accurate inferences can be made about the market factors and phenomena under investigation. Most researchers believe that descriptive research designs are for the most part quantitative in nature.

The final element in determining the use of descriptive research designs focuses on how to collect the primary data. There are two basic approaches to collecting primary data – and asking questions and observation. Although these approaches are used in any type of research design (exploratory, descriptive, causal), descriptive designs more frequently use data collection procedures that heavily emphasize asking respondents structured questions about what they think, feel, and do rather than observing what they do. In this sense, descriptive research designs can often be viewed as survey research methods for collecting quantitative data from large groups of people through the question/answer process.

Overview of Survey Method

Marketing researchers can survey respondents, observe behaviours, or conduct experiments. **Survey method** is the mainstay of marketing research in general and is typically associated with descriptive and causal research situations. One of the distinguishing features of survey research methods is the need to collect data from large groups of people (e.g. 200 or more). This size factor necessitates the use of 'bi-directional communication practices,' which means that individuals are asked questions and their responses are recorded in a structured, precise manner. Most marketing research is conducted through one or more of the various types of survey method.

Survey method Research procedures for collecting large amounts of raw data using question-and-answer formats.

Success in collecting primary data is more a function of correctly designing and administering a survey questionnaire than of relying on the communication and interpretive skills of an interviewer or observer. The main goal of quantitative survey research methods is to provide specific facts and estimates – from a large, representative sample of respondents – that decision makers can use to (1) more or less accurately understand the market phenomena concerned; and (2) identify possible relationships between market factors and behaviours of interested parties, who can be customers, consumers, or firms.

Survey research focuses on collecting data that enable the researcher to understand and resolve marketing problems. The advantages and disadvantages of survey research methods are summarized in Exhibit 7.1 and discussed more fully in the following sections.

Advantages of Survey Method

One major advantage of surveys is their ability to accommodate large sample sizes at relatively low costs. When implemented correctly, the data obtained from the survey method can increase the researcher's ability to make inferences about the target population as a whole. Moreover, the data can be analysed in many different ways based on the diversity of the variables. For example, data can be analysed according to gender, occupation, income, or any other relevant variable included in the survey. The analysis can also be based on multiple variables. For example, an analysis of product purchasing behaviours among households headed by female single parents in the northeast can be compared to the behaviours among households headed by female single parents in the southeast to reveal small differences in regional preferences that may not be apparent in simpler data analysis approaches. Thus, another factor in favour of surveys is they collect quantitative data that can be used with advanced statistical analysis to identify hidden patterns and trends in the data.

EXHIBIT 7.1 Advantages and Disadvantages of Survey Method

Advantages

- Can accommodate large sample sizes and generalize the results
- Can distinguish small differences
- Ability to use advanced statistical analysis
- Relative ease of administering and recording questions and answers
- Facilitate collection of standardized common data
- Factors and relationships not directly observable can be studied
- Cover all potential time frames

Disadvantages

- Potential difficulty in developing appropriate survey design
- Limit to the in-depth detail of data
- Limited control over timeliness
- Potentially low response rate
- Respondents may not be responding truthfully
- Inappropriate use of statistical techniques and misinterpretation of data

---

Another major advantage of surveys is their ease of administration. Most surveys are fairly easy to implement because there is no absolute need for sophisticated devices to record actions and reactions, as compared to observations or experiments. Surveys facilitate the collection of standardized common data since all respondents give answers to the same questions and have the same set of responses available to them. This allows direct comparisons between respondents.

A final advantage of surveys is their ability to tap into factors that are not directly observable (e.g. attitudes, feelings, preferences). Through both direct and indirect questioning techniques, people can be asked why they prefer, say, one package design over another. Predetermined questions determine what thought process a customer used to select a particular brand or how many brands were considered. Observation, for example, would show only that an individual selected a particular brand. Survey research methods enable the researcher to collect many different types of data and all potential time frames (i.e. the past, the present and the future).

Disadvantages of Survey Method

While quantitative research holds distinct advantages over qualitative exploratory research, the survey method is not without problems. Implementation is fairly easy, but developing the appropriate survey design for a particular study can be very difficult. To ensure precision, the researcher must resolve a variety of issues associated with construct development, scale measurements and questionnaire designs. Inappropriate treatment of these issues can produce many kinds of errors in survey findings. As the possibility of systematic error increases, so does the likelihood of collecting irrelevant or poor quality data. The development, measurement and design issues associated with surveys are discussed in Chapters 11, 12 and 13.

A second potential disadvantage of survey research methods relates to their limited use of probing questions. In general, surveys limit the use of extensive probing by the interviewer and rarely use unstructured or open-ended questions. Consequently, the data may lack the detail the researcher needs to address the initial research problems. A third disadvantage of surveys is the lack of control researchers have over their timeliness. Depending on the administration techniques, surveys can take significantly longer to complete than other methods. In direct mail surveys, for example, the researcher must carefully develop a questionnaire packet, disseminate the packets and wait for them to be returned via the postal service. The researcher can only estimate how long it will take the postal service to actually get the questionnaire packet to each selected respondent, how long the respondents will take to complete the survey, and how long it will take the postal service to return the packets. In reality, the researcher loses control of the process as soon as the questionnaire packets are given to the postal service. While the researcher may estimate that the process will take 14 days to complete, direct mail surveys can take far longer than the initial estimate. Getting the surveys out and back within a reasonable amount of time remains a great challenge for researchers using direct mail surveys. Associated with the problem of response time is the problem of guaranteeing a high response rate. As new data collection technologies emerge, the timeliness disadvantage will be reduced, but the response rate may not be much improved.

A fourth disadvantage of survey designs is that it can be difficult to know whether the selected respondents are being truthful. This difficulty varies depending on the actual method employed by the researcher. For example, in designs that incorporate a trained interviewer in a face-to-face communication process (e.g. personal in-home or shopping-intercept surveys) this problem is minimal since the interviewer can either observe facial expressions and other body language of the respondent or use probing techniques to judge the credibility of the answers. In contrast, in self-administered surveys (e.g. mail, fully automatic computer-assisted surveys, Internet surveys) truthfulness becomes a greater concern. Finally, although surveys are designed to collect quantitative data, the statistical techniques selected may introduce subtle levels of subjectivity to interpretation of data. Such subjectivity may not be as apparent in survey research as it is in qualitative research.

Types of Error in Survey Method

Before discussing the appropriate quantitative research methods and the types of descriptive research designs, it is important to understand the types of errors that can occur in any survey. Errors (also referred to as bias) and their sources can quickly reduce the accuracy and quality of the data the researcher collects. To select the best marketing strategy, decision makers must assess the overall accuracy of the research results being provided by the researcher. In any research design, whether qualitative or quantitative, numerous opportunities exist for careless researchers to let in errors. This is particularly true with survey designs.

Potential survey research errors can be classified as being either *sampling error* or *non-sampling error*. Exhibit 7.2 provides an overview of the various forms of survey errors researchers must be aware of and attempt to either reduce or at least control.

Sampling Error

Any survey design that involves collecting primary data from a sample will have a certain amount of error due to random fluctuations in the data. In simple terms, sampling error is the statistically measured difference between the actual random sample results and the true population results. With appropriate sampling approaches, this type of error is reduced by increasing the sample size. Sampling error is discussed in Chapters 9 and 10.

EXHIBIT 7.2 Types of Error

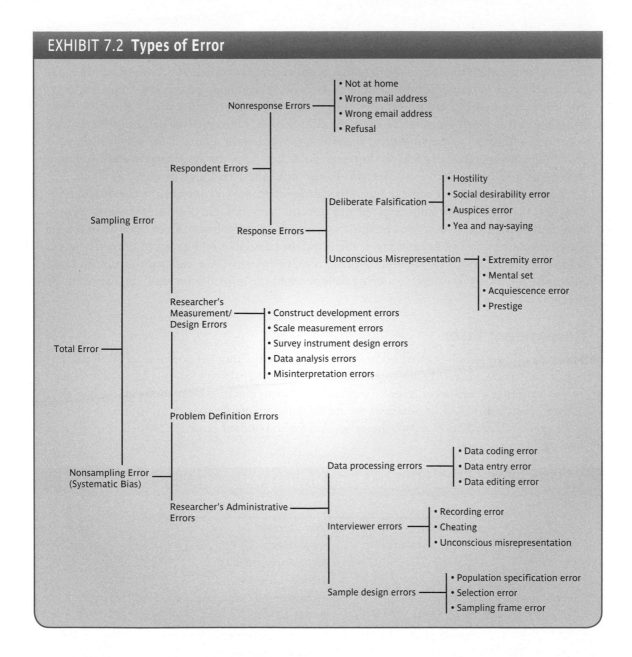

Non-Sampling Error

The counterpart to sampling error is non-sampling error. **Non-sampling error** represents all errors that can enter the survey design that are not directly related to the sampling technique used or sample size. Most types of non-sampling error can be traced back to four major sources: respondent errors, measurement/design errors, faulty problem definition and project administration errors.

> **Non-sampling error** All errors that can enter the survey design that are not directly related to the sampling method or sample size.

Regardless of the type of survey method used to collect primary data, there are several common characteristics among all types of non-sampling error. First, they tend to create some form of 'systematic variation' in the data that is not considered a natural occurrence or fluctuation on the part of the surveyed respondents. Hence non-sampling error is also termed systematic error. Systematic variations usually result from imperfections in the survey design or from mistakes in the execution of the research process. Second, non-sampling error is the result of some type of human mishap in either the design or execution of a survey. The responsibility for reducing non-sampling error falls on the researcher and requires that a set of controls be imposed during the design and execution processes of any type of survey research project.

Third, unlike sampling error that can be clearly identified and statistically measured, non-sampling error cannot be fully detected and directly measured. Finally, non-sampling error is interactive in nature. One type of error can potentially allow other types of error to enter the data collection process. For example, if the researcher designs a bad questionnaire, this questionnaire design error can potentially cause respondent error. Overall, non-sampling error lowers the quality level of the data being collected and the information being provided to the decision maker.

Respondent Error

This type of non-sampling error occurs when respondents either cannot be reached to participate in the survey process, do not cooperate, are unwilling to participate in the survey's question/answer exchange activities, or respond incorrectly or in an unnatural way to the questions asked in the survey. Exhibit 7.3 summarizes the major components that lead to respondent error in survey research practices. The two major sources for respondent error are termed *non-response error* and *response error*.

EXHIBIT 7.3 Types of Respondent Error in Survey Research

Type of Errors	Error Sources
Non-response error	Not at home
	Wrong mailing address
	Wrong email address
	Wrong/changed telephone number
	Refusal
Response error	Deliberate falsification:
	Feeling of hostility
	Social desirability
	Prestige imaging
	Auspices errors
	Yea and nay-saying
	Unconscious misrepresentation:
	Mental set errors
	Extremity errors
	Acquiescence errors
	Prestige

Non-response Error

Non-response error is a systematic bias that occurs when the final sample differs from the planned sample. This situation is likely to occur when a sufficient number of the preselected prospective respondents in the sample cannot be reached for participation. The major reasons for this type of error are not at home, wrong mailing address, wrong email address, and/or wrong/changed telephone numbers. Non-response error can also be caused when a sufficient number of the initial sampled respondents refuse to participate. No matter the cause, non-response errors can severely limit the generalizability of the findings. In addition, non-response errors can occur when individuals who do not respond have significantly different feelings and/or characteristics from those who do respond. When the non-response rate is high, the risk of biased results is increased. People choose to participate in a survey for a variety of reasons including social rewards, monetary incentives, boredom, or sometimes just for the experience.

> **Non-response error** A systematic bias that occurs when the final sample differs from the planned sample.

Non-response is caused by many factors. Some people do not trust the research sponsor and/or have little commitment towards responding, some prospective respondents resent what is perceived as an invasion of privacy, or the subject matter may be too sensitive. The differences between people who do and who do not respond can be striking. For example, some research has shown that for mail surveys, where the response rate tends to be lower than most other primary data collection methods, respondents tend to be more educated than non-respondents and have higher scores on other related variables such as income. In addition, respondents are more likely to be female. The effect of other sociodemographic variables is not well understood. But no matter what the data collection method, community size, gender, age, education and income of those who respond to second- and third-wave solicitations are different from nonrespondents.

To reduce the non-response rate, researchers attempt to be less intrusive on the respondent's life. Other practices for improving response rates include multiple callbacks, mailing waves, building credibility of the research sponsor and shorter questionnaires. Exhibit 7.4 further illustrates the impact of non-responses and some methods to improve survey response rates.

Response Error

When the researcher asks questions, one mechanism on the part of respondents begins operating. This is about the respondents searching their memory, retrieving their behavioural recollections and providing them as their response. If this doesn't happen automatically probably due to the respondents getting tired, or if respondents aren't motivated to search their memory probably because there may not be a good rapport with the interviewer, the responses may be biased in some manner. For example, the respondents may simply guess or just give a false response which fits either their ego or what the society deems desirable or what the interviewer wants to hear.

The human memory is also a source of response bias. People can have impaired memory and be unable to respond accurately. This is termed *faulty recall*. If the questions relate to a new attitude, the respondent may answer on the basis of some combination of short-term memory and the context of the question. Human memory is an inexact thing. It is subject to telescoping, selective perception and the compression of time, such that respondents may think they recall things that happened

EXHIBIT 7.4 Impact of Non-response Error

Two important points can be drawn from the discussion of non-response error:

1 Non-response error can occur even if there is no sampling frame error. Even selecting a probability sample from a representative sampling frame cannot guarantee there will be no non-response error.

2 Non-response error depends on the composition of the final sample compared to the planned sample. Remember, a response rate of less than 100 per cent does not automatically imply there is non-response error.

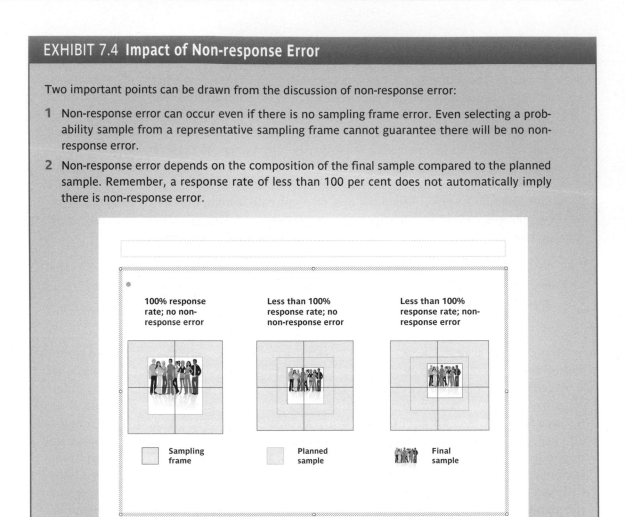

when they actually do not. Another memory problem is termed *averaging*. Averaging refers to assuming the norm behaviour or belief to be the actuality. For example, a person who commonly has fried chicken for Sunday dinner may be unable to recall that last week's Sunday dinner was a roast.

Researchers have found that measurement of the time between when a question is asked and the response is given is one technique that is useful to evaluate response bias. Responses that are expressed very fast and those that are given slowly may be biased. Fast response is indicative of a hurried response or a simple information request, while slow response is indicative of a question that the respondent may have difficulty in answering or one that the respondent is doubtful whether he should answer honestly.

Measurement and Design Error

In addition to respondent errors, researchers and decision makers must recognize that the quality of data can suffer from problems of bias resulting from inappropriate design of the constructs, scale measurements, and the survey questionnaire. Bias makes getting meaningful results from

EXHIBIT 7.5 Types of Measurement and Design Errors in Survey Research Methods

Type of Errors	Error Sources
Construct development error	Incomplete construct
	Low reliability of construct
	Low construct validity
Scale measurement error	Lack of precision
	Lack of discriminatory power
	Ambiguity of question
	Inappropriate use of scale descriptors
Survey instrument error	Inappropriate questionnaire design
	Leading question
	Improper sequence of questions
Data analysis error	Inappropriate analysis technique
	Predictive bias
Misinterpretation error	Interpretive bias
	Selective perception

the data problematic. Exhibit 7.5 summarizes the five major sources of measurement and design bias researchers must understand and attempt to reduce or control to enhance the collection of high quality data.

Construct Development Error

In any survey design, researchers must identify the different data requirements (i.e. concepts, objects, topics, etc.) that form the focus of the investigation. Non-sampling error can be introduced to the survey design when researchers are not careful in identifying the constructs to be used in the study. When critical constructs are not completely defined, for example, there is a strong likelihood that problems of inappropriate dimensionality will occur resulting in under-identifying the subcomponents that make up the construct. When data requirements are not fully developed, data quality, reliability, validity and ability to make generalizations about the defined target population become problematic.

Scale Measurement Error

Another area where non-sampling error can be introduced is in the process of creating the scale measurements used to collect data from groups of respondents. Once the constructs are identified, the researcher must create the appropriate scale measurements attached to those constructs. Measurement errors could be created through either the design of inappropriate questions, scale attributes, or scale point descriptors used to collect respondents' answers. In the design process, researchers must control for errors that might result from (1) a lack of precision in the measurement; (2) a lack of discriminatory power among the scale descriptors; (3) ambiguity of the scale's questions; or (4) use of inappropriate scale descriptors. These types of bias sources will negatively impact the reliability and validity of the data.

Survey Instrument Error

The survey instrument may induce some tainting of the data in several ways. Instrument bias can result from many things related to questionnaire design and the context in which the questions themselves are interpreted. In many cases, instrument bias is a result of leading questions – ones that suggest an appropriate answer. Leading questions put words in a respondent's mouth rather than drawing out what the respondent actually thinks. For example, asking a respondent 'Why do you think this is a high quality product?' encourages only positive responses. Leading questions do not encourage respondents to give their true feelings about the topic being investigated. Very often, leading questions elicit the responses we want to hear. While careful design of the individual measurements can reduce bias, it does not guarantee it. For example, improper sequencing of scale measurements used to make up a questionnaire can create systematic errors that are not directly related to scale measurement problems.

Data Analysis Error

One of the greatest types of non-sampling error is selecting an inappropriate analysis procedure. Incorrect statistical estimates invalidate the researcher's ability to test relationships between important factors. The researcher may also use an unsuitable analytical method that leads to wrong direction (e.g. from positive to negative) or magnitude of the coefficients for predictive purpose.

Misinterpretation Error

The two main bias sources are *interpretive bias* and *selective perception error*. First, interpretive bias is created when the wrong inference is made by the researcher about the real world or target population due to some type of extraneous factor. For example, the researcher might present the results in such a way that the findings appear to support the initial thoughts of the researcher. Selective perception error occurs in situations where the researcher uses only a selected portion of the survey results to give support to a tainted picture of reality. For example, leaders in the tobacco industry for years manipulated test results to hide the truth about the extent of harmful effects of nicotine as an ingredient in cigarettes.

Faulty Problem Definition Error

Survey research, like any other type of research methodology, can easily suffer when the initial problem situation and/or its corresponding research questions are not clearly or correctly identified. In these situations, *faulty problem definition error* occurs. The main causes that create faulty problem definition error are (1) lack of understanding of the real problem; (2) misinterpreting market performance factors (e.g. decrease in sales revenues) as being the problem rather than the symptom; or (3) the researcher inaccurately transforming the problem into research questions. Regardless of the cause, incorrectly defining the problems will make survey research results useless. For example, let's say the product manager for Nike requests a study to test the best media mix for athletic shoes. If the true problem is the company's pricing strategies, then any research conducted, no matter how technically correct, will not be helpful to the company.

Researcher's Administrative Error

In survey research, administrative error occurs from improper execution of the steps involved in gathering and processing data. In Exhibit 7.6, administrative errors are grouped into three basic sources: data processing error, interviewer error and sample design error.

EXHIBIT 7.6 Types of Administrative Error in Survey Research

Type of Errors	Error Sources
Data processing error	Data coding error
	Data entry error
	Data editing error
Interviewer error	Unconscious misrepresentation
	Cheating
	Recording error
Sample design error	Population specification error
	Sample selection error
	Sampling frame error

Data Processing Error

Non-sampling error that occurs in data processing is characterized as being either data *coding*, *entry*, and/or *editing* in nature. In any type of survey research method, the accuracy of data processed by computers can be compromised by mistreatment of any of these human activities. For example, coding error occurs when a person incorrectly assigns a computer code to a response. In turn, data entry error occurs when those codes are incorrectly entered into their designated column in the computer's data file. Editing error results from careless verifying procedures. These types or error can be minimized by establishing and implementing careful control procedures for verifying each step in data processing.

Interviewer Error

Interviewer error distorts information from respondents in a manner similar to survey instrument error. While instrument error is a result of an interaction between the measurement instrument and the respondent, interviewer error is a result of an interaction between the interviewer and the respondent. The three primary sources of interviewer error are *unconscious misrepresentation*, *cheating* and *recording error*. Unconscious misrepresentation can occur when the interviewer somehow induces a pattern of responses that is not indicative of the target population. For example, the respondent may interpret the interviewer's body language, facial expression, or tone of voice as a cue to how to respond to a question. It is important that interviewers remain as neutral as possible during surveys to reduce interviewer-induced bias. Proper training, supervision, and practice all help to reduce error due to unconscious misrepresentation.

In other situations, interviewer cheating involves *deliberate falsification* of responses by incorrectly recording responses, by making up entire questionnaires, or by filling in answers to questions that have been intentionally skipped by respondents. For example, some interviewers cheat to finish a survey as quickly as possible in order to complete their assignment or to avoid asking sensitive topic questions. On the other hand, recording error occurs when interviewers inadvertently check the wrong prelisted response or may be unable to write fast enough to capture the response verbatim. These are all examples of interviewer error. Quality control techniques that detect interviewer error whether deliberate or inadvertent should be used.

Sample Design Error

Critical to any survey design is asking questions and recording responses from the 'right' respondents. The 'right' respondents are those that are representative of the defined target population. To achieve this goal, most survey research projects incorporate a sampling design process to determine the 'right' respondents to represent the larger target population. A number of systematic errors can occur during the sampling process. The three primary types of error associated with developing and executing sample designs are population specification error, sampling frame error and sample selection error.

> **Sample design error** A family of non-sampling error that occurs when sampling plans are not appropriately developed and/or the sampling process is improperly executed.

Population specification error (also known as population frame error) is the term used to describe an incorrect definition of the target population of interest to the research question. Correctly defining the target population to be studied is a critical step in research. Imagine if we design and conduct a study thinking that only individuals who earn more than €50,000 are of interest and then discover that a large proportion of individuals earning €30,000 to €50,000 also use the product. The entire class of people earning €30,000 to €50,000 and their responses would not be represented. Population specification error is discussed in Chapters 9 and 10.

> **Population specification error** An incorrect definition of the true target population to the research question.

In sample designs, the sampling frame is the list of population elements or members from which the prospective respondents (or sampling units) are selected. **Sampling frame error** occurs when an incomplete or inaccurate sampling frame is used. The main problem with sampling frame error is that the sample is unlikely to be representative of the defined target population. An example of a sample design that is likely to include sampling frame error is one that uses a published telephone directory as the sampling frame for a telephone survey. Many individuals or households are not listed or not listed accurately in the current telephone directory because they either (1) do not want to be listed, (2) have recently moved and missed the publication deadline date, or (3) have recently changed their telephone number. Research has shown that people who are listed in telephone directories are systematically different from those who are not listed.

> **Sampling frame error** An error that occurs when a sample is drawn from an incomplete or inaccurate list of potential or prospective respondents.

In addition to population specification and sampling frame, error can occur due to drawing an inappropriate sample from the defined target population. **Sample selection error** occurs when incomplete or incorrect sampling procedures are executed or when the correct procedures have not been carried out. It can occur even if the target population is correctly specified. For example, interviewers may avoid some members of the target population in a shopping intercept survey because the individuals appear scruffy or unattractive in some way. Quality controls should include checks on the sample selected to ensure the data are collected from randomly selected members of the target population.

Sample selection error A specific type of sample design error that occurs when an inappropriate sample is drawn from the defined target population because of execution of incomplete or faulty sampling procedures or because the correct procedures have not been carried out.

Types of Survey Method

Recent improvements in computer hardware and software and telecommunications have created many new survey approaches. Nevertheless, almost all types of survey method can be classified as *person-administered*, *self-administered*, or *telephone-administered*. Exhibit 7.7 provides an overview of the types of survey method that can be used to collect data.

EXHIBIT 7.7 Types of Survey Method

Type of Survey Method	Description
Person-Administered	
In-home/in-office survey	A survey takes place in the respondent's home, or within the respondent's work environment.
Shopping-intercept survey	Shopping patrons are stopped and asked for feedback during their visit to a shopping mall.
Purchase-intercept survey	The respondent is stopped and asked for feedback at the point of purchase.
Telephone-Administered	
Traditional telephone survey	A survey takes place over the telephone. Interviews may be conducted from a central telephone location or the interviewer's home.
Computer-assisted telephone survey	A computer is used to conduct a telephone survey; respondents give answers by pushing buttons on their phone.
Completely automated telephone survey	The survey is completely administered by a computer without the use of any human interviewer.
Wireless phone survey	The survey is conducted over the respondent's wireless phone in either text-based or voice-based formats.
Self-Administered	
Mail survey	Questionnaires are distributed to and returned from respondents via the postal service.
Mail panel survey	Surveys are mailed to a representative sample of individuals who have agreed in advance to participate.
Drop-off survey	Questionnaires are left with the respondent to be completed at a later time. The surveys may be picked up by the researcher or returned via mail.
Fax survey	Surveys are distributed to and returned from respondents via fax by hand or computer.
Online	
Email survey	Surveys are distributed to and returned from respondents via electronic mail.
Internet survey	The Internet is used to ask questions of and record responses from respondents.

EXHIBIT 7.8 General Advantages and Disadvantages of Person-Administered Surveys

Advantages	Comments
Adaptability	Trained interviewers can quickly adapt to respondents' differences.
Rapport	Not all people are willing to talk with strangers when asked to answer a few questions. Interviewers can help establish a 'comfort zone' during the questioning process.
Feedback	During the questioning process, interviewers can answer respondents' questions and increase the respondents' understanding of instructions and questions, and capture additional verbal and non-verbal information.
Quality of responses	Sometimes the interviewer must screen to qualify prospective respondents based on a set of characteristics like gender, age, etc. Interviewers can help ensure respondents are correctly chosen. Respondents tend to be more truthful in their responses when answering questions in a face-to-face situation.
Disadvantages	
Speed of data acquisition	The requirement to meet each respondent face-to-face significantly slows the data collection process.
Possible recording error	Humans often use selective perception in listening to and recording responses to questions, which can cause inaccuracies in the respondent's answers. The interviewer may also incorrectly record the respondent's answers.
Interviewer-respondent interaction error	Respondents may interpret the interviewer's facial expression, tone of voice or body language as a clue to how to respond to a question.
High expense	Overall cost of data collection using an interviewer in a face-to-face environment is generally higher than other data collection methods.

Person-Administered Surveys

Person-administered survey is distinguished by the presence of a trained interviewer who asks questions and records the subject's answers. Once the primary survey method used by researchers to collect data, traditional person-administered survey methods are being seriously challenged today by the growing acceptance and use of sophisticated Internet and telecommunications technologies as well as decision makers' demands for faster data acquisition. Nevertheless, person-administered survey methods will continue to be used by researchers in the future, albeit at a lower frequency than in past years. Depending on the research problem and data requirement, different types of methods offer varying strengths and weaknesses to researchers. Exhibit 7.8 highlights some of the advantages and disadvantages associated with person-administered surveys.

> **Person-administered survey** A type of survey method that requires the presence of a trained human interviewer who asks questions and records the subject's answers.

In-Home/In-Office Survey

An **in-home survey** is a face-to-face structured question-and-answer exchange conducted in the respondent's home. Sometimes the interviewer/respondent exchange occurs in the respondent's work environment rather than in the home, in which case the term becomes **in-office survey**. This method has several advantages. The interviewer can explain confusing or complex questions, use visual aids or other stimuli to elicit responses, and assess contextual conditions. This helps generate large amounts of feedback from the respondent. In addition, respondents are in their own comfortable, familiar environments where many of them should feel safe and secure, thus increasing the likelihood of respondents' willingness to answer the survey's questions, and also potentially increasing the quality of their answers.

> **In-home/in-office survey** A structured question-and-answer exchange conducted in the respondent's home or work environment.

In the case of in-home survey, it is often accomplished through door-to-door canvassing of geographic areas. This canvassing process is one of its disadvantages. Interviewers who are not constantly supervised may skip homes they find threatening or may simply fabricate answers for the survey. To ensure the safety of the interviewer, researchers may have to provide training on how to avoid potentially threatening situations.

Shopping-Intercept Survey

Compared to in-home/in-office surveys, **shopping-intercept surveys** are a less expensive option. This type of survey is undertaken face-to-face with the respondents in a central location, frequently within shopping centres or similar shopping locations. Shoppers are stopped and asked to complete a survey.

> **Shopping-intercept survey** A face-to-face personal survey that takes place in a shopping mall or similar shopping locations.

Shopping-intercept surveys share the advantages of in-home and in-office surveys except for the familiarity of the environment for the respondent. However, the shopping-intercept is less expensive and more convenient for the researcher. A researcher spends less time and effort in securing a person's agreement to participate in the survey as both are already at a common location. In addition, the researcher benefits from reduced screening costs and time because interviewers can easily identify potential members of the target population by using their observation skills on location.

Shopping-intercept surveys are quite time consuming. However, as respondents are easier to recruit, the total time investment per respondent is lower than in-home/in-office surveys. One important point of caution is that mall patrons may not be representative of the general population. Individuals representative of the general population may shop at different stores or at different times during the day. Typically, shopping-intercept surveys are considered a non-probability sampling approach for selecting prospective respondents. As you will learn later, non-probability sampling approaches can have adverse effects on the ability to generalize survey results. Marketing researchers using shopping-intercept surveys need to be sensitive to these issues.

Purchase-Intercept Survey

As in a shopping-intercept, in a **purchase-intercept survey**, potential respondents are stopped and asked for feedback while on a shopping trip. However, purchase-intercepts are different in that the intercept takes place after the interviewer has observed a prespecified behaviour, usually the selection or purchase of a particular product or service. An advantage of this type of survey is that the recency of the behaviour aids the respondent's recall capabilities.

> **Purchase-intercept survey** A face-to-face survey that takes place immediately after the selection or purchase of a product or service.

There are two major disadvantages to purchase-intercept surveys in addition to those of shopping-intercepts. First, many stores are reluctant to allow their customers to be intercepted and their shopping interrupted in the store. Second, purchase-intercepts involve only those individuals who demonstrate some observable behaviour. Thus, consumers who are considering a purchase but do not buy are excluded from this type of data collection technique.

Telephone-Administered Surveys
Traditional Telephone Survey

Compared to face-to-face surveys, **telephone-administered surveys** are less expensive, faster, and more suitable for gathering data from large numbers of respondents. Interviewers working from their homes or from central locations use telephones to ask questions and record responses.

> **Telephone-administered survey** Question-and-answer exchanges that are conducted via telephone.

Advantages of Traditional Telephone Survey.   Traditional telephone survey has a number of advantages over face-to-face survey. One advantage is that interviewers can be closely supervised if they work out of a central location. Supervisors can record calls and review them later, and they can listen in on calls. Reviewing or listening to interviewers ensures quality control and can identify training needs. When interviewers work out of their own home, they can set hours that are convenient for them, within limits prescribed by the employer and the law.

Telephone surveys are less expensive than face-to-face surveys in a number of ways. They allow individual interviewers to do more surveys in a given time period, and they reduce travelling time and time spent on searching for respondents. Although there is the added cost of the telephone call and related equipment, wide area telephone service has made telephone calling a cost-efficient survey medium. Telephone surveys also facilitate data collection from respondents across a wide geographic area.

Another advantage of telephone surveys is that they enable interviewers to call back respondents who did not answer the telephone or respondents who found it inconvenient to cooperate with the survey when first called. Callbacks are very inexpensive compared to follow-up personal surveys. A fourth advantage is that respondents perceive telephone surveys to be more anonymous and may feel less threatened and therefore be more candid. Anonymity also reduces the opportunity for interviewer bias. Finally, telephone surveys may well be the last resort for collecting data from business professionals. While these people are usually busy and could not make time for a personal survey, they could take time for a telephone call. The same is true for many busy, hard-to-reach people. Using the telephone at a time convenient to the respondent facilitates collection of information from many individuals who would be almost impossible to survey personally.

Disadvantages of Traditional Telephone Survey. While some researchers believe the above advantages have made telephone surveys one of the dominant forms of collecting survey data, the traditional telephone survey, like any other type of survey method, has several drawbacks. One disadvantage is that pictures or other non-audio stimuli cannot be presented over the telephone. A second disadvantage is that it is difficult for telephone respondents to perform complex tasks. For example, imagine the confusion in the mind of a respondent asked to remember seven brands of a product, each with multiple variations, throughout an entire survey. Third is that telephone surveys tend to be shorter than personal surveys because people are likely to hang up on long telephone calls. Telephone surveys are also limited, in usual practice, by national borders – the telephone is seldom used in international research. Probably the greatest disadvantage, though, lies in the restrictions on the types of data that can be collected over the phone. For example, it is difficult to use multiple levels of agreement/disagreement, likes/dislikes, and so on, and all but impossible to accurately ask a brand image question that would require the respondent to answer using a semantic differential scale (see Chapter 13).

Ethics
Conducting Marketing Research for Non-Research Purpose

When a marketing research project is carried out, the tacit agreement between the researcher and the respondents/interviewees is that the project should be for research purpose only. According to Marketing Research Society, UK, a 'research purpose' is where information is collected purely to enhance understanding in a way that provides robust information on the population under study. It does not include data collection intended directly to create sales or to influence the opinions of the respondents/interviewees. Nor does it include data collection as a means of information gathering for use on future sales or direct marketing activities, such as to generate potential sales leads, contact details, or related details a particular respondent's/interviewee's usage and consumption patterns. Direct action should not be taken in relation to named respondents/interviewees as a result of the marketing research project.

On some occasions, market research companies may carry out a research project for non-research purpose, which is when data is collected for reasons other than for research purpose as defined above. For example, an office equipment supplier approaches a researcher to build a list of business contacts which the office equipment supplier can target for its products. The purpose of this project is to build a marketing list for direct marketing purpose. The researcher is asked to devise a questionnaire together with a prize draw that can be administered over the telephone.

In the above case, proper procedures should be undertaken by the researcher in order to conform to the marketing research ethics standard. The Marketing Research Society states that when conducting projects for non-research purpose, an ethical and responsible researcher should ensure that:

- the questions are fit for purpose and clients have been advised accordingly;
- the design and content of questionnaires are appropriate for the respondents/interviewees being researched;

- the respondents are able to answer the questions in a way that reflects the view they want to express;
- the respondents are not led towards a particular answer;
- the answers are capable of being interpreted in an unambiguous way;
- the personal data collected is relevant and not excessive;
- the questionnaire clearly defines the purpose, so that the respondent is not left with the impression that the project has a research purpose when it does not;
- the best practice advice contained in the Marketing Research Society Questionnaire Design Guidelines is considered;
- the relevant industry rules are adhered to.

Applying the above principles to the above case, the researcher should make sure that the questionnaire clearly states that the purpose of the data collection is for direct marketing purpose to establish the respondents'/interviewees' interest in purchasing office equipment, that the identifiable details will be passed to the office equipment supplier and that the client will be administering the prize draw. The researcher should also review the Direct Marketing Association Code of Practice to familiarize themselves with the relevant industry rules particularly regarding telephone direct marketing and the Marketing Research Society, Direct Marketing Association and Advertising Standards Association rules on conducting free prize draws.

Another disadvantage is the poor perception of telephone survey in some people's minds, due in part to the increased use of telemarketing practices and the misperception that this type of research is the same as telemarketing. The Ethics box describes the potentially unethical act of conducting marketing research for non-research purpose, which if not properly managed would no doubt contributes to this poor perception. Even the researcher has been following proper procedures, some people are still annoyed by telephone survey because it interrupts their privacy, their dinner, or their relaxation time. Generally, the most productive hours are during the day to reach non-working people. Evening hours during the week and mid-morning to early evening on weekends are good times to reach people who work during the week.

A difficult but critical task in being able to conduct telephone surveying is selecting the telephone number to be called. Using a telephone directory does not produce a random sample because many people choose to have unlisted numbers. In some cases, the client will supply the researcher with a customer list or another prescribed list, but most marketing research studies need a random sample. Three techniques – plus-one dialling, systematic random digit dialling, and random digit dialling – have been developed to overcome the telephone-number selection problem:

Plus-one dialling. In plus-one dialling, the researcher generates telephone numbers to be called by choosing numbers randomly from a telephone directory and adding 1. For example, suppose the telephone number 727-7119 is selected from the directory. Adding 1, we would dial 727-7120. This method is easy and allows for the possibility of unlisted telephone numbers to be included in the sample. But researchers should remember no telephone directory provides a sampling frame that covers the whole target population.

Systematic random digit dialling. Systematic random digit dialling is a technique in which researchers randomly dial telephone numbers, but only numbers that meet the 'sample interval' criterion. With this method, the marketing researcher randomly selects a telephone number as a starting point and uses a constant, or 'skip,' pattern in the selection process. The starting point, or seed number, is based on the sample interval. Specifically, the skip interval is added to the seed on the basis of the number of telephone numbers available divided by the number to be surveyed. For example, say that there are 10,000 telephone numbers in the 727 exchange. Assuming the researcher wants to conduct a survey on 500 households within that exchange, the skip interval would be $10,000/500 = 20$. The researcher would randomly choose a telephone number between 727-0000 and 727-0020, say 727-0009. Then, to generate additional numbers, the researcher would add the interval. Thus, the second number dialled in this example would be 727-0029, the third 727-0049, and so on.

The advantages of this method are that, prior to the selection of the first telephone number, each number has an equal chance of being called. In this sense, the selection of respondents is random. In principle, the sample will tend to share the attributes of the area and have an even geographic dispersion. Finally, the method is fairly simple to set up and administer.

Random digit dialling. Random digit dialling refers to a random selection of area codes and suffix numbers. All numbers have an equal chance of being called. This is the fundamental form of random sampling application in telephone surveys. With computer technology, the random choice of telephone numbers becomes automatic and simple.

Computer-Assisted Telephone Survey

Advances in telecommunication, computer and software technologies have totally revolutionized the administration of telephone survey. Most research companies have computerized the central location telephone surveying process. With faster, more powerful computers and affordable software, even small research companies can use **computer-assisted telephone survey** systems. Although different systems are available, the computer-assisted telephone survey system basically integrates advanced telecommunication technologies with the traditional telephone survey system. The interviewer is equipped with a 'hands-free' headset and is seated in front of a keyboard and a 'touch-screen' computer terminal or a personal computer. Upon activating the system, the computer dials the prospective respondent's phone number automatically and provides the interviewer with the appropriate introduction screen. When the qualified respondent is on the line, the interviewer activates the surveying process by pressing a key or series of keys on the keyboard or pressure-sensitive screen. Following the introductory comments, another simple keystroke brings up to the screen the first question and a prelisted set of choice responses.

> **Computer-assisted telephone survey** Integrated telephone and computer system in which the interviewer reads the questions off a computer screen and enters respondents' answers directly into the computer programme.

Many computer-assisted telephone survey systems are designed to have one question per screen. The interviewer then reads the question and records the respondent's answer. Note that depending on the question/scale design, the interviewer may read not only the question but also a list of possible answer choices. By recording the respondent's answer, the computer automatically skips ahead to the appropriate next question. For example, when Procter & Gamble conducts a clothes detergent purchasing behaviour study using a computer-assisted telephone survey system, one question asked by the interviewer may be 'In the past 30 days have you purchased any clothes cleaning products?' If the answer is yes, a series of specific questions focusing on the types of clothes cleaning products the person buys may follow. If the answer is no, those questions would be inappropriate to ask the respondent. The computer is programmed to skip to the next appropriate question on the basis of the respondent's answer. Here, the next question may be something like 'How often do you purchase clothes cleaning products?' When programmed to react in a predetermined way based on the respondent's initial response to the question, the computer can eliminate human error which exists in surveys conducted using the traditional paper-and-pencil telephone survey mode.

Computer-assisted telephone survey systems can be used to customize questions. Consider a study on car purchasers' satisfaction. In the early part of the survey, the respondent is asked to provide the years, makes and models of the cars owned in the past 10 years. Later in the survey, the interviewer may be prompted to ask the respondent to rate the safety features for a particular car owned. The question may appear as 'You said you owned this car model. How would you rate each of the following safety features of this model?' The process would continue until all the prelisted safety features have been rated. Although this type of questions can be handled in a traditional telephone survey mode, the computerized version handles them much more efficiently because the interviewer does not have to physically flip questionnaire pages back and forth or remember a respondent's previous responses. Today's computer-assisted telephone survey systems have alleviated most of the problems associated with manual systems of callbacks, complex quotas, skip logic, rotations, and randomization.

Advantages of computer-assisted telephone survey.   The advantages are not limited to the above – there are other advantages as well. In sophisticated systems, it is possible to switch from one questionnaire to another during the survey. Switching capabilities allow for surveying family members other than the head of household, for example. The advantage is that common information is shared between all the questionnaires, saving the need for multiple calls. Another advantage is ownership of the call. Sometimes people need to stop in the middle of a survey but are willing to finish at another time. Computer technology has the capability of routing inbound calls to a particular interviewer who 'owns' the survey with the particular respondent, resulting in the greater efficiency of the whole survey process.

Computer-assisted telephone survey systems also eliminate the need for separate editing and data entry tasks associated with manual systems. The researcher does not edit or clean complete questionnaires for errors or manually create electronic data files, because there is no physical questionnaire and the responses are automatically entered directly to a computer file at the end of the survey. The possibility for coding or data entry errors is eliminated with computer-assisted telephone survey systems because it is impossible to accidentally record an improper response from outside the set of prelisted responses established for a given question. Here is an easy example to illustrate this point. The respondent is asked the question 'How important is it for your new car to have an automatic seatbelt safety system?' The response choices are prelisted as (a) 'Extremely important,' (b) 'Important,' (c) 'Somewhat important,' and (d) 'Not at all important.' If the interviewer, by mistake, enters any code other than one of the four established codes, the computer will ask for the answer to be re-entered until an acceptable code is entered.

Given the sophistication of the computer-assisted telephone survey systems' software, tabulation of results can be run in real time at any point of the study. Real-time reporting of the results is not possible using traditional paper-and-pencil methods. Quick preliminary results can be beneficial in determining when some additional questions are needed because of unexpected patterns uncovered in the earlier part of the surveying process. Overall, use of computer-assisted telephone survey systems continues to grow at a rapid rate because decision makers have embraced the cost savings, quality control and time-saving aspects of these systems.

Disadvantages of computer-assisted telephone survey. Computer-assisted telephone survey systems have two problem areas. Setting up and activating them require substantial initial investment and operating costs. The investment in computers, especially for large and sophisticated systems, is still high, considering how quickly a computer system becomes obsolete. Software to control the hardware, monitor calls and record responses in real-time fashion is also expensive and rapidly changing, especially if customized, and can be time consuming to develop and debug. Second, in addition to having traditional skills, interviewers must have specific computer skills to effectively administer this type of survey. As the costs of both computer hardware and software go down and more people develop better computer literacy, these problems will be reduced.

Completely Automated Telephone Survey

Using more sophisticated software than computer-assisted telephone survey systems, some research companies have fully automated their telephone surveying process. This type of system is referred to as a **completely automated telephone survey** and uses no human interviewer. The survey is completely administered by a computer. After the system is activated, the computer dials a phone number and a recording is used to introduce the survey to the prospective respondent and give directions. The actual survey is conducted with the respondent who listens to the electronic voice and responds by pressing keys on the touch-tone telephone keypad. Although still relatively new, completely automated telephone survey systems have been successfully employed in service quality monitoring, product/warranty registrations, customer satisfaction studies, in-home product tests, and election day polls. One of the difficulties experienced in using this fully automated system is there is a high 'disconnect' rate among prospective respondents. While research is under way to investigate this disconnect behaviour, some informal evidence suggests the impersonal, one-way communication involved in responding to an unsolicited electronic voice is problematic.

> **Completely automated telephone survey** A telephone surveying system in which a computer dials a phone number and a recording is used to introduce and administer the survey, leaving the subject to interact with the computer directly.

Wireless Phone Survey

Wireless data networking and advanced database technologies offer researchers a promising new innovative data collection technique for doing marketing research studies – the wireless phone survey. With a **wireless phone survey** data are collected from wireless phone users. Researchers can survey in either text-based or voice-based formats or a combination of both. In a text-based format, the respondent can access the survey and display it as text messages on a wireless phone screen. The respondent uses the phone's dial pad to answer the questions.

All responses are sent, in real time, back to a backend database through the wireless network and the Internet. In contrast, a voice-based survey allows the respondent to listen to the questions on the wireless phone and answer them by speaking. All survey questions and answers are automatically processed and analysed by voice synthesis and recognition software on voice extensible markup language (VoiceXML) equipment. One of the unique characteristics of wireless phone surveys is their ability to allow respondents to deliver instant answers anywhere and anytime. They also enable researchers to capture data from respondents in their natural shopping and consumption environments.

> **Wireless phone survey** The method of conducting a marketing survey in which the data are collected on standard wireless phones.

Advantages of Wireless Phone Survey.   Although this data collection method is in infancy stage, there are a number of potential advantages over online, other telephone, and paper-and-pencil-based methods. First, wireless phone surveys are contemporaneous – they can capture consumers' real experiences at the moment of purchase or consumption. Another advantage is the mobility associated with wireless phones. Almost like a watch, a wireless phone is with the consumer wherever they go. This mobility factor brings a high degree of convenience for respondents, resulting in the possibility of higher response rate. Third, wireless surveys are less intrusive to the respondent because they can be sent without interrupting the lives of the respondents, who have full control of the time and place to fill out the survey. In cases where a respondent must complete the survey at a particular moment, such requirements are agreed upon by the respondent prior to sending the survey and are not viewed as obtrusive.

Capturing data via wireless phones increases the potential of implementing longitudinal types of studies. Normally, a wireless phone is a personal belonging and can be associated with each individual, thus making it easier for researchers to keep track of each respondent over time. In addition, the survey can be programmed similar to computer-assisted and completely automated telephone surveys to branch questions automatically based on previous answers. Finally, wireless phone surveys provide geographic flexibility and facilitate completing surveys on location-sensitive topics such as during a shopping trip at a particular mall or theme park.

Disadvantages of Wireless Phone Survey.   There are several challenges facing the use of wireless phone surveys. First, there are limited display spaces on wireless phone screens. Therefore, the questions must be kept short and simple in both text-based and voice-based formats. Consequently, wireless phone surveys are not suitable for research that involves long and/or complex questions and responses. Second, wireless phones have limited capacity to handle graphics. Therefore, wireless surveys may not be appropriate for studies that require visual stimuli for answering certain types of research questions. Third, the initial technology costs (both hardware and software) required for implementing wireless phone surveys are high. Finally, researchers conducting wireless phone surveys must be well trained in information technology skills in addition to other research skills.

Self-Administered Survey

The third type of surveying exchange is the **self-administered survey**. A self-administered survey is a data collection technique in which the respondent reads the survey questions and records their own responses without the presence of a trained interviewer. The advantages are low cost per survey and the absence of interviewer bias – but the latter comes at a price since there is no interviewer to probe for a deeper response. For example, on a self-administered survey a respondent may indicate that they did not purchase a certain product, but that respondent can also fail to answer 'Why not?'

> **Self-administered survey** A data collection technique in which the respondent reads the survey questions and records his or her own answers without the presence of a trained interviewer.

Exhibit 7.9 highlights some of the advantages and disadvantages associated with self-administered data collection methods. We discuss three types of self-administered surveys: direct mail, mail panel and drop-off.

EXHIBIT 7.9 General Advantages and Disadvantages of Self-Administered Surveys

Advantages	Comments
Low cost per survey	With no need for an interviewer or computerized assistance device, self-administered surveys are a much less costly method of data acquisition.
Respondent control	Respondents are in control of how fast, when and where the survey is completed; thus the respondent creates his/her own comfort zone.
No interviewer-respondent bias	There is no chance of introducing interviewer bias due to for example interviewer's body language, facial expression, or tone of voice.
Anonymity in responses	Respondents are more comfortable in providing honest and insightful responses because their true identity does not need to be revealed.
Disadvantages	
Lack of additional in-depth data	The type of data collected is limited to the specific questions placed initially on the survey. It is very difficult, if not impossible, to obtain additional in-depth data, because of the lack of chance for probing and observation.
High non-response rate	In many cases, it is impossible to guarantee that the respondent will complete and return the survey at all. The respondent may get frustrated with questions that need clarification.
Potential response error	The respondent may not fully understand a survey question and provide an erroneous response or mistakenly skip sections of the survey, resulting in inaccurate answers. Without an interviewer, respondents may unconsciously commit numerous errors while believing they are answering properly.
Slow data acquisition	Typically, the time required to acquire the data and enter it into a computer file for analysis is significantly longer than in many other data collection methods.
Lack of monitoring capability	Not having an interviewer present could lead to increases in misunderstanding of questions and instructions on how to respond to certain questions.

Mail Survey

In situations where the researcher decides that a **mail survey** is the best method, a questionnaire is developed and mailed to a list of people who return the completed surveys by mail. The researcher must be careful to select a list that accurately reflects the target population of interest. Sometimes obtaining the required mailing addresses is an easy task. But in other cases it can be time consuming and difficult. In addition, there are production considerations. For example, the envelope needs to be designed to stimulate the potential respondent's interest enough that the questionnaire is not simply thrown out. The questionnaire itself needs to be carefully designed to gather as much information as possible and still be short enough for people to complete in a reasonable length of time.

> **Mail survey** A self-administered questionnaire that is delivered to selected respondents and returned to the researcher by mail.

Advantages of Mail Survey.   This type of survey is inexpensive to implement. There are no interviewer-related costs such as remuneration, training, or travel costs. In addition, most of the production expenses are one-time costs that can be amortized over many surveys. The variable costs are primarily postage, printing and the cost of the incentive. Another advantage is that mail surveys can reach even hard-to-survey people.

Disadvantages of Mail Survey.   Mail surveys have several drawbacks. One major drawback is that response rates tend to be much lower than with face-to-face or telephone surveys. The risk of non-response bias is very real with mail surveys since the researcher gives up control over who responds. The researcher is never exactly sure who filled out the questionnaire, leaving the question of whether someone else provided the answers instead of the intended person. For example, in sending a mail survey to Mr Jones in Guildford, Surrey, the researcher cannot determine precisely whether Mr Jones or some other member of his household answered the survey.

Another problem is that of misunderstood or skipped questions. Mail surveys make it difficult to handle problems of both vagueness and potential misinterpretation in question-and-answer setups. People who simply do not understand a question may record a response that is actually incorrect. Or the respondent may skip one or more questions entirely. These are all problems associated with not having a trained interviewer available to assist the respondent. Finally, mail surveys are also slow as there can be a significant time lag between when the survey is mailed and when it is returned.

Mail Panel Survey

To avoid some of the drawbacks of a mail survey, a researcher may choose a **mail panel survey**. This is a questionnaire sent to a group of individuals who have agreed in advance to participate. The panel can be tested prior to the survey so the researcher knows that the panel is representative; the prior agreement usually produces high response rates. In addition, mail panel surveys allow for longitudinal research. That is, the same people can be tested multiple times over an extended period. This enables the researcher to observe changes in the panel members' responses over time.

> **Mail panel survey** A questionnaire sent to a group of individuals who have agreed in advance to participate.

The major drawback to mail panels is that members are very likely not to be representative of the target population at large. For example, individuals who agree to be on a panel may have a special interest in the topic or may simply have a lot of time available. There is little information on how much, if any, these aspects of mail panels bias the results of the research. Researchers should be cautious, therefore, regarding the degree of generalizability of the findings.

It is important to remember that the different types of survey method are not necessarily mutually exclusive. It is quite common for several methods to be employed on the same project. For example, the researcher may contact potential in-home respondents via telephone as a part of the screening process. Mail may then be used to inform people of impending personal survey.

Drop-Off Survey

One common combination technique is termed the **drop-off survey**. In this method, a representative of the researcher hand-delivers survey forms to respondents. Completed surveys are returned by mail or picked up by the representative. The advantages of drop-off surveys include the availability of a person who can answer general questions, screen potential respondents and spur interest in completing the questionnaire. The disadvantage to drop-offs is they are fairly expensive in comparison to mail surveys.

> **Drop-off survey** A self-administered questionnaire that a representative of the researcher hand-delivers to selected respondents; the completed surveys are returned by mail or picked up by the representative.

Fax Survey

A **fax survey** is essentially a mail survey sent by fax. The fax survey allows researchers to collect responses to visual cues, as in a mail survey, as well as semantic differential or constant sum scales (see Chapter 12), which are difficult to apply in telephone surveys. The potential benefit of fax surveys is that the flexibility of mail can be combined, to an extent, with the speed of the telephone.

> **Fax survey** A self-administered questionnaire that is sent to the selected subject via fax by hand or computer.

In comparison to mail surveys, the fax delivery facilitates faster delivery and response speed, and is generally less expensive. Administrative and clerical functions can also be reduced because there is no need to fold surveys and stuff envelopes. Finally, a fax survey implies urgency and is not perceived as being junk mail by many recipients. Even in a regular mail survey, merely offering the option to respond by fax can increase the response rate.

One disadvantage of fax surveys is that consumers and small businesses may not have fax machines and therefore cannot be contacted. In addition, respondents may have to pay to fax back their responses, which can reduce response rates. Sending a prepaid mailing label increases response time, while using a toll-free fax response line increases costs. In addition fax surveys can be delayed or not delivered because of operator error, equipment malfunctions, or busy signals. The relative lack of privacy may cause response problems as well. Finally, fax surveys may lack the clarity of image of a printed mail survey, and a colour fax may be too expensive.

Nevertheless, fax surveys offer an attractive alternative to direct mail surveys under proper conditions. Fax surveys can provide relatively faster responses, higher response rates and similar data quality. In addition, fax surveys can be cheaper due to low transmission and paper-handling costs. Still, the image-quality and limited-reach problems are not likely to be resolved in the foreseeable future.

Online Survey

Marketing research practices and the systems being used in collecting primary data have changed dramatically as people have increasingly accepted Internet technologies and telecommunications, while researchers are aiming for faster data acquisition and real-time reporting of results. Many traditional types of survey method have been revised by technology-savvy researchers to use new 'online' platforms. Although many of the fundamental principles that underlie traditional types of survey method remain the same, the speed of data acquisition and reporting systems has created new benchmarks for improving how primary data will be collected in years to come. Online advances that were just visions before the use of the Internet started to take off in the society are now part of reality. Exhibit 7.10 summarizes online data collection techniques that are in the process of replacing or augmenting traditional types of survey method. The following discussion focuses on the two online survey designs – email and Internet surveys – researchers increasingly are using to collect primary data.

Email Survey

An **email survey** is a self-administered data collection technique in which the survey is electronically delivered to and returned by email. Email surveys have become one of the popular methods within the 'family' of online surveys used by marketing researchers. Using the improvements of the batch feature associated with today's email systems, the researcher creates a standardized email message, sometimes in the format of a cover letter, and appends the online survey as an attachment. The email message and survey are then electronically transmitted as a 'mass mailing' to a large number of prospective respondents. Once the respondent opens the email, they are given an opt-in or opt-out approval option that serves to solicit the respondent's permission to participate in the study. The opt-in/opt-out option is a good ethical practice for protecting people from receiving 'spam' or 'sugging' mailings. *Spam* and *sugg* are terms for the illegal marketing practice of selling unsolicited products or services under the guise of conducting research. If respondents select the opt-out option, they do not participate in the attached survey, and their email addresses are supposed to be automatically removed from the researcher's mailing list, so they receive no future email from that originating source. In turn, respondents who select the opt-in option, granting permission, continue the survey following on-screen directions. After completing the survey, the respondent returns it via email. Today, returning an email survey is as easy as clicking a single Submit or Return button located normally at the end of the survey.

> **Email survey** A self-administered data collection technique in which the survey is delivered to and returned from the respondent by email.

Proponents of email surveys favour this method for its capability of collecting a variety of data at lightning speed at a very low cost-per-participant figure. In addition, as with other computer-assisted or online research methods, interviewer errors do not exist while data entry errors are

EXHIBIT 7.10 Online Computer Technology Integrates with Offline Survey Data Collection Methods

Offline Method	Online Method	Comments
Person-administered survey	Computer-assisted personal survey	The respondent sits with the interviewer, and the interviewer reads the respondent the questions from a laptop computer screen and directly keys in the responses.
Traditional telephone survey	Computer-assisted telephone survey	The interviewer phones the respondent, reads questions from a computer screen and directly enters the responses into the computer system.
Traditional telephone survey	Computer automated telephone survey	The computer calls respondents and an electronic voice gives directions and asks questions. The respondent uses the keypad of a touch-tone telephone to enter responses.
Mail survey	Mail survey by computer disk	A computer disk is mailed to the respondent, who completes the survey on their computer and returns the disk to the researcher by mail.
Mail panel survey	Online panel survey	Groups of people are invited and agree to become members of a selected panel of consumers. Initially these consumers fill out a form on background data on specific demographic and purchase factors. Later these respondents are sent surveys from time to time via email. They complete the survey and return it via email or direct mail.
Self-administered survey	Computer-assisted self-survey	The researcher directs a respondent to a specified computer terminal where the respondent reads questions from the screen and directly enters responses.
Self-administered survey	Fully automated self-survey	The respondent independently approaches a central computer station (kiosk) and reads and responds to the questions, all without researcher intervention.
Self-administered survey	Computer-generated fax survey	A computer is used to dial and send a survey to potential respondents via fax. The respondent completes the survey and returns it via fax.
Self-administered survey	Email survey	The batch feature available on most email systems is used to send a 'mass mailing' to potential respondents, the respondent completes an opt-in/opt-out option, and those respondents who opt in continue and complete the survey. Surveys are returned via email.
Self-administered survey	Internet survey	The survey is placed on a specified website, the respondent is contacted separately by letter or email about the survey and its website location and given a unique password in order to access the survey, and the respondent completes the survey and returns it by clicking the Send button.

reduced by technology-based controls. Email surveys have grown in popularity as a method of conducting fast and inexpensive research for international consumer products and services studies. Like any type of online survey method, there are still some difficulties that must be overcome.

First, not everyone has access to the Internet. Although Internet penetration rates are high in all developed countries, they are much lower in some other parts of the world. Therefore, online researchers will have to continue their efforts to establish legitimacy in generalizing their results to large target populations. The second significant problem revolves around data privacy. As noted above, research firms should provide opt-in/opt-out approval option to potential respondents. Yet it is always difficult to enforce this principle upon all the research firms in a country, and it is even more difficult to bind other countries into this principle.

Internet Survey

Internet surveys are another method gaining strong interest among many marketing research firms. This type of online survey method is tightly integrated into website technology. Some characteristics of Internet surveys are similar to email surveys, but there are some distinct differences. An **Internet survey** is a self-administered questionnaire that is placed on a website for prospective subjects to read and complete. After agreeing to participate, prospective respondents select unique 'login' and 'password' codes, which serve as entrance keys for participation. Following website instructions, respondents complete and submit their survey.

> **Internet survey** A self-administered questionnaire that is placed on a World Wide Web for prospective subjects to read and complete.

Another distinct difference is that respondents have the option of accessing the results of the survey in real time. Some companies, like Procter & Gamble through its 'Consumercorner.com' panel system, even encourage respondents to scroll through the results and have additional options that allow respondents to make and share testimonial comments about the products being surveyed with other panel members. Read the nearby Closer Look at Research box, which illustrates the use of computer simulations as a creative method of integrating computer technologies with survey research.

 ## A Closer Look at Research *(Using technology)*
Virtual Reality in Marketing Research

A computer programme can do a better job of tabulating what customers will actually do rather than what the customers think they will do. The problem is that people communicate in words but do not think or feel in words. People think and feel in pictures. Computer technology has the added bonus of reducing interviewer and consumer bias as well.

To illustrate the problem of consumer bias as a result of thinking in pictures and communicating in words, audiences are asked to think of the following sentence: 'You are standing by the water's edge.' Then, he produces four images: an ocean scene a lake scene, a river scene and a stream. Each image elicits different feelings. In practice, this consumer bias is the reason that people react differently to a can of Coca-Cola than they do to an old-style bottle of Coca-Cola.

The prescription is to take the consumer to the McDonald's restaurant instead of simply talking about a McDonald's. In this way, the researcher can get a truer picture of the consumer's reactions than time-lagged thoughts and feelings allow. The way to take the consumer to McDonald's is by computer simulation.

By using full-scale electronic simulations, the consumer can be exposed to the inside of the McDonald's restaurant and menus. The realism of the simulations allows for accurate communications with respondents and also for meaningful data collection. The simulation should be engaging and short enough to hold the respondent's attention. Let the respondent do, observe and question. And the computer can track and record the mental process step by step.

Consumer products companies can use simulations in many different ways. For example, a consumer might be asked to build a stereo system, spending only a given amount of money. The researcher using the computer simulation could see what the respondent would buy. Another example could be a sunglasses boutique. The consumer could have their face scanned into a computer and then electronically 'try on' sunglasses by clicking a mouse. Other researchers think that virtual reality may offer an exciting way of testing. The consumer could 'shop' the store, picking up items from shelves as they would in an ordinary store. The computer could track the respondent's actions and reactions. This virtual reality testing would allow companies to accurately pretest pricing changes, packaging, promotions, shelf layout, new product interest and substitution behaviours.

Proponents of the computer simulation research say the tests are becoming faster and the cost is decreasing as technology advances. Other benefits include a virtually realistic context for the respondent and a controlled, low-risk environment.

A Closer Look at Research *(Using technology)*
Paid Online Survey is Getting Popular

In recent years, paid online surveys have become a popular method of collecting data from consumers. In the UK, people can register with a market research website to receive a few 15- to 20-minute surveys by email every month. Each one completed – usually multiple-choice questions on brands and consumer goods – earns approximately between €1 and €10.

One of the most popular survey website is ciao.co.uk. Members are sent about four surveys a month on products that match their profile. The surveys, most of which pay approximately between €1 and €5, are on anything from holidays, breakfast habits and pets to cosmetics and white goods. Members can participate in as many or few as they like.

Another paid online survey website is itsyourview.com, which is run by the market research company ICM. The website sends members about two or three questionnaires each month and pays the equivalent of approximately €12 an hour.

Another one is valuedopinions.co.uk, which pays in vouchers for Amazon, HMV, Boots and Marks & Spencer, or makes donations to charities such as the British Red Cross and WWF, for remunerating its members' participations in its surveys.

For more cerebral surveys, people may prefer YouGov and join the panel at yougov.com to receive surveys on topics from politics to painkillers and pensions. Members receive approximately €1 for registering and €0.5 to €3 per survey. Each member receives about four to six surveys a month.

All these paid online surveys expect honest and thought-out answers. Their software can identify members who tick boxes at random.

While the benefits are many, there are still disadvantages. For example, response bias remains a problem because Internet surveys are available to everyone without being targeted to anyone. Internet surveys are initially passive in nature: a prospective respondent must seek out the website,

EXHIBIT 7.11 Types of Computer-Assisted Survey

	Personal	On-Site	On-Site	Telephone	Telephone	Mail	Online Panel	Email	Fax	Internet
	Computer-Assisted Personal Interview	Computer-Assisted Self-Interview	Fully Automated Self-Interview	Computer-Assisted Telephone Interview	Fully Automated Telephone Interview	Computer Disks by Mail	Online Panel Survey	Electronic-Mail Survey	Computer-Generated Fax Survey	Self-Administered Survey
Benefits										
No need for respondents to have computer-related skills	X			X	X		X		X	X
Allows respondents to choose own schedule for completing survey		X	X			X	X	X	X	X
Can incorporate complex branching questions into survey	X	X	X	X	X	X	X	X		X
Can incorporate respondent-generated words in questions	X	X	X	X	X	X	X	X		X
Can accurately measure response times to questions	X	X	X	X	X	X	X	X		X
Can display graphics and relate them directly to questions	X	X	X			X	X	X		X
Eliminates the need to encode data from paper survey forms	X	X	X	X	X	X	X	X		X
Errors in data less likely compared to manual methods	X	X	X	X	X	X	X	X		X
Speedier data collection and encoding compared to manual methods	X	X	X	X	X	X	X	X	X	X

and thus only those who have a prior interest or are attracted by provision of an incentive are likely to even find the survey, let alone complete it. Exhibit 7.11 summarizes the benefits of using computer-assisted and online surveys for collecting primary data. Refer to this book's website at www.mhhe.com/shiu09 for more discussion and examples of online survey.

Factors for Selecting the Appropriate Type of Survey Method

Merely selecting any type of survey method which the researcher finds interesting or convenient may not produce usable, cost-efficient data. In determining the appropriate type of survey method for a particular project, researchers should consider a number of important factors such as those listed in Exhibit 7.12.

EXHIBIT 7.12 Important Factors to Consider in Selecting an Appropriate Type of Survey Method

Factors	Important Issues and Questions
Situational	
Budget	What degree of appropriate resources can be committed to the project? What are the total amount of money and the number of staff hours available for committing to the research project's activities? What is the cost of collecting the required data?
Completion time frame	How much time is needed for completing the research project? How quickly do data gathering, data analysis and information generation activities have to be completed?
Quality requirement	How accurate is the derived information?
Completeness of data	How much data and what degree of detail are needed for the defined research problem?
Generalizability	At what level of confidence does the researcher want to make inferences about the defined target population from the data results?
Precision	What is the acceptable level of error that the data results may have in representing true population parameters?
Task	
Difficulty of task	How much effort is required by the respondent to answer the questions? How much preparation is required to create a desired environment for the respondents to answer the questions?
Stimuli needed to elicit a response	How much stimulus does a respondent need to be able to answer the questions? Do specific stimuli have to be used to elicit a response? How complex do the stimuli have to be?
Amount of data needed	How detailed do the respondent's answers have to be? Will probing activities be needed to obtain richer amount of data? How many questions should there be? How long should the respondent expect to take?
Research topic sensitivity	To what degree are the survey's questions socially, politically and/or personally sensitive?
Respondent	
Diversity in specified characteristics	How many prospective respondents share some common characteristics that are related to the implementation and quality of the type of survey method being considered or used?
Incidence rate	What percentage of the defined target population has the key characteristics to qualify for being included in the survey?
Participation rate	Are the selected respondents able to completely interact in the question-and-answer process? What is the person's ability to participate? What is the person's degree of willingness to participate? What is the knowledge level requirement for a person to participate in the survey process?

Situational Factors

In an ideal situation, the researcher's sole focus would be on the collection of accurate data. However, we live in an imperfect world and researchers must reckon with the competing objectives of budget, time and data quality. In most survey research methods, the goal is to produce usable data in as short a time as possible at the lowest cost. Finding the optimal balance between these three factors is frequently a ticklish task. It may not be difficult to generate large amounts of data in a short time if quality is ignored. But excellent data quality can be achieved only through expensive and time-consuming methods. In selecting a particular type of survey method, the researcher commonly considers all the situational factors in combination.

Budget

The budget is the amount of resources available to the researcher. While budgets are commonly thought of in terms of amount of money spending, other resources such as staff size can have similar constraining effects. Most researchers face budget constraints. The resources available for a study can greatly affect choice of the method. For example, if only 500 hours are available in the research department, it would be impossible to conduct a personal survey on more than 1,000 respondents of 30 minutes each. The researcher might select a mail survey because developing the survey form, mailing it and collecting the responses would take much less time than personal surveys. In a similar manner, a €10,000 budget for a 1,000-person study limits the researcher to spending €10 per person. Given this constraint, the researcher might elect to use a telephone survey. It should be noted that the researcher is not required to spend all the budgeted money or personnel resources in conducting any type of quantitative survey, but most researchers will try to keep the research design and activities cost-effective if at all possible.

In spite of the obvious importance of the budget factor, it is frequently taken as not the sole determinant of the choice of a particular type of survey method. In practice, the budget is often considered along with the data quality and time factors.

Completion Time Frame

For decisions to be effective, they often must be made within a specified time period. The time frame commonly has a direct bearing on the data gathering method. Long time frames allow the researcher the luxury of selecting the method that will produce the best data. In many situations, however, the affordable time frame is much shorter than desired, forcing the researcher to choose a method that may not be the researcher's ideal one. Some primary data surveys, such as direct mail or personal surveys, require relatively long time frames. Other methods, such as telephone surveys or shopping-intercepts, can be done more quickly.

Quality Requirement

Data quality is a complex issue that encompasses issues of scale measurement, questionnaire design, sample design, and data analysis. Data quality is too complex to discuss in this section, but a brief overview of three key issues will help explain the impact of data quality on the selection of a particular type of survey method.

Completeness of Data.   The first key data quality issue is the completeness of the data. Completeness refers to the depth and breadth of the data. Having complete data allows the researcher to paint a total picture, fully describing the information from each respondent. Incomplete data will lack some detail, resulting in a picture that is somewhat vague or unclear.

Personal surveys can be very complete, while mail surveys may not be. In some cases, the depth of information needed to make an informed decision will dictate that an in-depth personal survey be the appropriate method. In other cases, a telephone survey that allows for short calls and brief response times may be the appropriate choice.

Generalizability.   The second data quality issue is generalizability. Generalizability refers to the data being an accurate portrait of the defined target population. In principle, data that are generalizable accurately describe the population being studied. In contrast, data that are not generalizable cannot accurately reflect the population. In this situation, the data can lead only to less reliable estimates about the population and may truly reflect only the respondents who supplied it. For example, primary data from mail surveys are sometimes thought of as being relatively less generalizable due to low response rates or small samples.

Precision.   The third data quality issue is precision. Precision is related to, but still distinct from, completeness. Precision refers to the degree of exactness of the data in relation to some other possible response. For example, a car company may want to know what colours will be 'hot' for their new models. Respondents may indicate their preference for a bright colour for automobiles. The completeness issue refers to the respondents' preference for red, for example. Precision refers to the preference of red over blue by a two-to-one margin. If all we need to know is that bright colours are preferred, then fairly incomplete and imprecise data will suffice. If we need to know that red is preferred by a two-to-one margin, then both complete and precise data are needed. Mail surveys can frequently deliver precise results, but may not always produce the most generalizable results. Telephone surveys may be generalizable but may lack precision due to short questions and short interview times.

Task Factors

The characteristics of the task placed on respondents also influences the method used to collect data. The respondent's task characteristics can be categorized into four major areas: (1) the difficulty of the task; (2) the stimuli needed to elicit a response from the respondent; (3) the amount of information the respondent is asked to give; and (4) the sensitivity of the research topic.

Difficulty of Task

Task difficulty refers to how hard a respondent needs to work. Some marketing research questions involve very difficult tasks. For example, taste tests require respondents to sample foods prepared under very controlled conditions. In this example, the task difficulty is primarily in creating exactly the same stimulus for each respondent. In other cases, the respondent may have to work very hard to answer the questions. Sometimes product or brand preference testing involves many similar products and therefore can be laborious for the respondents. In general, the more complex the survey environment the greater the need for trained interviewers to help respondents complete the survey. Regardless of the difficulty of the survey task, the researcher should try to make it easy for the respondent to fully answer the questions.

> **Task difficulty** How hard a survey respondent needs to work and how much preparation the researcher needs to do.

Stimuli Needed to Elicit the Response

Frequently, researchers need to expose respondents to some type of stimulus in order to elicit a response. The stimuli may consist of products (as in taste tests), promotional visuals (as in advertising research), or some physical entity used to elicit the respondent's opinion. Some sort of personal involvement is needed in situations where respondents have to touch, see, or taste something. It is very difficult for the researcher to maintain control over such situations without a trained interviewer. In product concept research, for example, respondents frequently need to see and touch the product in order to form an opinion.

The actual form of the personal survey may vary. It is not always necessary to design a one-on-one survey. For example, people may come in groups to a central location for taste testing, or people in shopping-intercepts can be shown videotapes to elicit their opinions on advertising.

Amount of Data Needed

Researchers are always looking for ways to get more data from respondents. Yet respondents have limits in time, energy, patience and knowledge, among other things. Generally speaking, if a large amount of detailed data is required from respondents, a person-administered approach is usually more appropriate than a non-person-administered approach. Conversely, if very simple data is needed in small amounts, a telephone-administered approach can suffice.

The researcher's task is to achieve the best match between the type of survey method and the amount of data needed. In addition, the researcher has to assess the trade-off between getting more data and risking respondent fatigue and impatience. Ideally, prior to implementing the survey, an assessment of whether the respondent has the necessary knowledge to provide the amount of data needed will increase the quality of the data subsequently obtained.

Research Topic Sensitivity

In some cases, the problem may require researchers to ask some socially or personally sensitive questions. **Research topic sensitivity** is the degree to which a specific survey question leads the respondent to give a socially acceptable response. Examples of areas of sensitive questions are income, racial issues, environmental issues, politics, religion and personal hygiene. In these and other sensitive areas, the researcher should be careful. They should realize the fact that when asked about a sensitive issue, some respondents may feel they should give a socially acceptable response even if they actually feel or behave otherwise. In addition, some respondents simply refuse to answer those questions they consider too personal or sensitive. Others may even go further to terminate the whole interview. Typically, the less sensitive research topics are those that relate to issues such as brand preference, shopping behaviours and satisfaction levels. Such questions are usually viewed as being non-intrusive or otherwise not problematic.

> **Research topic sensitivity** The degree to which a survey question leads the respondent to give a socially acceptable response.

Respondent Factors

Since most marketing research projects target pre-specified types of people, the third major factor in selecting the appropriate type of survey method is the respondents' characteristics. The extent to which members of the target group of respondents share common characteristics will have some influence on the type of survey method selected. The following discussion will centre on three facets of respondent characteristics: diversity, incidence and participation.

Diversity in Specified Characteristics

Diversity in specified characteristics of respondents refers to the degree to which respondents share some characteristics that have impact on the implementation and quality of the type of survey method being adopted. The more diverse the respondents, the lower the proportion of respondents who share these characteristics. The less diverse the respondents, the higher this proportion and therefore the more beneficial for the use of the type of survey method that requires those characteristics.

For example, assume the defined target population is specified as people who own or have access to a fax machine. In a high fax machine penetration society, diversity is low and a computer-generated fax survey can be an effective and cost-efficient method. On the contrary, in societies where the target population does not have convenient access to a fax machine, fax surveys will fail.

> **Diversity in specified characteristics** The degree to which the respondents share characteristics that affects the implementation and quality of the type of survey method being adopted.

There are cases where the researcher may assume a particular survey type-related characteristic is shared by many people in the defined target population, when in fact significantly fewer than expected share that characteristic. For example, in some countries, judging from what is seen in big cities, the penetration rate of the Internet seems to be very high. In fact, the Internet penetration rate may be significantly lower in the rural parts of these countries.

In addition to the problem of gaining access to enough number of respondents, the diversity issue can also lead to another serious problem. In the cases of the fax machine or the Internet noted above, for example, people who do not own or have access to either of these may be different demographically, socio-economically or in other aspects from people who do. Under this circumstance, fax or Internet surveys will never be able to attain results that are representative of the target population.

Incidence Rate

The term **incidence rate** refers to the percentage of the general population who are the subject for the research topic of question. For example, in implementing a car owner survey, the incidence rate in Luxembourg is high because household car ownership there is more than 85 per cent. On the other hand, as in many other countries, the incidence rate in Luxembourg is low for an airplane pilot survey simply because the defined target group for the survey (airplane pilots) is very small in relation to the general population.

The incidence rate is expressed as a percentage. An incidence rate of 5 per cent means that 5 out of 100 members of the general population have the qualifying characteristic(s) sought in a given research study.

> **Incidence rate** The percentage of the general population who are the subject of the marketing research project in question.

As you may imagine, the incidence rate can have an impact on the cost of conducting survey research. When the incidence rate is very low, the researcher will spend considerably more time and money in locating enough respondents. In doing survey research, the researcher has the difficult goal to reduce the search time and expenditure of qualifying prospective respondents while attempting to maximize the number of responses within given time and budget constraints.

Participation rate

Respondent participation involves three basic forms: the respondent's ability to participate, the respondent's willingness to participate and the respondent's knowledge level of the topic or object. **Ability to participate** refers to the ability of the respondent to get together with the interviewer throughout a question-and-answer interchange. The ability of a respondent to share their thoughts with the researcher or interviewer is an important method-selection consideration. It is very frustrating for the researcher to find a qualified respondent who is willing to respond but for some reason is unable to participate in the study. For example, a busy business executive may be willing to participate but cannot find the time for the purpose. Similarly, while some shoppers might like to participate in a shopping-intercept survey, unfortunately they might be in a hurry to pick up children from day care or school and therefore have to decline the invitation. In such cases, a method such as a mail survey, in which the respondent can decide on the best time to complete the questions, may be an attractive option. As the above examples illustrate, the inability-to-participate problem is very common. To get around it, most telephone surveys, for example, allow for the respondent to be called back at a more convenient time. This illustrates the general rule that marketing researchers make every possible effort to respect the respondent's time constraints.

> **Ability to participate** The ability of both the respondent to get together with the interviewer throughout a question-and-answer interchange.

A second component of survey participation is the prospective respondent's **willingness to participate**, that is, the respondent's inclination to share their thoughts. Some people will respond simply because they have some interest in the subject or are instinctively more cooperative. Others will not respond because they are not interested, wish to preserve their privacy, find the topic objectionable, or simply have a negative or sceptical attitude towards marketing research in general. In any case, a self-selection process is in effect. The type of survey method selected affects the self-selection process. People find it much easier to ignore a mail survey than to refuse a person in a shopping-intercept or personal in-home/in office survey.

> **Willingness to participate** The respondent's inclination to share his or her thoughts.

Knowledge level is the degree to which the selected respondents have the knowledge or experience to answer questions about the survey topic. The respondents' knowledge level plays a

> **Knowledge level** The degree to which the selected respondents have knowledge of or experience with the survey's topic.

critical role in whether or not they agree to participate. The knowledge-level component also has a direct impact on the quality of the data collected. For example, a large manufacturer of computer software wanted to identify the key factors that small wholesalers use to decide what electronic inventory tracking system they would need for improving their just-in-time delivery services to retailers. The manufacturer decided to conduct a telephone survey among a selected group of 100 small wholesalers that did not currently use any type of electronic inventory tracking system. In the process of trying to set up the initial survey, the interviewers noticed that about 80 per cent of the responses were 'not interested'. In probing that response, they discovered that most of the respondents felt they were not familiar enough with the details of the system to be able to discuss the survey issues. As a general rule, the more detailed the information needed the higher the respondent knowledge level must be to get them to participate in the survey.

Over the years, researchers have developed various strategies to increase participation levels. One frequently used strategy is that of offering some type of incentive. Incentives can include both monetary gifts such as a €10 note and non-monetary items such as a pen, a coupon to be redeemed for a food product, or entry into a prize draw. To illustrate this point, let's take an example assuming that the researcher decides to collect data by executing a personal survey.

It is important to note that incentive strategies should ideally not be overly promoted as a reward for respondent participation. Over-emphasis on rewards is likely to attract an undesirably higher proportion of the respondents who participate overwhelmingly for what they can 'earn' afterwards, and can serve as the wrong motivator for people deciding to participate in a survey. Read the nearby Closer Look at Research box regarding respondent participation.

 ## A Closer Look at Research *(In the field)*
Respondent Cooperation

Downward Trend of Respondent Cooperation

Respondent cooperation has been declining, as evidenced in a variety of published sources relating to Government surveys and national surveys such as the National Readership Survey and the National Medical Readership Survey. This worry has been further affirmed in the results of an online survey with Marketing Research Society members undertaken by the Society in collaboration with the University of Strathclyde and the University of Westminster.

Nine hundred and thirty-three members completed the survey. On average, their perceptions of refusal rates ranged from 30 per cent of eligible respondents refusing during attempted in-home surveys through to 40 per cent for telephone surveys with the public. Perceived refusal rates were worse for business respondents ranging from 39 per cent in face-to-face surveys through to 45 per cent for telephone surveys. These figures were all expected to increase further over the next five years, leading to escalation in research costs and timescales.

Although increased direct marketing was cited as one of the main contributory factors, too many long, poorly designed questionnaires were seen as being equally to blame. Such questionnaires are resulting in members of the public becoming increasingly bored with market research. The relationship between market researchers and respondents was being viewed as unidirectional, providing little benefit or sense of fulfilment to the respondent.

One respondent suggested: 'We need to move to new innovative ways of engaging respondents, which makes it more fun for them to take part and enables them to see a real benefit.' Other respondents stated that more feedback should be provided to respondents about the outcomes of the research so that the value of their participation becomes clearer.

Source: Research Magazine, News Archive, www.research-live.com

Suggestions for Improving Respondent Cooperation

CMOR, a leading research organization focusing on respondent cooperation research, has conducted a Research Profession Image Study in 2006 looking into respondent attitudes, beliefs and behaviours. Five recommendations have been derived from this study:

- Value of research: Emphasis should be placed on communicating the value of research to respondents; this can be a powerful motivator to respondent cooperation.

- Length: Short, dynamic surveys are much more likely to be perceived in a positive light by respondents.

- Privacy: Privacy concerns are substantial throughout the public; it is therefore critical to communicate the confidential nature of research and your privacy policy to respondents.

- Motivation: Incentives are a large factor in panel research participation, but the knowledge that the respondent's opinion makes a difference is a greater motivating factor for other types of samples.

- Modality: Multimode surveys can be tailored to the respondent; respondents who refuse one particular type of mode (e.g. telephone) may be more likely to participate in a mode (e.g. mail) with characteristics that are personally more attractive to them.

Case 1: Finnish Sulake Company's Surveys on the Global Teen Market

Imagine asking 42,000 tech-savvy teenagers around the globe about their buying and spending habits and brand preferences. How long would it take to conduct such marketing research? If you wanted to zero in on kids who regularly played online games or engaged in networked communities in Web-based virtual worlds, how would your marketing research team target them and then verify their activity in these online parallel universes?

Sulake, the Finnish company that created Habbo, a popular 8-year-old virtual world aimed at teens, found a way to survey more than 42,000 such consumers in 22 countries, by soliciting responses to questions about real world global shopping preferences from Habbo avatars. Its first Global Habbo Youth Survey, conducted in association with Finnish market researcher 15/30, was published in the form of a 200-plus page report in 2007, and it's now available to curious corporations for about €2,500.

Habbo is a cartoony virtual world where teens create retro, highly pixelated alter egos. They can meet up in public spaces, build and participate in social networks, listen to streaming music and also create their own rooms and furnish them with digital versions of furniture and doodads that they pay real money for. Celebrities also enter Habbo as avatars: Heavy metal singer Ozzy Osbourne and pop star Lily Allen have visited Habbo's British site, while BMX champion Matt Hoffman's avatar hung out in the US site. And major corporations including Nintendo buy advertising space, such as a virtual billboard, or sponsor themed gathering spots for avatars. To date, more than 80 million avatars have been created since Habbo opened in 1999.

In the past, Sulake had used data on flesh-and-blood Finnish teens gathered by youth market research specialist 15/30 to help identify real life trends that they might apply to the design and development of Habbo site. But then Sulake realized it could tap its millions of avatars for information on real-life teen trends around the world. 'We wanted to focus on how users are behaving and how they are buying. At first, we thought we would simply use the information for internal purposes, for product development,' says Emmi Kuusikko, director of user and market insight at Sulake. 'Then we saw that we could do global research about teens' lives.' So Sulake and 15/30 solicited respondents in 22 countries across Europe, North America and Asia by sending a message to their avatars, which users received when they logged into their accounts. This linked to an external, Web-based questionnaire. The scope of the responses exceeded all expectations. As Kuusikko said, 'It is extremely rewarding to carry out this quantitative research. The teens were so eager to participate. They were in their own environment, an environment they can trust.' Besides, the process of surveying teens on this massive, global scale via their avatars is so efficient. 'We found we could gather this data in about a week,' says Kuusikko optimistically.

Some trend watchers think mining virtual worlds for teen trend data is a logical and timely marketing research strategy. 'The membrane between our real and our virtual worlds has become very thin, especially for teens today. Most of their social interaction takes place with a screen, whether it's on social networking sites, instant messaging, using a mobile phone to take photos or watch TV, or even just plain emailing,' observes Robyn Waters, the head of an eponymous trend watching firm. 'For this generation, interacting in the virtual world isn't just a trend. It's their life,' Waters continues. 'Trend watching in virtual worlds makes sense for any business in today's environment that wants to be around for the next generation.'

But other professional trend watchers warn that marketers should remember the demographics that are being represented, specifically, a teen who likes online games and prefers, or is at least comfortable with, having a digital alter ego. Teens who like to be authentic about their personalities and who lean towards uploading photographs to Facebook.com might differ in shopping

marketing research in action

habits from those who create cartoon-like selves in Habbo, cautions Heldi Dangelmaier, chief executive of 3iYing, a marketing firm that relies on teenage girls to develop marketing strategies for companies such as Virgin Mobile.

'With Facebook and MySpace, it's clear that many teen girls, at least, are interested in reality, rather than in virtual worlds,' says Dangelmaier, a former consultant to video game companies such as Electronic Arts and Sega, for which she researched girls' relationships to games. 'When surveying what kids want in the real world within an online multiplayer game or virtual world, it's important to ask, exactly who's in there?' she says.

Source: Business Week, 2007.

Questions

1 Do you agree or disagree with conducting surveys on the real world market for teenagers via their avatars in the virtual world? Give reasons for your response.

2 Is there any gender difference in the effectiveness of this survey approach?

3 Is there any cultural difference in the effectiveness of this survey approach?

4 Would the personality of the teenager influence the effectiveness of this survey approach?

5 Teenagers are officially defined as people aged between 13 and 19. Could this survey approach be adopted for people other than teenagers? If no, why? If yes, why and what are the people by age on whom this approach could work?

6 Would it be the case that this survey approach is more appropriate for some industries/products than others?

Case 2: Determining the Appropriate Type of Survey Method for the JP Hotel Preferred Guest Card Research Project

This illustration is designed to integrate the chapter's information on the types of survey method with the ongoing example of JP Hotel. The objective is to illustrate the activities a researcher undertakes in deciding which communication mode is appropriate when using the survey method to collect primary data. These activities normally begin Phase II of the research process (Select the Appropriate Research Design). To enhance understanding of this illustration, it will be helpful to review the information on the JP Hotel Preferred Guest Card research project presented in earlier chapters.

Background

Initially, the research objectives and data requirement identified in Phase I of the research process play a key role in determining whether a survey, an experiment, or an observation should be used to collect the needed primary data. Previously the researcher described the five research objectives of the JP Hotel research project as follows:

1 To determine card usage patterns among known JP Hotel Preferred Guest Card holders.

2 To identify and evaluate the privileges associated with the card programme and how important the card is as a factor in selecting a hotel for business purposes.

3 To determine business travellers' awareness of the card programme.

4 To determine whether or not JP Hotel should charge an annual fee for card membership.

5 To identify profile differences between heavy users, moderate users, light users and non-users of the card.

An assessment of these objectives shows that some type of descriptive research study should be conducted. The corresponding data requirement suggests the need for demographic, attitudinal and behavioural data from the respondents. These research objectives and data requirement led the researcher to decide that survey would be the most effective approach to collect the data. Now a decision had to be made regarding the most feasible mode for asking the questions and recording responses. Should the survey use a person-administered, telephone-administered, or self-administered approach?

Factors for Determining the Appropriate Type of Survey Method

While there are many factors to consider, the researcher conducted a comparison analysis of the three basic approaches using some of the situational, task and respondent factors displayed in Exhibit 7.12. He created an evaluation matrix (see Exhibit 7.13). Using his knowledge of the three alternative approaches and their strengths and weaknesses, he cross-evaluated the different types of survey method by ranking how well each method would achieve each of the listed factors. His ranking scheme consisted of using 1 to represent 'excellent,' 2 for 'good,' 3 for 'weak,' and N/A for 'not applicable'. As he did the actual evaluations, his rankings were influenced by such factors as cost and time considerations, the need to use multi-attribute scales (see Chapter 12), the difficulty of the question/response process, and the geographic diversity of the defined target population.

The Decision on the Type of Survey Method

After reviewing the results, the researcher determined the appropriate mode for conducting the survey would be a self-administered one where the selected respondents would read and respond to the survey's questions without the aid of any trained interviewer. How did he arrive at that decision? Initial interpretation of the cross-evaluation suggested that any of the three alternative modes for administering a descriptive survey could be appropriate. There is no one method that stands out as being the best. They all have their own benefits and weaknesses.

In this situation, the final decision was influenced by the fact that the defined target population was thousands of business travellers spread across different countries. The cost and time requirements in using a person-administered design outweighed the potential increased quality. Given the demographic, attitudinal and behavioural data requirement to fulfill the research objectives, the survey would have to include a significant number of question scales. In addition, some of the question scales would have to use multi-sensitive scale descriptors to meet the study's data requirement. Consequently, employment of a telephone-administered survey would not be desirable for two reasons. First, questions that use multi-sensitive scale descriptors are difficult for respondents to complete over the phone because they cannot easily visualize the different scale point alternatives. Second, the respondents are business people who generally will not answer a survey that takes more than 10 to 20 minutes to complete.

In this situation, a self-administered survey would not encounter the same problems associated with either person- or telephone-administered methods. Overall, self-administered surveys are less expensive than the alternatives. Major concerns are low response rates, control over possible non-response error, overall time frame for completing data collection activities and data quality. The researcher was concerned about these weaknesses, but felt that good planning and execution of the processes underlying the self-administered survey would minimize the weaknesses while still meeting the study's data requirement.

EXHIBIT 7.13 Factors Affecting the Selection of the Type of Survey Method

Factors	Person-Administered Survey	Telephone-Administered Survey	Self-Administered Survey
Budget			
Need for available money	3	2	1
Need for available staff	3	2	1
Completion time frame	3	1	2
Quality requirement			
Completeness of data	1	3	2
Generalizability	1	2	2
Precision	1	2	2
Difficulty of task			
Amount of thought	3	2	1
Preparation time	3	2	1
Information requirement			
Amount of information	1	3	2
Depth of information	1	3	2
Type of data	1	3	1
Length of survey	1	3	1
Research topic sensitivity	3	2	1
Diversity in specified characteristics	1	1	2
Geographic dispersion	3	1	1
Incidence rate	1	1	1
Search/contacting time	3	2	1
Participation rate			
Ability to participate	3	2	2
Willingness to participate	3	2	2
Knowledge level of topic	1	1	1
Overall cost per respondent	3	2	1
Likely response rate	1	2	2
Control of potential errors			
Interviewer error	3	2	[N/A]
Response error	2	2	2
Non-response error	1	2	2

Questions

Assume the role of the researcher in the JP Hotel Guest Card research project situation. Using your newfound knowledge about various types of online survey, create a new Exhibit 7.13 by adding the online survey discussed in the chapter, then go through and rank the four different survey approaches using the same three-point scheme described above. After creating the new ranking, analyse them and answer the following questions:

1   What type of survey approach would you now recommend to JP Hotel's management team? Why?

2   Should additional factors be included in your table of factors? If not, why not? If yes, what factors and why?

3   In this new situation, should the management team give final approval for this research project? Why or why not?

Summary of Learning Objectives

- **Explain the advantages and disadvantages of the survey method to collect primary data.**
  Some of the main advantages of the survey method are the ability to accommodate large sample sizes, generalizability of results, ability to distinguish small differences between diverse sampled groups and relative ease of administering and recording questions and answers. In contrast, some of the main disadvantages of this method are the potential difficulty in developing appropriate survey design, limit to the depth of the data structures, and limited control over timeliness.

- **Discuss the many types of survey method available to researchers. Identify and discuss the factors that drive the choice of different types of survey method.**
  Survey method is generally divided into four generic types. One is the person-administered survey, in which there is significant face-to-face interaction between the interviewer and the respondent. Second is the telephone-administered survey. In this type the telephone is used to conduct the question-and-answer exchanges. Computers are now used in many ways in telephone surveys, such as in telephone number selection and data recording. Third is the self-administered survey, where there is little, if any, actual face-to-face contact between the researcher and prospective respondents. The respondent reads the questions and records their answers. Many of the emerging technology's types of survey method are self-administered, although some, such as virtual reality, will require human intervention. The fourth is the online survey, which includes email survey and Internet survey.

  There are three major factors affecting the choice among different types of survey method: situational characteristics, task characteristics and respondent characteristics. With situational factors, consideration must be given to such elements as budget, completion time frame, and quality requirement. Also, the researcher must consider the overall task requirements and ask questions like 'How difficult are the tasks?' 'What stimuli will be needed to evoke responses?' 'How much data is needed from the respondent?' and 'To what degree are the questions sensitive?' Finally, researchers must be concerned about the diversity in specified characteristics of the prospective respondents, the likely incidence rate and the degree of survey participation. Maximizing the quantity and quality of data collected while minimizing the cost and time of the survey generally requires the researcher to make trade-offs.

- **Explain how the electronic revolution is affecting the administration of survey research.**
  With the continuous advances in telecommunication and computer technologies, many new survey techniques are available to researchers for collecting primary raw data from people.

The range of new techniques continues to grow and some obvious examples are computer-assisted personal survey, computer-assisted telephone survey, computer automated telephone survey, email survey and Internet survey. There is little doubt that the time requirement of data collection can be significantly decreased with these new survey techniques.

■ **Understand the strengths and weaknesses of each type of survey method.**
It is important to remember that all types of survey method have strengths as well as weaknesses. No single type is the best choice under all circumstances. A good researcher should not be limited to a single type of survey method. In some circumstances, innovative combinations of two or more survey types can produce excellent results, as the strengths of one type can be used to overcome the weaknesses of another.

■ **Identify and explain the types of errors that can occur in survey research.**
The researcher needs to evaluate the errors that potentially exist in the research results. All errors are either sampling error or non-sampling error. By far the greatest amount of error that can reduce data quality comes from non-sampling error sources. Three major sources of error are respondent error (i.e. non-response and response errors); measurement and design error (i.e. construct development, scale measurement, survey instrument design, data analysis and misinterpretation errors); faulty problem definition error and administrative errors (i.e. data processing, interviewer and sample design errors).

Key Terms and Concepts

1　Identify and discuss the advantages and disadvantages of using the survey method to collect primary data in marketing research.

2　What are the three critical components for determining data quality? How does achieving data quality differ in person-administered surveys and self-administered surveys?

3　Explain why survey designs that include a trained interviewer are more appropriate than computer-assisted survey designs in situations where the task difficulty and stimuli requirements are extensive.

4　Explain the major differences between in-home/in-office surveys and shopping-intercept surveys. Make sure you include their advantages and disadvantages.

5　How might measurement and design errors affect respondent errors? Develop three recommendations to help researchers increase the response rates in direct mail and telephone-administered surveys.

6　What possible issues associated with customer behaviour and consumption patterns might be extremely sensitive ones to directly question respondents about? How might researchers overcome the difficulties of collecting sensitive data?

7　What is 'non-response'? Identify four types of non-response found in surveys.

8　How does a wireless phone survey differ from computer-assisted and completely automated telephone surveys?

9　What are the advantages and disadvantages associated with online surveys?

10　How might a faulty problem definition error on the part of the researcher affect the implementation of a mail survey?

1　Develop a cross-table of the factors used to select from person-administered, telephone-administered, self-administered and online survey designs. Then discuss the appropriateness of those selection factors across each type of survey design.

2　What impact, if any, will advances in telecommunication and computer technologies have on survey research practices?

3　The regional sales manager for a national office furniture manufacturer interviews its sales representatives in the Midlands and asks them questions about the percentage of their time spent making presentations to new potential customers, talking on the telephone with current customers, working on the computer and engaging in on-the-job activities. What potential sources of error might be associated with the manager's line of questioning?

4　Revisiting Exhibit 7.2, which describes the different types of sampling and non-sampling errors found in survey designs, identify five potential sources of error that have direct ethical implications. Write a short report that discusses the ethical issues associated with each type of error source and the strategies that a researcher should implement to resolve each.

5   Go to the library. Find and read a market research report published by an internationally known market research company within the last two years. Evaluate the survey design being used in that report. Write a two-page report that points out the design's strengths and weaknesses.

6   What types of research studies lend themselves logically to using email as the communication method in surveying respondents? What are the advantages and disadvantages of using email surveys?

7   Comment on the ethics of the following situations:

- A researcher plans to use invisible ink to code his direct mail questionnaires to identify those respondents who return the questionnaire.
- A telephone interviewer calls at 10:00 pm on a Sunday and asks to conduct a survey.
- A manufacturer purchases 100,000 email addresses from a national email distribution house and plans to email out a short sales promotion under the heading 'We Want to Know Your Opinions'.

8   Recall from previous chapters the continuing example of Jimmy Spice's restaurant. The owner gained some preliminary insights into customers' attitudes and restaurant patronage behaviours from conducting 50 qualitative in-depth interviews. Now, they believe it is critical to obtain more descriptive detailed attitudinal and behavioural information representative of their larger potential target market of customers within the South East region. They decide they need to conduct some type of quantitative-based survey research, but are not sure which approach would be more effective in gathering the necessary data. Their budget is limited to about €5,000 and they need the information within the next 45 days. Using your understanding of the material in this chapter, respond to the following and provide support for your recommendations.

a   Develop a list of possible research questions that might be useful in helping the restaurant owner better understand the restaurant aspects that potential customers like and dislike, what creates a satisfying dining experience, the media/communication sources people use to gain knowledge of the different types of restaurants available to dine out at, as well as a demographic profile of who these potential customers typically are.

b   Select one offline and one online type of survey method which you would recommend as feasible methods to conduct a proposed survey that would gather the needed data for answering your listed research questions. Compare and contrast your selected methods based on the strengths and weaknesses of the methods.

c   What general or specific potential systematic errors should the owners be aware of with respect to the two methods that you have recommended above?

d   What particular concerns do these potential errors raise about the accuracy and quality of the data that could be collected using your recommended type of survey method?

e   Based on your responses to the above items, which of the two specific types of survey method would you recommend to the owner and why?

Chapter **8**

Quantitative Research Methods: Experimental Design and Test Marketing Design

LEARNING OBJECTIVES

After reading this chapter, you will be able to

☑ Describe and explain the importance of and differences between the variables used in experimental designs.

☑ Explain the theoretical importance and impact of internal, external and construct validity measures in experimental designs and interpreting functional relationships.

☑ Discuss the three major types of experimental designs used in marketing research. Explain the pros and cons of using causal designs as a means of assessing relationship outcomes.

☑ Explain what test marketing is, the importance and difficulties of executing this, and how the resulting data structures are used by researchers and marketing practitioners.

> Experimental investigations are the linemen of the game of scientific research. They don't gain much publicity, but scientific research cannot advance without them.
> —*Gregory Schadaberg*
> *Senior Research Analyst, EMI Corporation*

Weetos Multigrain Stars: Using Test Marketing to Gauge New Product Acceptance

Cambridge Market Research Ltd., based in Cambridge, England, carried out an independent small-scale market test as part of their Fast Foodfax Market Intelligence service on a new product branded Weetos Multigrain Stars. The product was developed by Weetabix Limited, a breakfast cereal products manufacturer headquartered in Northamptonshire.

The product is a mix of multigrain prebiotic caramel flavoured stars with chocolate flavour wheat hoops, sugar coated and fortified with vitamins and iron. This 500g box, at €1.19 each, was tested on 14 August 2006. The sample comprised 61 consumer panel testers, including 52 adults and 9 children.

Results showed that junior testers 'really loved' this cereal and all but one child were keen for their parents to buy this for them. One of the key attractions was the variety in appearance and taste offered by the combination of 'chocolatey Weetos' and 'crunchy wheaty stars'. The adult testers predicted that this cereal would be a hit with their kids and they were happy to include this in their children's repertoire because it was 'affordable' and 'quite healthy'. Some notable feedbacks were:

'just the right amount of Weetos' / 'lovely shapes'

'tasted nice' / 'not too sweet' / 'good chocolate taste to the Weetos'

'nice and crispy' / 'didn't go soggy'

'good as a dry snack'

The 'bright' purple pack was expected to stand out on the shelf and the size of the box was a welcome feature particularly for larger householders. The sugar coating was noted by health conscious parents, but the facts that the cereal did not taste sweet and a prebiotic was included boosted health perceptions. Purchase intention increased post test and a third of all adult testers considered adding this new product to their regular weekly or fortnightly shopping trips. Over half the total sample felt that this cereal was better than alternatives on the market. Detailed numerical results of the market test are shown below:

Characteristic	Mean Score Out of 5
Initial appeal	3.77
Appearance	3.90
Smell	3.74
Taste	3.73
Texture	3.93
Packaging	4.00
Health	3.71
Value for money	4.04
Overall impression	3.80
Post-test would-buy intention	3.67
Mean total	38.29
Pre-test would-buy intention	3.38
Difference between pre-test and post-test	0.29

Value of Experimentation and Test Marketing

The chapter opener illustrates a practical case of test marketing. Although the research design involved in this case is less sophisticated than many other test marketing cases conducted in a wide variety of business settings, it illustrates the insights that can be gleaned from the implementation of a test marketing design. Indeed, marketing research experimentation, and its main offshoot test marketing, are popular across many business sectors, including food, beverage, perfume and so on.

Test marketing consists of controlled field experiments usually conducted in limited market areas on plausible cause-and-effect relationships between specified marketing variables and market performance indicators. Its main objective is to predict sales, uncover valuable market information, or anticipate likely consequences of a marketing programme for a particular product. With growing popularity, experimental design procedures are employed to investigate potential cause-effect relationships regarding new products or improvements of existing products. Many practitioners use test marketing to determine customer attitudes towards new product ideas, service delivery alternatives, or marketing communication strategies. While exploratory qualitative and descriptive survey studies are extremely effective for collecting primary data in certain situations, they do not establish causal links between various events. Causal research designs are powerful in the sense that they can provide researchers with the appropriate data to understand why certain events occur. The primary focus of this chapter will be introducing and discussing experimental designs and test marketing designs. We also discuss reliability and validity issues that are closely linked to these kinds of designs.

The Nature of Experimentation

Marketing research requires the measurement of variables. **Variables** are the observable and measurable elements (or attributes) of an item or an event. They are the qualities the researcher specifies, studies and draws conclusions about. They can vary in different situations and at different times. To illustrate this concept, let's take the vehicle you are currently driving. Your car is really a composite of many different attributes. The colour, the make and model, the number of cylinders, the miles per gallon and the price are all variables. Any one car has one given set of variable values at any given time. Whenever an object, idea, or event is described, every element by which it can be observed and measured can be considered a variable, including where it is, how it is used and what surrounds it.

> **Variable** Any observable and measurable element (or attribute) of an item or event.

When conducting an experiment, the researcher attempts to identify the relationships among different variables. Let's consider, for example, the following research question: 'How long does it take a customer to place and receive an order from the drive-through at a McDonald's fast food restaurant?' The time it takes to receive a food order is a variable that can be measured quantitatively. That is to say, the different values of the time variable are determined by some method of measurement. But how long it takes a particular customer to receive a food order is complicated by a number of other variables. For instance, what if there were 10 cars waiting in line, or it was 12:00 noon, or it was raining? Additionally, such factors as the number of drive-up windows, the training level of order takers and the number of patrons waiting are all variables. Consequently, all of these variables can have some effect on the time variable.

In turn, the make of the car the person is driving, the number of brothers or sisters he has, and the quantity of food he orders are also variables. But the first two variables are unlikely to have much effect on order time. However, there is a relationship between the quantity of the order and the waiting time, because the more items in the order, the longer it takes to prepare. If it is true that the quantity of food ordered increases one's wait at a drive-through, the researcher can say that there is a **functional relationship** between food quantity ordered and waiting time. As such, it can be concluded that waiting time at a fast food drive-through is a function of the amount of food being ordered. In causal research designs that use experimental procedures, the researcher investigates the functional relationships between variables. The focus is on investigating the systematic change in one variable as another variable changes.

> **Functional relationship** An observable and measurable systematic change in one variable as another variable changes.

Types of Variables Used in Experimental Designs

In using experimental designs, researchers must be especially careful to confirm that the relationships they find between the variables being investigated actually do exist. Attempts must be made to hold constant the influence of extraneous variables so that accurate measures can be made of the variables under investigation. When designing causal research experiments, researchers must understand the four types of variables that are critical in the design process: independent, dependent, control and extraneous (see Exhibit 8.1).

EXHIBIT 8.1 Types of Variable Used in Experimental Designs

Type of Variable	Comments
Independent variable	Also called predictor or treatment variable (X). An attribute or element of an object, idea, or event whose values are directly manipulated by the researcher. The independent variable is assumed to be the causal factor of a functional relationship with a dependent variable.
Dependent variable	Also called criterion variable (Y). An observable attribute or element that is the outcome on specified test subjects that is derived from manipulating the independent variable(s).
Control variables	Variables the researcher controls so they do not affect the functional relationship between the independent and dependent variables included in the experiment.
Extraneous variables	Uncontrollable variables that should average out over a series of experiments. If not accounted for, they can have a confounding impact on the dependent variable measures that could weaken or invalidate the results of an experiment.

A Closer Look at Research *(Using Technology)*
MarketingScan System: a Case of Test Marketing in France

MarketingScan, a test marketing company based in France, has made use of the advance of information technology to set up the MarketingScan system to help its clients' new product marketing planning.

The MarketingScan system uses two French towns, Angers and Le Mans, as the test markets. There are three main reasons for this choice. First, both towns are of relatively large size and have respectively the sixteenth and nineteenth largest populations in France. This allows for greater exposure to test TV campaigns and ease of recruitment of panels. Second, the composition of their population is close to the national average without obviously atypical variations. This increases the representativeness of the data collected. Third, there is a wide variety of companies set up in these two towns, thereby eliminating the problem of skewness towards particular types of business as what could happen in other distributor panels.

The MarketingScan system has two types of panels, the distributor panel and the consumer panel. The distributor panel comprises 14 partner stores (7 hypermarkets, 5 supermarkets and two hard discount stores) in Angers and 10 partner stores (5 hypermarkets and 5 supermarkets) in Le Mans. All checkouts of these partner stores are equipped with the MarketingScan information technology system allowing daily collection of sales and purchase data. Data on in-store action, such as stocking, pricing and promotions, are also collected.

The consumer panel consists of 4,500 households each in Angers and Le Mans, who have been checked and confirmed to be representative of the national population. These 9,000 households make 95 per cent of their daily purchases within the distributor panel. As a panel household, each is equipped with a barcode card scanned at the checkout.

A new product to be tested with the MarketingScan system will be followed week by week. Its ongoing performance results in terms of sales volume, number of purchasers, average weekly sales and market share, will be monitored. They will be delivered to the client ten days after the end of each week. With these results, the strengths and weaknesses of the new product could be identified at an early stage of the test, and necessary adjustment of the marketing mix variables could be made.

During the test period of say 16 weeks, purchase behaviour data, including frequency of purchase, level of consumption and repurchase rate, are collected from point of sale scanning. These data can then be reliability extrapolated to make forecasts for the following 12 months. The forecast accuracy of the system has been proven to be within plus or minus 8 per cent.

In addition, the MarketingScan system incorporates a modelling function that allows an even more accurate measurement of the impact of a new marketing strategy on sales. In order to do so, the baselining model distinguishes, through two indicators, the base sales and the incremental sales. The former reflects the sales performance prior to the implementation of the new marketing strategy, while the latter is the result of the strategy such as promotional leaflets or displays within stores.

Independent variables are those whose values are directly manipulated by the researcher in an experiment. The researcher is interested in identifying functional relationships between independent and dependent variables. In many marketing research experiments, marketing mix variables such as price levels, product/package designs, distribution channel systems, and advertising themes are treated as independent variables. Let's say, for example, that Procter & Gamble (P&G) is interested in determining the relationship between several new package designs for its Ariel brand of laundry detergent and Ariel's unit sales. Using experimental design procedures, the researchers could observe customers' purchasing of the product on four different occasions. On each occasion, the researchers can change the package design from, say, round to square, to rectangular, to oval. Every time the package design is changed, sales can be measured. Since the researchers directly manipulated it, package design serves as the independent variable.

> **Independent variables** Variables whose values are directly manipulated by the researcher.

Dependent variables are measures of outcome that occur during the experiment. They are also referred to as measures of change in the conditions that exist after the experiment is completed. These variables may include such market performance indicators as unit sales, profit levels, and market shares. While values of independent variables are assigned before the experiment begins, this is not possible with dependent variables. Dependent variables are attributes or elements that are affected by the process of the experiment. Their specific outcome values cannot be measured before the experiment begins. In the P&G package design example, the dependent variable is Ariel's unit sales. This variable is measured under each manipulation of the package design. If the researchers want to state the results in terms of a functional relationship, they would say that Ariel's unit sales (the dependent variable) is a function of package design (the independent variable).

> **Dependent variables** Measures of outcome that occur during the experiment, or measures of change in the conditions that exist after the experiment is completed.

Control variables are the conditions or elements that make the research design a true experiment. These are variables that the researcher controls, or does not allow to vary freely or systematically with independent variables. Thus, the average value of a control variable or its impact should not change as the independent variable is manipulated. Researchers must design the experiment so that control variables cannot systematically affect the relationship between the independent and dependent variables. Control variables can present a major problem in using experimental designs to investigate hypothesized functional relationships. For example,

> **Control variables** Variables that the researcher does not allow to vary freely or systematically with independent variables; control variables should not change as the independent variable is manipulated.

if P&G wants to investigate the true relationship between Ariel's unit sales and package design alternatives, the researchers do not want any other variables to influence the measure of unit sales. They would want to make sure the conditions surrounding Ariel's unit sales (the dependent variable) are as similar as possible for each of the package design manipulations (the independent variable). For example, the customers should (1) shop at the same store during each package design manipulation; (2) shop at the same time of day with the same amount of store crowding; and (3) shop on successive days without being exposed to any advertised message for Ariel. In addition, the price and shelf location of Ariel should remain the same on all successive package design manipulations. This points to the problem that there are so many possible influences on Ariel's unit sales that the researchers cannot possibly control all of them. The researchers must, however, control as many as they can.

Extraneous variables, such as mood or instinctive shape preference of consumers, to name but two, cannot be controlled by the researchers. These types of variables may average out over the different manipulations of the independent variables, and thus not have systematic influences on the dependent variable. But they may still weaken the results of the experiment. One method P&G researchers could use to reduce the effects of extraneous variables is to randomize the manipulation conditions of the package design across a number of customers and then measure unit sales. This procedure would have to be accomplished across all of the package design manipulations until a significant number of customers were measured for Ariel unit sales under each manipulation. This procedure is referred to as **complete randomization** of subjects. The desired outcome is that the influence of the extraneous variables will average out over all manipulations of the independent variable. While the measured results under these conditions may not be very precise for any individual test subject, they should be acceptable enough to show a fairly accurate relationship between the independent and dependent variables.

> **Extraneous variables** Variables that cannot be controlled by researchers but that should average out over different trials and thus not systematically affect the results of the experiment.
>
> **Complete randomization** The procedure whereby many subjects are randomly assigned to different experimental treatment conditions, resulting in each group averaging out any systematic effect on the investigated functional relationship between the independent and dependent variables.

The Role of Theory in Experimental Designs

From an experimental design perspective, **theory** is a large body of interconnected propositions about how some portion of a phenomenon operates. Theory underpins the development of hypotheses about relationships. As such, hypotheses are smaller, untested versions of theories.

> **Theory** A large body of interconnected propositions about how some portion of a certain phenomenon operates.

Experimental research is primarily a hypothesis testing method and is often referred to as **deductive research**. Existing theoretical insights can help a researcher in identifying the critical independent variables that might bring about changes in dependent variables. Researchers derive a hypothesis from a theory, design an experiment and gather data to test the hypothesis. There are situations when researchers collect first hand data from which to generate hypotheses in order to create new theories or extend existing theories about a phenomenon. These are referred to as **inductive research**. In practice, researchers often use both deductive and inductive design methods. A researcher may begin an investigation using causal research procedures to test some hypotheses that focus on the cause-effect relationships between variables, but then develop new hypotheses when he sees the data results.

> **Experimental research** An empirical investigation that tests for hypothesized relationships between dependent variables and manipulated independent variables.
>
> **Deductive research** Investigations that are undertaken to test hypothesized relationships derived from the use of existing theories.
>
> **Inductive research** An investigation that collects and analyses primary data, from which to generate hypotheses and test them for creating new theories or extending existing ones.

It is important to understand that experimental and other causal research designs are most appropriate when the researcher wants to find out why certain events occur and why they happen under certain conditions and not others. Identifying and being able to explain cause-effect relationships enables marketing researchers to be in a position to make reasonable predictions about marketing phenomena.

Validity Concerns with Experimental Designs

To better understand causal research designs, we first must examine validity issues that directly affect these designs. Extraneous variables are numerous and difficult to control when using causal designs for testing hypothesized relationships. Their presence may result in contamination of the functional relationship. This contamination clouds the researcher's ability to conclusively determine whether the results of the experiment are valid. **Validity** refers to the extent to which the conclusions drawn from the experiment are true. In other words, do the differences in the dependent variable found through experimental manipulations of the independent variables really reflect a cause-effect relationship? While there are many ways to classify the validity of causal research designs, we will discuss three: *internal* validity, *external* validity and *construct* validity.

> **Validity** The extent to which the conclusions drawn from the experiment are true.

Internal Validity

Internal validity refers to the extent to which the research design accurately identifies causal relationships. In other words, internal validity exists when the researcher can rule out other explanations for the observed conclusions about the functional relationship. For example, in an experiment on the effects of electricity, if you shock someone (experimental treatment) and he jumps (observed effect), and he jumps only because of the shock and for no other reason, then internal validity exists.

> **Internal validity** The extent to which the research design accurately identifies causal relationships.

Why is establishing internal validity of causal research designs important to researchers? The following example illustrates the answer. Let's say a small bakery in Yorkshire, England wanted to know whether or not putting additional icing on its new cakes would cause customers to like the cakes better. Using an experimental design, it tested the hypothesis that its customers liked additional icing on their cakes. As the amount of icing was being manipulated, the bakery discovered the additional icing allowed the cakes to stay more moist. Consequently, it might have been the moistness and not the icing that caused the customers' positive reaction to the new cakes. In an attempt to assess internal validity, control groups were established consisting of customers who were not exposed to the treatment (original icing), but all other conditions (extra moistness) were kept the same. Adding the control group to the experimental design reduced the possibility that the observed effect of the new cakes was caused by something other than the treatment. In this case, if it was the icing, then the treated group should like the new cake more than the control group. But if it was the moistness, then both groups would like the new cake equally.

Exhibit 8.2 displays the types of threats that can negatively affect internal, external and construct validities associated with causal research designs. The latter two will be discussed in the next sections. Here we will discuss the threats to internal validity.

History threats would involve events that occur between the first measurement of the dependent variable and the second measurement. If the objective of the manipulation was to measure changes in a person's attitude about political integrity (dependent variable) resulting from a political history course, the results could be strongly affected if a major political scandal occurred between the first and second manipulation treatments (i.e. while the person was taking the political history course).

Without a doubt, our attitudes and behaviours change as we grow older, and these changes can represent a maturation threat to internal validity. The threat of testing refers to the second administration of the treatment whose scores may be affected by the subjects' experience with the first administration. Changes in observers' attitudes, reduced accuracy of scorers, or changed processes are all examples of the instrumentation threat to internal validity.

When strict random assignment to treatment and control groups is not followed, then selection bias resulting in noncomparable groups could occur, threatening internal validity. Mortality involves the loss of subjects from groups due to natural causes, thereby creating groups of subjects that are no longer comparable.

Ambiguity of causal direction may also be a problem. For instance, do higher family incomes result from higher education levels, or do higher income levels allow higher education levels? Such ambiguities reduce the researcher's ability to differentiate between cause and effect.

Statistical regression is where human beings score differently on each trial in an experiment, with the recorded scores regressing towards the true population mean. In other words, the errors balance out. In those cases where subjects are selected for particular groups based on extreme pre-treatment responses, the observed post-treatment measures will be even more biased.

EXHIBIT 8.2 Validity Types and Threats to Validity

THREATS TO INTERNAL VALIDITY

History	When extraneous factors that enter the experiment process between the first and later manipulations affect measures of the dependent variable.
Maturation	Changes in the dependent variable based on the natural function of time and not attributed to any specific event.
Testing	When learned understanding gained from the first treatment and measures of the dependent variable distort future treatments and measurement activities.
Instrumentation	Contamination from changes in measurement techniques, instruments and/or processes.
Selection bias	Contamination created by inappropriate selection and/or assignment processes of test subjects to experimental treatment and control groups.
Mortality	Contamination due to changing the composition of the test subjects in the experiment.
Ambiguity	Contamination from unclear determination of cause-effect relationship.
Statistical regression	Contamination created when experimental groups are selected on the basis of their extreme responses or scores.

THREATS TO EXTERNAL VALIDITY

Treatment vs. history	Contamination due to the experiment being held on a special day embedded in certain history traits.
Treatment vs. testing	When the pre-measurement process sensitizes test subjects to respond in an abnormal manner to treatment manipulations.
Treatment vs. setting	Generalizing the results to other environments beyond the one used in the experiment.
Treatment vs. selection	Generalizing the results to other categories of people beyond those types used in the experiment.
Treatment vs. treatment	When test subjects in different treatment groups are exposed to different numbers of manipulations.

THREATS TO CONSTRUCT VALIDITY

Inadequate pre-operationalization of variables	Contamination due to inadequate understanding of the complete makeup of the independent and dependent variables included in the experimental design.
Mono-method bias	Contamination due to assessing multi-attribute constructs using single-item measuring instruments.
Mono-operation bias	Contamination created by using only one method to measure the outcome of the dependent variable.
Demand characteristics	Contamination created by test subjects trying to guess the true purpose behind the experiment, thus giving abnormal socially acceptable responses.
Hypothesis guessing	Contamination by test subjects believing they know the desired functional relationship prior to the manipulation treatment.
Evaluation apprehension	Contamination caused by test subjects being apprehensive of the experiment to be taken.
Diffusion of treatment	Contamination due to test subjects discussing the treatment and measurement activities with individuals that have not received the treatment.

The primary weapon against threats to internal validity is random selection of subjects from a heterogeneous target population and then random assignment to treatment groups. This is considered standard practice in experimental research studies.

External Validity

External validity refers to the extent to which a causal relationship found in a study can be expected to be true for the target population. For example, let's say a Belgian food company wanted to find out if its new dessert would appeal to a commercially viable percentage of young Belgian citizens aged between 16 and 30. Obviously, it would be too costly for this company to ask each young person in the country to taste the product.

External validity The extent to which a causal relationship found in a study can be expected to be true for the entire target population.

By using experimental design procedures, the company could randomly select test subjects of the defined target population (aged between 16 and 30) and assign them to different treatment groups, varying one component of the dessert for each group. Different groups taste their 'own' desserts, and subsequently all the subjects taste the same new dessert.

If 60 per cent indicated they would purchase the product, and if in fact 60 per cent of the entire population did purchase the new product when it was marketed, then the results of the study would be considered perfectly externally valid.

Threats to external validity include interactions of treatment with history, testing, setting, selection and treatment exposures. Interactions with history that might lessen external validity could include testing on a special day such as Christmas or Halloween. If the researcher were interested in charitable behaviour, then a treatment manipulation and effect measures administered on Christmas Day might give quite different results than one given at some other less notable time.

After watching several movies emphasizing love for our country and fellow man, the average subject might react significantly differently to certain tested objects on this day than on some other. By the same token, polls on gun control might very likely be affected if taken immediately after the assassination of a major public figure. Generalizability to other time frames would therefore be considerably reduced.

Similar reductions in external validity might occur if the setting of the experiment is poised to influence the observed results. Surely, a fear-of-heights scale administered on top of a mountain would have different results than one administered in a classroom.

The threat of selection bias occurs when the sample is not truly representative of the target population. Asking subjects to participate in an experiment requiring several hours will limit the actual sample to only those who have the spare time and may not generate a truly representative sample.

Another possible threat to external validity can occur when some of the test subjects experience more than one treatment in the experimental setting. The conclusions drawn could not be generalized to situations where individuals received fewer or more treatments. For example, if an experiment was designed to study the effects of a price reduction on product sales in which the product was displayed in two separate locations, the results might fail to be generalized to situations where only one display was used. Here, the extra display competes against price reduction as an explanation of sales.

Construct Validity

Critical to all causal research designs is the ability to accurately identify and understand the independent and dependent variables included in the study. In addition, researchers must be able to accurately measure those variables in order to assess their true functional or cause-effect relationships. Consequently, researchers must attempt to assess the construct validity of both independent and dependent variables prior to executing their experimental or causal research design. **Construct validity** can simply be viewed as the extent to which the variables under investigation are completely and accurately identified prior to hypothesizing any functional relationships. Of the many approaches to establishing construct validity, one that is used widely consists of three steps.

> **Construct validity** The extent to which the variables under investigation are completely and accurately identified prior to hypothesizing any functional relationships.

First, the relationship between the constructs (or variables) of interest must be accurately identified. To illustrate, let's assume a researcher wants to use a construct called motivation to succeed (MTS) as an independent variable in predicting the likelihood of individuals' life success. Those who are measured the highest on the MTS construct will be hypothesized as those most likely to have succeeded in life. The fundamental question that must be addressed is 'What are the observable, real-life indicators of such success?' Using a process referred to as specifying the domain of observable subcomponents related to the construct, let's assume that peer respect, academic achievement and personal financial security represent success in the society being investigated. Knowing the precise nature of this specification is necessary so that the hypothesized relationship can be empirically tested with real data. Otherwise, the details collected will be insufficient to either support or refute the hypothesis.

Second, the researcher executes an experimental design that manipulates MTS and measures the outcome 'life success.' If the resulting data are both positive and substantial in support of the hypothesized functional relationship, then evidence of construct validity exists. Researchers should also attempt to determine what other constructs these observable subcomponents might be related to, such as social position and inherited wealth. To the extent the observable subcomponents are not related to MTS, but rather to other alternative constructs, then the evidence in support of construct validity will be weakened. For example, personal financial security may be the result of inherited wealth and have little to do with motivation to succeed. As a result, it will be necessary to find other observable subcomponents that are more closely related to MTS and that could not generally be caused by other variables.

Third, prior to executing the experiment, researchers compare the proposed measures of the independent and dependent variables with other similar measures. When existing measures of the same construct are highly correlated with the researcher's proposed measures, then there is evidence of **convergent validity** in support of the construct validity we seek. Additional evidence, called **discriminant validity**, may come from a negative correlation between the experiment's measures and those designed to measure completely different constructs.

> **Convergent validity** When the researcher's measures of a construct are highly correlated with known existing measures of the same construct.

> **Discriminant validity** The existence of a negative correlation between the experiment's measures and those measurements of completely different constructs.

Key Threats to Construct Validity

Construct validity can be threatened in many ways, including (1) inadequate pre-operationalization of constructs; (2) mono-operation bias; (3) mono-method bias; (4) hypothesis guessing; (5) demand characteristics; (6) evaluation apprehension; and (7) diffusion of treatment.

To avoid **inadequate pre-operationalization**, the researcher should carefully and completely define the construct as precisely as possible. Fear of heights cannot simply be defined as a fear of high places, since some people are afraid of being on high mountain roads but not in an office in a high rise building or on an aeroplane. As a researcher, it is essential that you know exactly what form of fear you are trying to measure. Then, once the definition has been refined in light of the purpose of the study, you can more precisely select measurable, observable constructs.

> **Inadequate pre-operationalization** Contamination to construct validity measures due to inadequate understanding of the complete makeup of the independent and dependent variables included in the experimental design.

Mono-method and mono-operation bias can threaten construct validity through contamination created by using only one method or single-item measurements. Where possible, researchers should use more than one measuring method and more than a single measure in each method to collect data.

> **Mono-method and mono-operation bias** A particular type of error source that is created when only a single method or a single-item measure is used to collect data for the experiment.

Researchers have found that many subjects try to guess the purpose of the research and respond as they feel the researcher wants them to respond. Called the **demand characteristic**, this threat can be reduced by making the research purpose difficult to guess. For example, one clever psychologist invited people to participate in an experiment, had them wait in an outer office, and then took them into a room where they were asked several questions. In actuality, the experiment involved inter-personal conversational patterns and took place in the waiting room. The conversations were facilitated by the psychologist's helpers posing as subjects, obviously without the knowledge of the real subjects.

Sometimes prior to attending the experiment, subjects may try to guess the functional relationship to be tested and desired by the researcher. They may then respond in an abnormal way to the experiment, thereby producing biased results. This type of threat is known as

hypothesis guessing. Wherever possible, researchers should strive to make the desired functional relationship very difficult if not impossible for their subjects to guess.

> **Demand characteristics** and **hypothesis guessing** Contamination to construct validity measures created by test subjects trying to guess the true purpose or the desired functional relationship behind the experiment and accordingly give socially acceptable responses.

Most of us have exhibited **evaluation apprehension** before an entrance exam or our first job interview. This can also happen to subjects going to the experiment. Because such apprehension can seriously bias the results of many studies, researchers should attempt to reduce it as much as possible. One approach frequently used in marketing research involves ensuring the anonymity of respondents. Careful briefing of respondents by the research team can also help reduce this threat.

> **Evaluation apprehension** Contamination to construct validity measures caused by test subjects' anxiousness of the experiment to be taken.

The final threat to construct validity involves the **diffusion of treatment**. Since it is rarely possible to completely isolate subjects, the control group may exchange information with the treatment group, or those who previously completed a questionnaire may discuss it with those who have yet to participate. Although the researcher cautions subjects not to discuss the research, such efforts are often unsuccessful. Taking several samples from the target population at various locations and under different conditions usually reduces this threat. In fact, using different samples from the population of interest is a good way to reduce threats to construct and other types of validity.

> **Diffusion of treatment** Contamination to construct validity measures due to test subjects discussing the treatment and measurement activities with individuals yet to receive the treatment.

Reliability of Experimental Research Designs

We must also understand reliability in causal research designs. For **experimental design reliability** to exist, researchers must be able to demonstrate that their experiment can be repeated and similar conclusions will be reached. For the same organization there can be benefits, in addition

> **Experimental design reliability** The degree to which the design and its procedures can be replicated and achieve similar conclusions about hypothesized relationships.

to reliability, through repeating the procedures used in causal research designs. For example, a company such as Sony, which has many different types of consumer electronics products, could standardize its design and testing procedures for investigating new product acceptance. Such standardization of procedures could lead to significant cost reductions within Sony's research and development activities.

Improving the Internal and External Validity of Experimental Designs

The ultimate goal of experimental research is determining the true causal or functional relationship between the independent and dependent variables. Researchers must minimize the extent to which extraneous variables confound experimental results. As a way to counter threats to internal and external validity, researchers can implement several techniques unique to experimental designs.

Inclusion of Control Groups

When designing an experiment, the researcher must determine who will be assigned to the groups that will be exposed to the manipulation and who will be assigned to the control group that does not receive the manipulation. Control groups represent the greatest strength of the experiment and the best way to ensure internal validity.

Time Order of the Manipulation Exposure

The researcher must also determine which variables, independent or dependent, will occur first. This can be accomplished by using pre-experimental measures of the variables prior to manipulation or by establishing experimental treatment and control groups that do not differ in terms of influencing the dependent variable before the manipulation takes place.

Exclusion of Non-similar Test Subjects

To increase internal validity, the researcher can select only those test subjects who have similar and controllable characteristics. Let's say, for example, that the researcher is interested in certain product purchasing behaviours among a targeted group of consumers. This study's results might be confounded by differences in age and occupational status of the test subjects. To counter this possibility, the researcher would select only those test subjects with age and occupational status characteristics similar to the target market. By doing so, the researcher is eliminating extraneous variation due to age and occupation.

Matching Extraneous Variables

Through the process of matching, the researcher measures certain extraneous variables on an individual basis. Those who respond similarly to the variables are then allocated to the experimental and control groups. This process can control for selection bias and enhance internal validity.

Randomization of Test Subjects to Treatment and Control Groups

Randomization of the assignment of test subjects to the experimental and control groups can help make the groups equivalent. The key to true randomization of test subjects is that the randomness must be secured in a carefully controlled manner. To enhance external validity, the researcher should also randomly select settings and times for the experiment based on the population or events under investigation. By ensuring the above procedures are followed in the experimental design, the researcher is in greater control of potential contamination of the relationships between the independent and dependent variables and increases the experiment's ability to accurately identify true causal or functional relationships.

Types of Experimental Research Designs

Experimental designs can be classified into three groups: (1) pre-experiments, (2) true experiments, and (3) quasi-experiments (See Exhibit 8.3). The main difference among these groups is the degree of control the researcher exercises in the design and execution. To facilitate understanding of the different types of experimental designs, we use the following set of symbols:

X = *The exposure of an independent variable (treatment manipulation) to a group of test subjects for which the effects are to be determined.*

O = *The process of observation or measurement of the dependent variable (outcome) on the test subjects.*

[R] = *The random assignment of test subjects to separate treatment groups.*

EG = *The experimental group of test subjects.*

CG = *The control group of test subjects.*

→ = *A movement through time, normally displayed as left-to-right movement.*

Note also that vertical alignment of symbols implies they refer to activities that occur simultaneously at a prescribed point in time, and that horizontal alignment of symbols implies all those symbols refer to a specific treatment group of test subjects.

Pre-experimental Designs

Three specific pre-experimental designs are available to marketing researchers: the one-shot study; the one-group pretest-posttest; and the static group comparison. These designs are commonly referred to as crude experiments and should be undertaken only when a stronger experimental design is not possible. These designs are characterized by an absence of randomization of test subjects. Their major weakness is the inability to meet internal validity criteria due to a lack of equivalent group comparisons.

One-Shot Study

The one-shot case study can be illustrated as follows:

$$(EG): X \rightarrow O_1$$

An example of this design would be when a researcher wishes to measure customer reactions to a product display in a single store. A design of this nature does not control extraneous variables. It ignores the process of group comparisons that is fundamental in the experimental process. The only comparisons made are those based on common knowledge, past experiences, or general impressions of what the condition would have been had the manipulation not occurred. In this instance, even careful development of accurate measures will not compensate for the inadequate design.

One-Group Pretest-Posttest

The value of the 'one-group pretest-posttest' design is its ability to provide the researcher with a comparison measure. It is diagrammed as follows:

$$(EG): O_1 \rightarrow X^1 \rightarrow O_2$$

EXHIBIT 8.3 Types of Experimental Research Designs in Marketing Research

Pre-experimental Designs

One-shot study	A single group of test subjects is exposed to the independent variable treatment X, and then a single measurement on the dependent variable is taken (O1).
One-group pretest-posttest	First a pre-treatment measure of the dependent variable is taken (O1), then the test subjects are exposed to the independent treatment X, and then a post-treatment measure of the dependent variable is taken (O2).
Static group comparison	There are two groups of test subjects: one group is the experimental group (EG) and is exposed to the independent treatment, and the second group is the control group (CG) and is not given the treatment. The dependent variable is measured in both groups after the treatment.

True Experimental Designs

Pretest-posttest control group	Test subjects are randomly assigned to either the experimental or control group, and each group receives a pre-treatment measure of the dependent variable. Then the independent treatment is exposed to the experimental group, after which both groups receive a post-treatment measure of the dependent variable.
Posttest-only control group	Test subjects are randomly assigned to either the experimental or the control group. The experimental group is then exposed to the independent treatment, after which both groups receive a post-treatment measure of the dependent variable.
Solomon Four Group	This design combines the 'pre test-post test control group' and 'post test-only control group' designs and provides both direct and reactive effects of testing. It is not commonly used in marketing research practices because of complexity and lengthy time requirements.

Quasi-experimental Designs

Nonequivalent control group	This design is a combination of the 'static group comparison' and the 'one-group pre test- post test' pre-experimental designs.
Separate-sample pretest-posttest	Two different groups of test subjects are drawn; neither group is directly exposed to the independent treatment variable. One group receives a pretest measure of the dependent variable. Then after the insignificant independent treatment occurs, the second group of test subjects receives a posttest measure of the dependent variable.
Field experiment	This is a causal design that manipulates the independent variables in order to measure the dependent variable in the natural setting of the event or test.
Factorial Designs	Experimental designs used to investigate the simultaneous effects of two or more treatment (independent) variables on single or multiple dependent (outcome) variables.
Latin square	This design manipulates one independent variable and controls for two additional sources of extraneous variations by restricting randomization to row and column.

The design is subject to the same extraneous confounding factors as with the one-shot study. In addition, history contamination is a major weakness, given events may occur between O_1 and O_2. It can be further affected by maturation and instrumentation problems. The effect of the pretest measure also introduces problems with the testing factor. Even environmental noise (sirens, thunder, phones) can affect results. The only way to control for the occurrence is to isolate the experiment in a controlled environment. Unfortunately, this is a widely used design in marketing research, such as for measuring advertising effects among consumers. Researchers take a pretest criterion measure of advertising recall, product involvement, media habits, or purchase history. Then an experimental independent treatment manipulation is delivered (e.g. exposure to an advertisement during a TV programme), followed by a posttest measure of the dependent variable, such as advertising recall.

One advantage of the 'one group pretest-posttest' design is its lack of selection bias. Since only one group exists, it automatically eliminates the problem of differential selection. Overall, this design has imperfect safeguards to internal validity and should be used only when nothing better is available.

Static Group Comparison

Static group comparison is a two-group experimental design consisting of an experimental group (EG) and a control group (CG) of test subjects, but it lacks any randomization. The experimental group receives the independent treatment manipulation, with the second operating as the control. It can be illustrated as follows:

$$(EG): X \rightarrow O_1$$
$$(CG): \quad O_2$$

Selection bias is the major defect of this design mainly because the groups are formed on a non-random basis. For example, many studies look at two store settings or two groups of consumers when comparing new product trials or sales. In theory there is no assurance the two groups are equivalent. Yet in comparison to the other pre-experimental designs, the static group comparison is substantially less susceptible to history, maturation, instrumentation and testing contaminations.

True Experimental Designs

There are three forms of true experimental designs: (1) pretest-posttest control group; (2) posttest-only control group; and (3) Solomon Four Group. The common denominator is that all three designs ensure equivalence between experimental and control groups by random assignment to the groups.

Pretest-Posttest Control Group – Completely Randomized Design

The 'pretest-posttest control group' design consists of one experimental group and one control group of test subjects, who are assigned to either group by the process of complete randomization. This process randomly assigns each experimental unit (subject) to the treatments. Randomization of experimental units is the researcher's attempt to control all extraneous variables while manipulating a single treatment variable. It can be illustrated as follows:

$$(EG): [R] O_1 \rightarrow X \rightarrow O_2$$
$$(CG): [R] O_3 \rightarrow O_4$$

with the treatment effect (TE) of the experimental manipulation being:

$$TE = (O_2 - O_1) - (O_4 - O_3)$$

This experimental design controls for extraneous factors contributing to the contamination of internal validity, but does not necessarily ensure true internal validity. For example, if extraneous history events occurred between O_2 and O_1, and between O_4 and O_3, one may assume the researcher has controlled for history contamination. Yet in reality the researcher cannot ascertain whether exactly the same history events exert impacts on both groups. Effects of certain events may have been felt in the experimental group and not the other. This can occur due to some disturbance factor influencing the test subjects in either the treatment or control group. To prevent this problem, the researcher should first randomly assign individuals into experimental and control groups, then have each individual tested for any such disturbance.

Maturation, testing and statistical regression threats are controlled since their inputs should be measured equally in experimental and control groups. An instrumentation problem might arise from the researcher knowingly modifying the measuring instrument between the pretest and posttest measures of the dependent variable. Differences in dropout rates among group members can also develop into a mortality issue. Selection is adequately handled through the process of randomization. Sometimes matching techniques are employed to improve equivalency. However, matching should be used only as a supplement to randomization.

Procedural operations of this design are quite simple. To illustrate this point, let's consider testing the impact of a promotional message on customers' preference towards a product. To begin, a sample of individuals is selected at random. Half are randomly assigned to the control group, the other half to the experimental group, i.e. the group that receives the promotional message. Firstly, everyone selected is measured on their degree of preference to the product concerned. The experimental group then receives the promotional message, and after an acceptable period of time, the product preference measure is again administered to all subjects.

Sources of extraneous variation might occur if differences occur between the measures of O_4 and O_3 (e.g., an actual product recall occurred during the experiment). If this type of extraneous effect did occur, it would be measured equally on those individuals in the experimental group.

While the design produces adequate control for internal validity, it does not necessarily do so for external validity. Two factors serve as threats to the external validity of this design: testing and selection. Pretests run the risk of introducing bias into the design based on the mere topic area being pretested. This can cause unusual attitudes to develop among experimental group subjects that can ultimately bias the posttest measures. In addition, a high mortality rate of subjects can destroy the intentions of sound randomization procedures. If this is a factor, replication of the experiment over time among different groups is necessary to ensure external validity.

Posttest-Only Control Group

This experimental design is identical to the previous completely randomized design except the pretest measures of the dependent variable are absent. This type of causal design works well if the process of randomization is totally assured. The design is illustrated as follows:

$$(\text{EG}): [\text{R}] \; \text{X} \rightarrow O_1$$
$$(\text{CG}): [\text{R}] \qquad O_2$$

Take for example a posttest only control group design that may be used by a research company in its efforts to examine the effects of various incentive alternatives used to increase the response rate of its new car owner satisfaction survey. The two incentive alternatives for subjects taking the experiment are personal monetary payments of €5 versus a Debenhams voucher of €10. With a control group being used in the design, there are actually three treatment groups: (1) no incentive offered to the control group of participants, (2) €5 personal monetary payment, and (3) €10 Debenhams voucher. Let's assume the researchers determine the overall sampling frame would need to be 1,500 new car owners resulting in 500 prospective participants being randomly assigned to each of the three treatment groups. Table 8.1 shows the hypothetical results of the experiment:

Table 8.1 Response Rates of the Three Experimental Treatment Groups

Groups	€5 Personal Incentive	€10 Debenhams Voucher	Control: No Incentive
Response Rates	39.4%	24.3%	25.7%
No. of Respondents	500	500	500

In comparing the above response rates (dependent variable) of each of the three treatment groups, the results suggest that personal payment incentives have the strongest influence on response rate. From a managerial perspective, the research company should expect a significantly higher survey response rate by including an offer of €5 personal payment with each of the new car owner satisfaction questionnaires mailed.

Solomon Four Group

Although a highly complex design, the Solomon Four Group enables the researcher to learn more about internal and external validity than any other experimental design does. But because of its complexity, marketing researchers do not use it as widely as the other design alternatives. It is illustrated as follows:

Design 1

$$\text{(EG): [R] } O_1 \rightarrow X \rightarrow O_2$$
$$\text{(CG): [R] } O_3 \ldots\ldots O_4$$

Design 2

$$\text{(EG): [R] } X \ldots\ldots \rightarrow O_5$$
$$\text{(CG): [R] } \quad O_6$$

The design is a combination of the 'pretest-posttest control group' and the 'posttest only control group' experimental designs. It provides both direct and reactive effects of testing, based on $O_1 \rightarrow X \rightarrow O_2$ and $X \rightarrow O_5$ respectively. External validity is enhanced, along with true experimental effect assurance by comparing $[O_2 \text{ less } O_1]$, $[O_2 \text{ less } O_4]$, $[O_5 \text{ less } O_6]$, and $[O_5 \text{ less } O_3]$. When these four comparisons agree, the researcher's ability to infer that the resulting change in outcome of the dependent variable is being caused by the experimental independent variable treatment dramatically increases.

Quasi-experimental Designs

Between the extremes of pre-experimental designs (which have little or no control) and true experimental designs (based on randomization), we have the quasi-experimental designs (See Exhibit 8.4). These designs are appropriate when the researcher can control some variables (e.g., price level, media vehicle, package design) but cannot establish equal experimental and control groups based on randomization. There are five major types of quasi-experimental designs as follows:

EXHIBIT 8.4   Summary of Other Quasi-experimental Designs Used in Marketing Research Practices

Non-equivalent dependent variable design	Single group of test subjects and pretest measures on two scales, one that is expected to change due to treatment manipulation and one that is not. This design is restricted to theoretical contexts where differential change is predicted. The design must be powerful enough to determine that the non-treated variable is reliably measured. The results are interpretable only when the two outcome measures are conceptually similar and both would be affected by the same non-treatment effect.
Removed treatment design with pretest and posttest	There could be an ethical problem in the removing of the treatment manipulation in the second scenario. There needs to be a noticeable discontinuity after the removal of the second treatment; otherwise, it could be that the initial treatment had no long-term effects.
Repeated treatment design	This design is interpretable when the results of the first experiment occur in the same direction as the second experiment and the initial pretest measure differs from any of the following test measures. This design is appropriate when there are unobservable treatments and long periods between a treatment and its reintroduction.
Reversed-treatment, non-equivalent control group design	This design requires both pretest and posttest measures and directional hypotheses. There is potential for high construct validity, but it depends on the research revealing the existence of an inverse relationship.
Cohort design with cyclical turnover	*Cohorts* are test subjects who follow each other through a formal institutional environment such as school or work. In this type of design, the researcher pretests a group of test subjects, then gives the treatment manipulation to the next group and collects posttest measures from the second group. The major underlying premise of this type of quasi-experimental design is that the samples are drawn from the same population. The design can eliminate the threats of history and testing by stratifying the treatment groups.
Regression discontinuity design	This causal design is used when the experimental groups are given rewards or those in special need are given extra assistance. The regressed lines for the treatment and non-treatment groups should be different due to the effect of the treatment. Interpretation of the results becomes difficult with the possibility of curvilinear relationships. Knowledge of the reward could lead to extra actions by the test subjects in order to receive it.

Non-equivalent Control Group

Commonly used in marketing research, the 'non-equivalent control group' design differs from true experimental designs in that the experimental and control groups are not equivalent. It can be illustrated as follows:

$$\text{Group 1 (EG): } O_1 \rightarrow X \rightarrow O_2$$

$$\text{Group 2 (CG): } O_3 \quad\quad O_4$$

In this type of quasi-experimental designs, experimental and control groups are formed in natural settings. For example, many marketing research quasi-experiments recruit test subjects from established organizations such as civic groups or church clubs. They also use customers who shop at similar stores. In this self-selected experimental group design, group membership is primarily based on the subject's willingness, interest or desire to participate. Many times, this is accomplished by selecting test subjects from particular organizations or retail locations, whereas control subjects are selected on the basis of availability. The difference between O_1 and O_3 becomes an indication of equivalency between the experimental and control groups. If pretest measures are significantly different, group compatibility must be seriously questioned. If the measures appear similar, then there is an increased certainty of internal validity. While this design may conform to sound validity practices, it is highly dependent on the circumstances that lead to the selection of test subjects.

Separate-Sample Pretest-Posttest

When it is virtually impossible to determine who is to receive the independent treatment manipulation, but when measures of the dependent variable can be determined, a 'separate sample pretest-posttest' design is an appropriate choice. This design can be illustrated as follows:

$$\text{Sample 1 } O_1 \rightarrow (X)$$

$$\text{Sample 2 } (X) \rightarrow O_2$$

Although this is a weak design, it is not an uncommon choice in marketing research practices. This type of quasi-design is often used when the population is large, a pretest measure will not produce any meaningful information, or there is no way to control for application of the experimental manipulation. This quasi-experimental framework is popular in advertising research. Let's say, for example, that the advertising agency for B&Q, a major home improvement and garden retailer with locations throughout the UK, is launching a major image campaign. First, it draws two samples of test subjects. One sample is interviewed about their perception of B&Q's image (dependent variable) prior to the image campaign. After the campaign ends, test subjects in the second sample are interviewed about their perception of the retailer's image.

Obviously, this design must deal with a number of threats to internal validity. History and mortality are the greatest concerns. Repetition of the experiment over several settings can reduce these effects somewhat.

On the other hand, this quasi-experimental design is considered superior to true experiments with regard to external validity. This is because of its natural setting and the use of large samples of test subjects who are representative of the target group. Overall, the reason why quasi-experimental designs are practised in marketing research is they are in a natural setting. In this way, they should be categorized as a type of field experiment. Field experiments, to which we devote the next section of this chapter, provide valuable information to researchers because they allow functional or causal relationships to be generalized to the target population.

Field Experiment

Field experiments are experimental research designs that manipulate the independent variables in order to measure the dependent variable in the natural setting of the test. Field experiments are commonly conducted in retail environments such as shopping centres or supermarkets. These settings tend to create a high level of realism. However, high levels of realism contribute to a lack of control of the independent variables and increase problems with extraneous variables.

Problems with control can occur in several ways. For example, conducting a field experiment of a new product in a supermarket requires the retailer's commitment to authorize the product in the store. Today, retailers are becoming more hesitant about adding new products, given the large number of new product introductions and the generally low rate of their success each year. Even if the product is authorized, proper display and retailer support are needed to appropriately conduct the experiment. Competition can also negatively influence a field experiment. In some field experiments of new products, competitors have negatively affected sales of the experimental product by using heavy price discounts and/or promotions to increase sales of their own products at the time of the test. When field experiments are used, there are two types of designs: *factorial* and *latin square* designs.

> **Field experiments** Causal research designs that manipulate the independent variables in order to measure the dependent variable in a natural setting of the test.

Factorial Design

In marketing, researchers are often interested in investigating the simultaneous effects of two or more independent (treatment) variables on single or multiple dependent (outcome) variables. When the effects of two or more independent variables are investigated in a field experiment situation, researchers should use factorial design. For example, SAP's management is interested in measuring the effects of the company's sales training procedure and the compensation plan (independent variables) on sales performance (dependent variable) for its sales representatives. There are two different types of sales training procedures (STP): (1) sales manager's on-the-job training and (2) video-based off-the-job self-training. The compensation plan (CP) also has two different types of schemes: (1) straight commission of 9 per cent and (2) salary plus a 4 per cent commission. So in this example there are two independent variables each consisting of two alternatives resulting in what is called a 2×2 factorial design. This design has four cells ($2 \times 2 = 4$) in the design matrix. Each cell can be considered a 'treatment' group. The overall experimental design matrix would look as shown in Table 8.2.

Table 8.2

Training Procedure (STP)	Compensation Plan (CP)	
	(CP$_1$) Salary+4% Commission	(CP$_2$) 9% Straight Commission
(STP$_1$) On-the-job training	STP$_1$, CP$_1$	STP$_1$, CP$_2$
(STP$_2$) Video self-training	STP$_2$, CP$_1$	STP$_2$, CP$_2$

A factorial design enables the researcher to measure the separate effect of each independent variable working alone. The sales training procedure (STP) effect is calculated similar to that of a completely randomized design but the researcher can also estimate the individual effect of the compensation plan (CP) concerned. The individual effect of each independent variable is referred to as the *main effect*. To illustrate the 'main effect' concept, hypothetical numbers for sales performance are used in the design matrix shown in Table 8.2.

The results suggest that regardless of the compensation plan used, the on-the-job training programme (STP$_1$) yields on average €60,000 more than the video self-training programme (STP$_2$). The main effect of STP$_1$ is €60,000. In turn, the main effect of the combination salary plus 4 per cent commission plan (CP_1), regardless of the type of training programme, yields on average €90,000 more than the straight commission of 9 per cent plan (CP_2). The total treatment effect STP_1, CP_2 is €150,000 (€60,000 + €90,000 = €150,000) and there is no interaction between sales training procedure and compensation plan (see Table 8.3).

Table 8.3

Training Procedure (STP)	Compensation Plan (CP)	
	(CP1) Salary + 4% Commission	(CP2) 9% Straight Commission
(STP_1) On-the-job training	€280,000	€190,000
(STP_2) Video self-training	€220,000	€130,000

The factorial design also allows the researcher to determine the magnitude of an *interaction effect* that may exist between the independent variables (STP and CP). This extra total effect combination of the independent variables working together is always greater than the sum of the variables' individual effects. An interaction effect occurs when the relationship between one of the independent variables, say STP, and the dependent variable (sales representative performance) is different for different levels of the compensation plan (CP) independent variable. In the SAP example, the relationship between salespeople's performance and the type of sales training programme may vary depending upon which compensation plan is used. Table 8.4 illustrates the interaction effect between the independent variables.

Table 8.4

Training Procedure (STP)	Compensation Plan (CP)	
	(CP1) Salary + 4% Commission	(CP2) 9% Straight Commission
(STP_1) On-the-job training	€280,000	€220,000
(STP_2) Video self-training	€220,000	€130,000

Here the effect of the training procedure depends on the compensation plan used. The on-the-job training programme (STP_1) is €60,000 better than video self-training (STP_2) when the combination salary plus 4 per cent commission compensation plan (CP_1) is used and €90,000 when the straight commission of 9 per cent compensation plan is employed. In turn, the combination of salary plus 4 per cent commission (CP_1) is €60,000 better than the straight commission plan (CP_2) when on-the-job training is used, and is €90,000 better when video self-training (STP_2) is the training programme.

Latin Square Design

The *Latin Square* design can be used in field experiment situations where the researcher wants to control the effects of two or more extraneous variables. Latin square designs manipulate one independent variable and control for two additional sources of extraneous variation by restricting randomization with respect to the row and column effects.

In order to employ a Latin square experimental design, several conditions must be met. First, the number of categories (levels) of each extraneous variable to be controlled must be equal to the number of treatments. For example, let's say management is now interested in three training procedures rather than two and wants to control for the 'age of the sales representative' and the 'potential sales performances per year'. Here STP_1 represents on-the-job training, STP_2 denotes video self-training and STP_3 stands for in-classroom training. Because there are now three treatment groups based on the type of training procedure, the researcher has to make sure the selected 'age' and 'sales performance' variables also have only three categorical levels. If this condition is not met, then a Latin square design is not appropriate. Applying Latin Square design to the above SAP example, the researcher would use a 3×3 design shown in Table 8.5.

Table 8.5

Age of Salespersons	Sales Potential per Year (in thousands)		
	€500 – €999	€1,000 – €3,999	€4,000 – €6,999
20–29	STP_1	STP_2	STP_3
30–45	STP_2	STP_3	STP_1
Over 45	STP_3	STP_1	STP_2

Another necessary condition for conducting a Latin Square design is the assignment of treatment levels in the cells of the square. While the assignment is random, each treatment can occur only once in each blocking situation. This means that because each row and column category defines a blocking situation, each type of training programme (STP) must appear only once in each row and each column. In conducting the experiment, each test subject is exposed to all three treatments in a preset random order.

Considerations in Using Field Experiments

Besides realism and control, there are at least three other issues to consider when deciding whether or not to use a field experiment: time frames, costs and competitive reactions. Field experiments take longer to complete than laboratory experiments.

The planning stage – which can include determining which test market cities to use, which retailers to approach with product experiments, securing advertising time, and coordinating the distribution of the experimental product – adds to the length of time needed to conduct field experiments.

Field experiments are more expensive to conduct than laboratory experiments because of the high number of independent variables that must be manipulated. For example, the cost of an advertising campaign alone can increase the cost of the experiment. Other items adding to the cost of field experiments are coupons, product packaging development, trade promotions and product sampling.

Because field experiments are conducted in a natural setting, competitors can learn about the new product almost as soon as it is introduced, and they can respond by using heavy promotional activity or by rushing similar products to market. If secrecy is desired, then laboratory experiments are a better alternative.

Validity Concerns

In deciding whether to use field experiments, researchers should consider the proposed experiment's desired internal validity and external validity. An ideal experiment would be high in both internal and external validity, however this is difficult to achieve in a field setting and usually a trade-off must be made. Researchers who want to be able to generalize an experiment's results to other settings, can select field experiments. On the other hand, if the lack of control over the independent variables associated with field experiments is a concern, then laboratory experiments are more appropriate to assess true causal relationships.

For researchers who opt for field experiments, they can choose from several types depending on the objectives of the experiment and the considerations mentioned above. The next section discusses the most common type of field experiment – test marketing – and includes overviews of its six different methods for conducting market tests.

Test Marketing

Test marketing is the use of controlled field experiments to gain information on usually a new product's predicted market performance and its contributory factors. Companies have several options available when choosing a test marketing method. Whichever method is used, test marketing measures the sales potential of a product and evaluates variables in the product's marketing mix. The cost of conducting test marketing experiments can be high. But with the high failure rate of new consumer products, many companies believe the expense of conducting test marketing can help them avoid the more expensive mistake of an unsuccessful product rollout. Exhibit 8.5 presents the six most popular test marketing designs: traditional, controlled, electronic, simulated, Web-based TV and virtual.

> **Test marketing** Using controlled field experiments to gain information on usually a new product's predicted market performance and its contributory factors.

Traditional Test Markets

One of the most frequently used form of test marketing is a traditional test market. This method tests a product's marketing mix variables through existing distribution channels. Companies select specific cities, or test markets, that have demographic and market characteristics similar to

EXHIBIT 8.5 The Six Most Popular Test Marketing Designs

Test Marketing Design	Comments
Traditional	Also referred to as 'standard' tests, these use experimental design procedures to test a product and/or its marketing mix variables through existing distribution channels.
Controlled	Tests that are performed by an outside research firm guaranteeing distribution of the test product through pre-specified outlets in selected cities.
Electronic	Tests that integrate the use of select panels of consumers who use a special identification card in recording their product-purchasing data.
Simulated	Also referred to as 'laboratory tests' or 'test market simulations,' these are quasi-experiments where test subjects are preselected, then interviewed and observed on their purchases and attitudes towards the test product.
Web-based TV	Similar to electronic test markets, these use broadband interactive TV (iTV) and advances in interactive multimedia communication technologies to conduct the field experiment. Preselected respondents are shown various stimuli and asked questions online through their iTV.
Virtual	Tests that are completely computerized, allowing the test subjects to observe and interact with the product as though they were actually in the test store's environment.

those of the targeted users of the product or service being tested. The most common application of a traditional test market is to evaluate consumer acceptance of a variation of an existing product or a more completely new product. Test marketing is also used to evaluate the potential of new marketing concepts, such as test marketing a women's theme shop in a selected number of sporting goods retail stores.

Advantages and Disadvantages of Traditional Test Markets

The primary advantage of traditional tests is they are conducted in actual distribution channels. Other test marketing methods attempt to simulate distribution channels, while traditional test markets place products in actual distribution outlets, typically retail outlets. In addition to measuring consumer acceptance of a product, standard test markets can determine the level of trade support for the tested item. If retailers are reluctant to give a company additional shelf space or displays for the new product, then plans for the product rollout may need to be reevaluated. Even products that have a high level of consumer appeal will have difficulty succeeding if minimum levels of distribution cannot be attained.

The limitations of traditional test markets are cost, time and exposure to competition. First, traditional test markets are much more expensive compared to laboratory experiments. Expenses incurred during a traditional test market include product development, packaging, distribution and advertising and promotion. Second, traditional test markets require more time to conduct than other forms of test marketing. Most standard test markets take between 12 and 18 months to complete. Third, because traditional test marketing uses actual distribution channels, other companies are able to observe a competitor's activity and can take action to hurt a test market. The combination of time and competitive pressures has changed the way in which many companies introduce new products. The need to introduce products more quickly than competitors is leading to large-scale rollouts of new products. The traditional approach of beginning with a test market and then increasing distribution region by region is being replaced by introducing a product in multiple regions simultaneously. In addition, test marketing does not always mean success, as illustrated in Exhibit 8.6, which describes the problems experienced by Coors.

EXHIBIT 8.6 Good Test Market Results Do Not Guarantee New-Product Success

Coors Gives the Cold Shoulder to Wine Coolers

Adolph Coors Company, manufacturer of Coors beer, suffered through a series of new-product disasters in the early 1980s, so when the company made a second attempt to enter the wine cooler market it relied on simulated test marketing to determine consumer acceptance for its new offering.

The company's test marketing woes began in 1978 when it introduced Coors Light. By the time the Coors product reached the market, Miller Lite was firmly entrenched as the number one light beer. The slow rollout did not seem to bother the company. In fact, it was consistent with their philosophy. Pete Coors remarked that his company let other companies do the pioneering work, referring to product development. 'Then we'll take what they've done, and do it better,' he added. Another product failure, Killian's Irish Red Ale, was introduced in 1982 using traditional test markets. The product stalled in the test marketing phase before national rollout could happen. Perhaps the worst experience was with Herman Josephs, a new beer positioned as a premium-priced beer that was supposed to compete with Michelob and Löwenbräu. Once again, Coors relied on traditional test marketing, planning to iron out bugs in the product and marketing mix before introducing the product in all markets. The test marketing for Herman Josephs began in 1981. Coors abandoned the product in 1989 after years of remaining in the test market phase.

▶ Coors had made a previous attempt to enter the wine cooler market with its Colorado Chiller coolers. The failure of Colorado Chiller was attributed in part to failure to get input from consumers about the product. Coors sought to correct this mistake when another cooler product, Crystal Springs Cooler, was tested in 1986. The company used simulated test marketing (STM) to find out how consumers would respond to the new product. Results of the STM were encouraging. Approximately 63 per cent of cooler drinkers surveyed were interested in purchasing Crystal Springs Cooler, and 74 per cent said they would buy the product after sampling it. Sales projections for Crystal Springs exceeded 300,000 barrels per year, which would have been Coors's third-largest product. In 1987, the company decided to discontinue its plans for Crystal Springs Cooler. Undoubtedly, its past new product failures left Coors with little confidence about rolling out a new product like Crystal Springs Cooler despite strong test marketing results.

Source: Burgess, 1993.

Controlled Test Markets

A second type of test market is a controlled test market. A **controlled test market** is performed by an outside firm that guarantees distribution of the test product through outlets in selected cities. AC Nielsen and Audits & Surveys are two firms that offer controlled test marketing services. These companies provide financial incentives to distributors to allow the test product to be added to the product line. The outside firm handles all distribution functions for its client during the test market, including inventory, stocking, pricing and billing. Sales data are gathered by the research firm. UPC scanner data and consumer surveys are used to compile information on trial and repeat rates, market penetration and consumer characteristics.

> **Controlled test market** A field experiment that guarantees the distribution of the test product through limited pre-specified outlets in selected test cities.

Advantages and Disadvantages of Controlled Test Markets

Controlled test markets overcome many of the disadvantages of traditional test markets. First, distribution of the test product is assured by the outside research firm handling the test market. Second, the cost of a controlled test market is generally less than that of a traditional test market. Third, competitive monitoring of a controlled test market is somewhat difficult compared with traditional test markets, given the level of control that can be implemented.

Controlled test markets are not without limits. First, the limited number of markets used makes accurate projections of sales and market penetration difficult. Second, the amount of actual trade support for a test product may be unclear if the research firm provides incentives to retailers to obtain shelf space. Will trade acceptance of the new product be the same without incentives? Third, the full effect of a proposed advertising campaign is difficult to evaluate. Despite these limitations, controlled test markets can be beneficial for marketers. Many companies use controlled test markets to determine whether a product warrants a full-scale standard test market. Also, controlled test markets can be used to test such pricing and promotional variables as coupons and displays.

Electronic Test Markets

An **electronic test market** gathers data from consumers who agree to carry an identification card they present when buying goods or services at participating retailers. This kind of test is usually performed by international and technologically well-equipped market research companies such as AC Nielsen or Information Resources, Inc. The advantage of this method is the identification card enables the researcher to collect demographic data on consumers who purchase the test product. A primary disadvantage of this method is the card-carrying consumers probably are not representative of the entire market because they are not chosen at random. In addition, there is a high cost associated with the use of advanced technologies. As a result, small businesses normally cannot afford electronic test marketing.

> **Electronic test market** A specific type of field experiment that requires the subject to use an electronic identification card and measures test product/service purchase results using universal product code scanner data.

Simulated Test Markets

Another type of test market that uses computer models to estimate consumer response to a new marketing programme is a **simulated test market** (STM). STMs project sales volume and evaluate the planned marketing mix. Some common STM services are Assessor and Bases II. While each of these methods uses its own approach to sampling, questionnaires and modelling, the overall process normally includes the following steps:

1 Potential participants are screened to satisfy certain demographic and product usage criteria.

2 Participants are shown commercials or print advertisements for the test product, as well as for other competitive or non-competitive products.

3 Participants are then allowed to purchase items in a simulated retail store. Regardless of whether the test item is selected, participants receive a free sample.

4 After a usage period, participants are contacted to gather information on the product as well as their repurchase intentions.

> **Simulated test market (STM)** A field experiment that uses computer models to estimate consumer responses to a new marketing programme.

Advantages and Disadvantages of Simulated Test Markets

Simulated test markets have several advantages. First, STMs offer substantial cost and time savings. They can be conducted at shorter time intervals than traditional test markets, and they cost much less than what a traditional test market costs. Second, a simulation can predict product trial rate repurchase rate and purchase cycle length with a good level of accuracy. Third, computer modelling allows several alternative marketing mix plans to be tested for their effect on sales volume. Finally, exposure to competition is minimized because the test market is not conducted in normal channels of distribution.

The isolation of STMs from the real-world environment leads to some weaknesses with this method. Trade acceptance of a new product cannot be measured using STMs – it must be assumed. A traditional test market would be more desirable if a company believes agreement for distribution with the trade will be difficult to secure and therefore should be dealt with as soon as possible. For example, Ore-Ida, a brand of potato-based frozen foods owned by H.J. Heinz Company, a global food giant, once conducted an STM for a new product assuming a 90 per cent distribution rate in the normal channels. However, the actual distribution rate was only 10 per cent, making the sales volume projections from the STM impossible to attain. Second, broad-based consumer reaction to a new product is impossible to measure using STMs, as opposed to traditional test markets where a larger number of consumers are allowed the opportunity to actually try a new product. In addition, STMs are more effective in estimating trial rates than repurchase rates. However, a good estimate of repurchase intentions is needed to determine a new product's potential for success. Finally, although STMs cost less than traditional test markets, they are still expensive. Usually only the larger companies can afford to use STMs.

STMs are an effective method for testing new products, especially variations of an existing brand or category of consumer packaged goods. For example, when Reynolds Metal Company, the third largest aluminum company in the world, introduced Reynolds Crystal Color plastic wrap, a variation of the traditional Reynolds clear plastic wrap, it used an STM to evaluate the potential of the new product. In the STM, 40 per cent of the participants indicated they would definitely try it, which is double the average predicted trial rate for new products.

Simulated test markets serve two important purposes. First, they can be used as either a substitute or a supplement to traditional test markets. They can be used as a substitute when the risk of product failure or cost is comparatively low. They can be used as a supplement to test combinations of marketing mix variables prior to a traditional test market introduction, when making changes would be too costly, if not impossible. Second, STMs can serve as a pilot test to determine whether a particular concept or product has the potential for success. If not, the idea can be dropped before further testing increases the cost of the mistake.

Web-based TV Test Markets

With consumers' growing acceptance of interactive TV (iTV) and the advances in multimedia communication technologies, larger technology-driven online research companies such as Harris Interactive, Burke, Inc., Lieberman Research Worldwide, M/A/R/C Research, NFO WorldGroup, and smaller speciality research companies, such as Critical Mix, POPULUS and DataStar, Inc., are investing heavily in the computer hardware and software to bring test marketing capabilities directly into the living rooms of consumers. **Web-based TV test markets** are a test market among consumers through Web-enabled television technology. This type of test market can literally bring consumers, manufacturers and sponsors together into a convenient 'living room' experience rather than a 'desk' experience. Basically, iTV computerizes the consumer's TV set with a 'set-top' box that has a hard drive for storing large amounts of data (e.g. a 60-second commercial, live or videotaped 30-minute interactive product

> **Web-based TV test market** The conducting of a test market among consumers through Web-enabled television technology.

demonstrations), allowing the consumer to watch at leisure for more in-depth product information.

Advantages and Disadvantages of Web-Based TV Test Markets

All the advantages associated with Web research practices are available through iTV. The big differences are the comfort of having the process delivered on a larger TV screen versus the smaller PC screen, using larger fonts, bigger graphics, and having interactive products, advertisements, and other test stimuli delivered in a digital format. For now, applications of this alternative have been limited to advertising copy testing and some infomercials of consumer-oriented products.

Several factors are slowing the acceptance and use of iTV test markets. The most pressing are that in-home demand for iTV technology is still to be expanded, and that the required hardware and software are costly. As many consumers still lack full knowledge of the iTV technologies, acceptance of iTV will remain to have sizable room for increase. In addition, this new technology is a difficult sell to many companies unfamiliar with web-based TV test marketing. Finally, much is dependent on iTV service providers for the potential widespread use of this test marketing technique.

Nevertheless, as time passes by, all the above inhibiting factors are expected to fade away. Indeed this form of test marketing is predicted to grow in the next few years to the point where it could overtake electronic test marketing activities.

Virtual Test Markets

In **virtual test markets**, not only can different marketing mixes be evaluated using computer modelling, but also even the simulated store itself appears on a computer screen. Using this method, participants can view store shelves stocked with many different kinds of products. The shoppers can pick up an item by touching its image on the monitor, and they can examine the product by moving a tracking ball device that rotates the image. Items are purchased by placing them in a shopping cart which appears on the screen. Information collected during this process includes the amount of time the consumer spends shopping in each product category, the time the consumer spends examining each side of a package, the product items purchased, and the quantity of each product item purchased.

> **Virtual test market** A high tech-driven field experiment that allows the subjects to manipulate different aspects of the test environment on a computer screen.

Advantages and Disadvantages of Virtual Test Markets

Although virtual test markets are similar to simulated test markets, they do have some unique advantages. First, the 'stores' that appear in virtual test markets more closely resemble actual stores than the ones created in simulated test markets. Second, researchers can make changes in the stores rather quickly. Different arrays of brands, pricing, packaging, promotions and shelf-space allocations can appear in a matter of minutes. Third, virtual test markets can be used for different purposes. They can be used to test entirely new concepts or products as well as to test for changes in existing products. As with simulated test markets, virtual test markets allow for these tests to be conducted without exposure to competition.

The disadvantages of virtual test markets are similar to those of simulated test markets. The primary concern for many companies is whether consumers will shop in virtual stores using the same patterns they use in actual stores. However, research into this concern suggests there is a high degree of correlation between virtual store and actual store sales. For example, a study in which 300 consumers took six trips through a virtual store and an actual store to purchase cleaning and health-and-beauty-aid products revealed similar market shares. Correlations were .94 for the cleaning product and .90 for the health-and-beauty-aid product. Another concern is the cost of the computer hardware and software needed to conduct virtual test markets. While the cost is still prohibitive for many companies, improvements in technology should lower it in the future. Finally, in a virtual store, consumers cannot feel, smell, or touch a product. Items that involve special handling from consumers may not be suited for virtual test marketing. Virtual test markets can be used to study questions such as:

1 What is our brand equity in a new retail channel?

2 Do we offer a sufficient variety of products?

3 How should products be displayed?

The Closer Look at Research box provides an example of how one company used virtual test markets.

A Closer Look at Research (*In the field*)
Goodyear Steps Out of Its Own Stores

Goodyear, the world's largest tyre company, used virtual test marketing to evaluate a major change in distribution strategy. For many years, the company sold its tyres through its own retail outlets. The new strategy was to sell Goodyear tyres through general merchandise stores and still maintain the current system of Goodyear stores. While such a move would no doubt allow Goodyear to reach more consumers, the new strategy would place Goodyear tyres in direct competition with other brands in the general merchandise stores. Goodyear questioned whether this increased competition would dictate a change in marketing strategy. Specifically, the company needed to determine what the level of brand equity was for its products. Was it strong enough to be able to charge a premium over other brands, or would it be forced to reduce prices and/or extend warranties to be competitive with other brands?

Goodyear turned to virtual test marketing to find answers to its questions. The company conducted a study of 1,000 consumers who had recently bought or planned to purchase passenger tyres, high-performance tyres, or light-truck tyres. Participants shopped several different virtual tyre stores, each store offering a different assortment of products, pricing, and warranties. Goodyear believed it achieved brand equity if a consumer purchased a Goodyear product at a higher price than competitors' products, if it captured sales from competitors when Goodyear products were reduced in price, and if it maintained sales levels despite competitors' price cuts. The results of the study assisted Goodyear in several ways. First, the company determined how shoppers in different product-market segments valued the Goodyear brand compared with competing brands. Second, the virtual market test allowed the company to test many different pricing strategies. This feature allowed Goodyear to evaluate how different prices, both its own and competitors' prices, affected consumer tendencies to switch brands. Third, major competitors were identified. Goodyear is aware of the companies it should consider its major competitors in general merchandise stores.

Other Issues in Test Marketing

Consumer versus Industrial Test Marketing

Our discussion of test marketing has centred on the evaluation of consumer products. However, test marketing practices are used by manufacturers of industrial products as well, though with different methods. Rather than develop a product for trial in the market, industrial manufacturers seek input from customers to determine the features and technologies needed for new products. Manufacturers develop prototypes based on customers' input, then evaluate and test them using selected customers. The manufacturers receive feedback from customers involved in the product test and use the feedback to make further changes to the product before introducing it to the entire market. As with consumer test markets, industrial test markets can be lengthy. The longer a test market runs, the more likely it is a competitor will learn of the new product and respond by rushing a similar product to market or by becoming more competitive with existing products.

Matching Experimental Method with Objectives

When selecting a test marketing method, researchers should consider the objective of the experiment.

Some field experiments may require more control over real-world variables. Consider a company that wants to evaluate the effectiveness of an advertising campaign for a new product. While the ability to generalize the results of the experiment to the entire market is important, equally important is that the company must determine whether a cause-and-effect relationship really exists between the advertising campaign and customers' acceptance of the new product. In other words, did the promotional campaign influence sales, or did the influence come from other variables, such as pricing or competition? This means that the experiment must have high internal validity. An experimental design for this objective can be an electronic test market that can record information about consumers' television viewing (did they view the advertisement?), purchase and repurchase behaviours (did they buy the advertised product and, if so, how many times?), and then determine whether a relationship exists between the advertising campaign and product sales. If the result is positive, the company could roll out the advertising campaign to other areas or even nationwide. If the result is not positive, the company can make changes in the advertising campaign, or drop it completely.

Once the researcher identifies the objective of the experiment, they can select the method that offers the greatest amount of the desired validity, internal or external. Some of the difficulties associated with standard test markets are leading to new trends in new product testing. First, companies that do not want to undertake the time and expense of standard test markets could turn to simulated and virtual test markets. There are some companies that find the standard test market process difficult, expensive or time consuming, but are not willing or able to use other methods. They may decide to roll out new products without any test marketing. This could be acceptable when the risk of product failure is low. The following case study illustrates recent developments in virtual test marketing.

marketing research in action

From Computer Gaming Technology to the Building of Virtual Test Store – Introducing the ShelfAware Package Developed in Oslo, Norway

Computer Gaming Technology

The technical development of the computer game industry has developed fast. Delivering realistic images in real-time, which was not possible only a few years ago, is now technically feasible. Kids, young adults and even some adults are spending much of their time playing computer games. One reason for this popularity is that computer games provide increasingly realistic and lifelike three-dimensional visual environments, which create a very engaging and immersing experience for the users.

This advance in computer game technology and the resulting user experience can also be adapted for non-game applications. Examples are simulators, educational or training tools, cultural heritage applications such as virtual museums and market research tools. With more and more people knowing how to use computer games in which they navigate and play, an increasing proportion of the population does not require specific training for using these non-game applications.

ShelfAware

ShelfAware is a specific market research tool that makes use of the technology available in the computer game industry. It is a software package developed in Norway and is used for virtual test marketing purpose.

Compared to other virtual test marketing tools, ShelfAware excels in its ability to replicate a shopping environment in a realistic and lifelike manner. Pictures from the real physical store are used to make (or replicate) the virtual test store. The ShelfAware package consists of an editor tool ShopEdit, which is used to design the virtual test store, and which is presented on a personal computer in a gaming environment. Building upon gaming technology, a three-dimensional experience of engagement and immersion can be created for the users (customers). As the shop environments on the computer screen are very realistic and lifelike, gloves, spectacles or other similar equipment are not needed.

The following figure is an example of a virtual test store built by ShelfAware. The contents of a shopping basket are shown at the bottom. When looking at the product in the centre of the screen, the price tag and a larger image of the item selected appears.

The virtual test store is actually assembled from 'modules', which are simple geometric shapes representing a shelf rack, refrigerator, or other object. The surfaces of the modules are texture-mapped, many with photo-textures taken from real shop interiors. Some of the surfaces have associated 'pickup points' from which the user (customer) may examine and pick up a particular product.

At the simplest level, editing a shop consists of arranging predefined modules from a library, with which modules can be placed, rotated and stacked in the shop.

Modules themselves are created and managed in the module editor. Here one can create new modules, alter existing modules, organize the library of modules and specify dimensions, as well as apply textures from a texture library.

Types of Data Collected

Upon completing the shopping trip, the user's shopping basket content, available in the logs of the virtual test store can be analysed. In addition to the shopping content, the movements of the users (customers) in the store are logged. Pure purchase figures can be imported to standard spreadsheets and statistical packages, but the logs contain a lot more information that is best presented and analysed in a more visual manner. For example, the movements of the users can be visualized by using the path tracker tool available within the ShelfAware package. An example is shown below.

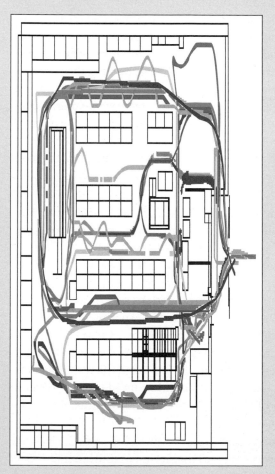

Other types of information collected after the shopping trip include the time spent in different areas of the shop, which helps identify traffic bottlenecks and hotspots of attention, movement vectors and mean gaze direction.

Source: Adapted from Leister, Tjostheim and Lous (2007).

Questions

Using your knowledge about market tests from reading the chapter and the above discussion of ShelfAware answer each of the following questions:

1 What are the key strengths of the use of ShelfAware for test marketing purpose?

2 What are the new features or functions that you would like the ShelfAware development team to add to in the future? Describe how these new features or functions could make this software package even better for conducting virtual test markets.

3 Do you envisage any weaknesses attached to the use of ShelfAware? If so, what are they?

Summary of Learning Objectives

- **Describe and explain the importance of and differences between the variables used in experimental designs.**

  To conduct causal research, the researcher must understand the four key types of variables in experimental designs (independent, dependent, extraneous, control) as well as randomization of test subjects and the role theory plays in developing experiments. The most important goal of any experiment is to determine which relationships exist among different variables. Functional (cause-effect) relationships require systematic change in one variable as another variable changes.

- **Explain the theoretical importance and impact of internal, external and construct validity measures in experimental designs and interpreting functional relationships.**

  Experimental designs are developed to control for contamination, which may confuse the true relationship being studied. Internal, external, and construct validities are the main types of validity that need to be evaluated for contamination. Internal validity refers to the accuracy of conclusions the researcher draws about a demonstrated functional relationship. The question is, 'Are the experimental results truly due to the experimental variables?' External validity is concerned with the interaction of experimental variables with extraneous factors causing a researcher to question the generalizability of the results to other settings. Construct validity is important in the process of correctly identifying and understanding both the independent and the dependent variables in an experimental design. Several techniques unique to experimental designs are used to control for problems of internal and external validity. These techniques centre on the use of control groups, pre-experimental measures, exclusion of subjects, matching subjects into groups and randomization of group members. These dimensions, built into the experimental design, provide true power for controlling contamination.

- **Discuss the three major types of experimental designs used in marketing research. Explain the pros and cons of using causal designs as a means of assessing relationship outcomes.**

  Pre-experimental designs do not meet internal validity criteria due to a lack of group comparisons. Despite this weakness, three designs are used quite frequently in marketing research: the one-shot study; the one-group pretest-posttest design; and the static group comparison. True experimental designs ensure equivalence between experimental and control groups by random assignment of subjects into groups. Three forms of true experimental designs exist: pretest-posttest control group; posttest only control group; and the Solomon Four Group. Quasi-experimental designs are appropriate when the researcher can control some of the variables but cannot establish true randomization of groups. While a multitude of these designs exist, two of the most common forms are the nonequivalent control group and the separate-sample pretest-posttest.

- **Explain what test marketing is, the importance and difficulties of executing this, and how the resulting data structures are used by researchers and marketing practitioners.**

  Test marketing is a specific type of field experiment commonly conducted in natural field settings. Most common in the marketing research field are traditional test markets, controlled test markets, electronic test markets, simulated test markets, Web-based TV test markets, and virtual test markets. Data gathered from test markets provide both researchers and practitioners with invaluable information concerning customers' attitudes, preferences, purchasing habits/patterns, and demographic profiles. This information can be useful in predicting new product/service acceptance levels and advertising and image effectiveness, as well as in evaluating current marketing mix strategies.

Key Terms and Concepts

Complete randomization 277	Field experiments 293
Construct validity 282	Functional relationship 274
Controlled test market 298	Hypothesis guessing 284
Control variables 276	Inadequate pre-operationalization 283
Convergent validity 282	Independent variables 276
Deductive research 278	Inductive research 278
Demand characteristic 284	Internal validity 279
Dependent variables 276	Mono-method bias 283
Diffusion of treatment 284	Simulated test market 299
Discriminant validity 283	Test marketing 296
Electronic test market 299	Theory 277
Evaluation apprehension 284	Validity 278
Experimental design reliability 284	Variable 273
Experimental research 278	Virtual test market 301
External validity 281	Web-based TV
Extraneous variables 277	test market 300

Review Questions

1. List the four types of experimental design variables and provide an explanation of each.
2. Identify the significant variables a consumer would consider when purchasing a computer.
3. Using university students as subjects for experimental studies is not a very uncommon occurrence in marketing research. What possible problems could arise from this practice?
4. Identify the tests used for (a) pre-experimental testing and (b) true experimental testing. What advantages and disadvantages are associated with each?
5. Explain the difference between internal validity and external validity. Discuss the problems associated with each type of validity.

1 Which of the six types of test marketing are likely to be adopted more frequently in future in the European advertising market? Why?

2 Why do the British food manufacturers often find that the new products they introduce are more likely to fail than succeed? What will you recommend they do to reduce this problem?

3 **Experience the Internet.** Go to the home page for the AC Nielsen research company. Examine the procedures and techniques the company uses for conducting test markets. Provide a brief explanation of the goals the company provides for its clients regarding test marketing.

4 The manager of a clothing store thinks that customers may stay in the store longer if slow, 'easy listening' music is played. The manager is considering whether he should hire a marketing researcher to design an experiment to test the influence of music tempo on shoppers' behaviours. Answer the following questions:

   a How would you operationalize the independent variable?

   b What dependent variables do you think might be important in this experiment?

   c Develop a hypothesis for each of your dependent variables.

5 Recall the continuing case about Jimmy Spice's restaurant from earlier chapters. The owner has launched new Indian flavour chicken wings, and is hoping to maximize their weekly sales. Currently customers have three options for ordering these wings (10 wings for €5.00, 20 wings for €9.00, or 50 wings for €20.00). Management would like to know what impact different promotional incentives would have on the weekly sales of their new chicken wings. The two experimental treatment incentives are 'a 25 per cent-off coupon' versus 'a free small-, medium-, or large-sized dessert depending on the size of the order', both on a single order only. On the advice of a marketing research expert, a control group would need to be included in the experiment, and thus there would be three treatment groups involved: (1) 25 per cent-off coupon, (2) free dessert and (3) no incentive. Design an experiment that would determine the impact of the proposed promotional incentives on the weekly sales of new Indian flavour chicken wings at Jimmy Spices restaurant. Make sure you address each of the following items:

   a Specify all the important details of your experiment, and present it in a diagram.

   b Assess the internal and external validity of your experiment.

   c What, if any, extraneous factors would you have to deal with?

Chapter 9

Qualitative and Quantitative Observation Techniques

LEARNING OBJECTIVES

After reading this chapter, you will be able to

- ☑ Understand the different types of qualitative and quantitative observation techniques.

- ☑ Discuss the characteristics, benefits and weaknesses of observation techniques.

- ☑ Elaborate the typical steps that can be followed to choose the most appropriate observation technique for a particular project.

> " Nothing is or exists in reality except truth. Without truth it is impossible to observe any principles or rules in life
>
> *—Gandhi* "

SPSL – Europe's Largest Company Specializing in Retail Observation Research

Established in 1989, SPSL, part of Synovate (www.synovate.com), has developed a technology-enabled observation system that can monitor and record retail store activities accurately. Retailers using its observation system are able to reliably measure customer traffic flow on an ongoing hour-by-hour basis, determine the in-store 'weather' periodically, assess the impacts of marketing initiatives and adjust staff levels according to customer demand rather than service supply.

SPSL runs its European operations from its head office in Milton Keynes, England. Supported by their technology-enabled observation system to count retail traffic, the company prides itself on no double counting, no counting of the shopper's shadow and no missing shoppers with ambient temperature outerwear.

SPSL is a believer in quantitative observation techniques and the company stresses the importance of footfall counting in the retail sector. This is the measurement of people visiting a shop or other public space, which serves as an important indicator of the popularity of the place being visited. Carrying out footfall counting repeatedly can provide an indication of customer behaviour patterns, which can empower businesses to better target their marketing efforts and therefore move towards maximizing their sales potential. A further benefit of footfall counting is its ability to forward-plan once trends in customer behaviour patterns are clearly understood. This is of particular use for staff scheduling, helping to ensure that customer demands are met without overheads getting excessive.

Overview of Observation Techniques

The real-world chapter opener illustrates a practitioner's successful implementation of quantitative observation techniques. Students should note that observation techniques, in contrast to all the other research methods discussed in previous chapters, can be either quantitative *or* qualitative. However, it is difficult to have a crystal clear categorization of qualitative and quantitative observation techniques because the same observation technique, such as human observation (through the observer's naked eyes only), can generate both qualitative data (such as the body language of the person being observed) and quantitative data (such as the number of times the person being observed has said a particular word or has behaved in a particular way). As a rule of thumb, if the observation technique you are using generates more qualitative than quantitative data, it should be regarded as a qualitative observation technique for your research project, and vice versa. This means that the same observation technique can become a quantitative one for another research project. However, there are some observation techniques which we can confidently categorize as qualitative or quantitative whatever the research project they are serving. Mystery shopper – which is where an observer disguised as a shopper observes the phenomena of interest usually at a particular retail setting – is usually regarded a qualitative technique. On the other hand, mechanical/electronic observation techniques, which can provide data in concrete figures about the phenomena of interest, are all treated as quantitative observation techniques.

Observation techniques are *tools* researchers can use to collect primary data about human behaviour and marketing phenomena regardless of the nature of research designs. The main characteristic of observation techniques is that researchers must rely heavily on their powers of observation rather than actually communicating with people. Basically, the researcher depends on watching and recording what people or objects do in different research situations. Much information about the behaviour of people and objects can be observed: *physical actions* (e.g. consumers' shopping patterns or automobile driving habits); *expressive behaviours* (e.g. the tone of voice and facial expressions of respondents during a personal interview); *verbal behaviour* (e.g. telemarketing phone conversations); *temporal behaviour patterns* (e.g. the amount of time spent online shopping or at a particular website); *spatial relationships and locations* (e.g. the number of vehicles that move through a traffic light or movements of people at a theme park); *physical objects* (e.g. which brand name items are purchased at supermarkets or which car makes/ models are driven), and so on. These types of data can be used alone to draw conclusion of a particular research study or to augment data patterns collected through other research designs by providing complementary evidence concerning individuals' true feelings.

Observation of non-verbal symbols exhibited by people can add much to the researcher's understanding of a given situation. For example, consider the focus groups used by a major European bank to examine customers' satisfaction and their behaviour toward switching accounts to competitors' banks. The videotapes of the focus groups can reveal distinct non-verbal communication symbols from the participants' facial expressions and hand gestures that support the existence of negative feelings and unhappiness when discussing bank switching behaviour.

In marketing research, **observation** refers to the systematic activities of observing and recording the behavioural patterns of objects, people, events and other phenomena without directly communicating with them. The main purpose for using observation techniques is to collect data structures about behavioural patterns. Observation techniques require two elements: a behaviour or event that is observable and a system of recording it. Researchers record the behaviour patterns by using trained human observers or devices such as videotapes, movie cameras, audiotapes, computers, handwritten notes, or some other recording mechanism. The main weakness of observation techniques is they cannot be used to capture cognitive elements such as attitudes, preferences, beliefs, or emotions.

> **Observation** The systematic activities of witnessing and recording the behavioural patterns of objects, people, and events without directly communicating with them.

Appropriate Conditions for Using Observation Techniques

Several conditions are required for the successful use of observation. The research objectives must clearly indicate that some type of event or behaviour is to be observed. In most of observation research studies, the event or behaviour is repetitive, frequent and relatively predictable. Finally, the behaviour should normally take place in some public or laboratory setting that enables the researcher to observe the behaviour directly. Exhibit 9.1 summarizes these important conditions.

Information Condition

Trying to collect current behaviour data using any other method may lessen the data's accuracy and meaningfulness due to faulty recall by subjects. For example, people may not accurately recall the

EXHIBIT 9.1 Conditions for Using Observation Techniques

Condition	Brief Description
Information	Current behaviour patterns must be part of the data requirements.
Type of data	Necessary data must be observable.
Time frame	In most cases, data patterns meet repetitiveness, frequency and predictability factors in a pre-specified time frame.
Setting	Behaviour is usually observable in some public or laboratory setting.

number of times they zap commercials while watching their favourite one-hour TV programme on Monday nights. New technology developed and used by companies like AC Nielsen Media Research can 'observe' and capture commercial zapping behaviour among members of its consumer panel groups.

Type-of-Data Condition

If the researcher wants to know why an individual purchased one brand of cereal over the other brands available, observation techniques will not provide the answers. Thus, observation is used only when a respondent's feelings are relatively unimportant to the research objective or believed to be readily inferrable from the behaviour. For example, in studying children playing with toys, it is possible to use facial expressions as an indicator of a child's preferences toward the toys because children often react with conspicuous physical expressions. However, this type of observation technique means the observer must have excellent interpretive skills.

Time-Frame Condition

For observation techniques to be cost and time effective, the behaviours or events being examined need to happen within a relatively short time span. That means they should be repetitive and relatively frequent. For example, attempting to observe all the activities involved in the process of buying a new home or automobile would not be feasible in terms of data collection costs and time. In turn, behaviours associated with someone purchasing food items in a supermarket, people waiting in line inside a bank, or children watching a TV programme are appropriate cases in which observation techniques are deployed.

Setting Condition

Activities are usually limited to those the investigator can readily observe firsthand with human eyes or through a device such as a video camera. Normally, activities such as private worshipping or using in-home products (e.g. products used when cooking, turning up and down air-conditioning controls, or washing clothes) are not readily observable without the permission of the person being observed.

It is important to recognize that all four conditions for using observation techniques apply to those situations involving *current* events. They do not hold for situations in which researchers are interested in collecting data on past events. In these situations, the main emphasis of the observer would be on interpreting the reported outcomes and making preliminary inductive statements about the actual behaviour.

Unique Characteristics of Observation Techniques

There are four general characteristics of observation techniques. Depending on the researcher's need for (1) directness, (2) subjects' awareness, (3) structure and (4) a specific type of observing/recording mechanism, they can choose from a number of ways to observe events and record primary data. These characteristics directly influence the framework for conducting the observations. With good designs, researchers can eliminate, or at least control for, methodological problems that could prevent the gathering of consistent and generalizable data. See Exhibit 9.2.

EXHIBIT 9.2 Unique Characteristics of Observation Techniques

Characteristic	Description
Directness of observation	The degree to which the researcher or trained observer actually observes the behaviour/event as it occurs. Researchers can use either direct or indirect observation
Subjects' awareness of being observed	The degree to which subjects consciously know their behaviour is being observed and recorded. Researchers can use either disguised or undisguised observation techniques.
Structuredness of observation	The degree to which the behaviour, activities, or events to be observed are specifically known to the researcher prior to doing the observations. Structured and unstructured techniques can be used to collect primary behavioural data.
Type of observing mechanism	How the behaviour, activities or events will be observed and recorded. Researchers have the option either of using a trained human observer or some type of mechanical or electronic device.

Directness of Observation

Direct observation is the process of observing actual behavioural activities or events and recording them as they occur. Direct observation uses a human being, rather than a mechanical device, for observing and recording actual behaviours. For example, if researchers were interested in conducting a field experiment to find out how often people read tabloid magazines while waiting to check out at a supermarket, they could use any of several different direct observation techniques. In contrast, some experts believe that indirect observation techniques can be used to capture subjects' past behaviours in special situations. **Indirect observation** focuses on directly observing the artifacts that represent specific behaviours from some earlier time. It can be easily argued that this direct observing of artifacts of past human behaviour is really nothing more than a trained investigator interpreting a form of secondary data. While indirect observation might allow a researcher some insights into past behaviours, those insights should be viewed as tenuous. For example, a large industrial equipment manufacturer can review and interpret the company's telephone logs to find out how many long-distance telephone calls its sales force made during the previous month. After interpreting the logs, management could make general inferences concerning the impact of cold-calling behaviours of each of its salespeople. Secondary sources that record past behaviour can be called archives or traces. These types of artifacts represent tangible evidence of some past event. For example, a retail chain looking to expand its operations to new locations might observe the amount of graffiti on existing buildings around proposed locations to estimate the likely degree of vandalism and unlawful behaviours in those areas.

> **Direct observation** The process of observing actual behaviours or events and recording them as they occur.
>
> **Indirect observation** The process of directly observing the recorded artifacts of past behaviours.

Subjects' Awareness of Being Observed

This characteristic refers to the degree to which subjects consciously know their behaviour is being observed and recorded. When the subjects are completely unaware they are being observed, the observation technique is termed **disguised observation**. A popular and easy-to-understand example of disguised observation is the 'mystery shopper' technique used by many retailers. A retailer such as Next might hire a research firm to send in observers disguised as ordinary shoppers to observe how well the stores' employees interact with customers. The observers might look for interpersonal behaviour that would demonstrate attributes like friendliness, courtesy, helpfulness and store/product knowledge. The resulting data can aid Next's management in determining how its employees' interpersonal skills can be enhanced to improve its customers' overall shopping experiences. Next's management can also use other methods (e.g. hidden cameras) to prevent its employees from finding out they are being observed.

Disguised observations are used because when people know they are being watched, they naturally tend to modify their normal behaviour. The resulting behaviour would therefore be atypical. For example, how would a sales person for Next act if told he or she is going to be watched for the next several hours? Most likely this sales person would be on his/her best possible behaviour for that time period.

> **Disguised observation** A data collection technique where the subjects of interest are completely unaware that they are being observed.

However, in future new consumer right-to-privacy legislation may be enacted which would limit the use of disguised observing techniques. These laws are likely to restrict the conditions for which disguised techniques are appropriate by requiring the approval of the subject.

Researchers may, however, face situations in which it is impossible to keep the subjects from knowing they may be being observed and monitored, for example, customer services representatives taking customers' calls in a bank's call centre. Similarly, AC Nielsen Media Research would find it difficult to use its audiometers on in-home TV sets without the subjects' knowledge. Whenever subjects are aware they are being watched, the process is termed **undisguised observation**. As a general practice, the researcher should minimize the presence of the observer to avoid the possibility of atypical behaviour by subjects.

> **Undisguised observation** The data recording method where the subjects are aware that they are being watched.

Structure of Observation

This characteristic refers to the degree to which the behaviours or events are specifically known to the researcher prior to the observation. When a researcher knows specifically which behaviours or events are to be recorded, a **structured observation** technique is appropriate. In these situations, the trained observer ignores all other behaviours. Researchers use some type of checklist or standardized recording form to help the observer restrict his or her attention to just those pre-specified behaviours or events. For example, the produce manager at a local Waitrose supermarket is deciding whether to pre-package the cherries or display them individually, because they are concerned about the extent to which customers handle and squeeze the cherries when selecting which ones to buy. Using a structured observation approach, the produce manager assigns a store employee to hang out in the produce department and observe 100 customers as they select cherries. The employee simply focuses on the following behaviours: number of times loose cherries are picked up and handled; number of times pre-packaged tomatoes are picked up and handled; and any noticeable squeezing of loose and pre-packaged cherries. The tallied results may show that 75 per cent of the customers observed picked up and handled the loose cherries, while only 35 per cent picked up and handled the pre-packaged ones. Also, 55 per cent of those observed actually squeezed the loose cherries, while only 40 per cent did the same to the pre-packaged ones. Do these numbers justify pre-packaging? Even though loose cherries got handled and squeezed more frequently, the produce manager feels uncomfortable going to the store manager to suggest that all cherries be pre-packaged to reduce spoilage. Now think about what other behaviours should have been recorded.

> **Structured observation** A method of recording specifically known behaviours and events.

In contrast, **unstructured observation** formats place no restrictions on the observer regarding what should be recorded. Ideally, all events would be observed and recorded. When an unstructured technique is used, what usually happens is researchers brief the trained observers on the research objectives and information requirements and then allow them to use their own discretion in determining what behaviours are actually recorded. For example, the government officials responsible for the 37 public parks and gardens in Paris want to develop a proposal for renovating several of the city's aging parks. Not sure what should be included in the renovations, they send out two park supervisors to observe people using the facilities at several of the city's most popular parks. The data collected could be useful not only in redesigning the ageing parks but also in providing ideas about how to make the parks safer for people.

> **Unstructured observation** The data recording format that does not place any restrictions on the observer regarding what behaviours or events should be recorded.

Type of Observing Mechanism

This characteristic relates to how the behaviours or events will be observed. The researcher can choose between human observers and mechanical or electronic devices. With **human observation**, the observer is either a person hired and trained by the researcher or is a member of the research team. To be effective, the observer must have a good understanding of the research objectives and strong observation and interpretive skills. For example, the teacher of a marketing research module

> **Human observation** Data collection by a researcher or trained observer who records text, subjects' actions, and behaviours.

can use observation skills to capture not only students' classroom behaviour but also non-verbal communication symbols exhibited by students during class (e.g. facial expressions, body postures, movement in chairs, hand gestures), which allows them to determine, in real time, if students are paying attention to what is being discussed, when students become confused about a concept, or if boredom begins to set in.

In many situations the use of a mechanical or electronic device is more suitable than employing a person in collecting the primary data. **Mechanical/electronic observation** is the use of some type of mechanical or electronic device (videotape camera, traffic counter, optical scanner, eye tracking monitor, pupilometer, audio voice pitch analyzer, psychogalvanometer, to name a few) to capture human behaviour, events, or marketing phenomena. Such devices may reduce the cost and improve the flexibility, accuracy, or other functions in the data collection process. For example, if the Department of Transportation in the UK conducts a traffic flow study, air pressure lines can be laid across the road and connected to a counter box that is activated every time a vehicle's tires roll over the lines. Although the data will be limited to the number of vehicles passing by within a specified time span, this method is less costly and more accurate than using human observers to record traffic flows. Other examples of situations where mechanical/electronic observation would be appropriate include using security cameras at self-service machines in library to detect problems that readers might have in using the machine, using optical scanners and bar-code technology (e.g. universal product code) to count, in real time, the number and types of products purchased at a retail establishment, and using turnstile tick-o-meters to count the number of fans at major sporting or entertainment events. The Closer Look at Research section below presents another example of the use of mechanical/electronic observation.

> **Mechanical/electronic observation** Data collection using some type of mechanical or electronic device to capture human behaviour, events, or marketing phenomena.

 ## A Closer Look at Research *(In the field)*
Heathrow Failed the Electronic Observation test

An electronic observation research issued in *The Times* on 4 August 2007 showed that Heathrow airport induces the same levels of stress and hypertension as being mugged at knifepoint or having a heart attack. Even standing motionless in a security queue can cause a passenger's heart rate to hit levels usually only attained by elite sportsmen.

Four passengers attached to probes and monitors flew out of Heathrow in order to provide researchers with statistical evidence of how travelling through the world's busiest international airport affects health. Their work has been funded by Silverjet, a business-class-only airline that operates out of Luton airport.

The study found that passenger heart rates accelerated from 55 beats per minute to 70 within minutes of arriving at Heathrow. Heart rates peaked at 200 beats per minute as stress levels rose. The blood pressure of passengers rose from an average of 123/81 to 170/99. Skin conductance, a stress measurement used in lie detector tests, reached levels 100 times higher than a typical relaxed state.

More than 68 million passengers a year use Heathrow despite its 1950s-era infrastructure designed to cope with only 45 million. The problems of overcrowding have been exacerbated by new security restrictions.

Willie Walsh, the chief executive of British Airways, Heathrow's largest user, estimates that domestic air travel has dropped by 10 per cent because passengers are put off by the new security rules and by airport overcrowding. Stephen Gill, one of the passengers in this observation experiment, said 'The airport is manic and passengers are treated like cattle. That's why it's stressful.'

With advances in technology, telecommunications and computer hardware and software, mechanical/electronic observation techniques are rapidly becoming very useful and cost-effective for monitoring human behaviours, events or marketing phenomena. For example, AC Nielsen has upgraded its Television Index system by integrating its People Meter technology into the system. The People Meter is a microwave-based, computerized television rating system that replaces the old passive meters and handwritten diary system with state-of-the-art electronic measuring. With AC Nielsen's TV household panel members, when the TV is turned on, a simple question mark symbol appears on the screen to remind the viewer to indicate who is watching the programme. Using a handheld electronic device similar to the TV's remote control, the viewer records who is watching. Another device attached to the TV automatically sends pre-specified information (e.g. viewer's gender, age, programme tuned in to, time of programme) to AC Nielsen's computers. These data are used by AC Nielsen to generate overnight ratings as well as demographic profiles for different programmes.

Another technology-driven device is the new software used to monitor people's interactive behaviour with Internet websites. Companies like Itracks, FocusVision Worldwide, Inc., HarrisInteractive and Burke have pioneered developments in new tracking software used to monitor people's interactive website behaviour and track popularity of participating websites and online Internet providers (e.g. Yahoo, MSN). This type of tracking software is installed on participating consumers' personal computers and allows for tracking websites consisting of multiple pages, page by page, as well as the paths or sequence of pages visitors follow.

Advances in scanner-based technology are quickly replacing traditional consumer purchasing diary methods. In brief, a **scanner-based panel** is made up of a group of participating households that are assigned a unique bar-coded card that is presented to the checkout clerk at the register. The household's code number is matched with information obtained from previous scanner transactions. The system enables the researcher to observe and build a purchase behaviour database on each household. Technology advances enable researchers to combine these tracking systems with demographic and psychographic information databases of the households, which provide more complete customer profiles. Scanner-based observation data provide marketers with information on how products are doing in individual stores; the extent sales has altered with price changes, local advertisements or promotion activities; and increasingly sophisticated purchase profiles of any particular customers.

Scanner-based panel A group of participating households which have a unique bar-coded card as an identification characteristic for inclusion in the research study.

Techniques Used in Measuring Physiological Actions and Reactions

For years, researchers have used mechanical observations to evaluate consumers' physiological reactions to various stimuli such as advertising copy, packaging, and new products. These techniques are used when the researcher is interested in recording actions and reactions the subjects are unaware of or when subjects are unwilling to provide honest responses to the effects of the stimulus being studied. Traditionally, there are four categories of mechanical observation devices used to measure physiological actions and reactions: voice pitch analysers, pupilometers, eye tracking monitors and psychogalvanometers.

The **voice pitch analyser** is a computer system that measures emotional responses by changes in the subject's voice. This technique uses sophisticated audio-adapted computers to detect abnormal frequencies in the subject's voice caused by changes in the person's autonomic nervous system. It is similar to a lie detector test, but the subject is not hooked up to a lot of wires. Computerized analysis compares the subject's voice pitch patterns during a warm-up session (benchmarked as the normal range) to those patterns obtained from the recorded verbal responses to a given stimulus (e.g. a TV commercial).

> **Voice pitch analyser** A computer system that measures emotional responses by changes in the subject's voice.

The **pupilometer** mechanically observes and records changes in the diameter of a subject's pupils. The subject is instructed to view a screen on which the stimulus is projected. As the distance and brightness of the stimulus to the subject's eyes are held constant, changes in pupil sizes are recorded and are interpreted as some type of unobservable cognitive activity. The assumption underlying the use of a pupilometer is the belief that increases in pupil size within a controlled environment reflect a specific attitude or interest in the stimulus.

> **Pupilometer** A mechanical instrument that observes and records changes in the diameter of a subject's pupils.

The **eye tracking monitor** is a device that observes and records a person's unconscious eye movements. Invisible infrared light beams record the subject's eye movements while reading or viewing the stimulus (e.g. a magazine ad, TV commercial, package design) and another video camera records what part of the given stimulus is being viewed at the movement. The two databases are overlaid and the system can determine what parts of the stimulus were seen and which components were overlooked. In advertising, this type of data can provide insights to possible points of interest and their likely impacts.

> **Eye tracking monitor** A mechanical device that observes and records a person's unconscious eye movements.

Finally, the **psychogalvanometer** measures involuntary changes in the electronic resistance of a subject's skin, referred to as the galvanic skin response (GSR). This mechanical observation technique indicates when the person's emotional arousal or tension level changes toward the stimulus, and these changes are assumed to be created by the presence of the stimulus.

Psychogalvanometer An electronic instrument that measures involuntary changes in the electronic resistance of a subject's skin; also referred to as the galvanic skin response (GSR).

While all these mechanical observation techniques are interesting, they are based on the unproven assumption that physiological actions and reactions are predictors of people's thoughts or emotions. There is no theoretical consensus this assumption is valid. Moreover, the accuracy of the measurements obtained from these techniques is questionable, and the technology needed is expensive. In addition, external validity remains an issue because use of these types of physiological observation requires that subjects be brought into controlled artificial laboratory environments, which do not represent reality.

Selecting an Appropriate Observation Technique

To determine the most appropriate type of observation technique for collecting primary data, researchers must integrate their knowledge and understanding of the research objectives, information requirements, conditions for using observations and characteristics of observation techniques.

The first step in determining the right observation technique is for the researcher to understand the information requirements that should be based on the research objectives, and consider how that information will be used later on. Without this understanding, the task of deciding a technique's appropriateness becomes significantly more difficult. The researcher must answer the following questions prior to method selection:

1 What types of behaviour are pertinent to the research problem?

2 How simple or complex are the behaviours?

3 How much detail of the behaviour needs to be recorded?

4 What is the most appropriate setting (natural or contrived) for the behaviour?

The second step involves integrating the researcher's knowledge of the conditions for observing behaviour and the characteristics of observation techniques in order to identify the most appropriate technique of observing and recording the specified behaviour. The issues that must be addressed include the following:

1 How complex is the required setting?

2 Is it available for observing the specified behaviours or events?

3 To what extent are the desired behaviours or events repetitious and frequently exhibited?

4 What degrees of directness and structure should be associated with observing the behaviours or events?

5   How aware should the subjects be that they and their behaviours are being observed?

6   Are the observable behaviours or events complex enough to require the use of a mechanical/ electronic device for observing the behaviour? If so, which specific method would be the most appropriate?

The last step focuses on the cost, flexibility, accuracy, efficiency and objectivity factors associated with observation techniques, as well as the ethical issues. Prior to implementing any observation technique, the researcher must evaluate the proposed method's ability to accurately observe and record the specified behaviour. The costs – time, money, manpower – involved must be determined and compared to the expected efficiency of collecting the data based in part on the number of subjects needed in the investigation. In addition, the researcher must consider the possible ethical issues that may exist with the proposed observation technique. The Ethics box (see p. 321) discusses ethical issues associated with observation techniques.

Strengths and Weaknesses of Observation Techniques

Observation techniques have several specific strengths and weaknesses (see Exhibit 9.3). Probably the most obvious strength is that they allow for very accurate gathering of consumers' actual behaviour patterns or events rather than reported activities. This is especially true in situations where the subjects are observed in a natural public setting using a disguised technique. Wherever possible and appropriate, mechanical/electronic observation techniques can be used to lessen the burden of the observer. In addition, observation techniques can help in reducing potential subject recall error, response bias, as well as non-response problem. In many situations, observation techniques enable the researcher to gather and record in-depth details about current behaviour or events.

Observation techniques have several weaknesses. One of the ongoing shortcomings of observation techniques is they produce data that are difficult to generalize beyond those test subjects who were actually observed. Typically, observation techniques are used in research projects that focus on a small number of subjects (typically between 5 and 60) under unique or special circumstances, thus reducing the representativeness of larger groups of people. Given the nature of observation techniques, it is extremely difficult for the researcher to explain logically why the observed behaviours or events took place. This inability to interrogate the subjects on their attitudes, motives, feelings and other non-observable factors means that any resulting insights into the behaviour should be considered subjective. Inferred meanings of the observed behaviour are therefore limited to 'educated guesses'.

In those situations where the natural public setting includes a large number of subjects, it is difficult even for trained observers to note all the activities occurring at the same time. While an observer is focused on the behaviour of one particular subject, they are likely to completely miss that of the other subjects in the setting during that same time frame. Disguised observation situations pose an

EXHIBIT 9.3 Major Strengths and Weaknesses of Observation Techniques

Major Strengths	Major Weaknesses
Accuracy of actual behaviour	Lack of generalizability of data
Reduction of confounding factors	Inability of explaining behaviours or events
Detail of the behavioural data	Complexity of setting and recording of behaviour(s) or events

Ethics

Subjects' Unawareness Can Raise Many Questions

Subjects' awareness of observation techniques raises some ethical questions worth noting. When using observations to collect primary behaviour data, should the subjects be informed that they are being observed? If so, what changes in their natural behaviour might occur? Remember, the researcher wants to capture the subjects' natural behaviour as it actually occurs and relates to the specified situation. Subjects being observed might feel uncomfortable about their true behaviour and try to behave in a more socially acceptable manner. For example, a marketing professor at a university is told by his department chair that as part of his annual performance review, an outside observer will be in class Monday to observe the professor's teaching style. How likely is it that the professor will modify his 'normal' classroom behaviour for that Monday's class session to make doubly sure his effectiveness meets or exceeds the required standard? Would you behave in a more socially acceptable manner if you know someone is going to be observe you? In disguised observations, the researcher uses some degree of deceit in order to observe behaviour without the subjects' knowledge. In this situation, the ethical questions focus on the subjects' right to privacy.

additional limitation in that human observers cannot instantaneously or automatically record the behaviour activities as they occur. There is some lag time between observing the behaviour or event and recording what was observed. With this natural lag time, there is the possibility of faulty recall on the part of the observer. One way to overcome these potential limitations is that the observations should be made with the appropriate mechanical/electronic device whenever possible.

marketing research in action

Thomas Pink Truly in the Pink

The original, classic style of Thomas Pink shirts that kick-started the company's fortune
Picture courtesy of Thomas Pink

It's a little known fact that the phrase 'in the pink' comes from the upmarket Mayfair tailor Thomas Pink who made the very best hunting coats. The expression 'hunting pink' for a coat which is actually red is also thought to be a reference to this talented man.

Today, Thomas Pink is the fashionable shirt, tie and accessory maker with branches from Jermyn Street in London to Madison Avenue, New York where it boasts the world's largest shirt store, as well as Brussels, Paris, Boston and San Francisco. The company has also opened a women's only store called, appropriately, Pink Woman on Sloane Street in London.

Thomas Pink's reputation for quality derives not only from its superb choice of fabrics and its unfailing attention to detail in the craftsmanship, but also from its relentless pursuit of excellence in its service to customers. Part of that relentless pursuit of service excellence is where SPSL, Europe's largest company in retail observation research belonging to Synovate, comes in. The research company has installed highly advanced customer counting and tracking equipment in several Thomas Pink stores, with more planned. The installation and the resulting data analysis are designed to provide Thomas Pink with key performance indicators that are vital for its business.

Thomas Pink Sales and Marketing Director, Alison Appel, takes up the story: 'At Thomas Pink we are highly focused on serving our customers to the best of our abilities. This means we must understand our demand patterns and that's where SPSL comes in. we can break down our retail traffic data into half hour segments and compare it to sales data, staff stretch and new promotions in order to see how well we are meeting the needs of both our customers and our targets. To that end, we have SPSL construct weekly league table reports with comparisons of sales versus traffic versus conversion rates. These reports are now a vital, mission-critical business tool, enabling constant fine tuning and improvement of our offer.'

Questions

1 What are the advantages and limitations of the observation technique that Thomas Pink has adopted for meeting its objective of customer service excellence?

2 What other observation techniques can Thomas Pink use for the same objective? Compare the pros and cons between these techniques and the observation technique already adopted.

Summary of Learning Objectives

■ **Understand the different types of qualitative and quantitative observation techniques.**
There are four major perspectives we can use to identify all the different types of qualitative and quantitative observation techniques. First is directness of observation. Second is whether the subject is aware of himself/herself being observed. Third is structure of observation, and the fourth is the observing mechanism to be used.

■ **Discuss the characteristics, benefits, and weaknesses of observation techniques.**
Observation techniques can be used by researchers in all types of research designs (exploratory, descriptive, causal). In addition to the general advantages of observation, major benefits are the accuracy of collecting data on actual behaviour, reduction of confounding factors and the amount of detailed behavioural data that can be recorded. The unique limitations of observation techniques are lack of generalizability of the data, inability to explain current behaviours or events and the complexity of observing the behaviour.

■ **Elaborate the typical steps that can be followed to choose the most appropriate observation technique for a particular project.**
The first step is to understand the information requirements and how that information will be used later on. The second step involves integrating the researcher's knowledge of the conditions for observing behaviour and the characteristics of observation techniques. The last step focuses on the cost, flexibility, accuracy, efficiency, objectivity and ethics issues associated with observation techniques.

Key Terms and Concepts

Review Questions

1 What are the major advantages and disadvantages of observation studies relative to surveys?

2 Discuss how you might combine the observation technique of data collection with the focus group method.

3 Discuss why disguised observation is an appropriate data collection technique for investigating how parents discipline their children when shopping at a supermarket.

4 Comment on the ethics of the following situations:

a You are unaware that a marketing researcher goes around on refuse collection day in your neighbourhood and collects your rubbish prior to the refuse person's arrival. The purpose is to assess your alcohol consumption behaviour during the previous three days.

b You are invited by a researcher to be a test user for a new food item at a shopping centre testing site and the researcher plans to secretly videotape your actions and reactions from behind a one-way mirror.

Discussion Questions

1 What type of observation technique and experimental design would you suggest for each of the following situations and why?

a The research and development manager at Calvin Klein suggests a new type of cologne for men that could be promoted by a sports celebrity like David Beckham.

b The housing manager at your university proposes some significant style changes to the physical configuration of the current on-campus accommodation.

c The management at Homebase must decide on the best location for a new store in your home town.

d The senior design engineer for Honda wants to identify desirable design changes for the next generation of its cars.

e A supermarket manager would like to know the popularity of a new brand of cereal.

2 Identify a restaurant situation and develop and execute a 'mystery shopper' method that will allow you to collect observation data to answer the research questions below. Write a brief (one to two page) summary report of your findings.

a How well do the restaurant servers and staff interact with their customers?

b How friendly are the restaurant's servers and staff to the customers?

c How courteous are the restaurant's servers and staff to the customers?

d How helpful are the restaurant's servers and staff in meeting customers' needs?

e What is the level of product/service knowledge exhibited by the restaurant's servers and staff?

f How satisfying or dissatisfying was the restaurant experience?

PART 3

Designs for Accurate Data

Part contents

Chapter 10

Questionnaire Design

LEARNING OBJECTIVES

After reading this chapter, you will be able to

- ☑ Identify and discuss the critical factors that can contribute to directly improving the accuracy of surveys, and explain why questionnaire development is not a simple process.

- ☑ Discuss the theoretical principles of questionnaire design, and explain why a questionnaire is more than just asking a respondent some questions.

- ☑ Identify and explain the communication roles of questionnaires in the data collection process.

- ☑ Explain why the type of information needed to address a decision maker's questions and problems will substantially influence the structure and content of questionnaires.

- ☑ List and discuss the 11 steps in the questionnaire development process, and tell how to eliminate some common mistakes in questionnaire designs.

- ☑ Discuss and employ the 'flowerpot' approach in developing scientific questionnaires.

- ☑ Discuss the importance of cover letters, and explain the guidelines to help eliminate common mistakes in cover letter designs.

> " The questionnaire represents one part of the survey process. It is, however, a very vital part of the process. A poorly written questionnaire will not provide the data that are required or, worse, will provide data that are incorrect.
>
> —Ian Brace
> Research Director at TNS UK "

Getting Prospective Respondents to Answer our Questions

Considerable time and effort needs to be involved in designing an acceptable questionnaire. However, if the number of respondents willing to fill in our questionnaire significantly falls short of our target, our questionnaire design process will be deemed a failure. Unfortunately, it is becoming increasingly likely that not enough respondents will answer our questions. Questionnaire survey refusal rates keep trending upward. For example, of China's major cities, refusal rates are estimated at 32 per cent in Guangzhou, 22 per cent in Beijing and 10 per cent in Shanghai.

Many factors contribute to questionnaires being refused. One of them is questionnaire length. After approximately 20 minutes, most respondents would become fatigued with the process and may terminate the interview. This questionnaire length factor is exacerbated in international studies, as different languages can shorten or lengthen the amount of time it takes to go through a questionnaire. For example, translated into Italian, a 20-minute American questionnaire will last only approximately 18 minutes. Translated into French, the same questionnaire will take 22 minutes.

Source: Adapted from Young and Javalgi, 2007.

Value of Questionnaires in Marketing Research

Many people believe that questionnaire design is not a difficult task. Perhaps they believe that it is simply a case of thinking of the questions you want to get answers to from respondents, writing down and organizing those questions in a questionnaire, and then going out to find people to fill in the questionnaire. However, the chapter opening example shows that designing a questionnaire that works well for a research project can be a very difficult task. The marketing researcher may want to include many questions in the questionnaire, but should be aware of the questionnaire length, among many other important issues in questionnaire design, because ignoring these issues may result in a high refusal rate and less accurate answers. These problems may be even more serious if the marketing researcher is involved in conducting questionnaire survey across different countries.

This chapter focuses on developing a clear understanding of the importance of questionnaire design, the process that should be undertaken and the issues that need to be carefully considered.

As a future marketing or management decision maker, you may never personally design a questionnaire, but for fulfilling your marketing/management responsibility, you need to be capable of determining whether a questionnaire you are reviewing is good or bad. Therefore, you should know about the considerations, preliminary activities and processes that should be undertaken in designing good quality questionnaires.

Much of the primary data necessary to create new information for resolving business and marketing problems requires the researcher to ask people questions and record their responses. If the problems were simple and required only one bit of raw data, questionnaires would not be necessary. A researcher could develop a single question measurement and administer it to a sample of respondents, collect the data, analyse it, and derive meaningful information. For example, let's say a retailer like Next wanted to know if having a '50 per cent off' sale on a particular Saturday would increase its sales revenue that day. A researcher could develop the following question: 'If Next had a 50 per cent off sale on all merchandise on that particular Saturday, would you come to Next and buy at least one item? ___YES ___NO'. Then the researcher could administer the question to 1,000 consumers representative of the general population. Let's assume that 650 people said yes (65 per cent) and 350 people said no (35 per cent) to the question, and the researcher interpreted the results as being 'the majority (65 per cent) of shoppers would come to Next and buy merchandise'. By having this one bit of information, would Next have enough information to decide whether or not to hold the sale?

In reality, it is highly unlikely that this one bit of information would be a good predictor of actual shopping behaviour. Some of the other factors that might also directly affect a person's decision to shop at Next include (1) attitude towards Next and its merchandise, (2) competitive activities, (3) economic climate, and (4) personal financial situation. The point is that many business problems are not unidimensional, and therefore a single piece of information about a problem often is not sufficient to resolve it.

A **questionnaire** is a formalized framework consisting of a set of questions and scales designed to generate primary data. Questionnaire construction involves taking established sets of scale measurements and formatting them into an instrument for collecting raw data from respondents. Prior to discussing questionnaire design, there are several key insights about questionnaires worth noting. First, the purpose of designing a 'good' survey instrument is to increase the probability of collecting high quality primary data that can be transformed into valid and reliable information for marketing managers and/or researchers. Construct and scale measurement validity and reliability issues should be addressed and assessed during the construct development stage by researchers prior to finalizing the questionnaire. The *layout* of the scale measurements used to collect primary data can influence any particular measurement's ability to provide valid and reliable data. Second, advances in communication systems, the Internet, and computer software programs have impacted the methods of asking questions and recording responses. Yet the critical decisions and processes that underlie the construction of good questionnaires basically remain unchanged. That is, whether designing a survey instrument for 'online' methods (i.e. computer assisted telephone survey, Internet survey) or 'offline' methods (i.e. personal or telephone survey), the rules and process steps researchers need to follow in designing questionnaires are essentially the same. Finally, questionnaires are always a key instrument used in collecting raw data, especially in descriptive and causal research.

> **Questionnaire** A formalized framework consisting of a set of questions and scales designed to generate primary raw data.

Theoretical Principles of Questionnaire Design

One of the great weaknesses of questionnaire design today is that many researchers still do not understand the theory behind questionnaire development. Many researchers believe that designing questionnaires is an art rather than a science. While there is some creativity in designing questionnaires, the process itself should be a scientific one that integrates established rules of logic, objectivity, and systematic procedures. Everyone understands that words go into questions and that questions go into questionnaires, but not everyone understands that writing questions does not necessarily give you an acceptable questionnaire.

Theoretical Components of a Questionnaire

Theoretically, a questionnaire consists of several components – words, questions, formats and hypotheses – that are integrated into a recognizable, hierarchical layer system.

Words

The most obvious component is words. Researchers must carefully consider which words to use in creating the questions and scales for collecting raw data from respondents. A few examples of wording problems include ambiguity, abstraction, and connotation. The words selected by the researcher can influence a respondent's answer to a given question. The following examples illustrate this point:

1 Do you think anything *could* be done to make it more convenient for students to register for classes at your university?

2 Do you think anything *should* be done to make it more convenient for students to register for classes at your university?

3 Do you think anything *might* be done to make it more convenient for students to register for classes at your university?

The different answers each of these questions would generate show how 'word phrasing' variations can become significant in questionnaire designs. Slight changes in wording can introduce different concepts into the questionnaire.

Question Setup

The next component is the question setup used to collect raw data from the respondent. Two important issues relating to question setup are (1) the type of question format (unstructured or structured) and (2) the quality of the question (good or bad).

Unstructured questions are open-ended questions that allow respondents to reply in their own words. There is no predetermined list of responses available to aid or limit the respondents' answers. This type of question requires more thinking and effort on the part of the respondents. An interviewer asking this kind of questions should be prepared to ask follow-up probing questions whenever appropriate. If administered correctly, unstructured questions can provide the researcher with a rich array of information. The format of open-ended questions can vary depending on the data collection method (e.g. personal survey, traditional telephone survey, computer-assisted telephone survey, online or offline self-administered survey). Exhibit 10.1 provides several examples to illustrate these format differences.

> **Unstructured questions** Open-ended questions formatted to allow respondents to reply in their own words.

Structured questions are closed-ended questions that require the respondent to choose the appropriate option(s) that apply from a predetermined set of options. This question format reduces the amount of thinking and effort required by respondents. In this type of question format, interviewer bias is largely reduced because the interviewer or the respondent simply checks a box or line, circles a category, hits a key on a keyboard, points and clicks a computer mouse, or records a number that best represents the respondent's response to the question.

> **Structured questions** Closed-ended questions that require the respondent to choose from a predetermined set of options.

EXHIBIT 10.1 Examples of Unstructured Question Setup Designs

Personal or Telephone Survey

What toppings, if any, do you usually add to a pizza when ordering a pizza for yourself from Pizza Hut? **(Interviewer: Record all mentioned toppings in the space provided below. Make sure you probe for specifics and clarity of responses.)**

_____

_____

_____

or

What toppings, if any, do you usually add to a pizza when ordering a pizza for yourself from Pizza Hut? **(Interviewer: DO NOT read the listed toppings; just record the toppings by checking the box next to the mentioned toppings below. Make sure you probe for specifics and clarity of responses.)**

❑ anchovies   ❑ bacon   ❑ barbecue beef
❑ black olives   ❑ extra cheese   ❑ green olives
❑ green peppers   ❑ ground beef   ❑ ham
❑ hot peppers   ❑ mushrooms   ❑ onions
❑ pepperoni   ❑ sausage   ❑ some other topping: _____

Self-Administered Survey (Online or Offline)

In the space provided below, please write the types of toppings, if any, that you usually add to a pizza when ordering a pizza for yourself from Pizza Hut. **(Please indicate as many toppings as apply.)**

_____

_____

_____

_____

Structured formats give the researcher greater opportunities to control the thinking respondents must do in order to answer a question. Exhibit 10.2 shows some examples.

Bad questions are any questions that prevent or distort the fundamental communication between the researcher and the respondent. A researcher may think an excellent question has been written because it accurately conveys a point of view or interest to the respondent, but if the respondent cannot answer it in a meaningful way, it is a bad question. Some examples of bad questions are those that are:

1 *Incomprehensible* to the respondent because the wording, the concept, or both cannot be readily understood. An example would be 'What is your attitude about the linkage between a company's approach to market visioning if any and its management's business philosophy?'

2 *Unanswerable* either because the respondent does not have access to the information needed or because none of the answer choices apply to the respondent. An example would be 'What was your parents' annual income two years ago?'

Bad questions Any questions that prevent or distort the fundamental communication between the researcher and the respondent.

EXHIBIT 10.2 Examples of Structured Question Setup Designs

Personal Survey

(HAND RESPONDENT CARD.) Please look at this card and tell me the letters that indicate what toppings, if any, you usually add to a pizza when ordering a pizza for yourself from Pizza Hut. **(Interviewer: Record all mentioned toppings by circling the letters below, and make sure you probe for any other toppings.)**

[a] anchovies	[b] bacon	[c] barbecue beef
[d] black olives	[e] extra cheese	[f] green olives
[h] green peppers	[i] ground beef	[j] ham
[k] hot peppers	[l] mushrooms	[m] onions
[n] pepperoni	[o] sausage	[p] some other topping: _____

Telephone Survey (Traditional or Computer Assisted)

I'm going to read you a list of pizza toppings. As I read each one, please tell me whether or not that topping is one that you usually add to a pizza when ordering a pizza for yourself from Pizza Hut. **(Interviewer: Read each topping slowly and record all mentioned toppings by circling their corresponding letter below, and make sure you probe for any other toppings.)**

[a] anchovies	[b] bacon	[c] barbecue beef
[d] black olives	[e] extra cheese	[f] green olives
[h] green peppers	[i] ground beef	[j] ham
[k] hot peppers	[l] mushrooms	[m] onions
[n] pepperoni	[o] sausage	[p] some other topping: _____

Self-Administered Survey (Online or Offline)

Among the pizza toppings listed below, what toppings, if any, do you usually add to a pizza when ordering a pizza for yourself from Pizza Hut?

(Please check as many boxes as apply.)

❑ anchovies	❑ bacon	❑ barbecue beef
❑ black olives	❑ extra cheese	❑ green olives
❑ green peppers	❑ ground beef	❑ ham
❑ hot peppers	❑ mushrooms	❑ onions
❑ pepperoni	❑ sausage	❑ some other topping: _____

3 *Leading* in that the respondent is led by the question wording to give a response that would not ordinarily be given. An example of this would be 'Do you agree that all the good citizens should support the concept of fair trade?'

4 *Double-barrelled* in that the respondent is asked to address more than one issue at a time. An example would be 'To what extent do you agree or disagree that iPhone is the most technologically advanced and user friendly mobile phone products in 2007?'

For more examples of bad questions go to the book's website at www.mhhe.com/shiu09 and follow the links.

Questionnaire Format

This component does not directly relate to the process of developing the individual questions but rather the layout of sets of questions. A good questionnaire format is one that allows for clear communication. Later in the chapter, we will discuss in detail the 'flowerpot' approach to designing questionnaires, which can improve the researcher's ability to collect accurate data.

Hypothesis Development

This final component focuses on the design of questionnaires for collecting meaningful data to test a **hypothesis** rather than merely to gather facts. The questions used in a questionnaire for this purpose should either directly or indirectly relate to a predetermined hypothesis that is relevant to the research objectives. Hypotheses can relate to

1 The nature of the respondent.

2 The sociological structures and their influence on the respondent.

3 The respondent's grasp of concepts being presented.

4 The relationships among a respondent's knowledge, attitudes, and marketplace behaviours.

5 The descriptive and predictive capabilities of attributes of the constructs (e.g. customer satisfaction, product or service quality).

> **Hypothesis** A formalized statement of a testable relationship between two or more constructs or variables.

By identifying the hypothesis associated with each of the questions on a questionnaire, researchers can improve their ability to determine which measurements are necessary for collecting primary data and which ones are nice but not necessary. The drawbacks of collecting 'nice but not necessary' data are that it will increase the length of the questionnaire and the likelihood of bias. Exhibit 10.3 displays some examples of different types of hypotheses a researcher can develop and connect to corresponding questions on a questionnaire.

Description Versus Prediction

While all good questionnaires are systematically structured, most surveys are designed to be descriptive or predictive. A descriptive design allows the researcher to collect raw data that can be turned into facts about a person or object. For example, the different European governments use questionnaires to collect state-of-being and state-of-behaviour data which can be translated into facts about their country population (e.g. income level, marital status, age, occupation, family size, usage rates, consumption quantities). In contrast, predictive questionnaires allow the researcher to collect a wide range of state-of-mind and state-of-intention data that can be used in predicting changes in attitudes and behaviours as well as in testing hypotheses.

Accuracy Versus Precision

Another theoretical principle that should guide the design of questionnaires is that of accuracy. This means a true report is obtained of the respondent's attitudes, preferences, beliefs, feelings, intentions, and/or actions. Questions and scales must be used that enable the researcher to gain an overall picture rather than just a fragment. **Accuracy** refers to the degree to which the data

> **Accuracy** The degree to which the data obtained from a questionnaire provide the researcher with a description of the true state of affairs.

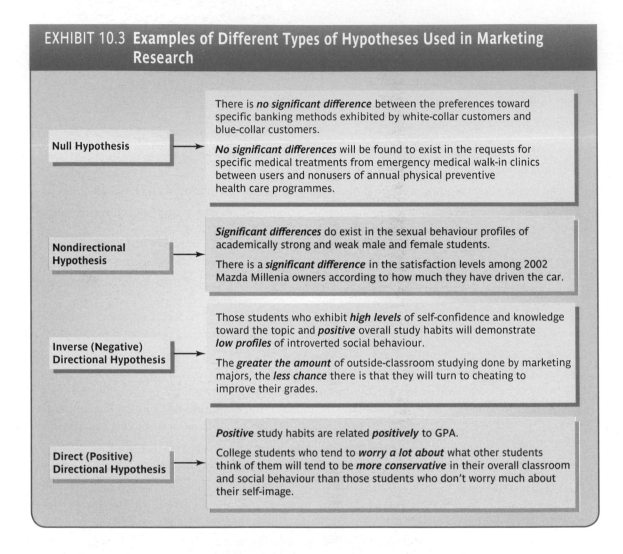

EXHIBIT 10.3 **Examples of Different Types of Hypotheses Used in Marketing Research**

Null Hypothesis

There is *no significant difference* between the preferences toward specific banking methods exhibited by white-collar customers and blue-collar customers.

No significant differences will be found to exist in the requests for specific medical treatments from emergency medical walk-in clinics between users and nonusers of annual physical preventive health care programmes.

Nondirectional Hypothesis

Significant differences do exist in the sexual behaviour profiles of academically strong and weak male and female students.

There is a *significant difference* in the satisfaction levels among 2002 Mazda Millenia owners according to how much they have driven the car.

Inverse (Negative) Directional Hypothesis

Those students who exhibit *high levels* of self-confidence and knowledge toward the topic and *positive* overall study habits will demonstrate *low profiles* of introverted social behaviour.

The *greater the amount* of outside-classroom studying done by marketing majors, the *less chance* there is that they will turn to cheating to improve their grades.

Direct (Positive) Directional Hypothesis

Positive study habits are related *positively* to GPA.

College students who tend to *worry a lot about* what other students think of them will tend to be *more conservative* in their overall classroom and social behaviour than those students who don't worry much about their self-image.

provide the researcher with a description of the true state of affairs. In contrast, **questionnaire design precision** focuses on whether questions and scales are narrowly and precisely defined.

> **Questionnaire design precision** The extent to which questions and scales are narrowly and precisely defined.

The Value of a Good Survey Instrument

The value of a well-constructed questionnaire cannot be overestimated by marketing researchers and practitioners. How a survey instrument is developed is a critical component in the process of creating information that can be used to solve business problems. Data collected through a questionnaire can be viewed as the key to unlocking understanding and truth about a problem situation.

In contrast, a bad questionnaire can be costly in terms of time, effort and money. It produces nothing more than 'garbage' data that, if used by decision makers, is likely to result in incorrect marketing actions. New technologies are providing a good way for designing good questionnaires and collecting the required data. Read the nearby Closer Look at Research box for a discussion of computerized questionnaire designs. For examples of 'good' and 'bad' questionnaires visit the book's website at www.mhhe.com/shiu09 and follow the links.

A Closer Look at Research (Using technology)
Computerized Questionnaires

'Smart' questionnaires are a very important development in marketing research. These questionnaires are structured with a mathematical logic that enables the computer to customize them for each respondent as the interview progresses. Through the use of interactive software, the computer constantly evaluates new information and presents the respondent with a new decision to make. In this type of survey, different respondents taking the same questionnaire would answer different sets of questions, each custom-designed to provide the most relevant data.

Before computerized questionnaires, corporations with diverse product lines would find it cumbersome and difficult to collect questionnaire data that can meet information requirements for each product line. With computerized questionnaires, collecting information specific to each product line becomes a lot easier.

Important advantages of computerized questionnaires over the pen-and-paper alternative include increased ease of participation, decreased time requirements and a reduction in resources needed to conduct the survey, thereby reducing the overall cost of survey administration. For corporations faced with constantly increasing time demands, computerized questionnaires are a natural choice for meeting their data collection needs.

The Flowerpot Approach to Questionnaire Designs

The process researchers follow to develop a questionnaire should be systematic. Exhibit 10.4 shows a set of steps for developing questionnaires. Each step can involve more than one activity.

With all these steps to understand, the development process can seem overwhelming at first. To simplify the questionnaire development process, we present the **flowerpot approach**. This approach involves a series of activities that have a logical, hierarchical order. The 'flowerpot' notion is symbolically derived from the natural shape associated with a clay pot used for growing flowers. The shape is wide at the top and narrower at the bottom – symbolizing a natural flow of data from general to specific.

> **Flowerpot approach** A specific framework for integrating sets of question/scale measurements into a logical, hierarchy-based questionnaire that ensures a general to specific data collection approach.

Although this approach is primarily used to create a good questionnaire structure, it has direct impacts on steps 1 and 3 of the development process outlined in Exhibit 10.4. The flowerpot approach helps the researcher make decisions regarding (1) construct development, (2) attributes of objects, (3) various question/scale formats, (4) wording of questions and (5) scale points. In situations where there are multiple research objectives, each objective will have its own pot of data. To reduce the likelihood of creating biased data, the size and width of the data requirements

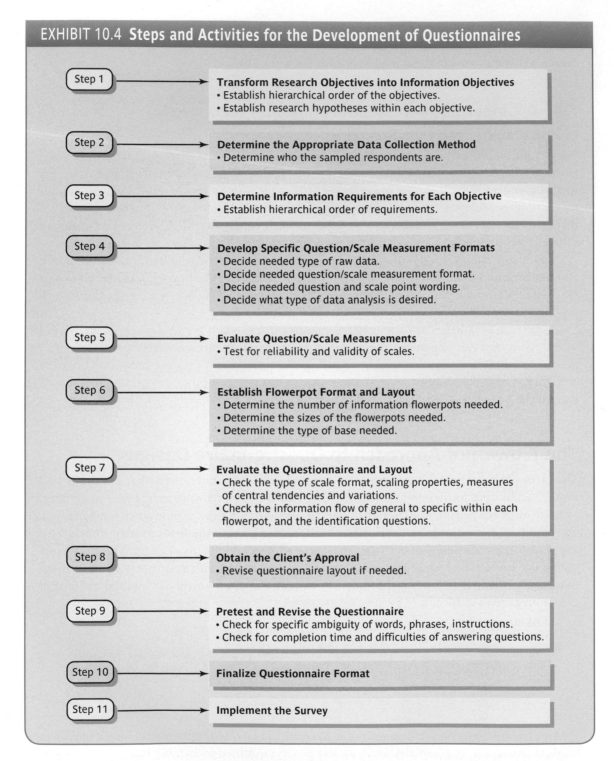

EXHIBIT 10.4 **Steps and Activities for the Development of Questionnaires**

Step 1 → **Transform Research Objectives into Information Objectives**
• Establish hierarchical order of the objectives.
• Establish research hypotheses within each objective.

Step 2 → **Determine the Appropriate Data Collection Method**
• Determine who the sampled respondents are.

Step 3 → **Determine Information Requirements for Each Objective**
• Establish hierarchical order of requirements.

Step 4 → **Develop Specific Question/Scale Measurement Formats**
• Decide needed type of raw data.
• Decide needed question/scale measurement format.
• Decide needed question and scale point wording.
• Decide what type of data analysis is desired.

Step 5 → **Evaluate Question/Scale Measurements**
• Test for reliability and validity of scales.

Step 6 → **Establish Flowerpot Format and Layout**
• Determine the number of information flowerpots needed.
• Determine the sizes of the flowerpots needed.
• Determine the type of base needed.

Step 7 → **Evaluate the Questionnaire and Layout**
• Check the type of scale format, scaling properties, measures
  of central tendencies and variations.
• Check the information flow of general to specific within each
  flowerpot, and the identification questions.

Step 8 → **Obtain the Client's Approval**
• Revise questionnaire layout if needed.

Step 9 → **Pretest and Revise the Questionnaire**
• Check for specific ambiguity of words, phrases, instructions.
• Check for completion time and difficulties of answering questions.

Step 10 → **Finalize Questionnaire Format**

Step 11 → **Implement the Survey**

must be determined for each objective, with the most general data requirements going into the biggest flowerpot and the next most general set of data going into a smaller pot. As illustrated in Exhibit 10.5, when multiple pots are stacked, the larger pot is always placed on top of a smaller pot to ensure that the overall general-to-specific flow of data is maintained.

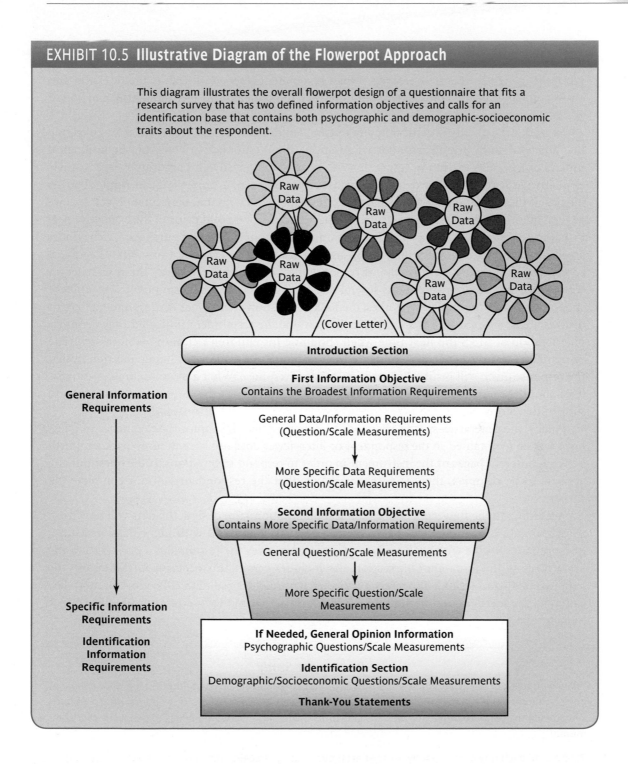

EXHIBIT 10.5 Illustrative Diagram of the Flowerpot Approach

This diagram illustrates the overall flowerpot design of a questionnaire that fits a research survey that has two defined information objectives and calls for an identification base that contains both psychographic and demographic-socioeconomic traits about the respondent.

Anyone learning to develop a proper questionnaire might raise this fundamental question: *Why should the questioning layout in the overall questionnaire as well as individual flowerpots always create a directional flow from general to more specific information?* The answer is threefold. First, logic has to be used in collecting primary data in the situation where the researcher (as well as the interviewer) and respondent begin the process as 'strangers' to each other. A survey that begins with general questions promotes the development of the necessary 'comfort zone' between the two parties. This comfort zone is similar to the one that has to be established in either focus group or in-depth interview settings. When respondents feel comfortable, the question and answer exchange process moves more smoothly and respondents are more thoughtful and honest with their responses.

Second, data quality is critical in any research study. Researchers run the risk of collecting low-quality data by asking respondents questions about an object or construct in an illogical order. For example, expecting respondents to be able to honestly and accurately express their evaluative judgements towards the performance of a particular object (e.g. an Apple iPod) is illogical if they have no knowledge of or personal experience with that particular object. A more general question about MP3 ownership or experience must be asked prior to the evaluative performance question. Asking a specific question about the attributes or purchasing behaviours associated with an object and then following up with more general questions about the object could cause ambiguity, confusion and response bias. For example, let's say the researcher, in conducting a retail store study, asks several questions concerning the respondent's *intention* of shopping at M&S for children's clothes, then asks a question about what the respondent likes or dislikes about shopping at M&S. Let's further assume the respondent indicated they *definitely plan* to shop at M&S the next time when shopping for children's clothing is necessary. The respondent's answer here could influence their response to the liking/disliking question in that the response given will justify the intention-to-shop response. What a respondent likes and dislikes about the store should be established prior to finding out the respondent's intention to shop at that store.

Finally, the general-to-specific sequence helps ensure that the appropriate sequence of questions will be maintained so the respondent or interviewer does not have to jump back and forth between different pages of the instrument in order to respond to questions. If the questionnaire appears to be complex, there is a greater chance that the respondent will not complete the survey.

According to the flowerpot concept, in a good questionnaire design, the data will flow from a general data level, down to a more specific data level, and end with identification data. A questionnaire begins with an *introductory section* that gives the respondent a basic idea of the main topic of the research. This section also includes general instructions for filling out the survey. The introduction's appearance will vary with the desired data collection method. For example, the introduction needed for a self-administered mode in a restaurant study might look as follows:

Restaurant Study

Thank you for your participation in this study. Your participation will aid us in determining what people in our community think about the present products and services offered by restaurants, which in turn will provide the restaurant industry with insights into how to better serve the needs of people in your community.

Please read each question carefully. Answer each question by checking the appropriate box(es) that represents your response or responses.

In contrast, an introduction for a housing study using the computer-assisted telephone survey mode might look as follows:

Housing Study

Verified   Phone # _____

By: _____   Date: _____

Date: _____   Time: _____ (a.m.) (p.m.)

Serial #: _____   Call Back Date and Time: _____

INTERVIEWER: Ask to speak with the head of household. If not available or none, ask for the next best alternative (relationship with the head of household): _____

Hello, I'm (Your Name) representing the Marketing Research Insights Group. Today, we are conducting an interesting study on housing in your county area and would like to include your opinions in it.

As was explained in the letter mailed to your residence about a week ago, we are not interested in selling you anything. We are only interested in your honest opinions about all the important issues of housing in your county area.

Notice how the two introductions differ. The computer-assisted telephone survey requires specific interviewer instructions.

Next, the researcher must determine how many different information objectives there are (i.e. the number of flowerpots needed to construct the questionnaire) and the breadth and depth of the information requirements (i.e. the different pot sizes).

First, working with the largest flowerpot (i.e. most general information), the researcher must identify the specific information requirements and arrange them from general to more specific. Then, going to the next largest flowerpot, the researcher again arranges the information requirements from general to specific. Because stacking the larger pots on top of smaller pots tends to create an unstable, top-heavy structure, a good questionnaire design should end with demographic and socioeconomic questions about the respondent to form a solid identification base. All questionnaires produced by the flowerpot approach should end with a thank-you statement.

The reasons underlying the placement of demographic and socioeconomic characteristics at the end of a questionnaire are twofold. First, in most consumer research studies, the primary information research objectives focus on collecting attitudinal emotional, and/or behavioural data about the consumer respondents. Demographic, socioeconomic, and physical characteristics about them, although important, are collected to mainly add a 'face' to those attitudes, feelings and behaviours. Seldom if ever is the purpose of the research expressed in terms of wanting to obtain demographic and socioeconomic information about people.

Second, these types of people characteristics are direct facts about a respondent often of a personal nature. In general, people are initially unwilling to provide these facts to strangers, who in this case are the researchers or interviewers. This unwillingness stems from the fact that most respondents do not understand their relevancy to the study's main information objectives and view them as inappropriate. Until the 'comfort zone' is established between the interviewer and respondent, asking personal questions could easily bring the interviewing process to a halt. To illustrate this point, suppose when you leave this class a student you don't know stops you and begins asking questions relating to your age, income, family members, occupation, marital status and so on. How would you react? Without knowing why this stranger was asking this kind of questions and how the information was going be used, this awkward situation would create uneasy feelings for you – powerful reasons for not responding and for ending the question/answer process.

The Flowerpot Approach's Impact on Questionnaire Development

Although the flowerpot approach is primarily used to determine the appropriate sequential order of the questions and scale measurements, it has a direct impact on several of the other development activities.

Determining the Information Objectives

After transforming the research objectives into information objectives, the researcher must evaluate each information objective for its broadness. This activity achieves two things for the researcher. First, it helps the researcher decide which information objectives represent a flowerpot of information. Second, it helps the researcher to determine how many flowerpots, and in what sizes, will need to be stacked up in the questionnaire design.

Determining the Information Requirements

Rather than developing all the data requirements for the information objectives within the same time interval, the flowerpot approach focuses on one information topic at a time before considering all other pending information topics. This decreases the likelihood of generating irrelevant or 'nice but not necessary' data. It also enhances the researcher's ability to determine the necessary order (general to specific) among the data requirements within a given pot.

Development of a Flowerpot-Designed Questionnaire

This section describes how the flowerpot approach influences the activities in the survey instrument development process described in Exhibit 10.4. The discussion is based on a banking study. Readers could then find the flowerpot approach is applicable and useful regardless of the mode used to collect the required survey data.

The Situation

The primary goal of the survey was to provide a selected European bank with relevant information regarding banking habits and patterns, as well as demographic and lifestyle characteristics of the bank's current customers.

Transform Research Objectives into Information Objectives

In the initial phase of the development process, the flowerpot approach guides the researcher not only in transforming the research objectives into information objectives but also in determining how many information objectives to include (the number of pots), along with the base stand and those objectives which represent testable hypotheses. The order, breadth and depth of the information objectives are also determined. The initial research objectives (in bold) were rewritten into information objectives (in italics) as follows:

1 **To obtain a demographic profile of the bank's current customers.** *(To collect data on selected demographic characteristics that can be used to create a profile of people who are current customers of the bank.)*
2 **To obtain a partial lifestyle profile of people who currently patronize the bank, with a particular emphasis on financial dimensions.** *(To collect data on selected financial-oriented*

lifestyle dimensions that can be used to create a profile that further identifies people who are current customers of the bank.)

3 **To determine banking habits and patterns of these customers.** *(To collect data to identify and describe desired and actual banking habits and patterns exhibited by the customers, as well as their selected attitudes and feelings towards those banking practices.)*

4 **To investigate the existence of possible differences between a blue-collar and a white-collar person with regard to their demographic and lifestyle dimensions.** *(To collect data that will enable the researcher to (1) classify customers as being either 'blue collar' or 'white collar' and (2) test for significant demographic and lifestyle profile differences between these two social classes.)*

5 **To determine the various geographic markets now being served by the bank on the basis of its customers' lengths of residence in the respective areas.** *(To collect selected state-of-being data that will enable the researcher to identify and describe the existing geographic service markets.)*

After transforming the research objectives into information objectives, the researcher determined that objectives 1 and 2 directly related to data that belong to the flowerpot's base. Objective 3 represents an information flowerpot. In contrast, objectives 4 and 5 do not represent information flowerpots but rather hypotheses about data structures that will be derived from data obtained within either the base or the identified information flowerpot. Although there were five initial information objectives, the actual structure consists of only one information flowerpot and its base.

Determine the Appropriate Data Collection Method

On the basis of the information objectives and target population (i.e. the bank's current customers), the management and the researcher jointly decided that a mail survey approach would be the most efficient mode of collecting data from the selected respondents. This step has a direct influence on creating the individual questions and scales, although these are designed only after the specific information items are determined for each objective.

Determine Information Requirements for Each Objective

The flowerpot approach has a significant impact on this step of the development process. Here the researcher interacts with the management to determine what specific data requirements are needed to achieve each of the information objectives as well as the respondent classification information. The researcher must establish the general-to-specific order among the identified data requirements. The study's data requirements and flow are detailed as follows:

1 *Flowerpot 1* (third objective): To collect data that can identify and describe desired and actual banking habits and patterns exhibited by customers as well as their selected attitudes and feelings towards those banking practices.

   a Consideration towards the bank patronized most often.

   b Bank characteristics deemed important in selecting a bank (e.g. convenience/location, operating hours, reasonable service charges, interest rates on savings, knew a person at the bank, bank's reputation, bank's promotional messages, interest rates on loans). Considerations towards having personal savings accounts at various types of financial institutions.

    c Preference considerations towards selected banking methods (e.g. inside the bank, 24-hour ATM, electronic banking, bank by mail, bank by phone).

    d Actual usage considerations towards various banking methods (e.g. inside the bank, 24-hour ATM, electronic banking, bank by mail, bank by phone).

2 *Flowerpot base – lifestyle dimensions* (second objective): To collect data on selected financial-oriented lifestyle dimensions that can be used to create a descriptive profile, which can help identify people who currently or potentially patronize at the bank.

    Belief statements that will classify the customer's lifestyle as being financial optimist, financially dissatisfied, information exchanger, credit card user, advertising viewer, family oriented, price conscious, or blue/white-collar oriented.

3 *Flowerpot base – demographic characteristics* (first objective): To collect data on selected demographic characteristics that can be used to create a descriptive profile identifying people who are current or potential customers of the bank. Include characteristics of gender, years in area, years at current residence, employment status, marital status, spouse's employment status, number of dependent children, education level, age, occupation, income level and postcode.

Notice that the fourth and fifth objectives have no direct bearing on determining the data requirements because they include factors that are covered either in the information flowerpot or its base. Therefore, the researcher does not have to integrate them into this particular aspect of the development process.

Develop Specific Question/Scale Measurement Formats

The flowerpot approach does not impact the activities that take place in this part of the development process. Nevertheless, these activities remain a crucial part of questionnaire design. Researchers must use their construct and scale measurement knowledge to develop appropriate scales, including questions/setups, dimensions/attributes and scale points/descriptions, for each individual data requirement. To do so, the researcher must make three key decisions: (1) the type of data (e.g. state of being, mind, behaviour, intention); (2) question format (open-ended or closed-ended format); (3) data type (nominal, ordinal, interval, or ratio); and (4) the question and specific scale point wording.

The flowerpot approach advocates that when developing the specific question/scale measurement formats, researchers should act as if they are two different people, one thinking like a technical, logical researcher and the other like a respondent. The results of this step can be seen in the final questionnaire displayed in Exhibit 10.6.

EXHIBIT 10.6 Consumer Banking Opinion Survey

THANK YOU for your participation in this interesting study. Your participation will aid us in determining what people in our community think about the present products and services offered by banks. The results will provide the banking industry with additional insights on how to better serve the needs of people. Your attitudes, preferences, and opinions are important to this study; they will be kept strictly confidential.

DIRECTIONS: PLEASE READ EACH QUESTION CAREFULLY. ANSWER THE QUESTION BY FILLING IN THE APPROPRIATE BOX(ES) THAT REPRESENT YOUR RESPONSE(S).

I. GENERAL BANKING HABITS SECTION

1. Which one of the following banks would you consider the one that you use most often in conducting banking or financial transactions? **(PLEASE FILL IN THE ONE APPROPRIATE BOX)**

   ❑ Abbey Bank   ❑ Alliance and Leicester Bank   ❑ Barclays Bank
   ❑ Halifax Bank   ❑ Lloyds TSB Bank   ❑ NatWest Bank
   ❑ Nationwide Building Society   ❑ Royal Bank of Scotland
   ❑ Another Institution (Please Specify): _____

2a. To what extent was each of the following bank items an important consideration to you in selecting your bank mentioned in Q.1 above? **(PLEASE FILL IN ONLY ONE RESPONSE FOR EACH BANK ITEM.)**

Bank Items	Extremely Important	Important	Somewhat Important	Not at All Important
Convenience of location	❑	❑	❑	❑
Operating hours	❑	❑	❑	❑
Reasonable service charges	❑	❑	❑	❑
Interest rates on savings	❑	❑	❑	❑
Personally knew someone at the bank	❑	❑	❑	❑
Bank's reputation	❑	❑	❑	❑
Bank's promotional messages	❑	❑	❑	❑
Interest rates on loans	❑	❑	❑	❑

2b. If there was some bank item you deemed important in selecting your bank mentioned in Q.1, please write it in the space below.

_____

3. At which of the following financial institutions do you or some member of your family have a bank account? **(PLEASE FILL IN AS MANY OR AS FEW AS ARE NECESSARY.)**

Financial Institutions	Both You and Some Other Member of Your Family	Some Other Member of Your Family	Yourself
Abbey Bank	❑	❑	❑
Alliance and Leicester Bank	❑	❑	❑
Barclays Bank	❑	❑	❑
Halifax Bank	❑	❑	❑
Lloyds TSB Bank	❑	❑	❑
NatWest Bank	❑	❑	❑
Nationwide Building Society	❑	❑	❑
Royal Bank of Scotland	❑	❑	❑
Another Institution: _____ (Please Specify)	❑	❑	❑

4. Concerning the different banking methods which you may or may not use, we would like to know your liking or disliking towards these methods. For each listed banking method, please

fill in the appropriate response that best describes your feeling towards using that method. **(PLEASE FILL IN ONE RESPONSE FOR EACH BANKING METHOD)**

Banking Methods	Definitely Like Using	Somewhat Like Using	Somewhat Dislike Using	Definitely Dislike Using
Inside the bank	❏	❏	❏	❏
24-hour machine	❏	❏	❏	❏
Bank by phone	❏	❏	❏	❏
Bank by mail	❏	❏	❏	❏
Electronic banking	❏	❏	❏	❏

5. Now we would like to know to what extent you actually use each of the following banking methods. **(PLEASE FILL IN THE APPROPRIATE RESPONSE FOR EACH LISTED BANKING METHOD.)**

Banking Methods	Usually	Occasionally	Rarely	Never
Inside the bank	❏	❏	❏	❏
24-hour machine	❏	❏	❏	❏
Bank by phone	❏	❏	❏	❏
Bank by mail	❏	❏	❏	❏
Electronic banking	❏	❏	❏	❏

II.   GENERAL OPINION SECTION

In this section, there is a list of general opinion statements for which there are no right or wrong answers. As such, the statements may or may not describe you or your feelings.

6. Next to each statement, please fill in the one response box that best expresses the extent to which you agree or disagree with the statement. Remember, there are no right or wrong answers – we just want your opinions.

Statements	Definitely Agree	Generally Agree	Somewhat Agree	Somewhat Disagree	Generally Disagree	Definitely Disagree
I often seek out the advice of my friends regarding a lot of different things.	❏	❏	❏	❏	❏	❏
I buy many things with credit cards.	❏	❏	❏	❏	❏	❏
I wish we had a lot more money.	❏	❏	❏	❏	❏	❏
Security for my family is the most important to me.	❏	❏	❏	❏	❏	❏
I am definitely influenced by advertising.	❏	❏	❏	❏	❏	❏
I like to pay cash for everything I buy.	❏	❏	❏	❏	❏	❏

	❑	❑	❑	❑	❑	❑
My neighbours or friends often come to me for advice on many different matters.	❑	❑	❑	❑	❑	❑
It is good to have an electronic banking account.	❑	❑	❑	❑	❑	❑
I will probably have more money to spend next year than I have now.	❑	❑	❑	❑	❑	❑
I like to shop around for bargains in order to save money.	❑	❑	❑	❑	❑	❑
For most products or services, I buy the ones that are the most popular.	❑	❑	❑	❑	❑	❑
Unexpected situations often catch me without enough money in my pocket.	❑	❑	❑	❑	❑	❑
Five years from now, my family income will probably be a lot higher than it is now.	❑	❑	❑	❑	❑	❑
Socially, I see myself more as a blue-collar person than a white-collar one.	❑	❑	❑	❑	❑	❑

III. CLASSIFICATION DATA SECTION

Now just a few more questions so that we can combine your responses with those of the other people taking part in this study.

7. Please indicate your gender. ❑ Female   ❑ Male

8. Please fill in the one response that best approximates how long you have lived in your community area.
   ❑ Less than 1 year   ❑ 4 to 6 years   ❑ 11 to 20 years
   ❑ 1 to 3 years   ❑ 7 to 10 years   ❑ Over 20 years

9. Approximately how long have you lived at your current address?
   ❑ Less than 1 year   ❑ 4 to 6 years   ❑ 1 to 20 years
   ❑ 1 to 3 years   ❑ 7 to 10 years   ❑ Over 20 years

10. Please indicate your current employment status.
    □ Employed   □ Employed part-time   □ Not currently employed   □ Retired full-time

11. Please indicate your current marital status.
    □ Married   □ Single (widowed, divorced, or separated)   →   **PLEASE SKIP TO Q.15**
                     □ Single (never married)_____   →   **PLEASE SKIP TO Q.15**

12. **IF MARRIED,** please indicate your spouse's current employment status.
    □ Employed   □ Employed part-time   □ Not currently employed   □ Retired full-time

13. **IF YOU HAVE CHILDREN,** please indicate the number of children under 18 years of age in your family.
    0   1   2   3   4   5   6   7   8   More than 8; please specify: _____   □ Do not have children
    □   □   □   □   □   □   □   □   □

14. Which one of the following categories best corresponds with your last completed year in school?
    □ Didn't Attend School Properly   □ Primary School
    □ Secondary School   □ Undergraduate Degree
    □ College   □ Doctoral Degree
    □ Master Degree

15. Into which one of the following categories does your current age fall?
    □ Under 18   □ 26 to 35   □ 46 to 55   □ 66 to 70
    □ 18 to 25   □ 36 to 45   □ 56 to 65   □ Over 70

16. What is your occupation; that is, in what kind of work do you spend the major portion of your time?

    _____

    □ Farming or Fishing or Forestry   □ Construction   □ Other Manufacturing   □ Education

    □ Legal   □ Medical   □ Creative Arts   □ Banking

    □ Finance (Other Than Banking)   □ Retailing   □ Retired or Unemployed   □ Student

    □ Others (please specify): _____

17. Into which of the following categories does your total income, before taxes, fall?
    □ Under €10,000   □ €40,001 to €50,000
    □ €10,000 to €20,000   □ €50,001 to €60,000
    □ €20,001 to €30,000   □ €60,001 to €70,000
    □ €30,001 to €40,000   □ Over €70,000

18. What is the postcode of your home address?

    Thank you very much for participation in this study. Your time and opinions are greatly and deeply appreciated.

Evaluate Questions and Scale Measurements

The flowerpot approach also does not impact the activities that take place in this aspect of the development process. Prior to laying out the actual survey instrument, the researcher should

---

EXHIBIT 10.7 Guidelines for Evaluating the Appropriateness of Questions

1 Questions should be as easy to understand as possible.

2 The question setups, attribute statements, and data response categories should be *unidimensional*.

3 Data response categories should be *mutually exclusive*.

4 *Arrangement* of response categories should be made to minimize the opportunity of bias in the respondent's answer.

5 Unless necessary, *undue stress* of particular words should be avoided.

6 *Double negatives should be avoided*.

7 Unless necessary, *technical* or *sophisticated language should be avoided*.

8 Wherever possible, questions and scale measurements should be phrased in a *realistic setting*.

9 Questions and scale measurements should always *avoid the use of-double-barreled items*.

Note: For examples, go to the book's website (www.mhhe.com/shiu09) and follow the links.

---

have already examined each question and scale measurement. See Exhibit 10.7 for a summary of the guidelines for evaluating the appropriateness of questions.

Establish Flowerpot Format and Layout

The activities undertaken here are at the centre of the flowerpot approach to questionnaire design. Taking all the individual questions and scales previously developed and tested, the researcher must present them in a logical order. After creating a title for the questionnaire, the researcher must include a brief introductory section and any instructions applicable to the whole questionnaire prior to asking the first question. The questions that make up the first information flowerpot must be asked in a natural general-to-specific order to reduce the potential for sequence bias.

All necessary instructions should be included within each question or scale, where appropriate. After completing the information flowerpot, the researcher must stabilize the structure by building a base. In the above bank example, there is a two-part base. The lifestyle belief (i.e. general opinions, psychographics) section is presented first, and then the more standardized classification section (i.e. demographics) is shown. The final part of any base is the thank you statement.

At the beginning of the classification section is this statement: 'Now just a few more questions so that we can combine your answers with those of the other people taking part in this study'. This is a 'transition phrase,' which serves three basic purposes. First, it communicates to the respondents that a change in their thinking process is about to take place. No longer do they have to think about their specific belief structures. They can clear their mind before thinking about their personal backgrounds. Second, it hints that the task of completing the survey is almost over. Third, it assures the respondent that the information they give will be used only for aggregate purposes – that is, it will be blended with the data provided by other respondents participating in the survey.

Evaluate the Questionnaire and Layout

After drafting the questionnaire, but before submitting it to the management team for approval, the researcher should review the whole questionnaire and its layout. Normally, the researcher focuses on determining whether each question is necessary and whether the overall length is acceptable. The adoption of the flowerpot approach would give more attention to (1) checking to make sure that the instrument meets all the information objectives; (2) checking the scale format and scaling properties; and (3) checking general-to-specific order.

An easy method of evaluating any questionnaire design is to answer the following five questions for each question or scale measurement:

1 What types of raw data (state of being, mind, behaviour, or intention) are being sought in the question, and for what purpose?

2 What types of questions or scale measurements (nominal, ordinal, true class interval, hybrid ordinally-interval, ratio) are being used?

3 What scaling properties (assignment, order, distance, origin) are being activated in the scale measurement?

4 What is the most appropriate measure of central tendency (mean, median, mode)?

5 What is the most appropriate measure of dispersion (frequency distribution, range, variance, standard deviation)?

Obtain the Client's Approval

The flowerpot concept does not impact this aspect of the development process. Copies of the questionnaire draft should be made and distributed to all parties that have authority over and interest in the project. Realistically, the client may step in at any time in the design process to express a need for some type of modification.

It is important to get final approval of the questionnaire prior to pretesting it. The logic behind client approval is that it commits management to the body of data and eventually to the information that will result from the specific questionnaire design. In addition, it helps reduce unnecessary surprises and saves time and money. If changes are necessary, this is where they should occur.

Pretest and Revise the Questionnaire

While fine-tuning the questionnaire can take place via discussions between the researcher and client, the final evaluation should come from people representing the individuals who will be asked to actually fill out the survey.

An appropriate pretest involves a simulated administration of the survey to a small, relevant group of respondents. How many respondents should be included in a pretest is open to debate. Some researchers will use as few as 10 respondents, while others may use as many as 50 depending on how the questionnaire was developed, the mode of administering the survey, and the purpose of the pretest. For example, if the questions were not properly tested for validity and reliability during the construct/scale measurement development process, then the pretest should include at least 50 respondents so that the researcher can possibly address validity and reliability issues. Other things being equal, a higher number of respondents is required in a self-administered survey than if a personal survey is used. The reason is that richer information can be obtained from a typical respondent in the latter than the former mode. If the main purpose of the pretest is to check for specific wording problems, then only about 10 respondents are enough for the pretest. In a pretest respondents are asked to pay attention to such elements as words, phrases, instructions, and question flow patterns and point out anything they feel is confusing, difficult to understand, or otherwise a problem.

In addition to addressing the validity/reliability and wording issues, the pretest can help the researcher determine how much time a typical respondent will need to complete the survey, whether to add any instructions, and what to say in the cover letter. If any problems or concerns arise in the pretest, modifications must be made and approved by the client prior to moving to the next step.

Finalize the Questionnaire Format

Here, the questionnaire is placed in a final format, which should convey a professional appearance about the questionnaire. Quality in appearance is more important in self administered surveys than in personal or telephone surveys. Any support materials – such as interviewer instructions, the cover letter, rating cards, mailing and return envelopes – should also be finalized and reproduced for distribution. Exhibit 10.10 (page 356) shows an example of the cover letter used in the bank study.

Implement the Survey

The focus here is on beginning the collection of the required raw data. Here the exact process involved will be dependent on the mode of data collection. Obviously, what needs to be done to implement the survey in the self-administered mode will be partially different from the telephone mode. In Exhibit 10.8, we offer a general summary of the major considerations in questionnaire design.

EXHIBIT 10.8 Summary of Important Considerations in Questionnaire Designs

1 Determine the *information objectives* and the *number of information flowerpots* required to meet those objectives.

2 Determine the *specific data requirements* for each information flowerpot, and stack the pots from *largest to smallest*.

3 Introduction section should include a *general description* of what the study is pertaining to; this may well be in a *disguised format*.

4 All types of *instructions*, if necessary, should be *clearly expressed*.

5 The *question and scale measurements* have to follow a *logical order* – an order that appears logical to the respondent rather than to the researcher or practitioner.

6 Begin a questionnaire with *general questions* that are usually easy to respond to, and then *gradually lead up* to the more specific and often more difficult questions.

7 Postpone *highly personal questions* (state-of-being data) *until late* in the survey. That is, place these questions in the base after the last information flowerpot.

8 Place questions that *involve psychographic traits* (i.e. lifestyle, beliefs) towards *the end* of the survey, but before the identification base.

9 *Do not ask too many questions of the same measurement format* in sequence. Otherwise the respondent's mind is less likely to be continuously switched on, leading to less accurate responses.

10 *Taper off* a survey with a *few relatively simple questions* that do not require extensive thoughts or expressions of feelings. The demographic data questions would be very appropriate here.

11 Always *end the survey* with a *thank-you statement*.

For those firms expanding into international markets, they must address whether the questionnaire design concepts they used in their own country can be directly applied in foreign countries. To illustrate this point log on to the book's website (www.mhhe.com/shiu09), follow the links to the Global Insight, read the Holiday Inn Resort example, and answer the questions.

Development of Cover Letters

The Role of a Cover Letter

A critical aspect associated with good questionnaire design is the development of an appropriate cover letter. Many marketing research textbooks offer little discussion of cover letter development. Usually, a **cover letter** is viewed as a letter accompanying a self-administered questionnaire that explains the nature of the survey. With personal or telephone surveys, researchers might not think to use a cover letter. However, they play several important roles in the successful collection of primary raw data, regardless of the survey mode being used. A cover letter is not the same as the introductory section on the actual questionnaire.

> **Cover letter** A separate written communication to a prospective respondent designed to mainly enhance that person's willingness to complete and return the survey in a timely manner.

The main role of the cover letter should be that of winning over the respondent's cooperation and willingness to participate in the research project. Many times a research project falls short of its goal because the response rate is very low. The cover letter can help persuade a prospective respondent to fill out the questionnaire and return it in a timely fashion, thus helping to increase the response rate.

Secondary roles that contribute to the performance of the above main role include (a) introducing the respondent to the research project and the researcher, (b) informing the respondent of the importance of the study, and (c) communicating the study's legitimacy and other particulars such as the deadline for returning the completed survey, and where to return it.

Having a standardized cover letter that will fit all survey situations is highly unlikely, but there are several factors that should be considered in any cover letter. Exhibit 10.9 outlines these factors and what they really mean. Each of these is discussed in the next section.

Factors for Developing Good Cover Letters

Regardless of a research project's mode of survey data collection, the researcher should include a well-developed cover letter. For self-administered questionnaires, a separate cover letter should be sent with the questionnaire. For telephone and personal surveys, a cover letter can be mailed to each prospective respondent before the initial contact by the interviewer.

Prior mailing of cover letters in telephone and personal survey situations is not a common practice among researchers, but this procedure can increase respondents' willingness to participate. The reason for this comes from an understanding of human behaviour. Before any initial contact takes place, the prospective respondent and the interviewer are strangers to each other.

EXHIBIT 10.9 Factors for Developing Good Cover Letters

Factor	Description
1 Personalization	Cover letter should be addressed to the specific prospective respondent; use research firm's professional letterhead stationery.
2 Identification of the organization doing the study	Clear identification of the name of the research firm conducting the survey; decide on disguised or undisguised approach of revealing the actual client (or sponsor) of the study.
3 Clear statement of the study's purpose and importance	Describe the general topic of the research and emphasize its importance to the prospective respondent.
4 Anonymity and confidentiality	Give assurances that the prospective respondent's name will not be revealed. Explain how the respondent was chosen, and stress that their input will be kept strictly confidential.
5 General time frame of doing the study	Communicate the overall time frame of the survey.
6 Reinforcement of the importance of the respondent's participation	Where appropriate, communicate the importance of the prospective respondents' participation.
7 Acknowledgement of reasons for non-participation in survey	Point out 'lack of time,' 'surveys classified as junk mail,' and 'forgetting the survey' reasons for not participating, and defuse them.
8 Time requirement and compensation	Clearly communicate the time required to complete the survey; describe incentive programme, if any.
9 Completion date and where and how to return the survey	Communicate to the prospective respondent all instructions for returning the completed questionnaire.
10 Advance thank-you statement for willingness to participate	Thank the prospective respondent for their cooperation.

People are more hesitant to express their opinions or feelings about a topic to a stranger than to someone they know, even to a limited extent. Mailing a cover letter to prospective respondents enables the researcher to break the ice prior to the actual survey.

The cover letter should introduce the potential respondent to the research project, stress its legitimacy, encourage participation, and let respondents know that a representative will be contacting them in the near future. Using a cover letter increases the initial cost of data collection, but the resulting increase in the response rate can reduce the overall cost of the project.

While the exact wording of a cover letter varies from researcher to researcher and from situation to situation, any cover letter should consider the factors displayed in Exhibit 10.9.

Factor 1: Personalization

Whenever possible, the cover letter should be addressed to the person who was selected as a prospective respondent. The cover letter should be typed on a professional letterhead that represents the research organization's affiliation.

Factor 2: Identification of the Organization Doing the Study

The cover letter should identify the research company conducting the survey. With regard to the decision on exposure of the actual client or sponsor of the study, there are two approaches available. In the undisguised approach, the actual client's (sponsor's) name will appear as part of the introduction statement. An example is as follows:

> The Nationwide Research Company is conducting a study for Nokia on people's mobile phone practices and would like to include your opinions.

In contrast, a disguised approach would not divulge the client's/sponsor's identity to the respondent and would appear like this:

> The Nationwide Research Company is conducting a study on people's mobile phone practices and would like to include your opinions.

Which approach to use will be determined by the overall research objectives and/or mutual agreement between the researcher and client regarding the possible benefits and drawbacks of revealing the client's/sponsor's name to the respondent. One reason for using a disguised approach is that it prevents competitors from finding out about the survey.

Factor 3: Clear Statement of the Study's Purpose and Importance

Statements must be included in any cover letter to describe the general nature or topic of the survey and emphasize its importance to the prospective respondents. In the above bank survey example, the researcher might use the following statements:

> Consumer banking practices are rapidly changing in recent years. With more players in the banking industry, many new banking services, new technologies, and the increased complexity of people's financial needs, financial institutions are indeed changing. These changes are having important effects on you and your family. We would like to gain insights into these changes and their impact from the consumer's perspective by better understanding your opinions about different banking services, practices, and habits. We think you will find the survey interesting.

When you state the purpose of the study, it is important that you introduce the general topic of the survey in an interesting manner using words that are familiar to the members of the target audience. The purpose of the study should be followed by a statement that conveys the importance of the topic to the respondents.

Factor 4: Anonymity and Confidentiality

After describing the purpose and importance of the survey, the researcher must let the respondent know how and why certain people were selected for the study. The researcher can use a statement like this:

> Your name was one of only 2,000 names randomly selected from a representative list of people living in our target survey area. Because the success of the survey depends upon the cooperation of all people who were selected, we would especially appreciate your willingness to help.

The phrasing should emphasize the importance of the respondent's participation to the success of the study.

If the researcher and client decide that assurances about anonymity and confidentiality are necessary, those factors should be incorporated at this point. **Anonymity** assures that the respondent's name or any identifiable designation will not be associated with his or her responses. Among the different survey data collection modes, anonymity statements are most appropriately associated with self-administered questionnaires. The researcher might use the following as an anonymity statement:

> The information obtained from the survey will in no way reflect the identities of the people participating in the study.

Anonymity The assurance that the survey respondent's name or any other identifiable designation will not be associated with the corresponding responses.

A statement of **confidentiality** assures the prospective respondent that his or her input, while known to the researcher, will not be divulged to a third party. A confidentiality statement might be phrased as follows:

> We are fully aware of the possible concern of our respondents regarding the confidentiality of the information that they provide to us. We can assure you that your opinions, attitudes, and other information as reflected in your responses to our questionnaire will be kept strictly confidential. They will only be used after being grouped with those of the other people participating in the survey.

Confidentiality The assurance that the respondent's input to the questionnaire will not be divulged to a third party.

Once the prospective respondent is promised confidentiality, the researcher should take up full responsibility in keeping that promise.

Factor 5: Time Frame

The cover letter should identify the time frame for the survey. To encourage a prospective respondent to participate, it should state the estimated completion time. An example is as follows:

> In the next couple of days, one of our trained representatives will be contacting you by phone …
> The survey will take less than 15 minutes of your time.

Factor 6: Reinforcement of the Importance of the Respondent's Participation

The researcher can incorporate simple phrases into any part of the cover letter to reinforce the point that the respondent's participation is critical to the success of the study. Such phrases should be worded positively, not negatively.

Factor 7: Acknowledgment of Reasons for Not Participating in the Study

People offer numerous reasons when declining the role of being a respondent in a survey. Research among a variety of different groups has identified three of the most common reasons for not participating in a survey: (1) not having enough time, (2) seeing surveys as junk mail and (3) forgetting the survey.

First, people treasure their leisure time and feel they do not have enough of it. Therefore, when they receive a mail survey or telephone call or are asked on the spot to answer a few questions, many potential respondents tend to use 'do not have the time' as a reason not to participate. The researcher should acknowledge the time factor in the cover letter. To do this, a researcher can use a statement like this:

> We realize that to most of us in the community our leisure time is scarce and important and that we do not like to spend it filling out a questionnaire for some unknown person's or organization's study. Please be informed that our organization is conducting this study for a good cause. You are among a carefully selected sample being asked to participate in this study and your participation is very important to helping us fulfill the cause.

This type of statement can be combined with statements about the importance of the topic to the respondent and the compensation to further effectively negate the time objection.

Second, many people have the tendency to classify surveys received as 'junk mail' or a telephone interviewer's call as an attempt to hard sell them. To acknowledge this, something like the following statement could be used:

> We realize that many of us in the community receive a lot of things which we classify as 'junk mail' and not important to respond to, but please do not consider the attached survey as being 'junk mail.' Your opinions, attitudes, and other responses to each question will help us know more precisely your banking needs and devise ways to better serve these needs.

And for telephone surveys, the researcher can incorporate a statement like the following:

> We realize that many of us in the community receive a lot of phone calls from strangers trying to sell us some product or service that we don't want. Let me assure you that I am not trying to sell you anything. I would just like to get your honest responses to some questions pertaining to your banking practices; they will help us know more precisely your banking needs and devise ways to better serve these needs.

Third is the issue of forgetting the survey. To help eliminate this problem, the researcher should incorporate a statement in the cover letter something like this:

> Past research has suggested that many questionnaires received, if not completed and returned within the first 36 hours, have a tendency to get misplaced or forgotten about. Upon receiving this survey, please take the time to complete it at your earliest convenience. Your participation is very important to us.

By acknowledging and negating these three main reasons for not participating in a research study, the researcher significantly improves the likelihood that the prospective respondent will complete and return the questionnaire or cooperate in a telephone survey.

Factor 8: Time Requirement and Compensation

In an effort to win over a prospective respondent, the researcher can emphasize in the cover letter that the survey will not take much time and effort. For a self-administered survey, the researcher can incorporate statements like the following:

> We have designed the questionnaire to include all the directions and instructions necessary to complete the survey without the assistance of an interviewer. The survey will take approximately 15 minutes to complete. Please take your time in responding to each question.

Indeed for any mode of survey, the researcher could use the following statement: 'The survey will take approximately 15 minutes to complete.' This type of statement helps to lessen the respondent's concern by stressing that the survey will not take up much of the person's time.

The researcher and client may decide that some form of compensation is needed to encourage the respondent's participation. A token amount (e.g. €3) can be offered to each prospective respondent and included in the questionnaire packet. The idea is that giving respondents a reward up front for participating will make them feel obligated to complete the survey and return it as requested. Experience with this method, however, suggests that people tend to assign a higher price than the token amount to their time. In many situations, non-monetary incentives (e.g. a sample product, tickets to a movie, a coupon redeemable for specific products or services) are a good alternative to encourage a respondent's participation.

An alternative to the individual reward system is the **lottery approach** in which the incentive money forms a significantly larger amount than the individual token amount, and everyone who completes and returns the survey has a chance of receiving the incentive. A significant reward is likely to increase the response rate. The lottery approach is not, however, restricted to direct monetary rewards. Alternative rewards might be the chance to win an expense-paid trip somewhere. For example, companies can use something like 'three-day, two-night all-expenses-paid weekend stay for two people' at a luxury hotel complex as the lottery incentive for respondents who have completed and returned their questionnaire by the specified date.

> **Lottery approach** The pooling of individual incentive offerings into a significantly larger offering for which those people who participate have an equal chance of receiving the incentive.

When a lottery is used, extra effort is required by the researcher to develop and include a separate identification form in the questionnaire packet that can be filled out and returned with a respondent's completed questionnaire. Descriptions of incentives in a cover letter look like the following:

> To show our appreciation for your taking the time to participate in this study, we are going to hold a draw for €1,500 among those who complete this survey. The drawing procedure has been designed in such a way that everyone who completes and returns the questionnaire will have an equal opportunity to receive the appreciation gift of €1,500.

Factor 9: Completion Date and Where and How to Return the Survey

In studies that collect data using a self-administered mail method, the researcher must give the respondent instructions for how, where, and when to return their completed survey. The how and where instructions can be simply expressed through the following type of statement:

> After completing all the questions in the survey, please use the enclosed stamped, addressed envelope to return your completed survey and appreciation gift card.

To deal with the return deadline date, the researcher should include a statement like this:

> To help us complete the study in a timely fashion, we need your cooperation in returning the completed questionnaire and incentive drawing card by no later than *30 November, 2008*.

For cover letters used with electronic surveys, the researcher must communicate the notion that after completing the survey by the due date, the respondent only needs to click the 'submit' button to send the completed survey to the researcher.

Factor 10: An Advance Thank You

Prior to closing the cover letter with a thank-you statement, the researcher might want to include a final reassurance that they are is not trying to sell the prospective respondent anything. In addition, the legitimacy of the study can be reinforced by supplying a name and telephone number if there are any doubts, concerns or questions, as follows:

Again, let me give you my personal guarantee that we are not trying to sell you something. If you have any doubts, concerns, or questions about this survey, please give me a call at 0121-4146529. Thank you in advance. We appreciate your cooperation in taking part in our study.

The researcher should sign the cover letter and include their title.

A good cover letter entails as much thought, care and effort as the questionnaire itself. While the actual factors will vary from researcher to researcher, these ten are standard elements of any good cover letter. The specific examples given above should not be viewed as standardized phrases that must be included in all cover letters, but they do show how a researcher could increase a prospective respondent's willingness to participate in a given study. To see how these factors fit together in a cover letter, see Exhibit 10.10. The bold number inserts refer to the factors listed in Exhibit 10.9 of the chapter.

EXHIBIT 10.10 Cover Letter Used with the Bank Survey

NATIONWIDE RESEARCH COMPANY
Regent's Park, London

15 November, 2008

[1]
Ms. Kathy V. Livingstone
48 Chedbrook Crest
Birmingham B15 3RL

Dear Ms. Livingstone:

[2]We at Nationwide Research Company in Regent's Park, London are conducting a study this month on people's banking practices **[5]**and would like to include your opinions.

[3]As you may know, consumer banking practices are rapidly changing in the last few years. With more players in the banking industry, many new banking services, new technologies, and the increased complexity of people's financial needs, financial institutions are indeed changing. These changes are having important effects on you and your family. We would like to gain insights into these changes and their impact from the consumer's perspective by better understanding your opinions about different banking services, practices and habits. We think you will find the survey interesting.

[4]Your name was one of only 600 names randomly selected from a representative list of people currently living in our target survey area. **[6]**Because the success of the survey depends upon the cooperation of all the people who were selected, we would greatly appreciate your willingness to help us in this study.

[4]The information obtained from the survey will in no way reflect the identities of the people participating. The information provided by you for our study will be kept strictly confidential. Your response will only be used after being grouped with those of the other people also taking part in the study. Let me give you my personal guarantee that we are not trying to sell you something.

[7]We realize that many of us in the community receive a lot of things which we classify as 'junk mail' and not important to respond to, but please do not consider the attached survey as being 'junk mail'. **[6]**Your opinions, attitudes, and other responses to each question will help us know more precisely your banking needs and devise ways to better serve these needs.

[7]To most of us our leisure time is scarce and important, and we do not like to spend it filling out a questionnaire for some unknown organization's survey. Please be informed that our organization is conducting this study for a good cause. You are among a carefully selected sample being asked to participate in this study and your participation is very important to helping us fulfil the cause.

[8]We have designed the questionnaire to include all the directions and instructions necessary to complete the survey without the assistance of an interviewer. You will find that the survey will take only about 15 minutes of your time. Please take your time in responding to each question.

[8]To show, in part, our appreciation for your taking the time to participate in this important study, we are going to hold a draw for €1,500 among the selected respondents including you who donate some of your leisure time to help us in completing this survey. The draw has been designed in such a way that everyone who completes and returns the questionnaire will have an equal opportunity to receive the appreciation gift of €1,500.

[7]Past research has suggested that many questionnaires that are received, if not completed and returned within the first 36 hours, have a tendency to be misplaced or forgotten about. Upon receiving this survey, please take the time to complete it at your earliest convenience. [6]Your participation is very important to us.

[9]After completing all the questions in this survey, please use the enclosed stamped and addressed envelope to return your completed survey and appreciation gift card by **no later than 30 November, 2008.**

If you have any doubts, concerns or questions about this survey, please feel free to give me a call at 0121-4146529.

[10]Thank you in advance. We deeply appreciate your cooperation in taking part in our study.
Sincerely,

Thomas L. Kirk
Director
Nationwide Research Company

Cover Letter Length

A rarely discussed question that affects the development of a cover letter is 'How long should the cover letter be?' There is no simple answer that is correct in all situations, and in fact there are two opposing views. First, many researchers believe that the cover letter should be simple, to the point, and no longer than one page. The nearby Closer Look at Research box illustrates a hypothetical cover letter for the bank survey that follows the direct, one-page approach.

While the one-page cover letter includes some of the factors we have discussed for influencing a prospective respondent's willingness to participate, it tends to be lower than a more comprehensively written cover letter in the levels of intensity and clarity needed to win over a stranger. Still, many researchers go with a one-page design because of the cost factor and because they believe people generally do not like to read detailed correspondence from organizations such as a research company. It is true that it costs less to develop, reproduce and mail a one-page cover letter than a multiple-page counterpart, but if the one-page cover letter is an important reason for not producing an adequate response rate, the study will cost more in the long run.

Regarding the notion that people generally do not like to read detailed correspondence from organizations such as a research company, a viable solution is to craft a sincere, interesting and emotion-laden cover letter that can persuade prospective respondents to cooperate. With such a well-crafted cover letter, the prospective respondent is likely to read not only the first page but the complete cover letter and move on to the questionnaire.

A Closer Look at Research *(In the field)*

NATIONWIDE RESEARCH COMPANY
Regent's Park, London

CONSUMER BANKING OPINION STUDY
1 November, 2008

If you have a bank account—

We need your opinion.

With more players in the banking industry, many new banking services, new technologies, and the increased complexity of people's financial needs, financial institutions are indeed changing. These changes will have an important effect on you and your family. We would like to gain insights into these changes and their impact from the consumer's perspective by better understanding your opinions relating to the changing banking industry.

Your name is among a selected sample of residents to determine what people in our community think about the present products and services offered by banks. Your opinions in this survey can never be traced back to you, and all results will be held strictly confidential. The results of the study will provide the banking industry with insight into how to better serve the needs of its customers.

The token amount enclosed with this letter is not enough to compensate you for your time in participating in the survey, but we hope you can realize how much we heartedly appreciate for your help.

Thank you for your assistance.

Sincerely,

Thomas L. Kirk
Director
Nationwide Research Company

P.S. Please return no later than 30 November, 2008. A postage-paid envelope is enclosed.

As always, the researcher should keep in mind the importance of ethical behaviour. The Ethics box shows where marketing researchers and questionnaire designers can rely on in order to upkeep the ethical standard of their questionnaires.

Ethics

Questionnaire Design Ethics: Key to Maintaining Respondents' Goodwill to Answer Our Questions

The future prospect of questionnaire survey depends upon the goodwill of members of the public to cooperate and give their time to answer our questions. In order to maintain the prospect of using questionnaires to collect data, marketing researchers need to maintain the public's goodwill to voluntarily continue to help our cause.

There are three main codes of conduct that marketing researchers can follow in designing their questionnaires. These are the European Society for Opinion and Marketing Research (ESOMAR) in Europe, the Market Research Society (MRS) in the UK, and the Council of American Survey Research Organizations (CASRO) in the US. Marketing researchers involved in the process of questionnaire design should familiarize themselves with the code that is appropriate to them. The codes can be found on the organizations' websites: www.esomar.org, www.mrs.org.uk and www.casro.org. In addition, the MRS has produced 'Questionnaire design guidelines', which are regularly updated and can be found at www.mrs.org.uk/standards/quant. htm#quest.

More and more countries now have laws defining the information that questionnaire designers are required to provide to prospective respondents. It should be noted that these laws, usually in the form of data protection laws, take precedence over the aforesaid codes of conduct, if there is any conflict between them.

Other Documents Associated with Questionnaire Design

Although the main focus of this chapter is the development process and flowerpot approach to designing questionnaires, several supplemental documents required to execute the survey fieldwork activities are worthy of discussion. There is a need to develop good supervisor and interviewer instructions as well as screening forms, rating cards, and call record sheets. These types of documents help increase the chance that the survey data collection process will be successful. We discuss the highlights of each of these forms in this section.

Supervisor Instructions

Many research companies collect much of their data using interviews that are conducted by specialty field interviewing companies located in selected geographic markets. These companies are the production line for collecting raw data within the research industry. This type of company completes the interviews and sends them to the client research company for further processing. A **supervisor instruction sheet** serves as a blueprint for training people on how to execute the interviewing process in a standardized fashion.

> **Supervisor instruction sheet** A document that serves as a blueprint for training people on how to execute the interviewing process in a standardized fashion.

The instructions outline the process for conducting the study and are vital to any research project that utilizes personal or telephone surveys. They include detailed information about the nature of the study, start and completion dates, sampling instructions, number of interviewers required, equipment and facility requirements, reporting forms, quotas and validation procedures. Exhibit 10.11 displays a sample page from a set of supervisor instructions for a banking study that uses trained student interviewers to administer personal surveys for collecting the data.

EXHIBIT 10.11 Example of Supervisor Instructions for a Banking Study

Purpose:	To understand students' banking practices and attitudes towards services provided by different banks.
Number of interviewers:	A total of 90 trained student interviewers (30 interviewers per class, three different classes).
Location and time of interviews:	Interviews will be conducted over a two-week period beginning 10 October and ending 24 October, 2008. They will be conducted between the hours of 10am and 9pm, Monday to Friday. The locations of the interviews will be outside the campus buildings housing the 14 colleges making up the university plus the Library and Student Union. There will be three shifts of interviewers, 30 interviewers per shift, working the time frames of 10am to 12noon or 12:01pm to 5pm or 5:01pm to 9pm.
Quota:	Each interviewer will conduct and complete 30 interviews, with 5 completed interviews for each of the following named banks: Barclays, NatWest, Lloyds TSB, and HSBC. The remaining required interviews should be done for any bank other than the above 'big four' banks. All the completed interviews should come from their assigned location and time period. For each shift of 30 interviewers, there will be 600 completed interviews for the four named banks in the study and 300 completed interviews representing the set of other banks.
Project materials:	For this study, you are supplied with the following materials: 2,701 questionnaires, 91 interviewer instruction-screening-quota forms, 91 sets of 'rating cards' with each set consisting of six different rating cards, 91 'verification of interview' forms, and 1 interviewer scheduling matrix form.
Preparation:	Review all the materials provided for complete understanding. Set a two-hour session for training your 90 student interviewers on how they should select a prospective respondent, screen for eligibility, and conduct the interviews. Make sure each interviewer understands the embedded 'interviewer instructions' in the actual questions making up the questionnaire. In addition, assign each interviewer to a specified location and time frame for conducting the interviews, making sure all the locations and time frames are appropriately covered.

Interviewer Instructions

To ensure data quality, the interviewing process must be consistent. Thus, it is very important to train the people who will actually be conducting the interviews. **Interviewer instructions** serve as the vehicle for training the interviewers to (1) correctly select a prospective respondent for inclusion in the study according to the predetermined sampling procedure, (2) screen prospective respondents for eligibility and (3) properly conduct the actual interview. Although these instructions cover many of the same points found in the supervisor's instructions, they are designed to be pertinent to the actual interview. The instructions include detailed information about the nature of the study; start and completion dates; sampling instructions; screening

> **Interviewer instructions** The vehicle for training the interviewer on how to select prospective respondents, screen them for eligibility, and conduct the actual interview.

procedures; quotas; number of interviews required; guidelines to asking questions, using rating cards, recording responses; reporting forms; and verification form procedures. Exhibit 10.12 displays a sample page from a set of interviewer instructions for a retail banking study that used personal surveys to collect the data.

EXHIBIT 10.12 Example of Interviewer Instructions for a Retail Bank Study Using Personal Surveys

Purpose:	To determine from students their banking practices and attitudes towards bank service quality across several different types of financial institutions.
Method:	All interviewing will be conducted in person at your assigned designated locations within your assigned interviewing time frames. These locations and times will be assigned to you by your supervisor.
Location and time of interviews:	Your interviews will be conducted over a two-week period beginning 10 October and ending 24 October, 2008. You will conduct the interviews during your assigned shift between the hours of 8am and 9pm, Monday through Friday. The locations of the interviews will be outside the campus buildings assigned to you by your supervisor.
Number of interviews/ quota:	You will conduct and complete 30 interviews, with 5 completed interviews for each of the following named banks: Barclays, NatWest, Lloyds TSB, HSBC and the 10 remaining interviews for any 'Other Banks'. All your completed interviews should come from your assigned location and time period.
Project materials:	For this study, you are supplied with the following materials: 30 personal questionnaires, 1 Interviewer Introduction-Screening-Quota form, 1 set of 'Rating Cards' consisting of six different rating cards, 1 'Verification of Interview' form, and 1 Interviewer Scheduling Matrix form.
Sampling procedure:	Once you are at your assigned location during your assigned interviewing shift (e.g., College of Education, 8am to 12noon), randomly select a person in that area and follow the 'introduction' instructions on your *Introduction-Screening-Quota form*. (First, politely walk up to that individual and introduce yourself. Then, politely explain to the person that: [read the given introduction statement on your *Introduction-Screening-Quota form*].) Follow the exact instructions. If the person is willing to be interviewed, continue to ask the 'screening' questions to determine that person's eligibility and check with quota requirements. Follow the instructions on your *Introduction-Screening-Quota form*. If the person qualifies, begin the actual survey. If you determine that the person is not eligible, follow the instructions for terminating the interview and selecting your next prospective respondent. All interviewer instructions will be denoted in **FULL CAPS** on your *Introduction-Screening-Quota form*.
Screening factors:	Prospective respondents will be eligible if:

    1. They are a current university student.
    2. They have not already participated in this survey.
    3. They are needed to fill any of the designated 'quotas' for the five specific named banks or the 'Other Banks' group.

Guidelines for actual interview:	Once the prospective respondent is determined eligible, you should begin the actual survey starting with question 1. Make sure you read each question as it is written on the questionnaire. All your instructions will appear in **FULL CAPS**; follow them carefully. After completing the interview, you must have the respondent fill out the required information on the 'Verification of Interview' form. Then randomly select your next prospective respondent and follow the procedures and instructions on your *Introduction-Screening-Quota form*.
Preparation:	Review the whole set of materials you have been given for complete understanding. Prior to beginning the actual interviews, do at least three practice interviews to become familiar with the procedures for selecting a prospective respondent, screening for eligibility, and conducting the interview. Make sure you understand the embedded 'interviewer instructions' in the actual questions making up the survey.

Although not explicitly displayed in Exhibit 10.12, many interviewer instructions list separately each general instruction as well as those within each question of the survey. In addition, the instructions include specific comments on procedures for asking each question and recording responses. It is important for all interviewers to read each survey question exactly as it was written, with no modifications. The interviewer instructions constitute a training tool to enhance the likelihood that all interviews will be conducted in the same manner, thus reducing the possibility that potential interviewer bias will enter the study and negatively impact the quality level of the data.

Screening Forms

Although screening forms are not involved in all surveys, when used they play an important role in ensuring that the sampled respondents of a study are what the researcher desires. Determining the eligibility of a prospective respondent up front increases the likelihood that the resulting data will be of acceptable quality. **Screening forms** are a set of preliminary questions used to determine the *eligibility* of a prospective respondent for inclusion in the survey. Normally, the researcher and the client group determine the set of special characteristics a person must have in order to be included into the pool of prospective respondents. The characteristics to be chosen for screening purpose are dependent mainly on the purposes of the study. A person's age, marital status, education level, number of purchases in a given time frame, or level of satisfaction towards a product or service might serve as a useful screener in a particular survey.

> **Screening forms** A set of preliminary questions that are used to determine the eligibility of a prospective respondent for inclusion in the survey.

Screening forms should also be used to ensure that certain types of respondents are *not* included in the study. This occurs when a person's occupation or a family member's occupation would exclude the person from being a respondent in the study. For example, let's assume that a marketing research company was hired to conduct a study regarding the impact of advertising on perceived quality of automobiles manufactured by BMW. To ensure objectivity in the results, the marketing research company would want to automatically exclude people who themselves or whose immediate family members work for a marketing research firm, an advertising firm, the BMW Company, or an automobile dealership that sells BMW vehicles. The reason behind excluding people who have an association with these particular types of occupations is that they normally hold inherent biases towards BMW vehicles or they are too professional in undertaking the role of a respondent to give unbiased and honest answers. Their responses are often not representative of those of other respondents who do not come from these particular occupational backgrounds.

Screening forms tend to be used mainly with personal or telephone surveysrather than with the self-administered option. The interviewer personally acts as a gatekeeper to control the screening process and make the final judgement about eligibility. On the other hand, self-administered questionnaires do not allow for this type of control. This does not mean that screening of prospective respondents is not possible in self-administered surveys. But it does require an additional process prior to administering the questionnaires. The process involves conducting a separate screening procedure either by telephone or with a personal interviewer before the prospective respondent receives their questionnaire. An exception to the need for a human being to serve as the control mechanism would be a survey that is self-administered through a computer or a television network (e.g. a hotel guest survey that is programmed on the TV in a guest's room). Here the questionnaire can be pre-programmed to automatically terminate the survey depending upon how respondents answered the initial screening questions. Exhibit 10.13 illustrates the screening form used in the banking study among university students.

EXHIBIT 10.13 Example of an Introduction-Screening-Quota Form for a Banking Opinion Study Using Personal Surveys

INTRODUCTION-SCREENING-QUOTA FORM
FOR THE UNIVERSITY STUDENT BANKING OPINION SURVEY

Approach to Selecting a Student

A. Politely walk up to an individual and introduce yourself.

B. Politely explain to the person that:

Your Marketing Research class is conducting a class project this semester on aspects related to students' banking behaviours and you would like to include their opinions in the study.

- IF THEY SAY **'NO'** or **'DON'T WANT TO PARTICIPATE'**, politely thank them and move on to select another person and repeat steps A and B.
- IF THEY ARE WILLING TO BE INTERVIEWED, ASK:

Q1. **Are you currently a university student this semester?**

If **YES,** continue with Q2.

If **NO,** thank them and **DISCONTINUE** the survey.

Q2. **Have you already participated in this survey?**

If **YES,** thank them and **DISCONTINUE** the survey.

If **NO,** continue with Q3.

> Q3. **Thinking about the various banks which you use, please tell me the name of the one bank that you would generally consider as being 'YOUR' primary bank.** (CHECK TO SEE IF THE RESPONDENT'S CHOICE FITS YOUR NEEDED QUOTA OF BANK NAMES BELOW)
>
> | Quota | | Possible 'Other' Banks | |
> |---|---|---|---|
> | 1 2 3 4 5 | Barclays | ☐ Write In _____ | Beneficial Savings |
> | 1 2 3 4 5 | NatWest | ☐ Write In _____ | Glendale Federal |
> | 1 2 3 4 5 | Lloyds TSB | ☐ Write In _____ | USF Credit Union |
> | 1 2 3 4 5 | HSBC | ☐ Write In _____ | Southeast Bank |
>
> - IF THE ANSWER **FITS** A NEEDED QUOTA
>   - (a) cross out one of the respective quota counts, and
>   - (b) record the answer in Question 1 of the survey and continue with Question 2 of the survey.
>
> - IF THE ANSWER **DOES NOT FIT** A NEEDED QUOTA
>   - (a) politely thank them and **DISCONTINUE** the survey, and
>   - (b) go back and repeat Steps A and B.

Quota Forms

In any type of research study there are situations when the researcher and client decide that the prospective respondents should automatically represent specifically defined subgroups or categories of prespecified sizes (or quotas). **Quota forms** are a simple tracking form that enhances the interviewer's ability to collect data from the right type of respondents. This form ensures that the identifiable respondent groups meet the prespecified requirements. Quotas also help an interviewer determine who is eligible for inclusion in the study. When a particular quota for a subgroup of respondents has been filled, it indicates to the interviewer that although an extra respondent may qualify on the basis of all the screening factors, they are not needed for the specific subgroup of respondents. In that case, the interview should be terminated.

> **Quota forms** A simple tracking form that enhances the interviewer's ability to collect raw data from the right type of respondents; the form helps ensure that representation standards are met.

In the above banking example, it was noted that 90 interviewers were used to collect the data for the study. Each interviewer was required to complete 30 interviews, for a total of 2,700 interviews. Among that total, a quota of 16.67 per cent was established for Barclays, NatWest, Lloyds TSB, and HSBC respectively. Once the quota was reached for a particular bank, let's say Barclays, any prospective respondent who qualified on the screening questions but indicated that Barclays was his or her primary bank would be terminated from the survey. Exhibit 10.13 illustrates how the quota system worked for the banking opinion survey.

Rating Cards

When collecting data by means of personal surveys, the researcher needs to develop another type of support document, referred to as a rating card. These cards serve as a tool to help the interviewer and respondent speed up the process of asking and answering the questions that make up the actual survey instrument. A **rating card** represents a reproduction of the set of actual scale points and their descriptions for specific questions on the survey. Whenever there is a question that asks the respondent to express some degree of intensity as part of the response,

---

Rating cards Cards used in personal surveys that represent a reproduction of the set of actual scale points and descriptions used to respond to a specific question in the survey. These cards serve as a tool to help the interviewer and respondent speed up the data collection process.

EXHIBIT 10.14 Example of the Question and the Corresponding Rating Card Used in Collecting Raw Data in a Banking Opinion Survey

RATING CARD A
(IMPORTANCE SCALE FOR Q2)

Rating Numbers	Description
6_____	**Extremely Important** Consideration to Me
5_____	**Definitely Important** Consideration to Me
4_____	**Generally Important** Consideration to Me
3_____	**Somewhat Important** Consideration to Me
2_____	**Only Slightly Important** Consideration to Me
1_____	**Not At All Important** Consideration to Me

Q2 Let's begin. I am going to read to you some bank features which may or may not have been important to you in selecting 'YOUR' bank.

Using this rating card **(HAND RESPONDENT RATING CARD A)**, please tell me the number that best describes how important you feel the bank feature was to you in helping select 'YOUR' bank.

To what extent was **(READ FIRST BANK FEATURE)** an important consideration to you in selecting 'YOUR' bank?

(INTERVIEWER: MAKE SURE YOU READ AND RECORD THE ANSWER FOR ALL LISTED BANK FEATURES)

Rating Number	Bank Features	Rating Number	Bank Features
_____	Convenience of branch locations	_____	Competitive service charges
_____	Flexibility of operating hours	_____	Friends' and family's recommendations
_____	Friendly/courteous bank personnel accounts	_____	Competitive interest rates on savings
_____	No minimum balance requirement	_____	Competitive interest rates on loans
_____	Promotional offer for opening an account with the bank	_____	Market status of the bank
_____	Overdraft facility	_____	Credibility of the bank

(UPON COMPLETION TAKE BACK RATING CARD A)

the interviewer provides the respondent with a rating card that reflects the possible scale responses. Before asking the survey question, the interviewer would hand the respondent the rating card and explain how to use the information on the card to respond to the question. Then the interviewer would read the question and each listed scale point and its description to the respondent and record the person's response. Typically, the respondent's answer would be in the form of a letter or number that was specifically assigned to represent each response on the card. Exhibit 10.14 offers a specific example of a question and the corresponding rating card used in a banking opinion survey administered using personal surveys.

Call Record Sheets

Call record sheets, also referred to as either *reporting or tracking sheets*, are used to help the researcher estimate the efficiency of their interviewers' performance. While there is no one best format for designing a call record sheet, it should indicate summary information regarding the number of contacts (i.e. attempts) made by each interviewer and the results of those attempts. Specifically, the types of information that are typically gathered from a call record sheet include number of contacts (attempts) made per hour, number of contacts per completed interview, length of time of each completed interview, degrees of completion by quota categories, number of terminated interviews, reasons for termination and number of callback attempts (see Exhibit 10.15). Typically, call record sheets are used in data collection modes that require the use of an interviewer.

> **Call record sheet** A recording document that gathers summary information about an interviewer's efforts and performance efficiency (e.g. number of contact attempts, number of completed interviews, length of time of interview).

A researcher or supervisor can examine the information for assessing an interviewer's effort and efficiency in gathering the required data, as well as identifying potential problem areas in the data collection process. For example, if the researcher/supervisor notices that an interviewer's number of contacts per completed interview is significantly above the average of those of all interviewers, he or she should investigate the reasons behind it. Perhaps the interviewer was not appropriately trained or was not using the proper approach in securing the prospective respondents' willingness to participate. From a cost perspective, the researcher might find that the high cost per interview associated with a particular field service operation was due to a larger number of contacts needed to get a completed interview. Further investigation might indicate that the field service company did a poor job in selecting the needed interviewers, or provided inadequate training.

Lastly, remember to visit the book's website (www.mhhe.com/shiu09) for more information and examples pertinent to questionnaire design.

EXHIBIT 10.15 An Example of an Interviewer's Call Record Sheet

Interviewer Code Number 076	Date 10/11	Date 10/13	Date 10/16	Date 10/18	Date 10/19	Date 10/20	Date 10/23
Total Contact Attempts	20	22	24	18	14	20	8
Number of initial attempts	8	12	10	8	12	14	4
Number of callbacks	12	10	14	10	2	6	4
Total Number of Noncontacts	4	2	5	0	6	2	2
No answer	1		1				
Reached a recording	2		1		3		1
Wrong phone number		1			1		
Phone no longer in service	1		3			1	1
Specific person not available					2		
Other reasons		1				1	
Total Number of Actual Contacts	4	10	5	8	6	12	2
Number of Completed Interviews	4	8	5	6	3	2	2
Barclays	2	1		1	1		
NatWest		2	1	2			
Lloyds TSB	1	1	2			1	
HSBC	1	1		3			
Other Banks		3	2		2	1	2
Contacts per Completed Interview	1	1.25	1	1.3	2	6	0
Number of Terminated Interviews	0	2	0	2	3	10	0
Screening ineligibility					1	2	
Refused participation				1		1	
Respondent break-off		1		1			
Quota requirement filled					3	7	
Language/hearing problems		1					
Other reasons							
Interviewing hours	4	4	4	5	4	4	4
Training hours	2						
Travel hours	4.5						
Mileage to interviewing centre	35						

Continuing Case Study: Designing a Questionnaire to Assess the Dining Out Habits and Patterns of Jimmy Spice's Restaurant's Customers

This illustration extends the chapter discussions on questionnaire development via the flowerpot approach. Read through this restaurant example, and answer the questions at the end.

EXHIBIT 10.16 Jimmy Spice's Restaurant Questionnaire

Below are the screening and follow-up questions asked and completed by the interviewer for each respondent.

_____

Hello. My name is _____ and I work for Marketing Intelligence and Research. We are talking to individuals today/tonight about dining out habits and patterns.

'Have you been living in the UK for over a year?'	__ Yes	__ No
'Are you living in Birmingham?'	__ Yes	__ No
'Do you usually eat out at a proper restaurant at least once every week?'	__ Yes	__ No

If respondent answers 'Yes' to all three questions, then say:

We would like you to answer a few questions about your experience today/tonight at this restaurant (Jimmy Spice's restaurant), and we hope you will be willing to give us your opinions. The survey will only take 15 minutes and your help will be very useful to the management at this restaurant in better serving its customers.

If the person says yes, give him/her a clipboard with the questionnaire on it, and briefly explain the questionnaire.

_____

When the respondent returns the questionnaire, check it for completeness and if there are missing items try to get him/her to complete them.

Look closely at the answers to questions 22, 23, and 24. If the respondent answers 1, 2, or 3, ask the following questions.

You indicated you are not too satisfied with this restaurant. Could you please tell me why?

Record answer here:

_____

You indicated you are not likely to recommend this restaurant. Could you please tell me why?

Record answer here:

_____

Could I please have your name and phone number for verification purposes?

_____   _____
        Name   **Phone #**

I hereby attest that this is a true and honest interview and complete to the best of my knowledge. I guarantee that all information relating to this interview shall be kept strictly confidential.

_____   _____
    Interviewer's Signature   **Date and Time completed**

_____

The following is the actual survey completed by respondents.

DINING OUT SURVEY

Please read all the questions carefully. If you do not understand a question, please don't hesitate to contact and ask us. In the first section a number of statements are given about interests and opinions. Using a scale from 1 to 7, with 7 being 'Strongly Agree' and 1 being 'Strongly Disagree'. Please indicate the extent to which you agree or disagree a particular statement describes you. Circle only one number for each statement. Please bear in mind that different people have different interests and opinions, so there is no right or wrong answer to each statement.

Section 1: Lifestyle Measures

1 I often try new and different things.

Strongly Disagree Strongly Agree
1 2 3 4 5 6 7

2 I like parties with music and lots of talk.

Strongly Disagree Strongly Agree
1 2 3 4 5 6 7

3 People come to me more often than I go to them for information about products.

Strongly Disagree Strongly Agree
1 2 3 4 5 6 7

4 I try to avoid fried foods.

Strongly Disagree Strongly Agree
1 2 3 4 5 6 7

5 I like to go out and socialize with people.

Strongly Disagree Strongly Agree
1 2 3 4 5 6 7

6 Friends and neighbours often come to me for advice about products brands.

Strongly Disagree Strongly Agree
1 2 3 4 5 6 7

7 I am self-confident about myself and my future.

Strongly Disagree Strongly Agree
1 2 3 4 5 6 7

8 I usually eat balanced, nutritious meals.

Strongly Disagree Strongly Agree
1 2 3 4 5 6 7

9 When I see a new product in stores, I often want to buy it.

Strongly Disagree Strongly Agree
1 2 3 4 5 6 7

10 I am careful about what I eat.

Strongly Disagree Strongly Agree
1 2 3 4 5 6 7

11 I often try new products before my friends and neighbours do.

Strongly Disagree Strongly Agree
1 2 3 4 5 6 7

Section 2: Perception Measures

Listed below is a set of characteristics that can be used to describe Jimmy Spice's restaurant. Using a scale from 1 to 7, with 7 being 'Strongly Agree' and 1 being 'Strongly Disagree', please indicate the extent to which you agree or disagree the restaurant possesses each of these characteristics. Circle only one number for each of them.

		Strongly Disagree						Strongly Agree
12	Has friendly employees	1	2	3	4	5	6	7
13	Is a fun place to eat	1	2	3	4	5	6	7
14	Generally provides large size portions off its menu	1	2	3	4	5	6	7
15	Offers fresh food	1	2	3	4	5	6	7
16	Charges reasonable prices	1	2	3	4	5	6	7
17	Has an attractive interior décor	1	2	3	4	5	6	7
18	Offers food of excellent taste	1	2	3	4	5	6	7
19	Has knowledgeable employees	1	2	3	4	5	6	7
20	Serves food at the proper temperature	1	2	3	4	5	6	7
21	Provides quick service	1	2	3	4	5	6	7

Section 3: Relationship Measures

Please indicate your view on each of the following questions:

22	How satisfied are you with Jimmy Spice's restaurant?	Not Satisfied At All						Very Satisfied
		1	2	3	4	5	6	7
23	How likely are you to return to Jimmy Spice's restaurant?	Definitely Will Not Return						Definitely Will Return
		1	2	3	4	5	6	7

24 How likely are you to recommend Jimmy Spice's restaurant to your friends?

Definitely Will Not Recommend						Definitely Will Recommend
1	2	3	4	5	6	7

25 How often do you patronize Jimmy Spice's restaurant?

1 = Less than once in last six months
2 = Less than once in last two months
3 = Less than once in last month
4 = 1–2 times a month
5 = 3 or more times a month

Section 4: Selection Factors

Listed below are some factors (reasons) many people use in selecting a restaurant whenever they want to dine. Think about your visits to restaurants in the last month and rank each listed factor below from 1 to 4, with 1 being the most important reason for selecting a particular restaurant and 4 being the least important reason.

Attributes	Ranking
26 Prices	
27 Food quality	
28 Atmosphere	
29 Service	

Section 5: Classification Questions

Please circle the number that classifies you best.

30 Distance driven to the Restaurant
1 Less than 1 mile
2 1–3 miles
3 More than 3 Miles

31 Do your recall seeing any advertisement in the last month for the restaurant?
0 No
1 Yes

32 Your gender
0 Male
1 Female

33 Number of children at home
1 None
2 1–2
3 More than 2 children at home

34 Your age in years
1 18–25
2 26–34
3 35–49
4 50–59
5 60 and Older

35 Your annual gross household income
1 €15,000–€30,000
2 €30,001–€50,000
3 €50,001–€75,000
4 €75,001–€100,000
5 More than €100,000

Thank you very much for your help. Please return your completed questionnaire to the interviewer.

Background to the Situation

A few years ago, two university business graduates (one with a degree in finance and the other in management) came together with a restaurant concept for a multi-ethnic casual dining experience with a wide variety of good food items and a friendly atmosphere. After six months of planning and creating detailed business and marketing plans the two entrepreneurs were able to get the necessary capital to build and open their first restaurant, branded as Jimmy Spice's, in Birmingham, UK (some of the information in this background section is hypothetical).

After the initial six months of success, they noticed that traffic flow and sales were declining and realized that they knew only the basics about their patrons. Neither of the owners had taken any marketing courses beyond basic marketing at university, so they turned to a friend who worked in marketing for some advice. Initially they were advised to hire a marketing research firm to collect some primary data about people's dining out habits and patterns. After some exploratory contacts with a number of marketing research firms, they found out that these firms charged a lot of money to willingly conduct the research. So they went to a high street bookstore and purchased a practitioner's book on how to do marketing research studies. Using their new understanding of how to do research and design questionnaires, the owners decided to adopt an experience intercept approach, i.e. stopping customers and asking them to be respondents as they were leaving the two owners' restaurant. This was to be carried out by trained interviewers, who needed to firstly qualify possible respondents using a set of three screening questions (see Exhibit 10.16), and then deliver a 35-question, self-administered questionnaire to actually collect the required data. Several follow-up questions the interviewers were to ask are also shown. As a whole, the following six research objectives were used to guide the design of their survey instrument shown in Exhibit 10.16.

Research Objectives

1 To identify the factors people deem important in making casual dining restaurant choice decisions.

2 To know the characteristics that customers use to describe Jimmy Spice's restaurant.

3 To develop a psychographic/demographic profile of Jimmy Spice's customer base.

4 To determine the patronage and positive word of mouth advertising patterns towards Jimmy Spice's.

5 To estimate the likelihood of the customer's willingness to return to Jimmy Spice's in future.

6 To assess the degree to which the customer is satisfied with their experience of Jimmy Spice's.

Questions

Using your understanding of the materials in this chapter, prepare answers to each of the following questions:

1 Based on the research objectives, does the owners' self-administered questionnaire, in its current form, correctly illustrate the 'flowerpot' approach? Please explain why or why not.

2 Overall, is the current survey design able to capture the required data needed to address all the stated research objectives? Why or why not? If changes are needed, how would you change the survey's design?

3 Evaluate the 'screener' used to qualify the respondents. Are there any changes needed? Why or why not?

4 Redesign questions 26–29 on the questionnaire as 'ordinal rating' scales that will enable you to capture the 'degree of importance' that a customer can attach to each of the four listed factors in selecting a restaurant to dine at.

Summary of Learning Objectives

- **Identify and discuss the critical factors that can contribute to directly improving the accuracy of surveys, and explain why questionnaire development is not a simple process.**

  Questionnaire development is much more than just writing a set of questions and asking people to answer them. Designing good surveys goes beyond just developing reliable and valid scales. A number of design factors, systematic procedural steps, and rules of logic must be considered in the development process. In addition, the process requires knowledge of sampling plans, construct development, scale measurement and types of data. It is important to remember that a questionnaire is a set of questions/scales designed to generate enough raw data to allow the researcher and decision maker to develop information to solve the business problem.

- **Discuss the theoretical principles of questionnaire design, and explain why a questionnaire is more than just asking a respondent some questions.**

  Many researchers, unaware of the underlying theory, still believe that questionnaire design is an art rather than a science. Questionnaires are, however, hierarchical structures consisting of four different components: words, questions, formats and hypotheses. Most surveys are descriptive instruments that rely heavily on the collection of state-of-being or state-of-behaviour data. Others are predictive instruments that focus on collecting state-of-mind and state-of-intention data that allow for predicting changes in people's attitudes and behaviours as well as testing hypotheses.

- **Identify and explain the communication roles of questionnaires in the data collection process.**

  Good questionnaires enable researchers to gain a true report of the respondent's attitudes, preferences, beliefs, feelings, behavioural intentions and actions/reactions in a holistic manner, not just a fragment. Through carefully worded questions and clear instructions, a researcher has the ability to control a respondent's thoughts and ensure objectivity. By understanding good communication principles, researchers can avoid bad questioning procedures that might result in unrealistic information requests, unanswerable questions, or leading questions that prohibit or distort the meaning of a person's responses.

- **Explain why the type of information needed to address a decision maker's questions and problems will substantially influence the structure and content of questionnaires.**

  Once research objectives are transformed into information objectives, determining the specific information requirements plays a critical role in the development of questionnaires. For each information objective, the researcher must be able to determine the types of data (state of being, mind, behaviour, or intentions); types of question/scale formats (nominal, ordinal, interval, or ratio); types of question structures (open-ended and closed-ended);

and the appropriate selection of scale point descriptors. Researchers must be aware of the impact that different data collection methods (personal, telephone, self-administered, computer-assisted, etc.) have on the wording of both questions and response choices.

- **List and discuss the 11 steps in the questionnaire development process, and tell how to eliminate some common mistakes in questionnaire designs.**
  Using their knowledge of construct development and scale measurement development (Chapter 11) and attitude measurement (Chapter 12), researchers can follow an 11-step process to develop scientific survey instruments. Refer back to Exhibit 10.4 which lists these steps.

- **Discuss and employ the 'flowerpot' approach in developing scientific questionnaires.**
  The flowerpot approach serves as a unique framework for integrating different sets of questions and scales into a scientific structure for collecting high-quality data. This ordered approach helps researchers make critical decisions regarding (1) construct development, (2) the appropriate dimensions and attributes of objects, (3) question/scale formats, (4) wording of actual questions and directives and (5) scale points and descriptors. Following the flowerpot approach assures that the data flow will correctly move from a general information level to a more specific level.

- **Discuss the importance of cover letters, and explain the guidelines to help eliminate common mistakes in cover letter designs.**
  While the main role of any cover letter should be winning over a prospective respondent, a set of secondary roles ranges from initial introduction to communicating the legitimacy and other important factors about the study. Ten critical factors should be included in most, if not all, cover letters. Including these will help the researcher counteract the three major reasons prospective respondents use to avoid participating in self-administered surveys and personal interviews. A lottery-based compensation system can significantly improve a prospective respondent's willingness to participate.

Key Terms and Concepts

Accuracy   333

Anonymity   353

Bad questions   331

Call record sheets   366

Confidentiality   353

Cover letter   350

Flowerpot approach   335

Hypothesis   333

Interviewer instructions   360

Lottery approach   355

Questionnaire   329

Questionnaire design precision   334

Quota forms   364

Rating card   365

Screening forms   362

Structured questions   330

Supervisor instruction sheet   359

Unstructured questions   330

Review Questions

1 Discuss the advantages and disadvantages of using unstructured (open-ended) and structured (closed-ended) questions in developing an online, self-administered survey instrument.

2 Explain the role of a questionnaire in the marketing research process. What should be the role of the client during the questionnaire development process?

3 Identify and discuss the guidelines available for determining the form and layout of a questionnaire. Discuss the advantages and disadvantages of using the flowerpot approach in developing a questionnaire.

4 What are the factors that constitute bad questions in questionnaire design? Develop three examples of bad questions. Then, using the information in Exhibit 10.7, rewrite your examples so they could be judged as good questions.

5 Discuss the value of a good questionnaire design.

6 Discuss the main benefits of including a brief introductory section in questionnaires.

7 Unless needed for screening purposes, why shouldn't classification questions be presented up front in most questionnaire designs?

8 Discuss the critical issues involved in pretesting a questionnaire.

Discussion Questions

1 Identify and discuss the guidelines for developing cover letters for a survey research instrument. What are some of the advantages of developing good cover letters? What are some of the costs of a bad cover letter?

2 Using the five specific questions that should be asked in evaluating any questionnaire design (see p. 348), evaluate Jimmy Spice's Restaurant questionnaire at the end of this chapter. Write a one-page assessment report.

3 **Experience the Internet.** Using any search engine of your choice, type in the search phrase 'questionnaire design'. Browse the various listings until you find a questionnaire of your liking. Evaluate the extent to which your selected questionnaire follows the flowerpot approach and write a two-page summary of your findings. Make sure you include in your report the website address used for reaching your selected questionnaire.

Construct Development and Scale Measurement

LEARNING OBJECTIVES

After reading this chapter, you will be able to

- ☑ Explain what constructs are, how they are developed, and why they are important to measurement and scale designs.

- ☑ Discuss the integrated validity and reliability concerns underlying construct development and scale measurement.

- ☑ Explain what scale measurement is and describe how to correctly apply it in collecting raw data from respondents.

- ☑ Identify and explain the five basic levels of scales and discuss the amount of information they can provide a researcher or decision maker.

- ☑ Discuss the hybrid ordinally-interval scale design and the types of information it can provide researchers.

- ☑ Discuss the components of scale development and explain why they are critical to gathering primary data.

" Success in predicting consumer sales for new Burger King stores came about after we understood how to better measure location site criteria using information research practices.

–C. Michael Powell
Former Director of Financial Analysis, Burger King Corporation "

Customer Loyalty Construct, Store Location and Sales Potential of Burger King Corporation

One of the most critical problems facing the Burger King Corporation is selecting sites for new restaurants that will attract sufficient customer loyalty for the new store to be profitable. Burger King's initial strategy to locate its stores no closer than about three miles from a McDonald's, on streets with high traffic, in neighbourhoods with schools, and in areas of predominantly middle-income families has proven to be no longer feasible. This traditional location strategy was based on management's early belief that these locations would produce the greatest probability of success.

Unfortunately, the previous decision-making process did not include any organized marketing research data or a clear understanding of the significance of customer loyalty, but rather relied heavily on the experience and knowledge of the Burger King senior management team. After years of using this traditional location model, it became increasingly difficult to meet the criteria established in the initial strategy and new stores' sales forecasts were often inaccurate.

To correct the problem, management began to seek a new formula for site location. Burger King's marketing research department added interview and survey data from customers to complement its use of sales and geographic data from existing Burger King stores. New research objectives included measuring customer loyalty and its impact on the relationship between the site location criteria and sales, and then seeking any other criteria that would predict sales more accurately. To gain a better understanding of customer loyalty, Burger King turned to Burke's Customer Satisfaction Division and its Customer Loyalty Index measures. New research quickly showed that while traffic density was a significant indicator of sales, neither the proximity of schools nor income levels of the surrounding area were good indicators. Moreover, it was found that customers preferred places where several fast food establishments were clustered together so that more choice was available. The study also found that customer loyalty toward new Burger King restaurants directly influenced the accuracy of sales potential estimates by store location. In the process, management learned that customer loyalty was a complex construct that required better understanding of consumers' satisfaction, positive word-of-mouth recommendations, and different levels of behavioural intentions.

Several insights about the importance of construct and measurement developments can be gained from the Burger King Corporation experience. First, not knowing the critical criteria, many of which are of multi-item constructs, for locating a business can lead to intuitive guess-work and counterproductive results. Second, making accurate location decisions requires identifying and precisely defining the patronage constructs (e.g. attitudes, emotions, behavioural factors) that consumers deem important to creating customer loyalty. Be sure to read the Marketing Research in Action at the end of this chapter to understand how Burke defines and measures customer loyalty.

Value of Measurement within Information Research

Measurement is an integral part of the modern world, yet the beginnings of measurement lie in the distant past. Before a farmer could sell his corn, potatoes, or apples, both he and the buyer had to decide on units of measurement. Over time this particular measurement became known as a bushel or four pecks or, more precisely, 2,150.42 cubic inches. In the early days, measurement was simply achieved by using a basket or container of standard size that everyone agreed was a bushel.

From such simple everyday devices as the standard bushel basket, we have progressed in the physical sciences to such an extent that we are now able to measure the rotation of a distant star, the altitude of a satellite in micro-inches, or time in picoseconds (1 trillionth of a second). Today, such precise physical measurement is critical to airline pilots flying through dense fog or physicians controlling a surgical laser.

In many marketing situations, however, the measurements are applied to things that are much more abstract than altitude or time. For example, most decision makers would agree that information about whether or not a firm's customers are going to like a new product is critically important prior to introducing that product. In many cases, such information has made the difference between business success and failure. Yet, unlike time or altitude, people's preferences can be very difficult to measure accurately. As we described earlier, the Coca-Cola Company introduced New Coke after inadequately measuring consumers' preferences, and thereby suffered substantial losses. In a similar fashion, such inadequate measurements of consumer attitudes quite often lead to the withdrawal of new products, and sometimes the failure of the entire companies.

Since accurate measurement of constructs is essential to effective decision making, the purpose of this chapter is to provide you with a basic understanding of the importance of measuring customers' attitudes and behaviours, and other marketplace phenomena. We describe the measurement process and the central decision rules for developing scale measurements. The focus here is on basic measurement issues, construct development, and scale measurements. Chapter 12 continues the topic of measurement and discusses several popular attitudinal, emotional and behavioural intention scales.

Overview of the Measurement Process

Measurement is the process of determining the amount (or intensity) of information about constructs, concepts or objects of interest and their relationship to a business problem or opportunity. In other words, researchers use the measurement process by assigning either *numbers* or *labels* to (1) people's characteristics, thoughts, feelings, and behaviours; (2) the features or attributes of objects; (3) the aspects of ideas; or (4) any type of phenomenon or event using specific rules to represent quantities and/or qualities of the factors being investigated. For example, to gather data that will offer insight about people who shop for automobiles online (a marketing phenomenon), a researcher collects information on the demographic characteristics, perceptions, attitudes, past online purchase behaviours, and other relevant factors associated with these people.

> **Measurement** An integrative process of determining the intensity (or amount) of information about constructs, concepts, or objects.

Critical to the process of collecting primary data is the development of well-constructed measurement procedures. The measurement process consists of two distinctly different development processes: *construct development* and *scale measurement*. To achieve the overall goal of collecting high quality data, researchers must understand what they are attempting to measure before developing the appropriate scale measurement. The goal of the construct development process is to precisely identify and define *what is to be measured*. In turn, the goal of the scale measurement process is to determine *how to precisely measure the construct of question*. We will begin with construct development, and then move to scale measurement.

Researchers interpret and use the terms objects and constructs in several ways. First, the term **object** refers to any tangible item in a person's environment that can be clearly and easily identified through the senses (sight, sound, touch, smell, taste). Remember that researchers do not measure the object per se but rather the elements that make up the object. Any object has what is called *objective properties* or features that are used to identify and distinguish it from another object. These properties represent attributes that make up an object of interest and are directly observable and measurable, such as the physical and demographic characteristics of a person (gender, age, income, occupational status, colour of eyes, etc.), or the actual number of purchases made of a particular product, or the tangible features of the object (horsepower, style, colour, stereo system of an automobile, etc.), to name a few.

> **Object** Refers to any tangible item in a person's environment that can be clearly and easily identified through their senses.

In turn, any object can also have *subjective properties* that are abstract, intangible characteristics that cannot be directly observed or measured because they are the mental images a person attaches to an object, such as perceptions, attitudes, feelings, expectations, or expressions of future actions (e.g. purchase intentions). Researchers refer to these intangible, subjective properties as abstract **constructs**. Measurement of constructs requires researchers to ask people to translate these mental features onto a continuum of intensity using carefully designed questions.

> **Construct** A hypothetical variable made up of a set of component responses or behaviours that are thought to be related.

Construct Development

The necessity for precise definitions in marketing research may appear to be obvious, but it frequently is the area where problems arise. Precise definition of marketing constructs begins with defining the purpose of the study and providing clear expressions of the research problem. Without a clear initial understanding of the research problem before the study begins, the researcher can end up collecting irrelevant data, thereby wasting a great deal of time, effort and money. Misguided research endeavours have contributed to many mistakes being made in such industries as music, fashion and food. Take the American automobile market as an example. Even after the first Volkswagens were introduced into the United States, many American automobile continued to invest in factories designed to produce large, inefficient automobiles. They ignored studies that suggested that increasing fuel prices, highway congestion and pollution controls favoured more modest vehicles. As a result, a significant proportion of automobile sales were lost to foreign competitors, notably Japanese carmakers including Toyota and Nissan. Such cases show that a very careful definition of the purpose of the study is essential.

Construct development is an integrative process in which researchers identify the subjective properties for which data should be collected to solve the defined research problem. Identifying these properties to investigate requires knowledge and understanding of constructs and their dimensionality, validity and operationalization.

> **Construct development** An integrative process in which researchers determine what specific data should be collected for solving the defined research problem.

Abstractness of the Construct

At the heart of construct development is the need to determine exactly what is to be measured. The objects that are relevant to the research problem are identified first. Then the objective and subjective properties of each object are specified. In cases where data are needed only about the concreteness of an object, the research focus is limited to measuring the object's objective properties. But when data are needed to understand an object's subjective properties, the researcher must identify measurable sub-components that can be used to clarify the abstractness associated with the object's subjective properties.

For instance, a hammer can easily be thought of as a concrete object. Researchers can easily measure a hammer's physical characteristics: the hardness of its head, its length and weight, the composition of the handle, and so on. Yet the hammer can also have a set of subjective properties, such as its quality and performance that are created from people's attitudes, emotions, and judgements towards the hammer. Due to level of abstractness associated with the hammer's intangible quality and performance features, there are no physical instruments that can directly measure these constructs. Exhibit 11.1 provides some examples of objects and their concrete, tangible properties and abstract, intangible properties, as well as some specific examples of marketing constructs. A rule of thumb is that if an object's features can be directly measured using physical instruments, then that feature is not a construct.

EXHIBIT 11.1 Examples of Concrete and Abstract Properties of Objects and Marketing Constructs

Objects

Aeroplane	**Concrete properties:** Number of engines, height, weight, length, seating capacity, physical characteristics of seats, type of aeroplane, etc.
	Abstract constructs: Quality of in-flight cabin service, comfortability of seating, smoothness of takeoff and landing, etc.
Consumer	**Concrete properties:** Gender, age, marital status, income, brand last purchased, amount of purchase, types of products purchased, etc.
	Abstract properties: Attitudes toward a product, level of involvement in purchase, emotions (love, fear, anxiety), brand loyalty, intelligence, personality, risk taking, etc.

Organization	**Concrete properties:** Name of company, total assets, number of employees, number of locations, total assets, operating capacity, types and numbers of products and service offerings, type of industry membership, etc.
	Abstract properties: Competence of employees, quality control, channel power, competitive advantages, company image, consumer-oriented practices, etc.
Marketing Constructs	
Brand loyalty	**Concrete properties:** A particular purchase pattern exhibited toward a specific brand name product or service, the frequency of purchases of a particular brand, amount of time needed in the store to select a brand.
	Abstract properties: The degree a person likes/dislikes a particular brand, the degree of satisfaction expressed towards a brand, a person's overall attitude towards the brand.
Customer satisfaction	**Concrete properties:** Identifiable attributes that make up a product, service, or experience.
	Abstract properties: Expressions of feelings (positive or negative) towards the product, service, or experience; liking/disliking of the individual attributes making up the product, service, or experience.
Service quality	**Concrete properties:** Identifiable attributes that make up a service encounter or experience. (e.g. customer waiting time for being served, percentage of customer queries that service staff can answer properly)
	Abstract properties: Expectations held about each identifiable attribute, evaluative judgement of performance.
Advertising recall	**Concrete properties:** Factual properties of the advertisement (e.g. message, symbols, movement), aided and unaided recognition of the facts.
	Abstract properties: Interpretations of the factual elements in the advertisement, favourable/unfavourable judgements, degree of affective attachment to advertisement.

Determining Dimensionality of the Construct

In determining exactly what is to be measured, researchers must keep in mind the need to acquire relevant, high-quality data to support management's decisions. For example, if the purpose is to assess the service quality of an automobile dealership, then what exactly should be measured? Since dealer service quality is an abstract construct, perhaps the most appropriate way to begin to answer this question is to indirectly identify those dealership attributes that are important to customers.

Researchers in this case can use a variety of qualitative data collection methods (e.g. focus groups or in-depth interviews) to develop preliminary insights into service quality and its **domain of observables**, which is the set of identifiable and measurable components associated with an abstract construct. To illustrate this point, researchers interested in identifying the domain of measurable components that represent the service quality construct conducted two different types of exploratory research, a secondary literature review of past research on service quality and several focus groups. The results suggested that the service quality construct can be indirectly represented by the

---

Domain of observables The set of identifiable and measurable components associated with an abstract construct.

domain of a service provider's ability to (1) *communicate* and *listen* to consumers; (2) demonstrate *excellent interpretative skills*; (3) *sincerely empathize* with consumers in interpreting their needs and wants; (4) be *tactful in responding* to customers' questions, objections, and problems; (5) create an impression of *reliability in performing* the services; (6) create an *image of credibility* by keeping promises; (7) demonstrate *sufficient technical knowledge* and *competence*; and (8) exhibit *strong interpersonal skills* in dealing with consumers. In turn, this preliminary information could then be used as a guideline for collecting data from a larger, representative sample of customers.

During the research process, it is necessary to ensure that the actions taken as a result of the preliminary insights fit the organization's goals and objectives. For instance, most customers desire lower service prices. Yet it may not be in the best interests of the dealership to reduce prices.

Assessing Construct Validity

Another important activity is assessing the validity of the construct, especially if the construct is believed to be multi-dimensional. It is important to note that assessing the validity of a construct is actually an after-the-fact activity because the process requires the researcher to create a set of scale measurements for each of the construct's components and collect data on each of those components. The researcher then needs to perform statistical analyses to test for content validity, convergent validity and discriminant validity.

Content validity (sometimes referred to as *face validity*) is the subjective yet systematic assessment of how well a construct's measurable components represent that construct. **Convergent validity** focuses on how well the construct's measurement positively correlates with different measurements of the same construct. For researchers to be able to evaluate convergent validity, they must know and use several different measurement approaches to evaluate the construct. For **discriminant validity**, researchers must determine whether the construct being investigated differs significantly from other constructs that are thought to be different from the construct of question. Finally, in some cases, **nomological validity** allows researchers to evaluate how well one particular construct theoretically compares with other established constructs that are related yet different.

> **Content validity** The subjective yet systematic assessment of how well a construct's measurable components represent that construct.
>
> **Convergent validity** When the researcher's measures of a construct are highly correlated with known existing measures of the same construct.
>
> **Discriminant validity** The existence of a negative correlation between the measurement of one construct and those measures of another clearly different construct.
>
> **Nomological validity** Assessment of how well one construct theoretically fits within a network of other established constructs that are related yet different.

Usually one of two approaches is used to collect data for assessing construct validity. If there are enough resources, researchers will conduct a pilot study among fifty or so people who are believed to be of characteristics similar to those of the defined target population. In situations where resources are not available for a pilot study, researchers will attempt to approximate content validity by having a panel of experts independently judge the dimensionality of the construct. While these approaches have become common measurement practices, they contain several weaknesses.

Inappropriate Scale Measurement Formats

When after-the-fact data are used to assess construct validity, the scale point descriptors used in collecting the data can cause inaccuracies. That is, using untested or inappropriate scale measurement indicators to measure the construct can create measurement artifacts that lead to misinterpretations of the true components as well as the true dimensionality traits of the construct. In this situation, the raw data are driving the researcher's theoretical framework instead of theory driving the measurement process. A procedure that can be used to overcome this type of weakness is **direct cognitive structural analysis**, in which respondents are simply asked to determine whether an attribute is part of the construct and, if so, how important it is to that construct.

> **Direct cognitive structural analysis** A data analysis technique that assesses how well the identifiable attributes of a construct reflect that construct and their importance to it.

Another element that impacts the assessment of construct validity but focuses more on scale measurement is *scale reliability*. Here the researcher determines the extent to which the scale used to measure the construct consistently measures what it was intended to measure. While reliability of scale measurements is a necessary but not, by itself, a sufficient condition for accurately determining construct validity, scale reliability remains an important element in the process of collecting high-quality data.

Inappropriate Set of Respondents

In academic research settings, for example, researchers too often rely on students' input in their process of determining the components of the construct being investigated. Although students are consumers and may have some knowledge and experience with certain products and services, in most cases their attitudes and buying behaviours are not representative of the general population or of many other specifically defined target populations.

A second problem that relates to using students in construct development is that student samples are typically drawn using a convenience sampling approach. Convenience sampling does not even guarantee true representation of a student population, let alone a larger defined target population. As a consequence, the components originally thought to make up the construct may be different when the study is extended to a more representative sample of the target population. The Closer Look at Research box (p. 385) offers an example of this problem as it occurred in a banking study.

Construct Operationalization

Operationalization is when the researcher explains a construct's meaning in measurement terms by specifying the activities or operations necessary to measure it. The process focuses on the design and use of questions and scale measurements to gather the needed data. Since many constructs, such as satisfaction, preferences, emotions, store images and brand loyalty cannot be directly observed or measured, the researcher attempts to indirectly measure them through operationalization of their components.

> **Operationalization** Explaining a construct's meaning in measurement terms by specifying the activities or operations necessary to measure it.

For example, one researcher developed over one hundred questions to determine if customers were satisfied with their respective dealer's service when they made their recent automobile purchase. Customers were asked to rate a number of components, including the salesperson's listening skills, the reliability/credibility of the service, the quality of the facilities and equipment and the serviceperson's personal social skills. Exhibit 11.2 illustrates two different measurement approaches used to capture data about the construct of automobile dealership service satisfaction.

EXHIBIT 11.2 Approaches to Measure Service Satisfaction with Automobile Dealerships

Example 1:
Now with all the knowledge, opinions, feelings, and personal experiences you have acquired as a customer with your *primary* automobile service provider (ASP), I would like to know how satisfied or dissatisfied you are concerning several service features. Using the scale described below, where:

6 = Completely satisfied	4 = Somewhat satisfied	2 = Definitely dissatisfied
5 = Definitely satisfied	3 = Somewhat dissatisfied	1 = Completely dissatisfied

please write a number from 1 to 6 in the space provided that best expresses how satisfied or dissatisfied you are with **each listed** service feature.

_____ Convenience of ASP's location	_____ ASP's communication skills
_____ Flexibility in ASP's operating hours	_____ Availability of quality service offerings
_____ Service provider's personal social skills	_____ Overall reputation of your primary ASP
_____ Personnel's understanding of customer needs	_____ ASP's concern of putting its customers 'first'
_____ Reliability/credibility of ASP's service providers	_____ ASP's listening skills
_____ Service provider's technical knowledge/competence	_____ Facilities and equipment at your primary ASP

Example 2:
Using the educational letter grading system of 'A', 'B', 'C', 'D', and 'F', please **circle** the one 'letter grade' that best expresses the overall grade that you would give to each of the following listed service factors at your primary ASP.

a. The communication skills of the service people at my primary ASP are ...	A	B	C	D	F
b. The listening capabilities of the service people at my primary ASP are ...	A	B	C	D	F
c. The ability of the service staff to understand my various repair/ maintenance service needs is ...	A	B	C	D	F
d. The ability of service employees to demonstrate understanding of my automobile service needs is ...	A	B	C	D	F
e. The service personnel's ability to respond quickly to my questions (or objections, problems) is ...	A	B	C	D	F
f. The reliability or credibility demonstrated by the service representatives is ...	A	B	C	D	F
g. The technical knowledge or competence demonstrated by the service personnel is ...	A	B	C	D	F
h. The personal social skills used by the service employees in dealing with me are ...	A	B	C	D	F
i. The facilities and equipment at my primary ASP are ...	A	B	C	D	F

The examples in Exhibit 11.2 suggest that assessing what appears to be a simple construct of service satisfaction can be more involved than it might seem at first. Here, the researcher was trying to fully capture information on all important dimensions that may affect a customer's service satisfaction at their automobile dealer. Certainly these multi-item approaches will give researchers a more accurate basis for evaluating how successful respective dealers have been in satisfying their customers. Moreover, this type of approaches provides a business with better opportunities to pinpoint areas of concern and take corrective actions. With only a single-question approach, corrective action would be very difficult if not impossible since the researcher would not be able to determine the exact problem area. After constructs and their possible traits have been adequately identified and understood, the researcher then needs to create appropriate scale measurements.

 ## A Closer Look at Research *(In the field)*
Problem in Construct Development

A marketing researcher wanted to identify the areas people might use in their process of judging banking service quality. The researcher conducted several focus groups among both undergraduate students in a basic marketing course and graduate students in a marketing management course to identify the service activities and offerings that might represent service quality. The researcher's rationale for using these groups was that they did have experience in conducting bank transactions, they were consumers, and the researcher had easy access to them for their opinions. The preliminary results of the focus groups revealed that the students used four dimensions for judging a bank's service quality: (1) interpersonal social skills of bank staff, (2) reliability of bank statements, (3) convenience of ATM delivery systems, and (4) diagnostic competence of bank tellers.

A month later, the researcher conducted four focus groups among known customers of a large bank. The preliminary results clearly suggested those customers used seven dimensions for judging a bank's service quality. Those dimensions were identified as the bank's ability to (1) communicate with and listen to consumers; (2) demonstrate diagnostic competence in understanding the customer's banking needs; (3) elicit sincere empathy by showing deep concern for customers' requirements; (4) be tactful in responding to customers' questions, objections, or problems; (5) create an impression of reliability and credibility inherent in a bank service encounter; (6) demonstrate sufficient competence in handling bank transactions; and (7) exhibit strong positive interpersonal social skills in conducting bank transactions.

The researcher was in a tentative position of not knowing for sure whether people perceive bank service quality as having four or seven crucial components. Which source of information should be used to better understand the construct of bank service quality? Which kind of focus group findings should the researcher rely on to conduct the empirical survey on bank service quality? These issues would directly affect the operationalization of construct development.

Basic Concepts of Scale Measurement
Types of Data Collected in Research Practices
Any data that could be useful for marketing research purpose can be classified as being one of four basic states of nature: verifiable facts, mental thoughts or emotional feelings, past or current behaviours and planned future behaviour intentions. In what follows, we will refer to verifiable facts as *state-of-being data*, mental thoughts and emotional feelings as *state-of-mind data*, past

and current behaviours as *state-of-behaviour data,* and planned future behaviour intentions as *state-of-intention data.*

State-of-Being Data (Verifiable Facts)

When the problem requires the researcher to collect responses that are relevant to the physical, demographic, or socioeconomic characteristics of individuals, organizations, or objects, the resulting data are considered verifiable facts, or state-of-being data. State-of-being data represent factual characteristics that can be verified through sources other than the person providing the responses. For example, a researcher can directly ask respondents their age, marital status, number of children, educational level, occupation, income level, height, weight, colour of eyes and telephone number – or the researcher could obtain some of these data through secondary sources such as electoral register, other types of public documents, and so on.

For organizations, data on total monetary/unit sales, number of employees, total assets, number and types of stores, and so on, can often be obtained through secondary sources, eliminating the need to ask direct questions about them. The same holds true for the physical characteristics of many objects. The main point to remember about state-of-being data is that the researcher is not limited to collecting the raw data by only asking questions.

> **State-of-being data** The physical, demographic, or socioeconomic characteristics of people, organizations, or objects.

State-of-Mind Data (Mental Thoughts or Emotional Feelings)

State-of-mind data represent the mental or emotional attributes of individuals that are not directly observable or available through external sources. State-of-mind data exist only within the minds of people. To collect such data, traditionally the researcher has to ask a person to respond to questions. Verification through secondary or external sources is all but impossible. Some examples of state-of-mind data would be a person's personality traits, awareness levels, perceptions, attitudes, feelings, beliefs, cognitive decision processes and product/service preferences. Therefore, data quality and accuracy are partly dependent on the degree of honesty of the person providing the responses to the researcher's questions.

> **State-of-mind data** The mental thoughts or emotional feelings of people.

In recent years, the advent of the functional Magnetic Resonance Imagery (fMRI) technique has caught the eye of the marketing research industry. The technique reveals fascinating data about brain activity. Many marketing researchers claim that use of these brain activity data can help us understand humans' thoughts or emotions, which can have a direct impact on their behaviour in the marketplace. Therefore, nowadays, at least part of the state-of-mind data are deemed to be obtainable not only through the traditional approach of asking the person concerned, but also through the use of the fMRI technique. The data collected with the new approach are also believed to be accurate, as they are devoid of the possibility of dishonesty of the concerned person's responses to the researcher's questions in the traditional approach.

However, whether the fMRI technique can really read all the important state-of-mind data for marketing research purpose in future is still a big unknown. Even more importantly, that scanning the brain activity through the use of the fMRI technique can explain consumer behaviour may be just a big myth. The fact is that our understanding of the brain and cognition is still very primitive. It is clear that the brain has organizing principles that we do not understand. Can the fMRI technique help us significantly understand the state of mind of human beings? And can the localized brain activities identified by the fMRI technique significantly explain human behaviour in the marketplace? So far human beings do not know enough to prove or disprove these hypothetical causal relationships.

State-of-Behaviour Data (Past and Current Behaviours)

State-of-behaviour data represent an individual's or organization's current observable actions or recorded past actions. The researcher has several options available to obtain state-of-behaviour data. A person can be asked questions about current or past behaviour. For example, a person can be asked to respond to questions such as 'In the past six months, how many times have you purchased breakfast cereal for your household?' or 'In a typical week, how often do you go grocery shopping?' To obtain current behaviour, a person can be asked to respond to such questions as 'Are you currently enrolled at a university?' or 'How many courses are you currently taking?'

> **State-of-behaviour data** A person's or organization's current observable or recorded past actions.

Another option is to use either a trained observer or some type of mechanical/electronic device to observe and record current behaviour. For example, a disguised observer or hidden camera can be used to selectively observe and record customers' frozen food selections at a local supermarket. Such behavioural data may include length of time in the frozen food section of the store, the specific brands and types of frozen foods inspected or selected, and the number of units of a product that were placed in the shopping cart.

A third option useful for collecting data on past behaviour is to find records of previously conducted behaviour. For example, a researcher could examine a restaurant's credit and debit card receipts over a specified period to determine how often a selected individual came in and ate at that particular restaurant, assuming the individual used only credit or debit cards to pay for their meals. There are limitations to the quality and accuracy of data using this option. In addition, verification of an individual's past behaviours through any type of external, secondary source is generally a difficult process in terms of time and effort involved. Feasibility and desirability of this option are heavily dependent on the existence of well-documented behaviours.

State-of-Intention Data (Planned Future Behaviours)

State-of-intention data represent an individual's or organization's expressed plans of future behaviour. State-of-intention data can be collected only by asking a person to respond to questions about behaviours that are yet to take place. For instance, a researcher can ask such questions as 'How likely are you to purchase a new car in the next six months?', 'Do you plan to tour outside Europe in your next overseas holiday travel?' or 'How likely would you be to buy ECover next time you need kitchen utensil washing liquid?'

> **State-of-intention data** A person's or organization's expressed plans of future behaviour.

The Nature of Scale Measurement

The quality of the responses depends much on the appropriateness of the scale measurements used by the researcher. **Scale measurement** is the process of assigning a set of descriptors to represent the range of possible responses to a question about a particular object or construct.

> **Scale measurement** The process of assigning descriptors to represent the range of possible responses to a question about a particular object or construct.

Within this process, the focus is on measuring the existence of various characteristics of a person's response. Scale measurement attempts to assign designated degrees of intensity to the responses. These degrees of intensity are commonly referred to as **scale points**. For example, a retailer might want to know how important a pre-selected set of store and service features is to consumers in deciding where to shop. The available levels of importance attached to each store or service feature would be determined by the researcher's assignment of a range of scale point descriptors each having a different level of intensity, thus representing the possible degrees of importance (e.g. definitely, moderately, slightly, not at all important) associated with each feature.

> **Scale points** Designated degrees of intensity assigned to the possible responses in a given questioning or observation method.

Properties of Scale Measurement

There are four properties a researcher can use in developing scales: assignment, order, distance and origin (see Exhibit 11.3).

EXHIBIT 11.3 Four Scaling Properties: Description and Examples

Scaling Properties	Description and Examples
Assignment property	The employment of unique descriptors to identify an object in a set.
	Examples: The use of numbers (10, 38, 44, 18, 23, etc.); the use of colours (red, blue, green, pink, etc.); yes and no responses to questions that identify objects into mutually exclusive groups.
Order property	Establishes 'relative magnitudes' between the descriptors, creating hierarchical rank-order relationships among objects.
	Examples: 1st place is better than a 4th-place finish; a 5-foot person is shorter than a 7-foot person; a regular customer purchases more often than a rare customer.
Distance property	Allows the researcher and respondent to identify, understand and accurately express absolute (or assumed) differences between objects.
	Examples: Family A with six children living at home, compared to family B with three children at home, has three more children than family B; differences in income ranges or age categories.

Origin property	A unique scale descriptor that is designated as being a 'true natural zero' or 'true state of nothing'. **Examples:** Asking a respondent his or her weight or current age; the number of times one shops at a supermarket; or the market share of a specific brand of hand soap.

Assignment

The **assignment property**, also referred to as *description* or *category property*, is where the researcher uses unique descriptors, or labels, to identify each object within a set. This property enables a researcher to categorize the responses into mutually exclusive groups, each with its own identity. Any descriptor can be used to represent a response. Some examples are the use of numbers (1, 7, 10, etc.) to identify the players in a football team so the referee can correctly record fouls committed; yes and no responses to the question 'Are you going to purchase a new automobile within the next six months?'; the use of colours (red, green, blue, etc.) to identify clothes or bathroom towels; and the use of size indicators (large, medium, small, etc.) to identify the quantity of soft drinks, fitting of clothes, or amount of pizza on offer.

Assignment property The employment of unique descriptors to identify each object in a set.

Order

The **order property** is the relative magnitude between the descriptors used as scale points. Relative magnitude between descriptors is based on the relationships between two or more descriptors. For example, there are only three relationships between responses A and B: A can be *greater than* B; A can be *less than* B; or A can be *equal to* B. When respondents can identify and understand a 'greater than' or a 'less than' relationship between two or more objects or responses, the order scaling property is established and a meaningful rank order can be identified among the reported responses. Some examples of the order property include the following: 1 is less than 5; 'extremely satisfied' is more intense than 'somewhat satisfied'; 'very important' has more importance than 'slightly important'; 'somewhat disagree' involves less disagreement than 'definitely disagree'; and a person holding a master of business administration (MBA) degree has more formal years of education than a person holding a bachelor's degree. When the order scaling property is included in a set of scale points, it enables the researcher to establish either a 'highest to lowest' or a 'lowest to highest' rank order among the raw responses. It is important to remember that the order scaling property, by itself, identifies only the relative differences between raw responses and not the absolute differences.

Order property The relative magnitude assigned to each scale point descriptor.

Distance

The **distance property** expresses the absolute difference between each of the descriptors or scale points. In other words, the distance property shows that the researcher knows the absolute magnitude that exists between each response to a question. For example, family A drives two cars, and family B drives four cars. Thus, family A has two fewer cars than family B. A person who has to travel 20 miles to work drives twice as many miles as their work colleague who drives only 10 miles to the same workplace. The distance scaling property is restricted to situations where the responses represent some type of natural numerical answer.

> **Distance property** The measurement scheme that expresses the absolute (or exact) difference between each of the descriptors or scale points.

In many cases researchers believe the scales associated with collecting state-of-mind data activate the distance property. For example, some researchers believe that 'extremely spicy' can be taken as one unit of spiciness away from 'very spicy', or that 'strongly agree' is two units of agreement away from 'somewhat agree', or that 'extremely important' is four units of importance away from 'slightly important'. However, in reality, as in all these examples, there is no way a researcher could statistically verify that the claimed absolute relationship between those scale point descriptors exists. This measurement problem will be discussed later in this chapter.

Origin

The **origin property** refers to the use of a unique starting point in a set of scale points that is designated as being a 'true natural zero' or true state of nothing. The origin property relates to a numbering system where zero is the displayed starting point in a set of possible responses. It must be noted that a response of 'don't know', 'no opinion', 'don't care', 'no response', and so on, to a question does not represent the zero origin property. Examples of questions that contain a true natural zero include current age, number of children, income, number of miles one travels to go for regular grocery shopping, and number of times a person usually purchases a specific product or service in a month.

> **Origin property** Having a unique starting point in a set of scale points that is designated as a true natural zero.

When developing scale measurements, the more scaling properties that can be simultaneously activated in a scale design, the more complete the collected data. Note that each scaling property builds on the previous one. This means that any scale will have the assignment property. A scale that includes the order property automatically possesses the assignment property. If the researcher designs a scale with the distance property, the scale has also assignment and order. Scales that are built with the origin property have assignment, order, as well as distance properties.

Levels of Scales

While scaling properties determine the amount of data obtained from any scale design, all scale measurements can be logically and accurately classified as one of five scale levels: nominal, ordinal, true class interval, hybrid ordinally-interval, or ratio. There are specific relationships between the level of scale and which scaling properties are activated within the scale (see Exhibit 11.4).

EXHIBIT 11.4 Relationships between Levels of Scales and Scaling Properties

Level of Scale	Scaling Properties			
	Assignment	Order	Distance	Origin
Nominal	Yes	No	No	No
Ordinal	Yes	Yes	No	No
True Class Interval	Yes	Yes	Yes	No
Hybrid Ordinally-Interval	Yes	Yes	Yes	No
Ratio	Yes	Yes	Yes	Yes

Nominal Scales

A **nominal scale** is the most basic level of scales. In this level of scale, the questions require respondents to provide only some type of descriptor as the response. The response does not contain any level of intensity. Therefore, it is impossible to establish any form of rank order among the set of given responses. That is, nominal scales provide data that cannot be arranged in a 'greater than/less than' or 'bigger than/smaller than' hierarchical pattern. Nominal scales allow the researcher only to categorize the responses into mutually exclusive subsets that do not illustrate distances between them. Some examples of nominal scales are given in Exhibit 11.5.

> **Nominal scale** The type of scale in which the questions require respondents to provide only some type of descriptor as the response.

EXHIBIT 11.5 Examples of Nominal Scale Structures

Example 1:
Please indicate your current marital status.
_____ Married _____ Single _____ Separated _____ Divorced _____ Widowed

Example 2:
Do you like or dislike chocolate ice cream?
_____ Like _____ Dislike

Example 3:
Please check those university facilities that you used at least once in the past academic year. (Check as many of them as they are applicable)
_____ Sports centre _____ Medical centre _____ Chaplaincy centre
_____ Student guild _____ University canteen _____ Campus bookshop
Some other facilities; Please specify _____

Example 4:
Please indicate your gender:
_____ Female _____ Male

Example 5:
Which of the following supermarkets have you shopped at in the last 30 days? (Please check all that apply)
_____ Asda _____ Coop _____ M&S _____ Morrisons
_____ Sainsbury's _____ Somerfield _____ Tesco _____ Waitrose

Ordinal Scales

An **ordinal scale** has both assignment and order scaling properties. This level of scale enables respondents to express relative magnitude between the answers to a question. The raw responses can be rank ordered into a hierarchical pattern. Thus, it is easy to determine 'greater than/less than', 'higher than/lower than', 'more often/less often', 'more important/less important', or 'less agreement/more agreement' types of relationships between the responses. But ordinal scales do not enable the researcher to determine the absolute difference in any of the ordinal relationships. Exhibit 11.6 provides several examples of ordinals.

> **Ordinal scale** A scale that allows a respondent to express relative magnitude between the answers to a question.

EXHIBIT 11.6 **Examples of Ordinal Scale Structures**

Example 1:
Which category best describes your knowledge about the services offered by your local government?
(Please check just one category.)
_____ Complete knowledge of services
_____ Good knowledge of services
_____ Basic knowledge of services
_____ Little knowledge of services
_____ No knowledge of services

Example 2:
The following list of library services, activities and resources may or may not be important to you when using a local public library. Using the scale provided below, for each listed item please check the response that best expresses how important you feel it is.

Services, Activities, Resources	Extremely Important	Definitely Important	Somewhat Important	Not at All Important
Variety of books that can be borrowed	____	____	____	____
Availability of current magazines	____	____	____	____
Availability of a designated area for children	____	____	____	____
Constant arrival of new books that can be borrowed	____	____	____	____
Computers with online access	____	____	____	____
Reference materials for business	____	____	____	____
Information resources related to your locality	____	____	____	____
General reference materials	____	____	____	____

Example 3:
We would like to know your preferences to different banking methods. Among the methods listed below, please indicate your top three preferences using '1' to represent your first choice, '2' for your second preference and '3' for your third choice of methods.
(Please write the numbers on the lines next to your selected methods.)
_____ Inside the bank   _____ Bank by telephone
_____ 24-hour ATM   _____ Online banking
_____ Bank by mail   _____ Banking at a bank-operated vehicle regularly visiting our community

Example 4:
For each pair of banks, circle the store you would be more likely to patronize:

Barclays or NatWest	Barclays or HSBC	Barclays or Lloyds TSB
NatWest or HSBC	NatWest or Lloyds TSB	HSBC or Lloyds TSB

Example 5:
Which one statement best describes your opinion of the quality of a Nokia N79 mobile phone?
(Please check just one statement.)

_____ Higher than iPhone
_____ About the same as iPhone
_____ Lower than iPhone

True Class Interval Scales

A **true class interval scale** has not only assignment and order scaling properties but also the distance property. Scales with the distance property can be used to measure absolute differences between each scale point. Also, because of the distance property, more powerful statistical techniques can be used to analyse the data. With true class interval scale structures, researchers can identify not only the hierarchical order in the data but also the specific differences between the data. In addition, it is possible to calculate means and standard deviations with interval data. True class interval scales are appropriate when the researcher wants to collect state-of-behaviour and certain types of state-of-being data. Exhibit 11.7 illustrates some examples of true class interval scale formats.

> **True class interval scale** A scale that demonstrates absolute differences between each scale point.

EXHIBIT 11.7 **Examples of True Class Interval Scales**

Example 1:
Approximately, how many charges for overdrawn cheques (NSF cheques) has 'your' bank imposed on you in the past year?

_____ None   _____ 1–2   _____ 3–7   _____ 8–15   _____ 16–25   _____ More than 25

Example 2:
Approximately how long have you lived at your current address?

_____ Less than 1 year	_____ 4 to 6 years	_____ 10 to 12 years
_____ 1 to 3 years	_____ 7 to 9 years	_____ Over 12 years

Example 3:
In which one of the following categories does your current age fall?

_____ Under 18	_____ 26 to 35	_____ 46 to 55	_____ Over 65
_____ 18 to 25	_____ 36 to 45	_____ 56 to 65	

Example 4:
Into which of the following categories does your total (approximate) current income, before taxes, fall?

_____ Under €10,000	_____ €40,000 to €49,999
_____ €10,000 to €19,999	_____ €50,000 to €59,999
_____ €20,000 to €29,999	_____ €60,000 to €69,999
_____ €30,000 to €39,999	_____ €70,000 or above

▶ **Example 5:**
In a typical week, how often do you access the Internet from a home computer?
(Please check the most appropriate response category)

_____ More than 20 times _____ 11 to 15 times _____ 1 to 5 times
_____ 16 to 20 times _____ 6 to 10 times _____ No Internet access at home

Hybrid Ordinally-Interval Scales

There are many situations in marketing research where it is useful to transform ordinal scaled data into what is generally assumed to be interval scaled data. To achieve this, researchers employ what are referred to as **hybrid ordinally-interval scale** designs. Ordinally-interval scales are ordinal but have an _assumed distance_ scaling property so the researcher can perform some type of advanced statistical analysis. The transformation is based on the assumption that the original scale point descriptors activated the distance scaling property. Strictly speaking, this transformation is a researcher artifact. But it is a widely accepted practice in marketing research.

> **Hybrid ordinally-interval scale** An ordinal scale that is artificially transformed into an interval scale by the researcher.

To create an ordinally-interval scale, the researcher uses two sets of scale point descriptors. The first set consists of narratively expressed indicators, referred to as **primary scale point descriptors**. The second set consists of whole integer numbers that are assigned to the primary set of descriptors and are referred to as **secondary scale point descriptors**. Let's take, for example, a situation in which the researcher originally develops an ordinal scale to collect general opinions from respondents. The original set of narrative scale points might range from 'definitely agree' to 'definitely disagree' (i.e. 'definitely agree', 'generally agree', 'slightly agree', 'slightly disagree', 'generally disagree', and 'definitely disagree'). These scale point indicators would be considered the primary descriptors, and the complete scale measurement might look as follows (example of an initial ordinal scale design):

For each of the following statements, please check the response that best expresses the extent to which you either agree or disagree with that statement.

Statement	Definitely Agree	Generally Agree	Slightly Agree	Slightly Disagree	Generally Disagree	Definitely Disagree
Immigration brings more benefits than costs to the country.	_____	_____	_____	_____	_____	_____
We should set an absolute limit on the number of asylum seekers accepted.	_____	_____	_____	_____	_____	_____
Immigration is the major factor contributing to social problems in the country.	_____	_____	_____	_____	_____	_____
The EU has been expanding too far and too fast.	_____	_____	_____	_____	_____	_____

> **Primary scale point descriptors** The set of narratively expressed scale point descriptors used in creating an ordinally-interval scale.
>
> **Secondary scale point descriptors** The set of cardinal numbers (whole integers) used as scale point expressions in an ordinally-interval scale design.

One option a researcher has is to redefine those scale points to include the distance property by assigning a secondary set of number descriptors to represent each of the original primary scale point descriptors. Usually the researcher will use a set of **cardinal numbers** as the secondary set of descriptors. In the simplest form, cardinal numbers are any set of consecutive whole integers (1, 2, 3, 4, 5, 6, 7, etc.). By combining the primary and secondary sets of descriptors, the researcher creates a relationship between the original scale point descriptors so that 'definitely agree' = 6, 'generally agree' = 5, 'slightly agree' = 4, 'slightly disagree' = 3, 'generally disagree' = 2, and 'definitely disagree' = 1. By using these secondary numerical values to represent the original scale points, the researcher can, on the assumption these cardinal numbers are really the respective integer values, now apply higher levels of data analysis techniques to the responses. This first approach would make the scale measurement resemble the following, which is a typical example of hybrid ordinally-interval design using full range of primary and secondary scale point descriptors:

For each of the following statements, please circle the response that best expresses the extent to which you either agree or disagree with that statement.

Statement	Definitely Agree	Generally Agree	Slightly Agree	Slightly Disagree	Generally Disagree	Definitely Disagree
Immigration brings more benefits than costs to the country.	6	5	4	3	2	1
We should set an absolute limit on the number of asylum seekers accepted.	6	5	4	3	2	1
Immigration is the major factor contributing to social problems in the country.	6	5	4	3	2	1
The EU has been expanding too far and too fast.	6	5	4	3	2	1

> **Cardinal numbers** Any set of consecutive whole integers.

Another option used quite frequently by marketing researchers involves having primary descriptors identify the extreme end points of a set of secondary cardinal numbers that make up the range of raw scale point descriptors. This approach leaves the interpretation of what the in-between numerical descriptors truly represent up to the imagination of the respondent. Again, such a method assumes there is a known distance property between each of the scale point descriptors. Using the above example, this second approach would make the scale measurement appear like the following, demonstrating an example of hybrid ordinally-interval scale design using primary descriptors as extreme end points only:

For each of the following statements, please circle the number that best expresses the extent to which you either agree or disagree with that statement.

Statements	Definitely Agree					Definitely Disagree
Immigration brings more benefits than costs to the country.	6	5	4	3	2	1
We should set an absolute limit on the number of asylum seekers accepted.	6	5	4	3	2	1
Immigration is the major factor contributing to social problems in the country.	6	5	4	3	2	1
The EU has been expanding too far and too fast.	6	5	4	3	2	1

In hybrid ordinally-interval scale designs, the absolute difference between a response of 'definitely agree' and that of 'generally agree' is assumed to be one unit of agreement. The assumption of an absolute difference of one unit cannot be confirmed. Therefore, researchers must be careful in interpreting findings obtained from this type of design. Additional examples of hybrid ordinally-interval type scales are provided in Exhibit 11.8.

EXHIBIT 11.8 Additional Examples of Hybrid Ordinally-Interval Scale Structures

Example 1:
For each of the brands of soft drinks listed below, please circle the number that best expresses your overall performance judgment of that brand.

Soft Drink Brands	Very Poor						Outstanding
Coke	1	2	3	4	5	6	7
Pepsi	1	2	3	4	5	6	7
Dr Pepper	1	2	3	4	5	6	7
Fanta	1	2	3	4	5	6	7
Sprite	1	2	3	4	5	6	7
Seven-Up	1	2	3	4	5	6	7

Example 2:
Using the scale provided below, select the number that best describes how important each of the listed attributes were in your deciding which restaurant to dine at. **Please place your numerical response on the line provided next to each attribute.**

Importance Scale

1 = Not at all important	3 = Somewhat important	5 = Definitely important
2 = Only slightly important	4 = Important	6 = Extremely important

Restaurant Attributes

_____ Taste of the food	_____ Quality of service	_____ Convenience of location
_____ Wide variety in menu	_____ Speed of service	_____ Décor of the restaurant
_____ Availability of reservation system	_____ Cheap price	_____ Convenience of parking

Example 3:

Concerning the different banking methods you may or may not use, we would like to know your feelings toward these methods. Next to each of the listed banking methods, please circle the number that best describes the degree to which you like or dislike using that method.

Banking Methods	Very Much Dislike Using									Very Much Like Using
Inside the bank	1	2	3	4	5	6	7	8	9	10
24-hour ATM	1	2	3	4	5	6	7	8	9	10
Bank by mail	1	2	3	4	5	6	7	8	9	10
Bank by phone	1	2	3	4	5	6	7	8	9	10
Online banking	1	2	3	4	5	6	7	8	9	10
Banking at a bank-operated vehicle regularly visiting our community	1	2	3	4	5	6	7	8	9	10

Ratio Scales

A ratio scale is the only level of scale that activates all the four scaling properties. A ratio scale is the most sophisticated scale because it enables the researcher to identify the absolute difference between any pair of scale points, and to make absolute comparisons between them. For instance, in collecting data about how many cars are owned by different households in Frankfurt, the researcher knows that the difference between owning one car and owning three cars is always going to be two. When comparing a one-car family to a three-car family, the researcher can assume that the three-car family will have significantly higher total car insurance and maintenance costs than the one-car family.

> **Ratio scale** A scale that allows the researcher to identify the absolute differences between each scale point, and to make comparisons between the raw responses.

Remember that ratio scale structures are designed to enable a 'true natural zero' or 'true state of nothing' response to be a valid raw response to the question. Normally, ratio scales request that respondents provide a specific numerical value as their response, regardless of whether or not a set of scale points is used. Exhibit 11.9 shows several examples of ratio scale structures. For more examples of the various types of scales go to www.mhhe.com/shiu09 and follow the links.

EXHIBIT 11.9 Examples of Ratio Scale Structures

Example 1:

Please circle the number of children under 18 years of age currently living in your household.

0   1   2   3   4   5   6   7   (If more than 7, please specify: _____.)

Example 2:

In the past seven days, how many times did you go shopping at a shopping centre?

_____ # of times

▶ **Example 3:**

In whole years, what is your current age?

_____ # of years old

Example 4:

To the best of your memory, how many times have you visited the following tourist attractions?

____ British Museum   ____ Tower of London   ____ St Paul's Cathedral

____ Westminster Abbey   ____ V&A Museum   ____ London Zoo

____ National Gallery   ____ Madame Tussaud's   ____ Science Museum

Example 5:

In a typical 12-month period, how many miles do you drive your car for personal activities?

____ # of miles driven

Development and Refinement of Scale Measurement

The keys to designing high-quality scales are (1) understanding the defined problem, (2) establishing detailed data requirements, (3) identifying and developing the constructs, and (4) understanding that a complete measurement scale consists of three critical components (the question, the attributes and the scale point descriptors). After the problem and data requirements are understood, the researcher must develop constructs. Next, the appropriate scale format (e.g. nominal, ordinal, interval, ordinally-interval, or ratio) must be selected. For example, if the problem requires interval data, but the researcher asks the questions using a nominal scale, the wrong level of data will be collected and the final information that can be generated will not be helpful in resolving the initial problem. To illustrate this point, Exhibit 11.10 offers examples of the different levels of data that are obtained on the basis of how the question is phrased to a respondent. These examples show that how the questions are phrased will directly affect the amount of raw data collected. It should be clear that nominal scale questions provide the least amount of raw data and ratio scale questions provide the richest data.

EXHIBIT 11.10 Example of the Five Basic Types of Question Phrasings

Information requirement: To determine how often consumers eat at Pizza Express.

NOMINAL QUESTION PHRASING:

When you are in the mood for pizza, do you usually enjoy a pizza at Pizza Express?

The logical raw response to this question would be a simple **Yes** or **No**.

ORDINAL QUESTION PHRASING:

When you are in the mood for pizza, how often do you enjoy a pizza from Pizza Express? **(Check only one response.)**

The logical raw responses might be as follows:

____ Never   ____ Seldom   ____ Occasionally   ____ Usually   ____ Every time

TRUE CLASS INTERVAL QUESTION PHRASING:

Thinking about your pizza consumption over the past six months, approximately how often have you consumed a pizza at Pizza Express? **(Check the one appropriate response.)**

The logical raw responses might be as follows:

____ Less than 3 times   ____ 7 to 9 times   ____ Over 12 times (Please specify: ____)

____ 4 to 6 times   ____ 10 to 12 times

HYBRID ORDINALLY-INTERVAL QUESTION PHRASING:

Thinking about your pizza consumption over the past six months, please circle the number that best expresses how often have you consumed a pizza at each of the following eating places that sell pizzas.

The logical raw responses might be as follows:

Pizza Eating Place	Never							Every Time
Pizza Express	0	1	2	3	4	5	6	7
Pizza Hut	0	1	2	3	4	5	6	7
Other Pizza Chain (Please Specify: ___)	0	1	2	3	4	5	6	7
Independent, Local Pizza Eating Place	0	1	2	3	4	5	6	7
Other Type of Eating Place (Please Specify: ___)	0	1	2	3	4	5	6	7

RATIO QUESTION PHRASING:

In the past 12 months, how many times did you consume a pizza at Pizza Express? **(Write the # of times on the line provided.)**

_____ # of times

Some Criteria for Scale Development

Once the importance of question phrasing is understood, the researcher can now focus on developing the most appropriate scale descriptors to be used. While there is no one agreed-on set of criteria for establishing the actual scale point descriptors, we suggest several key criteria in Exhibit 11.11.

EXHIBIT 11.11 Key Criteria in Scale Development

Scale Development Criteria	Description
Intelligibility of the questions	Use language in the questions and responses that the respondents are accustomed to, so as to ensure clarity and understanding.
Appropriateness of scale descriptors	Make sure that the narrative scale descriptors accurately reflect the type of data being sought in the setup part of the scale measurement.
Discriminatory power of the scale descriptors	Make sure that each scale descriptor used can be understood by the respondent as being mutually exclusive from each of the other scale descriptors, as well as the number of descriptors used is appropriate and can accurately represent the planned intensity levels of the descriptors.
Reliability of the scale	Use of procedures to ensure that each scale measure meets, at least, a desired minimum level of reproducible results in repeated trials.
Balancing positive/negative scale descriptors	In those cases where a 'symmetrical' scale design is required, objectivity must be maintained by assuring equal inclusion of both positive and negative response items.
Inclusion of a neutral response choice	When attempting to capture state-of-mind or certain types of state-of-intention raw data, consideration must be given towards including or excluding a 'neutral' or 'not applicable' response option.
Measures of central tendency and dispersion	Consideration must be given to the desired statistics and data analysis that will be used after the raw data are collected from respondents and understanding how different levels of scales activate the basic sample statistics (i.e. mean, median, mode, frequency distribution, range, and standard deviation).

Intelligibility of the Questions

The researcher must consider the intellectual capacity and language ability of those to whom the scale will be administered. Researchers should not automatically assume that respondents understand the questions being asked or the response choices. The **intelligibility** criterion is the degree to which questions are understood by respondents. Appropriate language must be used in both the questions and the answer choices.

> **Intelligibility** The degree to which the questions on a scale are understood by the respondents.

The researcher should try to eliminate guessing by respondents. Moreover, respondents should be able to understand what types of data are being asked for and how to respond. Refer back to scale example 3 in Exhibit 11.8. Suppose that in the setup portion of that scale the researcher had used only the first sentence ('Concerning the different banking methods you may or may not use, we would like to know your feelings towards these methods'). This would suggest that the researcher assumed the respondents would automatically understand how to complete the scale question. Without the second sentence (the exact instructions), respondents may not know what to do. Such assumptions on the part of the researcher could easily increase the likelihood of missing responses. The intelligibility factor thus promotes the use of 'respondent instructions' in scale measurement designs, especially in self-administered surveys. For personal or telephone surveys, it is quite possible that 'interviewer instructions' will also have to be included in the question/setup portion of the scale measurements.

Appropriateness of Scale Descriptors

Researchers must make sure the scale descriptors match the type of raw data they are seeking. Therefore, another criterion is the researcher must consider the **appropriateness of scale descriptors**. That is, the adjectives or adverbs used to indicate the relative magnitudes must be related to the scale descriptors. Let's say, for example, that the researcher wants to find out respondents' opinions about whether or not the Somerfield supermarket has 'competitive meat prices'. The task becomes one of determining which scale descriptors best represent the notion of 'competitive prices'.

> **Appropriateness of scale descriptors** The extent to which the scale descriptors match the type of raw data being sought.

There are several ways of representing competitive prices. First, if the researcher designs the question/setup to ask the respondents to agree or disagree that 'Somerfield has competitive meat prices', then the appropriate set of scale descriptors would be levels of agreement/disagreement (e.g. 'strongly agree', 'agree', 'neither agree nor disagree', 'disagree', 'strongly disagree'). Stating the question in terms of competitiveness would require an ordinal set of descriptors such as 'extremely competitive', 'definitely competitive', 'generally competitive', 'only slightly competitive', and 'not at all competitive'. In contrast, it would be inappropriate to try to represent respondents' opinions about 'competitive prices' using a performance-oriented set of descriptors like 'excellent', 'very good', 'good', 'average', 'fair', and 'poor'.

Discriminatory Power of the Scale Descriptors

This scale criterion relates to those situations when either (1) the problem requires the inclusion of relative magnitudes to the set of possible responses or (2) the researcher decides to establish sizes of differences between the scale points. The **discriminatory power** of a scale is the scale's ability to significantly differentiate between the scale responses. Researchers must decide how many scale points are necessary to represent the relative magnitudes of a response scale. Remember, the more scale points the greater the discriminatory power of the scale.

> **Discriminatory power** The scale's ability to significantly differentiate between the scale responses.

There is no clear rule about the number of scale points that should be used in creating a scale. But some researchers believe that scales should be between three and seven points because some respondents find it difficult to make a choice when there are more than seven levels. To illustrate this point, suppose Marriott International is interested in determining which hotel features patrons consider important in their process of choosing a hotel. In developing an 'importance' scale to capture the relative magnitude of importance attributed to each hotel feature, the researcher must subjectively decide how many recognizable levels of importance exist in the minds of travellers. The researcher must first understand that the basic dichotomous scale descriptors are simply 'important' and 'not important.' Second, the researcher must decide how detailed or how varied the raw importance data responses have to be to address the initial information problem. For example, an importance scale can consist of five different levels of importance. The five differential degrees can be expressed as 'extremely', 'definitely', 'generally', 'somewhat', and 'only slightly' important. But an importance scale can also use seven points and sometimes more. The more scale points you have, the greater the opportunity there is for variability in the data – an important consideration in data analysis. But one must always consider respondents' ability to discriminate when more scale points are used.

There are times when attempting to incorporate too many degrees of relative magnitude into the scale can decrease discriminatory power. Suppose in the above Marriott hotel example the researcher designs an importance scale that consists of 15 scale descriptors and presents the scale as follows:

IMPORTANCE SCALE

Not at All Important 1 2 3 4 5 6 7 8 9 10 11 12 13 14 15 Extremely Important

While this scale denotes 'not at all important' as being 1 and 'extremely important' as being 15, it is very unlikely that either the researcher or the respondent can attach any meaningful, differential descriptor interpretations to the scale points of 2 to 14.

Reliability of the Scale

Scale reliability refers to the extent to which a scale can reproduce the same measurement results in repeated trials. Any error in the scale produces inconsistency in scale measurements that leads

> **Scale reliability** The extent to which a scale can produce the same measurement results in repeated trials.

to lower scale reliability. Two of the techniques that can help researchers assess the reliability of scales are test-retest and equivalent form.

First, the **test-retest** technique involves repeating the scale measurement with either the same sample of respondents at two different times or two different samples of respondents from the same defined target population under as nearly the same conditions as possible. The idea behind this approach is simply that if variations are present, they will be revealed by variations in the scores between the two sampled measurements. If there are very few differences between the first and second administrations of the scale, the measuring scale is viewed as being stable and therefore reliable. For example, assume that determining the teaching effectiveness associated with your marketing research course involved the use of a 28-item scale designed to measure the degree to which respondents agree or disagree with each item. To gather the data on teaching effectiveness, your professor administers this scale to the class after the fourth week of the term and again after the eighth week. Using a mean analysis procedure on the items for each measurement period, the professor then runs correlation analysis on those mean values. If the correlations between the mean value measurements from the two assessment periods are high, the professor concludes that the reliability of the 28-item scale is high.

> **Test-retest** A technique of measuring scale reliability by administering the same scale to the same respondents at two different times or to two different samples of respondents under similar conditions.

There are several potential problems with the test-retest approach. First, some of the students who completed the scale the first time might be absent for the second administration of the scale. Second, students might become sensitive to the scale measurement and therefore alter their responses in the second measurement. Third, environmental or personal factors may change between the two administrations, thus causing changes in student responses in the second measurement. These factors can include the professor's levels of knowledge in different topics of the course, and the teaching and learning aids, if any, used in different teaching sessions.

Some researchers believe that the problems associated with test-retest reliability technique can be avoided by using the **equivalent form** technique. In this technique, the researcher creates two similar yet different (technically called 'equivalent form') scale measurements for the given construct (e.g. teaching effectiveness) and administers both forms to either the same sample of respondents or two samples of respondents from the same defined target population. In the 'teaching effectiveness' example, the professor would construct two 28-item scales whose main difference would lie in the wording of the item statements, not the agree/disagree scaling points. Although the specific wording of the statements would be changed, their meaning would remain constant. After administering each of the scale measurements, the professor calculates the mean values for each item and then runs correlation analysis. Equivalent form reliability is assessed by measuring the correlations of the scores on the two scale measurements. High correlation values are interpreted as meaning high scale measurement reliability.

> **Equivalent form** A technique to establish scale reliability by measuring and correlating the measures of two equivalent scaling instruments.

There are two potential drawbacks with the equivalent form reliability technique. First, usually substantial amounts of time, effort and expense are needed for developing two 'equivalent' scales to measure the same construct. Thus a question arises as whether this is worthwhile, considering that there are other options available to meet the same purpose, i.e. reliability testing. Second, it is very difficult and perhaps impossible to create two totally equivalent scale measurements. Questions may be raised as to which scale measurement is the most appropriate to use in measuring teaching effectiveness.

When investigating multi-dimensional constructs, summated scale measurements tend to be the most appropriate scales. In this type of scale, each dimension represents some aspect of the construct. Thus, the construct is measured by the entire scale, not just one component. **Internal consistency** refers to the degree to which the various dimensions of a multidimensional construct correlate with the scale. That is, the set of items that make up the scale must be internally consistent. There are two popular techniques used to assess internal consistency: split-half tests and coefficient alpha, also referred to as *Cronbach's alpha*. In a **split-half test**, the items in the scale are divided into two halves (odd versus even attributes, or randomly) and the resulting halves' scores are correlated against one another. High correlations between the halves indicate good (or acceptable) internal consistency. A **coefficient alpha** takes the average of all possible split-half measures that result from different ways of splitting the scale items. The coefficient value can range from 0 to 1, and, in most cases, a value of less than 0.6 would typically indicate marginal to low (unsatisfactory) internal consistency.

Internal consistency The degree to which the various dimensions of a multidimensional construct correlate with the scale.

Split-half test A technique that involves the division of the items in the scale into two halves and the correlation analysis of the resulting halves' scores.

Coefficient alpha A technique of taking the average of all possible split-half measures that result from all different ways of splitting the scale items.

Researchers need to remember that just because their scale measurement designs prove to be reliable, the data collected are not necessarily valid. Separate validity assessments must be made on the constructs being measured.

Balancing Positive/Negative Scale Descriptors

This scale development criterion relates to the researcher's decision to maintain objectivity in a scale that is designed to capture both positive and negative raw responses. To maintain scale objectivity, the researcher must design both positive and negative descriptors as scale points. For example, let's assume that a market research company wants to add to its 'New Vehicle Survey' a single-item scale that measures a purchaser's satisfaction with his or her new vehicle's overall performance. Since most people would consider the feeling of satisfaction to be positive and the feeling of dissatisfaction to be negative, the market research company would need to decide whether or not the scale measurement should be 'objective' and not bias the respondent's feeling one way or the other. By having equal relative magnitudes of satisfaction (positive) and dissatisfaction (negative), the scale measure would maintain a level of objectivity. Such a balanced scale measurement design can look like the following:

> Based on your experience with your new vehicle since owning and driving it, to what extent are you presently satisfied or dissatisfied with the overall performance of the vehicle?

(PLEASE CHECK THE ONE APPROPRIATE RESPONSE)

_____ Completely satisfied (no dissatisfaction)   _____ Slightly dissatisfied (some satisfaction)

_____ Definitely satisfied   _____ Generally dissatisfied

_____ Generally satisfied   _____ Definitely dissatisfied

_____ Slightly satisfied (some dissatisfaction)   _____ Completely dissatisfied (no satisfaction)

With a balanced scale measurement, objectivity is maintained. Now let's assume that the market research company is primarily interested in assessing new vehicle purchasers' satisfaction with their vehicles' overall performances and that dissatisfaction data are not that important. This type of data requirement is better met by using an unbalanced scale measurement that places heavier emphasis on the positive (satisfaction) scale descriptors than on the negative (dissatisfaction) ones. The unbalanced scale measurement design can look like the following:

> Based on your experience with your new vehicle since owning and driving it, to what extent are you presently satisfied with the overall performance of the vehicle?

(PLEASE CHECK THE ONE APPROPRIATE RESPONSE)

_____ Completely satisfied   _____ Generally satisfied   _____ Dissatisfied

_____ Definitely satisfied   _____ Slightly satisfied

It is important to remember that with an unbalanced scale measurement, objectivity is lower.

Inclusion of a Neutral Response Choice

In scale measurement design, the number of scale point descriptors becomes an important criterion only if the data requirements call for capturing either state-of-mind data or specific types of state-of-intention data that focus on positive/negative continuum ranges. The issue involves offering the respondent the opportunity to express a neutral response. Having an even number of positive/negative scale descriptors tends to force the respondent to select either a positive or negative answer.

A symmetrical scale that does not have a neutral descriptor to divide the positive and negative domains is referred to as a **forced-choice scale** measurement. In contrast, a symmetrical scale that includes a centre neutral response is referred to as a **free-choice scale** measurement. Exhibit 11.12 presents several different examples of both 'even-point, forced-choice' and 'odd-point, free-choice' descriptors.

Forced-choice scale A symmetrically designed polar scale that does not include a neutral response category.

Free-choice scale A symmetrically designed polar scale that does include a neutral response category.

EXHIBIT 11.12 Examples of 'Even-Point' (Forced-Choice) and 'Odd-Point' (Free-Choice) Scale Descriptors

'Even-Point, Forced-Choice' Itemized Rating Scale Descriptors

PURCHASE INTENTION (BUY/NOT BUY)

____ Definitely will buy   ____ Probably will buy   ____ Probably will not buy   ____ Definitely will not buy

PERSONAL BELIEFS/OPINIONS (AGREEMENT/DISAGREEMENT)

Definitely agree	Generally agree	Slightly agree	Slightly disagree	Generally disagree	Definitely disagree
____	____	____	____	____	____

MODERNITY (MODERN/OLD-FASHIONED)

____ Very modern   ____ Somewhat modern   ____ Somewhat old-fashioned   ____ Very old-fashioned

COST (EXPENSIVE/INEXPENSIVE)

Extremely expensive	Definitely expensive	Somewhat expensive	Somewhat inexpensive	Definitely inexpensive	Extremely inexpensive
____	____	____	____	____	____

'Odd-Point, Free-Choice' Itemized Rating Scale Descriptors

PURCHASE INTENTION (BUY/NOT BUY)

Definitely will buy	Probably will buy	Neither will nor will not buy	Probably will not buy	Definitely will not buy
____	____	____	____	____

PERSONAL BELIEFS/OPINIONS (AGREEMENT/DISAGREEMENT)

Definitely agree	Generally agree	Slightly agree	Neither agree nor disagree	Slightly disagree	Generally disagree	Definitely disagree
____	____	____	____	____	____	____

MODERNITY (MODERN/OLD-FASHIONED)

Very modern	Somewhat modern	Neither modern nor old-fashioned	Somewhat old-fashioned	Very old-fashioned
____	____	____	____	____

COST (EXPENSIVE/INEXPENSIVE)

Definitely expensive	Somewhat expensive	Neither expensive nor inexpensive	Somewhat inexpensive	Definitely inexpensive
____	____	____	____	____

Some researchers believe that scales used to collect state-of-mind data should be designed as 'odd-point, free-choice' scale measurements since not all respondents will have enough knowledge or experience with the given topic to be able to accurately assess their thoughts or feelings. If those respondents are forced to choose, the scale may produce lower quality data than the researcher desires. In free-choice scale designs, however, the so-called neutral scale point offers respondents an easy (and correct) way to express their feelings about the given topic.

An alternative approach to handling the situations, in which respondents have no knowledge of or experience with a topic and may feel uncomfortable if they are forced to express their thoughts or feelings about it, would be to incorporate a 'not applicable' response choice that would not be part of the actual scale measurement. The following example illustrates the *not applicable* (NA) response:

> Based on your experience with your new vehicle since owning and driving it, to what extent are you presently satisfied or dissatisfied with the overall performance of the vehicle? If you feel that you lack enough experience with your vehicle or that the statement is not pertinent to you, please check the 'NA'.

(PLEASE CHECK THE ONE APPROPRIATE RESPONSE)

____ Completely satisfied (no dissatisfaction) ____ Generally dissatisfied

____ Definitely satisfied ____ Definitely dissatisfied

____ Generally satisfied ____ Completely dissatisfied (no satisfaction)

____ Slightly satisfied (some dissatisfaction) ____ NA (Not Applicable)

____ Slightly dissatisfied (some satisfaction)

This approach allows the researcher to sort all the 'NA' responses out of the raw data and ensures that only quality data will be included in the data analysis.

Desired Measures of Central Tendency and Dispersion

In determining what levels of scale measurements should be developed, the researcher must consider the data analysis that will be used after the data are collected from respondents. The researcher must therefore have an understanding of the measures of central tendency and the measures of dispersion associated with different types of scale measurement designs.

Measures of central tendency refer to the basic sample statistics that are generated through analysing the collected data; these are the mean, the median, and the mode. The *mean* is nothing more than the arithmetic average of all the raw data responses. The *median* represents the sample statistic that splits the raw data into a hierarchical pattern where half the raw data are above the statistic value and half are below. The *mode* is the raw response that is the most frequently given among all of the respondents.

> **Measures of central tendency** The basic sample statistics that are generated through analysing raw data; these are the mean, the median and the mode.

Measures of dispersion relate to how the data are dispersed around a central tendency value. These basic sample statistics allow the researcher to report the diversity of the raw responses to a particular scale measurement. They include the frequency distribution, the range, and the standard deviation. A *frequency distribution* is a summary of how many times each possible response to a scale descriptor from the total group of respondents. This distribution can be

> **Measures of dispersion** The basic sample statistics that allow a researcher to report the diversity of the raw data collected from scale measurements; they are the frequency distribution, the range and the standard deviation.

EXHIBIT 11.13 Relationships between Scale Levels and Measures of Central Tendency and Dispersion

Measurements	Five Levels of Scales				
	Nominal	Ordinal	True Class Interval	Hybrid Ordinally-Interval	Ratio
Central Tendency					
Mean	*Inappropriate*	*Inappropriate*	**Most Appropriate**	**Most Appropriate**	**Most Appropriate**
Median	*Inappropriate*	**More Appropriate**	Appropriate	Appropriate	Appropriate
Mode	**Appropriate**	Appropriate	Appropriate	Appropriate	Appropriate
Dispersion					
Frequency Distribution	**Appropriate**	Appropriate	Appropriate	Appropriate	Appropriate
Range	*Inappropriate*	**More Appropriate**	Appropriate	Appropriate	Appropriate
Standard Deviation	*Inappropriate*	*Inappropriate*	**Most Appropriate**	**Most Appropriate**	**Most Appropriate**

easily converted into percentages or histograms for ease of comparison between raw data responses. The *range* represents a boundary that equals to the difference between the lowest and the highest numbers recorded from the respondents. The *standard deviation* is the statistical value that specifies the degree of variation in the data responses in such a way that allows the researcher to translate the variations into normal curve interpretations (e.g. 99 per cent of the responses fall between the mean value plus or minus 3 standard deviations).

Given the important role that these six basic sample statistics play in data analysis procedures, understanding how different levels of scales influence the use of a particular statistic becomes crucial in scale measurement design. Exhibit 11.13 displays these relationships. Remember that data collected through a nominal scale can only be analysed by modes and frequency distributions. For ordinal scales, you can analyse the data using medians and ranges as well as modes and frequency distributions.

A Closer Look at Research *(Using Technology)*

Call from British Advertisers to Establish a Standardized Measurement Scale of Website Audiences

Bob Wootton, director of media and advertising at the Incorporated Society of British Advertisers, has been frustrated by the lack of a standardized measurement of website audiences.

Fearing that younger audiences are deserting traditional media such as TV and print publications, advertisers have been chucking money at online advertising space. However, with no standardized, reliable measure of website audiences, they do not know the price they pay for buying an advertising space on a website is worth the money. On the other side of the transaction, website owners are in no hurry to back such a standardized measurement, as nowadays the most popular websites can pretty much name their price.

'This is why there needs to be a lot of downward pressure from advertising agencies and advertisers onto the media owners, as they are ultimately the guys that have to buy into this and fund the majority of its development', said Edward Ling, a member of the UK's Joint Industry Committee for Internet Measurement Systems (JICIMS) and strategy development director at digital advertising agency I-Level.

At first sight, the Internet may be one of the most measurable media out there – with Internet service providers and websites automatically collecting a wealth of data on web surfing habits. But at the same time, it is a continuously evolving, highly complex medium, unconfined by national borders. It is also a multi-media platform in itself – hosting websites, instant messaging applications, email, chatrooms, blogs, search engines, radio stations as well as streaming video. All these unique features render the establishment of a standardized measurement of website audiences that the Internet hosts much more difficult than first thought.

A standardized measurement of website audiences ideally needs to encompass data on how consumers access the Internet across different platforms – not jut on PCs, but also on TVs, PDAs and mobile phones.

It also needs to cover all the key criteria met by other media ratings systems in order to facilitate cross-media planning.

Dimensions that could constitute a standardized measurement of website audiences include unique visitors (although this dimension cannot differentiate between light and heavy users), minutes-of-use for communication tools such a email and instant messaging, audience engagement, and the number of distinct queries (useful for assessing how long people spend searching on the website).

In reality, these dimensions exist already, but they are not applied consistently by industry participants. For example, ComScore and NetRatings report on unique visitors as the number of unique persons that visit a website. But many publishers report internal numbers, which are a reflection of unique cookies not unique people. This phenomenon is like comparing apples and oranges. A definition of each candidate dimension to be consistently followed by all the parties concerned is therefore necessary before any work on establishing a standardized measurement of website audiences becomes feasible.

Source: Research Magazine, News Archive, www.research-live.com

For interval or ratio scale measurements, the most appropriate analysis procedures would be those that involve means and standard deviations as the sample statistics. In addition, interval and ratio data can be appropriately analysed using medians, modes, frequency distributions, or ranges.

Now that we have presented the basics of construct development as well as the rules surrounding scale measurements, we are ready to move forward to the popular attitudinal scales used by marketing researchers.

Chapter 12 focuses on more advanced scales. The Closer Look at Research box shows how a consulting firm integrates advanced technology to create high-quality segmentation measures.

Customer Loyalty Index – Part 1

This application is presented in a two-part format. In Part 1, you will read how researchers at Burke Customer Satisfaction Associates, an international market research enterprise renowned for its expertise in customer loyalty measurement, defines customer loyalty and how this construct is operationalized into a measurable index called the *Customer Loyalty Index*. The second part is presented in the European Case Study at the end of Chapter 12 and will focus on how this construct is actually measured by Burke Customer Satisfaction Associates.

The idea that loyal customers are especially valuable is not new to today's business managers. Loyal customers repeatedly purchase products or services. They recommend a company that they often patronize to others. And they stick with a business that they are fond of over time. Loyal customers are worth the special effort it may take to keep them. But how can you provide that special treatment if you don't know your customers and how their loyalty is won and lost?

Understanding loyalty – what makes your customers loyal and how to measure and understand loyal customers – enables your company to improve customer-driven quality. A customer loyalty index provides management with an easily understood tool that helps focus the organization towards improving satisfaction and retention.

What Customer Loyalty Is and Isn't

To better understand the concept of customer loyalty, let's first define what customer loyalty is not. Customer loyalty is not customer satisfaction. Satisfaction is a necessary component of loyal customers. However, the mere aspect of being satisfied with a company does not necessarily make customers loyal. Just because customers are satisfied with your company today does not mean they will continue to do business with you in the future.

Customer loyalty is not a response to trial offers or incentives. If customers suddenly begin buying your product or service, it may be the result of a special offer or incentive and not necessarily a reflection of customer loyalty. These same customers may be just as quick to respond to your competitors' incentives.

Customer loyalty is not strong market share. Many businesses mistakenly look at their sales numbers and market share and think, 'Those numbers are surrogates for direct measures of customer loyalty. After all, we wouldn't be enjoying high levels of market share if our customers didn't love us.' However, this may not be true. Many other factors can drive up market share, including poor performance by competitors or pricing issues. And high share doesn't mean low churn, which is the rate at which existing customers leave you – possibly to patronize your competition – and are replaced by new customers.

Customer loyalty is not repeat buying or habitual buying. Many repeat customers may be choosing your products or services because of convenience or habit. However, if they learn about a competitive product that they think may be less expensive, they may quickly switch to that product. Habitual buyers can defect; loyal customers usually don't.

EXHIBIT 11.14 Customer Loyalty Index

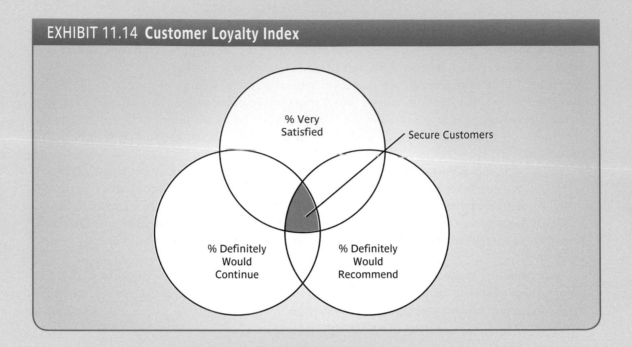

Now that we know what does not constitute customer loyalty, we can talk about what does. Customer loyalty is a composite of a number of qualities. It is driven by customer satisfaction, yet it also involves a commitment on the part of the customer to make a sustained investment in an ongoing relationship with a brand or company. Finally, customer loyalty is reflected by a combination of attitudes and behaviours. These attitudes include:

- The intention to buy again and/or buy additional products or services from the same company.
- A willingness to recommend the company to others.
- A commitment to the company demonstrated by a resistance to switching to a competitor.

Customer behaviours that reflect loyalty include:

- Repeat purchasing of products or services.
- Purchasing more and different products or services from the same company.
- Recommending the company to others.

Any one of these attitudes or behaviours in isolation does not necessarily indicate loyal customers. However, by recognizing how these indicators work together in a measurement system, we can derive an index of customer loyalty. Burke Customer Satisfaction Associates has developed a Customer Loyalty Index using three major components to measure customer loyalty: overall customer satisfaction, likelihood of repeat business and likelihood to recommend the company to others. Other elements may be included in the index depending upon the industry. In their experience, however, these three components are the core of a meaningful customer loyalty index.

Questions

Using the material from the chapter and the above information, answer each of the following questions:

1 Identify and provide a meaningful definition of each of the three constructs that researchers at Burke Customer Satisfaction Associates believe are the driving forces behind measuring the concept of customer loyalty.

2 What is the dimensionality of each of these three constructs? That is, are the constructs unidimensional or multidimensional? For each of those constructs that you believe is multidimensional, identify the possible domain of sub-components that would be representative of that construct. Also, explain why you feel your proposed domain set represents that construct.

3 In your judgement, what level of scale design would be the most appropriate in creating the necessary scale measurements for collecting primary data on each construct?

4 For each construct, design an example of the actual scale measurement that could be used by Burke Customer Satisfaction Associates to collect the data.

Summary of Learning Objectives

■ **Explain what constructs are, how they are developed, and why they are important to measurement and scale designs.**

Within the overall process of creating meaningful information for resolving both today's and future business/marketing problems, researchers must be able to develop appropriate questions and record the raw responses to those questions. Next to correctly defining the information problem, determining what type of data should be collected is the second most critical aspect in information research. Gaining access to raw data responses is achieved by the scale measurement incorporated into the questioning process. A construct can be viewed as any object that cannot be directly observed and measured by physical devices. Within the development process, researchers must consider the abstractness of the construct, its dimensionality, assessments of validity and its operationalization. Not knowing exactly what it is that one needs to measure makes it difficult to design the appropriate scale measurements.

■ **Discuss the integrated validity and reliability concerns underlying construct development and scale measurement.**

Regardless of the method used for data collection, researchers must strive to collect the most accurate data and information possible. Data accuracy depends heavily on the validity of the constructs and the reliability of the measurements applied to those constructs. Constructs can be assessed for content, convergent, discriminant and nomological validity. Testing for reliability of constructs is indirectly achieved by testing the reliability of the scale measurements used in data collection. Scale reliability test methods available to researchers include test-retest, equivalent form, and internal consistency. Although scale measurements may prove to be reliable, reliability alone does not guarantee construct validity.

■ **Explain what scale measurement is, and describe how to correctly apply it in collecting raw data from respondents.**

Scale measurement is the process of assigning a set of descriptors to represent the range of possible responses that a person gives in answering a question about a particular object, construct, or factor. This process aids in determining the amount of raw data that can be obtained from asking questions, and therefore indirectly impacts the amount of primary information that can be derived from the data. Central to the amount of data issue is understanding that there are four basic scaling properties (i.e. assignment, order, distance and origin) that can be activated through scale measurements. The rule of thumb is that as a researcher simultaneously activates more properties within the question/answering process, the greater the amount of raw data that can be gathered from people's responses. All raw data can be classified into one of four mutually exclusive types: state-of-being, state-of-mind, state-of-behaviour and state-of-intention. Understanding the categorical types of data that can be produced by individuals' responses to questions improves the researcher's ability in determining not only what questions should be asked, but also how to ask those questions.

■ **Identify and explain the five basic levels of scales, and discuss the amount of information they can provide a researcher or decision maker.**

The five basic levels of scales are nominal, ordinal, true class interval, hybrid ordinally-interval and ratio. Nominal scales are the most basic and provide the least amount of data. They activate only the 'assignment' scaling property; the raw data do not exhibit relative magnitudes between the categorical subsets of responses. The main data structures (or patterns) that can be derived from nominal raw data are in the form of modes and frequency distributions. Nominal scales would ask respondents about their religious affiliation, gender, type of dwelling, occupation, or last brand of cereal purchased, and so on. The questions require yes/no, like/dislike, or agree/disagree responses.

Ordinal scales require respondents to express their feelings of relative magnitude about the given topic. Ordinal scales activate both the assignment and order scaling properties and allow researchers to create a hierarchical pattern among the possible raw data responses (or scale points) that determine 'greater than/less than' relationships. Data structures that can be derived from ordinal scale measurements are in the forms of medians and ranges as well as modes and frequency distributions. An example of a set of ordinal scale descriptors would be 'complete knowledge', 'good knowledge', 'basic knowledge', 'little knowledge', and 'no knowledge'. While the ordinal scale measurement is an excellent design for capturing the relative magnitudes in respondents' raw responses, it cannot capture absolute magnitudes.

A true class interval scale activates not only the assignment and order scaling properties but also the distance property. This scale measurement allows the researcher to build into the scale elements that demonstrate the existence of absolute differences between each scale point. Normally, the raw scale descriptors will represent a distinct set of numerical ranges as the possible responses to a given question (e.g. 'less than a mile', '1 to 5 miles', '6 to 10 miles', '11 to 20 miles', 'over 20 miles'). With interval scaling designs, the distance between each scale point or response does not have to be equal. Disproportional scale descriptors (e.g. different-sized numerical ranges) can be used. With interval raw data, researchers can develop a number of more meaningful data structures that are based on means and standard deviations, or create data structures based on mode, median, frequency distribution and range.

Ratio scales are the only scale measurements that simultaneously activate all four scaling properties (i.e. assignment, order, distance and origin). Considered the most sophisticated scale design, they allow researchers to identify absolute differences between each scale point and to make absolute comparisons between the respondents' raw responses. Ratio question/ scale structures are designed to allow 'true natural zero' or 'true state of nothing' responses. Normally, though, the respondent is requested to choose a specific singular numerical value. The data structures that can be derived from ratio scale measurements are basically the same as those for interval scale measurements. It is important to remember that the more scaling properties simultaneously activated, the greater the opportunity to derive more detailed and sophisticated data structures and therefore more information. Interval and ratio scale designs are most appropriate to use when researchers want to collect state-of-behaviour or state-of-intention or certain types of state-of-being data.

- **Discuss the hybrid ordinally-interval scale design and the types of information it can provide researchers.**

Some researchers misidentify certain types of ordinal scales as being interval scales. They take an ordinal scale design and assume that the scale has activated the distance and origin scaling properties. This assumption comes about when the researcher assigns a secondary set of numerical scale descriptors (e.g. consecutive whole integers) to the original primary set of ordinal descriptors. There are two main approaches to developing an ordinally-interval scale measurement: (1) using a secondary set of cardinal number descriptors and redefining the complete set of primary scale descriptors (1 = definitely agree, 2 = generally agree, 3 = slightly agree, 4 = slightly disagree, 5 = generally disagree, and 6 = definitely disagree); or (2) using primary descriptors to identify only the extreme end points of a set of secondary cardinal numbers that make up the range of raw scale descriptors or scale points (definitely agree 1 2 3 4 5 6 definitely disagree). Regardless of the method used, for the researcher to believe that the absolute difference between a respondent's response of 'definitely agree' and another respondent's response of 'generally agree' is one unit of agreement is to some extent a leap of faith. Researchers should be careful how they interpret the data structures generated from this hybrid scale design.

- **Discuss the components of scale development and explain why they are critical to gathering primary data.**

In developing high-quality scale measurements, there are three critical components to any complete scale measurement: question/setup; dimensions of the object, construct, or behaviour; and the scale point descriptors. Some of the criteria for scale development are the intelligibility of the questions, the appropriateness of the primary descriptors, the discriminatory power of the scale descriptors, the reliability of the scale, the balancing of positive/ negative scale descriptors, the inclusion of a neutral response choice and desired measures of central tendency (mode, median, and mean) and dispersion (frequency distribution, range, estimated standard deviation). If the highest-quality raw data are to be collected to transform into useful primary information, researchers and practitioners alike must have an integrated understanding of construct development and scale measurement.

Key Terms and Concepts

Appropriateness of scale
    descriptors   400
Assignment property   389
Cardinal numbers   395
Coefficient alpha   403
Construct   379
Construct development   380
Content validity   382
Convergent validity   382
Direct cognitive structural
    analysis   383
Discriminant validity   382
Discriminatory power   401
Distance property   390
Domain of observables   381
Equivalent form   402
Forced-choice scale   404
Free-choice scale   404
Hybrid ordinally-interval scale   394
Intelligibility   400
Internal consistency   403
Measurement   378

Measures of central tendency   406
Measures of dispersion   406
Nominal scale   391
Nomological validity   382
Object   379
Operationalization   383
Order property   389
Ordinal scale   392
Origin property   390
Primary scale point descriptors   395
Ratio scale   397
Scale measurement   388
Scale points   388
Scale reliability   401
Secondary scale point descriptors   395
Split-half test   403
State-of-behaviour data   387
State-of-being data   386
State-of-intention data   387
State-of-mind data   386
Test-retest   402
True class interval scale   393

Review Questions

1 How does the activation of scaling properties determine the amount of data that can be derived from scale measurement designs?

2 Among the five basic levels of scale measurements, which one provides the researcher with the richest amount of data? Why is this particular scale the least used in research practices?

3 What are hybrid ordinally-interval scale measurements? Why do researchers insist on creating them to gather state-of-mind data from respondents? Make sure you also discuss their strengths and weaknesses in your answer.

4 Identify and explain the components that make up any level of scale measurement. What are the interrelationships between these components?

5 When developing the scale point descriptors for a scale measurement, what rules of thumb should the researcher follow?

6 Why should researchers complete construct development activities prior to actually designing a complete scale measurement?

7 What is scale measurement? In your response, explain the difference between an object's, such as a mobile phone's, 'concrete' properties and 'abstract' properties.

8 In construct/scale measurement development, how does discriminant validity differ from convergent validity? Make sure you include definitions of each of these two terms.

9 What are the major differences between ordinal, true interval and ordinally-interval scale measures? In your response include an example of each type of scale design.

10 Identify and discuss the differences between the four scaling properties that are used in scale measurement design. Include an example illustrating each property.

Discussion Questions

1 What are some of the weaknesses of using university students as respondents when developing constructs like 'retail store loyalty', 'telecommunication service quality', or 'attitudes towards kids' advertisements'?

2 For each of the listed scale measurements (A, B, and C), answer the following questions:

   a What type of raw data is being collected?
   b What level of scale measurement is being used?
   c What scaling properties are being activated in the scale?
   d What is the most appropriate measure of central tendency?
   e What is the most appropriate measure of dispersion?
   f What weakness, if any, exists with the scale?

   A How often do you travel for business or pleasure purposes?

For Business	**For Pleasure**
____ 0–1 times per month	____ 0–1 times per year
____ 2–3 times per month	____ 2–3 times per year
____ 4–5 times per month	____ 4–5 times per year
____ 6 or more times per month	____ 6 or more times per year

   B How do you pay for your air ticket that you last bought?

____ Cash	____ Debit card
____ Cheque	____ Air mile redemption
____ Credit card	____ Other _____

   C Please check the one category that best approximates your total personal annual income, before taxes. (Please check only one category.)

____ Under €10,000	____ €30,001–€40,000	____ €60,001–€70,000
____ €10,000–€20,000	____ €40,001–€50,000	____ €70,001–€100,000
____ €20,001–€30,000	____ €50,001–€60,000	____ Over €100,000

3 For each of the listed concepts or objects, design a scale measurement that would allow you to collect data on that concept/object.

   a An excellent long-distance runner.
   b A person's favourite Mexican restaurant.
   c Size of the listening audience for a popular radio station.
   d Public attitudes towards the AC Milan football team.
   e The satisfaction a person has towards his or her automobile.
   f Purchase intention for a new tennis racket.

4 Experience the Internet. Using a browser of your choice, log on to the Internet, go to one of the paid survey websites, and answer one of its questionnaires. Take only the first eight questions and evaluate each of them according to the following five scale measurement issues:

a What type of data is being sought?

b What level of scale measurement is being employed?

c What scaling properties are being activated?

d What would be the most appropriate measure of central tendency for analysing the data?

e What would be the most appropriate measure of dispersion?

5 Identify and discuss the key issues a researcher should consider when choosing a scale measurement for capturing consumers' expressions of satisfaction?

6 Orange is interested in capturing the evaluative judgements of its mobile phone service package. Determine and justify what service attributes should be used to capture the *performance* of its new package. Then design two scale measurements (one as an *ordinal* and the second as an *ordinally-interval*) that would allow Orange to capture the necessary performance data.

7 The local Volvo dealership is interested in collecting data to answer the following research question: 'How likely are young adults to purchase a new automobile within a year after graduating from university?' Design a nominal, ordinal, true class interval, hybrid ordinally-interval and ratio scale measurement that will allow the dealership to collect the required data. In your opinion, which one of your designs would be most useful to the dealership? And why?

8 Recall our continuing case about Jimmy Spices Restaurant. Management would like to capture some data from current customers that would help address the following set of research questions: (a) Which type of food items do customers most prefer? (b) How often do customers dine out at ethnic theme restaurants per month? (c) How important are food prices, food quality, restaurant atmosphere, and service in customers' process of selecting a restaurant to dine at? and (d) How many people make up their current household? Using your understanding from this chapter, develop the following scale measurements:

a Develop an *ordinal* scale measurement that would capture data for addressing 'Which type of food items do customers most prefer?'

b Develop a *true class interval* scale measurement that would capture data for addressing 'How often do customers dine out at ethnic theme restaurants per month?'

c Develop a *hybrid ordinally-interval* scale measurement that would capture data for addressing 'How important are food prices, food quality, restaurant atmosphere, and service in customers' process of selecting a restaurant to dine at?'

d Develop a *ratio* scale measurement that would provide the data to address the research question concerning 'current household size'.

Chapter 12

Attitude Scale Design

LEARNING OBJECTIVES

After reading this chapter, you will be able to

- ☑ Discuss what an attitude is and its three components.

- ☑ Design Likert, semantic differential and behaviour intention scales, and explain their strengths and weaknesses.

- ☑ Discuss the differences between noncomparative and comparative scale designs as well as the appropriateness of rating and ranking scale measurements.

- ☑ Identify and discuss the critical aspects of consumer attitudes and other marketplace phenomena that require measurement to allow us to make better decisions.

- ☑ Discuss the overall rules of measurement and explain the differences between single versus multiple measures of a construct as well as direct versus indirect measures.

> For the future, it would be relatively easy to 'type' any subsequent respondent as belonging to one or other of the nine mindsets by asking them to react to the most differentiating of the 20 attitudinal statements in this study.
>
> *–Vikki Schwebel*
> *Research Director, Healthcare Research Worldwide, Wallingford, England*

Attempts from Both Sides of the Atlantic to Define and Measure the Attitude Scale of 'Consumer Engagement'

Engagement: noun. Action of engaging; state of being engaged; appointment made with another person; moral commitment; battle
From the Concise Oxford Dictionary

Even a dictionary proves little help in settling the debate about what marketers actually mean when they talk about consumer engagement.

The word, the latest buzzword in the marketing industry, is on the lips of almost every advertiser, media buyer and media owner one talks to, but as Mark Greenstreet, managing director of communications research agency Carat Insight based in London, puts it: 'It's a word around an ill-defined concept. As it is currently used, engagement can mean pretty much what anyone wants it to mean.'

The importance of consumer engagement in marketing and advertising is that it relates to the efficiency at getting consumers to buy in to a brand message and, if luck presides with the seller, buy the brand itself.

Bob Barocci, president and CEO of the Advertising Research Foundation (ARF) in the US, urges studies in order to get some common understanding as to what it is and how it can be measured.

The ARF previously published a working definition: 'Engagement is turning on a prospect to a brand idea enhanced by the surrounding context.' However, it is likely to be more than just 'turning on a prospect'. 'How to turn on a mind is where engagement begins', says Bob Barocci.

This sounds like a quest to find the brain's 'buy button' – the holy grail for many advertisers.

'We don't quite know how the process goes from engagement to behaviour', says Bob Barocci. 'But there has to be an event or activity in the brain that happens as a result of contact with the marketing communication'.

Mark Greenstreet also put forward his view on the issue: 'In certain respects, this is something that is built into the UK industry standard measurement survey for posters and outdoor. All other media measure an opportunity to see. They measure the probability that someone was in the environs of the advertisement; that they were a reader of the newspaper; or they were in the room when the TV was switched on and the advertisement was playing; or that they were listening to a commercial radio station. With outdoor, they combine that probability of being in the environment of the advertisement and net it down through another study of 'probably have seen'. But that is about improving the likelihood of exposure to the advertisement. It is a long way from some of the grander concepts that have been used around engagement.'

As an offshoot of Carat Insight, Mark Greenstreet and his team hear first hand the importance of engagement. 'Probably our biggest concern – which relates to engagement – is 'holism': the ability to capture the effect of a wide range of communications,' he says.

'Capturing posters versus television versus radio is one problem, but then when you move into below-the-line, direct mail, public relations and the effect of competitive advertising, that's a wide range of contacts. And it's not just the fact that there are a wide range of contacts, it's that unless you measure a wide range, how can you be sure which of those things have had the influence that you're ultimately seeing.'

Erwin Ephron, a noted thinker on media and advertising in the US, comments: 'Engagement is more than search for accountability. It is a cry for help. Advertising has become more fragmented, more costly, and less effective. Many advertisers hope engagement will be the tool for making things better. A system for improving consumer response.'

That is still to be determined and answers to the two key questions – what is engagement, and how do we measure it? – could still be a long way off. 'We are hoping it's not a 10-year journey,' says Bob Barocci, 'but it could be.'

Source: Research Magazine, News Archive, www.research-live.com

Value of Attitude Measurement in Information Research

In today's business world, more and more marketers are attempting to better understand their customers' attitudes towards their products, services and delivery systems, as well as those of their competitors. However, as the opening example demonstrates, it may be very difficult, if not nearly impossible, to identify and measure a particular kind of attitude or feeling.

This chapter continues the discussion of scale measurement begun in Chapter 11 and builds on the concepts discussed in earlier chapters. The chapter focuses on scales used to collect attitudinal responses. As we will see below, attitude in its full definition encompasses emotions and behavioural intentions. These scales have a common link in that they are typically used to collect state-of-mind and state-of-intention data from respondents. They include non-comparative rating and comparative ranking scales.

In addition, there are several fundamental principles from earlier chapters that you need to think about as you read this chapter: (1) raw data, data structures and information are not the same things – they are unique concepts with different origins and uses (Chapter 2); (2) raw data are a given set of responses to a stated question (Chapters 2, 8, and 9); and (3) a complete scale measurement consists of three components: the question, the scale dimensions and attributes and the scale point descriptors (Chapter 11). The importance of the last principle cannot be overstated. If the overall goal is to collect high quality data to transform into useful primary information, researchers and practitioners alike must have a full understanding of the relationships that exist among the three components.

The Nature of Attitudes and Marketplace Behaviours

Many businesses today are attaching more importance to identifying consumers' attitudes as a way to determine their strengths and weaknesses. Attitudes are useful in explaining consumers' and industrial buyers' observable marketplace behaviours. Yet measuring attitudes and their components is a difficult process that uses less precise scales than those found in the physical sciences. Complete treatment of the theory of attitudes goes well beyond the scope of this chapter. For those who would like additional information, we suggest that you go to a consumer behaviour textbook or to the *Handbook of Consumer Behavior* by T. S. Robertson and H. H. Kassarjian or *Readings in Attitude Theory and Behavior* by Martin Fishbein.

An **attitude** is a learned predisposition to act in a consistent positive or negative way to a given object, idea, or set of information. Attitudes are state-of-mind constructs that are not directly observable. The true structure of an attitude lies in the mind of the individual holding that attitude. To accurately capture consumers' attitudes, researchers must be able to understand the dimensions of the relevant attitude construct.

> **Attitude** A learned predisposition to react in a consistent positive or negative way to a given object, idea, or set of information.

Components of Attitudes

Attitudes can be thought of as having three components: cognitive, affective and behavioural. Marketing researchers and decision makers need to understand all three components.

Cognitive Component

The **cognitive component** of an attitude is the person's beliefs, perceptions and knowledge about an object and its attributes. For example, as a university student you may believe that your university

- Is a prestigious place to get a degree.
- Has excellent teachers.
- Is a good value for the money.
- Needs more and better computer laboratories.

> **Cognitive component** The part of an attitude that represents a subject's beliefs, perceptions, and knowledge about a specified object and its attributes.

These beliefs represent the cognitive component of your attitude towards your university. Your beliefs may or may not be true, but they represent reality to you. The more positive beliefs you have of your university and the more positive each belief is, the more favourable the overall cognitive component is to be.

Affective Component

The **affective component** of an attitude is the person's emotions or feelings towards a given object. This component is the one most frequently expressed when a person is asked to verbalize his or her attitude towards some object, person, or phenomenon. For example, if you claim you 'love your university' or 'your university has the best athletes or smartest students' you are expressing your emotions or feelings. These emotions or feelings are the affective component of your attitude about your university. Your overall emotions or feelings about your university may be based on years of observing it, or they may be based on little actual knowledge. Your attitude could change as you are exposed to more information (e.g. from your first to your senior year), or it may remain essentially the same. Finally, two individuals may have different affective responses to the same experience (e.g. one student may like a particular lecturer teaching approach while another one may hate it).

> **Affective component** The part of an attitude that represents the person's emotional feelings held towards the given object.

Behavioural Component

The **behavioural component**, also sometimes referred to as a *conative* component, is a person's intended or actual behavioural response to an object. For example, your decision to apply to your university for a MSc degree programme is the behavioural component of your attitude. The behavioural component is an observable outcome driven by the interaction of a person's cognitive component (beliefs) and affective component (strength of beliefs) as they relate to a particular object. The behavioural component may represent future intentions (e.g. your plan to get an MSc degree after you finish your bachelor's degree), but it should usually be limited to a specific time period. Recommendations also represent a behavioural component (e.g. recommending that another student take a class from a particular professor).

> **Behavioural (conative) component** The part of an attitude that represents a person's intended or actual behavioural response to the given object.

Attitudes are a complex area to understand fully. For those who wish to learn more we have included Appendix 3 at the end of the book with more complete coverage. In the next section we discuss the different scales used to measure attitudes.

Scales to Measure Attitudes

Although the defined research problem and research objectives dictate which type of scale measurement a researcher should use, there are several types of attitudinal scaling formats that have proven to be useful in many different situations. The following section discusses three attitude scale formats: Likert scales, semantic differential scales and behaviour intention scales. Exhibit 12.1 shows the general steps in the construct development/scale measurement process.

Likert Scale

A **Likert scale** asks respondents to indicate the extent to which they either agree or disagree with a series of belief statements about a given object. Usually the scale format is balanced between agreement and disagreement scale point descriptors. Named after its original developer, Rensis Likert, this scale typically has five scale point descriptors: 'strongly agree', 'agree', 'neither agree

> **Likert scale** An ordinal scale format that asks respondents to indicate the extent to which they agree or disagree with a series of belief statements about a given object.

EXHIBIT 12.1 A General Construct Development/Scale Measurement Process

Process Steps	Key Activities
1. Identify and Define the Construct	Determine Dimensionality of Construct
2. Create Initial Pool of Attribute Items	Determine Theory, Secondary Data, Qualitative Research
3. Assess and Select a Reduced Set of Items	Perform Structural Analysis and Qualitative Judgement
4. Construct Initial Scale Measurement and Pretest	Conduct Pilot Study, Collect Data from Pretest Sample
5. Do Appropriate Statistical Data Analysis	Conduct Construct Validity and Scale Reliability Tests
6. Refine and Purify Scale Measurement	Eliminate Irrelevant Attribute Items
7. Collect More Data on Purified Scale Measurement	Select New Sample of Subjects from Defined Target Population
8. Statistically Evaluate Scale Measurement	Conduct Validity, Reliability, Generalizability Tests
9. Decide on Final Scale Measurement	Include Scale Measurement in Final Questionnaire

nor disagree', 'disagree', 'strongly disagree'. A series of hierarchical steps is followed in developing a Likert scale:

Step 1: Identify and understand the concept to be studied; let's assume the concept is political climate.

Step 2: Assemble a large number of belief statements (e.g. 50 to 100) concerning the general public's attitude towards political climate.

Step 3: Subjectively classify each statement as having either a 'favourable' or an 'unfavourable' relationship to the specific attitude under investigation. Then, the entire list of statements is pretested using a sample of respondents.

Step 4: Respondents decide the extent to which they either agree or disagree with each statement, using the intensity descriptors 'strongly agree', 'agree', 'neither agree nor disagree', 'disagree', and 'strongly disagree'. Each response is then given a numerical weight, such as 5, 4, 3, 2, 1. For favourable statements, a weight of 5 would be given to a 'strongly agree' response; for unfavourable statements, a weight of 5 could be given to a 'strongly disagree' response.

Step 5: A respondent's overall attitude score is calculated by the summation of the weighted values associated with the statements rated.

Step 6: Only statements that appear to discriminate between the high and low total scores are retained in the analysis. One possible method is a simple comparison of the top 25 per cent of the total mean scores with the bottom 25 per cent of total mean scores.

Step 7: In determining the final set of statements (e.g. 20 to 25), statements that exhibit the greatest differences in mean values between the top and bottom total scores are selected.

Step 8: Using the final set of statements, steps 3 and 4 are repeated in a full study.

By using the summation of the scores associated with all the statements, the researcher can tell whether a person's attitude towards the object is positive or negative. For example, the maximum favourable score on a 25-item scale would be 125 ($5 \times 25 = 125$). Therefore a person scoring 110 would usually be regarded as holding a positive (favourable) attitude. Another respondent who scores 45 would be taken as holding a negative attitude towards the object. The total scores do not identify any of the possible differences that might exist on an individual statement basis between respondents.

The Likert scale has been extensively modified by marketing researchers over the years. Today, the modified Likert scale expands the original five-point format to either a six-point forced-choice format with such scale point descriptors as 'definitely agree', 'generally agree', 'slightly agree', 'slightly disagree', 'generally disagree', 'definitely disagree' or a seven-point free-choice format with these same descriptors plus 'neither agree nor disagree' in the middle. In addition, many researchers treat the Likert scale format as an interval scale.

Despite the popular notion that Likert scales can measure a person's complete attitude, in reality they can capture only the cognitive components of a person's attitude and are therefore only partial measures. They do not capture the different possible intensity levels of expressed affective or behavioural components of a person's attitude. This misunderstanding of a Likert scale's capability may account for the scale's weak interpretive results in situations where identifying and measuring respondents' attitudes are critical to solving a particular marketing research problem.

Likert scales are feasible for research designs that use self-administered surveys, personal surveys or online surveys to collect the data. It is difficult to administer a Likert scale over the telephone because respondents have trouble visualizing and remembering the relative magnitudes of agreement and disagreement that make up the scale point descriptors. Exhibit 12.2 illustrates an example of a partially modified Likert scale in a self-administered survey.

EXHIBIT 12.2 **Example of a Partial Modified Likert Scale**

For each of the listed statements, please check the one response that best expresses the extent to which you agree or disagree with that statement.

Statement	Definitely Agree	Generally Agree	Slightly Agree	Slightly Disagree	Generally Disagree	Definitely Disagree
I buy **many things** with a credit card.	——	——	——	——	——	——
I wish we had **a lot more** money.	——	——	——	——	——	——
My friends **often come** to me for advice.	——	——	——	——	——	——
I am **never influenced** by advertisements.	——	——	——	——	——	——

To point out the interpretive difficulties associated with the Likert scale, we have used boldface in each of the statements in Exhibit 12.2 for the words that indicate a single level of intensity. For example, in the first statement (I buy many things with a credit card), the words 'many things' signify the intensity level. If the respondent checks the 'generally disagree' response, it would be a leap of faith for the researcher to interpret that response to mean that the respondent buys only a few things with a credit card. In addition, it would be a speculative guess on the part of the researcher to deduce that the respondent's attitude towards purchasing products or services with a credit card is unfavourable. The intensity level assigned to the agree/disagree scale point descriptors does not truly represent the respondent's attitude associated with the belief response. It identifies only the extent to which the respondent thinks the statement represents his or her own belief about credit card purchases.

Let's take the last statement in Exhibit 12.2 (I am never influenced by advertisements) as another example. The key words in this statement are 'never influenced'. If the respondent checks 'definitely disagree', it would again be the researcher's subjective guess that the response means that the respondent is very much influenced by advertisements. In reality, all that the 'definitely disagree' response indicates is that the statement is not one that the respondent would make. No measure of feeling can be attached to the statement.

Likert scales can also be used to identify and assess psychographic traits of individuals. To see how international marketing research companies use attitude and psychographic scale measurements to profile consumers across Latin American countries, visit the book's website at www.mhhe.com/shiu09 and follow the links.

Semantic Differential Scale

Another rating scale used quite often in marketing research endeavours is the **semantic differential scale**. This type of scale is unique in its use of bipolar adjectives (good/bad, like/dislike,

> **Semantic differential scale** A unique bipolar scale format that captures a person's thoughts or feelings about a given object.

competitive/noncompetitive, helpful/unhelpful, high quality/low quality, dependable/undependable, etc.) as the endpoints of a symmetrical continuum. Usually there will be one object and a related set of factors, each with its own set of bipolar adjectives to measure either a cognitive or an affective element. Because the individual scale point descriptors are not identified, each bipolar scale appears to be a continuum. More often than not, semantic differential scales will use between five and seven scale descriptors, though only the endpoints are identified. Respondents are asked to select the point on the continuum that best expresses their thoughts or feelings about the given object.

In most cases a semantic differential scale will use an odd number of scale points, thus creating a so-called neutral response that symmetrically divides the positive and negative poles into two equal parts. An interpretive problem that arises with an odd-number scale point format comes from the natural neutral response in the middle of the scale. A neutral response usually has little or no diagnostic value to the researcher or decision maker. Sometimes it is interpreted as meaning 'no opinion', 'don't know', 'neither/nor', or 'average'. None of these interpretations gives much information to the researcher. To overcome this problem, the researcher can use an even-point (or forced-choice) format and incorporate a 'not applicable' response out to the side of the bipolar scale.

A semantic differential scale is one of the few attitudinal scale formats that enables the researcher to collect both cognitive and affective data for any given factor. Although some researchers believe a semantic differential scale can be used to measure a person's complete attitude about an object, this scale format is more appropriate for identifying a 'perceptual image profile' about the object of concern.

The actual design of a semantic differential scale can vary from situation to situation. To help you understand the benefits and weaknesses associated with design differences, we present three different formats and discuss the pros and cons of each. In the first situation, the researcher is interested in developing a credibility scale that can be used by Nike to assess the credibility of Tiger Woods as a spokesperson in TV or print advertisements for Nike brands of personal grooming products. The researcher determines that the credibility construct consists of three factors – (1) expertise, (2) trustworthiness and (3) attractiveness – with each factor measured using a specific set of five bipolar scales (see Exhibit 12.3).

Randomization of the Positive and Negative Pole Descriptors

While the semantic differential scale format in Exhibit 12.3 appears to be correctly designed, there are several technical problems that may create response bias. First, notice that all the positive pole descriptors are arranged on the left side of each scale and the negative pole descriptors are all on the right side. This approach can cause a **halo effect bias**. That is, it tends to lead the respondent to react more favourably to the positive poles on the left side than to the negative poles on the right side. To prevent this problem, the researcher should randomly mix the positions of the positive and negative pole descriptors.

Halo effect bias A generalization from the perception of one outstanding factor, attribute, or trait to an overly favourable evaluation on the whole object.

EXHIBIT 12.3 Example of a Semantic Differential Scale Format for Tiger Woods as a Credibility Spokesperson

Now with respect to Tiger Woods as the spokesperson for Nike golf apparel, we would like to know your opinions about the expertise, trustworthiness, and attractiveness that you believe he brings to the advertisement. Each dimension has five factors. For each listed factor, **please check the line that best expresses your opinion about that factor**.

Expertise:

Knowledgeable	___	___	___	___	___	___	___	Unknowledgeable
Expert	___	___	___	___	___	___	___	Not an Expert
Skilled	___	___	___	___	___	___	___	Unskilled
Qualified	___	___	___	___	___	___	___	Unqualified
Experienced	___	___	___	___	___	___	___	Inexperienced

Trustworthiness:

Reliable	___	___	___	___	___	___	___	Unreliable
Sincere	___	___	___	___	___	___	___	Insincere
Trustworthy	___	___	___	___	___	___	___	Untrustworthy
Dependable	___	___	___	___	___	___	___	Undependable
Honest	___	___	___	___	___	___	___	Dishonest

Attractiveness:

Sexy	___	___	___	___	___	___	___	Not Sexy
Beautiful	___	___	___	___	___	___	___	Ugly
Attractive	___	___	___	___	___	___	___	Unattractive
Classy	___	___	___	___	___	___	___	Not Classy
Elegant	___	___	___	___	___	___	___	Plain

Lack of Extreme Magnitude Expressed in the Pole Descriptors

A second response problem with the scale format displayed in Exhibit 12.3 is that the descriptors at the ends of each scale do not express the extreme intensity associated with end poles. The respondent is asked to check one of seven possible lines to express his or her opinion, but only the two end lines are given narrative meaning. The researcher can only guess how the respondent is interpreting the other positions between the two endpoints. Let's take, for example, the 'dependable/undependable' scale for the trustworthiness factor. Notice the extreme left scale position represents 'dependable' and the extreme right scale position represents 'undependable'. Because dependable and undependable are natural dichotomous phrase descriptors, the scale design does not allow for any significant magnitudes to exist between them. The logical question is what do the other five scale positions represent, which in turn raises the question of whether or not the scale truly is a continuum ranging from dependable to undependable. This problem can be corrected by attaching a narratively expressed extreme magnitude to the bipolar descriptors (e.g. 'extremely' dependable and 'extremely' undependable).

Use of Non-bipolar Descriptors to Represent the Poles

A third response problem that occurs in designing semantic differential scales relates to the inappropriate narrative expressions of the scale descriptors. In a good semantic differential scale design, the individual scales should be truly bipolar so that a symmetrical scale can be designed. Sometimes the researcher will express the negative pole in such a way that the positive one is not really its opposite. This creates a skewed scale design that is difficult for the respondent to interpret correctly.

Take, for example, the 'expert/not an expert' scale in the 'expertise' dimension in Exhibit 12.3. While the scale is dichotomous, the words 'not an expert' do not allow the respondent to interpret any of the other scale points as being relative magnitudes of that phrase. Other than that one endpoint being described as 'not an expert', all the other scale points would have to represent some intensity of 'expert', thus creating a skewed scale towards the positive pole. Interpreting 'not an expert' as really meaning 'extremely' not an expert makes little or no diagnostic sense.

Researchers must be careful when selecting bipolar descriptors to make sure the words or phrases are truly extreme bipolar in nature and they allow for creating symmetrical scale designs. For example, the researcher could use pole descriptors such as 'complete expert' and 'complete novice' to correct the above-described scale point descriptor problem.

Matching Standardized Intensity Descriptors to Pole Descriptors

The scale design used by ABN AMRO Bank N.V. in a bank image study, as shown in Exhibit 12.4, eliminates the three problems we discussed in the example of Exhibit 12.3. In addition, this bank image example gives narrative expression to the intensity level of each scale point. Notice that all the separate poles and scale points in between them are anchored by the same set of intensity descriptors ('very', 'moderately', 'slightly', 'neither one nor the other', 'slightly', 'moderately', 'very'). In using standardized intensity descriptors, however, the researcher must be extra careful in determining the specific phrases for each pole – each phrase must fit the set of intensity descriptors in order for the scale points to make complete sense to the respondent. Take, for example, the 'makes you feel at home/makes you feel uneasy' scale in Exhibit 12.4. The intensity descriptor of 'very' does not make much sense when applied to that scale (i.e. 'very makes you feel at home' or 'very makes you feel uneasy'). Thus, including standardized intensity descriptors in a semantic differential scale design may force the researcher to limit the choice of bipolar phrases to describe or evaluate the object of concern. This in turn raises questions about the appropriateness of the data collected using this type of scale design.

The fundamentals discussed in Chapter 11 can help the researcher learn how to correctly develop customized scales to collect the most appropriate attitudinal data for the given marketing research problem. To illustrate this point, Exhibit 12.5 shows a semantic differential scale used by the AA (the Automobile Association) to collect attitudinal data about its performance perceived by its customers. Notice that each of the 14 different features that make up the AA's service profile has its own bipolar scale communicating the intensity level for the positive and negative poles. This reduces the possibility the respondent will misunderstand the scale's continuum range. This example also illustrates the use of an 'NA' – not applicable – response as a replacement for the more traditional midscale neutral response. After the data are collected from this scale format, the researcher can calculate the aggregate mean value for each of the 14 features, plot those mean values on each of their respective scale lines, and graphically display the results using 'profile' lines. The result is an overall profile that depicts the AA's service performance patterns (see Exhibit 12.6). In addition, the researcher can use the same scale and collect raw data on several competing automobile service providers, then show the semantic differential profile for each of the competitors under investigation.

EXHIBIT 12.4 Example of a Semantic Differential Scale Used by ABN AMRO Bank N.V. That Expresses Each Scale Point Descriptor

For each of the following banking features, please check the one line that best expresses your impression of that feature as it relates to ABN AMRO Bank N.V.

	Very	Moderately	Slightly	Neither One nor the Other	Slightly	Moderately	Very	
Courteous Employees	____	____	____	____	____	____	____	Discourteous Employees
Helpful Staff	____	____	____	____	____	____	____	Unhelpful Staff
Unattractive Exterior	____	____	____	____	____	____	____	Attractive Exterior
Competitive Rates	____	____	____	____	____	____	____	Noncompetitive Rates
Limited Service Offerings	____	____	____	____	____	____	____	Wide Variety of Service Offerings
Good Operating Hours	____	____	____	____	____	____	____	Bad Operating Hours
High Quality Service	____	____	____	____	____	____	____	Low Quality Service
Unreliable	____	____	____	____	____	____	____	Reliable
Successful Bank	____	____	____	____	____	____	____	Unsuccessful Bank
Makes You Feel at Home	____	____	____	____	____	____	____	Makes You Feel Uneasy

EXHIBIT 12.5 Example of a Semantic Differential Scale for AA

From your personal experiences with AA's service representatives, please rate the performance of AA on the basis of the following listed features. Each feature has its own scale ranging from 'one' (1) to 'six' (6). **Please circle the response number that best describes how AA has performed on that feature**. For any feature that you feel is not relevant to your evaluation, please circle the (NA) – Not applicable – response code.

Cost of Repair/ Maintenance Work	(NA)	Extremely High	6	5	4	3	2	1	Very Low, Almost Free
Appearance of Facilities	(NA)	Very Professional	6	5	4	3	2	1	Very Unprofessional
Customer Satisfaction	(NA)	Totally Dissatisfied	6	5	4	3	2	1	Truly Satisfied
Promptness in Delivering Service	(NA)	Unacceptably Slow	6	5	4	3	2	1	Impressively Quick
Quality of Service Offerings	(NA)	Truly Terrible	6	5	4	3	2	1	Truly Exceptional
Understands Customer Needs	(NA)	Really Understands	6	5	4	3	2	1	Doesn't Have a Clue

Credibility of AA	(NA)	Extremely Credible	6	5	4	3	2	1	Extremely Unreliable
AA's Keeping of Promises	(NA)	Very Trustworthy	6	5	4	3	2	1	Very Deceitful
AA's Services Assortment	(NA)	Truly Full Service	6	5	4	3	2	1	Only Basic Service
Prices/Rates/Charges of Services	(NA)	Much Too High	6	5	4	3	2	1	Great Rates
Service Personnel's Competence	(NA)	Very Competent	6	5	4	3	2	1	Totally Incompetent
Employee's Personal Social Skills	(NA)	Very Rude	6	5	4	3	2	1	Very Friendly
AA's Operating Hours	(NA)	Extremely Flexible	6	5	4	3	2	1	Extremely Restrictive
Convenience of AA's Locations	(NA)	Very Easy to Get to	6	5	4	3	2	1	Too Difficult to Get to

EXHIBIT 12.6 Example of AA's Performance Profile Compared with Two Hypothetical Competitors

Cost of Repair/Maintenance Work	:	Extremely High	6	5	4	3	2	1	Very low, Almost F
Appearance of Facilities	:	Very Professional	6	5	4	3	2	1	Very Unprofession
Customer Satisfaction	:	Totally Dissatisfied	6	5	4	3	2	1	Truly Satisfied
Promptness in Delivering Service	:	Unacceptably Slow	6	5	4	3	2	1	Impressively Quick
Quality of service offerings	:	Truly Terrible	6	5	4	3	2	1	Truly Exceptional
Understands Customer needs	:	Really Understands	6	5	4	3	2	1	Doesn't Have a Clu
Credibility of AA	:	Extremely Credible	6	5	4	3	2	1	Extremely Unrelial
AA's Keeping of Promises	:	Very Trustworthy	6	5	4	3	2	1	Very Deceitful
AA's Services Assortment	:	Truly Full Service	6	5	4	3	2	1	Only Basic Service
Prices/Rates/Charges of Services	:	Much Too High	6	5	4	3	2	1	Great Rates
Service Personnel's Competence	:	Very Competent	6	5	4	3	2	1	Totally Incompeter
Employee's Personal Social Skills	:	Very Rude	6	5	4	3	2	1	Very Friendly
AA's Operating Hours	:	Extremely Flexible	6	5	4	3	2	1	Extremely Limited
Convenience of AA's Locations	:	Very Easy to Get to	6	5	4	3	2	1	Too Difficult to Ge

AA ———— Competitor A - - - - - - Competitor B ————

Behaviour Intention Scale

Behaviour intention is the last stage of attitude, and **behaviour intention scale** is one of the most widely used scale formats in commercial marketing research. In using this scale the researcher or decision maker is attempting to obtain some idea of the likelihood that people would purchase a product or service, or adopt a specific action (e.g. attendance, shopping, usage), in a future time frame. In general, the behaviour intention scale has been found to be a good predictor of consumers' propensity to purchase non-durable and durable consumer products.

> **Behaviour intention scale** A type of rating scale designed to capture the likelihood that people would purchase a product or service, or adopt a specific action, in a future time frame.

Behaviour intention scales are easy to construct. Consumers are asked to make a subjective judgement on their likelihood of buying a product or service, or taking a specified action. The scale point descriptors typically used with a behaviour intention scale are 'definitely would', 'probably would', 'not sure', 'probably would not', and 'definitely would not'. For example, for a performing arts centre's interest in identifying how likely it is that people will attend a variety of performing arts events, see Exhibit 12.7, which illustrates the behaviour intention scale the centre management team could use to collect the raw behaviour intention data. Note that this scale uses a forced-choice design by not including the middle scale point of 'not sure.'

EXHIBIT 12.7 Example of Behaviour Intention Scale for Determining Attendance at Performing Arts Events

Now with respect to the next six months, we would like to know the extent to which you would consider attending various types of performing arts events if they were held in your region of residence.

Next to each type of event, please check the one box that best expresses the extent to which you would consider attending within the next six months.

Type of Event	Definitely Would Consider Attending	Definitely Would Consider Attending	Probably Would Not Consider Attending	Definitely Would Not Consider Attending
I. Music Concerts				
Popular Music	☐	☐	☐	☐
Jazz Music	☐	☐	☐	☐
Country Music	☐	☐	☐	☐
Bluegrass Music	☐	☐	☐	☐
Classical Music	☐	☐	☐	☐
Chamber Music	☐	☐	☐	☐
II. Theatrical Productions				
Drama	☐	☐	☐	☐
Comedy	☐	☐	☐	☐
Melodrama	☐	☐	☐	☐
Musical	☐	☐	☐	☐
III. Dance Productions				
Classical Dance	☐	☐	☐	☐
Modern Dance	☐	☐	☐	☐
Jazz	☐	☐	☐	☐
Folk Dance	☐	☐	☐	☐

It is important to remember that when designing a behaviour intention scale, you should include a specific time frame (e.g. 'would consider attending in the next six months') in the question portion of the scale. Without an expressed time frame, you increase the possibility that the respondents will bias their responses towards the 'definitely would' or 'probably would' scale categories.

To increase the clarity of the scale point descriptors, the researcher can attach a percentage equivalent expression to each one. To illustrate this concept, let's assume that a Norwegian researcher is interested in knowing how likely it is that consumers will shop at selected clothing stores within the following month in Norway. The following set of scale points can be used to obtain the intention data: 'definitely would shop at (90 per cent to 100 per cent chance)'; 'probably would shop at (50 per cent to 89 per cent chance)'; probably would not shop at (10 per cent to 49 per cent chance)'; and definitely would not shop at (less than 10 per cent chance).' Exhibit 12.8 shows what the complete shopping intention scale might look like.

For more examples of Likert, semantic differential, and behaviour intention types of scale designs visit the book's website at www.mhhe.com/shiu09 and follow the links.

Strengths and Weaknesses of Attitude Scale Measurements

Over the last decades, researchers have made significant advances in developing and validating attitudinal scale measurements that can capture the components making up people's attitudes. With these measurements, they can establish marketing models that aim at using attitudes to predict consumer behaviours.

EXHIBIT 12.8 Behaviour Intention Scale: Shopping at Selected Clothing Stores in Norway

When shopping for clothes for yourself or someone else, how likely are you to shop at each of the following stores withing the following month? **(Please check one response for each store type.)**

Clothing Store	Definitely Would Shop At (90 = 100 per cent chance)	Probably Would Shop At (50 = 89 per cent chance)	Probably Would Not Shop At (10 = 49 per cent chance)	Definitely Would Not Shop At (less than 10 per cent chance)
H&M (Hennes & Mauritz AB)	❏	❏	❏	❏
Benetton Group SpA	❏	❏	❏	❏
KappAhl Ab	❏	❏	❏	❏
Coop Norden	❏	❏	❏	❏
Grupo Inditex	❏	❏	❏	❏
Mango	❏	❏	❏	❏
Vivarte	❏	❏	❏	❏
Bestseller	❏	❏	❏	❏
JC	❏	❏	❏	❏
Lindex	❏	❏	❏	❏
Varner Gruppen	❏	❏	❏	❏

However, one must realize that no matter what type of scale measurements is used to capture people's attitudes, there is no one approach that can guarantee accurate prediction of consumer behaviour. The data provided from these scale measurements should not be interpreted as being facts about a given object. Instead, these data and any derived structures should be viewed only as insights into what might be reality at best.

As a rule of thumb, if the research problem involves predicting some type of purchase, consumption, or shopping behaviour, then behavioural intention scales, instead of cognitive and affective aspects of the attitude, would be a better predictor. However, an even stronger predictor of actual behaviour is past behaviour.

On the other hand, if the research problem is that of better understanding why consumers or customers behave or respond as they do in the marketplace, the researcher needs something other than a measurement of their behaviour intentions. Behaviours can be explained, directly or indirectly, by measuring both the cognitive and affective elements of the respondents' attitudes. Read the nearby Closer Look at Research box for a basic understanding of a new attitudinal measurement method called Best-Worst Scaling.

A Closer Look at Research *(Small-Business Implications)*
Online Best-Worst Scaling On the Up

Most small-business owners are constantly in search of different methods to evaluate customer attitudes towards their product and service offers. However, they may be bewildered by the conventional methods of attitudinal measurement as introduced in this chapter. With these conventional methods, prospective respondents may feel difficult to conceptualize, not to mention quantity, subtle differences in degrees of agreement or disagreement along the attitudinal scale. This difficulty can be an important problem for the small-business owners, who are in increasing need to build their brand positioning around precisely such subtleties in attitude and tone, in order to successfully differentiate from their larger counterparts and/or clinch a lucrative market niche.

Best-Worst Scaling, a new attitudinal measurement method which was popularized in a feature article by Marketing Research Society can be an answer to providing the reliable subtlety in responses to attitudinal scale questions. Attitudinal statements are presented in groups of four and individual respondents need only decide which one they agree with most (or consider the most important to them) and which they agree with least (or feel the least important). After responses to all the groups of attitudinal statements are collected, the order of the second and third can be readily determined.

It is the comparative aspect of the Best-Worst Scaling method that is crucial in preserving subtlety. However, it is also this aspect that becomes the main barrier in its adoption, because the number of possible four-way combinations of even 30 statements is vast.

Fortunately, nowadays with the advent of the Internet as an alternative platform to collect primary data from respondents, all of a sudden the Best-Worst Scaling method becomes very workable. As was commented by Chris Wright, director at qubiq-online, based in Wallingford, Oxfordshire, 'Respondents seem to find the Best-Worst Scaling process much more stimulating and engaging than merely rating statements for importance. Moreover, because it's so easy to do on screen, compliance and completion rates are usually very good!'

Source: Research Magazine, News Archive, www.research-live.com

Other Types of Comparative and Non-Comparative Scale Formats

Besides the rating scales discussed earlier, several variations, both comparative and non-comparative, remain popular among marketing research firms. Unfortunately, the terms used to identify these different scale formats vary from one researcher to the next. For example, some researchers refer to a *performance* rating scale format (e.g. example B in Exhibit 12.9) as an *itemized* rating scale format. Other researchers may refer to a similar format as a *numerical* scale, a *monadic* scale, a *composite* scale, or a *category* scale. For now, to avoid confusion, we classify any type of rating or ranking scale format as being either comparative or non-comparative in nature.

Overall, a non-comparative rating scale is used when the objective is to have a respondent express his or her attitudes about a specific object (which can be a product, a person, a

> Non-comparative rating scale A scale format that requires a judgement without reference to another object.

EXHIBIT 12.9 Different Forms of Non-comparative Rating Scales Used in Marketing Research

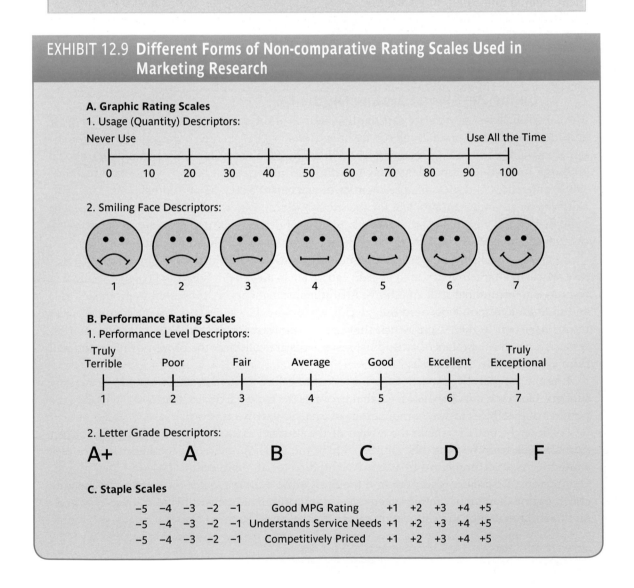

A. Graphic Rating Scales

1. Usage (Quantity) Descriptors:

Never Use   Use All the Time

0   10   20   30   40   50   60   70   80   90   100

2. Smiling Face Descriptors:

1   2   3   4   5   6   7

B. Performance Rating Scales

1. Performance Level Descriptors:

Truly Terrible	Poor	Fair	Average	Good	Excellent	Truly Exceptional
1	2	3	4	5	6	7

2. Letter Grade Descriptors:

A+   A   B   C   D   F

C. Staple Scales

−5	−4	−3	−2	−1	Good MPG Rating	+1	+2	+3	+4	+5
−5	−4	−3	−2	−1	Understands Service Needs	+1	+2	+3	+4	+5
−5	−4	−3	−2	−1	Competitively Priced	+1	+2	+3	+4	+5

phenomenon, etc.) or its attributes without making reference to another object or its attributes. In contrast, a scale format is **comparative rating** in nature when the objective is to have a respondent express their attitude about an object or its attributes on the basis of some other object or its attributes. Within the 'family' of non-comparative scale designs, we describe the three types – *graphic rating* scales, *performance rating* scales and *Stapel* scales – frequently used by marketing researchers. Exhibit 12.9 provides a few examples that illustrate these types of scale designs. Additional examples can be viewed by visiting the book's website at www.mhhe.com/shiu09 and following the links.

Comparative rating scale A scale format that requires a judgement comparing one object against another on the scale.

Graphic rating scales (also referred to as *continuous* rating scales) use a scale point format that presents a respondent with a graphic continuum as the set of possible responses to a question. For example, the first graphic rating scale (usage or quantity descriptors) displayed in Exhibit 12.9 is used in situations where the researcher wants to collect 'usage behaviour' data about an object. Let's say Yahoo wants to determine how frequently Internet users employ its search engine without making reference to any other available search engine alternatives (e.g. Google). In using this type of scale design, the respondents would simply place an 'X' along the graphic 'usage' line where the extreme endpoints of the line have narrative descriptors ('Never Use' and 'Use All the Time') and numerical descriptors (0 and 100), while the remainder of the line is sectioned and described in equally spaced numerical intervals (10, 20, 30, etc.).

Graphic rating scales A scale measure using a scale point format that presents the respondent with some type of graphic continuum as the set of possible raw responses to a given question.

Another popular type of graphic rating scale design is the 'Smiling Faces'. The smiling faces are arranged in a particular order and depict a continuous range from 'very sad' to 'very happy' without providing narrative meaning of the two extreme positions. Typically, the design uses a symmetrical format having equal numbers of happy and unhappy faces with a 'neutral' face in the middle position. This type of visual graphic rating scale design can be used to collect a variety of attitudinal data. It is popular in collecting data from children. For example, let's say Lego, the world famous Danish toy manufacturer, is product testing several new toys among children aged 6 to 10 years. Researchers can have the children play with the toys, then ask them questions about their likes and dislikes. The child answers by pointing to the face that best expresses their feelings about the particular toy.

Graphic rating scales can be constructed easily and are simple to use. They allow the identification of fine distinctions between responses, assuming the respondents have adequate discriminatory abilities. Graphic rating scales are appropriate in self-administered surveys (both online and offline) and personal surveys, but are difficult, if not virtually impossible, to use in telephone surveys.

Performance rating scales are a type of itemized rating scale using a scale point format that allows respondents to express some type of evaluative judgement about the object under investigation. Although these scale designs have the initial appearance of being very similar to a graphic rating scale, the primary difference is that each scale point included is given narrative meaning.

> **Performance rating scales** A scale measure that uses an evaluative scale point format that allows the respondent to express some type of postdecision or behaviour evaluative judgement about an object.

The examples in part B of Exhibit 12.9 illustrate two design possibilities among many a researcher can use. When using performance-level descriptors, the researcher asks respondents to select the response among a list of possible responses that best expresses their evaluative judgement towards the object of interest. The second design in Exhibit 12.9 illustrates the letter grade descriptor design. With this design, the researcher asks the respondent to express his or her performance judgement using a letter grade scheme. This type of design has an inherent flexibility factor in that researchers can easily expand the 6-point format as displayed in Exhibit 12.9 to, say, a 13-point scale ranging from A+ down to F (A+, A, A−, B+, B, B−, C+, C, C−, D+, D, D−, F).

However, this particular scale format has an obvious limitation. Performance rating scales are appropriate for use in self-administered questionnaires or interviewer-to-interviewee personal encounters, but are often problematic for telephone surveys, unless the number of scale point descriptors is kept to three or four. An exception to this is the shorter form of the letter grade design. Because of the inherent understanding and acceptance of this particular design, letter grade descriptors are fairly easy to administer in both traditional and computer-assisted telephone surveys.

A Stapel scale resembles a semàntic differential scale, but there are clear differences. Instead of using two dichotomous descriptive words or phrases as choices with semantic differential scales, Stapel scales use only one word or phrase. In addition, points are generally not visible on a semantic differential scale, yet they are visible on a Stapel scale. Lastly, while five- or seven-point scales are typically used with semantic differential scales, simply an even number of points are needed in the case of Stapel scales, with half of them above the word or phrase and half of them below.

Turning now to comparative rating scales, Exhibit 12.10 illustrates some of the scales associated with rank-order, paired comparison and constant sums rating scale formats. A common characteristic among all these types of comparative scale designs is that the scaling objective is to collect data that enable the researcher to identify and directly compare similarities and differences between two objects of concern, such as products (e.g. Mercedes versus Lexus cars), *people* (e.g. Gordon Brown versus David Cameron), *marketing phenomena* (e.g. shopping online versus shopping offline), *concepts* (e.g. product quality versus service quality), or any of the *attributes* that underline the object under investigation (e.g. importance of different attributes of a retail format). One important point to note here is that comparative scale designs can be used to collect any type of data, including state-of-being, mind, behaviour and intention data.

EXHIBIT 12.10 Different Forms of Comparative Rating Scales Used in Marketing Research

A. Rank-Order Rating Scales

Thinking about the different types of music, please rank your top three preferences of types of music you enjoy listening to by writing in your first choice, second choice, and third choice on the lines provided below.

First Preference: _____

Second Preference: _____

Third Preference: _____

B. Paired-Comparison Rating Scales

We are going to present you with several pairs of traits associated with a salesperson's on-the-job activities. For each pair, please indicate which trait you feel is more important for being a salesperson.

a. trustworthiness	b. competence
a. trustworthiness	b. communication skills
a. trustworthiness	b. personal social skills
a. competence	b. communication skills
a. competence	b. personal social skills
a. communication skills	b. personal social skills

Note: the researcher would want to scramble and reverse the order of these paired comparisons to avoid possible order bias.

C. Constant Sums Rating Scales

Below is a list of seven banking features. Please allocate 100 points among those features such that the allocation represents the importance each feature is to you in selecting 'your' bank. The more points you assign to a feature, the more important that feature is to your selection process. If the feature is 'not at all important', you should not assign it any points. When you have finished, please double-check to make sure your total adds to 100.

Banking Feature	Number of Points
Convenience of location	_____
Operating hours	_____
Charges on services provided	_____
The interest rates on loans	_____
The bank's reputation	_____
The interest rates on savings	_____
Customer services	_____
Operating efficiency	_____
	100 points

Rank-order rating scales use a scale format that enables respondents to compare their own responses by indicating the first preference, second preference, third preference, and so forth,

> **Rank-order rating scales** These allow respondents to compare their own responses by indicating their first, second, third preferences, and so forth, until all the desired responses are placed in a rank order.

until all the desired responses are placed in either a 'highest to lowest' or a 'lowest to highest' rank order. For example, consider the rank-order scale design in Exhibit 12.10. HMV, the largest high street entertainment specialist in the UK, Canada, Hong Kong and Singapore, could use this rank-order scale design to determine the types of music prospective customers would most likely purchase. This format allows for easy comparisons among all the possible responses (types of music), so that the responses that respondents have ranked highly, which can mean high preference, high importance or highly positive feelings, can be identified.

Rank-order rating scales are easy to use in personal surveys and all types of self-administered surveys. Use of rank-order rating scales in traditional or computer-assisted telephone surveys may be difficult, but it is possible as long as the number of items being compared is kept to four or five. When respondents are asked to rank an object's attributes, problems will occur if the respondent's preferred attributes are not part of the listed set of attributes being measured. Another limitation is that only ordinal data can be obtained using rank-order rating scales. Also, the researcher cannot learn anything about the reasoning used by the respondents in making their ranking choices.

Paired-comparison scales use a pre-selected group of tangible/intangible objects or their attributes (e.g. product or service characteristics) that are paired against one another. Respondents are asked to select which one in each pair matches what they should choose according to the question posed to them. Consequently, respondents make a series of paired judgements between the objects (or their attributes). It is important to remember that the number of paired comparisons increases geometrically as a function of the number of objects (or their attributes) being evaluated. For example, the paired-comparison scale shown in Exhibit 12.10 is one of several scales that a company such as Procter & Gamble's (P&G) recruiting team can use to administer to new university graduates seeking employment in its consumer-products sales division. Here, P&G is concerned with the traits of trustworthiness, competence, communication skills, and personal social skills of the new salespersons whom it is going to recruit. By asking a prospective applicant to make a series of paired judgements between these traits, the results can then be compared to P&G's standards to determine how well the applicant matches its desired profile of a salesperson. A potential weakness of this type of scale design is that respondent fatigue can set in if too many attributes and paired choices are included.

> **Paired-comparison scales** This format creates a pre-selected group of tangible/intangible objects or their attributes that are paired against one another; respondents are asked to select the one in each pair based on the question posed to them.

Constant sums scales require the respondent to allocate a given number of points, usually 100, among several objects (tangible or intangible) or their attributes. This format requires the respondent to determine the value of each separate object (or attribute) relative to all the other listed objects or attributes. The resulting value assignments indicate the relative magnitude that each object (or attribute) has to the respondent.

> **Constant sums scales** Require the respondent to allocate a given number of points, usually 100, among several objects or attributes based on the relative magnitude that each object or attribute imposes on the respondent.

Take, for example, the constant sums rating scale displayed in Exhibit 12.10. The hypothetical bank can use this type of scale design to identify which banking features are more important to consumers in influencing their decision of where to bank. This type of comparative scale design is appropriate for use in self-administered surveys and to a lesser extent in personal surveys. Caution must be used with constant sums scales when too many (e.g. more than seven) objects or attributes are included for evaluation, since this design requires a lot of mental energy on the part of the respondent.

For more examples of comparative and non-comparative scale designs, log on to the book's website at www.mhhe.com/shiu09 and follow the links.

Comments on Single-Item and Multiple-Item Scales

Before we conclude our discussion of advanced scale measures, it is worthwhile to make several comments about when and why researchers use single-item and multiple-item scaling formats. First, a scale design can be characterized as being a **single-item scale design** when the data requirement focuses on collecting data about only one attribute of the object or construct being investigated. An easy example to remember is collecting age data. Here the object is 'a person' and the single attribute of interest is that person's 'age'. Only one measure is needed to collect the required age data. The respondent is asked a single question about his or her age and supplies only one possible response to the question. In contrast, marketing research projects that involve collecting attitudinal data require some type of **multiple-item scale design**. Basically, when using a multiple-item scale to measure the object or construct of interest, the researcher will have to measure several attributes simultaneously rather than measuring just one attribute.

> **Single-item scale design** A scale format that collects data about only one attribute of an object or construct.
>
> **Multiple-item scale design** A scale format that simultaneously collects data on several attributes of an object or construct.

The decision to use a single-item versus a multiple-item scale is made in the construct development stage. Two factors play a significant role in the process. First, the researcher must assess the dimensionality of the construct under investigation. Any construct that is viewed as consisting of several different, unique multi-item dimensions will require the researcher to measure each of the items that make up a particular dimension. Second, researchers must deal with the validity and reliability issues of the scales used to collect data. To illustrate these two points, consider the Tiger Woods as a spokesperson example in Exhibit 12.3. Here the main construct of interest was 'credibility as a spokesperson'. Credibility was made up of three key dimensions (expertise, trustworthiness and attractiveness). Each of the dimensions was measured using five different seven-point scale items (e.g. the 'expertise' dimension – knowledgeable/unknowledgeable, expert/not an expert, skilled/unskilled, qualified/unqualified, experienced/inexperienced). Validity and reliability tests should be conducted to ensure the five scale items are reliably measuring what they are supposed to measure.

Another point to remember about multiple-item scales is that there are two types of scales: formative and reflective. A **formative composite scale** is used when each of the individual scale items measures some part of the whole construct. For example, to measure the *overall image* of a Fiat Bravo, the researchers would have to measure the different attributes that make up that automobile's image, such as performance, resale value, fuel efficiency, styling, price, safety features, sound system and craftsmanship. By creating a scale that measures each pertinent attribute, the researcher can sum the parts into a complete (formative) whole that measures the overall image held by respondents towards Fiat Bravo.

> **Formative composite scale** A scale format that uses several individual scale items to measure different parts of the whole construct.

With a **reflective composite scale** design, researchers use multiple items to measure an individual sub-component of a construct. For example, in isolating the investigation to the *performance* dimension of Fiat Bravo, the researcher can use a common performance rating scale and measure those identified attributes (e.g. trouble-free, MPG rating, comfort of ride, workmanship, overall quality, dependability, responsiveness) that make up the performance dimension. Each of these attributes reflects performance and an average of the reflective scale items can be interpreted as a measure of performance.

> **Reflective composite scale** A scale format that uses multiple scale items to measure one component of a construct.

Recap of Key Measurement Design Issues

The main design issues related to both construct development and scale measurement are reviewed below.

Construct Development Issues

Researchers should clearly define and operationalize constructs before they attempt to develop their scales. For each construct being investigated, the researcher must determine its dimensionality traits (i.e. uni- versus multi-dimensional). In a multidimensional construct, all relevant dimensions as well as their related attributes must be identified.

Avoid creating *double-barrelled dimensions*. That is, do not present two different dimensions of a construct as if they are one. For example, when investigating consumers' perceptions of service quality, do not attempt to combine the service provider's technological competence and diagnostic competence as one dimension. Within a singular dimension, avoid using double-barrelled attributes. For example, avoid asking a respondent to rate two attributes simultaneously (e.g. 'indicate to what extent you agree or disagree that European Union should have a more powerful European parliament and should have a president'). For a multidimensional construct, use scale designs in which multiple attribute items are used separately to measure each dimension independently from the other dimensions (see the Tiger Woods example in

Exhibit 12.3). Construct validity assessments should always be performed prior to creating the final scales.

Scale Measurement Issues

When phrasing the question part of a scale, use clear wording and avoid ambiguity. Also avoid using 'leading' words or phrases in any scale measurement's question part.

Regardless of the data collection method, all necessary instructions for both respondent and interviewer should be part of the scale measurement's setup. All instructions should be kept simple and clear. Make sure each attribute item is phrased *unidimensionally* (e.g. avoid double-barrelled item phrases). When determining the appropriate set of scale point descriptors, make sure the descriptors are relevant to the type of data being sought. Use only scale point descriptors and formats that have been pretested and evaluated for scale validity and reliability. Scale point descriptors should have adequate discriminatory power, be mutually exclusive, and make sense to the respondent.

Screening Questions

Screening questions (also referred to as *filter questions*) should always be used in any type of interview. Their purpose is to identify qualified prospective respondents and prevent unqualified respondents from being included in the study. However, bear in mind that it is difficult to use screening questions in self-administered questionnaires, except for computer-assisted surveys. Screening questions need to be separately administered before the beginning of the main interview.

Skip Questions

Skip questions (also referred to as *conditional* or *branching* questions) should be avoided if at all possible. If they are needed, the instructions must be clearly communicated to the respondent and interviewer. Skip questions can appear anywhere within the questionnaire and are used if the next question (or set of questions) should be responded to only by a respondent who meets a previous condition. A simple expression of a skip command might be: 'If you answered "yes" to Question 5, skip to Question 9'. Skip questions help ensure that only specifically qualified respondents answer certain items.

Ethical Responsibility of the Researcher

In the development of scale measurements, the researcher should use the most appropriate scales possible. Intentionally using scale measurements to produce biased information raises questions about the professional ethics of the researcher.

Any set of scale point descriptors used to frame a non-comparative rating scale can be manipulated to bias the results in any direction. Inappropriate scale point descriptors to collect brand image data can be used to create a positive view of one brand or a negative view of a competitor's brand, which does not paint a true picture of the situation. To illustrate this point, let's assume that in creating a seven-point semantic differential scale used to collect the image data for the seven attributes of Zara fashion retail chain's store image (i.e. quality, assortment, style, prices, reputation, location and sales staff's professionalism), the researcher decided not to follow many of the process guidelines for developing scale measurements, including no pretesting of the scales. Instead, he or she just used his intuitive judgement of what he thought the owner of

Zara was hoping for. Consequently, the following semantic differential scale measurement was developed:

For each of the following attributes, please circle the number that best expresses how you would rate that attribute for Zara fashion retail chain.

Quality of Merchandise	Truly Terrible	1	2	3	4	5	6	7	Outstanding
Merchandise Assortment	Limited	1	2	3	4	5	6	7	Extremely Wide
Style of Merchandise	Very Stylish	1	2	3	4	5	6	7	Not Stylish
Merchandise Prices	Extremely High	1	2	3	4	5	6	7	Reasonable
Overall Store Reputation	Very Good	1	2	3	4	5	6	7	Extremely Poor
Store's Location	Very Inconvenient	1	2	3	4	5	6	7	Definitely Convenient
Sales Staff	Very Professional	1	2	3	4	5	6	7	Very Unprofessional

Now, select a retail store of your choice, assume it to be Jackpot, the Danish fashion retail enterprise, and rate that store using the above scale. Interpret the image profile that you create. How objective were your ratings? Did you find yourself rating your store positively like Jackpot? What problems might you have encountered on each attribute?

Ethically, it is important to use balanced scales with comparable positive and negative descriptors. When a researcher does not follow scale development guidelines, responses can be biased. Using the above scale, a researcher can negatively bias evaluations of competitors' image by providing mildly negative descriptors against strong descriptors or vice versa. This example also hints at the need to pretest and establish scale measurements that have adequate validity, reliability and generalizability. Remember, scales that are invalid, are unreliable, or lack generalizability to the defined target population, will provide misleading findings. The principle of 'garbage in garbage out' clearly set in here.

Customer Loyalty Index – Part 2

This is the second part of the European Case Study that began at the end of Chapter 11. Recall that researchers at Burke measured the three main components (i.e. overall customer satisfaction, likelihood of repeat business and likelihood to recommend the company) making up their construct of Secure Customer Index (SCI).

Measuring Customer Loyalty

At Burke, these three components (i.e. overall customer satisfaction, likelihood of repeat business and likelihood to recommend the company) are measured by looking at the combined scores of three survey questions. For example, in examining the overall satisfaction of restaurant customers, we ask, 'Overall, how satisfied were you with your visit to this restaurant?' To examine their likelihood to recommend: 'How likely would you be to recommend this restaurant to your family, friends or colleagues?' And finally, to examine the likelihood of repeat purchases, we ask, 'How likely are you to choose to visit this restaurant again?'

With these three components, and the appropriate scales for each, secure customers would be defined as those giving the highly positive responses across all three components. All other customers would be considered vulnerable or at risk of defecting to a competitor. The degree of vulnerability can be determined from responses to these questions.

When we interpret a company's SCI, we typically compare it to other relevant SCI scores, such as the company's SCI scores in past years, the SCI scores of competitors, and the SCI scores of 'best-in-class' companies. While a company should always strive for higher scores, understanding how 'good' or 'bad' a given score might be is best done in comparative terms.

Customer Loyalty and Market Performance

Increasingly, we are able to link customer loyalty to bottom-line benefits. By examining customer behaviours over time and comparing them to SCI scores, we see a strong connection between secure customers and repeat purchasing of products or services. For example, we examined the relationship between customer loyalty survey data and repeat purchasing levels in the computer industry. Secure customers in this industry were twice as likely to renew contracts than were vulnerable customers. Secure customers were also twice as likely to expand their business with their primary vendor.

As we've continued to look at cases across customer and industry types, we've found other compelling illustrations that show a connection between the index scores and financial or market performance. These findings demonstrate the value of examining index scores not only across an industry but also over time within the same company to determine changes in the proportion of secure customers.

Competition, Customers, and Surveys

As with any measurement, a customer loyalty index may be influenced by other factors depending on the industry, market characteristics, customer types, or research methods. These factors should be considered when interpreting the meaning of any loyalty index. Industries with higher degree of competition tend to produce higher customer loyalty scores than industries with less competition which often means less choices for consumers.

A second factor that may contribute indirectly to a customer loyalty index score is the type of market being examined. In speciality markets where the product is tailored or customized for the customer, loyalty index scores tend to be higher than in general or non-customized markets.

For example, index scores for customers of a specialized software or network configuration would likely be higher than scores for customers of an airline.

The type of customers being measured may also influence the index score. For example, business-to-business customers may score differently from general consumers.

Finally, the data collection method may influence the customer's response. Researchers have long recognized that the different methods used to collect information, such as live interviews, mail surveys and telephone interviews, may produce varying results.

Recognizing these factors is important not only in collecting information but also in interpreting an index. Learning how to minimize or correct these influences will enhance the validity or true 'reading' of a customer loyalty index.

Using Data to Evaluate Your Own Efforts

Businesses committed to customer-driven quality must integrate the voice of the customer into their business operations. A customer loyalty index provides actionable information by demonstrating the ratio of secure customers to vulnerable customers. An index acts as a baseline or yardstick for management to create goals for the organization, and helps to focus efforts for continuous improvement over time. And as changes and initiatives are implemented in the organization, the index's score may be monitored as a way of evaluating those changes and initiatives.

Using a customer loyalty index helps companies better understand their customers. By listening to customers, implementing new actions and continuously monitoring the results, companies can move towards the optimization of their improvement efforts with the goal of winning and keeping customers.

Questions

Using your knowledge from the chapter and the information provided in this illustration, answer each of the following questions. Make sure you can defend your answers.

1 What are potential weaknesses associated with how Burke measured its Secure Customer Index (SCI)? Make sure you clearly identify each weakness and explain why you feel it is a weakness.

2 If you were the head researcher, what types of scale measurement designs would you have used to collect the needed data for calculating SCI? Why? Design a sample of the scale measurements that you would use.

3 Do you agree or disagree with Burke's interpretation of the value they provide their clients using the Customer Loyalty Index? Justify your answer.

Summary of Learning Objectives

■ **Discuss what an attitude is and its three components.**

An *attitude* is a learned predisposition to act in a consistent positive or negative way to a given object, idea, or set of information. Attitudes are state-of-mind constructs that are not directly observable. Attitudes can be thought of as having three components: cognitive, affective and behavioural. Marketing researchers and decision makers need to understand all three components. The *cognitive component* of an attitude is the person's beliefs, perceptions, and knowledge about an object and its attributes. The *affective component* of an attitude is the person's emotional feelings towards a given object. This component is the one most frequently expressed when a person is asked to verbalize his or her attitude towards some object, person, or phenomenon. The *behavioural component*, also sometimes referred to as a *conative component*, is a person's intended or actual behavioural response to an object.

■ **Design Likert, semantic differential and behaviour intention scales, and explain their strengths and weaknesses.**

Likert scale designs uniquely employ a set of agreement/disagreement scale descriptors to capture a person's attitude towards a given object or behaviour. Contrary to popular belief, a Likert scale format does not measure a person's complete attitude, only the cognitive structure. Semantic differential scale formats are exceptional in capturing a person's perceptual image profile about a given object or behaviour. This scale format is unique in that it uses a set of bipolar scales to measure several different yet interrelated factors (both cognitive and affective) of a given object or behaviour.

Multi-attribute affect scales use scale point descriptors that consist of relative magnitudes of an attitude (e.g. 'very important', 'somewhat important', 'not too important', 'not at all important', or 'like very much', 'like somewhat', 'neither like nor dislike', 'dislike somewhat', 'dislike very much'). With respect to behaviour intention scale formats, the practitioner is interested in obtaining some idea of the likelihood that people (e.g. actual or potential consumers, customers, buyers) will demonstrate some type of predictable behaviour towards purchasing an object or service. The scale point descriptors like 'definitely would', 'probably would', 'probably would not', and 'definitely would not' are normally used in an intentions scale format. If the information objective is that of collecting raw data that can directly predict some type of marketplace behaviour, then behaviour intention scales should be used in the study. In turn, if the objective is understanding the reasons that certain types of marketplace behaviour take place, then it is necessary to incorporate scale measurement formats that capture both the person's cognitive belief structures and feelings.

■ **Discuss the differences between noncomparative and comparative scale designs as well as the appropriateness of rating and ranking scale measurements.**

The main difference is that comparative scale measurements require the respondent to do some type of direct comparison between the attributes of the scale from the same known reference point, whereas noncomparative scales rate each attribute independently of the other attributes making up the scale measurement. The data from comparative scales must be interpreted in relative terms and only activate the assignment and order scaling properties. Noncomparative scale data are treated as interval or ratio, and more advanced statistical procedures can be employed in analysing the data structures. One benefit of comparative scales is that they allow for identifying small differences between the attributes, constructs, or objects. In addition, their comparative scale designs require fewer theoretical assumptions and are easier for respondents to understand and respond to than are many of the noncomparative scale designs. However, noncomparative scales provide opportunity for greater insights into the constructs and their components.

■ **Identify and discuss the critical aspects of consumer attitudes and other marketplace phenomena that require measurement to allow us to make better decisions.**

In order for organizations to make informed decisions regarding their suppliers, customers, competitors, employees, or organizational members, they must gather detailed, accurate information. The selection of a supplier may rest partially on their history of on-time delivery, reputation for quality and experience within the industry. Information concerning the preferences, purchase behaviour, shopping patterns, demographics, and attitudes of consumers can be vital to the success or failure of an organization.

Similarly, in-depth profiles of competitors may reveal opportunities or challenges facing the company and can lead to coherent plans designed to create a significant competitive advantage. If consumers prefer a competitor's product, then it would be quite valuable to understand through the use of proper measurement techniques why such preferences exist.

■ **Discuss the overall rules of measurement and explain the differences between single versus multiple measures of a construct as well as direct versus indirect measures.**

No single set of rules exists for all measurements; however, certain standards can be applied to the measurement process. For example, the rules for correctly using a thermometer to measure the temperature of water would be quite different from the rules for the use of a telescope to measure the distance to a star. Even so, the rules must be explicit and detailed so as to allow consistent application of the instrument.

Key Terms and Concepts

Review Questions

1 Conceptually, what is an attitude? Is there one best method of measuring a person's attitude? Why or why not?

2 Explain the major differences between 'rating' and 'ranking' scales. Which is a better scale measurement technique for collecting attitudinal data on salesforce performance of people who sell commercial laser printers? Why?

3 When collecting importance data about the features business travellers use to select a hotel, should a researcher use a balanced or an unbalanced scale measurement? Why?

4 Explain the main differences between using 'even-point' and 'odd-point' scale measurement designs for collecting purchase intention data. Is one approach better than the other? Why?

5 If a semantic differential has eight attribute dimensions, should all the positive pole descriptors be on the left side and all the negative pole descriptors be on the right side of the scale continuum? Why or why not?

6 What are the benefits and limitations of comparative scale measurements? Design a paired-comparison scale that will allow you to determine brand preference between Carlsberg, Stella Artois, Coors and Grolsch beers.

7 What are the weaknesses associated with the use of a Likert scale design to measure customers' attitudes towards the purchasing of products at Waitrose?

Discussion Questions

1 Develop a semantic differential scale that can identify the perceptual profile differences between Burger King and McDonald's fast food restaurants.

2 Explain the differences between a Likert summated scale format and a numeric rating scale format. Should a Likert scale ever be considered an interval scale? Why or why not? Now develop a forced-choice Likert scale measurement that can be used to measure consumers' perceptions about the movie *Titanic*.

3 Design a behaviour intention scale that can answer the following research question: 'To what extent are university students likely to purchase a new automobile within six months after graduating?' Discuss the potential shortcomings of your scale design.

4 Develop an appropriate set of attitudinal scales that would allow you to capture the cognitive and affective components of university students' overall attitude concerning environmentalism.

5 **Experience the Internet.** One company that has been heavily involved in research that uses scale measurements is SRI International, one of the world's largest contract research institutes. It has developed a segmentation technique that uses VALS-type data to classify people into different lifestyle categories. Go to SRI's website at www.future.sri.com:/valshome.html. Take their short survey to determine your VALS (Values and Lifestyles) type. While you are taking the survey, evaluate what scale measurements are being used. What type of possible design bias might exist?

6   What are the main differences between the Fishbein modelling approaches of 'attitude-towards-object' and 'attitude-towards-behaviour'? (see Appendix 3 discussions). Discuss in which situations each of these two modelling approaches would be more appropriate than trying to employ the 'affect global' approach in investigating consumer attitudes.

7   The results from two focus groups conducted on restaurant characteristics among 20 known customers suggested that the following features were thought about during their dining experiences: (1) friendly employees, (2) fun place to eat at, (3) size of portions served, (4) freshness of food, (5) prices, (6) attractiveness of interior, (7) food taste, (8) employees' knowledge, (9) food quality and (10) speed of service. With these insights, the owners of Jimmy Spice's Restaurant want to gain clearer insight into the following three questions: 'How important are those restaurant features to known and prospective customers when selecting a multi-ethnic themed restaurant to eat at?' 'How well does The Jimmy Spice's perform on those features?' and 'What is the likelihood that people will revisit the restaurant within the next 30 days?' To help the owners answer these three research questions, develop a specific scale measurement that could be used to capture the needed data for each of the stated research questions. Make sure that each of your scale measurements include all three components of a scale measurement, i.e. question, specific attributes/dimensions and scale point descriptors.

Chapter 13

Sampling Theory and Sample Size

LEARNING OBJECTIVES

After reading this chapter, you will be able to

☑ Discuss the concept of sampling and list reasons for sampling.

☑ Identify and explain the different roles of sampling in the overall information research process.

☑ Demonstrate the basic terminology used in sampling decisions.

☑ Understand the concept of error in the context of sampling.

☑ Discuss and calculate sampling distributions, standard errors and confidence intervals and how they are used in assessing the accuracy of a sample.

☑ Discuss the factors that must be considered when determining sample size.

☑ Discuss the methods of calculating appropriate sample sizes.

> The importance of sampling should not be underestimated, as it determines to whom the results of your research will be applicable. It is important, therefore, to give full consideration to the sampling strategy to be used and to select the most appropriate.
> *—Joanne Birchall*
> *Researcher, Rainbow Research Ltd., Preston, England*

Sampling Design of the Expenditure and Food Survey in the UK

The Expenditure and Food Survey is an annual sampling survey of private households in the UK, conducted by the Office for National Statistics and Department for Environment, Food and Rural Affairs. It covers various aspects of household income and expenditure for the year concerned. Categories of expenditure include housing, fuel and power, food and drink, tobacco, clothing and footwear, household goods and services, personal goods and services, motoring, fares and other travel costs, leisure goods and services, and miscellaneous items. It is a valuable source of the UK household income and expenditure information for the marketing research industry.

The survey uses a hybrid sampling technique – multi-stage stratified random sampling with clustering – to attain a nationally representative sample. The sample is drawn from the Small Users file of the Postcode Address File (PAF), i.e. the Post Office's list of addresses. It is a collection of over 27 million Royal Mail postal addresses, and is available in a variety of formats including Digital Audio Tape and compact disc.

Postcode sectors are the primary sampling unit. Altogether 672 are randomly selected during the year from a total of 11,598 postcode sectors (as of May 2005) in the UK, which comprise approximately 1.78 million postcodes. Each small user postcode typically has 15 postal addresses, although some postcodes can have up to 100 addresses.

Before the 672 postcode sectors are randomly selected, all the 11,598 postcode sectors should have been arranged in strata defined by Government Office Regions (sub-divided into metropolitan and non-metropolitan areas) and two Census variables – socio-economic group and ownership of cars. This is to ensure that the postcode sectors selected can represent each Government Office Region as well as each socio-economic classification. Car owners and non-owners can also be fairly represented.

There are nine Government Office Regions, including the North East, the North West, Yorkshire and the Humber, East Midlands, West Midlands, East of England, London, the South East and the South West.

The socio-economic classification consists of eight classes: higher managerial and professional occupations, lower managerial and professional occupations, intermediate occupations, small employers and own account workers, lower supervisory and technical occupations, semi-routine occupations, routine occupations and never worked and long-term unemployed.

For the Scottish part of the sample, all Scottish offshore islands and the Isles of Scilly are excluded because of excessive interview travel costs that would have been incurred.

For the Northern Ireland part of the sample, a different sampling frame, the Valuation and Lands Agency list, is used to draw a random sample.

Value of Sampling in Marketing Research

Sampling is an important concept that we practise in our everyday activities. Consider, for example, attending a job interview. We have been taught that making a good first impression in a job interview is extremely important, because after that initial exposure (i.e. sample), many times people will make judgements about the type of person we are. People sit in front of their TV with a remote control in their hand and rapidly flip through a number of different channels, stopping a few seconds to take a sample of the programme on each channel until they find a programme they decide to watch. Next time you have a free moment, go to a bookshop like Waterstone's. Readers there may pick up a book or magazine, look at its cover, and then read a few pages to get a feel for its content and writing style before deciding whether to buy the book. When people go car shopping, they want to test drive a particular car for a while to see how they feel about it and its performance before deciding whether to buy it. One commonality in all these situations is that a decision is based on the assumption that the smaller portion, or sample, is representative of the larger population. From a general perspective, **sampling** involves selecting a relatively small number of elements from a larger defined group of elements and expecting that the information gathered from the small group will enable accurate judgements about the larger group.

> **Sampling** Selection of a small number of elements from a larger defined target group of elements and expecting that the information gathered from the small group will allow accurate judgements to be made about the larger group.

Sampling as a Part of the Research Process

Sampling is often used when it is impossible or unreasonable to conduct a census. With a **census** primary data is collected from *every* member of a defined target population. The most comprehensive census in a country is the census done by its government, such as UK Census that takes place every 10 years.

> **Census** A research study that collects data from every member of the defined target population.

Intuitively, it is easy to see that sampling is less time consuming and less costly than conducting a census. For example, let's say the management of KLM wants to find out what business travellers like and dislike about flying KLM. Gathering data from 500 KLM business travellers would be much less expensive and time consuming than surveying all the ten of thousands of business travellers. No matter what type of research design is used to collect data, the time and money factors are usually critical to decision makers. For researchers, shorter projects are more likely to fit the decision maker's time frame.

The concept of sampling also plays an important role in the process of *identifying and developing* new marketing concepts. Consider a researcher helping the owner of a local doctor's walk-in clinic to understand the concept of service quality in medical practices. The researcher must identify the different important attributes that might make up service quality. By gathering responses from a sample of patients, the researcher could identify possible important attributes representing the service quality construct.

Samples also play an important indirect role in *designing questionnaires*. For example, by gathering opinions about the research topic from a sample of the target population and asking a different sample to fill in a draft questionnaire, researchers could ensure they include the necessary questions and exclude those questions that are surplus to requirement in the questionnaire, as well as ensure that the final questionnaire meets all the good principles of questionnaire survey.

In cases where the process of measurement results in the destruction of the elements being studied, sampling is the only alternative. For example, if every bag of Walker's crisps that came off the production line were tested for salt, oil, colour and so on, none would be left to package and sell. Although this reason for sampling is usually thought of in terms of quality control, it can be applied to marketing-related problems that require primary research in the testing of new products or ideas.

As the above examples illustrate, there are different reasons for the use of sampling in research. Whatever the reason is, the main objective of sampling is to enable researchers to make decisions about the target population using limited information. The concept of sampling involves two basic issues: (1) making the right decisions in selecting elements (e.g. people, organizations, or products) feeling confident that data from the sample can be transformed into accurate information about the target population.

Finally, this chapter sets the tone for better understanding topics later in the text: *construct development, scale measurement, questionnaire design, coding* and *data analysis.* We begin the chapter by introducing you to the basics of sampling theory. Then we discuss how to determine appropriate sample sizes for different marketing research projects.

Overview: The Basics of Sampling Theory

Basic Sampling Terminology

Population

A **population** is an identifiable group of elements of interest to the researcher. For example, let's say Tesco hired a market research company to measure customer satisfaction of its different types of business (grocery retailing, financial service, Internet provision, etc). This research project would suggest that the population of interest would be all the residents in the UK. It is unlikely, however, that the research company would use a sampling frame covering all the UK residents in order to draw a sample for the research project. Residents living in the outlying islands are too costly to reach. Also it may not be cost-effective to include residents such as short-term contract overseas workers or overseas students who stay in the UK for only one year as part of the sampling frame.

> **Population** The identifiable set of elements of interest to the researcher.

As a good practice, businesses conducting research projects that involve the use of sampling should not be really concerned with the population as such. Instead they should focus on the *target population.* A **target population** consists of the defined group of elements that are identified for investigation based on the evaluation of the research objectives, feasibility and cost-effectiveness.

> **Target population** The defined set of elements identified for investigation based on the evaluation of the research objectives, feasibility and cost-effectiveness.

Element

An **element** is usually a person, an organization or an object from which information is sought. Elements must be unique, countable, and when added together, make up the whole of the target population. Elements can be viewed collectively as the target population from which a sample will be drawn. Target population elements may include specific groups of people (e.g. females aged 18 to 34, or households with hi-tech home entertainment systems); specific organizations (e.g. FTSE 250 companies); or a particular consumer product (e.g. Volkswagen cars). When the initial definition of the target population incorrectly identifies the elements, it creates a bias referred to as target population frame error.

> **Element** Usually a person, an organization or an object from the target population from which information is sought.

Sampling Unit

Sampling units are the target population elements available for selection during the sampling process. In a single-stage sample, the sampling units and the target population elements can be the same. However, many studies involve more complex problems that require the use of a multi-stage sampling process.

> **Sampling units** The target population elements available for selection during the sampling process.

For example, assume Volkswagen wants to carry out a sampling survey to measure customer satisfaction towards its products. In this example, the owners of Volkswagen cars might be the target population elements of interest. However, it might be more to the German car company's interest to focus on only the owners who have purchased a new Volkswagen in the last two years. In that case the target population would need to be redefined. Refining the set of target population elements with a second factor modifies the sampling frame from which to draw a suitable sample for the research project.

Sampling Frame

After defining the target population, the researcher develops a list of all eligible sampling units, referred to as a **sampling frame**. Some common sources of sampling frames are lists of registered voters (electoral register) and customer lists from magazine publishers or credit card companies. There are also specialized commercial companies that sell databases containing names, addresses and telephone numbers of potential population elements.

> **Sampling frame** The list of all eligible sampling units.

A Closer Look at Research *(In the field)*
Two Versions of Electoral Register in the UK

The electoral register in the UK is a popular sampling frame to be used in the country. Researchers should note that there are two versions of the electoral register – the full register and the edited register.

The full register lists everyone who is entitled to vote. You can check it by calling at the Elections Office. However, only certain people and organizations can have copies of the full register and they can only use it for specified purposes. These include electoral purposes, the prevention and detection of crime and checking an applicant's identity when they have applied for credit. The law clearly says who can have a copy of the full register and what they can use it for. The full list of such people and purposes is given in the Representation of the People (England and Wales) (Amendment) Regulations 2002. It is a criminal offence for these permitted people to pass it on to anyone else or to use it for any other purpose.

The edited register, on the other hand, leaves out the names and addresses of people who have asked for them to be excluded from that version of the register. The edited register can be bought by anyone who asks for a copy and they may use it for any purpose.

Marketing researchers can only use the edited register, which does not include people who opt out of being listed.

Regardless of the source, it is often difficult and expensive to obtain accurate, representative and current sampling frames. It is doubtful, for example, that a list of individuals who have eaten an Indian meal in a particular city in the past month will be readily available. In this instance, a researcher would have to use an alternative method such as random-digit dialling (if conducting a telephone survey) to generate a sample of prospective respondents.

The Main Factors Underlying Sampling Theory

To understand sampling theory, you must be acquainted with its concepts and symbols. Exhibit 13.1 shows a summary of the basic concepts and their symbols. Descriptions and discussions of these concepts are provided in this chapter and revisited in later chapters.

In many statistics texts, sampling concepts and approaches are discussed for situations where the key population parameters are either known or unknown by the researcher prior to conducting the research project. Discussion here is limited to situations where the researcher does not know the true population parameters. This is because today's business environments are so complex and rapidly changing that it is highly unlikely business decision makers know the parameters of their target populations. For example, most retailers that added online shopping alternatives for consumers are scrambling to identify and describe the people who are now making their retail purchases over the Internet rather than at traditional 'brick and mortar' stores. One of the major goals of researching small, yet representative, samples of members of a defined target population is that of using sample results to determine what the true population parameters are within a certain degree of confidence.

If business decision makers had complete knowledge about their defined target populations, they would have perfect information about the realities of those populations. However, this is always

EXHIBIT 13.1 Concepts and Symbols Used in Sampling Theory

Population Parameters	Symbol	Sample Notations	Symbol
Size	N	Size	n
Mean value	μ	Mean value	$\bar{x}$
Percentage value (population proportion)	P	Percentage value (sample proportion)	$\bar{p}$
	Q or $[1-P]$		$\bar{q}$ or $[1-\bar{p}]$
Standard deviation	σ	Estimated standard deviation	$\bar{s}$
Variance	σ^2	Estimated variance	$\bar{s}^2$
Standard error (population parameter)	S_μ or S_p	Estimated standard error (sample statistics)	$S_{\bar{x}}$ or $S_{\bar{p}}$
Other Sampling Concepts			
Confidence interval	$CI_{\bar{x}}$ or $CI_{\bar{p}}$		
Tolerance level of error	e		
Critical z-value	Z_B		
Confidence level	CL		
Finite correction factor (the overall square root of $[N-n/N-1]$ (also referred to as 'finite multiplier' or 'finite population correction')	fcf		

Note: For a quick review of these concepts and symbols go to the book's website at www.mhhe.com/shiu09 and follow the links.

not the case. Today's marketing problems exist primarily because decision makers lack information about their problem situations and who their customers are, as well as customers' attitudes, preferences and marketplace behaviours. Appropriate use of the sampling theory and concepts can help decision makers draw up a more or less correct picture of their target populations.

An important assumption that underlies the sampling theory is that the population elements are randomly distributed. That is, if a researcher were able to do a census of the entire target population elements, then the probability distribution of the population (e.g. food spending per family) would be a normal bell-shaped distribution. Theoretically, this assumption enables the researcher to believe that if repeated random, representative samples of the known sampling elements were taken, then the resulting **sampling distribution** would be a normal distribution.

> **Sampling distribution** The frequency distribution of a specific sample statistic (e.g. sample mean or sample proportion) from repeated random samples of the same size.

For example, assume researchers are interested in determining the average household income in the East and West Midlands, England and there are approximately 4 million households in these two counties. The researchers are able to take 1,000 separate random samples, each the size of 500 households. Assume further that government statistics show the average household income (μ) of these 3 million households is €28,000 and the sampling distribution of average household income $\bar{x}$ from the 1,000 random samples ranges from €15,500 to €41,000. The frequency distribution of the means $\bar{x}$ of those samples would be a normal, bell-shaped curve with the population mean (μ) as the mean of the distribution, as shown in Exhibit 13.2. In reality, it would not be practical to take 1,000 different samples. The idea of a sampling distribution is a theoretical concept. However, it is a fundamental aspect of sampling. To deal with the reality, researchers rely on the central limit theorem in drawing a representative sample from a target population rather than many repeated samples.

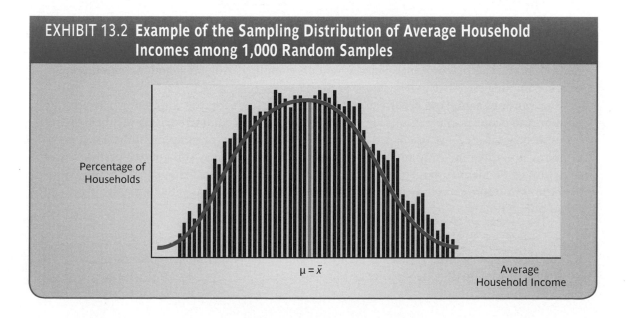

EXHIBIT 13.2 **Example of the Sampling Distribution of Average Household Incomes among 1,000 Random Samples**

Central Limit Theorem

The **central limit theorem (CLT)** is the theoretical backbone of survey research. The CLT is important in understanding the concepts of sampling error, statistical significance and sample sizes. In brief, the theorem states that theoretically for all defined target populations, the sampling distribution of the mean ($\bar{x}$) or the percentage ($\bar{p}$) value derived from a simple random sample will be pproximately normally distributed, provided the sample size is sufficiently large (i.e. when n is > or = 30). Moreover, the mean ($\bar{x}$) of the random sample with an estimated sampling error ($S_{\bar{x}}$) fluctuates around the true population mean (μ) with a standard error of $\sigma/\sqrt{n}$ and an approximately normal sampling distribution, regardless of the shape of the probability frequency distribution of the overall target population. In other words, there is a high probability that the mean of any sample ($\bar{x}$) taken from the target population will be a close approximation of the true target population mean (μ), as the size of the sample (n) is sufficiently large. With an understanding of the basics of the central limit theorem, the researcher can

1 Draw representative samples from any target population.

2 Obtain sample statistics from a random sample that serve as accurate estimates of the target population's parameters.

3 Draw one random sample, instead of many, reducing the costs of data collection.

4 Test more accurately the reliability and validity of constructs and scale measurements.

5 Statistically analyse data and transform them into meaningful information about the target population.

> **Central limit theorem (CLT)** Theorem that states that for almost all target populations, the sampling distribution of the means or the percentage value derived from a simple random sample will be approximately normally distributed provided that the sample size is sufficiently large.

Theoretical Tools Used to Assess the Quality of Samples

There are numerous opportunities to make mistakes that result in some type of bias in any research study. This bias can be classified as random sampling error, non-random sampling error, or non-sampling error.

The **random sampling error** can be detected by observing the difference between the random and proper sample results and the results of a census conducted using identical procedures. It happens because of chance variations in the selection of sampling units. Even if the sampling units are randomly and properly selected, those units may still not be a perfect representation of the defined target population. However, other things being equal, results generated from a random sample are generally reliable estimates of what is actually happening in the target population.

> **Random sampling error** A bias that occurs to random and proper samples because of chance variations in the selection of sampling units.

Based on the central limit theorem, the random sampling error can be reduced by increasing the size of the sample. Exhibit 13.3 illustrates the relationship between sample sizes and random sampling error.

The results show that doubling the size of the sample does not reduce the random sampling error by the same factor. In fact, the random sampling error can become so small that it raises questions concerning the overall costs involved with data collection. In short, increasing the sample size primarily to reduce the standard error may not be worth the cost.

Non-random sampling errors occur when a non-random sampling technique is adopted. Typical non-random sampling techniques include convenience sampling, judgemental sampling, quota sampling and snowball sampling. Results from the use of these techniques, no matter how robust they have been used, cannot confidently represent the target population. This is mainly because people of certain characteristics, rather than people randomly chosen from the target population, are often picked up as samples in these techniques. In addition, no matter how robust the research design using any of these non-random sampling techniques has been implemented,

---

EXHIBIT 13.3 Theoretical Example of the Relationship of Sample Sizes to Estimates of Random Sampling Error

In this example, the researcher is interested in better understanding the impact of sample size on predicted estimates of sampling error. Using the estimated standard error for a sample percentage where $(S_{\bar{p}})$ equals the overall square root of $(\bar{p})(\bar{q})/n$ and $\bar{p}$ is held constant at 50 per cent, the researcher calculates the predicted estimated standard error as the sample is doubled holding all other factors constant. The results would be as follows:

Sample Results $(\bar{p})$	Sample Size	Estimated Standard Error $(S_{\bar{p}})$	Change in $S_{\bar{p}}$
50%	10	±15.8%	—
50	20	±11.2	4.6%
50	40	±7.9	3.3
50	80	±5.6	2.3
50	160	±4.0	1.6
50	320	±2.8	1.2
50	640	±2.0	0.8

Graphically displaying the results:

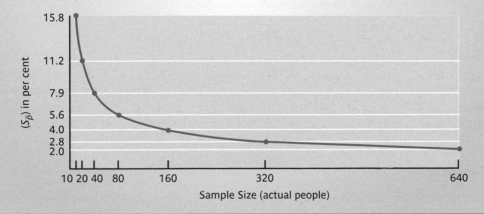

the researcher can never know exactly the extent of the error arising from the use of a particular non-random sampling technique.

> **Non-random sampling error** Any type of bias that is attributable to the use of a non-random sampling technique.

Non-sampling errors occur in a study regardless of whether a sample or a population is used. These errors can occur at any stage of the research process. For example, the target population may be inaccurately defined causing population frame error; inappropriate question/scale measurements can result in measurement error; a questionnaire may be poorly designed causing response error; or there may be other errors in gathering and recording data or when raw data are coded and entered for analysis. In general, the more extensive a study the greater the potential for non-sampling errors. Unlike sampling error, there are no statistical procedures to assess the impact of non-sampling errors on the quality of the data collected. Non-sampling errors are usually related to the accuracy of the data, whereas sampling errors relate to the representativeness of the sample to the defined target population.

> **Non-sampling error** A bias that occurs in a research study regardless of whether a sample or a population is used.

Statistical Precision

Knowing the sampling distributions and their shapes enables the researcher to make estimates of the target population. The critical level of error (i.e. allowable margin of error) is specified prior to doing a research study. This critical level of error (e) represents general precision (S) with no specific confidence level or precise precision [$(S)(Z_{B, CL})$] when a specific level of confidence is required. The **critical level of error** is the amount of observed difference between a sample statistical value($\bar{x}$ or $\bar{p}$)and the true target population parameter (μ or P).

> **Critical level of error** The observed difference between a sample statistical value and the corresponding true or hypothesized population parameter.

General precision can be viewed as the amount of general random sampling error associated with the sample data. **Precise precision** represents the amount of random sampling error associated with the data at a specified level of confidence. When attempting to measure the precision of data, researchers must incorporate the theoretical aspects of sampling distributions, the central limit theorem, and the estimated standard error in order to calculate the necessary confidence intervals.

> **General precision** The amount of general random sampling error associated with raw data.
>
> **Precise precision** The amount of random sampling error at a specified level of confidence.

Estimated Standard Error

Estimated standard error, also referred to as general precision, is a measure of the random sampling error and an indication of how far the sample result lies from the actual target population parameter. The formula to compute the estimated standard error of a sample mean $(S_{\bar{x}})$ is

$$S_{\bar{x}} = \bar{s} / \sqrt{n}$$

where
   $\bar{s}$ = Estimated standard deviation of the sample mean
   n = Sample size

For example, suppose Burger King conducts a survey among the general population to determine how many hamburgers (not limited to Burger King hamburgers) the average household in Britain consumes in a typical 90-day period. A sample of 950 telephone numbers is randomly selected from the corporation's newly purchased telephone number database that purports to cover the whole of Britain. The survey results show the average number of hamburgers consumed per household in the given period is 36 (i.e. $\bar{x} = 36$), and the estimated sample standard deviation is 12.5 hamburgers. Using the above formula, the researcher calculates the estimated standard error of the sample to be ±.406 hamburgers. Now assume the researcher had randomly sampled only 400 households and the average number of hamburgers and estimated standard deviation values were found to be the same as before. In this case, the calculated general random sampling error associated with the study increases to ±.625 hamburgers. Without considering a confidence factor, the results suggest there is a greater chance of random sampling error when the sample size is reduced. This further illustrates the inherent inverse relationship between sample size (n) and the estimated standard error of a sample mean $(S_{\bar{x}})$.

We can also find the estimated standard error of a sample percentage value $(S_{\bar{p}})$ by using the following formula:

$$S_{\bar{p}} = \sqrt{\frac{[(\bar{p})(\bar{q})]}{n}}$$

where
   $\bar{p}$ = The percentage of the sample possessing a specific characteristic
   $\bar{q}$ = The percentage of the sample not possessing the characteristic or $(1 - \bar{p})$
   n = Sample size

Barclays, for example, conducts a survey of customers with cheque accounts and finds that 65 per cent of those sampled have a savings account in addition to a cheque account (i.e. $\bar{p} = 65\,\text{per cent}$). The results are from a random sample of 489 currently known Barclays customers. Using the above $S_{\bar{p}}$ formula for sample percentages, the estimated standard error associated with the sample percentage would be ±2.16 percentage points.

The estimated standard error is a measure of variability since it measures the range the actual value of the target population can be expected to fall within. The more spread out the data, the greater the variability and the larger the estimated standard error. The more similar the survey results, the less the variability. The estimated standard error can be used to construct a confidence interval in which the actual target population's parameter is expected to fall. To see more examples of how estimated standard errors are used in determining statistical precision, visit the book's website at www.mhhe.com/shiu09 and follow the links.

Confidence Interval

A **confidence interval** represents a statistical range of values within which the true value of the target population parameter is expected to lie. The endpoints of a confidence interval (upper and lower values) are determined on the basis of the sample's results. The following formulas can be used to establish a confidence interval for a population's mean value (μ) and a population's proportion value (P). The confidence interval formula for a population mean parameter is

$$CI_\mu = \bar{x} \pm (S_{\bar{x}})(Z_{B,\,CL})$$

where

CI_μ = Confidence interval for a target population mean parameter
$\bar{x}$ = Sample mean value
$S_{\bar{x}}$ = Estimated standard error of the sample mean
$Z_{B,\,CL}$ = Level of confidence expressed in z-values (which are standardized)

> **Confidence interval** The statistical range of values within which the true value of the defined target population parameter is expected to lie.

The confidence interval formula for a population proportion parameter is

$$CI_P = \bar{p} \pm (S_{\bar{p}})(Z_{B,\,CL})$$

where

CI_P = Confidence interval for a target population propotion parameter
$\bar{p}$ = Sample proportion value
$S_{\bar{p}}$ = Estimated standard error of the sample proportion
$Z_{B,\,CL}$ = Level of confidence expressed in z-values (which are standardized)

In theory there are an infinite number of confidence levels, ranging from almost zero to almost 100 per cent. But the most commonly used confidence levels are the 90, 95, and 99 per cent levels. Since the central limit theorem enables researchers to assume a normal distribution, researchers can apply their knowledge of basic statistics regarding normal distributions and use a critical z-value of 1.65 for a 90 per cent level of confidence, 1.96 for a 95 per cent level of confidence, and 2.58 for a 99 per cent level of confidence. Since these are the standardized z-values, their values are the only ones represented for their respective confidence levels and do not change when calculating confidence intervals.

To use the above Barclays example, if the researcher wants to construct a 95 per cent confidence interval for the bank survey results, the above formula for a population proportion confidence interval can be used by incorporating the estimated standard error previously calculated, as shown below.

$$CI_P = 65 \text{ per cent} \pm (2.16)(1.96)$$
$$= 65 \text{ per cent} \pm 4.23 \text{ per cent}$$
$$= (65 \text{ per cent} - 4.23 \text{ per cent}), (65 \text{ per cent} + 4.23 \text{ per cent})$$
$$= 60.77 \text{ per cent} \leq P \leq 69.23 \text{ per cent}$$

In interpreting the confidence interval, we are 95 per cent confident that the actual percentage of Barclays customers who have a cheque account and a savings account will fall between 60.77 and 69.23 per cent. Stated another way, if the researcher had drawn repeated random samples of

Barclays cheque account customers, then 95 per cent of the time (19 out of 20 times, or 95 out of 100 times), the true percentage of customers holding both cheque and savings accounts with Barclays would be somewhere between 60.77 and 69.23 per cent.

The value generated by multiplying the estimated standard error by the critical z-value determines the amount of random sampling error that occurs due to the random sampling process. This is the precise precision at a given level of confidence. To see more examples of calculating confidence intervals, visit our Web site at www.mhhe.com/shiu09 and follow the links.

Random Sampling and Sample Sizes

Determining the random sample size is not an easy task. The researcher must consider how precise the estimates must be and how much time and money are available to collect the required data, since data collection is generally one of the most expensive components of a study. Three factors play an important role in determining sample sizes:

1 **The variability of the population characteristic under investigation (σ_μ or σ_p).** The greater the variability of the characteristic the larger the sample size necessary.

2 **The level of confidence desired in the estimate (CL).** The higher the level of confidence desired the larger the sample size needed.

3 **The degree of precision desired in estimating the population characteristic (e).** The more precise the required sample results (i.e. the smaller the e) the larger the sample size.

As with confidence intervals, there are separate formulas for determining sample size based on a predicted population mean (μ) and a population proportion (P). The formulas are used to estimate the sample size for a simple random sample. When the situation involves estimating a population mean, the formula for calculating the sample size would be

$$ n = (Z^2_{B,\,CL}) \left(\frac{\sigma^2}{e^2} \right) $$

where

$Z_{B,\,CL}$ = The standardized z-value associated with the level of confidence

σ = Estimate of the population standard deviation based on some type of prior information

e = Acceptable tolerance level of error (stated in percentage points)

In situations where estimates of a population proportion are of concern, the standardized formula for calculating the required sample size would be

$$ n = (Z^2_{B,\,CL}) \left(\frac{[P \times Q]}{e^2} \right) $$

where

$Z_{B,\,CL}$ = The standardized z-value associated with the level of confidence

P = Estimate of expected population proportion having a desired characteristic based on prior information or intuition

Q = $[1 - P]$, or the estimate of expected population proportion not holding the characteristic of interest

e = Acceptable tolerance level of error (stated in percentage points)

The formulas for determining the sample size are an extension of the standard formula for calculating the standard error of the population parameter, either S_μ or S_P, at a particular confidence level. Several general relationships are apparent between the formulas and the size of a sample. For example, when using the population mean formula, as the variability (σ_μ) of the probability distribution of the population mean (μ) increases, holding the other factors constant, the larger the required sample size. Fundamentally, this relationship holds because (σ_μ) is part of the numerator of the equation. In contrast, when the situation requires the use of a population proportion (P), any population proportion other than 50 per cent (e.g. $P = 70$ per cent or $P = 30$ per cent), holding the other factors constant, will result in a decrease in the required sample size.

There is a direct relationship between the desired level of confidence (e.g. 90 per cent, 95 per cent, 99 per cent) and the required sample size. Confidence levels are directly associated with corresponding critical z-values (i.e. 90 per cent CL ≈ 1.65; 95 per cent CL ≈ 1.96; 99 per cent CL ≈ 2.58). The higher the level of confidence required the larger the required number in the sample.

The last key consideration is the acceptable critical level of error (e). It is the amount of statistical precision specified by the researcher. This value is normally stated as a CL percentage (e.g. 2 per cent, 5 per cent, or 10 per cent), but it can be expressed as a mean value. The lower the percentage, the more precise the estimate and therefore the larger the required sample size.

The following example shows how to calculate the sample size where population parameter estimates from a pilot study are used. Assume you are the research analyst for Virgin Media, an entertainment and communications company based in the UK. Three months ago, to expand the business in the Welsh west coast, Virgin Media conducted a pilot study with 200 households in the area. Results showed that 50 per cent of the households in the area were users of broadband Internet. Virgin Media has decided to do a larger study so it can predict potential broadband Internet usage patterns as well as understand people's criteria for choosing between different broadband Internet service providers. Management wants data precision to be ±3 per cent with a 99 per cent confidence level. To determine the sample size, use the standard formula for a population proportion:

$$n = (Z^2_{\text{B, CL}})\left(\frac{[P \times Q]}{e^2}\right)$$

where
$Z_{\text{B, CL}} = 2.58$, the standardized z-value associated with the 99 per cent confidence level

$P = 50$ per cent, the estimated proportion of Virgin Media's potential customer base who are users of broadband Internet in the target area

$Q = 50$ per cent, $[1 - P]$ or the estimated proportion of Virgin Media's potential customer base who are not users of broadband Internet in the target area

$e = \pm 3.0$ per cent, the acceptable critical level of error (stated in percentage points)

Thus,

$$n = 2.58^2 \frac{(50 \times 50)}{3.0^2}$$

$$= 6.6564 \frac{(2.500)}{9.0}$$

$$= 6.6564(277.8) = 1{,}849.15, \text{ or } 1{,}850 \text{ households}$$

Virgin Media will have to randomly select and survey a sample of 1,850 households for the research results to meet the desired 3.0 per cent critical level of error at a 99 per cent confidence level. For more examples of calculating sample sizes, visit the Web site at www.mhhe.com/shiu09.

Sample Size and Small Finite Populations

There is often a misconception that a larger population requires a larger sample. But the size of the population is not a direct factor in determining sample size. If the sample size is large relative to the population, a **finite correction factor (fcf)** should be used to determine the sample size. Research industry standards suggest that sample size is considered large if it is more than 5 per cent of the population. The formula for the finite correction factor is:

$$\sqrt{\frac{N-n}{N-1}}$$

where

N = Known (or given) defined target population size
n = Calculated sample size using the original sample size formula

> **Finite correction factor (fcf)** An adjustment factor to the sample size that is made in those situations where the drawn sample is expected to be equal to or more than 5 per cent of the defined target population. fcf is equal to the overall square root of [$N-n/N-1$].

Using the finite correction factor is a two-step process. First, we determine whether the sample size is more than 5 per cent of the population by taking the calculated sample size and dividing it by the target population size. Second, if it is more than 5 per cent, we calculate the appropriate finite correction factor and multiply the originally calculated sample size by it to adjust the required sample size. To illustrate how the finite correction factor affects estimates of sample sizes, let's use the above Virgin Media example.

Initially not knowing how many households actually make up Virgin Media's Welsh west coast market, the researcher estimates that 1,850 randomly selected households would have to be included in the study, with data precision of ±3 per cent and a 99 per cent confidence level. Now let's assume that Virgin Media learns the initial target population size of the Welsh west coast market is expected to be about 15,000 households. To determine whether the initial sample size needs to be adjusted, the researcher would first determine if the initial sample size was greater than 5 per cent of the total defined target population size. This is achieved simply by dividing the estimated sample size (n = 1,850 households) by the target population size (N = 15,000 households). The results of this first step show the initial estimated sample size represents about 12.33 per cent of the defined target population. Therefore, the finite correction factor should be applied to adjust the sample size estimate.

Using the above formula, the correction factor is 0.93634. Now multiplying the initial sample-size estimate (1,850 households) by the correction factor, Virgin Media learns that the number of households needed in the larger study is only 1,733, a reduction of 117 households. When appropriately used, the single biggest benefit of the finite correction factor is that it reduces the overall costs of collecting data. Visit our website www.mhhe.com/shiu09 for more examples.

When the defined target population size in a consumer study is 500 elements or less, the researcher should consider doing a census of the population rather a sample. The logic behind this is based on the theoretical notion that at least 384 sampling units need to be included in theoretically all the studies to have a 95 per cent confidence level and a sampling error of ±5 percentage points.

Sample sizes in business-to-business research present a different problem than in consumer research where the population almost always is very large. With business-to-business research the population is likely to be only 200 to 300 individuals. In such cases an attempt can be made to contact and complete a survey from all individuals in the population. If a population survey is not possible for any reason and a sampling survey is the next best option, what then is an acceptable sample size?

An acceptable sample size can be as small as 30 per cent or so of the population, but the final decision should be made after examining the profile of the respondents. For example, you could look at position titles to see if you have a good cross section of respondents from all relevant categories. You may also check what proportions of firms in different levels of annual sales are in order to avoid having only smaller firms in the sample. Whatever approach you use, in the final analysis you must have a good understanding of who has responded so you can more accurately interpret the study's findings.

Non-Probability Sampling and Sample Size

Sample size formulas cannot be used for non-probability samples. Determining the sample size for non-probability samples is a more or less subjective judgement made by the researcher based on factors such as intuition, experience, past studies, industry standards and/or the amount of resources available. Regardless of the non-probability sampling technique used, the corresponding results cannot be used to make statistical inferences about the true population parameters. The best that can be offered is ideas about the directions of the target variables in the population.

 ## A Closer Look at Research (In the Field)

Impacts of Legal Environments on Future Sampling Decisions in Japan

Japan's Basic Resident Register has often been described as the most valuable sampling frame for probability sampling in the country. It lists household information to such detail as including the gender and age of each family member. For years, marketing researchers operating in Japan have been using the Register for their sampling survey projects. However, this is going to just become a good old thing of the past.

In 2005, the Japanese government began to review national laws governing the Basic Resident Register, and in November 2006, new legal restrictions blocking access to the Register for commercial market research projects came into force.

Before the enforcement of these legal restrictions, some local governments had already taken action to control the volume of access to the Register, by restricting the number of records one could access at one time. This made sampling frame building for marketing research purposes very difficult.

The legal restrictions do not apply to social and opinion research. Any research project whose objectives are considered 'public' in a nature can continue to gain access to the Register.

For commercial market research companies, in response to these restrictions, they are expected to increase their use of consumer panels, both online and offline, in order to generate valuable consumer data for their business.

In addition, with the trend of market fragmentation, restrictions of the use of the Register will not become a great pain for some market researchers whose projects rely on strictly defined and specific target groups, rather than on probability sampling.

Source: Research Magazine, News Archive, www.research-live.com

Final Versus Initial Sample Size

After the researcher determines the final desired sample size, they usually need to contact more potential respondents. In other words, this initial sample size to be contacted is always larger than the final sample size desired. There are three main factors contributing to this. They are expected reachable rate (ERR), expected incidence rate (EIR) and expected completion rate (ECR).

The expected reachable rate is the estimated percentage of the contacts that can be reached by the researcher or interviewer. It is not uncommon that not all the sampling units in a sampling frame are reachable. For example, in a mail survey, the mailing list that serves as the sampling frame may be dated or have some of the listed addresses may no longer be active. In this example, the percentage of active addresses on the mailing list is the ERR. You may now quickly deduce that the ERR rate can reflect the quality of the sampling frame used. The higher the ERR, the better the quality of the sampling frame.

The expected incidence rate (EIR) is the percentage of the defined target population elements that qualify for inclusion in the survey. Using the above Virgin Media example, assume researchers are doing a telephone survey for the company on people's broadband Internet usage habits. Also assume the needed sample size is estimated to be 1,500 people. In addition, Virgin Media decides that to qualify for the survey, individuals must meet the following set of requirements:

- Be between the ages of 20 and 60.
- Have broadband Internet connection.
- Do not work for an Internet service provision company, marketing research firm, or have anyone in their household who does.
- Have not participated in a marketing research study during the past six months.

The more qualifying requirements placed on prospective respondents, the greater the chance an individual will not qualify. As a result, the EIR will decrease.

In the marketing research industry, the expected completion rate (ECR) reflects the percentage of prospective respondents who will follow through and complete the survey. This factor is also referred to as the anticipated response rate.

Using the Virgin Media example, let's say the expected reachable rate was determined to be 90 per cent, the expected incidence rate was estimated to be 55 per cent, and the expected completion rate for telephone surveys of this nature was 85 per cent. Using the following formula,

$$\text{Initial sample size} = \text{Final sample size} / (\text{ERR}) * (\text{EIR}) * (\text{ECR})$$
$$= 1{,}500 / 0.9 * 0.55 * 0.85$$
$$= 1{,}500 / 0.42075$$
$$= 3{,}565.062 \text{ or } 3{,}566 \text{ people}$$

To ensure the final sample size of 1,500 will be obtained, this number must be adjusted by the expected reachable, incidence and completion rates. Consequently, this means that Virgin Media must contact 3,566 people. Prior to carrying out the field work, Virgin Media will have to consider the cost of contacting an extra 2,063 people in order to base the results on the needed 1,500 respondents.

Sampling and Non-Sampling Errors in the Expenditure and Food Survey

Dual Approach to Minimize Non-Response Error

The Expenditure and Food Survey is the largest continuous cross sectional survey of household income and expenditure in Britain. Results of the survey have been widely used by market researchers in both the commercial and academic sectors. A major reason for its widespread use is the fact that multi-stage stratified random sampling with clustering, a robust form of probability sampling, is always used to increase the representativeness of the survey data results so collected.

However, even such a large scale and properly designed survey could still be subject to all sorts of errors. As the survey is based on a planned sample of around 12,096 households, sampling error is unavoidable. In addition, since the survey asks each cooperating household expenditure and consumption of many different items, the occurrence of reporting error is likely. However, apparently the biggest threat to the representativeness of the survey is non-response error. This is because the overall response rate for the survey has been decreasing over the years, and was only 57 per cent in 2005–06. In other words, 43 per cent of the planned sample didn't respond to the survey. Some of them could not be contacted at all, while in other non-responding households one or more members declined to cooperate. Whatever the reasons for non-response, these households tend to differ from those who cooperated with regards to a number of household background characteristics, resulting in the possibility of significant differences in the answers to the survey between them.

In order to minimize the adverse impact of the non-response error on the quality of the data results, researchers of the Expenditure and Food Survey used a dual approach, i.e. sample-based weighting and population-based weighting.

The idea of sample-based weighting is to give each respondent a weight so that they represent the non-respondents that are similar to them in a number of household background characteristics. To operationalize this idea, results from the Census-linked study of non-respondents are used. The Census-linked study matches Census addresses with the sampled addresses of some of the large continuous surveys, including the Expenditure and Food Survey. Through this matching process, it would be possible to match the address details of the Expenditure and Food Survey respondents as well as non-respondents with corresponding information gathered from the Census for the same address. Results of the matching would be able to identify the types of households that have been under-represented in the survey.

Then a combination of household background variables (including government office region, metropolitan area, household composition, marital status and gender of household reference member) would be analysed to identify which of them would be most significant in distinguishing between responding and non-responding households. These variables would be used to produce ten weighting classes with different response rates. Households within each of the weighting classes would then be assigned a non-response weight, based on the inverse of their response rate. A weighting class with a low response rate would be given a high initial weight.

The second approach, population-based weighting, adjusts the non-response weights so that weighted totals match population totals, for males and females in different age groups and for regions. An important feature of population-based weighting is that it is done by adjusting the factors for households not individuals. Also worth noting is that this weighting procedure needs to be carried out for each quarter of the survey. This is mainly because sample sizes vary from quarter to quarter more than in the past. As a result it is necessary to re-issue addresses where there has been no contact or a refusal to cooperate, resulting in more interviews to be conducted in the later quarters than in the first quarter of the year. Conducting the weighting procedure quarter by quarter helps to counteract any bias from the uneven spread of interviews throughout the year. One side-effect of quarterly weighting is the small sample numbers in some of the gender/age categories, which require slight widening in order to ascertain acceptable sample numbers in all the categories.

Questions

1 What major points does this example bring to your attention about sampling?

2 What is the next most serious type of error that the Expenditure and Food Survey may have?

Summary of Learning Objectives

- **Discuss the concept of sampling and list reasons for sampling.**

  Sampling uses a portion of the population to make estimates about the entire population. The fundamentals of sampling are used in many of our everyday activities (e.g. selecting a TV programme to watch, test-driving a car before deciding whether to purchase it, determining if our food is too hot or if it needs some additional seasoning). The term *target population* is used to identify the complete group of elements (e.g. people or objects) that are identified for investigation. The researcher selects sampling units from the target population and uses the results obtained from the sample to make conclusions about the target population. The sample must be representative of the target population if it is to provide accurate estimates of population parameters.

  Sampling is frequently used in marketing research projects instead of a census because sampling can significantly reduce the amount of time and money required in data collection. When data collection destroys or contaminates the elements being studied, sampling is usually the only alternative.

- **Identify and explain the different roles of sampling in the overall information research process.**

  Sampling is necessary when there are short time frames for gathering the needed information. Sampling is useful in identifying, developing and understanding new marketing constructs, as well as in developing the scales used to collect primary data. Decisions concerning sampling indirectly affect the process of designing questionnaires.

- **Demonstrate the basic terminology used in sampling decisions.**

  A population is an identifiable group of elements (e.g. people, products, organizations, physical entities) of interest to the researcher and relevant to the information problem. An element is a person or object from which information is sought. Sampling units are the target population elements available for selection during the sampling process. After defining the target population, the researcher must assemble a list of eligible sampling units, referred to as a sampling frame.

- **Understand the concept of error in the context of sampling.**

  There are three types of error. Random sampling error is attributable to the difference between random sample results and census results because of chance variations when drawing the sample. Non-random sampling error is due to the use of non-random sampling technique, which usually draws a sample that is not representative of the population. Non-sampling error is the bias that occurs to a research study regardless of whether a sample or a population is used.

■ **Discuss and calculate sampling distributions, standard errors and confidence intervals and how they are used in assessing the accuracy of a sample.**

A sampling distribution is the frequency distribution of a sample statistic (e.g. sample mean $[\bar{x}]$ or sample proportion $[\bar{p}]$ that would result if we took repeated random samples of the same size). The central limit theorem suggests there is a high probability the mean of any random sample taken from a target population will closely approximate the actual population mean as the sample size increases. Formulas are used to compute the estimated standard error of a sample mean $(\bar{x})$ and the estimated standard error of a sample percentage $(\bar{p})$. The estimated standard error $S_{\bar{x}}$ or $S_{\bar{p}}$ gives us an indication of how far the sample data results lie from the actual population parameters.

Confidence intervals are based on the researcher's specified level of confidence and a given degree of sampling error for which estimates of the true value of the population parameter could be expected to fall.

■ **Discuss the factors that must be considered when determining sample size.**

Several factors must considered when determining the appropriate sample size. The amount of time and money available often affect this decision. In general, the larger the sample, the greater the amount of resources required to collect data. Three factors that are of primary importance in the determination of sample size are (1) the variability of the population characteristic under consideration (σ_μ or σ_p), (2) the level of confidence desired in the estimate (CL), and (3) the degree of precision desired in estimating the population characteristic (e). The greater the variability of the characteristic under investigation, the higher the level of confidence required. Similarly, the more precise the required sample results the larger the necessary sample size.

■ **Discuss the methods of calculating appropriate sample sizes.**

Statistical formulas are used to determine the final sample size in probability sampling. Final sample sizes for non-probability sampling designs are determined using subjective methods such as intuitive judgement, personal experience of the researcher, industry standards and past studies. In planning the sampling process, one must understand the difference between the final and the initial sample size. Factors of the difference are expected reachable rates, expected incidence rates and expected completion rates on the number of prospective respondent contacts.

Key Terms and Concepts

Review Questions

1 Why do many of today's research situations place heavy emphasis on correctly defining a target population rather than a total population?

2 Why is so much importance placed on the central limit theorem in survey research?

3 Identify, graph and explain the relationship between sample sizes and estimated standard error measures. What does the estimated standard error really measure in survey research?

4 The operations manager at an outdoor entertainment complex knows that 70 per cent of the patrons like roller coaster rides. He wishes to have an acceptable margin of error of no more than ±2 per cent and wants to be 95 per cent confident about the attitudes towards the 'Gwazi' roller coaster. What sample size would be required for a personal survey among on-site patrons?

5 What statistical factors must be considered in determining sample size?

6 How do ERC, EIC and ECC impact the relationship between initial and final sample sizes?

Discussion Questions

1 Summarize why a current telephone directory is not an ideal source from which to develop a sampling frame.

2 Why do researchers find it necessary to calculate confidence intervals? In a telephone survey of 700 people, 45 per cent responded positively to liking cats. Calculate a confidence interval, at the 95 per cent confidence level, that will reveal the interval estimate for the proportion of people who like cats within a target population of 60,000 people. How would you interpret the results?

3 You are doing a survey on beer consumption and beer prices during an annual beer festival. Last year, in the same festival, the average price per four-pack of beer was €3.75, with a standard deviation of €0.30, and average consumption of beer over the two days of the festival was 12 cans per person, with a deviation of 3.5 cans. Your survey requires a 90 per cent confidence level and allowable errors of €0.10 on the price of four-packs and 1.5 cans on beer consumption. Calculate the needed sample size for doing this year's survey.

4 **Experience the Internet.** Go to your university's electronic library and search for two academic journal articles that used sampling for their research. Read these two articles and comment on the sampling design they used.

5 What are the disadvantages of using exit interviews as a sampling technique for the Jimmy Spice's customer survey?

6 How would you improve the sampling approach for the Jimmy Spice's customer survey? Why is your approach better?

Chapter 14

Sampling Techniques and Sampling Plan

LEARNING OBJECTIVES

After reading this chapter, you will be able to

☑ Distinguish between probability and non-probability sampling techniques.

☑ Understand the advantages and disadvantages of probability sampling designs.

☑ Understand the advantages and disadvantages of non-probability sample designs.

☑ Illustrate the factors necessary for determining the appropriate sample design.

☑ Understand the steps in developing a sampling plan.

" It would be a huge, enormously expensive and indeed impractical task to collect all the figures that are needed from all the businesses. Sampling techniques render this unnecessary.

–Pam Davies
Researcher, Office of National Statistics, UK "

Tough Research Life!
Implementing a Multi-Country Quota Sampling Survey in France, Germany and Spain In a Weekend's Time

On a Friday, an International project manager at Survey Sampling International (SSI), a global market research specializing in sampling survey, received confirmation of a marketing research project that involved multi-country sampling survey. The client of the research project wanted quick results. Actually, they wanted them when they arrived at work the following Monday morning!

The company promptly assigned a French project manager to study the French market, a German project manager to do the German territory, while two Spanish project managers jumped on the Spanish version.

Using the company's established global Consumer Product Panel, the French study was conducted on Friday afternoon, the Spanish on Friday evening and the German on Saturday morning.

The client asked for 50 completes as a tested sample in each of the three countries. The client then checked the data from these tested samples and subsequently gave the company the go-ahead to obtain more completes but needed to have a temporary quota stop at half the required sample size of 250 – 500 per country.

On Saturday afternoon, the International project manager asked the client to lift the quota stops so she could email to more potential respondents to get the remaining 250 completes per country on Sunday. 'While I was waiting to receive a confirmation form the client', she continued, 'I received a call from Douglas Wayne (senior account executive of SSI). He informed me that the client had a technical problem on their end and we had to start Germany again'. The International project manager emailed more potential respondents to get the remaining 250 completes in France and Spain, and 500 in Germany on Sunday morning. During the sampling survey process, the International project manager emailed updates to the client every hour.

The younger age group (18 to 24) was difficult to get in France and Germany, while the older age group (45 to 54), surprisingly, was hard to get in Spain, the International project manager said. She had to pull additional sample to fill the required sample quotas by gender, age and packages of the product concerned. The sampling survey closed on Sunday afternoon for France and Germany, and Monday 3 am for Spain.

This challenging project required the International project manager to 'sit tight in my office all weekend and check the report link every hour, send updates, monitor the study and send more sample. The client had quota stops – one for 10 per cent at the soft launch, a second at 50 per cent, and lastly at 100 per cent. The client wanted to check the data after the 10 per cent and after the 50 per cent launch. I followed the client's instructions and fulfilled their requests. The client was very happy and very complimentary!'

Source: adapted with permission of SSI (Survey Sampling International).

The Value of Sampling Techniques in Marketing Research

As illustrated in the chapter opener example, adopting and implementing an appropriate sampling technique right through to the finish is crucial for the success of any marketing research project that requires the use of a sample for data collection.

Overall, there are two broad sampling designs: probability and non-probability, which are also referred to as random and non-random sampling respectively. Exhibit 14.1 lists the different types of both sampling techniques.

EXHIBIT 14.1 Types of Probability and Non-probability Sampling Techniques

Probability Sampling Techniques	Non-probability Sampling Techniques
Simple random sampling	Convenience sampling
Systematic random sampling	Judgemental sampling
Stratified random sampling	Quota sampling
Cluster random sampling	Snowball sampling

In **probability sampling**, each sampling unit in the defined target population has a known probability of being selected for the sample. The actual probability of selection for each sampling unit may or may not be equal depending on the type of probability sampling design used. Specific rules for selecting members from the population for inclusion in the sample are determined at the beginning of a study to ensure (1) unbiased selection of the sampling units and (2) proper sample representation of the defined target population. Probability sampling enables the researcher to judge the reliability and validity of data collected by calculating the probability that the sample findings are different from the defined target population. The observed difference can be attributed to the existence of sampling error. The results obtained by using probability sampling designs can be generalized to the target population within a specified margin of error.

> **Probability sampling** A technique of drawing a sample in which each sampling unit has a known probability of being included in the sample.

In **non-probability sampling**, the probability of selecting each sampling unit is not known. Therefore, sampling error is not known either. Selection of sampling units is based on some type of intuitive judgement or knowledge of the researcher. The degree to which the sample may or may not be representative of the defined target population depends on the sampling approach and how well the researcher executes and controls the selection activities. Although there is always a temptation to generalize non-probability sample data results to the defined target population, strictly speaking the results are limited to just the people who provided the survey data. Exhibit 14.2 provides a comparison of probability and non-probability sampling techniques based on selected comparison factors.

> **Non-probability sampling** A sampling process where the probability of selecting each sampling unit is unknown.

EXHIBIT 14.2 Summary of Differences between Probability and Non-probability Sampling Techniques

Comparison Factors	Probability Sampling	Non-probability Sampling
List of the Population Elements	Complete List Necessary	Not Necessary
Information about the Sampling Units	Each Unit Identified	Some essential Information Needed
Sampling Skill Required	Skill Required	Less Skill Required
Time Requirement	Time Consuming	Less Time Consuming
Cost per Unit Sampled	Moderate to High	Relatively Low
Estimates of Population Parameters	Unbiased	Biased
Sample Representativeness	Good, Assured	Suspect, Undeterminable
Accuracy and Reliability	Computed with Confidence Intervals	Unknown
Measurement of Sampling error	Statistical Measures	No True Measure Available

Types of Probability Sampling Designs
Simple Random Sampling

Simple random sampling (SRS) is a probability sampling procedure. With this approach, every sampling unit has a known and equal chance of being selected. For example, let's say a teacher decided to draw a sample of 10 students ($n = 10$) from among all the students in a marketing research class that consisted of 30 students ($N = 30$). The teacher could write each student's name on a separate, identical piece of paper and place all of the names in a jar. Each student would have an equal, known probability of selection for a sample of a given size that could be expressed by the following formula:

$$\text{Probability of selection} = \frac{\text{Size of sample}}{\text{Size of population}}$$

> **Simple random sampling (SRS)** A probability sampling procedure that ensures every sampling unit in the target population has a known and equal chance of being selected.

Here, each student in the marketing research class would have a 10/30 (or .333) chance of being randomly selected in the sample.

When the defined target population consists of a larger number of sampling units, a more sophisticated method is used to randomly draw the sample. One of the procedures commonly used in marketing research is to have a computer-generated table of random numbers to select the sampling units. A table of random numbers is just what its name implies – a table that lists randomly generated numbers (see Exhibit 14.3). Many of today's computer programmes can generate a table of random numbers.

Using the marketing research students again as the target population, a random sample could be generated (1) by using the last two digits of the students' bank account numbers or (2) by assigning each student a unique two-digit code ranging from 01 to 30. With the first procedure, we would have to make sure that no two students have the same last two digits in their bank account numbers;

EXHIBIT 14.3 A Partial Table of Random Numbers

31 25	81 44	54 34	67 03
14 96	99 80	14 54	30 74
49 05	49 56	35 51	68 36
99 67	57 65	14 46	92 88
54 14	95 34	93 18	78 27
57 50	34 89	99 14	57 37
98 67	78 25	06 90	39 90
40 99	00 87	90 42	88 18
20 82	09 18	84 91	64 80
78 84	39 91	16 08	14 89

Source: Kendall and Smith, 1946.

the range of acceptable numbers would be from 00 to 99. Then we could go to the table of random numbers and select a starting point, which can be anywhere on the table. Using Exhibit 10.3, let's say we select the upper-left-hand corner of the table (31) as our starting point. We would then begin to read down the first column (or across the first row) and select those two-digit numbers that matched the numbers within the acceptable range until 10 students had been selected. Reading down the first column, we would start with 31, then go to 14, 49, 99, 54, and so on.

If we had elected to assign a unique descriptor (01 to 30) to each student in class, we would follow the same selection procedure from the random number table, but use only those random numbers that matched the numbers within the acceptable range of 01 to 30. Numbers that fell outside the acceptable range would be disregarded. Thus, we would select students with numbers 14, 20, 25, 05, 09, 18, 06, 16, 08 and 30. If the overall research objectives call for telephone interviews, drawing the necessary sample can be achieved using a random-digit dialling (RDD) technique.

Advantages and Disadvantages

Simple random sampling has several noteworthy advantages. The technique is easily understood. It guarantees that every sampling unit has a known and equal chance of being selected, no matter the actual size of the sample, thereby often resulting in a valid representation of the defined target population with a pre-specified margin of error e. Another advantage is that simple random samples allow the researcher to obtain unbiased estimates of the population's characteristics.

The primary disadvantage of simple random sampling is the difficulty of obtaining an ideally complete and accurate listing of the target population elements. Simple random sampling requires that all sampling units be identified. For this reason, simple random sampling often works best for small populations or those where acceptable computer-derived lists are available.

Systematic Random Sampling

Systematic random sampling (SYMRS) is similar to simple random sampling but requires that the defined target population be ordered in some way. In research practices, SYMRS has become a popular alternative probability technique for drawing samples. Compared to simple random sampling, systematic random sampling is less costly, and it can be done relatively quickly. When executed properly, SYMRS can create a sample of prospective respondents or objects that is very similar in quality to a sample drawn using SRS.

> **Systematic random sampling (SYMRS)** A probability sampling technique that requires the defined target population to be ordered in some way.

To employ systematic random sampling, the researcher must be able to secure an acceptable listing of the potential sampling units that make up the defined target population. But unlike SRS, there is no need to give the sampling units any special code prior to drawing the sample. Instead, sampling units are selected according to their position using a skip interval. The skip interval is determined by dividing the number of potential sampling units in the defined target population by the number of units desired in the sample. The required skip interval is calculated using the following formula:

$$\text{Skip interval} = \frac{\text{Defined target population list size}}{\text{Desired sample size}}$$

For instance, if the researcher wants a sample of 100 to be drawn from a defined target population of 1,000, the skip interval would be 10 (1,000/100). Once the skip interval is determined, the researcher would then randomly select a starting point and take every 10th unit until he or she had proceeded through the entire target population list. Exhibit 14.4 displays the steps that a researcher would take in drawing a systematic random sample.

There are two important considerations when using systematic random sampling. First, the natural order of the defined target population list must be unrelated to the characteristic being studied. Second, the skip interval must not correspond to a systematic change in the target population. For example, if a skip interval of 7 was used in sampling daily sales or invoices from Galeries Lafayette, the high-end department store in France, and Saturday was randomly selected as the starting point, we would end up with data from the same day every week. We would not want to draw conclusions regarding overall sales performance based only on what happens every Saturday.

Advantages and Disadvantages

Systematic sampling is frequently used because it is a relatively easy way to draw a sample while ensuring randomness. The shorter time, less effort and lower cost required to draw a sample versus simple random sampling makes systematic sampling an attractive, economical technique for researchers. The greatest weakness of systematic random sampling is the potential for there to be hidden patterns in the data that are not noticed by the researcher. This could result in a sample that is not truly representative of the defined target population. Another difficulty is that the

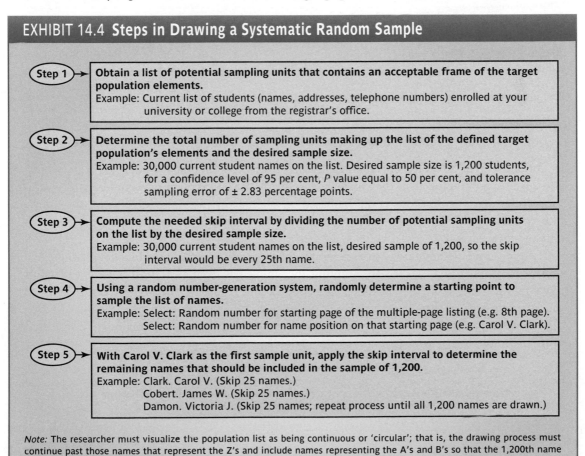

EXHIBIT 14.4 Steps in Drawing a Systematic Random Sample

Step 1 → Obtain a list of potential sampling units that contains an acceptable frame of the target population elements.
Example: Current list of students (names, addresses, telephone numbers) enrolled at your university or college from the registrar's office.

Step 2 → Determine the total number of sampling units making up the list of the defined target population's elements and the desired sample size.
Example: 30,000 current student names on the list. Desired sample size is 1,200 students, for a confidence level of 95 per cent, P value equal to 50 per cent, and tolerance sampling error of ± 2.83 percentage points.

Step 3 → Compute the needed skip interval by dividing the number of potential sampling units on the list by the desired sample size.
Example: 30,000 current student names on the list, desired sample of 1,200, so the skip interval would be every 25th name.

Step 4 → Using a random number-generation system, randomly determine a starting point to sample the list of names.
Example: Select: Random number for starting page of the multiple-page listing (e.g. 8th page).
Select: Random number for name position on that starting page (e.g. Carol V. Clark).

Step 5 → With Carol V. Clark as the first sample unit, apply the skip interval to determine the remaining names that should be included in the sample of 1,200.
Example: Clark. Carol V. (Skip 25 names.)
Cobert. James W. (Skip 25 names.)
Damon. Victoria J. (Skip 25 names; repeat process until all 1,200 names are drawn.)

Note: The researcher must visualize the population list as being continuous or 'circular'; that is, the drawing process must continue past those names that represent the Z's and include names representing the A's and B's so that the 1,200th name drawn will basically be the 25th name prior to the first drawn name (i.e. Carol V. Clark).

researcher must know exactly how many sampling units make up the defined target population. When the size of the target population is not clearly known, identifying the true number of units is difficult if not impossible, and estimates may not be accurate.

Stratified Random Sampling

Stratified random sampling (STRS) involves the separation of the target population into different groups, called strata, and the selection of samples from each stratum. Stratified random sampling is useful when the divisions of the target population are skewed or when extremes are present in the probability distribution of the target population. The goal in stratifying is to minimize the variability within each stratum and maximize the differences between strata. Stratified random sampling is similar to segmentation of the defined target population into smaller, more homogeneous sets of elements. Depending on the problem situation, there are cases in which the defined target population does not portray a normal symmetric distribution of its elements, and stratified random sampling would work well in these cases.

> **Stratified random sampling (STRS)** A probability sampling technique in which the defined target population is divided into groups, called strata, and samples are selected from each stratum.

To ensure that the sample maintains the required precision, representative samples must be drawn from each of the smaller population groups (each stratum). Drawing a stratified random sample involves three basic steps:

1 Dividing the target population into homogeneous groups or strata.
2 Drawing random samples from each stratum.
3 Combining the samples from each stratum into a single sample of the target population.

As an example, if researchers are interested in the market potential for home security systems in a specific geographic area, they may wish to divide the home owners/occupiers into several different strata. The divisions could be based on such factors as assessed value of the homes, household income, population density, or location (e.g. sections designated as high-, medium- and low-crime areas).

Two common methods are used to derive samples from the strata: *proportionate* and *disproportionate*. In **proportionate stratified sampling**, the sample size from each stratum is dependent on that stratum's size relative to the defined target population. Therefore, the larger strata are sampled more heavily because they make up a larger percentage of the target population. Exhibit 14.5 displays the fundamental steps a researcher should take in drawing a proportionately stratified random sample.

> **Proportionate stratified sampling** A stratified sampling technique in which each stratum is dependent on its size relative to the population.

In **disproportionate stratified sampling**, there are two approaches for researchers to choose. First is that the sample size selected from each stratum is independent of that stratum's proportion of the total defined target population. This approach is used when proportionate

EXHIBIT 14.5 Steps in Drawing a Proportionately Stratified Random Sample

Step 1 → **Obtain a list of potential sampling units that contains an acceptable frame of the defined target population elements.**
Example: List of known patrons (names, addresses, telephone numbers) from the current database of Symphony Hall in Birmingham, England. Total number of known patrons on the current database is 10,500 (this number is hypothetical).

Step 2 → **Using some type of secondary information or past experience with the defined target population, select a stratification factor for which the population's distribution is skewed (not bell-shaped) and can be used to determine that the total defined target population consists of separate sub-populations of elements.**
Example: Using patrons' addresses and attendance records, identify strata by geographic area and patronage frequency measured by number of events attended in the past year (i.e. regular, occasional, or rare). Total: 10,500 patrons with 5,900 'regular' (56.2 per cent); 3,055 'occasional' (29.1 per cent); and 1,545 'rare' (14.7 per cent) patrons.

Step 3 → **Using the selected stratification factor (or some other surrogate variable), segment the defined target population into strata. That is, use the stratification factor to regroup the prospective sampling units into mutually exclusive strata. Then determine both the actual number of sampling units and their percentage equivalents for each stratum.**
Example: Birmingham: 5,000 patrons with 2,500 'regular' (50 per cent); 1,875 'occasional' (37.5 per cent); and 625 'rare' (12.5 per cent) patrons.
West Midlands County other than Birmingham: 3,000 patrons with 1,800 'regular' (60 per cent); 580 'occasional' (19.3 per cent); and 620 'rare' (20.7 per cent) patrons.
Outside West Midlands County: 2,500 patrons with 1,600 'regular' (64 per cent); 600 'occasional' (24 per cent); and 300 'rare' (12 per cent) patrons.

Step 4 → **Determine whether there is a need to apply a disproportionate technique to the stratification process; otherwise, use the proportionate technique and then estimate the desired sample sizes.**
Example: Compare individual geographic area strata percentage value to overall target population strata values. Let's assume a proportionate technique and a confidence level of 95 per cent and a tolerance for sampling error of 2.5 percentage points. Estimate the sample size for total target population with no strata needed and assuming P = 50 per cent. The desired sample size would equal 1,537 people. Then proportion that size by the total patron percentage values for each of the three geographic areas determined in step 2, i.e. Birmingham = 5,000/10,500 (47.6 per cent); West Midlands country other than Birmingham = 3,000/10,500 (28.6 per cent); Outside West Midlands county = 2,500/10,500 (23.8 per cent). New sample sizes for each geographic area would be: Birmingham = 732; West Midlands county other than Birmingham = 439; Outside West Midlands county = 366. Now for sample size of each geographic area, proportion the sample sizes by the respective within-geographic-area estimates for 'regular', 'occasional', and 'rare' strata percentages determined in step 3.

Step 5 → **Select a probability sample from each stratum, using either the SRS or SYMRS procedure.**
Example: Follow the procedures discussed earlier for drawing SRS or SYMRS samples.

stratification of the target population produces sample sizes for groups that differ from their relative importance to the study. For example, stratification of manufacturers based on number of employees will usually result in a large segment of manufacturers with fewer than 50 employees and a very small proportion with, say, 500 or more employees. The obvious economic importance of those firms with 500 or more employees would dictate taking a larger sample from this stratum and a smaller sample from the group with fewer than 50 employees than indicated by the proportionality method.

> **Disproportionate stratified sampling** A stratified sampling technique in which the size of each stratum is independent of its relative size in the population, or is dependent on both its relative size and its variability.

An alternative approach of disproportionate stratified sampling technique is *optimal allocation*. In this technique, consideration is given to the relative size of the stratum as well as the variability within the stratum. The basic logic underlying optimal allocation is that the greater the homogeneity of the prospective sampling units within a particular stratum, the fewer the units that have to be selected to accurately estimate the true population parameter for that stratum. In contrast, the opposite would hold true for any stratum that has considerable variance among its sampling units or in other words that is perceived as heterogeneous.

Advantages and Disadvantages

Dividing the defined target population into strata provides several advantages, including: (1) further assurance of representativeness in the sample; (2) the opportunity to study each stratum and make comparisons between strata; and (3) the ability to make estimates for the target population with the expectation of greater precision and less error. Usually, the larger the number of relevant strata, the more precise the results will be.

The primary difficulty encountered with stratified sampling is determining the basis for stratifying. Secondary information relevant to the required stratification factors might not be readily available, therefore forcing the researcher to use less than desirable surrogate variables as the factors for stratifying the target population. This problem increases the likelihood of the adoption of irrelevant strata, which will waste time and money without providing meaningful results.

Sampling Ethics

A research company is conducting a public opinion survey on a European government's idea of investing its budget surplus in the stock market in order to stabilize its gradually failing economy. The government would like to seek public support for this idea. It believes that the parliament members who have the final say on the idea would respond in a manner consistent with the public opinion survey results.

The research company decides to use a telephone survey to ask the general public their opinions about three possible uses of the budget surplus: (1) invest a significant portion in the stock market; (2) reduce overall income taxes of the taxpayer; (3) redeem part of the national debt.

To conduct this survey, the government instructs the research company to develop a sampling plan for the telephone survey to be administered to 5,000 random selected members of the public that ensures representativeness across four defined age groups: (a) 20 to 35, (b) 36 to 50, (c) 51 to 65, and (d) 66 and older. Reminded of the importance of this survey's objective, the researchers choose to develop a disproportionate stratified random sampling plan that would place heavier emphasis on those people in the 36 to 50 and 51 to 65 age groups than on those people in the other two groups. To help ensure the desired outcome, interviewers are encouraged to 'work hard' on getting responses from respondents aged between 36 and 65. It has been further determined that no matter the actual within-age-group response rates, only the overall response rate and level of error would be released to parliament, the media and the general public.

- Is it ethical to conduct a study that knowingly misrepresents the true defined population for the purpose of seeking a pre-determined outcome?
- Is it ethical to encourage the interviewers to make disproportionate efforts in order to obtain responses from less than all the defined sampled strata?
- Is it ethical to report only the overall response rate and level of error when the disproportionate stratified random sampling technique is used to collect the data?
- Is it ethical not to report all these important aspects of the survey to parliament, the media and the general public, thereby causing them to misinterpret the results?
- Would it be more ethical to use the proportionately stratified random sampling technique?

Cluster Sampling

Cluster sampling is similar to stratified random sampling, but is clearly different in that the sampling units are divided into mutually exclusive and collectively exhaustive subpopulations, called clusters, rather than individually. Each cluster is assumed to be representative of the heterogeneity of the target population. Once the cluster has been identified, the prospective sampling units are selected for the sample by either using a simple random sampling technique or canvassing all the elements (i.e. a census) within the defined cluster.

> **Cluster sampling** A probability sampling technique in which the sampling units are divided into mutually exclusive and collectively exhaustive subpopulations, called clusters.

In marketing research, a popular form of cluster sampling is **area sampling**. In area sampling, the clusters are formed by geographic designations. Examples include Statistical Regions and counties. When using area sampling, the researcher has two additional options: the one-step approach or the two-step approach.

> **Area sampling** A form of cluster sampling in which the clusters are formed by geographic designations.

When deciding on a one-step approach, the researcher must have enough prior information about the various geographic clusters to reliably assume that all the geographic clusters are basically identical with regard to the specific factors that are used to initially identify the clusters. By assuming that all the clusters are identical, the researcher can focus his or her attention on surveying the sampling units within one designated cluster and then generalize the results from this cluster to the population. The probability aspect of this particular sampling technique is executed by randomly selecting one geographic cluster and performing a census on all the sampling units in that cluster.

As an example, assume the marketing manager of Debenhams plc wants to better understand shopping behaviours of people who shop at its 122 department stores located throughout England. Given a review of customer profile information in the database at corporate headquarters, the marketing manager assumes the same types of customers shop at Debenhams regardless of the store's geographic location or day of the week. The Debenhams store located in Guildford is randomly selected as the store site for conducting in-store personal surveys, and 300 such surveys are scheduled to be conducted on 17 February 2009.

The marketing manager's logic of using one store (a one-step cluster sampling technique) to collect data on customers' shopping behaviours has several weaknesses. His assumption that customers at the Guildford store are similar to customers that shop at the other 121 stores in England might well be unfounded. To assume that geographic differences in stores and consumers do not exist is a leap of faith. Limiting the sampling survey to only a certain day can also create problems. To assume that consumers' attitudes and shopping behaviours towards Debenhams department stores are the same on a weekday as they are on the weekend is likely to be misleading.

Another option is to use a two-step cluster sampling approach. First, a set of clusters could be randomly selected and then a probability sampling technique could be used to select individuals within each of the selected clusters. Usually, the two-step approach is preferable over the one-step approach, because there is a strong possibility a single cluster will not be representative of all other clusters.

To illustrate the basics of the two-step cluster sampling approach, let's use the same Debenhams plc example. In reviewing its database on customer profiles, Debenhams concludes that the 122 stores can be clustered on the basis of annual gross sales into three groups: (1) store type A (stores with annual gross sales in the bottom one-third within the full range of annual gross sales of all the 122 stores), (2) store type B (stores in the middle one-third), and (3) store type C (stores in the top one-third). The result is, hypothetically, 50 stores can be grouped as being type A, 30 stores as type B, and 42 stores as type C. In addition, sales have been clearly shown to be significantly heavier on weekends than during the week, which should be taken into account for sampling design purpose. Exhibit 14.6 shows the steps to take in drawing a two-step cluster sample for the Debenhams situation.

Advantages and Disadvantages

Cluster sampling is widely used in marketing research because of its cost-effectiveness and ease of implementation, especially in area sampling situations. In many cases, the only representative sampling frame available to researchers is one based on clusters (e.g. Statistical Regions, counties, universities). With the use of these types of clusters, researchers can avoid the need for compiling lists of all the individual sampling units making up the target population.

Cluster sampling techniques have several disadvantages. A primary disadvantage of cluster sampling is that the clusters chosen may not be representative of the target population. If this happens, even when simple random sampling or census is carried out in the clusters chosen, the result will still not be able to stand for the population. In reality, among the four probability sampling techniques, cluster sampling is likely to bring the least accurate results. Another disadvantage is that the people in a cluster are not as heterogeneous as desired. Ideally, the people in a cluster should be as heterogeneous as those in the population. In reality this is not unusually the case. For example, the people in a county (e.g. Surrey) chosen as the cluster are likely to share some common characteristics, which make them more homogeneous among themselves, and not as heterogeneous as people throughout England in general. Researchers should be aware that the more homogeneous the cluster is, the less precise the sample estimates will be.

Another concern with cluster sampling techniques – one that is not commonly addressed – is the appropriateness of the factors used to identify the clusters as well as the sampling units within clusters. While the defined target population remains constant, the subdivision of sampling units can be changed, for better or for worse, depending on the selection of the factors used. High caution must be used in selecting the appropriate factors.

EXHIBIT 14.6 Steps in Drawing a Two-Step Cluster Sample

Step 1 ➤ **Fully understand the problem situation and characteristics that are used to define the target population. Then determine the clustering factors to be used to identify the clusters of sampling units.**
Example: Initial sampling units would be the 122 known Debenhams department stores located throughout England. Using secondary data of stores' annual gross sales, establish the cluster categories (i.e. store types A, B and C) and weekday versus weekend sales figures.

Step 2 ➤ **Determine the number of sampling units that make up each cluster, obtain a list of potential sampling units for each cluster, and assign them with a unique designation code.**
Example: 50 type A stores – (01) to (50)
30 type B stores – (01) to (30)
42 type C stores – (01) to (42)
Weekday sales – (01) to (52)
Weekend sales – (01) to (52)

Step 3 ➤ **Determine whether to use a one-step or two-step cluster sampling technique.**
Example: Given that both store type and weekday/weekend sales factors are being used to designate the clusters, a two-step clustering approach will be used to draw the sampling units.

Step 4 ➤ **Determine how many sampling units in each cluster need to be sampled to achieve representativeness of that cluster.**
Example: Given the perceived relative homogeneity within each cluster group of stores and cost considerations, let's assume that the researcher feels comfortable in sampling only one store in each store type over two weekday periods and four weekend periods.

Step 5 ➤ **Using random numbers, select the sampling unit (i.e. store) within each cluster and the weekday and weekend time frames to be sampled.**
Example: For store type A: store numbered 01; weekday periods for weeks 10 and 34; weekend periods for weeks 03, 14, 26 and 41.
For store type B: store numbered 12; weekday periods for weeks 33 and 45; weekend periods for weeks 09, 24, 29 and 36.
For store type C: store numbered 10; weekday periods for weeks 22 and 46; weekend periods for weeks 04, 18, 32 and 37.

Step 6 ➤ **Determine the needed sample sizes for each cluster by weekday/weekend time frames.**
Example: Let's assume a desired confidence level of 95 per cent and a tolerance for sampling error of 2.5 percentage points. Estimate the desired sample size for total target population with no cluster grouping method and assuming P = 50 per cent. The desired sample size would equal 1,537 people. Then proportion that size by the percentage values for each type of store to total number of stores making up the defined target population frame (i.e. store type A = 50/122 (X per cent); store type B = 30/122 (X per cent); store type C = 42/122 (X per cent)). New sample sizes for each store type would be: store type A = Y; store type B = Y; store type C = Y. Then proportion these sample sizes by the respective within weekday and weekend estimates, determined in step 4. As a result, the required sample sizes by store type by weekday/weekend time frames would be:
Store type A: Weekday periods 43 people in week 10, 43 people in week 34; Weekend periods 43 people in week 03 and the same number for weeks 14, 26 and 41.
Store type B: Weekday periods 43 people in week 33, 43 people in week 45; Weekend periods 43 people in week 09 and the same number for weeks 24, 29 and 46.
Store type C: Weekday periods 43 people in week 22, 43 people in week 46; Weekend periods 43 people in week 04 and the same number for weeks 18, 32 and 37.

Step 7 ➤ **Select a probability sampling technique for selecting customers for in-store survey.**
Example: Randomize the weekday survey as well as the weekend survey so that in principle the data are represented across shopping days.

Types of Non-Probability Sampling Designs

Convenience Sampling

Convenience sampling is a technique in which samples are drawn based on convenience. For example, shopping-intercept interviews of individuals at shopping centres or other high-traffic areas is a common method of generating a convenience sample. The assumption that could be made by researchers using this method is that the individuals interviewed at the shopping centre or other chosen areas are similar to the overall defined target population with regard to the characteristic being studied. In reality, it is difficult to accurately assess the representativeness of the sample. Given self-selection and the voluntary nature of participating in the data collection, researchers should regard this method as non-representative, and should acknowledge and attempt to reduce the impact of any possible non-response error.

> **Convenience sampling** A non-probability sampling technique in which samples are drawn at the convenience of the researcher.

Advantages and Disadvantages

Convenience sampling enables a large number of respondents to be interviewed in a relatively short time. For this reason, it is commonly used in the early stages of research (i.e. construct and scale measurement development as well as pretesting of questionnaires). But using convenience samples to develop constructs and scales can be risky. For example, assume the researcher is developing a measure of service quality and in the preliminary stages uses a convenience sample of 300 undergraduate business students. While students are consumers of services, serious questions should be raised about whether they are truly representative of the general population. By developing and refining constructs and scales using data from a convenience sample of students, the construct and scale might later prove to be unreliable when used in investigations of other defined target populations. Even when non-students (e.g. shoppers at the shopping centre) are used as the convenience sample, serious doubts still arise as to whether shoppers at a particular shopping centre during specific interview times are representative of the target population, and whether the interviewer has picked their convenience sample from these shoppers in an objective manner. In any case, the representativeness of the sample simply can never be measured because sampling error estimates cannot be calculated. Review the nearby Closer Look at Research box on the use of convenience sampling in a Turkish market.

 A Closer Look at Research (in the field)

Using Convenience Sampling Survey to Study the Turkish Cola Market

The Turkish cola drink market is worth €500 million and is rapidly growing. In this market, Coca Cola and Pepsi Cola indisputably had been the major players. However, in recent years, Ulker Company, a well-known Turkish food giant traditionally specializing in confectionery and cookie products, launched a new indigenous cola product branded Cola Turka, and met with great success in its opening day sales.

Dilber Ulas and H. Bader Arslan, researchers at Ankara University, Turkey, conducted a sampling survey to study consumer attitudes specific to the booming and increasingly competitive Turkish cola market, with a focus on the future potential of Cola Turka.

With limited financial and time resources for the sampling survey, the researchers resorted to the use of a convenience student sample. In order to obtain greater diversity in the sample, they chose four different universities (Ankara, Gazi, Cukurova and Suleyman Demirel) from which to draw their sampling units. Three reasons were cited by them to support the use of student sub-samples from these four universities. First, the four universities are located in different regions of the country and thus students from them come from different subcultures and have different purchase habits. Second, cola drink consumption is evidently high among young people, including university students. Third, the students are comparatively easy to reach, as evidenced by the fact that 855 of 900 questionnaires were duly completed and received.

Results of the sampling survey show that Cola Turka has the potential to create a large loyal customer base. Despite Coca Cola still preserving it dominance, Pepsi Cola is predicted to be convincing overcome by the new indigenous brand.

Source: Ulas and Arslan, 2006.

Judgement Sampling

In **judgement sampling**, sometimes referred to as purposive sampling, sample respondents are selected because the researcher, based on their judgement, believes they meet the requirements of the study. In many industrial sales studies, the regional sales manager will survey sales representatives rather than customers to determine whether customers' wants and needs are changing or to assess the firm's product or service performance. Many consumer packaging manufacturers (e.g. Procter & Gamble) regularly select a sample of key accounts believed to be able to provide information about consumption patterns and changes in demand for selected products. The underlying assumption is that the opinions of a group of perceived experts are representative of the target population.

> **Judgement sampling** A non-probability sampling technique in which participants are selected according to the researcher's judgement that they will meet the requirements of the study.

Advantages and Disadvantages

If the judgement of the researcher is correct, the sample generated by judgement sampling will be better than one generated by convenience sampling. However, as with all non-probability sampling techniques, one cannot measure and prove the representativeness of the sample. At best, the data collected from judgement sampling should be interpreted cautiously.

Quota Sampling

Quota sampling involves the selection of prospective participants according to pre-specified quotas for either demographic characteristics (e.g. race, gender, age, income), specific attitudes (e.g. satisfied/dissatisfied, liking/disliking), or specific behaviours (e.g. regular/occasional/rare

> **Quota sampling** A non-probability sampling technique in which participants are selected according to pre-specified quotas that are thought to have major impacts on the findings of the survey.

customer, product user/non-user). The purpose of quota sampling is to assure that pre-specified subgroups of the target population are represented on selected variables which are deemed as having major impacts on the findings of the survey.

The variables to be selected as quotas should be dependent on the nature of the research objectives. For example, if a research study is conducted about fast food restaurants, the researcher may establish quotas using the age variable and the patronage behaviour of prospective respondents as follows:

Age	Patronage Behaviour
[1] Under 25	[1] Patronize a fast food restaurant at an average of once a month or more
[2] 25 to 54	[2] Patronize a fast food restaurant less frequently than once a month
[3] 55 and over	

Using these demographic and patronage behaviour variables, the researcher identifies six different subgroups of people to be included in the study. Determining the quota size for each of the subgroups is a systematic process. The researcher might use sales information to determine the percentage size of each subgroup according to how much each has contributed to the firm's total sales. This ensures that the sample will contain the desired number in each subgroup. Once the individual percentage sizes for each quota are established, the researcher segments the sample size by those percentage values to determine the actual number of prospective respondents to be included in each of the pre-specified quota groups. Let's say, for example, that a fast food restaurant wanted to interview 1,000 people and, using both industry-supplied sales reports and company sales records, determined that individuals aged 25 to 54 who patronize fast food restaurants at least once a month make up 50 per cent of its total sales. The researcher would then want that subgroup to make up 50 per cent of the total sample. Let's further assume that company records indicated that individuals aged 25 to 54 who frequent fast food restaurants less than once a month make up only 6 per cent of sales. This particular subgroup should consist of only 6 per cent of the total sample size.

Advantages and Disadvantages

The greatest advantage of quota sampling is that the sample generated contains specific subgroups in the proportions desired by researchers. The use of quotas ensures that the perceived appropriate subgroups are identified and included in the survey. Also, quota sampling should reduce selection bias caused by field workers. An inherent limitation of quota sampling is that the success of the study will again be dependent on subjective decisions, notably which quotas should be used, made by the researchers. Even assuming the quotas have been appropriately identified and used, the selection of respondents to meet each quota is still subject to the field workers' selection bias. Therefore, generalizing the results beyond the sampled respondents is questionable.

Snowball Sampling

Snowball sampling involves identifying and qualifying a set of initial prospective respondents who can, in turn, help the researcher identify additional people to include in the study. This technique of sampling is also called *referral sampling*, because one respondent refers other potential respondents to the researcher. Snowball sampling typically is used in situations where (1) the defined target population is small and unique, and (2) compiling a complete list of sampling units is very difficult. Consider, for example, researching the attitudes and behaviours of people who volunteer their time to charitable organizations like World Vision. While traditional sampling techniques require an extensive search effort (both in time and cost) to qualify a sufficient number of prospective respondents, the snowball technique yields better results at a much lower cost. Here the researcher interviews a qualified respondent, then solicits his or her help to identify other people with the same required characteristics. While membership in these types of social circles may not be publicly known, intracircle knowledge is largely accurate. The underlying logic of this technique is that rare groups of people tend to form their own unique social circles.

Advantages and Disadvantages

Snowball sampling is a reasonable technique for identifying respondents who are members of small, hard-to-reach, uniquely defined target populations. This technique is very useful in qualitative research practices. But snowball sampling allows bias to enter the study. If there are significant differences among people who are known in certain social circles, the findings from the snowball sample may significantly deviate from the true situation of the social circle from which the snowball sample is drawn. This representativeness problem is likely to be more acute if the snowball sample is used to stand for a general target population (such as population in the country concerned, or population in a geographic region).

Determining the Appropriate Sampling Design

Selection of the most appropriate sampling design should consider the seven factors displayed in Exhibit 14.7.

Research Objectives

An understanding of the research problem and objectives provides the initial guidelines for determining the appropriate sampling design. If the research objectives include the desire to generalize the sample results to the target population, then the researcher must probably use some type of probability sampling technique rather than a non-probability sampling technique.

EXHIBIT 14.7 Critical Factors in Selecting the Appropriate Sampling Design

Selection Factors	Questions
Research objectives	Do the research objectives call for the use of qualitative or quantitative research designs?
Degree of accuracy	Does the research call for making predictions or inductive inferences about the defined target population, or only preliminary insights?
Resources	Are there tight budget constraints with respect to both financial and human resources that can be allocated to the research project?
Time frame	How quickly does the research project have to be completed?
Knowledge of the target population	Are there complete lists of the defined target population elements? How easy or difficult is it to generate the required sampling frame of prospective respondents?
Scope of the research	Is the research going to be international, national, regional, or local?
Statistical analysis needs	To what extent are accurate statistical projections and/or testing of hypothesized differences in the data structures required?

Degree of Accuracy

The degree of accuracy required will vary from project to project, especially when cost savings or other considerations are evaluated. If the researcher wants to make predictions about members of the defined target population, then a probability sampling technique must be used. In contrast, if the researcher is interested only in preliminary insights about the target population, non-probability techniques might be appropriate.

Resources

If financial and human resources are limited, they most certainly will eliminate some of the more time-consuming, complex probability sampling techniques. If the budget is a substantial limitation, then it is likely that a non-probability sampling technique will be used rather than conducting no research at all.

Time Frame

Researchers with short deadlines will be more likely to select a simple, less time-consuming sampling technique rather than a more complex technique. For example, researchers with a tight work schedule tend to use convenience sampling to gather data for testing the reliability of a newly developed construct. However, one should bear in mind that, while data from this sampling technique might provide preliminary insights about the defined target population, there is no way to assess the representativeness of the results.

Knowledge of the Target Population

In cases where a complete list of the defined target population elements is not available and generation of the required sampling frame is difficult, the researcher may resort to the use of non-probability sampling techniques such as convenience sampling or snowball sampling.

Scope of the Research

The scope of the research project, whether international, national, regional, or local, will influence the choice of the sampling technique. Generally, the broader the geographical scope of the research project, the more complex the sampling technique may need to be to ensure proper representation of the target population.

Statistical Analysis Needs

The need for statistical projections based on the sample results is often a criterion. Only probability sampling techniques enable the researcher to use statistical analysis for reliable estimates beyond the immediate set of sampled respondents. While statistical analysis can also be performed on data obtained from non-probability samples, the ability to reliably generalize the findings to the target population is suspect.

Steps in Developing a Sampling Plan

Sampling is much more than just finding some people to participate in a research study. In an ideal scenario, researchers should consider a number of different concepts and procedures to successfully gather data from a group of people that can be used to make inferential predictions

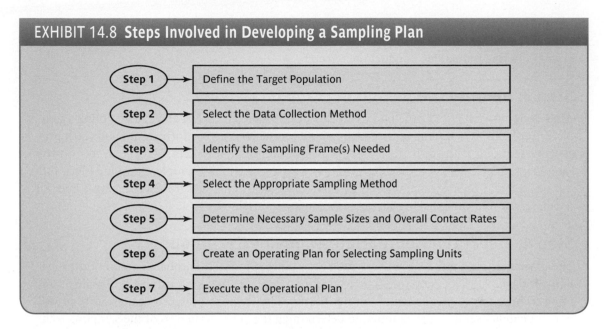

EXHIBIT 14.8 Steps Involved in Developing a Sampling Plan

Step 1 → Define the Target Population

Step 2 → Select the Data Collection Method

Step 3 → Identify the Sampling Frame(s) Needed

Step 4 → Select the Appropriate Sampling Method

Step 5 → Determine Necessary Sample Sizes and Overall Contact Rates

Step 6 → Create an Operating Plan for Selecting Sampling Units

Step 7 → Execute the Operational Plan

about a larger target population. After understanding the key components of sampling theory, the methods of determining sample sizes, and the various sampling designs available, the researcher is ready to use them to develop a **sampling plan**. A sampling plan is the blueprint to ensure that the data collected are representative of the target population. A good sampling plan includes the following steps: (1) define the target population, (2) select the data collection method, (3) identify the sampling frame(s) needed, (4) select the appropriate sampling technique (5) determine necessary sample sizes and overall contact rates, (6) create an operating plan for selecting sampling units, and (7) execute the operational plan.

> **Sampling plan** The blueprint or framework needed to ensure that the data collected are representative of the defined target population.

Exhibit 14.8 graphically presents the logical steps that make up a sampling plan. You are encouraged to revisit earlier parts of the chapter for more details of these activities.

Step 1: Define the Target Population

In any sampling plan, the first task of the researcher is to determine the group of people or objects that should be investigated. With the research problem and research objectives as guidelines, the target population should be identified using descriptors that represent the characteristics of the elements of the target population's frame. These elements become the sampling units from which a sample will be drawn. Clear understanding of the target population will help the researcher successfully draw a representative sample.

Step 2: Select the Data Collection Method

Using the research problem definition, the research objectives and the data requirements, the researcher chooses a method for collecting the data from the target population elements. Choices include some type of interviewing approach (e.g. personal or telephone) or a self-administered survey. The method of data collection guides the researcher in identifying and securing the necessary sampling frame(s) to conduct the research.

Step 3: Identify the Sampling Frame(s) Needed

After deciding what and the method to investigate, the researcher must aim at assembling a complete list of eligible sampling units. The list should contain enough information about each prospective sampling unit so the researcher can successfully contact them. Having an incomplete sampling frame decreases the likelihood of drawing a representative sample. Sampling frame lists can be created from a number of different sources (e.g. customer lists from a company's internal database, random-digit dialling, an organization's membership list).

Step 4: Select the Appropriate Sampling Technique

The researcher chooses between two types of sampling approaches: probability and non-probability. If the data will be used to estimate target population parameters, using a probability sampling technique will yield more accurate information about the target population than will non-probability sampling techniques. In determining the appropriateness of the sampling technique, the researcher must consider seven factors: (1) research objectives, (2) desired accuracy, (3) availability of resources, (4) time frame, (5) knowledge of the target population, (6) scope of the research, and (7) statistical analysis needs.

Step 5: Determine Necessary Sample Sizes and Overall Contact Rates

In this step of a sampling plan, the researcher decides how precise the sample estimates must be and how much time and money are available to collect the data. To determine the appropriate sample size, decisions have to be made concerning (1) the variability of the population characteristic under investigation, (2) the level of confidence desired in the estimates, and (3) the precision required. The researcher must also decide how many completed surveys are needed for data analysis, recognizing that initial sample size often is not equal to the final sample size.

At this point two important questions are: 'How many prospective sampling units will have to be contacted to ensure the estimated sample size is obtained, and at what additional costs?' To answer these, the researcher must be able to calculate the expected reachable rate, expected incidence rate and expected completion rate for the sampling situation.

Step 6: Create an Operating Plan for Selecting Sampling Units

In this step, the researcher must determine how to contact the prospective respondents who were drawn in the sample. Instructions should be clearly written so that interviewers know what to do and how to handle any problems contacting prospective respondents. For example, if the study data will be collected using a shopping-intercept survey, then instructions on how to select respondents and conduct the interviews must be given to the interviewer.

Step 7: Execute the Operational Plan

This step is in essence about actually collecting the data (e.g. calling prospective respondents to do a telephone survey). The important point at this stage is to maintain consistency and control.

Developing a Sampling Plan for a New Menu Initiative Survey for Jimmy Spice's Restaurant

Owners of Jimmy Spice's Restaurant realize that in order to remain competitive in the restaurant industry, new menu items need to be introduced periodically to provide variety for current customers and to attract new customers. Recognizing this, the owners of the restaurant preparing for a corresponding marketing research project believe three issues need to be addressed. One, should the menu be changed to include items beyond the current Indian, Thai, Chinese and Italian cuisines? For example, should items be added that would be considered French or Spanish cuisine? Second, regardless of the cuisine to be explored, how many new items (i.e. appetizers, entries, desserts, etc.) should be included in the survey? Third, what type of sampling plan should be developed for selecting respondents, and who should these respondents be (current customers, new customers, old customers, etc.)?

Understanding the importance of sampling and the impact it will have on the representativeness of the research results, the owners have asked a local university if a marketing research class could assist them in this project. Specifically, the owners have posed the following questions that need to be addressed:

- How many questions should the survey contain to adequately address all possible new menu items, including the notion of assessing the desirability of new cuisines?
- How should the potential respondents be selected for the survey? Should patrons be interviewed while they are dining? Should patrons be asked to participate in the survey upon exiting the restaurant? Or should a mail or telephone approach be used to collect information from patrons or non-patrons?

Questions

Based on the above questions, your task is to develop a procedure to address the following issues:

a From the total domain of possible new items to include on the menu, how many items can be put in the survey? Remember, all menu possibilities should be assessed but you must have a manageable number of questions so the survey can be performed in a timely and reasonable manner. Specifically, from a list of all possible menu items that can be included in the survey, what is the optimal number of menu items that should be used? Is there a sampling procedure one can use to determine the maximum number of menu items to place in the survey?

b Develop an appropriate sampling design proposal for Jimmy Spices that addresses the followings: Should a probability or non-probability sample be used? Given your answer, what type of sampling design should be employed (simple random, stratified, convenience, etc.)? Given the sampling design suggested, how will potential respondents be selected for the study? Finally, determine the necessary sample size and create an operating plan for selecting the sampling units.

marketing research in action

Summary of Learning Objectives

■ **Distinguish between probability and non-probability sampling techniques.**

In probability sampling, each sampling unit in the defined target population has a known probability of being selected for the sample. The actual probability of selection for each sampling unit may or may not be equal depending on the type of probability sampling design used. In non-probability sampling, the probability of selection of each sampling unit is not known. The selection of sampling units is based on some type of intuitive judgement or knowledge of the researcher.

■ **Understand the advantages and disadvantages of probability sampling designs.**

Probability sampling enables the researcher to judge the reliability and validity of data collected by calculating the probability that the findings based on the sample will differ from the defined target population. This observed difference can be partially attributed to the existence of sampling error. Each probability sampling technique – simple random, systematic random, stratified, and cluster – has its own inherent advantages and disadvantages.

■ **Understand the advantages and disadvantages of non-probability sample designs.**

In non-probability sampling, the probability of selection of each sampling unit is not known. Therefore, potential sampling error cannot be accurately known either. Although there may be a temptation to generalize non-probability sample results to the defined target population, for the most part the results are limited to the people who provided the data in the survey. Each non-probability sampling technique – convenience, judgement, quota, and snowball – has its own inherent advantages and disadvantages.

■ **Illustrate the factors necessary for determining the appropriate sample design.**

Selection of the most appropriate sampling design should incorporate the seven factors. These factors include: research objectives, degree of accuracy, availability of resources, time frame, advanced knowledge of the target population, scope of the research and statistical analysis needs.

■ **Understand the steps in developing a sampling plan.**

A sampling plan is the blueprint or framework needed to ensure that the data collected are representative of the defined target population. A good sampling plan will include, at least, the following steps: (1) define the target population, (2) select the data collection method, (3) identify the sampling frames needed, (4) select the appropriate sampling technique, (5) determine necessary sample sizes and overall contact rates, (6) create an operating plan for selecting sampling units, and (7) execute the operational plan.

Key Terms and Concepts

Area sampling   477
Cluster sampling   477
Convenience sampling   480
Disproportionate stratified
   sampling   476
Judgement sampling   481
Non-probability sampling   470
Probability sampling   470

Proportionate stratified sampling   474
Quota sampling   481
Sampling plan   485
Simple random sampling (SRS)   471
Snowball sampling   482
Stratified random sampling (STRS)   474
Systematic random sampling
   (SYMRS)   472

Review Questions

1 Briefly discuss the differences between probability and non-probability samples.

2 Explain the advantages and disadvantages of the following sampling techniques:

   a Simple random sampling

   b Systematic random sampling

   c Cluster sampling

   d Convenience sampling

3 Identify the major steps involved in developing a two-step cluster sample.

4 Discuss the critical factors necessary for determining an appropriate sample design.

5 Briefly discuss the seven steps involved in developing a sampling plan.

Discussion Questions

1 **Experience the Internet.** Log on to the Internet and go to Vacation Rentals by owners (VRBO) at www.vrbo.com. This website consists of thousands of vacation rentals worldwide. After getting to this website, select and click on 'Europe', then 'Netherlands', then 'Amsterdam'. First, how many vacation rentals are available in Amsterdam? Then using a systematic random sampling design, draw a sample of ten vacation rentals in Amsterdam.

2 **Experience the Internet.** Search the Internet to look for populations in different European Union countries. Use the proportionate stratified random sampling technique to develop a sample with 3,600 sampling units representing the overall European Union population. How many sampling units from each country should be included?

3 Over the past ten weeks, the number '9' was a winning number in the National Lottery 40 per cent of the time. If you pick a number for the upcoming lottery draw, and you select the number '9', will you be more or less likely to win the lottery? How would you explain your answer based on the concept of simple random sampling?

4 Outline the step-by-step process used to determine the following:

   a A systematic random sample of 200 students at your university.

   b A convenience sample of 150 shoppers at a local shopping centre.

   c A stratified random sample of 50 lawyers, 40 doctors and 60 dentists who subscribe to your local newspaper.

5 Vodaphone is interested in determining the heavy users of mobile phones. Which sampling technique would be best suited for this situation? Why?

PART 4

Data Preparation, Analysis and Reporting

Part contents

Chapter 15

Data Preparation

LEARNING OBJECTIVES

After reading this chapter, you will be able to

- ☑ Illustrate the process of preparing data for preliminary analysis.

- ☑ Demonstrate the procedure for assuring data validation.

- ☑ Describe the process of editing and coding data obtained through a questionnaire survey.

- ☑ Acquaint the user with data entry procedures.

- ☑ Illustrate a process for detecting errors in data entry.

- ☑ Discuss techniques used for data tabulation and data analysis.

> Data is the lifeblood of every business. Yet many businesses are still coming to terms with how to manage and utilize the vast amounts of critical data they hold in their databases.
>
> *Source: Case study of Italian services ICT company, Freedata, investing in the UK, which is posted on UK Trade & Investment web gateway*

Scanner Technology and Data Preparation

Scanner technology is widely used in the marketing research industry. Questionnaires can be prepared through any of a number of word-processing software packages and printed on a laser printer. Respondents can complete the questionnaire with any type of writing instrument. With the appropriate software and scanning device, the researcher can scan the completed questionnaires and the data are checked for errors, categorized, and stored within a matter of seconds. When a researcher expects to receive 400 to 500 completed surveys, scanner technology can be worth its weight in gold.

Value of Preparing the Collected Data

As the chapter opening quotation implies, recognizing the importance of data and thereby putting efforts into collecting relevant data are one thing; knowing how to manage and utilize these data is another. No matter how potentially powerful the collected data are, they are useless if the company concerned does not know how to deal with them or deals with them in the wrong way. One common malpractice is that companies do not prepare the collected data properly before they are put through to the data analysis stage. Because of this inadequate preparation, potential problems with the original collected data have not been detected and rectified, and therefore the undesirable garbage-in garbage-out outcome is liable to occur.

As the chapter opener example indicates, scanner technology has assisted marketing researchers in increasing not only the speed of data collection, but also the accuracy of the data collected. However, sources of data inaccuracy are varied and scanner technology cannot detect each of them. As marketing researchers, we need to have a well-rounded understanding of how to prepare the collected data properly. This chapter aims to nurture this understanding.

The fundamental rationale for data preparation is the principle of garbage-in garbage-out (GIGO). With today's advances in computer technology, data collection and data entry are much less time and labour consuming. However, this increase in efficiency is nothing if the data collected and entered are of poor quality. Properly preparing the collected data can enhance the quality of the data.

Converting data from a questionnaire so it can be transferred to a data warehouse is referred to as data preparation. This process usually follows a four-stage approach, beginning with data validation, then editing and coding, followed by data entry and finally data tabulation. Error detection begins in the first stage and continues throughout the process. The purpose of data preparation is to take data in its raw form and convert it to establish meaning and create value for the user.

The process of data preparation and analysis starts after the data is collected. Several interrelated tasks must be completed to ensure the data is accurately reported. The stages of data preparation and analysis are shown in Exhibit 15.1. This chapter discusses the data preparation process and Chapters 16 to 19 discuss major data analysis techniques which have been popular in the marketing research industry.

Data Validation

Data validation is concerned with determining, as far as possible, if a questionnaire survey was conducted in the right manner. If possible, each respondent's name and contact details can be recorded. While this information is not used for analysis, it does facilitate and improve the validation process.

> **Data validation** The process of determining, as far as possible, whether a questionnaire survey was conducted in the right manner.

Curbstoning is a term used in the marketing research industry to indicate falsification of data. As the name implies, curbstoning is when interviewers find an out-of-the-way location, such as a curbstone, and fill out the questionnaire themselves rather than follow the proper

EXHIBIT 15.1 Overview of the Stages of Data Preparation and Analysis

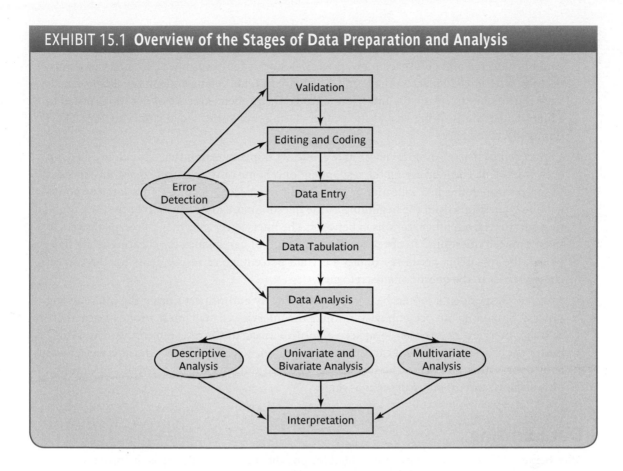

procedure with an actual respondent. With the likelihood for such falsification, data validation becomes a necessary step in the data preparation process.

> **Curbstoning** Cheating or falsification in the data collection process.

Typically marketing research professionals will target between 10 and 30 per cent of completed interviews for 'callbacks'. The percentage of respondents chosen will each be re-contacted by the research firm to check if the interview was conducted in the right manner. Normally through telephone recontact, respondents will be asked several short questions as a way of validating the questionnaire data obtained from the interview. The stage of data validation covers five areas:

1 *Fraud.* Was the person actually interviewed, or was the interview falsified? Did the interviewer contact the respondent simply to get a name and address, and then proceed to fabricate responses themselves? Did the interviewer use another person to conduct the interview?

2 *Screening.* Many times an interview must be conducted only with qualified respondents. For this purpose, potential respondents will be screened according to some pre-selected criteria, such as gender, age, income or recent purchase of a specific product or brand. A validation callback can verify these pre-selected criteria.

3   *Procedure.* It is always crucial that the data be collected according to a planned procedure. The questions should be asked properly and in the planned sequence, otherwise respondents could be affected and give inaccurate answers. Besides, many customer exit interviews must occur in a designated place as the respondent leaves a retail establishment. A validation call-back is necessary to ensure the interview followed the proper sequence of questions posed to respondents, and it took place at the proper setting, not some social gathering area like a dining place or a park.

4   *Correct completeness.* An interviewer may carelessly skip a question that should be asked, or, even worse still, cheat by asking the respondent only some of the requisite questions in order to speed through the data collection process. In the latter scenario, they may ask the respondent a few questions from the beginning of the questionnaire and then skip to the end, omitting questions from other sections in between. The interviewer may then make up answers to these omitted questions. To check whether this kind of carelessness or cheating really happened, the researcher could re-contact a certain percentage of respondents for the correct completeness in the questionnaires returned.

5   *Courtesy.* Respondents should be treated with courtesy and respect during the interviewing process. Situations can occur, however, where the interviewer may inject a tone of negativity into the interviewing process. To upkeep a positive image of the research company responsible for the process, respondent callbacks should be done to check whether the interviewer was courteous. Other aspects of the interviewer checked during callbacks include appearance, pleasantness, and proper manner as a whole.

Data Editing

After being validated, the data must be edited for possible mistakes. **Editing** is the process where raw data are checked for mistakes made by either the interviewer or the respondent. By scanning each completed questionnaire, the researcher can check two major areas of concern: (1) recording of responses to forced-choice questions, and (2) recording of responses to open-ended questions.

> **Editing** The process whereby the raw data are checked for mistakes made by either the interviewer or the respondent.

Recording of Responses to Forced-Choice Questions

Completed questionnaires sometimes contain wrong or unclear data. The interviewer may accidentally have recorded respondents' answers wrongly in the questionnaire; or they may not have recorded them in the proper location, which can lead to the recording of the answers in incorrect positions on the spreadsheet. With a careful check of all questionnaires, these problems can be identified. In such cases, respondents should be re-contacted in order to record the accurate answer in the correct place of the questionnaire.

Recording of Responses to Open-Ended Questions

Responses to open-ended questions often provide very meaningful data. Open-ended questions usually provide greater insight into the research questions than forced-choice questions. A major

EXHIBIT 15.2 Jimmy Spice's Restaurant Questionnaire

Below are the screening and follow-up questions asked and completed by the interviewer for each respondent.

_____

Hello. My name is _____ and I work for Marketing Intelligence and Research. We are talking to individuals today/tonight about dining out habits and patterns.

'Have you been living in the UK for over a year?'	___ Yes	___ No
'Are you living in Birmingham?'	___ Yes	___ No
'Do you usually eat out at a proper restaurant at least once every week?'	___ Yes	___ No

If respondent answers 'Yes' to all three questions, then say:

We would like you to ask for your permission to answer a number of questions about your experience today/tonight at Jimmy spice's restaurant, and we hope you could agree to help with this. Answering these questions will take approximately 15 minutes and it would be very helpful to the management of the restaurant in better serving its customers.

If the person says yes, give him/her clipboard with the questionnaire on it, and briefly explain the questionnaire.

_____

When the respondent returns the questionnaire, check it for completeness and if there is any question that should be answered but the respondent has not done so, try to get him/her to complete it.

Look closely at the answers to questions 22, 23 and 24. If the respondent answers 1, 2 or 3 ask the following questions.

You indicated you are not too satisfied with Jimmy spice's restaurant. Could you please tell me why?

Record answer here:

_____

You indicated you are not likely to return to Jimmy spice's restaurant. Could you please tell me why?

Record answer here:

_____

You indicated you are not likely to recommend Jimmy spice's restaurant. Could you please tell me why?

Record answer here:

_____

Also look closely at the answers to question 25. If the respondent answers 1 or 2 ask the following question.

You indicated in general you patronize Jimmy spice's restaurant at least once a month. Could you please tell me why?

Record answer here:

_____

> Could I please have your name and phone number for verification purposes?

_____   _____
              Name   **Phone #**

I hereby attest that this is a true and honest interview and has been completed to the best of my knowledge. I guarantee that all information relating to this interview shall be kept strictly confidential.

_____   _____
     Interviewer's Signature   **Date and Time Completed**

The following is the questionnaire to be filled in by the respondent.

DINING OUT QUESTIONNAIRE

Please read all the questions carefully. If you do not understand a question, ask the interviewer to help you. In the first section, a number of statements are given about yourself. Using a scale from 1 to 7, with 1 being 'Strongly Disagree' and 7 being 'Strongly Agree', please indicate the extent to which you agree or disagree a particular statement describes you. Circle only one number for each statement.

Section 1: Life Style Questions

		Strongly Disagree							Strongly Agree
1	I often try new and different things.	1	2	3	4	5	6	7	
2	I like parties with music and lots of talk.	1	2	3	4	5	6	7	
3	People come to me more often than I go to them for information about products.	1	2	3	4	5	6	7	
4	I try to avoid fried foods.	1	2	3	4	5	6	7	
5	I like to go out and socialize with people.	1	2	3	4	5	6	7	
6	Friends and neighbours often come to me for advice about products and brands.	1	2	3	4	5	6	7	
7	I am self-confident about myself and my future.	1	2	3	4	5	6	7	
8	I usually eat balanced, nutritious meals.	1	2	3	4	5	6	7	

9 When I see a new product in stores, I often want to buy it.

Strongly
Disagree
1 2 3 4 5 6 7

Strongly
Agree

10 I am careful about what I eat.

Strongly
Disagree
1 2 3 4 5 6 7

Strongly
Agree

11 I often try new products before my friends and neighbours do.

Strongly
Disagree
1 2 3 4 5 6 7

Strongly
Agree

Section 2: Perception Measures

Listed below is a set of characteristics that can be used to describe Jimmy spice's restaurant. Using a scale from 1 to 7, with 7 being 'Strongly Agree' and 1 being 'Strongly Disagree', to what extent do you agree or disagree that Jimmy Spice's

12 Has friendly employees

Strongly
Disagree
1 2 3 4 5 6 7

Strongly
Agree

13 Is a fun place to eat

Strongly
Disagree
1 2 3 4 5 6 7

Strongly
Agree

14 Has large size portions

Strongly
Disagree
1 2 3 4 5 6 7

Strongly
Agree

15 Has fresh food

Strongly
Disagree
1 2 3 4 5 6 7

Strongly
Agree

16 Has reasonable prices

Strongly
Disagree
1 2 3 4 5 6 7

Strongly
Agree

17 Has an attractive interior

Strongly
Disagree
1 2 3 4 5 6 7

Strongly
Agree

18 Has excellent food taste

Strongly
Disagree
1 2 3 4 5 6 7

Strongly
Agree

19 Has knowledgeable employees

Strongly
Disagree
1 2 3 4 5 6 7

Strongly
Agree

20 Serves food at the proper temperature

Strongly
Disagree
1 2 3 4 5 6 7

Strongly
Agree

21 Has quick service

Strongly
Disagree
1 2 3 4 5 6 7

Strongly
Agree

Section 3: Relationship Measures

Please indicate your view on each of the following questions:

22 How satisfied are you with Jimmy Spice's restaurant?

	Not Satisfied At All	Very Satisfied
	1 2 3 4 5 6 7	

23 How likely are you to return to Jimmy Spice's restaurant in the future?

	Definitely Will Not Return	Definitely Will Return
	1 2 3 4 5 6 7	

24 How likely are you to recommend Jimmy Spice's restaurant to a friend?

	Definitely Will Not Recommend	Definitely Will Recommend
	1 2 3 4 5 6 7	

25 How often do you patronize Jimmy Spice's restaurant?

1 = Occasionally (Less than once a month)
2 = Frequently (1–3 times a month)
3 = Very Frequently (4 or more times a month)

Section 4: Selection Factors

Listed below are some factors (reasons) many people use in selecting a restaurant where they want to dine. Think about your visits to casual dining restaurants in the last three month and please rank each attribute from from 1 to 4, with 1 being the most important reason for selecting the restaurant and 4 being the least important reason. There can be no ties so make sure you rank each attribute with a different number.

Attributes	Ranking
26 Prices	
27 Food Quality	
28 Atmosphere	
29 Service	

Section 5: Classification Questions

Please circle the number that classifies you best.

30 Distance driven

1 Less than 1 mile
2 1–3 miles
3 More than 3 miles

31 Do your recall seeing any advertisements in the last 60 days for Jimmy Spice's restaurant?

0 No
1 Yes

32 Your gender

0 Male
1 Female

33 Number of children at home

1 None
2 1–2
3 More than 2 children at home

34 Your age in years	1 18–25
	2 26–34
	3 35–49
	4 50–59
	5 60 and Older
35 Your annual gross household income	1 €15,000–€30,000
	2 €30,001–€50,000
	3 €50,001–€75,000
	4 €75,001–€100,000
	5 More than €100,000

Thank you very much for your help. Please return your completed questionnaire to the interviewer.

EXHIBIT 15.3 Responses to an Open-Ended Question

10 You indicated in general you patronize Jimmy spice's restaurant at least once a month? Could you please tell me why?

- They have good service.
- Found out how good the food is.
- Enjoy the food.
- We just moved here and where we lived there were no good ethnic restaurants.
- That part of town is building up so fast.
- They have a couple of promotional offers in the newspaper.
- It is right beside where my husband works.
- Tastes better.
- They started giving better value meal packages.
- We really like their spicy chicken dishes, so we go more often now.
- The good food.
- Only because there is no other good restaurant nearby.
- BLT and pulsating.
- Just opened lately.
- It is located right by the supermarket where I do most of my grocery shopping.
- Just moved into area and they have good food.
- It is close to where I work.

part of editing the answers to open-ended questions is interpretation. Exhibit 15.3 shows some typical responses to an open-ended question. These responses shed light on some potential problems associated with interpreting answers to open-ended questions.

One response to the question about why the respondent patronized Jimmy spice's restaurant at least once a month is simply 'They have good service'. This answer by itself is not sufficient to determine what the respondent means by 'good service'. The interviewer needs to probe for a more specific response. For example, are the employees friendly, helpful, courteous? Do they appear neat and clean? Do they smile when taking an order? Probes such as these would enable the researcher to better interpret the 'good service' answer.

Another response to the question is 'BLT and pulsating'. Here the respondent used an acronym and a word 'pulsating'. They may mean something valid but obviously they are a very unclear answer. They may even be a wrong answer because the respondent might misunderstand the question, answer it carelessly, or even play fun with it. To rectify the situation, re-contacts with the respondents concerned are necessary for clarification.

Data coding

Moving on from the editing process, data *coding* involves assigning values to responses to the questions on the survey instrument. Specifically, coding is the assignment of typically numerical values to each individual response for each question on the survey. Numerous coding is usually used because numbers are quick and easy to input and computers work better with numbers than alphanumerical values. Coding can be tedious if certain issues are not addressed prior to collecting the data. A well-planned and constructed questionnaire can reduce the amount of time spent on coding and increase the accuracy of the process.

Coding of Forced-Choice Questions

Exhibit 15.2 shows Jimmy spice's restaurant questionnaire that has pre-coded responses for all questions except the open-ended ones. In the 'Section 1: Life Style Questions', for example, a respondent has the option of responding from 1 to 7, based on their level of agreement or disagreement to a particular statement. Thus, if the respondent circles '5' as their choice, then the value of '5' will become the coded value for that particular statement.

> **Coding** Assigning value to various responses from the survey instrument.

In questionnaires that do not use pre-coded responses, the researcher can still apply the concept of coding by establishing a master code form on which the assigned coded values are shown for each response. Exhibit 15.4 illustrates what such a form looks like. Question 1 in Exhibit 15.4 illustrates all the coded values for responses to 'fast food restaurants visited in the past two months'. These values range from 01 to 12, with Burger King having the value of 01, Pizza Hut 02, Kentucky Fried Chicken 03, Pizza Moril 04, and so on.

Another example can be seen in Question 3. Here if the respondent checked '€4.01–€6.00', the coder would assign a value of 3 to that response. If another respondent checked 'more than €12,' the coder would assign a value of 7. The effective use of a master code serves as an additional safeguard for the coding rule to be followed correctly.

Coding of Open-Ended Questions

The above two examples are all forced-choice questions. However, open-ended questions sometimes appear in a questionnaire. These open-ended questions are much less easier than their forced-choice counterparts to be correctly coded. In Question 1 of the Master Code Form shown on Exhibit 15.4, the last possible response, 'Other, please specify', is an example of an open-ended question. It is different in nature from all the others in the same question and should be coded in a different way.

The key difference between 'Other, please specify' and all the other possible responses is that pre-coding is not possible in the former but feasible in the latter. The coder has to finish the data collection and then read all the possible answers to 'Other, please specify'. Based on all these possible answers, the coder can then develop a separate set of codes. For example, a respondent may have specified 'White Castle' for this response. Since 'White Castle' is not on the list of pre-coded responses for Question 1, a separate and unique value will have to be coded for 'White Castle'. Such coded values are customarily stored and listed on a separate code sheet, which can be entitled 'Code Sheet for 'Other' Responses'. Note that the coded value of 20 in Question 1 on the Master Code Form serves only as a temporary value before the coding of all the responses to the question takes place, and should be replaced by the subsequently decided coded values, such as '13' for 'White Castle', and so on.

EXHIBIT 15.4 An Illustration of a Master Code Form

Master Code Form

Questionnaire Identification Number 000 (1–3)

FAST FOOD RESTAURANT PATRONAGE BEHAVIOUR SURVEY IN PORTUGAL

This questionnaire pertains to a project being conducted by Marketing Research and Insight Company. The purpose of this project is to better understand the behaviours of consumers regarding their patronage at fast food restaurants. The questionnaire will take approximately 15 minutes to complete, and all responses will remain strictly confidential. Thank you for your help in this project.

1 **Below is a list of major fast food restaurants in Portugal. How many of these restaurants did you visit in the past two months? Check as many as may apply.**

Burger King	01	Lojadas Sopas	07
Pizza Hut	02	Burger Ranch	08
Kentucky Fried Chicken	03	Cascata	09
Pizza Moril	04	Joshua Shoarma Grill	10 ✓
McDonald's	05	Delifrance	11
Pans & Bacatta	06	Telepizza	12
		Other, please specify	→ see code sheet.
		Have not visited any of these restaurants	20

2 **In a typical month, how many times do you visit a fast food restaurant, such as the ones indicated above? (X ONE BOX)**

One ☐	Two ☐	Three ☑	Four ☐	Five ☐	Six ☐	Seven or more ☐
1	2	3	4	5	6	7

3 **On your last visit to a fast food restaurant, how much did you spend?**

Under €2	☐1	€8.01–€10.00	☐5
€2.01–€4.00	☐2	€10.01–€12.00	☐6
€4.01–€6.00	☑3	More than €12	☐7
€6.01–€8.00	☐4	Don't remember?	☐8

In order to ensure that answers to all the open-ended questions are coded properly, the researcher can follow through a four-phase process as illustrated below:

1   *Identification of responses.* The process begins by identifying a list of all the noteworthy responses to each question. These responses are then assigned values within a range determined by the actual number of responses identified.

2   *Consolidation of responses.* Consolidation of responses is the second phase of the process. Exhibit 15.5 illustrates several actual responses to the question 'Why are you dining less frequently at the _____ restaurant?' Four of these are 'I do not like their food', 'I got tired of their burgers. I don't like the spices', 'Family doesn't like it. My husband didn't like the way the burgers tasted', and 'Cannot eat their food', are all related to not liking the food. Therefore they can be consolidated into a single response category because they all have the same shared meaning. Wherever possible, the development of consolidated categories should be made by an experienced research analyst with input from the project's sponsor.

3   *Determination of a list of coded values.* The third step of the process is to determine a typically numerical value as a code. In performing this step, the number of consolidated responses per open-ended question needs to be taken into account. For example, if a question has more than 10 consolidated responses, and if numerical values are used for coding, then double-digit codes must be used, such as '01', '02', … '12'.

Another common practice is to assign higher-value codes to positive responses and lower-value codes to negative responses. For example, 'no' responses are coded '0' and 'yes' responses

---

EXHIBIT 15.5 Illustration of Response Consolidation Using Open-Ended Questions

Q10a Why are you dining less frequently at the _____ restaurant?

Respondent # 72113

- I look for bargains. (Need) more specials.
- Because I'm no longer close to a _____.

Respondent # 72114

- I do not like their food.

Respondent # 72116

- They often get my order wrong.
- I got tired of their burgers. I don't like the spices.
- Prices (are) too high. They should give more with their meal than they do. (Need) more fries.
- Because they are rude.
- Family doesn't like it. My husband didn't like the way the burgers tasted.
- Health reasons.
- I work longer hours, and don't think about food.
- Cannot eat their food.
- We started using _____.
- My work location was moved so I'm not near _____.

coded '1'; dislike' responses are coded as '1' and 'like' responses coded as '5'. Coding of this nature can facilitate subsequent data analysis. For example, the researcher will find it easier to interpret means if higher values occur as the average moves from 'dislike' to 'like'.

If the researcher is going to use correlation or regression in data analysis, then for categorical data there is another consideration. The researcher may wish to create 'dummy' variables, which contain the codes of '0' and '1' only.

Assigning a coded value to missing data is very important. If, for example, a respondent completes a questionnaire except for the very last question and a recontact is not possible, how do you code the response to the unanswered question? A good practice in this situation is to first consider how the response is going to be used in the analysis phase. In certain types of analysis, if the response is left blank and has no numerical value, the entire questionnaire (not just the individual question) will be deleted. The best way to handle the coding of omitted responses is first to check on how your data analysis software will handle missing data. This should be the guide for determining whether omissions are coded or left blank.

4 *Assignment of coded values to actual responses.* The fourth step in the coding process is to assign a coded value, out of a list of coded values determined in the previous step, to each actual response. This is probably the most tedious step because it has to be done manually. Unless an optical scanning approach is being used to enter the data, this task is almost always necessary to guard against problems in the data entry phase. First, each questionnaire needs to be assigned a numerical value. The numerical value typically is a three-digit code if there are fewer than 1,000 questionnaires to code, and a four-digit code if there are 1,000 or more. For example, if 452 completed questionnaires were returned, the first would be coded 001, the second 002, and so on, finishing with 452. Questionnaire coding will be discussed again when we cover data entry.

Immediately following each questionnaire code, a numbered reference should be included in parentheses next to the code. This informs the data entry operator to place the questionnaire code in the corresponding data fields of the data record. It is important to realize that throughout the questionnaire the numbers in parentheses indicate the data field where each coded response will be added on the data record. The researcher should proceed through the entire questionnaire, assigning the appropriate numerical codes to each response.

Data Entry

Data entry follows validation, editing and coding. Data entry involves entering the data into the computer for subsequent data analysis. It includes those tasks involved with the direct input of the coded data into a software package that enables the research analyst to manipulate and transform the raw data into useful information.

> **Data entry** Those tasks involved with the direct input of the coded data into some specified software package that ultimately allows the research analyst to manipulate and transform the raw data into useful information.

There are several ways of entering coded data into a computer. The most common option is to key in each coded data onto an appropriate cell of the spreadsheet. SPSS, SAS and Excel all provide the spreadsheet facility for users to key in their coded data. However, this is a time-consuming option. For a long questionnaire survey on 1,000 respondents, one should expect to use a number of full days to key in all the coded data onto the spreadsheet.

There are less time-consuming options though. For example, some computer terminals have touch-screen capabilities that allow the data entry personnel to simply touch an appropriate area of the screen for entering a coded data. Another similar option uses a light pen – a handheld electronic pointer that enters data through the terminal screen.

EXHIBIT 15.6 Example of Optical Character Recognition Questionnaire

WELLNESS ASSESSMENT QUESTIONNAIRE

Risk Assessment Systems, Inc.
5846 Distribution Drive
Memphis, Tennessee 38141

INSTRUCTIONS

To ensure an accurate Personal Wellness Assessment, please answer all of the following questions as accurately and completely as possible.

USE A NO. 2 PENCIL ONLY   Example: ▭ ▭ ▬ ▭ ▭   Erase *completely* to change

Name _____

Street address _____

City _____

State _____

Phone # (_____) _____

Zip Code
Social Security Number

PHYSICAL DATA/CURRENT HEALTH STATUS

Sex — Date of Birth (Month – Day – Year) — Height (ft. in.) — Weight (lbs.) — Blood Pressure (If you know your Blood Pressure, enter it here) — Systolic (High) — Diastolic (Low)

Male
Female

If not, which best describes it?
▭ High
▭ Normal or Low
▭ Don't Know

1. In general, would you say your current state of health is:
▭ Excellent   ▭ Very Good   ▭ Good   ▭ Fair   ▭ Poor

2. During the past 12 months, how many days of work have you missed due to your own injury or sickness?
▭ None   ▭ 1 to 3   ▭ 4 to 6   ▭ 7 or more   ▭ Does not apply

PERSONAL/FAMILY MEDICAL HISTORY

3. How often are you given a routine physical examination by a physician?
▭ More than once a year   ▭ Once a year   ▭ Once every 2 years   ▭ Every 3 years or longer   ▭ Never had one

4. How long has it been since your last electrocardiogram (EKG)?
▭ Less than 1 year ago   ▭ 1 to 2 years ago   ▭ 2 to 3 years ago   ▭ 3 or more years ago   ▭ Never had one

5. Have you or has anyone in your family (parents, grandparents, brother or sister) had any of the following health problems? If so, please mark the corresponding box. *(Please mark all that apply.)*

	Self	Brother	Sister	Father	Mother	Father's side Grandfather	Father's side Grandmother	Mother's side Grandfather	Mother's side Grandmother
Heart disease before age 55	▭	▭	▭	▭	▭	▭	▭	▭	▭
Heart disease age 55 to 64	▭	▭	▭	▭	▭	▭	▭	▭	▭
Heart disease age 65 or later	▭	▭	▭	▭	▭	▭	▭	▭	▭
High blood pressure	▭	▭	▭	▭	▭	▭	▭	▭	▭
Stroke	▭	▭	▭	▭	▭	▭	▭	▭	▭
Diabetes	▭	▭	▭	▭	▭	▭	▭	▭	▭
Breast cancer	▭	▭	▭	▭	▭	▭	▭	▭	▭
Colon cancer	▭	▭	▭	▭	▭	▭	▭	▭	▭
Cancer (except breast/colon)	▭	▭	▭	▭	▭	▭	▭	▭	▭
Kidney disease	▭	▭	▭	▭	▭	▭	▭	▭	▭
Tuberculosis	▭	▭	▭	▭	▭	▭	▭	▭	▭
Mental illness	▭	▭	▭	▭	▭	▭	▭	▭	▭
Suicide	▭	▭	▭	▭	▭	▭	▭	▭	▭
Drug/alcohol addiction	▭	▭	▭	▭	▭	▭	▭	▭	▭

Continued on Page 2

© 1992 Risk Assessment Systems, Inc. 11/92   **1**   ✦ SCANTRON FORM NO. F-5414-RAS   P4 3593-G C1530-5.4 92

Improved scanning technology has created another option of data entry. Questionnaires prepared on any form of Microsoft Windows software and printed on a laser printer can be readily scanned through optical scanning. This method of data entry is quite common in the USA but less common in Europe. Exhibit 15.6 shows a questionnaire from a US company that has been designed for optical character recognition. Through a scanning device, alphabetic, numeric and special character codes can all be read. On the questionnaire in Exhibit 15.6, the respondent would use a number two pencil to fill in their responses, which would then be scanned directly into a computer.

All the above options are concerned with respondents providing answers on a paper questionnaire. However, with marketing researchers relying more and more on conducting their questionnaire survey online, and with the powerful online function to automatically transfer all the questionnaire responses to a spreadsheet (typically in Excel) format, the data entry step can be eliminated entirely.

Error Detection

Throughout the entire process of data preparation and analysis, the responsible personnel should always detect whether there is any error lurking in the shadows. Some sources of error have already been discussed previously. This section focuses on the error detection tactics that can be deployed to minimize errors within the data entry step.

One approach to error detection is for the researcher to review a printed representation of the entered data. Exhibit 15.7, for instance, shows the coded values for respondents with ID numbers from 398 to 427 in Jimmy spice's restaurant survey database. The top row indicates the names assigned to each variable (e.g. 'id' is the label for the respondent ID number, 'x_s1' represents the first screening question, x1 is the first question on the survey after the three screening questions). The numbers in the columns are the coded values representing the respective respondents' answers. The dots indicate missing responses. While the process is somewhat tedious, the researcher can view all the actual entered data on the same spreadsheet for accuracy and can then tell exactly where any errors occurred.

Another approach to error detection is to determine whether the software used for data entry and tabulation will allow the researcher to perform 'error edit routines', thereby making it impossible for data entry personnel to make certain types of mistakes. These routines can identify any wrong data existing in the data record or its concomitant tabulated results. For example, say that for a particular variable on a given data record, only the code of 1 or 2 should appear. An error edit routine can display an error message on the data output if any number other than 1 or 2 has been entered. A separate error edit routine can be established for every variable derived from the questionnaire.

The final approach to error detection is to use statistical analysis-enabled software, such as SPSS, for producing frequency tables that can be translated into a corresponding data/column list table for the entered data. A sample data/column list table is shown in Exhibit 15.8. The rows indicate the fields of the data record, with each field standing for a particular variable. The columns indicate the frequency of responses for each field concerned. In data field 40, for example, 50 responses of 1 were entered, 20 responses of 2 were entered, and so on. A quick viewing of this data/column list table can indicate to the researcher whether any inappropriate response was entered. If so, the researcher can then find the corresponding questionnaire and correct the error as needed.

EXHIBIT 15.7 SPSS Data View of Coded Values for Jimmy Spice's Restaurant Survey

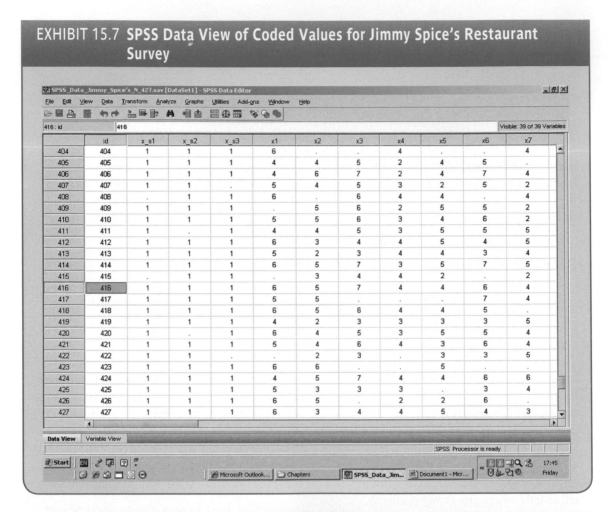

EXHIBIT 15.8 Example of Data/Column List Table

Data Field	1	2	3	4	5	6	7
40	50	20	33	81	0	2	1
41	5	9	82	77	36	8	0
42	10	12	11	15	0	0	0
43	15	16	17	80	1	3	5
44	0	0	7	100	2	11	0
45	17	42	71	62	1	3	5
46	100	2	5	18	16	2	12
47	22	25	62	90	10	30	15
48	0	0	25	18	13	17	35
49	61	40	23	30	18	22	17
50	10	11	62	73	10	21	0
51	7	11	21	17	52	47	5
52	82	46	80	20	30	6	7

A Closer Look at Research *(In the field)*
Data Collection Should Not Be Manual Labour

With the computerization of survey design and dissemination, manual questionnaires have become a thing of the past. Computer-based surveys can accommodate vast and complex arrays of data, greatly increasing the capacity for data collection and substantially reducing confusion and errors by interviewers and respondents. Three of the major benefits are as follows:

1 **Encoding data without transcribing from paper.** The interviewer or respondent can enter encoded data directly into a computer database. Numerous hours of tedious effort can be eliminated by avoiding transcription from paper surveys.

2 **Minimizing errors in data.** Errors in data are less likely with computer data collection than with manual transcriptions of paper surveys. Researchers no longer have to decipher illegible interviewer or respondent handwriting.

3 **Speeding up data collection and coding.** Computer surveys can speed the process of gathering data at any or all of five points in the data collection process: (*a*) getting the questions to the respondent, (*b*) asking questions of the respondent, (*c*) recording the respondent's answers, (*d*) getting the answers back to the researcher, and (*e*) entering the answers into a computer database. Clearly, all of these add up to time savings and potential cost savings.

By scanning actual raw data input, initiating error edit routines, or producing a data/column list table, the researcher should have increased confidence in the accuracy of the entered data, and can then consider performing data tabulation and data analysis. The nearby Closer Look at Research box addresses additional issues of error detection.

Data Tabulation

Tabulation is the process of counting the number of respondents who are classified into each different category of a variable. Therefore only those variables which are categorical or have been categorized can be used for tabulation purposes.

> **Tabulation** The process of counting the number of respondents who are classified into each different category of a variable.

Tabulation takes two common forms: one-way tabulations and cross-tabulations. A one-way tabulation is the categorization of only one selected variable at a time. It shows the number of respondents who belong to each one of the different categories of the selected variable.

Cross-tabulation simultaneously compares two or more variables in the study. It categorizes the number of respondents based on their responses to two categorized or to-be-categorized variables. For example, a cross-tabulation could involve the number of respondents who spent more than €10 last month on using a mobile phone versus those who spent less.

The use of tabulations ranges from further validation of the accuracy of the data to the reporting of research results. What follows is an illustration of different uses of one-way tabulations and cross-tabulations.

One-Way Tabulation

One-way tabulations serve several purposes in the research project. First, they can be used to determine the amount of non-response to individual questions. Based on the coding scheme used for missing data, one-way tabulations identify the actual number of respondents who did not answer various questions on the questionnaire.

> **One-way tabulation** Categorization of a single variable at a time.

Second, one-way tabulations can be used to locate simple blunders in data entry. If a specific range of codes has been established for all possible non-missing responses to a question, say 1 to 5, a one-way tabulation can illustrate if an inaccurate code was entered, say, a 7 or 8. It does this by providing a list of all actual coded responses to a particular question.

Finally, one-way tabulations can also be used to communicate the results of the research project. They can profile sample respondents, as well as identify characteristics that distinguish between groups (e.g. heavy users versus light users).

The most common way to illustrate a one-way tabulation is to construct a one-way frequency table. A one-way frequency table shows the numbers of respondents who chose any one of the available options provided by the question. An example of this type of table is shown in Exhibit 15.9, which shows which income category each respondent belonged to. The information indicates that 93 individuals (21.8 per cent) earned between €10,000 and €20,000, 113 (26.5 per cent) took between €20,001 and €30,000, and so on.

In addition to listing the numbers of responses corresponding to different options provided by the question, one-way frequency tables also identify missing data, valid percentages and summary statistics, as explained below.

1 *Missing data.* One-way frequency tables show the number of missing responses for the question being investigated. As shown in Exhibit 15.10, a total of 27 respondents, or 6.3 per cent of

EXHIBIT 15.9 **Example of One-Way Frequency Table**

X35 – Income

		Frequency	Per cent	Valid Per cent	Cumulative Per cent
Valid	10,000 – 20,000	93	21.8	21.8	21.8
	20,001 – 30,000	113	26.5	26.5	48.2
	30,001 – 40,000	52	12.2	12.2	60.4
	40,001 – 50,000	91	21.3	21.3	81.7
	50,001 or more	78	18.3	18.3	100.0
	Total	427	100.0	100.0	

the sample, did not respond to how frequently they patronized Jimmy spice's restaurant. It is important to recognize the number of missing responses when calculating percentages from a one-way frequency table.

2   *Valid percentages.* To determine valid percentages one must remove missing responses. For example, in Exhibit 15.10, while the total number of responses for question X25 is 427, only 400 are used to develop the valid percentages of responses across categories because the 27 missing responses were subtracted.

3   *Summary statistics.* Finally, one-way frequency tables can also illustrate a variety of summary statistics, which include the mean, median, mode, and standard deviation. These statistics help the researcher gain further insights from the responses to a particular variable. For example, in Exhibit 15.10, the mean of 2.00 indicates that many respondents are frequent patrons of Jimmy spice's restaurant.

EXHIBIT 15.10 One-Way Frequency Table Illustrating Missing Data, Valid Percentages and Summary Statistics.

Statistics

X25 – Frequency of Patronage of Jimmy Spice's Restaurant

N	Valid	400
	Missing	27
	Mean	2
	Median	2
	Mode	2
	Std. Deviation	1

X25 – Frequency of Patronage of Jimmy Spice's Restaurant

		Frequency	Per cent	Valid Per cent	Cumulative Per cent
Valid	Occasionally (Less Than Once a Month)	111	26.0	27.8	27.8
	Frequently (Once a Month)	178	41.7	44.5	72.2
	Very Frequently (2 or More Times a Month)	111	26.0	27.8	100.0
	Total	400	93.7	100.0	
Missing	System	27	6.3		
Total		427	100.0		

Cross-Tabulation

After producing and analysing one-way frequency tables, the next logical step is often to perform **cross-tabulation**. Cross-tabulation is extremely useful when the researcher wishes to study relationships between variables. The purpose of cross-tabulation is to determine whether responses to a variable differ because of responses to other selected variables. In fact, cross-tabulation is the primary form of data analysis in some marketing research projects.

> **Cross-tabulation** Simultaneously treating two or more variables in the study; categorizing the number of respondents who have responded to two or more variables in a questionnaire.

Development of cross-tabulations

It is essential to note here that, in developing cross-tabulations, the selection of variables should be based on the objectives of the research project. In other words, the selection should be based on whether the pair or bunch variables chosen can meet one or more of the research objectives. Inexperienced or lesser quality researchers sometimes perform cross-tabulation analysis by picking the pair or bunch variables without any valid reason. This trial hit and miss opportunistic tactic should be discouraged.

Personal background variables including demographics, lifestyles and psychographics are typically the starting point in developing cross-tabulations. These variables are usually the columns of the cross-tabulation table, while the rows are consumer behaviour variables such as purchase intention, purchase or usage data. Cross-tabulation tables such as these calculate percentages on the basis of column personal background variable totals. This allows the researcher to understand the relationships between consumer behaviours and respective respondents' backgrounds such as income, gender and marital status.

A variety of software and statistical packages can be used to generate cross-tabulation tables. Spreadsheets such as Excel, along with statistical packages like SPSS and SAS, can all generate cross-tabulations.

Interpretation of cross-tabulations

Exhibit 15.11 shows a simple cross-tabulation between gender and recall of Jimmy Spice's advertisements. The cross-tabulation shows frequencies and percentages, with percentages occurring for both rows and columns. One way to interpret this table would be to identify those individuals by gender who do not recall advertisements for Jimmy spice's restaurant. These individuals represent 65.3 per cent of the overall sample, with 39.5 per cent being male and 25.8 per cent female.

Looking at Exhibit 15.11, percentages are calculated for each cell of the cross-tabulation table. These cell percentages represent different kinds of insights that can be obtained from reading the same table.

The top number within each cell represents the frequency of responses for each variable (e.g. 158 male respondents do not recall advertisements). Below the absolute frequency is the row percentage per cell. For example, the 158 male respondents who did not recall Jimmy Spice's advertisements represented 60.5 per cent of the total in the 'Do Not Recall Advertisements'

EXHIBIT 15.11 Example of a Cross-Tabulation: Gender by Advertisement Recall

X31 – Advertising Recall * X32 – Gender Crosstabulation

			X32 – Gender		
			Male	Female	Total
X31 – Advertising Recall	Do Not Recall Advertisements	Count	158	103	261
		% within X31 – Advertising Recall	60.5%	39.5%	100.0%
		% within X32 – Gender	66.9%	62.8%	65.2%
		% of Total	39.5%	25.8%	65.2%
	Recall Advertisements	Count	78	61	139
		% within X31 – Advertising Recall	56.1%	43.9%	100.0%
		% within X32 – Gender	33.1%	37.2%	34.8%
		% of Total	19.5%	15.2%	34.8%
	Total	Count	236	164	400
		% within X31 – Advertising Recall	59.0%	41.0%	100.0%
		% within X32 – Gender	100.0%	100.0%	100.0%
		% of Total	59.0%	41.0%	100.0%

category, to which 261 respondents belonged. Below the row percentages are the column percentages. To illustrate, one can see there were 238 males in the sample. Among this gender group, 66.9 per cent belonged to the 'Do Not Recall Advertisements' category, while 33.1 per cent were in the 'Recall Advertisements' category. Further down are the total percentages, calculations of which are based on the total sample. For example, with a total sample of 400, 39.5 per cent of the sample were males who did not recall advertisements, and 19.5 per cent are males who did recall advertisements.

As a data analysis technique, cross-tabulation provides the researcher with a useful tool to extract meanings from the raw survey data. It is easy to understand and interpret, and can provide a valid description of both aggregate and subgroup data. Chapter 15 will discuss various statistical techniques often used with cross-tabulation, as well as tests of association, significant differences, and measures of central tendency.

Descriptive Statistics

Descriptive statistics are used to summarize and describe the data obtained from the respondents. There are two types of measures in descriptive statistics. One of those is measures of central tendency and the other is measures of dispersion. Both are described in detail in the next chapter. For now we refer you to Exhibit 15.12, which provides an introductory overview of the major types of descriptive statistics used by marketing researchers.

EXHIBIT 15.12 **Introductory Overview of Descriptive Statistics**

A simple data set is presented below, which helps to illustrate each of the major types of descriptive statistics. The data set is concerned with the ten students'/respondents' satisfaction with their MP3 player. Satisfaction is measured on a 7-point scale with the end points labelled 'Highly Satisfied = 7' and 'Not Satisfied at All = 1'.

Respondent	Satisfaction Rating
1	7
2	5
3	6
4	4
5	6
6	5
7	7
8	5
9	4
10	5

DESCRIPTIVE STATISTICS

Frequency = the number of times a number (raw response) is in the data set.

To compute it, count how many times the number is in the data set. For example, the number 7 is in the data set twice.

Frequency distribution = a summary of how many times each possible number (raw response) to a question appears in the data set.

To develop a frequency distribution, count how many times each number appears in the data set and make a table demonstrating the results, such as what is shown below:

Satisfaction Rating	Respondent
7	2
6	2
5	4
4	2
3	0
2	0
1	0
Total	10

Percentage distribution = the result of converting a frequency distribution into percentages.

To develop a percentage distribution, divide each frequency count for each rating by the total count.

Satisfaction Rating	Count	Percentage
7	2	20%
6	2	20%
5	4	40%
4	2	0%
3	0	0%
2	0	0%
1	0	0%
Total	10	100%

Cumulative percentage distribution = each individual percentage added to the previous to get a total. To develop a cumulative percentage distribution, arrange the percentages in descending order and sum the percentages one at a time and show the result.

Satisfaction Rating	Count	Percentage	Cumulative Percentage
7	2	20%	20%
6	2	20%	40%
5	4	40%	80%
4	2	20%	100%
3	0	0%	
2	0	0%	
1	0	0%	
Total	10	100%	

Mean = the arithmetic average of all the raw responses.

To calculate the mean, add up all the values of a distribution of responses and divide the total by the number of valid responses.

The mean is: $(7+5+6+4+6+5+7+5+4+5)*54/10 = 5.4$

Median = the descriptive statistic that splits the raw data into a hierarchical pattern where half the raw data is above the median value and half is below.

To determine the median, look at the cumulative percentage distribution and find either where the cumulative percentage is equal to 50 per cent or where it includes 50 per cent. The median in the above data set is 4.

Mode = the most frequently occurring raw response.

To determine the mode, find the number that has the highest frequency (count). In the above data set, the number 5 has the highest count and therefore is the mode.

Range = a statistic that represents the spread of the data and is the distance between the largest and the smallest values of a frequency distribution.

For the above data set, to calculate the range, subtract the lowest rating point from the highest rating point and get the difference. As the maximum number is 7 and the minimum number is 4, the range is $7-4=3$.

Standard deviation = the measure of the average dispersion of the values in a set of responses about their mean. It provides an indication of how similar or dissimilar the values are in the set of responses.

To calculate the standard deviation, subtract the mean from each value and get the difference, square the difference and sum all the squared differences. Then divide that sum by the total number of responses minus one, and finally take the square root of the result.

Graphical Illustration of Data

For many researchers, the next logical step following the construction of one-way tabulations and cross-tabulations is to translate them into graphical illustrations. These, as opposed to tables, can be very useful for communicating key research results to the client. A detailed discussion of graphical illustrations will be provided in Chapters 15 to 17.

Data Analysis Case: Delicatessen Delight

Towards the end of this chapter, a number of basic techniques for analysing data have been introduced. More advanced statistical techniques will be demonstrated in later chapters. To help readers develop a better understanding of the techniques available to them for analysing their data, and following the principle of practice makes perfect, we have prepared several databases that readers can work on. The case and its corresponding database shown in this chapter is about 'Delicatessen Delight', a sandwich restaurant chain operating in a few western European countries. The fictitious brand name 'Delicatessen Delight' is used for business confidentiality reasons. The database is available at www.mhhe.com/shiu09.

Delicatessen Delight sells cold and hot sandwiches, pies, cookies, soups, yoghurts and drinks. The restaurant is positioned in the fast food market to compete directly with similar sandwich restaurants. Its competitive advantages include special sauces on sandwiches, supplementary menu items like pies and soups, and quick delivery within specified zones.

As agreed between the director of a marketing degree programme and the Delicatessen Delight headquarters, a chosen student was assigned to conduct a survey for the owner of a local Delicatessen Delight restaurant near her campus, which became the primary data for her dissertation. The survey was undertaken inside the restaurant. A sample of customers were approached to seek their cooperation to be interviewed.

The survey included 17 questions (Exhibit 15.13). Sampled customers were first asked their perceptions of the restaurant on six factors (variables X1–X6) and then asked to rank the same six factors in terms of their importance in selecting a restaurant for their dining purpose (variables X12–X17). Finally, respondents were asked to write down their gender, how satisfied they were with the restaurant, how likely they were to recommend it to a friend, how often they eat there, and how far they drove to have a meal there. The main variables and their coding are shown below under three different sections.

Perception Factors – Assessing Delicatessen Delight's Performance

Listed below is a set of factors that could be used to describe Delicatessen Delight. On a scale from 1 to 10, with 10 being 'Strongly Agree' and 1 being 'Strongly Disagree', to what extent do you agree or disagree that Delictessen Delight has:

    X1 – Friendly employees
    X2 – Competitive prices
    X3 – Competent employees
    X4 – Excellent food quality
    X5 – A wide variety of food
    X6 – Fast service

If a respondent chose a 10 on 'friendly employees', this would indicate strong agreement that Delicatessen Delight has friendly employees. On the other hand, if a respondent chose a 1 for 'fast service', this would indicate strong disagreement, signifying that the restaurant was perceived as offering very slow service.

Perception Factors – Their Importance in Selecting Restaurants for Dining Purposes

Listed below is a set of factors people often use when selecting a fast food restaurant to dine at. Please rank each factor from 1 to 6, with 6 being the most important factor for selecting a fast food restaurant and 1 being the least important. There can be no ties, so please make sure you rank each factor with a different number.

X12 – Friendly employees
X13 – Competitive prices
X14 – Competent employees
X15 – Excellent food quality
X16 – A wide variety of food
X17 – Fast service

Classification Variables

Data for the classification variables were to be acquired at the end of the survey, but in the database it is recorded as variables X7–X11. Responses were coded as follows:

X7 – Gender (1 = Male; 0 = Female)
X8 – Recommend to friend (7 = Definitely recommend; 1 = Definitely not recommend)
X9 – Satisfaction level (7 = Highly satisfied; 1 = Not very satisfied)
X10 – Usage level (1 = Heavy user [eats at Delicatessen Delight 2 or more times each week]; 0 = Light user [eats at Delicatessen Delight fewer than 2 times a week])
X11 – Distance travelled (1 = Within 1 mile; 2 = 1–3 miles; 3 = More than 3 miles)

EXHIBIT 15.13 Delicatessen Delight Questionnaire

RAPPORT AND SCREENING QUESTIONS

Hello. My name is ___ and I'm a postgraduate marketing student at European First University. For my dissertation research purpose, I would like to request your cooperation in answering some questions about your thoughts and experience today/tonight at Delicatessen Delight. I hope you will accept my request, which will take approximately 15 minutes of your time.

If you are kind enough to accept my request, please be assured that I will keep your information confidential during the research process, and will not disclose it to any organization or individual whatsoever. Your information will be aggregated with those provided by other cooperating customers in order to enable me to do aggregate analysis. Results of the aggregate analysis will be used for my dissertation research purpose. Also as agreed with the owners of this restaurant, the same results of the aggregate analysis will be provided to them so that they could use them to improve the service they offer their customers. Your information, as well as individual information provided by other cooperating customers, will be destroyed after the announcement of assessment of my dissertation.

As a token of appreciation for your prospective cooperation, we will be delighted to give you a voucher that you can use to claim any of the main courses on the menu free of charge for you and another person you bring with you next time you visit this restaurant.

If the customer agrees to your request, then ask the following three screening questions:

1 'How often do you eat out?' ___ Often ___ Occasionally ___ Very infrequently
  'Often' = 'Equal to or more than twice a week'
  'Occasionally' = 'More or less once a week'
  'Very infrequently' = 'Less than once a week'

2 'Are you a resident in this city?' ___ Yes ___ No

3 'Have you completed a questionnaire on
  Delicatessen Delight before?' ___ Yes ___ No

If the respondent answers 'Often or Occasionally' to the first question, 'Yes' to the second question and 'No' to the third question, then:

Give them a clipboard with the questionnaire on it, briefly explain the questionnaire, ask them to complete the survey, and affirm that you will be there to answer any questions the respondent may have while completing the questionnaire.

If the respondent does not answer 'Often or Occasionally', 'Yes' and 'No' respectively to the above three questions, then say that they are not the type of respondent you are looking for, thank them for their initial cooperation and abort the survey.

THE QUESTIONNAIRE

Please read all the following questions carefully. If you do not understand any of these questions, please ask me for clarification.

Section 1: Performance of Delicatessen Delight on the Six Perception Factors

Listed below is a set of factors that could be used to describe Delicatessen Delight. On a scale from 1 to 10, with 10 being 'Strongly Agree' and 1 being 'Strongly Disagree', to what extent do you agree or disagree that Delicatessen Delight has: (Circle the correct response)

1 Friendly employees

Strongly Disagree — Strongly Agree

1 2 3 4 5 6 7 8 9 10

2 Competitive prices

Strongly Disagree — Strongly Agree

1 2 3 4 5 6 7 8 9 10

3 Competent employees

Strongly Disagree — Strongly Agree

1 2 3 4 5 6 7 8 9 10

4 Excellent food quality

Strongly Disagree — Strongly Agree

1 2 3 4 5 6 7 8 9 10

5 A wide variety of food

Strongly Disagree — Strongly Agree

1 2 3 4 5 6 7 8 9 10

6 Fast service

Strongly Disagree — Strongly Agree

1 2 3 4 5 6 7 8 9 10

Section 2: Importance of the Six Perception Factors in Selecting Restaurants for Dining purposes

Listed below is a set of factors people often use when selecting a fast food restaurant to dine at. Please rank each of these factors from 1 to 6, with 6 being the most important factor for selecting a fast food restaurant and 1 being the least important. There can be no ties so please make sure you rank each factor with a different number.

Factor	Ranking
7 Friendly employees	
8 Competitive prices	
9 Competent employees	
10 Excellent food quality	
11 A wide variety of food	
12 Fast service	

Section 3: Classification Variables

Please circle the response below that best describes you.

13 Your Gender   1   Male
                                 0   Female

14 How likely are you to recommend Delicatessen Delight   Definitely   Definitely
                                                                  Not Recommend   Recommend
                                                                  1 2 3 4 5 6 7

15 How satisfied are you with Delicatessen Delight?   Not Very   Highly
                                                                  Satisfied   Satisfied
                                                                  1 2 3 4 5 6 7

16 How often do you patronize Delicatessen Delight?   1 = eat at Delicatessen Delight
                                                           2 or more times each week.
                                                        0 = eat at Delicatessen Delight
                                                           fewer than 2 times each week.

17 How far did you drive to get to Delicatessen   1 = Within 1 mile
    Delight for having a meal there?   2 = 1–3 miles
                                                        3 = More than 3 miles

Thank you very much for your cooperation. Please accept this voucher as a token of our appreciation.

Questions

1 Identify how the the Delicatessen Delight survey and questionnaire described above affects the analysis of its corresponding data. How would you further improve the restaurant's survey and questionnaire?

2 What are the competitive advantages and disadvantages of Delicatessen Delight over its competitors in general?

Summary of Learning Objectives

■ **Illustrate the process of preparing data for preliminary analysis.**

Marketing research is valued for its ability to provide decision making information to the user or client. To accomplish this, the raw data must be converted into usable information. After collecting data through the appropriate method, the task becomes one of ensuring that the data is accurate and will provide intended meaning and value. Data preparation is the first part of the process of transforming raw data into usable information. This part of the process takes into account five steps: (1) data validation, (2) editing and coding, (3) data entry, (4) error detection and (5) data tabulation.

■ **Demonstrate the procedure for assuring data validation.**

Data validation attempts to determine whether a questionnaire survey was conducted correctly and free from fraud. In re-contacting selected respondents, the researcher asks whether the survey (1) was falsified, (2) was conducted with a qualified respondent, (3) took place in the proper procedural setting, (4) was correctly completed and (5) was accomplished in a courteous manner.

■ **Describe the process of editing and coding data obtained through a questionnaire survey**

The editing process involves the manual scanning of questionnaire responses to determine whether the proper questions were asked, proper answers recorded and proper screening questions employed, as well as whether open-ended questions were recorded accurately. Once edited, all questionnaires are coded by assigning numerical value to all responses. Coding is the process of providing numeric labels to the data so they can be conveniently entered into a computer for subsequent statistical analysis.

■ **Acquaint the user with data entry procedures.**

There are four principal methods of entering coded data into a computer. First is the keyboard terminal or PC keyboard. Data may also be entered through terminals having touchscreen capabilities, or through the use of a handheld electronic pointer or light pen. Finally, data from certain questionnaires can be entered through a scanner using optical character recognition.

■ **Illustrate a process for detecting errors in data entry.**

Unfortunately, error detection normally occurs after the data have been entered into computer storage. Entry errors can be detected through the use of error edit routines built or developed into the data entry software. An additional approach is to visually scan the actual data after entry. A data table is one approach for visually scanning entered data.

■ **Discuss techniques used for data tabulation and data analysis.**

Two common forms of data tabulations are used in marketing research. A one-way tabulation indicates the number of respondents who gave each possible answer to a particular question on a questionnaire. Cross-tabulation provides categorization of respondents by treating two or more variables simultaneously. Categorization is based on the number of respondents who have responded to two or more questions.

Key Terms and Concepts

Coding   502

Cross-tabulation   512

Curbstoning   495

Data entry   505

Data validation   494

Editing   496

One-way tabulation   510

Tabulation   509

Review Questions

1 Briefly describe the process of data validation. Specifically discuss the issues of fraud, screening, procedure, completeness and courtesy.

2 What are the differences between data validation, data editing and data coding?

3 Explain the differences between establishing codes for open-ended questions and for closed-ended questions.

4 What is the role of probing questions and why are they an important part of the research process?

5 Briefly describe the process of data entry. What changes in technology have simplified this procedure?

6 What are the three approaches to error detection? In your discussion be sure to describe the data/column list procedure.

7 What is the purpose of a simple one-way tabulation? How does this relate to a one way frequency table?

8 What is the advantage of cross-tabulation over one-way tabulation?

Discussion Questions

1 Obtain a copy of a marketing research questionnaire and on the basis of your knowledge of developing codes, convert the questionnaire into a master code illustrating the appropriate values for each question and corresponding responses.

2 Look back at the beginning of this chapter. On the basis of what you now know about gatekeeping data for analysis, give marketing research scenarios under which 'garbage in, garbage out' may happen.

3 Have a closer look at Jimmy spice's restaurant database and develop three research questions that could be answered by running one-way tabulations. Then run these one-way tabulations. Write a one-paragraph explanation of your findings for each one-way tabulation.

4 Now develop another three research questions that could be addressed by corresponding cross-tabulations. Write a one-paragraph explanation of your findings for each cross-tabulation. Discuss the value of cross-tabulations over one-way tabulations.

16

Basic Data Analysis and Hypothesis Testing Techniques

> " The more I know, the more I know I don't know.
>
> —*Anonymous* "

Statistical Software Makes Data Analysis Easy

Firms of all sizes are increasingly paying attention to the collection and storage of data relevant to their activities. These data may come from surveys of customers or be internally gathered by the sales force. But to be useful for decision making, the data must be organized, categorized, analysed and shared among responsible employees. Tom Peters, in his book *Thriving on Chaos*, said, 'We are drowning on information and starved for knowledge'. To convert this ocean of information into knowledge, we need user-friendly, powerful software packages. Many software packages can help us accomplish this conversion, including the popular Excel programme that is part of Microsoft Windows. But as the amount of information increases exponentially, we need comprehensive, sophisticated packages that are relatively inexpensive and easy to use. Fortunately, at least two are available and can be used with most PCs: SPSS and SAS. Both are very powerful and provide statistical processing capabilities for a variety of tasks, from calculating means and modes to executing neural networking and other sophisticated data mining tasks. Each package is briefly described below. We rely on SPSS in many chapters to analyse the data collected in a customer survey of a restaurant called Jimmy Spice's.

SPSS

The SPSS software package is designed to be user-friendly, even for novice computer users. Released in the Microsoft Windows format and touted as 'Real Stats, Real Easy', SPSS delivers easy data access and management, highly customizable output, complete just-in-time-training, and a revolutionary system for working with charts and graphs. The producers of SPSS proudly claim that 'you don't have to be a statistician to use SPSS', an important characteristic for individuals who are somewhat afraid of statistics. Available in almost any format, SPSS provides immense statistical analysis capability while remaining one of the most user-friendly statistical packages available today. Information concerning SPSS is available online at www.spss.com.

SAS

The SAS system provides extensive statistical analysis capabilities, including tools for both specialized and enterprise-wide analytical needs. Universities, research institutes, laboratories, marketing research firms, pharmaceutical companies, banks and government agencies all take advantage of the power offered by SAS. From traditional analysis of variance to exact methods of statistical visualization, the SAS system provides the tools required to analyse data and help organizations make the right statistical choices. Many heavy users of statistical software packages feel that SAS offers greater statistical analysis capabilities than SPSS. However, this increased statistical power is sometimes compromised by applications less user-friendly than those of SPSS. Information concerning SAS is available online at www.sas.com.

Value of Testing for Differences in Data

Once the data have been collected and prepared for analysis, there are some basic statistical analysis procedures the marketing researcher will want to perform. An obvious need for these statistics comes from the fact that it's hard to find out from a particular data set what its entire set of responses means because there are 'too many numbers' to look at. Consequently, almost every data set needs some summary information developed that describes the numbers it contains. Basic statistics and descriptive analysis were developed for this purpose.

Some of the statistics common to almost all marketing research projects are described in this chapter. The chapter also explains how to display the data graphically so decision makers can understand it. For example, if you conducted a study of people who buy Domino's pizza you would be able to use graphs to clearly show who the most frequent purchasers are compared to the least frequent purchasers, and perhaps why.

First, we describe measures of central tendency and dispersion. The advantages and pitfalls of each measure need to be understood so that the distribution of the data being looked at can be reasonably well described. Next, we discuss relationships of the sample data. The *t* distribution and associated confidence interval estimation are discussed in this second section. Third, we describe hypothesis testing, including tests for examining hypotheses related to differences between two sample means, as well as the corresponding terminology. Finally, the chapter closes with an introduction to analysis of variance, a powerful technique for detecting differences between three or more sample means.

Guidelines for Graphics

Graphics should be used whenever they are helpful in communicating the data and results more clearly. They help the information user to quickly grasp the essence of the information developed in the research project. Charts, a particular kind of graphics, are an effective visual aid to enhance the communication process. In this section we will show the value of bar charts, line charts and pie charts. We will use the variable X25 – Frequency of Patronizing Jimmy Spice's restaurant database to develop the frequency distribution in Exhibit 16.1. Note that 400 respondents indicated how frequently they patronize the restaurant using a 3-point scale, with 1 = Occasionally, 2 = Frequently and 3 = Very Frequently. The total sample was 427, but 27 respondents did not answer this question and therefore are considered missing data. The numbers in the Per cent column are calculated using the total sample size of 427, while the numbers in the Valid per cent and Cumulative per cent columns are calculated using the total sample size minus the number of missing responses to this question $(427 - 27 = 400)$.

Bar Charts

A *bar chart* shows the data in the form of bars that may be horizontally or vertically oriented. Bar charts are excellent tools to depict both absolute and relative magnitudes, differences, and change. Exhibit 16.2 is an example of a vertical bar chart that displays the information in Exhibit 16.1. For example, the frequency for the value label of Very Infrequently = 1 ($N = 49$) is the first vertical bar on the left side of the chart. The remaining bars are developed in the same way.

A *histogram* is similar to a bar chart and often there is confusion among users between the two types of charts. A histogram for variable X22 – Satisfaction is shown in Exhibit 16.3. Note the bars in a bar chart have space between them whereas in a histogram they do not. An additional feature of the histogram is that a normal line has been drawn over the frequency distribution to provide an indication of whether the data approximates a normal curve. The distribution of X22 is skewed a little to the right but still closely approximates a normal curve.

EXHIBIT 16.1 Frequency Distribution for Variable X25 – Frequency of Patronizing Jimmy Spice's Restaurant

Statistics

X25 – Frequency of Patronage of Jimmy Spice's Restaurant

N	Valid	400
	Missing	27
	Mean	2
	Median	2
	Mode	2
	Std. Deviation	1

X25 – Frequency of Patronage of Jimmy Spice's Restaurant

		Frequency	Per cent	Valid Per cent	Cumulative Per cent
Valid	Occasionally (Less Than Once a Month)	111	26.0	27.8	27.8
	Frequently (Once a Month)	178	41.7	44.5	72.2
	Very Frequently (2 or More Times a Month)	111	26.0	27.8	100.0
	Total	400	93.7	100.0	
Missing	System	27	6.3		
Total		427	100.0		

EXHIBIT 16.2 Bar Chart for Variable X25 – Frequency of Patronizing Jimmy Spice's Restaurant

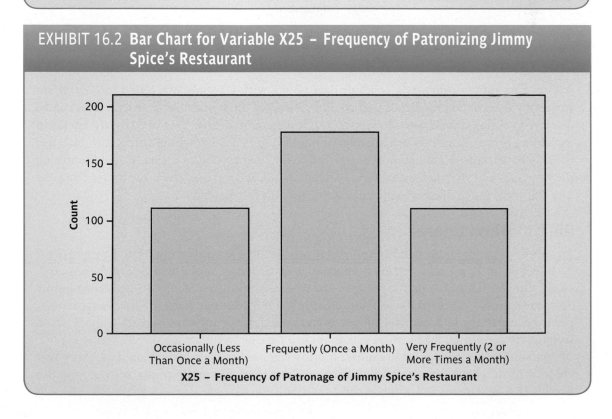

X25 – Frequency of Patronage of Jimmy Spice's Restaurant

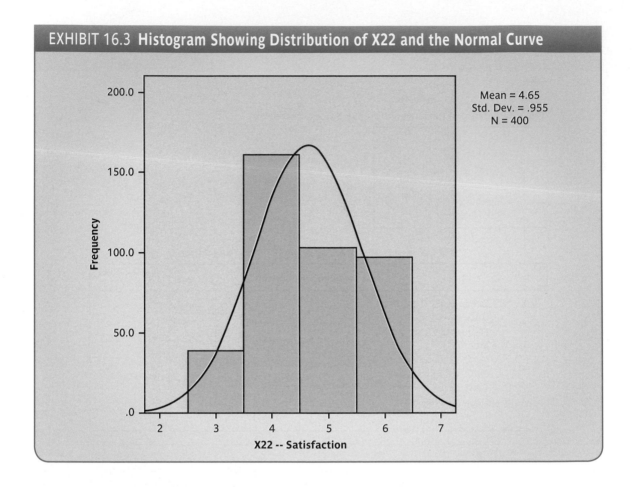

EXHIBIT 16.3 **Histogram Showing Distribution of X22 and the Normal Curve**

Mean = 4.65
Std. Dev. = .955
N = 400

Frequency

X22 -- Satisfaction

Line Charts

A *line chart* simply connects a series of data points with a continuous line. Line charts are frequently used to portray trends over several periods of time. In addition, several lines can be displayed on the same chart, allowing for multiple comparisons. This can be very useful in explaining comparisons between variables. If multiple lines are used in the same chart, each line needs to have its own label and must be clearly different in form and/or colour to avoid confusing the viewer. Exhibit 16.4 is a special form of a line chart, called an *area chart*. In an area chart, the area below the line is filled in to dramatically display the information.

Pie or Round Charts

Pie charts, sometimes also called round charts, are excellent for displaying relative proportions. Each section of the pie is the relative proportion, as a percentage of the total area of the pie, associated with the value of a specific variable. The relative proportions of X25 – Patronizing Jimmy Spice's restaurant were used to create the chart in Exhibit 16.5. Pie charts are not useful for displaying comparative information between several variables or changes over time. Generally, seven sections are considered the practical maximum in a pie chart.

Marketing researchers need to exercise caution when using charts to explain data. It is possible to misinterpret information in a chart and lead users to inappropriate conclusions. See Exhibit 16.6 for a discussion of this pitfall.

EXHIBIT 16.4 Area Chart for X22 – Satisfaction with Jimmy Spice's Restaurant

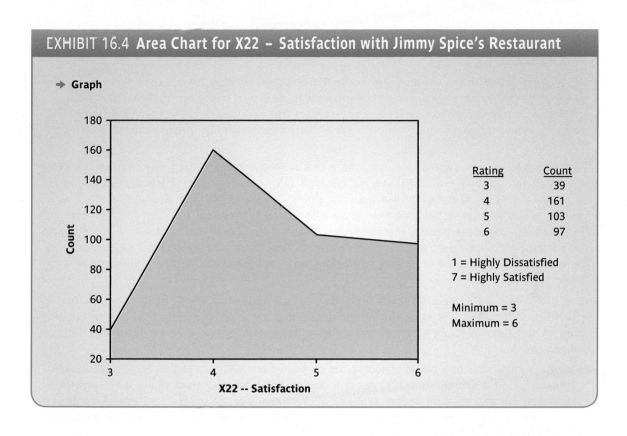

→ **Graph**

Rating	Count
3	39
4	161
5	103
6	97

1 = Highly Dissatisfied
7 = Highly Satisfied

Minimum = 3
Maximum = 6

EXHIBIT 16.5 Pie Chart for X25 – Frequency of Patronizing Jimmy Spice's Restaurant

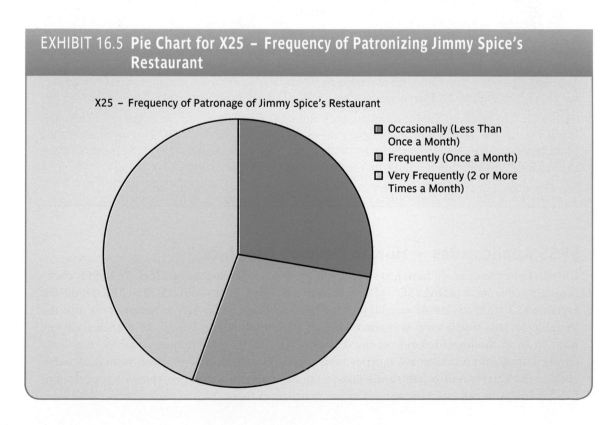

X25 – Frequency of Patronage of Jimmy Spice's Restaurant

◼ Occasionally (Less Than Once a Month)
◼ Frequently (Once a Month)
◻ Very Frequently (2 or More Times a Month)

EXHIBIT 16.6 A Good Picture Is Worth a Thousand Words

Many people panic when confronted with mounds of statistics, but they are quick to rely on charts and graphs. The old saying 'A good picture is worth a thousand words' seems especially appropriate when applied to charts intended to simplify tables of numbers. The problem is, however, that the saying lacks one very important qualifier: a good picture is worth a thousand words. A bad picture is worth very little.

Unfortunately, we are all exposed to many charts that are bad pictures. A chart may be colourful, artistic, eye-catching, and even accurate but can still fail in its mission. Charts are supposed to dramatize the facts, but some – called 'gee-whiz' charts – overstate the facts. *Gee-whiz chart* is a term coined by Darrell Huff in his book *How to Lie with Statistics*. No doubt Huff intended his book to help readers recognize misleading representations of data, though some readers may have misappropriated it as a primer for data muddling instead. Politicians, economists, marketing researchers and others with an axe to grind or a cause to promote have used gee-whiz charts to overdramatize their point.

It is simple to make a gee-whiz chart. Draw the chart correctly and cut off the bottom part. Insert a little jog in the vertical scale on the left to indicate that the scale is incomplete and you have created a chart that overdramatizes any trend, up or down, and makes it appear to be much more impressive.

Suppose annual sales of a brand of toothpaste dropped from 420 tons to 295 tons, a 30 per cent decline. A good picture will show a 30 per cent decline, but a gee-whiz chart would show something that looked like a 90 per cent decline. While close examination of the numbers will reveal the actual decline to be 30 per cent, the picture creates an exceedingly stronger, and thus misleading, impression. The numbers tell, the picture shows – a sort of twisted version of a children's show-and-tell exercise.

Thomas Semon, a research consultant, bemoans the fact that he has seen many gee-whiz charts in research presentations. He notes that it is less likely that a marketing researcher would deliberately distort the actual results when expressed in numbers, yet some will distort the results visually in charts. A misleading chart is disinformation according to Semon. It is a deliberate attempt to create an erroneous impression or to make a trend appear more dramatic and noteworthy.

He suggests the following course of action. Look closely at every chart you see in the newspaper and magazines for the next month, and identify those that may be gee-whiz charts. Imagine what they would look like if they were correctly drawn. If after your 'corrective' action many of the trends in these charts appear insignificant, it is likely that the trend really is insignificant.

As a final note, Semon says that while a lot of news is hype, research shouldn't be.

SPSS Applications – How to Develop Graphics

Graphics like the ones we have just shown you are easy to develop using SPSS. The SPSS 'click-through' sequence is ANALYSE → DESCRIPTIVE STATISTICS → FREQUENCIES. Highlight variable X25 from the list of variables on the left-hand side of the screen and move it into the Variable(s): box. If you want only the frequency table as shown in Exhibit 15.1, then click OK now. Note on the lower left side of the dialogue box that 'Display frequency tables' is already checked. If you do not want a frequency table you can uncheck it here. If you want bar charts, click on the 'Charts' button, which will take you to the dialogue box shown in the right portion of Exhibit 16.7. You can select histograms or pie charts from there.

EXHIBIT 16.7 SPSS Dialogue Boxes for Graphics with Bar Charts

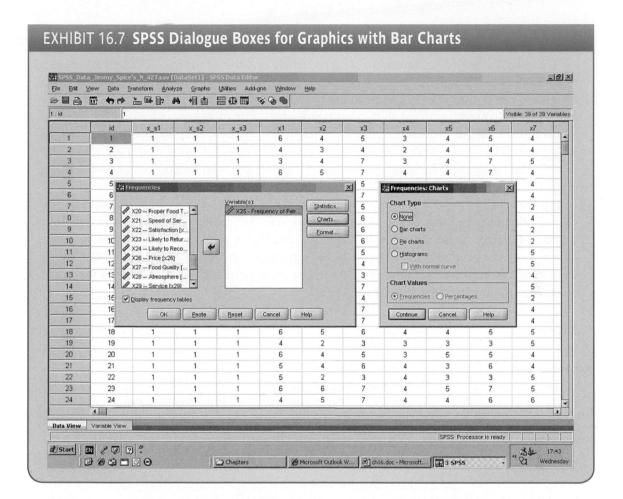

Measures of Central Tendency

As described above, frequency distributions can be useful for examining the different values of a given variable. Frequency distribution tables are easy to read and provide a great deal of basic information. There are times, however, when the amount of detail is just too much. In such situations the researcher needs a way to summarize and condense all the information in order to get at the underlying meaning. Descriptive statistics, which incorporate measures of central tendency, are commonly used to accomplish this task. Three typical central tendency measures are the mean, the median and the mode. These measures locate the centre of the distribution. For this reason, the mean, median, and mode are sometimes also called *measures of location*.

Mean

The **mean** is the arithmetic average value within the distribution, and is the most commonly used measure of central tendency. The mean tells us, for example, the average number of cups of coffee

> **Mean** The arithmetic average within the distribution of data; all values of a distribution of responses are added up and divided by the number of valid responses.

a typical student may drink during the two-week examination period. The mean can be calculated when the data scale is either interval or ratio.

The mean is a very robust measure of central tendency. Most of the time it is fairly insensitive to data values being added or deleted. Occasionally the mean can be subject to distortion when extreme values are included in the distribution. For example, suppose you ask four students how many cups of coffee they drank during the two-week examination period. Respondent answers are as follows: Respondent A = 1 cup; Respondent B = 10 cups; Respondent C = 5 cups; and Respondent D = 6 cups. Let's also assume we know that respondents A and B are males and respondents C and D are females, and we want to compare consumption of coffee between males and females. Looking at the males first (Respondents A and B), we calculate the mean number of cups to be 5.5 (1 + 10 = 11; 11/2 = 5.5). Looking at the females next (Respondents C and D), we calculate the mean number of cups to be 5.5 (5 + 6 = 11; 11/2 = 5.5). If we look only at the mean number of cups of coffee consumed by males and females, we would conclude there is no difference between the two groups. Looking at the underlying distribution, however, we must conclude the data presented by two groups are different. The mean actually distorts our understanding of coffee consumption patterns of males and females.

Mode

The **mode** is the value that appears in the distribution most often, and represents the highest peak in the distribution's graph. For example, the average number of cups of coffee students drank during the examination period may be 5 (the mean), while the number of cups of coffee that most students drink is only 3 (the mode). The mode is especially useful as a measure for data that have been somehow grouped into categories. The mode of the data distribution in Exhibit 16.1 is Occasionally (Coded 3) because when you look in the Frequency column you will note that the largest number of responses is 111 for the 'Occasionally' value label.

> **Mode** The most common value in the set of responses to a question; that is, the response most often given to a question.

Median

The **median** is the middle value of the distribution which is ordered in either an ascending or a descending sequence. For example, if you interviewed a sample of students to determine their coffee drinking behaviour during the examination period, you might find that the median number of cups of coffee consumed is four. The number of cups of coffee consumed above and below this number would be the same. If there are an odd number of observations, the median is the middle value. In case the number of data observations is even, the median is the average of the two middle values. The median is especially useful as a measure of central tendency for ordinal data.

> **Median** The middle value of a rank-ordered distribution; exactly half of the responses are above and half are below the median value.

Each measure of central tendency describes a distribution in its own manner, and each measure has its own strengths and weaknesses. For nominal data, the mode is the best measure. For ordinal data, the median is generally best. For interval or ratio data, the mean is generally used. If there are extreme values within the interval or ratio data, however, the mean can be distorted. In those cases, the median and the mode should be considered. SPSS and other statistical software packages are designed to incorporate the calculation of these central tendency measures.

SPSS Applications – Measures of Central Tendency

Jimmy Spice's restaurant database can be used with the SPSS software to calculate measures of central tendency. The SPSS 'click-through' sequence is ANALYSE → DESCRIPTIVE STATISTICS → FREQUENCIES. Let's use X25 – Frequency of Patronage of Jimmy Spice's restaurant as a variable to examine. Click on X25 to highlight it and then on the arrow box for the Variables box to use in your analysis. Next open the Statistics box and click on Mean, Median and Mode, and then Continue and OK. Recall that if you want to create charts, open the Charts box. Your choices are Bar, Histograms and Pie. For the Format box we will use the defaults, so click on OK to execute the programme. The dialogue boxes for this sequence are shown in Exhibit 16.8.

EXHIBIT 16.8 Dialogue Boxes for Calculating the Mean, Median and Mode

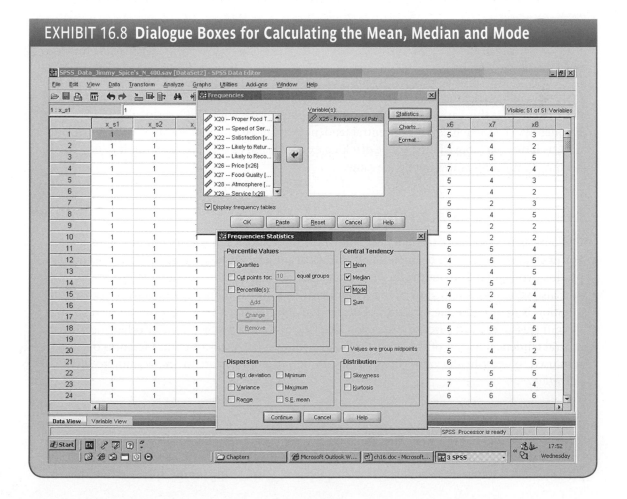

EXHIBIT 16.9 Output for Mean, Median and Mode for X25 – Frequency of Patronage

Statistics

X25 – Frequency of Patronage
of Jimmy Spice's Restaurant

N	Valid	400
	Missing	0
	Mean	2
	Median	2
	Mode	3

Let's look at the output for the measures of central tendency shown in Exhibit 16.9. In the Statistics table we see the mean is 2.17, the median is 2.00, the mode is 3, and there is no missing data. Recall that this variable is measured on a 3-point scale, with 1 = Occasionally and 3 = Very Frequently. The three measures of central tendency can all be different within the same distribution, as illustrated above in the coffee drinking example, and as they are here. But it is also possible that all three measures can be the same.

Measures of Dispersion

Often measures of central tendency cannot tell the whole story about a distribution of responses. For example, if data have been collected about consumers' attitudes towards a new brand of a product, you could find out the mean, median and mode of the distribution of answers, but you may also want to know if most of the respondents had similar opinions. One way to answer this question is to examine the measures of dispersion associated with the distribution of responses to your questions. Measures of dispersion describe how close to the mean or other measure of central tendency the rest of the values in the distribution fall. Two common measures of dispersion used to describe the variability in a distribution of numbers are the *range* and the *standard deviation*.

Range

The **range** defines the spread of the data. It is the distance between the smallest and largest values of the variable. Another way to think about it is that the range identifies the endpoints of the distribution of values. For variable X25 – Frequency of Patronizing Jimmy Spice's restaurant, the range is the difference between the response category 3 (largest value) and response category 1 (smallest value); that is, the range is 2. In this example, since we defined the response categories to begin with, the range doesn't tell us much. However, if we asked people questions, such as how often in a week they eat out, or how much they would pay to buy a DVD player, the range would be more informative. In this case, the respondents, not the researchers, would be defining the range by their answers. For this reason, the range is often used to describe the variability of responses to such open-ended questions as our eating out and DVD examples above.

> **Range** The distance between the smallest and largest values in a set of responses.

Standard Deviation

The **standard deviation** describes the average distance of the distribution values from the mean. The difference between a particular response and the distribution mean is called a *deviation*. When we subtract each value in a distribution from the mean and add them up, the result will be close to zero. This is because the positive and negative results will cancel each other out.

> **Standard deviation** Describes the average distance of the distribution values from the mean.

The solution to this difficulty is to square the individual deviations before we add them up. Remember that squaring a number of a positive sign and the same number of a negative sign produce the same result. Once the sum of the squared deviations is determined, it is divided by the number of respondents minus 1. The result of dividing the sum of the squared deviations is the average squared deviation. To get the result back to the same type of unit of measure as the mean, we simply take the square root of the answer. This produces the standard deviation of the distribution. Sometimes the average squared deviation, called the **variance**, is also used as a measure of dispersion for a distribution.

> **Variance** The average squared deviation about the mean of a distribution of values.

As the standard deviation is the square root of the average squared deviations, it can logically be used to represent the average distance of the values in a distribution from the mean. A distribution with a large standard deviation signifies that its constituent values do not fall very close to the mean. On the other hand, if the standard deviation is small, you can be sure that the distribution values are close to the mean.

Another way to think about the standard deviation is that its size tells you something about the level of agreement among the respondents when they answered a particular question. For example, in Jimmy Spice's Restaurant database, respondents were asked to rate the restaurant on the friendliness and knowledge of its employees (X12 and X19). We will use the SPSS programme later to examine the standard deviations for these questions. The formula for calculating the standard deviation is available on the book's website, www.mhhe.com/shiu09.

Together with the measures of central tendency, these descriptive statistics can reveal a lot about the distribution of a set of values representing the answers to an item on a questionnaire. Often, however, marketing researchers are also interested in questions that involve more than one variable at a time. The next section, on hypothesis testing, provides some ways to analyse those types of questions.

SPSS Applications – Measures of Dispersion

Jimmy Spice's Restaurant database can be used with the SPSS software to calculate measures of dispersion, just as we did with the measures of central tendency. The SPSS click-through sequence is ANALYSE → DESCRIPTIVE STATISTICS → FREQUENCIES. Let's use X22 – Satisfaction as a variable to examine. Click on X22 to highlight it and then on the Arrow box to move X22 to the Variables box. Next open the Statistics box, go to the Dispersion box in the lower-left-hand corner, and click on Standard deviation, Variance, Range, Minimum and Maximum, and then Continue. If you would like to create charts, then open the Charts box – your choices are Bar, Histograms and Pie. For the Format box we will use the defaults, so click on OK to execute the programme.

Let's look at the output for the measures of dispersion shown in Exhibit 16.10 for variable X22. First, the highest response on the 7-point scale is 6 (maximum) and the lowest response is 3 (minimum). The range is 3 ($6 - 3 = 3$), the standard deviation is .955, and the variance is .911. A standard deviation of .955 on a 7-point scale tells us the responses are dispersed fairly closely around the mean of 4.64.

EXHIBIT 16.10 Output for Measures of Dispersion

Frequencies

Statistics

X22 -- Satisfaction

N	Valid	400
	Missing	0
Mean		4.64
Median		4.50
Mode		4
Std. Deviation		.955
Variance		.911
Range		3
Minimum		3
Maximum		6

X22 -- Satisfaction

		Frequency	Per cent	Valid Per cent	Cumulative Per cent
Valid	3	39	9.8	9.8	9.8
	4	161	40.3	40.3	50.0
	5	103	25.8	25.8	75.8
	6	97	24.3	24.3	100.0
	Total	400	100.0	100.0	

Hypothesis Testing

Marketing researchers often have some preconceived notion of the relationships between different variables in the dataset they are working on. This preconception is called a hypothesis. An example of a hypothesis would be 'The average number of cups of coffee students consume during the two-week examination period will be greater than the average they consume at other times.' In this section of the chapter, we introduce the concept of hypothesis testing, explain some related terms and discuss some types of possible errors.

> **Hypothesis** An empirically testable though yet unproven statement developed in order to explain phenomena.

Independent Versus Related Samples

Often the marketing researcher wants to compare the means of two groups. There are two possible situations when means are compared. The first is when the means are from independent samples, and the second is when the samples are related. An example of independent samples would be the results of surveys on male and female coffee drinkers. The researcher may want to compare the average number of cups of coffee consumed by male students to the average number of cups of coffee consumed by female students. An example of the second situation, related samples, is when the researcher compares the average number of cups of coffee consumed by male students with the average number of soft drinks consumed by the same sample of male students.

> **Independent samples** Two or more groups of responses that are tested as though they come from different populations.
>
> **Related samples** Two or more groups of responses that originated from the same population.

In the related-sample situation, the marketing researcher must take special care when analysing the data. Although the questions are independent, the respondents are the same. This is called a *paired sample*. When testing for differences in related samples the researcher must use what is called a *paired samples* t-*test*.

Developing Hypotheses

The first step in testing a hypothesis is, of course, to develop the hypothesis itself. As we have said in earlier chapters, hypotheses are developed not only prior to the collection of data but also as a part of the research plan. Hypotheses allow the researcher to make comparisons between two groups of respondents and to determine if there are important differences between the groups. For example, if the average number of cups of coffee consumed by female students during the exam period is 6.1, and the average number of cups of coffee consumed by males is 4.7, is there any statistical difference between the two means?

In the independent-sample situation, the groups to be compared may be from two different surveys or they may be different subsets of the total sample in a particular survey. In either of these two cases, the research is conducted under the assumption that the two groups potentially are from separate populations.

To illustrate, let's consider the fast food industry. Suppose you have conducted research on fast food restaurant patronage and found that of the 1,000 people surveyed this year, 18 per cent say they visit fast food establishments at least 15 times per month. These people can be regarded as heavy users of fast foods. But in a survey conducted last year, only 12 per cent said they visited fast food restaurants at least 15 times per month. In this example, the samples are independent. The question is whether or not the difference in the number of visits per month is meaningful. Stated another way, 'Did the percentage of persons eating at fast food restaurants at least 15 times per month increase from 12 per cent last year to 18 per cent this year?'

The answer appears to be straightforward, but as we have previously pointed out, some type of sampling error could have distorted the results enough so there may not be any real difference between this year's percentage of heavy users of fast food restaurants and last year's. If the difference between the percentages is very large, one would be more confident that there is in fact a true difference between the groups. However, there would still be some uncertainty as to whether the difference is meaningful. In this instance we have intuitively factored in one of the most important components in determining whether important differences exist between two sample means: the magnitude of the difference between the means. But another important component to consider is the size of the sample used to calculate the means.

In hypothesis development, the **null hypothesis** states that there is no difference between the group means in the comparison. In this case, the null hypothesis states there is no difference between the 12 per cent visiting fast food restaurants at least 15 times a month last year and the 18 per cent found this year. The null hypothesis is the one that is always tested by statisticians and marketing researchers. Another hypothesis, called the **alternative hypothesis**, states that there is a true difference between the group means. If the null hypothesis is accepted, there is no change to the status quo. If the null hypothesis is rejected, we automatically conclude the alternative hypothesis should be right, and conclude that there has been a true difference between the group means under investigation.

Null hypothesis A statement that asserts the status quo; that is, that any change from what has been thought to be true is due to random sampling error.

Alternative hypothesis A statement that is the opposite of the null hypothesis; that is, that the difference should exist in reality and is not simply due to random sampling error.

You should remember that a null hypothesis refers to a population parameter, not a sample statistic. Results of hypothesis testing indicate that either there is a meaningful difference between the two groups (reject the null hypothesis) or there is not a large enough difference between the groups to conclude that the groups are different (fail to reject the null hypothesis). It is important to bear in mind that failure to reject the null hypothesis does not necessarily mean that the null hypothesis is true. This is because data from another sample of the same population could produce different results.

In marketing research the null hypothesis is developed in such a way that its rejection leads to an acceptance of the alternative situation to be preconceived. In other words, the alternative hypothesis represents the situation being assumed to be true. Usually, the null hypothesis is notated as H_0 and the alternative hypothesis is notated as H_1. If the null hypothesis (H_0) is rejected, then the alternative hypothesis (H_1) should be accepted. The alternative hypothesis always bears the burden of proof.

Small businesses need to test hypotheses just as large ones do. SPSS and SAS can help them do this, as shown in the Closer Look at Research box below.

A Closer Look at Research *(Small Business Implications)*
SPSS and SAS

Small business owners and managers can use information from the SPSS and SAS websites for a variety of marketing research purposes. The sites provide a wealth of information that can lead to idea generation for marketing research opportunities.

In many small businesses, owners and managers possess limited statistical ability. SPSS and SAS offer convenient-to-follow guidance on how to use statistical analysis to benefit their business in a number of ways. Examples include uncovering trends in a particular niche market, identifying potential outliers (companies not following the standard path in that particular market), and graphical representations of all market participants (which allows for easy visual comparison of competitors). Small businesses can rely on SPSS and SAS to learn and gradually build sophisticated statistical models within their organization one small step at a time.

Statistical Significance

Whenever the marketing researcher draws an inference regarding a population, there is a risk that the inference may be incorrect. In other words, the test the marketing researcher performs in order to decide whether or not to reject the null hypothesis may produce incorrect results.

There are two types of error associated with hypothesis testing that the marketing researcher needs to be aware of when forming conclusions based on the data analysis. The first type of error is termed Type I. Type I error is associated with rejecting the null hypothesis and accepting the alternative hypothesis in error. This type of error, frequently called *alpha* (α), occurs when the sample data lead to rejection of a null hypothesis that is in fact true. The probability of such an error is termed the level of significance. The level of significance is equivalent to the amount of

> **Type I error** The error made by rejecting the null hypothesis when it is true; the probability of alpha.
>
> **Level of significance** The amount of risk regarding the accuracy of the test that the researcher is willing to accept.

risk regarding the accuracy of the test that the researcher is willing to accept. Put another way, the level of significance is the probability that the rejection of the null hypothesis is in error. Marketing researchers usually accept a level of significance of .10, .05, or .01. This means that the researcher is willing to accept some risk of incorrect rejection of the null hypothesis, and that level of risk is prespecified.

The second type of error, termed **Type II error**, is the error that occurs when the sample data produce results that fail to reject the null hypothesis when in fact the null hypothesis is false and should be rejected. Type II error is frequently called *beta* (β).

> **Type II error** The error of failing to reject the null hypothesis when the alternative hypothesis is true; the probability of beta.

In some research situations, the researcher may be much more concerned about controlling one type of error than the other. For example, if a new, potentially life-saving drug is being tested, the researcher would probably want to minimize the error or possibility of concluding that the drug is effective (i.e. rejecting the null hypothesis) when in fact the drug is not effective. In this case, Type I error is of the much greater importance than Type II error.

Analysing Relationships of Sample Data

Once the researcher has developed hypotheses and calculated the means of the groups, the next step is to analyse the relationships of the sample data. In this section we will discuss the methods used to test hypotheses. We will introduce the *t* distribution and describe its function for testing hypotheses. This requires a review of some basic statistical terminology.

Sample Statistics and Population Parameters

The purpose of inferential statistics is to make a determination about a population on the basis of a sample from that population. As we explained in Chapter 9, a sample is a subset of all the elements within the population. For example, if we wanted to determine the average number of cups of coffee consumed by students during the examination period at your university, we probably would not interview all the students. This would be costly, take a long time and probably be impossible since we might not be able to find them all or some would decline to participate. Instead, if there were 16,000 students at your university, we might decide that a sample of 200 females and 200 males is sufficiently large to provide rather accurate information about the coffee drinking habits of all 16,000 students.

Sample statistics are measures obtained directly from the sample or calculated from the data in the sample. A population parameter is a variable or some sort of measured characteristic of the entire population. Sample statistics are useful in making inferences regarding the population's parameters. The actual population parameters are usually unknown since the cost to perform a census of almost any large population is often prohibitive.

A frequency distribution displaying the data obtained from the sample is commonly used to summarize the results of the data collection process. When a frequency distribution displays a variable in terms of percentages, then this distribution is representing proportions within a population. For example, a frequency distribution showing that 40 per cent of the people patronize

Burger King indicates the percentage of the entire population eating at the fast food restaurant. The proportion may be expressed as a percentage, a fraction, or a decimal value.

Univariate Tests of Significance

In many situations a marketing researcher will form hypotheses regarding population means based on sample data. This involves going beyond the simple tabulations incorporated in a frequency distribution and calculation of averages. In these instances, the researcher may conduct univariate tests of significance. These tests involve hypothesis testing using one variable at a time.

Suppose a marketing researcher has agreed to help Jimmy Spice's restaurant's owners determine whether customers think their menu prices are reasonable. Respondents have answered this question using a 7-point scale on which 1 = 'Strongly Disagree' and 7 = 'Strongly Agree'. The scale is assumed to be an interval scale, and previous research using this measure has shown the responses to be approximately normally distributed.

The researcher must perform a couple of tasks before attempting to answer the question posed above. First, the hypotheses to be compared (the null and alternative hypotheses) have to be developed. Then the level of significance for rejecting the null hypothesis and accepting the alternative hypothesis must be selected. Thereafter the researcher can conduct the statistical test and determine the answer to the research question.

In this example, the owners think the customers consider the prices of food at Jimmy Spices' restaurant to be average. That means responses to the question on reasonable prices will have a mean close to 4, which is approximately halfway between 1 and 7 on the response scale. The null hypothesis is that the mean of the X16 – Reasonable Prices will not be significantly different from 4. Recall that the null hypothesis asserts the status quo: any difference from what is thought to be true is due to random sampling. The alternative hypothesis is that the mean of the answers to X16 – Reasonable Prices will not be 4: there is in fact a true difference between the sample mean we find and the mean we think it is, i.e. 4.

Assume also the owners want to be 95 per cent certain the mean is not 4. Therefore, the significance level will be set at .05. Using this significance level means that if the survey of Jimmy Spice's customers is conducted many times, the probability of incorrectly rejecting the null hypothesis when it is true would be less than 5 times out of 100, i.e. .05.

Two tests could be used to examine this hypothesis – the *t*-test and the *z*-test. A **t-test** utilizes the *t* distribution; it is most appropriate when the sample size is smaller than 30 and the standard deviation is unknown. In contrast, a **z-test** utilizes the *z* distribution. This test is used when the sample size is larger than 30 and the standard deviation is unknown. Use of the *z*-test assumes the data have a normal distribution. But if the sample size is 30 or less the assumption of a normal distribution must not be held and the *t*-test should be used. Fortunately, in most situations we do not have to deal with the issue about which test should be used. Popular computerized software such as SPSS or SAS is set up to compute the correct statistic. That means the software determines whether the *t* or z is appropriate and calculates the correct one. In SPSS you should know, however, that the statistic is always referred to as a *t*-test. But if the sample is larger than 30 a *z*-test has been used.

> **t-test** A hypothesis test that utilizes the *t* distribution; used when the sample size is smaller than 30 and the standard deviation is unknown.

> **z-test** A hypothesis test that utilizes the z distribution; used when the sample size is larger than 30 and the standard deviation is unknown.

SPSS Application – Univariate Hypothesis Tests

Using the SPSS software, you can test the responses in Jimmy Spice's restaurant database to find the answer to the research question posed above. The click-through sequence is: ANALYSE → COMPARE MEANS → ONE-SAMPLE *T*-TEST. When you get to the dialogue box, click on X16 – Reasonable Prices to highlight it. Then click on the arrow to move X16 into the Test Variables box. In the box labelled Test Value, enter the number 4. This is the number you want to compare the respondents' answers against. Click on the Options box and enter 95 in the confidence interval box. This is the same as setting the significance level at .05. Then, click on the Continue button and OK to execute the programme.

The SPSS output is shown in Exhibit 16.11. The top table is labelled One-Sample Statistics and shows the mean, standard deviation and standard error for X16 – Reasonable Prices. The One-Sample Test table below shows the results of the *t*-test for the null hypothesis that the average response to X16 is 4 (Test Value = 4). The *t*-test statistic is 5.537, and the significance level is .000. This means that the null hypothesis can be rejected and the alternative hypothesis accepted with a high level of confidence from a statistical perspective.

From a practical standpoint, in terms of Jimmy Spice's restaurant, the results of the univariate hypothesis test mean respondents perceived that menu prices were somewhat reasonable. The mean of 4.34 is somewhat higher than the mid-point of 4 on the 7-point scale. Thus, the restaurant owners can conclude that their prices are not perceived as unreasonable. But, on the other hand, there is a lot of room to improve between the mean of 4.34 on the 7-point scale and the highest value of 7. This is clearly an area that needs to be examined. The owners also need to know if the respondents' answers are based on reality or incorrect perceptions.

EXHIBIT 16.11 Univariate Hypothesis Test Using X16 – Reasonable Prices

➔ **T – Test**

One-Sample Statistics

	N	Mean	Std. Deviation	Std. Error Mean
X16 -- Reasonable Prices	400	4.34	1.228	0.61

One-Sample Test

	Test Value = 4				95 per cent Confidence Interval of the Difference	
	t	df	Sig. (2-tailed)	Mean Difference	Lower	Upper
X16 -- Reasonable Prices	5.537	399	.000	.34	.22	.46

Bivariate Hypothesis Tests

In many instances the marketing researcher will want to test hypotheses that compare the mean of one group to the mean of another group. For example, the marketing researcher may be interested in determining whether there is any difference between older and younger respondents in terms of the importance of in-house fitness facilities when they are booking a hotel room. In situations where more than one group is involved, bivariate hypothesis tests are needed. In the following section we describe two bivariate hypothesis tests: the *t*-test (to compare two means) and analysis of variance (a method to compare three or more group means).

In nearly all cases the null hypothesis is that there is no difference between the group means. This null hypothesis is specifically stated as follows:

$$\mu_1 = \mu_2 \text{ or that } \mu_1 - \mu_2 = 0$$

Using the *t*-Test to Compare Two Means

Just as with the univariate *t*-test, the bivariate *t*-test requires interval or ratio data. Also, the *t*-test is especially useful when the sample size is small ($n < 30$) and when the population standard deviation is unknown. Unlike the univariate test, however, we assume that the samples are drawn from populations with normal distributions and that the variances of the populations are equal.

Essentially, the *t*-test for differences between group means can be conceptualized as the difference between the means divided by the variability of random means. The *t* value is a ratio of the difference between the two sample means and the standard error. The *t*-test tries to provide a rational way of determining if the difference between the two sample means occurred by chance. The formula for calculating the *t* value is:

$$z = \frac{\overline{X}_1 - \overline{X}_2}{S\overline{x}_1 - \overline{x}_2}$$

where

$\overline{x}_1$ = mean of sample 1
$\overline{x}_2$ = mean of sample 2
$S\overline{x}_1 - \overline{x}_2$ = standard error of the difference between the two means

SPSS Application – Independent Samples *t*-Test

To illustrate the use of a *t*-test for the difference between two group means, let's turn to Jimmy Spice's Restaurant database. The restaurant owners want to find out if there are differences in the level of satisfaction between male and female customers. To do that we can use the SPSS Compare Means programme.

The SPSS click-through sequence is ANALYSE → COMPARE MEANS → INDEPENDENT-SAMPLES *t*-Test. When you get to this dialogue box click variable X22 – Satisfaction into the Test Variables box and variable X32 – Gender into the Grouping Variable Box. For variable X32 you must define the range in the Define Groups box. Enter a 0 for Group 1 and a 1 for Group 2 (males are coded 0 and females are coded 1 in the database) and then click Continue. For the Options we will use the defaults, so just click OK to execute the programme.

Results are shown in Exhibit 16.12. The top table shows the Group Statistics. Note that 236 male customers and 164 female customers were interviewed. Also, the mean satisfaction level for males was a bit higher at 4.83, compared to 4.38 for the female customers. The standard deviation for females was somewhat smaller (.874) than for the males (.966).

EXHIBIT 16.12 Using the Independent-Samples *t*-Test to Compare Two Means

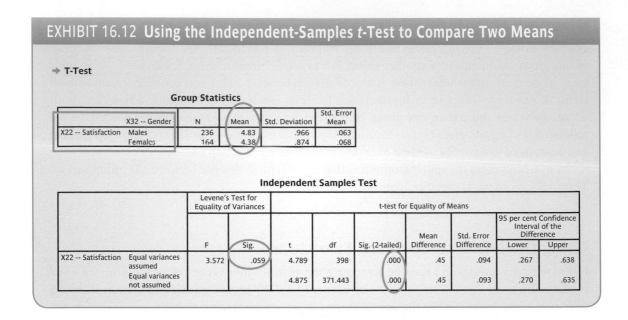

➡ **T-Test**

Group Statistics

	X32 -- Gender	N	Mean	Std. Deviation	Std. Error Mean
X22 -- Satisfaction	Males	236	4.83	.966	.063
	Females	164	4.38	.874	.068

Independent Samples Test

		Levene's Test for Equality of Variances		t-test for Equality of Means					95 per cent Confidence Interval of the Difference	
		F	Sig.	t	df	Sig. (2-tailed)	Mean Difference	Std. Error Difference	Lower	Upper
X22 -- Satisfaction	Equal variances assumed	3.572	.059	4.789	398	.000	.45	.094	.267	.638
	Equal variances not assumed			4.875	371.443	.000	.45	.093	.270	.635

To find out if the two means are significantly different, we look at the information in the Independent Samples Test table. The statistical significance of the difference in two means is calculated differently if the variances of the two means are equal versus unequal. The Levene's test for equality of variances is reported on the left side of the table. In this case the test shows the two variances are equal (Sig. value of .059), but almost significantly different. In all cases where this value is <.05 you would use the 'Equal variances not assumed' test. In the column labelled Sig. (2-tailed) you will note that the two means are significantly different (<.000), whether we assume equal or unequal variances. Thus, there is no support for the null hypothesis that the two means are equal, and we conclude that male customers are significantly more satisfied than female customers. There is other information in this table, but we do not need to concern ourselves with it at this time. As a researcher, however, you must always interpret statistical findings cautiously before drawing conclusions.

SPSS Application – Paired Samples *t*-Test

Sometimes marketing researchers want to test for differences in two means for variables in the same sample. For example, the owners of Jimmy Spice's restaurant noticed in their survey that the taste of their food was rated 5.31 while the food temperature was rated only 4.57. Since the two food variables are obviously related, they want to know if the ratings for taste really are significantly higher (more favourable) than for temperature. To examine this, we use the paired samples *t*-test for the difference in two means. This test examines whether two means from two different questions using the same scaling and answered by the same respondents are significantly different. The null hypothesis is the mean ratings for the two food variables (X18 and X20) are equal.

To test this hypothesis we use the SPSS paired-samples *t*-test. The click-through sequence is ANALYSE → COMPARE MEANS → PAIRED-SAMPLES *t*-Test. When you get to this dialogue box, highlight both X18 – Food Taste and X20 – Food Temperature and then click on the arrow button to move them into the Paired Variables box. For the Options we will use the defaults, so just click OK to execute the programme.

Results are shown in Exhibit 16.13. The top table shows the Paired Samples Statistics. The mean for food taste is 5.31 and for food temperature is 4.57. The t value for this comparison is 17.649 (see Paired Samples Test table) and it is significant at the .000 level. Thus we can reject the null hypothesis that the two means are equal and conclude that Jimmy Spices' customers definitely have more favourable perceptions of food taste than food temperature.

EXHIBIT 16.13 Paired Samples *t*-Test

T-Test

Paired Samples Statistics

		Mean	N	Std. Deviation	Std. Error Mean
Pair 1	X18 -- Excellent Food Taste	5.31	400	1.088	0.54
	X20 -- Proper Food Temperature	4.57	400	1.104	0.55

Paired Samples Test

		Paired Differences							
					95 per cent Confidence Interval of the Difference				
		Mean	Std. Deviation	Std. Error Mean	Lower	Upper	t	dt	Sig. (2-tailed)
Pair 1	X18 -- Excellent Food Taste - X20 -- Proper Food Temperature	.74	.841	.042	.66	.83	17.649	399	.000

Best Western

Best Western is the world's biggest hotel chain, with some 3,300 independently owned hotels. By using marketing research, Best Western has been able to identify its market segments. The hotel chain has discovered that business travellers tend to shy away from unknown, less-expensive brands of hotels in favour of consistent-quality brands, such as Best Western. The first table here shows the composition of the worldwide hotel market, and the second shows the source of business (domestic or foreign) by world region.

Composition of Worldwide Hotel Market

Market Segment Group	Per cent of Total Market
Business travellers	36.0%
Individual travellers	24.5
Tour groups	13.5
Conference participants	12.7
Other groups	9.2
Government officials	4.1

Composition of Business Traveller Market

Source of Business	Worldwide	Africa/ Middle East	Asia/ Australia	North America	Europe
Domestic	50.7%	24.6%	35.0%	84.6%	47.3%
Foreign	49.3	75.4	65.0	15.4	52.7
Total	100.0	100.0	100.0	100.0	100.0

Using marketing research to uncover facts about its market segments such as the ones above, Best Western has been able to focus its marketing strategy on business travellers. In addition, the hotel chain emphasizes domestic business in North America; focuses on both domestic and foreign business in Europe; and targets foreign business in Africa, Asia, Australia and the Middle East.

Questions

1 What are the different types of graphics that can be used to illustrate the above results? Use Choose one of these graphics types to illustrate the results in the form of SPSS output.

2 What other data you would like to have for Best Western's market segmentation strategy? What are the basic data analysis techniques that you would use to analyse these additional data?

Summary of Learning Objectives

■ **Understand how to prepare graphical presentations of data.**

Distributions of numbers can be illustrated by several different types of graphs. Histograms and bar charts display data in either horizontal or vertical bars. Line charts are a good choice for communicating trends in data, while pie charts are well suited for illustrating relative proportions.

■ **Calculate the mean, median and mode as measures of central tendency.**

The mean is the most commonly used measure of central tendency and describes the arithmetic average of the values in a sample of data. The median represents the middle value of an ordered set of values. The mode is the most frequently occurring value in a distribution of values. All these measures describe the centre of the distribution of a set of values.

■ **Explain the range and standard deviation of a frequency distribution as measures of dispersion.**

The range defines the spread of the data. It is the distance between the smallest and largest values of the distribution. The standard deviation describes the average distance of the distribution values from the mean. A large standard deviation indicates a distribution in which the individual values are spread out and are relatively farther away from the mean.

■ **Understand the difference between independent and related samples.**

In independent samples the respondents come from different populations, so their answers to the survey questions do not affect each other. Questions about mean differences in independent samples can be answered by using a student t-test statistic. In related samples, the same respondent answers several questions, so comparing answers to these questions requires the use of a paired-samples t-test.

■ **Explain hypothesis testing and assess potential error in its use.**

A hypothesis is an empirically testable though yet unproven statement about a set of data. Hypotheses allow the researcher to make comparisons between two groups of respondents and to determine whether there are important differences between the groups.

Hypothesis tests have two types of error connected with their use. The first type of error (Type I error) is the risk of rejecting the null hypothesis on the basis of your sample data when it is, in fact, true for the population from which the sample data was selected. The second type of error (Type II error) is the risk of not detecting a false null hypothesis. The level of statistical significance (alpha) associated with a statistical test is the probability of making a Type I error.

■ **Understand t-tests and z-tests.**

t-tests of mean values should be used when the sample size is small (less than 30) and the standard deviation of the population is unknown; z-tests are statistical tests of mean values best used when sample sizes are above 30 and the standard deviation of the population is known. Both tests involve the use of the sample mean, a t or z value selected from the respective distribution, and the standard deviation of either the sample or the population.

Tests of the differences between two groups require the use of t-tests for small samples (less than 30) and unknown population standard deviations. For larger samples and known population standard deviations, either the t-test or z-test can be used.

Key Terms and Concepts

Alternative hypothesis 536	Range 533
Hypothesis 535	Related samples 535
Independent samples 535	Standard deviation 533
Level of significance 537	t-test 539
Mean 529	Type I error 537
Median 530	Type II error 538
Mode 530	Variance 533
Null hypothesis 536	z-test 540

Review Questions

1 Why are graphic approaches to reporting marketing research better than simply reporting numbers?
2 Explain the difference between the mean, the median and the mode.
3 Why do we use hypothesis testing?
4 Why and how would you use t- and z-tests in hypothesis testing?
5 Why and when would you want to use ANOVA in marketing research?
6 What will ANOVA tests not tell you, and how can you overcome this problem?

Discussion Questions

1 The measures of central tendency discussed in this chapter are designed to reveal information about the centre of a distribution of values. Measures of dispersion provide information about the spread of all the values in a distribution around the centre values. Assume you are conducting an opinion poll on voters' approval ratings of the job performance of the mayor of the city where you live. Do you think the mayor would be more interested in the central tendency or the dispersion measures associated with the responses to your poll? Why?
2 If you are interested in finding out whether or not young adults (21–34 years old) are more likely to buy products online than older adults (35 or more years old), how would you phrase your null hypothesis? What is the implicit alternative hypothesis accompanying your null hypothesis?
3 The level of significance (alpha) associated with testing a null hypothesis is also referred to as the probability of a Type I error. Alpha is the probability of rejecting the null hypothesis on the basis of your sample data when it is, in fact, true for the population you are interested in. Since alpha concerns the probability of making a mistake in your analysis, should you always try to set this value as small as possible? Why or why not?
4 Analysis of variance (ANOVA) allows you to test for the statistical difference between two or more means. Typically, there are more than two means tested.

If the ANOVA results for a set of data reveal that the four means that are being compared are significantly different from each other, how would you find out which individual means are statistically different from each other? What statistical techniques would you apply to answer this question?

5 **Experience the Internet.** Nike, Adidas, Reebok and Converse are strong competitors in the athletic shoe market. The four use different advertising and marketing strategies to appeal to their target markets. Use one of the search engines on the Internet to identify information relevant to this market. Go to the websites for these four companies (www.Nike.com; www.adidas.com; www.Reebok.com; www.Converse.com). Gather background information on each, including its target market and market share. Design a questionnaire based on this information and survey a sample of students. Prepare a report on the different perceptions of each of these four companies, their shoes and related aspects. Present the report in class and defend your findings.

6 **SPSS Exercise.** Form a team of three to four students in your class. Select one or two fast food restaurants, such as Subway or McDonald's, to conduct a survey on. Design a brief questionnaire (10–12 questions) including questions like ratings on quality of food, speed of service, knowledge of employees, attitudes of employees and price, as well as several demographic variables such as age, address, how often the respondents eat there and day of week and time of day. Obtain permission from the fast food restaurant selected to interview their customers at a convenient time, usually when they are leaving. Assure the restaurant you will not bother customers and that you will provide it with a valuable report on your findings. Develop frequency tables, pie charts and other types of graphic displays of your findings, where appropriate. Use statistics to test hypotheses, such as 'Perceptions of speed of service differ by day of week or time of day'. Prepare a report and present it to your class; particularly point out where statistically significant differences exist and why.

7 **SPSS Exercise.** Using SPSS and Jimmy Spice's restaurant database, provide frequencies, means, medians and modes for the relevant variables on the questionnaire. The actual questionnaire is presented in Chapter 14. In addition, develop bar charts and pie charts where appropriate for the data you analysed. Run an ANOVA using the lifestyle and restaurant perceptions variables to identify any group differences that may exist. Be prepared to present a report on your findings.

Chapter 17

Bivariate Correlation and Regression Analysis Techniques

LEARNING OBJECTIVES

After reading this chapter, you will be able to

- ☑ Understand and evaluate the types of relationships between variables.

- ☑ Explain the concepts of covariation and association.

- ☑ Discuss the differences between Chi-square, Pearson correlation and Spearman correlation.

- ☑ Explain the concepts of statistical significance versus practical significance.

- ☑ Understand when and how to use bivariate regression analysis.

> " Correlation does not imply causation.
>
> *–Darrell Huff*
> *In How To Lie With Statistics* "

Companies Are Not Analysing their Customer Data

A report commissioned by Royal Mail and quoted by blogcrm.com has found that a staggering 90 per cent of companies in the UK are not making the best use of their own customer data and in the process they are collectively losing out on millions of pounds in sales. If these companies put more effort into analysing these data so as to gain better customer insights, they could increase sales and profit, and subsequently the value of their business, by as much as 30 per cent.

According to Colin Bredshaw, head of data strategy at Royal Mail, only 15 per cent of the companies that they investigated regarded their customer data as an important asset. For companies that try to conduct some data analysis, most of them only use simple data analysis techniques in order to find something meaningful from their data.

We believe that this 'data analysis inertia' is not just happening in the UK, but is also common in Europe and beyond.

Relationships between Variables

Data analysis is crucial to any type of organization. Yet as the chapter opening example shows, most businesses do not realize its importance. For those that try to make some use of their customer data, simple data analysis is the norm. This simple data analysis, such as finding the mean of a single variable, does not look beyond dealing with only one variable at a time. This chapter represents a move above this simple data analysis, by exploring potential relationships between variables in a given dataset.

Relationships between variables can be described in several ways, including presence, direction, strength of association and type. We will describe each of these concepts in turn.

> **Relationship** A consistent and systematic link between two or more variables.

The first issue, and probably the most obvious, is whether two or more variables are related at all. If a consistent and systematic relationship exists between two or more variables, this is referred to as the presence of a relationship. To measure whether a relationship is present, we rely on the concept of statistical significance. By choosing and conducting an appropriate statistical test, we can find out whether a relationship between the variables of question exists. If a relationship exists, we can confidently claim that knowledge about the behaviour of one variable allows us to make a useful prediction about the behaviour of another. For example, if we found a statistically significant relationship between respondents' perceptions of the quality of Jimmy Spice's food and their satisfaction levels, we would say a relationship is present and that perceptions of the quality of the food can tell us what the levels of satisfaction are likely to be.

If a relationship is present between two variables, it is important to know the direction. The direction of a relationship can be either positive or negative. Using the Jimmy Spice's example, we can say that a positive relationship exists if respondents who rate the quality of the food high also are highly satisfied. Similarly, a negative relationship exists if respondents say the speed of service is slow (low rating) but they are still satisfied (high rating).

An understanding of the strength of association is also important. We generally categorize the strength of association as non-existent, weak, moderate, or strong. If a consistent and systematic relationship is not present, then the strength of association is non-existent. A weak association means the variables concerned are only loosely related to each other. A strong association means there is a a close relationship between the variables under investigation.

A fourth concept that is important to understand is the type of relationship. If two variables can be described as related, then we would pose this as a question: 'What is the nature of the relationship?' How can the link between Y and X *be* best described? There are two broad ways in which two variables can share a relationship. Variables Y and X can have a **linear relationship**, which means that the strength and direction of the relationship between them remains the same over the entire range of both variables, and can best be described using a straight line. Conversely, Y and X could have a **non-linear relationship**, which means that the strength and/or direction of their relationship changes over the range of both variables. For instance, Y's relationship with X first gets stronger as X increases, but then gets weaker as the value of X continues to increase.

> **Linear relationship** A relationship between two variables whereby the strength and direction of the relationship remains the same over the range of both variables.
>
> **Non-linear relationship** A relationship between two variables whereby the strength and/or direction of their relationship changes over the range of both variables.

It may occur to you that a linear relationship would be much simpler to work with than a non-linear relationship and that is true. If we know the value of variable X, then we can apply the formula for a straight line ($Y = a = bX$) to determine the value of Y. But when two variables have a non-linear relationship, the formula that best describes that linkage will be more algebraically complex and possibly hard to determine. For these reasons, most marketing researchers tend to work with relationships that they believe are linear, or are close approximations to linearity. In fact, many of the statistics you learned about in this textbook are based on the assumption that a linear relationship is an acceptable way to describe the link between two variables under investigation.

Marketers are very often interested in describing the relationship between a marketing mix variable (e.g. price) and a marketing performance variable (e.g. sales). To test a possible relationship like this, following what we have discussed previously in this section, we need to answer the following four fundamental questions. First, 'Is there a relationship between the two variables we are interested in?' Interest in questions two to four depend upon the answer to the first. If there is a relationship, then one can further examine 'What is the direction of that relationship?', 'How strong is that relationship?', and 'How can that relationship be best described?'

Using Covariation to Describe Variable Relationships

Since we are interested in finding out whether two variables describing our customers are related, the concept of covariation is a very useful idea. **Covariation** is defined as the amount of change in one variable that is consistently related to a change in another variable of interest. For example,

> **Covariation** The amount of change in one variable that is consistently related to the change in another variable of interest.

if we are convinced that younger people purchase more DVDs, we may want to know further the extent to which younger persons purchase more DVDs. Another way of stating the concept of covariation is that it is the degree of association between two items. If two variables are found to change together on a consistent basis, then we can use that information to make decisions on different marketing strategy aspects.

One easy way of visually describing the covariation between two variables is with the use of a **scatter diagram**. A scatter diagram plots the relative position of two variables using a horizontal and a vertical axis to represent the values of the respective variables. Exhibits 17.1 to 17.4 show some examples of possible relationships between two variables that might show up on a scatter diagram. In Exhibit 17.1, the best way to describe the visual impression left by the collection of dots representing the values of each variable is probably a circle. This implies there is no particular skewness or direction regarding the collection of dots. Thus, if you take a number of sample values of variable Y from the scatter diagram, you won't find any discernible pattern with regard to the values for X. Knowing the values of Y or X would not tell you very much (maybe nothing at all) about the possible values of the other variable. Exhibit 17.1 suggests that there is no systematic relationship between Y and X and accordingly there is virtually no covariation shared by the two variables. If we measured the amount of covariation shared by these two variables, it would be very close to zero.

Scatter diagram A graphic plot of the relative position of two variables using a horizontal and a vertical axis to represent the values of the respective variables.

In Exhibit 17.2, the two variables present a very different picture from that of Exhibit 17.1. There is a distinct pattern to the dots. As the values of Y increase, so do the values of X. This pattern could be very effectively described using the idea of a straight line, which signifies the presence of linearity. We could also describe this relationship as positive, because increases in the value of Y are associated with increases in the value of X. in other words, the values of Y and X change in

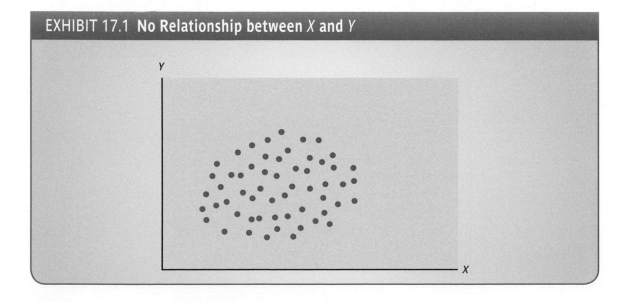

EXHIBIT 17.1 No Relationship between X and Y

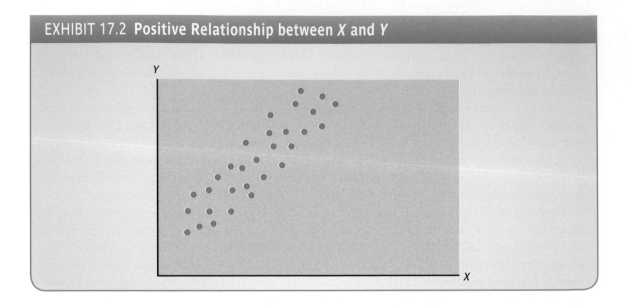

EXHIBIT 17.2 **Positive Relationship between *X* and *Y***

the same direction. Similarly, if the values of *Y* decrease, the values of *X* should decrease as well. If we try to measure the amount of covariation shown by the values of *Y* and *X*, it would be relatively high. Thus, changes in the value of *Y* are systematically related to changes in the value of *X*.

Exhibit 17.3 shows the same type of distinct pattern between the values of *Y* and *X*, but the direction of the relationship is opposite the one in Exhibit 17.2. There still seems to be the same linear pattern, but now increases in the value of *Y* are associated with decreases in the values of *X*. The values of *Y* and *X* change in the opposite direction. This type of relationship is known as a negative relationship. The amount of covariation shared between the two variables is still high, because *Y* and *X* still change together, though in a direction opposite from that shown in Exhibit 17.2. The concept of covariation refers to the amount of shared movement, not the direction of the relationship between two variables.

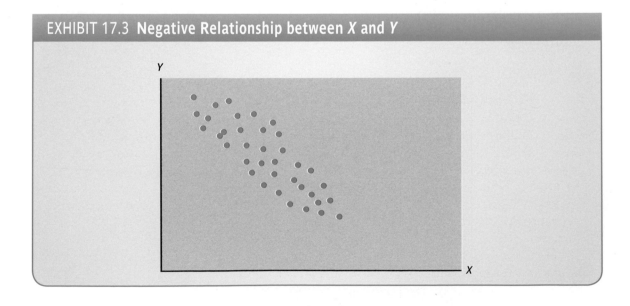

EXHIBIT 17.3 **Negative Relationship between *X* and *Y***

EXHIBIT 17.4 **Curvilinear Relationship between *X* and *Y***

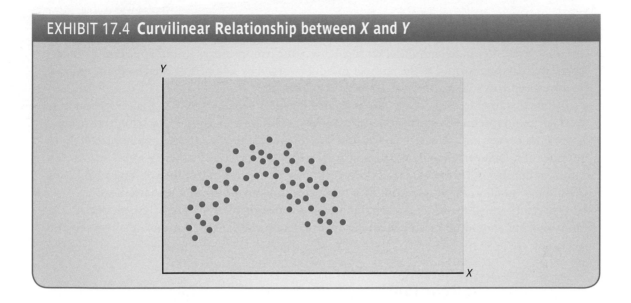

Finally, Exhibit 17.4 shows a more complicated type of relationship between the values of *Y* and *X*. This pattern of dots can be described as *curvilinear*. That is, the relationship between the values of *Y* and the values of *X* is different for different values of the variables. In the case of Exhibit 17.4, part of the relationship is positive (increases in the small values of *Y* are associated with increases in the small values of *X*), but then the relationship becomes negative (increases in the larger values of *Y* are now associated with decreases in the larger values of *X*).

This pattern of dots clearly cannot be described as a linear relationship. However, many of the statistics marketing researchers use to describe association assume the two variables have a linear relationship. These statistics won't perform effectively when used to describe a curvilinear relationship. In Exhibit 17.4, we can still say the covariation exhibited by the two variables is strong. However, now we can't talk very easily about the direction (positive or negative) of the relationship, because the direction can change depending on which range of the values of Y and X we are talking about. The Closer Look at Research box provides an insight into how correlations can be used in small businesses.

A Closer Look at Research *(Small Business Implications)*
Correlation Does Not Identify Causation

Situations often arise where many small-business owners and managers collect data from two relevant samples yet do not know how to statistically compare the two measures. When this occurs, the most frequently used statistical technique available to the small-business owner is correlation analysis.

Correlation analysis describes the degree of relationship between the two variables, often stated as an absolute value score between 0 and 1. The higher the correlation score, the stronger the relationship between the two variables. Through the use of correlation procedures, small-business owners can identify trends in their particular market.

A brief description of correlation analysis in action is described below. This example is only one of a variety of possible applications of correlation analysis.

A small-business owner might have information on the exact number of hours worked by salespeople in his company last year and the amount of advertising sold by each sales representative that year. After initial graphical representation, the two measures would appear to be highly correlated. In other words, as the number of hours worked by salespeople increased, the amount of advertisements sold per individual would also increase.

While this brief example shows the possible inferences from correlation analysis, a common mistake in interpreting the correlation score for two variables is to assume that a high correlation score implies causation. No such conclusion is automatic. In the previous example, although the number of hours worked and sales productivity are highly correlated, other factors – such as territory or number of representatives in that area – play an important role in analysing correlation. Assuming causation based solely on these two factors might ignore other important variables.

Therefore, small-business owners should use correlation analysis to analyse potential relationships but should be careful in attempting to determine causal relationships between two variables.

Measuring the Relationship

The use of a scatter diagram gives us a visual way to describe approximately the relationship between two variables and a sense of the amount of covariation they share. For example, a scatter diagram can tell us that as a person's income increases the average consumption of fruits and vegetables increases too. But even though a picture is worth a thousand words, it is often better to use a more precise quantitative measure of the covariation to measure the relationship between two variables.

One of the bivariate correlation analysis techniques that can provide a quantitative measure of the covariation between two variables is Pearson correlation analysis. The covariation measure in this analysis is called the **Pearson correlation coefficient**. It varies between -1.00 and 1.00, with 0 representing absolutely no association between two variables and -1.00 or 1.00 representing a perfect link between two variables. The higher the correlation coefficient, the stronger the level of association between two variables. The correlation coefficient can be either positive or negative, depending on the direction of the relationship between two variables. As we explained earlier, if there is a negative correlation coefficient between Y and X, that means that increases in the value of Y are associated with decreases in the value of X, and vice versa.

> **Pearson correlation coefficient** A statistical measure of the strength of a linear relationship between two metric variables.

The null hypothesis for the Pearson correlation states that there is no association between the two variables in the population and that the correlation coefficient is zero. For example, we may hypothesize that there is no relationship between Starbucks coffee consumption and income levels. If you take measures of two variables (coffee consumption and income) from a sample of the population and estimate the correlation coefficient for that sample, the basic question is 'What is the probability that I would get a correlation coefficient of this size in my sample if the correlation coefficient in the population is actually zero?' That is, if you calculate a large correlation coefficient between the two variables in your sample, and your sample was properly selected from the population of interest, then the chances that the population correlation coefficient is really zero are relatively small. Therefore, if the correlation coefficient is statistically significant, the null hypothesis is rejected, and you can conclude with some confidence that the two variables you are examining do share some association in the population. In other words, Starbucks coffee consumption is related to income.

Earlier in the chapter we stated that the first question of interest is 'Does a relationship between Y and X exist?' Statistically speaking, this question is equivalent to asking whether the correlation coefficient quantifying the relationship between Y and X is statistically significant. If so, then the researcher can move on to the following three questions: 'How strong is that relationship?' 'What is the direction of the relationship?' and 'What is the best way to describe that relationship?'

The most critical of these questions is the first one. This is because if there is no statistically significant relationship between Y and X, there is no point in probing further into the size of the relationship, the direction of the relationship and the best way to describe the relationship.

So how to find out whether there is any statistically significant relationship between two variables. Researchers can refer to published tables, which are replicated in most marketing research and statistics textbooks, indicating which correlation coefficients are significant at various sample sizes. Another way is to rely on statistical software, such as SPSS, which shows the significance level for a computed correlation coefficient. The significance level, identified as the 'Sig.' Value in the SPSS output, is referred to as the probability that the null hypothesis is true. To explain this point, let's take an example: The null hypothesis is no relationship between coffee consumption and income. Results show that the correlation coefficient is .71 with a significance level of .045. This means there are less than five chances out of 100 that there is no relationship between the two variables. Therefore the null hypothesis of no relationship should be rejected.

Having found a statistically significant relationship between the two variables, the researcher should address the second 'relationship' question, i.e. how strong is that relationship? This question can be answered by looking at the size of the correlation coefficient. There are some rules of thumb to interpret the size of a correlation coefficient. As Exhibit 17.5 suggests, correlation coefficients between .81 and 1.00 are considered very strong. At the other extreme, if the correlation coefficient is between .00 and .20, then there is a good chance the null hypothesis of no relationship between the two variables won't be rejected. However, these rules of thumb are not absolute, and researchers should take account of the specific situation of their research project when making use of these suggested rules. For example, a correlation coefficient of .65 should probably not regarded as strong enough if the researcher is relying on it to make recommendations of huge importance to the marketing decision maker. Also a correlation coefficient of .75 may be viewed as solidly strong in social science research, but may not be seen as strong enough in physical science research.

EXHIBIT 17.5 Rules of Thumb about the Strength of Correlation Coefficients

Range of Coefficient	Description of Strength
± .81 to ± 1.00	Very strong
± .61 to ± .80	Strong
± .41 to ± .60	Moderate
± .21 to ± .40	Weak
± .00 to ± .20	None

The third 'relationship' question, the direction of the relationship, can be answered by simply looking at the sign of the correlation coefficient. A positive sign signifies a positive relationship between the two variables under investigation, which means if the value of one variable goes up, the value of another variable will also go up and vice versa. On the other hand, if the sign is negative, then the relationship between the two variables is negative. Put another way, the two variables are said to be inversely proportional to each other, i.e. if the value of one variable goes up, the value of another variable is expected to go down and vice versa.

The last question 'What is the best way to analyse and describe the relationship?' relates to the choice of an appropriate correlation analysis technique in a particular research context. Such a choice depends on the type of data of the two variables to be analysed. In view of the statistical knowledge required for understanding the different available choices, this last 'relationship' question will be dealt with below under three different headings representing three different correlation analysis techniques, i.e. Pearson correlation analysis, Spearman correlation analysis and Chi-square analysis for correlation testing purpose.

Pearson Correlation Analysis

The covariation measure of Pearson correlation analysis has been explained in the above section. To use this correlation analysis technique, you should remember that it requires the fulfilment of an assumption that the two variables to be measured must be interval- or ratio-scaled measures (ordinally-interval are acceptable; see Chapter 11).

A second implicit assumption for the Pearson correlation analysis is that the nature of the relationship to be measured is linear. That is, a straight line will do a reasonably good job of describing the relationship between the two variables of interest.

Use of the Pearson correlation analysis technique also assumes that the variables at hand come from a bivariate normally distributed population. That is, the population is such that all the observations with a given value of one variable have values of the second variable that are normally distributed. In fact, this assumption of normal distributions for the variables under study is a common requirement for many parametric statistical techniques used by marketing researchers. Although it is a common assumption, satisfying it for the sample data you are working with is sometimes difficult and often taken for granted.

SPSS Application – Pearson Correlation Analysis

We can use the Jimmy Spice's database to further understand the **Pearson correlation analysis** technique. The owners anticipate that the relationship between satisfaction with the restaurant and likelihood to recommend the restaurant would be significant and positive. Looking at the database, you should be able to find that information was collected on Satisfaction Level (variable X22) and Likely to Recommend (variable X24).

> **Pearson correlation analysis** A statistical technique for measuring the relationship between two variables where both have been measured using interval or ratio scales.

It is often good practice to develop an initial understanding of the separate variables before probing into their possible relationship. One typical type of measure for this purpose is the measure of central tendency. As the Pearson correlation analysis requires the data to be of interval- or ratio-scale nature, it is therefore logical to use the means to represent the measure of central tendency of each of the two variables being investigated.

Exhibit 17.6 shows that the means of 'satisfaction level' (4.64) is higher than 'likely to recommend (3.46), while the standard deviations of the two are more similar. As these two variables are measured on a 7-point scale and both are quite near the mid-point of 4, there is room for improvement in both measures. Although it looks as if the two means may be significantly different from each other, it doesn't imply respondents' answers to one variable question are independent of those to the other variable. Indeed it is still possible that the pattern of responses to these two variable questions is similar. To find out whether this is the case, we need to look at the results of Pearson correlation analysis.

With SPSS it is convenient to get Pearson correlation analysis results. The SPSS click-through sequence is ANALYSE → CORRELATE → BIVARIATE, which leads to a dialogue box where you select the variables to be involved. Transfer variables X22 and X24 into the Variables box. Note that we will use all three default options shown below: Pearson correlation, two-tailed test of significance, and flag significant correlations. Next go to the Options box, and after it opens click on Means and Standard Deviations and then continue. Finally, when you click on OK at the top right of the dialogue box it will execute the Pearson correlation analysis.

The SPSS Pearson correlation analysis results are shown in Exhibit 17.6. As you can see in the Correlations table, the correlation between variable X24 – Likely to Recommend and X22 – Satisfaction Level is .672. The statistical significance of this correlation is .000. Thus, we have confirmed Jimmy Spice's restaurant owners' anticipation that satisfaction is significantly and positively related to likely to recommend.

EXHIBIT 17.6 SPSS Pearson Correlation Example

Correlations

Descriptive Statistics

	Mean	Std. Deviation	N
X22 -- Satisfaction	4.64	.955	400
X24 -- Likely to Recommend	3.46	.930	400

Correlations

		X22 -- Satisfaction	X24 -- Likely to Recommend
X22 -- Satisfaction	Pearson Correlation	1	.672**
	Sig. (2-tailed)	.	.000
	N	400	400
X24 -- Likely to Recommend	Pearson Correlation	.672**	1
	Sig. (2-tailed)	.000	.
	N	400	400

**. Correlation is significant at the 0.01 level (2–tailed).

Coefficient of Determination

When you square the Pearson correlation coefficient, you arrive at the **coefficient of determination,** or r^2. This number ranges from 0 to 1 and shows the proportion of variation explained or accounted for in one variable by another. The larger the size of the coefficient of determination, the stronger will be the explanatory relationship between the two variables being examined.

> **Coefficient of determination (r^2)** A number measuring the proportion of variation in one variable explained or accounted for by another. The r^2 ranges from 0 to 1 and can be thought of as a percentage showing the degree of explanatory power.

In our Jimmy Spice's example, the correlation coefficient for 'likelihood to recommend' and 'satisfaction' was .672. Thus, the $r^2 = .452$, meaning that approximately 45.2 per cent of the variation in 'likelihood to recommend' can be accounted for by 'satisfaction'. Therefore we have accounted for almost one-half of the variation in 'likelihood to recommend' by relating it to 'satisfaction'.

Spearman Correlation Analysis

If the type of data to be analysed is ordinal, one cannot use the **Spearman correlation analysis** technique discussed in the previous section. The Spearman correlation analysis technique should be used instead in this situation. Take an example. A sports market researcher may be interested in finding out whether the performance in ranking of a soccer team is related to the financial investment in the team as ranked against other teams in the same league. In this case, using the Pearson correlation analysis technique and assuming the soccer teams' performance rankings or financial investment rankings have interval or ratio scale properties (when they actually do not) will possibly produce misleading or overstated results. The Spearman correlation analysis technique, which tends to produce the lowest correlation coefficient and is therefore a more conservative measure than its Pearson counterpart, is the appropriate technique to be used. Adopting the more conservative Spearman technique reflects the lower order of the type of data (from interval or ratio scale to ordinal scale) being studied.

> **Spearman correlation analysis** A statistical technique for measuring the relationship between two variables where both have been directly measured or adjusted to be measured using ordinal (rank order) scales.

SPSS Application – Spearman Correlation Analysis

Prior to conducting Spearman correlation analysis, researchers can first perform some basic analysis to grasp an understanding of the results of the two variables involved for correlation analysis purpose. As both of the variables are of ordinal scale the mean, which is used in the Pearson correlation analysis, is not suitable here. The median should be used instead.

As Jimmy Spice's restaurant owners are interested in finding out whether there is any correlation among the four selection factors affecting consumers' choice of restaurants, all these four factors will be included for getting their respective medians. This will enable us to examine the overall relative rankings of all the four factors. To do this, the SPSS click-through sequence is ANALYSE → DESCRIPTIVE STATISTICS → FREQUENCIES. Click on variables X26–X29 to highlight the four factors and then on the arrow box for the Variables box to use them in your analysis. Next, open the Statistics box and click on Median and then Continue. For the Charts and Format options we will use the defaults, so click on OK to execute the programme.

The SPSS results for median rankings are shown in the Statistics table in Exhibit 17.7. Recall that the four selection factors were ranked from 1 to 4, with 1 = most important, and 4 = least important. Therefore the variable with the lowest median is ranked the highest and is the most important, and the variable with the highest median is the least important. Note that food quality is ranked as the most important (median = 1.00) while atmosphere and service are the least important. Our Spearman correlation analysis example shown below will involve two of the four selection factor: food quality (median = 1.00) and service (median = 3.00). From the above median ranking analysis, we've found that food quality is a significantly more important restaurant selection factor than is service.

Performing correlation analysis of the Food Quality factor and the Service factor can provide insights into consumers' thinking behind their restaurant selection decision. The SPSS click-through sequence is ANALYSE → CORRELATE → BIVARIATE, which leads to a dialogue box where variables can be selected. Transfer variables X27 (Food Quality) and X29 (Service) into the Variables box. You will note that the Pearson correlation is the default along with the two-tailed test of significance. 'Unclick' the Pearson correlation and then click on Spearman. Then click on OK at the top right of the dialogue box to execute the programme.

The SPSS results for the Spearman correlation are shown in Exhibit 17.8. As you can see in the Correlations table, the correlation between variable X27 – Food Quality and X29 – Service is −.130, and the significance value is .01 There is therefore a statistically significant relationship between the two restaurant selection factors. However, the size of the correlation is so small that it is not considered substantively significant (refer back to Exhibit 17.5 for the rules of thumb

EXHIBIT 17.7 SPSS Median Ranking Analysis of Restaurant Selection Factors

Frequencies

Statistics

		X26 – Price	X27 – Food Quality	X28 – Atmosphere	X29 – Service
N	Valid	400	400	400	400
	Missing	0	0	0	0
Median		2.00	1.00	3.00	3.00

EXHIBIT 17.8 SPSS Spearman Correlation Example

Nonparametric Correlations

Correlations

			X27 – Food Quality	X29 – Service
Spearman's rho	X27 – Food Quality	Correlation Coefficient	1.000	– .130**
		Sig. (2 – tailed)		.009
		N	400	400
	X29 – Service	Correlation Coefficient	– .130**	1.000
		Sig. (2 – tailed)	.009	.
		N	400	400

**. Correlation is significant at the .01 level (2 – tailed).

---

about the strength of correlation coefficients). Furthermore, the correlation coefficient is accompanied with a negative sign. Assume a significant and substantive relationship exists, a negative correlation indicates that a customer who ranks food quality high in importance tends to rank service significantly lower.

Chi-Square Analysis

If the variables involved in correlation testing analysis are of nominal scale nature, neither Pearson nor Spearman techniques are suitable. In this scenario, Chi-square test should be used. The test will tell you whether there is any significant relationship between the two variables. If a significant relationship is confirmed, the researcher should use Cramer's V to find the size of the correlation. As with Pearson or Spearman correlation coefficient, the possible range of value of Cramer's V is from 0 to 1. The higher the value, the greater will be the strength of the relationship between the two nominal variables.

In Chi-square analysis, the main research question, from a purely statistical point of view, is 'Do the numbers of responses that fall into different categories differ from what is expected?' For example, the owners of Jimmy Spice's restaurant might believe there is no difference in the percentage of men and women who recall advertisements about their restaurant. Thus, the null hypothesis would be that the number of men and women customers who recall Jimmy Spice's Restaurant advertisements is the same. This question and similar ones could be answered by using chi-square analysis.

Chi-square (χ^2) analysis permits us to test for significance between the frequency distributions for two nominally scaled variables in a cross-tabulation table to determine if there is any

Chi-square (χ^2) analysis Assesses how closely the observed frequencies fit the pattern of the expected frequencies and is referred to as a 'goodness-of-fit' test.

association. It is therefore logical to say that a cross-tabulation, which allows us to see results for one variable by each different level of the other variable, is about an integration of two frequency distributions. Categorical data from questions about gender, education, or other nominal variables can be examined to provide tests of hypotheses of interest. Chi-square analysis compares the observed frequencies (counts) of the responses with the expected frequencies. The expected frequencies are based on our ideas about the population distribution or our predicted proportions. Chi-square analysis assumes that no association exists between the nominal-scaled variables being examined. It tests whether or not the observed data are distributed the way we expect them to be. For example, if we observe that women recall advertisements more than men, we would compare it to the expected frequency to see if it differs.

The use of the chi-square statistic is very helpful in answering questions about data that are all nominally scaled. There is one word of caution though. The Chi-square results will be distorted if more than 20 per cent of the cells have an expected count of less than 5, or if any cell has an expected count of less than 1. In such cases, you should not use this test. SPSS will tell you if these conditions have been violated. One solution to small counts in individual cells is to collapse them into fewer cells to get larger counts.

Calculating the χ^2 Value

To help you to better understand the Chi-square statistic, we will show you how to calculate it. The Chi-square formula is shown below:

$$\chi^2 = \sum_{i-1}^{n} \frac{(\text{Observed}_i - \text{Expected}_i)^2}{\text{Expected}_i}$$

where
  Observed$_i$ = observed frequency in cell i
  Expected$_i$ = expected frequency in cell i
      n = number of cells

When you apply the above formula to Jimmy Spice's restaurant data shown in Exhibit 16.5, you get the following calculation of Chi-square value:

$$\text{Chi-square value} = \frac{(88-108)^2}{108} + \frac{(95-75)^2}{75} + \frac{(58-57.8)^2}{57.8}$$
$$+ \frac{(40-40.2)^2}{40.2} + \frac{(90-70.2)^2}{70.2} + \frac{(29-48.8)^2}{48.8} = 22.616$$

As you can see from the above equation, the expected frequency is subtracted from the observed frequency and then squared to eliminate any negative values. The resulting value is divided by the expected frequency to take into consideration cell size differences. Then these amounts are summed over all cells to arrive at the Chi-square value. The Chi-square value tells you how far the observed frequencies are from the expected frequencies. The computed Chi-square statistic is compared to a table of Chi-square values to determine if the differences are statistically significant. In general, larger Chi-square values indicate greater differences.

Some marketing researchers call Chi-square a 'goodness-of-fit' test. That is, the test evaluates how closely the actual frequencies 'fit' the expected frequencies. When the differences between observed and expected frequencies are large, you have a poor fit and you reject your null hypothesis. When the differences are small, you have a good fit.

SPSS Application – Chi-square

Based on their conversations with customers, the owners of Jimmy Spice's restaurant have begun to think that male customers are coming to the restaurant from farther away than are female customers. The Chi-square statistic can be used to determine if this is true. The null hypothesis is that the same proportion of male and female customers would make up each of the response categories for X30 – Distance Driven.

To conduct this analysis, the click-through sequence is ANALYSE → DESCRIPTIVE STATISTICS → CROSSTABS. Click on X30 – Distance Travelled for the Row variable and on X32 – Gender for the Column variable. Click on the Statistics button and the Chi-square box, and then Continue. Next click on the Cells button and on Expected frequencies (Observed frequencies is usually already checked). Then click Continue and OK to execute the programme.

The SPSS results are shown in Exhibit 17.9. The top table shows the actual number of responses (count) for males and females for each of the categories of X30 – Distance Driven. Also shown in this table are the expected frequencies under the null hypothesis of no difference. For example, 88 males drove a distance of less than 1 mile while 95 females drove from this same distance.

The expected frequencies (count) are calculated on the basis of the proportion of the sample represented by a particular group. For example, the total sample of Jimmy Spice's customers is 400 and 236 are males and 164 are females. This means 59 per cent of the sample is male and

EXHIBIT 17.9 SPSS Chi-Square Crosstab Example

x30 -- Distance Driven 'X32 -- Gender Crosstabulation

| | | | X32 -- Gender | | |
			Males	Females	Total
x30 -- Distance Driven	Less than 1 mile	Count	88	95	183
		Expected Count	108.0	75.0	183.0
		% within x30 -- Distance Driven	48.1%	51.9%	100.0%
	1 -- 3 miles	Count	58	40	98
		Expected Count	57.8	40.2	98.0
		% within x30 -- Distance Driven	59.2%	40.8%	100.0%
	More than 3 miles	Count	90	29	119
		Expected Count	70.2	48.8	119.0
		% within x30 -- Distance Driven	75.6%	24.4%	100.0%
Total		Count	236	164	400
		Expected Count	236.0	164.0	400.0
		% within x30 -- Distance Driven	59.0%	41.0%	100.0%

Chi-Square Tests

	Value	df	Asymp. Sig. (2-sided)
Pearson Chi-Square	22.616[a]	2	.000
Likelihood Radio	23.368	2	.000
Linear-by-Linear Association	22.343	1	.000
N of Valid Cases	400		

a. 0 cells (0%) have expected count less than 5. The minimum expected count is 40.18.

41 per cent is female. When we look in the Total column for the distance driven category labelled 'Less than 1 mile' we see that there are a total of 183 male and female respondents. To calculate the expected frequencies, you multiply the proportion a particular group represents times the total number in that group. For example, with males you calculate 59 per cent of 183 and the expected frequency is 107.97. Similarly, females are 41 per cent of the sample so the expected number of females = 75.03 (.41 × 183). The other expected frequencies are calculated in the same way.

Look again at the observed frequencies. Note that a higher proportion than expected of male customers drive further to get to Jimmy Spice's. That is, we would expect only 70.2 men to drive to Jimmy Spice's from more than three miles, but actually 90 men drove from this far away. Similarly, there are fewer female customers than expected who drive from more than three miles away, as the expected is 48.8 but the actual is only 29.

Information in the Chi-Square Tests table, as displayed in Exhibit 17.9, shows the results for this test. The Pearson Chi-Square value is 22.616 and it is significant at the .000 level. Since this level of significance is much higher than our standard criterion of .05, we can reject the null hypothesis with a high degree of confidence. The interpretation of this finding suggests that there is a high probability that male customers drive from farther away to get to the Jimmy Spice's. There also is a tendency for females to drive shorter distances to get to the restaurant.

One final important note regarding the choice of bivariate correlation techniques is that if the types of data of the two variables concerned are different, for example one variable is measured in ratio scale while the other variable is of ordinal scale nature, then the responsible researcher should adopt the relationship testing technique that matches the lowest measurement scale prevalent among the two variables concerned.

Substantive Significance versus Statistical Significance

Assuming statistical significance of relationship has been firstly affirmed, if the correlation coefficient is also strong, one can be confident that the two variables are strongly associated in a linear fashion. However, if the correlation coefficient is weak, then two possibilities must be considered: (1) there simply is no consistent, systematic relationship between the two variables in the population one is interested in; or (2) the association exists, but it is not linear, and other types of relationships must be explored further.

A very important concept that we hope you will remember is that finding only the statistical significance of a correlation coefficient is not sufficient. You also need to assess the substantive significance – do the numbers you calculate mean anything practically useful? The statistical procedure for identifying significance levels includes information on the sample size. This means that the results of statistical significance are affected by the number of sampling elements involved. It is indeed possible to find statistical significance, but the correlation coefficient is really too small to be of much practical use. For example, if we had compared satisfaction with the likelihood to recommend and the correlation coefficient was .30 at .05 significance level, the coefficient of determination would be .09. Can we conclude this result is practically useful?

Therefore any researcher must always look at both types of significance (statistical and substantive) before jumping to any conclusion for practical use, e.g. for developing marketing strategies. This is particularly important when assessing information from more complex issues and larger markets.

Bivariate Regression Analysis

We have just discussed correlation as a way of determining the existence, strength and direction of a relationship between two variables. We have also introduced the different correlation techniques to analyse and describe the relationship. There are instances, however, when answers from correlation analysis are not enough for the marketing researcher. For example, the marketing researcher may need to make predictions about future sales levels or how a potential price increase will affect the profit or market share of the company. Making this kind of prediction is conceptually different from analysing and describing relationships, and requires a more sophisticated statistical technique called *regression analysis*.

There are a number of ways to make predictions such as the examples in the preceding paragraph: (1) guesses (educated or otherwise); (2) extrapolation from past behaviour of the variable concerned; and (3) use of a regression equation that connects information about related variables to assist in the prediction. Guesses (educated or otherwise) and extrapolation usually assume that past conditions and behaviours will continue into the future. They do not examine the influences behind the behaviour of interest. Consequently, when sales levels, profits, or other variables of interest to a manager differ from those in the past, extrapolation and guessing do not provide any means of explaining why.

Bivariate regression analysis is a statistical technique that uses information about the predictive, linear relationship between an independent or predictor variable and a dependent or criterion variable, and combines it with the algebraic equation for a straight line to make predictions. Particular values of the independent variable are considered, and the behaviour of the dependent variable is observed. These data are then applied to the equation for a straight line. For example, if you want to find the current level of your company's sales volume, you would apply the following straight line equation:

$$\text{Sales volume } (Y) = €0 + (\text{Price per unit} = b) \,(\text{Number of units sold} = X)$$

> **Bivariate regression analysis** A statistical technique that analyses the predictive, linear relationship between two variables by estimating coefficients for a straight line equation. One variable is designated as a dependent or criterion variable and the other is called an independent or predictor variable.

You would not expect any sales volume if nothing were sold. Price per unit (b) determines the amount that sales volume (Y) increases with each unit sold (X). The relationship between Y and X is of predictive nature rather than of purely descriptive nature that we discussed in the previous correlation analysis sections. The relationship is also linear, which means it is consistent over the values of both Y and X.

Once a regression equation has been developed to predict values of Y_i we are interested in trying to find out how good that prediction is. An obvious place to begin will be the actual value collected from the sample. By comparing this actual value Y_i to our predicted value Y_i we can tell how far away our prediction is. This procedure of comparing actual values from a sample to predicted values from a regression equation is a commonly used method of determining the accuracy of a regression equation.

A couple of points should be made about the assumptions behind regression analysis. First, just like correlation analysis, regression analysis assumes that a linear relationship will provide a good representation of the relationship between two variables. If the scatter diagram showing the positions of the values of both variables looks like the scatter plot in Exhibit 17.2 or 17.3, we could say this assumption is held. If the plot looks like Exhibit 17.1 or 17.4, then regression analysis isn't a good choice.

Second, even though the common terminology of regression analysis uses the labels *dependent* and *independent* for the variables, those names don't mean that we can say one variable causes the behaviour of the other. Regression analysis uses knowledge about the association between two variables to make predictions. Statements about the ability of one variable to cause changes in another must be based on conceptual logic or information other than just statistical techniques.

There are three more assumptions that have to be satisfied for the use of a standard regression model: (1) the variables of interest are measured on interval or ratio scales (except in the case of dummy variables, which we will discuss later); (2) these variables come from a bivariate normal population (the same assumption made by correlation analysis); and (3) the error terms associated with making predictions are normally and independently distributed (we will also talk about this particular assumption and its validation later in this chapter).

Fundamentals of Regression Analysis

Regression analysis assumes a straight line predictive relationship between the independent and dependent variables. This relationship is illustrated in Exhibit 17.10. The general formula for a straight line regression equation is:

$$Y = a + bX + e_i$$

where

Y = the dependent variable
a = the intercept (point where the straight line intersects the *y*-axis when $X = 0$)
b = the slope (the change in Y for every 1-unit change in X)
X = the independent variable used to predict Y
e_i = the error for the prediction

EXHIBIT 17.10 **The Straight Line Predictive Relationship in Regression**

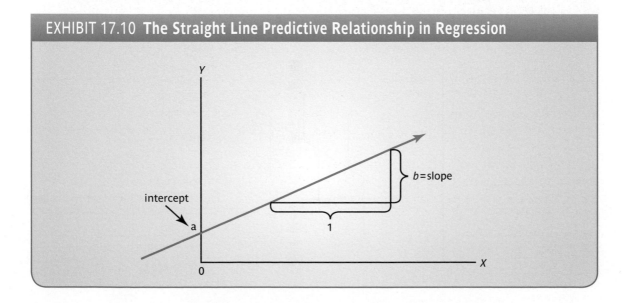

In applying regression analysis, we examine the hypothetical predictive relationship between the independent variable X and the dependent variable Y. To do so, we use the known values of X and Y and the computed values of a and b. The calculations are based on the least squares procedure. The *least squares procedure* determines the best-fitting line by minimizing the vertical distances of all the points from the line, as shown in Exhibit 17.11. This best-fitting line is the regression line. Any point that does not fall on the line is unexplained variance. This unexplained variance is called error and is represented by the vertical distance between the regression straight line and the points not on the line. The distances of all the points not on the line are squared and added together to determine the sum of the squared errors, which is a measure of the total error in the regression.

After we compute the values of a and b, we must test their statistical significance. The calculated a (intercept) and b (slope) are sample estimates of the true population parameters α (alpha) and β (beta). The t-test is used to determine whether the computed intercept and slope are significantly different from zero. In the SPSS regression examples discussed later, the significance of these tests is reported in the Sig. column for each of these coefficients. The a is referred to as a 'Constant' and the b is associated with each independent variable.

In the case of bivariate regression analysis, we are looking at one independent variable and one dependent variable. For example, an information technology company operating in the business-to-business market may want to know whether and if so to what extent increasing the investment in sales force training can increase sales.

However, in many other marketing situations, managers may want to look at the combined influence of several independent variables on one dependent variable. For example, would DVD purchases be predicted by a person's age and only by age, or would they also be accounted for by income, ethnicity, gender, geographic location, education level, and so on? Similarly, referring to Jimmy Spice's restaurant database, we might ask whether customer satisfaction is predicted only by customer perception of the restaurant's food taste (X18), or is satisfaction also accounted for by perceptions of friendly employees (X12), reasonable prices (X16) and speed of service (X21)? Multiple regression is the appropriate technique to test and measure these hypothetical

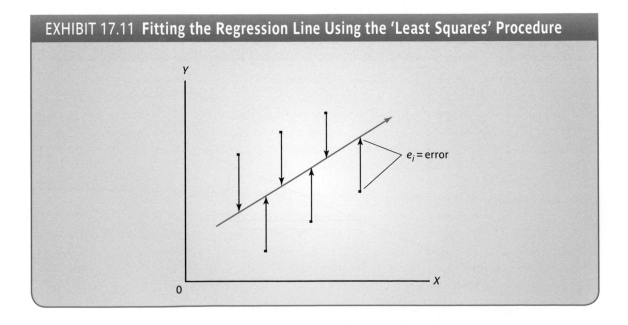

EXHIBIT 17.11 Fitting the Regression Line Using the 'Least Squares' Procedure

relationships and is basically a straightforward extension of bivariate regression. We will go through the mechanics of conducting a bivariate or simple regression analysis before turning to a discussion of multiple regression analysis.

Regression Coefficients

A regression equation is used to examine and mathematically describe the predictive relationship between the dependent and independent variables. The slope coefficient b tells us how much we can expect Y to change, given a 1-unit change in X. Once this equation is developed from sample data, we can use it to make predictions about Y, given different values of X.

This regression equation is the best-fitting straight line developed through an application of the least square procedure, which has been introduced in the earlier section. More specifically, the least square procedure is what statisticians call ordinary least squares (OLS), which guarantees that the straight line it estimates to describe the data is the best one. We said earlier that the best-fitting line is one in which the difference between the actual value of Y and the predicted value of Y *is* the smallest. Ordinary least squares is a statistical procedure that produces predictions with the lowest sum of squared differences between actual and predicted values, and the predictions are represented by the computed coefficients (a and b).

> **Ordinary least squares** A statistical procedure involved in the estimation of regression equation coefficients that produce the lowest sum of squared differences between the actual and predicted values of the dependent variable.

Regression Errors

The differences between actual and predicted values of Y are represented by e^i (the error term of the regression equation). If we square these regression errors for each observation and add them up, the total will represent an aggregate or overall measure of the accuracy of the regression equation. Regression equations calculated through the use of the ordinary least squares procedure will always give the lowest squared regression error totals, and this is why both bivariate and multiple regression analyses are sometimes referred to as *OLS regression.*

Besides allowing the researcher to evaluate the quality of the prediction produced by a regression equation, the regression error terms can also be used to diagnose potential problems caused by the data used that do not meet the assumptions described above. The pattern of regression errors produced by comparing actual Y values to predicted Y values can tell us whether the regression errors are normally distributed and/or have equal variances across the range of X values. Exhibits 17.12, 17.13 and 17.14 illustrate several possible patterns of *residuals* (another term for the regression error between actual and predicted Y values).

In Exhibit 17.12 there is no discernible pattern of residuals, which are plotted against their respective predicted values. This will be the desired outcome because the assumptions relating to the residuals for the validity of the regression equation have been met.

In Exhibit 17.13 there is an apparent pattern; the predictions made for small values of Y are more precise than the predictions made for large values of Y. This means the corresponding regression equation is more accurate for some values of the independent variable X than for others. There are transformation techniques that can be applied to this kind of data to potentially help this problem.

EXHIBIT 17.12 Random Pattern of Residuals

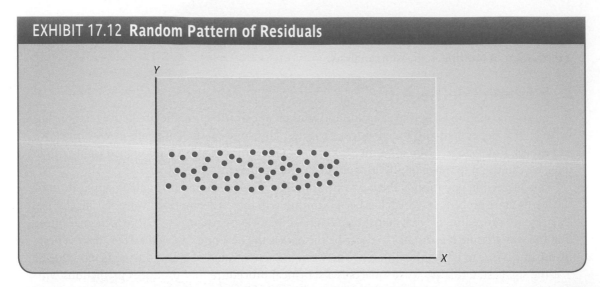

EXHIBIT 17.13 Increasing Pattern of Residuals

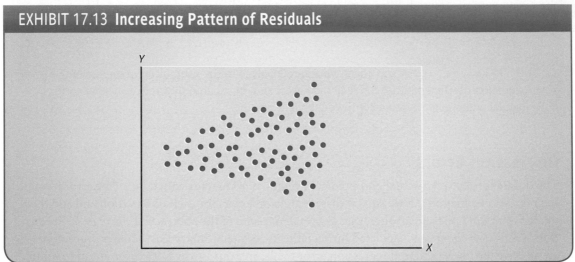

EXHIBIT 17.14 Nonlinear Pattern of Residuals

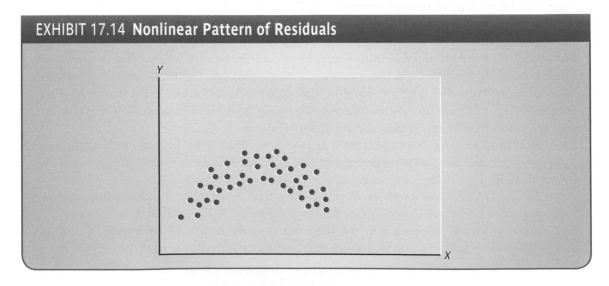

Exhibit 17.14 portrays a pattern of residuals that suggests a non-linear relationship between Y and X. In this case, the researcher's initial thought that a straight line would be the best way to describe the potential predictive relationship would need to be changed. The approach suitable for fitting this kind of data would be a non-linear predictive relationship-based technique.

Examination of the residuals and the pattern obtained by comparing the predicted values of Y against these residuals can tell us whether our initial assumptions about the appropriateness of using regression analysis to examine predictive relationships between variables are correct. In addition, the evidence obtained from this examination can sometimes suggest the next type of analysis to undertake, given the characteristics of the data we have collected. We illustrate the estimation and use of regression coefficients and residuals in a SPSS multiple regression application using Jimmy Spice's restaurant database later in this chapter.

SPSS Application – Bivariate Regression

An example at this point will help illustrate the procedures for completing a bivariate regression analysis. Suppose the owners of Jimmy Spice's restaurant want to know if more favourable perceptions of their prices are accounting for higher customer satisfaction. The common sense answer would be 'of course it would'. But how much improvement would be expected in customer satisfaction if the owners improved the perceptions of prices to a certain extent? Bivariate regression analysis can provide information to help answer this question.

In Jimmy Spice's restaurant database X22 is a measure of customer satisfaction level, with 1 = Not Satisfied at All to 7 = Highly Satisfied. Variable X16 is a measure of respondents' perceptions of the reasonableness of the restaurant's prices (ranging from 1 = Strongly Disagree to 7 = Strongly Agree). The null hypothesis in this case is there is no relationship between X22 – Satisfaction and X16 – Reasonable Prices. The alternative hypothesis is that X22 and X16 are significantly related and X22 can be predicted to a certain degree by X16.

The formulas to calculate the regression equation components are provided in Appendix 2. We will use the SPSS programme to perform these calculations.

The SPSS click-through sequence is ANALYSE → REGRESSION → LINEAR. Click on X22 – Satisfaction and move it to the Dependent Variable box. Click on X16 – Reasonable Prices and move it to the Independent Variables box. We will use the defaults for the other options so click OK to run the bivariate regression.

Exhibit 17.15 contains the results of the bivariate regression analysis. The table labelled Model Summary has three types of 'Rs' in it. The R on the far left is the correlation coefficient (.321). The R-square is .103; you get it by squaring the correlation coefficient (.321) for this regression. The third R – **Adjusted R-Square** – reduces the R^2 by taking into account the sample size and the number of independent variables in the regression equation. It should be used when the multiple regression equation has too many independent variables. As you recall from our earlier discussion, R-square figures show the percentage of variation in one variable that is accounted for by another variable. In this case, the customer perception of Jimmy Spice's restaurant's prices accounts for 10.3 per cent of the total variation in customer satisfaction with the restaurant.

> **Adjusted R-square** This adjustment reduces the R^2 by taking into account the sample size and the number of independent variables in the regression equation.

The final number in the table – Std. Error of the Estimate – is a measure of the accuracy of the predictions of the regression equation. The smaller the standard error of the estimate, the better the fit of the regression line and therefore the better the predictive power of the regression.

The ANOVA table, as displayed in Exhibit 17.15, shows the F ratio for the regression model that indicates the statistical significance of the overall regression model. The F ratio is calculated the same way for regression analysis as it was for the ANOVA technique described in Chapter 15. The variance in X22 – Customer Satisfaction that is accounted for by X16 – Reasonable Prices is referred to as **explained variance**. The remainder of the total variance in X22 that is not associated with X16 is referred to as **unexplained variance**. The F ratio is the result of comparing the amount of explained variance to the unexplained variance. The larger the F ratio the more variance in the dependent variable that is accounted for by the independent variable. In our example, the F ratio $= 45.810$. The statistical significance is .000 – the 'Sig.' value on the SPSS output – so we can reject the null hypothesis that no relationship exists between the two variables.

Explained variance Is the amount of variation in the dependent variable that can be accounted for by the independent variables.

Unexplained variance Is the amount of variation in the dependent variable that cannot be accounted for by the independent variables.

EXHIBIT 17.15 **SPSS Results for Bivariate Regression**

Regression

Model Summary

Model	R	R Square	Adjusted R Square	Std. Error of the Estimate
1	.321[a]	.103	.101	.905

a. Predictors: (Constant), X16 -- Reasonable Prices

ANOVA[b]

Model		Sum of Squares	df	Mean Square	F	Sig.
1	Regression	37.530	1	37.530	45.810	.000[a]
	Residual	326.060	388	.819		
	Total	363.590	399			

a. Predictors: (Constant), X16 -- Reasonable Prices

b. Dependent Variable: X22 -- Satisfaction

Coefficients[a]

Model		Unstandardized Coefficients		Standardized Coefficients	t	Sig.
		B	Std. Error	Beta		
1	(Constant)	3.561	.166		21.400	.000
	X16 -- Reasonable Prices	.250	.037	.321	6.768	.000

a. Dependent Variable: X22 -- Satisfaction

The Coefficients table (See Exhibit 17.15) shows the regression coefficient for X16. The **regression coefficient** is an indicator of the importance of an independent variable in predicting a dependent variable. Large coefficients are good predictors and small coefficients are weak predictors. In bivariate regression, the regression coefficient is considered 'unstandardized'. The column labelled Unstandardized Coefficients indicates the unstandardized regression coefficient for X16 is .250. The column labelled Sig. shows the statistical significance of the regression coefficient for X16, as measured by the *t*-test. The *t*-test examines the question of whether the regression coefficient is different enough from zero to be statistically significant. The *t* statistic is calculated by dividing the regression coefficient by its standard error (labelled Std. Error in the Coefficients table of Exhibit 17.15). If you divide .250 by .037, you will get a *t* value of 6.768, which is significant at the .000 level.

Regression coefficient An indicator of the importance of an independent variable in predicting a dependent variable. Large coefficients are good predictors and small coefficients are weak predictors.

The Coefficients table also shows the result for the Constant component in the regression equation. It shows the value of the dependent variable if all the independent variables have no significant effects on the dependent variable, i.e. the values of all the independent variables are zero. In the current example, if the independent variable took on a value of 0, the dependent measure (X22) would have a value of 3.561. Combining the results of the Coefficients table into a regression equation, we have

Predicted value of X22 = 3.561 + .250 (value of X16) + .905 (avg. error in prediction)

Therefore the predictive relationship between customer satisfaction and reasonable prices is positive and moderately strong. The regression coefficient for X16 is interpreted as 'For every unit that X16 increases, X22 will increase by .250 units'. Recall that Jimmy Spice's owners wanted to know: 'If the prices in our restaurant are perceived as being reasonable, will this improve customer satisfaction?' The answer is yes, somewhat, because the model is significant at the .000 level and the R-square was .103. For every unit increase in X16, X22 goes up .250 units.

One additional note must be mentioned. The Coefficients table contains a column labelled Standardized Beta Coefficients. This number is not particularly meaningful in a bivariate regression. However, when multiple independent variables are used, the scales used to measure each one may not always be the same (e.g. using years of age and annual income to predict frequency of dining out). Standardization is a method of removing the individual units of measure from each variable and placing all of these variables on the same scale.

Significance

Once the statistical significance of the regression coefficients is determined, we can be sure that our independent variables account for our dependent variable in some way. But how much they account for? The output of the regression analysis includes the coefficient of determination, or r^2. As we noted earlier, the coefficient of determination describes the amount of variation in the dependent variable accounted for by the variation in the independent variables. Another way of thinking about it is that this r^2 tells you what percentage of the total variation in your dependent variable you can explain by using the independent variable. The r^2 measure varies between .00 and 1.00, and is calculated by dividing the amount of variation you have been able to explain with your regression equation (found by summing the squared differences between your predicted value and the mean of the dependent variable) by the total variation in the dependent variable. In Jimmy Spice's restaurant example that examined the predictive relationship between reasonable prices and satisfaction, the r^2 was .107. That means approximately 10.7 per cent of the variation in customer satisfaction is accounted for by the variation in price reasonableness. Remember, we cannot say that price reasonableness causes changes in satisfaction. We can only say that price reasonableness accounts for satisfaction, and therefore price reasonableness can be used to predict satisfaction.

When examining the substantive significance of a regression equation, you should look at not just the size of the r^2, but also the strength of the regression coefficient. The regression coefficient may be statistically significant, but still relatively small, meaning that your dependent measure won't change very much for a given unit change in the independent measure. In our Jimmy Spice's restaurant example, the unstandardized regression coefficient was .254, which indicates the predictive relationship is not very strong. When regression coefficients are significant but small, we say a predictive relationship is present in our population, but that it is weak. Therefore Jimmy Spices' owners may need to consider additional independent variables that will help them to better understand and predict customer satisfaction. We will show you how to do that in the next section.

QualKote Manufacturing's Customer Satisfaction Study

The plant manager of QualKote Manufacturing, a hypothetical manufacturing firm located in central Europe, is interested in the impact his year-long effort to implement a quality improvement programme is having on the satisfaction of his customers. The plant foreman, assembly-line workers and engineering staff have closely examined the operations they are responsible for, in order to determine which activities have the most impact on product quality. Together, the plant employees of all levels have worked to better understand how each particular task affects the final delivered quality of the product as the customer perceives it.

To answer his questions about customer satisfaction, the plant manager conducted an internal survey on plant employees of all levels using a 7-point Likert scale (endpoints – 1 = 'Strongly Disagree' and 7 = 'Strongly Agree'). His plans are to get opinions from within the company first and then do a customer survey on the same topic. He has collected completed surveys from 57 plant employees. The following are examples of the issues that were covered in the questionnaire:

- Data from a variety of external sources (customers, competitors, suppliers, etc.) are used in the strategic planning process. Independent variable A10.
- Customers are involved in the product quality planning process. Independent variable A12.
- Customer requirements and expectations of the company's products are used in developing strategic plans. Independent variable A17.
- There is a systematic process to translate customer requirements and expectations into new/ improved products. Independent variable A23.
- There is a systematic process to accurately determine customers' requirements and expectations. Independent variable A31.
- The company's product quality programme has improved the level of customer satisfaction. Dependent variable A36.
- The company's product quality programme has improved the likelihood that customers will recommend us. Dependent variable A37.
- Gender of the plant employee responding: Male = 1; Female = 0. Classification variable A40.

A multiple regression was run using SPSS with responses of the 57 plant employees. The output is shown in Exhibits 17.16 and 17.17. There is an actual database of QualKote employee responses to these questions available in SPSS format at www.mhhe.com/shiu09. The database is labelled C_16_Qualkote MRIA.sav.

The results indicate there is a statistically significant predictive relationship between the metric dependent variable (A36 – Satisfaction) and the metric independent variables. The R^2 for the relationship is .670. Results suggest favourable perceptions by employees about the implementation of the quality improvement programme.

Questions

1 Will the results of this multiple regression model be useful to the QualKote plant manager? If yes, how?

2 Which independent variables are helpful in predicting A36 – Customer Satisfaction?

3 What other hypothetical regression models can be tested with the questions from this survey?

EXHIBIT 17.16 Descriptive Statistics and Correlations for Variables Used in QualKote Manufacturing's Customer Satisfaction Study

Descriptive Statistics

	Mean	Std. Deviation	N
A36	4.81	.953	57
A10	5.00	1.414	57
A12	3.60	1.334	57
A17	2.28	1.176	57
A23	4.53	1.104	57
A31	2.89	.838	57

Correlations

		A36	A10	A12	A17	A23	A31
Pearson Correlation	A36	1.000	.490	.626	.065	.472	.354
	A10	.490	1.000	.435	-.494	-.080	-.030
	A12	.626	.435	1.000	-.188	.171	.073
	A17	.065	-.494	-.188	1.000	.324	.266
	A23	.472	-.080	.171	.324	1.000	.736
	A31	.354	-.030	.073	.266	.736	1.000
Sig. (1-tailed)	A36	.	.000	.000	.315	.000	.003
	A10	.000	.	.000	.000	.277	.412
	A12	.000	.000	.	.080	.102	.295
	A17	.315	.000	.080	.	.007	.023
	A23	.000	.277	.102	.007	.	.000
	A31	.003	.412	.295	.023	.000	.
N	A36	57	57	57	57	57	57
	A10	57	57	57	57	57	57
	A12	57	57	57	57	57	57
	A17	57	57	57	57	57	57
	A23	57	57	57	57	57	57
	A31	57	57	57	57	57	57

EXHIBIT 17.17 Multiple Regression Model for QualKote Manufacturing's Customer Satisfaction Study

Model Summary

Model	R	R Square	Adjusted R Square	Std. Error of the Estimate
1	.819[a]	.670	.638	.574

a. Predictors: (Constant), A31, A10, A12, A17, A23

ANOVA[b]

Model		Sum of Squares	df	Mean Squares	F	Sig.
1	Regression	34.095	5	6.819	20.723	.000[a]
	Residual	16.782	51	.329		
	Total	50.877	56			

a. Predictors: (Constant), A31, A10, A12, A17, A23
b. Dependent Variable: A36

Coefficients[a]

Model		Unstandardized Coefficients		Standardized Coefficients	t	Sig.	Correlations		
		B	Std. Error	Beta			Zero-order	Partial	Part
1	(Constant)	.309	.496		.624	.535			
	A10	.314	.068	.466	4.587	.000	.490	.540	.369
	A12	.294	.066	.411	4.451	.000	.626	.529	.358
	A17	.208	.080	.257	2.614	.012	.065	.344	.210
	A23	.296	.108	.343	2.744	.008	.472	.359	.221
	A31	1.980E-02	.136	.017	.145	.885	.354	.020	.012

a. Dependent Variable: A36

Summary of Learning Objectives

■ **Understand and evaluate the types of relationships between variables.**

Relationships between variables can be described in several ways, including presence, direction, strength of association and type. Presence tells us whether a consistent and systematic relationship exists. Direction tells us whether the relationship is positive or negative. Strength of association tells us whether we have a weak or strong relationship, and the type of relationship is usually described as either linear or nonlinear.

Two variables may share a linear relationship, in which a change in one variable is accompanied by some change (not necessarily the same amount of change) in the other variable. As long as the amount of change stays constant over the range of both variables, the relationship is termed linear. Relationships between two variables that change in strength and/or direction as the values of the variables change are referred to as nonlinear.

■ **Explain the concepts of covariaton and association.**

The terms covariation and association are referred to an attempt to quantify the strength of the relationship between two variables. Covariation is the amount of change in one variable of interest that is consistently related to a change in another variable under study. The degree of association is a numerical measure of the strength of the relationship between two variables. Both these terms are referred to linear relationships only.

■ **Discuss the differences between Chi-square, Pearson correlation, and Spearman correlation.**

The Chi-square statistic permits us to test for significance between the frequency distributions of two groups. Categorical data from questions such as gender, race, profession, and so forth, can be examined and tested for statistical differences through Chi-square analysis. Pearson correlation coefficients are a measure of linear association between two variables of interest. The Pearson correlation coefficient is used when both variables are measured on an interval or ratio scale. When one or more variables of interest are measured on an ordinal scale, the Spearman rank order correlation coefficient should be used.

■ **Explain the concepts of statistical significance versus practical significance.**

Because some of the procedures involved in determining the statistical significance of a statistical test include consideration of the sample size, it is possible to have a very low degree of association reflecting a low practical significance between two variables, but which are shown up as statistically significant (i.e. the population parameter is not equal to zero). However, by considering the absolute strength of the relationship in addition to its statistical significance, the researcher is better able to draw the appropriate conclusion about the data and the population from which they were selected.

■ **Understand when and how to use bivariate regression analysis.**

Bivariate regression analysis is useful in answering questions about the strength of a predictive relationship between a dependent variable and an independent variable. The results of a bivariate regression analysis indicate the amount of change in the dependent variable that is associated with a one-unit change in the independent variable. The accuracy of a regression equation can be evaluated by comparing the predicted values of the dependent variable to the actual values of the dependent variable drawn from the sample.

Key Terms and Concepts

Adjusted R-square   569
Bivariate regression analysis   564
Chi-square (χ^2) analysis   560
Coefficient of determination (r^2)   558
Covariation   550
Explained variance   570
Linear relationship   550
Non-linear relationship   550

Ordinary least squares   567
Pearson correlation analysis   556
Pearson correlation coefficient   554
Regression coefficient   571
Relationship   549
Scatter diagram   551
Spearman correlation analysis   558
Unexplained variance   570

Review Questions

1 Explain the difference between testing for significant differences and testing for association.

2 Explain the difference between association and causation.

3 What is covariation? How does it differ from correlation?

4 Which statistical tests should be used with nominal and ordinal data? Which can be used with interval and ratio data?

5 What are the differences between univariate, bivariate and multivariate statistical techniques?

6 What is regression analysis? When would you use it? What is the difference between simple regression and multiple regression?

7 How do we use beta coefficients in multiple regression analysis?

8 What is the value of dummy variables in multiple regression analysis?

Discussion Questions

1 Regression and correlation analysis both describe the strength of linear relationships between variables. Consider the concepts of education and income. Many people would say these two variables are related in a linear fashion. As education increases, income usually increases (although not necessarily at the same rate). Can you think of two variables that are related in such a way that their relationship changes over their range of possible values (i.e. in a curvilinear fashion)? How would you analyse the relationship between two such variables?

2 Is it possible to conduct a regression analysis on two variables and obtain a significant regression equation (significant F ratio), but still have a low r^2? What does the r^2 statistic measure? How can you have a low r^2 yet still get a statistically significant F ratio for the overall regression equation?

3 The ordinary least squares (OLS) procedure commonly used in regression produces a line of 'best fit' for the data to which it is applied. How would you define best fit in regression analysis? What is there about the procedure that guarantees a best fit to the data? What assumptions about the use of a regression technique are necessary to produce this result?

4 When multiple independent variables are used to predict a dependent variable in multiple regression, multicollinearity among the independent variables is often a concern. What is the main problem caused by high multicollinearity among the independent variables in a multiple regression equation? Can you still achieve a high r^2 for your regression equation if multicollinearity is present in your data?

5 **Experience the Internet.** A trend in marketing is to shop for products and services on the Internet. Identify a product or service that you think is commonly sold on the Web. Search the Web to choose three to five retailers that sell the product or service you identified. Note that these retailers can be purely online retailers or brick-and-mortar retailers expanding their sales channel to the Web. Then identify at least five online store attributes that you believe are important to consumers' decision making when they are doing online shopping. Design a questionnaire trying to compare between your chosen retailers on the attributes that you've identified. Ask a sample (at least 50) of students to visit the online stores of the three to five retailers that you've chosen, and then to complete the questionnaire. Enter the data into a SPSS and assess your finding statistically. Prepare a report and be able to defend your conclusions.

6 **SPSS Exercise.** Choose one or two other students from your class and form a team. Identify the different retailers from your community where DVD players, TVs and other electronics products are sold. Team members should divide up and visit all the different stores and describe the products and brands that are sold in each. Also observe the layout in the store, the store personnel and the type of advertising the store uses. All these efforts should help you familiarize with each retailer's marketing mix. Use the knowledge gathered to design a questionnaire. Interview 100 people each of whom has heard of all the retailers you selected and collect their responses. Analyse the responses using SPSS. Prepare a report of your findings, including whether the perceptions of each of the stores are similar or different, and particularly whether the differences are statistically and substantively different. Present your findings in class and be prepared to defend your conclusions and your use of the statistical techniques.

7 **SPSS Exercise.** In Chapter 15, the European Case Study for La Brioche Dorée and its two competitors included numerous categorical variables. Run a Chi-square analysis to compare the three competitors on the categorical segmentation variables (X16–X21) and prepare a profile of each restaurant's customers. Next, run a multiple regression analysis between the restaurant selection factors and satisfaction, and present your findings. A database for the La Brioche Dorée case is available in SPSS format at www.mhhe.com/shiu09. The database is labelled C_15_LaBriocheDoree.sav.

8 **SPSS Exercise.** Jimmy Spice's restaurant owners believe one of their competitive advantages is that the restaurant is a fun place to eat. Use the Jimmy Spice's database and run a bivariate correlation analysis between X13 – Fun Place to Eat and X22 – Satisfaction to test this hypothesis. Could this hypothesis be further examined with multiple regression?

Chapter 18

Multivariate Analysis: An Overview and Dependence Techniques

LEARNING OBJECTIVES

After reading this chapter, you will be able to

- ☑ Define multivariate analysis.

- ☑ Understand how to use multivariate analysis in marketing research.

- ☑ Distinguish between dependence and interdependence techniques.

- ☑ Apply metric dependence techniques including multiple regression analysis, ANOVA, MANOVA and conjoint analysis to marketing research.

- ☑ Apply non-metric dependence techniques including discriminant analysis, logistic regression, Poisson regression and conjoint analysis to marketing research.

 A flood of data should never be allowed to wash away your common sense and your own feeling for the market.

—Jack Trout
Columnist, Forbes

Multivariate Methods Impact Our Lives Every Day

The amount of information available for business decision making has grown tremendously since the late 1990s. Until recently, much of that information just disappeared. It either was not used or was discarded because collecting, storing, extracting and interpreting it was not economical. Now, decreases in the cost of data collection and storage, development of faster data processors and user-friendly client–server interfaces, and improvements in data analysis and interpretation made possible through data mining enable businesses to convert what had been a 'waste by-product' into a great new resource to provide added value to customers and to improve business decisions.

Data mining facilitates the discovery of interesting patterns in databases and data warehouses that are difficult to identify and have a high potential for improving decision making and creating knowledge. It does this first through an automated process involving 'machine-learning' methods which emerged mostly from artificial intelligence. Examples include neural networking and genetic algorithms. After this first phase, the identified relationships are confirmed using 'human-learning' approaches many of which are multivariate techniques. The use of data mining and multivariate analysis will continue to expand because the amount of data will increase exponentially, applications will become increasingly real-time, the quality of some type of data will improve and data mining tools will be more powerful and easier to use.

Multivariate techniques are widely used in marketing research. GIM, one of the largest marketing research companies in Germany, has been making effective use of multivariate analysis for its research projects. The company has its headquarters in Heidelberg, and owns and manages a number of research institutes in Berlin, Lyon, Moscow and Zurich.

The types of quantitative studies that GIM has been conducting include advertisement testing (measurement of advertising recall, message transfer, liking, evaluation profile, acceptance, purchase stimulus), segmentation (e.g. automotive market being segmented on product requirements, attitudes towards driving, personal values, lifestyles). For these and other types of studies, GIM makes use of a variety of multivariate techniques, such as conjoint analysis, cluster analysis, perceptual mapping and structural equation modelling.

The company is also adept at combining different multivariate techniques for the same project. For example, conjoint analysis is normally used for product optimization purposes. GIM goes beyond this application by combining conjoint analysis and cluster analysis in order to ascertain specific sub-target segment groups, such as consumer groups having an affinity to brands, or those who are price sensitive.

To make accurate business decisions in today's increasingly complex environment, we must analyse intricate relationships with many intervening variables. Multivariate techniques are worth considering as tools for addressing such issues.

Value of Multivariate Analysis

The chapter opener highlights the important role that multivariate analysis plays in today's business world. This has been much attributable to the technology development leading to lower cost and greater benefit of conducting multivariate analysis. There have been remarkable advances in computer hardware and software since the mid-1980s. Generally speaking, according to Moore's law, the speed and storage capability of computers have been doubling every 18 months or so, while prices have tumbled. We can now analyse large quantities of complex data with relative ease. For many years data came mostly from surveys, which belong to the external primary data category. Now, increasingly data warehouses are stocked with mountains of internal secondary data that can be mined to identify valuable relationships about customers and employees. Some of these data can be analysed using simple statistics like those discussed in earlier chapters. But in many situations we need more complex techniques. Indeed, many marketing researchers believe that unless we use more complex multivariate techniques we may be only superficially examining marketing problems.

Today most of the problems marketing researchers are interested in understanding involve more than two variables and therefore require multivariate statistical techniques. Moreover, business decision makers as well as consumers tend to use a lot of information to make choices and decisions. Consequently, potential influences on business reactions and consumer behaviours abound.

Multivariate techniques have been increasingly used partly because of the need of businesses to address such complexity. The ability to determine the relative influence of different independent variables, as well as to assess the behaviour of groups of dependent measures simultaneously, has become an important asset in the marketing researcher's toolbox. In addition, tremendous increases in computing power have encouraged the adoption of multivariate analysis by individuals who were unable to realistically consider such approaches in earlier years.

What is multivariate analysis? **Multivariate analysis** refers to a group of statistical techniques that simultaneously analyse multiple measurements on each individual or object being investigated. The multivariate statistical procedures we will highlight in this chapter are extensions of the univariate and bivariate statistical procedures discussed in previous chapters. It should be emphasized that, in order not to oversize this textbook and also considering that what we are writing is a marketing research textbook rather than a multivariate data analysis textbook, we've decided to provide only a short, but concise, overview of the major multivariate analysis techniques in this chapter. Interested readers are encouraged to consult textbooks focusing on multivariate data analysis for a more complete coverage of all the techniques.

> **Multivariate analysis** A group of statistical techniques that simultaneously analyse multiple measurements on each individual or object being investigated.

To recap, multivariate analysis is indispensable and irreplaceable in marketing research because most business problems involve the interplay of multiple variables and their measurements. It is often insufficient to analyse corporations and their customers by only one or two variables. The nearby Closer Look at Research box illustrates how multivariate techniques can aid small businesses.

 ## A Closer Look at Research *(Small Business Implications)*
XLSTAT

Many small businesses may not be prepared to spend on the rather expensive statistical packages like SPSS or SAS. XLSTAT is a less expensive, but still user-friendly, statistical package that small businesses can consider adopting. It is an add-on for Microsoft Excel. It allows the small business user, working in an Excel worksheet, to transfer stored data into the programme for data analysis purposes.

XLSTAT offers more than 40 different functions to empower Excel and make it an everyday statistical solution package for small businesses. The package can perform very simple techniques like box plots, frequencies and other descriptive statistics. But it can also perform many of the more complex statistical techniques, such as factor analysis, cluster analysis, discriminant analysis and multiple regression. To see examples of data analysed, and how XLSTAT performs various statistical analysis functions, readers can consult the XLSTAT webpage at www.xlstat.com.

Classification of Multivariate Techniques

One challenge facing marketing researchers is determining the appropriate statistical technique for a given business problem. To facilitate their decision making in this aspect, a classification of major multivariate analysis techniques is presented in Exhibit 18.1. This chapter focuses on dependence techniques, while interdependence techniques and structural equation modelling (a technique integrating both dependence and interdependence techniques) will be discussed in the following chapter.

Dependence and Interdependence Techniques

As can be seen from Exhibit 18.1, other than structural equation modelling which is a hybrid integrating dependence and interdependence techniques, multivariate techniques can be broadly divided into dependence and interdependence techniques.

A **dependence technique** can be defined as one in which one or more variables is/are identified as dependent variables to be predicted or explained by other independent variables. Many businesses today are very interested in predicting dependent variables such as customer loyalty or customer usage on the basis of numerous independent variables. Depending on the types of data

> **Dependence technique** A category of multivariate techniques; used when one or more of the variables can be identified as dependent variables to be predicted or explained by other independent variables.

EXHIBIT 18.1 Classification of Major Multivariate Analysis Techniques

Dependence Techniques with Metric Dependent Variables	Interdependence Techniques
Multiple regression	Factor analysis
ANOVA	Cluster analysis
MANOVA	Perceptual mapping
Conjoint analysis	
Dependence Techniques with Non-metric Dependent Variables	**Techniques Integrating Dependence and Interdependence Techniques**
Discriminant analysis	Structural Equation Modelling
Logistic regression	
Poisson regression	
Conjoint analysis	

Note: Conjoint analysis can deal with both metric and non-metric dependent variables.

involved, these businesses can choose an appropriate dependence technique, such as multiple regression or discriminant analysis, for their business interest.

In contrast, an **interdependence technique** is one in which no single variable or group of variables is defined as being independent or dependent. In this case, the multivariate procedure involves the analysis of all variables in the data set simultaneously. A common goal of interdependence techniques is to examine a whole set of interdependent relationships among the variables under investigation, thereby enabling the researcher to statistically and objectively classify respondents or objects into different groups. Factor analysis, cluster analysis and perceptual mapping are some of the most frequently used interdependence techniques for marketing research purposes. For example, of a marketing manager in the fast food industry who wants to identify various customer segments on the basis of a number of selected customer characteristics, might utilize cluster analysis.

> **Interdependence technique** Another one of the two categories of multivariate techniques; used when a whole set interdependent relationships is examined.

Influence of Measurement Scales

Just as with other data analysis techniques – such as correlation analysis techniques discussed in the last chapter – the nature of the measurement scales will determine which multivariate technique is appropriate to analyse the data.

Selection of a proper technique requires consideration of the types of measures used for both dependent and independent sets of variables. When the dependent variable is measured non-metrically, a suitable technique could be discriminant analysis. When the dependent variable is measured metrically, eligible techniques include multiple regression, ANOVA and MANOVA. Multiple regression and discriminant analysis typically require metric independents, but they can use non-metric dummy variables. ANOVA and MANOVA are appropriate with non-metric independent variables. For the interdependence techniques of factor analysis and cluster analysis, by default, researchers should use metrically measured variables, but non-metric adaptations can be acceptable.

Multivariate statistical techniques help marketers make better decisions than is possible with univariate or bivariate statistics. But regardless of which type of technique is selected, the outcome of the analysis is the key point. Review the Global Insights box to see how outcomes can change across markets.

Global Insights
Analysis from Global Research May Yield Interesting Findings

Just Kids Inc., a marketing research firm specializing in the 2- to 12-year-old market, uncovered some interesting findings among youngsters in Great Britain. Children in Great Britain seem to shed their childhood much earlier than their peers elsewhere. McDonald's and Coke are universally loved, but the same advertising that attracts a 9-year-old American child may not appeal to a 9-year-old British counterpart. Asked to identify their favourite TV programmes, children in

Great Britain named adult shows. Their responses also demonstrated more teen behaviour than those youngsters from other countries. For example, many of the 9-year-olds around the globe said they wanted to be like their mum and dad when they grow up. In Britain, 9-year-olds wanted to be rock stars and entertainers. The conclusion: If you're a marketer with a clown and a happy meal, you may have a problem in Britain.

Dependence Techniques with Metric Dependent Variables

We now focus our discussion on the multivariate techniques that deal with analysis of dependence. The purpose of these techniques is to predict a variable from a set of independent variables. In this section, we will cover three major dependent techniques that can manage metric dependent variables. These are multiple regression analysis, analysis of variance (ANOVA), multivariate analysis of variance (MANOVA), and conjoint analysis.

Multiple Regression Analysis

Recall that in the last chapter we discussed bivariate regression analysis. The fundamental knowledge components underpinning bivariate and multiple regression analysis are the same. The main difference is that in bivariate regression analysis, there are only two variables included. One is dependent variable and the other is independent variable. On the other hand, at least two independent variables must be present in multiple regression analysis, which falls within the family of multivariate analysis.

In most of the marketing problems faced by managers, there are several independent variables that need to be examined for their influence on a dependent variable of interest. **Multiple regression analysis** is the appropriate technique to use for these situations. The technique is a straightforward extension of the bivariate regression analysis discussed in Chapter 17. Multiple independent variables are entered into the same type of regression equation, and for each variable a separate regression coefficient is calculated that describes its predictive relationship with the dependent variable. These coefficients allow the marketing researcher to examine the relative influence of each independent variable on the dependent variable. For example, Jimmy Spice's restaurant owners may want to examine not only customers' perceptions of price reasonableness, but also their perceptions of employees, atmosphere, service, and so forth. This could give them a more accurate picture of what to focus on in developing marketing strategies to compete more effectively.

> **Multiple regression analysis** A straightforward extension of the bivariate regression analysis; it hypothesizes that the dependent variable of question is influenced by two or more independent variables, and estimates a separate regression coefficient for each of these independent variables.

Now with multiple independent variables we have to think of multiple independent dimensions instead of just a single one. The logical way to examine these multiple independent dimensions is to estimate the regression coefficients for each independent variable. These coefficients still describe the average amount of change to be expected in Y given a unit change in the value of the particular independent variable you are examining.

However, with more than one independent variable, we have a couple of new issues to consider. One is the possibility that each independent variable may be measured using a different scale. For example, let's assume a marketing research company has been commissioned by a Canon copier distributor to predict the distributor's annual sales revenue. To predict the dependent variable, sales revenue, we could use size of sales force ($X1$), amount of advertising budget ($X2$), and consumer attitude towards the distributor's products ($X3$). Each of these independent variables is likely to be measured using a different scale, that is, different units. The size of the sales force would be measured by the number of salespeople, the amount of the advertising budget would be in Euros, and the consumer attitude might be measured on a five-point scale from 'Very poor' to 'Excellent'. When multiple independent variables are measured with different scales, it is not possible to make relative comparisons between normal regression coefficients in order to see which independent variable has the most influence on the dependent variable.

To solve this problem, we calculate the *standardized regression coefficient*. It is called a **beta coefficient**, and is calculated from the normal or unstandardized regression coefficient. The regression coefficient is recalculated to have a mean of 0 and a standard deviation of 1. Standardization removes the effects of using different scales of measurement. Beta coefficients will range from .00 to 1.00. Use of the beta coefficient enables direct comparisons between independent variables to determine which variables have the most influence on the dependent measure.

> **Beta coefficient** An estimated regression coefficient that has been recalculated to have a mean of 0 and a standard deviation of 1. This enables independent variables with different units of measurement to be directly compared on their relative influence on the dependent variable.

Statistical Significance

After the regression coefficients have been estimated, you still must examine the statistical significance of each coefficient. This is done in the same manner as the bivariate regression case. Each regression coefficient will be divided by its standard error to produce a t statistic, which is compared against the critical value to determine whether the null hypothesis can be rejected. The basic question we are trying to answer is still the same: 'What is the probability that we would get a coefficient of this size in our sample if the real regression coefficient in the population were zero?' You should examine the t-test statistics for each regression coefficient. Many times not all the independent variables in a regression equation will be statistically significant. Practically speaking, if a regression coefficient is not statistically significant, that means the independent variable does not have a relationship with the dependent variable and the slope describing that relationship is relatively flat (i.e. the value of the dependent variable does not change at all as the value of the statistically insignificant independent variable changes).

When using multiple regression analysis, it is important to examine the overall statistical significance of the regression model. The amount of variation in the dependent variable that you have been able to explain with the independent measures is compared with the total variation in the dependent measure. This comparison results in a statistic called a **model F statistic**. This measure is compared against a critical value to determine whether or not to reject the null hypothesis. If the F statistic is statistically significant, it means that the chances of the regression model for your sample producing a large r^2 when the population r^2 is actually 0 are acceptably small.

> **Model F statistic** A statistic that compares the amount of variation in the dependent measure 'explained' or associated with the independent variables to the 'unexplained' or error variance. A larger F statistic indicates that the regression model has more explained variance than error variance.

Substantive Significance

Once we have estimated the regression equation describing the relationships between our independent variables and the dependent variable, we need to assess the strength of the association that exists. From an overall perspective, the multiple r^2 or multiple coefficient of determination describes the strength of the relationship between all the independent variables in our equation and the dependent variable. If you recall our discussion of r^2 from the section on correlation analysis, the coefficient of determination is a measure of the amount of variation in the dependent variable associated with the variation in the independent variable. In the case of multiple regression analysis, the r^2 measure shows the amount of variation in the dependent variable associated with (or explained by) all of the independent variables considered together.

The larger the r^2 measure, the more of the behaviour of the dependent measure is associated with the independent measures we are using to predict it. For example, if the multiple r^2 in our Canon copier example above were .78, that would mean that we can account for, or explain, 78 per cent of the variation in sales revenue by using the variation in sales force size, advertising budget and customer attitudes toward our copier products. Higher values for r^2 mean stronger relationships between the group of independent variables and the dependent measure. As before, the measure of the strength of the relationship between an individual independent variable and the dependent measure of interest is shown by the regression coefficient or the beta coefficient for that variable.

To summarize, the elements of a multiple regression model to examine in determining its significance include the r^2; the model F statistic; the individual regression coefficients for each independent variable; their associated t statistics; and the individual beta coefficients. The appropriate procedure to follow in evaluating the results of a regression analysis is as follows: (1) assess the statistical significance of the overall regression model using the F statistic and its associated probability; (2) evaluate the obtained r^2 to see how large it is; (3) examine the individual regression coefficients and their t statistics to see which are statistically significant; and (4) look at the beta coefficients to assess relative influence. Taken together, these elements should give you a comprehensive picture of the answers to our basic three questions about the relationships between your dependent and independent variables.

SPSS Application – Multiple Regression

Regression can be used by the marketing researcher to examine the relationship between a single metric dependent variable and one or more metric independent variables. If you examine Jimmy Spice's restaurant database you will note that the first 21 variables are metric independent variables. They are lifestyle variables and perceptions of the restaurant, measured using a 7-point

Likert-type rating scale with 7 representing the positive dimension and 1 the negative dimension. Variables X22, X23, and X24 are metric dependent variables measured on a seven-point Likert-type rating scale. Variable X25 – Frequency of Patronage, X30 – Distance Driven, X31 – Ad Recall, and X32 – Gender are nonmetric. Variables X26 to X29 also are nonmetric variables because they are ranking data, and cannot therefore be used in regression.

A simple problem to examine with multiple regression would be to see if perceptions of the food in the restaurant are related to satisfaction. In this case, the single metric dependent variable is X22 – Satisfaction, and the independent variables would be X15 – Fresh Food, X18 – Food Taste, and X20 – Food Temperature. The null hypothesis would be that there is no relationship between the three food variables and X22. The alternative hypothesis would be that X15, X18, and X20 are significantly related to X22 – Customer Satisfaction.

The SPSS click-through sequence to examine this relationship is ANALYSE → REGRESSION → LINEAR. Highlight X22 and move it to the Dependent Variables box. Highlight X15, X18, and X20 and move them to the Independent Variables box. We will use the defaults for the other options so click OK to run the multiple regression.

The SPSS output for the multiple regression is shown in Exhibit 18.2. The Model Summary table shows R-square for this model is .381. This means that 38.1 per cent of the variation in satisfaction (dependent variable) can be explained from the three independent variables. The table

EXHIBIT 18.2 SPSS Multiple Regression Example

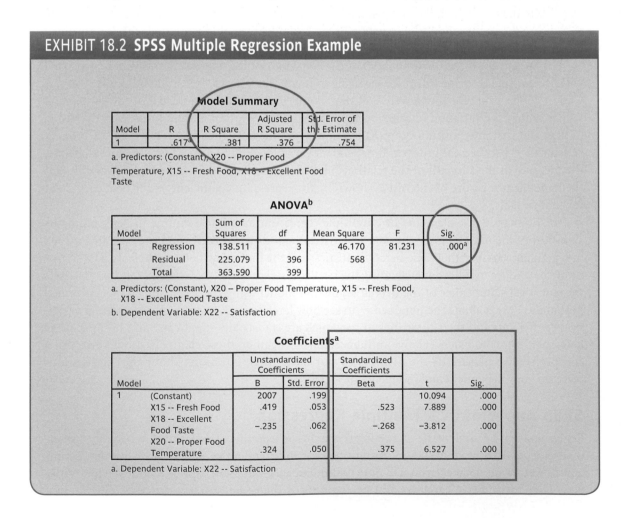

Model Summary

Model	R	R Square	Adjusted R Square	Std. Error of the Estimate
1	.617[a]	.381	.376	.754

a. Predictors: (Constant), X20 -- Proper Food Temperature, X15 -- Fresh Food, X18 -- Excellent Food Taste

ANOVA[b]

Model		Sum of Squares	df	Mean Square	F	Sig.
1	Regression	138.511	3	46.170	81.231	.000[a]
	Residual	225.079	396	568		
	Total	363.590	399			

a. Predictors: (Constant), X20 – Proper Food Temperature, X15 -- Fresh Food, X18 -- Excellent Food Taste

b. Dependent Variable: X22 -- Satisfaction

Coefficients[a]

Model		Unstandardized Coefficients		Standardized Coefficients		
		B	Std. Error	Beta	t	Sig.
1	(Constant)	2007	.199		10.094	.000
	X15 -- Fresh Food	.419	.053	.523	7.889	.000
	X18 -- Excellent Food Taste	–.235	.062	–.268	–3.812	.000
	X20 -- Proper Food Temperature	.324	.050	.375	6.527	.000

a. Dependent Variable: X22 -- Satisfaction

also shows the adjusted R-square for the model as .376. Any time another independent variable is added to a multiple regression model, the R-square will increase (even if only slightly). Consequently, it becomes difficult to determine which models do the best job of explaining variation in the same dependent variable. The adjusted R-square does just what its name implies. It adjusts the R-square by the number of predictor variables in the model. This adjustment allows the easy comparison of the explanatory power of models with different numbers of predictor variables. It also helps us decide how many variables to include in our regression model.

The regression model results in the ANOVA table show that the overall model is significantly different from 0 (F ratio = 81.231; probability level ('Sig.') = .000). This probability level means there are .000 chances the regression model results come from a population where the R-square actually is .00. That is, there are zero chances out of 1,000 that the correlation coefficient is .00.

To determine if one or more of the food independent variables are significant predictors of satisfaction we examine the information provided in the Coefficients table. Looking at the Standardized Coefficients Beta column reveals that X15 – Fresh Food has a beta coefficient of .523 which is significant (.000). Similarly, X18 – Food Taste and X20 – Food Temperature have beta coefficients of −0.268 and 0.375, respectively (Sig. level of .000). This means we can reject the null hypothesis that the three food variables are not related to X22 – Customer Satisfaction. Thus, this regression analysis tells us that customer perceptions of food in Jimmy Spice's restaurant are a good predictor of the level of satisfaction with the restaurant.

A word of caution is needed at this point regarding the beta coefficients. Recall that the size of the individual coefficients show how strongly each independent variable is related to the dependent variable. The signs (negative or positive) are also important. A positive sign indicates a positive relationship (higher independent variable values are associated with higher dependent variable values). A negative sign indicates a negative relationship. The negative sign of X18 – Food Taste suggests, therefore, that less favourable perceptions of food taste are associated with higher levels of satisfaction. This result is clearly not logical, and points out one of the weaknesses of multiple regression. When the independent variables are highly correlated with each other the signs of the beta coefficients may be reversed in a regression model, which happened in this case.

For this reason, the analyst must always examine the logic of the signs for the regression betas when independent variables are highly correlated. If the sign is the opposite of what is anticipated, one must look at a simple bivariate correlation of the two variables. This can be seen in the table below, which clearly shows the true positive correlation of .409. So always be careful in using the beta coefficient signs to interpret regression results.

Correlations		
		X22 – Satisfaction
X18 – Food Taste	Pearson Correlation	.409*
	Sig. (2-tailed)	.000
	N	400

*Correlation is significant at the 0.01 level (2-tailed).

Examination of the SPSS tables reveals that there is a lot of information provided that we did not discuss. Researchers may use this information, but managers typically do not. One of the challenges for you will be to learn which information to use and which to discard.

At this point we recommend you start to learn by actually doing the analysis yourself. For example, the next problem you can examine may be to change the dependent variable from X22 – Satisfaction to X23 – Likely to Return, and run the regression with the same independent variables. Another possibility is to keep X22 – Satisfaction as the dependent and use either the lifestyle variables or the other restaurant perceptions as independent variables. By doing this you will learn how to use the SPSS package and also see if any relationships exist between the variables.

The Use of Dummy Variables in Multiple Regression

Sometimes the particular independent variables you may want to use to predict a dependent variable are not measured using interval or ratio scales (a basic assumption for the use of regression analysis). It is still possible to include such variables through the use of **dummy variables**. For example, if you wanted to include the gender of customers of Jimmy Spice's restaurant to help explain their satisfaction with the restaurant, it is obvious your measure for gender would include only two possible values – male or female.

> **Dummy variables** Artificial variables introduced into a regression equation to represent the categories of a nominally scaled variable.

The use of dummy variables involves choosing one category of the variable to serve as a reference category and then adding as many dummy variables as there are possible values of the variable, minus that reference category. The categories are coded as either 0 or 1. In the example above, if you choose the male category as the reference category, you would have one dummy variable for the female category. That dummy variable would be assigned the value of 1 for females and 0 for males. In Jimmy Spice's restaurant database, X32 – Gender is already coded as a dummy variable for gender, with males as the reference category.

SPSS Application – Use of Dummy Variables in Regression

To see how multiple regression works with dummy variables, let's use Jimmy Spice's restaurant database to investigate into the question of whether the satisfaction of customers is related to X15 – Fresh Food and X16 – Reasonable Prices, and whether this relationship is different for X32, male and female customers. The null hypothesis would be that X22 – Customer Satisfaction is not related to X15, X16, or X32.

The SPSS click-through sequence is ANALYSE → REGRESSION → LINEAR. Click on X22 – Satisfaction and move it to the Dependent Variables box. Click on X15 – Fresh Food, X16 – Reasonable Prices, and X32 – Gender and move them to the Independent Variables box. Now click OK to run the multiple regression.

The SPSS results are shown in Exhibit 18.3. In the Model Summary table, you can see the R^2 for the model is .392. Thus, 39.2 per cent of the total variation in X22 is associated with X15 – Fresh Food, X16 – Reasonable Prices, and X32 – Gender. The ANOVA table indicates the regression model is significant – the 'Sig.' value indicates a probability level of .000.

The Coefficients table shows that X15 – Fresh Food is a significant predictor of satisfaction, with a beta coefficient of .525. Reasonable prices (X16), with a beta of .193, is also significantly related to customer satisfaction (i.e., probability level of .000). Now, the question of interest is

EXHIBIT 18.3 **SPSS Multiple Regression with a Dummy Variable**

Model Summary

Model	R	R Square	Adjusted R Square	Std. Error of the Estimate
1	.626a	.392	.387	.747

a. Predictors: (Constant), X32 -- Gender, X15 -- Fresh Food, X16 -- Reasonable Prices

ANOVAb

Model		Sum of Squares	df	Mean Square	F	Sig.
1	Regression	142.445	3	47.482	85.024	.000a
	Residual	221.145	396	.558		
	Total	363.590	399			

a. Predictors: (Constant), X32 -- Gender, X15 -- Fresh Food, X16 -- Reasonable Prices

b. Dependent Variable: X22 -- Satisfaction

Coefficientsa

Model		Unstandardized Coefficients		Standardized Coefficients		
		B	Std. Error	Beta	t	Sig.
1	(Constant)	1.699	.226		7.531	.000
	X15 -- Fresh Food	.420	.032	.525	13.252	.000
	X16 -- Reasonable Prices	.150	.033	.193	4.615	.000
	X32 -- Gender	−.303	.080	−.156	−3.775	.000

a. Dependent Variable: X22 -- Satisfaction

'Does the satisfaction level of Jimmy Spice's customers differ depending on whether they are male or female?' According to the results in the Coefficients table, the beta coefficient of −.156 for X32 – Gender is significant (i.e. Sig. level of .000). This means the female and male customers exhibit significantly different levels of satisfaction with Jimmy Spice's restaurant. The negative beta coefficient means that a lower number for gender are associated with a higher value for satisfaction. Since males were coded 0 in our database this means males are more satisfied with Jimmy Spice's restaurant than females.

It is also possible to use categorical independent variables with more than just two categories. Let's say you wanted to use consumers' purchase behaviour of coffee to help predict their purchase behaviour for cakes and biscuits, and you had separated your sample into non-users, light users and heavy users. To use dummy variables in your regression model, you would pick one category as a reference group (non-users) and add two dummy variables for the remaining categories. The variables would be coded as follows, using 0 and 1:

Category	D_1	D_2
Non-user	0	0
Light user	1	0
Heavy user	0	1

The use of dummy variables in regression models allows different types of independent variables to be included in prediction efforts. The researcher must keep in mind the difference in the interpretation of the regression coefficient and the identity of the reference category that is represented by the intercept term.

Multicollinearity and Multiple Regression Analysis

One common problem area for marketing researchers involves the situation in which the independent variables are highly correlated among themselves, which is referred to as **multicollinearity**. The general definition of the regression coefficient that describes the relationship between one independent variable and the dependent variable of interest is that it signifies the average amount of change in the dependent variable associated with a unit change in the independent variable, assuming all other independent variables in the equation remain the same. If several independent variables are highly correlated (say, for example, the education level and annual income of a respondent), then clearly income level is not going to remain the same as the education level of a respondent changes.

> **Multicollinearity** A situation in which several independent variables are highly correlated with each other. This characteristic can result in difficulty in estimating separate or independent regression coefficients for the correlated variables.

The effect of high levels of multicollinearity is to make it difficult or impossible for the regression equation to separate out the independent contributions of the independent or predictor variables. The practical impact of multicollinearity relates to the statistical significance of the individual regression coefficients, as well as their signs (negative or positive). While multicollinearity does not affect the size of r^2 or your ability to predict values of the dependent variable, it inflates the standard error of the coefficient and lowers the t statistic associated with it (recall that the regression coefficient is subtracted from the null hypothesis coefficient and divided by its standard error to calculate the t statistic). Therefore, it may be possible, if the multicollinearity is severe enough, for your regression model to have a significant F statistic, a reasonably large r^2, and still have no regression coefficients that are statistically significant from zero.

In addition to its impact on the statistical significance of the individual regression coefficients, multicollinearity may also reverse the signs of the individual coefficients on the SPSS output. When results look suspicious, always check the signs using a bivariate correlation procedure.

SPSS Application – Multicollinearity

The SPSS output from the Jimmy Spice's example described earlier provides some results to help you determine whether multicollinearity is a potential problem in the data. Recall that the click-through sequence is ANALYSE → REGRESSION → LINEAR. Highlight X22 and move it to the Dependent Variable box. Highlight X15 and X16 and move them to the Independent Variable box. In the Methods box we will keep Enter, which is the default. Similarly, click on the Statistics button and keep Estimates in the Regression Coefficients box Model Fit as defaults (already checked). Now click Collinearity Diagnostics and then Continue.

The results are shown in Exhibit 18.4. First, the R2 for this regression model is .37 and it is significant at the .000 level. To assess multicollinearity, look at the columns labelled Tolerance and VIF under the heading Collinearity Statistics on the right side of the Coefficients table. These are both measures of collinearity among the variables (VIF stands for *variance inflation factor*). They tell us the degree to which each independent variable is explained by the other independent variables.

For the tolerance small values indicate the absence of collinearity. The VIF is the inverse of tolerance, so we look for large values. If the tolerance value is smaller than .10, we conclude that multicollinearity is a problem. Similarly, if the VIF is 5 or larger, then multicollinearity is a problem. In the Jimmy Spice's output, the tolerance between X15 and X16 is .978 and the VIF is 1.022. Since the tolerance value is substantially above .10 and the VIF is much smaller than 5, we conclude that multicollinearity among the independent variables is not a problem.

EXHIBIT 18.4 SPSS Results for Multicollinearity

Model Summary

Model	R	R Square	Adjusted R Square	Std. Error of the Estimate
1	.608[a]	.370	.367	.760

a. Predictors: (Constant), X16 -- Reasonable Prices, X15 -- Fresh Food

ANOVA[b]

Model		Sum of Squares	df	Mean Square	F	Sig.
1	Regression	134.487	2	67.244	116.523	.000[a]
	Residual	229.103	397	.577		
	Total	363.590	399			

a. Predictors: (Constant), X16 -- Reasonable Prices, X15 -- Fresh Food
b. Dependent Variable: X22 -- Satisfaction

Coefficients[a]

Model		Unstandardized Coefficients		Standardized Coefficients	t	Sig.	Collinearity Statistics	
		B	Std. Error	Beta			Tolerance	VIF
1	(Constant)	1.418	.216		6.550	.000		
	X15 -- Fresh Food	.417	.032	.522	12.962	.000	.978	1.022
	X15 -- Reasonable Prices	.190	.031	.244	6.056	.000	.978	1.022

a. Dependent Variable: X22 -- Satisfaction

To avoid the problem of multicollinearity in regression, you should examine the correlations between the independent variables ahead of time. If they are too high (>.70), then you should remove one of the highly correlated variables. Another approach to deal with multicollinearity is to submit the variables to a factor analysis. We discuss how to do this in Chapter 19.

Analysis of Variance (ANOVA)

Analysis of variance (ANOVA) is used to determine the statistical difference between three or more means. For example, if a sample finds that the average number of cups of coffee consumed by freshmen during the exam period is 3.7, while the average number of cups of coffee consumed by seniors and graduate students is 4.3 cups and 5.1 cups, respectively, are these observed differences statistically significant? The ability to make such comparisons is useful for the marketing researcher.

> **Analysis of variance (ANOVA)** A statistical technique that determines whether three or more means are statistically different from each other.

While the name ANOVA can be disconcerting to many students, the technique is really quite straightforward. In this section we shall describe a one-way ANOVA. The term *one-way* is used since there is only one independent variable. ANOVA can be used in cases where multiple independent variables are considered, and it allows the analyst to estimate both their individual and their joint effects on the dependent variable.

Multiple dependent variables can be analysed together using a related procedure called *multivariate analysis of variance (MANOVA)*. The objective in MANOVA is identical to that in ANOVA – to examine group differences in means. The difference is that in the former technique, the comparisons are considered for a group of dependent variables. While a detailed discussion is beyond the scope of this text, a brief description of MANOVA is included on page 597.

An example of an ANOVA problem may be to compare light, medium and heavy drinkers of Starbucks coffee on their attitude towards a particular Starbucks advertising campaign. In this instance there is one independent variable – consumption of Starbucks coffee – but it is divided into three different levels. Our earlier *t* statistics won't work here, since we have more than two groups to compare.

ANOVA requires that the dependent variable, in this case the attitude towards the Starbucks advertising campaign, be metric. That is, the dependent variable must be either interval or ratio scaled. A second data requirement is that the independent variable, in this case the coffee consumption variable, be categorical.

In this example, the null hypothesis for ANOVA should state that there is no difference between the advertising campaign attitudes of the three groups of Starbucks coffee drinkers. In specific terminology, the null hypothesis would be

$$\mu_1 = \mu_2 = \mu_3$$

The ANOVA technique focuses on the behaviour of the variances within a set of data. If you remember the earlier discussion of measures of dispersion, the variance of a variable is equal to the average squared deviation from the mean of the variable. The logic of the ANOVA technique says that if we calculate the variance between the groups and compare it to the variance within the groups, we can make a rational determination as to whether the means (attitudes towards the advertising campaign) are significantly different.

Determining Statistical Significance in ANOVA

In ANOVA, the *F*-test is used to statistically evaluate differences between the group means. For example, suppose the heavy users of Starbucks coffee rate the advertising campaign 4.4 on a five-point scale, with 5 = very favourable. The medium users of Starbucks coffee rate the campaign 3.9, and the light users of Starbucks coffee rate the campaign 2.5. The *F*-test in ANOVA tells us if these observed differences are meaningful.

> ***F*-test** The test used to statistically evaluate differences between the group means in ANOVA.

The total variance in a set of responses to a question can be separated into between-group and within-group variance. The *F* distribution is the ratio of these two components of total variance and can be calculated as follows:

$$F \, \mathrm{ratio} = \frac{\text{Variance between groups}}{\text{Variance within groups}}$$

The larger the difference in the variance between groups, the larger the *F* ratio. Since the total variance in a data set is divisible into between and within components, if there is more variance explained or accounted for by considering differences between groups than there is within groups, then the independent variable is likely to have a significant impact on the dependent variable. The larger the *F* ratio, the more likely it is that the null hypothesis will be rejected.

ANOVA, however, is able to tell the researcher only that statistical differences exist somewhere between the group means. The technique cannot identify which pairs of means are significantly different from each other. In our example of Starbucks coffee drinkers' attitudes towards the advertising campaign, we can conclude that differences in attitudes towards the advertising campaign exist among light, medium, and heavy coffee drinkers, but we are unable to determine if the differences are between light and medium, or between light and heavy, or between medium and heavy. Thus, the marketing researcher is still saddled with the task of determining where the mean differences lie. Follow-up tests have been designed for just that purpose.

There are several **follow-up tests** available in statistical software packages such as SPSS and SAS, including comparison tests by Tukey, Duncan, Dunn and Scheffé. All of these methods involve multiple comparisons, or simultaneous assessment of confidence interval estimates of differences between the means. All means are compared two at a time. The differences between the techniques lie in their ability to control the error rate. We shall briefly describe the Scheffé procedure, although a complete discussion of these techniques is beyond the scope of this book. Relative to the other follow-up tests mentioned, the Scheffé procedure is a more conservative method of detecting significant differences between group means.

> **Follow-up test** A test that flags the means that are statistically different from each other; follow-up tests are performed after an ANOVA determines there are differences between means.

The Scheffé follow-up test essentially establishes simultaneous confidence intervals, holding the entire experiment's error rate to a specified level. The test exposes differences between all pairs of means to a high and low confidence interval range. If the difference between each pair of means falls outside the range of the confidence interval, then we reject the null hypothesis and conclude that the pairs of means falling outside the range are statistically different. The Scheffé test may show that one, two, or all three pairs of means in our Starbucks example are different. This type of test is equivalent to simultaneous two-tailed hypothesis tests. Because the technique holds the experimental error rate to α, the confidence intervals tend to be wider than in the other methods, but the researcher has more assurance that true mean differences exist.

n-Way ANOVA

The entire discussion of ANOVA to this point has been devoted to one-way ANOVA. In a one-way ANOVA there is only one independent variable. In the foregoing example, the consumption category (consumption of Starbucks coffee) was the independent variable. However, it is not at all uncommon for the researcher to be interested in several independent variables simultaneously. In those cases, an *n*-way ANOVA should be used.

Using the same Starbucks coffee example, the marketing researcher may be interested in the region of the country where the product is sold, in addition to the consumption category. Using multiple independent factors allows for an interaction effect, which is the effect of the multiple independent factors acting in concert to affect group means. For example, heavy customers of Starbucks coffee in the Northeast may have attitudes about a Starbuck advertising campaign that are different from those of heavy customers of Starbucks coffee in the Southeast, and there may also be differences between the various coffee-consumption-level groups, as shown earlier.

Another situation that may require *n*-way ANOVA is the use of experimental designs, where the researcher may provide different groups in a sample with different information to see how their responses change. For example, a marketer may be interested in finding out whether consumers prefer a humorous advertisement to a serious one and whether that preference varies across gender. Each type of advertisement can be shown to the two groups of consumers, i.e. male and female groups. Then, questions about their preferences for the advertisement and the product it advertises can be asked. An *n*-way ANOVA can be used to find out whether the advertising execution difference (humorous versus serious) helped cause differences in advertisement and product preferences, as well as whether gender contributes to these differences.

From a conceptual standpoint, *n*-way ANOVA is very similar to one-way ANOVA, but the mathematics behind it is more complex. However, statistical packages such as SPSS and SAS can allow the marketing researcher to conveniently perform *n*-way ANOVA.

SPSS Application – ANOVA

To help you further understand the ideas involved in using ANOVA techniques to answer research questions, we will use Jimmy Spice's restaurant database to answer some predetermined questions. The owners want to know first whether customers who come to the restaurant from greater distances differ from customers who live nearby in their willingness to recommend the restaurant to a friend. They also want to know whether that difference in willingness to recommend, if any, is influenced by the gender of the customers. The database variables are X24 – Likely to Recommend, measured on a 7-point scale, with 1 = 'Definitely Will Not Recommend' and 7 = 'Definitely Recommend'; X30 – Distance Driven, where 1 = 'Less than 1 mile', 2 = '1–3 miles', and 3 = 'More than 3 miles'; and X32 – Gender, where 0 = 'male' and 1 = 'female'.

On the basis of informal comments from a handful of customers, the owners think customers who come from more than 3 miles are more likely to recommend the restaurant. They also think female customers are more likely to recommend the restaurant than males. The null hypotheses are there would be no difference in the mean ratings for X24 – Likely to Recommend between customers who travelled different distances to come to the restaurant (X30) and between females and males (X32).

The purpose of the ANOVA analysis is to see if the differences that do exist are statistically significant. To examine the differences, an F ratio is used. The bigger the F ratio, the bigger the difference among the means of the various groups with respect to their likelihood of recommending the restaurant.

SPSS can help you conduct the statistical analysis to test the null hypotheses set up above. The best way to analyse the Jimmy Spice's data to answer the owners' questions is to use a factorial model. A factorial model is a type of ANOVA in which the individual effects of each independent variable on the dependent variable are considered separately and then the combined effects (an interaction) of the independent variables on the dependent variable are analysed. The click-through sequence is ANALYSE → GENERAL LINEAR MODEL → UNIVARIATE. Highlight the dependent variable X24 – Likely to Recommend by clicking on it and move it to the Dependent Variable box. Next, highlight X30 – Distance Driven and X32 – Gender, and move them to the Fixed Factors box. Click OK, since we don't need to specify any other options for this test.

The SPSS output for ANOVA is shown in Exhibit 18.5. The Tests of Between-Subjects Effects table shows that the F ratio for X30 – Distance Driven is 80.452, which is statistically significant at the .000 level. This means that customers who come from different distances to eat at the restaurant vary in their likelihood of recommending the restaurant. The F ratio for X32 – Gender is 49.421, which is also statistically significant at the .000 level. This means the gender of customsers influences their likelihood of recommending the restaurant.

We now know that both X30 – Distance Driven and X32 – Gender influence customers' likelihood of recommending Jimmy Spice's restaurant. But we do not know how. To answer this question we must look at the means for these two variables. The SPSS means programme helps us to do this. The click-through sequence is ANALYSE → COMPARE MEANS → MEANS. Highlight the dependent variable X24 – Likely to Recommend by clicking on it and move it to the Dependent List box. Next, highlight X30 – Distance Driven and X32 – Gender, and move them to the Independent List. Then click OK. The results are shown in Exhibit 18.6.

Look at the table under the Mean heading on the SPSS output and you will see that the average likelihood of recommending the restaurant to a friend increases as the Distance Driven by the respondent increases. In short, customers who come from within 1 mile of the restaurant show an average likelihood to recommend of 2.90, compared to a 3.62 and 4.18 average likelihood for customers who come from 1–3 and more than 3 miles away, respectively.

As previously noted, the restaurant's owners are also interested in knowing whether there is a difference in the likelihood of males versus females recommending Jimmy Spice's restaurant. The F ratio for gender is again quite large (49.421; see Exhibit 18.5) and statistically significant (.000). Looking at the means of the customer groups based on gender (see Exhibit 18.6), we see that indeed males are more likely to recommend the restaurant (mean = 3.77) as compared to females (mean = 3.01). The null hypothesis is rejected, and we conclude there is a difference in the average likelihoods to recommend the restaurant between male and female customers.

The interaction variable (interaction between distance travelled and gender) has an F ratio of .456, with a probability level of .634, meaning that the difference in the likelihood of recommendation when both independent variables are considered together is very small. This means there

EXHIBIT 18.5 ANOVA for X24 – Likely to Recommend, X30 – Distance Driven, and X32 – Gender

Univariate Analysis of Variance

Between-Subject Factors

		Value Label	N
x30 -- Distance Driven	1	Less than 1 miles	183
	2	1 – 3 miles	98
	3	More than 3 miles	119
X32 -- Gender	0	Males	236
	1	Females	164

Tests of Between-Subject Effects

Dependent Variable: X24 -- Likely to Recommend

Source	Type III Sum of Squares	df	Mean Square	F	Sig.
Connected Model	149.397[a]	5	29.879	60.100	.000
Intercept	4018.202	1	4018.202	8082.330	.000
X30	79.995	2	39.997	80.452	.000
X32	24.570	1	24.570	49.421	.000
X30*X32	.454	2	.227	.456	.634
Error	195.881	394	.497		
Total	5127.000	400			
Corrected Total	345.278	399			

a. R Squared = .443 (Adjusted R Squared = .425)

EXHIBIT 18.6 Comparison of Likely to Recommend for Male and Female Customers Who Drove Different Distances to Dine at Jimmy Spice's Restaurant

Means

X24 -- Likely to Recommend *X30 -- Distance Driven

X24 -- Likely to Recommend

X30 -- Distance Driven	Mean	N	Std. Deviation
Less than 1 mile	2.90	183	.691
1 – 3 miles	3.62	98	.914
More than 3 miles	4.18	119	.676
Total	3.46	400	.930

X24 -- Likely to Recommend *X32 -- Gender

X24 -- Likely to Recommend

X32 -- Gender	Mean	N	Std. Deviation
Males	3.77	236	.845
Females	3.01	164	.862
Total	3.46	400	.930

is no effect on the likelihood to recommend the restaurant that is due to the interaction between distance driven and gender.

Multivariate Analysis of Variance (MANOVA)

A related technique, MANOVA, is designed to examine multiple dependent variables across single or multiple independent variables. The technique considers the mean differences for a group of dependent measures. For example, a researcher may want to measure customers' use of several types of related products, such as golf balls, golf shoes, golf clubs and golf clothing. Since use of one of these types of products is logically related to use of the others, MANOVA will be a good choice for examining the effect of independent variables like income or gender on use of the entire group of golf-related products. The statistical calculations for MANOVA are similar to n-way ANOVA and are typically included in the statistical software packages mentioned earlier.

Conjoint Analysis

The conjoint analysis technique originated in mathematical psychology, but is now being commonly used in marketing research. Examples of its marketing research applications include testing of consumer acceptance of new product designs, evaluation of new service design, assessment of appeal of competing advertisements and identification of the best possible positioning of the product.

Conjoint analysis is a multivariate technique that can be used in marketing research to determine how consumers value different attributes that make up a given product, service, marketing communication message, or any other object. One big assumption for the effective use of conjoint analysis is that consumers evaluate the value of an object (such as a product) by aggregating the separate amounts of value provided by each attribute of the product.

Key Terms and Issues Involved in Conjoint Analysis

Utility, a measure of an individual's subjective preference to an object or an attribute of an object, is the conceptual basis for measuring value of product attributes in conjoint analysis. To define utility for each chosen product attribute assigned by each individual involved in a study, the researcher must be able to describe the object in terms of both its attributes and all relevant values for each of these attributes. This requires the researcher to address the following three important issues:

1 A product can have numerous attributes, such as shape, colour, having a particular new function or not, and price level levied on it. It will be ineffective, if not impossible, to include all the attributes in a conjoint analysis. Therefore, the researcher must be able to identify all those attributes that have a significant bearing on an individual's feeling of preference or utility towards the product. These attributes are called determinant attributes. All the determinant attributes should be included in the conjoint analysis.

2 To conduct conjoint analysis, the levels of each determinant attribute must be determined. Levels are the possible values that the researcher wants to use in conjoint analysis. The researcher can then use these values to describe the object being studied to the respondents. For instance, 'packaging material' and 'ingredients used' can be two attributes of a new food product to be tested in conjoint analysis. 'Packaging material' can have three levels: plastic, metal, and glass, whereas 'ingredients used' can have two levels: organic and non-organic.

3   After the researcher specifies the attributes and the levels to describe an object, they have to draw up all the possible combinations, each of which is commonly known as a stimulus or treatment. In the above example of 'packaging material' and 'ingredients used', there are six stimuli, i.e. plastic and organic, plastic and non-organic, metal and organic, metal and non-organic, glass and organic, and glass and non-organic.

Collecting Preference Evaluation from Respondents

After drawing up all the possible stimuli, the researcher can start to collect information about preference to each combination from each respondent in the sample. Respondents can either rank order all the stimuli provided to them, or they can rate each stimulus on a pre-determined scale (such as a 7-point or 10-point scale). When the respondents rank order or rate the stimuli, they must weigh all attributes in a stimulus simultaneously in order to make a judgement on that stimulus. In other words, they must make a trade-off decision because it is often the case that a stimulus has the characteristics, some of which are favourable whilst some others some unfavourable to the respondent of question.

The preference or utility that a respondent gives to a stimulus can be thought of as the sum of what the parts of the object are worth, called part-worths. A conjoint analysis model can be written in the following form:

(Total worth for object with a given stimulus)$_{ij}$ = n_{ij} = Part worth of level i for attribute 1 + Part worth of level j for attribute 2 + $\cdots$ + Part-worth of level n for attribute m

where the object has m attributes, each having n levels. The object with a given stimulus comprises level i of attribute 1, level j of attribute 2, and so on, up to level n of attribute m.

With the part-worth estimates, the researcher can calculate the preference or utility for any stimulus given to a respondent. They can also identify the relative importance of each attribute in determining the utility. By combining and analysing the preference evaluation information of all the respondents involved, the researcher can have a clearer picture about the competitive environment that the tested object will face in reality.

Estimation of Part-Worths

Each level of a given attribute exerts an impact on a respondent's evaluation of the preference to a given stimulus. The impact of each level for a particular respondent can be calculated as the difference from the overall average ranking for that level.

For example, to evaluate a beer product in glass bottle, a respondent is given eight stimuli and is asked to rank order each of them. Each stimulus contains, among others, one attribute that is the same, say colour of the bottle, and this attribute has two levels, say brown colour and green colour. Four of the eight stimuli will have the same level of green colour, and four others will have the red-colour level. Assuming this respondent is very fond of the colour brown and hates the colour green, it is likely that they will rank the four stimuli with brown colouring above all the other four stimuli with green colouring. So what are the part-worths of the brown colour and the green colour?

We should first calculate the average rank for each of the two colour levels. For the brown colour, the average rank is $(1 + 2 + 3 + 4)/4 = 2.5$, while the average rank for the green colour is $(5 + 6 + 7 + 8)/4 = 6.5$. Then we should calculate the overall average rank, which is obviously $(1 + 2 + 3 + 4 + 5 + 6 + 7 + 8)/8 = 4.5$. Therefore, the brown colour level will have a difference (deviation) of -2.0 $(2.5 - 4.5)$ from the overall average rank, whereas the green colour level will have a deviation of +2.0 (6.5–4.5). Note that in this example, we use smaller numbers to represent higher ranks. As a result, a negative deviation means higher utility and a positive deviation actually means lower utility. We can reverse the signs of the deviations in the above example so that positive deviations indicate higher utility and therefore higher part-worth.

Using a step-by-step approach, the estimation of part-worths can be carried out by following the five steps below:

1 Calculate the impact of each level, measured by deviation, as illustrated above. Reverse the signs of the deviations if smaller numbers are used to represent higher ranks.

2 Square the deviations and calculate the sum for each level used in the analysis.

3 Calculate the standardized value, which is the total number of levels divided by the sum of squared deviations.

4 Multiply each squared deviation by the standardized value calculated in step 3 to get the standardized squared deviation.

5 Take the square root of the standardized squared deviation to get the part-worth.

An illustrative Example of Conjoint Analysis

With the permission of Elsevier, we have adapted Moore, Louviere and Verma's (1999) work published in the *Journal of Product Innovation Management* to explain how conjoint analysis can be applied to help companies in their product design strategies. The company used is a small one (a real company, but its real name is not disclosed here for business confidentiality reasons), which we will call 'Alpha'. The company is a leader in several niches of the electronic equipment tester market. Its customers include big names in the electronic equipment market, such as IBM, HP and 3M.

Alpha is considering launching two new products, X and Z, which compete in different niches of the market. X costs more to produce but is priced a few times higher than Z. They share a common technological platform, but each of them has a number of unique attributes.

Calculation of Utilities

A different questionnaire was developed for each of the two products. Questionnaires were faxed to selected individuals who play a key role in the purchase decisions of electronic equipment testers. The names of these individuals were drawn from a list of companies that constitute about 80 per cent of the market.

A fractional factorial design was used to create 16 hypothetical tests, which would be used for conducting conjoint analysis. Some levels of certain attributes cost significantly more to produce. These levels were associated with an increment added to the base price. Logically the utility for these levels represents the respondent's corresponding preference at the known higher price.

Respondents rated their likelihood of purchasing each of the 16 hypothetical testers presented to them. Individual-level utilities for attribute levels were estimated from these likelihood ratings. These attribute levels were used to calculate their average utilities by following the formula below and the results are provided in Exhibit 18.7.

$\breve{u}_{ij} = \sum_l \beta_{lj} x_{ij}$, *which means the utility of the ith product to person j, $\breve{u}_{ij}$, is modelled as a linear function of the preferences (or utilities) of the levels of product I.*

EXHIBIT 18.7 Attribute Levels and Average Utilities for the Two Electronic Equipment Testers

Attribute	Level 1	Level 2	Level 3	Level 4
Brand	**Alpha**	**Other**		
Product X	0.462	−0.462		
Product Z	0.032	−0.032		
Display	**Current Display**	**Larger Line Display**	**Largest Line Display**	**Graphic Display**
Product X	−0.356	0.091	−0.166	0.431
Product Z	−0.319	0.138	0.008	0.173
Backlight	**Yes**	**No**		
Product X	0.039	−0.039		
Product Z	0.015	−0.015		
Data I/O Method	**Connect to Single PC**	**Floppy Disk**	**Memory Module**	**Networked**
Product X	−0.206	−0.283	0.123	0.366
Product Z	−0.036	−0.255	−0.055	0.316
Accuracy	**Current**	**More Accurate**		
Product X	−0.103	0.103		
Product Z	−0.062	0.062		
Speed	**Current**	**Faster**		
Product X	−0.246	0.246		
Product Z	−0.136	0.136		
Connection Method	**Method One**	**Method Two**		
Product X	0.433	−0.433		
Product Z	0.357	−0.357		
Stress Level Applied	**Current**	**Higher**		
Product X	−0.052	0.052		
Maximum Size Tested	**Current**	**Larger**		
Product Z	0.076	−0.076		
Price (per cent of current)	**84%**	**92%**	**100%**	**108%**
Product X	0.028	0.001	−0.001	−0.028
Product Z	0.085	0.029	−0.029	−0.085

The first seven attributes in Exhibit 18.7 were common to both questionnaires. For the 'Brand' attribute, respondents were asked to name another supplier from whom they would also consider purchasing, apart from 'Alpha', the dominant supplier in the market. As can be seen from the table, the utility for Alpha is higher than for 'Other' for both products.

There are four levels for the 'Display' attribute. The first three are 'Current Display', 'Larger Line Display' and 'Largest Line Display'. They all contain varying numbers of lines and characters per line. The last one is 'Graphic Display' and results indicate that this last Display level is the most preferred. In contrast, the 'Current Display' level is the least preferred.

Regarding the 'Backlight' attribute, respondents showed a small preference for a backlight, which can improve visibility in poor lighting conditions, for both products X and Z.

For a typical electronic equipment tester, relevant data need to be input to carry out the testing, and be output for statistical process control. There are four levels in this 'Data I/O Method' attribute: 'Connect to Single PC', 'Floppy Disk', 'Memory Module' (such as a PCMCIA card) and 'Networked'. The last level is the most preferred.

The 'Accuracy' and 'Speed' attributes are specified in technical terms in the questionnaires, but they are disguised here. Exhibit 18.7 demonstrates that respondents preferred more accurate and faster testers.

Regarding the 'Connection Method' attribute, there are two levels, again disguised as 'Method One' and 'Method Two' here. 'Method One' was pioneered by Alpha, and it has earned respondents' much higher preference as opposed to 'Method Two'.

The following two attributes, 'Stress Level Applied' and 'Maximum Size Tested', are applied to only Product X and Product Z respectively. Results show that the higher stress level applied for Product X is preferred, while the current maximum size for Product Z is chosen by the respondents.

Lastly, we can find the respective utilities for different 'Price' (expressed as a percentage of the current price) levels for both products X and Z in Exhibit 18.7. As expected, the higher the price, the lower the utility.

Overall, the utilities estimated in Exhibit 18.7 make intuitive sense as brand Alpha (the market leader), the method of connection (Method One) that it pioneered, the more user-friendly graphic display, higher accuracy, faster speed, as well as lower price are preferred.

Market Simulations

The utilities shown in Exhibit 18.7 were combined with managerial judgements concerning market size and likely competitive actions, as well as fixed and variable cost estimates. All these data were input into a Fortran programme, which searched for the optimal product configuration through complete enumeration. For each combination of attribute levels, the programme forecast which tester each respondent would purchase. The forecast information so derived was then integrated in order to forecast industry sales, market shares, contribution and profit. Profit will be used as the criterion of performance of different configurations being considered.

Determination of Optimal Product Design Strategy

The forecast data of profit can then be used to identify which combination of attribute levels (technically called product configurations) for a particular product (product X or product Z) can provide the highest level of profit. The best product configurations that can maximize the profits for products X and Z respectively are shown in Exhibit 18.8. You may notice that the profit maximizing X and Z product configurations are quite similar: graphic display, connection to a single PC for data I/O, current level of accuracy, faster speed, connection method one and price 8 per cent higher than current level. The only difference is that the optimal product Z has a backlight.

However, after taking into account the fixed and variable cost estimates, even though the Z product configuration is a profit maximizing one, it still records the negative profit of 1052.2 per cent because it has to bear all the high fixed cost alone. Therefore, if Z is the only product considered, the optimal decision is not to design and launch it. On the contrary, as product X is expected to yield a profit of 100 per cent, the decision about whether to design and launch Product X if it is considered alone should be a clear yes.

Column 3 assumes that product X and Z are designed independently, but fixed cost is shared wherever possible. Again, the only difference in common attribute levels between products X and Z is the backlight. The two products designed and launched in this 'quasi-cooperative' way can generate a total expected profit that is four times higher than if X is the only product considered. Even though this is not the optimal product design strategy, it shows the significantly beneficial impact of spreading the fixed cost over two products.

Finally, you may recall that earlier in this section we noted that the profit maximizing X and Z product configurations are quite similar. This similarity information can actually inform the company of the viability of setting up a technological platform strategy. A technological platform is a foundation for a range of individual product variations, i.e. something that is developed once and used in multiple applications, and its relevance to this study will be discussed towards the end of this section. In Exhibit 18.8, a potential technological platform consisting of graphic display, presence of backlight, data I/O method, accuracy, speed and connection method one is examined and outlined in column 4. When the platform is optimized over two products simultaneously, it is equipped with a backlight, networking capability and the capacity to apply a higher stress level. Most importantly, if the platform strategy is adopted, it can generate an expected profit nearly six times that of product X alone and almost 50 per cent above that generated from independent designs and shared fixed cost.

EXHIBIT 18.8 Product Design Strategy Options

	Design Product X Alone	Design Product Z Alone	Design Products X and Y Separately But Share Fixed Cost	Design and Nurture a Technological Platform
Forecast Profit (%)	100.0%	−1052.2%	401.7%	578.6%
Decision	Yes	No	Yes	Yes
Product Attributes				
Brand	Alpha	Alpha	Alpha	Alpha
Display	Graphic Display	Graphic Display	Graphic Display	Graphic Display
Backlight	No	Yes	No	Yes
I/O Method	Connect to PC	Connect to PC	Connect to PC	Networked
Accuracy	Current	Current	Current	Current
Speed	Faster	Faster	Faster	Faster
Connection Method	Method One	Method One	Method One	Method One
Stress Level Applied	Current	N/A	Current	Higher
Maximum Size Tested	N/A	Current	Current	Current
Price	108%	108%	108%/108%	108%/108%

Dependence Techniques with Non-Metric Dependent Variables

In this section, we will discuss three major dependence techniques useful in circumstances of non-metric dependent variables. As noted in Exhibit 18.1, conjoint analysis is a dependence technique that can deal with both metric and non-metric dependent variables. We have covered this technique in the former section, and therefore won't repeat it here. Instead we will elaborate discriminant analysis, logistic regression and Poisson regression.

Discriminant Analysis

Discriminant analysis is a multivariate technique used for predicting group membership on the basis of two or more independent variables. There are many situations where the marketing researcher's purpose is to classify objects into groups by a set of independent variables. Thus, the dependent variable in discriminant analysis is non-metric or categorical. In marketing, consumers are often categorized on the basis of heavy versus light users of a product, or buyers versus non-buyers of a service. Conversely, the independent variables in discriminant analysis are metric and often include characteristics such as demographics and psychographics. Additional insights into discriminant analysis can be found in the Closer Look at Research box.

> **Discriminant analysis** A technique for predicting group membership based on two or more independent variables. In this technique, the criterion or dependent variable is non-metric and categorical and the predictor or independent variables are metric.

A Closer Look at Research *(Using Technology)*
Discriminant Analysis – SPSS

Discriminant analysis is used primarily to classify individuals or other types of objects into two or more uniquely defined populations. An example of the use of discriminant analysis is a credit card company that would like to classify credit card applicants into two groups: (1) individuals who are considered good credit risks, and (2) individuals who are considered poor credit risks.

On the basis of this classification, individuals considered good credit risks would be offered credit cards, while individuals considered poor credit risks would not be offered credit cards. Different factors that could help the credit card company in determining which of the two groups applicants would fall into include salary, past credit history, level of education and number of dependents. The statistical software package SPSS could be used to determine where the line should be drawn between these two groups.

To learn more about the use of discriminant analysis in SPSS, go to the SPSS website at www.spss.com.

Let's elaborate the concept and use of discriminant analysis in greater detail with an example. A fast food restaurant, abbreviated as BYB for business confidentiality reasons, wants to see whether a lifestyle variable such as eating nutritious meals (X_1) and a demographic variable

EXHIBIT 18.9 Discriminant Analysis Scatter Plot of Lifestyle and Income Data about Fast Food Restaurant Patronage

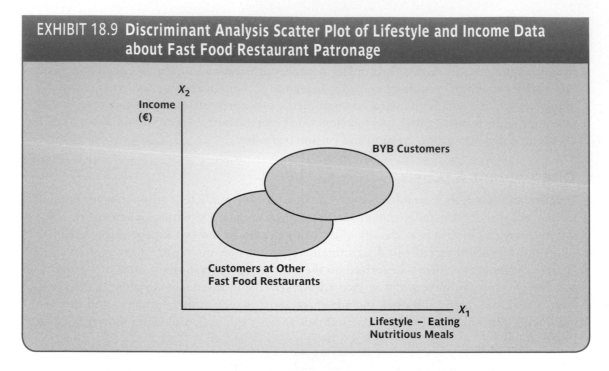

such as household income (X_2) are useful in distinguishing households visiting their restaurant from those visiting other fast food restaurants. Marketing researchers gathered data on X_1 and X_2 from a random sample of households that eat at fast food restaurants, including BYB. Discriminant analysis procedures would plot these data on a two-dimensional graph, as shown in Exhibit 18.9.

The scatter plot in Exhibit 18.9 yields two groups, one containing primarily BYB's customers and the other containing primarily households that patronize other fast food restaurants. From this example, it appears that X_1 and X_2 are critical discriminators of fast food restaurant patronage. Although the two areas overlap, the extent of the overlap does not seem to be substantial. This minimal overlap between groups is an important requirement for a successful discriminant analysis. Generally the plot tells us that BYB customers are more nutrition conscious and have relatively higher incomes.

Let us now turn to the fundamental statistics of discriminant analysis. As noted previously, the prediciton of group membership is the purpose of discriminant analysis. From a statistical perspective, this involves studying the direction of group differences based on finding a linear combination of independent variables – the **discriminant function** – that shows large differences in group means. Thus, discriminant analysis is a statistical tool for determining linear combinations of those independent variables and using this to discriminate between the categories of the dependent variable, i.e. predict group membership.

> **Discriminant function** The linear combination of independent variables as developed by discriminant analysis, which will best discriminate between the categories of the dependent variable.

To illustrate how a discriminant function is developed, our previous fast food restaurant example will be used. Recall that BYB is considering the possibility to predict whether a customer will or will not patronize their restaurant on the basis of lifestyle (X_1) and income (X_2). This is a case of two-group discriminant analysis in which the responsible researcher aims at finding a linear function of the independent variables that can show large differences in means between the two groups, i.e. patrons and non-patrons of BYB. The plots in Exhibit 18.9 show this is possible.

The **discriminant score**, or the Z score, is the basis for predicting to which group a particular individual belongs and is represented by a linear function. This Z score will be derived for each individual by means of the following equation:

$$Z_i = b_1 X_{1i} + b_2 X_{2i} \cdots + b_n X_{ni}$$

where

Z_i = ith individual's discriminant score

b_n = Discriminant function coefficient for the nth independent variable

X_{ni} = Individual's value on the nth independent variable

> **Discriminant score** In discriminant analysis, the Z score derived for each individual on the discriminant function.

Discriminant weights (b_n), or more formally called **discriminant function coefficients**, are estimates of the discriminatory power of a particular independent variable. These coefficients can be computed by means of a discriminant analysis software such as SPSS. The size of the coefficient associated with a particular independent variable is determined by the variance structure of the variables in the equation. Independent variables with large discriminatory power will have large weights, and those with little discriminatory power will have small weights.

> **Discriminant function coefficients** Also called discriminant weights, which are the multipliers of variables in the discriminant function, with the variables in their respective units of measurement.

Returning to our fast food restaurant example, suppose the researcher finds the standardized weights or coefficients in the equation to be

$$Z = b_1 X_1 + B_2 X_2$$
$$= .32 X_1 + .47 X_2$$

These results show that income (X_2) with a coefficient of .47 is the more important variable in discriminating between those patronizing BYB and those who patronize other fast food restaurants. With a coefficient of .32, the lifestyle variable (X_1) is also a variable of good discriminatory power.

EXHIBIT 18.10 Classification Matrix for BYB Patrons and Non-patrons

Classification Results[a]

			Predicted Group Membership		Total
	BYB Patrons = 1 ys. Non-Patrons = 2		1	2	
Original	Count	1	214	2	216
		2	0	80	80
	%	1	99.1	.9	100.0
		2	0	100.0	100.0

a. 99.3% of original grouped cases correctly classified.

Another important goal of discriminant analysis is classification of individuals or other types of objects into groups. In our example, the corresponding goal was to correctly classify consumers into BYB patrons and those who patronize other fast food restaurants. To determine whether the estimated discriminant function is a good predictor, a **classification (prediction) matrix** is developed. The classification matrix in Exhibit 18.10 shows that the discriminant function correctly classified 214 of the BYB patrons (99.1 per cent) and 80 of the non-patrons (100 per cent). The classification matrix also shows that the number of correctly classified consumers (214 patrons and 80 non-patrons) out of a total of 296 equals 99.3 per cent correctly classified. This resulting percentage is much higher than would be expected by chance.

> **Classification (or prediction) matrix** A table showing the number of correctly classified and misclassified cases.

Discriminant Analysis Applications in Marketing Research

While our example illustrated how discriminant analysis helped classify patrons and non-patrons of a restaurant based on selected lifestyle and demographic variables, the technqiue has many other applications such as the following:

- *Product research.* Discriminant analysis can help to distinguish between heavy, medium and light users of a product in terms of their consumption habits and lifestyles.
- *Image research.* Discriminant analysis can discriminate between customers who exhibit favourable perceptions of a store or company and those who do not.

- *Advertising research*. Discriminant analysis can assist in distinguishing how market segments differ in media consumption habits.
- *Direct marketing*. Discriminant analysis can help in distinguishing characteristics of consumers who respond to direct marketing solicitations and those who don't.

SPSS Application – Discriminant Analysis

The usefulness of discriminant analysis can be further demonstrated with our Jimmy Spice's restaurant database. Recall that with discriminant analysis the single dependent variable is a non-metric variable and the multiple independent variables are measured metrically. In the database, variables X30 – Distance Driven, X31 – Advertising Recall, and X32 – Gender are non-metric variables. The latter two are two-group variables, while the former is a three-group variable. We could use discriminant analysis to see if there are differences in perceptions of Jimmy Spice's restaurant between male and female customers or between the two different levels of advertising recall, or we could see if the perceptions differ depending on how far customers drove to eat at the restaurant.

Recently, Jimmy Spice's has been running an advertising campaign emphasizing its fresh, nice tasting food and good service. The owners want to know if the advertisments have been effective. One way to assess this is to see if recall of the advertisements influences customer perceptions of foods offered by the restaurant. Looking at variables X12–X21, there are three variables associated with customer perceptions of Jimmy Spice's restaurant foods – variables X15, X18 and X20.

The task is to determine if perceptions of Jimmy Spice's restaurant's foods are different between customers who recall advertisements and those who do not (X31 – Advertising Recall). Another way of stating this is, 'Can perceptions of Jimmy Spice's restaurant foods predict whether or not customers recall advertisements?'

The SPSS click-through sequence is ANALYSE → CLASSIFY → DISCRIMINANT, which leads to a dialogue box where you select the variables (see Exhibit 18.11). The dependent, non-metric variable is X31 and the independent, metric variables are X15, X18 and X20. The next thing you should do is transfer variable X31 to the Grouping Variable box at the top, and then click on the Define Range box just below it. You must tell the programme what the minimum and maximum numbers are for the grouping variable. In this case the minimum is 0 = Do Not Recall Advertisements and the maximum is 1 = Recall Advertisements, so just put these numbers in and click on Continue. Then you should transfer the food perception variables into the Independents box (X15, X18 and X20). Then click on the Statistics box and check Means, Univariate ANOVAS, and Continue. The Method default is Enter, and we will use this. Now click on Classify and Compute from group sizes. We do not know if the sample sizes are equal, so we must check this option. You should also click Summary Table and then Continue. We do not use any option under Save, so click OK to run the programme. Exhibit 18.11 shows the SPSS screen where you move the dependent and independent variables into their appropriate dialogue boxes. The Exhibit also shows the Statistics box.

There is a lot of SPSS output from discriminant analysis. Not every piece of this output information has to be used for a particular project. Here we will introduce five tables from the SPSS discriminant analysis output.

The first two tables are shown in Exhibit 18.12. The first important information to consider is in the Wilks' Lambda table. The Wilks' Lambda is a statistic that assesses whether the discriminant analysis is statistically significant. If this statistic is significant, as it is in our case (.000), then we look at the Classification Results table. At the bottom we see that the overall ability of

EXHIBIT 18.11 A SPSS Screen for Discriminant Analysis

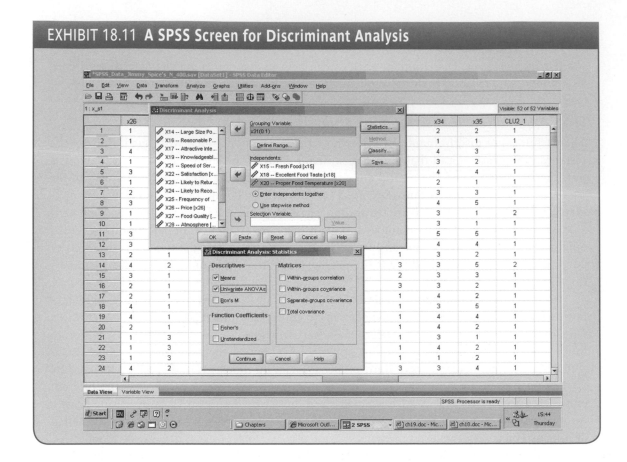

our discriminant function to predict group membership is 77.5 per cent. This is good because without the discriminant function we could predict with only 65.5 per cent accuracy (our sample sizes are recall advertisements = 139 and do not recall advertisements = 261, so if we placed all respondents in the do not recall advertisements group, we would predict with 65.5 per cent accuracy).

To find out which of the independent variables help us to predict group membership we look at the information from the two tables in Exhibit 18.13. Results in the table labelled Tests of Equality of Group Means show which food perception variables differ between advertising recall groups on a univariate basis. Note that variables X15, X18 and X20 are all statistically very significant (look at the numbers in the Sig. column). Thus, on a univariate basis all three food perception variables differ significantly between the different advertising recall groups.

To consider the variables from a multivariate perspective (discriminant analysis), we look at the information in the Structure Matrix table. First we identify the numbers in the Function column that are .30 or higher. This cut-off level is determined in a manner similar to a factor loading. All variables .30 or higher are considered to be helpful in predicting group membership. Like the univariate results, all three food perception variables help us to predict advertising recall group membership. X15 (.875) and X20 (.810) are very strong predictors while X18 (.607) is a moderately strong predictor.

EXHIBIT 18.12 SPSS Discriminant Analysis for X31 - Advertising Recall

Discriminant

Wilks' Lambda

Test of Function(s)	Wilks' Lambda	Chi-square	df	Sig.
1	.641	176.206	3	.000

Classification Results[a]

		X31 -- Ad Recall	Predicted Group Membership: Do Not Recall Ads	Predicted Group Membership: Recall Ads	Total
Original	Count	Do Not Recall Ads	221	40	261
		Recall Ads	50	89	139
	%	Do Not Recall Ads	84.7	15.3	100.0
		Recall Ads	36.0	64.0	100.0

a. 77.5% of original grouped cases correctly classified.

EXHIBIT 18.13 SPSS Discriminant Analysis for X31 - Advertising Recall Continued (1)

Discriminant

Tests of Equality of Group Means

	Wilks' Lambda	F	df1	df2	Sig.
X15 -- Fresh Food	.700	170.327	1	398	.000
X18 -- Excellent Food Taste	.829	82.117	1	398	.000
X21 -- Proper Food Temperature	.732	145.99	1	398	.000

Structure Matrix

	Function 1
X15 -- Fresh Food	.875
X20 -- Excellent Temperature	.810
X18 -- Excellent Food Taste	.607

Pooled within-groups correlations between discriminating variables and standardized canonical discriminant functions
Variables ordered by absolute size of correlation within function.

EXHIBIT 18.14 SPSS Discriminant Analysis for X31 – Advertising Recall Continued (2)

Discriminant

Group Statistics

X31 -- Ad Recall		Mean	Std. Deviation	Valid N (listwise) Unweighted	Weighted
Do Not Recall Ads	X15 -- Fresh Food	5.28	1.169	261	261.000
	X18 -- Excellent Food Taste	4.98	1.070	261	261.000
	X20 -- Proper Food Temperature	4.15	1.030	261	261.000
Recall Ads	X15 -- Fresh Food	6.65	.561	139	139.000
	X18 -- Excellent Food Taste	5.93	.822	139	139.000
	X20 -- Proper Food Temperature	5.35	.760	139	139.000
Total	X15 -- Fresh Food	5.76	1.194	400	400.000
	X18 -- Excellent Food Taste	5.31	1.088	400	400.000
	X20 -- Proper Food Temperature	4.57	1.104	400	400.000

To further interpret the discriminant function we look at the group means in the Group Statistics table (Exhibit 18.14). For all three variables (X15, X18 and X20) we see that customers who recalled advertisements had more favourable perceptions of the Jimmy Spice's foods (mean values for recalled advertisements group all higher). Thus, perceptions of the restaurant's foods are significantly more favourable for customers who recalled advertisements versus those who didn't. This finding can be used by the owners of the restaurant to further develop their advertising campaign.

Logistic Regression

In many marketing decision problems, the issue of concern is a dichotomous dependent variable. For example, the marketing researcher may be interested in predicting whether a person will buy a product. They may like to collect background information (such as gender, age, region of residence) from a sample of say 1,000 people and use these background variables to do the prediction.

You have learned that multiple regression is an appropriate technique for predicting the value of a dependent variable based on the given values of independent variables in the regression equation. However, for the above scenario concerning whether a person will buy a product, multiple regression cannot be used. This is because when we try to predict the values of a dependent variable coded, say, 0 or 1, we can consider the predicted values to be probabilities, i.e. the probability of getting a predicted value of 1. In multiple regression where the analyst tries to find a straight line that best fits the data, it is obviously often the case that values less than 0 or greater than 1, which are beyond the possible range allowed for in a dichotomous dependent variable.

EXHIBIT 18.15 The Logistic Curve

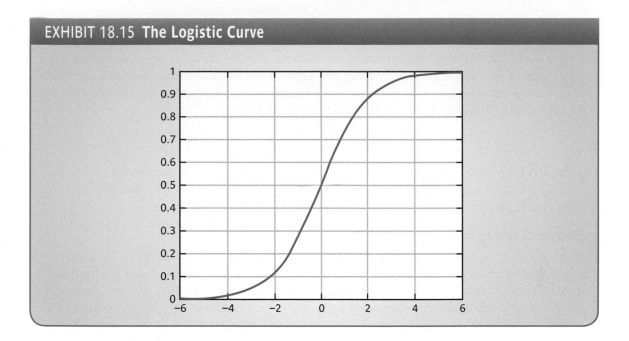

The second reason why multiple regression cannot be used for predicting the values of a dichotomous dependent variable is concerned with the issue of homogeneity of variance, one of the key assumptions of regression. In the case of a dichotomous dependent variable, the mean and the standard deviation are related because the standard deviation is where p is the mean of the variable. Considering the obvious functional relationship between the mean and the standard deviation, the assumption of homogeneity of variance across values of the dependent variable cannot be met.

Logistic regression was developed in the 1960s to deal with the above data analysis problem. To predict the value of a variable that ranges from 0 to 1, we can try to fit the data to an S-shaped curve. In this S-shaped curve, called the logistic curve, the probabilities of the dichotomous dependent variable can be any value from 0 to 1 (see Exhibit 18.15, where the values of the vertical axis are hypothetical).

Logistic Regression Equation

When fitting a logistic regression equation, you should note that the dependent variable is not the raw data values (i.e. 0 or 1), but the odds of the event of interest occurring. The general equation for logistic regression is:

$$\ln(\text{Odds}) = \alpha + \beta_1 X_1 + \beta_2 X_2 + \cdots - \beta_K X_K$$

where the terms on the right are the terms for the intercept and independent variables as they are in a multiple regression equation. However, on the left-hand side of the equation is the natural log of the odds, and the quantity ln(Odds) is called a logit. It can vary from minus to plus infinity, thereby eradicating the problem of the predicting outside the bounds (0 to 1) of the dichotomous dependent variable. Expressed in terms of the probability value, the odds are:

$$\text{Odds} = \frac{\text{Prob}}{1 - \text{Prob}}$$

Now, you may be confused by the fact that the logistic regression equation depicts a linear relationship but the logistic function is S-shaped. You should realize that the linear relationship is in the log odds, not in the original probabilities. Because what we are ultimately interested is the probability of an event (e.g. the probability that a person will buy a particular product), we need to do a transformation process that converts the logistic regression equation into an equation in the probability. This converted equation is in the form as follows.

$$P = \frac{1}{1 + e^{-(a + bX)}}$$

where P is the probability of an event of question occurring (which is the proportion of 1s in the binary dependent variable Y or the mean of Y), e is the base of the natural logarithm, X is the independent variable, and a and b are the parameters of the model.

Elements of Logistic Regression

Steps in logistic regression analysis are mostly similar to those for multiple regression. The analyst needs to identify a set of independent variables that are hypothesized to influence the probability of a particular outcome of the dichotomous dependent variable. In most cases, the particular outcome in which we are interested is the desired outcome (e.g. would a person of a given set of background characteristics buy my product?) or the one that is of the central concern in a study (e.g. would a person default on their loan repayment to my bank?) The analyst also needs to check the data for any unusual patterns, outliers and non-negligible missing data problems. He should make sure that the data meet the assumptions required by logistic regression analysis. It is also a good practice to derive a logistic regression model on half of the sample, and test the derived model on a holdout sample. This model validation process is particularly important when the analyst wants to predict the category membership (e.g. 'buy' or 'not buy' category) on future cases.

Aside from the above elements in which logistic and multiple regressions share their similarities, the two types of regression are also different in a number of respects. Because the mean and variance are related in the logistic regression scenario, it would be problematic to use the R^2, which is commonly used in multiple regression, to measure the amount of explained variance in logistic regression. Pseudo R^2, which can be derived by using SPSS, should be used in the logistic scenario. In addition, other things being equal, logistic regression requires a larger sample size than multiple regression for correct inference. A reasonable rule of thumb is that the number of cases should be at least thirty times of the number of parameters being estimated in the model.

Assumptions of Logistic Regression

Logistic regression requires that the independent variables be of scale, interval, or dichotomous nature. The form of the relationship to be estimated is assumed to be linear. The expected value of the error term is zero. There should be no autocorrelation, as well as no correlation between the error and any of the independent variables. There should also be no perfect multicollinearity between any pair of the independent variables. All these assumptions also apply to multiple regression.

On the other hand, there are two assumptions in multiple regression that logistic regression does not need to abide by. First is normality of errors, that is, the errors are assumed to be binomially distributed, which only approximates a normal distribution when the sample gets larger and larger. Second is homogeneity of variance, which can never be upheld in logistic regression given the dichotomous nature of its dependent variable.

An Illustrative Example of Logistic Regression

There are a number of factors contributing to the potential growth of both online usage and online purchase. One such factor is the assertion that Internet technology and its concomitant products are so internationalized that they appeal to consumers irrespective of national culture. As such, spatial cultural values become subsumed within global technology values. Technological products, including the Internet, are assumed as having values that are more global than local in nature. Stores (2000) noted that Internet technology is 'captivating people on every continent in virtually every national culture, and in many languages', while Hamel and Sampler (1998) declared the beginning of 'a world where customers are no longer hostages to geography'.

However, a common characteristic of the studies above is the use of educated conjecture and/ or macro-level evidence – i.e. from an overall supply or demand viewpoint – to support the internationalization claim of the Internet. There has been de facto no research whose major objective is to assess the existence and degree of internationalization from a micro-level perspective, i.e. from the individual consumer viewpoint. This is surprising because individual consumers, in aggregate, hold the key to deciding whether Internet technology has permeated the national culture in which they live. The Internet internationalization studies so far might only demonstrate that the Internet is successful in generating sizable usage in other cultures, but cannot go further to validate whether the success of the product is so deep as to transcend cultures.

In order to find an externally valid micro-level means to assess the relative impact of Internet technology and national culture in the internationalization process of online usage and online purchase, Shui and Dawson (2004) uses nationally representative samples to analyse the relative impacts of within-culture and between-culture dimensions on each of the two. The within-culture dimension is represented by a selection of national culture-excluded personal factors, while the between-culture dimension is broadly reflected by the degree of functioning of the national culture factor.

The nature of this study necessitates a cross-cultural research perspective. Four countries – Britain, Germany, Japan and Taiwan – have been selected to represent four different national cultures for two reasons. First, they are similar and comparable in respect of the internationalization level of Internet technology from a macro-level perspective. Second, Britain and Germany are located in Europe, while Japan and Taiwan are in Asia. This renders a balanced mix of countries in terms of geographical spread.

The data have been obtained from Taylor Nelson Sofres and comprise, among others, four nationally representative survey datasets. These datasets are of omnibus nature with the same questions and same measurements for each question. The questions are in three categories. First is about overall online usage and purchase, such as 'have you personally used the Internet in the past month?' and 'have you bought or ordered goods through the Internet in the past month?', and each is measured as a dichotomous yes or no variable. Second is about online purchase of different product types, such as groceries/food and music/CDs, and is also expecting a yes or no answer. Third is respondents' background information of gender, age and country of residence.

The British survey involved 2,240 interviews, and the Japanese survey comprised 1,532 respondents. A smaller sample size is found in both Taiwanese and German datasets, with 1,000 and 996 respectively.

Two hypothetical models have to be developed, with the dependent variable of each as online usage and online purchase respectively. As the survey data of both online usage and online purchase are collected in a binary form, i.e. respondents are asked whether they are engaged in online usage/purchase activities in the last month or not, logistic regression becomes an appropriate technique for testing the hypothetical models. These models consist of two types of independent variables: within-culture variables and between-culture variables. The former are represented by gender and age, while the latter use three dummy country variables as proxies. All these dummy variables are dichotomous, denoted as 1 if the respondent comes from a particular country or 0 if they do not come from this country. In this connection, the first dummy variable is 'Country1', which separates the British from the non-British; the second is 'Country2' dividing the German from the non-German; and the third is 'Country3', distinguishing the Japanese from the non-Japanese. A respondent is expected to be denoted as 1 in only one of the three dummy variables, or 0 in all of them. In the later case, the respondent is a Taiwanese. Greater details are illustrated as follows:

$y1 (online\ usage) = b_0 + b_1{}^*Gender + b_2{}^*Age + b_3{}^*Country1 + b_4{}^*Country2 + b_5{}^*Country3$

$y2 (online\ purchase) = b_0 + b_1{}^*Gender + b_2{}^*Age + b_3{}^*Country1 + b_4{}^*Country2 + b_5{}^*Country3$

where:

$y1 = 1$ if the respondent is engaged in online usage activities in the last month, and 0 if otherwise;

$y2 = 1$ if the respondent is engaged in online purchase activities in the last month, and 0 if otherwise;

$b_0 =$ the intercept;

Gender $= 1$ if the respondent is male, and 0 if otherwise;

Age $= 1$ if the respondent is aged $<= 20$, 2 if aged between 21 and 30, 3 if aged between 31 and 40, 4 if aged between 41 and 50, 5 if aged between 51 and 60, and 6 if aged 61–70;

Country1 $= 1$ if the respondent is a British, and 0 if otherwise;

Country2 $= 1$ if the respondent is a German, and 0 if otherwise;

Country3 $= 1$ if the respondent is a Japanese, and 0 if otherwise;

b_1, b_2, b_3, b_4, and b_5 are logistic regression coefficients for their corresponding variables.

The degree of performance of the two logistic regression models is subject to two fundamental questions. First, how well does a particular model classify the observed data? Second, how likely is it that the sample results are given the parameter estimates? The classification test will be adopted to address the first question, while the likelihood test will be employed to hit the second question. Results are shown in Exhibit 18.16.

At the SPSS default cut-off point of 0.5, both models have achieved an overall correct rate of approximately 70 per cent or above. This indicates that most of the respondents in the two

EXHIBIT 18.16 Tests for Diagnosing Logical Regression Model Performance

Test Type	Test Variable	Online Usage Model	Online Purchase Model
Classification test	Overall correct	68.9%	94.8%
	Alpha	30.8%	4.9%
	Proportional chance criterion	57.4%	90.7%
Likelihood test	-2 log likelihood	6262.424	2123.866
	Chi-square	616.580	105.718
	p-value	0.000	0.000

models, especially the online purchase model, have been correctly classified. In considering a baseline measure against which the classification results can be further assessed, Shiu and Dawson uses the proportional chance criterion, which acknowledges unequal prior probabilities caused by unequal group sizes, and therefore takes into account the actual group size of the observed frequencies. Results show that both models outperform their respective proportional chance criteria, signifying a satisfactory classification capability of the models.

A likelihood test on both models shows that, under the customary rule of 95 per cent confidence level, both models show significant improvement over a hypothetical model with only the intercept.

Results of the four-country logistic regression model on online usage, as in Exhibit 18.17, show that the within-culture dimension represented by gender and age is significantly influencing whether respondents are engaged in online usage with 95 per cent confidence level. On the contrary, none of the three country variables are significant with the same confidence level. This is further evidenced by only a slight change in probabilities of online usage, from 55.18 per cent to 57.71 per cent, between four typical respondents from each of the four countries with the same demographic backgrounds as males aged at twenties. The same analysis on the four nationalities, again keeping the demographic backgrounds constant but this time focusing on females aged 31 to 40, also typifies a narrow range of online usage probabilities, this time from 54.21 per cent to 56.76 per cent. This indicates that, for respondents of the same gender and age backgrounds, the probability change in online usage does not change significantly between countries.

Between the two significant within-culture variables, gender seems to be a bigger contributor to consumer online usage decisions than age as evidenced by a comparison between their odds ratios.

Results of the four-country logistic regression model on online purchase, as in Exhibit 18.18, show a strongly contrasting picture. All the within-culture and between-culture variables are found to be significantly influencing consumer decision on whether to buy through the Internet. What is more, all the between-culture variables have a larger magnitude of odds ratio than each of the within-culture variables, signifying that national culture is more influential than Internet technology in consumer online purchase decisions. For example, among all the male respondents aged 21 to 30 across the four countries, the average probability change of online purchase is more than 6 per cent from 62.41 per cent in Taiwan to 68.95 per cent in Germany. As another example, among all female respondents aged 31 to 40, the average probability change is again more than 6 per cent from 60.49 per cent in Taiwan to 67.19 per cent in Germany.

EXHIBIT 18.17 Four-Country Logistic Regression Model on Online Usage

	Intercept	Gender	Age	Country1	Country2	Country3
Beta coefficient	0.598	0.584	−0.483	−0.141	0.160	0.017
Standard error	0.099	0.062	0.022	0.088	0.102	0.091
Wald statistic	36.188	89.609	461.293	2.550	2.444	0.034
Significance	0.000	0.000	0.000	0.110	0.118	0.854
Odds ratio	1.818	1.793	0.617	0.869	1.174	1.017

EXHIBIT 18.18 Four-Country Logistic Regression Model on Online Purchase

	Intercept	Gender	Age	Country1	Country2	Country3
Beta coefficient	−3.595	0.482	−0.288	1.390	1.744	1.583
Standard error	0.293	0.125	0.043	0.280	0.291	0.281
Wald statistic	150.932	14.936	44.667	24.614	35.907	31.789
Significance	0.000	0.000	0.000	0.000	0.000	0.000
Odds ratio	0.027	1.619	0.750	4.015	5.721	4.870

Therefore we can conclude that the between-culture dimension, represented by the three dummy country variables, is more influential than the within-culture dimension in consumer choice of online purchase. This implies that national culture has been playing a significant role in mitigating the internationalization capability of the transaction/consumption function of the Internet. Second, online usage is more successful than online purchase in internationalizing across national cultures. This indicates the functioning of cultural impediments on business-to-consumer electronic commerce in an international context (Shiu and Dawson, 2004).

Poisson Regression

Consider this scenario. A cinema manager would like to know whether the frequency of a person going to the cinema can be predicted by a set of demographic and attitudinal variables. She believes that if such a predictive relationship can be established, she will be in a position to utilize her marketing resources for promotion and segmentation purposes in a better way. For data analysts, the problem of this scenario is that the dependent variable is neither an interval/ratio variable, nor a dichotomous variable. Therefore, neither multiple regression nor logistic regression can be used.

Fortunately, there is an unconventional type of regression, called Poisson regression, which is appropriate in dealing with the above scenario. Poisson regression is used to model the number of occurrences of an event of interest (such as the number of times a person goes to the cinema in a given time period say six months) as a function of a set of independent variables. Therefore, if your dependent variable is of count data type, you can consider using this type of regression.

Major Assumptions of Poisson regression

As can be inferred by its name, Poisson regression assumes that the dependent variable has a Poisson distribution. Another important assumption is that the nth and $n+1^{th}$ time of occurrence of an event of interest must be independent of each other. That is, using the above scenario as an example, a person's patronage of a cinema this time will not make patronage next time more or less likely. However, the probability of the number of occurrences of an event per unit time can be related to covariates such as time of day.

Poisson regression also assumes that the logarithm of the dependent variable's predicted value can be modelled by a linear combination of parameters. In its simplest form, a Poisson regression equation is written like the following:

$$\log(E(Y)) = a + bx$$

Application of Poisson Regression

As already stated, Poisson regression is appropriate when the dependent variable is of count data type, such as the number of times of visiting the cinema or the number of times of buying new clothes.

Another type of application of Poisson regression is when the dependent variable is of rate data type. Here 'rate' refers to a count of occurrences of an event within a particular unit of observation divided by some particular measure of that unit's exposure. For example, sustainable marketers may like to model plant species survival rates in different forests of the world, and the rate would be the number of plant species per square kilometre. Commerce policy planners may like to count the number of small businesses in different industrial districts, and in this case the rate could be the number of small businesses per square kilometre of floor area within each industrial district being studied. In both of the above examples, the exposure is the unit area, which can be handled as an offset during Poisson regression analysis. An offset is where the exposure variable is put on the right-hand side of the equation, but its parameter estimate is constrained to 1, as shown below:

$$\log(E(Y)) = \log(\text{exposure}) + a + bx$$

which implies

$$\log(E(Y)) - \log(\text{exposure}) = \log[(E(Y)/\text{exposure})] = a + bx$$

Overdispersion Problem

Any data set that follows Poisson distribution must have its mean equal to its variance. When we are attempting to fit a set of data to a Poisson regression equation, it is possible that the observed variance is much greater than the mean. In statistical terms, this is called 'overdispersion', which arises from the absence of a random disturbance term that can take account of unexplained variation. Although overdispersion does not affect the regression coefficients, it can significantly overestimate test statistics and underestimate standard errors, which can lead to incorrect conclusions. Therefore, marketing researchers using this special type of regression should always check the Poisson regression model so derived, and if overdispersion really occurs, they need to make corresponding adjustments. The illustrative example below demonstrates how a Poisson regression model should be checked and adjusted for solving the overdispersion problem.

An Illustrative Example of Poisson Regression

Convenience and health are arguably the two prevailing consumption trends in the British food market, with single-adult households as keener followers than many other household types. In the light of the increasing importance of these trends, Shiu and Dawson (2004b) conducted a study to attempt a corresponding segmentation analysis.

To identify the food products that can reliably represent the convenience and health trends respectively in the industry, Shiu and Dawson carried out a consumer face-to-face sampling survey that aimed to obtain a list of food products considered as convenience- or health-oriented. Respondents were asked to evaluate whether a food product in question is convenience- or health-oriented on a five-point Likert scale (from strongly agree to strongly disagree). A food product is regarded as convenience- or health-oriented if 70 per cent or more of the respondents choose 'strongly agree' or 'agree'. Results, as illustrated in Exhibit 18.19, show that 19 convenience-oriented

EXHIBIT 18.19 **The Convenience- and Health-Oriented Food Products Defined in this Study**

Convenient-Oriented Food Product	Health-Oriented Food Product
Bacon and ham, cooked, including canned	Yoghurt (90%)
Cooked poultry, not purchased in cans	Fully skimmed milk (73.4%)
Takeaway cooked poultry (100%)	Semi and other skimmed milk (83.3%)
Other cooked meat, not purchased in cans	Reduced fat spreads (73.3%)
Other canned meat and canned meat	Low fat spreads (73.3%)
Meat pies, ready to eat (90%)	Vegetable juice (76.7%)
Sausage rolls, ready to eat (96.7%)	Bread, wholemeal, sliced (93.3%)
Pate (70%)	Bread, wholemeal, unsliced (90%)
Delicatessen type sausages (80%)	Oatmeal and oat products (86.6%)
Meat pastes and spreads (76.7%)	Muesli (86.7%)
Meat pies, pasties and puddings (80%)	Other high fibre breakfast cereals (86.7%)
Takeaway meat pies, pasties and puddings	
Ready meals (96.7%)	
Takeaway ready meals (89.7%)	
Fish, cooked (73.3%)	
Takeaway fish products (72.4%)	
Baked beans in sauce (93.1%)	
Other canned beans and pulses (70%)	
Soups, canned (90%)	

Note: Number in each bracket refers to the proportion of the number of respondents who strongly agree or agree to the corresponding food product as convenience- or health-oriented.

and 11 health-oriented food products pass the 70 per cent cut-off test, which are therefore used for representing the convenience and health trends respectively. Based on the data collected from the National Food Survey in Britain, each of these food products will be recorded as either 'consumed' or 'not consumed' for this study. You should now realize that the dependent variables – convenience and health trends respectively – are in essence a total of the responses of a number of dichotomous variables. In other words they are a count number. The value of the dependent variables can be any integer from 0 to 19 for the convenience trend, and from 0 to 11 for the health trend. As the distribution of a collection of these non-negative, integer-valued count numbers is always highly skewed and far from normal, the standard regression technique is not suitable. These count numbers are not categorical so logistic regression technique is also not appropriate. Poisson regression, which has been developed by Nelder and Wedderburn (1972) and McCullagh and Nelder (1989) among many others and which fits a dependent variable of count number type, is adopted. Although the dependent variable of Poisson regression is supposedly Poisson distribution, it is not always necessary.

There is ample evidence of the relationship between demographic variables and food market segmentation. Davis and Worrall (1998) are also confident in stating that 'demographic characteristics play a large part in determining food purchases'. In light of this, Shiu and Dawson decided to use six demographic variables as segmentation variables of the convenience and health trends in Britain. These variables are:

Gender: male is labelled as '1', and female as '0'.

Age group (abbreviated as Age): coded number from 1 to 6 representing respective age group, with 15 to 20 coded as 1, 21–30 coded as 2, 31–40 coded as 3, 41–50 coded as 4, 51–60 coded as 5, 61–70 coded as 6.

Occupation: two dummy variables are created. Occ1 is '1' if the respondent is an employer, manager or professional, and '0' if otherwise. Occ2 is '1' if the respondent is involved in clerical or manual work, and '0' if otherwise. Respondents not belonging to Occ1 or Occ2 are categorized as economically inactive.

Income: two dummy variables are created. Inc1 is '1' if the respondent belongs to lower one-third income category, and '0' if otherwise. Inc2 is '1' if the respondent falls into middle one-third income category, and '0' if otherwise. Respondents not categorized so far belong to upper one-third income category. The categorization is based on the calculation of weekly net family income divided by number of members in the family.

Household size (abbreviated as Hhsize): number of available members in the household. To contain the outlier effect, households with more than 7 members are all coded as 7.

Region of residence (abbreviated as Region): living in Greater London is labelled as '1', and living in other areas is labelled as '0'.

The two hypothetical Poisson regression models are as follows:

Convenience food trend $= b_0 + b_1{}^*Gender + b_2{}^*Age + b_3{}^*Occ1 + b_4{}^*Occ2 + b_5{}^*Inc1 + b_6{}^*Inc2 + b_7{}^*Hhsize + b_8{}^*Region$

Health food trend $= b_0 + b_1{}^*Gender + b_2{}^*Age + b_3{}^*Occ1 + b_4{}^*Occ2 + b_5{}^*Inc1 + b_6{}^*Inc2 + b_7{}^*Hhsize + b_8{}^*Region$

where:

– Convenience and health food trends are referred to the number of varieties of food products representing each of the two trends consumed during a Survey period in 1998;

– b_0 is the intercept;

– $b_1, b_2 \ldots b_7, b_8$ are regression coefficients for their respective variables.

Besides multicollinearity, which has been checked and passed with satisfaction, overdispersion is another potential problem of Poisson regression that needs to be checked. When doing the checking, the focus point of concern should be the scaled deviation relative to the degrees of freedom of the regression results. A ratio significantly greater than 1 signifies the presence of the problem. This is found in one of the two Poisson regression models, as evidenced by a large scaled deviation relative to degrees of freedom, leading to the said ratio of 1.4525 of the model. To tackle this problem, the scale parameter, which has a value of 1 by default, is adjusted to be the square root of the ratio of the Pearson's Chi-square to its degrees of freedom. As a result, the ratio of the scaled deviance to its degrees of freedom decreases from 1.45 to 1.16, thereby bringing any regression results so derived to a reliable condition. See Exhibit 18.20 for details of the adjustment results.

Results are outlined in Exhibit 18.21 and 18.22, where we can see household size and region of residence are significant in segmenting the convenience-oriented food product market among single adult households. Two different variables – gender and age – are effective segmentation criteria for the health-oriented food product market of the same household type.

EXHIBIT 18.20 Scaled Deviation per Degree of Freedom for Checking Over-Dispersion

		Convenience Food Trend Model	Health Food Trend Model
	Degrees of freedom	1,372	1,372
Before adjustment	Scaled deviation	1,992.8574	1,600.6242
	Scale parameter	1	1
	Scaled deviance/degree of freedom	1.4525	1.1666
After adjustment	Scaled deviation	1,550.5661	1,601.8027
	Scale parameter	1.1337	0.9996
	Scaled deviance/degree of freedom	1.1302	1.1675

EXHIBIT 18.21 Poisson Regression Model for the Convenience Food Trend

Parameter	Coefficient	Chi-square[1]		Probability>Chi-square[1]	
		Before	After	Before	After
Intercept	−0.0586	0.2461	0.1915	0.6198	0.6617
Gender	0.0780	2.2651	1.7624	0.1323	0.1843
Age group	0.0302	2.9702	2.3110	0.0848	0.1285
Occupation1	−0.1732	3.0489	2.3723	0.0808	0.1235
Occupation2	0.0303	0.3068	0.2387	0.5796	0.6251
Income1	0.0741	1.2100	0.9415	0.2713	0.3319
Income2	−0.0746	1.2369	0.9624	0.2661	0.3266
Household size	0.1889	44.0743	34.2925	0.0001	0.0001
Region of residence	−0.3079	16.0646	12.4992	0.0001	0.0004

Notes: Number of observations=1,381.

[1]'Before' and 'After' refer to analysis results before and after an adjustment has been made to solve the overdispersion problem, if any, respectively.

EXHIBIT 18.22 Poisson Regression Model for the Health Food Trend

Parameter	Coefficient	Chi-square[1]		Probability>Chi-square[1]	
		Before	After	Before	After
Intercept	−0.0323	0.0664	0.0665	0.7966	0.7965
Gender	−0.2691	24.2543	24.2722	0.0001	0.0001
Age group	0.0714	15.0186	15.0297	0.0001	0.0001
Occupation1	0.0025	0.0007	0.0007	0.9792	0.9792
Occupation2	0.0536	0.8565	0.8571	0.3547	0.3545
Income1	−0.1367	3.7098	3.7125	0.0541	0.0540
Income2	−0.0424	0.4150	0.4154	0.5194	0.5193
Household size	0.1044	10.4031	10.4108	0.0013	0.0013
Region of residence	−0.0086	0.0145	0.0145	0.9042	0.9042

Notes: Number of observations=1,381.

[1]'Before' and 'After' refer to analysis results before and after an adjustment has been made to solve the overdispersion problem, if any, respectively.

Examining Restaurant Image Positions for LBD in France

LBD is a popular fast food restaurant brand in France. The restaurant has successfully blended the prevailing fast food concept with the traditional delicacy of French cuisine. It offers a selection of foods to its customers, including brioches, Viennese buns, pastries, savoury snacks, sandwiches, salads and hot dishes.

Recently, the management team of LBD began asking themselves some fundamental questions about the restaurant's operations and its way forward. The restaurant discussed these questions with a local marketing research firm and subsequently decided to appoint the firm to conduct marketing research in order to better understand their customers' attitudes and feelings. More specifically, the restaurant wanted to gain information and insights into the following set of questions:

1 What are the major factors customers use when selecting a restaurant to dine at, and what is the relative importance of each of these factors?

2 What image do customers have of LBD and its two major competitors?

3 Is LBD providing quality and satisfaction to its customers?

4 Do any of LBD's current marketing strategies need to be changed, and if so in what ways?

To address these questions, the marketing research firm recommended conducting a survey using an Internet panel approach. Initial contact was made with potential respondents using a random digit dialling telephone survey to screen for individuals who were patrons of LBD as well as customers of its major competing restaurants (i.e. MD and CC). Respondents had to have eaten at fast food restaurants in last two months, have patronized MD, CC and LBD restaurants before, and also have a minimum annual household income of €15,000. If an individual passed all these three screening questions, they would be directed to a website to complete the survey.

Since this was the first time LBD conducted any marketing research, it was considered exploratory and the marketing research firm recommended a sample size of 200. If the results from this sample were helpful, a larger sample size would be contemplated in order to increase the precision of the findings. The questionnaire collected data on the importance ratings of restaurant selection factors, perceptions of the images of the three restaurants being studied on the same set of factors, and selected classification information on the respondents. When the quota of 200 completed questionnaires was reached, the sample included 86 respondents most familiar with MD, 65 most familiar with CC, and 49 most familiar with LBD. This last criterion was used to determine which restaurant a particular respondent should evaluate.

A database for the questions in this case study is available in SPSS format at www.mhhe.com/shiu09. The name of the database is SPSS_Data_LBD.sav. Please note that to observe business confidentiality, the raw data provided in this case have been significantly altered and therefore do not reflect the reality about LBD or its major competitors.

The initial analysis of the data focused on the importance ratings of the restaurant selection factors. The importance ratings are variables X1–X6 in the LBD's database. Exhibit 18.23 shows that food quality and speed of service were the two most important factors. To derive this exhibit, the click-through sequence is ANALYSE → DESCRIPTIVE STATISTICS → FREQUENCIES. Highlight variables X1–X6 and move them to the Variable(s) box. Then go to the Statistics box and check Mean, and then click Continue and OK. The least important factor was competent employees, which had a mean of 3.12. This does not mean employees aren't important. It simply means they are relatively less important compared to the other factors respondents were asked about in the survey. To sum up, these respondents wanted good food, fast service and reasonable prices.

The next task was to examine respondents' perceptions of the three restaurants being studied. Using the restaurant perceptions variables, the marketing research firm conducted an ANOVA to see if there were any differences in the perceptions of the three restaurants. Results are shown in Exhibits 18.24 and 18.25. To derive these exhibits, the click-through sequence is ANALYSE → COMPARE MEANS → ONEWAY ANOVA. Highlight variables X7–X12 and move them to the Dependent List box, and then highlight variable X22 and move it to the Factor Box. Next go to the Options box and check Descriptive, and then click Continue and OK.

EXHIBIT 18.23 Importance Ratings of Restaurant Selection Factors

Frequencies

Statistics

		X1 -- Large Portions	X2 -- Competent Employees	X3 -- Food Quality	X4 -- Speed of Service	X5 -- Atmosphere	X6-- Reasonable Prices
N	Valid	200	200	200	200	200	200
	Missing	0	0	0	0	0	0
Mean		4.95	3.12	6.09	5.99	4.74	5.39

EXHIBIT 18.24 One-Way ANOVA for the Three Restaurants being Studied

Descriptives

		N	Mean	Std. Deviation	Std. Error	95% Confidence Interval for Mean		Minimum	Maximum
						Lower Bound	Upper Bound		
X7 – Large Portions	MD	86	3.57	.805	.087	3.40	3.74	2	4
	CC	65	2.77	.880	.109	2.55	2.99	1	4
	LBD	49	3.39	.862	.123	3.14	3.64	1	4
	Total	200	3.26	.910	.064	3.14	3.39	1	4
X8 – Competent Employees	MD	86	5.15	.623	.067	5.02	5.28	4	6
	CC	65	3.25	.919	.114	3.02	3.47	2	5
	LBD	49	2.49	.617	.088	2.31	2.67	2	4
	Total	200	3.88	1.355	.096	3.69	4.07	2	6
X9 – Food Quality	MD	86	6.42	.659	.071	6.28	6.56	5	7
	CC	65	5.12	.839	.104	4.92	5.33	4	7
	LBD	49	6.86	.354	.051	6.76	6.96	6	7
	Total	200	6.10	.969	.069	5.97	6.24	4	7
X10 – Speed of Service	MD	86	4.35	.943	.102	4.15	4.55	3	6
	CC	65	3.02	.857	.106	2.80	3.23	2	5
	LBD	49	2.27	.670	.096	2.07	2.46	1	3
	Total	200	3.40	1.216	.086	3.24	3.57	1	6
X11 – Atmosphere	MD	86	6.09	.890	.096	5.90	6.28	4	7
	CC	65	4.35	.799	.099	4.16	4.55	3	6
	LBD	49	6.59	.537	.077	6.44	6.75	5	7
	Total	200	5.65	1.210	.086	5.48	5.82	3	7
X12 – Reasonable Prices	MD	86	5.50	.763	.082	5.34	5.66	4	6
	CC	65	5.00	.810	.100	4.80	5.20	4	6
	LBD	49	5.49	.767	.110	5.27	5.71	4	6
	Total	200	5.34	.810	.057	5.22	5.45	4	6

EXHIBIT 18.25 One-Way ANOVA for the Differences in Restaurant Perceptions Variables

Oneway

ANOVA

		Sum of Squares	df	Mean Square	F	Sig.
X7 -- Large Portions	Between Groups	24.702	2	12.351	17.349	.000
	Within Groups	140.253	197	.712		
	Total	164.955	199			
X8 -- Competent Employees	Between Groups	259.779	2	129.889	242.908	.000
	Within Groups	105.341	197	.535		
	Total	365.120	199			
X9 -- Food Quality	Between Groups	98.849	2	49.425	110.712	.000
	Within Groups	87.946	197	.446		
	Total	186.795	199			
X10 -- Speed of Service	Between Groups	150.124	2	75.062	102.639	.000
	Within Groups	144.071	197	.731		
	Total	294.195	199			
X11 -- Atmosphere	Between Groups	169.546	2	84.773	136.939	.000
	Within Groups	121.954	197	.619		
	Total	291.500	199			
X12 -- Reasonable Prices	Between Groups	10.810	2	5.405	8.892	.000
	Within Groups	119.745	197	.608		
	Total	130.555	199			

An overview of the findings presented in Exhibits 18.23, 18.24 and 18.25 is provided in Exhibit 18.26, which is quite revealing. On the most important factor (food quality), LBD was rated the highest (mean = 6.86; see Exhibit 18.24), but MD's was a close second (mean = 6.42). LBD was also rated the highest on atmosphere (mean = 6.59) but this factor was only fifth most important. For speed of service (second most important) and competent employees (least important), LBD was rated the lowest of the three restaurants.

A concise way to convey the results of the above analysis is to prepare an importance performance chart (IPC). An IPC has quadrants (A–D) that are described as follows:

Quadrant A: Modifications are needed.
Quadrant B: Good job – no need to modify.
Quadrant C: Don't worry – low priority.
Quadrant D: Rethink – a possible overkill.

The IPC for LBD is shown in Exhibit 18.27. The chart shows that in terms of food quality and prices, the restaurant is doing well. But in comparison to the competition, there are several areas for improvement.

EXHIBIT 18.26 Summary of Findings from Exhibits 18.23, 18.24 and 18.25

Attributes	Rankings[a]	Competitor Means			Sig.
		MD	CC	LBD	
X7 – Large portions	4	3.57	2.77	3.39	.000
X8 – Competent employees	6	5.15	3.25	2.49	.000
X9 – Food quality	1	6.42	5.12	6.86	.000
X10 – Speed of service	2	4.35	3.02	2.27	.000
X11 – Atmosphere	5	6.09	4.35	6.59	.000
X12 – Reasonable prices	3	5.50	5.00	5.49	.000
N = 200 total		86	65	49	.000

[a]Rankings are based on mean importance ratings.

EXHIBIT 18.27 Importance Performance Chart for LBD

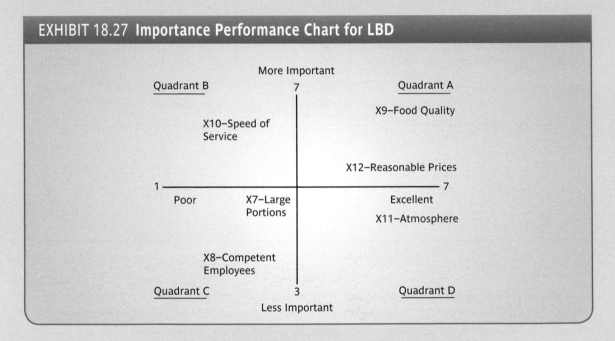

Questions

1 What are the other areas of improvement for LBD?

2 Run post hoc ANOVA tests among the three restaurants. What additional problems or challenges do the results of the tests reveal?

3 What new marketing strategies would you suggest to LBD?

4 Understand how to use multivariate analysis in marketing research.

5 Distinguish between dependence and interdependence techniques.

6 Apply metric dependence techniques including multiple regression analysis, ANOVA, MANOVA and conjoint analysis to marketing research.

7 Understand when and how to use discriminant analysis.

8 Identify the peculiarities of logical regression and Poisson regression analysis.

Summary of Learning Objectives

■ **Define multivariate analysis.**

Multivariate analysis is about a group of statistical procedures used to simultaneously analyse three or more variables. Multiple regression, discriminant analysis, factor analysis and cluster analysis are some of the popular multivariate statistical techniques used in marketing research.

■ **Understand the importance of multivariate analysis in marketing research.**

Multivariate analysis is very important in marketing research because most business problems are multidimensional. Marketing managers are often concerned about various aspects of the consumer (e.g. demographics, lifestyles), consumers' purchasing process (e.g. motives, perceptions) and competition. Suitable multivariate techniques can be deployed to assist marketing managers in simultaneously assessing a set or sets of variables.

■ **Distinguish between dependence and interdependence techniques.**

Multivariate techniques can be classified into dependence and interdependence techniques. A dependence technique is one in which a variable or set of variables is identified as the dependent variable to be predicted or explained by other, independent variables. An interdependence technique is one in which no single variable or group of variables is defined as being independent or dependent. The goal of interdependence techniques is data reduction, or grouping things together.

■ **Apply metric dependence techniques including multiple regression, ANOVA, MANOVA and conjoint analysis to marketing research.**

Multiple regression is an extension of the bivariate regression analysis we discussed in Chapter 17. It is an appropriate technique when the researcher wishes to examine the relative influence of several independent variables on a dependent variable. For each independent variable a separate regression coefficient is calculated that describes its predictive relationship with the dependent variable.

ANOVA is used to determine the statistical significance of the difference between two or more means. The ANOVA technique calculates the variance of the values between groups of respondents and compares it to the variance of the values within the groups. If the between-group variance is significantly greater than the within-group variance as indicated by the F ratio, the means are significantly different. The statistical significance between means in ANOVA is detected through the use of a follow-up test. The Scheffé test is one type of follow-up test. The test examines the differences between all possible pairs of sample means against a high and low confidence range. If the difference between a pair of means falls outside the confidence interval, then the means can be considered statistically different.

MANOVA is designed to examine multiple dependent variables across single or multiple independent variables. It would be a good choice for assessing the effect of independent variables like income or gender on the entire group of products such as golf-related products within the same product family.

Conjoint analysis can be used in marketing research to determine how consumers value different attributes that make up a given product, service, marketing communication message, or any other object. One big assumption for the effective use of conjoint analysis is that consumers evaluate the value of an object (such as a product) by aggregating the separate amounts of value provided by each attribute of the product. Utility, a measure of an individual's subjective preference to an object or an attribute of an object, is the conceptual basis for measuring value of product attributes in conjoint analysis.

■ **Apply non-metric dependence techniques including discriminant analysis, logistic regression, Poisson regression and conjoint analysis to marketing research.**
The purpose of discriminant analysis is to predict a variable from a set of independent variables. Discriminant analysis uses independent variables to classify observations into mutually exclusive categories. It can also be used to determine whether statistically significant differences exist between the average discriminant score profiles of two or more groups.

When the issue of concern is a dichotomous dependent variable, logistic regression will be an appropriate option. This multivariate technique aims at predicting the value of a dichotomous dependent variable that ranges from 0 to 1, and in doing so, tries to fit the data to an S-shaped curve.

Poisson regression is used to model the number of occurrences of an event of interest (such as the number of times a person goes to the cinema in a given time period say six months) as a function of a set of independent variables. Therefore, it will be a suitable choice if the dependent variable is of count data type.

Conjoint analysis can deal with both metric and non-metric dependent variables.

Key Terms and Concepts

Analysis of variance (ANOVA) 592	Dummy variables 588
Beta coefficient 584	*F*-test 593
Classification (or prediction) matrix 606	Follow-up test 593
	Interdependence technique 582
Dependence technique 581	Model *F* statistic 585
Discriminant analysis 603	Multicollinearity 590
Discriminant function 604	Multivariate analysis 580
Discriminant function coefficients 605	Multiple regression analysis 583
Discriminant score 605	

Review Questions

1 Why are multivariate techniques so important to managers today?
2 How do multivariate techniques differ from univariate and bivariate techniques?
3 What is the difference between dependence and interdependence techniques?
4 What is the purpose of discriminant analysis?
5 How might discriminant analysis be used to solve a marketing problem or identify a marketing opportunity?

Discussion Questions

1 **SPSS Exercise.** Review the Marketing Research in Action for this chapter. There were three restaurant competitors – MD, CC and LBD. Results for a one-way ANOVA of the restaurant image variables were provided. Now run post hoc ANOVA tests to see where the group differences are. Make recommendations regarding new marketing strategies for LBD after taking into account its major competitors.

2 Discriminant analysis is a frequently used multivariate technique when the objective is to find out important variables that can identify group membership of some type. What is the role of the discriminant function coefficients in identifying these important variables? In the chapter on regression, multicollinearity among the independent variables in a regression equation was highlighted as a potential problem for interpretation of the results. Do you think multicollinearity would also pose a problem for interpreting discriminant analysis results? Why or why not?

3 **Experience the Internet.** Access the Internet and select a particular search engine. Use appropriate keywords of your choice in order to identify five major marketing research companies with operations in Europe that provide data analysis services. Compare and contrast the information in their websites, and identify the strength and weaknesses of each in terms of their data analysis services. Which would you choose to conduct a marketing research project that incorporates data analysis for you? Why? Prepare a two-page report so that you can share your findings and opinions with other students in the class.

Multivariate Analysis: Interdependence Techniques and Structural Equation Modelling

LEARNING OBJECTIVES

After reading this chapter, you will be able to

☑ Apply factor analysis to marketing research.

☑ Apply cluster analysis to marketing research.

☑ Apply perceptual mapping to marketing research.

☑ Understand the fundamentals of structural equation modelling.

> " Proper analysis of business data can lead to a ROI of around 112 per cent in a very short time.
>
> *–Robert Blumstein*
> *Research Director of CRM, IDC* "

Uncover the True Scene of the Forest from the Mountain of Trees

Tukey (1977), a worldwide known statistician, noted that the basic challenge with any body of data is to make it effectively understood. There are many data analysis techniques for researchers to uncover the information that is carried by data. However, most of these techniques are vulnerable to anomalies in data, which can easily lead to erroneous conclusions.

Tukey therefore advocated a philosophical approach to data analysis that postpones the usual pre-determined assumptions about what kind of model the data follow but instead allows the data itself to reveal its underlying structure and model. He suggested the use of exploratory data analysis, much of which is about graphics, such as histograms, mean plots and standard deviation plots. These graphical results could entice the data to reveal its structural secrets, and help the researcher to gain serendipity from the data.

In brief, what Tukey proclaimed is to open-mindedly explore the data and let the data speak for itself. In so doing, the researcher has a greater opportunity to uncover the true scene of the forest of information from the mountain of trees of data.

Interdependence Techniques

The chapter opener points out that many data analysis techniques, including the multivariate techniques we cover in the previous and current chapters, are vulnerable to anomalies in data, and therefore Tukey rightly advocated going back to basics to conduct exploratory data analysis of the data collected. However, this does not mean that multivariate techniques and other data analysis techniques are problematic themselves. Appropriately used, they can be very powerful tools for businesses and indeed any form of organization. What you should bear in mind is that we should be knowledgeable enough about these techniques in order to be able to use them correctly and effectively, and this chapter and other data analysis chapters are to help you gain a correct understanding of the techniques being discussed.

Recall that as we said in Chapter 18, interdependence techniques are ones in which no single variable or group of variables is defined as being independent or dependent, and a common goal of this kind of technique is to investigate a whole set of interdependent relationships among the variables put to analysis, so that the researcher can statistically and objectively classify respondent or objects into different groups. In this chapter, we will first introduce three interdependence techniques that have been popular in marketing research. These are factor analysis, cluster analysis and perceptual mapping. We will then end by introducing one of the most sophisticated multivariate techniques, structural equation modelling, which is technically speaking a hybrid technique integrating the dependence techniques covered in Chapter18 and the interdependence techniques in this chapter.

Factor Analysis

Factor analysis is a multivariate statistical technique that is used to uncover underlying factors through summarizing the information contained in a large number of variables into a smaller number of subsets called factors. With factor analysis there is no distinction between dependent and independent variables; rather, all variables under investigation are analysed together in order to identify underlying factors.

> **Factor analysis** Used to uncover underlying factors through summarizing the information contained in a large number of variables into a smaller number of subsets called factors.

Many problems facing businesses today are often the result of a combination of several variables. For example, if a local fast food restaurant is interested in assessing customer satisfaction, many variables of interest must be measured. Variables such as freshness of the food, speed of service, food taste, food temperature, cleanliness and how friendly and courteous the personnel are would all be measured by means of a number of rating questions.

Let's explain how to apply the factor analysis technique in details by referring to an example. In a marketing research study, customers were asked to rate a local fast food restaurant on six characteristics or variables. On the basis of the pattern of their responses, these six measures were combined into two summary measures, or factors: service quality and food quality (see Exhibit 19.1).

By using factor analysis to summarize the information contained in a large number of variables into a smaller number of factors, marketing researchers can help marketing managers simplify their decision making because they have to consider only two broad areas – service quality and food quality – instead of six different variables. Our example has reduced six variables to two factors, but in typical business situations it is common for marketing researchers to use factor analysis to reduce, for example, 50 variables to only less than 10 factors. The convenience of simplicity brought by factor analysis is even more evident.

EXHIBIT 19.1 Example of a Factor Analysis Application to a Local Fast Food Restaurant

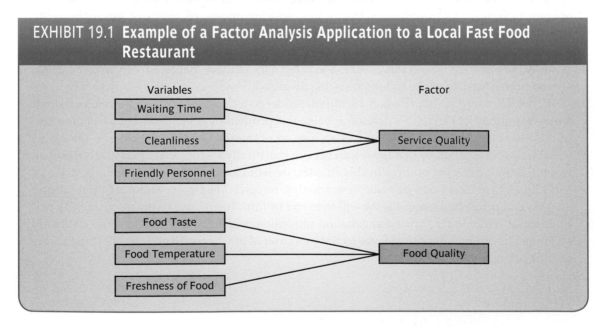

The starting point in interpreting results of factor analysis is factor loadings. **Factor loading** refers to the correlation between each of the original variables and the newly developed factors. Each factor loading is a numerical representation of the importance of the variable in measuring each factor. Factor loadings, like correlations, can vary from 0.00 to 1.00. If variable A_4 (food taste) is closely associated with factor 2, the factor loading or correlation would be high.

> **Factor loading** The correlation between each of the original variables and the newly developed factors.

Factor analysis would produce factor loadings between each factor and each of the original variables. An illustration of the output is given in Exhibit 19.2. Variables A_1, A_2, and A_3 are highly correlated with factor 1 and variables A_4, A_5, and A_6 are highly correlated with factor 2. In technical terms, variables A_1, A_2, and A_3 have 'high loadings' on factor 1, which means that they help define that factor to a large extent. Similarly, a research analyst would also say that variables A_4, A_5, and A_6 have 'high loadings' on factor 2.

The next step in factor analysis is to name the resulting factors. The researcher examines the variables that have high loadings on a particular factor. There is often a certain consistency among the variables that load high on a given factor.

As the ratings on waiting time (A_1), cleanliness (A_2) and friendly personnel (A_3) all load on the same factor, we have chosen to name this factor service quality. This is because although the three variables deal with three different aspects, all these aspects are about customers' service experience with the restaurant. On another front, variables A_4, A_5, and A_6 all load highly on factor 2, which we named food quality. Naming factors in this fast food restaurant example is straightforward. However, doing the same in the real-life business scenario is sometimes a daunting task because the mental picture arising from the factor loadings table like that presented in Exhibit 19.2 may not be so clear cut. To name the factor as appropriate as possible, researchers often need to rely on a combination of their intuition (which can be subjective) with an inspection of the variables loaded highly on a particular factor in order to optimize the factor naming process.

A final aspect of factor analysis concerns the number of factors to retain. While our fast food restaurant example comes up with two factors only, real-life situations can involve many more factors. Deciding on how many factors to retain is actually a very complex process because

EXHIBIT 19.2 Factor Loadings for the Two Factors

	Correlation with:	
Variable	**Factor 1**	**Factor 2**
A_1 (waiting time)	.79	.07
A_2 (cleanliness)	.72	.10
A_3 (friendly personnel)	.72	.05
A_4 (food taste)	.09	.85
A_5 (food temperature)	.11	.70
A_6 (freshness of food)	.04	.74

there can be more than one possible solution to any factor analysis problem. A discussion of the technical aspects of this part of factor analysis is beyond the scope of this book, but we will provide an example showing how a research analyst can decide on the number of factors to be retained.

An important measure to consider in deciding how many factors to retain is the percentage of the variation in the original data that is explained by each factor. A factor analysis computer programme will produce a table of numbers that will give the percentage of variation explained by each factor. A simplified illustration of these numbers is presented in Exhibit 19.3. In this example, we should definitely keep the first two factors, because they explain a total of 96.8 per cent of the variability in the five measures. The last three factors combined explain only 3.2 per cent of the variation, and each accounts for only a small portion of the total variance. In non-technical terms they contribute little to our understanding of the data and thus should not be retained. Most marketing researchers stop factoring when additional factors no longer make sense, because the variance they explain often contains a large amount of random and error variance.

Factor Analysis Applications in Marketing Research

While our fast food restaurant example illustrated the power of factor analysis in simplifying customer perceptions towards a local fast food restaurant, the technique has many other important applications in marketing research:

- *Product.* Factor analysis can be used to identify product attributes that influence consumer choice.
- *Pricing.* Factor analysis can help identify the characteristics of price sensitive and prestige sensitive customers.
- *Advertising.* Factor analysis can be used to better understand media habits of various customers.
- *Distribution.* Factor analysis can be employed to better understand channel selection criteria among distribution channel members.

SPSS Application – Factor Analysis

The continuing Jimmy Spice's restaurant case will be used here to demonstrate how to conduct factor analysis under SPSS environment. Looking at Jimmy Spice's restaurant database, you can find many variables are measured metrically. Note that in order to use the factor analysis technique, the researcher has to make sure that all the variables involved have to be of metric scale.

EXHIBIT 19.3 Percentage of Variation in Original Data Explained by Each Factor

Factor	Percentage of Variation Explained
1	50.3%
2	46.5%
3	1.8%
4	0.8%
5	0.6%

Now let's focus on variables X12 to X21, which represent customers' perceptions of Jimmy Spice's restaurant on eleven dimensions or variables. For the purpose of this section, the task now is to determine if we can simplify our understanding of the customers' perceptions of the restaurant by reducing the number of these eleven perception-oriented variables to significantly fewer than eleven. If this is feasible, the owners of the restaurant can then simplify their decision making by focusing on fewer aspects of their restaurant in developing appropriate marketing strategies.

The SPSS click-through sequence is ANALYSE → DATA REDUCTION → FACTOR, which leads to a dialogue box where you select variables X12–X21. After you have put these variables into the Variables box, look at the data analysis options below. First click on the Descriptives box and unclick the Initial Solution box because we do not need it at this point. Now click Continue to return to the previous dialogue box. Next go to the Extraction box. In this one you leave the default of principal components and unclick the unrotated factor solution under Display. You should keep the other defaults, so now click the Continue box. Next go to the Rotation box. The default is None. We want to rotate, so click on Varimax as your rotational choice and then Continue. Finally, go to the Options box and click Sorted by Size, and then change the Suppress Absolute Values from .10 to .30. These last choices eliminate unneeded information, thus making the solutions printout much easier to read. We do not need Scores at this point, so we can click on OK at the top of the dialogue box to execute the factor analysis. Exhibit 19.4 shows examples of the dialog boxes you will encounter when running factor analysis, with the upper one as the main box and the lower one as the rotation box.

EXHIBIT 19.4 SPSS Dialogue Box Examples for Factor Analysis

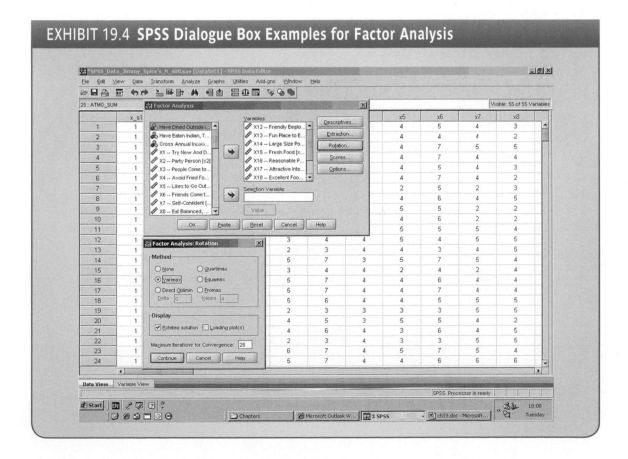

The SPSS output regarding factor analysis of customers' perceptions of Jimmy Spice's restaurant is reproduced in Exhibit 19.5. The first table on the output is the Rotated Component Matrix table. Labels for the eleven variables analysed (X12–X21) are shown in the left column. To the right are four columns of numbers containing the factor loadings for the four factors that resulted from the factor analysis. By suppressing loadings under .30 we see only three numbers under column one (Component 1, or factor 1), three numbers under column two (Component 2, or factor 2), and two numbers under columns three and four (Components 3 and 4). For example, X18 – Excellent Food Taste has a loading of .910 on factor 1 and X12 – Friendly Employees has a loading of .949 on factor 2. We prefer a factor solution in which each original variable loads on only one factor, as in our Jimmy Spice's restaurant working example. But in many cases this may not happen.

Before trying to name the factors we must decide if four factors are enough or if we need more. Our preference here is to have as few factors as possible yet account for a reasonable amount of the information contained in the eleven original variables. To determine the number of factors, we look at information in the Total Variance Explained table (bottom of Exhibit 19.5).

EXHIBIT 19.5 SPSS Output regarding Factor Analysis of Customers' Perceptions of Jimmy Spice's Restaurant

Rotated Component Matrix[a]

	Component			
	1	2	3	4
X18 -- Excellent Food Taste	.910			
X15 -- Fresh Food	.891			
X20 -- Proper Food Temperature	.862			
X12 -- Friendly Employees		.949		
X21 -- Speed of Service		.941		
X19 -- Knowledgeable Employees		.749		
X16 -- Reasonable Prices			.978	
X14 -- Large Size Portions			.978	
X17 -- Attractive Interior				.897
X13 -- Fun Place to Eat				.834

Extraction Method: Principal Component Analysis.
Rotation Method: Varimax with Kaiser Normalization.
a. Rotation converged in 5 iterations.

Total Variance Explained

Compo nent	Rotation Sums of Squared Loadings		
	Total	% of Variance	Cumulative %
1	2.493	24.927	24.927
2	2.418	24.184	49.112
3	1.994	19.936	69.048
4	1.663	16.628	85.676

Extraction Method: Principal Component Analysis.

It shows the four factors accounted for 85.676 per cent of the variance in the original eleven variables. This is a substantial amount of the information to account for, and we have reduced the number of original variables by two-thirds, from eleven to four. So let's consider four factors acceptable and see if our factors sound logical.

To determine if our factors are logical, look at the information in the Rotated Component Matrix (Exhibit 19.5). First, examine which original variables are combined to make each new factor. Factor 1 is made up of X18 – Excellent Food Taste, X15 – Fresh Food, and X20 – Proper Food Temperature. Factor 2 is made up of X12 – Friendly Employees, X21 – Speed of Service, and X19 – Knowledgeable Employees. Factor 3 is made up of X16 – Reasonable Prices and X14 – Large Size Portions. Factor 4 is made up of X17 – Attractive Interior and X13 – Fun Place to Eat. To analyse the logic of these combinations we look at the variables with the highest loadings, i.e. largest absolute size. That is why we suppressed loadings of less than .30. Factor 1 looks to be related to food, whereas factor 2 is related to service. On the other hand, factor 3 looks to be related to value, while factor 4 is related to atmosphere. Therefore now we have developed a four-factor solution that accounts for a substantial amount of variance. We have also demonstrated the logic in the combinations of the original eleven variables. With this four-factor solution, instead of having to think about the eleven original variables, the owners of Jimmy Spice's restaurant can now concentrate on only four variables – food, service, value and atmosphere – when they are developing and revising their marketing strategies.

Using Factor Analysis with Multiple Regression

Sometimes we may want to use the results of factor analysis with another multivariate technique, such as multiple regression in the dependence techniques category. We can show how to conduct integrated factor analysis-multiple regression techniques by following up the previous factor analysis example, where we combined the eleven customer perception variables into four factors.

To use the resulting four factors in a multiple regression, we must first calculate factor scores. Factor scores are composite scores estimated for each respondent on each of the derived factors. Return to the SPSS dialogue box for the four-factor solution. Looking at the dialogue box you see the Scores box, which we did not use before. Click on this box and then click Save as Variables. When you do this there will be more options, but just click the Regression option. Now click Continue and then OK, and the corresponding factor scores will be automatically calculated with the SPSS. The result will be four factor scores for each of the 400 respondents. They will appear at the far right side of your original database and will be labelled fac1_1 (scores for factor 1), fac2_1 (scores for factor 2), and so on. See Exhibit 19.6 to view the factor scores.

Now we want to see if customers' perceptions of the restaurant, as measured by the four factors, account for the same customers' satisfaction with the restaurant. To meet this research objective, multiple regression will be an appropriate technique. As multiple regression is one of the dependence techniques, both dependent and independent variables have to be clearly identified. By default they should be metrically measured. Now, as we expect, you should be able to find out the single dependent metric variable is X22 – Satisfaction, while the independent metric variables are the factor scores.

The SPSS click-through sequence is ANALYSE → REGRESSION → LINEAR, which should lead you to a dialogue box where you can select the variables. You should select X22 as the dependent and fac1_1, fac2_1, fac3_1, and fac4_1 as the independents. Now click on the Statistics button and check Descriptives. There are several additional types of analysis that can be selected, but at this point we will use the programme defaults. Click OK to execute the regression. The dialogue boxes for this regression are shown in Exhibit 19.7.

EXHIBIT 19.6 **Factor Scores for the Four Derived Factors Reflecting the Eleven Original Jimmy Spice's Restaurant Customer Perception Variables**

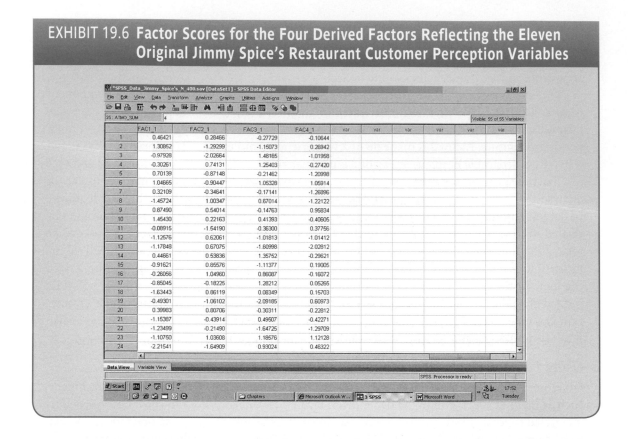

EXHIBIT 19.7 **SPSS Dialogue Boxes for Regression with Factor Scores**

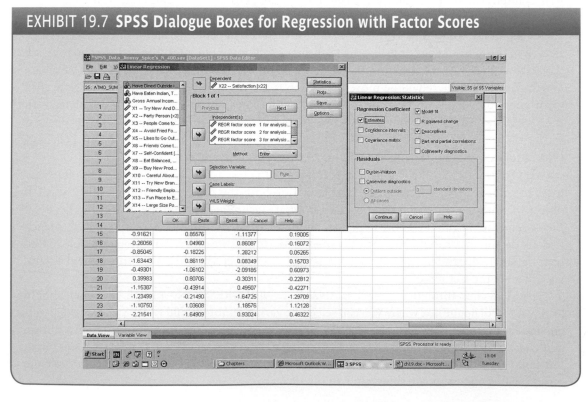

The SPSS output for regression with factor scores is shown in Exhibit 19.8. The Model Summary table reveals that R-square is .492 and the ANOVA table indicates the regression equation model is statistically significant at the .000 level. This means that 49.2 per cent of the variation in satisfaction (dependent variable) can be accounted for by the four independent variables – the factor scores. Underneath the table, the footnote says that the regression equation includes a constant and that the predictor (independent) variables are factor scores for the four variables, i.e. the four derived factors of Atmosphere, Value, Service and Food, developed in the previous factor analysis section.

To determine if one or both of the factor score variables are significant predictors of satisfaction we must examine the Coefficients table (Exhibit 19.8). Looking at the Standardized Coefficients Beta column, you can find that Factor 1 – Food is .480, Factor 2 – Service is .325, Factor 3 – Value is .258, and Factor 4 – Atmosphere is .300. The statistical significance is .000 for all the four factors. Thus, we know from this regression analysis that customer perceptions represented by the four aforesaid derived factors are strong predictors of customer satisfaction, with Factor 1 being somewhat better than the other three factors because its beta size is somewhat larger.

In this section we have demonstrated how you can integrate one multivariate technique – factor analysis – with another technique – multiple regression – to better understand your data. Indeed it is also possible to use other multivariate techniques in combination. For example, if

EXHIBIT 19.8 **SPSS Output for Regression with Factor Scores**

Model Summary

Model	R	R Square	Adjusted R Square	Std. Error of the Estimate
1	.702[a]	.492	.487	.684

a. Predictors: (Constant), REGR factor score   4 for analysis 1, REGR factor score   3 for analysis 1, REGR factor score   2 for analysis 1, REGR factor score   1 for analysis 1

ANOVA[b]

Model		Sum of Squares	df	Mean Square	F	Sig.
1	Regression	179.047	4	44.762	95.809	.000[a]
	Residual	184.543	395	.467		
	Total	363.590	399			

a. Predictors: (Constant), REGR factor score   4 for analysis 1, REGR factor score   3 for analysis 1, REGR factor score   2 for analysis 1, REGR factor score   1 for analysis 1

b. Dependent Variable: X22 – Satisfaction

Coefficients[a]

Model		Unstandardized Coefficients		Standardized Coefficients	t	Sig.
		B	Std. Error	Beta		
1	(Constant)	4.645	.034		135.914	.000
	REGR factor score 1 for analysis 1	.458	.034	.480	13.396	.000
	REGR factor score 2 for analysis 1	.310	.034	.325	9.054	.000
	REGR factor score 3 for analysis 1	.246	.034	.258	7.189	.000
	REGR factor score 4 for analysis 1	.287	.034	.300	8.374	.000

a. Dependent Variable: X22 – Satisfaction

your dependent variable is non-metric, such as gender, you can use discriminant analysis in a manner similar to our use of multiple regression as shown above. You can also use cluster analysis in combination with multiple regression or discriminant analysis. You should be able to have clearer understanding of these potential combined usages after reading about other multivariate techniques later in this chapter.

Cluster Analysis

Cluster analysis is another multivariate interdependence technique. As the name implies, the fundamental purpose of cluster analysis is to classify objects (e.g. customers, products, market areas) into groups so that objects within each group are similar to one another on a variety of variables. Speaking in greater detail, cluster analysis seeks to classify objects such that there will be as much similarity within groups and as much difference between groups as possible. As such this technique strives to identify natural groupings of objects among variables without designating any of the variables as a dependent variable.

Cluster analysis A multivariate interdependence technique whose fundamental purpose is to classify objects into relatively homogeneous groups based on a prescribed set of variables.

We will start our discussion of cluster analysis with this intuitive example. A fast food chain is considering opening a restaurant in a new, growing suburb of a cosmopolitan city. The marketing research company working for the fast food chain surveyed a large sample of households in this suburb and collected data on characteristics such as demographics, lifestyles, and expenditures on eating out. The chain wants to identify one or more household segments that are likely to visit its new restaurant. Once the segment(s) is/are identified, the firm's marketing communication activities would be tailored to them.

A target segment can be identified for the company by conducting a cluster analysis of the data its marketing research company has gathered. Results of cluster analysis will identify segments, each containing households that have similar characteristics but differing considerably from the other segments. Exhibit 19.9 identifies four potential clusters or segments for our fast food chain, which are drawn up based on two characteristics or variables, i.e. extent of eating out at dine-in restaurants and extent of patronizing a fast food restaurant. As the exhibit implies, the new, growing suburb contains households who rarely visit restaurants (cluster 1), households who tend to frequent dine-in restaurants exclusively (cluster 2), households frequenting fast food restaurants exclusively (cluster 3) and households patronizing both dine-in and fast food restaurants (cluster 4). By examining the characteristics associated with each of the clusters, management can decide which clusters to target and how best to reach them through marketing communications.

Statistical Procedures for Cluster Analysis

Several cluster analysis procedures are available, each based on a somewhat different set of complex computer programmes. The general approach in each procedure is the same, however, and involves measuring the similarity between objects on the basis of their ratings on the various variables. The degree of similarity between objects is usually determined through a distance measure. This process can be illustrated with our earlier example involving two variables:

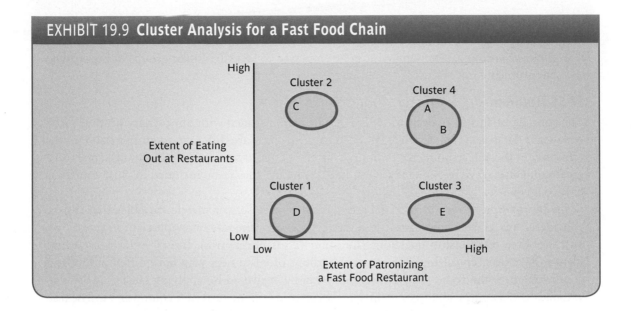

EXHIBIT 19.9 Cluster Analysis for a Fast Food Chain

V1 = Frequency of eating out at fancy restaurants
V2 = Frequency of eating out at fast food restaurants

Data on V1 and V2 are shown on the two-dimensional plot in Exhibit 19.9. Five respondents are plotted with the letters A, B, C, D and E. Each letter represents the position of one respondent with regard to the two variables V1 and V2. The distance between any pair of letters is positively related to how similar the two respondents are when the two variables are considered together. Thus, respondent A is more like B than either C, D, or E.

This analysis can inform the management of the proposed new restaurant outlet in the new, growing suburb that potential customers are more likely to be among those who tend to eat at both dine-in and fast food restaurants (cluster 4). To develop an effective marketing communication strategy to reach this cluster of households, management would need to identify demographic, psychographic, and behavioural profiles of the respondents in cluster 4.

Clusters are often developed from scatter plots, as what we have shown with our fast food restaurant example. This is a complex trial-and-error process. Fortunately, computer algorithms are available, and should be used if the clustering is to be done in an efficient, systematic fashion. While the more detailed mathematics behind the analysis are beyond the scope of this chapter, readers should note that the algorithms are all based on the idea of starting with some arbitrary cluster boundaries and modifying the boundaries until a point is reached where the average distances within clusters are as small as possible relative to the average distances between clusters.

Cluster Analysis Applications in Marketing Research

Our fast food chain example illustrated how cluster analysis can be used to develop distinct market segments. The technique has also many other important applications in marketing research:

- *New product research.* Clustering brands can help a firm examine its position in the competitive marketplace. Brands in the same cluster often compete more fiercely with each other than with brands in other clusters.

- *Test marketing.* Cluster analysis groups test cities into homogeneous clusters for test marketing purposes.
- *Buyer behaviour.* Cluster analysis can be employed to identify similar groups of buyers who have similar choice criteria.

SPSS Application – Cluster Analysis

The running of cluster analysis with SPSS can be demonstrated with our plenary Jimmy Spice's restaurant database. The task here is to determine if there are different, identifying subgroups (clusters) of the 400 respondents to Jimmy Spice's restaurant survey. To fulfil this task, one technical point that must be remembered is that all the variables to be included in cluster analysis have to be metrically measured.

In Jimmy Spice's restaurant database, there are three sets of metric variables that can be considered for cluster analysis – the lifestyle questions, the customer perception questions, and the three relationship questions (question #25 is nonmetric). Jimmy Spice's restaurant owners have been enquiring if there are subgroups of customers who have different levels of commitment to the restaurant. This enquiry can be answered by applying cluster analysis to variables 22, 23 and 24, all three of which represent measures of customer commitment. The task then is to see if there are clusters of customers that have distinctly different levels of commitment to the restaurant.

The SPSS click-through sequence is ANALYSE → CLASSIFY → HIERARCHICAL CLUSTER, which leads to a dialogue box where you select variables X22, X23 and X24. After you have put these variables into the Variables box, look at the other options in the dialogue box. Keep all the defaults that are shown on the dialogue box. You should also use the defaults for the Statistics and Plots options. Click on the Method box and select Ward's under the Cluster Method (you have to scroll to the bottom of the list), but use the default of squared Euclidean distances under Measure. We do nothing with the Save option at this point, so you can click OK at the top of the dialogue box to run the programme of cluster analysis. Exhibit 19.10 shows the SPSS dialogue boxes that have to be dealt with for running the programme.

The SPSS output has a table called Agglomeration Schedule, a portion of which is shown in Exhibit 19.11. This table has lots of numbers in it, but we look only at the numbers in the Coefficients column (middle of table). Go to the bottom of the table and look at the numbers in the Coefficients column (circled in red). The number at the bottom will be the largest, and the numbers get smaller as you move up the table. The bottom number is 1139.868, the one right above it is 576.104, and the next above is 358.468. The coefficients in this column show how much you reduce your error by moving from one cluster to two clusters, from two clusters to three clusters, and so on. As you move from one cluster to two clusters there always will be a large drop (difference) in the coefficient of error, and from two clusters to three clusters another drop. Each time you move up the column the drop in the numbers will get smaller. What you are looking for is where the difference between two numbers gets substantially smaller. This means that going from, say, X clusters to X+1 clusters has not substantially reduced the coefficient of error.

It is apparent, in the case of Exhibit 19.11, that going from three clusters to four clusters does not lead to substantial decrease in the coefficient of error. You can see that the change is only from 358.468 to 277.687. It is therefore sensible to choose three clusters instead of four. However, some researchers may argue for the choice of two clusters instead of three. This is also logical because the error is reduced by a huge amount when going from one to two clusters, and significantly less when adding one more cluster. Moreover, two clusters are likely to be easier to interpret

EXHIBIT 19.10 SPSS Dialogue Boxes for Cluster Analysis

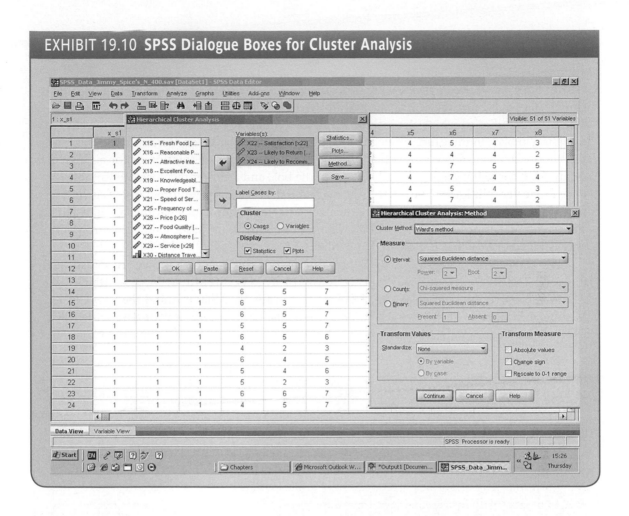

EXHIBIT 19.11 Cluster Analysis Agglomeration Schedule

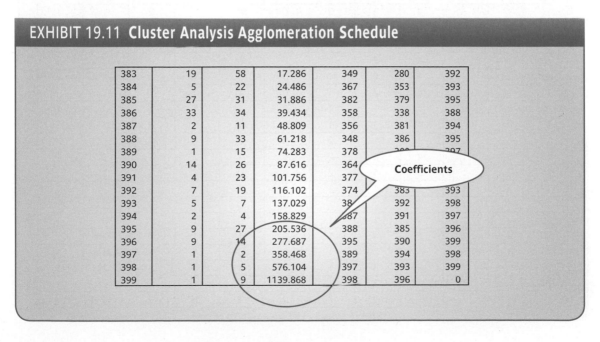

383	19	58	17.286	349	280	392
384	5	22	24.486	367	353	393
385	27	31	31.886	382	379	395
386	33	34	39.434	358	338	388
387	2	11	48.809	356	381	394
388	9	33	61.218	348	386	395
389	1	15	74.283	378		
390	14	26	87.616	364		
391	4	23	101.756	377		
392	7	19	116.102	374	383	393
393	5	7	137.029	38	392	398
394	2	4	158.829	87	391	397
395	9	27	205.536	388	385	396
396	9	14	277.687	395	390	399
397	1	2	358.468	389	394	398
398	1	5	576.104	397	393	399
399	1	9	1139.868	398	396	0

Coefficients

and manage than three. Therefore, one can see that there is some softer issue in cluster analysis that different researchers may decide on differently, all based on their different, but logical, arguments.

Now let's say we decide to adopt the two-cluster solution. Before attempting to name the two clusters, let's make sure they are significantly different. To do so, you must first create a new variable that identifies which cluster each of the 400 respondents has been assigned to by cluster analysis. Go back to the Cluster dialogue box and click on the Save box. When you do this, you can choose to create a new cluster membership variable for a single solution or for a range of solutions. Choose the single solution, put a 2 in the box, and a cluster membership variable for the two-cluster solution will be created when you run the cluster analysis programme again. The new cluster membership variable will be the new variable in your data set at the far-right-hand side of your data labelled clu2_1. It will show a 1 for respondents in cluster 1 and a 2 for respondents assigned to cluster 2, as illustrated in Exhibit 19.12.

Now you can run a one-way ANOVA between the two clusters to see if they are statistically different. The SPSS click-through sequence is ANALYSE → COMPARE MEANS → ONE-WAY ANOVA. Next you put variables X22, X23 and X24 in the Variables box and the new Cluster Membership variable in the Factor box. This will be the new variable in your data set labelled CLU2_1. Next click on the Options box and then on Descriptive under Statistics, and Continue.

EXHIBIT 19.12 New Cluster Variable To Identify Cluster Membership

	x26	x27	x28	x29	x30	x31	x32	x33	x34	x35	CLU2_1
1	1	2	4	3	1	0	1	1	2	2	1
2	1	2	4	3	2	0	0	2	1	1	1
3	4	2	3	1	1	0	0	1	4	3	1
4	1	2	3	4	2	0	0	3	3	2	1
5	3	2	4	1	1	0	0	1	4	4	1
6	1	3	4	2	2	0	0	2	2	1	1
7	2	1	4	3	1	0	1	1	3	3	1
8	3	1	4	2	1	0	0	1	4	5	1
9	1	3	4	2	2	0	0	2	3	1	2
10	1	2	3	4	1	0	0	1	3	1	1
11	3	1	4	2	1	0	1	1	5	5	1
12	3	2	4	1	1	0	1	1	4	4	1
13	2	1	4	3	1	0	1	1	3	2	1
14	4	2	3	1	2	0	0	3	3	5	2
15	3	1	4	2	2	0	1	2	3	3	1
16	2	1	3	4	2	0	0	3	3	2	1
17	2	1	3	4	1	0	1	1	4	2	1
18	4	1	3	2	1	0	0	1	3	5	1
19	4	1	3	2	1	0	0	1	4	4	1
20	2	1	3	4	1	0	1	1	4	2	1
21	1	3	4	2	1	0	0	1	3	1	1
22	1	3	4	2	1	0	1	1	4	2	1
23	1	3	4	2	1	0	0	1	1	2	1
24	4	2	3	1	2	0	1	3	3	4	1

EXHIBIT 19.13 Comparing Cluster Means Using ANOVA

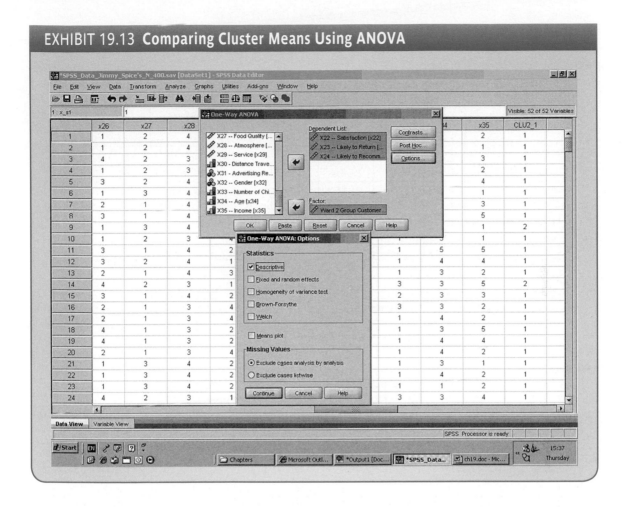

Now click OK and you will get an output with a Descriptives and an ANOVA table. The dialogue boxes for running this procedure are shown in Exhibit 19.13.

The SPSS ANOVA output of the cluster solution is shown in Exhibit 19.14. When you look at the Descriptives table you will see the sample sizes for each cluster (N) and the means of each variable for each cluster, as well as a lot of other numbers we will not use. For example, the sample size for cluster 1 is 269 and for cluster 2 it is 131. Similarly, the mean for satisfaction in cluster 1 is 4.11, and in cluster 2 it is 5.74; the mean for likely to return in cluster 1 is 3.81, and in cluster 2 it is 5.45; and the mean for likely to recommend in cluster 1 is 3.12, and in cluster 2 it is 4.15.

We interpret the two clusters by looking at the means of the variables for each of them. By looking at the means we see that respondents in cluster 1 are relatively less satisfied, less likely to return, and less likely to recommend (lower mean values). In contrast, cluster 2 respondents are relatively more satisfied, more likely to return, and more likely to recommend Jimmy Spice's restaurant (higher mean values). Thus, cluster 2 has much more favourable perception of the restaurant than does cluster 1.

Next, look at the ANOVA table to see if the differences between the cluster means are statistically significant. You will see that for all three variables the differences between the means of the two clusters are statistically very significant (Sig. .000). Thus, we have two very different groups of restaurant customers with cluster 2 being moderately committed to the restaurant and cluster 1

EXHIBIT 19.14 SPSS ANOVA Output – Results for the Two Clusters Measured by X22-X24

Descriptives

		N	Mean	Std. Deviation	Std. Error	95% Confidence Interval for Mean		Minimum	Maximum
						Lower Bound	Upper Bound		
X22 -- Satisfaction	1	269	4.11	.625	.038	4.04	4.19	3	5
	2	131	5.74	.440	.038	5.66	5.82	5	6
	Total	400	4.64	.955	.048	4.55	4.74	3	6
X23 -- Likely to Return	1	269	3.81	.719	.044	3.73	3.90	2	5
	2	131	5.45	.659	.058	5.34	5.56	4	6
	Total	400	4.35	1.039	.052	4.25	4.45	2	6
X24 -- Likely to Recommend	1	269	3.12	.787	.048	3.02	3.21	2	5
	2	131	4.15	.808	.071	4.01	4.29	3	5
	Total	400	3.46	.930	.047	3.37	3.55	2	2

ANOVA

		Sum of Squares	df	Mean Square	F	Sig.
X22 -- Satisfaction	Between Groups	233.760	1	233.760	716.604	.000
	Within Groups	129.830	398	.326		
	Total	363.590	399			
X23 -- Likely to Return	Between Groups	235.866	1	235.866	481.079	.000
	Within Groups	195.134	398	.490		
	Total	431.000	399			
X24 -- Likely to Recommend	Between Groups	94.138	1	94.138	149.187	.000
	Within Groups	251.140	398	.631		
	Total	345.277	399			

only somewhat committed. Based on the mean values and significance levels, we will name cluster 1 'Somewhat Committed' and cluster 2 'Moderately Committed'.

SPSS Application – Combining Cluster Analysis and Discriminant Analysis

We can use cluster analysis in combination with other multivariate techniques. This section demonstrates how to combine cluster analysis and discriminant analysis.

In the cluster analysis example earlier in this chapter, we identified customer commitment groups based on information on variables X22, X23 and X24. Of the two clusters identified, cluster 1 respondents were moderately committed while cluster 2 respondents were highly committed to Jimmy Spice's restaurant. We can use the results of this cluster analysis solution as the dependent variable in a discriminant analysis.

Now we must identify which of the database variables we would use as metric independent variables. We have used the consumer perception variables (X12–X21) in an earlier example but we have not used the lifestyle variables (X1–X11). Let's, therefore, see if we can find a predictive relationship between the metric lifestyle variables and the non-metric customer commitment clusters.

There are 11 lifestyle variables that can be used as independent variables. Three of the variables are related to nutrition – X4 – Avoid Fried Foods, X8 – Eat Balanced Meals, and X10 – Careful About What I Eat. Using these three variables as independents, we can determine if nutrition predicts customer commitment, i.e. whether a customer is moderately committed or highly committed.

The SPSS click-through sequence is ANALYSE → CLASSIFY → DISCRIMINANT, which leads to a dialogue box where you select the variables. The dependent, non-metric variable is clu2_1, and the independent, metric variables are X4, X8 and X10. First transfer variable clu2_1 to the Grouping Variable box at the top, and then click on the Define Range box just below it. Insert the minimum and maximum numbers for the grouping variable. In this case the minimum is 1 = cluster 1 and the maximum is 2 = cluster 2, so just put these numbers in and click on Continue. Then transfer the food perception variables into the Independents box (X4, X8 and X10). Then click on the Statistics box at the bottom and check Means, Univariate ANOVAS, and Continue. The Method default is Enter, and we will use this. Now click on Classify and Compute from group sizes. We do not know if the sample sizes are equal, so we must check this option. We should also click Summary Table and then Continue. We do not use any options under Save, so click OK to run the programme.

As already noted above, the SPSS discriminant analysis programme gives you a lot of output some of which you may not use for a particular project. Here we look at only five tables. The first two tables to look at are shown in Exhibit 19.15. Note that the discriminant function is highly significant (Wilks' Lambda of .000) and that the predictive accuracy is very high (86.8 per cent correctly classified). Recall that group 1 of our cluster analysis solution had relatively less favourable perceptions of Jimmy Spice's restaurant than did group 2. The overall predictive accuracy of 86.8 per cent indicates that this is a very good predictive function.

To find out which of the independent variables help us to predict group membership we look at the information in two tables (shown in Exhibit 19.16). Results from the table labelled Tests of Equality of Group Means show which nutrition lifestyle variables differ on a univariate basis. Note that all the independent variables are highly significant.

To consider the variables from a multivariate perspective, use the information from the Structure Matrix table. Identify the numbers in the Function column that are .30 or higher. This cut-off level is determined in a manner similar to a factor loading. All variables .30 or higher are considered to be helpful in predicting group membership. Like the univariate results, all of the independent variables help us for the prediction. The strongest nutrition variable is X4 (.775), the second best predictor is X10 (.644), and the least predictive but still helpful is X8 (.377).

EXHIBIT 19.15 Discriminant Analysis of Customer Commitment Clusters and Nutrition Lifestyle Variables

Discriminant

Wilks' Lambda

Test of Function(s)	Wilks' Lambda	Chi-square	df	Sig.
1	.479	291.451	3	.000

Classification Results[a]

		Ward Method	Predicated Group Membership 1	2	Total
Original	Count	1	235	34	269
		2	19	112	131
	%	1	87.4	12.6	100.0
		2	14.5	85.5	100.0

a. 86.8% of original grouped cases correctly classified.

EXHIBIT 19.16 Discriminant Analysis – Customer Commitment Clusters

Discriminant

Wilks' Lambda

Test of Function(s)	Wilks' Lambda	Chi-square	df	Sig.
1	.479	291.451	3	.000

Classification Results[a]

		Ward Method	Predicated Group Membership		Total
			1	2	
Original	Count	1	235	34	269
		2	19	112	131
	%	1	87.4	12.6	100.0
		2	14.5	85.5	100.0

a. 86.8% of original grouped cases correctly classified.

EXHIBIT 19.17 Nutrition Variable Means for Customer Commitment Clusters

Discriminant

Tests of Equality of Group Means

	Wilks' Lambda	F	df1	df2	Sig.
X4 -- Avoid Fried Foods	.605	259.467	1	398	.000
X8 -- Eat Balanced, Nutritious Meals	.866	61.390	1	398	.000
X10 -- Careful About What I Eat	.689	179.342	1	398	.000

Structure Matrix

	Function
	1
X4 -- Avoid Fried Foods	.775
X10 -- Careful About What I Eat	.644
X8 -- Eat Balanced, Nutritious Meals	.377

Pooled within-groups correlations between discriminating variables and standardized canonical discriminant functions
Variables ordered by absolute size of correlation within function.

To interpret the meaning of the discriminant analysis results we examine the means of the nutrition variables shown in the Group Statistics table of Exhibit 19.17. From this examination, we can see all the means for the nutrition variables in group 2 are lower than the means in group 1. Moreover, based on the information provided in Exhibit 19.16 we know all of the nutrition variables are significantly different. Thus, customers in group 1 are significantly more nutrition conscious than those in group 2.

Recall that cluster 1 (more nutrition conscious) was somewhat satisfied with Jimmy Spice's restaurant while cluster 2 (less nutrition conscious) was moderately satisfied. Thus, the overall results indicate an interesting finding: the more satisfied customers are less nutrition conscious. One insight derived from this finding is that the owners of Jimmy Spice's restaurant should consider putting some 'Heart Healthy' entrées on the menu in order to appeal to the somewhat satisfied cluster. These new entrées could also appeal to the moderately satisfied cluster who had favourable perceptions of the restaurant.

Perceptual Mapping

Perceptual mapping is a process that is used to develop maps that show the perceptions of respondents. The maps are visual representations of respondents' perceptions of a company, product, service, brand, or any other object in two dimensions. A perceptual map typically has a vertical and a horizontal axis that are labelled with descriptive adjectives. Possible adjectives for our restaurant example are food freshness, food temperature, speed of service, good value for money, and so on.

> **Perceptual mapping** A process that is used to develop maps showing the perceptions of respondents. The maps are visual representations of respondents' perceptions of a company, product, service, brand, or any other object in two dimensions.

Several different approaches can be used to develop perceptual maps. These include rankings, mean ratings and multivariate techniques. To illustrate perceptual mapping, data from an example involving ratings of six major fast food restaurants in the Europe are presented in Exhibit 19.18. The names of these restaurants have been changed for business confidentiality reasons. Respondents are given a set of the six restaurants and asked to express how they perceive each restaurant. The perceptions of the respondents are then plotted on a two-dimensional map using two of the adjectives, food freshness and food temperature. Inspection of the map, shown in Exhibit 19.19, illustrates that WD and BYB were perceived as quite similar to each other, as were MD and BK. AB and HD were also perceived as somewhat similar, but not as favourable as the other restaurants. However, BYB and MD were perceived as very dissimilar.

EXHIBIT 19.18 Ratings of Six Fast Food Restaurants

	Food Freshness	Food Temperature
MD	1.8	3.7
BK	2.0	3.5
WD	4.0	4.5
BYB	4.5	4.8
AB	4.0	2.5
HD	3.5	1.8

Food temperature: 1=Warm, 5=Hot; Food freshness: 1=Low, 5=High.

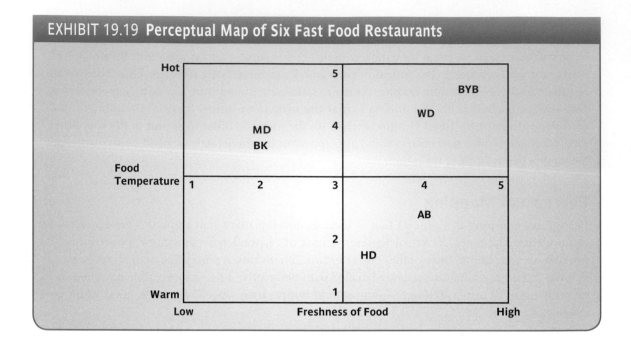

EXHIBIT 19.19 Perceptual Map of Six Fast Food Restaurants

Perceptual Mapping Applications in Marketing Research

While our fast food restaurant example illustrates how perceptual mapping grouped pairs of restaurants together based on perceived ratings, perceptual mapping has many other important applications in marketing research. These include

- *New product development.* Perceptual mapping can identify gaps in perceptions and thereby help to position new products.
- *Image measurement.* Perceptual mapping can be used to identify the current image of the company and its desired image relative to the competition.
- *Advertising.* Perceptual mapping can assess advertising effectiveness in enhancing the brand's reputation.
- *Branding.* Perceptual mapping can be deployed to position different brands in the market.
- *Distribution.* Perceptual mapping can be used to assess similarities of channel outlets.

Structural Equation Modelling

The dependence techniques covered in Chapter 18 render marketing researchers with powerful tools to conduct sophisticated data analysis. However, all these techniques share one common limitation – each technique can examine only one relationship at a time.

There are dependent techniques, such as multivariate analysis of variance covered in Chapter 18 and canonical analysis (not covered in this text due to space constraints), which take into account multiple dependent variables. However, even these techniques address only a single relationship between the dependent and independent variables.

With the increasing sophistication of the marketing environment, marketing researchers are increasingly required to deal with a set of interrelated questions in a marketing research project.

For instance, what variables determine a consumer's perception of a retail store environment? How does that perception combine with other variables to affect the consumer's selection of navigational search strategy? How does navigational search strategy selection team up with other variables to influence the consumer's retail search behaviour, and how does retail search behaviour lead to the extent of shopper search satisfaction? This series of issues, as illustrated in Exhibit 19.20, can have immense managerial and theoretical implications. However, none of the techniques we discussed so far can address all these issues altogether at the same time and help the researcher to establish an entire theory of consumer retail search process. Structural equation modelling – an extension of a number of multivariate techniques notably factor analysis and multiple regression – is regarded as a hybrid multivariate technique that integrates both dependence and interdependence techniques, and is therefore the answer.

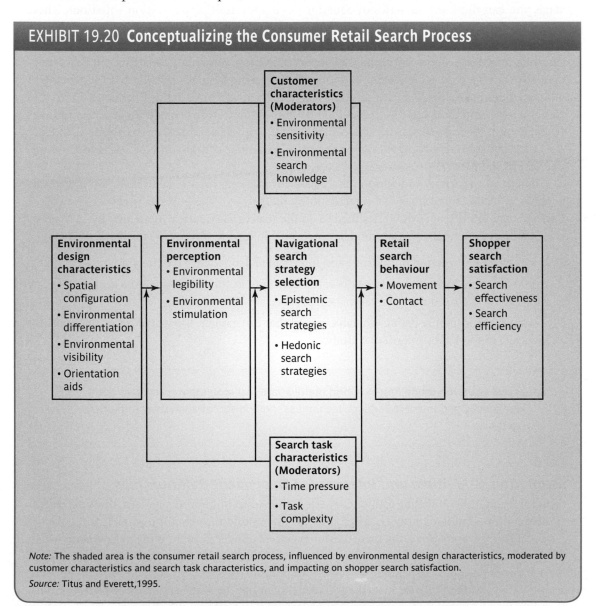

EXHIBIT 19.20 Conceptualizing the Consumer Retail Search Process

Note: The shaded area is the consumer retail search process, influenced by environmental design characteristics, moderated by customer characteristics and search task characteristics, and impacting on shopper search satisfaction.

Source: Titus and Everett, 1995.

Structural equation modelling can examine a series of dependence relationships simultaneously. Using the above retail example to illustrate this point, if we believe that navigational search strategy selection affects retail search behaviour and retail search behaviour affects shopper search satisfaction, then we know that retail search behaviour is both a dependent and an independent variable in the same theory. This means a hypothesized dependent variable becomes an independent variable in a subsequent dependence relationship.

Application of Structural Equation Modelling

Structural equation modelling examines the structure of interrelationships among a diverse set of variables, and expresses the structure in a series of equations. To help you conceptualize at this stage, you can think of this series of equations as one of multiple regression equations. These equations depict all of the relationships among constructs used in the analysis. These constructs are unobservable or latent factors represented by a set of manifest variables, which are very like variables found to be representing a factor in factor analysis. Any single construct can be an independent variable only, a dependent variable only, or taking a dual role as both an independent and dependent variable (such as the 'retail search behaviour' construct in Exhibit 19.20. As you can now see, structural equation modelling combines the workings of dependence techniques (notably multiple regression) and interdependent techniques (notably factor analysis). Therefore structural equation modelling should be regarded as a unique combination of both types of multivariate techniques.

Structural equation modelling is also called covariance structure analysis or latent variable analysis. It is also sometimes just referred to by the name of the popular specialized software package (e.g. LISREL or AMOS) destined to do the structural equation modelling job. Whatever it is called, all structural equation models possess the following three characteristics:

1 It involves an estimation of multiple and interrelated dependence relationships.

2 It must be able to incorporate unobserved concepts in these relationships and specify any measurement error during the estimation process.

3 It should subsequently define a reliable model that can explain the whole set of relationships involved and tested in a particular study.

> **Structural equation modelling** A hybrid multivariate technique that integrates both dependence and interdependence techniques, notably factor analysis and multiple regression.

Estimation of Multiple and Interrelated Dependent Relationships

Structural equation modelling estimates a series of separate, but interdependent, multiple regression equations simultaneously by specifying the corresponding structural model. To do so, the researcher first draws up existing theory, prior experience and logical thinking to figure out which independent variables predict each dependent variable. During this process, the researcher should be well aware that some dependent variables can become independent variables in a subsequent relationship, and therefore we have the interdependent nature of the structural equation model. It should also be noted that many of the same variables can affect, with differing effects, each of many of the dependent variables.

The proposed relationships so developed are then expressed in a series of structural equations, which are similar to multiple regression equations, for each dependent variable. This unique feature of simultaneously multiple relationships fundamentally distinguishes structural equation modelling from other multivariate techniques that accommodate multiple dependent variables, as the latter allow only a single relationship between dependent and independent variables at a time.

Incorporation of Unobserved Concepts and Specification of Measurement Error

Structural equation modelling can incorporate unobserved concepts in its analysis of multiple, interrelated relationships. These unobserved concepts are called latent constructs, which are represented by observable or measurable variables, also called manifest variables, which are usually gathered through various primary research methods.

The main rationale for using unobserved concepts or latent constructs in marketing research is that some concepts to be measured (such as customer satisfaction or customer loyalty) are abstract concepts that are impossible to measure directly by asking customers a simple satisfaction or loyalty question. You may argue that we can ask customers a question such as 'how satisfied are you with a particular food retail store?' or 'how many times out of the last ten food shopping occasions have you visited a particular food retail store?' The answer you get from these questions can give you an indication of customer satisfaction with or customer loyalty to a particular retailer. However, the indication you get is certainly not precise, because the concepts of both satisfaction and loyalty are multi-faceted. For example, a customer may be satisfied with the store layout but not the customer service. It is therefore much better to identify all the important facets that are poised to contribute to a typical customer's feeling of satisfaction towards the retailer, measure all these facets, and then represent the scores of different facets by an overall concept of customer satisfaction.

Like the results of any other multivariate techniques, structural equation models always have some degree of measurement error. It can be caused by inaccurate responses from the respondents, different interpretations of the same question by different respondents, and so on. To account for measurement error, structural equation modelling enables the establishment of the measurement model, which specifies the rules of correspondence between latent constructs and manifest variables. The measurement model allows the researcher to try any number of variables for an unobserved concept (independent or dependent concept) and then estimate or specify the resulting measurement error (or reliability, as measurement error and reliability are two sides of the same coin).

Definition of a Reliable Model

A **theory** can be thought of as a systematic set of relationships that can explain some real-world phenomena in a consistent and comprehensive manner, and can be represented by a corresponding model.

> **Theory** A systematic set of relationships that can explain some real-world phenomena in a consistent and comprehensive manner, and can be conceptually captured by a corresponding model.

In structural equation modelling, there are actually two models that will be developed. First is measurement model, which shows how the manifest variables are placed together to represent different latent constructs. Second is structural model, which illustrates how different latent constructs are associated with each other.

EXHIBIT 19.21 **A Typical Path Diagram**

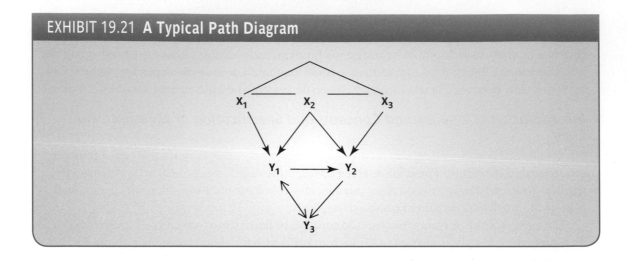

A complete structural equation model, which consists of measurement and structural models, can be quite complex to read and comprehend. One way to simplify it is to portray a model in a visual form, known as a path diagram. An example of a path diagram is given in Exhibit 19.21.

Exhibit 19.21 actually demonstrates a rather complicated model. There are three independent constructs (denoted as X_1, X_2, and X_3), each related to the others (a line linking each pair of them). There are three dependent constructs (Y_1, Y_2, and Y_3), with Y1 predicting Y_2, Y_1 predicting Y_3, Y_2 predicting Y_3, and Y_3 predicting Y_2. Each of these dependent constructs is also a predictor, directly or indirectly, of the independent constructs. The most complicated part is the relationship between Y_1 and Y_3, which is shown by a two-headed arrow. This mean a reciprocal relationship between them, i.e. Y_1 is a predictor of Y_2, and Y_2 is also a predictor of Y_1. As you can see, there are a number of relationships occurring simultaneously in the path diagram in Exhibit 19.21. Expressing this interrelated set of relationships in a single path diagram can make the model more easily read and comprehended by readers and users, especially those who are not familiar with the structural equation modelling technique.

An Illustrative Example of Structural Equation Modelling

The ever-upgrading mobile commerce technology leads many existing and potential sellers to contemplate all sorts of new product and market opportunities. However, the extent to which the mobile commerce technology-enabled products are successful in the market largely depends on consumer willingness to adopt new products arising from this technology. Bruner and Kumar (2005) borrowed the technology acceptance model (TAM) from the work environment and applied it to the consumer context (c-TAM) in order to study the consumer acceptance of mobile commerce technology. They used the structural equation modelling technique for this study, and their finished work was published in the *Journal of Business Research*. With the permission of *Journal of Business Research* to use this finished work, we have done some rewriting and focus on only the model development and data analysis aspects of Bruner and Kumar's work, in order to show the readers how structural equation modelling has been carried out in practice.

According to Bruner and Kumar, the fundamental idea underlying TAM is that a person's behavioural intention to use a new system (e.g. a new hardware, a new software, or mobile commerce technology as in this study) is determined mainly by two constructs – its usefulness and its ease of use. Usefulness is concerned with the degree to which a person believes that the system in focus will help perform a particular task, while ease of use is about the extent to which a person believes the use of that system will be relatively free of effort.

Exhibit 19.22 outlines the hypothetical e-TAM for mobile commerce technology to be tested by Bruner and Kumar. The model shows the predictive relationships among the different constructs involved. These predictive relationships are based on the theoretical reasoning developed through literature review and commonsense logic. The following shows the reasoning of each predictive relationship included in the model.

Predictive Relationships of the Hypothetical Model

Ease of use -> Usefulness
It is expected that if consumers believe the system concerned is easier to use, they are also likely to perceive the system to be more useful as they have a higher chance to fully utilize the functions offered by the system.

Ease of use -> Fun
Consumers are likely to derive greater enjoyment and have more fun from using the system compared to a system that is more cumbersome to use.

Ease of use -> Usefulness -> Attitude towards the system
Attitude towards the system is about an overall evaluation of the system concerned. This overall evaluation comprises two components: utilitarian and hedonic components. The predictive relationships of Ease of use -> Usefulness -> Attitude towards the system constitute the utilitarian component.

Ease of use -> Usefulness -> Attitude towards the system
These predictive relationships represent the hedonic component of Attitude towards the system.

Usefulness ->Attitude towards the system -> Behavioural intention
It is expected that Attitude towards the system would mediate the relationship between Usefulness and Behavioural intention. The rationale is that people would develop intentions to engage in certain behaviours towards which they have positive attitudes that arise from their satisfaction with the usefulness of the system.

EXHIBIT 19.22 The Hypothetical e-TAM for Mobile Commerce Technology

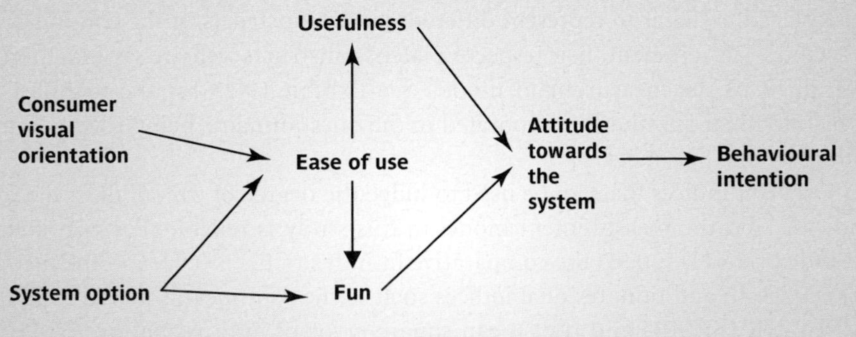

The numbers near the arrows are path coefficients. In the case of the two paths from 'System option', the first number in each pair is the path coefficient of the mobile phone/desktop computer comparison and the second number is the PDA/desktop computer comparison.
Source: Bruner and Kumar, 2005.

Fun -> Attitude towards the system -> Behavioural intention

Higher levels of fun associated with the system would lead to more positive attitudes towards the system, resulting in a greater intention to purchase the system.

Style of processing -> Ease of use

People tend to follow either a visual or verbal modality to process information. For those people who are more predisposed towards a visual mode of processing, they would find it easier to use devices where clicking on icons and symbols are a natural way to move from one piece of information to another in an interactive manner. Compared to people who are more verbally than visually predisposed, they are more likely to rely on visual cues and also more comfortable with the use of mental imagery to process information. It is therefore expected that if a person has a greater inclination towards a visual mode of processing, they will find the system (mobile commerce technology in this study) easier to use.

System option -> Ease of use

Until recently traditional desktop computers and laptop computers were the only means for individuals to access the Internet, which is a major reason for people adopting mobile commerce technology. Consumers non have access to a growing number of new system options to access the Web. Examples include mobile phones and PDAs. Generally speaking they are small in size, rendering them more difficult for the user to decipher the text and graphics and more time-consuming to enter the data. They are therefore expected to be less easy to use than the traditional system options (desktop computer and laptop computer). Therefore the degree of ease of use of mobile commerce technology is dependent on the system option used to access the Internet.

System option -> Fun

Mobile phones and PDAs may be less easy to use, but they provide greater intrinsic motivation to consumers. This is because the relative novelty and mobility of this kind of option would result in an element of discovery associated with their usage, and subsequently lead to greater fun for consumers than a traditional computer.

Results

Measurement model

As explained in a preceding section, structural equation modelling produces two models: the measurement model and the structural model. The measurement model shows how the manifest variables are placed together to represent different latent constructs. If the combinations of the manifest variables can represent their respective latent constructs well, we say that there is a satisfactory overall fit of the measurement model. See Exhibit 19.23 for the manifest variables, expressed as individual questions incorporated in the questionnaire, being used to represent the corresponding latent constructs.

There are several indices that can be used to judge the degree of overall fit of the model, and they all indicate that the measurement model in this study is reliable. For example, the non-normed fit index (NNFI) is 0.97, the comparative fit index (CFI) is 0.98, and the incremental fit index (IFI) is 0.98. In addition, residual indices such as the root mean squared residual (RMR), standardized RMR (SRMR) and root mean square error of approximation (RMSEA) are all <0.05, while the average absolute standardized residual is 0.035. The values of all these indices suggest satisfactory fit of the model. Greater details of these indices are beyond the scope of the current text. (Readers who wish to learn more are encouraged to read texts focused on structural equation modelling.)

EXHIBIT 19.23 Latent Constructs and their Constituent Manifest Variables

Consumer visual orientation
When listening to someone describing their experiences, I try to mentally picture what was happening.
When I think of someone I know, I often 'picture' in my mind what they look like.

Usefulness
It helped me be more effective.
It helped me be more productive.

Ease of use
It was easy to use.
I learned to use it quickly.

Fun to use
I have fun using it.
I found using it to be enjoyable.

Attitude towards the system
For me, using the ___ to ___ is bad (1) / good (5)
For me, using the ___ to ___ is negative (1) / positive (5)

Behavioural intention
Assuming you have access to such a device in the future, what is the probability that you would use it to accomplish a similar task?
Unlikely (1) / likely (5)
Improbable (1) / probable (5)

Further proof of the fit of the model is that every item has loaded significantly on the construct it is supposed to measure ($p < 0.01$), and that composite reliabilities are found to be greater than 0.70 for all constructs. Exhibit 19.24, which is part of the outcome of the measurement model, demonstrates that the average variance extracted by the items measuring a construct is greater than 0.50 for all constructs and the average variance extracted by each construct is greater than the squared correlations between that construct and every other construct in the study. Therefore, we can be confident that all the constructs have met the requirements of unidimensionality, internal consistency, covergent validity and discriminant validity, so they are ready to be incorporated in the structural model.

Structural model

The structural model is shown in Exhibit 19.25. Dummy variables, with desktop computers as the baseline for comparison, have been created to capture the effect of the Internet-access system option being used. The overall fit of the model is assessed using both incremental and absolute fit indices. The incremental fit indices (e.g. CFI, IFI, NNFI) are all >0.95, while the absolute fit indices (such as RMSEA) are all <0.05. All these indices indicate a satisfactory fit of the model to the data.

Path coefficients

Realizing the overall fit of the measurement model and structural model, we would like to know the exact details of the predictive relationships incorporated in the structural model. We like to

EXHIBIT 19.24 Construct Correlations and Average Variance Extracted

	Consumer visual orientation	Usefulness	Ease of use	Fun	Attitude towards the system	Behavioural intention
Consumer visual orientation	**0.53**	0.23	0.21	0.18	0.06	0.17
Usefulness		**0.60**	0.70	0.61	0.41	0.21
Ease of use			**0.74**	0.57	0.31	0.15
Fun				**0.70**	0.47	0.22
Attitude towards the system					**0.74**	0.33
Behavioural intention						**0.82**

Note: The numbers in bold are the average variance extracted by each construct.

EXHIBIT 19.25 The Structural Model Showing the c-TAM

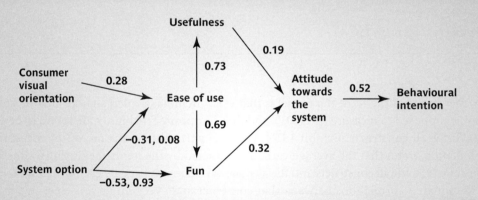

Note: The numbers near the arrows are path coefficients. In the case of the two paths from 'System option', the first number in each pair is the path coefficient of the mobile phone/desktop computer comparison and the second number is the PDA/desktop computer comparison.
Source: Bruner and Kumar, 2005.

know whether the hypothetical predictive relationships really exist, and if they exist, how strong are those relationships.

The path coefficients of all the predictive relationships involved in the model are shown in Exhibit 19.25. By examining these path coefficients and their corresponding t values, we are assured that all the paths shown are statistically significant.

In more microscopic detail, results show that the higher a person's inclination to process information visually, the easier it is for them to use mobile commerce technology (b = 0.28, t = 3.74). Concerning the predictive relationship between system options and ease of use, it is found that mobile phones are significantly less easy to use than desktop computers to access the mobile commerce system (b=−0.31, t=−2.46). However, PDAs are found to be as easy to use as the desktop computers (b=0.08, t<1.0). PDAs are found to be more fun to use than desktop computers (b=0.93, t=7.61) but contrary to the researchers' expectations, mobile phones are found to be less fun to use than desktop computers (b=−0.53, t=−3.75). All these results demonstrate that people perceive significant differences between the Internet-access system options in terms of their ease of use and the fun associated with the use of the system.

Results also show strong predictive relationships of the ease of use of mobile commerce technology on people's perceptions of its usefulness (b=0.73, t=8.65), as well as the ease of use of the system on the extent to which the system is perceived to be fun to use (b=0.69, t=7.91). On the other hand, people's perceptions of the usefulness of the system exerts a significant effect (b=0.19, t=2.17) on their attitude towards the system. Also the extent of fun associated with the system has a significant effect on people's attitude towards the system (b=0.32, t=4.86). Lastly, as expected, people's attitude towards the system significantly influences their intention to purchase the system (b=0.52, t=4.76).

Case 1: Cluster Analysis of Spanish Retail Landscape

MOSAIC, a standard geodemographic classification, was first introduced in Chapter 3 where it was used to conduct the European case study into geodemographic segmentation of Spanish supermarket chains for their retail location strategy.

MOSAIC is an example of the use of cluster analysis. It uses seven geodemographic factors to put each of the 506,329 urban geography areas in Spain into the most appropriate cluster. These factors are professional activity, habitat, tourism and commerce, families, employment, type of household, and business. Exhibit 19.26 summarizes the interpretation of these factors, which are measured on a scale between 0 and 10.

Note that data for all the above seven factors can be obtained from secondary sources. Cluster analysis was then carried out. Results show that Spain's retail landscape can be classified into 14 distinct groups and 48 separate typologies. Exhibit 19.27 names each of these groups and typologies and the percentage of population in each. Mean values of the factors within each group and type were used to characterize the supermarket chains as noted in the Marketing Research in Action Case 1 of Chapter 3 (page 125).

EXHIBIT 19.26 MOSAIC Factors Characterizing Each Urban Geography Area in Spain

Factor	Minimum point on the 10-point scale	Maximum point on the 10-point scale
Professional activity	Primary sector / building	Services sector
Habitat	Intensive urban development	Extensive urban development
Tourism and commerce	Low linking with tourism and commerce	High linking with tourism and commerce
Families	Older families	Young families
Employment	Active economies	Unemployment
Type of household	Households in transition	Settled households
Businesses	Low economic activity	High economic activity

EXHIBIT 19.27 MOSAIC Groups and Typologies in Spain

Group	Per cent of population	Typology	Per cent of population
A. Elite	5.4	A01 Classic elite	2.5
		A02 Urban elite	1.8
		A03 Residential elite	1.1
B. Urban well-off	4.0	B04 Settled well-off	1.4
		B05 Consummate well-off	1.2
		B06 Pre-retirement well-off	1.3

C. Provincial well-off	7.1	C07 Well-off in tourist area	1.4
		C08 Provincial well-off	2.6
		C09 Industrial well-off	2.0
		C10 Well-off in mixed areas	1.1
D. Qualified professionals	7.0	D11 Newly settled professionals	1.7
		D12 New emerging professionals	1.4
		D13 Professionals from the 80s	2.3
		D14 Professionals from the 90s	1.6
E. Mid-level professionals	9.6	E15 Satisfied immigrants	1.7
		E16 Autochthonous residents	2.8
		E17 Apparent white collar	2.4
		E18 Provincial white collar	2.7
F. Consolidated	10.6	F19 Stable employees	1.1
		F20 Apparent employees	2.4
		F21 Traditional employees	1.2
		F22 Mid-level employees	2.7
		F23 Modest employees	3.2
G. Tourist	3.3	G24 Summer resorts	1.5
		G25 Tourist areas	1.8
H. Industrial	14.3	H26 Older workers	3.2
		H27 Modern workers	1.6
		H28 Workers in SME	2.9
		H29 Classic workers	2.7
		H30 Traditional workers	1.2
		H31 Modest workers	2.7
I. Non-qualified	5.4	I32 Unskilled stable workers	1.6
		I33 Unskilled large households	2.3
		I34 Unskilled modest workers	1.5
J. Sectorial mix	7.5	J35 Local business	2.7
		J36 Territorial services centre	2.6
		J37 Small mixed city	2.2
K. Diversified rural	5.3	K38 Rural in expansion	1.3
		K39 Older rural	1.8
		K40 Rural border	2.2
L. Agricultural	10.5	L41 Young farmers	2.5
		L42 Traditional farmers	4.5
		L43 Mature agricultural workers	3.5
M. Passive areas	9.1	M44 Retired urban professionals	2.1
		M45 Older people on their own	0.6
		M46 Unskilled retired	0.6
		M47 Rural aged	5.8
N. Security and defence	0.9	N48 Security and defence	0.9

Source: Based on an adaptation of a study by Gonzalez-Benito and Gonzalez-Benito, 2005.

Questions

1 Find out whether similar geodemographic classification also exists in your country. If so, describe the factors your country's geodemographic classification uses to conduct cluster analysis.

2 If there is available standard geodemographic classification in your country, find out the type and typology of the area where you live. Do you agree that the type and typology describing your area is correct?

3 If the type and typology describing your area is incorrect, what are the possible reasons for the incorrectness?

Case 2: Combining Cluster Analysis and Discriminant Analysis to Study European Consumer Adoption of DVD Recorders

The latest DVD recorders do a lot more than just record material on DVDs. The latest models let you play and record VHS video, while others include hard drives and programming guides to give you TiVo-like functionality. Stand-alone DVD recorders use the same drive technology as PCs, and they provide a home theatre platform. The DVD discs take up less physical space than bulky VHS tapes, plus they have menus that let the user easily jump to specific points within a recording. Moreover, the quality is much better than is the case of a VCR, with the ability to record up to several times more horizontal lines of resolution compared to only 250 with a VCR.

The DVD market is huge and rapidly getting much larger. No longer limited to its original free standing use as a replacement of VCR, DVD is being combined with increasing numbers of consumer electronics products such as computers and personal portable electronic devices – DVD is virtually everywhere!

DVD hit the market in the late 1990s and has enjoyed very fast growth, as evidenced by meteoric global sales shortly after its mass market introduction. Indeed, DVD has enjoyed the most rapid rise of any consumer electronics technology ever introduced. To date the total market for all types of DVD systems (players, recorders, set-tops, PCs, etc.) shows no sign of abating.

DVD players and player/recorders have caught the interest of consumers. DVD set-top box players have also boomed in sales due not only to their functionality, but also to their rapidly falling prices.

Two of the biggest challenges of today's marketers are (1) the successful introduction of new technology-based product innovations into consumer markets, and (2) stimulating the diffusion of those innovations to profitable penetration levels. To meet these challenges, researchers must be able to gain clearer insights into the key factors people often use in deciding whether to adopt technological innovations, many of which occur in consumer electronics.

In recognition of the above challenges and the respective measures that can be undertaken, consumer electronics researchers conducted a pan-European research project in the mid-2000s to look into factors influencing consumer decision-making process in the market for consumer electronics products, and more specifically DVD products. In order to provide more detailed and usable findings, they focused on the innovator and early adopter segments, and aimed at comparing them on the basis of issues of concern such as product usage, purchase likelihood and demographics.

The two primary research questions addressed were: 'Are there attitudinal and behavioural differences between innovators and early adopters?' and 'Can these differences be associated with purchase likelihood of DVDs?' A copy of the questionnaire for the project is shown in Exhibit 19.28.

Data were collected over a two-week period, using an Internet panel approach from a sample of 200 individuals. The sample frame was consumers with annual household incomes €20,000 or more and ages 18 to 35 years. The questionnaire included a variety of topics such as innovativeness,

EXHIBIT 19.28 Consumer Survey on Electronics Products

This is a project being conducted by Consumer Marketing Research Company. The purpose of this project is to better understand the attitudes, interests, opinions and activities of consumers towards consumer electronics products. The questionnaire will take approximately 15 minutes to complete, and all responses will be kept strictly confidential. Thank you for your help in this project.

I. Attitudes

The following questions are related to your attitudes, interests, opinions and activities about consumer electronics products, things you like to do, and so forth. On a scale of 1 to 7, with 7 being Strongly Agree, and 1 being Strongly Disagree, please circle the number that best expresses the extent to which you agree or disagree to each of the following statements.

		Strongly Disagree						Strongly Agree
1	The Internet is a good place to get lower prices.	1	2	3	4	5	6	7
2	I don't shop for specials.	1	2	3	4	5	6	7
3	People come to me for advice.	1	2	3	4	5	6	7
4	I often try new brands before my friends and neighbours.	1	2	3	4	5	6	7
5	I would like to take a trip around the world.	1	2	3	4	5	6	7
6	My friends and neighbours come to me for advice and consultation.	1	2	3	4	5	6	7
7	Coupons are a good way to save money	1	2	3	4	5	6	7
8	I seldom look for the lowest price when I shop.	1	2	3	4	5	6	7
9	I like to try new and different things.	1	2	3	4	5	6	7

10 To what extent do you believe you need a DVD player? Please indicate on the scale provided below:

	Product I Definitely Do Not Need					Product I Would Like to Try
1	2	3	4	5	6	7

11 How likely are you to purchase a DVD player? Please indicate whether you are moderately likely or highly likely to purchase a DVD player. (Note: respondents who are not likely to purchase a DVD player will be screened out of the survey.)

0 = Moderately Likely
1 = Highly Likely

II. Classification Information

We need some information for group classification purposes. Please tell us a little about yourself. As previously promised, your information will be kept strictly confidential, used for aggregate analysis purpose only and discarded once this project is completed.

12 What is the highest level of education you have attained? (Check only ONE box.)
__ High school graduate or below
__ College graduate or above

13 Electronics Products Ownership. Please indicate the level of electronics products ownership that best describes you.
__ Own few electronics products
__ Own a moderate amount of electronics products
__ Own lots of electronics products

14 Please check the category that best indicates your total annual household income before taxes. (Check only ONE box.)
— €20,000 – €35,000
— €35,001 – €50,000
— €50,001 – €75,000
— €75,001 – €100,000
— More than €100,000

15 Innovators vs. Early Adopters – this classification will be developed using the statistical technique called cluster analysis. In the database, participants will be classified into either one of the following two groups:
0 = Early Adopters
1 = Innovators

16 Price Consciousness – this classification will be developed using questions 1, 2, 7 and 8 from the survey. In the database, participants will be classified as below:
0 = Less Price Conscious
1 = More Price Conscious

Thank you for sharing your attitudes, interests, opinions and experiences of electronic products with us. Your responses will be key to our success in this project.

lifestyles, product and brand image, and classification questions. Some of the questions were intervally measured while others were nominal and ordinal. There is a database for the questions in this case available in SPSS format at www.mhhe.com/shiu09. The database is labelled CH19_DVDSurvey.sav.

To examine the first primary research question as stated previously, it was necessary to classify respondents as either an innovator or an early adopter. The Innovativeness scale consisted of five variables: X3, X4, X5, X6 and X9. A cluster analysis was run to identify respondents who rated themselves higher on this scale, that is, relatively more innovative. The result was 137 Innovators and 63 Early Adopters. This categorical variable (X15) was then used as the dependent categorical variable in a discriminant analysis. The independent variables were X10 – DVD Product Perception, X11 – Purchase Likelihood, X12 – Education, X13 – Electronic Products Ownership, X14 – Income, and X16 – Price Consciousness.

The results are shown in Exhibit 19.29. Based on the Wilks' Lambda, the discriminant function is found highly significant in predicting innovators versus early adopters. Moreover, the Classification Results indicate the predictive accuracy of the discriminant function is very high, at 92.0 per cent.

The significant independent variable predictors are shown in Exhibit 19.30. On a univariate basis (see Tests of Equality of Group Means table) all of the independent variables are highly significant. Looking at the information in the Structure Matrix table, variables X11, X10 and X14 are the most significant in predicting innovators versus early adopters.

The comparison of group means is shown in Exhibit 19.31. The group means indicate that for all variables except X16 – Price Consciousness, the means are higher for innovators than they are for early adopters. This can be interpreted as follows. Innovators:

- Have more positive perceptions of DVD player-recorders.
- Are more likely to purchase a DVD player-recorder.
- Are more highly educated.

EXHIBIT 19.29 Discriminant Analysis of Innovators vs. Early Adopters

Wilks' Lambda

Test of Function(s)	Wilks' Lambda	Chi-square	df	Sig.
1	.323	220.177	6	.000

Classification Results[b,c]

		X15 – Innovators vs. Early Adopters	Predicted Group Membership		
			Early Adopters	Innovators	Total
Original	Count	Early Adopters	63	.0	63
		Innovators	19	118	137
	%	Early Adopters	100.0	.0	100.0
		Innovators	13.9	86.1	100.0
Cross–validated[a]	Count	Early Adopters	62	1	63
		Innovators	19	118	137
	%	Early Adopters	98.4	1.6	100.0
		Innovators	13.9	86.1	100.0

a. Cross validation is done only for those cases in the analysis. In cross validation, each case is classified by the functions derived from all cases other than that case.

b. 90.5% of original grouped cases correctly classified.

c. 90.0% of cross-validated grouped cases correctly classified.

EXHIBIT 19.30 Significant Predictors of Innovators vs. Early Adopters

Tests of Equality of Group Means

	Wilks's Lambda	F	df1	df2	Sig.
X10 -- DVD Product Perceptions	.527	178.053	1	198	.000
X11 -- Purchase Likelihood	.512	188.856	1	198	.000
X12 -- Education	.921	17.006	1	198	.000
X13 -- Electronic Product Ownership	.954	9.505	1	198	.002
X16 -- Price Conscious	.968	6.643	1	198	.001

Structure Matrix

	Function 1
X11 -- Purchase Likelihood	.679
X10 -- DVD Product Perceptions	.660
X12 -- Education	.204
X13 -- Electronic Products Ownership	.152
X16 -- Price Conscious	−.127

Pooled within-groups correlations between discriminating variables and standardized canonical discriminant functions
Variables ordered by absolute size of correlation within function.

- Own relatively more electronic products.
- Have higher incomes.

The price consciousness mean is lower for innovators than for early adopters (0 = less price conscious; 1 = more price conscious). The interpretation of this is:

- Innovators are less price conscious than early adopters.

To sum up, this case study has shown that combining cluster analysis and discriminant analysis can help DVD marketers gain a better understanding of their potential market segments. The study demonstrated that DVDs have left the innovator stage of the product diffusion process and are making inroads into the early adopter stage. But DVD manufacturers and retail marketers alike must focus on developing strategies that can attract more potential early adopters as well as create awareness and desire among the early majority.

EXHIBIT 19.31 Mean Profiles of Innovators vs. Early Adopters

Group Statistics

X15 -- Innovators vs. Early Adopters		Mean	Std. Deviation
Early Adopters	X10 -- DVD Product Perceptions	3.17	1.115
	X11 -- Purchase Likelihood	.10	.296
	X12 -- Education	.40	.493
	X13 -- Electronic Products Ownership	1.49	.669
	X14 -- Income	2.48	.965
	X16 -- Price Conscious	.59	.496
Innovators	X10 -- DVD Product Perceptions	5.45	1.124
	X11 -- Purchase Likelihood	.83	.375
	X12 -- Education	.69	.463
	X13 -- Electronic Products Ownership	1.82	.727
	X14 -- Income	4.04	.906
	X16 -- Price Conscious	.39	.490
Total	X10 -- DVD Product Perceptions	4.74	1.542
	X11 -- Purchase Likelihood	.60	.491
	X12 -- Education	.60	.491
	X13 -- Electronic Products Ownership	1.72	.724
	X14 -- Income	3.55	1.177
	X16 -- Price Conscious	.46	.499

Questions

1 What other issues can be examined with this survey?

2 What problems do you see with the questionnaire shown in Exhibit 19.28, and how would these problems affect data analysis?

Summary of Learning Objectives

■ **Apply factor analysis to marketing research.**

Factor analysis is used to summarize the information contained in a large number of variables into a smaller number of factors. The purpose of this technique is to simplify the data. The result is that managers can then simplify their decision making because they can now consider a smaller number of factors rather than many variables.

■ **Apply cluster analysis to marketing research.**

Cluster analysis classifies observations into a small number of mutually exclusive groups. These groups should have as much similarity within each group and as much difference between groups as possible. In striving to identify mutually exclusive groupings on a variety of defined variables, this technique does not designate any of the variables as a dependent variable.

■ **Apply perceptual mapping to marketing research.**

Perceptual mapping is used to develop maps that show perceptions of respondents visually. These maps are graphic representations that can show how companies, products, brands, or other objects are perceived as relative to each other on two key attributes. The two key attributes are presented along the vertical and horizontal axes respectively of the graph.

■ **Understand the fundamentals of structural equation modelling.**

With the increasing sophistication of the marketing environment, marketing researchers are increasingly required to deal with a set of interrelated questions in a marketing research project. Structural equation modelling, an extension of a number of multivariate techniques notably factor analysis and multiple regression, and therefore is regarded as a hybrid multivariate technique that integrates both dependence and interdependence techniques, is suitable for projects containing a set of interrelated questions. In structural equation modelling, there are actually two models that will be developed. First is measurement model, which shows how the manifest variables are placed together to represent different latent constructs. Second is structural model, which illustrates how different latent constructs are associated with each other.

Key Terms and Concepts

Cluster analysis 638	Perceptual mapping 647
Factor analysis 630	Structural equation modelling 650
Factor loading 631	Theory 651

1 What is the goal of factor analysis? Give an example of a marketing situation that would call for factor analysis.

2 How does cluster analysis differ from factor analysis? Give an example of how cluster analysis is used in marketing research.

3 Why would a marketing researcher use cluster analysis?

4 Why would a marketing researcher want to use both discriminant analysis and cluster analysis on the same project to analyse the data?

5 What is perceptual mapping and what are the approaches that can be used to collect data for perceptual mapping?

6 What is structural equation modelling? How is it different from other popular multivariate techniques?

1 The primary objective of cluster analysis is to classify objects into relatively homogeneous groups based on a set of defined variables. Once those groups are identified by a cluster analysis, what is the next logical data analysis step a marketing researcher might want to take? Will the results of a cluster analysis also reveal the characteristics of the members in each group? Why or why not?

2 **SPSS Exercise.** Using Jimmy Spice's restaurant dataset and the questionnaire shown in Chapter 14, carry out the following two tasks:

a Submit the data for questions 22, 23 and 24 to an SPSS cluster analysis. Create a new variable called 'Customer Commitment'. Develop a three-group cluster solution identifying three levels of customer commitment.

b Using these new clusters as the dependent variable and questions 12 to 21 (consumer perception variables) as the independent variables, perform a three-group discriminant analysis.

3 **SPSS Exercise.** Using Jimmy Spice's restaurant dataset and questionnaire again, perform a factor analysis on the lifestyle variables. Are the results of the factor analysis acceptable, and if so why?

4 **SPSS Exercise.** Continue to use Jimmy Spice's restaurant dataset and questionnaire, perform the following tasks:

a Conduct a factor analysis using the consumer perception variables (X_{12}–X_{21}). After you find the best factor solution, label the factors based on which variables load on each factor.

b Calculate factor scores for the factor solution you've developed. Use the factors scores as independent variables in a multiple regression with variable X_{22} – Satisfaction as the dependent variable. Use SPSS to run the multiple regression analysis. Interpret your findings and develop conclusions.

c Now run another regression using the same independent and dependent variables as in b. above, but now add variables X_{31} and X_{32} as independent dummy variables. What have you learned from this task?

Chapter

20

Report Preparation and Presentation

LEARNING OBJECTIVES

After reading this chapter, you will be able to

- ☑ Understand the primary objectives of a research report.
- ☑ Explain how a marketing research report is organized.
- ☑ List problems that can be encountered when preparing the report.
- ☑ Understand the importance of presentations in marketing research.
- ☑ Identify different software options available for developing presentations.
- ☑ Understand the advantages and disadvantages of different software options available for developing presentations.

 Many times what you say may not be as important as how you say it.

—Anonymous

How Would you Score on your Research Presentation?

After the marketing researcher has finished the analysis of the data and got the findings, conclusions and recommendations for his client company, they are normally required to make a research presentation orally to the management of the company. How good will they be in making that presentation? We all know that some people are good presenters while some others present badly.

Rick Altman, author of *The Tyranny of Presentation Software* (2007), gives his ratings on different quality levels of presentations:

The Best presentation: Truly excellent speaker, great ideas, and slides that amplify on the points made, instead of repeating them.

Very Good presentation: Truly excellent speaker, great ideas, and no slides.

Still OK presentation: Excellent speaker, redundant slides that don't add anything.

No So Good presentation: Bad speaker, good slides.

Pretty Bad presentation: Bad speaker, no slides.

The Worst presentation: Bad speaker, redundant slides.

Value of Report Preparation and Presentation

The chapter opener demonstrates that a good research presentation requires a combination of good speaker, good content and good presentation aids. No matter how perfectly a marketing research project is designed and implemented, if the results cannot be effectively communicated to the client, the research project is not a success. An effective marketing research presentation, whether visual or written or both, is one way to ensure that the time, effort and money that went into the project will be completely realized.

The purpose of this chapter is to introduce the style and format of the marketing research presentation. We will identify how the marketing research report is designed, and explain the specific objectives of each section of the report. We then discuss best industry practices regarding effective visual presentation of the research report, focusing on the use of computer technology for that purpose. You will then be able to put concepts into practice by addressing the questions arising from the 'Mobile Phone Consumer Research in Switzerland' project in the Marketing Research in Action section at the end of the chapter (pp. 683–8).

Objectives of the Marketing Research Report

A professional written marketing research report has four primary objectives: (1) to effectively communicate the findings of the marketing research project, (2) to provide an accurate interpretation of those findings, (3) to establish the credibility of the research project, and (4) to serve as a future reference document for strategic or tactical decisions.

(1) Effective Communication of the Findings

The first objective of the research report is to effectively communicate the findings of the marketing research project. Since a key purpose of the research project is to obtain information for answering questions about a specific business problem, the report must explain both how the information was obtained and what relevance it has to the research questions.

A detailed description of the following factors should be communicated to the client:

1 The research objectives.
2 The research questions the study is to answer.
3 Procedural information about the collection of secondary data (if necessary).
4 A description of the research methods used.

5 Findings displayed in tables, graphs or charts.

6 Interpretation of the findings.

7 Conclusions based on data analysis.

8 Recommendations for implementation.

(2) Accurate Interpretation of the Findings

Too often researchers are so concerned about communicating results they forget to provide an accurate, clear and logical interpretation of those results. To a larger or smaller extent, researchers are generally knowledgeable in statistics, data analysis computer output, questionnaire design, and other project-related material. However, they must recognize that their clients may have problems in understanding even the basics of sampling techniques and statistics. Thus, researchers must present technical or complex information in a manner that is understandable to all parties. In presenting such information to the client, researchers should always keep the original research objectives in mind. The task is to focus on the objectives and communicate how each part of the project is related to the fulfilment of that objective.

For example, Exhibit 20.1 illustrates a research objective that identifies significant predictors of moderate versus heavy users of family-style restaurants. While much numerical data is necessary to fulfill this objective, the use of non-technical and concise terminology provides an understandable interpretation of the data and its findings. Exhibit 20.1 reveals that compared with moderate users, heavy users are less concerned about nutrition, particularly salt and fat, have a high child orientation, are innovators in terms of buying new and different things, are less concerned about food prices, have a lower preference for combo meals, and consider food quality and service relatively more important.

EXHIBIT 20.1 Simple Interpretation of Data and its Findings

Significant Predictors of User Groups: Family Dining Segments		
Predictors **Opinions**	**Moderate Users**	**Heavy Users**
Nutritious meals	High	Low
Information	Seekers	Leaders
Eating	Skip lunch	Routine
Children	Less child oriented	Highly child oriented
Eating	Sometimes avoid fat and salt	Little concern about fat and salt
Novelty	Sometimes buy new and different things	Often buy new and different things
Leadership	Follower	Leader
Attitudes towards Restaurants		
Food prices	Important	Less important
Food quality	Less important	Important
Combo meals	High preference	Lower preference
Advertising impact	Moderate importance	High importance
Service	Moderate importance	High importance

(3) Establishment of Credibility of the Research Project

The research report must establish **credibility** for the research project including its research methods, findings and conclusions. This can be accomplished only if the report is accurate, believable and professionally organized. These three dimensions cannot be treated separately because they collectively operate to build credibility in the research document.

> **Credibility** The quality of a research report that is related to its accuracy, believability and professional organization.

To ascertain **accuracy** of the report, all of the input must be accurate. No degree of carelessness in handling of data, use of statistics, or interpretation of findings can be tolerated. Mathematical calculation errors, grammatical mistakes and incorrect terminology are just a few types of inaccuracy that can serve to diminish the credibility of the entire report.

> **Accuracy** Related to the accuracy of the research report, which necessitates accuracy of all of its input.

Logical thinking, clear explanation and precise presentation create **believability**. When the underlying logic is fuzzy, explanation is unclear or presentation is imprecise, readers may have difficulty understanding what they read. If readers do not understand what they read, they may not believe in the research report altogether. For example, a client may believe that half of all respondents find the company's store locations very convenient. If the actual results deviate from this expectation, the client may question the research results. In such cases, the researcher needs to communicate his/her thinking logically, explain the findings clearly and present the report precisely. These tactics are to convince the client that, although the findings are unexpected, they are believable.

> **Believability** Related to the believability of the research report, which necessitates logical thinking, clear explanation and precise presentation.

Finally, the credibility of the research report is affected by the degree of **professional organization** of the document itself. The report must be organized in a manner that can deliver the image of professional quality to its readers. Also, to the extent possible it should appropriately reflect the background and knowledge of the reader.

> **Professional organization** Related to the professional organization of the research report, which necessitates the delivery of professional quality image and the appropriate reflection of the background and knowledge of the reader.

(4) Use as a Future Reference Document

The fourth objective of the research report is to be a future reference document. Once it is completed and used for its original purpose, the research report should still have a life of its own as a reference. Many marketing research studies cover a variety of different objectives and seek to answer several research questions. This is accomplished with large volumes of information in both statistical and narrative formats. The studies and their accompanying information can still be a useful reference document to be cited over an extended period in future.

Some marketing research reports are a part of a larger research project conducted in various stages over time. It is not uncommon for one marketing research report to serve as a baseline for additional studies.

***

The following is helpful in preparing the report: Make an outline of all major points, with supporting details in their proper position and sequence. Always keep the reader informed of where the topical development of the report is going. Use short, concise sentences and paragraphs. Always say exactly what you intend to say – don't leave the reader 'grasping' for more information. Always select wording that is consistent with the background and knowledge of the reader. If necessary, rewrite the report several times. This will force you to remove clutter and critically evaluate the document for possible errors.

Format of the Marketing Research Report

Every marketing research report is unique in some way – due to client needs, research objectives, and so on – yet all reports contain some common elements. Although their terminologies may differ among industry practices, the common elements occurring in all marketing research reports are the following:

1 Title page
2 Table of contents
3 Executive summary
   a   Research objectives
   b   Concise statement of research methods
   c   Summary of findings
   d   Conclusions and recommendations
4 Introduction
5 Research design
6 Data analysis and findings
7 Conclusions and recommendations
8 Limitations
9 Appendixes

Title Page

The title page indicates the subject of the report and the name of the recipient, along with their position, department and employing organization. It should also contain the name, position, employing organization, address and telephone number of the person or persons submitting the report, as well as the date the report is submitted.

Table of Contents

The table of contents lists the topics of the report in sequential order. Wherever available, it also lists the sub-topics. Starting page numbers of each topic and sub-topic are stated as well.

After showing the table of contents in terms of topics and sub-topics, it is also a common practice for the researcher to continue to have two tables, one listing the titles of each table and the other listing the titles of each figure, and the pages where they can be found, in the report.

Executive Summary

The **executive summary** is the most important part of the report. Many consider it the soul of the report, insofar as many busy executives may read only the executive summary. It presents the major points of the report, and must be complete enough to provide a true representation of the entire document but in summary form.

> **Executive summary** The part of a marketing research report that presents the major points; it must be complete enough to provide a true representation of the document but in summary form.

The major purposes of an executive summary are: (1) to convey why and how the research was undertaken, (2) to summarize the findings, and (3) to suggest future actions. In other words, the executive summary must contain the research objectives, a concise statement of the research methods used, a summary of the findings, and specific conclusions and recommendations.

Research objectives should be as precise as possible. The research questions that guided the project should also be stated in this section. Next, a brief description of the research design including research methods, sampling techniques and any concomitant procedural aspects is addressed. Following this is a statement of findings. Include only key findings that relate to the research objectives. Finally, the executive summary should contain a brief statement of conclusions and recommendations. Conclusions are given as opinions based on the findings. They are statements of what the research generated and what meaning can be attached to the findings. Recommendations, in contrast, are for appropriate future actions. Recommendations focus on specific marketing strategies or tactics the client can use to gain a competitive advantage in the market.

Introduction

The introduction contains information necessary for a preliminary understanding of the different major issues related to the report. Background information contributing to the development of the research project, research problems identified, definition of key terms deployed in the report and the study's scope and emphasis are communicated in the introduction.

This section should also list specific research objectives and questions the study was designed to answer. Hypotheses (if any), analytical models (if any), theoretical frameworks (if any) and the duration of the study are also contained in the introduction. Upon reading the introduction, the client should be able to know exactly what the report is about, why the research was conducted, and what relationships exist between the current study and past or future research endeavours.

Research Design

The research design section is to communicate how the research was conducted. Issues addressed in this section include the following:

1 The type of research design used: exploratory, descriptive, and/or causal.

2 Types of secondary data included in the study.

3 If primary data had been collected, what research methods were used (e.g. observation, questionnaire) and what concomitant research-related administrative procedures were employed (e.g. personal, mail, telephone, Internet).

4 Sampling decisions made. The following issues should be addressed:

    a The population defined and profiled?

    b Sampling units used (businesses, households, individuals, etc.).

    c The sampling frame used in the study.

    d The sampling technique adopted.

    e The sample size determined.

When generating the methods-and-procedures section, the writer can often get bogged down in presenting too much detail. If on completing of this section the reader can say how the research was conducted, clearly covering all the above issues, the writer's objective has been fulfilled. The Marketing Research in Action at the end of the chapter will exemplify further.

Data Analysis and Findings

Many data analysis techniques may be too technical for the clients to understand properly. Therefore the writer of the report (usually the main researcher for the project) should write the data analysis part as easily understandable as possible. Nonetheless, a number of important issues relating to the data analysis conducted should still be covered in this section.

For example, if the researcher is reporting the output of a Chi square they should cover the concepts of statistical and practical significance of the test, the general rationale for performing the test and the assumptions associated with the data analysis technique adopted.

For more sophisticated data analysis techniques, such as multiple regression or ANOVA, it is always good practice to additionally provide a brief description of the technique along with what outcomes can occur.

The actual results of the study – the findings – will constitute the majority of this section of the report. All the findings must be logically arranged so as to correspond to each research objective and research question indicated earlier in the report. These findings should always include a detailed presentation with supporting tables and figures. The tables and figures generated should provide a summation of the data in a concise and non-technical manner. For example, Exhibit 20.2 contains a table illustrating the results for the research question, 'How frequently do you patronize Jimmy Spice's restaurant?' This table illustrates the data output in a concise and non-technical manner, enabling the reader to easily view how frequently respondents patronize the restaurant.

More sophisticated or technical tables or figures should be reserved for the appendixes of the report. Unlike the table in Exhibit 20.2, the information contained in Exhibit 20.3 is more complex and more difficult to explain. While this information is directly related to the research objective concerning factors influencing the image of Jimmy Spice's restaurant, it needs detailed explanation to help the reader understand. Information such as this is better suited for the appendix section of the report.

EXHIBIT 20.2 Findings Illustrating Concise and Non-Technical Results

How frequently do you patronize Jimmy Spice's restaurant?

	Frequency	Percentage	Cumulative Percentage
Occasionally (less than once a month)	111	27.8	27.8
Frequently (1–3 times a month)	178	44.5	72.3
Very Frequently (4 or more times a month)	111	27.8	100.0
Total	400	100.0	

EXHIBIT 20.3 Findings Illustrating More Sophisticated and Technical Results

Rotated Component Matrix[a]

	Component			
	1	2	3	4
X18 -- Excellent Food Taste	.910			
X15 -- Fresh Food	.891			
X20 -- Proper Food Temperature	.862			
X12 -- Freindly Employees		.949		
X21 -- Speed of Service		.941		
X19 -- Knowledgeable Employees		.749		
X16 -- Reasonable Prices			.978	
X14 -- Large Size Portions			.978	
X17 -- Attractive interior				.897
X13 -- Fun Place to Eat				.834

Extraction Method: Prinicpal Component Analysis.
Rotation Method: Varimax with Kaiser Normalization.
  a. Rotation converged in 5 iterations.

Total Variance Explained

	Rotation Sums of Squared Loadings		
Component	Total	% of Variance	Cumulative %
1	2.493	24.927	24.927
2	2.418	24.184	49.112
3	1.994	19.936	69.048
4	1.663	16.628	85.676

Extraction Method: Principal Component Analysis.

Conclusions and Recommendations

Conclusions and recommendations are condensed pieces of information derived mainly from the findings. Conclusions, as illustrated in Exhibit 20.4, are descriptive statements generalizing the results of the study, not necessarily the numbers generated by statistical analysis. Each conclusion is made in reference to the research objectives.

Recommendations are generated by critical thinking. The task is one where the researcher must critically evaluate each conclusion and develop specific areas of applications for strategic or tactical actions. Recommendations should focus on how the client can solve the problem at hand through the creation or enhancement of a competitive advantage, and/or the eradication or minimization of an existing competitive disadvantage.

EXHIBIT 20.4 Examples of Conclusions in a Marketing Research Report

Conclusions

- Four primary factors are related to satisfaction with and patronage of Jimmy Spice's restaurant – food quality, service, value and atmosphere.
- Food quality is the most important factor influencing satisfaction with and patronage of Jimmy Spice's restaurant.
- Perception of service level is the second most important factor influencing satisfaction with and patronage of the restaurant.
- Customers have favourable perceptions of Jimmy Spice's restaurant's food quality and service.
- Customer perceptions of value and atmosphere are relatively less favourable.
- Customer perceptions of Jimmy Spice's restaurant on all four factors – food quality, service, value, and atmosphere – are significantly less favourable for the less frequent patrons.
- More frequent patrons of Jimmy Spice's restaurant have lifestyles that characterize them as innovators and influencers.

EXHIBIT 20.5 Examples of Recommendations in a Marketing Research Report

Recommendations

- Advertising messages should emphasize food quality and service, since these are the most important factors influencing customer satisfaction.
- If advertisements include people, they should be characterized as innovative in their lifestyles.
- Focus group research needs to be conducted to learn why customer perceptions of value and atmosphere are less favourable than perceptions of food quality and service.
- The focus group research also needs to examine why perceptions of less frequent Jimmy Spice's patrons are significantly less favourable than those of more frequent patrons.
- The current study collected data from customers of Jimmy Spice's Restaurant. In the future, data should be collected from non-customers.

Exhibit 20.5 outlines the recommendations that correspond to the conclusions displayed in Exhibit 20.4. You will notice that each recommendation, unlike the conclusions, is in the form of a clear action statement.

Limitations

Good researchers always strive to develop and implement a flawless study for the client. But extraneous factors often place **limitations** on the project. Researchers must be able to reflect on the limitations of a project and communicate them to the client. Common limitations associated with marketing research include the sampling error, non-sampling error, financial constraints, time pressures, scale development and geographical scope of the study.

> **Limitations** Extraneous factors placing certain restrictions on the report that influence its quality level.

Every study has limitations and it is the responsibility of the researcher to make the client aware of them. Researchers should not be embarrassed by limitations but rather admit openly that they exist. Treatment of limitations in the research report usually involves a discussion of results and accuracy. For example, researchers should tell clients about the generalizability of the results beyond the sample used in the study. Weaknesses of specific scales should be addressed, along with potential sources of non-sampling error. If limitations are not stated and later discovered by the client, mistrust and scepticism towards the entire report may result. Limitations rarely diminish the credibility of the report but rather serve to improve the perceptions clients hold towards the integrity of the researcher and the project.

Appendixes

An **appendix** usually contains information not absolutely necessary for the report. Many pieces of this information are of complex, detailed or technical nature, and inclusion of them in the main body may adversely the flow of the report as well as the reader's ability to understand. Some common pieces of information contained in appendixes are statistical calculations, detailed sampling maps, questionnaires, interviewer forms and tables such as the one in Exhibit 20.6.

> **Appendix** A section following the main body of the report; often used to house complex, detailed or technical information.

EXHIBIT 20.6 Example of Detailed Results Table Suitable for the Appendix Section

Descriptives

		N	Mean	Std. Deviation	Std. Error	95 per cent Confidence Interval for Mean Lower Bound	Upper Bound	Minimum	Maximum
X22 -- Satisfaction	Occasionally	111	3.81	.694	.066	3.68	3.94	3	6
	Frequently	111	4.54	.829	.079	4.38	4.70	3	6
	Very Frequently	178	5.23	.735	.055	5.12	5.34	4	6
	Total	400	4.64	.955	.048	4.55	4.74	3	6
X23 -- Likely to Return	Occasionally	111	3.61	.822	.078	3.46	3.77	2	5
	Frequently	111	3.98	.820	.078	3.83	4.14	3	6
	Very Frequently	178	5.04	.833	.062	4.92	5.16	4	6
	Total	400	4.35	1.039	.052	4.25	4.45	2	6
X24 -- Likely to Recommend	Occasionally	111	2.88	.735	.070	2.74	3.02	2	5
	Frequently	111	3.14	.962	.091	2.96	3.33	2	5
	Very Frequently	178	4.01	.681	.051	3.91	4.11	3	5
	Total	400	3.46	.930	.047	3.37	3.55	2	5

ANOVA

		Sum of Squares	df	Mean Square	F	Sig.
X22 -- Satisfaction	Between Groups	139.439	2	69.720	123.482	.000
	Within Groups	224.151	397	.565		
	Total	363.590	399			
X23 -- Likely to Return	Between Groups	159.969	2	79.984	117.159	.000
	Within Groups	271.031	397	.683		
	Total	431.000	399			
X24 -- Likely to Recommend	Between Groups	102.129	2	51.064	83.375	.000
	Within Groups	243.149	397	.612		
	Total	345.278	399			

Researchers know the appendix is usually not read as intensively as the main body of the report. In fact, most appendixes are treated as points of reference in the report. That is, many times information in the appendix is cited in the report in order to guide the reader, if they wish, to further technical or non-technical detail.

Common Problem Areas in Preparing the Marketing Research Report

Often we get so involved with the writing of a research report that we fail to keep in mind key issues that may later present themselves as problems. Such simple things as language may even get overlooked in some cases. Industry best practices suggest five common problem areas that may arise in writing a marketing research report.

1 *Lack of data interpretation.* In some instances, we get involved in constructing results tables but fail to provide proper interpretation of the data in the tables. A good researcher always provides unbiased interpretation of the data and the related findings.

2 *Unnecessary use of multivariate statistics.* To impress clients, many researchers unnecessarily use sophisticated multivariate statistical techniques. In many research reports, tests such as a Chi-square test may be sophisticated enough for data analysis purposes. Avoid showing off your ability to use sophisticated statistical techniques unless they are essential to derive meaning from the data.

3 *Emphasis on packaging instead of quality.* Many researchers go out of their way to make reports look classy or flamboyant using sophisticated computer-generated graphics. While graphic representation of the results is often beneficial for the clarity of the report, never lose sight of the primary reason for writing the report – to provide valid and credible information to the client.

4 *Lack of relevance.* Reporting data, statistics and information that are not consistent with the study's objectives can be a major problem when writing the report. Always develop the report with the research objectives clearly in focus. Avoid adding unnecessary information just to make the report bigger. Always remain in the realm of practicality. Suggest ideas that are doable and consistent with the results of the study. A further discussion of relevance appears in the Closer Look at Research box.

5 *Placing too much emphasis on a few statistical outcomes.* Never base all conclusions or recommendations on one or a few statistically significant results. Always attempt to find additional evidence for any conclusion and recommendation.

The final research document is the end product of the researcher. Individual credibility can be enhanced or damaged by the report, and credibility is what helps a researcher gain repeat business and referrals from clients. The quality, dedication and honesty one places into the report have the potential to generate future business, career promotions and salary increases.

A Closer Look at Research (*In the field*)
Development of the Presentation Component of Marketing Research

Technology advances, including the convergence of computers, software and telephones, have led to the acceleration of the speed of getting answers from the respondents. However, presentation of results, another important component of marketing research, has been slow in benefiting from the technological improvement. While the speed of data collection has leapt ahead, the results are often still printed out on paper in too much detail and clients are bombarded with information.

Progress in results presentation is essential. Nowadays most clients have PCs on their desks. The voice of the consumer should be made available to them in an interactive format that allows for immediate action. This is far from what conventional presentation can do. It means quickly identifying what matters in the data, comparing it to past data for any change and giving the client what is needed. In this way data could be used to make swift decisions and match the almost daily changes in the marketplace. To provide useful research, suppliers must know their clients' business. They can no longer be providers of results tables only, but must provide data specifically tailored to the needs of their clients.

The future will see more specialization by research companies, including research companies collecting data and research companies using the data to inform clients. And many of the new developments in marketing research will be in the area of presenting data in a form that clients can access easily, quickly, and use interactively. That's a long way from the old-style presentation of data in large bound volumes of tables.

The Critical Nature of Presentations

Presentation of marketing research results can be as important as, if not more important than, the results of the research itself. This is true for several reasons. First, any research, no matter how well done or how important, cannot be properly acted upon if the results are not effectively communicated to those who will use the information in making decisions. Managers need clear and accurate information if they are going to make good decisions, and if they do not understand the marketing research findings because of improper presentation, they may well make poor decisions that lead to difficulty not only for the organization but also for individuals in the organization affected by those decisions. Second, the presentation is sometimes the only part of the marketing research project that will be seen by those commissioning the report. Senior managers often do not have the time to review all aspects of a research project, so they rely on the researcher to carry out the research properly and then present the findings concisely. Third, the form of the presentation and the perceived quality of the content are closely intertwined. Poorly organized presentations in an unclear and lengthy format often lead audiences to discount the content. Presentations that use high-technology applications and methods are often perceived as having more merit than presentations that rely on older and lower technology

Presenting Marketing Research Results

Traditional presentation methods include chalkboards, whiteboards (dry-erase boards), and overhead projectors. These tried-and-true methods used to be acceptable. Today, however, they do not effectively communicate nearly as well. The desire to create cleaner, more professional-looking presentations of marketing research results has led to the development of a wide variety of computer-based presentation applications, from computer-generated overhead transparencies to full-blown multimedia presentations, complete with text, graphics, sound and video or animation.

General Guidelines for Preparing the Visual Presentation

The visual presentation is a separate but equal component of the marketing research report. Equal because the visual presentation must reflect the exact content of the written marketing research report. Separate because based on the type of presentation and style preference of the presenter, it may not adhere to the same basic outline of the written research report. Regardless of the presentation style used, the visual presentation has one primary goal: to provide a visual summary of the marketing research report, designed in a manner that will complement and enhance oral communication of the written marketing research report.

In many cases, Microsoft PowerPoint is the preferred method of preparing the visual marketing research presentation. Given the versatility of PowerPoint, the visual presentation can be as simple as multiple slides reflecting summary statements of the written report, or as complex as a total multimedia presentation including the use of sound, animation, colour graphics and streaming video. Regardless of the complexity in the presentation, industry practices suggest the following guidelines:

1 Begin with a slide showing the title of the presentation and the individual(s) doing the presentation. In addition, the client and the marketing research firm should also be identified.

2 A sequence of slides should be developed indicating the objectives of the research and the specific research questions to be addressed, followed by the research methodology employed and a description of the sample used.

3 A visual presentation often includes ancillary material such as environmental trends, market activities, customer behaviours and other forms of secondary data.

4 Additional slides should be developed that highlight the research findings or particular results of the study which the researcher deems important for communicating with the audiences.

5 Finally, the presentation should conclude with conclusions, recommendations, and if applicable research implications.

A PowerPoint presentation illustrating many of the above suggestions can be reviewed at www.mhhe.com/shiu09.

Using Computer Software to Develop Presentations

There are many computer software packages for presentation purposes. We focus on two major formats useful in presenting marketing research findings: computer screen projection and Web pages. Projecting the computer screen has several advantages. Researchers often find it easy to develop the presentation on a computer and import information from the computer files of the research project as needed. The computer helps the researcher stay organized during presentations, with little chance of lost or out-of-order transparencies. It also facilitates the use of sound, colour and other graphics. Finally, it enables presenters to reduce costs, since they no longer need to pay for costly colour transparencies, and its electronic format means it can easily be emailed to clients ahead of time for review.

One of the most widely used presentation software packages is Microsoft's **PowerPoint**. PowerPoint can develop transparencies, 35-mm slides and on-screen electronic presentations. It can also be used to develop notes, audience handouts and outlines, all from the same information.

PowerPoint A software package used to develop slides for electronic presentation of research results.

Thus, the presenter has to type or import information only once to develop the presentation. Presentation software packages such as PowerPoint can be used to develop eye-catching, organized presentations that convey research findings concisely and smoothly.

Another emerging format for presentations is the use of **hypertext markup language (HTML)** to create Web pages. This is the format for communication over the Internet. By using the Internet, researchers are able to communicate marketing research results to their audiences around the world, without the restrictions of time or geography. No longer do all members of the audience need to be at a given time in the same location to receive information during a presentation. Marketing research results can be posted on Web pages and viewed at leisure. Furthermore, not only the presentation itself but also the supporting materials – including text, sound, graphics, and animation or movie files – are available for viewers to download and see, and articles on similar topics can be linked together for easy reference. Also, technology has made it possible to conduct real-time video conferencing where participants in different geographical locations take part in meetings, seeing and hearing each other through their computers over the Internet.

Hypertext markup language (HTML) Computer language used to create Web pages for communicating results on the Internet.

In developing Internet-based presentations, researchers have several options. They can put their information on a server for the world to view, and let those interested in the information know where and how to access it so they can receive the information independently, at their convenience. Or, if the researcher wants to present the information at a given time and location, they can place the information either on a server or on their own computer, and then personally lead the presentation of information to the audience, adding input and guiding the presentation along.

In this section, we focus on the creation and development of Internet-based presentations that will be placed on a server for geographically dispersed audiences to view independently. But keep in mind that the presenter can just as easily use this format in actual presentations of research results to a local audience. The flexibility and power of Internet-based presentations makes them an attractive format for use where time or distance is a problem in disseminating information.

One easy-to-use software package is **Claris Home Page** (www.learningspace.org/tech/clrs_hmpg/chintro.html), which is used to create Web pages and can integrate text, graphics and other types of computer files. While there are several software packages available for Web page development, they are similar enough in operation that an understanding of Claris Home Page should provide a sound foundation for using any of the other packages.

Claris Home Page A software package used to create Web pages that can integrate text, graphics and other types of computer files.

Advantages and Disadvantages of Computer Formats

Computer screen projection and Web page presentation formats each have their own advantages and disadvantages. Both formats enable presenters to easily import text outlines into the presentation software. Both formats also enable the integration of text, graphics and other types of computer files to create eye-catching presentations and the use of colouring, background shading and textures to highlight certain topics or major points. However, both formats require at least the use of computers and their basic power requirements – it would be difficult to give a computer-based presentation to a group of farmers in a wheat field without a nearby source of electricity. Both formats also require the presenter, or both the presenter and the audience, to have some basic level of computer competence.

The use of software packages such as Microsoft PowerPoint in computer screen projection enables presenters to control their presentation in terms of timing, highlighting key points and making transitions between topics. A disadvantage, however, is that it requires the audience to be physically present at a given time and location. Also, the amount of information presented is usually limited to the main points, with supporting documentation usually distributed in printed form, requiring added printing expense. Finally, animations and other high-tech graphics are not easily integrated into this presentation format.

Internet-based presentations of marketing research have the primary advantage of not requiring the audience to be physically present at any given time or location. Members of the audience can access the information at any time, from many different locations. For example, a member of the marketing division at a multinational enterprise can access a designated website and download the reading materials while travelling from Paris to Vienna, using a laptop computer and a mobile phone. Furthermore, additional information with supporting documentation, graphics, animations or sounds can be readily available on request through the computer. Also, information from other websites can be linked so that the audience can quickly and easily access a wealth of relevant information. Finally, the Web itself can be used to conduct further investigations. Computer searches can be conducted to find out what other information is available and where it can be found.

Using the Internet has its drawbacks, however. The main drawback is that the presenter loses some control over the presentation, so the information must be presented in a more self-explanatory fashion. This requires presenters to spend more time on developing their presentations, with greater organization and an eye towards avoiding all possible misunderstandings. Another consideration is that the speed at which files are transmitted over the Internet can be a problem, particularly if large graphics files must be transmitted. Finally, creating Internet-based presentations requires presenters to have the relevant computer skills, since, for example, graphics files must often be converted and saved in particular file formats for use in Web pages.

A Closer Look at Research *(In the field)*
Development of the Presentation Component of Marketing Research

Assume you are asked to do this exercise – you are shown eight words (such as plate, elephant, bicycle) for a few seconds and are asked to remember them, and then, after they are taken away, you are required to recall them. Results should show that those who can undertake this task well can do so by creating stories around the data (the eight words in this case). The results of this exercise corresponds with what Daniel Chandler wrote in his book *Semiotics* (2007): 'We seem as a species to be driven by a desire to make meanings; above all, we are surely homo significans – meaning-makers'. Information without a story is easier to forget. On the contrary, people can recall information if they are able to create a story around it.

In a workshop organized by the European Pharmaceutical Marketing Research Association, Alexis Puhan from skillbuild inc. in Switzerland demonstrated how to use a Think Story Line approach to present marketing research results.

Alexis firstly highlighted the importance of the concepts of 'summarizing' and 'synthesizing' in marketing research presentation. Summarizing is about selecting the key facts, while synthesizing is concerned with discussing the implications of what should be done. These two concepts are not necessarily polar opposites – some comments can be parts of each.

He then emphasized how to build a story, or message, by selecting evidence in two different types of pyramid structures. The first could be considered a 'grouping/logical structure' where your message is supported by three major arguments, and each of these arguments could then be subdivided. The other could be an 'argument/chain structure' where the main message is reached towards the end of a reasoned assessment of the evidence.

Mobile Phone Consumer Research in Switzerland: Writing a Marketing Research Report and Preparing a PowerPoint Slide Presentation

After some documentary research and interviews with several experts, Cyril Ruchonnet, assistant professor at HEC University of Geneva, decided to investigate customers' attitudes towards mobile phone providers in the Geneva context. He decided to limit his study to a survey of the attitudes of a group of undergraduate students at the University of Geneva. His objective was to focus on respondents' perception and knowledge of the three providers established in the market, namely Sunrise, Orange and Swisscom. He had in mind to proceed with a survey of a full class of some sixty third-year undergraduate students. The questionnaire would be administered in class.

He intended to take the position of a hypothetical marketing manager employed at any of these three firms who wonders whether the targeting, positioning and advertising content of their firm should be altered as a result of any possibly significant confusion among customers.

His first task was to formulate the research problems that had to be investigated and to delineate the corresponding information needs. After some thought and discussion with several experts in mobile telephony, Cyril decided first to formulate the decision problems that a mobile phone provider would have to consider in case of consumer confusion and second to formulate the corresponding research questions that would lead to the definition of the information needs that would have to be specified prior to the writing of a questionnaire. These issues are presented below.

First decision problem:

1. Should the targeting strategy which has been adopted be altered?

Cyril reasoned that the targeting adopted by the providers might not be appropriate, and felt that the profile of the customers for each provider should be investigated. He formulated the research problem as follows:

1. What is the targeting of each provider by comparison to the targeting adopted by the other competitors?

He felt that he needed to get data on:

- The provider(s) respondents subscribe to;
- The age group of the customers of each provider;
- The gender of the customers of each provider.

Second decision problem:

2. Should the positioning strategy which has been adopted be altered?

Cyril thought it was a major issue. He formulated the corresponding research problem as follows:

2. What is the present positioning of each brand in comparison to the other brands?

Data needed was:

- Respondent's perception of each provider including the one he/she is subscribing to;
- Respondent's perception of the services offered by each provider.

Third decision problem:

3. Should communication content be modified?

The research problem was formulated as follows:

3.1. What is the respondents' knowledge regarding the services offered by the three competing brands?

Corresponding information needs are:

- Knowledge of services offered by the three competitors;
- Technical services;
- Commercial services.

3.2. What is the level of knowledge of competitive position of each provider?

Corresponding information needs are:

- Perceived market share of each provider.

In addition, Cyril felt that he needed the following information on the respondents for classification purposes:

- Age;
- Gender;
- Subscriber/non-subscriber;
- Operator subscribed to;
- Pre-paid cardholder or subscriber.

Having specified the research questions and information needs, Cyril proceeded with the drafting of a questionnaire (see below), which was administered as planned to a class of some sixty undergraduate students at the University of Geneva. Results were then computed. Below are these results, including frequencies for all questions and other more sophisticated analysis.

1 There are three mobile phone providers in Switzerland, namely Swisscom, Sunrise and Orange. Which one do you think holds the largest market share?
[1.6 per cent] Orange
[79.7 per cent] Swisscom
[10.9 per cent] Sunrise
[1.6 per cent] No difference between the operators
[6.3 per cent] Don't know

2 Which operator provides customers with the largest amount of information on its services in its advertisements?
[30.2 per cent] Orange
[23.8 per cent] Swisscom
[28.1 per cent] Sunrise
[17.5 per cent] Don't know

3 Which of the services listed below are offered by each of the three operators? (Tick several cases if necessary):

	Proposed by Orange	Proposed by Swisscom	Proposed by Sunrise	Don't Know
WAP	[77.8%]	[85.7%]	[68.3%]	[14.3%]
Fax	[41.3%]	[54.0%]	[36.5%]	[46.0%]
Voice mail	[93.7%]	[95.2%]	[92.1%]	[4.8%]
Conferencing	[33.3%]	[44.4%]	[30.2%]	[55.6%]
GPRS	[27.0%]	[30.2%]	[28.6%]	[69.8%]
SMS	[96.8%]	[100.0%]	[96.8%]	[0%]

Data transmission	[38.1%]	[42.9%]	[36.5%]	[57.1%]
Display of calling number	[90.5%]	[98.4%]	[88.9%]	[1.6%]
Call transfer	[73.0%]	[82.5%]	[76.2%]	[7.5%]
24-hour customer service	[71.4%]	[74.6%]	[74.6%]	[15.4%]
Detailed billing	[71.4%]	[47.6%]	[69.8%]	[28.6%]
Loyalty programme	[61.9%]	[38.1%]	[38.1%]	[38.1%]
Mail information service	[49.2%]	[61.9%]	[55.6%]	[38.1%]
SMS information service	[66.7%]	[55.6%]	[49.2%]	[33.3%]

4 Please indicate to what extent you agree with the following statements (1 = does not agree at all, 5 = completely agree):

	1	2	3	4	5
Sunrise offers high-level knowhow	[4.8%]	[17.5%]	[55.6%]	[17.5%]	[4.8%]
Swisscom is a strong company	[0%]	[7.8%]	[31.3%]	[40.6%]	[20.3%]
Orange listens to the customers	[6.5%]	[9.7%]	[37.1%]	[30.6%]	[16.1%]
Swisscom listens to the customers	[7.8%]	[25.0%]	[39.1%]	[26.6%]	[1.6%]
Orange is a dynamic company	[1.6%]	[11.1%]	[15.9%]	[49.2%]	[22.2%]
Sunrise is a strong company	[1.6%]	[25.4%]	[46.0%]	[27.0%]	[0%]
Orange is a cheap operator	[11.1%]	[22.2%]	[30.2%]	[30.2%]	[6.3%]
Sunrise listens to the customers	[4.7%]	[10.9%]	[48.4%]	[31.3%]	[4.7%]
Swisscom focuses on user friendliness	[14.1%]	[46.9%]	[34.4%]	[4.7%]	[0%]
Swisscom offers high-level knowhow	[0%]	[3.1%]	[18.8%]	[46.9%]	[31.3%]
Sunrise is a dynamic company	[0%]	[7.9%]	[46.0%]	[36.5%]	[9.5%]
Orange offers reliable services	[11.1%]	[15.9%]	[39.7%]	[28.6%]	[4.8%]
Orange offers high-level knowhow	[1.6%]	[23.8%]	[44.4%]	[22.2%]	[7.9%]
Sunrise focuses on user friendliness	[1.6%]	[15.9%]	[44.4%]	[30.2%]	[7.9%]
Swisscom is a cheap operator	[39.1%]	[37.5%]	[15.6%]	[4.7%]	[3.1%]
Orange is a strong company	[3.2%]	[17.5%]	[49.2%]	[23.8%]	[6.3%]
Sunrise is a cheap company	[3.2%]	[11.1%]	[25.4%]	[39.7%]	[20.6%]
Swisscom offers reliable services	[0%]	[3.1%]	[20.3%]	[48.4%]	[28.1%]
Swisscom is a dynamic company	[6.3%]	[29.7%]	[42.2%]	[20.3%]	[1.6%]
Orange focuses on user friendliness	[1.6%]	[7.9%]	[46.0%]	[27.0%]	[17.5%]
Sunrise offers reliable services	[6.3%]	[25.4%]	[41.3%]	[23.8%]	[3.2%]

5 Which of the following age groups does each of the operators target? (only one answer by operator)

	15–25	25–35	Over 35	Don't Know
Orange	[57.6%]	[36.4%]	[0%]	[3.0%]
Swisscom	[0%]	[28.8%]	[63.6%]	[4.5%]
Sunrise	[54.5%]	[31.8%]	[3.0%]	[7.6%]

6 Do you feel that the operators are primarily targeting men or women?

	Primarily Women	Primarily Men	Don't Know
Orange	[34.8%]	[13.6%]	[48.5%]
Swisscom	[6.1%]	[51.5%]	[39.4%]
Sunrise	[12.1%]	[25.8%]	[57.6%]

7 Do you feel that mobile telephony is easy or difficult to understand (1 = very easy to understand, 5 = very difficult to understand)?

1	2	3	4	5
[13.6%]	[39.4%]	[28.8%]	[13.6%]	[1.5%]

8a Do you own a mobile phone?
[92.4 per cent] Yes
[4.5 per cent] No
If your answer is << No >> go to question 9

8b If yes, how long for?
mean = 37 months

8c Do you subscribe to a monthly service or do you hold a prepaid card?

	Monthly Service	Pre-Paid Card	None
With Orange	[30.3%]	[ ]	[ ]
With Swisscom	[33.3%]	[ ]	[ ]
With Sunrise	[34.8%]	[ ]	[ ]

8d Have you subscribed to any other operator before?
[43.9 per cent] Yes
[53.0 per cent] No

8e If yes, which was (were) your previous operators?
[19.7 per cent] Orange
[25.8 per cent] Swisscom
[9.1 per cent] Sunrise

8f How please are you with your present operator?

	Not Client	Very Unsatisfied	Rather Unsatisfied	Neither Unsatisfied Nor Satisfied	Rather Satisfied	Very Satisfied
Orange	[56.9%]	[3.1%]	[1.5%]	[13.8%]	[10.8%]	[3.1%]
Swisscom	[55.4%]	[1.5%]	[4.6%]	[3.1%]	[18.5%]	[6.2%]
Sunrise	[58.5%]	[1.5%]	[4.6%]	[3.1%]	[23.1%]	[1.5%]

9 Female [34.8 per cent] or Male [65.2 per cent]?

10 How old are you?
mean = 23 years

Comparison of respondent age by mobile provider (Orange, Sunrise, Swisscom)
Test used: ANOVA (analysis of variance)

	Sum of Squares	Degrees of Freedom	Sum of Squares	F	p-Value
Between groups	1.152	2	.576	.180	.836
Within groups	166.230	52	3.197		
Total	167.382	54			

Comparison of respondent gender by mobile provider (Orange, Sunrise, Swisscom)

Test used: Pearson chi-square test

	Orange	Swisscom	Sunrise	Total
Female	5	3	10	18
Male	13	13	11	37
Total	18	16	21	55

Pearson chi-square value $= 3.735$, p-value $= .154$

Perceived age groups targeted by each operator

Test used: Friedman chi-square test

	Mean Rank
Orange	1.51
Swisscom	2.90
Sunrise	1.59

Friedman chi-square value $= 78.677$, p-value $= .000$

Perceived gender groups targeted by each operator

	Female	Male
Orange	17	8
Swisscom	4	21
Sunrise	8	17

Cochran's $Q = 14.000$, p-value $= .001$

Perceived image of the three operators

Test used: Friedman chi-square test

	Swisscom	Orange	Sunrise	p-Value
High level of knowhow	2.63	1.79	1.58	.000
Strong company	2.39	1.85	1.76	.000
Reliable services	2.55	1.75	1.71	.000
Listens to the customers	1.77	2.19	2.05	.020
Dynamic company	1.56	2.40	2.04	.000
Focuses on user friendliness	1.41	2.37	2.21	.000
Cheap operator	1.40	2.16	2.40	.000

Knowledge of services offered by the three operators

Test used: Cochran's Q

	Swisscom	Orange	Sunrise	p-Value
WAP	77.80	85.70	68.30	.003
Fax	41.30	54.00	36.50	.002
Voice mail	93.70	95.20	92.10	.549
Conferencing	33.30	44.40	30.20	.035
GPRS	27.00	30.20	28.60	.687
SMS	96.80	100.00	96.80	.135
Data transmission	38.10	42.90	36.50	.236

Display of calling number	90.50	98.40	88.90	.021
Call transfer	73.00	82.50	76.20	.097
24-hour customer service	71.40	74.60	74.60	.695
Detailed billing	71.40	47.60	69.80	.001
Loyalty programme	61.90	38.10	38.10	.000
Mail information service	49.20	61.90	55.60	.191
SMS information service	66.70	55.60	49.20	.007

Questions

1 On the basis of the results above, use the knowledge you've learned from this chapter to write a corresponding marketing research report.

2 Then prepare PowerPoint slides for presentation of these results.

Summary of Learning Objectives

■ **Understand the primary objectives of a written marketing research report.**
There are four primary objectives. First is to effectively communicate the findings of the marketing research project. Second is to provide an accurate interpretation of those findings. Third is to establish the credibility of the research project, and fourth is to serve a future reference document for strategic or tactical decisions.

■ **Explain how a marketing research report is organized.**
A marketing research report generally starts with a title page, a table of contents and an executive summary. Following the executive summary are the introduction of the report, a description of the research design employed, and a discussion of data analysis and findings. The final elements are conclusions and recommendations, and a description of limitations. If necessary appendixes can be added, which can include technical explanations or documentation.

■ **List problems that can be encountered when preparing a marketing research report.**
Problem areas that may arise in the preparation of a marketing research report are (1) lack of data interpretation, (2) unnecessary use of multivariate statistics, (3) emphasis on packaging instead of quality, (4) lack of relevance and (5) placing too much emphasis on a few statistical outcomes.

■ **Understand the importance of presentations in marketing research.**
Presentations are important because research results must be effectively communicated to those seeking to use the information in decision making. Managers need clear and accurate information if they are going to make good decisions, and if they do not understand the marketing research findings because of improper presentation, they may well make poor decisions that lead to difficulty not only for the organization but also for individuals in the organization affected by those decisions. Sometimes the presentation is the only part of the marketing research project that will be seen by those commissioning the report. The form of the presentation and the perceived quality of the content are closely intertwined. Poorly organized presentations in an unclear and lengthy format often lead audiences to discount the content.

- **Identify different software options available for developing presentations.**
  There are many computer software packages for presentation purposes. The two major software-based formats for presenting information are (1) computer screen projection, in which computer slides are projected to a live audience, and (2) Internet-based presentation or Web pages.

- **Understand the advantages and disadvantages of different software options available for developing presentations.**
  Computer screen projection requires the audience to be physically present at a given time and location but allows the presenter to control the presentation, receive immediate feedback from the audience, and answer any questions. Internet-based presentations or Web pages enable audiences to review the information anytime from anywhere they have computer access. Yet the drawbacks of this option are that the presenter loses some control over the presentation, the speed at which files are transmitted can be a problem, and the presenter is required to have the relevant computer skills.

Key Terms and Concepts

Accuracy   670
Appendix   676
Believability   670
Claris Home Page   680
Credibility   670
Executive summary   672

**Hypertext markup language
(HTML)**   680
Limitations   675
PowerPoint   679
Professional organization   670

Review Questions

1   What are the primary objectives of the marketing research report? Briefly discuss each objective and why they are so important.

2   In the context of the marketing research report, what is the primary goal of the executive summary?

3   What is the primary purpose of the research methods-and-procedures section of a marketing research report?

4   Why are conclusions and recommendations included in a marketing research report?

5   What are some common problems in preparing the marketing research report?

6   What are some general guidelines for preparing a visual presentation?

7   What is the value of computer software in developing marketing research presentations?

8   Why is Microsoft PowerPoint such a valuable tool for preparing marketing research presentations?

1 **Experience the Internet.** Go to the Website www.intelliquest.com/resources, click on presentations and select a presentation of your choice. Identify the presentation you selected and provide a critical review of the effectiveness of that presentation.

2 **Experience the Internet.** Go to the Website www.microsoft.com/Education/ Tutorials. aspx. Complete the Tutorials dialogue box by typing in higher education in the Grade Level box, technology in the Learning Area box, and PowerPoint in the Product box. After selecting and completing the tutorial, provide written comments on the benefits you received by taking this tutorial.

3 On the basis of what you have learned about marketing research presentations, select Jimmy Spice's restaurant data or one of the other databases provided with this text (see Deli Depot, MRIA, Chapter 14; Remingtons, MRIA, Chapter 15; Qualkote, MRIA, Chapter 16; or DVD Survey, MRIA, Chapter 17). Analyse the data using the appropriate statistical techniques, prepare a PowerPoint presentation of your findings, and present it to your research class.

4 How can the Internet be used to facilitate communication of marketing research results?

5 **SPSS Exercise.** Using Jimmy Spice's restaurant data set and the questionnaire found in Chapter 14, conduct the following tasks:

   a Conduct a factor analysis using the restaurant perceptions variables ($X_{12} - X_{21}$). After you find the best factor solution, label the factors based on which variables load on each factor.

   b Develop a PowerPoint presentation that visually displays the results.

6 **SPSS Exercise.** Using Jimmy Spice's restaurant dataset and the questionnaire found in Chapter 14, conduct the following tasks:

   a Run a regression using the restaurant perceptions variables ($X_{12} - X_{21}$) as independent variables and variable X_{22} – Satisfaction as the dependent variable. Develop the best multiple regression solution (i.e. the one that has only the significant independent variables in the regression model) for this set of data.

   b Prepare a PowerPoint presentation that visually displays the results.

Appendix 1

Careers in Marketing Research

Career opportunities in marketing research vary by industry, company and size of company. Different positions exist in consumer products companies, industrial goods companies, internal marketing research departments and professional marketing research firms. Marketing research tasks range from the very simple, such as tabulation of questionnaires, to the very complex, such as sophisticated data analysis.

In addition to the skills discussed previously in this chapter, which are regarded as very important for becoming a successful marketing researcher, here are a few real-life examples to demonstrate what kinds of qualities recruiters are actually looking for to fill their marketing research job vacancies.

First, a job advertisement via the ESOMAR website in May 2008 for a research manager of Cataliz Company based in Paris specifies that a suitable candidate should possess a number of characteristics, including (1) a university degree, preferably with a strong mathematics and statistics component; (2) fluency in English and French both verbally and in writing; (3) 3 to 5 years' experience in ad hoc market research, the majority of it in an agency; (4) good communication skills; and (5) the ability to oversee the project but not become immersed in details.

Second, via the Marketing Research Society website in April 2007, a suitable person for the post of market research executive in Birmingham, UK should (1) be of graduate calibre; (2) have a proven ability to effectively interpret continuous panel data; (3) possess a working understanding of primary qualitative and quantitative market research techniques; and (4) be equipped with excellent analytical, project management and interpersonal skills.

Third, on the ESOMAR website in May 2008, there was a vacancy announcement for the post of research project manager of HTP Concept Company headquartered in Berlin. Interested applicants for this post should check whether they (1) have 3–5 years of experience working in a qualitative marketing research company, in the marketing or market research department of a corporation, or in planning within an advertising agency; (2) have been trained in classical and modern methods of market research, and have the ability to decide which method fits best with which type of research project; (3) have good presentation skills and be well-versed in Engish; (4) have experience in conducting international projects, be comfortable with coordinating and supervising international marketing projects, and don't see regular travel as a burden; and (5) have an active interest in brands as well as cultural and social trends.

Besides the characteristics noted in the above three examples, an increasing number of European marketing research firms, particularly in the UK, are using some form of psychometric or aptitude testing in recruitment and development. At MORI, candidates are required to attend an hour-long job interview and do a one-and-a-half hour psychometric test. The candidate's eye for detail, report writing ability and numerical skills are measured, and the suitability for the type of role within a team setting to be undertaken by the successful candidate would be assessed. At NOP World, candidates also need to do a one-and-a-half hour test for assessing their attitude and critical thinking skills. They are also required to analyse a given set of market research data for understanding their analytical skills. All these tests aim at reducing the subjectivity that may occur in job interviews. As John Gotting, former HR Director for Estée Lauder and Heron International, said, the insight these tests give can highlight a candidate's important character trait that may otherwise take three months on the job to reveal.

In the UK, if you are interested in a job in marketing research, a good way to start is to look at the Marketing Research Society website for the listing of jobs offered by marketing research companies. If you are pursuing a professional qualification in marketing research, the Society offers the programme of Advanced Certificate in Marketing and Social Research Practice, which is linked to the UK's National Qualifications Framework. The Society also provides a variety of training programmes for current and would-be marketing researchers. These include, among others, qualitative research, quantitative research, moderating skills, ethnic minority research, children and young people research, and building client relationships.

In Europe as a whole, interested readers can look at ESOMAR's website, which is physically located in Amsterdam and which sells the *Directory of Research Organizations*. From this, you can ascertain further details of marketing research organizations in different parts of the world. The Directory categorizes them into four groups: fieldwork and tabulation, full service agency, consultant, and qualitative agency/consultant. At times these organizations are recruiting marketing researchers and will put their job advertisements on their websites. Year on year, ESOMAR also organizes a number of workshops on topics such as interviewing, ethnography and observational research, for interested people to enhance their marketing research knowledge and skills.

In the US there is the Marketing Research Association in Connecticut, which published a useful guidebook, *Career Guide: Your Future in Marketing Research*. Another useful reference is the *Marketing and Sales Career Directory* published by Gale Research Inc. in Detroit. This career directory is available at many university libraries.

1 Go to the home Web page for Research International, one of the world leaders in custom market research services, and identify the requirements that Research International is seeking in marketing research personnel. Write a brief description of these requirements and report your findings to your learning group.

2 If you were seeking a marketing research position at Research International, how would you prepare yourself through training and education for such a position? Put together a one-year plan for yourself identifying the college courses, special activities, interests and related work experience you would engage in to obtain a marketing research position at Research International.

Using SPSS with Jimmy Spice's Restaurant Database

The SPSS software package is very user-friendly and enables you to easily learn the various statistical techniques without having to use formulas and calculate the results. The approach is a simple Windows-based 'point-and-click' process. In this appendix, we provide a brief overview of how to use the package and click-through sequences for the techniques you will be using. This will be a quick reference point for you to refresh your memory on how to run the various techniques.

When you run the SPSS software, you will see a screen like that in Exhibit A2.1. It may be slightly different from your screen, because you may be running a newer or an older version than the one that this book refers to at the time of publishing.

The case study database is available from our website at www.mhhe.com/shiu09 or from your instructor. You will note the columns are blank because the data have not been entered into the SPSS software.

When you load SPSS a screen in the top left-hand corner labelled Untitled – SPSS Data Editor should be visible in the background. In the foreground is a dialogue box called SPSS for Windows Student Version. If you have never run SPSS you will have to tell the programme where to find the data. If you have previously run the SPSS programme you can simply highlight the location of the database and click on OK at the bottom of the screen. The SPSS Data Editor screen without the dialogue box in the foreground is shown in Exhibit A2.1.

EXHIBIT A2.1 SPSS Data Editor Window with No Data

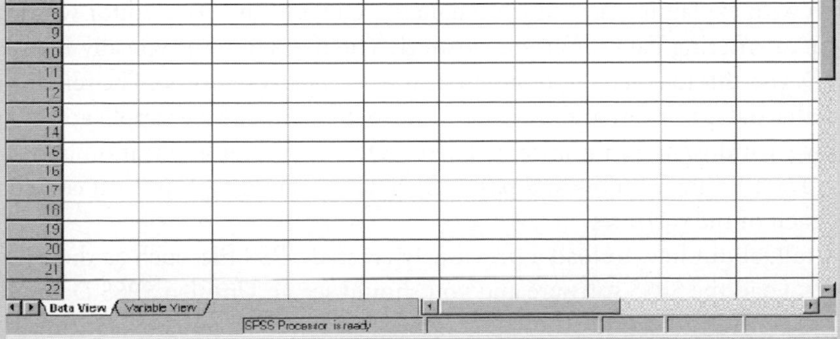

Across the top of the screen is a toolbar with a series of pull-down menus. Each of these menus leads you to several functions. An overview of these menu functions is shown below.

Menus

There are 10 'pull-down' menus across the top of the screen. You can access most SPSS functions and commands by making selections from the menus on the main menu bar. Below are the major features accessed from each of the menus on the Student Version 12 of the SPSS software.

File = create new SPSS files; open existing files; save a file; print; and exit.

Edit = cut and/or copy text or graphics; find specific data; change default options such as size or type of font, fill patterns for charts, types of tables, display format for numerical variables, and so forth.

View = modify what and how information is displayed in the window.

Data = make changes to SPSS data files; add variables and/or cases; change the order of the respondents; split your data file for analysis; and select specific respondents for analysis by themselves.

Transform = compute changes or combinations of data variables; create new variables from combinations of other variables; create random seed numbers; count occurrences of values within cases; recode existing variables; create categories for existing variables; replace missing variables; and so on.

Analyse = prepare reports; execute selected statistical techniques such as frequencies, correlation and regression, factor, cluster, and so on.

Graphs = prepare graphs and charts of data, such as bar, line, and pie charts; also boxplots, scatter diagrams, and histograms.

Utilities = information about variables such as missing values, column width, measurement level, and so on.

Window = minimize windows or move between windows.

Help = a brief tutorial of how to use SPSS; includes a link to the SPSS home page at www.spss.com.

Entering Data

There are two ways you can enter data into SPSS files. One is to enter data directly into the Data Editor window. This can be done by creating an entirely new file or by bringing data in from another software package such as Excel. The other is to load data from a file that has been created in another SPSS application.

Let's begin with explaining how to enter data directly into the Data Editor window. The process is similar to entering data into a spreadsheet. The first column typically is used to enter a respondent ID. Use this to enter a respondent number for each response. The remaining columns are used to enter data. You can also 'cut and paste' data from another application. Simply open the Data Editor window and minimize it. Then go to your other application and copy the file, return to the Data Editor window and paste the data in it, making sure you correctly align the columns for each of the variables.

Now let's talk about how to load a previously created SPSS file, such as the one that comes with your text. Load the SPSS software and you should see an Untitled SPSS Data Editor screen. Click on the Open File icon and you will get an Open File dialogue box. Click on 'Look in' to indicate where to look for your file. For example, look on your CD or other storage device.

This will locate your SPSS files and you should click on Jimmy Spice's restaurant survey. This will load up your file and you will be ready to run your SPSS analysis.

Data View

When you load up your SPSS file it will show the Data View screen. Exhibit A2.2 shows the Data View screen for Jimmy Spice's restaurant survey. This screen is used to run data analysis and to build data files. The other view of the Data Editor is Variable View. The Variable View shows you information about the variables. To move between the two views go to the bottom left-hand corner of the screen and click on the view you want. We discuss the Variable View screen in the next section.

The survey database is set up in columns. The first column on the far left labelled 'id' is a unique number for each of the 400 respondents in your database. The remaining columns are the data from the interviews conducted at the restaurant. In the first 3 columns to the right of the id you have the values for the three screening questions. Then, you have the first six variables of the survey – the lifestyle variables (X_1–X_6). For example, respondent 1 gave the restaurant a '6' on the 7-point scale for the first variable (X_1). Similarly, that same respondent rated the restaurant a '4' on the second variable (X_2) and a '5' on the third one (X_3). Exhibit A2.2 shows only the id, the three screening variables, and the first six variables of the survey. But on your SPSS screen if you scroll to the right you will see the data for all of the survey variables.

EXHIBIT A2.2 Data View of Jimmy Spice's Restaurant Survey Database

SPSS_Data_Jimmy_Spice's_N_427.sav [DataSet1] - SPSS Data Editor

File Edit View Data Transform Analyze Graphs Utilities Add-ons Window Help

1 : id   1   Visible: 39 of 39 Variables

	id	x_s1	x_s2	x_s3	x1	x2	x3	x4	x5	x6	x7
1	1	1	1	1	6	4	5	3	4	5	4
2	2	1	1	1	4	3	4	2	4	4	4
3	3	1	1	1	3	4	7	3	4	7	5
4	4	1	1	1	6	5	7	4	4	7	4
5	5	1	1	1	4	4	5	2	4	5	4
6	6	1	1	1	4	6	7	2	4	7	4
7	7	1	1	1	5	4	5	3	2	5	2
8	8	1	1	1	6	4	6	4	4	6	4
9	9	1	1	1	6	5	6	2	5	5	2
10	10	1	1	1	5	5	6	3	4	6	2
11	11	1	1	1	4	4	5	3	5	5	5
12	12	1	1	1	6	3	4	4	5	4	5
13	13	1	1	1	5	2	3	4	4	3	4
14	14	1	1	1	6	5	7	3	5	7	5
15	15	1	1	1	6	3	4	4	2	4	2
16	16	1	1	1	6	5	7	4	4	6	4
17	17	1	1	1	5	5	7	4	4	7	4
18	18	1	1	1	6	5	6	4	4	5	5
19	19	1	1	1	4	2	3	3	3	3	5
20	20	1	1	1	6	4	5	3	5	5	4
21	21	1	1	1	5	4	6	4	3	6	4
22	22	1	1	1	5	2	3	4	3	3	5
23	23	1	1	1	6	6	7	4	5	7	5
24	24	1	1	1	4	5	7	4	4	6	6

Data View | Variable View

SPSS Processor is ready

Variable View

Exhibit A2.3 shows the Variable View screen for Jimmy Spice's restaurant survey. In this view the variable names appear in the far left-hand column. Then each of the columns defines various attributes of the variables as described below:

Name = This is an abbreviated name for each variable.

Type = The default for this is numeric with 2 decimal places. This can be changed to express values as whole numbers or it can do other things such as specify the values as 5 dates, dollar, custom currency, and so forth. To view the options click first on the Numeric cell and then on the three shaded dots to the right of the cell.

Label = In this column you give a more descriptive title to your variable. For example, with Jimmy Spice's restaurant survey variable X_1 is labelled as X_1 – Try New and Different Things and variable X_2 is labelled as X_2 – Party Person. When you have longer labels and want to be able to see all of them you can go to the top of the file and click between the Label and Values cells and make the column wider.

Values = In the values column you can assign a label for each of the values of a variable. For example, with Jimmy Spice's restaurant survey data variable X_1 – Try New and Different Things we have indicated that a 1 = Strongly Disagree and a 7 = Strongly Agree. To view the options click first on the Values cell and then on the three shaded dots to the right of the cell. You can add new labels or change existing ones.

Missing = Missing values are important in SPSS. If you do not handle them properly in your database it will cause you to get incorrect results. Use this column to indicate values that are assigned to missing data. A blank Numeric cell is designated as system-missing and a full stop (.) is placed in the cell. The default is no missing data but if you have missing data then you should use this column to tell the SPSS software what is missing. To do so, you can record one or more values that will be considered as missing data and will not be included in the data analysis. To use this option, click on the Missing cell and then on the three shaded dots to the right. You will get a dialogue box that shows the default of no missing data. To indicate one or more values as missing click on Discrete missing values and place a value in one of the cells. You can record up to three separate values. The value most often used for missing data is a 9. If you want to specify a range of values click on this option and indicate the range to be considered as missing.

Column = Click on the Column cell to indicate the width of the column. The default is 8 spaces but it can be increased or decreased.

Align = The default for alignment is initially left, but you can change to either centre or right alignment.

Let's look at the Variable View screen for Jimmy Spice's restaurant survey database. It is shown in Exhibit A2.3. To see the Variable View screen go to the bottom left-hand corner of the screen and click on 'Variable View.' The name of the variable will be in the first column, but if you look at the fifth column it will tell you more about the variable. For example, variable X_1 is 'Try New and Different Things' while X_2 is 'Party Person.' All of the remaining variables have a similar description. Also, if you look under the Values column it will tell you how the variable is coded; for example, 1 = Strongly Disagree and 7 = Strongly Agree.

Running a Programme

The two menus you will use most often are 'Analyse' and 'Graphs'. Let's do a simple chart to show you how easy it is to use SPSS. Click on the 'Graphs' pull-down menu first. When you do, select

EXHIBIT A2.3 Variable View of Jimmy Spice's Restaurant Survey Data

SPSS_Data_Jimmy_Spice's_N_427.sav [DataSet1] - SPSS Data Editor

File Edit View Data Transform Analyze Graphs Utilities Add-ons Window Help

	Name	Type	Width	Decimals	Label	Values	Missing	Columns	Align	Measure
1	id	Numeric	4	0	ID	None	None	8	Center	Nominal
2	x_s1	Numeric	4	0	Have Dined Out...	None	None	8	Center	Nominal
3	x_s2	Numeric	4	0	Have Eaten Indi...	None	None	8	Center	Nominal
4	x_s3	Numeric	4	0	Gross Annual I...	None	None	8	Center	Nominal
5	x1	Numeric	4	0	X1 -- Try New A...	{1, Strongly ...	None	8	Center	Scale
6	x2	Numeric	4	0	X2 -- Party Per...	{1, Strongly ...	None	8	Center	Scale
7	x3	Numeric	4	0	X3 -- People Cu...	{1, Strongly ...	None	8	Center	Scale
8	x4	Numeric	4	0	X4 -- Avoid Frie...	{1, Strongly ...	None	8	Center	Scale
9	x5	Numeric	4	0	X5 -- Likes to G...	{1, Strongly ...	None	8	Center	Scale
10	x6	Numeric	4	0	X6 -- Friends C...	{1, Strongly ...	None	8	Center	Scale
11	x7	Numeric	4	0	X7 -- Self-Confi...	{1, Strongly ...	None	8	Center	Scale
12	x8	Numeric	4	0	X8 -- Eat Balan...	{1, Strongly ...	None	8	Center	Scale
13	x9	Numeric	4	0	X9 -- Buy New ...	{1, Strongly ...	None	8	Center	Scale
14	x10	Numeric	4	0	X10 -- Careful A...	{1, Strongly ...	None	8	Center	Scale
15	x11	Numeric	4	0	X11 -- Try New ...	{1, Strongly ...	None	8	Center	Scale
16	x12	Numeric	4	0	X12 -- Friendly ...	{1, Strongly ...	None	8	Center	Scale
17	x13	Numeric	4	0	X13 -- Fun Plac...	{1, Strongly ...	None	8	Center	Scale
18	x14	Numeric	4	0	X14 -- Large Si...	{1, Strongly ...	None	8	Center	Scale
19	x15	Numeric	4	0	X15 -- Fresh Food	{1, Strongly ...	None	8	Center	Scale
20	x16	Numeric	4	0	X16 -- Reasona...	{1, Strongly ...	None	8	Center	Scale
21	x17	Numeric	4	0	X17 -- Attractive...	{1, Strongly ...	None	8	Center	Scale
22	x18	Numeric	4	0	X18 -- Excellent...	{1, Strongly ...	None	8	Center	Scale
23	x19	Numeric	4	0	X19 -- Knowled...	{1, Strongly ...	None	8	Center	Scale
24	x20	Numeric	4	0	X20 -- Proper F...	{1, Strongly ...	None	8	Center	Scale
25	x21	Numeric	4	0	X21 -- Speed of...	{1, Strongly ...	None	8	Center	Scale
26	x22	Numeric	4	0	X22 -- Satisfacti...	{1, 1 = Not ...	None	8	Center	Scale

Data View Variable View

SPSS Processor is ready

Bar and you will get a dialogue box called Bar Charts. There are three options on the top left but for now use 'Simple,' which is the default (already checked). We also use the default in the 'Data in Chart are:' box. This default tells the programme to create a bar chart showing the count of the number of responses in each of the categories of the 7-point scale for this question. Now click Define and use the default $= N$ of cases. Your database variables are shown in a window to the left of the screen. Highlight variable X_{22} – Satisfaction and then click on the 'arrow button' to the left of the Category Axis box to move this variable into the box. Now click OK and you will get the bar chart shown in Exhibit A2.4.

There are several things we can learn about this variable from the bar chart. First, the highest rating on the 7-point scale is a 6 and the lowest rating is a 3 (7 = Very Satisfied and 1 = Not Satisfied At All). Second, the rating given most often is a 5 and the one given least often is a 2. Recall the question for this variable read: 'Please indicate your view on each of the following questions: How satisfied are you with Jimmy Spice's restaurant?' Based on how the respondents answered this question, the bar chart tells us that overall the respondents are somewhat satisfied. We recommend you explore some of the other pull-down menus at this point and take the tutorial to begin familiarizing yourself with the SPSS software. As you go through the chapters we will give you the 'Click-through' sequence for each of the problems we ask you to examine. But for a quick reference to the major procedures, we provide an alphabetic listing of these sequences in the following section. This will help you to easily apply and learn the statistical techniques that are most often used in analysing data for business research reports and managerial decision making.

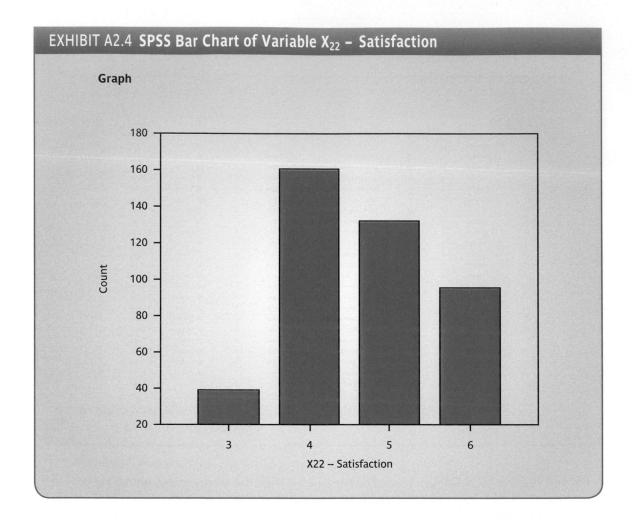

EXHIBIT A2.4 SPSS Bar Chart of Variable X_{22} – Satisfaction

Click-through Sequences for Selected Data Analysis Techniques

ANOVA

The click-through sequence is ANALYSE → GENERAL LINEAR MODEL → UNIVARIATE. Highlight the dependent variable X_{24} – Likely to Recommend by clicking on it and move it to the Dependent Variable box. Next, highlight X_{30} – Distance Driven and X_{32} – Gender, and move them to the Fixed Factors box. Click OK, since we don't need to specify any other options for this test.

Bar Charts

The click-through sequence to prepare a bar chart for variable X_{22} – Satisfaction is: ANALYSE → DESCRIPTIVE STATISTICS → FREQUENCIES. Highlight X_{22} and click on the arrow box to move it into the Variables box. Click on Charts and Bar Charts, and then Continue. Next click OK to execute the program.

Bivariate Regression

The click-through sequence for bivariate regression is ANALYSE $\rightarrow$ REGRESSION $\rightarrow$ LINEAR. Click on X_{22} – Satisfaction and move it to the Dependent Variable box. Click on X_{16} – Reasonable Prices and move it to the Independent Variables box. We will use the defaults for the other options, so click OK to run the bivariate regression.

Compare Means

The click-through sequence is ANALYSE $\rightarrow$ COMPARE MEANS $\rightarrow$ MEANS. Highlight the dependent variable X_{24} – Likely to Recommend by clicking on it, and move it to the Dependent List box. Next, highlight X_{30} – Distance Driven and X_{32} – Gender, and move them to the Independent List. Then click OK.

Chi-Square

The click-through sequence for Chi-Square is ANALYSE $\rightarrow$ DESCRIPTIVE STATISTICS $\rightarrow$ CROSSTABS. Click on X_{30} – Distance Travelled for the Row variable and on X_{32} – Gender for the Column variable. Click on the Statistics button and the Chi-Square box, and then Continue. Next click on the Cells button and on Expected frequencies (Observed frequencies is usually already checked). Then click Continue and OK to execute the programme.

Cluster Analysis

The SPSS click-through sequence is ANALYSE $\rightarrow$ CLASSIFY $\rightarrow$ HIERARCHICAL CLUSTER, which leads to a dialogue box where you select variables X_{22}, X_{23} and X_{24}. After you have put these variables into the Variables box, look at the other options below. Keep all the defaults that are shown on the dialogue box. You should also use the defaults for the Statistics and Plots options below. Click on the Method box and select Ward's under the Cluster Method (you have to scroll to the bottom of the list), but use the default of squared euclidean distances under Measure. We do nothing with the Save option at this point, so you can click OK at the top of the dialogue box to execute the cluster analysis.

Discriminant Analysis

The SPSS click-through sequence is ANALYSE $\rightarrow$ CLASSIFY $\rightarrow$ DISCRIMINANT, which leads to a dialogue box where you select the variables (see Exhibit 18.11, page 608). The dependent, non-metric variable is X_{31} and the independent, metric variables are X_{15}, X_{18} and X_{20}. The first thing you do is transfer variable X_{31} to the Grouping Variable box at the top, and then click on the Define Range box just below it. You must tell the programme what the minimum and maximum numbers are for the grouping variable. In this case the minimum is 0 = Do Not Recall Ads and the maximum is 1 = Recall Ads, so just put these numbers in and click on Continue. Next you must transfer the food perceptions variables into the Independents box (X_{15}, X_{18}, and X_{20}). Then click on the Statistics box at the bottom and check Means, Univariate ANOVAS, and Continue. The Method default is Enter, and we will use this. Now click on Classify and Compute from group sizes. We do not know if the sample sizes are equal, so we must check this option. You should also click Summary Table and then Continue. We do not use any options under Save, so click OK to run the programme.

Discriminant Analysis with Cluster Analysis

The SPSS click-through sequence is ANALYSE → CLASSIFY → DISCRIMINANT, which leads to a dialogue box where you select the variables. The dependent, nonmetric variable is clu2_1, and the independent, metric variables are X_4, X_8, and X_{10}. First transfer variable clu2_1 to the Grouping Variable box at the top, and then click on the Define Range box just below it. Insert the minimum and maximum numbers for the grouping variable. In this case the minimum is 1 = cluster one and the maximum is 2 = cluster two, so just put these numbers in and click on Continue. Next you must transfer the food perceptions variables into the Independents box (X_4, X_8, and X_{10}). Then click on the Statistics box at the bottom and check Means, Univariate ANOVAS, and Continue. The Method default is Enter, and we will use this. Now click on Classify and Compute from group sizes. We do not know if the sample sizes are equal, so we must check this option. You should also click Summary Table and then Continue. We do not use any options under Save, so click OK to run the program.

Factor Analysis

The SPSS click-through sequence is ANALYSE → DATA REDUCTION → FACTOR, which leads to a dialogue box where you select variables $X_{12} - X_{21}$. After you have put these variables into the Variables box, look at the data analysis options below. First click on the Descriptives box and unclick the Initial Solution box because we do not need it at this point. Now click Continue to return to the previous dialogue box. Next go to the Extraction box. In this one you leave the default of principal components and unclick the unrotated factor solution under Display. We will keep the other defaults, so now click the Continue box. Next go to the Rotation box. The default is None. We want to rotate, so click on Varimax as your rotational choice and then Continue. Finally, go to the Options box and click Sorted by Size, and then change the Suppress Absolute Values from .10 to .30. These last choices eliminate unneeded information, thus making the solutions printout much easier to read. We do not need Scores at this point, so we can click on OK at the top of the dialogue box to execute the factor analysis. Exhibit 17.6 shows examples of some of the dialogue boxes for running this factor analysis.

Independent Samples *t*-test

The SPSS click-through sequence is ANALYSE → COMPARE MEANS → INDEPENDENT SAMPLES T-TEST. When you get to this dialogue box click variable X_{22} – Satisfaction into the Test Variables box and variable X_{32} – Gender into the Grouping Variable box. For variable X_{32} you must define the range in the Define Groups box. Enter a 0 for Group 1 and a 1 for Group 2 (males were coded 0 in the database and females were coded 1) and then click Continue. For the Options we will use the defaults, so just click OK to execute the program.

Mean, Median and Mode

The SPSS click-through sequence is ANALYSE → DESCRIPTIVE STATISTICS → FREQUENCIES. Let's use X_{25} – Frequency of Patronage of Jimmy Spice's restaurant as a variable to examine. Click on X_{25} to highlight it, and then on the arrow box for the Variables box to use in your analysis. Next open the Statistics box and click on Mean, Median, and Mode, and then Continue and OK. Recall that if you want to create charts, open the Charts box. Your choices are Bar, Pie, and Histograms. For the Format box we will use the defaults, so click on OK to execute the program.

Multiple Regression

The SPSS click-through sequence to examine this relationship is ANALYSE → REGRESSION → LINEAR. Highlight X_{22} and move it to the Dependent Variables box. Highlight X_{15}, X_{18} and X_{20} and move them to the Independent Variables box. We will use the defaults for the other options so click OK to run the multiple regression.

Multiple Regression with Factor Analysis

The SPSS click-through sequence is ANALYZE → REGRESSION → LINEAR, which leads you to a dialog box where you select the variables. You should select X_{22} as the dependent and fac1_1, fac2_1, fac3_1, and fac4_1 as the independents. Now click on the Statistics button and check Descriptives. There are several additional types of analysis that can be selected, but at this point we will use the program defaults. Click OK at the top right of the dialogue box to execute the regression.

Paired Samples *t*-test

The click-through sequence is ANALYSE → COMPARE MEANS → PAIRED SAMPLES T-TEST. When you get to this dialogue box, highlight both X_{18} – Food Taste and X_{20} – Food Temperature, and then click on the arrow button to move them into the Paired Variables box. For the Options we will use the defaults, so just click OK to execute the program.

Pearson Correlation

The SPSS click-through sequence is ANALYSE → CORRELATE → BIVARIATE, which leads to a dialogue box where you select the variables. Transfer variables X_{22} and X_{24} into the Variables box. Note that we will use all three default options shown below: Pearson correlation, two-tailed test of significance, and flag significant correlations. Next go to the Options box, and after it opens click on Means and Standard Deviations and then continue. Finally, when you click on OK at the top right of the dialogue box it will execute the Pearson correlation.

Range, Standard Deviation and Variance

Jimmy Spice's restaurant survey database can be used with the SPSS software to calculate measures of dispersion, just as we did with the measures of central tendency. The SPSS click-through sequence is ANALYSE → DESCRIPTIVE STATISTICS → FREQUENCIES. Let's use X_{22} – Satisfaction as a variable to examine. Click on X_{22} to highlight it and then on the arrow box to move X_{22} to the Variables box. Next open the Statistics box, go to the Dispersion box in the lower-left-hand corner, and click on Standard deviation, Variance, Range, Minimum and Maximum, and then Continue. If you would like to create charts, then open the Charts box – your choices are Bar, Pie, and Histograms. For the Format box we will use the defaults, so click on OK to execute the program.

Sample Subgroups

To split the sample into groups, the click-through sequence is: DATA → SPLIT FILE. First click on the Data pull-down menu and scroll down and highlight and click on Split File. You will now see in the Split File dialogue box where the default is Analyse all cases. Click on the Compare groups option, highlight the variable you want to split the groups with (e.g. X_{32} – Gender), and click on the arrow box to move it into the Groups Based on: box. Next click on OK and you will be analysing the males versus females groups separately. That is, your output will have the results for males and females separately.

Spearman Rank Correlation

The SPSS click-through sequence is ANALYSE → CORRELATE → BIVARIATE, which leads to a dialogue box where you select the variables. Transfer variables X_{27} and X_{29} into the Variables box. You will note that the Pearson correlation is the default along with the two-tailed test of significance, and flag significant correlations. 'Unclick' the Pearson correlation and then click on Spearman. Then click on OK at the top right of the dialogue box to execute the program.

Summated Scores

The restaurant perceptions variables include three measures related to satisfaction. They are variables X_{22}, X_{23}, and X_{24}. To calculate the summated score, the click-through sequence is TRANSFORM → COMPUTE. First type a variable name in the Target Variable box. In this case we are calculating a summated score for the satisfaction variables so let's use the abbreviation Sum_Sat for Summated Satisfaction. Next click on the Numeric Expression box to move the cursor there. Look below at the buttons and click on the parenthesis to place it in the Numeric Expression box (make sure cursor is between parentheses). Now highlight variable X_{22} and click on the arrow box to move it into the parenthesis. Go to the buttons below and click on the plus (+) sign. Go back and highlight variable X_{23} and click on the arrow box to move it into the parenthesis. Again click on the plus (+) sign. Finally, go back and highlight variable X_{24} and click on the arrow box to move it into the parenthesis. Now put the cursor at the right end of the parentheses and click on the divide sign (/) and then 3 to get the average. Next click on OK and you will get the average summated score for the three variables. You can find the new variable at the far right-hand side of your data editor screen.

Univariate Hypothesis Test

The click through sequence is ANALYSE → COMPARE MEANS → ONE SAMPLE T-TEST. When you get to the dialog box, click on X_{16} – Reasonable Prices to highlight it. Then click on the arrow to move X_{16} into the Test Variables box. In the box labelled Test Value, enter the number 4. This is the number you want to compare the respondents' answers against. Click on the Options box and enter 95 in the confidence interval box. This is the same as setting the significance level at .05. Then, click on the Continue button and OK to execute the program.

Trilogy and Affect Global Approaches

This appendix provides an overview of the theoretical trilogy and affect global approaches to explaining the structure of an attitude. The discussion illustrates how different attitude scaling formats yield different results about the same attitude construct.

The Trilogy Approach

The **trilogy approach** suggests that understanding of a person's complete attitude towards an object (e.g. a person, a product/service, or a phenomenon) requires an understanding of the *cognitive, affective* and *conative* components that make up that attitude. It is the integration of these three components that allows a person to create an overall perception of a given object. Exhibit A3.1 illustrates the integrative nature of these components.

The *cognitive component* of an attitude represents the person's beliefs, perceptions, and knowledge about the specified object and its attributes. These aspects are the key elements and outcomes of learning. For example, think back to the 39 days that followed the US presidential election on November 7, 2000. In retrospect, we know that the outcome of these 39 days has had a huge impact not only on global politics alone, but also on global marketing environments.

Let's consider the unproven but widely discussed notion at the time that George W. Bush stole the election with the help of his younger brother Jeb, then governor of Florida. Many people held

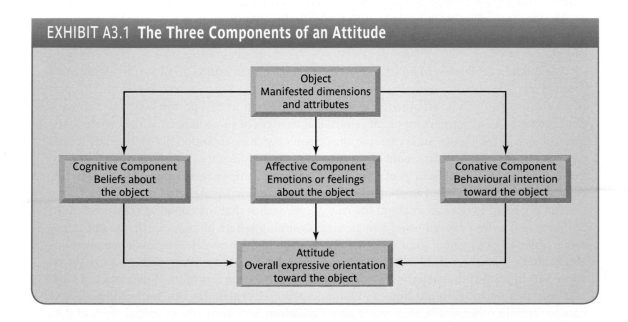

EXHIBIT A3.1 **The Three Components of an Attitude**

a variety of different beliefs about this, which they developed as they learned more about the situation. Here is a sample of those beliefs:

- Al Gore received more votes in Florida than did George W. Bush.
- Florida did not count all the votes that were cast by its citizens.
- Florida's voting process disenfranchised a significant number of key voters.
- Al Gore and the Democratic Party were outmanoeuvred by the Republicans.
- George W. Bush won the state in accordance with Florida voting laws.
- People in Florida cannot count ballots.

These statements are selected beliefs about some of the attributes that people formed regarding the Florida voting phenomenon. Although any one of these beliefs by itself would provide a poor representation of the people's attitude concerning Bush's possible stealing the US presidency from Gore, in combination they form the basis for identifying people's overall attitude on the vote–recount phenomenon. A key point to remember here is that most state-of-mind objects or constructs investigated by researchers have a multi-dimensional aspect requiring researchers to include sets of attributes in their scale measurement designs. In reality, people have hundreds of beliefs about many different objects that make up their everyday environment.

An attitude's *affective component* represents the person's emotions or feelings towards the given object. This is the component most frequently expressed when a person is asked to verbalize their attitude towards some object, such as a person, a product or service, or a phenomenon. A simple way to view this affective component is to think of it as being the amount of emotion or feeling a person attaches to each of their individual beliefs. This component serves as a mechanism that enables a person to create some type of hierarchical order among a set of beliefs about an object. For example, a person considering the purchase of a new Toyota Auris might identify several common attributes about cars that are generally important in the selection process. The affective component of that person's attitude towards Toyota cars allows them to decide which of the car's attributes (engine power, safety system, fuel economy, price, exterior design, etc.) holds more importance (or less importance) to them. At this point, remember that people's emotions or feelings towards an object are anchored to a set of recognizable beliefs about that object.

The *conative component* of an attitude relates to a person's intended behavioural response to a given object. The conative component is also referred to as the *behavioural component*. This part of an attitude tends to be an outcome driven by the interaction of a person's cognitive component (beliefs) and affective component (emotional strength of those beliefs) as they relate to the given object. In the Toyota Auris example, the person's purchase intention decision to buy (conative component) this new car would be directly influenced by the set of beliefs (cognitive components) and the emotional feelings of importance (affective components) attached to those beliefs concerning each of the listed attributes that are part of the new Toyota Auris.

The key point to remember about the trilogy approach is that the complete measurement of attitudes cannot be achieved using a single-item or multiple-item global scale design but rather requires the development of some type of multiplicative-additive model. The fundamental rationales behind the need for this kind of model are that most objects are really nothing more than a composite of many different parts (or attributes). People have the capability of developing a separate attitude towards each attribute, and attitudes themselves tend to consist of distinguishable components. In other words, to measure attitudes, researchers must collect several types of data (cognitive, affective, and conative) about the object and its attributes of interest and then, through a modelling process, derive a composite attitude score. Several types of multiplicative-additive model have been developed within the trilogy framework, but we will limit our discussion to two of the most frequently used models: attitude-towards-object and attitude-towards-behaviour.

Attitude-towards-Object Model

One popular attitudinal model is Fishbein's *attitude-towards-object model,* which is presented in the form of the following equation:

$$Attitude_O = \sum_{i-1}^{k} b_i e_i$$

where *Attitude$_O$* is a separate, indirectly derived composite measure (sometimes considered a global measure) of a person's combined thoughts and feelings for or against the given object (e.g. product, service, brand, manufacturer, retail establishment); b_i is the strength of the belief that the person holds towards the *i*th attribute of the object (e.g. the Toyota Auris has a satisfactory mileage rating); e_i is the person's affect evaluation (expressed emotional feeling of importance) of the belief towards that *i*th attribute of the object (e.g. it is very important that my car has an excellent mileage rating); and $\sum_{i=1}^{k}$ indicates that there are *k* salient attributes making up the object over which the multiplicative combinations of b_i and e_i for those attributes are summated.

To illustrate the development processes for the scales researchers use to collect the data to capture a person's overall attitude towards an object through the attitude-towards-object modelling approach, we expand the Toyota Auris example. Let's say the overall research objective is to collect data that will enable management to better understand the attitudes owners hold towards the *performance* of a Toyota Auris. Assume Toyota's marketing department worked with a reputable market research company to develop a two-phase research plan that includes both qualitative and quantitative research activities to create the different scale measurements needed to collect the cognitive components (b_i) and corresponding affective components (e_i) that relate to assessing respondents' attitudes towards the performance of car. First, using qualitative research practices, several focus groups were conducted among a cross section of people who were known to have purchased a new car within the past 12 months. One topic of those focus groups was the attributes people use to judge the performance of car. This part of the research discovered and identified the following seven attributes:

1 The perception of the car as *trouble-free.*
2 The actual *miles per gallon (MPG) rating* of the car.
3 The *comfort* of the ride provided by the car.
4 The *craftsmanship* built into the car.
5 The *overall quality* of the car.
6 The *reliability* of the car.
7 The *responsiveness* of the car in different weather conditions.

To validate these seven attributes as meaningful ones people use to assess their attitudes towards the performance of cars, the researchers conducted a pilot study where 300 randomly selected respondents were given a survey that included these seven attributes and were asked to judge them using a four-point scale scheme where 4 = 'definitely a factor of performance', 3 = 'generally a factor of performance', 2 = 'only somewhat a factor of performance', and 1 = 'not at all a factor of performance'. The researchers then analyzed the data collected from the pilot study. The results demonstrated that all seven attributes should be considered factors people used in assessing the performance of cars, all having mean values of 3.5 or higher.

Using the information generated from the first phase of the research project, researchers planned and executed the second phase by conducting a more elaborate quantitative study where surveys were administered to 1,500 known Toyota Auris owners who were randomly selected from Toyota's customer data bank. To capture these respondents' emotional importance (e_i) associated with each of the seven performance attributes, the affective scale measurement displayed in Exhibit A3.2 was developed and tested for reliability (internal consistency). Using this scale measurement, respondents were asked to write a number from 1 to 6 in the space provided that best expressed how emotionally important they felt each listed attribute was to them in assessing the performance of a new car.

On the other hand, the six-point cognitive scale measurement displayed in the exhibit was developed, tested for reliability (internal consistency), and used to capture the respondents' evaluative performance beliefs (b_i) about the Toyota Auris. In applying the cognitive scale measurement, respondents were asked to circle a number from 1 to 6 that best expressed how well their Toyota Auris performed on each listed attribute. In those cases where a particular attribute might

---

EXHIBIT A3.2 Scale Measurements used in Determining the Attitude towards the *Performance* of Toyota Auris

AFFECTIVE (IMPORTANCE) SCALE MEASUREMENT

Using the scale below, please write a number from one (1) to six (6) in the space provided that best expresses how emotionally important you feel each listed attribute is to you in assessing the performance of a car.

Not at all Important	Only Slightly Important	Somewhat Important	Important	Definitely Important	Extremely Important
(1)	(2)	(3)	(4)	(5)	(6)

ATTRIBUTES

_____ The perception of the car as trouble-free.
_____ The actual miles per gallon (MPG) rating of the car.
_____ The comfort of the ride provided by the car.
_____ The craftsmanship built into the car.
_____ The overall quality of the car.
_____ The reliability of the car.
_____ The responsiveness of the car in different weather conditions.

COGNITIVE (BELIEF) SCALE MEASUREMENT

Thinking about all experiences with driving your Toyota Auris, we would like to know your opinion about each of the following factors. For each factor, please circle the number that best expresses how you believe your Toyota Auris has performed on that factor. For any factor(s) that are not relevant to your assessment, please circle the 'N/A', which means 'not applicable'.

Toyota Auris	Truly Terrible	Fair	Average	Good	Excellent	Truly Exceptional	N/A
Trouble-free	1	2	3	4	5	6	0
Miles per gallon (MPG) rating	1	2	3	4	5	6	0
Comfort of the ride	1	2	3	4	5	6	0
Craftsmanship	1	2	3	4	5	6	0
Overall quality	1	2	3	4	5	6	0
Reliability	1	2	3	4	5	6	0
Responsiveness	1	2	3	4	5	6	0

not be relevant in their assessment, respondents were instructed to circle the zero (0) response, which meant 'not applicable' (N/A).

After collecting the cognitive (b_i) and corresponding affective (e_i) data on the seven attributes, researchers can apply the multiplicative-additive model to determine a respondent's overall composite attitude towards the performance of the Toyota Auris or the respondent's individual attitudes for each of the separate seven attributes. To see how researchers can determine a respondent's individual attitude towards a particular attribute, let's use attribute 1, perception of the car *as being a trouble-free* car. We simply multiply the respondent's raw belief score (b_i) assigned to this attribute by the corresponding raw importance score (e_i), resulting in a possible score range of 1 ($1 \times 1 = 1$) to 36 ($6 \times 6 = 36$). The score would be interpreted to mean that the lower the value, the weaker the attitude and the higher the value, the stronger the attitude.

In determining a respondent's overall attitude towards the *performance* of the Toyota Auris, the researchers would take each of the individually derived attitude scores for each attribute and simply add them together into one composite score that could range between 7 (7 attributes $\times 1 = 7$) on the low end and 252 (7 attributes $\times 36 = 252$) at the high end. Again, interpretation of the composite scores would be that the lower the composite value, the weaker the overall attitude, and the higher the value, the stronger the attitude.

This modelling approach also allows the researchers to determine the average attitudes held by all the respondents included in the study for each attribute as well as the comprehensive performance attitude held towards Toyota Auris. To analyse the group attitude towards a particular attribute, the researchers with the use of a computer would calculate the 1,500 individual attitude scores for that attribute, then add those scores together, then divide that total by the total number of respondents who contributed in deriving that total score. The average group attitude score for any of the individual attributes would range between 1 and 36 and be interpreted similarly to an individual attitude score. A similar procedure would be used to determine the group's overall composite performance attitude towards Toyota Auris. Researchers would calculate the individual composite scores for each of the seven attributes among the 1,500 respondents, add those scores together, then divide that total by the sample size of respondents used to derive the total attitude score. Interpretation of the group's average composite attitude score would be the same as the interpretation of an individual's composite score described earlier.

It is important to remember that in this measurement approach, equal emphasis is given to measuring both a person's beliefs (cognitive) and a person's emotional feelings (affective) towards the attributes of the object under investigation. This modelling approach provides researchers and decision makers with a lot of diagnostic insight into the components that make up the customer's or consumer's attitude. Researchers and decision makers can learn how and what the customer or consumer used to evaluate either the actual or potential performance of a given object (e.g. Toyota Auris).

Attitude-towards-Behaviour Model

Another popular multiplicative-additive attitude model is Fishbein's *attitude-towards-behaviour model*. This model captures a person's attitude towards their *behaviour* with a given object rather than the attitude towards the object itself. One benefit of this approach is that it gives researchers a picture that more closely demonstrates the actual behaviour of individuals than does the attitude-towards-object model. Normally, the attitude-towards-behaviour model is presented by the following equation:

$$Attitude_{(beh)} = \sum_{i=1}^{n} b_i a_i$$

where $Attitude_{(beh)}$ is an indirectly derived composite measure of a person's combined thoughts and feelings for or against carrying out a specific action (e.g. the purchasing and driving of Toyota Auris); b_i is the strength of the person's belief that the ith specific action will lead to a specific outcome (e.g. that driving a Toyota Auris will increase the person's social standing in the community); a_i is the person's expressed feeling (affect) towards the ith action outcome (e.g. the 'favourableness feeling' of knowing friends admire Toyota Auris); and $\sum_{i=1}^{n}$ indicates that there are n salient action outcomes making up the behaviour over which the multiplicative combinations of b_i and a_i for those outcomes are summated.

Exhibit A3.3 illustrates the scales and procedures that might be used in an attitude-towards-behaviour model to capture a person's overall attitude towards *purchasing* a Toyota Auris. The key thing to remember here is that behaviour-oriented beliefs are used and that greater emphasis is placed on measuring the person's affective evaluation of the behavioural outcome. This approach can help the researcher or decision maker understand why customers behave as they do towards a given object. For example, collecting this type of attitudinal data offers the researcher insights into how and why customers judge the 'service quality' construct associated with purchasing a new car.

From a scale measurement perspective, deciding which affective or cognitive scale point descriptors to use for an attitudinal scale measurement can be difficult. To help make that decision a little easier, we advocate the following *rules for deciding the use of an affective or cognitive based scale* measurement:

1 If the measurement objective is one of collecting data that enable you to identify *how the respondent is feeling*, then the focus should be on using scale point descriptors that reflect the *affective* component.

2 If the measurement objective is one of collecting data that enable you to describe *how the respondent is thinking*, then the focus should be on using scale point descriptors that emphasize the *cognitive component*.

EXHIBIT A3.3 Scale Measurements used in Determining the Attitude towards *Purchasing* a Toyota Auris

In this example, qualitative and quantitative research activities were employed to create the different scale measurements needed to collect both the cognitive components (b_i) and the affective components (a_i) that relate to assessing respondents' attitude towards the purchasing of car (attitude-towards-behaviour).

   I. **Qualitative research activities**

   A. Several general focus group sessions were conducted among a cross section of people who were known to be considering the purchase of a new car within the next six months. One of the topics of these sessions was the items people deemed as factors in purchasing a new car. The study discovered and identified the following 15 factors.

   1. The car is viewed as being a generally trouble-free car.
   2. The car's miles per gallon (MPG) rating.
   3. The comfort in the car's ride.
   4. The craftsmanship built into the car.
   5. The overall quality of the car.
   6. The reliability of the car.
   7. The car's responsiveness in different weather conditions.

8. The car's potential resale value.
9. The warranty guarantee programme associated with the car.
10. The car's styling features.
11. The price of the car.
12. Overall reputation of the dealership.
13. Reputation of the dealer's service department.
14. The car's safety features.
15. The quality reputation of the manufacturer.

B. To validate the 15 items as the meaningful factors that people consider in their purchase of a new car, 250 randomly selected respondents were given a survey that included the 15 factors and were asked to express the degree to which each one was a factor of consideration they would use in purchasing a new car, using the following five-point scale: (5) 'a critical factor'; (4) 'definitely a factor'; (3) 'generally a factor'; (2) 'only somewhat of a factor'; (1) 'not at all a factor'. Results demonstrated that all the 15 items were reasonable factors of consideration that people used in car purchase decision making, all having mean values of 3.5 or higher.

[Importance Scale]

Not at all Important	Only Slightly Important	Somewhat Important	Important	Definitely Important	Extremely Important
(1)	(2)	(3)	(4)	(5)	(6)

Buying a car …

__ that is generally *trouble-free*.

__ with an *acceptable miles per gallon (MPG) rating*.
__ that provides a *comfortable ride*.
__ that has the *craftsmanship* built into it.

__ that is built with *overall quality*.

__ that is *reliable*.
__ that has satisfactory *responsiveness* in different weather conditions.
__ that has good potential *resale* value.

__ that is backed by a *solid warranty* guarantee program.
__ that has the *styling* features I want.
__ that has a *price that is affordable*.
__ from a dealership having *overall* reputation *excellence*.

__ from a dealership whose service department is *reputable*.
__ that has the *safety features* I want.
__ that is made by a manufacturer with a *quality reputation*.

II. Quantitative research activities

A. To capture respondents' affective importance (a_i) associated with each of the 15 purchasing attributes, the following scale measurement was developed and tested for internal consistency.

Using the affective importance scale below, please circle a number from 1 to 6 in the space provided that best expresses how emotionally important you feel each listed factor is to you in purchasing a new car.

B. To capture respondents' evaluative beliefs (b_i) about the Toyota Auris being able to meet the individual's requirements, the following scale measurement was developed and tested for internal consistency.

Regarding all your expectations about a new car, we would like to know your opinions about each of the following factors as they relate to the Toyota Auris. For each factor please circle the number that best expresses the extent to which you agree or disagree that buying a Toyota Auris will meet that factor. For any factor(s) that are not relevant to your assessment, please circle '(0)', which means 'not applicable' (NA).

Buying a 2005 Acura 3.2 TL Will …	Definitely Agree	Generally Agree	Slightly Agree	Slightly Disagree	Generally Disagree	Definitely Disagree	(NA)
	(6)	(5)	(4)	(3)	(2)	(1)	(0)
Give me a generally *trouble-fee* mode of transportation	6	5	4	3	2	1	0
Give me a car with acceptable *miles per gallon (MPG)* rating	6	5	4	3	2	1	0
Allow me a *comfortable ride*	6	5	4	3	2	1	0
Give me a car with *great craftsmanship*	6	5	4	3	2	1	0
Give me a car with the *overall quality* I was looking for	6	5	4	3	2	1	0
Give me a car that is *reliable*	6	5	4	3	2	1	0
Give me a car that has satisfactory *responsiveness* in different weather conditions	6	5	4	3	2	1	0
Give me a car that has good potential *resale value*	6	5	4	3	2	1	0
Give me a solid *warranty guarantee programme*	6	5	4	3	2	1	0
Give me a car that has the *styling features* I want	6	5	4	3	2	1	0
Give me a car I can *afford*	6	5	4	3	2	1	0
Give me a car from a dealership with an *overall reputation of excellence*	6	5	4	3	2	1	0
Give me a car from a dealership whose service department is *reputable*	6	5	4	3	2	1	0
Give me a car that has the *safety features* I want	6	5	4	3	2	1	0
Give me a car made by a manufacturer with a *quality reputation*	6	5	4	3	2	1	0

The Affect Global Approach

In contrast to the trilogy approach to attitude measurement, the **affect global approach** maintains that an attitude is nothing more than a person's global (i.e. overall) expression of favourable or unfavourable feelings towards a given object. The idea here is that a person's *feelings* can have dominant influence on their overall judgement of a given object. In other words, affect equals attitude. Within this approach, heavy emphasis is placed on capturing a person's global evaluative feelings of an object as being either positive or negative (i.e. liking/disliking, good/bad, satisfied/dissatisfied). Rating scale formats use a set of affective descriptors to capture the necessary responses. A limitation to the affect global approach is that it does not give the researcher insights into what beliefs contribute to the formation of the overall attitude. At best, the researcher can

EXHIBIT A3.4 Examples of Affect Scale Formats for Measuring Attitudes

Example 1:

For each of the following listed items, please *fill in* the box that best expresses the extent to which you were satisfied or dissatisfied with that item in relation to the vehicle you purchased last time.

Items	Very Satisfied	Somewhat Satisfied	Somewhat Dissatisfied	Very Dissatisfied
Customer service	❑	❑	❑	❑
Fuel efficiency	❑	❑	❑	❑
Quality of craftsmanship	❑	❑	❑	❑
Reputation of manufacturer	❑	❑	❑	❑
Purchase price	❑	❑	❑	❑
Resale value	❑	❑	❑	❑

Example 2:

Now we would like you to think about your driving experience, then read each of the following statements and fill in the box that best expresses your feelings about that statement.

Statement	Like Very Much	Like Somewhat	Neither Like nor Dislike	Dislike Somewhat	Dislike Very Much
Driving in my own way	❑	❑	❑	❑	❑
Changing the oil myself	❑	❑	❑	❑	❑
Driving on a long trip	❑	❑	❑	❑	❑
Letting someone else do the driving	❑	❑	❑	❑	❑
Observing the speed limit at all times	❑	❑	❑	❑	❑

Example 3:

Overall, how angry or happy were you with the US and UK's decision to start the Iraq war in 2003? **(Please check only one response.)**

Very Angry	Somewhat Angry	Neither Angry Nor Happy	Somewhat Happy	Very Happy
❑	❑	❑	❑	❑

only speculate about the beliefs underlying the expressed emotional ratings. Exhibit A3.4 displays several affect based attitude scale formats.

Overview of the Links between Measurements of Cognitive and Affective Behavioural Components

Researchers have made mixed comments on the strength of the relationships between the cognitive and affective components as they are used to explain or predict marketplace behaviours. Some researchers have found that when people's beliefs towards an object (e.g. Toyota Auris) coincide with their associated feelings, then attitude consistency exists and behaviour is more likely to be explainable or predictable. Yet others have found only limited relationships among the three components. Today's marketers should be aware of several factors that can operate to reduce the consistency between measures of beliefs, feelings and observations of marketplace behaviour: Elements that might create attitude measurement bias are:

1 A favourable attitude requires a need or motive before it can be translated into action.

2 Translating favourable beliefs and feelings into ownership requires ability.

3 The environment in which the attitude is formed is changing rapidly.

4 The attitudinal responses obtained are based on incomplete information of the respondents.

5 The attitude of the respondent to be measured is liable to influences from their family and friends.

6 The object (e.g. product) based on which attitudinal information is obtained is unfamiliar to the respondent (e.g. a very innovative product not yet launched to the market).

7 It is difficult to identify and measure all of the relevant aspects of a particular attitude of question.

Appendix 4

The La Brioche Doree Questionnaire

Hello. My name is _____ and I work for Brest Marketing Research Company. We are talking to individuals today/tonight about their dining out experiences.

1 'Do you regularly dine at fast food restaurants?'   __ Yes   __ No

2 'Have you eaten at other casual restaurants in the last six months?'   __ Yes   __ No

3 'Is your gross annual income Euro 15,000 or more?'   __ Yes   __ No

4 There are three major fast food restaurants in you neighbourhood – McDonald's, Casino Cafeteria, and La Brioche Doree. Which of these restaurants are you most familiar with?
  a McDonald's __
  b Casino Cafeteria __
  c La Brioche Doree __
  d None __

If respondent answers 'Yes' to first three questions, and is familiar with one of the three restaurants, then say:

We would like you to answer a few questions about your recent dining out experiences at McDonald's/Casino Cafeteria/La Brioche Dorée. The survey will only take approximately 15 minutes and it will be very helpful for the restaurant owners to better serve their customers in this area.

If the person says yes, give them instructions on how to access the website and complete the survey.

DINING OUT SURVEY

Please read all questions carefully. If you do not understand a question, stop the survey and email us so we can help you to understand it.

In the first section a number of factors are listed that people often use in choosing a fast food restaurant to dine at. Using a scale from 1 to 7, with 7 being 'Very Important' and 1 being 'Very Unimportant,' please indicate the extent to which a particular factor is important or unimportant. Circle only one number for each factor.

Section 1: Importance Ratings

How important is each of the following factors in choosing a restaurant to dine at?

1 Large portions

Very Unimportant						Very Important
1	2	3	4	5	6	7

2 Competent employees

Very Unimportant						Very Important
1	2	3	4	5	6	7

3 Food quality

Very Unimportant						Very Important
1	2	3	4	5	6	7

4 Speed of service

Very Unimportant 1 2 3 4 5 6 7 Very Important

5 Atmosphere

Very Unimportant 1 2 3 4 5 6 7 Very Important

6 Reasonable prices

Very Unimportant 1 2 3 4 5 6 7 Very Important

Section 2: Perceptions Measures

Listed below is a set of characteristics that can be used to describe McDonald's/Casino Cafeteria/ La Brioche Dorée. Using a scale from 1 to 7, with 7 being 'Strongly Agree' and 1 being 'Strongly Disagree', to what extent do you agree or disagree that _____ : (one of the three restaurants' name appears on the screen based on the respondent's answer to the familiarity question in the screening and rapport questions)

7 Has large portions

Strongly Disagree 1 2 3 4 5 6 7 Strongly Agree

8 Has competent employees

Strongly Disagree 1 2 3 4 5 6 7 Strongly Agree

9 Has excellent food quality

Strongly Disagree 1 2 3 4 5 6 7 Strongly Agree

10 Has quick service

Strongly Disagree 1 2 3 4 5 6 7 Strongly Agree

11 Has a good atmosphere

Strongly Disagree 1 2 3 4 5 6 7 Strongly Agree

12 Charges at reasonable prices

Strongly Disagree 1 2 3 4 5 6 7 Strongly Agree

Section 3: Relationship Measures

Please indicate your view on each of the following questions:

13 How satisfied are you with _____?

Not Satisfied At All 1 2 3 4 5 6 7 Very Satisfied

14 How likely are you to return to _____ in the future?

Definitely Will Not Return 1 2 3 4 5 6 7 Definitely Will Return

15 How likely are you to recommend _____ to a friend?

Definitely Will Not Recommend 1 2 3 4 5 6 7 Definitely Will Recommend

16 Frequency of Patronage
       How often do you eat at _____?

1 = Occasionally (Less than once a month)
2 = Frequently (1 – 3 times a month)
3 = Very Frequently (4 or more times a month)

Section 4: Classification Questions

Please circle the number that classifies you best.

17 Number of children at home

1   None
2   1 – 2
3   More than 2

18 Do you recall seeing any
       advertisement in the last
       month for McDonald's/Casino Cafeteria/
       La Brioche Dorée?

0   No
1   Yes

19 Your gender

0   Male
1   Female

20 Your age in years

1   18 – 25
2   26 – 34
3   35 – 49
4   50 – 59
5   60 and older

21 Your annual gross income

1   €20,000 – €35,000
2   €35,001 – €50,000
3   €50,001 – €75,000
4   €75,001 – €100,000
5   More than €100,000

Thank you very much for your help. Click on the submit button to exit the survey.

Appendix 5

Formulas for Calculating Correlation and Regression Issues

Pearson Product Moment Correlation

$$r_{xy} = \frac{\sum\limits_{i=1}^{n} (x_i + \bar{x})(y_i - \bar{y})}{n s_x s_y}$$

where

X_i = the X values

Y_i = the Y values

$\bar{X}$ = mean of the X values

$\bar{Y}$ = mean of the Y values

n = number of paired cases

$s_x s_y$ = standard deviation of X and Y

Regression

The general equation for regression is:

$$y = a + bx + e_i$$

where

Y = the dependent variable

a = the intercept for the regression line, or constant (point where the straight line intersects the y-axis when $x=0$)

b = the slope of the regression line, or regression coefficient (the change in y for every 1-unit change in x)

x = the independent variable used to predict y

e_i = the error for the prediction (the difference between the predicted value and the true value)

Values for a and b can be calculated using the following formulas:

The formula for computing the regression parameter b is:

$$b = \frac{n\sum_{i=1}^{n} x_i y_i - \left(\sum_{i=1}^{n} x_i\right)\left(\sum_{i=1}^{n} y_i\right)}{n\sum_{i=1}^{n} x_i^2 - \left(\sum_{i=1}^{n} x_i\right)^2}$$

where

n = the number of pairs

y_i = a y value paired with each x_i value

x_i = an x variable value

The formula for computing the intercept is:

$$a = \bar{y} - b\bar{x}$$

Appendix 6

Examining Residuals

Earlier in the chapter we discussed the need to examine error terms (residuals) in order to diagnose potential problems caused by data observations that do not meet the assumptions of regression. Remember, residuals are the difference between the observed value of the dependent variable and the predicted value of the dependent variable produced by the regression equation. We can use SPSS to examine the residuals.

The click-through sequence is ANALYSE → REGRESSION → LINEAR. Highlight X22 and move it to the Dependent Variable box. Highlight X15 and X16 and move them to the Independent Variable box. In the Methods box we will keep Enter, which is the default.

This is the same sequence as earlier regression applications, but now we also must click on the Plots button. To produce plots of the regression residuals for checking on potential problems, click on ZPRED and move it to the Y box. Then click on ZRESID and move it to the X box. These two items stand for Standardized Predicted Dependent Variable and Standardized Residual. Comparing these two quantities allows us to determine whether the hypothesized relationship between the dependent variable X22 and the independent variables X15 and X16 is linear, and also whether the error terms in the regression model are normally distributed (one of the assumptions of a regression model).

To fully evaluate the regression results, we need to examine two other graphs. To do so, go to the lower left-hand portion of the dialog box where it says Standardized Residual Plots. Click on the Histogram and Normal probability options. Now click on Continue and then OK to run the regression procedure.

The SPSS output is shown in Exhibit A6.1. The information in the Model Summary table shows the R-square is .370. From the ANOVA table you can see that this R-square is significant at the .000 level. Finally, in the Coefficients table we see that both independent variables have significant betas and are therefore related to the dependent variable of satisfaction.

Now go to the Charts section at the end of the output to evaluate whether the data we used in the regression model violated any of the assumptions (linear relationship, normally distributed errors, etc.). Exhibits A6.2 to A6.4 present information about the distribution of the residuals. If the regression model predicts equally well over the entire range of the independent variables, there should be no unexpectedly discernible pattern or shape in the residuals and their distribution should be normal. The results shown in these residual charts will help you determine whether the residuals produced by our regression analysis conform to this standard.

Exhibit A6.2 shows the frequency distribution of the standardized residuals compared to a normal distribution. As you can see, most of the residuals are fairly close to the normal curve. There are some observations at −1.50 and +1.00 that exceed the curve, but this result is not of significant concern at this point. Examination of only this table does not suggest there is a problem – but you need to look at all three tables to make a final judgement.

Exhibit A6.3 shows the observed standardized residuals compared against the expected standardized residuals from a normal distribution. If the observed residuals are normally distributed, they will fall directly on the 45° line shown on the graph. As you can see, the residuals from our

EXHIBIT A6.1 Examining Residuals in Multiple Regression

Model Summary[b]

Model	R	R Square	Adjusted R Square	Std. Error of the Estimate
1	.608[a]	.370	.367	.760

a. Predictors: (Constant), X16 – Reasonable Prices, X15 – Fresh Food

b. Dependent Variable: X22 – Satisfaction

ANOVA[a]

Model		Sum of Squares	df	Mean Square	F	Sig.
1	Regression	134.487	2	67.244	116.533	.000[a]
	Residual	229.103	397	.577		
	Total	363.3590	399			

a. Predictors: (Constant), X16 – Reasonable Prices, X15 – Fresh Food

b. Dependent Variable: X22 – Satisfaction

Coefficients[b]

Model		Unstandardized Coefficients		Standardized Coefficients		
		B	Std. Error	Beta	t	Sig.
1	(Constant)	1.418	.216		6.550	.000
	X15 – Fresh Food	.417	.032	.522	12.062	.000
	X10 – Reasonable Prices	.190	.031	.344	6.056	.000

a. Dependent Variable: X22 – Satisfaction

EXHIBIT A6.2 Standardized Residuals versus Normal Distribution

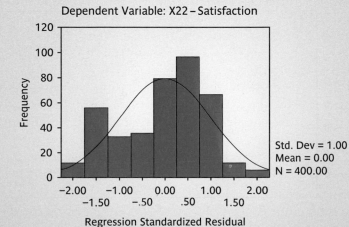

Histogram

Dependent Variable: X22 – Satisfaction

Std. Dev = 1.00
Mean = 0.00
N = 400.00

Regression Standardized Residual

regression model are fairly close to the 45° line so there does not seem to be a problem. Finally, Exhibit A6.4 compares the standardized predicted values of the dependent variable with the standardized residuals from the regression equation. The scatter plot of residuals shows no large difference in the spread of the residuals as you look from left to right on the chart. Again, this result suggests the relationship we are trying to predict is linear and that the error terms are normally distributed.

EXHIBIT A6.3 Observed versus Expected Standardized Residuals

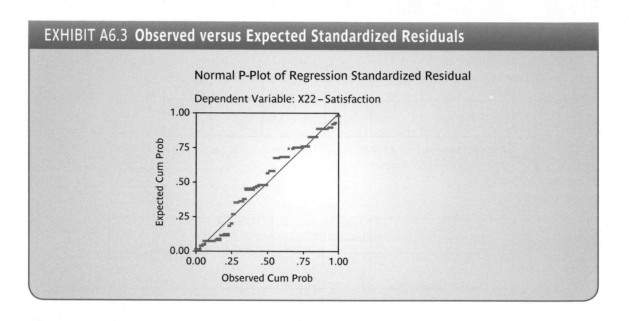

EXHIBIT A6.4 Standardized Predicted Values versus Standardized Residuals

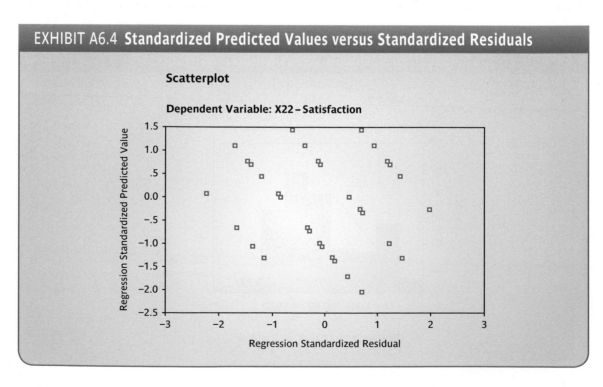

Thus, from an examination of the information presented in all three exhibits we can conclude that there are no significant data problems prohibiting us from saying the assumptions of multiple regression have been seriously violated. Indeed regression is a robust statistical technique and substantial violations of its assumptions are necessary to create problems.

There is one last issue that is worthy of examination from the printout – the Residual Statistics table (see Exhibit A6.5). It includes columns across the top showing the minimum, maximum, mean and standard deviation for the predicted value of the dependent variable, X22. Down the left side are references to the predicted value of X22, the residual, the standardized predicted value and the standardized residual. Note that the standardization process produces scores with a mean of 0 and a standard deviation of 1.00.

You should look closely at the Minimum and Maximum columns. The numbers in these columns will tell you if the data have any distinctive outliers. Distinctive outliers are individual responses that are probably valid responses, but are clearly different from the rest of the responses to a particular question.

The entries in the Minimum and Maximum columns for the standardized predicted value and standardized residual represent the number of standard deviations from the mean of 0. For example, the largest value of the standardized predicted value for X22 is −2.030 standard deviations below the mean value of 0. Likewise, the largest value of the standardized residual is −2.212 standard deviations below its mean of 0. The best way to utilize these numbers is to search for minimum and maximum values greater than 3.0. If these large values really comes from the search, that would mean that some of the predicted values and residuals are further than three standard deviations away from their means and could indicate the presence of outliers in the data.

EXHIBIT A6.5 Residual Statistics for Regression

Residuals Statistics[a]

	Minimum	Maximum	Mean	Std. Deviation	N
Predicted Value	3.47	5.48	4.64	.581	400
Residual	−1.68	1.51	.00	.758	400
Std. Predicted Value	−2.030	1.434	.000	1.000	400
Std. Residual	−2.212	1.986	.000	.997	400

a. Dependent Variable: X22 -- Satisfaction

Glossary

A

ability to participate The availability of both the interviewer and the respondent to get together in a question-and-answer interchange.

accuracy The degree to which the data obtained from a questionnaire provide the researcher with a description of the true state of affairs.

acquiescence error A specific type of response bias that can occur when the respondent perceives what answer would be the most desirable to the sponsor.

active data Data acquired by a business when customers interact with the business's website.

adjusted R-square This adjustment reduces the R_z by taking into account the sample size and the number of independent variables in the regression equation.

administrative error Bias that can stem from data processing mistakes, interviewer distortion of the respondents' answers, or systemic inaccuracies created by using a faulty sampling design.

advertising agencies Businesses that design, implement and evaluate advertising campaigns for individual clients.

affect global approach The theoretical approach of viewing the structure of a person's attitude as nothing more than the overall (global) expression of their favourable or unfavourable feeling towards a given object or behaviour.

affective component That part of an attitude which represents the person's feelings towards the given object, idea, or set of information.

alpha factor The desired or acceptable amount of difference between the expected and the actual population parameter values; also referred to as the *tolerance level of error.*

alternative hypothesis A statement that is the opposite of the null hypothesis, where the difference in reality is not simply due to random error.

ambiguity Contamination of internal validity measures due to unclear determination of cause–effect relationships between investigated constructs.

analysis of variance (ANOVA) A statistical technique that determines whether two or more means are statistically different from each other.

anonymity The assurance that the prospective respondent's name or any identifiable designation will not be associated with his or her responses.

appendix A section at the end of the final research report used to house complex, detailed, or technical information.

appropriateness of descriptors The extent to which the scale point elements match the data being sought.

area sampling A form of cluster sampling where clusters are formed by geographic designations such as cities, subdivisions and blocks. Any geographic unit with boundaries can be used, with one-step or two-step approaches.

articulative interview A qualitative-oriented interviewing technique that focuses on the listening for and identifying of key conflicts in a person's orientation values towards products, services or concepts.

assignment The scaling property that allows the researcher to employ any type of descriptor to identify each object (or response) within a set; this property is also known as *description* or *category.*

assignment property The employment of unique descriptors to identify each object in a set.

attitude A learned predisposition to react in some consistent positive or negative way to a given object, idea, or set of information.

attitude-towards-behaviour model A multiplicative-additive model approach that attempts to capture a person's attitude towards a behaviour rather than to the object itself; where the attitude is a separate, indirectly derived composite measure of a person's combined thoughts and feelings for or against carrying out a specific action or behaviour.

attitude-towards-object model A multiplicative-additive model approach that attempts to capture a person's attitude about a specific object; where the attitude is a separate indirectly derived composite measure of a person's combined thoughts and feelings for or against a given object.

attribute-importance estimate The importance of an attribute of an object as estimated by conjoint analysis. It is calculated by subtracting the minimum part-worth estimate from the maximum part-worth estimate.

auspices error A type of response bias that occurs when the response is dictated by the image or opinion of the sponsor rather than the actual question.

automatic replenishment system (ARS) A continuous, automated inventory control system designed to analyse inventory levels, merchandise order lead times and forecasted sales.

availability of information The degree to which the information has already been collected and assembled in some type of recognizable format.

B

bad questions Any question or directive that obscures, prevents, or distorts the fundamental communications between respondent and researcher.

balancing positive/negative scale descriptors The researcher's decision to maintain objectivity in a scale that is designed to capture both positive and negative state-of-mind raw data from respondents; the same number of relative magnitudes of positive and negative scale descriptors are used to make up the set of scale points.

bar code A pattern of varied-width electronic-sensitive bars and spaces that represents a unique code of numbers and letters.

behaviour intention scale A special type of rating scale designed to capture the likelihood that people will demonstrate some type of predictable behaviour towards purchasing an object or service.

behavioural (conative) component That part of an attitude which refers to the person's behavioural response or specific action/reaction

towards the given object, idea, or set of information; it tends to be the observable outcome driven by the interaction of a person's cognitive and affective components towards the object or behaviour.

believability The quality achieved by building a final report that is based on clear, logical thinking, precise expression and accurate presentation.

benefit and lifestyle studies Studies conducted to examine similarities and differences in needs; used to identify two or more segments within a market for the purpose of identifying customers for the product category of interest to a particular company.

beta coefficient An estimated regression coefficient that has been recalculated to have a mean of 0 and a standard deviation of 1. This statistic enables the independent variables with different units of measurement to be directly compared on their association with the dependent variable.

bias A particular tendency or inclination that skews results, thereby preventing accurate consideration of a research question.

bivariate regression analysis A statistical technique that analyses the linear relationship between two variables by estimating coefficients for an equation for a straight line. One variable is designated as a dependent variable, and the other as an independent (or predictor) variable.

Boolean operators Key words that form a logic string to sort through huge numbers of sites on the World Wide Web.

brand awareness The percentage of respondents having heard of a designated brand; brand awareness can be either unaided or aided.

business ethics The moral principles and standards that guide behaviour in the world of business.

business intelligence A procedure for collecting daily operational information pertinent to the company and the markets it serves.

C

call record sheet A recording document that gathers basic summary information about an interviewer's performance efficiency (e.g. number of contact attempts, number of completed interviews, length of time of interview).

cardinal numbers Any set of consecutive whole integers.

cartoon (balloon) test A qualitative data collection method in which the subject is given a cartoon drawing and suggests the dialogue in which the character(s) might engage.

causal research Research that focuses on collecting data structures and information that will allow the decision maker or researcher to model cause–effect relationships between two or more variables under investigation.

census A study that includes data about or from every member of a target population. Sampling is often used because it is impossible or unreasonable to conduct a census.

central limit theorem (CLT) The theoretical backbone of sampling theory. It states that the sampling distribution of the sample mean ($\bar{x}$) or the sample proportion ($\bar{p}$) value derived from a simple random sample drawn from the target population will be approximately normally distributed provided that the associated sample size is sufficiently large (e.g. when n is greater than or equal to 30).

In turn, the sample mean value ($\bar{x}$) of that random sample with an estimated sampling error (S_g) (estimated standard error) fluctuates around the true population mean value (μ) with a standard error of σ/n and has a sampling distribution that is approximately a standardized normal distribution, regardless of the shape of the probability frequency distribution curve of the overall target population.

cheating The deliberate falsification of respondents' answers on a survey instrument.

Chi-square (χ^2) analysis Assesses how closely the observed frequencies fit the pattern of the expected frequencies and is referred to as a 'goodness-of-fit' test.

Claris Home Page A specific software programme that can be used to create Web pages that can integrate both text and graphics with other types of computer files.

classification (or prediction) matrix The classification matrix in discriminant analysis that contains the number of correctly classified and misclassified cases.

cluster analysis A multivariate interdependence technique whose primary objective is to classify objects into relatively homogeneous groups based on the set of variables considered.

clusters The mutually exclusive and collectively exhaustive subpopulation groupings that are then randomly sampled.

cluster sampling A method of probability sampling where the sampling units are selected in groups (or clusters) rather than individually. Once the cluster has been identified, the elements to be sampled are drawn by simple random sampling or all of the units may be included in the sample.

code of ethics A set of guidelines that states the standards and operating procedures for ethical decisions and practices by researchers.

coding The activities of grouping and assigning values to various responses from a survey instrument.

coefficient alpha See *Cronbach's alpha*.

coefficient of determination (r^2) A statistical value (or number) that measures the proportion of variation in one variable accounted for by another variable; the r^2 measure can be thought of as a percentage and varies from .00 to 1.00.

cognitive component That part of an attitude which represents the person's beliefs, perceptions, preferences, experiences, and knowledge about a given object, idea, or set of information.

commercial/syndicated data Data that have been compiled and displayed according to some standardized procedure.

company ethics programme The framework through which a firm establishes internal codes of ethical behaviour to serve as guidelines for doing business.

comparative rating scale Scale used when the scaling objective is to have a respondent express an attitude, feeling, or behaviour about an object (or person, or phenomenon) or its attributes on the basis of some other object (or person, or phenomenon) or its attributes.

competitive intelligence analysis Specific procedures for collecting daily operational information pertaining to the competitive companies and markets they serve.

complete randomization The procedure whereby many subjects are randomly assigned to different experimental conditions, resulting in each

group averaging out any systematic effect on the investigated functional relationship between the independent and dependent variables.

completely automated telephone survey (CATS) A survey administered by a computer with no human interviewer. The computer dials a telephone number and the respondent listens to the electronic voice, responding by pushing keys on the Touch-Tone telephone pad.

completeness The depth and breadth of the data.

completion deadline date Part of the information included in a cover letter that directly communicates to a prospective respondent the date by which his or her completed questionnaire must be returned to the researcher.

complexity of the information One of the two fundamental dimensions used to determine the level of information being supplied by the information research process; it relates to the degree to which the information is easily understood and applied to the problem or opportunity under investigation.

computer-administered survey A survey design that incorporates the use of a computer to ask questions and record responses.

computer-assisted personal survey A survey in which the interviewer reads respondents the questions from a computer screen and directly keys in the response.

computer-assisted self-survey A survey in which respondents are directed to a computer where they read questions from the computer screen and directly enter their responses.

computer-assisted telephone survey A survey that uses a fully automated system in which the respondent listens to an electronic voice and responds by pushing keys on a Touch-Tone telephone keypad.

computer-generated fax survey A survey procedure in which a computer is used to send a survey to potential respondents via fax; the respondent completes the survey and returns it via fax or mail.

computerized secondary data sources Data sources designed by specific companies that integrate both internal and external data with online information sources.

concept and product testing Information for decisions on product improvements and new product introductions.

confidence interval A statistical range of values within which the true value of the target population parameter of interest is expected to fall based on a specified confidence level.

confidence levels Theoretical levels of assurance of the probability that a particular confidence interval will accurately include or measure the true population parameter value. In information research, the three most widely used levels are 90 per cent, 95 per cent, and 99 per cent.

confidentiality The expressed assurance to the prospective respondent that their name, while known to the researcher, will not be divulged to a third party, especially the sponsoring client.

confirmation/invitation letter A specific follow-up document sent to prospective focus group participants to encourage and reinforce their willingness and commitment to participate in the group session.

conformance to standards The researcher's ability to be accurate, timely, mistake free

and void of unanticipated delays.

conjoint analysis A multivariate technique that can be used in marketing research to determine how consumers value different attributes that make up a given product, service, marketing communication message, or any other object.

connect time The length of time, frequently measured in minutes and seconds, that a user is logged on to an electronic service or database. The amount of connect time is generally used to bill the user for services.

connectors Logic phrases and symbols that allow search terms to be linked together in a Boolean logic format.

consent forms Formal signed statements of agreement by the participants approving the taping or recording of the information provided in group discussions and releasing that data to the moderator, researcher, or sponsoring client.

constant sums rating scale A scale format that requires the respondents to allocate a given number of points, usually 100, among several attributes or features based on their importance to the individual; this format requires a person to value each separate feature relative to all the other listed features.

construct development An integrative process of activities undertaken by researchers to enhance understanding of what specific data should be collected for solving defined research problems.

construct development error A type of nonsampling (systematic) error that is created when the researcher is not careful in fully identifying the concepts and constructs to be included in the study.

constructs Hypothetical variables composed of a set of component responses or behaviours that are thought to be related.

construct validity The degree to which researchers measure what they intended to measure, and to which the proper identification of the independent and dependent variables were included in the investigation.

consumer-generated media A collective name applied to different forms of digital communications whereby consumers openly share their opinions and experiences, often about their reactions to products and services.

consumer panels Large samples of households that provide certain types of data for an extended period of time.

content analysis The technique used to study written or taped materials by breaking the data into meaningful aggregate units or categories using a predetermined set of rules.

content validity That property of a test which indicates that the entire domain of the subject or construct of interest was properly sampled. That is, the identified factors are truly components of the construct of interest.

control group That portion of the sample which is not subjected to the treatment.

controlled test markets Test markets performed by an outside research firm that guarantees distribution of the test product through pre-specified outlets in selected cities.

control variables Extraneous variables that the researcher is able to account for according to their systematic variation (or impact) on the functional relationship between the independent and dependent variables included in the experiment.

convenience sampling A method of nonprobability sampling where the samples are drawn on the basis of the convenience of the researcher or interviewer; also referred to as *accidental sampling*. Convenience sampling is often used in the early stages of research because it allows a large number of respondents to be interviewed in a short period of time.

convergent validity The degree to which different measures of the same construct are highly correlated.

cost analysis An analysis of alternative logistic system designs that a firm can use for achieving its performance objective at the lowest total cost.

covariation The amount of change in one variable that is consistently related to the change in another variable of interest.

cover letter A separate letter that either accompanies a self-administered questionnaire or is mailed prior to an initial interviewer contact call and whose main purpose is to secure a respondent's willingness to participate in the research project; sometimes referred to as a *letter of introduction*.

cover letter guidelines A specific set of factors that should be included in a cover letter for the purpose of increasing a prospective respondent's willingness to participate in the study.

credibility The quality that comes about by developing a final report that is accurate, believable and professionally organized.

critical level of error The observed difference between a sample statistic value and the corresponding true or hypothesized population parameter.

critical questions Questions used by a moderator to direct the group to the critical issues underlying the topics of interest.

critical *z* value The book *z* value and the amount of acceptable variability between the observed sample data results and the prescribed hypothesized true population values measured in standardized degrees of standard errors for given confidence levels.

Cronbach's alpha A widely used measurement of the internal consistency of a multi-item scale in which the average of all possible split-half coefficients is taken.

cross-tabulation The process of simultaneously treating (or counting) two or more variables in the study. This process categorizes the number of respondents who have responded to two or more questions consecutively.

curbstoning Cheating or falsification of data during the collection process that occurs when interviewers fill in all or part of a survey themselves.

curvilinear relationship An association between two variables whereby the strength and/or direction of their relationship changes over the range of both variables.

customer-centric approach Use of granular data to anticipate and fulfil customers' desires.

customer interaction The relationship between the enterprise and the customer.

customer knowledge The collection of customer interaction information used to create customer profiles that can be used to tailor interactions, segment customers and build strong customer relationships.

customer knowledge information Information volunteered by customers that might be outside the marketing function of an organization.

customer relationship management (CRM) Management of customer relationships based on the integration of customer information throughout the business enterprise in order to achieve maximum customer satisfaction and retention.

customer satisfaction studies Studies designed to assess both the strengths and weaknesses customers perceive in a firm's marketing mix.

customer-volunteered information Data provided by the customer without solicitation.

cycle time The time that elapses between taking a product or service from initial consumer contact to final delivery.

cycle time research A research method that centres on reducing the time between the initial contact and final delivery (or installation) of products.

D

data Facts relating to any issue or subject.

data analysis error A 'family' of nonsampling errors that are created when the researcher subjects the raw data to inappropriate analysis procedures.

database A collection of secondary information indicating what customers are purchasing, how often they purchase and how much they purchase.

database technology The means by which data are transformed into information.

data coding errors The incorrect assignment of computer codes to the raw responses.

data editing errors Inaccuracies due to careless verifying procedures of raw data to computer data files.

data enhancement The process of weaving data into current internal data structures for the purpose of gaining a more valuable categorization of customers relative to their true value to the company.

data entry The direct inputting of the coded data into some specified software package that will ultimately allow the research analyst to manipulate and transform the raw data into data structures.

data entry errors The incorrect assignment of computer codes to their pre-designated location on the computer data file.

data field A basic characteristic about a customer that is filled in on a database.

data interaction matrix A procedure used to itemize the type and amount of data required by each functional area of the company regardless of the cost of data collection.

data mining The process of finding hidden patterns and relationships among variables/characteristics contained in data stored in the data warehouse.

data processing error A specific type of nonsampling error that can occur when researchers are not accurate or complete in transferring raw data from respondents to computer files.

data silo Collection of data by one area of a business that is not shared with other areas.

data structures The output analysis results of combining a group of reported raw data using some type of quantitative or qualitative analysis procedure.

data validation A specific control process that the researcher undertakes to ensure that his or her representatives collected the data as required. The process is normally one of recontacting about 20 per cent of the selected respondent group to determine that they did participate in the study.

data warehouse A central repository for all significant pieces of information that an organization collects.

debriefing analysis The technique of comparing notes, thoughts and feelings about a focus group discussion between the moderator, researcher and sponsoring client immediately following the group interview.

decision opportunity The presence of a situation in which market performance can be significantly improved by undertaking new activities.

decision problem A situation in which management has established a specific objective to accomplish and there are several courses of action that could be taken, each with its own risks and potential benefits.

deductive research Investigations that are undertaken to test hypothesized relationships derived from the use of existing theories.

defined target population A specified group of people or objects for which questions can be asked or observations made to develop the required data structures and information; also referred to as the *working population*. A precise definition of the target population is essential when undertaking a research project.

degree of manipulation The extent to which data structures and results have been interpreted and applied to a specific situation.

deliberate falsification When the respondent and/or interviewer intentionally gives wrong answers or deliberately cheats on a survey.

demand analysis The estimating of the level of customer demand for a given product as well as the underlying reasons for that demand.

demand characteristics Contamination to construct validity measures created by test subjects trying to guess the true purpose behind the experiment and therefore give socially acceptable responses or behaviours.

demographic characteristics Physical and factual attributes of people, organizations, or objects.

deontologists Individuals who emphasize good intentions and the rights of the people involved in an action; they are much less concerned with the results from any ethical decision.

dependence techniques Appropriate multivariate procedures when one or more of the variables can be identified as dependent variables and the remaining as independent variables.

dependent variable A singular observable attribute that is the measured outcome derived from manipulating the independent variable(s).

depth The overall number of key data fields or variables that will make up the data records.

description The process of discovering patterns, associations and relationships among key customer characteristics.

descriptive questionnaire design A questionnaire design that allows the researcher to collect raw data that can be turned into facts about a person or object. The questions and scales primarily involve the collecting of state-of-being and state-of-behaviour data.

descriptive research Research that uses a set of scientific methods and procedures to collect data structures that are used to identify, determine and describe the existing characteristics of a target population or market structure.

diffusion of treatment Contamination to construct validity measures due to test subjects discussing the treatment and measurement activities with individuals yet to receive the treatment.

direct cognitive structural analysis A data analysis procedure in which respondents are simply asked to determine the extent to which an attribute is part of the construct's structural makeup and its importance to construct.

direct (positive) directional hypothesis A statement about the perceived relationship between two questions, dimensions, or subgroups of attributes that suggests that as one factor moves in one direction, the other factor moves in the same direction.

directed data Comprehensive data about customers collected through the use of computers.

direct mail survey A questionnaire distributed to and returned from respondents via the postal service.

directness of observation The degree to which the researcher or trained observer actually observes the behaviour/event as it occurs; also termed *direct observation.*

direct observation The process of observing actual behaviours or events and recording them as they occur.

direct self-administered questionnaire A survey instrument designed to have the respondent serve as both an interviewer and a respondent during the question-and-answer encounter.

discretion of primary descriptors The carefulness that a researcher must use in selecting the actual words used to distinguish the relative magnitudes associated with each of the primary descriptors in a scale design.

discriminant analysis A multivariate technique for analysing marketing research data when the dependent variable is categorical and the independent variables are interval.

discriminant function The linear combination of independent variables developed by discriminant analysis which will best discriminate between the categories of the dependent variable.

discriminant function coefficient The multipliers of variables in the discriminant function when the variables are in the original units of measurement.

discriminant score In discriminant analysis, this represents the score of each respondent on the discriminant function.

discriminant validity The degree to which measures of different constructs are uncorrelated.

discriminatory power The scale's ability to significantly differentiate between the categorical scale responses (or points).

disguised observation An observation technique in which the test subjects are completely unaware that they are being observed and recorded.

disguised sponsorship When the true identity of the person or company for which the research is being conducted is not divulged to the prospective respondent.

disproportionate stratified sampling A form of stratified sampling in which the size of

the sample drawn from each stratum is independent of the stratum's proportion of the total population.

distance property The scaling property that when activated allows the researcher and respondent to identify, understand, and accurately express in a unit measurement scheme the exact (or absolute) difference between each of the descriptors, scale points, or raw responses.

diversity in specified characteristics The degree to which the respondents share characteristics that affect the implementation and quality of the type of survey method being adopted.

diversity of respondents The degree to which the respondents in the study share some similarities.

domain of observables The set of observable manifestations of a variable that is not itself directly observable. A domain represents an identifiable set of components that indirectly make up the construct of interest.

drop-off survey A questionnaire that is left with the respondent to be completed at a later time. The questionnaire may be picked up by the researcher or returned via some other mode.

dummy variables Artificial variables introduced into a regression equation to represent the categories of a nominally scaled variable (such as sex or marital status). There will be one dummy variable for each of the nominal categories of the independent variable, and the values will typically be 0 and 1, depending on whether the variable value is present or absent for a particular respondent (e.g. male or female).

E

editing The process in which the interviews or survey instruments are checked for mistakes that may have occurred by either the interviewer or the respondent during data collection activities.

electronic database A high-speed, computer-assisted information source or library.

electronic data interchange (EDI) A specific system designed to speed the flow of information as well as products from producer to distributor to retailer.

electronic test markets Test procedures that integrate the use of selected panels of consumers who use a special identification card in recording their product purchasing data.

element The name given to the object about which information is sought. Elements must be unique, countable, and, when added together, make up the whole of the target population.

email survey A survey in which electronic mail is used to deliver a questionnaire to respondents and receive their responses.

empirical testing The actual collection of data in the real world using research instruments and then subjecting that data to rigorous analysis to either support or refute a hypothesis.

ending questions Questions used by a focus group moderator to bring closure to a particular topic discussion; encourages summary-type comments.

enterprise The total business unit, including all facets of the business as well as suppliers and retailers.

environmental forecasting The projection of environmental occurrences that can affect the long-term strategy of a firm.

environmental information Secondary information pertaining to a firm's suppliers and/or distributors.

equivalent form A method of assessing the reliability associated with a scale measurement; the researcher creates two basically similar yet different scale measurements for the given construct and administers both forms to either the same sample of respondents or two samples of respondents from the same target population.

error The difference between the true score on a research instrument and the actual observed score.

estimated sample standard deviation A quantitative index of the dispersion of the distribution of drawn sampling units' actual data around the sample's arithmetic average measure of central tendency; this sample statistical value specifies the degree of variation in the raw data responses in a way that allows the researcher to translate the variations into normal curve interpretations.

estimated sample variance The square of the estimated sample standard deviation.

estimated standard error of the sample statistic A statistical measurement of the sampling error that can be expected to exist between the drawn sample's statistical values and the actual values of all the sampling units' distributions of those concerned statistics. These indexes are referred to as *general precision*.

estimates Sample data facts that are transformed through interpretation procedures to represent inferences about the larger target population.

ethical dilemmas Specific situations in which the researcher, decision maker, or respondent must choose between appropriate and inappropriate behaviour.

ethics The field of study that tries to determine what behaviours are considered to be appropriate under certain circumstances by established codes of behaviour set forth by society.

evaluation apprehension Contamination to construct validity measures caused by test subjects being fearful that their actions or responses will become known to others.

executive interview A person-administered interview of a business executive. Frequently, these interviews will take place in the executive's office.

executive summary The part of the final research report that illustrates the major points of the report in a manner complete enough to provide a true representation of the entire document.

expected completion rate (ECR) The estimated percentage of prospective respondents who are expected to participate and complete the survey; also referred to as the *anticipated response rate*.

expected incidence rate (EIR) The estimated percentage of the defined target population elements who qualify for inclusion into the survey.

expected reachable rate (ERR) The estimated percentage of the contacts that can be reached by the researcher or interviewer.

experience interview Informal gathering of information from individuals thought to be knowledgeable on the issues relevant to the research problem.

experimental design reliability The degree to which the research design and its procedures can be replicated and achieve similar conclusions about hypothesized relationships.

experimental research An empirical investigation that tests for hypothesized relationships between dependent variables and manipulated independent variables.

expert systems Advanced computer-based systems that function in the same manner as a human expert, advising the analyst on how to solve a problem.

explained variance In multivariate methods, it is the amount of variation in the dependent construct that can be accounted for by the combination of independent variables.

exploratory research Research designed to collect and interpret either secondary or primary data in an unstructured format using sometimes an informal set of procedures.

external secondary data Data collected by outside agencies such as the federal, state, or local government; trade associations; or periodicals.

external validity The extent to which the measured data results of a study based on a sample can be expected to hold in the entire defined target population. In addition, it is the extent that a causal relationship found in a study can be expected to be true for the entire defined target population.

extraneous variables All variables other than the independent variables that affect the responses of the test subjects. If left uncontrolled, these variables can have a confounding impact on the dependent variable measures that could weaken or invalidate the results of an experiment.

extremity error A type of response bias when the clarity of extreme scale points and ambiguity of midrange

options encourage extreme responses.

eye tracking monitor A device that observes and records a person's unconscious eye movements.

F

facilitating agencies Businesses that perform a marketing research function as a supplement to a broader marketing research project.

factor analysis A class of statistical procedures primarily used for data reduction and summarization.

factor loadings Simple correlations between the variables and the factors.

factor scores Composite scores estimated for each respondent on the derived factors.

facts Pieces of information that are observable and verifiable through a number of external sources.

faulty recall The inability of a person to accurately remember the specifics about the behaviour under investigation.

fax survey A questionnaire distributed to the sample via fax machines.

field experiments Causal research designs that manipulate the independent variables in order to measure the dependent variable in a natural test setting.

field service providers Businesses that schedule, supervise and complete field work studies assigned by individual clients.

finite correction factor (fcf) An adjustment factor to the sample size that is made in those situations where the drawn sample is expected to equal 5 per cent or more of the defined target population. The fcf is equal to the overall square root of $N - n/N - 1$.

flowerpot approach A specific, unique framework or blueprint for integrating different sets of

questions and scale measurements into an instrument that is capable of collecting the raw data needed to achieve each of the established information objectives.

focus group facility A professional facility that offers a set of specially designed rooms for conducting focus group interviews; each room contains a large table and comfortable chairs for up to 13 people, with a relaxed atmosphere, built-in audio equipment, and normally a one-way mirror for disguised observing by the sponsoring client or researcher.

focus group incentives Specified investment programmes to compensate focus group participants for their expenses associated with demonstrating a willingness to be a group member.

focus group moderator A special person who is well trained in interpersonal communications; listening, observation, and interpretive skills; and professional mannerisms and personality. His or her role in a session is to draw from the participants the best and most innovative ideas about an assigned topic or question.

focus group research A formalized qualitative data collection method for which data are collected from a small group of people who interactively and spontaneously discuss one particular topic or concept.

follow-up test A statistical test that flags the means that are statistically different from each other; follow-up tests are performed after an ANOVA determines there are differences between means.

forced-choice scale measurements Symmetrical scale measurement designs that do not have a logical 'neutral' scale descriptor to divide the positive and negative domains of response descriptors.

formal rating procedures The use of structured survey instruments or questionnaires to gather information on environmental occurrences.

formative composite scale Scale used when each of the individual scale items measures some part of the whole construct, object, or phenomenon.

F-ratio The statistical ratio of between-group mean squared variance to within-group mean squared variance; the *F* value is used as an indicator of the statistical difference between group means in an ANOVA.

free-choice scale measurements Symmetrical scale measurement designs that are divided into positive and negative domains of scale-point descriptors by a logical centre 'neutral' response.

frequency distributions A summary of how many times each possible raw response to a scale question/setup was recorded by the total group of respondents.

F-test The test used to statistically evaluate the difference between the group means in ANOVA.

full-text Option of having the entire document, news story, article, or numerical information available for downloading.

fully automated self-survey A procedure in which respondents independently approach a central computer station or kiosk, read the questions, and respond – all without researcher intervention.

completely automated telephone survey A data collection procedure in which the computer calls respondents and asks questions; the respondent records his or her answers by using the keypad of a touch-tone telephone.

functional relationship An observable and measurable systematic change in one variable as another variable changes.

G

garbage in, garbage out A standard phrase used in marketing research to represent situations where the process of collecting, analysing, and interpreting data into information contains errors or biases, creating less than accurate information.

gatekeeper technology Any device used to help protect one's privacy against intrusive marketing practices such as telemarketing solicitors, unwanted direct marketers, illegal scam artists, and 'sugging' (caller ID, voice messengers, answering machines).

generalizability The extent to which the data are an accurate portrait of the defined target population; the representativeness of information obtained from a small subgroup of members to that of the entire target population from which the subgroup was selected.

generalizability of data structures The degree to which sample data results and structures can be used to draw accurate inferences about the defined target population, that is, the extent to which the research can extrapolate results from a sample to the defined target population.

general precision The amount of general sampling error associated with the given sample of raw data that was generated through some type of data collection activity; no specific concern for any level of confidence.

granular data Highly detailed, highly personalized data specifically structured around an individual customer.

graphic rating scale A scale point format that presents respondents with some type of graphic continuum as the set of possible raw responses to a given question.

group dynamics The degree of spontaneous interaction among group members during a discussion of a topic.

H

hits The number of documents or other items that meet the search terms in an online search.

human observation Data collection by a researcher or trained observer who records text subjects' actions and behaviours.

hybrid ordinally-interval scale An ordinal scale that is artificially transformed into an interval scale by the researcher.

hypertext markup language (HTML) The language used to create Web pages for communicating the research results as well as other information on the Internet.

hypothesis A yet-unproven proposition or possible solution to a decision problem that can be empirically tested using data that are collected through the research process; it is developed in order to explain phenomena or a relationship between two or more constructs or variables.

hypothesis guessing Contamination to construct validity measures due to test subjects' believing they know the desired functional relationship prior to the manipulation treatment.

I

iceberg principle The general notion indicating that the dangerous part of many marketing decision problems is neither visible nor well understood by marketing managers.

importance-performance analysis A research and data analysis procedure used to evaluate a firm's and its competitors' strengths and weaknesses, as well as future actions that seek to identify key attributes that drive purchase behaviour within a given industry.

inadequate pre-operationalization of variables Contamination to construct validity measures due to inadequate understanding of the complete makeup of the independent and dependent variables included in the experimental design.

inappropriate analysis bias A type of data analysis error that creates the wrong data structure results and can lead to misinterpretation errors.

incidence rate The percentage of the general population who are the subject of the marketing research project in question.

independent samples Two or more groups of responses that are tested as though they may come from different populations.

independent variable An attribute of an object whose measurement values are directly manipulated by the researcher, also referred to as a *predictor* or *treatment variable*. This type of variable is assumed to be a causal factor in a functional relationship with a dependent variable.

in-depth interview A formalized, structured process of a subject's being asked a set of semistructured, probing questions by a well-trained interviewer usually in a face-to-face setting.

indirect observation A research technique in which researchers or trained observers rely on artifacts that, at best, represent specific reported behavioural outcomes from some earlier time.

inductive research An investigation that collects and analyses primary data, from which to generate hypotheses and test them for creating new theories or extending existing ones.

information The set of facts derived from data structures when someone – either the researcher or decision maker – interprets and attaches narrative meaning to the data structures.

informational data Data collected through On-Line Analytical Processing (OLAP) software for analysis purposes as a decision-making tool for marketing programmes.

information requirements The identified factors, dimensions, and attributes within a stated information objective for which raw data must be collected.

in-home survey A person administrated survey that takes place in the respondent's home.

instrumentation Contamination to internal validity measures from changes in measurement processes, observation techniques, and/or measuring instruments.

intelligibility The degree to which questions can be understood by the respondents making up the defined target population to whom the scale will be administered.

intention to purchase A person's planned future action to buy a product or service.

interdependence techniques Multivariate statistical procedures in which the whole set of interdependent relationships is examined.

internal consistency The degree to which the various dimensions of a multidimensional construct correlate with the scale.

internal consistency reliability The extent to which the items of a scale represent the same domain of content and are highly correlated both with each other and summated scale scores. It represents the degree to which the components are related to the same overall construct domain.

internal quality movement One of the underlying factors for which many organizations are restructuring away from old traditional functional control/power systems of operating to new cross-functional structures where team building, decision teams and sharing of information and responsibility are the important factors, not control and power.

internal secondary data Facts that have been collected by the individual company for accounting and marketing activity purposes.

internal validity The certainty with which a researcher can state that the observed effect was caused by a specific treatment; exists when the research design accurately identifies causal relationships.

International Standard Industrial Classification of All Economic Activities (ISIC) Numerical industrial listings designed to promote uniformity in data reporting procedures by governments and businesses in different countries.

Internet A network of computers and technology linking computers into an information superhighway.

Internet survey The method of using the Internet to ask survey questions and record responses of respondents.

interpersonal communication skills The interviewer's abilities to articulate the questions in a direct and clear manner so that the subject understands what they are responding to.

interpretive bias Error that occurs when the wrong inference about the real world or defined target population is made by the researcher or decision maker due to some type of extraneous factor.

interpretive skills The interviewer's capabilities of accurately understanding and recording the subject's responses to questions.

interval scales Any question/scale format that activates not only the assignment and order scaling properties but also the distance property; all scale responses have a recognized absolute difference between each of the other scale points (responses).

interviewer error A type of nonsampling error that is created in situations where the interviewer distorts information, in a systematic way, from respondents during or after the interviewer/respondent encounter.

interviewer instructions The vehicle for training the interviewer on how to select prospective respondents, screen them for eligibility, and conduct the actual interview.

interviewer/mechanical devices The combination of highly skilled people who are aided by high-technology devices during the questioning/responding encounters with respondents.

introductory questions Questions used by a focus group moderator to introduce the general topic of discussion

and opportunities of reflecting their past experiences.

inverse (negative or indirect) directional hypothesis A statement about the perceived relationship between two questions, dimensions, or subgroupings of attributes that suggests that as one factor moves in one direction, the other factor moves in an opposite fashion.

J

judgement sampling A non-probability sampling design that selects participants for a sample based on an experienced individual's belief that the participants will meet the requirements of the research study.

junk mail A categorical descriptor that prospective respondents attach to surveys that are administered through the direct mail delivery system or an unwanted telephone interview that is viewed as being nothing more than a telemarketing gimmick to sell them something they do not want or need.

K

knowledge level of respondent The degree to which the selected respondents feel they have experience (or knowledge) with the topics that are the focus of the survey's questioning.

L

lead country test markets Field test markets that are conducted in specific foreign countries.

leading question A question that tends to purposely elicit a particular answer.

level of significance The amount of risk regarding the accuracy of the test that the researcher is willing to accept.

library A large group of related information.

lifetime value models Procedures developed using historical data, as well as actual purchase behaviour, not probability estimates, to predict consumer behaviour.

Likert scale A special rating scale format that asks respondents to indicate the extent to which they agree or disagree with a series of mental belief or behavioural belief statements about a given object; it is a cognitive-based scale measurement.

limitations A section of the final research report in which all extraneous events that place certain restrictions on the report are fully communicated.

linear relationship An association between two variables whereby the strength and nature of the relationship remains the same over the range of both variables.

listening skills The interviewer's capabilities of understanding what the respondent is communicating.

logistic assessment Information in logistics that allows market researchers to conduct total cost analysis and service sensitivity analysis.

logistic regression A multivariate technique that can accommodate dichotomous or other categorical dependent variables.

lottery approach A unique incentive system that pools together either individual small cash incentives into a significantly larger dollar amount or a substantial nonmonetary gift and then holds a drawing to determine the winner or small set of winners. The drawing procedure is designed so that all respondents who complete and return their survey have an equal chance of receiving the larger reward.

M

mail panel survey A representative sample of individual respondents who have agreed in advance to participate in a mail survey.

mail survey A self-administered questionnaire that is delivered to selected respondents and returned to the researcher by mail.

mail survey by computer disk A survey procedure in which computer disks are mailed to respondents; the respondents complete the survey on their own computer and return the disk to the researcher via the mail.

managerial function software system A computer-based procedure that includes forecasting, brand management and promotional budget capabilities.

market intelligence The use of real-time customer information (customer knowledge) to achieve a competitive advantage.

market performance symptoms Conditions that signal the presence of a decision problem and/or opportunity.

marketing The process of planning and executing pricing, promotion, product, and distribution of products, services, and ideas in order to create exchanges that satisfy both the firm and its customers.

marketing decision support system (MDSS) A computer-based system intended for use by particular marketing personnel at any functional level for the purpose of solving information and/or semistructured problems. Within this system databases are developed and used to analyse the firm's performance as well as control its marketing activities.

marketing knowledge A characteristic that complements a researcher's technical competency.

marketing research The function that links an organization to its market through the gathering of information. The information allows for the identification and definition of market-driven opportunities and problems. The information allows for the generation, refinement, and evaluation of marketing actions.

marketing research codes of ethics A set of ethical codes formulated by marketing research industry governing institutions, such as ESOMAR. These ethical codes are used by many marketing research companies for establishing their internal company codes of ethics.

marketing research database A collection of information indicating what customers are purchasing, how often they purchase, and the amount they purchase.

marketing research process The ten systematic task steps involved in the four phases of gathering, analysing, interpreting and transforming data structures and results into information for use by decision makers.

maturation Contamination to internal validity measures due to changes in the dependent variable based on the natural function of time and not attributed to any specific event.

mean The arithmetic average of all the raw responses; all values of a distribution of responses are summed and divided by the number of valid responses.

measurement Rules for assigning numbers to objects so that these numbers represent quantities of attributes.

measurement/design error A 'family' of nonsampling errors that result from

inappropriate designs in the constructs, scale measurements, or survey measurements used to execute the asking and recording of people's responses to a study's questions.

measures of central tendency The basic sample statistics that could be generated through analysing the collected raw data; they are the mode, the median and the mean.

measures of dispersion The sample statistics that describe how all the raw data are actually dispersed around a given measure of central tendency; they are the frequency distribution, the range and the estimated sample standard deviation.

mechanical devices High-technology instruments that can artificially observe and record either current behavioural actions or physical phenomena as they occur.

mechanical observation Some type of mechanical or electronic device is used to capture human behaviour, events, or marketing phenomena.

median The sample statistic that splits the raw data into a hierarchical pattern where half the raw data is above the median statistic value and half is below.

media panels Selected households that are primarily used in measuring media viewing habits as opposed to product/brand consumption patterns.

method bias The error source that results from selecting an inappropriate method to investigate the research question.

misinterpretation error An inaccurate transformation of data structures and analysis results into usable bits of information for the decision maker.

mode The most frequently mentioned (or occurring) raw

response in the set of responses to a given question/setup.

model *F* statistic A statistic which compares the amount of variation in the dependent measure 'explained' or associated with the independent variables to the 'unexplained' or error variance. A larger *F*-statistic value indicates that the regression model has more explained variance than error variance.

moderator's guide A detailed document that outlines the topics, questions, and subquestions that serve as the basis for generating the spontaneous interactive dialogue among the focus group participants.

modified Likert scale Any version of the agreement/disagreement-based scale measurement that is not the original five-point 'strongly agree' to 'strongly disagree' scale.

monetary compensation An individual cash incentive used by the researcher to increase the likelihood of a prospective respondent's willingness to participate in the survey.

mono-method bias A particular type of error source that is created when only a single method is used to collect data about the research question.

moral philosophy A person's basic orientation towards problem solving. Within the ethical decision-making process, philosophical thinking will come from teleology, deontology and/or relativity orientations.

mortality Contamination to internal validity measures due to changing the composition of the test subjects in the experiment.

multicollinearity A situation in which several independent variables are highly correlated with each other. This characteristic can result in difficulty in estimating separate or independent regression coefficients for the correlated variables.

multiple-item scale designs Method used when the researcher has to measure several items (or attributes) simultaneously in order to measure the complete object or construct of interest.

multiple regression analysis A statistical technique which analyses the linear relationships between a dependent variable and multiple independent variables by estimating coefficients for the equation for a straight line.

multivariate analysis (techniques) A group of statistical techniques used when there are two or more measurements on each element and the variables are analysed simultaneously.

mystery shopper studies Studies in which trained, professional shoppers visit stores, financial institutions, or companies and 'shop' for various products and assess service quality factors or levels.

N

nominal scales Question/scale structures that ask the respondent to provide only a descriptor as the raw response; the response does not contain any level of intensity.

nomological validity The extent to which one particular construct theoretically networks with other established constructs which are related yet different.

non-comparative scale Scale used when the scaling objective is to have a respondent express an attitude, emotion, action, or intention about one specific object (person, phenomenon) or its attributes.

non-directional hypothesis A statement regarding the existing relationship between two questions, dimensions, or subgroupings of attributes as being significantly different but lacking an expression of direction.

non-equivalent control group A quasi-experimental design that combines the static group comparison and one-group, pretest-posttest pre-experimental designs.

non-monetary compensation Any type of individual incentive excluding direct cash (e.g. a free T-shirt) used by the researcher to encourage a prospective respondent's participation.

non-probability sampling Sampling designs in which the probability of selection of each sampling unit is not known. The selection of sampling units is based on the judgement or knowledge of the researcher and may or may not be representative of the target population.

non-response error An error that occurs when the portion of the defined target population not represented or underrepresented in the response pool is systematically and significantly different from those that did respond.

non-sampling error A type of bias that occurs in a research study regardless of whether a sample or census is used.

not at home A specific type of non-response bias that occurs when a reasonable attempt to initially reach a prospective respondent fails to produce an interviewer/respondent encounter.

null hypothesis A statement of the perceived existing relationship between two questions, dimensions, or sub-groupings of attributes as being not significantly different; it asserts the status quo condition, and any change from what has been thought to be true is due to random sampling error.

O

object Any tangible item in a person's environment that can be clearly and easily identified through the senses.

objectivity The degree to which a researcher uses scientific procedures to collect, analyse and create nonbiased information.

observation The systematic process of witnessing and recording the behavioural patterns of objects, people, and occurrences without directly questioning or communicating with them.

observing mechanism How the behaviours or events will be observed; *human observation* is when the observer is either a person hired and trained by the researcher or the researcher himself; *mechanical observation* refers to the use of a technology-based device to do the observing rather than a human observer.

odd or even number of scale points When collecting either state-of-mind or state-of-intention data, the researcher must decide whether the positive and negative scale points need to be separated by a neutral scale descriptor; even-point scales (known as *forced-choice scales*) do not require a neutral response, but odd-point scales (known as *free-choice scales*) must offer a neutral scale response.

one-group, pretest-posttest A pre-experimental design where first a pre-treatment measure of the dependent variable is taken (O_1), then the test subjects are exposed to the independent treatment (X), then a post-treatment measure of the dependent variable is taken (O_2).

one-shot study A single group of test subjects is exposed to the independent variable treatment (X), and then a single measurement on the dependent variable is taken (O_1).

one-way tabulation The categorization of single variables existing in the study.

online focus groups A formalized process whereby a small group of people form an online community for an interactive, spontaneous discussion on one particular topic or concept.

online services Providers of access to electronic databases and other services in real time.

opening questions Questions used by a focus group moderator to break the ice among focus group participants; identify common group member traits; and create a comfort zone for establishing group dynamics and interactive discussions.

operational data Data collected through online transaction processing (OLTP) and used for the daily operations of the business.

operationalization The process of precisely delineating how a construct is to be measured. The variables are specified in such a manner as to be potentially observable or manipulable.

opportunity assessment The collection of information on product-markets for the purpose of forecasting how they will change in the future. This type of assessment focuses on gathering information relevant to macroenvironments.

optical scanner An electronic device that optically reads bar codes; this scanner captures and translates unique bar code numbers into product information.

order property The scaling property that activates the existence of relative magnitudes between the descriptors used as scale points (or raw responses); it allows the researcher to establish either a higher-to-lower or lower-to-higher rank order among the raw responses.

ordinally interval scales Ordinal questions or scale formats that the researcher artificially redefines as being interval by activating an assumed distance scaling property into the design structure; this hybrid-type scale format incorporates both primary ordinal scale descriptors and a secondary set of cardinal numbers used to redefine the original primary descriptors.

ordinal scales A question/scale format that activates both the assignment and order scaling properties; the respondent is asked to express relative magnitudes between the raw responses to a question.

ordinary least squares A statistical procedure that estimates regression equation coefficients which produce the lowest sum of squared differences between the actual and predicted values of the dependent variable.

origin property The scaling property that activates a unique starting (or beginning) point in a set of scale points that is designated as being a 'true zero' or true state of nothing.

overall reputation The primary dimension of perceived quality outcomes.

over-registration When a sampling frame contains all of the eligible sampling units of the defined target population plus additional ones.

P

paired-comparisons A scale format in which pre-selected groups of product characteristics or features are paired against one another and the respondents are asked to select which feature in each pairing is more important to them.

part-worth estimates Estimates of the utility survey that respondents place on each individual level of a particular attribute or feature.

passive data Data supplied to a business when a consumer visits the company's website.

Pearson correlation coefficient A statistical measure of the strength and direction of a linear relationship between two metric variables.

perceptual map A graphic representation of respondents' beliefs about the relationship between objects with respect to two or more dimensions (usually attributes or features of the objects).

performance rating scale descriptors A scale that uses an evaluative scale point format that allows the respondents to express some type of postdecision evaluative judgement about an object.

person-administered survey A survey in which an individual interviewer asks questions and records responses.

phantom respondents A type of data falsification that occurs when the researcher takes an actual respondent's data and duplicates it to represent a second (nonexisting) set of responses.

physical audits (or traces) Tangible evidence (or artifacts) of some past event or recorded behaviour.

picture test A qualitative interviewing method where subjects are given a picture and asked to describe their reactions by writing a short narrative story about the picture.

plus-one dialling The method of generating telephone numbers to be called by choosing

numbers randomly from a telephone directory and adding one digit.

poisson regression A multivariate technique to model the number of occurrences of an event of interest as a function of a set of independent variables.

population The identifiable total set of elements of interest being investigated by a researcher.

population mean value The actual calculated arithmetic average parameter value based on interval or ratio data of the defined target population elements (or sampling units).

population proportion value The actual calculated percentage parameter value of the characteristic of concern held by the target population elements (or sampling units).

population size The determined total number of elements that represent the target population.

population specification error An incorrect definition of the true target population to the research question.

population standard deviation A quantitative index of the dispersion of the distribution of population elements' actual data around the arithmetic average measure of central tendency.

population variance The square of the population standard deviation.

positioning The desired perception that a company wants to be associated with its target markets relative to its products or brand offerings.

posttest-only, control group A true experimental design where the test subjects are randomly assigned to either the experimental or control group; the experimental group is then exposed to the independent treatment after which both groups receive a posttreatment

measure of the dependent variable.

PowerPoint A specific software package used to develop slides for electronic presentation of the research results.

precise precision The amount of measured sampling error associated with the sample's raw data at a specified level of confidence.

precision The degree of exactness of the raw data in relation to some other possible response of the target population.

predictions Population estimates that are carried into a future time frame; they are derived from either facts or sample data estimates.

predictive bias A specific type of data analysis error that occurs when the wrong statistical facts and estimates invalidate the researcher's ability to predict and test relationships between important factors.

predictive questionnaire design A design that allows the researcher to collect raw data that can be used in predicting changes in attitudes and behaviours as well as testing hypothesized relationships. The question/scales primarily involve the collecting of state-of-mind and state-of-intention data.

predictive validity The extent to which a scale can accurately predict some event external to the scale itself.

pre-experimental designs A family of designs (one-shot study, one-group pretest-posttest, static group comparison) that are crude experiments that are characterized by the absence of randomization of test subjects; they tend not to meet internal validity criteria due to a lack of equivalent group comparisons.

pretesting The conducting of a simulated administering of a designed survey (or questionnaire) to a small, representative group of respondents.

pretest-posttest control group A true experimental design where the test subjects are randomly assigned to either the experimental or the control group and each group receives a pre-treatment measure of the dependent variable. Then the independent treatment is exposed to the experimental group, after which both groups receive a posttreatment measure of the dependent variable.

primary data Data structures of variables that have been specifically collected and assembled for the current research problem or opportunity situation; they represent 'firsthand' structures.

primary information Firsthand facts or estimates that are derived through a formalized research process for a specific current problem situation.

primary scale point descriptors The set of narratively expressed scale point descriptors used in creating an ordinally-interval scale.

probability distribution of the population The relative frequencies of a population's parameter characteristic emulating a normal bell-shaped pattern.

probability sampling Sampling designs in which each sampling unit in the sampling frame (operational population) has a known, nonzero probability of being selected for the sample.

probing questions The outcome of an interviewer's taking the subject's initial response to a question and using that response as the framework for asking the next question.

problem definition A statement that seeks to determine precisely what problem management

wishes to solve and the type of information necessary to solve it.

product analysis Methods that identify the relative importance of product selection criteria to buyers and rate brands against these criteria.

project costs The price requirements of doing marketing research.

projective techniques A family of qualitative data collection methods where subjects are asked to project themselves into specified buying situations and then asked questions about those situations.

proportionate stratified sampling A form of stratified sampling in which the sample size from each stratum is dependent on that stratum's size relative to the total population.

protocol interviewing A technique that takes respondents into a specified decision-making situation and asks them to verbally express the process and activities considered when making the decision.

psychogalvanometer A device that measures a subject's involuntary changes in the electronic resistance of his or her skin, referred to as galvanic skin response (GVR).

pupilometer A device that observes and records changes in the diameter of a subject's pupils. Changes are interpreted as the result of unobservable cognitive activity.

purchase-intercept survey A survey similar to a mall intercept except that the respondent is stopped at the point of purchase and asked a set of pre-determined questions.

Q

qualitative research Selective types of research methods used in exploratory research designs

where the main objective is to gain a variety of preliminary insights to discover and identify decision problems and opportunities.

quality of the information One of the two fundamental dimensions that is used to determine the level of information being provided by the research process; it refers to the degree to which the information can be depended on as being accurate and reliable.

quantitative research Data collection methods that emphasize using formalized, standard, structured questioning practices where the response options have been predetermined by the researcher and administered to significantly large numbers of respondents.

quasi-experimental designs Designs in which the researcher can control some variables in the study but cannot establish equal experimental and control groups based on randomization of the test subjects.

query Part of an MDSS that enables the user to retrieve information from the system without having to have special software requirements.

questionnaire A set of questions and scales designed to generate enough raw data for accomplishing the information requirements that underlie the research objectives.

questionnaire design precision The extent to which questions and scales are narrowly and precisely defined.

questionnaire development process A specific yet integrative series of logical activities that are undertaken to design a systematic survey instrument for the purpose of collecting primary raw data from sets of people (respondents).

questionnaire format/layout The integrative combination of sets of question/scale measurements into a systematic structured instrument.

question/setup The question and/or directive that is asked of the respondent for which the respondent is to supply a raw response; it is one of the three elements that make up any scale measurement.

quota sampling The selection of participants based on specific quotas regarding characteristics such as age, race, gender, income, or specific behaviours.

quota sheets A simple tracking form that enhances the interviewer's ability to collect raw data from the right type of respondents; the form helps ensure that representation standards are met.

R

random-digit dialling A random selection of area code, exchange, and suffix numbers.

random error An error that occurs as the result of chance events affecting the observed score.

randomization The procedure whereby many subjects are assigned to different experimental treatment conditions, resulting in each group's averaging out any systematic effect on the investigated functional relationship between the independent and dependent variables.

random sampling error The statistically measured difference between the actual sampled results and the estimated true population results.

ranges Statistics that represent the grouping of raw data responses into mutually exclusive subgroups with each having distinct identifiable lower and upper boundary designation values in a set of responses.

rank-order rating scale A scale point format that allows respondents to compare their responses to each other by indicating their first preference, then their second preference, then their third preference, etc., until all the desired responses are placed in some type of rank order, either highest to lowest or lowest to highest.

rating cards Cards used in personal interviews that represent a reproduction of the set of actual scale points and descriptions used to respond to a specific question/setup in the survey. These cards serve as a tool to help the interviewer and respondent speed up the data collection process.

ratio scales Question/scale formats that simultaneously activate all four scaling properties; they are the most sophisticated scale in the sense that absolute differences can be identified not only between each scale point but also between individuals' raw responses. Ratio scales request that respondents give a specific singular numerical value as their response to the question.

raw data The actual firsthand responses that are obtained about the investigated object by either asking questions or observing the subject's actions.

reader-sorter An electronic mechanism located at the point-of-purchase (POP) that resembles a miniature automated bank teller machine. This device enables consumers to pay for transactions with credit cards, ATM cards, or debit cards.

real-time transactional data Data collected at the point of sale.

reflective composite scale Scale used when a researcher measures an individual subcomponent (dimension) of a construct, object, or phenomenon.

refusal A particular type of nonresponse bias that is caused when a prospective respondent declines the role of a respondent, or simply is unwilling to participate in the question/answer exchange.

regression coefficient The statistical measure of the slope coefficient (b) of an independent variable (x) that tells how much the researcher can expect the dependent variable (y) to change, given a unit change in (x).

related samples Two or more groups of responses that originated from the sample population.

relational database system A database in table format of rows and columns, with tables (not data fields) being linked together depending on the output requirements.

relationship marketing A management philosophy that focuses on treating each customer as uniquely different with the overall goal of building a long-term, interactive relationship and loyalty with each customer.

relationships The degree (relative magnitude) and direction of a consistent and systematic linkage (dependence) between two or more variables; this type of information can be derived from either facts or sample data estimates; in special cases, the researcher can determine the existence of cause–effect associations between two or more variables.

relativists Individuals who let present practice set the standard for ethical behaviour.

reliability The extent to which the measurements taken with a particular instrument are repeatable.

reliability of data Data structures that are consistent across observations or interviews.

reliability of the scale The extent to which the designed scale can reproduce the same measurement results in repeated trials.

reliability of service The researcher's ability to be consistent and responsive to the needs of the client.

reputation of the firm The culmination of a research firm's ability to meet standards, reliability of service, marketing knowledge and technical competency for purposes of providing quality outcomes.

research instrument A microscope, radiation meter, ruler, questionnaire, scale, or other device designed for a specific measurement purpose.

research objectives Statements that the research project will attempt to achieve. They provide the guidelines for establishing a research agenda of activities necessary to implement the research process.

research proposal A specific document that serves as a written contract between the decision maker and researcher.

research questions Specific statements that address the problem areas the research study will attempt to investigate.

respondent characteristics The attributes that make up the respondents being included in the survey; three important characteristics are diversity, incidence and participation.

respondent error The type of nonsampling errors that can occur when selected prospective respondents cannot be initially reached to participate in the survey process, do not cooperate, or demonstrate an unwillingness to participate in the survey.

respondent participation The overall degree to which the selected people have the ability and the willingness to participate as well as the knowledge of the topics being researched.

response error The tendency to answer a question in a particular and unique systematic way. Respondents may consciously or unconsciously distort their answers and true thoughts.

response rate The percentage of usable responses out of the total number of responses.

retailing research Research investigations that focus on topics such as trade area analysis, store image/perception, in-store traffic patterns and location analysis.

role-playing activities A technique in which participants are asked to take on the identity of a third person and are placed into a specific pre-determined situation. They are then asked to verbalize how they would act in the situation.

S

sales forecasting A research method that uses variables that affect customer demand to provide estimates of financial outcomes for different price strategies.

sample A randomly selected group of people or objects from the overall membership pool of a target population.

sample design error A family of nonsampling errors that occur when sampling plans are not appropriately developed and/or the sampling process is improperly executed by the researcher.

sample mean value The actual calculated arithmetic average value based on interval or ratio data of the drawn sampling units.

sample percentage value The actual calculated percentage value of the characteristic of concern held by the drawn sampling units.

sample selection error A specific type of sample design bias that occurs when an inappropriate sample is drawn from the defined target population because of incomplete or faulty sampling procedures or because the correct procedures have not been carried out.

sample size The determined total number of sampling units needed to be representative of the defined target population; that is, the number of elements (people or objects) that have to be included in a drawn sample to ensure appropriate representation of the defined target population.

sampling The process of selecting a relatively small number of elements from a larger defined group of elements so that the information gathered from the smaller group allows one to make judgements about that larger group of elements.

sampling distribution The frequency distribution of a specific sample statistic value that would be found by taking repeated random samples of the same size.

sampling error Any type of bias in a survey study that is attributable to mistakes made in either the selection process of prospective sampling units or determining the size of a sample required to ensure its representativeness of the larger defined target population.

sampling frame A list of all eligible sampling units for a given study.

sampling frame error An error that occurs when a sample is drawn from an incomplete list of potential or prospective respondents.

sampling gap The representation difference between the population elements and sampling units in the sample frame.

sampling plan The blueprint or framework used to ensure that the raw data collected are, in fact, representative of a larger defined target population structure.

sampling units Those elements that are available for selection during the sampling process.

satisfaction of experience A person's evaluative judgement about their postpurchase consumption experience of a specified object.

scale dimensions and attributes element The components of the object, construct, or concept that is being measured; it identifies what should be measured and is one of the three elements of a scale measurement.

scale measurement The process of assigning a set of descriptors to represent the range of possible responses that an individual gives in answering a question about a particular object, construct, or factor under investigation.

scale points The set of assigned descriptors that designate the degrees of intensity to the responses concerning the investigated characteristics of an object, construct, or factor; it is one of the three elements that make up scale measurements.

scale reliability The extent to which a scale can produce the same measurement results in repeated trials.

scanner-based panel A group of participating households which have a unique bar-coded card as an identification characteristic for inclusion in the research study.

scatter diagram A graphic plot of the relative position of two variables using a horizontal and a vertical axis to represent the values of the respective variables.

scientific method The systematic and objective process used to develop reliable and valid firsthand information by using the information research process.

scoring models Procedures that attempt to rank customer segments by their potential profitability to the company.

screening forms A set of preliminary questions that are used to determine the eligibility of a prospective respondent for inclusion in the survey.

screening questions Specific questions that are used to qualify prospective respondents for a survey or eliminate unqualified respondents from answering questions in a study.

search A computer-assisted scan of the electronic databases.

search engine An electronic procedure that allows the researcher to enter keywords as search criteria for locating and gathering secondary information off the Internet.

search words The terms that the computer looks for in electronic databases.

secondary data Historical data structures of variables that have been previously collected and assembled for some research problem or opportunity situation other than the current situation.

secondary information Information (facts or estimates) that has already been collected, assembled and interpreted at least once for some other specific situation.

selection bias Contamination of internal validity measures created by inappropriate selection and/or assignment processes of test subjects to experimental treatment groups.

selective perception bias A type of error that occurs in situations where the researcher or decision maker uses only a selected portion of the survey results to paint a tainted picture of reality.

self-administered survey A survey in which respondents read the survey questions and record their responses without the assistance of an interviewer.

semantic differential scale A special type of symmetrical rating scale that uses sets of bipolar adjectives and/or adverbs to describe some type of positive and negative poles of an assumed continuum; it is used to capture respondents' cognitive and affective components of specified factors and create perceptual image profiles relating to a given object or behaviour.

semi-structured question A question that directs the respondent towards a specified topic area, but the responses to the question are unbounded; the interviewer is not looking for any preconceived right answer.

sentence completion test A projective technique where subjects are given a set of incomplete sentences and asked to complete them in their own words.

separate sample, pretest-posttest A quasi-experimental design where two different groups of test subjects are drawn for which neither group is directly exposed to the independent treatment variable. One group receives the pretest measure of the dependent variable; then after the insignificant independent treatment occurs, the second group of test subjects receives a posttest measure of the dependent variable.

sequential database system
A sorting procedure that displays data in a very simple pattern, usually where the data are organized by a simple path, linkage, or network.

service quality studies Studies designed to measure the degree to which an organization conforms to the quality level expected by customers; they concentrate on attributes determined to be most important to customers.

service sensitivity analysis
A procedure that helps an organization in designing a basic customer service programme by evaluating cost-to-service trade-offs.

shopping-intercept survey An interview technique in which mall patrons are stopped and asked for feedback. The interview may take place in the mall's common areas or in the research firm's offices at the mall.

silo Data in one functional area of a business not shared with other areas of the business.

similarity judgements A direct approach to gathering perceptual data for multidimensional scaling; where the respondents use a Likert scale to rate all possible pairs of brands in terms of their similarity.

simple random sampling (SRS)
A method of probability sampling in which every sampling unit has an equal, nonzero chance of being selected. Results generated by using simple random sampling can be projected to the target population with a pre-specified margin of error.

simulated test markets Quasi-test market experiments where the test subjects are pre-selected, then interviewed and observed on their purchases and attitudes towards the test products; also referred to as *laboratory*

tests or *test market simulations.*

single-item scale design A scale used when the data requirements focus on collecting data about only one attribute of the object or construct being investigated.

situation analysis An informal process of analysing the past, present and future situations facing an organization in order to identify decision problems and opportunities.

situational characteristics
Factors of reality such as budgets, time, and data quality that affect the researcher's ability to collect accurate primary data in a timely fashion.

skip interval A selection tool used to identify the position of the sampling units to be drawn into a systematic random sample design. The interval is determined by dividing the number of potential sampling units in the defined target population by the number of units desired in the sample.

snowball sampling
A non-probability sampling method that involves the practice of identifying a set of initial prospective respondents who can, in turn, help in identifying additional people to be included in the study.

social desirability A type of response bias that occurs when the respondent assumes what answer is socially acceptable or respectable.

Solomon Four Group A true experimental design that combines the pretest-posttest, control group and posttest only, control group designs and provides both 'direct' and 'reactive' effects of testing.

Spearman rank order correlation coefficient A statistical measure of the linear association between two variables where

both have been measured using ordinal (rank-order) scale instruments.

split-half test A technique used to evaluate the internal consistency reliability of scale measurements that have multiple attribute components.

standard deviation The measure of the average dispersion of the values in a set of responses about their mean.

standard error of the population parameter A statistical measure used in probability sampling that gives an indication of how far the sample result lies from the actual population measure we are trying to estimate.

staple scales Considered a modified version of the semantic differential scale; they symmetrically centre the scale point domain within a set of plus (+) and minus (−) descriptors.

state-of-behaviour data Raw responses that represent an individual's or organization's current observable actions or reactions or recorded past actions/reactions.

state-of-being data Raw responses that are pertinent to the physical and/or demographic or socioeconomic characteristics of individuals, objects, or organizations.

state-of-intention data Raw responses that represent an individual's or organization's expressed plans of future actions/reactions.

state-of-mind data Raw responses that represent the mental attributes or emotional feelings of individuals which are not directly observable or available through some type of external source.

static group comparisons
A pre-experimental design of two groups of test subjects; one is the experimental group (EG) and is exposed to the

independent treatment; the second group is the control group (CG) and is not given the treatment; the dependent variable is measured in both groups after the treatment.

statistical conclusion validity The ability of the researcher to make reasonable statements about covariation between constructs of interest and the strength of that covariation.

statistical regression Contamination to internal validity measures created when experimental groups are selected on the basis of their extreme responses or scores.

statistical software system A computer-based system that has capabilities of analysing large volumes of data and computing basic types of statistical procedures, such as means, standard deviations, frequency distributions and percentages.

store audits Formal examinations and verifications of how much of a particular product or brand has been sold at the retail level.

strata The subgroupings that are derived through stratified random sampling procedures.

stratified random sampling (STRS) A method of probability sampling in which the population is divided into different subgroups (called strata) and samples are selected from each stratum.

structural equation modelling A sophisticated multivariate technique that can examine a series of dependence relationships simultaneously. A hypothesized dependent variable can become an independent variable in a subsequent dependence relationship.

structured observation A method of recording specifically known behaviours and events.

structured questions Questions that require the respondent to make a choice among a limited number of pre-listed responses or scale points; they require less thought and effort on the part of the respondent; also referred to as closed-ended questions.

structuredness of observation The degree to which the behaviours or events are specifically known to the researcher prior to doing the observations.

subjective information Information that is based on the decision maker's or researcher's past experiences, assumptions, feelings, or interpretations without any systematic assembly of facts or estimates.

subject's awareness The degree to which subjects consciously know their behaviour is being observed; *disguised observation* is when the subject is completely unaware that they are being observed, and *undisguised observation* is when the person is aware that they are being observed.

supervisor instructions A form that serves as a blueprint for training people on how to execute the interviewing process in a standardized fashion; it outlines the process by which to conduct a study that uses personal and telephone interviewers.

survey instrument design error A 'family' of design or format errors that produce a questionnaire that does not accurately collect the appropriate raw data; these nonsampling errors severely limit the generalizability, reliability, and validity of the collected data.

survey instrument error A type of error that occurs when the survey instrument induces

some type of systematic bias in the response.

survey method Research procedures for collecting large amounts of raw data using question-and-answer formats.

symptoms Conditions that signal the presence of a decision problem or opportunity; they tend to be observable and measurable results of problems or opportunities.

syndicated data Data that have been compiled according to some standardized procedure which provides customized data for companies such as market share, advertising effectiveness and sales tracking.

systematic error The type of error that results from poor instrument design and/or instrument construction causing scores or readings on an instrument to be biased in a consistent manner; creates some form of systematic variation in the raw data that is not a natural occurrence or fluctuation on the part of the surveyed respondents.

systematic random-digit dialling The technique of randomly dialling telephone numbers, but only numbers that meet specific criteria.

systematic random sampling A method of probability sampling that is similar to simple random sampling but requires that the defined target population be ordered in some way.

T

table of random numbers A table of numbers that have been randomly generated.

tabulation The simple procedure of counting the number of observations, or data items, that are classified into certain categories.

target market analysis Information for identifying

those people (or companies) that an organization wishes to serve.

target population A specified group of people or objects for which questions can be asked or observations made to develop required data structures and information.

task characteristics The requirements placed on the respondents in their process of providing answers to questions asked.

task difficulty How hard the respondent needs to work to respond, and the level of preparation required to create an environment for the respondent.

technical competency The degree to which the researcher possesses the necessary functional requirements to conduct the research project.

technology-enabled market intelligence The use of real-time customer information (customer knowledge) to achieve a competitive advantage, which can be made possible only by the deployment of appropriate technology.

teleologists Individuals who follow a philosophy that considers activities to be ethical if they produce desired results.

telephone-administered survey A survey in which individuals working out of their homes or from a central location use the telephone medium to ask participants questions and record the responses.

test marketing A controlled field experiment conducted for gaining information on specified market performance indicators or factors.

test-retest A procedure used to assess the reliability of a scale measurement; it involves repeating the administration of the scale measurement to either the sample set of sampled

respondents at two different times or two different samples of respondents from the same defined target population under as nearly the same conditions as possible.

test-retest reliability The method of accumulating evidence of reliability by using multiple administrations of an instrument to the same sample. If those administrations are consistent, then evidence of test-retest reliability exists.

thematic apperception test (TAT) A specific projection technique that presents the subjects with a series of pictures and asks them to provide a description of or a story about the pictures.

theory A large body of interconnected propositions about how some portion of a certain phenomenon operates.

topic sensitivity The degree to which a specific question or investigated issue leads the respondent to give a socially acceptable response.

touchpoint Specific customer information gathered and shared by all individuals in an enterprise.

traditional test markets Test markets that use experimental design procedures to test a product and/or a product's marketing mix variables through existing distribution channels; also referred to as *standard test markets*.

trained interviewers Highly trained people, with excellent communication and listening skills, who ask research participants specific questions and accurately record their responses.

trained observers Highly skilled people who use their various sensory devices to observe and record either a person's current behaviours or physical phenomena as they take place.

transactional data Secondary information derived from transactions by consumers at the retail level.

transition questions Questions used by a moderator to direct a focus group's discussion towards the main topic of interest.

trilogy approach The theoretical approach of viewing a person's attitude towards an object as consisting of three distinct components: cognitive, affective, and conative.

true class interval scale A scale that demonstrates absolute differences between each scale point.

true experimental designs Designs that ensure equivalence between the experimental and control groups of subjects by random assignment of subjects to the groups ('pretest-posttest, with control group,' 'posttest-only, with control group,' Solomon Four Group).

*t***-test (also referred to as** *t* **statistic)** A hypothesis test procedure that uses the *t*-distribution: *t*-tests are used when the sample size of subjects is small (generally less than 30) and the standard deviation is unknown.

Type I error The error made by rejecting the null hypothesis when it is true; represents the probability of alpha error.

Type II error The error of failing to reject the null hypothesis when the alternative hypothesis is true; represents the probability of beta error.

U

under-registration When eligible sampling units are left out of the sampling frame.

undisguised observation The data recording method where the subjects are aware that they are being watched.

undisguised sponsorship When the true identity of the person or company for which the research is being conducted is directly revealed to the prospective respondent.

unexplained variance In multivariate methods, it is the amount of variation in the dependent construct that cannot be accounted for by the combination of independent variables.

unstructured observation The data recording format that does not place any restrictions on the observer regarding what behaviours or events should be recorded.

unstructured questions Question/scale formats that require respondents to reply in their own words; this format requires more thinking and effort on the part of respondents in order to express their answers; also called *open-ended questions*.

V

validity The degree to which a research instrument serves the purpose for which it was constructed; it also relates to the extent to which the conclusions drawn from an experiment are true.

validity of data The degree to which data structures actually do represent what was to be measured.

variability A measure of how data are dispersed; the greater the dissimilarity or 'spread' in data, the larger the variability.

variable Any observable, measurable element (or attribute) of an event.

variance The average squared deviations about a mean of a distribution of values.

virtual test markets Completely computerized systems that allow the test subjects to observe and interact with the product as though they were actually in the test store's environment.

voice pitch analyser A computerized system that measures emotional responses by changes in the subject's voice.

W

Web-based TV test markets Use of broadband interactive TV (iTV) and advances in interactive multimedia communication technologies to conduct field experiments. Pre-selected respondents are shown various stimuli and asked questions online through their iTV.

Web home page The guide to a website; generally the home page is the first Web page accessed at the website.

Web page A source of secondary information that is likely to be linked to other complementary pages; includes text, graphics and even audio.

Website An electronic location on the World Wide Web.

Web 2.0 A concept describing the trend in the use of Web technology and Web design that strives to enhance information sharing and collaboration among users.

width The total number of records contained in the database.

willingness to participate The respondent's inclination or disposition to share his or her thoughts and feelings.

wireless phone survey The method of conducting a marketing survey in which the data are collected on standard wireless phones.

word association test A projective technique in which the subject is presented with a word, or a list of words or short phrases, one at a time, and asked to respond with the first thing comes to mind.

World Wide Web (WWW) A graphical interface system that allows for text linkage between different locations on the Internet.

wrong mailing address A type of nonresponse bias that can occur when the prospective respondent's mailing address is outdated or no longer active.

wrong telephone number A type of nonresponse bias that can occur when the prospective respondent's telephone number either is no longer in service or is incorrect on the sample list.

Z

z-test (also referred to as z statistic) A hypothesis test procedure that uses the z distribution; z-tests are used when the sample size is larger than 30 subjects and the standard deviation is unknown.

Bibliography

Chapter 1

Advertising Age, 1997, Survey of Top Marketing Research Firms, June 27.

Boddy, C., 2001, Perceived reasons for success of the UK market research industry, *International Journal of Market Research*, 43(1): 29–41.

ECCH, Red Bull case

ESOMAR website, www.esomar.org

Flores, L., Weill, G. and Heck, O., The 2006 FIFA World Cup Case, ESOMAR Congress 2007.

Guinness website, www.guinness.com

Irish Independent, Great Irish Brands, November 2007.

Jimmy Spice's website, www.jimmyspices.co.uk

Keller, K.L., 2003, *Strategic Brand Management*, 2nd edn, Upper Saddle River, NJ: Prentice Hall.

Lamb, C., Hair, J. and McDaniel, C., 2004, *Marketing*, 7th edn, Cincinnati: Southwestern, pp. 592–3.

Marketing Research, 1997a, Value Added Research, Fall edition.

Marketing Research, 1997b, Fostering Professionalism, Spring edition.

Marketing Research Society website, www.mrs.org.uk

Nielsen website, www.nielsen.com

Redbull website, www.redbull.com

Solomon, M., 2004, *Consumer Behavior*, 6th edn, Upper Saddle River, NJ: Pearson/Prentice Hall, pp. 242–5.

The Times (Travel Section), 28 June 2008, p. 14.

University of Memphis (Center for Cycle Time Research), 2003, Research Topics in Cycle Time Research.

Chapter 2

Cir, J., Pawle, J. and Patterson, S., Rexona, ESOMAR Congress 2007.

Coca-Cola Company, Form 10-K, Washington, DC: Securities and Exchange Commission, 16 September, 1996.

Perreault, W.D., 1992, The shifting paradigm in marketing research, *Journal of the Academy of Marketing Science*, 20 (4): 369.

Playstation website, www.playstation.com

Shields, M.J., 1985, Coke's research fizzles, fails to factor in customer loyalty, *Adweek,* July 15, p. 8.

Wade, R.K., 1993, The when/what research decision guide, *Marketing Research: A Magazine and Application*, 5 (3): 24–7.

Chapter 3

Admap, 2006, Research as a management tool, November edition, p. 7.

Baltic Sea Region GIS website, www.grida.no/baltic

Bell, S., 2000, Launching profits with customer loyalty, *Customer Relationship Management,* April edition, p. 58.

Blue Sheep website, www.bluesheep.co.uk

Experian website, www.qas.co.uk

Fickel, L., 1999, Know your customer, *CIO Magazine,* 15 April.

Fung, D., 1995, Managing by the map, *Business Perspectives* 8 (2), The University of Memphis.

GIS website, www.gis.com

Inmon, B., 2001, Building the data warehouse, *The Data Warehousing Information Center,* 21 June.

IRIS website, www.iris.co.uk

Johnson, A., 1999, Viewing data in real time, *CIO Magazine,* 1 December.

Lamb, C., Hair, J. and McDaniel, C., 2004, *Marketing,* 7th edn, Cincinnati: Southwestern, p. 685–7.

Levinson, M., 2004, Getting to know them, *CIO Magazine,* 15 February.

Lodish, L., 1997, On measuring advertising effects, *Journal of Advertising Research,*
    September–October edition.

Marketing Direct Magazine, 2007, Customer insight: the big picture, 4 April.

MDSS website, www.mdss.net

MDSS World website, www.mdssworld.com

Nolan, P., 2001, Getting started and finishing well, *Intelligent Enterprise Magazine,* 7 May.

Research Magazine website, www.research-live.com

Roberts, D., 2000, Turning lemons to lemonade, *Customer Relationship Management,* July
    edition, p. 64.

The Business Intelligence and Data Warehousing Glossary, www.sdgcomputing.com

Chapter 4

AC Nielsen Media Research website, www.nielsenmedia.com

Arbitron website, www.arbitron.com

Bell, S., 2000, Launching profits with customer loyalty, *Customer Relationship Management,* April
    edition, p. 58.

Corporate Information website, www.corporateinformation.com

de Ruyck, T., Schillewaert, N., van Belleghem, S. and Distare, S., Dove case, ESOMAR
    Congress 2007.

Edgar Online website, www.freeedgar.com

Eurostat website, www.epp.eurostat.ec.europa.eu

Gonzalez-Benito, O. and Gonzalez-Benito, J., 2005, The role of geodemographic segmentation in
    retail location strategy, *International Journal of Market Research,* 47 (3) pp. 295–316.

Marketing Research Magazine, 1997, Secondary Research, Fall edition.

Marketing UK website, www.marketinguk.co.uk

NPD Group website, www.npdgroup.com

Pride, W. and Ferrell, O.C., 2003, *Marketing,* 10th edn, Boston: Houghton Mifflin.

Sales & Marketing Management Magazine, Survey of Buying Power, 2003,
    www.salesandmarketing.com

UK Data Archive website, www.data-archive.ac.uk

United Nations Statistics Division, 2007, ISIC Draft Revision 4.

WARC website, www.warc.com

Chapter 5

Achenbaum, A.A., 2001, When good research goes bad, *Marketing Research,* Winter edition, pp: 13–15.

Beistell, G. and Nitterhouse, D., 2001, Asking all the right questions, *Marketing Research,*
    Fall edition, pp. 14–20.

Cooper, P., 1991, Comparison between the UK and US: the qualitative dimension, *Journal of the Marketing Research Society*, 31(4), pp. 509–20.

ECCH (European Case Clearing House) website, www.ecch.com

EuroPHEN (European Public Health Ethics Network) website, www.shef.ac.uk/europhen

Focusvision Worldwide website, focusvision.com

Greenbaum, T.L., 1988, It's possible to reduce cost of focus groups, *Marketing News*, August 29, p. 43.

Greenbaum, T.L., 1991, Do you have the right moderator for your focus groups? Here are ten questions to ask yourself, *Bank Marketing*, 23(1), p. 43.

Greenbaum, T.L., 1996, Understanding focus group research aboard, *Marketing News*, 2 June, p. H16 & pp. H36.

Henderson, N.R., 2002, The many faces of qualitative research, *Marketing Research*, Summer edition, pp. 13–17.

Kinnear, T.C. and Taylor, J.A., 1996, *Marketing Research: An Applied Approach*, 5th edn, New York: McGraw-Hill.

Krueger, R.A., 1994, *Focus Groups: A Practical Guide for Applied Research*, 2nd edn, Thousand Oaks, CA: Sage.

Lonnie, K., 2001, Combine phone and web for focus groups, *Marketing News*, 19 November, pp. 15–16.

Marketing News, 1991, Focus group moderators should be well versed in interpretative skills, 18 February, p. 23.

Orient Pacific Century website, www.orientpacific.com

Ortinau, D.J. and Brensinger, R.P., 1993, An empirical investigation of perceived quality's intangible dimensionality through direct cognitive structural (DCS) analysis, In: King, R.L. (ed.), *Marketing Perspectives for the 1990s*, Richmond, VA: Society for Marketing Advances.

Research magazine, News Archive, research-live.com

Rook, D.W., 2003, Out-of-focus groups, *Marketing Research*, Summer edition, pp. 10–15.

Shiu, E., 2003, Profiling traditional market shoppers in Britain – the elderly men syndrome. Proceedings of the 3rd Hawaii International Conference on Business, Honolulu.

Wansink, B., 2000, New techniques to generate key marketing insights, *Marketing Research*, Summer edition, pp. 28–36.

Welch, J.L., 1985, Research marketing problems and opportunities with focus groups, *Industrial Marketing Management*, p. 248.

Winters, L., 1999, What's new in focus group research, *Marketing Research*, December edition, pp. 69–70.

Yovovick, B.G., 1991, Focusing on consumers' needs and motivations, *Business Marketing*, March edition, pp. 41–3.

Zinchiak, M., 2001, Online focus groups FAQs, *Quirk's Marketing Research Review*, July/August edition, pp. 38–46.

Chapter 6

Cir, J., Pawle, J. and Patterson, S., 2007, Rexona case, ESOMAR Congress 2007.

Letelier, M.F., Sinosa, C. and Calder, B.J., 2000, Taking an expanded view of consumers' needs: qualitative research for aiding innovation, *Marketing Research*, Winter edition, pp. 4–11.

Ramsey, E., Ibbotson, P. and McCole, P., 2006, Application of projective techniques in an e-business research context, *International Journal of Market Research*, 48 (5): 551–73.

Research magazine, News Archive, research-live.com

The Times, Magazine, pp. 29–32, 7 June 2008.

Wyner, G.A., 1999, Anticipating customer priorities, *Marketing Research*, Spring edition, pp. 36–8.

Chapter 7

Assael, H. and Keon, J., 1982, Nonsampling vs. sampling errors in survey research, *Journal of Marketing*, Spring edition, pp. 114–23.

Bagozzi, R.P., 1994, Measurement in marketing research: basic principles of questionnaire design, In: Bagozzi, R.P.(ed.), *Principles of Marketing Research*, Cambridge, MA: Blackwell, pp. 1–49.

Bertagnoli, L., 2001, Middle East Muddle, *Marketing News*, 16 July, pp. 1 & 9.

Bowers, D.K., 1995, Sugging banned, at last, *Marketing Research*, Fall edition, p. 40.

Bush, A.J. and Hair, J.F. Jr., 1985, An assessment of the mall intercept as a data collect method, *Journal of Marketing Research*, May edition, pp. 158–67.

Business Week, 2007, Mining virtual worlds for market research, 13 August.

Childers, T.L. and Skinner, S.J., 1996, Toward a conceptualization of mail survey response behavior, *Psychology and Marketing*, March edition, pp. 185–225.

CMOR website, www.cmor.org

Colombotos, J., 1969, Personal vs. telephone interviews effect responses, *Public Health Reports*, September edition, pp. 773–820.

Crowley, A., 1995, E-mail surveys elicit fast response, cut costs, *PC Week*, 30 January.

Czinkota, M.R. and Ronkainen, I.A., 1995, Conducting primary market research: market research for your export operations, Part 2, *International Trade Forum*, January edition, p.18.

Dacko, S., 1995, Data collection should not be manual labor, *Marketing News*, 28 August, p. 31.

Dalecki, M.G., Ilvento, T.W. and Moore, D.E., 1988, The effect of multi-wave mailings on the external validity of mail surveys, *Journal of Community Development Society*, pp. 51–70.

dePaulo, P.J. and Weitzer, R., 1994, Interactive phone technology delivers survey data quickly, *Marketing News*, 4 January, p.15.

Dickson, J.P. and MacLachlan, D.L., 1992, Fax surveys? *Marketing Research: A Magazine of Management & Applications*, September edition, pp. 26–30.

Dickson, J.P. and MacLachlan, D.L., 1996, Fax surveys: return patterns and comparison with mail survey, *Journal of Marketing Research*, February edition, pp. 108–13.

Gjestland, L., 1996, Net? Not yet: CATI is still superior to internet interviewing but enhancements are on the way, *Marketing Research: A Magazine of Management & Applications*, 8 (1): 26+.

Green, K.E., 1996, Sociodemographic factors and mail survey response rates, *Psychology and Marketing*, March edition, pp. 171–84.

Groves, R.M., Cialdini, R.B. and Couper, M.P., 1992, Understanding the decision to participate in a survey, *Public Opinion Quarterly*, pp. 475–95.

Hartke, D., 1996, What farmers think of market research, *Agri Marketing*, March edition, pp. 54–8.

James, D., 2000, Old, new make up today's surveys, *Marketing News*, 5 June, p. 4.

James, D., 2000, The future of online research, *Marketing News*, 3 January, p. 11.

Kraus, M., 1998, Research and the web: eyeballs or smiles, *Marketing News*, 7 December, p.18.

Lilien, G., Brown, R. and Searls, K., 1991, Cut errors, improve estimates to bridge biz-to-biz info gap, *Marketing News*, 7 January, pp. 20–2.

Long, J., Whinston, A.B. and Tomak, K., 2002, Calling all customers, *Marketing Research: A Magazine of Management & Applications*, Fall edition, pp. 28–33.

Lucus, W.A. and Adams, W.C., 1997, An assessment of telephone survey methods, *Rand Report R-2135-NSF*.

Marketing Research Society website, www.mrs.org.uk

Moberg, P.E., 1982, Biases in unlisted phone numbers, *Journal of Advertising Research*, August–September edition, p. 55.

Murphy, P.R. and Daley, J.M., 1995, Mail surveys: to fax or not to fax, *Proceedings of the Association of Marketing Theory and Practice Annual Meetings,* Chicago, IL: American Marketing Association, p. 152–7.

Ossip, A., 1986, Likely improvements in data collection methods—what do they mean for day-to-day research management? *Journal of Advertising Research,* October–November edition, p. RC9–RC12.

Remington, T., 1992, Rising refusal rates: the impact of telemarketing, *QUIRKS Marketing Research Review,* May edition, pp. 8–15.

Remington, T.D., 1993, Telemarketing and declining survey response rates, *Journal of Advertising Research,* p. RC-6 & RC-7.

Research magazine, News Archive, reseach-live.com.

Rogers, T.F., 1976, Interviewing by telephone and in-person quality of response and field performance, *Public Opinion Quarterly,* Spring edition, pp. 51–65.

Saltzman, A., 1993, Improving response rates in disk-by-mail surveys, *Marketing Research: A Magazine of Management and Applications,* Summer edition, pp. 32–9.

Shuptrine, F.K., 1992, Survey research: respondent attitudes response and bias, In: King, R.L. (ed.), *Marketing Perspectives for the 1990s,* Southern Marketing Association Proceedings, November edition, pp. 197–200.

Stem, D.E. Jr. and Lamb, C.W. Jr., 1981, The marble-drop technique: a procedure for gathering sensitive information, *Decision Sciences,* October edition, pp. 702–8.

Tourangeau, R. and Rasinski, K.A., 1988, Cognitive process underlying content effects in attitude measurement, *Psychological Bulletin,* pp. 299–314.

Yu, J. and Cooper, H., 1983, Quantitative review of research design effects on response rules to questionnaires, *Journal of Marketing Research,* February edition, pp. 36–44.

Chapter 8

Banks, S., 1965, *Experimentation in Marketing,* New York: McGraw-Hill, pp. 168–79.

Bernstein, A., 1985, Spalding and four major chains launch women's theme shops, *Sporting Goods Business,* November edition.

Brennan, L., 1988, Test marketing, *Sales and Marketing Management Magazine,* March edition, p. 140 & 150–2.

Burgess, R., 1993, Coors chiller fiasco costs brewer dearly, *Denver Business Journal,* 23 April, p. 1A.

Burke, R., 1996, Virtual shopping: breakthrough in marketing research, *Harvard Business Review,* March/April edition.

Calder, B.J., Phillips, L.W. and Tybour, A.M., 1992, The concept of external validity, *Journal of Consumer Research,* December edition, pp. 240–4.

Cambridge Market Research website, www.cambridge-market-research.co.uk

Campbell, D.T. and Stanley, J.C., 1966, *Experimental Designs for Research,* Skokie, IL: Rand-McNally.

Carmines, E.G. and Zeller, R.A., 1979, *Reliability and Validity Assessment,* Newbury Park, CA: Sage, pp. 9–48.

Churchill, G.A. Jr., 1979, A paradigm for the development of better measures of marketing constructs, *Journal of Marketing Research,* February edition, pp. 64–73.

Cook, T.D. and Campbell, D.T., 1979, *Quasi-Experimentation: Design and Analysis Issues for Field Settings,* Boston, MA: Houghton Mifflin, pp. 39–41, 51, 59, 64 & 70–3.

Crano, W.D. and Brewer, M.B., 1986, *Principles and Methods of Social Research,* Boston, MA: Allyn and Bacon, pp. 23–38.

Fishbein, M., 1967, Attitude and the prediction of behavior, In:, Fishbein, M. (ed.), *Readings in Attitude Theory and Behavior,* New York: John Wiley and Sons, pp. 477–92.

Gleason, M., 1995, P&G tests smoothie, *Advertising Age,* 30 October.

Hellebursch, S.J., 2000, Don't read research by the numbers, *Marketing News,* 11 September, pp. 19, 25 & 34.

Jarvis, S., 2001, iTV finally comes home, *Marketing News,* 27 August, pp. 1, 19 & 20.

Kerlinger, F.N. and Lee, H.B., 2000, *Foundations of Behavior Research,* 4th edn, Cincinnati: Wadsworth-Thomas Learning, pp. 324–6 & 461–3.

Leister, W., Tjostheim, I. and Lous, J., 2007, Market research using virtual test store on gaming technology, In: Schulze, T. et al. (eds), *Simulation und Visualisierung,* pp. 399–411.

MarketingScan website, www.marketingscan.fr

Peterson, B., 1995, Trends turn around, *Marketing Research,* Summer edition.

Prince, M., 1992, Choosing simulated test marketing systems, *Marketing Research,* September edition, pp. 14–16.

Chapter 9

Becker, B., 1999, Guidelines to direct observation, *Marketing News,* 27 September, pp. 20, 29, 31 & 33.

Cote, J.A., McCullough, J. and Reilly, M., 1985, Effects of unexpected situations on behavior-intention differences: a garbology analysis, *Journal of Consumer Research,* September edition, pp. 188–94.

Sinkula, J.M., 1986, Status of company usage of scanner-based research, *Journal of the Academy of Marketing Science,* Spring edition, pp. 63–71.

Sinkula, J.M., 1991, Some factors affecting the adoption of scanner-based research in organizations, *Journal of Advertising Research,* April/May edition, pp. 50–5.

SPSL website, www.customercounting.com

Synovate website, www.synovate.com

Webb, E.J., Campbell, D.T., Schwartz, R.D. and Sechrest, L., 1971, *Unobtrusive Measures: Nonreaction Research in the Social Sciences,* Chicago: Rand-McNally, pp. 113–14.

Whalen, B., 1983, Marketing detective reveals competitive-intelligence secrets, *Marketing News,* 16 September, p. 1.

Chapter 10

Alreck, P.L. and Settle, R.B., 1995, *The Survey Research Handbook,* 2nd edn, New York: McGraw-Hill/Irwin, pp. 120–2.

Barns, J.H. and Dotson, M.J., 1989, The effects of mixed grammar chains on response to survey questions, *Journal of Marketing Research,* 26(4) pp. 468–72.

Carroll, S., 1994, Questionnaire's design affects response rate, *Marketing News,* 3 January, pp. 14 & 23.

Diamantopoula, A., Schlegelmilch, B. and Wilcox, N., 1994, Pretesting in questionnaire design: the impact of respondent characteristics on error detection, *Journal of Marketing Research Society,* April edition, pp. 295–314.

Dillman, D., Sinclair, M. and Clark, J., 1993, Effects of questionnaire length, respondent friendly design, and a difficult question on response rates for occupant-addressed census mail surveys, *Public Opinion Quarterly,* pp. 289–304.

Hubbard, R. and Little, E., 1988, Cash prizes and mail response rates: a threshold analysis, *Journal of the Academy of Marketing Science,* Fall edition, pp. 42–4.

Patten, M., 2001, *Questionnaire Research,* Los Angeles, CA: Pyrczak, pp. 8–12.

Payne, S., 1951, *The Art of Asking Questions,* Princeton, NJ: Princeton University Press.

Peterson, R.A., 2000, *Constructing Effective Questionnaires,* Thousand Oaks, CA: Sage, pp. 1–2.

Sanchez, M.E., 1992, Effects of questionnaire design on the quality of survey data, *Public Opinion Quarterly*, pp. 208–17.

Young, R.B. and Javalgi, R.G., 2007, International marketing research: a global project management perspective, *Business Horizons*, pp. 113–22.

Chapter 11

Albaum, G., Best, R. and Hawkins, D.I., 1977, Measurement properties of semantic scales data, *Journal of the Marketing Research Society*, 25(1): 21–8.

Barnard, N.R. and Ehrenberg, A.S.C., 1990, Robust measures of consumer brand beliefs, *Journal of Marketing Research*, November edition, pp. 477–84.

Brensinger, R.P., 1993, An empirical investigation of consumer perceptions of combined product and service quality: the automobile, unpublished doctoral dissertation, Tampa, FL: The University of South Florida, pp. 54–60.

Carmines, E.G. and Zeller, R.A., 1979, *Reliability and Validity Assessment*, Newbury Park, CA: Sage, pp. 9–48.

Churchill, G.A. Jr., 1979, A paradigm for the development of better measures of marketing constructs, *Journal of Marketing Research*, February edition, pp. 64–73.

Churchill, G.A. and Peter, J.P., 1984, Research design effects on the reliability of rating scales: a meta-analysis, *Journal of Marketing Research*, February edition, pp. 360–75.

Crano, W.D. and Brewer, M.B., 1986, *Principles and Methods of Social Research*, Boston, MA: Allyn and Bacon, pp. 23–38.

Crask, M.R. and Fox, R.J., 1987, An exploration of the interval properties of three commonly used marketing research studies: a magnitude estimation approach, *Journal of the Marketing Research Society*, 29(3), pp. 317–39.

Cronbach, L.J., 1951, Coefficient alpha and internal structure of tests, *Psychometrika*, pp. 297–334.

Gaito, J., 1980, Measurement scales and statistics: resurgence of an old misconception, *Psychological Bulletin*, pp. 564–7.

Garner, W.R. and Creelman, C.D., 1967, Problems and methods of psychological scaling, In: Bevan, H. and Bevan, W. (eds), *Contemporary Approaches to Psychology*, New York: van Nostrand, p. 4.

Goetz, E.T., Alexander, P.A. and Ash, M.J., 1992, *Educational Psychology*, New York: Macmillian, p. 670–4.

Hawkins, D.I. and Coney, K.A., 1981, Uninformed response error in survey research, *Journal of Marketing Research*, August edition, pp. 370–4.

Holdaway, E.A., 1971, Different response categories and questionnaire response patterns, *Journal of Experimental Education*, Winter edition, p. 59.

Jacoby, J. and Matell, M.S., 1971, Three Point Likert Scales are good enough, *Journal of Marketing Research*, November edition, pp. 495–506.

Kerlinger, F.N. and Lee, H.B., 2000, *Foundations of Behavioral Research*, 4th edn, Cincinnati: Wadsworth-Thomas Learning, p. 403.

Nunnally, J.C., 1978, *Psychometric Theory*, 2nd edn, New York: McGraw-Hill, p. 102.

Ortinau, D.J. and Brensinger, R.P., 1992, An empirical investigation of perceived quality's intangible dimensionality through direct cognitive structural (DCS) analysis, In: King, R.L. (ed.), *Marketing: Perspectives for the 1990s*, New Orleans, LA: Southern Marketing Association, pp. 214–9.

Perreault, W.D. Jr. and Young, F.W., 1980, Alternating least squares optimal scaling: analysis of nonmetric data in marketing research, *Journal of Marketing Research*, February edition, pp. 1–13.

Research Magazine, News Archive, www.research-live.com

Schneider, K.C., 1985, Uninformed response rate in survey research, *Journal of Business Research*, April edition, pp. 153–62.

Schuman, H. and Pesser, S., 1981, *Questions and Answers in Attitude Survey,* New York: Academic Press, pp. 179–201.

Schwarz, N. et al., 1991, Rating scales: numeric values may change the meanings of scale labels, *Public Opinion Quarterly,* Winter edition, pp. 570–82.

Segal, M.N., 1984, Alternate form conjoint reliability, *Journal of Advertising Research,* pp. 31–8.

Spagna, G.J., 1984, Questionnaire: which approach do you use? *Journal of Advertising Research,* February–March edition, pp. 67–70.

Spector, P.E., 1992, *Summated Rating Scale Construction: An Introduction,* Newbury Park, CA: Sage, pp. 12–17 & 46–65.

Stevens, S.S., 1946, On the theory of scales of measurement, *Science,* 7 June, pp. 677–80.

Stevens, S.S., 1951, Mathematics, measurement and psychophysics, In: Stevens, S.S. (ed.), *Handbook of Experimental Psychology,* New York: John Wiley and Sons.

Taylor, M., 1977, Ordinal and interval scaling, *Journal of the Marketing Research Society,* 25(4): 297–303.

Wildt, A.R. and Mazis, M.B., 1978, Determinants of scale response: labels versus position, *Journal of Marketing Research,* May edition: pp. 261–7.

Chapter 12

Ajzen, I. and Fishbein, M., 1977, Attitude-behavior relations: a theoretical analysis and review of empirical research, *Psychological Bulletin,* September edition: 888–948.

Ajzen, I. and Fishbein, M., 1980, *Understanding and Predicting Social Behavior,* Englewood Cliffs, NJ: Prentice Hall, pp. 53–89.

Beatty, S.E. and Kahle, L.R., 1988, Alternative hierarchies of the attitude-behavior relationship, *Journal of the Academy of Marketing Science,* Summer edition, pp. 1–10.

Cote, J.A., McCullough, J. and Reilly, M., 1985, Effects of unexpected situations on behavior-intention differences, *Journal of Consumer Research,* 12 (3): 185–93.

Dabholkar, P.A., 1994, Incorporating choice into an attitudinal framework, *Journal of Consumer Research,* 21(1): 100–18.

Fishbein, M., 1967, Attitude and the prediction of behavior, In: Fishein, M. (ed.), *Readings in Attitude Theory and Behavior,* New York: John Wiley and Sons.

Fishbein, M., 1967, *Readings in Attitude Theory and Behavior,* New York: John Wiley and Sons.

Fishbein, M., 1983, An investigation of the relationships between beliefs about an object and the attitude toward that object, *Human Relations,* pp. 233–40.

Garg, R.K., 1996, The influence of positive and negative wording and issues involvement on response to Likert Scales in Marketing Research, *Journal of the Marketing Research Society,* 38 (3): 235–46.

Hawkins, D.I., Best, R.J. and Coney, K.A., 1998, *Consumer Behavior: Building Marketing Strategy,* 7th edn, New York: McGraw-Hill/Irwin, pp. 401–3.

Ohanian, R., 1990, Construction and validation of a scale to measure celebrity endorsers' perceived expertise, trustworthiness, and attractiveness, *Journal of Advertising,* 19 (3): 39–52.

Prus, A. and Brandt, D.R., 1995, Understanding your customers—what you can learn from a customer loyalty index, *Marketing Tools,* July/August edition, pp. 10–14.

Research Magazine, News Archive, www.research-live.com

Robert, T., Wu, W. and Petroshius, S.M., 1987, The halo effect in store image management, *Journal of Academy of Marketing Science*: 44–51.

Robertson, T.S. and Kassarjian, H.H., 1991, *Handbook of Consumer Behavior,* Englewood Cliffs, NJ: Prentice Hall.

Sahni, A., 1994, Incorporating perceptions of financial control in purchase prediction, In: Allen, C.T. and John, D.R. (eds), *Advances in Consumer Research*, Provo, UT: Association for Consumer Research, pp. 442–8.

Siciliano, T., 1993, Purchase intent: facts from fiction, *Marketing Research,* Spring edition, p. 56.

Solomon, M.R., 2004, *Consumer Behavior,* 6th edn, Upper Saddle River, NJ: Pearson/Prentice Hall, pp. 242–5.

Tsai, Y., 1985, On the relationship between cognitive and affective processes, *Journal of Consumer Research,* 12(3): 358–62.

Chapter 13

ClickZ website, www.clickz.com/stats

Kephart, P., 1995, The leader of the pack: how Dannon Yogurt put research to work – and came out a winner, *Marketing Tools,* September edition, pp. 16, 18 & 19.

Office for National Statistics website, www.statistics.gov.uk

Research Magazine, News Archive, www.research-live.com

Chapter 14

Kendall, M.G. and Smith, B.B., 1946, Table of random sampling numbers, *Tracts for Computers,* Cambridge: Cambridge University Press.

SSI (Survey Sampling International) website, www.surveysampling.com

Ulas, D. and Arslan, B., 2006, An empirical investigation of Turkish cola market, *British Food Journal,* 108(2/3): 156–68.

Chapter 15

Deville, B., 1995, The data assembly challenge, *Marketing Research Magazine,* Fall/Winter edition, p. 4.

UK Trade and Investment web gateway, www.uktradeinvest.gov.uk

Chapter 16

Gruca, T.S., 1996, Reporting poll results: focusing on point spreads instead of percentages can be misleading, *Marketing Research,* Winter edition, p. 29.

Huff, D., 1993, *How to Lie with Statistics,* reissue edn, New York: W.W. Norton & Co.

Peters, T., 1989, *Thriving on Chaos: Handbook for a Management Revolution,* US: Harper Business.

SAS website, www.sas.com

Semon, T.T., 1993, A bad picture is worth very few words, *Marketing Research,* 24 May, p. 11.

SPSS website, www.spss.com

Tufte, E.R., 1983, *The Visual Display of Quantitative Information,* Cheshire, CT: Graphics Press.

Chapter 17

BlogCRM website, www.blogcrm.com

Huff, D., 1993, *How to Lie with Statistics,* reissue edn, New York: W.W. Norton & Co.

Ingram, J.A. and Monks, J.G., 1989, *Statistics for Business and Economics,* San Diego, CA: Harcourt Brace Janovich.

Moore, W.L., Louviere, J.J. and Verma, R., 1999, Using conjoint analysis to help design product platforms, *Journal of Product Innovation Management,* 27–39.

Chapter 18

Davis, B. and Worrall, S., 1998, Basket analysis profiling British customers, *British Food Journal,* 100(2), pp. 102–9.

Gesellschaft für Innovative Marktforschung website, www.g-i-m.com

Hair, J.A. Jr. et al., 2005, *Multivariate Data Analysis,* 6th edn, Upper Saddle River, NJ: Prentice Hall.

Hamel, G. and Sampler, J., 1998, The e-corporation, Fortune, 138(11), p.80.

Iversen, G.R. and Norpoth, H., 1987, *Analysis of Variance,* Newbury Park, CA: Sage.

McCullagh, P. and Nelder, J.A., 1989, Generalized linear models, 2nd edn, Chapman and Hall, London.

Moore, W.L., Louviere, J.J. and Verma, R., 1999, Using conjoint analysis to help design product platforms, *Journal of Product Innovation Management,* pp. 27–39.

Nelder J.A. and Wedderburn, R.W.M., 1972, Generalized linear models, *Journal of Royal Statistical Society A,* 135, pp. 370–84.

Shiu, E. and Dawson, J., 2004a, Comparing the impacts of Internet technology and national culture on online usage and purchase from a four-country perspective, *Journal of Retail and Consumer Services,* 11 (6): 385–94.

Shiu, E., Dawson, J. and Marshall, D., 2004b, Segmenting the convenience and health trends in the British food market, *British Food Journal,* 106 (2): 106–27.

Stores, 2000, Understanding the online customer, Stores, 82(1), pp. 11–21.

Chapter 19

Bruner, G.C. and Kumar, A., 2005, Explaining consumer acceptance of handheld Internet devices, *Journal of Business Research,* 58 (5): 553–8.

Gonzalez-Benito, O. and Gonzalez-Benito, J., 2005, The role of geodemographic segmentation in retail location strategy, *International Journal of Market Research,* 47(3): 295–316.

Hair, J.A. Jr. et al., 2005, *Multivariate Data Analysis,* 6th edn, Upper Saddle River, NJ: Prentice Hall.

Titus, P.A. and Everett, P.B., 1995, The consumer retail search process: a conceptual model and research agenda, *Journal of the Academy of Marketing Science,* pp. 106–119.

Tukey, J.W., 1877, Exploring data analysis. Addison-Wesley Series in Behavioral Science: Quantitative Methods, Reading, Mass: Addison-Wesley.

Chapter 20

Altman, R., 2007, *The Tyranmy of Presentation Software,* www.desktop Publishing. com/altman/ presentation.html, accessed 30 June 2008.

Chandler, D., 2007, *Semiotics: The Basics,* 2nd edn, London: Routledge.

ECCH (European Case Clearing House) website, www.ecch.com

European Pharmaceutical Marketing Research Association website, www.ephmra.org

Index